THE PRACTICE OF
CHILD THERAPY

Related Titles of Interest

**Working with Linguistically and Culturally Different Children:
Innovative Clinical and Educational Approaches**
Sharon-ann Gopaul-McNicol and Tania Thomas-Presswood
ISBN: 0-205-19986-0

Handbook of Pediatric and Adolescent Health Psychology
Anthony J. Goreczny and Michel Hersen (Editors)
ISBN: 0-205-15624-X

**Approaches to Child Treatment: Introduction to Theory, Research,
and Practice, Second Edition**
James H. Johnson, Wiley C. Rasbury, and Lawrence J. Siegel
ISBN: 0-205-15604-5

The Child Clinician's Handbook
William G. Kronenberger and Robert G. Meyer
ISBN: 0-205-14752-6

Child and Adolescent Therapy
Margaret Semrud-Clikeman
ISBN: 0-205-15026-8

**Child Neuropsychology: Assessment and Interventions for
Neurodevelopmental Disorders**
Phyllis Anne Teeter and Margaret Semrud-Clikeman
ISBN: 0-205-16331-9

For more information or to purchase a book, please call 1-800-278-3525.

THE PRACTICE OF CHILD THERAPY

Third Edition

Edited by

RICHARD J. MORRIS
University of Arizona

THOMAS R. KRATOCHWILL
University of Wisconsin—Madison

Allyn and Bacon

Boston   London   Toronto   Sydney   Tokyo   Singapore

Series Editor: Carla F. Daves
Series Editorial Assistant: Susan Hutchinson
Marketing Manager: Joyce Nilsen
Advertising Manager: Anne Morrison
Manufacturing Buyer: Suzanne Lareau

Copyright © 1998 by Allyn & Bacon
A Viacom Company
Needham Heights, MA 02194

Internet: www.abacon.com
America Online: keyword: College Online

Library of Congress Cataloging-in-Publication Data

The practice of child therapy / edited by Richard J. Morris, Thomas R.
   Kratochwill.—3rd ed.
      p.   cm.
   Includes bibliographical references and index.
   ISBN 0-205-16818-3
   1. Child psychotherapy. I. Morris, Richard J. II. Kratochwill,
Thomas R.
RJ504.P68   1998
618.92'8914—dc21
                                          97-18367
                                          CIP

Printed in the United States of America

10 9 8 7 6 5 4 3 2 1   02 01 00 99 98

To our children:

Stephanie, Michael, and Jacqueline Morris

and

Tyler Thomas Kratochwill

We thank you for enriching our lives and those of others.

CONTENTS

PREFACE

We are delighted to produce a third edition of *The Practice of Child Therapy*. Research, theory, and practice continue to grow rapidly in the area of treatment of childhood learning and behavior disorders. Nevertheless, there are still relatively few books that have presented a systematic review and detailed discussion of existing treatment procedures for children's learning and behavior disorders. In our volume we tried to present a broad range of child treatment approaches in which systematic and detailed discussion of available treatment techniques takes precedence over conceptual and theoretical issues.

Our book is again intended to be a treatment-oriented reference volume for individuals who work and intend to work directly in the area of childhood learning and behavior disorders. The third edition has been enlarged and expanded. This book contains 17 chapters covering obsessive compulsive disorders, childhood depression, childhood fears and phobias, attention-deficit hyperactivity disorder, academic problems, conduct disorder, somatic disorders, childhood autism, mental retarda-

tion, children medically at risk, posttraumatic stress syndrome, sexual and other abuse of children, psychopharmacotherapy, the use of computer technology in child therapy, prevention, and legal and ethical issues in child therapy.

The book is designed to assemble in one volume summaries of the treatment literature and related treatment procedures on some of the more common childhood behavior disorders. As was true in the first and second editions, we have not included all possible childhood disorders. On the other hand, we have attempted to sample those most often encountered by individuals who practice in applied settings (e.g., clinic and counseling centers; classroom and school settings; home, residential, and hospital settings). Each chapter is written by an individual or individuals who are well-qualified to discuss the treatment practices for the specific topic under consideration. Although the authors have generally adopted a broad-based behavioral orientation in their respective chapters, the reader will also note that we have asked them to take an empirical approach toward inclusion of treatment techniques that have been applied to the disorder. Authors were again encouraged to sample widely from existing sources in the treatment literature and to construct their presentation on the basis of empirically supported treatment techniques and procedures. Some chapters include a discussion of theoretical issues, but the primary emphasis is on intervention techniques and strategies for changing various problem behaviors. Case examples are often used to elucidate treatment procedures presented in the chapter. The addition of the chapter on behavior informatics reflects the changing nature of the practice of child therapy with the integration of computers into a therapist's practice.

This book is intended for individuals who have entered or plan to enter mental health and related applied professions, including special education, nursing, and rehabilitation. This book will be especially useful for individuals taking child therapy and child intervention courses and practicum courses, as well as for those professionals who work in applied settings, including clinics, schools, and counseling centers, as well as psychiatric hospitals and residential treatment centers.

A number of individuals made major contributions to the completion of this work. Thanks are given to Jerry Frank (deceased) at Pergamon Press for his support in the development of the first edition of the book, as well as his continuing support in the preparation of the second edition. The publication of the second edition, as well as the early guidance surrounding the preparation of the third edition was expertly performed at Allyn and Bacon by Mylan Jaixen and, later, by Carla Daves. We very much appreciate their support of this book. Our appreciation goes also to Edward S. Shapiro, Ph.D., Lehigh University, for his comments on reviewing this manuscript. In addition, we express our appreciation to Shirley Biamonte for her secretarial assistance during various phases of this project. Primarily, we express our special thanks to our wives, Vinnie Morris and Carol Kratochwill, who have constantly served as inspirations for our scholarly and professional work with children and adolescents.

ABOUT THE EDITORS AND CONTRIBUTORS

ABOUT THE EDITORS

Thomas R. Kratochwill (Ph.D., University of Wisconsin, 1973) is Professor of Educational Psychology and Director of the Educational and Psychological Training Center at the University of Wisconsin—Madison. He has authored and edited several books including *Single-Subject Research: Strategies for Evaluating Change, Selective Mutism: Implications for Research and Treatment,* and *Treating Children's Fears and Phobias: A Behavioral Approach* (with Richard J. Morris); he also co-edits the *Advances in School Psychology,* an annual series. Dr. Kratochwill has published numerous journal articles and book chapters on behavior therapy in assessment and research methodology. He has received the Lightner Witmer Award and the Senior Scientist Award from Division 16 of the American Psychological Association. He has served as Associate Editor for *Behavior Therapy,* the *Journal of Applied Behavior Analysis,* and *School Psychology Review.* In addition to being on numer-

ous editorial boards, he has edited the American Psychological Association Division 16 journal, *Professional School Psychology,* now *School Psychology Quarterly.* He has also been a practitioner in several applied settings and a consultant to numerous schools and other applied clinical treatment settings.

Richard J. Morris (Ph.D., Arizona State University, 1970) is Professor and Director of the School Psychology Program, College of Education, Department of Special Education and Rehabilitation, The University of Arizona. Previous to this position he was Professor of Educational Psychology, The University of Arizona; Assistant to Associate Professor of Psychology, Clinical Psychology Training Program, Syracuse University; and Clinical Assistant Professor of Pediatrics, Upstate Medical Center, State University of New York at Syracuse. He has authored and edited several books, including *Behavior Modification With Children: A Systematic Guide, Perspectives in*

Abnormal Behavior, and *Behavior Modification With Exceptional Children: Principles and Practices,* has coauthored with Thomas R. Kratochwill *Treating Children's Fears and Phobias: A Behavioral Approach,* has coedited with Burton Blatt *Perspectives in Special Education and Special Education: Research and Trends,* and has coedited with Thomas R. Kratochwill *Handbook of Psychotherapy with Children and Adolescents.* He has published numerous journal articles and book chapters on children's behavior disorders and on behavior therapy. He is a member of several professional associations, a Fellow of the American Psychological Association, and serves on the editorial boards of a number of professional journals. He has been President of the Division of Rehabilitation Psychology of the American Psychological Association, Vice-President of the National Register of Health Service Providers in Psychology, and has been a consultant to a number of publishing companies, child mental health and developmental disabilities treatment facilities, and schools.

ABOUT THE CONTRIBUTORS

Heather Applegate is a doctoral student in clinical psychology at Louisiana State University. Her clinical and research interests include dual diagnosis, psychopharmacology, and staff/parent training of individuals with developmental disabilities.

Steven L. Bair, Psy.D., is a licensed Clinical Psychologist and Associate Clinical Professor of Psychology in the Medical Psychology Graduate program at the University of Alabama in Birmingham. He has been in private practice for 20 years and is a managing partner of Meredith, Bair and Peacock, P.C. Dr. Bair earned his doctoral degree from Baylor University in 1977 and completed his clinical internship at the University of Alabama Medical Center. He has been honored for professional advocacy efforts with the Karl F. Heiser Presidential Award from the American Psychological Association. Dr. Bair has developed software applications for behavioral health care. Dr. Bair is a consultant to The Psychological Corporation in the areas of behavioral health care and behavioral informatics.

Russell Barkley, Ph.D., is Director of Psychology and Professor of Psychiatry and Neurology at the University of Massachusetts Medical Center. He has published numerous widely acclaimed books, video programs, book chapters, and journal articles related to ADHD and he is the editor of *The ADHD Report.*

Judith V. Becker, Ph.D., is a Professor of Psychology and Psychiatry and Associate Dean of Academic Affairs at the College of Social and Behavioral Sciences, University of Arizona. Clinical and research interests include sexual offenders and victimization.

Jeffery P. Braden, Ph.D., NCSP, is an Associate Professor of Educational Psychology and Director of the School Psychology Program, University of Wisconsin—Madison. He has consulted with educational systems in the U.S. and abroad to promote academic achievement and prevent academic and social failure. His current projects include large-scale service delivery reform in Chicago Public Schools via school-based problem-solving teams, and research on the efficacy of psychoeducational treatments and the role of assessment in educational consultation.

Barbara L. Bonner, Ph.D., a Clinical Child Psychologist, is an Associate Professor and Director of the Center on Child Abuse and Neglect in the Department of Pediatrics at the University of Oklahoma Health Sciences Center.

Marjorie H. Charlop-Christy, Ph.D., is Professor of Psychology and Director of The Claremont Autism Center, her research and treatment program. A graduate of UCLA, she received her M.A. and Ph.D. from Claremont Graduate University, and was awarded a Postdoctoral Fellowship at The Johns Hopkins School of Medicine. Her published research focuses on speech and language, social skills, behavior problems, and motivation. Her treatment program is a blend of direct treatment, parent training, and incidental paradigms, and is presented in her manual, "How to Treat the Child with Autism."

Stephanie Sergent Daniel, Ph.D., received her doctoral degree in Clinical Psychology from The University of North Carolina at Greensboro. She completed her predoctoral internship at The University of Alabama at Birmingham in Birmingham, Alabama. Dr. Daniel is currently at The Bowman Gray School of Medicine in Winston-Salem, North Carolina, in the Department of Psychiatry and Behavioral Medicine. Her clinical and research interests are in the areas of child and adolescent psychopathology and developmental disabilities, and in longitudinal and treatment outcome research methodologies.

Mark DeKraai, J.D., Ph.D., is the Children's Mental Health Administrator and Child and Adolescent Service System Program Director at the Nebraska Department of Health and Human Services. He is currently a member of the State Mental Health Representatives of Children and Youth (Division of National Association of State Mental Health Program Directors), the Nebraska Child and Family Leadership Commission, the Nebraska Child and Family Council, and the Nebraska Commission on the Protection of Children.

George DuPaul, Ph. D., is an Associate Professor in the School Psychology program at Lehigh University. He has written numerous journal articles and book chapters related to ADHD. His primary research interest is the development of school-based interventions for students with ADHD.

Greg R. Ford, Ph.D., was born in Anacortes, WA. He received his Ph.D. in Medical (Clinical Psychology) Psychology from the University of Alabama at Birmingham. He completed his internship at the University of North Carolina-Chapel Hill. He is currently completing a post doctoral fellowship in rehabilitation psychology at the University of Washington.

Kenneth D. Gadow received his Ph.D. from the University of Illinois at Urbana-Champaign and is currently Professor of Psychiatry, Professor of Special Education, and Professor of Education at the State University of New York at Stony Brook. Dr. Gadow is the author or editor of over 20 books about childhood learning and behavior disorders, and his numerous publications appear in journals in psychology, psychiatry, pediatrics, and special education.

Susan R. Hall, J.D., is a doctoral student in the Psychology, Policy and Law Program and the Clinical Psychology Program at the University of Arizona. Her clinical practice and research interests are in family violence and child victimization. She currently serves as a member of the State of Arizona Governor's Task Force on Children's Justice.

Daniel P. Hallahan is the Virgil S. Ward Professor of Education at the University of Virginia. He has published extensively in special education. He is the president-elect of the Division for Learning Disabilities of CEC and is the co-principal investigator of the Center of Minority Research in Special Education.

A. Dirk Hightower, Ph.D., is the Director of the Primary Mental Health Project, Associate Director of the Center for Community Study, and a Senior Research Associate at the University of Rochester. Dr. Hightower is on the editorial board of school and community psychology journals. He has been active in NASP and APA Division 16.

Nadine J. Kaslow, Ph.D., ABPP, an Associate Professor at Emory University School of Medicine in the Department of Psychiatry and Behavioral Sciences, holds joint appointments in the Departments of Pediatrics, Psychology, and Rollins School of Public Health. She is also Chief Psychologist at Grady Health System. Dr. Kaslow is on a number of child psychopathology and family therapy editorial boards, and is an elected member of the Association of Predoctoral and Postdoctoral Internship Centers.

James M. Kauffman is Professor of Education at the University of Virginia. He received his Ed.D. degree in special education from the University of Kansas in 1969. He is a past president of the Council for Children with Behavioral Disorders and has published numerous journal articles, chapters, and books.

Alan E. Kazdin, Ph.D., is Professor of Psychology at Yale University, Professor in the Child Study Center (Child Psychiatry) at the School of Medicine, and Director of the Yale Child Conduct Clinic, an outpatient clinic for children with aggressive and antisocial behavior.

Clayton Keller, who received his doctorate from the University of Virginia, is an associate professor and the coordinator of the special education program at the University of Minnesota, Duluth. His major research interests include educators who have disabilities and the integration of students with disabilities in general education classrooms.

Patricia F. Kurtz received her M.A. and Ph.D. from Claremont Graduate School. She is an Assistant Professor at the Kennedy Krieger Institute and the Johns Hopkins University School of Medicine. Her research interests include assessment and treatment of children with autism and the functional analysis of severe behavior problems.

John Wills Lloyd is Associate Professor of Education at the University of Virginia. He received a Ph.D. in special education from the University of Oregon in 1976. He is interested in the nature, development, and assessment of learning and behavior problems, and most of his academic work has focused on treatments for those problems. He is past president of the Division for Research of the Council for Exceptional Children.

Johnny L. Matson, Ph.D., is a professor of Psychology at Louisiana State University and Director of the Clinical Psychology Ph.D. program. He has also served on the faculties of Northern Illinois University and the University of Pittsburgh. He is author of over 325 publications including 26 books with a primary emphasis on children and adults with developmental disabilities.

Ronald L. Meredith, Psy.D., received the Doctor of Psychology Degree from Baylor University in 1975. He completed a clinical internship at the University of Alabama Medical Center. Dr. Meredith has been a clinical practitioner for 20 years and is a managing partner of Meredith, Bair and Peacock, P.C. He is a Clinical Professor of Psychology in the Medical Psychology program at the University of Alabama at Birmingham and is a consultant to The Psychological Corporation in the areas of behavioral health care and behavioral informatics.

Mary K. Morris, Ph.D., is an Assistant Professor of Psychology and Director of Assessment at the Regents Center for Learning Disorders at Georgia State University. She is a clinical psychologist with training in clinical child psychology and neuropsychology, with interests in the impact of developmental and acquired disabilities on the developing child.

Karen L. Pierce, Ph.D., is a researcher at the University of California, San Diego. Dr. Pierce received her B.A. from the State University of New York at Stony Brook, and her M.A. and Ph.D. from UC San Diego. She has taught psychology courses at UC San Diego and has written several book chapters and research articles in the area of autism. Her research interests include both the assessment and treatment of social deficits in children with autism as well as the investigation of a wide range of cognitive abilities in these children. Scholarly papers summarizing her work can be found in both the *Journal of Applied Behavior Analysis* and the *Journal of Autism and Developmental Disorders*.

John C. Pomeroy completed his medical and psychiatric training at the University of London. Currently, he is Associate Professor of Psychiatry at the State University of New York at Stony Brook. His clinical and research interests have been in the areas of childhood psychopathology, psychopharmacology, autism, and mental retardation. Dr. Pomeroy is the director of a recently created Division of Developmental Disabilities at Stony Brook.

Lynn P. Rehm, Ph.D., is a Professor of Psychology at the University of Houston. He is well-known for his research in depression in both children and adults. His work has focused on the assessment, psychopathology, and intervention of depression. He is the developer of the self-management treatment program for depression that has been applied to adults and children.

Philip A. Saigh, Ph.D., is a Professor at the Graduate Center of the City University of New York. Since 1977 he has conducted research on the epidemiology, assessment, and treatment of traumatized youth. Dr. Saigh also directs the Child-Adolescent PTSD Clinic at Bellevue Hospital. He is a Fellow of the American Psychological Association and was a member of the American Psychiatric Association's work group for PTSD in the DSM-IV.

Bruce D. Sales, Ph.D., J.D., is founder of the first Law and Psychology, J.D.-Ph.D. Program in the United States, is joint appointed as a Professor of Psychology, Psychiatry, Sociology, and Law, and Director of the Psychology, Policy and Law Program, at the University of Arizona. Having served as the first Editor of the journals, *Law and Human Behavior* and *Psychology, Public Policy, and Law*, Professor Sales is the recipient of a number of awards and honors, including The Distinguished Contributions Award to Psychology and Law from the American Psychology-Law Society. Having more than 160 publications, Professor Sales' recent books include: *Finding the Law for Social Science Research and Mental Health Practice* (1996), and *Law, Mental Health, and Mental Disorder* (1996).

Laura Schreibman, Ph.D., is Professor of Psychology at the University of California, San Diego. Professor Schreibman is the author of over 100 books, research articles, and chapters all dealing with the experimental analysis and behavioral treatment of autism. Her main research emphases include parent training, design of naturalistic teaching strategies, and treatment evaluation.

Lawrence J. Siegel, Ph.D., is Dean and Professor of the Ferkauf Graduate School of Psychology at Yeshiva University. Previously, he was Director of the Division of Pediatric Psychology at the University of Texas Medical Branch at Galveston and a member of the clinical psychology faculty at the University of Florida and at the University of Missouri-Columbia. He received his Ph.D. from Case Western Reserve University in 1975. Dr. Siegel is past President of the Society of Pediatric Psychology (Section 5, Division 12) of the American Psychological Association. He is co-author of *Behavioral Medicine: Practical Applications in Health Care* and *Approaches to Child Treatment: Introduction to Theory, Research, and Practice* (2nd edition).

Brandi B. Smiroldo, M.A., is a doctoral student at Louisiana State University. Her research interests include dual diagnosis, behavioral treatment of individuals with developmental disabilities, functional analytic approaches to treatment, and staff training issues.

Sydney Stallings, M.A., received her masters degree in clinical psychology from Louisiana State University. She is currently involved in a behavioral treatment team project in conjunction with the University of Mississippi Medical Center's Psychology Department.

CHAPTER 1

HISTORICAL CONTEXT OF CHILD THERAPY

Richard J. Morris
Thomas R. Kratochwill

Although we currently find a great deal of interest in the understanding, care and treatment of children having emotional and behavior disorders, this is a relatively recent event within the history of the mental health field. Unlike the adult treatment literature—which can be traced back to ancient civilizations, with reliance on such practices as trephining and exorcism—the child mental health treatment literature can be traced with any clarity only to the early twentieth century (Achenbach, 1974; Kanner, 1948). The one notable exception is the literature on children who were diagnosed as having mental retardation.

Concern for the systematic and organized care of children with mental retardation can be traced to Jean Itard and his attempts, beginning in 1799, to educate the "Wild Boy of Aveyron." These initial treatment approaches were continued by Edward Seguin in the mid-1800s, with research concerned with the causes, nature, and treatment of mental retardation (Achenbach; 1974). This work was followed by the building of residential schools for persons with mental retardation—the first in Massachusetts in 1848 and the second in New York in 1851. These facilities were initially established on an experimental basis as educational institutions, almost like boarding schools, rather than as custodial asylums. The assumption here was that after receiving training to assist them in their functioning in society, these children would be returned to their homes. This assumption, however, was found to lack empirical support since few students/residents actually returned home. By the end of the nineteenth century, the state residential "educational" institution, although still typically called a "state school" for the mentally retarded (or, as the children were referred to then, as mentally deficient, or as idiots and feebleminded), had become a custodial treatment institution.

Other notable developments in the early twentieth century that contributed to the concern with the treatment of children having emotional and behavior problems were: the mental hygiene movement, the establishment of child guidance clinics, and the introduction of dynamic psychiatry. Within the mental hygiene movement, Clifford Beers is credited with changing the direction of the treatment of mentally ill persons in America. Beers, a law student at Yale University, had become clinically depressed and suicidal and was hospitalized. Following his hospitalization, Beers published *A Mind That Found Itself* (1908), describing the mistreatment that he and others received while they were patients at a state mental hospital. The book gained considerable popularity and raised the level of public awareness of the terrible conditions in the state hospitals and the inadequate treatment received by mental patients. With the help of a number of prominent professionals (for example, Adolph Meyer and William James), Beers formed the National Committee for Mental Hygiene to inform the public of the conditions in state hospitals, to promote the establishment of better treatment methods, and to sponsor research on the prevention and treatment of mental illness. This led to the establishment of mental hygiene programs in schools and the advancement of the child guidance movement (Kauffman, 1981).

The child guidance movement had actually started prior to the publication of Beers's book, because of the establishment of a psychological clinic in 1896 by Lightner Witmer at the University of Pennsylvania. However, the movement gained impetus following the publication of Beers's book and the establishment, in 1909, of the Juvenile Psychopathic Institute (now called the Institute for Juvenile Research) in Chicago, under the leadership of William Healy. The institute staff worked directly with juvenile offenders and stressed an interdisciplinary approach to studying them. Psychiatrists, psychologists, and social workers worked together on particular cases, emphasizing the multiple contributing factors to any given child's behavior disorder(s).

Aided by Beers's National Committee for Mental Hygiene, other child guidance clinics developed across the country to work with a broader range of children's behavior disorders. Kanner (1948) reports that by 1930, there were about 500 such clinics in the United States.

The introduction of dynamic psychiatry in the early twentieth century also substantially contributed to our current emphasis on treatment services to children. Sigmund Freud, in Vienna, and Adolph Meyer, in the United States, are often credited with introducing the dynamic approach. Individuals affiliated with this approach maintained that the origins of behavior problems lay in the past (typically, childhood) experiences of the person (Kanner, 1948). With adult patients, these experiences were explored retrospectively by the psychiatrist, who attempted to draw causal relationships between these past experiences and the patients' present behavior. It should be emphasized that, during these early years, children were usually not seen in treatment by psychiatrists. In fact, as Kanner (1948) states, "Even Freud, who so clearly understood the influence of early experiences on emotional development, had his theory of infantile sexuality all worked out and published [in 1905] three years before he even saw one single child "professionally" (p. 7). However, the retrospective search for the relationship between early childhood events and present functioning aroused sufficient interest among professionals that some began to acquaint themselves specifically with the behavior problems of children as well as with the dynamics that contribute to their difficulties.

This psychodynamic interest in children was not formally realized in the literature until the publication, in 1909, of Freud's detailed case of "Little Hans." Interestingly, although Freud formulated his etiological theory of phobias on the basis of Hans's symptoms and experiences, he did not treat Hans directly. Hans's father treated him under Freud's direction and supervision (Morris & Kratochwill, 1983).

Although Hans's problem was treated successfully, it was not until 15 to 20 years later that Freudian psychoanalytic child therapy came into existence. This was largely due to the contributions and adaptations of his treatment for children by Melanie Klein, Freud's student, and Anna Freud, his daughter. Their changes made his therapeutic approach more applicable to children and contributed to its increasing popularity in subsequent years. Some of the changes were the substitution of play activities for the technique of free association and the use of drawings and dreams to understand a child's problem more completely (Knopf, 1979). These changes and the emphasis on the child's internal dynamics from Freud's psychoanalytic theory made psychoanalytic play therapy popular and influential in the development of many later forms of child therapy.

Thus, these three major developments—and the earlier concerns by professionals for the care and treatment of children and adults who were mentally retarded—contributed substantially to our present focus on the provision of clinical services to children having emotional and behavior disorders. Other developments also contributed to the current focus and should be mentioned briefly. The intelligence testing movement, begun by Alfred Binet at the beginning of the twentieth century, had a tremendous influence on the study of children. As a result, it became possible to learn the extent to which a particular child differed from the norm in cognitive ability. It also demonstrated clearly the diversity of children in terms of their comprehension of classroom instruction (Kanner, 1948).

The formation of three professional associations, in addition to Clifford Beers's National Committee for Mental Hygiene, also contributed to the increasing emphasis on the treatment of children. The first association was the Association of Medical Officers of American Institutions for Idiots and Feeble-minded Persons, founded in 1876, which evolved into the present-day American Association on Mental Retardation. Its first president was Edward Seguin. In 1922, the second association, The Council for Exceptional Children, was formed. It consisted primarily of educators and other professionals, although parents were members too. The third early association was the American Orthopsychiatric Association, founded in 1924 and consisting primarily of psychiatrists, applied psychologists, and social workers, although educators as well as other professionals and parents were also members. Each of these groups encouraged the formulation and conduct of research with behavior disordered children as well as the sharing of information regarding effective psychological and/or educational interventions.

In addition, following the emerging changes in the early twentieth century in the predominant and very rigid and structured philosophy surrounding the education of students, and in recognition of Alfred Binet's work, a movement to provide more individualized instruction and special education classes for mentally and emotionally handicapped students began. These classes were to be taught by teachers who had studied the particular behavior disorders and developed specific methods for modifying them. As a result, teacher-training programs began to develop—the earliest appearing in 1914, in Michigan.

Finally, in addition to the work of Anna Freud and Melanie Klein regarding applying Freudian psychoanalysis to children, a second treatment approach emerged which was initially much less popular than psychoanalytic child therapy. This approach was called *behaviorism* and later became known as the behavior modification movement (Kazdin, 1994; Morris, 1985). Behavior modification emerged largely from the experimental psychology laboratory rather than from direct interaction with patients, and was based on theories concerning how people and animals learn to behave through stimulus-response learning and conditioning rather than through the conscious or unconscious thinking found in psychoanalytic writings. Perhaps, the two most famous behaviorists associated with this movement were John B. Watson (e.g., Watson, 1913, 1919), often referred to as the "Father of Behaviorism," and B. F. Skinner (e.g., Skinner, 1938, 1953), the behavioral researcher and theorist who extended Watson's behavioristic views and developed a learning paradigm that Skinner referred to as "operant conditioning." The behavior modification and behavior therapy procedures that were derived from various learning theories were largely confined for many years to research settings. In fact, it was not until the mid-1960s to mid-1970s that these procedures began being applied on a regular basis in children's residential treatment settings, regular and special education classrooms, and outpatient mental health settings (Morris, 1985). As was the case with child psychoanalysis 50 years earlier and the child guidance movement 30 years earlier, the impact of the child behavior modification movement in the mid-1960s to mid-1970s was profound in that it further contributed to society's thinking that children having various emotional and behavior disorders could be treated successfully.

In considering all these developments, one begins to realize that concern with the understanding, care and treatment of children did not stem from one or two major activities. Rather, many events, occurring over 80–90 years, set the stage for our present-day psychotherapy services for children. The authors of the remaining chapters provide a brief historical perspective on their respective topics and then present a detailed account of various therapeutic methods for helping children and adolescents change their behavior. We hope that readers will find these chapters of great interest and practical value.

REFERENCES

Achenbach, T. M. (1974). *Developmental psychopathology*. New York: Ronald Press.

Beers, C. (1908). *A mind that found itself*. New York: Longmans, Green.

Freud, S. (1963, 1909). The analysis of a phobia in a five-year-old boy. *Standard edition of the complete psychological works of Sigmund Freud* (Vol. 10). London: Hogarth Press.

Kanner, L. (1948). *Child psychiatry*. Springfield, IL: Charles C. Thomas.

Kauffman, J. M. (1981). *Characteristics of children's behavior disorders*. Columbus, OH: Merrill.

Kazdin, A.F. (1994). *Behavior modification in applied settings* (rev. ed.). Homewood, IL: Dorsey Press.

Knopf, I. J. (1979). *Childhood psychopathology*. Englewood Cliffs, NJ: Prentice-Hall.

Morris, R. J. (1985). *Behavior modification with exceptional children: Principles and practices*. Glenview, IL: Scott, Foresman and Company.

Morris, R. J., & Kratochwill, T. R. (1983). *Treating children's fears and phobias: A behavioral approach*. Elmsford, NY: Pergamon Press.

Skinner, B.F. (1938). *The behavior of organisms*. New York: Appleton-Century-Crofts, Inc.

Skinner, B. F. (1953). *Science and human behavior*. New York: MacMillan.

Watson, J. B. (1919). *Psychology from the standpoint of a behaviorist*. Philadelphia: Lippincott.

Watson, J. B. (1913). Psychology as the behaviorist views it. *Psychological Review, 20,* 158–177.

CHAPTER 2

OBSESSIVE COMPULSIVE DISORDERS

Jesse B. Milby
Shirley L. Robinson
Stephanie Daniel

OVERVIEW AND LITERATURE REVIEW METHOD

This chapter reviews research and clinical findings on childhood Obsessive Compulsive Disorders (OCD) in a historical perspective. It reviews assessment and treatment strategies and procedures for use by practitioners and describes a successfully treated case. Reviews of epidemiology, etiology, and theories of obsessive compulsive disorder are placed in a clinical context. A variety of assessment and treatment strategies and procedures are described, including recommendations for those that seem most useful and effective. Lastly, costs and benefits of treatment are discussed.

The scientific and professional literature on Obsessive Compulsive Disorder has greatly expanded during the past decade with more than a two fold increase in published medical research since 1969. In fact, most of the literature in this area has been published since the 1980s, including a large increase in the number of publications on child and adolescent OCD. To access the wealth of literature now available, the authors employed a computer-assisted search of PsycLIT and Medline databases using the same key words for both searches: obsessive compulsive disorder, obsessive compulsive neurosis, human, English language, child, children, or adolescents. For this chapter, PsycLIT and Medline intervals searched were 1988 through March, 1995, overlapping by several years the intervals searched for the previous chapter (Milby & Weber, 1989). Additional recent references were also selected.

HISTORICAL PERSPECTIVE

Religious and medical conceptualizations of OCD antedated Freud's postulation that obsessions stem from defensive reactions to psychosexual anxiety. Earliest concepts of obsessions likely had religious origins stemming from demonic influence (Rachman & Hodgson, 1980). Early medical conceptualizations of OCD involved the role of fevers and disordered imagination. There has been a historical transition from religious and medical to psychoanalytic and psychological conceptualizations of OCD with most contemporary work utilizing the medical and psychological models. Those interested in further historical background are directed to Rachman and Hodgson (1980) and Hunter and MacAlpine (1963), and to Skoog (1959), who reviews the early psychiatric literature.

The study of OCD has been hampered over the years by the lack of agreement on concepts and terms as well as the lack of agreement on uniformly applied operational definitions for OCD or uniform diagnoses with explicit diagnostic criteria. Terms like "obsessionality," "obsessive compulsive personality," "obsessive compulsive traits," "obsessive compulsive neurosis," and "obsessive compulsive disorder" were often used interchangeably. The use of terms interchangeably complicates the search for trends in patient types. Consequently, the assumption that such terms refer to obsessive compulsive neurosis or OCD may be erroneous, unless a careful description of symptoms was included. In order not to perpetuate this problem, the authors used terms defined by Rachman and Hodgson (1980) and emphasized the use of the diagnostic criteria, including the clinical definition and terms outlined in the fourth edition of the *Diagnostic and Statistical Manual of Mental Disorders* (*DSM-IV*; American Psychiatric Association, 1994).

The study of OCD has been further complicated by the lack of a common instrument by which to measure the presence of OCD symptoms. One of the first attempts at developing such a standardized instrument was that of Cooper (1970) with his work on the Leyton Obsessional Inventory. Since his original work, there has been considerable improvement in conceptualizing the diagnostic criteria via several editions of the *International Classification of Diseases* (e.g., see ninth revision, *ICD-9*; World Health Organization, 1977) and several editions of the *DSM* as discussed in *DSM-IV* (American Psychiatric Association, 1994). Recently, several other instruments have been developed and a few have been used in multiple studies, strengthening the scientific basis of patient and treatment comparisons. New developments in assessment are reviewed in a subsequent section.

The historical development of the conceptualization of OCD is outlined below in the section titled, "Diagnosis of Obsessive Compulsive Disorder," with an emphasis on the changes in diagnostic criteria in recent versions of the *DSM*, from *DSM-III* to *DSM-III-R*, and *DSM-IV* (American Psychiatric Association, 1980; 1987; 1994).

KEY TERMS AND CONCEPTS

Obsession—an intrusive, repetitive thought, image or impulse. It is unacceptable, associated with subjective resistance, and usually produces distress. The function of the obsession can be further delineated by describing the obsession as anxiety elevating or anxiety reducing.

Compulsion—a repetitive, stereotyped act, completely or partly unacceptable, but regarded as excessive and/or exaggerated. It is accompanied by a subjective need to perform the act and provokes and usually reduces distress.

Compulsive ritual—a prescribed performance for some act. Though under voluntary control, the ritual's urge is strong and a sense of diminished volition is experienced.

Four other OCD phenomena are defined and described in the following section on behavioral assessment issues. They are *compulsive rituals, cognitive compulsions, primary obsessional slowness,* and *obsessive doubting*.

ON THE RELATIONSHIP BETWEEN OBSESSIONS AND COMPULSIONS

There is usually a close relationship between obsessions and compulsions such that the former predisposes the latter. While the presence of one implies the other, there may be exceptions. In primary obsessional slowness found in adults, there is dissociation between the ritualized behavior and identifiable obsessions (Rachman, 1974). In obsessive doubting, cognitive activities dominate the conscious state without provoking overt behavior. One adult study reported that 25 percent of reported obsessions were not associated with compulsions (Akhtar, Pershad, & Verma, 1975). Obsessions and compulsions in adults can run independent courses within the same patient or obsessions may irrevocably lead to some compulsive activity (Milby, Meredith, & Rice, 1981). Although there is little research on this in children, such independence has been observed by child clinicians and may be attributable to inability of young children to verbalize their thoughts.

DIAGNOSIS OF OBSESSIVE COMPULSIVE DISORDER

Diagnosis of OCD in children is hampered by several factors. First, children often do not realize that their obsessions and compulsions are excessive or unreasonable, and as such, do not report OCD symptoms as ego-dystonic. Thus, children usually do not request help for OCD symptoms, but rather are brought to the attention of professionals by parents, other family members, or teachers. Another factor that makes initial recognition of OCD symptoms difficult is the fact that children and adolescents are more likely to refrain from rituals in front of peers in school or other social situations, engaging in them primarily at home or when they are alone and unobserved. Thus, impairment can be worse at home, although symptoms may occur in school and other social situations when the disorder worsens. OCD may be first recognized when symptoms begin to occur outside the home.

The *DSM-III-R* attempted to clarify diagnostic criteria for obsessive compulsive disorder (American Psychiatric Association, 1987). Both the *DSM-III* (American Psychiatric Association, 1980) and the *DSM-III-R* required the presence of either obsessions or compulsions that cause distress sufficient to interfere with normal social and occupational functioning. However, *DSM-III-R* made the additional requirement that obsessions or compulsions are time-consuming, requiring more than 1 hour per day. *DSM-III-R* also subdivided, and made more explicit, the individual criteria for obsessions and compulsions. Diagnostic criteria for OCD in *DSM-III-R* were retained in *DSM-IV* (American Psychiatric Association, 1994) with important changes, however, in the definitions of obsessions and compulsions. *DSM-IV* acknowledges that

thoughts can be *either* obsessions or compulsions, depending on whether they increase (obsessions) or decrease (compulsions) subjective anxiety. This distinction has often been made by clinicians and researchers in the field over the last two decades and will likely displace, by conventional clinical use, the equally logical conceptualization of anxiety elevating or anxiety diminishing obsessions. The definition of obsessions has been revised to exclude the terms "ego-dystonic" and "senseless" used in *DSM-III-R*. *DSM-IV* eliminates the definition of compulsions as purposeful and intentional. *DSM-IV* also directs the clinician to specify the patient "with poor insight," if for most of the time during the current episode, the person does not recognize that the obsessions and compulsions are excessive or unreasonable (American Psychiatric Association, 1994). This concern and direction is primarily applicable for adults.

The *DSM-IV* diagnostic criteria for 300.3 Obsessive Compulsive Disorder are listed below (American Psychiatric Association, 1994, pp. 422–423):

A. Either obsessions or compulsions:
Obsessions as defined by 1., 2., 3. and 4.:
1. recurrent and persistent thoughts, impulses, or images that are experienced, at some time during the disturbance, as intrusive and inappropriate and that cause marked distress.
2. the thoughts, impulses, or images are not simply excessive worries about real-life problems.
3. the person attempts to ignore or suppress such thoughts, impulses, or images or to neutralize them with some other thought or action.
4. the person recognizes that the obsessional thoughts, impulses, or images are a product of his or her own mind, (not imposed from without as in thought insertion).
Compulsions as defined by 1. and 2.:
1. repetitive, behaviors (e.g., hand washing, ordering, checking) or mental acts (e.g., praying, counting, repeating words silently) that the person feels driven to perform in response to an obsession, or according to rules that must be applied rigidly.
2. the behaviors or mental acts are aimed at preventing or reducing distress or preventing

some dreaded event or situation; however, these behaviors or mental acts either are not connected in a realistic way with what they are designed to neutralize or prevent, or are clearly excessive.

B. At some point during the course of the disorder, the person has recognized that the obsessions or compulsions are excessive or unreasonable. **Note:** This does not apply to children.

C. The obsessions or compulsions cause marked distress, are time-consuming (take more than 1 hour per day), or significantly interfere with the person's normal routine, occupational (or academic) functioning, or usual social activities or relationships.

D. If another Axis I disorder is present, the content of the obsessions or compulsions is not restricted to it, (e.g., preoccupation with food in the presence of an Eating Disorder; hair-pulling in the presence of Trichotillomania; concern with appearance in the presence of Body Dysmorphic Disorder; preoccupation with drugs in the presence of a Substance Use Disorder; preoccupation with having a serious illness in the presence of Hypochondriasis; preoccupation with sexual urges or fantasies in the presence of a Paraphilia; guilty ruminations in the presence of Major Depressive Disorder).

E. The disturbance is not due to the direct physiological effects of a substance (e.g., a drug of abuse, a medication) or a general medical condition.

Specify if:

With Poor Insight: if, for most of the time during the current episode, the person does not recognize that the obsessions and compulsions are excessive or unreasonable (American Psychiatric Association, 1994, pp. 422–423).

These criteria exclude the psychotic child who may also have troubling obsessions and rituals. The diagnosis should not be dismissed with a brain-injured individual with known pre-injury OCD or with Mental Retardation where OCD may coexist. OCD or obsessive compulsive personality styles may coexist with other psychiatric syndromes. Generally, however, Obsessive Compulsive Personality Dis-

order (OCPD) should not be diagnosed in children since the *DSM-IV* criteria generally refer to "… an enduring pattern of inner experience and behavior that deviates markedly from the expectations of the individual's culture, is pervasive and inflexible, has an onset in adolescence or early adulthood, is stable over time, and leads to distress or impairment." (American Psychiatric Association, 1994, p. 629). However, in unusual instances where the maladaptive OC pattern appears to be stable in adolescence, it may be used. The clinician should understand that in such cases there is less certainty that the personality disorder will persist through adolescence and emerge relatively unchanged in adulthood.

Montgomery (1993) argues that OCD should be conceptualized and diagnosed as a separate illness apart from, and independent of, other anxiety disorders. As evidence, he cites OCD's unique phenomenology, incidence, sex ratio, response to anxiolytic drug treatment differences and specific efficacious response to serotonin reuptake inhibitors, in comparison to other anxiety disorders. He contends that one reason OCD should be classified as a separate disorder from anxiety disorders is while both anxiety and depression seem integral to OCD, they make no contribution to drug treatment. However, this argument is not without flaws. He also argues, but without citing empirical data, that OCD can occur without the presence of anxiety. If anxiety is integral as he acknowledges, it would seem that it is ample rationale for classifying OCD as an anxiety disorder. Most clinicians would argue that if OCD symptoms appear without the presence of anxiety, the disorder as conceptualized in *DSM-III-R* and *DSM-IV* should not be diagnosed, and some other diagnosis such as OC Personality Disorder should be considered. Lastly, he faults the *DSM-IV* conceptualization of the functional nature of obsessions, which increase anxiety and compulsions which prevent or reduce anxiety as putting explanation ahead of observation. There is an extensive literature, however, which documents the functional relationship between anxiety-elevating obsessions and anxiety-reducing compulsive behaviors and their stimulus control. For examples, see Foa, Steketee, and Milby (1980); Foa & Tillman, (1978); Milby, Meredith, and Rice, (1981); and Mills, Agras, Barlow, and Mills, (1973).

DIFFERENTIAL DIAGNOSIS

OCD is frequently comorbid with phobic disorders including social phobia. OCD is relatively easily discriminated from phobias because of the lack of distress in the absence of the phobic object or situation and by the specific nature of the phobia (i.e., snakes, heights, dark, etc.). Social phobia and separation anxiety are common comorbid conditions with childhood OCD. Bulimia and anorexia have obsessional and compulsive features usually focused on food and/or exercise, but are distinguishable from OCD because the obsessions and compulsions are not typical washing, counting, arranging, etc., rituals. Distinguishing between compulsions and tics in Tourette's Disorder where the tics often have a complex behavioral component can be difficult. The difficulty is compounded by the fact that in several recent studies 20–80% of patients with Tourette's Disorder have had either obsessive compulsive symptoms or OCD (Frankel et al., 1986; Grad, Pelcovitz, Olson, Matthews, & Grad, 1987; Pauls, Towbin, Leckman, Zahner, & Cohen, 1986). The *DSM-IV* criteria of personal distress and functional impairment distinguishes OCD from normal range excessive thoughts and repetitive habits. These criteria, when applied to children, must take into account the child's developmental stage and age-appropriate functional behaviors that are disrupted by OCD symptoms.

Research on the diagnosis of OCD in children and adolescents has also been complicated by the many definitions, terms, assumptions, and idiosyncratic diagnostic practices employed by clinicians and researchers. For example, in a chart review of 4,594 nonretarded patients treated at the Children's Psychiatric Hospital in Risskov, Denmark, from 1970-1986, Thomsen and Mikkelsen (1991) found that 61 children met *DSM-III* criteria for OCD but only 8 were given a discharge diagnosis of OCD. They attribute this under-diagnosis to clinicians' formulation of OCD symptoms as transient phenomena and their unwillingness to diagnose OCD because of its bad prognosis. The diagnoses given to most instead of OCD was neurosis infantilis, followed by maladjustment.

Vitiello, Spreat, and Behar, (1989) found that 10 of 283 (3.5%) patients with mild to profound mental retardation had compulsions that met *DSM-III-R* criteria for OCD except for the absence of expressed resistance to compulsions or feelings of anxiety. This study has implications for current diagnostic procedures since the ego-dystonic features have been eschewed as a criterion from *DSM-IV*. Thus, it would appear that more children with mental retardation may now be diagnosed with OCD.

OCD AS AN IMPULSE CONTROL DISORDER

Recently, some researchers have made a case for subtypes of OCD as part of a spectrum of disorders, including Trichotillomania, characterized by pathological grooming (Swedo & Leonard, 1992). Trichotillomania is currently classified in *DSM-IV* as one of the Impulse-Control Disorders Not Elsewhere Classified, 312.39. Support for classifying some types of OCD with grooming compulsions with Trichotillomania and others stems, in part, from the clinical presentation. Persons with Trichotillomania describe strong urges to pull their hair and urges to pull out certain targeted hairs perceived to be different in texture or other characteristics. More importantly, when the hairs are pulled out, patients report momentary relief of emotional tension, which, however, is soon replaced by another compulsive urge to pull hair repeating the cycle. However, it does not appear that those with Trichotillomania have an analogous cognitive component for what those with OCD report as obsessions. Persons with Trichotillomania also seem to have a much more fixed response pattern of hair-pulling, which doesn't seem to change much over time, unlike persons with OCD, whose rituals commonly change over time.

PRIMARY OBSESSIVE SLOWNESS

Primary obsessive slowness seems to have first been described in the literature by Rachman (1974) based on a series of 10 patients who showed extreme slowness in execution of routine tasks of daily living such as dressing, bathing, or eating. It seems to be a phenomenon and variant of OCD reported in the adult OCD research literature. The authors did not find any reference to it in the child research literature reviewed. However, one of the authors (JBM) has treated severe OCD in a young man whose primary obsessive slowness developed in adolescence. Recently, Frost and Shows (1993) studied what is often a component of obsessive slowness found in OCD, a phenomena called compulsive indecisiveness. In three studies they have examined the phenomenon using the newly developed Indecisiveness Scale.

Several other mental disorders can present with OCD type symptoms: Obsessive Compulsive Personality Disorder is perhaps the most difficult for clinicians to differentiate; Schizophrenia, especially when manifested by ritualized behavior; phobias that present with ritualized avoidance and escape behavior patterns; and depressive disorders. Certain forms of addictive behavior such as pathological gambling, obsessive and ritualized sexual behavior, and klepto-mania, all share obsessive characteristics with OCD, but lack the functional relationship between the obsessions that instigate or raise a dysphoric state (i.e., anxiety) and ritualized behavior which reduces that state. However, the discrimination between OCD and sexual dysfunction or addictive behavior may be difficult. Where certain forms of addictive behavior serve to alleviate a dysphoric state, such as anxiety or sexual craving, and circumscribed, even ritualized behaviors occur in response to such dysphoric states, addictive behaviors associated with substance abuse should clearly be diagnosed as Substance Use Disorders.

Other disorders that emulate OCD are Tourette's Disorder and other tics. Also, some forms of temporal lobe epilepsy, occasionally post- traumatic and postencephalitic complications, and Body Dysmorphic Disorder produce a symptom picture similar to OCD. OCD and Tourette's Disorder have a similar age of onset and similar compulsive-like symptoms. However, instead of obsessions and compulsions as primary symptoms, Tourette's is characterized by motor and vocal tics that occur frequently and virtually every day. Also, in Tourette's, there is not reported anxiety reduction following the tics. The distinction is difficult because the majority of patients with Tourette's have compulsive symptoms. Kaplan, Sadock, and Grebb (1994) report that as many as two thirds of patients with Tourette's meet diagnostic criteria for OCD as a comorbid disorder. Leonard,

Lenane, Swedo, Rettew, Gershon, and Rapoport (1992) report that 14.7% of 54 patients with childhood OCD met criteria for Tourette's Disorder and 57% of the sample had lifetime histories of tics.

Body Dysmorphic Disorder (BDD) was classified in *DSM-III-R* as a somatoform disorder with usual onset in adolescence and manifested by persistent repetitive thoughts of perceived body defects existing with minimal, objectively verified, disfigurement. Differential diagnosis is difficult due to the occasional presentation of compulsive checking behavior in persons diagnosed with BDD. It is estimated that 2% of cosmetic surgery patients are diagnosed with this disorder (Andreasen & Bardach, 1977). The preoccupation is obsession-like and similar to OCD obsessions, but not usually linked to compulsive behavior or rituals. Like OCD, BDD has a high rate of comorbid affective anxiety and personality disorders associated with it, and impairments in social and occupational functioning have been noted.

ETIOLOGICAL FACTORS IN OCD

The Natural History and Course of OCD

Though descriptive data on the natural history of any disorder is useful, and there are such data on OCD, a caveat must be registered. The data are obfuscated by the unreliable application of variable diagnostic concepts and definitions and the tendency to under-diagnose OCD in children and adolescents (Thomsen & Mikkelsen, 1991). Despite such difficulties, there is surprising agreement on the essential features of OCD.

Swedo, Leonard, and Rapoport's (1992) study of clinical interviews of 70 children and adolescents enrolled in National Institute of Mental Health (NIMH) treatment studies and 18 additional patients with OCD considered together, described the common clinical presentation of childhood onset OCD. Children generally presented with both rituals and obsessions and the content of the obsessive compulsive behaviors changed over time in 85% of the sample. Children with only obsessions were rare (3 of 70 subjects), whereas children with rituals in the absence of obsessions were fairly common. Rituals only were especially common in very young children (ages 6–8 years).

Washing rituals were the most common, affecting over 85% of the sample. In 48% of the sample, excessive washing was accompanied by obsessional concern with dirt, germs, body excretions, or environmental toxins. A lifetime history of repeating rituals was present in 51% of the sample. Checking rituals were common and reported in 46% of the sample, and obsessional symmetry, ordering, or exactness were reported in 17% of the sample. Other common obsessions included aggressive or sexual images (4%) and scrupulosity (13%). Obsessions regarding scrupulosity seemed to occur in adolescents and involved worry about going to Hell if they were not able to always do the right thing and have only good thoughts. Miscellaneous compulsions included rituals of writing, moving, or speaking (26%), and ordering and arranging (17%). Vocal, ocular, and touching rituals were experienced by 20% of the sample and closely resembled motor and vocal tics of Tourette's Disorder; thus, the two were difficult to distinguish. However, in most cases, children were able to verbalize an obsessional thought preceding the ritual and considered the ritual a response to that thought rather than a motor response to an nondefined urge.

Hollingsworth, Tanguay, Grossman, and Pabst (1980) reported serious problems with social life and peer relationships in their study. None were married and only 30% were dating. In a prospective follow-up study of 25 patients with childhood onset OCD, Flament et al. (1990) reported that 74% of patients continued to live with their families versus 57% of controls. Only 59% of patients were enrolled in school while 86% of controls continued in school. Eleven percent were currently not enrolled in school or employed. Thirty percent had been hospitalized since the initial study, whereas no controls had been hospitalized.

"Fixedness" of OC Symptoms in Children

Several follow-up studies of OCD in childhood have provided valuable information on the fixedness or stability of OC symptoms (Allsopp & Verduyn, 1988; Goodwin, Guze, & Robins, 1969; Hollingsworth et al., 1980). Berg et al. (1989) attempted to determine the stability of OC symptoms in adolescents and young adults over time. They screened and identified high school students with possible OC symptoms on the basis of information obtained from self-report questionnaires. Once identified, students participated in semistructured clinical interviews. Two years later, subjects were assessed again. Fifty percent of persons diagnosed with either current or a lifetime history of OCD were given the diagnosis at the 2-year follow-up. Persons initially diagnosed with OC symptoms did not develop OCD. Flament et al. (1990) followed patients treated successfully with clomipramine and found that approximately 68% still met criteria for OCD. Only 28% no longer met criteria for a psychiatric diagnosis at follow-up.

Childhood Versus Adult Presentation of OCD

Clinical presentation of OCD in childhood is quite similar to that of adults, with one possible exception. The content of rituals and obsessions in adults seems to follow consistent themes even though the actual ritualized behavior may change over time, whereas, in youths, there is a shifting symptom pattern over time with a particular symptom pattern lasting for months or a few years then shifting to new symptoms. As Rettew, Swedo, Leonard, Lenane, and Rapoport (1992) found, the most common progression of symptoms was a gradual increase in the number of symptoms followed by a decrease by late adolescence and early adulthood. None of their patients at follow-up presented with the same constellation of symptoms as at baseline. Swedo, Rapoport, Leonard, Lenane, and Cheslow (1989) had also reported changes in symptom patterns over time for 90% of their NIMH sample.

Khanna and Srinath (1988) also found some consistent differences between adult and childhood forms of OCD in India. Obsessions and compulsions noted in 16 children with OCD were compared to 389 adult cases over the previous decade. A majority of OC symptoms in the children were compulsive rituals. Most prevalent were washing and repeating compulsions. Obsessions in children were significantly less reported than in adults.

In general, it seems that most studies have reported continued OCD symptoms into adulthood for approximately half of the total number of persons diagnosed with OCD during childhood and adolescence. In addition, most studies report some change in symptom pattern over time. Data on the continuity of OCD from childhood to adulthood and changes in symptom patterns are difficult to obtain due to the variety of definitions and assessment methods used and the tendency of clinicians to under-diagnose childhood OCD.

Comorbidity

Several psychiatric diagnoses have frequently been found to be comorbid with OCD in children. In a 2- to 7- year follow-up of 54 children diagnosed with OCD, Leonard et al. (1992) evaluated lifetime and current rates of tics and Tourette's Disorder among child cohorts and their first-degree relatives. They found 59% of the children had a lifetime history of tics with approximately one third of the children presenting with a current diagnosis. Although the lack of methodologically sound population studies made it difficult to make direct comparisons for the prevalence of OCD and Tourette's Disorder, the authors suggested that the lifetime prevalence rates for persons in their study with OCD and Tourette's Disorder (11–15%) or tics (59%) and their first-degree relatives (1.8% and 14%, respectively) was higher than in most other published studies (.03%–.40% and 4–12%, respectively).

Leonard et al. (1992) also attempted to determine what variables would differentiate persons with comorbid OCD and Tourette's Disorder or OCD and tics from persons with OCD only. They found that an early age of onset and male gender were more predictive of persons comorbid for OCD and Tourette's than of persons with OCD only. Persons comorbid for tics and OCD were distinguished by an earlier onset of OCD, higher baseline anxiety, and higher cerebrospinal fluid concentrations of 5-hydroxyindoleacetic acid and homovanillic acid (5-HIAA/HVA) than persons with OCD only.

Many studies have reported comorbidity of OCD with other *DSM-IV* Axis I Disorders. In approximately 70 children and adolescents diagnosed with OCD, Swedo, Rapoport, Leonard, Lenane, and Cheslow (1989) found that only 26% had OCD as their only diagnosis. Most frequent associated diagnoses were: depression (35%), other anxiety disorders (40%), developmental disabilities (24%), oppositional disorder (11%), and attention-deficit disorder (10%). In approximately half of the cases comorbid for OCD and depression or OCD and an anxiety disorder, onset of OCD predated the depression or anxiety diagnosis. Tourette's was an exclusionary criterion in the NIMH studies. At 2–7-year follow-up, however, 12% met criteria for Tourette's Disorder.

Flament and colleagues reported a high rate (48%) of comorbid OCD and anxiety or OCD and depression in their 2-7 year follow-up of 25 children and adolescents diagnosed with OCD (Flament et al., 1990). Likewise, in a 2–7-year follow-up of 54 children and adolescents, Leonard et al. (1993) found 22% of their sample with an affective disorder, 30% with an anxiety disorder, 31% with a tic disorder, 2% with a substance abuse disorder, and 2% with a psychotic disorder.

In a more recent epidemiological study of adolescents using a community sample, Valleni-Basile et al. (1994) found major depression in 45% of persons with OCD, dysthymia in 29% of persons with OCD, separation anxiety in 34%, and phobias in 8%. In a study of 31 children and adolescents referred to a clinic, Hanna (1995) noted that 32% had a lifetime affective disorder, 26% had a lifetime anxiety disorder in addition to OCD, 29% had a disruptive behavior disorder, and 26% had a lifetime diagnosis of tic disorders. In contrast to the findings reported on comorbid depression and OCD, Last and Strauss (1989) reported that comorbid anxiety disorders were most common, whereas depressive disorders were rare in their study of 20 children and their families.

The comorbidity of OCD and various *DSM-IV* Axis II personality disorders has also been assessed. Thomsen and Mikkelsen (1993) followed 47 children with previous psychiatric admissions for OCD and 49 control children with other psychiatric diagnoses from 6 to 22 years following initial admission in an effort to establish the rate of comorbid personality disorders and OCD. Avoidant, Dependent, and

Obsessive Compulsive Personality Disorders were more common in the OCD group. In contrast, Paranoid Personality Disorder was least common among the OCD group. Obsessive Compulsive Personality Disorder was not more common in adults with OCD than child OCD patients with no OCD at the time of follow-up. The authors concluded that the presence of OCD is not a necessary condition for the diagnosis of Obsessive Compulsive Personality Disorder.

Comorbidity of mental retardation (also assessed on Axis II of the *DSM*) and OCD has also been evaluated. Vitiello et al. (1989) found that 10 of 283 (3.5%) patients with mild to profound mental retardation presented with compulsions that met all criteria for *DSM-III-R* OCD except for the absence of expressed resistance to compulsions or feelings of anxiety. This study has implications for current diagnostic procedures since the ego-dystonic features have been eschewed as a criterion from *DSM-IV*. Thus, it would appear that more children with mental retardation would now be diagnosed with OCD.

In addition to psychiatric disorders comorbid with childhood OCD, studies have examined comorbidity of pediatric medical conditions and illnesses and childhood OCD. For example, Burke et al. (1989) examined the frequency of OC symptoms in children with inflammatory bowel disease or with Cystic Fibrosis. Results indicated OC symptoms are not specific to inflammatory bowel disease or Cystic Fibrosis. However, OC symptoms may be secondary to the demands of such illnesses (e.g., self-care and monitoring).

Others have evaluated the comorbidity of OCD and Sydenham's Chorea (Swedo et al., 1993; Swedo, Rapoport, Cheslow, et al., 1989). In one study, 11 children with Sydenham's Chorea underwent physical, neuropsychological, and psychiatric evaluations (Swedo et al., 1993). They found that 9 children displayed OC symptoms with 4 of the 9 meeting diagnostic criteria for OCD. The OC symptoms reportedly occurred days to weeks before the chorea, and waxed and waned with motor abnormalities.

Pine, Shaffer, and Schonfeld (1993) have also empirically pursued the hypothesis that disorders involving neurological difficulties are comorbid with OCD. In 11 children with neurological soft signs, they found 3 children who displayed OC behaviors. The authors contend that children with neurological soft signs and anxious behaviors are at risk for "persistent emotional disorders" in adolescence.

Thus, it seems clear that OCD is comorbid with a variety of other psychiatric and medical conditions. In most instances of comorbidity, however, it remains an empirical question as to the specific nature of the relationship between one disorder and another. In addition, the implications for treatment are unclear when OCD in children is comorbid with another disorder. Future research is needed to address these empirical issues.

Only one research group known to the authors (Leonard, Goldberger, Rapoport, Cheslow, & Swedo, 1990) attempted to empirically evaluate the notion that normal childhood superstitions and rituals may reflect an early manifestation of OCD and/or pre-clinical markers for OCD. In a literature review and small empirical study, these researchers could not distinguish between OCD and normal control groups, and OCD was not on a continuum with nonpsychotic superstitions. However, they did note more ritualized behaviors for OCD persons in childhood than for normal controls. It was not clear to them whether the increased frequency of rituals in children with OCD should be considered early manifestations of OCD or as clinical markers or signs that a child may be at risk for OCD. Future prospective longitudinal studies may provide information to address such questions.

Many developmentalists would argue that some ritualized behavior in children is normal and is a means of controlling and imposing structure on the environment for children. Such behavior may first be noticed as early as the age of 2 years, and continues into adolescence with the specific content of the rituals changing with age. Thus, normal child development is important to consider in the assessment and diagnosis of childhood OCD.

Incidence of OCD

Until the 1980s Obsessive Compulsive Disorder was reported to be uncommon and was infrequently diagnosed (Milby, Meredith, & Wendorf, 1983; Rachman & Hodgson, 1980). In addition, OCD was considered poorly responsive to treatment except among behavior therapists. One decade later, it is now considered relatively common (Kaplan, Sadock & Grebb, 1994). Since 1980, one study has shown over a threefold increase in diagnostic frequency at a psychiatric hospital and more than a twofold increase in publication rate on the disorder among all published medical research from 1969—1990 (Stoll, Tohen, & Baldessarini, 1992).

Kaplan et al. (1994) estimated lifetime prevalence rates between 2% and 3%, with the disorder found in up to 10% of outpatients in psychiatric clinics. These authors do not cite original empirical prevalence studies, but if their notions of prevalence are accurate, Obsessive Compulsive Disorder would be the fourth most common psychiatric diagnosis, after phobias, substance use disorders, and major depression.

Table 2.1 summarizes prevalence rates for recent studies on child and adolescent OCD. As shown in Table 2.1, for those reporting prevalence rates, rates for OCD in community samples are higher than rates for psychiatric samples.

Age of Onset

Goodwin et al. (1969) found that about 65% of persons with OCD develop their disorder before age 25 and fewer than 15% developed OCD after age 35. In Beech's (1974) review of 357 cases, one third were discovered before age 15. These data suggest that between one third and one half of those with treated OCD seek treatment before age 20. Thus, a significant proportion experience onset of symptoms during early adolescence and childhood. These figures may be conservative. All of these data were collected in treatment centers where the patient or the parents first had to recognize the disorder as one needing treatment. Consequently, a higher incidence of OCD may exist because of failure to identify the disorder and relatively low rates of referral to treatment centers.

Rapoport, Swedo, and Leonard (1992) reported that OCD in children has been documented in children as young as 2 years old. Average age of onset in the NIMH treated sample was 10.1 yrs. + 3.5 yrs., with OC symptoms in eight children having onset

before age 7 (Swedo, Rapoport, Leonard, et al., 1989). Rettew et al. (1992) noted the symptom picture for children with earlier onset may differ from that for children with later onset. They reported that children with an onset at 6 years or younger displayed more compulsions than obsessions. Swedo, Leonard, and Rapoport (1992) also reported that rituals without obsessions were more common among very young children (ages 6–8). However, other than these observations, differences in symptom patterns between children with an early age versus later age of onset have not been empirically addressed in controlled studies. One hypothesis to account for such differences, however, is that children with an earlier age of onset experience obsessions but lack the verbal or cognitive abilities to identify and label them.

The mean age of onset of OCD for 43 child and adolescent studies published from 1988 to March, 1995 and reviewed here, ranged from 9.9 to 19.1 years of age, with most studies reporting age of onset as approximately 10 years of age. However, some investigators could not determine specific times for onset. Goodwin et al. (1969) found that 30% of their adult patients could give no specific onset and Black (1974) found the same for 50% of their adult patients. Accurate data are difficult to collect, as many studies are retrospective in nature and may be unreliable.

Gender Ratio

Goodwin et al. (1969) found that although gender ratios differed among 13 studies they reviewed, the ratio for the combined sample approached unity. At that time, it appeared that gender ratios for incidence of adult OCD were about the same. More recently, additional evidence has accumulated on the gender ratios of OCD in childhood. Data from 43 studies from child and adolescent psychiatric samples (1988 to March, 1995) indicate that gender ratios differ between studies. In contrast to the data on the gender ratio for adult OCD, the gender ratio for the combined sample of child and adolescent psychiatric studies is approximately 3:2 (males: females).

TABLE 2.1. Prevalence Rates in Reviewed Studies of Childhood OCD for Community and Psychiatric Samples

STUDY	PREVALENCE RATES (%)	COMMUNITY SAMPLE	PSYCHIATRIC SAMPLE
1. Hamburger, Swedo, Whitaker,Davies, & Rapoport (1989)	20 w/5, 596 students .0035	X	
2. Sher, Martin, Raskin, & Perrigo (1991)	11.000	X	
3. Thomsen & Mikkelsen (1991)	1.3300		X
4. Thomsen & Mikkelsen (1993)	1.3000		X
5. Valleni-Basile et al. (1994)	3.0000		X
6. Thomsen (1991)	1.3300		X
7. Zohar et al. (1992)	4.0000	X	
8. Flament et al. (1988)	1.0000 (current) 1.9000 (lifetime)		X

Note: Not all reviewed studies reported prevalence rates.

Childhood Precursors and Precipitating Events

While there has been interest in describing precursors for OCD in children, investigators have not typically identified specific precursors. This may be in part due to the difficulties inherent in research attempting to identify etiological factors. Researchers and clinicians have, however, attempted to describe some of the precipitating events of OCD during childhood and to identify the child-rearing patterns and practices shown by parents of children with OCD.

Rachman and Hodgson (1980) reviewed seven studies with a total of 655 patients, almost all adults, and found 40% to 90% with precipitating factors. One retrospective review found 17 patients with OCD that onset in childhood. Significant life stress was reported in 82% of the parents, and in 15 of the 17, obsessive thoughts and phobic reactions appeared to be clearly related to realistically frightening home situations or family distress (Hollingsworth et al., 1980).

In an NIMH study, Swedo and colleagues noted that one third of their sample indicated that certain stimuli related to or involved in the ritual served as cues for their rituals (Swedo, Rapoport, Leonard, et al., 1989). Toro, Cervera, Osejo, and Salamero (1992) also reported specific stressful situations preceding

the onset of OCD in 53% of the 72 children and adolescents evaluated in their study. Likewise, Rettew et al. (1992) reported that either family members of their participants or the participants themselves contended that a specific event cued their OC behavior. These events were reported as early as age 2 years, and most often were related to a stressful family event or a reaction to viewing a television program. OC symptoms often initially reflected content of the triggering event. However, content of the OC symptoms was less specific to the triggering event at follow-up.

In contrast to the notion that specific events trigger OC symptoms, 70% of the OCD patients described in Rasmussen and Tsuang's (1986) study were unable to identify a particular precipitating stress or environmental precipitant that triggered their illness. Almost all of their patients, however, reported experiencing a worsening of symptoms in times of stressful life events. In addition to stressful life events, negative affect has also been reported to precipitate and/or exacerbate OCD symptoms in adults diagnosed with OCD (Ristvedt, Mackenzie, & Christenson, 1993).

Thus, it may be prudent to search for a precipitating stress factor(s) in cases of sudden onset OCD in children. However, the search for precipitating factors does not imply causality, as an underlying and largely unnoticed pattern of OC behaviors may be exacerbated by current stressors.

Birth Order

The only quasi-controlled study of birth order effects known to the authors was by Kayton and Borge (1967). They studied 40 children with OCD and compared them with 40 controls. Of the 40 children with OCD, 31 were firstborn or only children, compared to 11 of 40 controls. This difference is statistically significant. Of 30 males in the group, 26 were firstborn, a statistically significant difference, but birth order was not found to be significant in the females.

More recent studies have provided descriptive information, or frequency data, on the birth order of children and adolescents. In a study of 21 children and adolescents diagnosed with OCD, Riddle, Scahill, et al. (1990) reported that 5 were firstborn, 13 were last born, 2 were middle siblings, and 1 was an only child. Likewise, Hanna (1995) reported that the majority of children and adolescents in a study attempting to describe clinical presentation and demographic characteristics of 31 youths were firstborn. Fourteen youths were firstborn, 12 last born, 2 middle siblings, 2 were children, and the birth order of 1 adopted youth was unknown. These results are interesting in view of Toman's (1969) theorizing on firstborn and only children as being more performance and achievement oriented.

Intelligence

None of the studies we reviewed have reported consistently low measured intelligence for children, adolescents, or adults with OCD (Flament et al., 1990 ; Rachman & Hodgson, 1980; Swedo, Rapoport, Leonard et al., 1989; Templer, 1972). Generally, the literature shows intelligence to be average or higher, with most of the evidence supporting higher than average intelligence. However, OC symptoms have been identified in persons well below the average range of intelligence and in patients with mental retardation (Vitiello et al, 1989).

Genetics of OCD

There are at least four methods that can be used to evaluate genetic contributions to OCD: (a) comparisons between monozygotic and dizygotic twins, (b) studies of adopted parents and children, (c) studies of familial incidence, and (d) genetic transmission studies (Rachman & Hodgson, 1980). These types of studies have clarified the genetic contribution to psychiatric disorders in general, especially schizophrenia and bipolar disorders. Efforts to determine the genetic contribution to OCD have increased during the last decade. However, it is difficult to disentangle the role of the environment, especially family practices and modeling, from genetic effects in many studies. Thus, although there are numerous studies showing higher incidence of anxiety states in families of patients and in twins (Dilsaver & White, 1986), few exclude the effect of the family environment. The best case for a genetic etiology based on twin concordance would be made by studies of adoptive twins reared together and apart with blind and independent assessment of the twins. No studies were identified using this strategy.

To summarize, since the last review in the second edition of this book, there have been a number of new genetic studies, several of which have been well-controlled (see especially Lenane et al., 1990; Lenane et al., 1992; Pauls et al., 1995; Riddle, Scahill et al., 1990). These have still yielded mixed results, with the majority of them supportive of a genetic transmission of OCD, if only a nonspecific transmission of anxiety vulnerability. Current research accommodates the notion that what is currently diagnosed as OCD may include a genetically transmitted form, perhaps associated with Tourette's Disorder, (Leonard, Lenane, Swedo, Rettew, Gershon, & Rapoport, 1992), a genetically transmitted form with anxiety vulnerability only, and a nongenetically transmitted form. Thus, the full nature and limitations of genetic transmission of OCD remain to be clarified by further research.

Family Characteristics and Child-Rearing Practices

As in studies cited previously that have attempted to determine the genetic contribution of OCD, one approach to the study of family characteristics has involved determining the occurrence of OCD, other anxiety disorders, and general psychopathology in first-degree relatives of persons with OCD. A second approach has involved evaluating specific child-rearing practices and parental characteristics (e.g., Adams, 1973; Clark & Bolton, 1985; Manchanda & Sharma, 1986; Tseng, 1973).

A series of studies have attempted to assess the role of "expressed emotion"(EE) or the degree or over-involvement and criticism in family members of persons with OCD by comparing them to family members of persons with disruptive behavior disorders, and to family members of normal controls (Hibbs, Hamburger, Kruesi, & Lenane, 1993; Hibbs et al., 1991; Hibbs, Zahn, Hamburger, Kruesi, & Rapoport, 1992). Hibbs et al. (1991) found that high EE and psychiatric disorders occurred frequently in the parents of children and adolescents with OCD when compared to normal controls. In another study, Hibbs et al. (1993) evaluated the relationship between EE, family environment, and marital relationships. Satisfaction with marital relationships and family environments were related to low EE, whereas mothers (particularly mothers from the OCD group) with high orientations for achievement, and families with greater conflict and psychiatric disorders, demonstrated high EE.

Merkel, Pollard, Weiner, and Staebler (1993) asked patients diagnosed with OCD to complete an adjective checklist to describe their parents. They speculated that persons diagnosed with OCD would describe parents using adjectives consistent with obsessive compulsive personality (e.g., strictness, cleanliness, meticulousness). This hypothesis was not supported. Results indicated persons with OCD were more likely to see their mothers as overprotective, but not as disorganized as parents of depressed patients.

A third approach to the study of family characteristics has involved evaluating the child-rearing practices of parents of children with OCD. Rachman and Hodgson (1980) observed that parental reactions to OCD in childhood are of two types: (a) rejection, or (b) over-indulgence of the child's fears and problems. The family involved in a pattern of overindulgence to ritualistic behavior demands may become preoccupied with the obsessive compulsive behavior of the child. For example, the family may react to the child's washing and cleaning compulsions by trying to meet the child's demands for a clean and sterile home. As a result, others may be discouraged from visiting.

It is possible that overt rejection may occur more often with OCD in young adults due to the significant burden placed on families. In a study evaluating areas impacted in families of patients with OCD and other disorders, Chakrabarti, Kulhara, and Verma (1993) reported that families experience financial stress and disruptions in their routines and leisure activities, with no differences noted between the families with OCD versus other psychiatric disorders.

When there is OCD in parents, child-rearing practices are likely to lead to widespread psychological dysfunction, but not necessarily OCD, compared to children of parents with other psychiatric disorders (Cooper & McNeil, 1968; Rutter, 1972). Sawyer et al. (1992) found that the 10–18-year old offspring of adults with OCD did not exhibit any more problems than the children and adolescents of normal controls from the community. Lastly, it should be noted that any causal link between child-rearing practices and OCD, if there is one, may be bidirectional.

Cross-Cultural Considerations

Researchers and clinicians have investigated whether there are differences in epidemiology and the clinical presentation of OCD in childhood between various cultures and races (Okasha, Saad, Khahil, El Dawla, & Yehia, 1994). In a study of 90 Egyptian outpatients, Okasha et al. (1994) noted the influence of religious upbringing on OCD symptoms. They reported a higher prevalence of religious obsessions and repeating compulsions, suggesting that clinical manifestations might be accounted for by the emphasis placed on ritualized prayer and cleanliness in the Muslim religion. Compared to Christians, who comprised approximately one-tenth of the Egyptian population, rituals were more common in Muslims with no significant differences noted in the frequency of obsessions for the two groups. In a study of 61 Danish children and adolescents, Thomsen (1991) and Thomsen and Mikkelsen (1991) concluded that there were no cross-cultural differences in the clinical presentation of OCD symptoms between Danish patients and the findings previously reported for other cultures such as Japan and India.

Overall, it appears that unique cultural features may influence the manifestation and presentation of symptoms within OCD diagnosed groups, but the prevalence of OCD across cultural and ethnic groups appears relatively uniform.

THEORIES OF ETIOLOGY

Theories of OCD etiology can be broadly classified according to the domain of their explanatory variables. Biological theories hypothesize a disease or neurophysiological malfunction as the cause of OCD. Psychological models propose etiologies stemming from environment-person interactions. However, it should be noted that logic does not preclude models that propose more than one causal factor or models that include both biological and psychological variables like Rachman and Hodgson's (1980).

Neurophysiological Dysfunction Theories

No theory specifies a specific neurological defect as a cause of OCD. Instead, multiple mechanisms, systems and brain functioning substrates are proposed with more or less specificity to explain the etiology of OCD. Though these are presented as separate etiological theories, they may or may not prove to be independent of other explanatory factors. For example, it is possible that an identified malfunction of a neurophysiological system may account for the etiology of OCD symptoms in a subgroup of OCD or for most persons with OCD. It is also possible that such a malfunctioning system may be inherited and thus genetically transmitted.

In the last decade, there has been a convergence of neurochemical, neurophysiological, and genetic findings, which strongly suggests that biological factors may contribute to the etiology of OCD. Once more, studies of cerebral metabolism and anatomic anomalies stemming from developments in computer-enhanced brain-scanning have suggested that the central nervous system (CNS) focus of dysfunction may be in the frontal cortex and basal ganglia. More converging evidence has stemmed from studies showing that among patients with OCD, normal metabolic levels return after successful treatment with clomipramine and fluoxetine. The role of neurological dysfunction in OCD also has been strengthened by the findings of increased OCD symptoms following basal ganglia lesions (Laplane et al., 1989) and in other basal ganglia disorders, that is, Tourette's Disorder, Sydenham's Chorea, and post-encephalitic parkinsonism (Baxter et al., 1992; Modell, Mountz, Curtis, & Greden, 1989; Rapoport, 1991).

Brain imaging studies of metabolism and blood flow have implicated involvement of several brain areas, frontal lobes, left orbital gyrus, basal ganglia, and cingulum in patients with OCD (Adams, Warneke, McEwan, & Fraser, 1993; Baxter et al., 1987; Leckman et al., 1994; Luxenberg et al., 1988; Machlin et al., 1991). At least one study has shown metabolic rate changes with both drug and behavior therapy for OCD (Baxter et al., 1992).

Several studies have focused on possible abnormalities in the regulation of vasopressin and corticotropin-releasing factor secretion in the etiology of OCD (Altemus et al., 1992; Altemus et al., 1994; Leckman et al., 1994; Swedo, Leonard, Kruesi, et al., 1992). If these prove to be reliable findings, some of these phenomena (e.g., oxytocin levels), could become subtyping variables for OCD in the future and prove useful as partitioning variables to reanalyze previous data sets.

While largely unsupported empirically, there have been several neurophysiological dysfunction theories proposed over the last two decades. Wise and Rapoport's (1989) model proposed that the striatum functions as a feature detector or filter, triggering release of species-typical behaviors like ritualized washing and grooming. However, they found no studies of trigger stimuli in childhood OCD. Lieberman (1984) proposed a biological link to explain co-morbidity of depression and OCD. Studies classifying patients with OCD as normal or abnormal on the dexamethasone suppression test have sought to evaluate this possibility (Jenike et al., 1987; Lieberman et al., 1983; Monteiro, Marks, Noshirvani, & Checkley, 1986). All found that most patients with OCD suppressed normally. Thus, little evidence from this research supports such a link.

The notion that cognitive deficits in patients with lesions in basal ganglia as in Huntington's Disease might be found in OCD patients, where basal ganglia dysfunction has been recently implicated, has also been evaluated. Martin et al. (1993) used an extensive battery of neuropsychological tests and age- and education-matched normal controls. Neither the groups with OCD or trichotillomania showed impairment on battery components. They suggest that the occasional co-occurrence of OCD and Huntington's Disease-like cognitive deficits reported occasionally in the literature result from dysfunction of proximal, but anatomically, functionally, and neurochemically distinct CNS systems. In considering this research area, Luxenberg et al. (1988) remind us that though many neuroanatomical findings are consistent with a neurobiological etiology of childhood-onset OCD, the role of a third factor producing both anatomical anomalies and caudate nuclei or other focal findings can not be ruled out.

Serotonergic Defect Hypothesis

A serotonergic defect has been proposed as an explanatory mechanism for OCD (Yaryura-Tobias, Bebirian, Neziroglu, & Bhagavan, 1977). Clomipramine has been found to relieve OC symptoms in controlled studies, with animal research showing it to be a potent and relatively selective blocker of serotonin reuptake. Blood serotonin has been lower in drug-free OCD patients than in controls and after clomipramine therapy in which OC symptoms were reduced. Flament, Rapoport, Murphy, Berg, and Lake (1987) found that clomipramine reduced obsessional symptoms and platelet serotonin concentration, which seemed closely correlated with the therapeutic response. However, they also cautioned, other neuropharmacologic properties of clomipramine could account for its efficacy.

Some of the strongest evidence for serotonergic involvement in OCD comes from over 20 studies of adults showing 40–70% improvement in OC symptoms from use of various 5-hydroxytryptamine (5-HT) reuptake blockers, including clomipramine

hydrochloride, fluoxetine hydrochloride, fluvoxamine, and zimeldine hydrochloride. These studies are briefly reviewed and cited by Hollander et al. (1992). The therapeutic response noted in them was compared to the relatively ineffective response to treatment with noradrenergically selective antidepressants like desipramine hydrochloride. This group added their finding of a differential response of M-chlorophenylpiperazine (m-CPP) but not fenfluramine or placebo in a well-controlled study. However, the complexity of their findings suggests the role of this system in OCD involves complex mechanisms including multiple neurotransmitter and neuromodulator systems and not simple up- or down-regulation of the 5-hydroxytryptamine receptor system. Thus, recent findings support conclusions that inhibition of serotonin may be necessary but not sufficient in the pharmacotherapy of OCD (Greist, Jefferson, Kobak, Katzelnick, & Serlin, 1995; Jenike, Baer, & Greist, 1990; Jenike, Baer, Summergrad, et al., 1990; Jenike, Hyman, et al., 1990; Stanley & Turner, 1995).

Kaplan et al. (1994) provide a succinct summary of research to date in this field. They report that data show serotonergic drugs are more effective than drugs that affect other neurotransmitter systems. They conclude that studies generally support the hypothesis that dysregulation of serotonin is involved in symptom formation of obsessions and compulsions. However, they note that caution is warranted in concluding that serotonin is involved in the *cause* of OCD at this time.

The Genetic Model

In the genetic model obsessive compulsive disorders are proposed to be due to some inherited defect or polygenetic abnormality. Research conducted before the 1980s on a genetic etiology for OCD showed mixed results with inheritance rates as high as 35% and as low as 0%. This work is difficult to interpret because of the lack of uniformity in populations studied and in the number of OCD defining criteria and assessment methods and instruments in use.

Black, Noyes, Goldstein, and Blum (1992) studied first-degree relatives of OCD adult probands diagnosed with the Diagnostic Interview Schedule

(Robins, Helzer, Cottler, & Goldring, 1989). Risk for anxiety disorders was increased among the relatives compared to normal controls, but risk for OCD was not. These results suggest an anxiety disorder predisposition is inherited in families with OCD, but its expression is variable.

Pauls et al. (1995) summarized several twin studies that found concordance rates ranging from 53–87% for monozygotic twins and 22–47% for dizygotic twins. Two other twin studies suggested that genetic factors are important for manifestation of anxiety disorders in general. They also cite five studies during the 1990s that addressed the previous studies' shortcomings.

Pauls et al. (1995) add weight to this evidence in their study of OCD versus a comparison group of screened normal controls. Rates of OCD and subthreshold OCD were significantly greater among proband relatives (10.3% and 7.9%, respectively) than among comparison subjects (1.9% and 2.0%, respectively). Rates of Tourette's Disorder and chronic tics were also significantly greater among proband relatives than comparisons, 4.6% versus 1.0%. They conclude that OCD is a heterogenous condition in which some cases are familial and related to tic disorders, some cases are familial and unrelated to tic disorders, and other cases seem to have no familial history for either OCD or tics. Again, it is important to note that even if evidence for some inherited defect or polygenetic abnormality were convincing, arguing genetic causality from an identified inherited defect is risky on logical grounds. Some third factor could be causally related to both the inherited defect and the OCD.

Biological Models: A Critique

Since the previous edition of this chapter, the evidence for a neurophysiological defect and multiple neurophysiological correlates of OCD has steadily mounted and is increasingly more scientifically compelling. Careful work is showing that biological factors contribute to the understanding of this disorder and appear to be important substrates for it. However, it seems inappropriate to reconceptualize OCD as a "treatment-resistant disease" (Elkins, Rapoport, & Lipsky, 1980, p. 521). There is little evidence to support OCD as a "disease" as yet, and much evidence to suggest it is not treatment resistant in most cases.

Psychological Models

Psychoanalytic Theory

Psychoanalytic theory of OCD is subsumed within Freud's overall theory of personality developed in several scholarly works, *The Interpretation of Dreams* in 1900, *Psychopathology of Everyday Life* in 1904; and in his theory of psychosexual development, which formed the basis for a theory of psychoanalysis in Freud's *Three Contributions to the Theory of Sex*. Concepts from all three of these sources are concisely discussed in Kimble and Garmezy (1968, chap. 20).

According to psychoanalytic theory, the genesis of OCD is within the anal stage of development during which toilet training occurs. Persons with OC behaviors allegedly had difficulties during this stage that later led to the characteristic rigidity, over-control, scheduling, and other OC traits and behaviors. However, in three empirical studies that tested the hypothesis of toilet-training problems in children with OCD, 17 of 18 cases showed no evidence of strict toilet training (Dai, 1957; Judd, 1965; Tseng, 1973).

Some psychoanalytic theorists propose that needs for control and object mastery are central characteristics of OCD. These needs are proposed as defense mechanisms that seek control over repressed impulses of hostility, violence, and sexuality, which stem from a fixation at the anal stage of development. Though the need for control may be revealed in many interpersonal domains of functioning, Staebler, Pollard, and Merkel (1993) looked for effects in the sexual history, sexual satisfaction, and marital adjustment of OCD patients versus two comparison groups with depression and panic disorder. They could not distinguish the OCD patients from either comparison group. Thus, to date there seems to be little supporting evidence from empirical research to support the psychoanalytic theory of etiology for OCD.

Learning Theory and Conditioning Models

Several learning theories have been used to explain OCD. One of the most frequently cited theories is the two-factor learning theory (Mowrer, 1960). This theory proposes that obsessive thought produces anxiety because the thought has been previously associated with unconditioned, anxiety-arousing stimuli. Obsessions then elicit conditioned anxiety, the reduction of which is reinforcing. Compulsions become established and maintained as they follow and serve to reduce anxiety. They become elaborated via response chaining. Thus, factor one is classical conditioning of the anxiety response, and factor two is instrumental conditioning of compulsive behavior reinforced by reduction of anxiety (i.e., negative reinforcement). Two-factor theory parsimoniously accounts for major symptoms of OCD, and implications from the theory have provided the rationale for the development of response prevention and exposure treatment shown to be effective with adults and children. These procedures are reviewed in more detail in the section on treatment.

Rachman–Hodgson Model

Rachman and Hodgson (1980) proposed four determinants of OCD: (a) a genetic component of hyperarousability, (b) mood disturbances, (c) social learning, and (d) specific learning exposures. They postulated a continuum of OC behavior with the OCD maladaptive pattern at the extreme. For them, the most important questions for understanding OCD become: (a) What generates the behavior?, and (b) What maintains it?. Multiple determinants are assumed instead of a particular cause. They suggest that it is most helpful to determine what conditions promote compulsive behaviors such as excessive talkativeness or hand washing.

Family-Systems Model

One early attempt to describe OCD from a family-systems perspective was by Watzlawick, Weakland, and Fisch (1974). This approach and theoretical system is now widely used and accepted for a variety of disorders (Gurman & Kniskern, 1981). There is no one definitive family-systems theory. However, various theories share some fundamental assumptions. Symptoms are understood as existing within an interpersonal context (i.e., the person's family). Symptoms represent dysfunction of a system. The system consists of the relationships or patterns of interactions between its members. The individual and the symptoms are influenced by others' actions and, in turn, influence both in a circular rather than linear fashion. Causality is seen as a mutually causative sequence or may even be rejected as a concept in favor of describing a "coherent pattern" in a self-recursive cycle of events with no real beginning or end (Dell, 1981; Dell & Goolishian, 1979). Therapy is primarily aimed at altering patterns of relating within the system.

TREATMENT OF OBSESSIVE COMPULSIVE DISORDERS

This section provides a review of OCD treatment for children and adolescents from 1991 to 1995. Included is a brief overview of adult treatment from which most treatment for childhood OCD has been derived. This overview benefitted greatly from an excellent review of the adult literature by Stanley and Turner (1995).

Behavioral Treatment with Adults

By 1980, the literature reflected that 90% of exposure with response prevention (ERP) treated patients showed at least moderate (39%) to much improvement or were symptom free at post-treatment (51%) (Foa, Steketee, & Ozarow, 1985). Treatment typically consisted of no more than 20 sessions. Since then, other studies have suggested that about 80% of patients are classified as improved with up to 80% symptom reduction (Stanley & Turner, 1995). When rates for treatment-refusers and dropouts are also considered, these reviewers predict that 30% of patients will not complete behavioral therapy, 36% will show at least 70% symptom reductions, 27% will show 31% to 69% improvement, and 7% will fail to benefit. Overall, it appears that about 63% of patients might benefit from ERP. Most of the patients treated with ERP (79%) maintained about

60% symptom reductions for periods of 1 to 6 years, although up to 18% received additional ERP and 33% received some type of treatment for depression during follow-up intervals. These researchers estimate conservatively that about 55% of OCD patients receiving ERP would be considered treatment responders at long-term follow-up and conclude that ERP treatment has a robust effect on OCD. They note, however, that the disorder is often chronic with ongoing needs for treatment even among treatment responders.

Stanley and Turner (1995) observed that ERP studies have focused primarily on washing rituals, with exposure primarily effecting obsessions and response prevention primarily effecting compulsive behaviors and rituals (e.g., see Foa et al., 1980). Other treatment variables associated with maintaining gains included use of self-exposure training and cognitive restructuring, involving a significant other in treatment, weekly telephone contacts, supportive psychotherapy, and social support from family. Active treatment of comorbid disorders appeared helpful, including both psychotherapy and psychopharmacology. Patient characteristics that predict maintained improvement at follow-up included status at post-treatment, age at symptom onset, pretreatment anxiety and depression, and primary ritual type. Poorer outcomes may be associated with intense, negative relationships, and ERP may be more helpful for primary cleaning compulsions than those with checking compulsions. Comorbid depression may not predict poorer outcome as earlier research suggested. Data are still inconclusive regarding treatment variations such as therapist versus patient-directed exposures, use of group therapy for milder OCD with less comorbidity, added cognitive strategies, and treatment for obsessions without compulsions and "fixed" obsessions such as overvalued ideation and schizotypal characteristics. Studies that include cognitive therapy, social-skills training, and neuroleptics need to be conducted.

Behavioral Treatment with Children and Adolescents

Several review articles were helpful in understanding the pediatric behavioral literature (March, 1995; Milby & Weber, 1991; Piacentini et al., 1992). Milby and Weber (1991) concluded that advocates of both ERP and clomipramine (CMI) treatment have "overstepped their data in describing their methods as the 'treatment of choice'" (p. 27). They recommend problem-oriented idiographic assessment of the child and family system to identify multiple determinants of the child's OC behaviors, espousing goal-oriented and more directive treatment approaches over more time-consuming and expensive psychodynamic strategies. Within such a comprehensive format, a multimodal approach can include psychotherapeutic techniques, medications, and family interventions to produce specific clinical results.

March (1995) identified 32 articles from three databases published between 1967 and 1994, excluding articles on the OC spectrum disorders, impulse disorders, and mental retardation. Most were single case reports lacking empirical data and a conceptual framework, while a few were more rigorous case studies or series with very small sample sizes. With the exception of one study, all attributed some benefit to cognitive behavioral interventions, with 26 claiming successful use of response prevention, 10 incorporating cognitive strategies, 9 utilizing concurrent family and supportive therapies to help address comorbidity and compliance with ERP (particularly in hospital settings), and 1 utilizing anxiety management or relaxation strategies. March also discussed other therapeutic strategies such as cartographic and story metaphors that he and his colleagues have integrated with cognitive behavioral strategies (March, Mulle, & Herbel, 1994). March (1995) concluded that abundant clinical and empirical data are emerging to suggest that CBT alone or in combination with drug treatment is an effective treatment for pediatric OCD.

In their review of pediatric psychopharmacologic studies, Piacentini et al. (1992) briefly summarized the behavioral literature, noting that some researchers predict youngsters with OCD may be more responsive to behavior therapy than their adult counterparts with chronic symptoms and secondary disabilities. Despite early and encouraging successes in drug treatments with children and adolescents, alternative and complementary treatment approaches are important to identify, particularly given individual differences in response to medication and the high relapse rates associated with OCD. These researchers speculated that a multimodal approach, similar to current practice standards for the treatment of Attention Deficit Hyperactivity Disorder (ADHD), may emerge as the treatment of choice for pediatric OCD. Clearly, more controlled behavioral studies with larger sample sizes, between group components, and longer-term follow-up are needed.

The authors identified two evolving clinical research programs including behavioral treatments, one originating at Duke University (March, 1995; March et al., 1994) and one at Columbia University/New York State Psychiatric Institute (Graae, Gitow, Piacentini, Jaffer, & Liebowitz, 1992; Piacentini, Gitow, Jaffer, Graae, & Whitaker, 1994; Piacentini et al., 1992). Both groups published review papers and standardized treatment protocols that could help clinicians develop treatment plans. Other literature yielded several other interesting case studies and reports that relied primarily on ERP with varying components and procedures (Fisman & Walsh, 1994; Harris & Wiebe, 1992; Kearny & Silverman, 1990).

Piacentini et al. (1994) reported results for three of five children (ages 9 to 13) with moderate to severe *DSM-III-R* OCD who received therapist-supervised outpatient ERP adapted for youngsters from guidelines by Foa and Rowan (1990). These youngsters reported obsessions about contamination, fear of harm, fear of saying certain words, and of having one's clothes not fit "just right." Compulsions included washing rituals, avoiding contamination, elaborate praying rituals, substituting nonsense words for feared words, frequent safety checks, rearranging clothing, and stereotypical dressing, bathing, grooming, studying, arranging, and avoidance behaviors. Outcome measures included the Child Yale-Brown Obsessive Compulsive Scale (CY-BOCS; Goodman, Price, Rasmussen, Mazure, Delgado, et al., 1989; Goodman, Price, Rasmussen, Mazure, Fleischman et al., 1989), the NIMH Global OCD Scale (Insel et al., 1983), the Clinical Global Impression Scale (National Institute of Mental Health [NIMH], 1985), global improvement ratings, and Subjective Units of Discomfort Scale (SUDS) ratings.

Adaptations for youngsters included use of psychoeducational sessions with family, facilitating disengagement from the child's OCD behaviors, and helping to restructure the family system more adaptively. Treatment consisted of parallel assessment sessions for the child and family members (2 each) and 10 weekly 2-hour sessions, with the child receiving either in vivo or imaginal exposures. Youngsters were taught coping strategies such as cognitive self-statements and humorous visualizations to manage anxiety during ERP. Homework assignments consisted of 2 hours of ERP, with the therapist conducting home visits at weeks 5 and 10. Therapists used individualized contingency management and charts for recording target behaviors. From treatment onset, families were instructed to ignore OCD behaviors and to distinguish inappropriate OCD behaviors from normal child noncompliance and oppositionality. Preliminary results suggested marked improvements for moderately disturbed children with 60% to 78% symptom reductions overall. The authors noted potential for limited successes or longer treatment courses to facilitate a therapeutic alliance in markedly dysfunctional families. Incorporating rewards, visual performance feedback, and concurrent family sessions helped compliance and motivation in less severe cases.

March et al. (1994) reported preliminary results using a copyrighted self-help/treatment manual, "How I Ran OCD Off My Land." The manual was designed to improve compliance, exportability, and empirical evaluations of outpatient treatment in youngsters with OCD. Fifteen youngsters (ages 8–18) with *DSM-III-R* diagnoses of OCD participated. Symptoms included obsessions about contamination and fear of harm, and compulsions included washing and checking behaviors. Concurrent therapies including serotonin transport inhibitors (STIs), other medications, and other psychotherapies were allowed for the majority of the patients for at least part of the study. Outcome measures included the Yale-Brown Obsessive Compulsive Scale the NIMH Global Obsessive Compulsive Scale and the Clinical Global Impression Scale (citing versions from Leonard, Swedo et al., 1989).

Treatment consisted of 4 phases administered over 16 sessions. Week 1 consisted of psychoeducation, during which story metaphors were introduced so that the child would begin to "author" OCD out of his or her life. Week 2 consisted of "mapping" OCD and week 3 of teaching the concept of a "transition zone" at the lower end of the child's stimulus hierarchy. Weeks 4–15 consisted of cognitive behavioral therapy (anxiety management training and ERP). Session materials included reviews, goal-planning, educational information, ERP targets, practice, hand-outs, and monitoring procedures (informal symptom diaries, fear thermometer ratings for use during exposures, etc.). Parent sessions were recommended for weeks 1, 6, and 12. Week 16 consisted of a graduation ceremony and week 22 was a booster session.

The authors reported that 66% of their patients showed greater than 50% symptom reduction at follow-up, with 40% asymptomatic at post-treatment and 60% at follow-up. With booster sessions, 67% were able to discontinue medications with little or no return of symptoms. The mean number of behavioral therapy sessions was 10.4 over an average of 8 months, with an average of 7.3 months to follow-up. There were three nonresponders (20%) and two responders who dropped out early (13%), citing "enough improvement" or family concerns. The authors concluded that positive outcomes were not likely due to medication alone, citing average improvements of about 37% in clomipramine multicenter trials (DeVeaugh-Geiss et al., 1992). March et al. (1994) suggested that cognitive behavioral therapy, specifically ERP, is the psychotherapeutic treatment of choice, which likely has an independent or positive interaction effect. They suggested that in the absence of accessible behavioral therapists, their "how to" manual should ensure replication and exportability of treatments while improving compliance. However, it remains unclear whether the ERP was either independent or interactive with medication effects and whether such treatment can be safely and effectively administered by untrained individuals.

Two single-subject case studies may be of help to clinicians considering the use of therapist-directed versus staff-directed, self-directed, or family-assisted ERP procedures (Harris & Wiebe, 1992; Kearny & Silverman, 1990). Both studies limited parent participation to assessment or monitoring. Kearny and Silverman (1990) successfully treated a 14-year-old boy with severe OCD by alternating therapist-directed response prevention (RP) and cognitive therapy (CT) in a 12-week, 24-session course. Window and body checking were eliminated by week 5 and maintained at 6-month follow-up, with reductions in comorbid depression and anxiety. Harris and Wiebe (1992) treated a 15-year-old boy with previously treated, refractive, OC symptoms who received a 28-month course of inpatient and outpatient staff- and self-directed graded exposure, flooding, and RP. His symptoms at the onset of this study included obsessions about cancer, AIDS, and contamination, compulsive handwashing, (up to 40 times daily), refusal to touch others and their belongings, school refusal, becoming housebound, and unusual neck and head posturing. Improvements in handwashing (61%) were attributed to graded exposure and a combination of therapist-guided flooding and self-guided home exposures. Atypical neck and head posturing increased during treatment, but were not a focus of ERP.

Finally, Fisman and Walsh (1994) presented brief, less rigorous case histories of two preteens exhibiting AIDS-related OC symptoms after identifiable trigger events. Symptoms included contamination obsessions and compulsions including food inspection, avoidance of school washrooms and water, and involving family members in reassurance rituals. ERP appeared effective in both preteens over courses of 6 weeks or 1 year, although results may have been confounded by other concurrent and follow-up treatments. In one case, thought-stopping appeared to facilitate ERP.

Case Illustration Using ERP With an Adolescent

Meredith and Milby (1980) offer a case example of a successful course of ERP. Selected techniques from this research model could be modified for individual behavioral therapy with the child, such as including more conceptualization for parents and other family members, use of homework, and adjunctive in-home exposure and response prevention sessions, behavioral observation, and data gathering. In addition, some of the strategies for exposure using contaminants such as human feces, urine, and semen would likely need to be modified given changes in clinical procedures for handling these materials over the decade and a half since this model was first published.

The youngster was a 15-year-old male of above average intelligence enrolled in a suburban Catholic high school and working parttime as a busboy. He presented excessive handwashing and showering rituals related to a fear of contamination from feces, body fluids, and related materials. Rituals averaged 30 minutes for handwashing and 65 minutes for showering per day. He was also obsessed about punishment from God and prayed ritualistically to allay these fears. The ritualistic praying ceased spontaneously during the pretreatment assessment. Washing rituals began two years prior to treatment. No precipitating events were recalled.

At the time of treatment, the patient's fears and rituals began to interfere with scholastic performance, but not work functioning. Sexual development, family relationships, and peer relationships appeared normal. No previous psychiatric treatment had been attempted.

The behavioral assessment was completed in three and a half two-hour sessions. In addition to detailed interviewing, assessment included a daily log of the number, type, duration, and time at which ritual behavior occurred and the antecedent and consequent events associated with the rituals. It revealed that ritualized washing occurred when the patient was exposed to contamination from feces, body fluids, and other related items. A SUDS analysis of various types of contamination (Wolpe, 1973) revealed the hierarchy in Table 2.2.

During assessment, details of the treatment plan involving two weeks of exposure followed by two weeks of response prevention were agreed upon. In addition, the patient signed a consent form to participate in a clinical study that also described major aspects of treatment.

Contamination materials were provided by the patient at the start of treatment, each in a separate plastic container with lid. The first behavioral avoidance test, described later, was administered in the

TABLE 2.2. SUDS Analysis of Types of Contamination

SOURCE	SUDS
Human feces, other	100
Animal feces	95
Own feces	90
Human urine, other	85
Own urine	80
Pubic hair, other	75
Pubic hair, own	60
Bird droppings	55
Semen	50
Washing machine water	45
Rain-sewer water	40
Shoe-sole bottom	35
Vomit	30
Bellybutton lint	25
Bathroom doorknob	20
Dirty floor	15
Fingernail dirt	10

same session, but before exposure treatment began. In vivo exposure began using a moderate SUDS level contaminant, washing machine water (SUDS = 45). After initial review of progress and problems, the two-hour session was divided into 15-minute exposure segments. Every 15 minutes washing machine water was spread on the patient's hands and face. He was permitted to wash immediately after exposure, but chose not to. His SUDS levels were recorded every 10 minutes throughout the session. Between exposures, discussion of progress and problems would often continue. However, effort was made to direct conversation to topics that did not arouse anxiety and could serve a counterconditioning role. When the patient showed clear diminution of SUDS levels during exposure, semen was added to the washing machine water. When SUDS levels diminished, urine and bird droppings were added. Last, human feces were used. Homework exposure involved the same procedure and schedule of spreading contamination materials on his face and hands every 15 minutes for 2 consecutive hours, twice per day. Between exposures, he was encouraged to engage in his normal routine. Homework also involved self-monitoring and recording of washing activities and any avoidance behavior. Exposure sessions were scheduled 5 days per week for 2 weeks. Homework continued 7 days per week until the final weekend, when exposure homework was eliminated while self-monitoring continued.

Because this patient was treated as part of a research protocol, response prevention was administered in a second 2-week period. Aside from supervised response prevention (i.e., no bathing or washing for a week at a time), this plan of treatment was essentially the same as the first 2 weeks. During the last 5 days, therapist-supervised showers and handwashing were introduced. Showering was limited to 10 minutes and handwashing to 30 seconds, both without rituals. Therapist supervision was phased out over the last 3 days of treatment.

Two weekly follow-up sessions were scheduled to monitor progress, detect any rituals or other avoidance behavior, and work on a conflict situation between the patient and his mother. Additional follow-up sessions were scheduled at 1-, 2-, and 3-month intervals.

Handwashing and showering ritual behavior are illustrated in Figure 2.1. At the start of exposure, handwashing averaged 30 minutes and showering 65 minutes per day. Ritualized behavior tended to increase during exposure, an understandable and predictable result since the patient was exposed to contamination for as long as 6 hours per day. After

exposure, but before response prevention was introduced, ritual behavior reduced to baseline levels although it was still above what was considered normal limits. With the introduction of exposure plus response prevention, ritual behavior dropped to zero, remaining until supervised normal washing and showering was introduced during the second week of treatment.

Following exposure plus response prevention and up to 3 months follow-up, there was no ritualized behavior. The data shown in Figure 2.1 from follow-up represent normal time to wash hands (2 to 3 minutes per day) and to bath or shower (8 to 10 minutes per day).

Behavioral exposure test data are illustrated in Figure 2.2. In this test, the patient was asked to touch contamination materials, a combination of human feces and urine, using a glove and then starting with eight paper towels, progressing with fewer towels until he touched materials with his bare hand. With each progression, his SUDS levels for anxiety, contamination, and urge to wash were assessed. The first exposure test was given before treatment began.

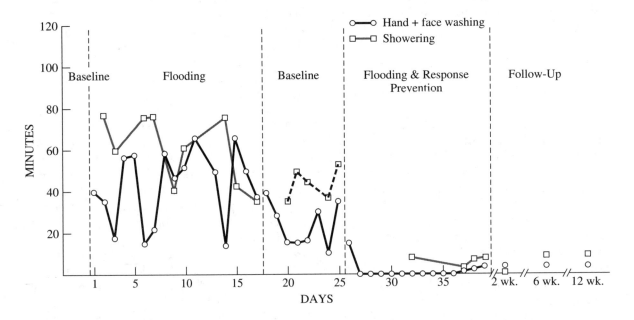

Figure 2.1. Daily washing time for a single subject treated by exposure only, followed by the combination of exposure and response prevention. From "Differential effects of exposure and response prevention in obsessive compulsive washers" by E. B. Foa, G. Steketee, and J. B. Milby, 1980. *Journal of Consulting and Clinical Psychology, 48,* 71–79. Copyright 1980 © by the American Psychological Association. Adapted with permission.

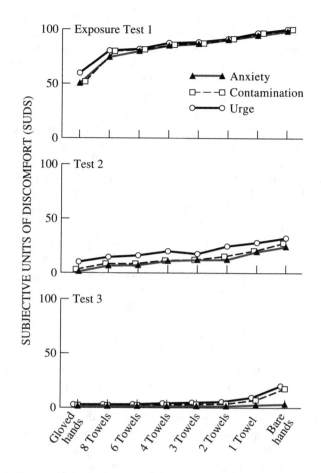

Figure 2.2. Subjective anxiety during the exposure test reported by a single subject treated by exposure only, followed by the comgination of exposure ad response prevention. From "Differential effects of exposure and response prevention in obsessive compulsive washers" by E. B. Foa, G. Steketee, and J. B. Milby, 1980. *Journal of Consulting and Clinical Psychology, 48,* 71–79. Copyright 1980 © by the American Psychological Association. Adapted with permission.

He did not touch the contamination materials with his bare hand, but completed the rest of the progression showing higher SUDS levels through the progression. Test 2 was conducted after flooding, but before the combination treatment was given. SUDS levels at this point were reduced significantly, but still above zero. In both tests 2 and 3, he touched contamination materials with his bare hand. In test 3, SUDS are near zero except when he touched materials using one towel and with his bare hand. These are interpreted as normal level reactions.

Drug Treatment Studies

Sources generally concurred that the serotonergic transport inhibitors (STIs) are currently the most potent, efficacious, and well-tolerated of drugs available for the treatment of OCD in adults. This class of drugs includes the serotonin-specific tricyclic antidepressant clomipramine (CMI; Anafranil), fluoxetine (Prozac), fluvoxamine (Luvox), sertraline (Zoloft), and paroxetine (Paxil), all of which share common antidepressant and serotonergic effects, but may differ structurally with individual differences in dose ranges, adverse effects, and clinical responses (Greist et al., 1995; Kaplan & Sadock, 1993; Kaplan & Sadock, 1996; Kaplan et al., 1994; Maxmen & Ward, 1995; Stanley & Turner, 1995). There are a variety of other drugs yielding limited or inconsistent results, including serotonergic drugs such as imipramine (Tofranil), trazodone (Desyrel), and clonazepam (Klonipin), and nonserotonergic drugs such as buspirone (BuSpar) and clonidine (Catapres) (Fogelson & Bystritsky, 1991; Hollander et al., 1992; Kaplan & Sadock, 1993; Kaplan & Sadock, 1996; Kaplan et al., 1994; Leonard et al., 1994; Pigott et al., 1992).

Several drug comparison studies using meta-analytic techniques have recently been published (Greist et al., 1995; Jenike, Baer, & Greist, 1990; Jenike, Hyman, et al., 1990; Pigott et al., 1992; Stanley & Turner, 1995). Effect sizes or ranges were reported for several drugs using the Y-BOCS as the primary outcome measure (from highest to lowest): CMI (1.42 to 1.50), fluoxetine (.69 to 1.34), buspirone (1.28), fluvoxamine (.50 to 1.09), sertraline (.35 to .80), placebo (.54), and trazodone (.37). These data suggest an inverse relationship between effect sizes and serotonin-specificity for a subset of the STIs, with CMI showing greater efficacy despite being classed as the least specific and potent of the STIs (Jenike, Baer & Greist, 1990; Jenike, Hyman, et al., 1990). Overall treatment dropout rates, as well as dropout rates due to adverse effects, appear to favor CMI in the adult literature (Greist et al., 1995). Greist et al. (1995) noted that significantly more subjects were identified as treatment responders to clomipramine (60%) than to fluoxetine (38%), fluvoxamine (43%), or sertraline (39%).

Drug Treatment Studies with Youngsters

Clomipramine (CMI)

The most convincing results on efficacy and tolerability of CMI were from the Ciba-Geigy multicenter trial. DeVeaugh-Geiss et al. (1992) reported results from five sites utilizing a 10-week, fully randomized, double-blind, parallel groups, placebo-controlled design. Subjects included 60 youngsters (ages 10 to 17 years) with *DSM-III-R* primary diagnoses of OCD. Exclusionary criteria included other major comorbid diagnoses and concurrent behavioral or drug treatments. Subjects received placebo treatment under single-blind conditions during the first 2 weeks to allow drug washout, then were randomized to either the CMI or placebo for the remaining 8 weeks of treatment. After completion of an 8-week double-blind phase, patients were eligible for a 1 year open-label CMI continuation trial. Maximum daily CMI doses ranged from 75 mg/day to 200 mg/day, depending on body weight. Outcome measures included the Yale-Brown Obsessive Compulsive Scale (Y-BOCS; Goodman, Price, Rasmussen, Mazure, Delgado, et al., 1989; Goodman, Price, Rasmussen, Mazure, Fleischman, et al., 1989) and the NIMH Global Obsessive Compulsive Scale (Insel et al., 1983).

Results did not differ by center. For the 8-week treatment, mean symptom reductions of 38% were observed for CMI versus 8% with placebo, with significant reductions observed as early as week 3. Ninety percent of subjects completed 8 weeks of CMI or placebo, 87% agreed to participate in the 1-year open-label extension, and 53% completed the full year. Discontinuation rates due to adverse reactions were 13% and 8%, respectively. The study demonstrated CMI's superiority over placebo and the safety and efficacy of the drug for up to a year. The authors observed that CMI appeared to have antiobsessional properties independent of its antidepressant effects. A subsequent study of physiological responses to CMI in 15 youngsters (Hanna, McCracken, & Cantwell, 1991) reported significant increases in basal prolactin levels following 8-week open and controlled CMI trials. Changes also appeared to be related to previous tic history and the duration and severity of OCD over time, although small group sizes and lack of statistical power compromise these findings.

There are multiple NIMH studies typically consisting of small samples of youngsters with severe, recalcitrant OCD, many of whom had previous trials of CMI or another STI, and some participated in more than one study. Early short-term, double-blind, placebo-controlled, and crossover trials demonstrated CMI's efficacy over placebo and desipramine (Flament et al., 1985; Leonard et al., 1991; Leonard, Swedo, et al., 1989). The first two yielded mean treatment response rates of 26% to 35% over 5- and 10-week courses for CMI doses ranging from 50 to 250 mg/day. Leonard, Swedo, et al. (1989) also demonstrated high relapse rates for both OCD and depression symptoms upon substitution of desipramine for CMI, with 36% of the sample "surviving" and 64% relapsing at the 5-week crossover. Leonard et al. (1991) found that 11% of their sample survived a 3-month crossover to desipramine, while 82% of the CMI patients continued on CMI, survived without relapse in an 8-month, double-blind, desipramine substitution and CMI discontinuation study.

Two 2–7-year prospective follow-up studies have been reported in recent literature (Flament et al., 1990; Leonard et al., 1993). In the former, 68% of patients were still diagnosed as OCD and the number of comorbid diagnoses had increased at final follow-up. Leonard et al. (1993) further reported that although 80% of their sample had improved from baseline, significant impairments were still evident at follow-up with 70% of the patients on psychoactive medications, 37% still on CMI, and 91% qualifying for OCD and comorbid diagnoses. An average of two interim courses of psychotherapy were reported, with 19% also reporting interim hospitalizations. Significant outcome predictors were identified: severity at week 5 after initial treatment response, parental psychopathology, and comorbid tic disorders.

A recent NIMH study focused on physiological findings associated with behavioral outcomes. Altemus et al. (1994) found monoamine metabolite and neuropeptide changes associated with treatment gains over a 19-month CMI trial in 17 youngsters. However, results were compromised by very small sample sizes, use of extrapolation, and significant findings that did not hold over multiple comparisons. If replicated with larger samples, this work may have implications for understanding the neurophysiological substrates of CMI treatment response.

Fluoxetine

Two programs of research on fluoxetine were identified that led to two controlled studies that were discontinued prematurely for various reasons as discussed below, one at Yale University (Riddle et al., 1992) and one at the University of Rochester (Kurlan, Como, Deeley, McDermott, & McDermott, 1993). There were several other supporting studies and independent open trials at other sites. At Yale, researchers attempted a 20-week randomized, placebo-controlled study of 20 mg/day fixed dose fluoxetine in 14 youngsters (ages 8 to 15) with DSM-III-R diagnoses of moderately severe OCD and selected comorbid diagnoses (Riddle et al., 1992). Unlike many CMI studies, subjects were naive to psychiatric drug use, and concurrent medications and behavioral therapies were not provided.

During the first 8-week phase, 30% to 45% symptom reductions were reported and overall functioning improved significantly on fluoxetine (21%) but not placebo (14%). Discontinuation was attributed to a high dropout rate (57%) due to noncompliance and relapses upon crossover to fluoxetine (after initially high placebo response rates). A high rate of generally well-tolerated side effects was reported, including motoric activation, insomnia, fatigue, nausea, and exacerbations of pre-existing chronic motor tic severity in two subjects. Suicidal ideation in one subject reportedly resolved upon discontinuation. Although the trial was discontinued prematurely after consultation with other colleagues about variations in dosage nationally, Riddle et al. (1992) concluded that fluoxetine appeared generally safe and effective for short-term treatment.

Earlier at Yale, Riddle, Hardin, King, Scahill, and Woolston (1990) had discontinued a 20-week open trial of 20 mg/day fluoxetine in 10 youngsters (ages 8 to 15) with *DSM-III-R* diagnoses of either OCD or Tourette's Disorder. A 60% dropout rate in that study was attributed to completed inpatient hospitalization and lack of efficacy rather than to side effects, with about 50% of the subjects classed as treatment responders. Additionally, King et al. (1991) reviewed case histories of 6 of 42 youngsters who developed self-destructive and suicidal behaviors during 20 to 60 mg/day fluoxetine trials, concluding that suicidality could be coincidental and secondary to high psychiatric risk, or might reflect drug-induced disorganization in high-risk children.

At Rochester, lower dropout rates (18% to 19%) were reported and attributed to noncompliance, lack of benefits, and adverse effects. Kurlan et al. (1993) failed to confirm the efficacy of fluoxetine in an attempt to pilot a four month double-blind, randomized, placebo-controlled trial of 20 to 40 mg/day fluoxetine in children with Tourette's Disorder and mild OC symptoms. Como & Kurlan (1991) suggested the drug was safe and efficacious in 13 children (ages 6 to 17) with Tourette's Disorder and moderately severe OC symptoms over open trial courses of 20 to 40 mg/day. Similar mild side effects were reported, and in this case the overall dropout rate (19%) was attributed to lack of benefits in 4 of 6 youngsters and to adverse effects, including skin rash and impotence, in 2 of 6 youngsters.

Other researchers have also reported results of successful open trials of 20 mg/day to 80 mg/day fluoxetine over 10-day to 2-year courses that should be considered in developing clinical protocols for youngsters with primary OCD (Bouvard & Dugas, 1993; Geller, Biederman, Reed, Spencer, & Wilens, 1995; Liebowitz, Hollander, Fairbanks, & Campeas, 1990) and those with autism or mental retardation associated with OC symptoms (Cook, Rowlett, Jaselskis, & Leventhal, 1992). The Geller et al. (1995) study reported a 74% overall response rate and a 47% improvement from baseline for 38 youngsters with OCD who received open trials with average doses of 50 mg/day fluoxetine over an average 19-month course. This study is particularly important in highlighting the utility of calculating weight-corrected doses and the overall rates of side effects. About 39% of these youngsters reported no side effects and in others, mild side effects appeared well-tolerated with higher incidences of behavioral activation and dyscontrol among 8 children who received lower average doses.

Fluvoxamine

No controlled studies of fluvoxamine were identified although the side-effect profiles of two recent open-trial studies may be of interest to clinicians (Apter et al., 1994; Fennig, Fennig, Pato, & Weitzman, 1994). Apter et al. (1994) reported an 8-week, 100 to 300 mg/day open-label trial of fluvoxamine in 20 adolescents (ages 13 to 18) with *DSM-III-R* OCD or depression, some with comorbid disruptive behavior disorders, Tourette's Disorder, or eating disorders. Side effects were systematically recorded using the Dosage Record Treatment Emergent Symptom Scale (DOTES; Campbell & Palij, 1985). Subjects with comorbid anorexia or borderline personality showed the poorest OCD symptom reduction. Eight subjects (40%) reported transient or dose-related major side effects including dermatitis, excitement, hyperactivity, anxiety, insomnia, and/or nausea, and 4 (20%) discontinued the trial after developing serious but reversible dermatitis, confusion and delirium, hallucinations, or hypomania. The authors concluded that fluvoxamine may be safe and useful in some adolescents who are unlikely to benefit from standard drug protocols. Fluvoxamine was also used to augment loxapine in a 14-year-old boy with a *DSM-III-R* diagnosis of OCD (Fennig et al., 1994). These studies demonstrate a need for closely monitoring fluvoxamine use in youngsters until more is understood about its side effects and interactions with other drugs.

Other Drugs

The literature did not yield any controlled studies of sertraline or paroxetine in children and adolescents with OCD. Two successful open trials using buspirone and clonazepam were identified, but none for imipramine, trazodone, or clonidine (Alessi & Bos, 1991; Leonard et al., 1994). OCD and depressive symptoms in an 11-year-old girl improved markedly following fluoxetine augmented with 30 mg/day buspirone after unsuccessful trials of imipramine and fluoxetine augmented by trazodone (Alessi & Bos, 1991). More recently, fluoxetine was augmented with 6 mg/day clonazepam in a 20-year-old male with severe, recalcitrant OCD (Leonard et al., 1994). After an 11-month drug holiday and 10 months of fluoxetine and buspirone without further relief, buspirone was replaced by clonazepam with improvements maintained for at least 1 year. Further research is needed on the safety and efficacy of these drugs and combinations.

Meta-analyses and Challenge Studies with Youngsters

No meta-analyses or drug challenge studies specific to the pediatric population were identified in our review of the literature. However, some adolescent participants in multicenter fluoxetine trials were included in calculating effect size in one meta-analytic study (Greist et al., 1995) and one boy exhibiting emergent Tourette's-like side effects upon fluvoxamine augmentation was deliberately rechallenged with higher doses that elicited similar atypical side effects (Fennig et al., 1994).

Clinical Guidelines for Drug Treatments with Youngsters

Green (1991) offered an informative chapter on the general principles of child and adolescent clinical psychopharmacology addressing issues such as maturational factors, developing a treatment plan, compliance, premedication work-ups, laboratory and diagnostic procedures, generic versus trade preparations, drug holidays, and so forth. Interested clinicians are referred to this chapter for further details.

Kaplan and Sadock (1996) recommended that clinicians utilize "five Ds" to optimize drug therapy: diagnosis, drug selection, dose, duration, and dialogue (pp. 275–276). They noted that a careful diagnosis, the past history of drug response, and overall medical status should be considered in developing an individualized drug treatment protocol. In drugs with similar efficacy, side-effect profiles, tolerability, and lethality should be considered. Nonsedative drugs and those with less abuse potential are preferred. Once drug therapy is initiated, the clinician should attempt to achieve therapeutic dose levels. Underdosing and inadequate trials are the most common causes of treatment failure. When possible, clinical trials should continue at least 4 to 6 weeks since therapeutic response is often delayed. It is preferable to discuss potential side effects with children and caretakers, clearly differentiating expected and rare adverse effects. Information to children should be at a developmentally appropriate level. Children and caretakers need assurance child patients will not become addicted. In children, doses typically begin small and are increased until clinical effects are observed, although adult doses may be used if effective and well-tolerated. Because knowledge about drugs changes rapidly, those responsible for treatment should consult package inserts for updated information.

Some tricyclics such as CMI function differently in youngsters than adults (Kaplan & Sadock, 1993; Kaplan & Sadock, 1996). Youngsters typically have faster metabolism than adults and may reach higher and faster peak levels and lower and earlier trough levels. More frequent doses may improve therapeutic stability. CMI has been approved by the FDA for treatment of OCD in youngsters at least 10 years old (Green, 1991). It is generally started in children at 50 mg/day and can be titrated upwards by not more than 3 mg/kg/day to 200 mg/day (Kaplan & Sadock, 1996). Typical tricyclic side effects include dry mouth, constipation, tachycardia, drowsiness, postural hypotension, hypertension, and mania. In youngsters, electrocardiogram (ECG) monitoring is recommended because of risk for cardiac conduction slowing, and a baseline electroencephalogram (EEG) is advised since CMI can lower seizure thresholds. Blood levels may also be useful clinical feedback (Kaplan & Sadock, 1996). Emergent side effects can be measured systematically using the DOTES (Campbell & Palij, 1985) or some similar organized charting.

Fluoxetine, fluvoxamine, and sertraline should be started at lower than adult recommended doses (Kaplan & Sadock, 1996). Adult doses for OCD are often higher than for depression, at 20–120 mg/day fluoxetine, 200–300 mg/day fluvoxamine, 100–200 mg/day sertraline, and 20–50 mg/day paroxetine (Maxmen & Ward, 1995). Side effects include nausea, headache, nervousness, insomnia, dry mouth, diarrhea, and drowsiness (Kaplan & Sadock, 1996). The most common side effects of each include mild agitation with fluoxetine, a higher rate of nausea in fluvoxamine, fewer side effects in sertraline, and slightly higher somnolence in paroxetine.

Candidates for drug augmentation may include treatment-resistant patients, those not tolerating certain compounds, patients with known comorbid diagnoses, and some with obsessive compulsive spectrum disorders. Individualized protocols for augmentation are beyond the scope of this chapter but those interested can find discussions in Green (1991) and Kaplan and Saddock (1996).

Summary of Pediatric Drug Treatment Studies

It appears that CMI and fluoxetine continue to demonstrate greater utility than other STIs in treating pediatric OCD. However, the data on fluoxetine's efficacy are not as convincing as those on CMI given small sample sizes, high dropout rates, and discontinued controlled studies. Further research including maintenance and discontinuation studies, meta-analyses, challenge studies, and controlled multicenter studies, including less severe and drug-naive youngsters, appear warranted before the relative efficacy and tolerability of the two can be adequately compared. CMI continues to be the most widely used of the STIs, with side-effect profiles generally mild and consistent with those of the tricyclic antidepressants. Fluoxetine appears to have potential for lower side effects and for demonstrating more null side-effect profiles among adult treatment responders, but more controlled studies are needed in youngsters to draw similar conclusions for them. Variations in dose ranges and length of treatment courses for fluoxetine need further exploration, whether used alone, with an augmenting agent, or with other psychotherapies.

Drugs and Behavior Therapy: Comparisons and Combined Approaches

Several researchers have suggested that in addition to meta-analyses, direct comparisons of behavior therapy and drug treatments are needed, as well as study designs that combine or partial out these treatments (Apter et al., 1994; Geller et al., 1995; Jenike, Baer, & Greist, 1990; Leonard & Rapoport, 1989; Leonard et al., 1991; Leonard et al., 1993; March et al., 1994; Milby & Weber, 1991; Piacentini et al.,

1992; Stanley & Turner, 1995). These recommendations seem appropriate for researchers in both the adult and pediatric arenas. Most of the pediatric studies reviewed for this chapter allowed concurrent drug or behavioral therapies without controlling for the effects of either.

Effect Size

In the relative absence of comparison studies to date, pediatric researchers could utilize meta-analytic techniques to discern promising future research directions. Within adult meta-analyses, use of an effect size statistic allowed for comparisons across diverse studies and measures, although not without criticism of the methodology (Rosenthal, 1991). Effect size statistics can be used along with a variety of other indicators such as drop-out rates, side-effect profiles, and so forth, to provide additional information for clinicians assessing individual differences in treatment responses across a variety of treatment modalities.

Summary and Future Directions

Together, Meredith and Milby's (1980) ERP case example and the general clinical guidelines for drug treatments (Green, 1991; Kaplan & Sadock, 1996; Maxmen & Ward, 1995) have utility for developing a multimodal treatment model from which clinicians could formulate and apply idiographic behavioral assessments of the child, the family system, and the family environment. This would facilitate multimodal but problem-oriented, goal-directed interventions in treatment applications and outcome research. A comprehensive model would retain the capacity to expand or contract to accommodate individual ERP treatment alone or in conjunction with family-oriented behavioral treatments, drug treatments, and other supportive interventions, also accommodating treatment strategies from clinicians with differing etiological perspectives.

Reviewed studies suggest that the efficacy of CMI, fluoxetine, and ERP are now well-established and supported within the adult literature. CMI continues to demonstrate an edge for efficacy while fluoxetine has achieved similar efficacy in some studies but appears to have better tolerability and the potential for a higher rate of null side-effect profiles. Within the child literature, CMI has been convincingly demonstrated as efficacious for up to a year in youngsters with moderately severe to severe OCD that appears to take a chronic, fluctuating course even among CMI treatment responders followed for up to 7 years. Research on fluoxetine in youngsters is less convincing than in adults or in CMI use in children. In the pediatric literature, we identified proportionately more fluoxetine studies than those for CMI, other STIs, and other drugs. However, controlled studies have been prematurely terminated for various reasons and there are a lack of multicenter data on fluoxetine.

Behavioral and drug therapy researchers appear to support the efficacy and utility of ERP, some touting it as the overall treatment of choice, some as the psychotherapeutic treatment of choice, and most speculating that combination treatment packages offering STIs (especially CMI or fluoxetine) with adjunctive behavior therapy may prove to be the treatment(s) of choice for adult and pediatric OCD. Some pediatric researchers appear poised to attempt standardized applications of ERP within the context of multimodal treatment packages, to contribute to treatment outcome research. Further research using comprehensive behavioral treatment strategies and research methodologies to facilitate multimodal treatment outcome studies is clearly needed. Gaps in current treatment outcome knowledge could be addressed in future combined and comparison studies of behavioral and drug treatments.

Costs and Benefits of Treatment

In the literature review, the authors found no cost effectiveness or cost benefit analysis studies. Therefore, comments are based on clinical experience and judgement and on our knowledge of the treatment outcome and follow-up literature. In the consideration of cost and benefits for treatment of OCD, one can identify two kinds of costs to be weighed against each other: (a) costs to the child and his or her family, and (b) costs to society. Both these costs can be considered when treatment is provided versus when not provided. Costs to the child, family, and society when treatment is not provided are in the domain of consequences suffered. Costs of treatment can be conceptualized along a continuum from least to most expensive, ranging from less expensive outpatient school interventions and counseling, to infrequent to frequent individual behavioral therapy with family interventions, to more expensive intense inpatient psychiatric and psychological interventions with extended follow-up.

When OCD in a child is mild, family distress and disruption are more tolerable. Up to the last decade, most cases of OCD in children were not recognized as a treatable condition and were not treated. Thus, children probably suffered some impairment in social development, school performance, and family adjustment and consequent mild to moderate impairments in adult functioning. Some of these types of costs, health policy analysts now are estimating and ascribing monetary values to, but certainly, if calculated, costs of no treatment would be many times less than costs of treatment in the case of moderate to severe OCD. Since mild OCD can be treated on an outpatient basis with several types or combinations of effective treatment reviewed earlier, the benefits of treatment can be weighed against the costs of 15–20 outpatient sessions for assessment, family conferences, ERP, and follow-up along with a course of pharmacotherapy coordinated by an additional practitioner. Costs would differ depending on the area of the country, practitioners, and number of interventions involved, but would be in the range of $1,500–$2,300 including costs of medication for four months (costs assume professional fees at $100/hr. and medication costs at $75/mo.). Assuming typical successful treatment response of 50–60% for mild OCD with such treatments, would the probability of benefit be worth the cost to the family and to society? Most people would answer yes.

With more severe OCD, the costs of no treatment to the child, the family, and to society, and costs of more expensive, intense treatments, all rise together against the likelihood that a fully successful treatment response will not be as great and the expectation that more frequent, intensive, follow-up and recurring treatment will be needed for the foreseeable future. Costs of a 3-week hospitalization for intensive multimodal assessment, behavioral, family, and pharmacotherapy intervention followed by a year-long, once-per-week follow-up and continuing medication would cost at least $22,000 (assuming costs as above plus $750/day for hospitalization). These costs are in the range of 10 times that for mild OCD. Are they worth it? Though the risks of treatment failure are greater, perhaps as high as 50%, the potential benefits from avoided costs of future treatment and costs to society from having to partially cover costs with public support and services are also greater. Perhaps fewer, but still most people would probably answer yes, expected benefits are worth the increased cost.

ASSESSMENT ISSUES

Behavioral assessment with OCD children and adolescents should address four basic goals. The first is to provide a detailed definition of problem behaviors. This is accomplished through a focused clinical interview with the child and family. An attempt should be made to develop a comprehensive list of behaviors perceived by the child and family as problematic. The result should be a detailed description of functioning in the cognitive, motoric, and affective modalities that addresses the specific nature of the obsessions and/or ritualized behavior. Attention should be given to the interpersonal and perceptual dimensions. It is also useful to examine the role of imagery (particularly with reference to fantasies about dire consequences or catastrophic outcomes) and to develop a clear understanding about the general level of arousal, the presence of a major affective component (e.g., depression), or acute panic attacks.

The authors clinical experience and knowledge of the literature suggest that the primary types of obsessive compulsive disorder requiring specific examination include the following: (a) *Compulsive rituals* that often assume the form of washing, checking, or other forms of repetitive motoric behavior; (b) *Cognitive compulsions* consisting of words, phrases, prayers, sequence of numbers, or other forms of counting, and so forth.; (c) *Primary obsessional slowness* in which simple tasks of living require excessive time to complete; and, (d) *Obsessive doubting* and other anxiety-elevating

obsessions in which specific cognitive patterns (e.g., questioning the adequacy of specific behaviors) increase distress or discomfort.

Compulsive rituals and cognitive compulsions typically are anxiety-reducing in that their performance decreases aversive levels of arousal. Doubting, in contrast, is anxiety-elevating and seems to be more clearly a cognitive component of a general anxiety response to specific stimuli. Primary obsessional slowness may be anxiety-decreasing in a general sense as the various types of behaviors involved serve to avoid confrontation of more threatening stimuli. For example, excessively slow dressing and preparation for school may delay or even allow the child to avoid school completely. The positive reinforcers should be identified that support primary obsessional slowness (e.g., parental attention, satisfaction with personal appearance, etc.)

Assessment should also focus on a number of other dimensions of functioning. In the interpersonal modality, it is important to examine basic communication skills, assertion skills, heterosocial skills, and interpersonal emotional responsivity. Frequently, children and adolescents with OCD have major difficulty with basic interpersonal transactions. Their speech and interpersonal posture may be pedantic, stilted, intellectualized, and self-preoccupied. Expression of feeling may be constricted to discussion of dysphoria or distress associated with their particular problematic behavior. The direct expression of anger and even more positive and intimate patterns of communication may not be a comfortable part of their interpersonal repertoire. Once problem behaviors have been specified across modalities, it is then desirable to determine both antecedent and consequent events that elicit or maintain the problematic behavior.

Subjective scaling of fears using the Subjective Units of Discomfort Scale (SUDS) is useful (Wolpe, 1973). This scale simply asks the child to rate anxiety-producing stimuli (distress) on a continuum from 0 (absolute calm) to 100 (absolute panic). Careful specification of antecedent events using this scale is an effective way to identify problem patterns and to develop hierarchies for use later in treatment. By carefully identifying antecedent events, it is also possible to develop a clear understanding of the relationship between obsessive compulsive behaviors and the role they play with respect to either eliciting or reducing discomfort. It is extremely important to examine other potential sources of reinforcement in addition to anxiety reduction that influence the obsessive compulsive behavior. The interpersonal response to others is especially important. Obsessive Compulsive behaviors can exert tremendous control over family members and significant others. They may promote interpersonal reinforcement by eliciting caring, sympathetic, and supportive responses from others and serve as a means to express anger or hostility passively (i.e., obsessive compulsive behavior occasionally may be analogous to passive-resistive behavior).

The assessment of the problem behaviors and examination of antecedent and consequent events is time-consuming and should not be equated with the typical clinic intake evaluation of one hour. For the first session, a focus on collecting relevant history is recommended to obtain an overview of the problem, early development, relationships with immediate and extended family, educational history, sexual development, moral-religious development, and medical history. This more general intake evaluation is important to avoid omission of significant information, (e.g., academic deficiencies, recent psychosocial stressors, medical problems, etc.), which might be of value in the overall treatment plan. The next several hours in the evaluative sequence would then address examination of family functioning and completing a behavioral assessment.

The second goal of assessment is to devise behavioral objectives in concert with the child and family and to detail an intervention plan. The objectives may address specific types of changes required of the family and significant others in addition to changes in obsessive compulsive behaviors. It is essential that treatment objectives be discussed with the child and family, as their expectations will directly influence the course and approach to treatment.

The third goal of assessment is to establish ongoing objective evaluation of treatment. Ongoing assessment follows directly from treatment objectives and implies detailing methods to assess relative attainment of treatment objectives. These measures may range from family ratings of success

with homework assignments to recording frequencies of obsessive compulsive behaviors.

The last goal of a detailed assessment involves increasing expectations/motivation for change by the child and family members. As the child and family begin to articulate problems and controlling variables, they develop understanding of the disorder. They see the development of a specific plan and begin to experience positive effects resulting from collaborating with the therapist. Motivation is enhanced and trust in the therapeutic alliance develops.

ASSESSMENT INSTRUMENTS

Since the first edition of this chapter, several additional assessment instruments have been made available for children: Leyton Obsessional Inventory-Child Version, Survey Form (Berg, Whitaker, Davies, Flament, & Rapoport, 1988; Berg, Rappoport, & Flament, 1986); Obsessive Compulsive Rating Scale (Rapoport, Elkins, & Mikkelson, 1986); Comprehensive Psychopathological Rating Scale (Thoren, Asberg, & Cronholm, 1980); and the NIMH Self-rating Scale (Post, Korin, & Goodwin, 1983). Each of these are purported to provide workable and valid assessments for children (Wolff & Rapoport, 1988). In addition, The Yale-Brown Obsessive Compulsive Scale (Y-BOCS) has been widely used in adult clinical trials (Goodman, Price, Rasmussen, Mazure, Delgado, et al., 1989; Goodman, Price, Rasmussen, Mazure, Fleischmann, et al., 1989). It has a core section 10-item scale, with each item rated on a four-point scale for 0 (no symptoms) to 4 (extreme symptoms). The scale also has a children's version, the abbreviated CY-BOCS, which simplifies technical terms and provides definitions of obsessions and compulsions which are easy to understand. It has been used as an outcome measure in several multicenter drug trials for OCD.

The Padua Inventory (PI) is a self-report inventory facilitating accurate quantification of OCD symptoms and distinguishes obsessional from compulsive dimensions (Sanavio, 1988). It contains items that measure intrusive thoughts, doubts, checking and cleaning behaviors as well as urges perceived as senseless or unacceptable, repetitive thinking of improbable dangers, and recurrent repugnant images. The scale was highly correlated (0.70) with the Maudsley Obsessive Compulsive Inventory (.070) (MOCI; Hodgson & Rachman, 1977) and the Leyton Obsessional Inventory (0.71) (Cooper, 1970) and is reported to have satisfactory test-retest reliability in a student sample with a 30-day interval and to have satisfactory internal consistency (Van Oppen, 1992).

The Indecisiveness Scale has been developed by Frost and Shows (1993) as a measure of indecisiveness associated with general psychopathology and OCD characteristics of perfectionism and compulsive hoarding. Their three studies provide evidence for its reliability and validity.

Thomsen and Jensen (1991) used a dimensional approach to assessing OCD in childhood and adolescence. They contend that the scale is capable of measuring OC symptomatology along a continuum because the items constitute a one-dimensional latent structure of OCD. While this scale may be useful as a brief screening instrument, it is unlikely to provide the detailed information needed to plan behavioral treatments. To date it has not been used as an outcome measure to assess the results of treatment.

Space does not permit a detailed review of the psychometric properties of these assessment instruments. It is recommended, however, that readers evaluate each measure's reliability and validity before adopting them for clinical use.

INDIVIDUAL BEHAVIORAL INTERVENTION

Behavioral intervention may assume several different forms depending on the results of the behavioral analysis. Many times the behavioral intervention would be only one part of the overall treatment. Application of behavioral programs in the family can be conducted in the context of family-interpersonal strategies. However, the focus of this section will be on the review and illustration of promising behavioral techniques. Most often, such techniques would be used concurrently with strategies designed to deal with the interpersonal context of OCD.

Exposure Treatment

The review of a moderately severe case (Meredith & Milby, 1980) of OCD treated by exposure and response prevention, described earlier, illustrates these techniques. Although this case illustrates these techniques, it does not represent as well the multimodal approach that is often required in the clinical setting. Successful treatment was conducted without the necessity of a more comprehensive treatment package. Although occasionally this is the case, readers should not assume that these procedures used alone will be sufficient to produce efficacious treatment.

Other Behavioral Procedures

A number of additional treatment approaches may be useful in particular situations, but they may lack the solid research foundation of ERP. Cognitive-behavioral therapy has been utilized with what appears to be reasonable success with older children and adolescents to alter irrational beliefs and attitudes about specific obsessive compulsive behaviors. The practitioner attempts to provide accurate information and empirically anchored interpretations of symptoms to alter both beliefs and affect of OCD manifestations.

Treatment for anxiety-decreasing cognitive compulsions should generally assume the same basic format as with compulsive rituals. Exposure, by necessity, involves the use of covert techniques. Anxiety-eliciting cognitions are identified and presented via exposure in imagery, using similar hierarchies as those discussed for compulsive rituals. Repeated exposure to the cognitions is demanded until anxiety diminishes. One shortcoming of this approach is the lack of control over the performance of the cognitive compulsions as a means of avoiding the anxiety associated with distressing cognitions (hierarchy items). More appropriate self-statements, verbalized during exposure, can be substituted. For example, with a child who is frightened by sexual thoughts and who exhibits repetitive covert praying to allay anxiety, more positive thoughts about sexuality can be introduced (e.g., "feeling anxious about sex is okay for right now," and "this will be less of a problem as I feel more comfortable talking with girls/boys"). Although no data on efficacy presently exist, homework assignments involving adaptive overt verbal behavior (discussions with family and friends) may be useful to promote these more positive cognitive patterns.

Treatment of anxiety-elevating obsessions is less well-developed and has not received much research attention. At this point, no specific treatments of choice exist. The treatments described in the literature include prolonged exposure (negative practice), thought stopping, faradic disruption, and cognitive flooding. With children, procedures that minimize aversive stimulation seem more desirable. It is possible that systematic desensitization or variations of this technique (e.g., anxiety management training) may prove to be useful. No studies used cognitively oriented behavioral approaches. These may be useful when combined with treatments that also reduce the affective response to the anxiety-elevating cognitive pattern.

Thought-stopping was used by Campbell (1973) in successful treatment of a 12-year-old boy with obsessions of the violent death of his sister, which he witnessed 9 months prior to treatment. The youngster described, in detail, how he had watched his sister become entangled in a machine used to grind grain. Behavioral analysis revealed that he averaged 15 daily rumination periods and that these periods lasted approximately 20 minutes each. Treatment involved training the child "to evoke a negative thought and then to stop the thought pattern by loudly counting backwards from 10 to 0 as rapidly as possible." Following his counting, he was instructed to switch his thoughts to one of a number of pleasant scenes previously identified. Following mastery of this procedure, he was instructed to repeat the methodology utilizing the subvocal counting verbalization. Practice occurred in the therapy session, outside of therapy, whenever anxiety-arousing obsessions occurred, and prior to retiring each evening. Three-year follow-up with the mother suggested a good response to this intervention. At the time this treatment was provided, there was not a *DSM* diagnosis for Post Traumatic Stress Disorder (PTSD). If a similar case were presented today, comorbid symptoms of PTSD and the OCD should both be addressed.

Cognitive flooding (Milby et al., 1981) may be useful with anxiety-elevating obsessions. In the treatment of an obsessive adult, repeated videotaped exposure to anxiety-arousing stimuli produced a relatively quick and rapid response. Procedurally, the technique involves videotaping the child's own description of anxiety-producing obsessions with discussion of associated catastrophic events. These monologues are then edited so separate tapes repeat a particular theme every few seconds for the duration of a one-hour tape. Training involves sitting with the child and helping the youngster focus attention on a television screen in which he or she repeatedly discusses a particular obsessive theme. In the case of obsessive concerns of harm befalling a family member, the child's description of his thoughts would be videotaped, edited, and played back to him. The child would then be encouraged to listen and watch himself repeat the same performance 30 to 40 times within the therapy hour. The prolonged exposure seems to produce extinction or habituation of the emotional component of the obsessive thought. This technique may be useful with youngsters experiencing anxiety-elevating obsessional thinking, however, more research is clearly needed. For some children, depending on their cognitive abilities, this technique could be easily combined with others designed to promote more adaptive cognitive patterns.

A final treatment consideration involves intervention with primary obsessional slowness. This pattern is not well researched, but is commonly observed in the clinical situation. The only treatment approach identified was a combination of prompting, shaping, and pacing of responses suggested by Rachman and Hodgson (1980). Based on such a model, after providing instructions and modeling, the therapist prompts quicker behavior while the child carries out the task. Shaping, instructions, and verbal reinforcement are used to encourage a faster pace and to discourage persistent slowness. External pacing by timing devices is used.

OTHER TREATMENT CONSIDERATIONS

Other Presenting Problems

Other presenting problems besides OCD may need to be addressed. Of particular importance are approaches to develop more effective general interpersonal and heterosocial skills. A focus on increasing "emotional freedom" through assertive training is also often a necessary component. Cognitively-oriented strategies that deal with perfectionistic striving and problem-solving skills may also have application with OCD youngsters. These techniques and approaches are beyond the scope of this discussion but should not be omitted in a comprehensive treatment plan. Successful and lasting treatment in most cases will demand a working knowledge of these approaches.

The most important tasks for the clinician in completing the assessment after establishing a differential diagnosis of OCD is to diagnose associated disorders, especially those that may impact treatment planning and outcome. For example, depression and other anxiety disorders, especially phobias commonly co-occur with OCD in children. In adults, having a lifetime diagnosis of OCD is associated with increased likelihood of depression, alcohol and drug abuse, phobias and antisocial personality disorder (Kolada, Bland, & Newman, 1994).

The child practitioner's best assessment tool is still the sensitive clinical interview, perhaps aided by an outline or standardized format. However, several OCD assessment instruments are excellent for three purposes: (a) to screen for OCD symptoms that a diagnostic interview can confirm and elaborate (b) to provide details of OCD symptomatology that can be confirmed by interview and observational methods and used to evaluate the ongoing effectiveness and outcome of treatment and (c) to evaluate treatment outcome. Goodman and Price (1992) provide a brief review of several of these assessment tools.

The authors' preference and recommendation is to use the Y-BOCS for adolescents or the CY-BOCS for children after establishing the differential diagnosis by clinical interview and other psychometric measures. This could include instruments such as the Child Depression Inventory (Kovacs, 1985; Kovacs & Beck, 1977), which might facilitate further assessment of other disorders. A brief assessment of intellectual ability and educational functional level is helpful in selecting further assessment instruments and in determining appropriate levels of explanation and instruction for the client.

Along with the CY-BOCS or Y-BOCS the authors recommend use of target behavior logs that include 10-point or 100-point Subjective Units of Discomfort Scales (SUDS) to record frequency of ritualized behaviors, the strength of obsessional thoughts or beliefs, and the level of emotional discomfort associated with these events before and after ritualized behavior occurs. In most cases, the older child or adolescent can keep these logs themselves. Logs can be designed to capture most OCD activity or merely to sample it depending on the degree of cooperation and motivation of the child. For very young children, some with cognitive delays, and some with oppositionality, parents may have to assist in keeping such logs. A sampling method may be the best approach to use when the child is not under constant observation. Where the child or adolescent is being assessed and treated in a hospital or residential setting, logs can be kept by staff after some explanation and training by the practitioner. Such logs should be designed specifically for the child (i.e., idiosyncratic, although they can be elaborated from a general format).

Treatment Generalization

The generalization of treatment effects with OCD involves several issues. The first is how to promote generalization across settings. For children with OCD, this involves transfer of effects from the treatment setting (clinic or hospital) to the home or school. Generalization procedures are not guided by firm empirical data. From the authors' viewpoint, however, treatment generalization across settings demands treatment involvement of family members and school personnel. With the family, this may assume several forms, ranging from family therapy sessions to utilizing parents in administering behavioral programs in the home. School personnel also should be involved in treatment programming in cases in which consent has been granted by the parents and the child's problematic behaviors are manifested in school. Practically speaking, it is usually not possible to develop elaborate behavioral programs in the school. It is usually possible, however, to inform teachers, counselors, and the school psychologist of problems and treatment goals and methods that they might utilize in the educational setting to support treatment. Such discussions should emphasize what teachers can do to promote treatment success. A general premise is that to promote generalization across settings, involvement of representatives of these various settings is necessary.

A second issue concerns generalization across behavioral modalities. It is clear that generalization across behaviors should not be anticipated. The literature on adult OCD suggests a specific association between treatment choice and type of therapeutic change (i.e., a relative independence of treatment effects). Several examples are suggested from the literature. Milby et al. (1981) found it necessary to design a specific treatment for obsessive ideation that did not diminish after exposure/response prevention successfully decreased compulsive rituals. In a related example, Foa et al. (1980) demonstrated response prevention had more impact on the operant response of compulsive rituals, while exposure treatment clearly had more effect on decreasing the emotional response. A third example is provided by Marks, Stern, Mawson, Cobb, and McDonald (1980) who demonstrated independent treatment effects for depressed persons with OCD for whom antidepressant medication clearly decreased depressive symptoms but did not significantly influence compulsive rituals. Exposure and response prevention techniques also were effective in alleviating the compulsive rituals, but did not substantially modify depressive symptoms.

Consequently, evaluation of treatment effects must utilize multiple outcome measures across settings to assess accurately the impact of treatment. Assessment should be sensitive to generalization of treatment across response modalities (e.g., What effect does exposure for compulsive rituals have on cognitive compulsions?). It should also be sensitive to generalization of treatment from specific obsessive compulsive responses to associated problems (e.g., What impact does exposure for compulsive rituals have on mood or interpersonal behavior?). At this point in our clinical understanding, it makes sense to treat discrete problems (family problems or OC symptoms) and to monitor the impact of this focus on remaining problems. It should be realized that multitreatment packages are needed for most

clinical cases. In the absence of the development of more robust techniques, this will likely continue to be the case.

Limitations and Pitfalls

Since the approach advocated is one that not only involves the child, but also the family and, in some cases, the school, multiple opportunities for problems, misunderstandings, inconsistency, and noncompliance could arise. The best antidote known for this is thorough ground work and follow-up consultations with all who are supporting the intervention. However, in spite of the best efforts and intentions of all concerned, the treatment may not be effective. Based on success rates of about 75% for behavioral therapy in adults with OCD, the clinician might expect that one child in four may not respond well to behavioral interventions. In such cases, a thorough review of the assessment data and implementation of the treatment plan may help to identify correctable flaws. Where none are found, adjunctive or alternative treatment approaches should be entertained, including the consideration of medication.

Medication side effects are sometimes a limitation on treatment effectiveness, as such side effects may be intolerable despite the reduction of OC symptomatology. Also, the medication itself may not produce the therapeutic effect desired. In both cases, a trial of another medication can be tried. Parents will often have strong concerns about giving the child medication, and some may even be responsible for noncompliance and subsequent relapse in the child. The concerns of parents may need to be assessed further, and if it is determined they are unwilling to support the medication regimen prescribed even after education and support, alternative means of treatment may be attempted (i.e., behavioral and/or family-systems therapy).

Consultation and Referral

No clinician likes to "give up" on the treatment of a child even if treatment is not going well. When systematic assessment has been followed by systematic and multimodal intervention and the child and/or family system are still unresponsive, a consultant can often add to the conceptualization of the case and make suggestions to increase treatment efficacy. Lastly, referral to another clinician may facilitate therapeutic efficacy. Though often the last resort, a new clinician, starting fresh with the child and family, especially if a more acceptable or believable treatment approach is attempted, may be successful.

SUMMARY

This chapter reviewed available literature on epidemiology, theories of etiology, assessment, and treatment of OCD with children and adolescents. A continuum of treatment approaches was discussed, ranging from family -level interventions to interventions focused on modifying the behavior of an individual child with OCD. Assessment strategies were reviewed, and behavioral assessment was strongly recommended. The model of treatment suggested incorporates idiographic assessment with prescriptive treatments that address family and interpersonal functioning, specific obsessive compulsive behaviors, and treatment for associated problems that are often a part of the clinical picture (e.g., assertive deficits, etc.).

The authors recommend the use of a multimodal approach to case conceptualization and treatment. The most significant aspects of effective treatment appear to be careful idiographic assessment of child and family, development of an accepting and nurturing therapeutic alliance, and active, directive, interventions that focus on changing specific problems in the interpersonal system of the child, as well as addressing the child's individual obsessive compulsive behaviors. In short, an empirical, data-based approach coupled with ongoing assessment to monitor the impact of treatment approaches developing from clinical hypotheses is strongly recommended.

REFERENCES

Adams, B. L., Warneke, L. B., McEwan, A. J. B., & Fraser, B. A. (1993). Single photon emission computerized tomography in obsessive compulsive disorder: A preliminary study. *Journal of Psychiatry & Neuroscience, 18*, 109–112.

Adams, P. L. (1973). *Obsessive children.* New York: Brunner/Mazel.

Akhtar, S., Pershad, D., & Verma, S. K. (1975). A Rorschach study of obsessional neurosis. *Indian Journal of Clinical Psychology, 2*, 139–143.

Alessi, N., & Bos, T. (1991). Buspirone augmentation of fluoxetine in a depressed child with obsessive compulsive disorder. *American Journal of Psychiatry, 148*, 1605–1606.

Allsopp, M., & Verduyn, C. (1988). A follow-up of adolescents with obsessive compulsive disorder. *British Journal of Psychiatry, 154*, 829–834.

Altemus, M., Pigott, T., Kalogeras, K. T., Demitrack, M., Dubbert, B., Murphy, D. L., & Gold P. W. (1992). Abnormalities in the regulation of vasopressin and corticotropin releasing factor secretion in obsessive compulsive disorder. *Archives of General Psychiatry, 49*, 9–20.

Altemus, M., Swedo, S. E., Leonard, H. L., Richter, D., Rubinow, D. R., Potter, W. Z., & Rapoport, J. L. (1994). Changes in cerebrospinal fluid neurochemistry during treatment of obsessive compulsive disorder with clomipramine. *Archives of General Psychiatry, 51*, 794–803.

American Psychiatric Association. (1980). *Diagnostic and statistical manual of mental disorders* (3rd ed.). Washington, DC: Author.

American Psychiatric Association. (1987). *Diagnostic and statistical manual of mental disorders* (3rd ed., rev.). Washington, DC: Author.

American Psychiatric Association. (1994). *Diagnostic and statistical manual of mental disorders* (4th ed.). Washington, DC: Author.

Andreasen, N. C., & Bardach, J. (1977). Dysmorphophobia: Symptom or disease? *American Journal of Psychiatry, 134*, 673–676.

Apter, A., Ratzoni, G., King, R. A., Weizman, A., Iancu, I., Binder, M., & Riddle, M. A. (1994). Fluvoxamine open-label treatment of adolescent inpatients with obsessive compulsive disorder or depression. *Journal of the American Academy of Child and Adolescent Psychiatry, 33*, 342–348.

Baxter, L. R., Jr., Phelps, M. E., Maziotta, J. C., Guze, B.H., Schwartz, J. M., & Selin, C. E. (1987). Local cerebral glucose metabolic rates in obsessive compulsive disorder. *Archives of General Psychiatry, 44*, 211–218.

Baxter, L. R., Schwartz, K. S., Bergman, J. P., Szubba, B. H., Guze, B. H., Mazziotta, J. C., Allazraki, A., Selin, C. E., Ferng, H. K., Munford, P., & Phelps, M. E. (1992). Caudate glucose metabolic rate changes with both drug and behavior therapy for obsessive compulsive disorder. *Archives of General Psychiatry, 49*, 685.

Beech, H. R. (Ed.). (1974). Obsessional states. London: Methuen & Co.

Berg, C. J., Rapoport, J. L., & Flament, M. F. (1986). The Leyton obsessional inventory-child version. *Journal of the American Academy of Child and Adolescent Psychiatry, 25*, 84–91.

Berg, C. Z., Rapoport, J. L., Whitaker, A., Davies, M., Leonard, H., Swedo, S. E., Braiman, S., & Lenane, M. (1989). Childhood obsessive compulsive disorder: A two-year prospective follow-up of a community sample. *Journal of the American Academy of Child and Adolescent Psychiatry, 28*, 528–533.

Berg, C. Z., Whitaker, A., Davies, M., Flament, M. F., & Rapoport, J. L. (1988). The survey form of the Leyton Obsessional Inventory-Child Version: Norms from an epidemiological study. *Journal of the American Academy of Child and Adolescent Psychiatry, 27*, 759–763.

Black, A. (1974). The natural history of obsessional neurosis. In H.R. Beech (Ed.), *Obsessional states*. London: Methuen & Co.

Black, D. W., Noyes, R., Jr., Goldstein, R. B., & Blum, N. (1992). A family study of obsessive compulsive disorder. *Archives of General Psychiatry, 49*, 362–368.

Bouvard, M., & Dugas, M. (1993). Fluoxetine in obsessive compulsive disorder in adolescents. *International Clinical Psychopharmacology, 8*, 307–310.

Burke, P., Meyer, V., Kocoshis, S., Orenstein, D., Chandra, R., & Sauer, J. (1989). Obsessive compulsive symptoms in childhood inflammatory bowel disease and cystic fibrosis. *Journal of the American Academy of Child and Adolescent Psychiatry, 28*, 525–527.

Campbell, L. M. (1973). A variation of thought stopping in a twelve-year-old boy: A case report. *Journal of Behavior Therapy and Experimental Psychiatry, 4*, 69–70.

Campbell, M., & Palij, M. (1985). Measurement of side effects including tardive dyskinesia. *Psychopharmacology Bulletin, 21*, 1063–1072.

Chakrabarti, S., Kulhara, P., & Verma, S. K. (1993). The pattern of burden in families of neurotic patients. *Social Psychiatry and Psychiatric Epidemiology, 28*, 172–177.

Clark, D. A., & Bolton, D. (1985). Obsessive compulsive adolescents and their parents: A psychometric study. *Journal of Child Psychology and Psychiatry, 26*, 267–276.

Como, P. G., & Kurlan, R. (1991). An open-label trial of fluoxetine for obsessive compulsive disorder in Gilles de la Tourette's Syndrome. *Neurology, 41*, 872–874.

Cook, E. H., Jr., Rowlett, R., Jaselskis, C., & Leventhal, B. L. (1992). Fluoxetine treatment of children and adults with autistic disorder and mental retardation. *Journal of the American Academy of Child and Adolescent Psychiatry, 31*, 739–745.

Cooper, J. (1970). The Leyton obsessional inventory. *Psychological Medicine, 1*, 48–64.

Cooper, J., & McNeil, J. (1968). A study of houseproud housewives and their interaction with children. *Journal of Child Psychology and Psychiatry, 9*, 173–188.

Dai, B. (1957). Obsessive compulsive disorders in Chinese culture. *Social Problems, 4*, 313–321.

Dell, P. F. (1981). *Beyond homeostasis: Toward a concept of coherence*. Unpublished manuscript.

Dell, P. F. & Goolishian, H. A. (1979). *"Order through fluctuation": An evolutionary epistemology for human systems*. Paper presented at the Annual Scientific Meeting of the A.K. Rice Institute, Houston.

DeVeaugh-Geiss, J., Moroz, G., Biederman, J., Cantwell, D., Fontaine, R., Greist, J. H., Reichler, R., Katz, R., & Landau, P. (1992). Clomipramine hydrochloride in childhood and adolescent obsessive compulsive disorder—A multicenter trial. *Journal of the American Academy of Child and Adolescent Psychiatry, 31*(1), 45–49.

Dilsaver, S. C., & White, K. (1986). Affective disorders and associated psychopathology: A family history study. *Journal of Clinical Psychiatry, 47*, 162–169.

Elkins, R., Rapoport, J. L., & Lipsky, A. (1980). Obsessive compulsive disorder of childhood and adolescence: A neurological viewpoint. *Journal of the American Academy of Child Psychiatry, 19*, 511–524.

Fennig, S., Fennig, S. N., Pato, M., & Weitzman, A. (1994). Emergence of symptoms of Tourette's Syndrome during fluvoxamine treatment of obsessive compulsive disorder. *British Journal of Psychiatry, 164*, 839–841.

Fisman, S. N., & Walsh, L. (1994). Obsessive compulsive disorder and fear of AIDS contamination in childhood. *Journal of the American Academy of Child and Adolescent Psychiatry, 33*, 349–353.

Flament, M. F., Koby, E., Rapoport, J. L., Berg, C. J. Zahn, T., Cox, C., Denckla, M., & Lenane, M. (1990). Childhood obsessive compulsive disorder: A prospective follow-up study. *Journal of Child Psychology and Psychiatry, 31*, 363–380.

Flament, M. F., Rapoport, J. L., Berg, C. J., Sceery, W., Kilts, C., Mellstrom, B., & Linnoila, M. (1985). Clomipramine treatment of childhood obsessive compulsive disorder: A double-blind controlled study. *Archives of General Psychiatry, 42*, 977–983.

Flament, M. F., Rapoport, J. L., Murphy, D. L., Berg, C. J., & Lake, C. R. (1987). Biochemical changes during clomipramine treatment of childhood obsessive compulsive disorders. *Archives of General Psychiatry, 44*, 219–225.

Flament, M, F., Whitaker, A., Rapoport, J. L., Davies, M., Berg, C. Z., Kalikow, K., Sceery, W., & Shaffer, D. (1988). Obsessive compulsive disorder in adolescence: An epidemiological study. *Journal of the American Academy of Child and Adolescent Psychiatry, 27*, 764–771.

Foa, E., & Rowan, V. (1990). Behavior therapy of OCD. In A. E. Bellack and M. Hersen (Eds.), *Handbook of comparative treatments for adult disorders*. New York: John Wiley & Sons.

Foa, E. B., Steketee, G., & Milby, J. B. (1980). Differential effects of exposure and response prevention in obsessive compulsive washers. *Journal of Consulting and Clinical Psychology, 48*, 71–79.

Foa, E. B., Steketee, G., & Ozarow, B. J. (1985). Behavior therapy with obsessive compulsives: From theory to treatment. In M. Mavissakalian, S. M. Turner, & L. Michelson (Eds.), *Obsessive compulsive disorder: Psychological and pharmacological treatments* (pp. 49–120). New York: Plenum Press.

Foa, E., & Tillman, A. (1978). The treatment of obsessive compulsive neurosis. In E. Foa & A. Goldstein (Eds.), *The handbook of behavioral interventions* (pp. 415–500). New York: Wiley Interscience.

Fogelson, D. L., & Bystritsky, A. (1991). Imipramine in the treatment of obsessive compulsive disorder with and without major depression. *Annals of Clinical Psychiatry, 3*, 233–237.

Frankel, M., Cummings, J. L., Robertson, M. M., Trimble, N. R., Hill, M. A., & Benson, D. F. (1986). Obsessions and compulsions in Gilles de la Tourette's syndrome. *Neurology, 36*, 378–382.

Frost, R. O., & Shows, D. L. (1993). The nature and measurement of compulsive indecisiveness. *Behaviour Research and Therapy, 31*, 683–692.

Geller, D. A., Beiderman, J., Reed, E. D., Spencer, T., & Wilens, T. E. (1995). Similarities in response to fluoxetine in the treatment of children and adolescents with obsessive compulsive disorder. *Journal of the American Academy of Child and Adolescent Psychiatry, 34*(1), 36–44.

Goodman, W. K., & Price, L. H. (1992). Assessment of severity and change in obsessive compulsive disorder. *Psychiatric Clinics of North America, 15*, 861–869.

Goodman, W. K., Price, L. H., Rasmussen, S. A., Mazure, C., Delgado, P., Heninger, G. R., & Charney, D. S. (1989). The Yale-Brown Obsessive Compulsive Scale: II. Validity. *Archives of General Psychiatry, 46*, 1012–1016.

Goodman, W. K., Price, L. H., Rasmussen, S. A., Mazure, C., Fleischmann, R. L., Hill, C. L., Henniger, G. R., & Charney, D. S. (1989). The Yale-Brown Obsessive Compulsive Scale: I. Development, use, and reliability. *Archives of General Psychiatry, 46*, 1006–1011.

Goodwin, D. W., Guze, S. B., & Robins, E. (1969). Follow-up studies in obsessional neurosis. *Archives of General Psychiatry, 20*, 182–187.

Graae, F., Gitow, A., Piacentini, J., Jaffer, M., & Liebowitz, M. (1992). Response of obsessive compulsive disorder and trichotillomania to serotonin reuptake blockers. *American Journal of Psychiatry, 149*(1), 149–150.

Grad, L. R., Pelcovitz, D., Olson, M., Matthews, M., & Grad, G. J. (1987). Obsessive compulsive symptomatology in children with Tourette's syndrome. *Journal of the American Academy of Child and Adolescent Psychiatry, 26*, 69–73.

Green, W. H. (1991). *Child and adolescent clinical psychopharmacology*. Baltimore, MD: Williams & Wilkins.

Greist, J. H., Jefferson, J. W., Kobak, K. A., Katzelnick, D. J., & Serlin, R. C. (1995). Efficacy and tolerability of serotonin transport inhibitors in obsessive compulsive disorder: A meta-analysis. *Archives of General Psychiatry, 52*, 53–60.

Gurman, A. S. & Kniskern, D. P. (1981). Family therapy outcome research: Knowns and unknowns. In A. S. Gurman & D. P. Kniskern (Eds.), *Handbook of family therapy* (pp. 742–775). New York: Brunner/Mazel.

Hamburger, S. D., Swedo, S., Whitaker, A., Davies, M., & Rapoport, J. L. (1989). Growth rate in adolescents with obsessive compulsive disorder. *American Journal of Psychiatry, 146*, 652–655.

Hanna, G. L. (1995). Demographic and clinical features of obsessive compulsive disorder in children and adolescents. *Journal of the American Academy of Child and Adolescent Psychiatry, 34*(1), 19–27.

Hanna, G. L., McCracken, J. T., & Cantwell, D. P. (1991). Prolactin in childhood obsessive compulsive disorder: Clinical correlates and response to clomipramine. *Journal of the American Academy of Child and Adolescent Psychiatry, 30*, 173–178.

Harris, C. V., & Wiebe, D. J. (1992). An analysis of response prevention and flooding procedures in the treatment of adolescent obsessive compulsive disorder. *Journal of Behavior Therapy and Experimental Psychiatry, 23*, 107–115.

Hibbs, E. D., Hamburger, S. D., Kruesi, M. J. P., & Lenane, M. (1993). Factors affecting expressed emotion in parents of ill and normal children. *American Journal of Orthopsychiatry, 63*(1), 103–112.

Hibbs, E. D., Hamburger, S. D., Lenane, M., Rapoport, J. L., Kruesi, M. J. P., Keysor, C. S., & Goldstein, M. J. (1991). Determinants of expressed emotion in families of disturbed and normal children. *Journal of Child Psychology and Psychiatry, 32,* 757–770.

Hibbs, E. D., Zahn, T. P., Hamburger, S. D., Kruesi, M. J. P., & Rapoport, J. L. (1992). Parental expressed emotion and psychophysiological reactivity in disturbed and normal children. *British Journal of Psychiatry, 160,* 504–510.

Hodgson, R. J., & Rachman, S. (1977). Obsessional-compulsive complaints. *Behaviour Therapy, 15,* 389–395.

Hollander, E., DeCaria, C. M., Nitescu, A., Gully, R., Suckow, R. F., Cooper, T. B., Gorman, J. M., Klein, D. F., & Liebowitz, M. R. (1992). Serotonergic function in obsessive compulsive disorder: Behavioral and neuroendocrine responses to oral m-chlorophenylpiperazine and fenfluramine in patients and healthy volunteers. *Archives of General Psychiatry, 49,* 21–28.

Hollingsworth, C. E., Tanguay, P. E., Grossman, L., & Pabst, P. (1980). Long-term outcome of obsessive compulsive disorder in childhood. *Journal of the American Academy of Child Psychiatry, 19,* 134–144.

Hunter, R., & MacAlpine, T. (Eds.). (1963). *Three hundred years of psychiatry.* London: Oxford University Press.

Insel, T. R., Murphy, D. L., Cohen, R. M., Alterman, I., Kilts, C., & Linnoila, M. (1983). Obsessive compulsive disorder: A double–blind trial of clomipramine and clorgyline. *Archives of General Psychiatry, 40,* 605–612.

Jenike, M. A., Baer, L., Brotman, A. W., Goff, C., Minichiello, W. E., & Regan, N. J. (1987). Obsessive compulsive disorder, depression, and the dexamethasone suppression test. *Journal of Clinical Psychopharmacology, 7,* 182–184.

Jenike, M. A., Baer, L., & Greist, J. H. (1990). Clomipramine versus fluoxetine in obsessive compulsive disorder: A retrospective comparison of side effects and efficacy. *Journal of Clinical Psychopharmacology, 10,* 122–124.

Jenike, M. A., Baer, L., Summergrad, P., Minichiello, W. E., Holland, A., & Seymour, R. (1990). Sertraline in obsessive compulsive disorder: A double-blind comparison with placebo. *American Journal of Psychiatry, 147,* 923–928.

Jenike, M. A., Hyman, S., Baer, L., Holland, A., Minichiello, W. E., Buttolph, L., Summergrad, P., Seymour, R., & Ricciardi, J. (1990). A controlled trial of fluvoxamine in obsessive compulsive disorder: Implications for a serotonergic theory. *American Journal of Psychiatry, 147,* 1209–1215.

Judd, L. L. (1965). Obsessive compulsive neurosis in children. *Archives of General Psychiatry, 12,* 136–142.

Kaplan, H. I., & Sadock, B. J. (1993). *Pocket handbook of psychiatric drug treatment.* Baltimore, MD: Williams & Wilkins.

Kaplan, H. I., & Sadock, B. J. (1996). *Pocket handbook of clinical psychiatry* (2nd ed.). Baltimore, MD: Williams & Wilkins.

Kaplan, H. I., Sadock, B. J., & Grebb, J. A. (1994). Anxiety disorders: 16.4/Obsessive compulsive disorder. In H. I. Kaplan, B. J. Sadock, & J. A. Grebb (Eds.), *Kaplan and Sadock's synopsis of psychiatry: Behavioral sciences & clinical psychiatry* (7th ed., pp. 598–606). Baltimore, MD: Williams & Wilkins.

Kayton, L., & Borge, G. F. (1967). Birth order and the obsessive compulsive character. *Archives of General Psychiatry, 17,* 751–753.

Kearney, C. A., & Silverman, W. K. (1990). Treatment of an adolescent with obsessive compulsive disorder by alternating response prevention and cognitive therapy: An empirical analysis. *Journal of Behaviour Therapy and Experimental Psychiatry, 21*(1), 39–47.

Khanna, S., & Srinath, S. (1988). Childhood obsessive compulsive disorder: 1. Psychopathology. *Psychopathology, 21,* 254–258.

Kimble, G. A., & Garmezy, N. (1968). Personality: Theory and measurement. In G. A. Kimble and N. Garmezy (Eds.), *Principles of general psychology* (3rd ed.) (pp. 568–597). New York: Ronald Press.

King, R. A., Riddle, M. A., Chappell, P. B., Hardin, M. T., Anderson, G. M., Lombroso, P., & Scahill, L. (1991). Case study: Emergence of self-destruction phenomena in children and adolescents during fluoxetine treatment. *Journal of the American Academy of Child and Adolescent Psychiatry, 30,* 179–186.

Kolada, J. L., Bland, R. C., & Newman, S. C. (1994). Obsessive compulsive disorder. *Acta Psychiatrica Scandinavica,* (Suppl. 376), 24–35.

Kovaks, M. (1985). The Children's Depression Inventory (CDI). *Psychopharmacology, 21,* 995–1000.

Kovaks, M., & Beck, A. T. (1977). An empirical-clinical approach toward a definition of childhood depression. In J. G. Schultebrandt & A. Raskin (Eds.), *Depression in children: Diagnosis, treatment, and conceptual models.* New York: Raven Press.

Kurlan, R., Como, P. G., Deeley, C., McDermott, M., & McDermott, M. P. (1993). A pilot controlled study of fluoxetine for obsessive compulsive symptoms in children with Tourette's Syndrome. Clinical *Neuropharmacology, 16,* 167–172.

Laplane, E., Levasseur, M., Pillon, Dubois, B., Baulac, M., Mazoyer, B., Tran Dinh, S., Sette, G., Danze, F., & Baron, J. C. (1989). Obsessive compulsive and other behavioral changes with bilateral basal ganglia lesions. *Brain, 112,* 699–725.

Last, C. G., & Strauss, C. C. (1989). Obsessive compulsive disorder in childhood. *Journal of Anxiety Disorders, 3,* 295–302.

Leckman, J. F., Goodman, W. K., North, W. G., Chappell, P. B., Price, L. H., Pauls, D. L., Anderson, G. M., Riddle, M. A., McSwiggan-Hardin, M., McDougle, C. J., Barr, L. C., & Cohen, D. J. (1994). Elevated cerebrospinal fluid levels of oxytocin in obsessive compulsive disorder: Comparison with Tourette's Syndrome and healthy controls. *Archives of General Psychiatry, 51,* 782–792.

Leckman, J. F., Towbin, K. E., Ort, S. I., & Cohen, D. J. (1988). Clinical assessment of tic disorder severity. In J. Cohen, R. Brunn, & J. F. Leckman (Eds.). *Tourette syndrome and tic disorders: Clinical understanding and treatment* (pp. 55–78). New York: Wiley.

Lenane, M. C., Swedo, S. E., Leonard, H., Pauls, D. L., Sceery, W., & Rapoport, J. L. (1990). Psychiatric disorders in first degree relatives of children and adolescents with obsessive compulsive disorder. *Journal of the American Academy of Child and Adolescent Psychiatry, 29,* 407–412.

Lenane, M. C., Swedo, S. E., Rapoport, J. L., Leonard, H., Sceery, W., & Guroff, J. J. (1992). Rates of obsessive compulsive disorder in first degree relative of patients with trichotillomania: A research note. *Journal of Child Psychology and Psychiatry and Allied Disciplines, 33,* 925–933.

Leonard, H. L., Goldberger, E. L., Rapoport, J. L., Cheslow, D. L., & Swedo, S. E. (1990). Childhood rituals: Normal development or obsessive compulsive symptoms? *Journal of the American Academy of Child and Adolescent Psychiatry, 29*(1), 17–23.

Leonard, H. L., Lenane, M. C., Swedo, S. E., Rettew, D. C., Gershon, E. S., & Rapoport, J. L. (1992). Tics and Tourette's Disorder: A 2- to 7-year follow-up of 54 obsessive compulsive children. *American Journal of Psychiatry, 149,* 1244–1251.

Leonard, H. L., & Rapoport, J. L. (1989). Pharmacotherapy of childhood obsessive compulsive disorder. *Psychiatric Clinics of North America, 12,* 963–970.

Leonard, H. L., Swedo, S. E., Lenane, M. C., Rettew, D. C., Cheslow, D. L., Hamburger, S. D., & Rapoport, J. L. (1991). A double-blind desipramine substitution during long-term clomipramine treatment in children and adolescents with obsessive compulsive disorder. *Archives of General Psychiatry, 48,* 922–927.

Leonard, H. L., Swedo, S. E., Lenane, M. C., Rettew, D. C., Hamburger, S. D., Bartko, J. J., & Rapoport, J. L. (1993). A 2- to 7-year follow-up study of 54 obsessive compulsive children and adolescents. *Archives of General Psychiatry, 50,* 429–439.

Leonard, H. L., Swedo, S. E., Rapoport, J. L., Koby, E. V., Lenane, M. C., Cheslow, D. L., & Hamburger, S. D. (1989). Treatment of obsessive compulsive disorder with clomipramine and desipramine in children and adolescents: A double-blind crossover comparison. *Archives of General Psychiatry, 46,* 1088–1092.

Leonard, H. L., Topol, D., Bukstein, O., Hindmarsh, D., Allen, A. J., & Swedo, S. E. (1994). Clonazepam as an augmenting agent in the treatment of childhood-onset obsessive compulsive disorder. *Journal of the American Academy of Child and Adolescent Psychiatry, 33,* 792–794.

Lieberman, J. (1984). Evidence for a biological hypothesis of obsessive compulsive disorder. *Neuropsychobiology, 11,* 14–21.

Lieberman, J. A., Breener, R., Lesser, M., Coccaro, E. Borenstein, M., & Kane, J. M. (1983). Dexamethasone suppression tests in patients with panic disorder. *American Journal of Psychiatry, 140,* 917–919.

Liebowitz, M. R., Hollander, E., Fairbanks, J., & Campeas, R. (1990). Fluoxetine for adolescents with obsessive compulsive disorder. *American Journal of Psychiatry, 147,* 370–371.

Luxenberg, J. S., Swedo, S. E., Flament, M. F., Friedland, R. P., Rapoport, J., & Rapoport, S. I. (1988). Neuroanatomical abnormalities in obsessive compulsive disorder detected with quantitative X-Ray computed tomography. *American Journal of Psychiatry, 145,* 1089–1093.

Machlin, S. R., Harris, G. J., Pearlson, G. D., Hoehn-Saric, R., Jeffery, P., & Camargo, E. E. (1991). Elevated medial-frontal cerebral blood flow in obsessive compulsive patients: A SPECT study. *American Journal of Psychiatry, 148,* 1240–1242.

Manchanda, R., & Sharma, M. (1986). Parental discipline and obsessive compulsive neurosis. *Canadian Journal of Psychiatry, 31,* 698.

March, J. S. (1995). Cognitive-behavioral psychotherapy for children and adolescents with OCD: A review and recommendation for treatment. *Journal of the American Academy of Child and Adolescent Psychiatry, 34*(1), 7–18.

March, J. S., Mulle, K., & Herbel, B. (1994). Behavioral psychotherapy for children and adolescents with obsessive compulsive disorder: An open trial of a new protocol-driven treatment package. *Journal of the American Academy of Child and Adolescent Psychiatry, 33,* 333–341.

Marks, I. M., Stern, R., Mawson, D. J., Cobb, J., & McDonald, R. (1980). Clomipramine and exposure for obsessive compulsive rituals: I. *British Journal of Psychiatry, 136,* 1–25.

Martin, A., Pigott, T. A., Lalonde, F. M., Dalton, I., Dubbert, B., & Murphy, D. L. (1993). Lack of evidence for Huntington's Disease-like cognitive dysfunction in obsessive compulsive disorder. *Biological Psychiatry, 33,* 345–353.

Maxmen, J. S., & Ward, N. G. (1995). *Psychotropic drugs: Fast facts* (3rd ed.). New York: W. W. Norton & Company.

Meredith, R. L., & Milby, J. B. (1980). Obsessive compulsive neurosis: Behavioral approaches to evaluation and intervention. In R. J. Daitzman (Ed.), *Clinical behavior therapy and behavior modification* (pp. 21–80). Stanford, CT: Garland Press.

Merkel, W. T., Pollard, C. A., Wiener, R. L., & Staebler, C. R. (1993). Perceived parental characteristics of patients with obsessive compulsive disorder, depression, and panic disorder. *Child Psychiatry and Human Development, 24,* 49–57.

Milby, J. B., Meredith, R. L., & Rice, J. (1981). Videotaped exposure: A new treatment for obsessive compulsive disorders. *Journal of Behavioral Therapy and Experimental Psychiatry, 12,* 249–255.

Milby, J. B., Meredith, R. L., & Wendorf, D. (1983). Obsessive compulsive disorders. In R. J. Morris & T. R. Kratochwill (Eds.), *Practice of child therapy: A textbook of methods* (pp. 1–26). New York: Pergamon Press.

Milby, J. B., & Weber, A. (1989). Obsessive compulsive disorders. In T. R. Kratochwill & R. J. Morris (Eds.), *The practice of child therapy* (pp. 9–42). New York: Pergamon Press.

Milby, J. B., & Weber, A. (1991). Obsessive compulsive disorders. In T. R. Kratochwill & R. J. Morris (Eds.), *The practice of child therapy* (2nd ed.) (pp. 9–42). Boston: Allyn & Bacon.

Mills, H. L., Agras, W. S., Barlow, D. H. & Mills, J. R. (1973). Compulsive rituals treated by response prevention: An experimental analysis. Archives of *General Psychiatry, 28,* 524–529.

Modell, J. G., Mountz, J. M., Curtis, G. C., & Greden, J. F. (1989). Neurophysiologic dysfunction in basal ganglia/limbic striatal and thalamocortical circuits as a pathogenetic mechanism of obsessive compulsive disorder. *Journal of Neuropsychiatry, 1,* 27–36.

Monteiro, W., Marks, I. M., Noshirvani, H., & Checkley, S. (1986). Normal dexamethasone suppression test in obsessive compulsive disorder. *British Journal of Psychiatry, 148,* 326–329.

Montgomery, S. A. (1993). Obsessive compulsive disorder is not an anxiety disorder. *International Clinical Psychopharmacology, 8* (Suppl. 1), 57–62.

Mowrer, O. H. (1960). *Learning theory and behavior.* New York: Wiley.

National Institute of Mental Health (1985). CGI (Clinical Global Impressions) Scale. *Psychopharmacology Bulletin, 21,* 839–843.

Okasha, A., Saad, A., Khalil, A. H., El Dawla, A. S., & Yehia, N. (1994). Phenomenology of obsessive compulsive disorder: A transcultural study. *Comprehensive Psychiatry, 35,* 191–197.

Pauls, D. L., Alsobrook, J. P., II, Phil, M., Goodman, W., Rasmussen, S., & Leckman, J. F. (1995). A family study of obsessive compulsive disorder. *American Journal of Psychiatry, 152*(1), 76–84.

Pauls, D. L., Towbin, K. E., Leckman, J. F., Zahner, G. E., & Cohen, D. J. (1986). Gilles de la Tourette's syndrome and obsessive compulsive disorder: Evidence supporting a genetic relationship. *Archives of General Psychiatry, 43,* 1180–1182.

Piacentini, J., Gitow, A., Jaffer, M., Graae, F., & Whitaker, A. (1994). Outpatient behavioral treatment of child and adolescent obsessive compulsive disorder. *Journal of Anxiety Disorders, 8,* 277–289.

Piacentini, J., Jaffer, M., Gitow, A., Graae, F., Davies, S. O., Del Bene, D., & Liebowitz, M. (1992). Psychopharmacologic treatment of child and adolescent obsessive compulsive disorder. *Psychiatric Clinics of North America, 15*(1), 87–107.

Pigott, T. A., L'Heureux, F., Rubenstein, C. S., Bernstein, S. E., Hill, J. L., & Murphy, D. L. (1992). A double-blind, placebo controlled study of trazodone in patients with obsessive compulsive disorder. *Journal of Clinical Psychopharmacology, 12,* 156–162.

Pine, D., Shaffer, D., & Schonfeld, I. S. (1993). Case study: Persistent emotional disorder in children with neurological soft signs. *Journal of the American Academy of Child and Adolescent Psychiatry, 32,* 1229–1236.

Post, R., Korin, J. V., & Goodwin, F. K. (1983). Tetrahydrocannabinol (THC) in depressed patients. *Archives of General Psychiatry, 28,* 345–352.

Rachman, S. (1974). Primary obsessional slowness. *Behavioral Research and Therapy, 12,* 9–18.

Rachman, S. J., & Hodgson, R. J. (1980). *Obsessions and compulsions.* Englewood Cliffs, New Jersey: Prentice-Hall.

Rapoport, J. L. (1991). Recent advances in obsessive compulsive disorder. *Neuropsychopharmacology, 2,* 23–28.

Rapoport, J., Elkins, R., & Mikkelson, E. (1986). Clinical controlled trial of chlorimipramine in adolescents with obsessive compulsive disorder. *Psychopharmacology Bulletin, 16,* 61–63.

Rapoport, J. L., Swedo, S. E., & Leonard, H. L. (1992). Childhood obsessive compulsive disorder. *Journal of Clinical Psychiatry, 53* (Suppl. 4), 11–16.

Rasmussen, S. A., & Tsuang, M. T. (1986). Clinical characteristics and family history in DSM-III obsessive compulsive disorder. *American Journal of Psychiatry, 143,* 317–322.

Rettew, D. C., Swedo, S. E., Leonard, H. L., Lenane, M. C., & Rapoport, J. L. (1992). Obsessions and compulsions across time in 79 children and adolescents with obsessive compulsive disorder. *Journal of the American Academy of Child and Adolescent Psychiatry, 31,* 1050–1056.

Riddle, M. A., Hardin, M. T., King, R., Scahill, L., & Woolston, J. L. (1990). Fluoxetine treatment of children and adolescents with Tourette's and obsessive compulsive disorders: Preliminary clinical experience. *Journal of the American Academy of Child and Adolescent Psychiatry, 29*(1), 45–48.

Riddle, M. A., Scahill, L., King, R. A., Hardin, M. T., Anderson, G. M., Ort, S. I., Smith, J. C., Leckman, J. F., & Cohen, D. J. (1992). Double-blind, crossover trial of fluoxetine and placebo in children and adolescents with obsessive compulsive disorder. *Journal of the American Academy of Child and Adolescent Psychiatry, 31,* 1062–1069.

Riddle, M. A., Scahill, L., King, R., Hardin, M. T., Towbin, K. E., Ort, S. I., Leckman, J. F., & Cohen, D. J. (1990). Obsessive compulsive disorder in children and adolescents: Phenomenology and family history. *Journal of the American Academy of Child and Adolescent Psychiatry, 29,* 766–772.

Ristvedt, S. L., Mackenzie, T. B., & Christenson, G. A. (1993). Cues to obsessive compulsive symptoms: Relationships with other patient characteristics. *Behaviour Research and Therapy, 31,* 721–729.

Robins, L. N., Helzer, J. E., Cottler, L., & Goldring, E. (1989). *NIMH Diagnostic Interview Schedule,* (Version III, Rev.). St. Louis: Washington University School of Medicine, Department of Psychiatry.

Rosenthal, R. (1991). Replication in behavioral research. In J. W. Neuliep (Ed.), *Replication research in the social sciences* (pp. 1–30). Newbury Park: Sage Publications.

Rutter, M. L. (1972). Relationships between child and adult psychiatric disorders. *Acta Psychiatrica Scandinavica, 48,* 3–21.

Sanavio, E. (1988). Obsessions and compulsions: The Padua inventory. *Behaviour Research and Therapy, 28,* 341–345.

Sawyer, M. G., Slocombe, C., Kosky, R., Clark, J., Mathias, J., Burfield, S., Faranda, I., Hambly, H., Mahar, A., Tang, B. N., & Baghurst, P. (1992). The psychological adjustment of offspring of adults with obsessive compulsive disorder: A brief report. *Australian and New Zealand Journal of Psychiatry, 26,* 479–484.

Sher, K. J., Martin, E. D., Raskin, G., & Perrigo, R. (1991). Prevalence of DSM-III-R disorders among nonclinical compulsive checkers and noncheckers in a college student sample. *Behaviour Research and Therapy, 29,* 479–483.

Skoog, G. (1959). The anacastic syndrome. *Acta Psychiatrica Scandinavia, 34,* 134.

Staebler, C. R., Pollard, C. A., & Merkel, W. T. (1993). Sexual history and quality of current relationships in patients with obsessive compulsive disorder: A comparison with two other psychiatric samples. *Journal of Sex & Marital Therapy, 19,* 147–153.

Stanley, M. A., & Turner, S. M. (1995). Current status of pharmacological and behavioral treatment of obsessive compulsive disorder. *Behavior Therapy, 26,* 163–186.

Stoll, A. L., Tohen, M. & Baldessarini, R. J. (1992). Increasing frequency of the diagnosis of obsessive compulsive disorder. *American Journal of Psychiatry, 149,* 639.

Swedo, S. E., & Leonard, H. L. (1992). Trichotillomania: An obsessive compulsive spectrum disorder? *Psychiatric Clinics of North America, 15,* 777–790.

Swedo, S. E., Leonard, H. L., Kruesi, M. J. P., Rettew, D. C., Listwak, S. J., Berrettini, W., Stipetic, M., Hamburger, S., Gold, P. W., Potter, W. Z., & Rapoport, J. L. (1992). Cerebrospinal fluid neurochemistry in children and adolescents with obsessive compulsive disorder. *Archives of General Psychiatry, 49,* 29–36.

Swedo, S. E., Leonard, H. L., & Rapoport, J. L. (1992). Childhood-onset obsessive compulsive disorder. *Psychiatric Clinics of North America, 15,* 767–775.

Swedo, S. E., Leonard, H. L., Schapiro, M. B., Casey, B. J., Mannheim, G. B., Lenane, M. C., & Rettew, D. C. (1993). Sydenham's Chorea: Physical and psychological symptoms of St. Vitus Dance. *Pediatrics, 91,* 706–713.

Swedo, S. E., Rapoport, J. L., Cheslow, D. I., Leonard, H. L., Ayoub, E. M., Hoosier, D. M., & Wald, E. R. (1989). High prevalence of obsessive compulsive symptoms in patients with Sydenham's Chorea. *American Journal of Psychiatry, 146,* 246–249.

Swedo, S. E., Rapoport, J. L., Leonard, H., Lenane, M., & Cheslow, D. (1989). Obsessive compulsive disorder in children and adolescents: Clinical phenomenology of 70 consecutive cases. *Archives of General Psychiatry, 46,* 335–341.

Templer, D. (1972). The obsessive compulsive neurosis: Review of research findings. *Comprehensive Psychiatry, 13,* 375–383.

Thomsen, P. H. (1991). Obsessive compulsive symptoms in children and adolescents: A phenomenological analysis of 61 Danish cases. *Psychopathology, 24,* 12–18.

Thomsen, P. H., & Jensen, J. (1991). Dimensional approach to obsessive compulsive disorder in childhood and adolescence. *Acta Psychiatrica Scandinavica, 83,* 183–187.

Thomsen, P. H., & Mikkelsen, H. U. (1991). Children and adolescents with obsessive compulsive disorder: The demographic and diagnostic characteristics of 61 Danish patients. *Acta Psychiatrica Scandinavica, 83,* 262–266.

Thomsen, P. H., & Mikkelsen, H. U. (1993). Development of personality disorders in children and adolescents with obsessive compulsive disorder: A 6- to 22-year follow-up study. *Acta Psychiatrica Scandinavica, 87,* 456–462.

Thoren, P., Asberg, M., & Cronholm, B. (1980). Clomipramine treatment of obsessive compulsive disorder: I. A controlled clinical trial. *Archives of General Psychiatry, 37,* 1281–1285.

Toman, W. (1969). Family constellation. New York: Springer.

Toro, J., Cervera, M., Osejo, E., & Salamero, M. (1992). Obsessive compulsive disorder in childhood and adolescence: A clinical study. *Journal of Child Psychology and Psychiatry, 33,* 1025–1037.

Tseng, W. (1973). Psychopathologic study of obsessive compulsive neurosis in Taiwan. *Comprehensive Psychiatry, 14,* 139–140.

Valleni-Basile, L. A., Garrison, C. Z., Jackson, K. L., Waller, J. L., McKeown, R. E., Addy, C. L., & Cuffe, S. P. (1994). Frequency of obsessive compulsive disorder in a community sample of young adolescents. *Journal of the American Academy of Child and Adolescent Psychiatry, 33,* 782–791.

Van Oppen, P. (1992). Obsessions and compulsions: Dimensional structure, reliability, convergent and divergent validity of the Padua Inventory. *Behaviour Research and Therapy, 30,* 631–637.

Vitiello, B., Spreat, S., & Behar, D. (1989). Obsessive compulsive disorder in mentally retarded patients. *The Journal of Nervous and Mental Disease, 177,* 232–236.

Watzlawick, P., Weakland, J. & Fisch, R. (1974). *Change: Principles of problem formation and problem resolution.* New York, W.W. Norton & Company.

Wise, S., & Rapoport, J. L. (1989). Obsessive compulsive disorder: Is it basal ganglia dysfunction? In Rapoport, J. L. (Ed.), *Obsessive compulsive disorder in children and adolescents* (pp. 327–334). Washington, DC: American Psychiatric Press.

Wolff, R., & Rapoport, J. (1988). Behavioral treatment of childhood obsessive compulsive disorder. *Behavior Modification, 12,* 252–266.

Wolpe, J. (1973). *The Practice of Behavior Therapy.* Elmsford, NY: Pergamon Press.

World Health Organization (1977). *Manual of the international statistical classification of diseases, injuries, and causes of death: Based on the recommendations of the Ninth Revision Conference, 1975, and adopted by the Twenty-ninth World Health Assembly.* Geneva: Author.

Yaryura-Tobias, J. A., Bebirian, R. J., Neziorglu, F. A. & Bhagavan, H. N. (1977). Obsessive compulsive disorders as a serotonergic defect. *Research Communications in Psychology, Psychiatry and Behavior, 2,* 5–6.

Zohar, A. H., Ratzoni, G., Pauls, D. L., Apter, A., Bleich, A., Kron, S., Rapoport, M., Weizman, A., & Cohen, D. J. (1992). An epidemiological study of obsessive compulsive disorder and related disorders in Israeli adolescents. *Journal of the American Academy of Child and Adolescent Psychiatry, 31,* 1057–1061.

CHAPTER 3

CHILDHOOD DEPRESSION

Nadine J. Kaslow
Mary K. Morris
Lynn P. Rehm

Developing and implementing empirically validated interventions for depressed children and adolescents is a budding field of endeavor. Although there have been years of research in therapeutic approaches for depressed adults (Antonuccio, Danton, & DeNelsky, 1995; Robinson, Berman, & Neimeyer, 1990), there are only a few studies assessing the efficacy of intervention and prevention programs with depressed youth. However, the study of child and adolescent depression has become increasingly popular and productive in recent years, with particular focus on epidemiology, diagnostic issues, comorbid conditions and correlates, and the relation between depression in parents and children. Thus, this chapter represents a significant revision from the previous edition of this book, rather than primarily an update on the progress in the field in the past six to eight years.

This chapter reviews current developments and outlines strategies for the conceptualization, assessment, intervention, and prevention of depression in youth. We argue that current diagnostic practices identify children with a correlated set of presenting behaviors for whom special treatment strategies will be appropriate. Prominent among the characteristics of the population is a set of maladaptive cognitive and behavioral skills for self-management, impairments in interpersonal competence with peers and family members, and neurobiological abnormalities. We make the case that these attributes can be assessed individually and may be the target for intervention and prevention strategies. Finally, we believe that all interventions should be informed by a developmental perspective and conducted within a family context.

HISTORICAL PERSPECTIVE

Historically, little empirical work was done in the area because of the controversy that surrounded the very existence and nature of depression in children. A number of perspectives characterized this debate. More recently, a consensus position has emerged in which depression in youths is considered to be similar to depression in adults. This consensus view has enabled research in the field to burgeon.

Psychodynamic Perspectives

The first psychodynamic view emerged from classical psychoanalytic theory. Proponents of this model maintained that for structural reasons, depression cannot exist in children. Specifically, they asserted that depression could not occur in children because of immature superego development and lack of a stable self-concept (Rie, 1966). According to ego-analytic models, which do not depend heavily on structural development, depression is possible in children (see Bemporad, 1994). Sandler and Joffee (1965) hypothesized that children become depressed when they feel they have lost or are unable to attain adequate nurturance and support to develop healthy narcissism, and as a result they feel helpless and deprived. Bemporad (1978) posited that depressed children's cognitive distortions are a function of problematic parent-child interactions. Recently, object relations and attachment theorists (e.g., Bowlby, 1980) have underscored the role of early parent-child attachment in increasing one's predisposition to depression in the face of loss. Specifically, Bowlby (1980) hypothesized that depression emerges in those youth who feel helpless and develop negative self- and object-representations as a function of insecure or disrupted attachment bonds.

Depression in Childhood Is Masked

An early dominant perspective was coined "masked" depression or "depressive equivalents." This position argues that depression exists in children as an internal, unobservable pathological entity, the external manifestations of which are depressive equivalents. The assumption is that children may be depressed, but display this depression in diverse behavioral complaints typical of childhood (e.g., Cytryn & McKnew, 1974). Frequently cited "masking" symptoms include many nonpsychotic disorders: enuresis, temper tantrums, hyperactivity, disobedience, truancy, run-ning away, delinquency, fire setting, phobias, somatization, irritability, learning disabilities, and school failures.

The logical problems inherent in this position made it untenable. The major criticisms were that the construct of masked depression is not of clinical or heuristic significance, because every possible symptom has been considered an indicator of depression, and there is no way to be certain that depression underlies these symptoms. Further, these "symptoms" may be developmentally and culturally determined ways of expressing or coping with distress (Kovacs & Beck, 1977). Although the masked depression concept largely has been abandoned, it may have emerged as a reflection of the high rates of comorbid internalizing and externalizing symptoms and disorders associated with childhood depression (Hammen & Compas, 1994; Kovacs, 1989). These comorbid conditions make it more difficult to diagnose depression and raise questions about the independence of depressive disorders in youth (Hammen & Compas, 1994).

Depression in Childhood Is Transitory

A third perspective regarding the nature of depression in children was provided by Lefkowitz and Burton (1978). They assumed that: (a) the behaviors that constitute the syndrome of depression are prevalent in normal children, and therefore not deviant; (b) the symptoms that comprise the syndrome of depression are transitory developmental phenomena that dissipate with time, and thus cannot be considered pathological; and (c) if symptoms remit spontaneously, clinical intervention is not necessary. Based on these observations, they argued that the syndrome of child depression does not exist. A number of criticisms were made about this work (e.g., Costello, 1980). Specifically, data reveal that although single symptoms may be prevalent in a given population, it is the constellation of symptoms that defines the syndrome. In fact, prevalence rates for depressive disorders in youth range from 2–5% in community samples (Fleming & Offord, 1990). Additionally, even though specific symptoms may be prevalent, the degree to which a given symptom may impact negatively on a child's development or sense of well-being is not diminished by its frequency in the population. The second assumption fails to adopt a developmental perspective (Kaslow & Rehm, 1991) and is inconsistent with empirical findings regarding the course of depressive disorders in youth. Specifically, depressive disorders are of relatively long duration, recur throughout the life span, and are associated with impaired psychological, psychosocial, and physical functioning (Hanna, 1992; Harrington, 1993; Kovacs, 1989). Given new evidence from longitudinal studies of the persistence of depressive disorders, the assumption that intervention is unnecessary can not be supported.

Depression in Childhood Parallels Depression in Adulthood

The most common view is that depression in children is a distinct clinical entity whose defining characteristics are isomorphic with its adult counterpart (Mitchell, McCauley, Burke, & Moss, 1988). This perspective has been adopted by the American Psychiatric Association's *Diagnostic and Statistical Manual of Mental Disorder* in its recent versions, DSM-III-R (APA, 1987) and DSM-IV (APA, 1994). The DSM-IV states that the essential features of mood disorders in children are the same as those in adults. The four sets of complaints used by Beck (1967) to characterize adult depression are evident in the DSM-IV criteria for major depressive episode in youth: (a) affective – e.g., depressed mood, anhedonia; (b) cognitive—e.g., feelings of worthlessness or guilt, diminished ability to think or concentrate, recurrent thoughts of death; (c) motivational —e.g., fatigue or loss of energy; and (d) vegetative and psychomotor—e.g., significant weight loss or weight gain, insomnia or hypersomnia, psychomotor agitation or retardation.

The DSM-IV does note differences in characteristic features of depression, and in the duration of symptoms necessary to diagnose youth. In children and adolescents, mood may be irritable rather than depressed, and failure to make expected weight gains may be observed rather than weight loss. Further, whereas adults must exhibit symptoms over a two year period to meet diagnostic criteria for dysthymic disorder, those under age 18 may receive this diagnosis with a symptom duration of one year. The DSM-IV also notes that somatic complaints and social withdrawal are depressive symptoms that are more prominent in depressed children than adults, whereas psychomotor retardation, hypersomnia, and delusions are less common in prepubertal depressed youth than their adolescent or adult counterparts.

Developmental Psychopathology Perspective

The basic tenet underlying the organismic-developmental approach is the orthogenetic principle (i.e., whenever development proceeds from a state of relative globality and lack of differentiation to one of increasing differentiation, articulation, and hierarchic integration) (Werner, 1957). Depression results when there is a lack of organization or integration of social, cognitive, or emotional competencies, preventing the successful resolution of salient developmental tasks (Cicchetti & Schneider-Rosen, 1986). The developmental perspective complements standard diagnostic classification schemas by providing a broader framework for addressing the etiology and clinical manifestations of psychopathology over the life span. This view also highlights new dimensions, variables, and parameters essential for a comprehensive, developmentally relevant nosology (Carlson & Garber, 1986; Rutter, 1986).

Developmentally oriented writers express concerns about adopting the unmodified adult, DSM-IV criteria for youth (Carlson & Garber, 1986). These criteria do not account for age-related differences in the defining attributes or manifest expressions of depression, fail to take into account children's cognitive, affective, and interpersonal competencies, and do not consider ways that developmental advances in cognitive abilities influence the manner in which children experience, interpret, and express emotions (Cicchetti & Schneider-Rosen, 1986). Future diagnostic systems should address similarities and differences in depression across the life span, and identify age-appropriate signs and symptoms taking into account the individual's level of cognitive, affective, and interpersonal development in relation to normative age-appropriate functioning.

ETIOLOGICAL MODELS IN THE UNDERSTANDING OF DEPRESSION IN CHILDREN AND ADOLESCENTS

A number of models have been proposed to account for the development and maintenance of depression in youth. Rather than review the myriad influences, this section provides an in-depth discussion of those models that underlie current intervention approaches and that have received empirical support. Thus, we address behavioral and cognitive models, interpersonal and family perspectives, and neurobiological approaches.

Behavioral and Cognitive Models

A number of models of adult depression postulate that behavioral (activity level, social skills) and cognitive (attributional style, cognitive distortions, self-control behaviors) variables are associated with depressive symptoms. During the past decade these models have been applied to the treatment of depressed youth.

Activity Level

Activity-increase programs for depression are an outgrowth of early behavioral conceptualizations in which depression was seen as reduced activity caused by low rates of environmental reinforcement (Costello, 1972; Ferster, 1971; Lewinsohn, 1974; Lewinsohn, Youngren, & Grosscup, 1979; Skinner, 1953). According to Lewinsohn, who built on the work of Skinner, Ferster, and Costello, the etiology of depression is a lack of response-contingent positive reinforcement that may be the result of a reinforcement-poor environment or an environment that has changed, so that prior reinforcement is no longer present. Activity-increase programs assume that increasing pleasant or rewarding activities will increase the general level of response-contingent reinforcement in a person's life, leading to a reduction in depression.

Research with adults shows an association between depressive symptoms and engagement in pleasant and unpleasant activities in multiple samples (e.g., students, community volunteers, psychi-

atric patients, medical patients) (e.g., Grosscup & Lewinsohn, 1980; Rehm, 1978). In general, these studies reveal a positive correlation between depressed mood and unpleasant activities and a negative correlation between depressed mood and participation in pleasant activities. Additionally, empirical work indicates that adults engage spontaneously in a variety of activities designed to counter and cope with depressive symptoms (Rippere, 1977).

Researchers have begun to examine the association between activity level and depression in children (e.g., Wierzbicki & Sayler, 1991) and adolescents (e.g., Carey, Kelley, Buss, & Scott, 1986; Larson, Raffaelli, Richards, Ham, & Jewell, 1990). In 8–14 year-olds, Wierzbicki and Sayler (1991) found a positive correlation between depressed mood and engagement in unpleasant activities; that is, those youth with elevated depressive symptoms engaged in more unpleasant activities according to both child and parent report. However, the predicted negative correlation between depressive symptoms and participation in pleasant activities only was supported by parent ratings of the child's level of depression. Similarly, depressed adolescents report more unpleasant activities than their nondepressed counterparts (Carey et al., 1986), however, a correlation between participation in pleasant activities and depression has not been supported in this age group (e.g., Carey et al., 1986; Larson et al., 1990). A related finding that may be of particular significance in the development of activity-increase programs for depressed youth is that depressed children generate fewer counterdepressive activities than their nondepressed peers (Wierzbicki, 1989). The reason(s) for differences in the child/adolescent and adult data remain unclear, but may be attributable in part to developmental differences in the ability to self-select activities and to generate alternative solutions (Wierzbicki & Sayler, 1991)

Social Skills

There are several variations on the theme of deficits in social skills as the basis for depression in adults. According to Lewinsohn and colleagues (e.g., Lewinsohn, Biglan, & Zeiss, 1976), depressed adults often lack the social skills necessary to obtain reinforcement from others resulting in a low rate of response-contingent social reinforcement. In a related vein, Wolpe (1979) argued that one cause of depression is an inability to control interpersonal situations. Nezu, Nezu, and Perri (1989) see interpersonal problem-solving as the focal deficit associated with depression.

Social skills deficits interpersonal difficulties contribute to the emergence of depressive symptoms, reflect the presence of depression, persist after recovery from a depressive episode, and predict future depressive episodes (Hammen, 1992; Puig-Antich et al., 1985a; 1985b; 1993; Wierzbicki & McCabe, 1988). Depressed children display deficits in social functioning with their parents, siblings, teachers, and peers (e.g., Altmann & Gotlib, 1988; Blechman, McEnroe, Carella, & Audette, 1986; Fauber, Forehand, Long, Burke, & Faust, 1987; Kazdin, Esveldt-Dawson, Sherick, & Colbus, 1985; Nolen-Hoeksema, Girgus, & Seligman, 1986; Puig-Antich et al., 1985a), and often are rejected or viewed negatively by their peers and teachers (e.g., Bell-Dolan, Reaven, & Peterson, 1993; Dalley, Bolocofsky, & Karlin, 1994; Rudolph, Hammen, & Burge, 1994). These youth are rated by peers as less likable and attractive, as emitting fewer positive behaviors, and as being in greater need of therapy than are nondepressed children (Peterson, Mullins, & Ridley-Johnson, 1985). Depressed youth experience others as less friendly, often report wanting to be alone, and spend less time in public places and more time in their bedrooms (Larson et al., 1990). In addition, they are cognizant of their interpersonal difficulties, report dissatisfaction with their interpersonal skills, and rate their social problem-solving skills negatively (Marton, Connolly, Kutcher, & Korenblum, 1993).

Only a handful of studies have assessed directly the social problem-solving skills of depressed children. Although some studies find that depressed children have impaired social problem-solving, social information-processing, and conflict-negotiation skills (Quiggle, Garber, Panak, & Dodge, 1992; Rudolph et al., 1994), other studies have failed to demonstrate an association between depression and interpersonal problem-solving skills, (e.g., Doerfler, Mullins, Griffin, Siegel, & Richards, 1984; Joffe,

Dobson, Fine, Marriage, & Haley, 1990; Marton et al., 1993; Rotheram-Borus, Trautman, Dopkins, & Shrout, 1990). This lack of an association may be attributable in part to the limited ecological validity of paper- and pencil-measures used to assess social problem-solving skills (Dujovne, Barnard, & Rapoff, 1995). One study did find, however, that social problem-solving skills moderate the association between negative life stress and depressive symptoms (Goodman, Gravitt, & Kaslow, 1995). Specifically, children with limited social problem-solving skills who experience a high impact of negative life events are more likely to evidence depressive symptoms than those with more effective social problem solving abilities.

Attributional Theory

According to the original learned helplessness model (Seligman, 1975), individuals become helpless and depressed when they perceive environmental events as uncontrollable. There is a significant body of literature supporting learned helplessness theory in humans (Garber & Seligman, 1980). A number of studies support the application of the original learned helplessness theory to depression in children and adolescents. A series of studies indicate that depressive symptoms in youth are associated with "personal helplessness" (i.e., perceived incompetence) and "universal helplessness" (i.e., perceived noncontingency) (Weisz, Sweeney, Proffitt, & Carr, 1993). Additionally, depressed youth have deficits in instrumental responding (e.g., Bodiford, Eisenstadt, Johnson, & Bradlyn, 1988; Kaslow, Tanenbaum, Abramson, Peterson, & Seligman, 1983). After several empirical investigations with humans, an attributional reformulation of the learned helplessness model was proposed (Abramson, Seligman, & Teasdale, 1978). This reformulation postulates an insidious attributional style that produces the deficits in affectivity, motivation, and self-esteem associated with depression. When a person experiences an aversive event, the way in which the person attributes the cause of the event will determine whether or not he or she becomes depressed. Individuals who make more internal, stable, and global attributions for negative events are at greater risk for developing depressive symptoms than are those who make more external, unstable, and specific attributions for these same events. Causal explanations for positive events have also been associated with depressive symptoms. Specifically, people who attribute positive events to external, unstable, and specific causes are likely to manifest depressive cognitions (Sweeney, Anderson, & Bailey, 1986).

As predicted by the reformulated model of learned helplessness, higher levels of depressive symptoms and depressive disorders in children and adolescents are associated with an attributional style similar to that of depressed adults (for reviews see Garber & Hilsman, 1992; Gladstone & Kaslow, 1995; Joiner & Wagner, 1995; Kaslow, Brown, & Mee, 1994). This cross-sectional attribution-depression link appears consistent across age, gender, and sample type. However, evidence supporting the hypothesis that maladaptive attributional patterns mediate the association between negative life events and depression in youth is mixed (Joiner & Wagner, 1995).

Abramson and colleagues (Abramson, Metalsky, & Alloy, 1989) revised further the attributional reformulation to highlight the construct of hopelessness. According to the hopelessness theory of depression, a diathesis-stress model, attributional style moderates the relation between negative life events and the subsequent development of hopelessness and later depression. Prospective studies offer support for the hopelessness theory in adults (e.g., Metalsky & Joiner, 1992). Although no published study has tested the hopelessness theory of depression in youth, some data support the diathesis-stress component of the theory (e.g., Garber & Hilsman, 1992; Nolen-Hoeksema, Girgus, & Seligman, 1992).

Cognitive Distortions

In Beck's (1967; Beck, Rush, Shaw, & Emery, 1979) cognitive model of depression, depressive cognitions—the "negative cognitive triad"—are regarded as the essential features of the depressive syndrome. Depressed individuals have a systematically negative bias in their thinking, resulting in a negative view of self, world, and future. They also use dysfunctional schemas to interpret their experiences and evaluate their behavior. These dysfunctional

schema, combined with negative automatic thoughts, lead to symptoms of depression. These depressive symptoms exacerbate further the negative cognitions, such that a debilitating feedback loop emerges between distorted thoughts and dysphoric feelings. Considerable data support the association between distorted cognitions and the development and maintenance of depressive symptoms and disorders in adults (for review see Kwon & Oei, 1994).

Consistent with the cognitive model, depressed children, as compared to their nondepressed counterparts (a) have lower self-esteem and perceived competence; (b) rate themselves more negatively despite comparable task performance; and (c) manifest more negative cognitions, particularly regarding loss and self-concept, than do their nondepressed peers. However, data regarding the presence of more negative schemata in depressed than nondepressed children is inconsistent. Finally, depressed youth feel hopeless about their futures, and thus are at increased risk for suicidal behavior (for reviews see Garber & Hilsman, 1992; Kaslow et al., 1994).

Self-Control Deficits

Rehm's (1977) self-control model of depression incorporates aspects of the cognitive model (Beck, 1967), the activity level and social-skills models (Lewinsohn, 1974; Lewinsohn et al., 1979), and the attributional model (Abramson et al., 1978), and self-control theory (Kanfer & Karoly, 1972). Self-control, a three-stage feedback-loop process, includes self-monitoring, self-evaluation, and self-reinforcement. Depressed individuals have deficits in one or more of these phases, resulting in depressive symptoms (for review see Rehm, 1988). Self-control deficits of depressed adults include: (a) selective monitoring or attending to negative events to the exclusion of positive events, (b) selective monitoring to immediate as opposed to delayed consequences of one's behavior, (c) setting overly stringent self-evaluation criteria, (d) making negative attributions of responsibilities for one's behavior, (e) utilizing insufficient contingent self-reinforcement and (f) administering excessive self-punishment (Rehm, 1977). The few studies examining self-control deficits in depressed children and adolescents reveal that these youth set overly stringent self-evaluative criteria, endorse maladaptive causal attributions, and engage in self-punishment (Kaslow, Rehm, & Siegel, 1984; Kaslow, Rehm, Pollack, & Siegel, 1988). They also report more overall self-control problems than their nondepressed peers (Kaslow et al., 1988).

Interpersonal/Family Factors

Interpersonal Perspective

Similar to the social-skills model articulated above, the interpersonal perspective focuses on social relationships. However, while the social-skills approach emphasizes social-skill deficits as the primary cause of depression, the interpersonal model takes a more interactional view. For example, according to Klerman, Weissman, Rounsaville, and Chevron (1984), the interpersonal approach focuses on dysfunction in past and current social roles and interpersonal interactions as the key etiologic factors in depression. Similarly, in Coyne's (1976) interpersonal formulation of depression, depressive symptoms initially are reinforced by the increased support and concern of others. As a person displays more depressive symptoms, others experience them as aversive and respond with a combination of anger, guilt, and superficial support. In response, the depressed person becomes more symptomatic and significant others withdraw further, maintaining and intensifying the vicious interpersonal cycle. Gotlib and Hammen (1992) proposed a cognitive-interpersonal integrative model of depression. According to this diathesis-stress model, cognitive variables that mediate the stress-depression relation must be understood in a context of social and environmental resources and behavioral competencies. Specifically, individuals who acquire dysfunctional cognitive schema regarding self and others, secondary to problematic parent-child and family relations (including attachment difficulties), are likely to exhibit poor interpersonal skills and impaired self-esteem. This combination of factors increases vulnerability to depression, particularly in response to experiences that activate negative interpretations of interpersonal events.

The data described in the social skills section regarding the interpersonal functioning of depressed youth also support the interpersonal etiological models of depression. Thus, these findings will not be reiterated here.

Family Perspective

Since the family serves as a child's primary social contact, the salient role of the family in the etiology and maintenance of depression in children and adolescents must be considered (for reviews see Chiariello & Orvaschel, 1995; Hammen, 1991; Kaslow, Deering, & Racusin, 1994; Kaslow, Deering, & Ash, 1996). Several family risk factors are associated with an increased vulnerability to depression in a child or adolescent, most notably family history of mood disorders, other family psychiatric conditions (e.g., substance abuse, anxiety disorders), family structure variables (e.g., single parent families, divorced families), and acute and chronic negative family life events (e.g., loss, maltreatment, poverty). Family relational patterns associated with depressive symptoms in youth include: insecure parent-child attachment, low levels of family cohesion and support, inappropriate levels of family control, high levels of conflict and poor conflict resolution skills, difficulties with affect regulation, dysfunctional communication patterns, and a poorness of fit between child temperament and family interactional style (Kaslow et al., 1996). Mechanisms proposed to account for the transmission of depression from parents to children include genetic predisposition, maladaptive parent-child interactions, impaired parenting skills, and marital discord (for reviews see Hammen, 1991; Kaslow et al., 1994; 1996).

Biological Factors

Genetic Contribution

Data support a genetic contribution to depressive disorders in children and adolescents. Children with a family history of depression, particularly parental depression, are at increased risk for depression (Hammen, 1991). Monozygotic twins, even when reared apart, have a higher concordance rate for mood disorder than dizygotic twins. Further, adopted children of biologic parents with a positive history for depression have more depression than do adopted controls.

Neurobiological Factors

Studies of adults demonstrate associations between depression and a number of neurobiological variables (Schatzberg & Nemeroff, 1995). Dysfunction of the neuroendocrine system has been documented as evidenced by increased cortisol activity, decreased secretion of growth hormone, diminished responsivity to thyroid releasing hormone, and sleep cycle abnormalities. Abnormalities in neurotransmitter systems (e.g., acetylcholine, norepinephrine, serotonin, neuropeptides) are postulated to be of etiological significance in adult depression (Schatzberg & Nemeroff, 1995).

Attempts to identify specific neuroanatomic structures that may result in depression when damaged or dysfunctional have met with more limited success. Sleep and neuroendocrine abnormalities in depressed adults may indicate dysfunction of the limbic system and the hindbrain (Puig-Antich, 1987). Studies of patients with lateralized hemisphere damage secondary to stroke reveal an association between damage to the left frontal region and subsequent depression symptoms (Robinson, Kubos, Starr, Rao, & Price, 1984). Other researchers report focal left-sided motor abnormalities in depressed adults consistent with right hemisphere dysfunction (Freeman, Galaburda, Cabal, & Geschwind, 1985). Functional neuroimaging studies also have conflicting data regarding hemispheric dysfunction in depressed adults; one study reported decreased cerebral blood flow in the right hemisphere (Ross & Rush, 1981), while another found global cortical blood flow reduction (Sackeim et al., 1990). Further, electrophysiological studies document increased activation in right frontal regions in depressed patients relative to nondepressed individuals (Davidson & Tomarken, 1989). Finally, neuropsychological studies of depressed adults have revealed nonverbal cognitive deficits suggestive of

right hemisphere dysfunction (Fromm & Schopflocher, 1984; Gray, Dean, D'Amato, & Rattan, 1987). However, these findings may reflect global problems with attention, concentration, and psychomotor speed (Tramontana & Hooper, 1989).

Only recently have scientists explored the neurobiological correlates of depression in children and adolescents (for reviews see Emslie, Weinberg, Kennard, & Kowatch, 1994; Kennard, Emslie, & Weinberg, 1992). Most neurobiological research has focused on the neuroendocrine functioning and sleep physiology in depressed youth. Abnormal neuroendocrine markers in depressed youth include growth hormone abnormalities and elevated serum thyrotropin (for review see Emslie et al., 1994). The dexamethasone suppression test (DST) may have some utility in identifying abnormality in the hypothalamic-pituitary-adrenal axis (Casat, Arana, & Powell, 1989). Although early studies failed to demonstrate sleep abnormalities in depressed prepubertal children (e.g., Puig-Antich et al., 1982), prepubertal children studied after recovery from depression have improved sleep continuity, decreased rapid eye movement (REM) latency, and increased REM density compared to normal and nondepressed controls (e.g., Emslie, Rush, Weinberg, Rintelmann, & Roffwarg, 1990; Puig-Antich et al., 1983). Polysomnography findings with adolescents have been less consistent (Goetz et al., 1987).

Data on neurotransmitter systems in depressed children is sparse and inconclusive (for reviews see Dujovne et al., 1995; Emslie et al., 1994). The most sophisticated study revealed dysregulation of central serotonergic symptoms in children with major depressive disorder (Ryan et al., 1992). Similarly, there are limited data on the neuroanatomic correlates of depression in children (Hendren, Hodde-Vargas, Vargas, Orrison, & Dell, 1991) and functional neuroimaging techniques have not yet been used to characterize depressed children. Finally, although several early studies suggested that depressed youth manifested relative impairment on the Performance subtests of the Wechsler Intelligence Schedule for Children—Revised (WISC-R), consistent with nonverbal processing deficits (e.g., Blumberg & Izard, 1985; Kaslow et al., 1983; Mullins, Siegel, & Hodges, 1985), more recent and sophisticated neuropsychological evaluations have not identified specific patterns of cognitive strengths and weaknesses in depressed youth (for review see Tramontana & Hooper, 1989).

OVERVIEW OF ASSESSMENT AND TREATMENT/INTERVENTION METHODS

Studies of interventions emphasize comprehensive assessment of depressive symptoms and disorders, comorbid psychiatric conditions, and constructs hypothesized to be associated with the development and maintenance of depressive disorders in youth. This section overviews the assessment literature and summarizes the treatment literature.

Assessment

The past 20 years have witnessed a proliferation of assessment techniques for use in clinical and research settings. These diverse techniques include self-report structured interviews, parent reports, clinician/staff, teacher ratings, and peer nominations (for reviews see Clarizio, 1994; Hodges, 1994; Reynolds, 1994). A summary of measures of depressive symptoms and disorders, and comorbid conditions, is presented in Table 3.1.

We recommend that the assessment of depression in youth employ a multitrait, multimethod, multiinformant approach to examine both individual and contextual factors, using interviews with the child/adolescent, caretakers, and other family members, and behavior ratings scales completed by multiple informants (e.g., child, parents, teachers, peers, clinicians). This strategy enhances diagnostic reliability and validity and addresses inter-informant discrepancies (Kazdin, 1994). It is essential that a comprehensive assessment include an evaluation of the child's cognitive and interpersonal competencies and impairments, as well as environmental factors. Consistent with the etiological models described above, assessment of activity level, social skills and interpersonal functioning, interpersonal problem solving, attributional style, cognitive distortions (negative cognitive triad, automatic thoughts, negative schema), self-control behav-

iors, self-esteem and perceived competence, family functioning, and life events may be included. These constructs may serve as the direct targets of intervention. Table 3.2 lists representative measures of several relevant constructs.

The development of new assessment techniques should be informed by a developmental perspective. Most current instruments are modeled after adult scales, and often do not adequately consider the child's developmental level. Future scales might be enhanced by incorporating items pertinent to different developmental levels and by developing age-appropriate norms.

When evaluating a youth for depression, a medical work-up is essential. In addition to a physical examination, laboratory work should include a hematologic profile with differential to look for signs of infection or anemia, a thyroid panel to evaluate for thyroid disease, and an electrolyte panel (including liver and kidney function tests) to evaluate for potential metabolic abnormalities and kidney disorders (Weller & Weller, 1991). Other tests may include an EEG to rule out seizures, and an electrocardiogram (ECG) if a tricyclic antidepressant trial is likely. Since depression may be substance induced, a drug screen may be appropriate. Further, because many prescribed medications have depressive symptoms as a side effect, a thorough medication history should be obtained (Kashani & Breedlove, 1994).

Treatment and Intervention

A range of psychosocial interventions for depressed youth have been articulated. Commonly proposed interventions include psychodynamic (Bemporad, 1988), cognitive (Wilkes, Belsher, Rush, & Frank, 1994), cognitive-behavioral (Kaslow & Rehm, 1991; Stark, 1990), interpersonal (Mufson, Moreau, Weissman, & Klerman, 1993), group (Beeferman & Orvaschel, 1994), and family (Kaslow & Racusin, 1994) therapies. Empirical investigations of treatments for depression in youth are relatively recent. The earliest published reports were case studies in which traditional psychodynamic approaches were described (Bemporad, 1978; Beres, 1966; Boverman & French, 1979; Cohen, 1980; Furman, 1974; Gilpin, 1976; Sacks, 1977). Case reports of

TABLE 3.1. Assessment Instruments

SCALE	AUTHOR	DESCRIPTIONS	SAMPLES AND PSYCHOMETRICS
Children's Depression Inventory (CDI	Kovacs & Beck (1977) Kovacs (1992)	27-item self-report, modified version of Beck Depression Inventory for adults. Measures severity of depressive symptoms. Subscales for negative mood, interpersonal problems, ineffectiveness, anhedonia, and negative self-esteem.	Psychiatric, medical, and normal children ages 7–17. Standardized composite and subscale scores are available. Internal consistency and test-retest reliabilities are good. The scale has adequate discriminant and concurrent validity, and is sensitive to change.
Children's Depression Scale (CDS)	Tisher & Lang (1983)	66-item self-report. Alternate forms for parents, teachers, and siblings. Subscales for affective response, social problems, self-esteem, sickness and death, guilt, pleasure, and enjoyment.	Psychiatric and normal samples ages 9–16. Internal consistency and discriminant reliability is high, test-retest reliability is moderate, and criterion validity is adequate.
Children's Depression Scale-Revised (CDS-R)	Reynolds, Anderson, & Bartell (1985)	30-item self-report scale with 29 items measuring depressive symptoms and 1 item being a global rating of depression.	Normal children ages 8–13. Demonstrated high internal consistency, high correlatin with CDI and with teacher's global ratings.
Depression Self-Rating Scale (DSRS)	Birleson (1981)	18-item original scale and 21-item original modified scale. Self-report scale patterned after the Zung.	Psychiatric inpatients, children 7–13. Adequate criterion validity, and concurrent validity. Good test, retest, split-half, and internal consistency reliability.
Reynolds Child Depression Scale (RADS)	Reynolds (1989)	30-item self-report scale measuring depressive symptomatology.	Large sample of normal children ages 8–13. Good internal consistency and test-retest, reliability, and good criterion related validity, content validity, discriminant validity, and clinical utility.
Reynolds Adolescent Depression Scale (RADS)	Reynolds (1986)	30-item self-report scale reflecting DSM-III symptomatology for major depression and dysthymic disorder.	Large ethnically diverse normative sample of 12–18-year-olds. Good internal consistency and test-retest reliability and concurrent and discriminative validity.
Center for Epidemiological Depression Studies– Depression Scale modified for Children (CES-DC)	Weissman, Orvaschel, & Padian (1980)	20-item self-report scale that is a derivative of the adult CES-D.	Normal sample and inpatients, ages 6–17. Low test-retest reliability, low adequate internal consistency, reliability, and limited discriminative validity.
Back Depression Inventory	Beck et al. (1961)	21-item self-report scale measuring depressive symptoms.	Normal and clinical (inpatient and outpatient) samples of 13–18-year-olds. Adequate internal consistency reliability, low to moderate test-retest reliability, reasonable sensitivity and specificity in normal but not clinical samples, and low criterion validity.
Depression Adjective Checklist (C-DACL)	Sokoloff & Lubin (1983)	Both forms of C-DACL self-report scale contain 34 adjectives pertaining to presence or absence of depressed mood	Emotionally disturbed youth. Excellent internal consistency, alternate form, and split-half reliabilities. Good concurrent validity.

TABLE 3.1. Assessment Instruments (continued)

SCALE	AUTHOR	DESCRIPTIONS	SAMPLES AND PSYCHOMETRICS
Youth Self Report (YSR)	Achenbach & Edelbrock (1987)	Includes a competence scale and 112 items that load on 7 subscales. Also yields broad band internalizing and externalizing scale scores and a total problem score.	Normal and clinical samples of 11–18 year-olds. Adequate test-retest reliability and criterion related validity.
Rating Scale for Dysphonia (RSD)	Lefkowitz, Tesiny, & Solodow (1989)	12-item self-report Likert response scale parallels the Peer Nomination Inventory for Depression.	Used with school children and adolescents. Adequate test-retest and internal consistency reliabilities, and criterion-related validity.
Kiddie-SADS-Epidemiologic Version (K-SADS-E)	Orvaschel & Puig-Antich (1987)	Structured interview to assess past and current episodes of depression and other forms of psychopathology. Based on the SADS interview and DSM-III-R.	Psychiatric and normal samples ages 6–17. Adequate test-retest reliability and moderate criterion-related validity.
Kiddie-SADS-Present Episode	Revised by Puig-Antich & Ryan (1986)	Structured interview for depression, other diagnoses, and psychiatric history. Focuses on present episode. Modified version of Schedule for Affective Disorders and Schizophrenia. DSM-III-R compatible revised version. Interview Administered to parent and child.	Psychiatric and normal samples, ages 6–17. Interrater reliability high, good convergent validity, but low to moderate interinformant reliability.
NIMH Diagnostic Interview Schedule for Children (DIS-2.3)	Costello, Edelbrock, Dulcan, Kalas, & Klavic (1984); Shaffer et al. (in press)	Clinical interview based on DSM-IV diagnostic categories.	Can be administered by lay interviewers to children ages 6–17 and their parents. Adequate test-retest reliability and criterion related validity.
Child Assessment Schedule (CAS)	Hodges, Cools, & McKnew (1989)	Scale includes a clinical interview and clinician rating of depression and other forms of psychopathology. Administered to the child.	Outpatients, inpatients, and normal latency-age children and offspring of affectively disturbed and normal mothers. Satisfactory interrater reliability and concurrent validity.
Diagnostic interview for Children and Adolescents–Revised (DICA-R)	Herjanic, Herjanic, Brown, & Wheatt (1975)	Interview with parent and child forms to assess school progress, social behavior, somatic and psychiatric symptoms. Parent form also assesses early development, family history, and socioeconomic status.	Adequate psychometrics.
Interview Schedule for Children (ISC)	Kovacs (1980/1981)	Structured interview covering mental status, behavioral observations, and DSM diagnoses. Child and parent administered interviews.	Psychiatric and normal samples, ages 8–13. Adequate interrater reliability for most items. Correlates with CDI.
Children's Depression Rating Scale-Revised (CDRS-R)	Poznanski et al. (1984)	Clinician-rated instrument. The severity-of-depression scale has 17 items. 14 scored on verbal observation and 3 on nonverbal observation. Revision of Hamilton Depression Rating Scale.	Psychiatric and pediatric samples of children, ages 6–12. Scale has good test-retest reliability, interrater reliability, and concurrent validity.

TABLE 3.1. Assessment Instruments (continued)

SCALE	AUTHOR	DESCRIPTIONS	SAMPLES AND PSYCHOMETRICS
Bellevue Index of Depression (BID)	Petti (1978)	Structured interview with 40 items under 19 headings. Assesses severity on basis of Weinberg criteria. Parent and child report used.	Inpatient and outpatient samples, ages 6–12. Good interrater reliability and adequate convergent validity.
Children's Affective Rating Scale (CARS)	McKnew Cytryn, Efron, Gershon, & Bunney (1979)	Clinical interview assessing mood, behavior, verbal expression, and fantasy on 10-point scales.	Psychiatric inpatients, medical patients, normals, and children of depressed parents, ages 5–15. Adequate interrater reliability and concurrent validity.
School Aged Depressed Listed Interview (SADLI)	Petty & Law (1982)	28-item interview to measure change in severity of depressive symptomatology.	Psychiatric inpatients, ages 6–13. Psychometric properties not explored, although there is high interrater reliability on videotaped interviews.
Dysthymic Check List (DCL)	Fine, Moretti, Haley, & Marriage (1984)	Clinician rating scale to assess each criterion of dysthymia on a 3-point severity scale.	Outpatient, inpatient, and medical populations, ages 8–17. Good interrater reliability.
Child Behavior Check List (CBCL)	Achenbach (1991)	Includes a competence scale and 112 behavior problems that yield 7 narrow band and 2 broad band factors, plus a total problem score.	Appropriate for parents of clinic and normal children, ages 4–16. Good psychometric properties.
Personality Inventory for Children-Depression Scale (PIC)	Wirt, Lachar, Klinedinst, & Seat (1977)	600-item parent report inventory, 46-item depression scale; symptoms identified by clinicians.	Designed for ages 3–16. Good test-retest reliability. Factor analysis yields clusters directly comparable to DSM-III-associated symptoms of depression.
Staff Nomination Inventory of Depression	Saylor, Finch, Baskin, Furey, & Kelly (1984)	20-item scale by which staff members nominate children who best fit each description.	Staff member on inpatient unit rating, 7–11-year-olds. No psychometrics reported.
Teacher's Report Form (TRF)	Achenbach (1991)	Parallel form to YSR and CBCL.	Appropriate for teachers of 4–16-year-olds. Adequate psychometrics data.
Teacher Rating Inventory of Depression-Modified (TRID-M)	Lefkowitz & Tesiny (1980); Bell-Dolan, Reaven, & Peterson (1993)	12-item rating scale parallels Peer Nomination Inventory for Depression.	None reported.
Teacher Rating Scale (TRS)	Lefkowitz & Tesiny (1980)	5-item rating scale of depressive symptoms.	None reported.
Peer Nomination Inventory for Depression (PNID)	Lefkowitz & Tesiny (1980)	Peer nomination ratings for depression (13), happiness (4), and popularity roles (2).	Given to fourth and fifth graders. Good internal consistency, test-retest, and interrater reliability; good content and concurrent validity.

TABLE 3.2. Assessment of Correlates of Child and Adolescent Depression

DOMAIN	INSTRUMENT	REFERENCES
Activity level	Children's Reinforcement Survey Schedule	Cautela (1977)
	Adolescent Activities Checklist	Cole, Kelly, & Carey (1988)
Social and interpersonal skills	Social Adjustment Inventory for Children and Adolescents (SAICA)	John, Gammon, Prusoff, & Warner (1987)
	Matson Evaluation of Social Skills with Youngsters (MESSY)	Matson, Rotatori, & Helsel (1983)
	Behavioral Assertiveness Test for Children (BAT-C)	Bornstein, Bellack, & Hersen (1977)
Social problem solving	Alternative Solutions Test (AST)	Caplan, Weissberg, Bersoff, Ezekowitz, & Wells (1986)
Attributional style	Children's Attributional Style Questionnaire (CASQ)	Seligman, Peterson, Kaslow, Tanenbaum, & Abramson (1984)
Cognitive distortions	Cognitive Triad Inventory for Children (CTI-C)	Kaslow, Stark, Printz, Livingston, & Tasi (1992)
	Automatic Thoughts Questionnaire (ATC)	Hollon & Kendall (1980); Kazdin (1990)
	Children's Negative Cognitive Error Questionnaire	Leitenberg, Yost, & Carroll-Wilson (1986)
	Hopelessness Scale for Children (HPLS)	Kazdin, Rodgers, & Colbus (1986)
Self concept/self-esteem/ perceived competence	Piers-Harris Children's Self Concept Scale	Piers (1984)
	Self-Perception Profile for Children	Harter (1985)
Self-control	Usually That's Me	Humphrey (1982)
Life events	Life Events Checklist (LEC)	Brand & Johnson (1982); Johnson & McCutcheon (1980)
	Family Inventory of Life Events and Changes (LIFE)	McCubbin, Patterson, & Wilson (1985)
Family functioning	Family Adaptability and Cohesion Evaluation Scales III (FACES-III)	Olson, Portner, & Lavee (1985)
	Family Environment Scale (FES)	Moos & Moos (1981)
	Family Assessment Device	Epstein, Baldwin, & Bishop (1983)
	Family Assessment Measure	Skinner, Steinhauer, & Santa-Barbara (1983)
	Family Strengths	Olson, Larsen, & McCubbin (1985)
	Living and Familial Environments Coding System (LIFE)	Arthur, Hops, & Biglan (1982)

behavioral interventions for depressed youth, particularly social-skills training, also emerged (e.g., Bornstein, Bellack, & Hersen, 1977; Frame, Matson, Sonis, Fialkov, & Kazdin, 1982; Matson et al., 1980; Petti, Bornstein, Delamater, & Connors, 1980). More recently, psychosocial treatment outcome studies for depressed children (for review see Stark, Rouse, & Kurowski, 1994) and depressed adolescents (for review see Lewinsohn, Clarke, & Rohde, 1994) have appeared.

Consistent with the psychosocial literature, the early pharmacological treatment reports were case studies using antidepressant medications (for reviews see Campbell & Spencer, 1988; Puig-Antich, 1982). More recently, methodologically rigorous research designs have been used to examine the efficacy of various medications (for reviews see Dujovne et al., 1995; Johnston & Fruehling, 1994).

SPECIFIC INTERVENTION AND PREVENTION METHODS

Consistent with the etiological models discussed above, this section will describe empirical studies of specific interventions organized into three categories: cognitive-behavioral; interpersonal/family; and biological. Only group-design studies that incorporate treatment manuals or clearly defined intervention techniques and that provide pre-post intervention data are reviewed. Illustrative case examples will be provided, and applications of the methods across settings and providers will be discussed. Recent prevention programs designed for youth at-risk for depression will also be reviewed. In presenting these studies, we realize that few, if any, meet the recently delineated criteria for either "well-established" or "probably efficacious" treatments (Task Force on Promotion and Dissemination of Psychological Procedures, 1995), however, they represent the best efforts of the field to date, and significant advances have been made in the past few years.

Cognitive-Behavioral Interventions

The majority of treatment outcome studies for depressed children and adolescents have investigated cognitive-behavioral techniques. Most studies have not assessed specific cognitive-behavioral interventions, but rather have been guided by multiple models of depression and have targeted myriad cognitive and behavioral symptoms.

The first empirical investigation of treatment for depressed children compared the efficacy of 10-session role play, cognitive restructuring, attention placebo, and waiting list conditions for fifth and sixth graders with elevated self-reported depression scores and teacher referrals (Butler, Miezitis, Friedman, & Cole, 1980). This study was undertaken in an elementary school; the interventions were conducted by graduate students in applied psychology. The role-play intervention, devised for this study, targeted social problem-solving training and rehearsal of social skills. In the cognitive restructuring condition, influenced by the work of Beck, Rush, Shaw, and Emery (1979) and Ellis (1962), depressive and cognitive patterns were identified, and the children were taught to develop more adaptive cognitions. Although both experimental conditions were effective, children in the role-play group showed comparatively fewer self-reported depressive symptoms and better functioning in the classroom. No follow-up was conducted.

Stark, Reynolds, and Kaslow (1987) compared 12-session group interventions of self-control therapy based on the work of Rehm (1977), behavior problem-solving therapy based on the work of Lewinsohn (1974), and a waiting list control condition for fourth through sixth graders with elevated self-reported depression scores. This study was implemented in a school setting; interventions were led by graduate students and postdoctoral fellows in clinical and school psychology. The self-control groups were taught adaptive self-monitoring, self-evaluating, self-consequating, and appropriate causal attributions. The behavioral problem-solving group consisted of education, self-monitoring of pleasant events, and group problem solving directed toward improving social behavior. Post-intervention and 8-week follow-up assessments found that children in both active interventions reported a reduction of depressive symptoms; participants on the waiting list endorsed minimal change.

In a subsequent study in which the primary treatment intervention was based on a combination of

Rehm's self-control model and Lewinsohn's behavioral model, Stark, Rouse, and Livingston (1991) evaluated self-control therapy for fourth through seventh graders with high levels of depressive symptoms. This 24–26 session cognitive-behavioral treatment, conducted in a school setting by graduate students in school psychology, included self-control and social-skills training, cognitive restructuring, and problem-solving techniques. This experimental intervention was compared to a traditional counseling condition designed to control for nonspecific elements of therapy. Both conditions incorporated monthly family contacts. At post-intervention and 7-month follow-up, both groups revealed decreased self-reported depression on a paper- and pencil-measure. Interestingly, however, at post-intervention, children in the cognitive-behavioral group were rated by graduate students blind to treatment condition as more improved on a semi-structured interview than were youth in the counseling condition. Children in the cognitive-behavioral intervention also endorsed fewer depressive cognitions at post-intervention than their peers in the counseling condition. These data suggest that interventions that target cognitions may enhance adaptive cognitive processing more than interventions not designed to address directly dysfunctional cognitions.

Rehm and Sharp (1996) examined a psychoeducational intervention based on self-control theory in a large, urban multicultural school setting. The sample consisted of fourth and fifth graders nominated by school personnel based on descriptions of depressed behavior and who had elevated depressive symptom scores. The intervention was conducted by school psychology interns and graduate students in clinical and counseling psychology. At post-intervention, there were significant decreases in self-reported depressive symptoms, significant improvements in social skills, and more adaptive attributional styles. No follow-up data are reported.

Liddle and Spence (1990) randomly assigned 7- to 11-year-olds with elevated depressive symptoms on self-report measures and a diagnostic interview to 8-week social competence training, attention placebo control, and no treatment control groups. This study was conducted in private Catholic schools by postdoctoral fellows in clinical psychol-

ogy. The social competence training condition, based on a combination of cognitive and behavioral models, included social-skills training, interpersonal problem-solving techniques, and cognitive restructuring regarding social situations. Although all groups reported fewer depressive symptoms at post-intervention and 3-month follow-up, no differential treatment effects were found and no changes in social competence were revealed.

Kahn, Kehle, Jenson, and Clark (1990) compared three psychoeducational group interventions (cognitive-behavioral, relaxation training, self-modeling) and a wait-list control for 10- to 14-year-olds selected on self-reports and parent reports, and clinical interview. These psychoeducational groups took place in a large, suburban middle school, and were led by a school psychologist or school counselor. The cognitive-behavioral intervention incorporated the Coping with Depression course of Lewinsohn and colleagues (Lewinsohn, Antonuccio, Steinmetz, Teri, 1984), a relaxation training program similar to that used by Reynolds and Coats (1986), and a self-modeling approach in which individuals repeatedly view videotapes of themselves exhibiting only positive behaviors (Dowrick, 1983). Decreases in depressive symptoms and improved self-esteem were noted in children in all three experimental conditions relative to the wait-list control. Improvements were maintained at 1-month follow-up. There were no significant differences between the experimental conditions.

Reynolds and Coats (1986) conducted the first treatment outcome study of adolescent depression. Nonreferred high school students who self-reported high levels of depressive symptoms were assigned randomly to self-control therapy akin to the treatment delineated by Rehm (10 sessions), relaxation training in accord with the strategies articulated by Lewinsohn (10 sessions), or a wait-list control condition. All sessions were conducted in the high school and were led by graduate students in school psychology. Post-treatment and 5-week follow-up results revealed that both experimental conditions were more effective than the control condition in reducing depression and anxiety and enhancing academic self-concept. No differences were found between the active treatment conditions.

Fine, Forth, Gilbert, and Haley (1991) compared a 12-week social-skills training group to a therapeutic support group for psychiatric outpatient adolescents who met diagnostic criteria for major depressive disorder or dysthymic disorder. Both groups were conducted by a male-female co-therapy dyad, that included an experienced and less experienced mental health professional (psychiatrist, psychologist, social worker, psychiatric nurse). The social-skills groups, based on Lewinsohn's social-skills model, taught specific skills including recognizing feelings, assertiveness, communication skills, and social problem solving. In the therapeutic support groups, discussions of common concerns were facilitated and adaptive ways to address difficult situations were addressed. At post-treatment, youth in the support groups had less clinical depression and higher self-concepts than those in the social-skills groups. At 9-month follow-up, between-group differences were no longer evident; adolescents in the support groups maintained their gains and those youth who had participated in the social skills group continued to improve.

The most sophisticated cognitive-behavioral treatment outcome study has been conducted by Lewinsohn, Clarke, Hops, and Andrews (1990) with depressed adolescents in schools. These interventions were led by graduate students in clinical, counseling, or educational psychology or social work. Lewinsohn and colleagues (1990) assigned high school students, ages 14–18 with DSM depressive disorders, to 14-session cognitive-behavioral group treatment for the adolescent only, concurrent cognitive-behavioral treatment groups for the depressed adolescent and his or her parents, and a wait-list control. The cognitive-behavioral intervention, based on the Coping with Depression course for adults (Lewinsohn et al., 1984), was adapted to address the concerns and competencies of adolescents, and focused on experiential learning and skills training (increasing pleasant activities, relaxation, controlling depressive thoughts, improving social interaction and communication, and negotiation and conflict resolution skills). The 7-session complementary parent intervention aimed at enhancing parents' capacity to reinforce and promote their adolescent's adaptive changes to increase

the likelihood that treatment effects would be maintained and generalized. Post-therapy, fewer adolescents in the active treatment groups met criteria for depression, and they showed greater reductions in self-reported depressive and anxious symptoms and maladaptive cognitions, and more involvement in positive events compared to youth in the wait-list condition. Gains were maintained at 2-year follow-up. Although a trend indicated that the adolescent-and-parent condition was more effective than the adolescent-only condition, only a few between-group differences reached statistical significance.

While these studies suggest that a variety of cognitive-behavioral intervention approaches may be efficacious in ameliorating depressive symptoms, and are more effective than no intervention, no single treatment appears superior for depressed children and adolescents. Most studies were conducted in schools with nonreferred youth with depressive symptoms and used relatively inexperienced clinicians. Thus, the generalizability of the findings across populations, settings, and clinician-experience level remains unclear (Asarnow, 1990). Further, there are no data regarding which specific component(s) of these multifaceted interventions may be most beneficial for which problems (Asarnow, 1990; Harrington, 1993). Finally, these outcome studies fail to accommodate developmental differences in children's competencies and do not assess the effectiveness of various intervention strategies for youth at different ages and developmental level. Future research should: (a) integrate developmental research findings on the cognitive, affective, and social functioning of youth in devising and implementing cognitive-behavioral therapies for depressed children; (b) explore the efficacy of specific components of those multimodal interventions for which positive findings have been reported; and (c) be designed consistent with the recommendations for empirically validated interventions set forth by the Task Force on Promotion and Dissemination of Psychological Procedures (1995).

Case Illustration

J., an 8-year-old male was referred to the school psychologist for a psychological evaluation by his teacher who reported that he seemed sad, increasingly withdrawn socially, less active in classroom activities, and more self-deprecatory for the past few months, ever since his best friend had moved out of the school district. Upon evaluation of the child, and after gathering data from J.'s parents and peers, and observing him in the school setting, the school psychologist determined that he met diagnostic criteria for a major depressive disorder, single episode. He did not show evidence for a significant sleep or appetite disturbance, and he denied active suicidal intent. What was most prominent in interviews with J. was his description of himself as "a failure." He stated, "I hate myself and everyone hates me. I can't do anything right. Nothing is fun anymore and nobody likes me." His parents appeared kind and loving, but it was evident that his father was depressed and had low self-esteem and his mother also noted "feeling insecure" and commented, "I blame myself for J.'s problems and for everything that goes wrong in the family." The school psychologist used a cognitive-behavioral approach to address J.'s depressive symptoms. Specific attention was paid to addressing his maladaptive attributional patterns (i.e., he made internal-stable-global attributions for negative events) and helping him make more adaptive causal statements regarding both positive and negative events in his life (e.g., blame himself less for negative events, and understand the causes of these events as less stable over time and less generalizable across situations). In a related vein, the school psychologist used a number of techniques to challenge J.'s negatively distorted view of himself and his world. As J. began to use these techniques, he acknowledged "feeling better" and "being more with other kids." He began to report, however, that "no matter what I do, it's never good enough for my parents." Thus, to help address the parents' own low self-esteem, maladaptive attributions for their own behavior and for J.'s behavior, and their tendency to be overly critical and not sufficiently reinforcing of either themselves or J., a referral was made for concurrent family therapy. The family intervention focused on addressing the family's depressive cognitive style, which influenced each family member's view of him or her self, as well as their interactions with one another. Within a few months, the family reported communicating with one another in a more supportive and less critical fashion. This shift in the family patterns was associated with improved school performance and social involvement on the part of J.

Interpersonal/Family

As noted above, some of the cognitive-behavioral intervention programs have incorporated a parent program (e.g., Lewinsohn et al., 1990; Stark et al., 1991), but there is limited data to support the enhanced efficacy of cognitive-behavioral interventions when parent involvement is included. Other studies have evaluated treatments that emphasize the role of interpersonal and family factors in depression including: interpersonal psychotherapy for depression and family psychoeducational programs.

Interpersonal therapy for adolescents (IPT-A) (Mufson et al., 1993), modified from interpersonal therapy for adults (Klerman et al., 1984), is a psychoeducational treatment approach designed for use with adolescents ages 12–18 with an acute onset major depression. Its goals are to decrease the depressive symptoms and interpersonal problems associated with depression. IPT-A uses a developmental perspective to address common interpersonal issues of adolescence, including age-appropriate independence from family-of-origin, authority and peer conflicts, and romantic relationships with peers. After a 12-week open trial of individual interpersonal psychotherapy for clinically depressed adolescents in an outpatient psychiatric clinic, adolescents treated by a clinical child psychologist reported decreases in depressive symptoms, no longer met criteria for a depressive disorder, and evidenced improvements in other psychological symptoms and physical distress (Mufson et al., 1994). IPT-A also appeared to improve overall social functioning. No follow-up data on this cohort of 14 adolescents has been reported thus far.

Brent, Poling, McKain, and Baugher (1993) examined a 2-hour psychoeducational program for parents of suicidal adolescents with mood disorders followed in an outpatient clinic. This psychoeducational program was led jointly by a psychiatrist and a social worker, and emphasized knowledge and coping strategies (Poling, 1989). For some parents, attendance at this program was associated with a small increase in knowledge about mood disorders and a slight modification of dysfunctional beliefs about the etiology, course, and treatment of adolescent depression. No follow-up data are reported.

In sum, the limited data regarding interpersonal psychotherapy for depression in youth are promising. But, the small sample size and absence of follow-up data make it premature to comment on the efficacy of this approach. Given the dearth of empirical studies focusing on family interventions for depressed youth, despite data suggesting that family variables play a critical role in the development and maintenance of depression in youth, no conclusions about the efficacy of this treatment approach can be drawn. We recommend that future research focus on the development, implementation, and evaluation of interpersonal and/or family-systems interventions for depressed children and adolescents.

Case Illustration

S., an intelligent, articulate 15-year-old female requested to see a therapist, informing her parents, who were in the midst of a divorce, that she was "depressed." During the evaluation, it became evident that S.'s depression (dysphoric and irritable mood, appetite decrease and 10-pound weight loss, anhedonia, low self-esteem, concentration difficulties, decreased concentration) was associated with her feeling triangulated during her parent's divorce. Her mother had become profoundly depressed prior to the divorce, and S. felt like she had to "mother my mother. She doesn't act like a mother to me anymore." She felt more cared for by her father, but experienced him as critical and demanding of perfection and a high level of achievement, but rarely complimentary when she did achieve. Given that S.'s depressive symptoms emerged in the context of family turmoil, it appeared that some structural family interventions to detriangulate and de-parentify S. were indicated. Additionally, S. appeared interested in some individual sessions to help her "grow up and become my own person." "I feel depressed about my family situation and my parents can't help me because they have too many of her own problems." Since S. did not evidence particular skill deficits, a

course of IPT-A was initiated once the major structural family interventions had been put into place.

Biological Interventions

There are two biological interventions for depressed youth: pharmacotherapy and electroconvulsive therapy. Pharmacological intervention targets neurotransmitter systems implicated in depression (see Schatzberg & Nemeroff, 1995). It is believed that the mechanism of action of antidepressant medications involves both increasing intrasynaptic serotonin/norepinephrine, and the down-regulation of neuroreceptors and other effects on the neurons via second messenger systems.

Initially, open trials of TCAs (e.g., imipramine, nortriptyline, amitriptyline) yielded encouraging results for prepubertal youth. However, findings were less clear for adolescents (for reviews see Harrington, 1993; Ryan, 1992). Open trials of two SSRIs, fluoxetine (prozac) and fluvoxamine (luvox), yielded positive results in adolescent depression (e.g., Apter et al., 1994; Boulous, Kutcher, Gardner, & Young, 1992). In more methodologically sophisticated double-blind studies, however, TCAs were not found to be superior to placebo medication (e.g., Geller et al., 1992; Puig-Antich et al., 1987). Similarly, a placebo-controlled double-blind study of fluoxetine failed to demonstrate superiority of medication over placebo (Simeon, DiNicola, Ferguson, & Copping, 1990). The disparity of findings between youth and adult populations may be related to developmental differences in pharmacokinetics and brain neurochemistry (Ryan, 1992).

Although TCAs and SSRIs are the two major classes of drugs that have been used to treat youth depression, other pharmacological agents have been studied. For example, some adolescents who fail to have a complete recovery with TCAs alone, may benefit from lithium augmentation (e.g., Strober, Freeman, Rigali, Schmidt, & Diamond, 1992). Additionally, although monoamine oxidase inhibitors (MAOIs) may be used, they rarely are prescribed for youth due to the required dietary restrictions (e.g., Ryan, 1992).

Despite equivocal empirical support for antidepressant medications, many child psychiatrists advocate their use. However, TCAs are associated with problematic side effects in children (e.g., cardiac changes) and may be lethal in overdose (Ryan, 1992). Similarly, there are enumerable problems associated with the use of MAOIs in youth. However, SSRIs, the newest class of antidepressants, have few harmful side effects and tend not to be dangerous in overdose (Rosenberg, Holttum, & Gershon, 1994). These medications are, however, more expensive than other antidepressants, and may be cost prohibitive for some families. Fortunately, some pharmaceutical companies offer programs for low income individuals.

An alternative treatment that may impact neurotransmitter function is electroconvulsive therapy (ECT). In this medical procedure, an electrical current is applied to the brain to elicit a generalized seizure in an anesthetized patient. ECT has been hypothesized to result in changes in neurotransmitter function and may alter the metabolic activity of some regions of the brain. Some case reports document the efficacy of ECT in 80% of depressed youth (e.g., Bertagnoli & Borchardt, 1990). However, there is a reluctance to use this treatment due to the limited documentation of treatment efficacy with youth and the potential negative sequelae (e.g., brief organic impairment and long-term cognitive deficits, alteration of seizure threshold, anxiety, disinhibition) (Bertagnoli & Borchardt, 1990). The American Psychiatric Association Task Force on ECT (1990) recommends that ECT be used only for youth for whom other treatments are not effective or safe.

Case Illustration

P., a 14-year-old male, was referred for an evaluation by his pediatrician who was concerned about his nonspecific somatic complaints, lethargy and psychomotor retardation, marked weight gain and frequent need to nap following the murder of his father. An evaluation with P., which included meetings with his family (e.g., maternal grandmother, mother, two older siblings), as well as P. individually revealed a marked deterioration in his interpersonal and academic functioning for the three months since his father's death. P., who had been quite close to his father, spent hours alone in his room, "wishing I'm dead." He reported feeling "too sad to cry"

and his family was "afraid for his safety." His mother and older brother had been on antidepressant medications since the father's death, and both reported the medications to be "helpful." The family also reported a family psychiatric history significant for depression, alcohol abuse, and anxiety. Given the severity of P.'s vegetative symptoms, the presence of significant suicidal ideation, and the positive response on the part of family members to antidepressant medications, P. was started on a medication trial concurrent with the institution of a family oriented cognitive-behavioral intervention for P.'s depression. Since the family was supportive and P. was willing to contract not to harm himself, at least on a session by session basis, it was decided that hospitalization was not indicated.

Prevention Programs

When devising and implementing intervention programs for depressed children and adolescents, we recommend consideration of the relatively new prevention literature. A number of the approaches used to treat depression in youth have been used in a preventative context. For the most part, these prevention efforts have been psychoeducational in nature (Rehm & Sharp, 1996). While many of these prevention programs have been conducted in school settings, some efforts that have targeted at-risk youth (e.g., children of depressed parents) have been undertaken in clinical settings. Some of the prevention efforts conducted to date have incorporated universal interventions, delivered to all members of a population, whereas others have used targeted interventions, delivered to a subgroup of high-risk youth (e.g., individuals with early signs of a mood disorder; children of depressed parents). Prevention trials for depression are recent, although a number of programs designed for youth following stressful events (e.g., divorce, bereavement) have implications for preventing depression (Asarnow, 1990). These programs have targeted children as young as first grade through high school. The major empirical prevention studies are discussed below.

Kellam and colleagues (Kellam, Rebok, Mayer, Ialongo, & Kalodner, 1994) instituted a classroom-based prevention program to enhance academic competence among urban, lower middle to low socioeconomic status first graders of mixed ethnicity. One program targeted reading achievement and the other program targeted aggressive behavior; both targets were considered to be antecedents to later depressive symptoms. These two prevention programs were compared to education as usual. The reading intervention yielded improved reading skills, which were linked to a marked reduction of depressive symptoms, most notably in boys. All girls who showed achievement gains, regardless of group status, also evidenced reductions in depressive symptoms. Due to the complexity of the study design and the resultant findings, it is premature to draw conclusions about the efficacy of these prevention approaches for depression in youth.

Jaycox, Reivich, Gillham, and Seligman (1994) explored the efficacy of a group cognitive and social problem solving program for 10- to 13-year-olds with elevated depressive symptoms and parental conflict. The cognitive component of the program was based on the work of Ellis (1962) and Beck (1967; Beck et al., 1979). This study was conducted in suburban schools, and the preventive intervention was led by doctoral students in clinical psychology. Results revealed greater diminution of symptoms for youth in the experimental condition than for those in the condition; this finding was true at both post-intervention and 6-month follow-up.

Rice, Herman, and Petersen (1993) used a psychoeducational approach to teach adaptive cognitive and behavioral skills to seventh graders in both rural (working class) and suburban (middle to upper-middle class) school settings. The 16-session preventive intervention was based primarily on Clarke and Lewinsohn's (1986) Coping with Depression manual and the work of Goldstein and colleagues (Goldstein, Sprafkin, Gershaw, & Klein, 1980) on teaching prosocial skills. Participants in the preventive intervention reported increases in perceived coping ability and perceived control over challenging events, improved peer relationships, and enhanced family relationships, whereas no significant improvements were noted in those youth who did not receive the intervention. Additionally, while the preadolescents in the preventive intervention condition noted a decrease in negative life events,

control subjects revealed a notable increase in negative life events. No follow-up data were reported.

Clarke and colleagues (1995) compared a 15-session after-school preventive intervention program (a modification of the Coping with Depression course: Adolescent version; Clarke & Lewinsohn, 1986) versus a treatment-as-usual control condition for ninth and tenth graders with self-reported depressive symptoms who did not meet diagnostic criteria for a mood disorder. The groups were held in suburban high schools and were led by master's level school psychologists and school counselors with considerable experience and training. A survival analysis indicated that at a 12-month follow-up, adolescents in the experimental group were less likely than controls to meet diagnostic criteria for a mood disorder. These findings support the utility of prevention programs in reducing the risk for mood disorders in vulnerable youth.

Related prevention efforts focus on children at high risk for depression (e.g., children of affectively ill parents). In an outpatient clinic, Beardslee and colleagues (1993) compared clinician-based versus lecture-based cognitive psychoeducational prevention programs for addressing family members' behaviors and attitudes toward depression. Families in the clinician-based group were more positive about the program and developed more adaptive attitudes and behaviors for coping with stress than did families in the lecture-based program. These changes may be associated with improved parental management of high-risk children and more adaptive child coping, both of which may decrease the child's risk for depression (Beardslee et al., 1993).

Taken together, these prevention efforts, which are in their infancy, yield promising results. Given that depressive disorders recur and interfere with a child's development and functioning, clinical researchers need to design and implement prevention programs aimed at reducing the risk of childhood mood disorders and their impact on adaptive functioning. Attention should be paid to developing preventive intervention programs for children and adolescents at risk for depression (e.g., low levels of persistent dysphoria; children of depressed parents). Additional efforts should be devoted to relapse prevention. These prevention efforts should be grounded in clear theoretical frameworks that address risk factors for child and adolescent depression.

TREATMENT PRESCRIPTIONS

Given that our empirically based knowledge about effective treatments for depressed youth is in its early stages, there are virtually no data that address specifically which treatment, for which depressed child or adolescent, in which setting(s), and under what conditions. Consistent with the model articulated in earlier editions of this chapter (e.g., Kaslow & Rehm, 1991), it is our belief that optimal treatment for depressed youth is both theory-driven and developmentally appropriate. Intervention begins with a thorough and careful assessment of the child and his or her family across multiple behavioral domains hypothesized by the various models to be associated with depression in youth. Based on the deficits identified in the assessment, optimal interventions should incorporate therapeutic strategies targeting these specific behaviors into a comprehensive treatment plan.

When treating children and adolescents, it is desirable to identify which deficit(s) seem to be most prominent. One could approach this problem by attempting to assess all potential deficits and then choosing specific interventions, or by developing a very large treatment package that would attempt to cover all potential targets systematically. Either of these approaches would be cumbersome, time-consuming, and cost-ineffective, and would fail to take each child or adolescent's unique difficulties and competencies into account. Kaslow and Rehm (1991) assert that a more rational strategy might be to order the potential treatments in a logical sequence and then to make step-wise decisions regarding selection and implementation. The following discussion of treatment prescription builds on and expands the prior work of Kaslow and Rehm (1991). We begin with an overview of the context within which treatment decisions should be made and implemented, emphasizing the child's social network and biological functioning. The next section describes specific treatment strategies for target behaviors that have been linked theoretically to child and adolescent depression, as discussed in pre-

vious sections of this chapter. To illustrate the recommended decision-making process, Figure 3.1 provides an illustrative flow chart that can aid in treatment planning.

Biopsychosocial Context

In treating depressed children, it is important to attend to family functioning, including the possibility of depression and related forms of psychopathology in the parents, family stress, family interaction patterns, family-support systems, and the implications of these factors for the child's psychological development and functioning. For those families in which the parents also manifest difficulties, the family work should address the parents' needs as well. Families in which the family dynamics appear linked intimately with the development and/or maintenance of the child's depression should received family-systems oriented interventions and/or parent-training methods. Finally, for those families in which the child's difficulties appear relatively separate from the family situation, parents can be encouraged to facilitate specific intervention strategies to help remediate their depressed child's deficits. For example, parents might be incorporated into an activity-increase strategy as the managers of external reinforcement and might help the child become involved in the various activities. In self-control programs, parents may model the various self-management strategies; support their children in utilizing these strategies; and utilize appropriate monitoring, evaluation, attribution, and reinforcement of their children's behavior (Lewinsohn & Clark, 1986). For more detailed discussion of family involvement in the treatment of depressed youth, the reader is referred to Kaslow and Racusin (1994).

Although empirical support for pharmacological interventions for child and adolescent depression is equivocal, clinical practice reveals that medication in conjunction with psychosocial and psychological interventions may be helpful for certain youth. Specifically, children who exhibit significant neurovegetative symptoms (e.g., sleep disturbance, appetite disturbance, concentration difficulties, psychomotor agitation or retardation) may not be able

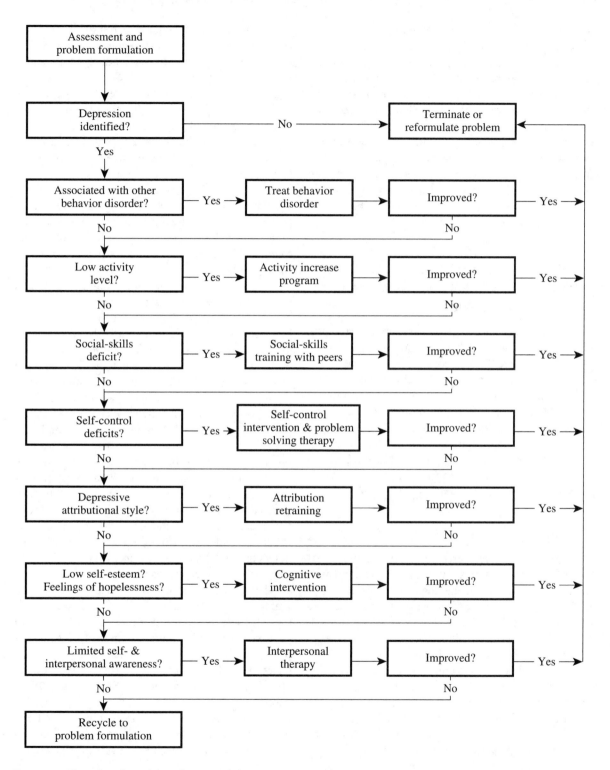

Figure 3.1. Flow chart for ordering decisions about intervention targets in treating depression in children and adolescents.

to benefit from more psychologically oriented approaches until some symptom remission can be achieved. For these youth, early pharmacologic intervention may be indicated. For other youth, minimal response to psychological interventions or deterioration in functioning may signal the need for a medication consultation trial. Throughout the treatment course, ongoing monitoring of the symptom severity and need for medication is recommended. For those depressed youth who appear acutely suicidal, either during the evaluation or at some point during the treatment, inpatient hospitalization may be necessary to insure safety.

Cognitive-Behavioral and Interpersonal Targets and Associated Intervention Srategies

This section reviews briefly those treatment outcome studies with depressed adults that have informed, or may inform, cognitive and behavioral intervention programs with depressed youth. The intent of this section is to provide sufficient information about each approach to allow the clinician or clinical researcher to incorporate in an age-appropriate manner those intervention strategies most useful to target the specific, behavioral, cognitive, or interpersonal deficits manifested by a given depressed child or adolescent.

Activity Level Increase Programs

Lewinsohn and colleagues conducted a number of group studies with adults in which increasing pleasant activities and decreasing negative activities were the major goals of at least one of the treatment conditions (for reviews see Rehm & Kaslow, 1984; Lewinsohn & Gotlib, 1995). The therapeutic interventions in these programs include: (a) monitoring mood and activity level to obtain a baseline; (b) identifying positive activities in an individual's repertoire that correlate with daily pleasant mood, (c) instigating increases in those activities that are potentially reinforcing, (d) decreasing negative activities that correlate with negative mood, and (e) setting up environmental contingencies to reinforce increased positive activity and decreased negative activity. The activity level increase studies conducted with adults have yielded partially successful results, though many subjects are still depressed at post-testing (Rehm & Kaslow, 1984). Changes in activity level do correlate with changes in depression.

The assumption underlying activity-increase programs is that behaviors associated with reinforcing consequences are not being produced.

Target behaviors for activity-increase programs should be intrinsically reinforcing or have a high probability of producing external reinforcement. First, targeted behaviors may be those that were found to be enjoyable in the past. For example, social withdrawal in a child who formerly had enjoyed good peer relationships might suggest that certain social activities should be the target of an activity-increase program. Second, an activity might be targeted if it could be empirically shown to be associated with improved mood. Third, self-report events schedules (i.e., lists of potentially rewarding activities have been used to survey possible targets). Fourth, the Premack principle—whereby more frequent positive behavior is used to increase the frequency of less probable behaviors—may be employed. Parallel to the adult programs, activity increases may be prompted merely by scheduling the activities, or external or self-managed reinforcement programs may be used. Initially developed for younger children, external reinforcement may be preferable to self-reinforcement. Major techniques found to be effective in increasing children's activity level include modeling, individual and group contingencies and social reinforcement, and social-skills training.

There are no reports of activity-increase programs as the sole treatment for depression in children. However, monitoring and increasing of positive events has been a component of a number of the empirical treatment studies with youth (e.g., Clark et al., 1995; Kahn et al., 1990; Lewinsohn et al., 1990; Stark et al., 1987; Stark et al., 1991) described above. Given empirical evidence that depressed adults have a reduced activity level and benefit from activity-increase programs, and that depressed youth evidence low levels of engagement in positive activities, it behooves clinical researchers to evaluate activity level in depressed children and adolescents and to intervene with this symptom when indicated.

Social Skills Training

The goal of social-skills training is to enhance the depressed individuals' social skills and ability to elicit reinforcement from others. Numerous studies have been conducted with depressed adults to improve their social skills (for review, see Lewinsohn & Gotlib, 1995). In these programs participants are taught appropriate assertive social skills to use in problematic interpersonal situations. Skills taught vary from the specific details of voice quality and posture, to the more general goals of improving the individual's overall social skills and social perceptions. Methods include instruction, modeling, rehearsal and role play, feedback, and homework. According to Rehm and Kaslow's (1984) and Lewinsohn and Gotlib's (1995) reviews of this literature, social-skills training is superior to control conditions, but equivalent or inferior to more complex cognitive and behavioral programs.

Depressed youth may have deficits in eliciting contingent positive reinforcement from significant others in the social environment. A prerequisite to using social-skills training with children and adolescents is the identification of specific skills that, in natural settings, are rewarding to children at different levels of development. Research in childhood depression would be enhanced by naturalistic study of the social skills of clinical, normal, and socially adept samples of children.

In a recent handbook of child and adolescent treatment manuals, LeCroy (1994) discusses the utility of social-skills training as an approach to treating a variety of childhood internalizing and externalizing disorders, in addition to providing a manualized, step-by-step social-skills training program for youth across multiple settings (e.g., schools, residential treatment centers, day treatment centers, and community-based agencies). The literature on social-skills training procedures with children suggests that three main strategies have been

used: (a) shaping procedures that use adult reinforcement, (b) modeling or combined modeling and reinforcement procedures, and (c) direct training procedures to make use of the child's cognitive and verbal skills. Contingent adult reinforcement can be useful in shaping the amount of interaction between children but these positive effects may not be maintained. Modeling techniques appear to have dramatic effects in increasing the child's social interaction, with superior maintenance of changes. The more recent verbal-cognitive approaches emphasize teaching both relatively specific social skills (e.g., asking a peer for help) as well as general problem-solving techniques.

A number of case studies have been reported that specifically examine social-skills training for depressed children (e.g., Bornstein et al., 1977; Frame et al., 1982; Matson et al., 1980; Petti et al., 1980) (for review of these studies, see Kaslow & Rehm, 1991). For the most part, these reports of both hospitalized and outpatient depressed youth, yield promising findings, suggesting the utility of this approach for those depressed children and adolescents who manifest social-skills deficits. Further support for this training strategy can be gleaned from those group design studies that incorporated a social-skills training component (e.g., Clark et al., 1995; Fine et al., 1991; Kahn et al., 1990; Lewinsohn et al., 1990; Liddle & Spence, 1990; Reynolds & Coats, 1986; Rice et al., 1993; Stark et al., 1987; 1991).

Attribution Retraining

Based on the attributional reformulation of the learned helplessness model, Seligman (1981) described four therapeutic strategies for treating depression: (a) environmental enrichment—use of environmental manipulation to reduce the estimated likelihood of aversive outcomes and increase the estimated likelihood of desired outcomes, (b) personal control training—the strategy of changing expectations from uncontrollability to controllability, (c) resignation training—the strategy of making highly preferred outcomes less preferred, and (d) attribution retraining—the use of methods to change an individual's unrealistic attributions. According to

Seligman (1981), individuals should be retrained to attribute failure to more external, unstable, and specific factors and success to more internal, stable, and global factors. To date, little research has been conducted using attribution retraining strategies alone for treating depressed adults. However, in conjunction with other cognitive and behavioral strategies, attribution retraining appears efficacious in ameliorating depressive symptoms in adults and enhancing adaptive attributional patterns (for review, see Rehm & Kaslow, 1984). Similarly, a few of the multicomponent cognitive-behavioral treatment studies with children and adolescents that yielded positive outcomes included an attribution retraining component (e.g., Rehm & Sharp, 1996; Stark et al., 1987).

Another approach, which is akin to Seligman's (1981) attribution retraining, is described by Dweck (1975) in her work with children who had extreme reactions to failure. These children received one of two training procedures. One group was given success experiences only, similar to the environmental enrichment proposed by Seligman (1981). The second group was given attributional retraining, which taught these children to take responsibility for their failure and to attribute it to lack of effort (i.e., an internal-unstable-specific attribution for failure). Results revealed that the post-intervention performance of children in the success-only condition continued to deteriorate when they were confronted with failure. However, the children in the attribution retraining group maintained or improved their performance, and showed an increase in the degree to which they emphasized lack of effort versus lack of ability as a determinant of their failure. It is notable that Dweck has children learn to make internal-unstable-specific attributions for their failure; this may be appropriate to instigate greater effort on solvable problems. Dweck's attribution retraining program demonstrates that an adaptive coping response can be taught to children as an alternative to helplessness and lends further support to the potential utility of using attribution retraining with those depressed children with a "depressogenic" attributional style.

More recently, Seligman and coworkers (Seligman, Reivich, Jaycox, & Gillham, 1995) have advocated the use of attribution training as a preventative strategy for depression, and to enable children and adolescents to feel more optimistic and hopeful in order to cope more effectively with life stresses. A recent prevention trial with school children incorporated an attribution retraining program (e.g., Jaycox et al., 1994), and with positive results.

Cognitive Therapy

Cognitive therapy for depression in adults, has been described in a lengthy therapy manual (Beck et al., 1979). The techniques are designed to help the patient identify, reality-test, and modify distorted conceptualizations and dysfunctional attitudes and beliefs. The cognitive techniques proposed include the following: (a) recognizing the connection between cognition, affect, and behavior; (b) monitoring negative automatic thoughts; (c) examining evidence for and against distorted automatic thoughts; (d) substituting more reality-oriented interpretations for distorted cognitions; and (e) learning to identify and modify dysfunctional beliefs. The behavioral techniques used in cognitive therapy (e.g., scheduling activities, mastery and pleasure techniques, graded task assignment, cognitive-behavioral rehearsal, assertiveness training, role playing) also aim to change the patient's cognitions.

Cognitive therapy for depressed adults has been evaluated in a number of reports by Beck and his colleagues and in independent evaluations, and a number of researchers have used modifications of Beck's therapy with depressed adults (Beck, 1961; Beck et al., 1979). Additionally, the large, National Institute of Mental Health Depression Treatment Collaborative study included cognitive therapy as one of its treatment conditions (e.g., Elkin et al., 1989). In general, these studies document the efficacy of cognitive therapy for depression, but few have found it to be superior to other active interventions.

A number of authors have suggested methods for adapting cognitive therapy for adult depression to the treatment of nonpsychotic depressed children and adolescents (e.g., DiGiuseppe, 1986; Emery, Bedrosian, & Garber, 1983; Wilkes et al., 1994). These authors have enumerated a number of ways in which cognitive therapy for depressed youths differs from cognitive therapy for depressed adults. First, the therapist should be well trained in conducting child psychotherapy, in order to establish an effective therapeutic alliance with the patient. Second, it is important to involve the child's or adolescent's family in the assessment and treatment process. The family's cognitions interact with those of the depressed child and may reinforce and perpetuate the child's depression. Parents can be aided in arranging more appropriate contingencies that will extinguish the child's depressive behaviors and increase more socially adaptive behaviors. In those instances in which the family holds distorted cognitions, it is necessary to challenge and change these distortions and to alter parenting techniques that may be reinforcing and perpetuating their child's depression. Parents may also become involved in actively providing opportunities that will enable their child to acquire new information and test new hypotheses to modify their cognitive distortions. Third, it is crucial to take into account the youth's level of cognitive development. In the concrete-operational stage, children have the capacity to experience many of the cognitive symptoms associated with depression—such as guilt, low self-esteem, misattributions of negative events, and feelings of rejection. However, given their lack of fully developed time perspective, they may not be able to experience hopelessness fully. Children at the concrete-operational stage can make inaccurate inferences about concrete reality. However, they are also cognitively capable of generating and testing propositions, but may require help from adults in identifying alternative inferences. Adolescents at the formal-operational level are cognitively capable of experiencing all the cognitive symptoms associated with depression; they can generate hypotheses and logically deduce the relations among two or more propositions. Thus, many of the techniques that cognitive therapists utilize with adults are potentially effective with depressed adolescents. However, the difficulties that adolescents sometimes encounter in communicating with a therapist, as well as the key features of adolescent depression (e.g., anhedonia, self-esteem and identity issues, feelings of helplessness, rejection, and loss) call for the modification of cognitive therapy methods. Wilkes and coworkers (1994) have provided a

treatment manual for cognitive therapy with depressed outpatient and inpatient adolescents, with and without comorbid psychiatric conditions. Although there are no treatment studies with children or adolescents that use only cognitive therapy techniques, many of the multicomponent intervention and prevention programs with youth have incorporated the collaborative empiricism designed to help children and adolescents identify and evaluate their cognitions regarding self, world, and future that is the hallmark of the cognitive therapy approach (e.g., Butler et al., 1980; Clark et al., 1995; Jaycox et al., 1994; Lewinsohn et al., 1990; Liddle & Spence, 1990; Stark et al., 1991).

Another cognitively oriented treatment that targets symptoms associated with child and adolescent depression is presented in the book *Self-Esteem Enhancement with Children and Adolescents* by Pope, McHale, and Craighead (1988). These authors describe treatment modules covering topics relevant to all the approaches described in this chapter. Social problem solving, self-statements, attributional style, self-control, social understanding and skills, and communication skills, are all addressed as means of enhancing self-esteem. Additionally, in her treatment guide for coping skills interventions for children and adolescents, Forman (1993) describes techniques for decreasing irrational beliefs and developing stress reducing thought patterns.

Self-Control Therapy

Based on the self-control model of depression, Rehm and his colleagues have conducted a series of treatment outcome studies with depressed adults, and independent replications of this treatment approach also have been reported (for review see Rehm, 1990). The specific techniques used in self-control therapy are designed to improve the individual's self-control skills. Participants are taught to: (a) monitor their positive activities and self-statements, (b) increase those positive behaviors and cognitions associated with improved mood, (c) identify the delayed versus immediate consequences of their behavior, (d) attend to the positive and delayed consequences that result from performing a difficult behavior, (e) set more realistic and attainable standards, (f) break goals down into attainable subgoals, (g) make more appropriate attributions for success and failure, and (h) increase contingent overt and covert self-reinforcement and decrease both overt and covert self-punishment.

Self-control therapy has been found to be superior to a waiting-list control group, nonspecific group therapy, and to assertion training (Rehm and Kaslow, 1984). Although a significant portion of the clients remain mildly depressed at the end of treatment, a large number are nondepressed at the completion of therapy and at follow-up. According to Rehm (1990), the effectiveness of this intervention approach does not depend on the inclusion of all three components (i.e., self-monitoring, self-evaluation, self-reinforcement) of the model. It also appears to be equally effective in ameliorating cognitive and behavioral deficits associated with depression, suggesting a nonspecificity of treatment effects.

The self-control model of depression (Rehm, 1977) differs from other models in that it postulates that a sequence of related, but semi-independent, behaviors are central to depression. It assumes that depression is associated with deficits at one or more stages of self-control. Thus, in adapting this model for children and adolescents, it is important to use those strategies that target the particular self-control deficit(s), as well as overall self-control skills, manifested by a given youth.

A major intervention approach for improving overall self-control skills in children is self-instruction training (e.g., Forman, 1993; Kendall & Braswell, 1985; Meichenbaum, 1977), which has received considerable attention as a training method in the literature on cognitive-behavioral therapy with children. Self-instruction training aims to teach children to use self-verbalization strategies to control their behavior, monitor their progress, and self-reinforce contingently. Self-verbalizations are developed through cognitive modeling, overt external guidance, overt and covert rehearsal, prompts, feedback, and reinforcement. Most self-control training programs help children with problem definition, problem approach, focusing attention on the problem and considering options, choosing an answer, taking action on a chosen plan, and using self-reinforcement or coping statements. These self-

control training programs for youth use strategies similar to those found effective in problem-solving therapy for adult depression in which depressed individuals are taught to: identify previous and current life-situations that may be antecedents of a depressive episode, minimize the negative impact of depressive symptoms on current and future coping attempts, increase the effectiveness of problem-solving efforts at coping with current life stresses, and develop skills that will facilitate dealing with future problems (Nezu et al., 1989).

There are a number of major advantages of self-instruction training and problem-solving approaches (e.g., Cole & Kazdin, 1980; Nezu et al., 1989). First, these approaches represent a form of self-control that children can use to interrupt or inhibit a sequence of thoughts or actions. The use of self-instruction enables the child to become less dependent on external contingencies and more reliant on internal control. This facilitates generalization and maintenance of treatment effects. Second, verbal self-instruction training and problem solving are components of the natural developmental sequence by which children gain control of their verbal behavior (Vygotsky, 1962). It may be that a remedial procedure for children with self-control deficits may enhance the development of self-control skills and may lead to the growth of automatic covert verbal self-control. Third, self-instruction training and problem-solving therapy provide the basic skills for adaptive problem solving that may allow children to avoid depression and other problems later in their development.

Self-instruction training has been used effectively for children with a variety of behavior problems including impulsivity, hyperactivity, delinquency, social withdrawal (an aspect of depression), and learning disabilities. A meta-analytic review of outcome studies using self-instruction training for childhood behavioral disorders yielded positive results (Dush, Hirt, & Schroeder, 1989). Based on the data from this meta-analysis, the authors concluded that programs conducted in clinical settings (e.g., outpatient clinics, special education programs) were more effective than those implemented in regular school environments. Additionally, results indicated that therapist experience was associated with more positive outcome.

Unfortunately, however, data on the long-term effects of this intervention approach is limited.

Most relevant to the current chapter is the fact that a number of treatment studies for depressed youth have been based on Rehm's (1977) self-control therapy for depression (e.g., Reynolds & Coats, 1986; Stark et al., 1987; 1991). These intervention programs have modified Rehm's (1977) treatment manual in a manner that takes into account children's cognitive developmental capacities and requires the therapist to play a more active role in effecting the desired change by utilizing more action-oriented techniques and concrete task assignments. Overall, self-control as a model for assessing and treating depression in children seems to have promise. As with the other models, however, continued systematic work is necessary.

Interpersonal Therapy

Whereas the aforementioned treatments target primarily cognitive and behavioral deficits, interpersonal psychotherapy (IPT) is a major non-cognitive-behavioral psychological therapy of depression that has been well-articulated (e.g., Klerman et al., 1984) and has been subjected to experimental investigation with depressed adults. This treatment approach stresses identifying central relationship problems and developing approaches to resolve these difficulties. The treatment with depressed adults focuses on the problem areas of grief, interpersonal role disputes, role transitions, and interpersonal deficits. IPT incorporates traditional psychotherapy techniques along with cognitive and behavioral strategies, and is based on attachment theory, interpersonal psychiatry, and findings from epidemiological studies revealing the association between social "exit events" and the onset of depressive episodes. The approach has been evaluated in a number of studies and has been included in the national collaborative study of therapy for depression (Elkin et al., 1989). Results from these investigations reveal that IPT is associated with a reduction in depressive symptoms and an improvement in social adjustment. In the large collaborative study, IPT was as effective as cognitive therapy, both of which were less effective than medication management and more effective than a placebo plus clinical management

control condition (Elkin et al., 1989). As noted earlier, preliminary data support the efficacy of interpersonal therapy for adolescents (IPT-A) (Mufson et al., 1994) and a treatment manual designed specifically for depressed adolescents has been published (e.g., Mufson et al., 1993). It is reasonable to posit that those youth whose primary difficulties are in the interpersonal domain, and who do not respond adequately to social-skills training, may benefit from IPT-A. Additionally, those youth who are able to benefit to some degree from skills training, but whose interpersonal awareness limits capacity to utilize these skills, also may be helped by this approach.

Recommended Treatment Sequence for Depressed Youth

The flow chart shown in Figure 3.1 is an attempt to suggest a sequential decision process for incorporating specific cognitive, behavioral, and interpersonal strategies for targeting specific symptoms into a treatment plan. The first step in the chart is a thorough assessment and problem formulation. If based on this assessment, evidence of syndromal depression is found, the first consideration should be whether or not the depressive complaints may be secondary to another major childhood problem (e.g., enuresis, school phobia, impulsivity, aggression) and/or a secondary consequence of one of the disorders that often appear to be comorbid with depression (e.g., anxiety disorders, conduct disorders, attention deficit disorders, substance use disorders, eating disorders) (e.g., Angold & Costello, 1993; Kashani et al., 1987). In such cases, treatment should first be aimed at alleviating the primary behavioral disorder. Depression should be monitored and, if it persists after these problems have been remedied, treatment strategies targeted at specific depressive behaviors should be considered. Reviews of methods for the treatment of these other childhood problems can be found elsewhere in this book. If the depression appears to be primary, the behavioral, cognitive, and interpersonal intervention strategies articulated above should be considered.

The model assumes that some skills may be prerequisites to others and that some deficits may be more fundamental than others. For example, the model places targets of overt behavioral change (e.g., activity level, social skills) prior to covert or cognitive targets (e.g., cognitive distortions, self-control deficits) based on the assumption that accuracy of self-control skills probably cannot be well-evaluated unless some level of appropriate overt behavior is present. The next series of steps in the flow chart are ordered according to the degree to which cognitions, rather than behaviors, are the intervention target. Specifically, as one progresses through the sequence, the focus of intervention becomes increasingly cognitive in nature. Finally, increased self-awareness may be important to solidify those behavioral and cognitive changes associated with the aforementioned targeted treatments. Thus, interpersonal therapy may be the final step in the sequence for those youth who possess the necessary skills, but lack the capacity to effectively utilize these cognitive and behavioral strategies.

As noted earlier, this sequence of targeted interventions is most likely to be beneficial to the child or adolescent if conducted with active family involvement. Depending on the child's particular difficulties and competencies, as well as the setting, a combination of individual and/or group therapy in conjunction with family work may be indicated. Additionally, when neurovegetative symptoms are severe and/or persist, pharmacotherapy may be a useful adjunctive intervention.

ADDITIONAL CONSIDERATIONS ASSOCIATED WITH THE TREATMENT OF CHILD AND ADOLESCENT DEPRESSION

When designing and implementing treatments for depressed youth, there are two additional considerations that deserve attention: developmental factors and the sex of the child.

Developmental Factors

Depression manifests itself differently across the life span. The types of symptoms exhibited by children of different ages are dependent on the attainment of cognitive, interpersonal, and affective skills (e.g.,

Cole & Kaslow, 1988; Rehm & Carter, 1990) necessary to report depressive cognitions, self-reflect, and regulate affect. Specifically, observation of distressed infants reveals symptoms commonly associated with depression including: lethargy; feeding and sleep problems; irritability; sad or expressionless faces; decreased affective responsivity, attentive behavior, and curiosity; and increased frowning and crying (Carlson & Kashani, 1988). Symptoms commonly associated with depressive behavior in preschoolers include anger and irritability, sad facial expression, labile mood, somatic complaints, feeding and sleep problems, lethargy, excessive crying, hyper- or hypo- activity, decreased socialization, tantrums, separation anxiety, and anhedonia (Carlson & Kashani, 1988). There is a relatively stable pattern of depressive symptoms in 6- to 8-year-olds that includes prolonged unhappiness, decreased socialization, sleep problems, irritability, lethargy, poor school performance, accident-proneness, phobias, separation anxiety, and attention-seeking behaviors (Carlson & Kashani, 1988; Edelsohn, Ialongo, Werthamer-Larsson, Crockett, & Kellam, 1992). Children at this age typically do not verbalize hopelessness and self-deprecation; rather, they express their inner experiences through behavioral problems. In contrast, 9- to 12-year-olds, who are more self-aware often verbalize feelings of low self-esteem and helplessness when depressed. They also evidence irritability, depressed mood, sad expression, aggression, lethargy, guilt, poor school performance, phobias, and separation anxiety (Carlson & Kashani, 1988; Weiss et al., 1992). More severe symptoms may emerge at this time, such as suicidal ideation (Poznanski, 1982), hallucinations (Ryan et al., 1987), and self-destructive behaviors (Bemporad & Lee, 1984). Studies comparing the phenomenology of depression in child and adolescent samples indicate that the similarities in symptom expression exceed the differences (Mitchell et al., 1988; Ryan et al., 1987). Both groups evidence somatic complaints, social withdrawal, hopelessness, and irritability. However, as a result of the cognitive developmental shift that accompanies formal operations, compared to depressed elementary school children, depressed adolescents report more concern about the future in conjunction with pessimism, worthlessness, and apathy (Weiss et al., 1992). Increased autonomy and peer comparison contribute to depressed adolescents' tendency to engage in more lethal suicide attempts, substance abuse, eating disorders, and antisocial behavior (Reinherz, Frost, & Pakiz, 1991; Ryan et al., 1987).

Given the differences in symptom presentation and cognitive, interpersonal, and affective competencies that characterize depressed youth at different developmental stages, it is essential that any treatment intervention be developmentally sensitive. Since the cognitive-behavioral and interpersonal intervention programs to date have focused on children during the middle childhood and adolescent years, the following comments address treatment modifications appropriate for these age groups.

The developmental literature highlights several challenges associated with treating depressed youth. First, children have limited memory and attentional capacities. As such, they may benefit from short and repetitious treatment sessions. Second, because of children's limited verbal capacities, they may be engaged most effectively when games, activities, and stories are incorporated into treatment protocols (Stark et al., 1994). Finally, because children are dependent on, and influenced by their families, family involvement in treatment may be beneficial and even necessary (Kaslow & Racusin, 1994).

As with children, in evaluating treatment procedures for use in adolescence, it is important to consider the challenges associated with this developmental stage. First, adolescence is characterized by the transition from concrete to formal operational thought, and adolescents often are excited by their newly developing abilities for meta-cognition. As a result, therapies that exercise these new abilities may be met with less resistance than is found with many adults (Rush & Nowels, 1994). In addition, adolescence is characterized by biological, psychological, and social developmental changes that occur during puberty (Rutter & Hersov, 1985; Wilkes et al., 1994). Thus, treatment approaches must consider not only the adolescent's cognitive and internal psychological processes, but also his or her psychosocial environment (e.g., peers, family, social activities).

Sex Differences

Research on sex differences in depression indicates a sex X age interaction. Among prepubertal children, some researchers report higher rates of depression in prepubertal boys than girls (Anderson, Williams, McGee, & Silva, 1987), while others report an absence of sex differences in depression (Fleming & Offord, 1990). However, studies consistently reveal that, by age 15, females are twice as likely as males to receive a depressive diagnosis (Angold & Rutter, 1992; Nolen-Hoeksema & Girgus, 1994). Explanations for sex differences in depression among adolescents include differences in sex-role socialization, cognitive styles, the presence and timing of negative life events during early adolescence, and differential hormonal changes associated with puberty (e.g., Brooks-Gunn & Warren, 1989; Nolen-Hoeksema & Girgus, 1994; Petersen et al., 1993).

When considering gender-sensitive treatment modifications, clinicians must consider the specific sociocultural factors associated with the development and maintenance of depressive episodes in females versus males, the tasks and challenges that their current life stage present, and the centrality of interpersonal relationships in females' construction of self and achievement concerns in males' identity formation. These gender-sensitive treatment modifications may be guided by the work of Carter and Kaslow (1992), who recommend specific ways to tailor cognitive-behavioral, interpersonal, and pharmacological interventions separately for females and males.

GENERALIZABILITY OF TREATMENTS FOR CHILD AND ADOLESCENT DEPRESSION

Given that the treatment literature for child and adolescent depression is in its early stages, it may not be surprising that little information is available regarding the generalizability of treatment across settings, providers, behaviors, developmental stage, sociocultural context, and time. Thus, the following is a brief review of the pertinent literature on treatment generalization.

Although interventions for depressed youth have been conducted in several settings, including schools, outpatient clinics, and inpatient units, specific studies examining the efficacy of a given intervention approach across two or more of these settings have not yet been conducted. Additionally, the pre- and post-intervention assessment of depressed youth's functioning has paid little attention to the generalization of behavior change across settings. The one exception to this is the study by Butler and colleagues (1980), in which involvement in a cognitive-behavioral group was associated with improved classroom functioning. In a related vein, there is a paucity of information about the generalization of treatment effects across therapists and service providers of different orientations and experience levels. The treatment interventions studied empirically to date predominantly have been conducted by relatively inexperienced clinicians (primarily graduate students in psychology), although some studies have used more experienced professionals, as well as therapists from different mental health disciplines. Additionally, there is virtually no information addressing the impact of treatment on symptoms or behaviors other than those targeted directly by the intervention.

There also is a dearth of information regarding the generalizability of depression treatments across a range of client attributes, including age, developmental level, cognitive ability, socioeconomic status, and ethnicity. However, different studies have targeted different age groups, and have specified the ages and/or grades of the participants. As noted in the previous section, it is essential that intervention programs be developmentally sensitive. Thus, treatment programs may need to take into account the child's age, developmental, and cognitive level, limiting the value of generalizing a given treatment across childhood. However, it may be the case that certain model-driven intervention programs, modified to be developmentally appropriate, may generalize across groups.

There is no data regarding the degree to which treatments for child and adolescent depression generalize across diverse cultural and socioeconomic backgrounds. Again, the importance of culturally

sensitive interventions for youth (e.g., Canino & Spurlock, 1994) may preclude the use of a uniform treatment package for all children, adolescents, and their families. Additionally, in light of research that questions the universality of the expression of depression, and suggests that culture influences the manifestation of depressive symptoms in youth (e.g., Manson, Ackerson, Dick, Baron, & Fleming, 1990), it is important to examine ethnic and socioeconomic differences and similarities in the etiology, expression and phenomenology of depressive disorders as these impact the treatment process (Marsella, Sartorius, Jablensky, & Fenton, 1985).

Some data have been presented addressing the issue of the generalization across time. Findings from a number of treatment outcome studies have demonstrated maintenance of treatment gains across time (e.g., Fine et al., 1991; Kahn et al., 1990; Lewinsohn et al., 1990; Liddle & Spence, 1990; Reynolds & Coats, 1986; Stark et al., 1987; 1991). The time interval between post-intervention assessment and the collection of follow-up data has ranged from one month (e.g., Kahn et al., 1990) through two years (Lewinsohn et al., 1990).

COMORBIDITY ISSUES ASSOCIATED WITH TREATMENT

Depressed children and adolescents are more likely than adults to exhibit comorbid disorders (Cantwell, 1992), and depressed youth are 20 to 80 times more likely to experience another internalizing or externalizing disorder (Angold & Costello, 1993). A review of studies of clinic-referred children revealed that 30% to 75% of clinically depressed youth had a diagnosable anxiety disorder (Kovacs, 1989). Puig-Antich (1982) reported rates of comorbid depression and conduct disorder among his clinical sample to be 33%. Empirical evidence suggests that comorbid diagnoses exist in community as well as clinic samples. Kashani and colleagues (1987) found that in a community sample of depressed adolescents, 75% had concurrent anxiety disorders, 33% received a conduct disorder diagnosis, and 50% had oppositional defiant disorder. Depression co-occurs with myriad other disorders, notably attention deficit disorder, substance use disorders, and eating disorders (Angold & Costello, l993; Kashani et al., l987).

Despite the proliferation of data regarding the comorbidity of depression and other emotional and behavioral problems in childhood, information regarding treatment considerations due to the high rates of comorbidity is sparse. One possible strategy for addressing the issue of comorbid conditions has been articulated by Kaslow and Rehm (1991) and is underscored in the flow chart depicted in Figure 3.1. Specifically, this approach suggests that if a depressive disorder appears secondary to another behavior problem, the intervention approach should begin by addressing the other condition first. If this results in an alleviation of depressive symptoms, no further intervention is indicated. However, if such a strategy does not yield significant amelioration of depressive symptoms, then interventions targeting specific cognitive, behavioral, and interpersonal problems associated with depression are the treatment of choice.

A second possible, albeit not mutually exclusive strategy, has been recommended by Kendall and colleagues (Kendall, Kortlander, Chansky, & Brady, 1992). This strategy involves the modification of treatment strategies for children and adolescents with comorbid conditions in a manner that addresses symptoms of multiple disorders. These authors suggest that clinicians treating youth with comorbid disorders may need to shift from designing and implementing interventions based on diagnostic categories toward an approach that is designed to address the individual child or adolescent's unique constellation of symptoms and difficulties. For example, when working with youth with comorbid depression and anxiety, Kendall and coworkers (1992) recommend exploring whether the child's lack of interest in attempting new activities with peers is secondary to anhedonia consistent with depression or to social inhibitions consistent with anxiety. If the former is the case, then strategies targeting dysphoric affect and associated cognitions are indicated, whereas if the latter is the case, the use of gradual exposure techniques to reduce social anxiety would be warranted. In some children, both strategies may be indicated.

CONCLUDING COMMENTS

Depression in children has been a topic of increasing theoretical, clinical, and empirical interest for the past two decades. Evidence supports the idea that some youth manifest the syndrome of depression and that depressive behavior is not reducible to mere transient reactions to life's situations or to other problematic behavior. Based on research examining the applicability of current behavioral, cognitive, and interpersonal models of depression, there is evidence that depressed youth have low activity level, poor social skills and interpersonal functioning, maladaptive attributions, distorted cognitions, deficits in self-control behaviors, and limited self- and interpersonal-awareness. Additionally, these youth often reside in families characterized by high levels of stress, discord, and maladaptive communication patterns. Further, many of these youth exhibit neurovegetative symptoms of depression indicative of underlying neurobiological abnormalities.

The cognitive-behavioral, interpersonal, and biological models of child and adolescent depression have guided the development of intervention and prevention programs and some empirical studies of their efficacy have been conducted. Taken together, treatment studies conducted with nonreferred children evidencing depressive symptoms indicate that, relative to nontreatment controls, a variety of intervention approaches (typically with a cognitive-behavioral orientation) are helpful in decreasing depressive symptoms. However, few differences have been found between treatment conditions. Although recent studies reflect greater developmental sensitivity than earlier studies, the treatment outcome literature for child and adolescent depression remains limited in several ways. First, since most studies involved nonreferred children, it is unclear whether or not these findings generalize to clinical populations (Asarnow, 1990; Harrington, 1993). Second, many intervention approaches consist of multiple components; however, there are limited data regarding which specific component(s) may be most beneficial (Asarnow, 1990). Third, although these studies appropriately examine depressive symptoms as the outcome variable, they fail to investigate changes in the target behaviors and cognitions (e.g., social skills, depressive cognitions that may precipitate and maintain depression). Fourth, these outcome studies fail to assess the effectiveness of intervention strategies for youth at different developmental levels and of different genders. Thus, research may benefit from continued efforts to incorporate a developmental and gender-sensitive perspective in designing and implementing psychosocial treatments for depressed children. Fifth, intervention programs to date have failed to take into account the child's sociocultural context and it behooves future clinical researchers to devise and implement more culturally sensitive interventions, as well as interventions that more actively include key members of the child's social network. Finally, more information is needed about the extent to which treatment programs generalize across settings, providers, and behaviors.

In closing, although data regarding a cost-benefit analysis of treatments for depressed youth are not available, there is clear and abundant evidence that left untreated, depression in youth is associated with significant cost. Specifically, depressed youth exhibit deficits in affective, cognitive, interpersonal, family, and adaptive behavior functioning that are manifested across academic, social, and ultimately, vocational settings. Additionally, depression in youth is associated with an increased risk of suicide attempts and completions. Given that current treatment approaches are more efficacious than no treatment, it is essential that we identify and intervene promptly when children and adolescents manifest signs and symptoms of depression.

REFERENCES

Abramson, L. Y., Metalsky, G . I., & Alloy, L. B. (1989). Hopelessness depression: A theory-based subtype of depression. *Psychological Bulletin, 96,* 358–372.

Abramson, L. Y., Seligman, M. E. P., & Teasdale, J. (1978). Learned helplessness in humans: Critique and reformulation. *Journal of Abnormal Psychology, 87,* 49–74.

Achenbach, T. M. (1991). *Manual for the Child Behavior Checklist/4–18 and 1991 profile.* Burlington, VT: University of Vermont Department of Psychiatry.

Achenbach, T. M. (1991). *Manual for the Teacher's Report Form and 1991 profile.* Burlington, VT: University of Vermont Department of Psychiatry.

Achenbach, T. M., & Edelbrock, C. (1987). *Manual for the Youth Self-Report Profile.* Burlington, Vt: University of Vermont Department of Psychiatry.

Altmann, E. O., & Gotlib, I. H. (1988). The social behavior of depressed children: An observational study. *Journal of Abnormal Child Psychology, 15,* 29–44.

American Psychiatric Association (1987). *Diagnostic and Statistical Manual of Mental Disorders—Third Edition—Revised (DSM-III-R).* Washington DC: American Psychiatric Association.

American Psychiatric Association (1994). *Diagnostic and Statistical Manual of Mental Disorders—Fourth Edition (DSM-IV).* Washington DC: American Psychiatric Association.

American Psychiatric Association Task Force on ECT (1990). The practice of ECT: Recommendations for treatment, training, and privileging. *Convulsive Therapy, 6,* 85–120.

Anderson, J. C., Williams, S., McGee, R., & Silva, P. A. (1987). DSM-III disorders in preadolescent children. *Archives of General Psychiatry, 44,* 69–76.

Angold, A. & Costello, E. J. (1993). Depressive comorbidity in children and adolescents: Empirical, theoretical, and methodological issues. *American Journal of Psychiatry, 150,* 1779–1791.

Angold, A., & Rutter, M. (1992). Effects of age and pubertal status in a large clinical sample. *Development and Psychopathology, 4,* 5–28.

Antonuccio, D. O., Danton, W. G., & DeNelsky, G. Y. (1995). Psychotherapy versus medication for depression: Challenging the conventional wisdom with data. *Professional Psychology: Research and Practice, 26,* 574–585.

Apter, A., Ratzoni, G., King, R., Weizman, A., Iancu, I., Binder, M., & Riddle, M. (1994). Fluvoxamine open-label treatment of adolescent inpatients with obsessive compulsive disorder or depression. *Journal of the American Academy of Child and Adolescent Psychiatry, 33,* 342–348.

Arthur, J. A., Hops, H., & Biglan, A. (1982). *LIFE (Living in Familial Environments) coding system.* Unpublished manuscript, Oregon Research Institute.

Asarnow, J. R. (1990). Psychosocial intervention strategies for the depressed child: Approaches to treatment and prevention. *Child and Adolescent Psychiatric Clinics of North America, 1,* 257–283.

Beardslee, W. R., Salt, P., Porterfield, K., Rothberg, P. S., van de Velde, P., Swatling, S., Hoke, L., Moilanen, D. L., & Wheelock, I. (1993). Comparison of preventive interventions for families with parental affective disorder. *Journal of the American Academy of Child and Adolescent Psychiatry, 32,* 254–263.

Beck, A. T. (1967). *Depression: Clinical, experimental, and theoretical.* New York: Hoeber.

Beck, A. T., Rush, A. J., Shaw, B. F., & Emery, G. (1979). *Cognitive therapy of depression.* New York: Guilford Press.

Beck, A. T., Ward, C. H., Mendelson, M., Mock, J. E., & Erbaugh, J. (1961). An inventory for measuring depression. *Archives of General Psychiatry, 4,* 561–571.

Beeferman, D., & Orvaschel, H. (1994). Group psychotherapy for depressed adolescents: A critical review. *International Journal of Group Psychotherapy, 44,* 463–475.

Bell-Dolan, D. J., Reaven, N. M., & Peterson, L. (1993). Depression and social functioning: A multidimensional study of the linkages. *Journal of Clinical Child Psychology, 22,* 306–315.

Bemporad, J. R. (1978). Psychotherapy of depression in children and adolescents. In S. Arieti and J. Bemporad (Eds.), *Severe and mild depression: A psychotherapeutic approach* (pp. 344–357). New York: Basic Books.

Bemporad, J. R. (1988). Psychodynamic treatment of depressed adolescents. *Journal of Clinical Psychology, 49,* 26–31.

Bemporad, J. R. (1994). Dynamic and interpersonal theories of depression. In W. M. Reynolds and H. F. Johnston (Eds.), *Handbook of depression in children and adolescents* (pp. 81–95). New York: Plenum Press.

Bemporad, J. R., & Lee, K. W. (1984). Developmental and psychodynamic aspects of childhood depression. *Child Psychiatry and Human Development, 14,* 145–157.

Beres, D. (1966). Superego and depression. In R. M. Lowenstein, L. M. Newman, M. Scherr, and A. J. Solnit (Eds.), *Psychoanalysis—a general psychology* (pp. 479–498). New York: International Universities Press.

Bertagnoli, M. W., & Borchardt, C. M. (1990). A review of ECT for children and adolescents. *Journal of the American Academy of Child and Adolescent Psychiatry, 29,* 302–307.

Birleson, P. (1981). The validity of depressive disorder in childhood and the development of a self-rating scale: A research report. *Journal of Clinical Child Psychology and Psychiatry, 22,* 73–88.

Blechman, E., McEnroe, M., Carella, E., & Audette, D. (1986). Childhood competence and depression. *Journal of Abnormal Psychology, 95,* 223–227.

Blumberg, S. H., & Izard, C. E. (1985). Affective and cognitive characteristics of depression in 10- and 11-year-old children. *Journal of Personality and Social Psychology, 49,* 194–202.

Bodiford, C. A., Eisenstadt, T. H., Johnson, J. H., & Bradlyn, A. S. (1988). Comparison of learned helpless cognitions and behavior in children with high and low scores on the Children's Depression Inventory. *Journal of Clinical Child Psychology, 17,* 152–158.

Bornstein, M. R., Bellack, A. S., & Hersen, M. (1977). Social skills training for unassertive children: A multiple baseline analysis. *Journal of Applied Behavior Analysis, 10,* 183–195.

Boulous, C., Kutcher, S., Gardner, D., & Young, E. (1992). An open naturalistic trial of fluoxetine in adolescents and young adults with treatment-resistant major depression. *Journal of Child and Adolescent Psychopharmacology, 2,* 103–111.

Boverman, H., & French, A. P. (1979). Treatment of the depressed child. In A. French and I. Berlin (Eds.), *Depression in children and adolescents* (pp. 129–139). New York: Human Sciences press.

Bowlby, J. (1980). *Attachment and loss: Vol. 3. Loss.* New York: Basic Books.

Brand, A. H., & Johnson, J. H. (1982). Note on reliability of the Life Events Checklist. *Psychological Reports, 50,* 1274.

Brent, D. A., Poling, K., McKain, B., & Baugher, N. (1993). A psychoeducational program for families of affectively ill children and adolescents. *Journal of the American Academy of Child and Adolescent Psychiatry, 32,* 770–774.

Brooks-Gunn, J., & Warren, M. P. (1989). Biological and social contributions to negative affect in young adolescent girls. *Child Development, 60,* 40–55.

Butler, L., Miezitis, S., Friedman, R., & Cole, E. (1980). The effect of two school-based intervention programs on depressive symptoms in preadolescents. *American Educational Research Journal, 17,* 111–119.

Campbell, M., & Spencer, E. K. (1988). Psychopharmcology in child and adolescent psychiatry: A review of the past five years. *Journal of the American Academy of Child and Adolescent Psychiatry, 27,* 269–279.

Canino, I. A., & Spurlock, J. (1994). *Culturally diverse children and adolescents: Assessment, diagnosis, and treatment.* New York: Guilford Press.

Cantwell, D. P. (1992). Clinical phenomenology and nosology. *Child and Adolescent Psychiatric Clinics of North America, 1,* 1–11.

Caplan, M., Weissberg, R. P., Bersoff, P. M., Ezekowitz, W., & Wells, M. L. (1986). *The middle school alternative solutions test (AST) scoring manual.* Unpublished manuscript. New Haven, CT: Yale University, Department of Psychology.

Carey, M. P., Kelley, M. L., Buss, R. R., & Scott, W. O. N. (1986). Relationship of activity to depression in adolescents: Development of the Adolescent Activities Checklist. *Journal of Consulting and Clinical Psychology, 54,* 320–322.

Carlson, G. A., & Garber, J. (1986). Developmental issues in the classification of depression in children. In M. Rutter, C. E. Izard, and P. B. Read (Eds.), *Depression in young people: Developmental and clinical perspectives* (pp. 399–435). New York: Guilford Press.

Carlson, G. A., & Kashani, J. H. (1988). Phenomenology of major depression from childhood through adulthood: Analysis of three studies. American Journal of *Psychiatry, 145,* 1222–1225.

Carter, A. S., & Kaslow, N. J. (1992). Phenomenology and treatment of depressed women. *Psychotherapy: Theory, Research, Practice, and Training, 29,* 603–609.

Casat, C. D., Arana, G. W, & Powell, K. (1989). The DST in children and adolescents with major depressive disorder. *American Journal of Psychiatry, 146,* 503–507.

Cautela, J. R. (1977). Children's Reinforcement Survey Schedule (CRSS). In J.R. Cautela (Ed.), *Behavior analysis forms for clinical intervention* (pp. 45–52). Illinois: Research Press.

Chiariello, M. A., & Orvaschel, H. (1995). Patterns of parent-child communication: Relationship to depression. *Clinical Psychology Review, 15,* 395–407.

Cicchetti, D., & Schneider-Rosen, K. (1986). An organization approach to childhood depression. In M. Rutter, C. E. Izard, and P. B. Read (Eds.), *Depression in young people: Developmental and clinical perspectives* (pp. 71–134). New York: Guilford Press.

Clarizio, H. F. (1994). Assessment of depression in children and adolescents by parents, teachers, and peers. In W. M. Reynolds and H. F. Johnston (Eds.), *Handbook of depression in children and adolescents* (pp. 235–248). New York: Plenum Press.

Clarke, G. N., Hawkins, W., Murphy, M., Sheeber, L. B., Lewinsohn, P. M., & Seeley, J. R. (1995). Targeted prevention of unipolar depressive disorder in an at-risk sample of high school adolescents: A randomized trial of a group cognitive intervention. *Journal of the American Academy of Child and Adolescent Psychiatry, 34,* 312–321.

Clarke, G. N., & Lewinsohn, P. M. (1986). *The Coping with depression course: Adolescent version.* Eugene: Oregon Research Institute.

Cohen, D. J. (1980). Constructive and reconstructive activities in the analysis of a depressed child. In A. J. Solnit, R. Eissler, A. Freud, M. Kris, and P. B. Neubauer (Eds.), *The psychoanalytic study of the child, 35* (pp. 237–266). New Haven, CT: Yale University Press.

Cole, P. M., & Kaslow, N. J. (1988). Interactional and cognitive strategies for affect regulation: A developmental perspective on childhood depression. In L. B. Alloy (Ed.), *Cognitive processes in depression* (pp. 310–343). New York: Guilford Press.

Cole, P. M., & Kazdin, A. E. (1980). Critical issues in self-instruction training with children. *Child Behavior Therapy, 2,* 1–21.

Cole, T. L., Kelley, M. L., & Carey, M. P. (1988). The adolescent activities checklist: Reliability, standardization data, and factorial validity. *Journal of Abnormal Psychology, 16,* 475–484.

Costello, C. G. (1972). Depression: Loss of reinforcers or loss of reinforcer effectiveness? *Behavior Therapy, 3,* 240–247.

Costello, C.G. (1980). Childhood depression: Three basic but questionable assumptions in the Lefkowitz and Burton critique. *Psychological Bulletin, 87,* 185–190.

Costello, A. J., Edelbrock, L. S., Dulcan, M. K., Kalas, R., & Klaric, S. H. (1984). *Report on the NIMH Diagnostic Interview Schedule for Children (DISC).* Washington DC: National Institute of Mental Health.

Coyne, J. C. (1976). *Toward an interactional description of depression. Psychiatry, 39,* 28–40.

Cytryn, L., & McKnew, D. H. (1974). Factors influencing the changing clinical expression of the depressive process in children. *American Journal of Psychiatry, 131,* 879–881.

Dalley, M. B., Bolocofsky, D. N., & Karlin, N. J. (1994). Teacher-ratings and self-ratings of social competency in adolescents with low- and high- depressive symptoms. *Journal of Abnormal Child Psychology, 22,* 477–485.

Davidson, R. J., & Tomarken, A. J. (1989). Laterality and emotion: An electrophysiological approach. In F. Boller and J. Grafman (Eds.), *Handbook of neuropsychology* (Vol. 3) (pp. 419–441). Amsterdam: Elsevier Science.

DiGiuseppe, R. (1986). Cognitive therapy for childhood depression. In A. Freeman, N. Epstein, & K. M. Simon (Eds.). *Depression in the family* (pp. 153–172). New York: Haworth Press.

Doerfler, L., Mullins, L., Griffin, N., Siegel, L., & Richards, C. (1984). Problem-solving deficits in depressed children, adolescents, and adults. *Cognitive Therapy and Research, 8,* 489–500.

Dowrick, D. W. (1983). Self-modeling. In P. W. Dowrick and S. J. Biggs (Eds.), *Using video: Psychological and social applications* (pp. 105–124). New York: John Wiley & Sons.

Dujovne, V. F., Barnard, M. U., & Rapoff, M. A. (1995). Pharmacological and cognitive-behavioral approaches in the treatment of childhood depression: A review and critique. *Clinical Psychology Review, 15,* 589–611.

Dush, D. M., Hirt, M. L., & Schroeder, H. E. (1989). Self-statement modification in the treatment of child behavior disorders: A meta-analysis. *Psychological Bulletin, 106,* 97–106.

Dweck, C. S. (1975). The role of expectations and attributions in the alleviation of learned helplessness. *Journal of Personality and Social Psychology, 31,* 674–685.

Edelsohn, G., Ialongo, N., Werthamer-Larsson, L., Crockett, I., & Kellam, S. (1992). Self-reported depressive symptoms in first-grade children: Developmentally transient phenomena? *Journal of the American Academy of Child and Adolescent Psychiatry, 31,* 282–290.

Elkin, I., Shea, T., Watkins, J. T., Imber, S.D., Sotsky, S. M., Collins, J. G., Glass, D. R., Pilkonis, P. A., Leber, W. R., Docherty, J. P., Flester, S. J., & Parloff, M. B. (1989). National Institute of Mental Health Treatment of Depression Collaborative Research Program: General effectiveness of treatments. *Archives of General Psychiatry, 46,* 971–982.

Ellis, A. (1962). Reason and emotion in psychotherapy. New York: Lyle Stuart.

Emery, G., Bedrosian, R., & Garber, J. (1983). Cognitive therapy with depressed children and adolescents. In D.P. Cantwell and G.A. Carlson (Eds.), *Affective disorders in childhood and adolescence: An update* (pp. 445–471). New York: Spectrum Publications.

Emslie, G. J., Rush, A. J., Weinberg, W. A., Rintelmann, J.W., & Roffwarg, H.P. (1990). Children with major depression show reduced rapid eye movement latencies. *Archives of General Psychiatry, 47,* 119–124.

Emslie, G. J., Weinberg, W. A., Kennard, B. D. & Kowatch, R. A. (1994). Neurobiological aspects of depression in children and adolescents. In W. M. Reynolds, W. M. and H. F. Johnston (Eds.), *Handbook of depression in children and adolescents* (pp. 143–165). New York: Plenum Press.

Epstein, N.B., Baldwin, L.M., & Bishop, D.S. (1983). The McMaster Family Assessment Device. *Journal of Marital and Family Therapy, 9,* 171–180.

Fauber, R., Forehand, R., Long, N., Burke, M., & Faust, J. (1987). The relationship of young adolescent Children's Depression Inventory (CDI) scores to their social and cognitive functioning. *Journal of Psychopathology and Behavioral Assessment, 9,* 161–172.

Ferster, C.B. (1971). The use of learning principles in clinical practice and training. *Psychological Record, 21,* 353–361.

Fine, S., Forth, A., Gilbert, M., & Haley, G. (1991). Group therapy for adolescent depressive disorder: A comparison of social skills and therapeutic support. *Journal of the American Academy of Child and Adolescent Psychiatry, 30,* 79–85.

Fine, S., Moretti, M., Haley, G., & Marriage, K. (1984). Depressive disorder in children and adolescents: Dysthymic disorder and the use of self-rating scales in assessment. *Child Psychiatry and Human Development, 14,* 223–229.

Fleming, J. E., & Offord, D. R. (1990). Epidemiology of childhood depressive disorders: A critical review. *Journal of the American Academy of Child and Adolescent Psychiatry, 29,* 571–580.

Forman, S. G. (1993). *Coping skills interventions for children and adolescents.* San Francisco: Jossey-Bass Publishers.

Frame, C., Matson, J. L., Sonis, W. A., Fialkov, M. J., & Kazdin, A. E. (1982). Behavioral treatment of depression in a prepubertal child. *Journal of Behavioral Therapy and Experimental Psychiatry, 3,* 239–243.

Freeman, R. L., Galaburda, A. M., Cabal, R. D., & Geschwind, N. (1985). The neurology of depression: Cognitive and behavioral deficits with focal findings in depression and resolution after electroconvulsive therapy. *Archives of Neurology, 42,* 289–291.

Fromm, D., & Schopflocher, D. (1984). Neuropsychological test performance in depressed patients before and after drug therapy. *Biological Psychiatry, 19,* 55–72.

Furman, E. (1974). *A child's parent dies: Studies in child bereavement.* New Haven, CT: Yale University Press.

Garber, J., & Hilsman, R. (1992). Cognitions, stress, and depression in children and adolescents. *Child and Adolescent Psychiatric Clinics of North America, 1,* 129–167.

Garber, J., & Seligman, M. E. P. (Eds.). (1980). *Human helplessness: Theory and applications.* New York: Academic Press.

Geller, B., Cooper, T. B., Graham, D., Fetner, H., Marstellar, F., & Wells, J. (1992). Pharmacokinetically designed double-blind placebo-controlled study of nortriptyline in 6- to 12-year-olds with major depressive disorder. *Journal of the American Academy of Child and Adolescent Psychiatry, 31,* 34–44.

Gilpin, D. C. (1976). Psychotherapy of the depressed child. In A. J. Anthony and D. C. Gilpin (Eds.), *Three clinical faces of childhood* (pp. 229–245). New York: Spectrum Publications.

Gladstone, T. R. G., & Kaslow, N. J. (1995). Depression and attributions in children and adolescents: A meta-analytic review. *Journal of Abnormal Child Psychology, 23,* 597–606.

Goetz, R. R., Puig-Antich, J., Ryan, N., Rabinovich, H., Ambrosini, P. J., Nelson, B., & Krawiec, V. (1987). Electroencephalographic sleep of adolescents with major depression and normal controls. *Archives of General Psychiatry, 44,* 61–68.

Goldstein, A. P., Sprafkin, R. P., Gershaw, N. J., & Klein, P. (1980). *Skill-streaming the adolescent.* Champaign, IL: Research Press.

Goodman, S. H., Gravitt, G. W., & Kaslow, N. J. (1995). Social problem solving: A moderator of the relation between negative life stress and depression symptoms in children. *Journal of Abnormal Child Psychology, 23,* 473–485.

Gotlib, I. H., & Hammen, C. L. (1992). *Psychological aspects of depression: Toward a cognitive-interpersonal integration.* New York: John Wiley & Sons.

Gray, J. W., Dean, R. S., D'Amato, R. C., & Rattan, G. (1987). Differential diagnosis of primary affective depression using the Halsted-Reitan Neuropsychologi-cal Battery. *International Journal of Neuroscience, 35,* 43–49.

Grosscup, S. J., & Lewinsohn, P. M. (1980). Unpleasant and pleasant events and mood. *Journal of Clinical Psychology, 36,* 252–258.

Hammen, C. (1991). *Depression runs in families: The social context of risk and resilience of children of depressed mothers.* New York: Springer-Verlag.

Hammen, C. (1992). Cognitive, life stress, and interpersonal approaches to a developmental psychopathology model of depression. *Development and Psychopathology, 4,* 189–206.

Hammen, C., & Compas, B. E. (1994). Unmasking unmasked depression in children and adolescents: The problem of comorbidity. *Clinical Psychology Review, 14,* 585–603.

Hanna, G. L. (1992). Natural history of mood disorders. *Child and Adolescent Psychiatric Clinics of North America, 1,* 169–181.

Harrington, R. (1993). *Depressive disorder in childhood and adolescence.* West Sussex, England: John Wiley & Sons, Ltd.

Harrington, R. (1992). Annotation: The natural history and treatment of child and adolescent affective disorders. *Journal of Child Psychology and Psychiatry, 33,* 1287–1302.

Harter, S. (1985). *Manual for the Self-Perception Profile for Children (Revision of the Perceived Competence Scale for Children).* Unpublished manuscript. University of Denver, Denver, CO.

Hendren, R. L., Hodde-Vargas, J. E., Vargas, L. A., Orrison, W. W., & Dell, L. (1991). Magnetic resonance imaging of severely disturbed children: A preliminary study. *Journal of the American Academy of Child and Adolescent Psychiatry, 30,* 466–470.

Herjanic, B., Herjanic, M., Brown, F., & Wheatt, T. (1975). Are children reliable reporters? *Journal of Abnormal Child Psychology, 3,* 41–48.

Hodges, K. (1994). Evaluation of depression in children and adolescents using diagnostic clinical interviews. In W.M. Reynolds and H.F. Johnston (Eds.), *Handbook of depression in children and adolescents* (pp. 183–208). New York: Plenum Press.

Hodges, K., Cools, J., & McKnew, D. (1989). Test-retest reliability of a clinical research interview for children: The Child Assessment Schedule (CAS). *Psychological Assessment: A Journal of Consulting and Clinical Psychology, 1,* 317–322.

Hollon, S. D., & Kendall, P. C. (1980). Cognitive self-statements in depression: Development of an Automatic Thoughts Questionnaire. *Cognitive Therapy and Research, 4,* 383–395.

Humphrey, L. L. (1982). Children's and teacher's perspectives on children's self-control: The development of two rating scales. *Journal of Consulting and Clinical Psychology, 50,* 624–633.

Jaycox, L. H., Reivich, K. J., Gillham, J., & Seligman, M. E. P. (1994). Prevention of depressive symptoms in school children. *Behavioral Research and Therapy, 32,* 801–816.

Joffe, R. D., Dobson, K. S., Fine, S., Marriage, K., & Haley, G. (1990). Social problem-solving in depressed, conduct-disordered and normal adolescents. *Journal of Abnormal Child Psychology, 18,* 565–575.

John, K., Gammon, D., Prusoff, B., & Warner, V. (1987). The Social Adjustment Inventory for Children and Adolescents (SAICA): Testing a new semi-structured interview. *Journal of the American Academy of Child and Adolescent Psychiatry, 26,* 898–911.

Johnson, J. H., & McCutcheon, S. M. (1980). Assessing life stress in older children and adolescents: Preliminary findings with the Life Events Checklist. In I.G. Sarason and C.D. Spielberger (Eds.), *Stress and anxiety* (Vol. 7) (pp. 111–125). Washington DC: Hemisphere.

Johnston, H. F., & Fruehling, J. J. (1994). Pharmacotherapy for depression in children and adolescents. In W.M. Reynolds and H.F. Johnston (Eds.), *Handbook of depression in children and adolescents* (pp. 365–397). New York: Plenum Press.

Joiner, T. E., & Wagner, K. D. (1995). Attributional style and depression in children and adolescents: A meta-analytic review. *Clinical Psychology Review, 15,* 777–798.

Kahn, J. S., Kehle, T. J., Jenson, W. R., & Clark, E. (1990). Comparison of cognitive- behavioral, relaxation, and self-modeling interventions for depression among middle-school students. *School Psychology Review, 19,* 196–211.

Kanfer, F. H., & Karoly, P. (1972). Self-control: A behavioristic excursion into the lion's den. *Behavior Therapy, 3,* 398–416.

Kashani, J. H. & Breedlove, L. (1994). Depression in medically ill youngsters. In W.M. Reynolds and H.F. Johnston (Eds.), *Handbook of depression in children and adolescents* (pp. 427–443). New York: Plenum Press.

Kashani, J. H., Carlson, G. A., Beck, N. C., Hoeper, E. W., Corcoran, C. M., McAllister, J. A., Fallahi, C., Rosenberg, T. K., & Reid, J. C. (1987). Depression, depressive symptoms, and depressed mood among a community sample of adolescents. *American Journal of Psychiatry, 144,* 931–934.

Kaslow, N. J., Brown, R. T., & Mee, L. L. (1994). Cognitive and behavioral correlates of childhood depression: A developmental perspective. In W. M. Reynolds and H. F. Johnston (Eds.), *Handbook of depression in children and adolescents* (pp. 97–121). New York: Plenum Press.

Kaslow, N. J., Deering, C. G., & Racusin, G. R. (1994). Depressed children and their families. *Clinical Psychology Review, 14,* 39–59.

Kaslow, N. J., Deering, C. G., & Ash, P. (1996). Relational diagnosis of child and adolescent depression. In F.W. Kaslow (Ed.), *Handbook of relational diagnosis and dysfunctional family patterns* (pp. 171–185). New York: John Wiley & Sons.

Kaslow, N. J., Racusin, G. R. (1994). Family therapy for young people. In W.M. Reynolds and H.F. Johnston (Eds.), *Handbook of depression in children and adolescents* (pp. 345–363). New York: Plenum Press.

Kaslow, N. J., & Rehm, L. P. (1991). Childhood depression. In T.R. Kratochwill and R.J. Morris (Eds.), *The practice of child therapy* (2nd ed.) (pp. 43–75). New York: Pergamon Press.

Kaslow, N. J., Rehm, L. P., & Siegel, A. W. (1984). Social cognitive and cognitive correlates of depression in children. *Journal of Abnormal Child Psychology, 12,* 605–620.

Kaslow, N. J., Rehm, L. P., Pollack, S. L., & Siegel, A. W. (1988). Attributional style and self-control behavior in depressed and nondepressed children and their parents. *Journal of Abnormal Child Psychology, 16,* 163–175.

Kaslow, N. J., Stark, K. D., Printz, B., Livingston, R., & Tsai, S. L. (1992). Cognitive Triad Inventory for Children: Development and relation to depression and anxiety. *Journal of Clinical Child Psychology, 21,* 339–347.

Kaslow, N. J., Tanenbaum, R. L., Abramson, L. Y., Peterson, C., & Seligman, M. E. P. (1983). Problem-solving deficits and depressive symptoms among children. *Journal of Abnormal Child Psychology, 14,* 499–515.

Kazdin, A. E. (1990). Evaluation of the automatic thoughts questionnaire: Negative cognitive processes and depression among children. *Psychological Assessment: A Journal of Consulting and Clinical Psychology, 2,* 73–79.

Kazdin, A. E. (1994). Informant variability in the assessment of childhood depression. In W.M. Reynolds and H.F. Johnston (Eds.), *Handbook of depression in children and adolescents* (pp. 249–271). New York: Plenum Press.

Kazdin, A. E., Esveldt-Dawson, K., Sherick, R. B., & Colbus, D. (1985). Assessment of overt behavior in childhood depression among psychiatrically disturbed children. *Journal of Consulting and Clinical Psychology, 51,* 504–510.

Kazdin, A. E., Rodgers, A., & Colbus, D. (1986). The Hopelessness Scale for Children: Psychometric characteristics and concurrent validity. *Journal of Consulting and Clinical Psychology, 54,* 241–245.

Kellam, S. G., Rebok, G. W., Mayer, L. S., Ialongo, N., & Kalodner, C. R. (1994). Depressive symptoms over first-grade and their response to a developmental epidemiologically based preventive trial aimed at improving achievement. *Development and Psychopathology, 6,* 463–481.

Kendall, P. C., & Braswell, L. (1985). *Cognitive-behavioral therapy for impulsive children.* New York: Guilford Press.

Kendall, P. C., Kortlander, E., Chansky, T.E., & Brady, E.U. (1992). Comorbidity of anxiety and depression in youth: Treatment implications. *Journal of Consulting and Clinical Psychology, 60,* 869–880.

Kennard, B. D., Emslie, G. J., & Weinberg, W. A. (1992). Mood, affect, and their disorders in children and adolescents. In S. J. Segalowitz and I. Rapin (Eds.), *Handbook of neuropsychology* (Vol. 7) (pp. 331–355). Amsterdam: Elsevier Science.

Klerman, G. L., Weissman, M. M., Rounsaville, B. J., & Chevron, E. S. (1984). *Interpersonal psychotherapy of depression.* New York: Basic Books.

Kovacs, M. (1980/1981). Rating scales to assess depression in school-aged children. *Acta Paedopsychiatrica, 46,* 305–315.

Kovacs, M. (1989). Affective disorder in children and adolescents. *American Psychologist, 44,* 209–215.

Kovacs, M. (1992). *Children's Depression Inventory.* North Tonawanda, New York: Multi-Health Systems.

Kovacs, M., & Beck, A. T. (1977). An empirical-clinical approach toward a definition of childhood depression. In J.G. Schulterbrandt and A. Raskin (Eds.), *Depression in childhood: Diagnosis, treatment, and conceptual models* (pp. 1–25). New York: Raven Press.

Kwon, S., & Oei, T. P. S. (1994). The roles of two levels of cognitions in the development, maintenance, and treatment of depression. Clinical Psychology Review, 14, 331–358.

Larson, R. W., Raffaelli, M., Richards, M. H., Ham, M., & Jewell, L. (1990). Ecology of depression in late childhood and early adolescence: A profile of daily states and activities. *Journal of Abnormal Psychology, 99,* 92–102.

LeCroy, C. W. (1994). Social skills training. In C.W. LeCroy (Ed.), *Handbook of child and adolescent treatment manuals* (pp. 126–169). New York: Lexington Books.

Lefkowitz, M. M., & Burton, N. (1978). Childhood depression: A critique of the concept. *Psychological Bulletin, 85,* 716–726.

Lefkowitz, M. M., & Tesiny, E. P. (1980). Assessment of childhood depression. *Journal of Consulting and Clinical Psychology, 48,* 43–50.

Lefkowitz, M.M., Tesiny, E.P., & Solodow, W. (1989). A rating scale for assessing dysphoria in youth. *Journal of Abnormal Child Psychology, 17,* 337–347.

Leitenberg, H., Yost, L.W., & Carroll-Wilson, M. (1986). Negative cognitive errors in children: Questionnaire development, normative data, and comparisons between children with and without self-reported symptoms of depression, low self-esteem, and evaluation anxiety. *Journal of Consulting and Clinical Psychology, 54,* 528–536.

Lewinsohn, P. M. (1974). A behavioral approach to depression. In R.M. Friedman and M.M. Katz (Eds.), *Psychology of depression: Contemporary theory and research* (pp. 157–185). New York: John Wiley & Sons.

Lewinsohn, P. M., Antonuccio, D. O., Steinmetz, J., & Teri, L. (1984). *The Coping With Depression course: A psychoeducational intervention for unipolar depression.* Eugene, OR: Castalia Press.

Lewinsohn, P. M., Biglan, A., & Zeiss, A. M. (1976). Behavioral treatment of depression. In P. O. Davidson (Ed.), *The behavioral management of anxiety, depres-

sion, and pain* (pp. 91–146). New York: Brunner/Mazel.

Lewinsohn, P. M., & Clarke, G. (1986). *The coping with depression course: A psychoeducational intervention for unipolar depression.* Eugene, OR:Castalia Press.

Lewinsohn, P.M., Clarke, G.N., Hops, H., & Andrews, J. (1990). Cognitive-behavioral treatment for depressed adolescents. *Behavior Therapy, 21,* 385–401.

Lewinsohn, P. M., Clarke, G. N., & Rohde, P. (1994). Psychological approaches to the treatment of depression in adolescents. In W.M. Reynolds and H.F. Johnston (Eds.), *Handbook of depression in children and adolescents* (pp. 309–344). New York: Plenum Press.

Lewinsohn, P. M., & Gotlib, I. H. (1995). Behavioral theory and treatment of depression. In E.E. Beckham and W.R. Leber (Eds.), *Handbook of depression* (pp. 352–375). New York: Guilford Press.

Lewinsohn, P. M., Youngren, M. A., & Grosscup, S. J. (1979). Reinforcement and depression. In R. A. Depue (Ed.), *The psychobiology of the depressive disorders: Implications for the effects of stress* (pp. 291–315). New York: Academic Press.

Liddle, B. & Spence, S. H. (1990). Cognitive-behaviour therapy with depressed primary school children: A cautionary note. *Behavioural Psychotherapy, 18,* 85–102.

Manson, S. M., Ackerson, L. M., Dick, R. W., Baron, A. E., & Fleming, C. M. (1990). Depressive symptoms among American Indian adolescents: Psychometric characteristics of the Center for Epidemiologic Studies—Depression Scale (CES-D). *Psychological Assessment: A Journal of Consulting and Clinical Psychology, 2,* 231–237.

Marsella, A. J., Sartorius, N., Jablensky, A., & Fenton, F. R. (1985). Cross-cultural studies of depressive disorders: An overview. In A. Kleinman & B. Good (Eds.), *Culture and depression* (pp.299–324). Berkeley: University of California Press.

Marton, P., Connolly, J., Kutcher, S., & Korenblum, M. (1993). Cognitive social skills and social self-appraisal in depressed adolescents. *Journal of the American Academy of Child and Adolescent Psychiatry, 32,* 739–744.

Matson, J. L., Esveldt-Dawson, K., Andrasik, F., Ollendik, T. H., Petti, T.A., & Hersen, M. (1980). Observation and generalization effects of social skills training and emotionally disturbed children. *Behavior Therapy, 11,* 522–531.

Matson, J. L., Rotatori, A. F., & Helsel, W. J. (1983). Development of a rating scale to measure social skills in children: The Matson Evaluation of Social Skills with Youngsters (MESSY). *Behaviour Research and Therapy, 21,* 335–340.

McCubbin, H. I., Patterson, J. M., & Wilson, L. R. (1985). *FILE: Family Inventory of Life Events and Changes.* In D. Olson, H. McCubbin, H. Barnes, A. Larsen, M. Muxen, and M. Wilson (Eds.), Family inventories (rev. ed.). St Paul: Family Social Science, University of Minnesota.

McKnew, D. H., Cytryn, L., Efron, A. M., Gershon, E. S., & Bunney, W. E. (1979). Offspring of patients with affective disorders. *British Journal of Psychiatry, 134,* 148–152.

Meichenbaum, D. (1977). *Cognitive-behavior modification: An integrative approach.* New York: Plenum.

Metalsky, G. I., & Joiner, T. E. (1992). Vulnerability to depressive symptomatology: A prospective test of the diathesis-stress and causal mediation components of the hopelessness theory of depression. *Journal of Personality and Social Psychology, 63,* 667–675.

Mitchell, J., McCauley, E., Burke, P. M., & Moss, S. J. (1988). Phenomenology of depression in children and adolescents. *Journal of the American Academy of Child and Adolescent Psychiatry, 27,* 12–20.

Moos, R. H., & Moos, B. S. (1981). *Family Environment Scale manual.* Palo Alto:CA: Consulting Psychological Press.

Mufson, L., Moreau, D., Weissman, M. M., Klerman, G. L. (1993). *Interpersonal psychotherapy for depressed adolescents.* New York: Guilford Press.

Mufson, L., Moreau, D., Weissman, M., Wickramaratne, P., Martin, J., & Samoilov, A. (1994). Modification of interpersonal psychotherapy with depressed adolescents (IPT-A): Phase I and II studies. *Journal of the American Academy of Child and Adolescent Psychiatry, 33,* 695–705.

Mullins, L. L., Siegel, L. J., & Hodges, K. (1985). Cognitive problem-solving and life event correlates of depressive symptoms in children. *Journal of Abnormal Child Psychology, 13,* 305–314.

Nezu, A. M., Nezu, C. M., & Perri, M. G. (1989). *Problem solving therapy for depression: Theory, research, and clinical guidelines.* New York: Wiley.

Nolen-Hoeksema, S., & Girgus, J. S. (1994). The emergence of gender differences in depression during adolescence. *Psychological Bulletin, 115,* 424–443.

Nolen-Hoeksema, S., Girgus, J. S., & Seligman, M. E. P. (1986). Learned helplessness in children: A longitudinal study of depression, achievement, and explanatory style. *Journal of Personality and Social Psychology, 51,* 435–442.

Nolen-Hoeksema, S., Girgus, J., & Seligman, M. E. P. (1992). Predictors and consequences of childhood depressive symptoms: A five year longitudinal study. *Journal of Abnormal Psychology, 101,* 405–422.

Olson, D. H., Larsen, A. S., & McCubbin, H. I. (1985). Family Strengths. In D. Olson, H. McCubbin, H. Barnes, A. Larsen, M. Muxen, and M. Wilson (Eds.), *Family inventories* (rev. ed.). St Paul: Family Social Science, University of Minnesota.

Olson, D. H., Portner, J., & Lavee, Y. (1985). Family Adaptability and Cohesion Evaluation Scale (FACES III). In D. Olson, H. McCubbin, H. Barnes, A. Larsen, M. Muxen, and M. Wilson (Eds.), *Family inventories* (rev. ed.). St Paul: Family Social Science, University of Minnesota.

Orvaschel, H., & Puig-Antich, J. (1987). *Schedule for Affective Disorder and Schizophrenia for School-Age Children-Epidemiologic version (Kiddie-SADS-E [K-SADS-E].* Pittsburgh: Western Psychiatric Institute and Clinic.

Petersen, A. C., Compas, B. E., Brooks-Gunn, J., Stemmler, M., Ey, S., & Grant, K.E. (1993). Depression in adolescence. *American Psychologist, 48,* 155–168.

Peterson, L., Mullins, L. L., & Ridley-Johnson, R. (1985). Childhood depression: Peer reactions to depression and life stress. *Journal of Abnormal Child Psychology, 13,* 597–609.

Petti, T. A. (1978). Depression in hospitalized child psychiatry patients. *Journal of the American Academy of Child Psychiatry, 17,* 49–59.

Petti, T. A., Bornstein, M., Delamater, A., & Connors, C. K. (1980). Evaluation and multimodal treatment of a depressed pre-pubertal girl. *Journal of the American Academy of Child Psychiatry, 19,* 690–702.

Petti, T., & Law, W. (1982). Imipramine treatment of depressed children: A double-blind pilot study. *Journal of Clinical Psychopharmacology, 2,* 107–110.

Piers, E. V. (1984). *Revised manual for the Children's Self-Concept Scale.* Los Angeles: Western Psychological Services.

Poling, K. (1989). *Living with depression: A survival manual for families.* Pittsburgh: University of Pittsburgh, Western Psychiatric Institute and Clinic.

Pope, A. W., McHale, S. M., & Craighead, W. E. (1988). *Self-esteem enhancement with children and adolescents.* New York: Pergamon Press.

Poznanski, E. O. (1982). The clinical phenomenology of childhood depression. *American Journal of Orthopsychiatry, 52,* 308–313.

Poznanski, E. O., Grossman, J. A., Buchsbaum, Y., Banges, M., Freeman, L., & Gibbons, R. (1984).

Preliminary studies of the reliability and validity of the Children's Depression Rating Scale. *Journal of the American Academy of Child Psychiatry, 23,* 191–197.

Puig-Antich, J. (1982). Major depression and conduct disorder in prepuberty. *Journal of the American Academy of Child Psychiatry, 21,* 118–128,

Puig-Antich, J. (1987). Sleep and neuroendocrine correlates of affective illness in childhood and adolescence. *Journal of Adolescent Health Care, 8,* 505–529.

Puig-Antich, J., Goetz, R., Hanlon, C., Davies, M., Thompson, J., Chambers, W. J., Tabrizi, M. A., & Weitzman, E. D. (1982). Sleep architecture and REM sleep measures in prepubertal children with major depression: A controlled study. *Archives of General Psychiatry, 39,* 932–939.

Puig-Antich, J., Goetz, R., Hanlon, C., Tabrizi, M. A., Davies, M., & Weitzman, E. D. (1983). Sleep architecture and REM sleep measures in prepubertal major depressives: Studies during recovery from the depressive episode in a drug-free state. *Archives of General Psychiatry, 40,* 187–192.

Puig-Antich, J., Lukens, E., Davies, M., Goetz, D., Brennan-Quattrock, J., & Todak, G. (1985a). Psychosocial functioning in prepubertal major depressive disorder. *Archives of General Psychiatry, 42,* 500–507.

Puig-Antich, J., Lukens, E., Davies, M., Goetz, D., Brennan-Quattrock, J., & Todak, G. (1985b). Psychosocial functioning in prepubertal major depressive disorder. II. Interpersonal relationships after sustained recovery from affective episode. *Archives of General Psychiatry, 42,* 511–517.

Puig-Antich, J., Kaufman, J., Ryan, N.D., Williamson, D., Dahl, R.E., Lukens, E., Todak, G., Ambrosini, P., Rabinovich, H., & Nelson, B. (1993). The psychosocial functioning and family environment of depressed adolescents. *Journal of the American Academy of Child and Adolescent Psychiatry, 32,* 244–253.

Puig-Antich, J., Perel, J. M., Lupatkin, W., Chambers, W. J., Tabrizi, M. A., King, J., Goetz, R., Davies, M., & Stiller, R. L. (1987). Imipramine in prepubertal major depressive disorders. *Archives of General Psychiatry, 44,* 81–89.

Puig-Antich, J., & Ryan, N. (1986). Schedule for Affective Disorder and Schizophrenia for School-Age Children (6–18 years)—Kiddie-SADS (K-SADS). Unpublished manuscript. Western Psychiatric Institute and Clinic, Pittsburgh, PA.

Quiggle, N. L., Garber, J., Panak, W. F., & Dodge, K. A. (1992). Social information processing in aggressive and depressed children. *Child Development, 63,* 1305–1320.

Rehm, L. P. (1977). A self-control model of depression. *Behavior Therapy, 8,* 787–804.

Rehm, L. P. (1978). Mood, pleasant events, and unpleasant events: Two pilot studies. *Journal of Consulting and Clinical Psychology, 46,* 854–859.

Rehm, L. P. (1988). Self-management and cognitive processes in depression. In L. B. Alloy (Ed.), *Cognitive processes in depression* (pp. 143–176). New York: Guilford Press.

Rehm, L. P. (1990). Cognitive and behavioral theories. In B.B. Wolman and G. Stricker (Eds.), *Depressive disorders: Facts, theories and treatment methods* (pp. 64–91). New York: John Wiley & Sons.

Rehm, L. P., & Carter, A. S. (1990). Cognitive components of depression. In M. Lewis and S. M. Miller (Eds.), *Handbook of developmental psychopathology* (pp. 341–351). New York: Plenum Press.

Rehm, L. P., & Kaslow, N. J. (1984). Behavioral approaches to depression: Research results and clinical recommendations. In C.M. Franks (Ed.), *New developments in behavior therapy* (pp. 155–229). New York: Haworth Press.

Rehm, L. P., & Sharp, R. N. (1996). Strategies for childhood depression. In M. A. Reinecke, F. M. Dattilio, and A. Freeman (Eds.), *Cognitive therapy with children and adolescents: A casebook for clinical practice* (pp. 103–123). New York: Guilford Press.

Reinherz, H. Z., Frost, A. K., & Pakiz, B. (1991). Changing faces: Correlates of depressive symptoms in late adolescence. *Family and Community Health, 14,* 52–63.

Reynolds, W. M. (1986). *Assessment of depression in adolescents: Manual for Reynolds Adolescent Depression Scale.* Odessa, FL: Psychological Assessment Resources.

Reynolds, W. M. (1989). *Reynolds Child Depression Scale: Professional Manual.* Odessa, FL: Psychological Assessment Resources.

Reynolds, W. M. (1994). Assessment of depression in children and adolescents by self-report questionnaires. In W.M. Reynolds and H.F. Johnston (Eds.), *Handbook of depression in children and adolescents* (pp. 209–234). New York: Plenum Press.

Reynolds, W. M., Anderson, G., & Bartell, N. (1985). Measuring depression in children: A multimethod assessment investigation. *Journal of Abnormal Child Psychology, 13,* 513–526.

Reynolds, W. M., & Coats, K. I. (1986). A comparison of cognitive-behavioral therapy and relaxation training for the treatment of depression in adolescents. *Journal of Consulting and Clinical Psychology, 54,* 653–660.

Rice, K. G., Herman, M. A., & Petersen, A. C. (1993). Coping with challenge in adolescence: A conceptual model and psycho-educational intervention. *Journal of Adolescence, 16,* 235–251.

Rie, H. E. (1966). Depression in childhood: A survey of some pertinent contributions. *Journal of the American Academy of Child Psychiatry, 5,* 653–685.

Rippere, V. (1977). "What's the thing to do when you're feeling depressed?": A pilot study. *Behavior Research and Therapy, 15,* 185–191.

Robinson, L. A., Berman, J. S., & Neimeyer, R. A. (1990). Psychotherapy for the treatment of depression: A comprehensive review of controlled outcome research. *Psychological Bulletin, 108,* 30–49.

Robinson, R. G., Kubos, K. L., Starr, L. B., Rao, K., & Price, T. (1984). Mood disorders in stroke patients: Importance of location of lesion. *Brain, 107,* 81–93.

Rosenberg, D. R., Holttum, J., & Gershon, S. (1994). *Textbook of pharmacotherapy for child and adolescent psychiatric disorders.* New York: Brunner/Mazel.

Ross, E.D., & Rush, A. J. (1981). Diagnosis and neuroanatomical correlates of depression in brain-damaged patients. *Archives of General Psychiatry, 38,* 1344–1354.

Rotheram-Borus, M. J., Trautman, P. D., Dopkins, S. C., & Shrout, P. E. (1990). Cognitive style and pleasant activities among female adolescent suicide attempters. *Journal of Consulting and Clinical Psychology, 58,* 554–561.

Rudolph, K. D., Hammen, C., & Burge, D. (1994). Interpersonal functioning and depressive symptoms in childhood: Addressing the issues of specificity and comorbidity. *Journal of Abnormal Child Psychology, 22,* 355–371.

Rush, A.J., & Nowels, A. (1994). Adaptation of cognitive therapy for depressed adolescents. In T. C. R. Wilkes, G. Belsher, A. J. Rush, and E. Frank (Eds.), *Cognitive therapy for depressed adolescents* (pp. 3–21). New York: Guilford Press.

Rutter, M. (1986). The developmental psychopathology of depression: Issues and perspectives. In M. Rutter, C. E. Izard, and P. B. Read (Eds.), *Depression in young people: Developmental and clinical perspectives* (pp. 3–30). New York: Guilford Press.

Rutter, M., & Hersov, L. (Eds.) (1985). *Child and adolescent psychiatry.* London: Blackwell.

Ryan, N. D. (1992). The pharmacologic treatment of child and adolescent depression. *Psychiatric Clinics of North America, 15,* 29–40.

Ryan, N. D., Birmaher, B., Perel, J.M., Dahl, R. E., Meyer, V., Al-Shabbout, M., Iyengar, S., & Puig-Antich, J.

(1992). Neuroendocrine response to L–5-hydroxytryptophan challenge in prepubertal major depression: Depressed versus normal children. *Archives of General Psychiatry, 49,* 843–851.

Ryan, N. D., Puig-Antich, J., Ambrosini, B., Rabinovich, H., Robinson, D., Nelson, B., Iyengar, S., & Twomey, J. (1987). The clinical picture of major depression in children and adolescents. *Archives of General Psychiatry, 44,* 854–861.

Sackeim, H. A., Prohovnik, I., Moeller, J. R., Brown, R. P., Apter, S., Prudic, J., Devanand, D. P., & Mukherjee, S. (1990). Regional cerebral blood flow in mood disorders. *Archives of General Psychiatry, 47,* 60–70.

Sacks, J. M. (1977). The need for subtlety: A critical session with a suicidal child. *Psychotherapy: Theory, Research, and Practice, 14,* 434–437.

Sandler, J. & Joffee, N. G. (1965). Notes on childhood depression. *International Journal of Psychoanalysis, 46,* 88–96.

Saylor, C.F., Finch, A.J., Baskin, C.H., Furey, W., & Kelly, M.M. (1984). Construct validity for measures of childhood depression: Application of multitrait-multimethod methodology. *Journal of Consulting and Clinical Psychology, 52,* 977–985.

Schatzberg, A.S., & Nemeroff, C.B. (1995). *Textbook of psychopharmacology.* Washington DC: American Psychiatric Press, Inc.

Seligman, M.E.P. (1975). *Helplessness: On depression, development, and death.* San Francisco: W.H. Freeman.

Seligman, M.E.P. (1981). A learned helplessness point of view. In L.P. Rehm (Ed.), *Behavior therapy for depression* (pp. 123–141). New York: Academic Press.

Seligman, M.E.P., Peterson, C., Kaslow, N.J., Tanenbaum, R.L., & Abramson, L.Y. (1984). Attributional style and depressive symptoms among children. *Journal of Abnormal Psychology, 93,* 235–238.

Seligman, M.E.P., Reivich, K., Jaycox, L., & Gillham, J. (1995). *The optimistic child.* Boston: Houghton Mifflin.

Shaffer, D., Fisher, P., Dulcan, M., Davies, M., Piacentini, J., Schwab-Stone, M., Lahey, B. B., Bourdon, K., Jensen, P., Bird, H., Canino, C., & Regier, D. (in press). The second version of the Diagnostic Schedule for Children (DISC-2). *Journal of the American Academy of Child and Adolescent Psychiatry.*

Simeon, J., DiNicola, V., Ferguson, H., & Copping, W. (1990). Adolescent depression: A placebo controlled fluoxetine treatment study and follow-up. *Progress in Neuro-psychopharmacology and Biological Psychiatry, 14,* 791–795.

Skinner, B. F. (1953). *Science and human behavior.* New York: Free Press.

Skinner, H. A., Steinhauer, P. D., & Santa-Barbara, J. (1983). The family assessment measure. *Canadian Journal of Community Mental Health, 2,* 91–105.

Sokoloff, M. R., & Lubin, B. (1983). Depressive mood in adolescent, emotionally disturbed females: Reliability and validity of an adjective checklist (C-DACL). *Journal of Abnormal Child Psychology, 11,* 531–536.

Stark, K. D. (1990). *Childhood depression: School-based intervention.* New York: Guilford Press.

Stark, K. D., Reynolds, W. R., & Kaslow, N. J. (1987). A comparison of the relative efficacy of self-control therapy and a behavioral problem-solving therapy for depression in children. *Journal of Abnormal Child Psychology, 15,* 91–113.

Stark, K. D., Rouse, L. W., & Kurowski, C. (1994). Psychological treatment approaches for depression in children. In W. M. Reynolds and H.F. Johnston (Eds.), *Handbook of depression in children and adolescents* (pp. 275–307). New York: Plenum Press.

Stark, K. D., Rouse, L. W., & Livingston, R. (1991). Treatment of depression during childhood and adolescence: Cognitive-behavioral procedures for the individual and family. In P. Kendall (Ed.), *Child and adolescent therapy* (pp. 165–206). New York: Guilford Press.

Strober, M., Freeman, R., Rigali, J., Schmidt, S., & Diamond, R. (1992). The pharmacotherapy of depressive illness in adolescents: II. Effects of lithium augmentation in nonresponders to imipramine. *Journal of the American Academy of Child and Adolescent Psychiatry, 31,* 16–20.

Sweeney, P. D., Anderson, K., & Bailey, S. (1986). Attributional style in depression: A meta-analytic review. *Journal of Personality and Social Psychology, 50,* 974–991.

Task Force on Promotion and Dissemination of Psychological Procedures, Division of Clinical Psychology, American Psychological Association (1995). Training in and dissemination of empirically-validated psychological treatments: Report and recommendations. *Clinical Psychologist, 8,* 3–24.

Tisher, M., & Lang, M. (1983). The Children's Depression Scale: Review and further developments. In D.P. Cantwell and G.A. Carlson (Eds.), *Affective disorders in childhood and adolescence: An update* (pp. 375–415). New York: Spectrum Publications.

Tramontana, M. G., & Hooper, S. R. (1989). Neuropsychology of child psychopathology. In C. R. Reynolds and E. Fletcher-Janzen (Eds.), *Handbook of clinical child neuropsychology* (pp. 87–106). New York: Plenum Press.

Vygotsky, L.S. (1962). *Thought and language.* New York: John Wiley and Sons.

Weiss, B., Weisz, J. R., Politano, M., Carey, M., Nelson, W. M., & Finch, A. J. (1992). Relations among self-reported depressive symptoms in clinic-referred children versus adolescents. *Journal of Abnormal Psychology, 101,* 391–387.

Weissman, M. M., Orvaschel, H., & Padian, N. (1980). Children's symptom and social functioning self-report scales: Comparison of mother's and children's reports. *Journal of Nervous and Mental Disease, 168,* 736–740.

Weisz, J. R., Sweeney, L., Proffitt, V., & Carr, T. (1993). Control-related beliefs and self-reported depressive symptoms in late childhood. *Journal of Abnormal Psychology, 102,* 411–418.

Weller, E. B. & Weller R. A. (1991). Mood disorders. In M. Lewis (Ed.), *Child and adolescent psychiatry: A comprehensive textbook* (pp. 646–664). Baltimore: Williams and Wilkins.

Werner, H. (1957). The concept of development from a comparative and organismic point of view. In D. Harris (Ed.), *The concept of development.* Minnesota: University of Minnesota Press.

Wierzbicki, M. (1989). Children's perceptions of counter-depressive activities. *Psychological Reports, 65,* 1251–1258.

Wierzbicki, M., & McCabe, M. (1988). Social skills and subsequent depressive symptomatology in children. *Journal of Clinical Child Psychiatry, 17,* 203–208.

Wierzbicki, M., & Saylor, M. K. (1991). Depression and engagement in pleasant and unpleasant activities in normal children. *Journal of Clinical Psychology, 47,* 499–505.

Wilkes, T. C. R., Belsher, G., Rush, A. J., & Frank, E. (Eds.). (1994). *Cognitive therapy for depressed adolescents.* New York: Guilford Press.

Wirt, R. D., Lachar, D., Klinedinst, J. K., & Seat, P. D. (1977). *Multidimensional description of child personality: A manual for the Personality Inventory for Children.* Los Angeles: Western Psychological Services.

Wolpe, J. (1979). The experimental model and treatment of neurotic depression. *Behavior Research and Therapy, 17,* 555–566.

CHAPTER 4

CHILDHOOD FEARS AND PHOBIAS ·

Richard J. Morris
Thomas R. Kratochwill

Concern with children's fears and phobias has increased tremendously on the part of mental health professionals over the past three decades— although there has been a strong tradition in psychology of study and interest in this area since the early 1900s (see Freud, 1909; Jones, 1924a, b; King, Hamilton, & Ollendick, 1988; Morris & Kratochwill, 1983; Watson & Rayner, 1920).

NORMATIVE AND PREVALENCE DATA

Fears are found in children from infancy through adolescence. Those fears seen in infancy typically occur as a reaction to something taking place in the infant's environment. As the child grows older, into the early school years, fears broaden and involve the dark, supernatural figures and particular persons, objects, and events. With increasing age, fears turn more toward imaginary figures, objects, and events as well as the future (e.g., school and social performance) (Jersild, 1968). These "age-related" fears

are typically transitory in nature and of short duration; they vary in intensity both in any given child and from one child to another. Some typical childhood fears are listed in Table 4.1.

A number of studies have examined the incidence rates of children's fears within particular age ranges. For example, in one of the early normative studies on children's fears, Jersild and Holmes (1935) found that children between 24 and 71 months of age had an average of 4.6 fears. In addition, they found the fading-out of some high-percentage fears (e.g., of dark rooms, large dogs, strange persons, walking across high boards) as the children grew older and maintenance of other fears (e.g., snakes). Although Jersild and Holmes (1935) found that children's fears were relatively transient, some later research findings have questioned these investigators' conclusions. For example, Eme and Schmidt (1978) conducted a 1-year longitudinal study of 27 children. These authors found that the fears in these children were quite stable in type iden-

TABLE 4.1. Normative Data on Children's Fears

AGE	FEARS
0–6 months	Loss of support, loud noises.
7–12 months	Fear of strangers; fear of sudden, unexpected, and looming objects.
1 year	Separation from parent, toilet injury, strangers.
2 years	A multitude of fears including loud noises (e.g., vacuum cleaners, sirens/alarms, trucks, thunder), animals (e.g., large dogs), dark rooms, separation from parent, target objects/machines, change in personal environment, strangers.
3 years	Masks, dark, animals, separation from parent, being left alone.
4 years	Separation from parent, animals, dark, noises (including at night), insects.
5 years	Animals, "bad" people, dark, thunder, separation from parent, bodily harm, ghosts.
6 years	Supernatural beings (e.g., ghosts, witches, ghouls), bodily injuries, thunder and lightning, dark, sleeping or staying alone, separation from parent.
7–8 years	Supernatural beings, dark, fears based on media events, staying alone, bodily injury, school performance.
9–12 years	Tests and examinations in school, school performance, social performance, bodily injury, nuclear war, physical appearance, thunder and lightning, death, dark (low percentage).

Source: Ilg & Ames, 1955; Ferrari, 1986; Jersild & Holmes, 1935; Kellerman, 1981; Lapouse & Monk, 1959; Scarr & Salapatek, 1970. Adapted from *Treating children's fears and phobias: A behavioral approach* (p. 2) by R. J. Morris, & T. R. Kratochwill, 1983. Elmsford, NY: Pergamon Press. Copyright 1983 by Pergamon Press. Reprinted by permission of Allyn and Bacon, Inc.

tified and number. Specifically, 83% of the fears identified by these children were still present at the end of a year. Subsequent research by others (e.g., Dong, Xia, Lei, Yang, & Ollendick, 1995; King, Ollier, Iacuone, Schuster, Bays, Gullone, & Ollendick, 1989; Ollendick, Matson, & Helsel, 1985) has also suggested that children's fears tend to be stable over time.

With respect to the number of fears that children experience, Ollendick, Yang, King, Dong, and Akande (1996) found in their study involving children between 7 and 17 years of age in four different countries that American children manifested a mean number 13.60 fears, Australian children 14.29 fears, Chinese children 15.52 fears, and Nigerian children 26.08 fears. In addition, consistent with previous studies (e.g., King et al., 1989; King, Gullone, & Tonge, 1991; Ollendick et al., 1985), these researchers found that American and Australian children who were below 11 years of age had appreciably more fears and higher levels of fear than children who were 11 years of age or older. This was not

the case, however, for the children in the Chinese or Nigerian sample. Specifically, Chinese children between the ages of 11 and 13 years were found to have a higher number of fears and a higher level of fear than children below 11 years or above 13 years of age. Nigerian children, on the other hand, were found to have a similar number of fears and level of fear across the various age ranges.

Ollendick, et al., (1996) also found that consistent with other research literature (e.g., Dong, Yang & Ollendick, 1994; Erol & Sahin, 1995; Graziano & Mooney, 1984; King et al., 1988; Morris & Kratochwill, 1983; Ollendick, Yule, & Ollier, 1991) girls in the American, Australian, and Chinese samples reported appreciably more fears and had a higher level of fear than did boys. Inconsistent with these findings were the results from the Nigerian sample in which it was found that boys and girls did not differ with regard to either the number of fears or level of fear.

With respect to some of the most common fears that children report, a number of studies (e.g., Erol &

Sahin, 1995; Ollendick, et al., 1991; Ollendick, et al., 1996) have found the following fears to be amongst the more frequent: being hit by a car or truck, not being able to breathe, falling from a high place, earthquakes, death and/or dead people, bombing attacks, fire—getting burned, failing a test, having my parents argue, getting poor grades, getting a serious illness, and a burglar breaking into the house.

With regard to phobias and/or severe fears, the literature is more sparse. For example, Miller, Barrett, and Hampe (1974) report that intense or excessive fears occurred in about 5% of their sample of children ranging in age from 7 to 12 years. Similarly, Graham, as cited in Marks (1969), reports that only 4% of the children referred for treatment had phobias. Rutter, Tizard, and Whitmore's (1970) prevalence data were only slightly higher (about 7%), as were those of Graziano and DeGiovanni (1979) regarding those children with clinical fears or phobias who were referred to behavior therapists for treatment. A later study by Anderson, Williams, McGee, and Silva (1987) found that of 792 New Zealand children sampled who were 11 years old, 3.5% were reported to have a diagnosis of separation anxiety disorder, 2.4% had a diagnosis of simple phobia, and .9% had social phobia—with more girls than boys having these disorders. By combining these latter percentages, the resulting 6.8% is consistent with the Rutter et al., (1970) findings. Adding the presence of "panic attacks" to these percentages does not appear to increase these numbers appreciably, since, as King, Ollendick, and Mattis (1994) report, panic attacks or disorders are infrequent or rare among children and "fairly infrequent and of short duration" in adolescents.

With regard to "school phobia," Kennedy (1965) reports that 17 out of 1,000 children (1.7%) experience this problem. This rate, however, has been questioned by Trueman (1984) because no source for this rate was provided by Kennedy. Other estimates of "school phobia" in those children referred to clinics have ranged from 0.04% (Eisenberg, 1958) to 8% (Kahn & Nursten, 1962) of all referrals. Even though these various incidence studies differ in their definitions of severe fear, clinical fear, phobia, and related problems, each study reports that the prevalence of intense fears (i.e., those necessitating

clinical intervention) and/or phobias among children is equal to or less than 8% of the number of referrals to a clinician or in the general child population.

FEARS VERSUS PHOBIAS

Although the meaning of the terms "phobia" and "phobic reaction" might seem clear, the literature reveals a good deal of confusion between them and others, such as "fear," "anxiety," "stress," "panic," "refusal behavior," and "avoidance behavior." All these terms are used differently at different times. The term "fear," for example, is often used in the child development literature to refer to a *normal* reaction to a real or perceived threat. For instance, a child may develop a fear of dentists' offices because of actual pain experienced during a dental procedure. However, in the child behavior disorders/psychopathology literature, the term "fear" is sometimes used within the context of a normal developmental reaction and at other times as a clinical problem.

In an attempt to differentiate the terms "fear" and "phobia," Marks (1969) suggested that phobia should be considered a subcategory of fear that:

1. Is out of proportion to demands of the situation.
2. Cannot be explained or reasoned away.
3. Is beyond voluntary control.
4. Leads to avoidance of the feared situation.

To these criteria, Miller et al., (1974) add that a phobia "persists over an extended period of time...is unadaptive...[and] is not age or, "stage specific" (p. 90). This differentiation between fear and phobia—with the additional Miller et al., criteria—is among the most widely used definition of "phobia" (e.g., King et al., 1988; Morris & Kratochwill, 1983). Phobias have also been referred to as *clinical fears*—usually also on the basis of the above criteria. Graziano, DeGiovanni, and Garcia (1979), however, suggest that such fears "be defined as those with a duration of over 2 years, or an intensity that is debilitating to the client's routine "lifestyle" (p. 805).

Although phobias involve the observing of or direct involvement with a traumatic or aversive event, this is not always the case. In some instances, no observable aversive antecedent event precedes the phobic response. For example, some preadolescent children who refuse to stay alone in their homes have never had an identified negative experience associated with being alone. Similarly, many adolescent children who refuse to sleep in their bedroom at night without having a lamp on (versus having on a small night light) have never had any traumatic event associated with their bedroom lights being off. In such cases, an unpleasant fantasy/image/movie may be the antecedent factor. Again, all these fears fall into the subcategory of phobic behavior according to the Marks (1969) and Miller et al., (1974) criteria. However, controversy does exist regarding the differentiation of "fear" from "phobia." Suffice it to say that there is no unanimity among researchers and/or practitioners regarding the denotative operations associated with the definition of each term (King et al., 1988; Kratochwill & Morris, 1985).

ASSESSMENT OF FEARS AND PHOBIAS

Typically, the area of childhood fears and phobias is divided into two assessment categories: behavioral and traditional. However, this is somewhat of an oversimplification, because there is often a great deal of overlap in actual techniques and practice. Nevertheless, the major differences between these two positions emanates from the assumptions underlying each approach's view of human behavior (e.g., Barrios, 1988; Nelson & Hayes, 1979). For example, individuals working within the traditional view typically focus fear assessment toward identifying underlying causes. In contrast, behavioral assessors typically focus on environmental or person-environmental events as they relate to the development of a treatment program. Behavioral assessment can be further distinguished from more traditional forms of assessment on many other dimensions. For example, within the context of childhood fears and related problems, traditional assessment approaches have tended to emphasize intraorganismic variables to account for these disorders. In such assessment, traditional approaches focus more heavily on constructs where overt behavior (e.g., behavioral avoidance) is considered a *sign* of underlying pathology and the *sit-uation* in which the client is assessed is of less or little importance. It is important to recognize, however, that traditional assessment is not a uniform approach with consistent models and techniques (Knoff, Batsche, & Carlyon, 1993; Korchin & Schuldberg, 1981). For example, traditional approaches include both psychodynamic and trait models.

Behavioral Assessment: A Conceptual Framework

A diverse set of procedures and techniques characterize contemporary behavioral assessment (see, for example, Bellack & Hersen, 1988; Frame & Matson, 1987; Mash & Terdal, 1988; Shapiro & Skinner, 1993). An increasingly popular conceptualization of fear (and/or anxiety) assessment in the child (and adult) literature was formally introduced by Lang (1968) and has been variously labeled the "triple response mode" (e.g., Cone, 1979), "multiple response components" (e.g, Nietzel & Bernstein, 1981), or "three-response system" (e.g., Kozak & Miller, 1982). The position is that fear and/or anxiety is a complex multichannel response pattern of behavior or emotion that includes motoric, cognitive, and physiological components (e.g., Barrios & Hartmann, 1988; Francis & Ollendick, 1987; Shapiro & Skinner, 1993). These response patterns are not always highly correlated, but they are often related to some extent (e.g., Barrios & O'Dell, 1989; Hodgson, & Rachman, 1974; Rachman & Hodgson, 1974). This relationship implies that changes in one response channel may not be effected by or lead to changes in another response channel, but also that results obtained in one channel may have important implications for the type of data one might obtain from a different channel.

A child or adolescent may therefore display his or her fear or phobia in any one or in all three channels. Therefore, a thorough behavioral assessment should tap responses in all three areas. Moreover, the clinician should be aware that the response channel that is most troublesome to a significant adult in the child's life may not necessarily be the one that is of most concern to the child. Thus, assessment data must be gathered from at least the target child and his or her parent (or, in the school setting, his or her teacher).

To provide a perspective on this approach for assessing child and adolescent fears and phobias, we briefly review the three response channels.

Cognitive Channel

One system or channel used to define anxiety is the cognitive system. This is regarded as a subjective system in that it depends upon the self-report of the client to validate its existence. The self-report may come through direct statements to another, through self-monitoring data, or from retrospective responses to structured questionnaire items (e.g., fear surveys).

Virtually every therapeutic approach reviewed in this chapter considers self-report as an important source of data to define the concept of fear, phobia, and anxiety. There is, however, considerable variation in the emphasis placed on this system in definition of fear within the behavior therapy field. For example, cognitive behavioral therapists (see, for example, Kendall & Sessa, 1993) have tended to place much greater emphasis on self-report data than applied behavior analysts, who have generally been critical of the exclusive use of cognitive assessment. However, we regard the self-report channel as important to the definition, assessment, and treatment efforts of behaviorally oriented service providers.

Physiological Channel

The physiological channel focuses on measurement of the sympathetic portion of the autonomic nervous system (e.g., Nietzel & Bernstein, 1981; Shapiro & Skinner, 1993). Fear in this channel is assessed by a variety of measures that focus on the autonomic nervous system (heart rate, blood pressure, galvanic skin response or GSR). Usually, more than one physiological measure is used to define fear and anxiety in this system. The reason for this assessment is that different physiological measures may not correlate highly (Haynes, 1978).

Motor Channel

The third channel is referred to as motor or overt behavior. Measurement here focuses on the client's actual overt behavior (King et al., 1991). This channel has been divided into *direct* and *indirect* measures (Paul & Bernstein, 1973; Shapiro & Skinner 1993). Direct measures involve the overt behavioral consequences of physiological arousal. For example, if a child was trembling in the presence of a particular stimulus (e.g., a dog, water), this would be a direct measure defining the presence of anxiety. Indirect measures include escape and/or avoidance behaviors from certain stimuli (e.g., running away from a horse).

Considerations

The three-channel perspective is gaining wide acceptance in the research on and behavioral treatment of fears and phobias (e.g., Barrios, 1988; Barrios & O'Dell, 1989; Shapiro & Skinner 1993). Indeed, a multiple-response framework has been suggested as one of the major characteristics of behavior therapy in general (Kazdin & Hersen, 1980). Despite the popularity of this approach, many writers have raised important questions in its use (e.g., Cone, 1979; Hugdahl, 1981; Kozak & Miller, 1982; Shapiro & Skinner 1993). For example, a major problem raised by the three-response system relates to the criteria used for definition. When the three systems are monitored, it cannot be assumed that they are highly correlated (Cone, 1979; Bellack & Hersen, 1977a, 1977b), and this may be especially true with clinically significant emotions such as fears. Another major concern with the three-system approach is that different writers have used different terms and meanings in defining aspects of the systems. This has particularly been the case in regard to the subjective status of the fear experience (Kozak & Miller, 1982). For example, researchers and practitioners may equate verbal expression with cognitions, but there may be great differences between what people "say and do." When verbal and cognitive behaviors are equated, cognition or emotion may be empirically untenable. Aside from this problem with variation in definitions of certain systems, comparisons across studies become very difficult (Hugdahl, 1981). A third problem raised by the three-system model is the limited number of dimensions for fear assessment that might be used in clinical research and practice. As

Kozak and Miller (1982) note, "the *assessor* may be tempted to think that there are only three *things* to be measured and that getting a number for each system sufficiently measures fear" (p. 352). Thus, the usual methods for assessing the three channels (i.e., physiological arousal, overt behavior, verbal reports) do not measure unitary phenomena.

A final concern with this approach relates to matching treatments to the systems. A common assumption has been that different treatments may be necessary for different levels of fear within the three-response system. For example, a child with high "cognitive" fear may be exposed to a cognitive intervention, while a person with behavioral avoidance ("motoric" fear) could be treated with reinforced practice (e.g., Leitenberg & Callahan, 1973). Yet, such a conclusion may be problematic, because avoidance behavior is usually present in all clinical phobias. Thus, one could question whether the behavioral component is a discrete system (Hugdahl, 1981). In the future, it may be possible to develop specific treatments based on certain response patterns within each system. Currently, there is a paucity of research in this area involving children and adolescents.

Assessment Methods

The assessment methods or procedures used to gather data can be ordered along a continuum of directness representing the extent to which they measure a behavior at the time and place of its natural occurrence (Cone, 1978; Shapiro & Skinner 1993). Within this framework, interviews, self-report questionnaires, and behavior checklist and rating scales are regarded as indirect measures because they are verbal representations of more clinically relevant activities that occur at some other time and place. However, self-monitoring observations, direct observation, and physiological recordings represent direct measures of behavior because the assessment occurs at the time of the natural occurrence of the behavior.

In using any of these assessment procedures within the three-channel system, it is important to draw a distinction between the mode of measurement and the content response channel that it is designed to assess (Barrios, Hartmann, & Shigetomi, 1981; Cone, 1978). In this regard, the three behavioral content areas can be measured by a technique or device whose mode is motor, cognitive, or physiological. For example, a child might be assessed on the motor component of a fear of water through an interview in which he or she was asked questions regarding approach behaviors toward a lake or pond. Data obtained through the interview therefore assess motor behavior indirectly. The child may also be assessed through direct observation via an *in vivo* behavioral avoidance test, wherein the clinician accompanies the child to a lake.

It is also important to note that many questionnaires and rating scales may actually measure more than one channel within the same instrument. Thus, a self-report scale may include items that provide a measure of the motoric response channel, but it may also include items that refer only to cognitions or physiological responses.

Finally, it is important to emphasize that some measurement strategies represent only theoretical possibilities within the framework presented by Cone (1977). For example, cognitive activities cannot be measured using ratings or direct observation by others.

FEAR REDUCTION METHODS

In recent years, there has been a rapid proliferation of research on the development and application of fear reduction methods with children (see, for example, reviews by Barrios & O'Dell, 1989; Francis & Ollendick, 1987; Graziano et al., 1979; Hatzenbuehler & Schroeder, 1978; Johnson, 1979; King et al., 1988, 1991; Kratochwill et al., 1988; Miller, Barrett, & Hampe, 1974; Morris, Kratochwill, & Dodson, 1986; Morris, Kratochwill, & Aldridge, 1988; Ollendick, 1979b, 1986; Ramirez, Kratochwill, & Morris, 1997). The assumptions underlying these approaches have generally taken a behavioral orientation. There are currently four major behavior therapy methods of fear reduction in children; systematic desensitization (including variations of this procedure), contingency management procedures, modeling procedures, and cognitive-behavioral interventions (King et al.,

1988; McReynolds, Morris, & Kratochwill, 1989; Morris & Kratochwill, 1983; Ramirez et al., 1997).

Systematic Desensitization

Systematic desensitization, developed in the early 1950s by Joseph Wolpe, is one of the most frequently used behavior therapy procedures for reducing children's fears and phobias (King et al., 1988; Morris & Kratochwill, 1983, 1985; Morris et al., 1988). The basic assumption of this technique is that a fear response can be inhibited by substituting an activity that is antagonistic to it. The response that is most typically inhibited by this treatment process is anxiety, and the response frequently substituted for it is relaxation and calmness.

The desensitization process involves exposing the child in small, graduated steps to the feared situation or event as she or he is performing an activity antagonistic to anxiety. The gradual exposure to the feared (or avoided) stimulus can take place either in the child's cognitions, where she or he is asked to imagine being in various target fear-related situations. Or the child may be asked to pretend that he or she is a popular superhero who approaches the feared situation while performing his or her "usual" superhero-related activities. Finally, the exposure can occur in real life (i.e., *in vivo*). Wolpe (1958) termed the principle that underlies the desensitization process *reciprocal inhibition*. He described this principle in the following way: "If a response inhibitory to anxiety can be made to occur in the presence of anxiety-evoking stimuli, it will weaken the connection between these stimuli and the anxiety responses" (Wolpe, 1962, p. 562).

There are essentially three phases to systematic desensitization: relaxation training, development of the anxiety hierarchy, and systematic desensitization proper.

Relaxation Training

The first step in relaxation training is to let the child become very comfortable within the setting in which the desensitization procedure will be performed. Following this, the relaxation steps used in Table 4.2 are initiated by the therapist. These steps represent a modified version of a technique devel-oped by Jacobson (1938) for inducing deep muscle relaxation. The wording of each step should be adapted to each child's developmental level. The whole procedure usually takes about 20 to 25 minutes to complete, each step taking about 6 to 10 seconds, with a 10- to 15-second pause between each step. During the first few relaxation training sessions, it is often helpful for the therapist to practice the relaxation procedure with the child, so that he or she can observe how to perform a particular step correctly. It may also be helpful, before training begins, for the therapist to explain to the child what changes he or she will begin to experience in his or her body during relaxation training. This explanation becomes especially important for those children or adolescents the therapist feels have never (or rarely) had a waking "relaxed state."

The therapist may also have to guide the child physically at first in performing some of the steps, gradually letting this assistance fade out. Also, the therapist should make sure that she or he paces the presentation of each step to the child's readiness to perform each step. It may be found that certain steps will have to be presented and practiced many times before the child achieves mastery.

Once the child has gained a medium level of proficiency at relaxation training (usually after three or more sessions), the therapist should encourage the child to practice the relaxation method at home or during a quiet time at school (e.g., Bergland & Chal, 1972; King et al., (1988). The practice sessions should last 10 to 15 minutes per session and take place at least twice per day. To enhance the child's practice, some therapists record the relaxation procedure on an audio cassette tape and have the child or adolescent play the tape during each day's practice. Others (e.g., Koeppen, 1974) include fantasy play in the relaxation exercise to maintain the child's involvement in the task. For example, to help the child relax the jaw and lower facial muscles, the therapist might have the child pretend that she or he is a big tired lion who is taking "a great big yawn" because he or she is so sleepy. Some therapists also provide the child, where it seems appropriate, with a list of the muscle groups and encourage the child's parents and/or teachers to practice the relaxation procedure with the child.

TABLE 4.2. Relaxation Protocol

STEPS IN RELAXATION

1. Take a deep breath and hold it (for about 10 seconds). Hold it. Okay, let it out.
2. Raise both of your hands about halfway above the couch (or arms of the chair) and breathe normally. Now drop your hands to the couch (or arm).
3. Now hold your arms out and make a tight fist. Really tight. Feel the tension in your hands. I am going to count to three and when I say "three" I want you to drop your hands. One...two...three.
4. Raise your arms again and bend your fingers back the other way (toward your body). Now drop your hands and relax.
5. Raise your arms. Now drop them and relax.
6. Now raise your arms again, but this time "flap" your hands around. Okay, relax again.
7. Raise your arms again. Now relax.
8. Raise your arms above the couch (chair) again and tense your biceps. Breathe normally and keep your hands loose. Relax your hands. (Notice how you have a warm feeling of relaxation.)
9. Now hold your arms out to your side and tense your triceps. Make sure that you breathe normally. Relax your arms.
10. Now arch your shoulders back. Hold it. Make sure that your arms are relaxed. Now relax.
11. Hunch your shoulders forward. Hold it and make sure that you breathe normally and keep your arms relaxed. Okay, relax. (Notice the feeling of relief from tensing and relaxing your muscles.)
12. Now turn your head to the right and tense your neck. Relax and bring your head back into in its natural position. Turn your head to the left and tense your neck. Relax and bring your head back again to its normal position.
13. Turn your head to the left and tense your neck. Relax and bring your head back again to its natural position.
14. Now bend your head back slightly toward the chair. Hold it. Okay, now bring your head back slowly to its natural position.*
15. This time bring your head down almost to your chest. Hold it. Now relax and let your head come back to its natural resting position.
16. Now open your mouth as much as possible. A little wider, okay, relax (mouth should be partly open afterwards).
17. Now tense your lips by closing your mouth. Okay, relax.
18. Now put your tongue at the roof of your mouth. Press hard. (Pause.) Relax and allow your tongue to come to a comfortable position in your mouth.
19. Now put your tongue at the bottom of your mouth. Press down hard. Relax and let your tongue come to a comfortable position in your mouth.
20. Now just lie (sit) there and relax. Try not to think of anything.
21. To control self-verbalizations, I want you to go through the motions of singing a high note—not aloud. Okay, start singing to yourself. Hold that note. Okay, relax. (You are becoming more and more relaxed.)
22. Now sing a medium tone and make your vocal cords tense again. Relax.
23. Now sing a low note and make your vocal cords tense again. Relax. (Your vocal apparatus should be relaxed now. Relax your mouth.)
24. Now close your eyes. Squeeze them tight and breathe naturally. Notice the tension. Now relax. Notice how the pain goes away when you relax.
25. Now let your eyes relax and keep your mouth open slightly.
26. Open your eyes as much as possible. Hold it. Now relax your eyes.
27. Now wrinkle your forehead as much as possible. Hold it. Okay, relax.
28. Now take a deep breath and hold it. Relax.
29. Now exhale. Breathe all the air out...all of it out. Relax. (Notice the wondrous feeling of breathing again.)
30. Imagine that there are weights pulling on all your muscles making them flaccid and relaxed...putting your arms and body down into the couch.
31. Pull your stomach muscles together. Tighter. Okay, relax.
32. Now extend your muscles as if you were a prizefighter. Make your stomach hard. Relax. (You are becoming more and more relaxed.)
33. Now tense your buttocks. Tighter. Hold it. Now relax.
34. Now search the upper part of your body and relax any part that is tense. First the facial muscles. (Pause 3 to 5 sec.) Then the vocal muscles. (Pause 3 to 5 sec.) The neck region. (Pause 3 to 5 sec.) Your shoulders...relax any part that is tense. (Pause.) Now the arms and fingers. Relax these. Becoming very relaxed.
35. Maintaining this relaxation, raise both your legs (about a 45%angle). Now relax. Notice how this further relaxes you.
36. Now bend your feet back so that your toes point toward your face. Relax your mouth. Bend them hard. Relax.
37. Bend your feet the other way...away from your body. Not far. Notice the tension. Okay, relax.
38. Relax. (Pause.) Now curl your toes together as hard as you can. Tighter. Okay, relax. (Quiet— silence for about 30 seconds.)
39. This completes the formal relaxation procedure. Now explore your body from your feet up. Make sure that every muscle is relaxed. Say slowly—first your toes, your feet, your legs, buttocks, stomach, shoulders, neck, eyes, and finally your forehead—you should be relaxed now. (Quiet—silence for about 10 seconds.) Just lie there and feel very relaxed, noticing the warmness of the relaxation. (Pause.) I would like you to stay this way for about 1 minute, and then I am going to count to five. When I reach five, I want you to open your eyes feeling very calm and refreshed. (Quiet—silence for about 1 minute.) Okay, when I count to five I want you to open your eyes feeling very calm and relaxed. One...feeling very calm; two...very calm, very refreshed; three...very refreshed; four...and five.

*The child or adolescent should not be encouraged to bend his or her neck either all the way back or forward.

Note: Adapted in part from Jacobson, 1938, Rimm (1967, personal communication), and Wolpe and Lazarus (1966). From *Treating children's fears and phobias: A behavioral approach* (p. 135) by R. J. Morris and T. R. Kratochwill, 1983, Elmsford, NY: Pergamon Press. Copyright 1983 by Pergamon Press. Reprinted by permission of Allyn & Bacon Inc.

Some children and adolescents cannot relax using this training method. No matter how motivated they are, they just find it difficult to respond—or find the training instructions too complex to comprehend and/or carry out. A few children and adolescents even avoid relaxation and/or report feeling tense when they engage in relaxation training. Some behaviors associated with clients who are *not* relaxed, are rapid and/or uneven breathing, hands clenching chair, finger tapping, giggling, smiling, fidgeting, repeatedly opening eyes and/or squeezing eyes closed, and frequent yawning (e.g., Luiselli, 1980; Morris & Kratochwill, 1983). To deal with a person's difficulty, in learning to relax, Morris (1973) proposed a shaping procedure to teach children and adults to close their eyes for increasingly longer periods of time during the relaxation training session. Similarly, Cautela and Groden (1978) discuss the use of shaping to assist children in learning how to tense and then relax particular muscle groupings. They also suggest using various squeeze toys to help children (especially some special-needs children) in learning how to tense their arms and hands, as well as the use of certain air-flow toys (e.g., whistles, party horns, harmonicas, bubble pipes, etc.) to teach the breathing-step portions of relaxation training programs. Although adjunctive methods such as biofeedback-assisted relaxation (e.g., Javel & Denholtz, 1975; Reeves & Maelica, 1975; Tarler-Benlolo, 1978), hypnosis, or carbon dioxide-oxygen (Wolpe & Lazarus, 1966; Wolpe, 1973) and the administration of medication (e.g., Brady, 1966, 1972; Friedman, 1966) have been recommended by some writers to assist adult clients in achieving relaxation, there is currently no organized body of literature that supports their use with children and adolescents.

Development of the Anxiety Hierarchy

During the relaxation phase, the therapist should begin planning an anxiety hierarchy with the child or adolescent (and, where appropriate, with his or her parents) for each of the target fears identified as needing to be reduced. A hierarchy is usually constructed on only those fears that the client and therapist agree on as being in need of change during or immediately following the initial assessment and diagnosis period. The therapist should not impose treatment on a child for a fear that she or he has not agreed is in need of being reduced.

Typically, the client and/or the parents are given 10 3- by 5-inch index cards and asked to write down on each card a brief description of different situations regarding the fear that produces certain levels of anxiety or tension. Specifically, the child or adolescent is asked to describe on the cards those situations that are related to his or her fear and that she or he feels produce increasing amounts of anxiety, tension, or discomfort. Each of the 10 cards is assigned a number that is a multiple of 10 (i.e., 10, 20, 30, 40,…100), with the card having the value of 100 containing a description of the most anxiety-provoking situation.

When the client returns with the prepared hierarchy, the therapist goes through it with the child and adds intermediate items whenever it seems appropriate. The hierarchies of children and adolescents often differ markedly from each other—even those having to do with the same type of fear. Hierarchies vary on such factors as the person's unique interpretation of the events occurring in the feared situations, the number and type of people present in the feared situations, temporal and/or spatial considerations, type of environment or space in which the fear might occur, level of embarrassment that the person might feel if placed in or exposed to the fear situation, and degree to which the child or adolescent feels she or he can escape from or leave the feared situation without being noticed by others.

The final hierarchy usually takes at least, or part of, two or three sessions to develop and should represent a slow and smooth gradation of anxiety-provoking situations, each of which the child or adolescent can easily imagine. Most hierarchies contain 20 to 25 items. It is not unusual however, for those hierarchies that represent a very specific fear (e.g., fear of becoming sick while riding in a car, fear of being alone in the house, fear of sleeping alone in one's own room, fear of entering a pool) to contain fewer items, while those representing a more complex fear (e.g., fear of being evaluated, fear of robbers entering the home, fear of school, fear of being away from the home, fear of losing control, fear of using a public toilet) contain more items.

While developing the final hierarchy, the therapist should also determine what the child or adolescents considers to be a very relaxing situation, one that the child can easily imagine and that she or he would rate as a zero on the hierarchy. Some examples of "zero-level" scenes are:

Reading a good novel in bed before going to sleep.
Watching a favorite television program.
Having my daddy read to me when I go to bed at night.
Playing in the swimming pool.
Laying in bed and listening to music on my stereo.
Out riding my bicycle in the neighborhood.
Playing a video game on our home computer.
Going hiking in the woods.
Playing with my train set (Adapted from Morris & Kratochwill, 1983, p. 141)

Although most children and adolescents who understand and master relaxation training are capable of constructing an anxiety hierarchy, on rare occasions a person does not comprehend the notion of an anxiety hierarchy, and, therefore, is not able to assist the therapist in formulating his or her hierarchy (e.g., Stedman & Murphey, 1984). In such cases, the therapist should switch to an alternative fear reduction method that is more concrete in nature.

Systematic Desensitization Proper

By the time the therapist is ready to begin the desensitization proper sessions, the child or adolescent should have had sufficient time to practice relaxation and be proficient at relaxing on command. If the child or adolescent has developed several hierarchies, the therapist should first work on the one that is most distressing to the client. Then, if time allows, the therapist can work on others.

The first desensitization session starts with having the client spend about 3 to 5 minutes relaxing on a couch or in a recliner. The client is also asked to indicate, by raising his or her right index finger, when a very relaxing and comfortable state has been achieved.

After the child or adolescent signals, the therapist asks him or her to visualize a number of scenes from the hierarchy that the two of them have developed over the past few sessions. The therapist asks the client to imagine each scene as clearly and as vividly as possible—"As if you were really there,"—while still maintaining a very relaxed state. If the child or adolescent feels the least bit of anxiety or tension in imagining a particular scene, she or he is told to signal immediately with the right finger. If the client signals, the therapist presents the zero-level scene and then reviews with the client the steps in the relaxation sequence until the feeling of tension is gone.

Each hierarchy scene is presented three to four times, with a maximum exposure time of 5 seconds for the first presentation, and with a gradual increase up to 10 seconds for subsequent presentations. The hierarchy items are presented first in ascending order, starting with the least feared item with relaxation periods between each scene varying from 10 to 15 seconds. In most cases, three to four different scenes are presented per session. This means that a particular desensitization session will last between 15 and 20 minutes.

After the last scene for a particular session is presented, and if the decision is not to go on to another fear hierarchy, the therapist usually asks the child or adolescent to relax for a short time before entering the session.

The same general format is followed for all subsequent desensitization sessions. Each scene should be presented until the client has had three consecutive successes. If, however, the child or adolescent has two consecutive failures (indications of anxiety), the therapist should go back to the previous successfully passed scene and work back up the hierarchy again. If failure occurs again, the previously successful scene should be presented again so that the child or adolescent ends the session with a positive experience. Following this, it is often helpful to review with the client the problems she or he was having with the difficult scene.

Additional Considerations

Although there has been a substantial amount of clinical and "analogue" research conducted with adults on those factors that contribute to the effectiveness of systematic desensitization, relatively little controlled research of this nature has been done with children and adolescents (see, for example, Barrios & O'Dell, 1989; Graziano et al., 1979; King et al., 1988; Morris & Kratochwill, 1983; Ollendick & King, 1994). Current factors that may contribute to the effectiveness of systematic desensitization therapy with children and adolescents include the following: age of child receiving treatment, child's level of visual imagery, his or her ability to relax, child's and parents' motivation level regarding a desire to reduce the fear or phobia, child's ability to follow instructions, child's level of acquiescence, and child's threshold of fatigue (see, for example, Kissel, 1972). Regarding the age factor, very few studies report the successful use of systematic desensitization with children under 9 years of age. Little if any research has been conducted on the other client factors listed above (see, for example, Morris & Kratochwill, 1983; 1985).

As in the case of client variables, little research with children or adolescents has studied variables involving the therapist or the setting and their effect on the outcome of systematic desensitization. Some research of this type has been conducted with adults (see, for example, Morris & Magrath, 1983; Morris & Suckerman, 1974a, 1974b, 1976), but it is not clear whether these findings can be transferred to the conduct of systematic desensitization with children and adolescents.

Supportive Research

As stated earlier in this chapter, systematic desensitization is one of the most frequently used procedures to reduce the fears and phobias of children and adolescents (see, for example, Barrios & O'Dell, 1989; Graziano et al., 1979; King et al., 1988; Morris & Kratochwill, 1983; Ollendick & King, 1994). Mann and Rosenthal (1969), for example, compared direct (systematic) and vicarious (children observing other children receiving treatment) desensitization in individual and group treatment settings with a no-treatment control group. The participants in the treatment groups consisted of 50 seventh graders, while the participants in the control

group were 21 eighth graders. Compared to the control group, the treatment groups showed a significantly greater reduction in their respective self-report test anxiety scores and a sufficient improvement in their performance in a reading test. No significant differences, however, were found between the individual or group, direct or vicarious desensitization methods.

With regard to other school-related fears, Taylor (1972) reported the successful use of systematic desensitization with a 15-year-old girl who was "school-phobic." The case was especially interesting since the girl engaged in excessive urination during school and in school-related activities, contributing to her avoidance of school and withdrawal from social relationships. Her anxiety hierarchies involved three themes: riding in the school bus, being in school, and participating in class activities. A 4-month follow-up evaluation indicated that she was no longer experiencing frequent urination and that she had satisfactory relationships in school.

Miller (1972) treated a 10-year-old boy who was reluctant to go to school and experienced "extreme fear" of being separated from his mother as well as a fear of his own death. Using systematic desensitization, Miller found that the child's fear of separating from his mother decreased gradually over the 11 treatment weeks. Systematic desensitization was also effective in reducing the boy's school phobia, but failed to decrease his fear of his own death. Lazarus (1960) also treated a school-phobic child with systematic desensitization. Following her ninth birthday, the girl became enuretic and afraid of the dark. She also developed "violent" abdominal pains at school, which eventually resulted in her being excused from class and her mother having to come to school. It was determined that her multiple fears were the result of her fear of being separated from her mother. Desensitization took five sessions over a 10-day period. A 15-month follow-up revealed a "very occasional" enuretic incident with no reported school-related problems.

In another case study, Kushner (1965) used systematic desensitization to reduce the fears of a 17-year-old youth who feared driving his car, being driven by others, and being around cars. After three treatment sessions, the client reported feeling better.

At the sixth and last session the client felt he had improved. At the three-month follow-up, there was further improvement and no recurrence of his fears. MacDonald (1975) also reported the successful use of systematic desensitization with an 11-year-old boy who had a dog phobia, which had lasted for eight years. By the sixth session, the boy reported staying outdoors without worrying about dogs, and at the fourteenth session, his parents reported that he was engaging in appropriate interactions in both benign and threatening dog encounters. In addition to the use of desensitization, MacDonald added some adjuncts to treatment: for example, dog pictures in the boy's room, asking the boy to write a happy story about himself and a dog, listening to an audiotape recording of barking dogs, providing skill training regarding interacting with dogs, and engaging in programmed outdoor activity. The results were maintained at 2-year follow-up.

An adjunct to systematic desensitization was also used in a study by Saunders (1976) involving a 13-year-old boy who developed motion sickness and vomiting during trips in cars or buses. In addition to the standard desensitization method, Saunders added an in vivo relaxation component, where the boy approached and sat in a vehicle. Treatment was completed in 11 sessions over a 4-month period. At the 19-month follow-up period, the child reported feeling no nausea, that he was able to take a long trip with his family, and that he was able to ride the bus to school.

Each of the studies described can best be described as clinically descriptive case studies. Only a very few controlled single-case time series experiments have been published. For example, Van Hasselt, Hersen, Bellack, Rosenblum, and Lamparski (1979) used systematic desensitization with an 11-year-old boy who had fears of blood, heights, and taking tests. The authors measured the boy's motoric, cognitive, and physiological responses to each fear. Treatment lasted for four relaxation sessions and four to six desensitization sessions for each fear. Although relaxation training did not appreciably change any of the dependent measures, systematic desensitization was found to effect changes on all but the physiological measure. A second controlled study by Ollendick (1979a) also

demonstrated the effectiveness of systematic desensitization. Using a withdrawal design, Ollendick treated a 16-year-old anorexic youth who feared gaining weight and subsequent criticism from his peers. When the desensitization procedure was in effect, the adolescent gained weight, and when the procedure was withdrawn, he began to lose weight. When desensitization was reinstated, he began gaining weight again, thereby demonstrating experimental control of the desensitization procedure. Following the completion of the use of desensitization, an adjunctive weight-maintenance-enhancing procedure was introduced. At the 18-month follow-up, the weight gain was maintained, while at the 2-year follow-up a slight decrease in weight was found.

Systematic desensitization treatment has also been used with children and adolescents who are handicapped (e.g., King, Ollendick, Gullone, Cummins, & Josephs, 1990; Obler & Terwilliger, 1970). For example, Obler and Terwilliger (1970) worked with a group of neurologically impaired children who had a "severe monophobic disorder" involving either dogs or the use of a public bus. The 30 children were assigned randomly either to a treatment or to a no-treatment control condition, with each condition subdivided further into retarded ("minimally aware" of treatment procedures) and nonretarded ("aware" of treatment procedures) groups. The participants in each condition were also matched for age, sex, intelligence, and phobic diagnosis. The IQ of the children ranged from 50 to 70 in the treatment condition and 57 to 73 in the control condition. The authors used a modified Wolpean systematic desensitization procedure, involving *in vivo* exposure plus social (and later, tangible) reinforcement for approaching the feared object. Although no formal anxiety hierarchy was constructed, Obler and Terwilliger (1970) indicated that a hierarchy "was determined arbitrarily" by the therapist. The results showed that all the children in the treatment condition were rated by parents as improved, whereas only 30% of the no-treatment children were so rated. When a more stringent, success criterion was used, 53.3% of the treatment children were rated as improved, whereas none of the control children were so rated. Approximately the same result was also found, using the more stringent criterion, between the two subgroups of mentally retarded children with the treatment participants rated as 60% improved and the control participants rated as 60% improved. Obler and Terwilliger (1970), concluded, that the modified systematic desensitization procedure "significantly affected" the treatment outcome. Unfortunately, no follow-up or generalization data were provided.

In vivo desensitization has also been used successfully in the reduction of an "extreme toilet phobia" in a 5-year-old boy who was diagnosed as autistic and borderline mentally retarded (Wilson & Jackson, 1980), in a 21-year-old moderately mentally retarded man with a long-standing mannequin phobia (Waranch, Iwata, Wohl & Nidiffer, 1981), and in a 7-1/2-year-old mildly retarded boy who had a fear of physical examinations (Freeman, Roy, & Hemmick, 1976). In addition, a modified systematic desensitization procedure using *in vivo* components, was implemented successfully in the reduction of a 13-year-old borderline mentally retarded boy's phobia regarding body hair (Rivenq, 1974).

With respect to research comparing systematic desensitization to other therapeutic approaches, only a few studies have been reported. For example, Miller, Barrett, Hampe, and Noble (1972) compared the relative effectiveness. of systematic desensitization and conventional psychotherapy to a waiting-list control condition with children having various phobias. The desensitization condition lasted for 24 sessions and at times included assertiveness training, presence of parents at the desensitization sessions, and assistance of parents in developing alternative responses to fear and anxiety. This method, therefore, included elements that were additional to standard systematic desensitization. The conventional psychotherapy condition also lasted for 24 sessions and included having the child talk out feelings and conflicts, with emphasis on effective expression of and subsequent cognitive awareness of preconditions for fear. As in the desensitization condition, parent training was involved. Parents were taught to alter their child's home environment and to remove any potential contributing factors to the child's fear. It thus appeared that the two treatment approaches contained many

common elements. The outcome was assessed in terms of the clinician's ratings of the intensity and extent of each child's fear and, by the ratings of parents on the Louisville Behavior checklist and the Louisville Fear Survey for Children. No child's actual fear responses were systematically observed by the researchers. The overall results for the clinicians' ratings showed that neither treatment method was superior to the waiting-list control condition; however, when age was considered, it was found that children between 6 and 10 years of age in both therapy groups significantly improved over the waiting-list control children. No differences were found between the desensitization and psychotherapy conditions for the 6- to 10-year-olds or the 11- to 15-year-olds. In addition, the level of experience of the clinician (clinician with 20 years experience vs. recently graduated clinician with minimal child therapy experience) did not have a significant effect on the outcome of the study, nor did such factors as sex of child, IQ, or chronicity of fears. With respect to parent ratings, parents of children in both treatment groups and across age groups reported significantly more improvement in their children than did parents of children in the waiting-list control condition. No significant differences, however, were found between the two treatment groups. The results on each of the dependent measures were maintained at a 6-week follow-up. A 21-month follow-up (Hampe, Noble, Miller, & Barrett, 1973) showed that the improvement found in the children had been maintained. It was also found that most of those children who were in the waiting-list control group or who did not respond to treatment also improved over the 21-month period. In some cases, however, this improvement was due to additional therapy. Given the "impure" nature of the systematic desensitization group, the fact that no overt fears were observed, and that this study has not been replicated, it is difficult to interpret the meaningfulness of these findings.

In another comparison study, Ultee, Griffioen, and Schellekens (1982) compared over a four-session period *in vitro* desensitization (i.e., graduated minimal exposure to anxiety-provoking scenes plus relaxation training) to *in vivo* desensitization (i.e., gradual exposure to anxiety-provoking stimuli in the actual or real situation plus relaxation training) and a no-treatment control group. Following this, the authors added an *in vivo* desensitization component to the previous *in vitro* group and compared this combination procedure (four sessions *in vitro* followed by four sessions of *in vivo* desensitization) with the *in vivo* and no-treatment control groups. The children in the study were 12 boys and 12 girls between 5 and 10 years of age who had a fear of water. The results showed that at the end of four sessions, the *in vivo* group improved significantly more than either the *in vitro* or no-treatment groups on at least two of the three dependent measures. At the end of eight sessions, the *in vivo* group was found to improve more significantly, more than the no-treatment group on two out of three of the dependent measures and to improve significantly more than the *in vitro* plus *in vivo* group on one out of three measures. On the other hand, the *in vitro* group or the *in vitro* plus *in vivo* condition did not show any significant differences from the no-treatment group on any of the three dependent measures. Ultee et al., concluded that the *in vivo* condition was better than the *in vitro* condition and that imaginal desensitization does not add significantly to the overall effectiveness of real-life exposure to a feared situation.

Although the findings from the Ultee et al., (1982) study are certainly noteworthy, it should be pointed out that no follow-up data were reported by the authors nor were any transfer of training effects assessed in other settings. In addition, a possible developmental artifact was noted by the authors that may be responsible for the findings: namely, the possible lack of anticipatory "imaginative capacity" in the children in this study, which would have prevented them from developing "a dynamic image of one's own behavior in the phobic situation" (Ultee et al., 1982, p. 66) and, thus, transferring this information to the actual feared situation. This point is also made by Morris and Kratochwill (1983), who point to research evidence suggesting that children cannot form visual images until they are approximately 9 years of age. Therefore, these authors tentatively recommend that the use of imaginal systematic desensitization be limited to children who have reached this age.

Interestingly, the only other controlled comparison study that has been published, (e.g., Sheslow, Bondy, & Nelson, 1983) has also found, working with 4- and 5-year-old children who were afraid of the dark, that the only two treatment conditions that were effective in reducing children's fears were those that included in vivo exposure. The verbal-coping-alone condition did not differ from the control group on the dependent measures. Other than this suggestion (that in vivo exposure should be included in any desensitization treatment with children below 9 years of age), few conclusions can be drawn at this time from the research literature on this method. The volume of uncontrolled case studies and controlled research in this area, however, does suggest that this procedure is an effective fear-reduction method that can be used with children and adolescents who are intellectually normal; however, its efficacy with children and adolescents having mental retardation and/or other handicapping conditions has not been firmly established (King, et al., 1990).

Variations of Systematic Desensitization

Various alternatives to individual systematic desensitization have been proposed by researchers; each involves variations of the desensitization procedure previously discussed.

Group systematic desensitization. This procedure, involves the same basic phases as individual systematic desensitization, but the phases are adapted for group administration. Typically, groups of five to eight persons are included in this procedure. Hierarchy construction is conducted in the group, with the group rank-ordering the hierarchy items. An alternative approach involves having the therapist bring to the group a listing of potential hierarchy items: The group rank-orders them after deciding which are appropriate and/or need modification. In this variation, the desensitization proper stage is conducted in a slightly different manner from the individual approach. Here, the general rule is that desensitization proper is geared to the person in the treatment group who is progressing most slowly.

In terms of supportive research, we again find a disproportionate amount of it being conducted on group desensitization with adults as opposed to children and, in both instances, mostly in the area of school-related problems (e.g., test anxiety, speech anxiety, reading difficulties, etc.). For example, Kondas (1967) used group systematic desensitization with test-anxious (oral examination) 11- to 15-year-old students. Compared to the relaxation or hierarchy-only groups, the desensitization group showed significant decreases in self-reported fears and measures of palmar perspiration. Barabasz (1973) also studied the relative effectiveness of group desensitization with test-anxious students. He found that highly test-anxious treated participated, as compared with highly test-anxious no-treatment control participants—showed significant reductions on autonomic measures of anxiety and performed better on a group test. In addition, no differences were found on either dependent measure for the experimental and control low test-anxious participants. Other studies on test anxiety (see, for example, Deffenbacher & Kemper, 1974a, 1974b; King, et al., 1991; Laxer, Quarter, Kooman, & Walker, 1969), using a variety of different dependent measures, have also reported group treatment by systematic desensitization to be effective.

In vivo desensitization. In this method, as discussed above, the child is exposed to the items on the hierarchy in the raw or actual situation rather than through his or her imagination. Relaxation training is not always used as the counterconditioned response to the feared situation. Instead, those feelings of comfort, security, and trust that the child has developed for the therapist and which have emerged from the therapeutic relationship are used as the counterconditioning agent. The therapist goes into the real life situation with the child and encourages him or her to go through each item on the hierarchy.

In terms of corroborating research, a number of studies over the past 30–35 years have used *in vivo* desensitization either alone or in combination with some other procedure to reduce fears in children (e.g., Bentler, 1962; Craghan & Musante, 1975; Freeman et al., 1976; Garvey & Hegrenes, 1966; Jones, 1924a; King, et al., 1988; Kuroda, 1969;

O'Reilly, 1971; Sheslow et al., 1983; Tasto, 1969; Ultee et al., 1982; Van der Ploeg, 1975; Wilson & Jackson, 1980). Few of these studies, however, are well controlled, and none have systematically examined the relative effectiveness of only *in vivo* desensitization (e.g., Sheslow et al., 1983; Ultee et al., 1982). Freeman et al., (1976), for example, presented a case study of a 7-year-old boy who had a fear of having a physical examination. The therapist was a nurse who had a good relationship with the child. The nurse took the child to the examining room and gradually exposed him to the 11-step physical examination hierarchy. Treatment lasted over a 7-session period, with the child permitting, in the last session, an examination of his entire body. Physicians were introduced gradually and, after some additional sessions, the boy permitted the physician to examine him entirely. Craghan and Musante (1975) used this method with a 7-year-old boy who had a fear of high buildings. Treatment lasted for six sessions and involved both *in vivo* desensitization and game-playing with the therapist (e.g., jumping over sidewalk cracks, kicking buildings, throwing snowballs at buildings). Following treatment and at the 3-month and 1-year follow-up, the child showed no indication of being afraid of high buildings. This approach was also used by Kuroda (1969) in eliminating fears of frogs and earthworms in 3- and 4-year-old children.

In vivo desensitization approaches have also been used by parents of phobic children under the supervision of a therapist (e.g., Bentler, 1962; Stableford, 1979; Tasto, 1969). For example Bentler (1962) reports a case involving an 11-month-old girl who was afraid of water. With the mother, he established a hierarchy involving increasing exposure to water and found that by age $12\frac{3}{4}$ months, the child "was thoroughly recovered," with no additional fears reported at either 13, months or 18 months of age.

In summary, although a number of case/descriptive studies have reported successful use of *in vivo* desensitization, there have been only a few well-controlled research studies on this method, and none of these has included both follow-up and transfer of training data. Furthermore, most of the case studies in the literature have used this method in combination with other procedures. Nevertheless, this procedure does appear to be potentially effective in reducing a variety of fears and phobias.

Automated systematic desensitization. In this procedure, the client goes through the desensitization process by listening to a series of audio tape-recorded scene presentations prepared by the therapist with the client's assistance. Developed by Lang (as cited in Wolpe, 1969), this procedure allows clients to pace themselves through the desensitization process. A variation of this automated procedure is called *self-directed desensitization* (e.g., Baker, Cohen, & Saunders, 1973; Rosen, 1976). In this procedure patients use instructional materials typically provided by the therapist and conduct the treatment at their own pace at home. The major difference between these methods is that the automated method is structured by the therapist and uses recording devices and/or computers in the therapist's office to present treatment. In self-directed treatment, on the other hand, the client develops the treatment package at home, with minimal therapist control. Both procedures have been used mainly with adults, but a few studies have involved children. For example, Wish, Hasazi, and Jurgela (1973) report the use of a self-directed procedure with an 11-year-old boy who had a fear of loud noises. Following the construction of the hierarchy and relaxation training, a tape of the child's favorite music was made with sounds from the fear hierarchy superimposed on the music. The child was instructed to relax in a dark room at home and to listen to the tape with the volume gradually increased over the 8-day, 3-session-per-day period. By the end of treatment, the child could listen comfortably to the sounds he feared most at a loud intensity. In addition, the child did not show any fear responses to other noises (e.g., balloon pop, firecracker, etc.). The child's behavior was maintained at a 9-month follow-up. This is an interesting treatment approach and one that is in need of a good deal more research before any definitive statement can be made about its efficacy in reducing children's fears.

Emotive imagery. This method was first used by Lazarus and Abramovitz (1962) to adapt the desensitization proper phase to children. It involves the use of those anxiety-inhibiting images in children that arouse feelings of excitement associated with adventure as well as feelings of pride, mirth, and so on. It consists of the following steps:

1. As in the usual method of systematic desensitization, a graduated hierarchy is drawn up.
2. By sympathetic conversation and inquiry, the clinician establishes the nature of the child's hero images and the wish fulfillments and identifications that accompany them.
3. The child is asked to close his eyes and imagine a sequence of events that is close enough to his everyday life to be credible, within which is woven a story concerning his favorite hero or alter ego.
4. When the clinician judges that these emotions have been maximally aroused, he introduces as a natural part of the narrative, the lowest item in the hierarchy. If there is evidence that anxiety is being inhibited, the procedure is repeated as in ordinary systematic desensitization until the highest item in the hierarchy is tolerated without distress (Wolpe & Lazarus, 1966, p. 143).

Relatively few studies have been published that have used this procedure (e.g., Boyd, 1980; Chudy, Jones, & Dickson, 1983; Jackson & King, 1981; Lazarus & Abramovitz, 1962; Stedman & Murphy, 1984). For example, Boyd (1980) used this method with a 16-year-old "school-phobic" youth who was mildly retarded. After two weeks of therapy, the boy was able to attend school for the full day and finished the school year with no recurrence of the school phobia. In addition, Lazarus and Abramovitz (1962) report in a series of case/descriptive studies the successful use of the procedure with a dog-phobic 14-year-old, a 10-year-old who was afraid of the dark, and an 8-year-old who was enuretic and afraid of going to school. Although this approach, is innovative and has some clinical support, systematic controlled research has not yet been published to support its effectiveness.

Contact desensitization. Developed by Ritter (1968), this method has been used with children and adults, and combines elements of desensitization and modeling approaches. The desensitization process is carried out by exposing the child to each step on the fear hierarchy only after each step has first been demonstrated/modeled by the therapist. Upon modeling a particular step, the therapist helps the client perform that step—touching the client, for example, on the shoulder to help guide him or her, encouraging the client with various motivating statements, and praising the client for making progress. The therapist then gradually removes the prompts until the child or adolescent can perform each step on his or her own. Rimm and Masters (1974) and Morris (1985) have suggested a fourth component of this procedure, namely, the therapist's presence/relationship with the client, although the relative contribution of one aspect of this factor (therapist warmth) in contact desensitization treatment with adult acrophobic persons has been questioned by Morris and Magrath (1979).

In terms of supportive research, studies have been published suggesting the efficacy of this procedure (e.g., Glasscock & MacLean, 1990; Ritter, 1968, 1969). For example, Ritter (1968) assigned 44 snake-avoidant children to one of three groups: contact desensitization, live-modeling, and a no-treatment control condition. The children in the two treatment groups received two 35-minute small-group sessions. The results showed that both treatment conditions were superior to the no-treatment group in the behavior avoidance test, and that the children in the contact desensitization group showed more improvement than the children in the modeling group. In a second study with snake-avoidant children, Ritter (1969) found, that contact desensitization was superior to a contact desensitization treatment without a touch condition. Murphy and Bootzin (1973) discovered that the outcome of their study was not influenced by whether the children in their experiment approached a few snakes in the standard contact desensitization manner (active condition) or whether this experimenter/therapist gradually approached the children with the snake (passive condition).

Self-control desensitization. In this approach, the desensitization procedure is construed as training the client in coping skills, that is, teaching the client to cope with anxiety (Goldfried, 1971; Meichenbaum,

1974; Meichenbaum & Genest, 1980). Clients are told, for example, to apply relaxation training whenever they become aware of an increase in their feelings of anxiety and tension. They are also encouraged, during the desensitization proper phase, to continue imagining a scene that produced anxiety and to "relax away" the anxiety and/or to imagine themselves becoming fearful and then seeing themselves coping with the anxiety and tenseness that they feel. This variation is based on the view that clients will not always be in a position where they can readily leave a fearful and tension-arousing situation— that they must learn to cope with the situation on their own. In this regard, it is not important for the anxiety hierarchy to be theme-oriented as in standard systematic desensitization (Goldfried & Goldfried, 1977). The hierarchy need only be composed of situations arousing increasing amounts of anxiety, independent of theme.

In terms of corroborating research, there is little that supports this approach with children (e.g., Bornstein & Knapp, 1981; DiNardo & DiNardo, 1981). Bornstein and Knapp (1981) used this procedure with a 12-year-old boy who had fears of separation, travel, and illness. Treatment effects were assessed using a multiple-baseline design across these fears. The authors report that the child's fear-related verbal comments, as well as the ratings on the, *Fear Survey Schedule for Children* for each fear, showed "marked reductions" following treatment. In addition, these changes were maintained at 1-year follow-up. This is another interesting treatment approach, but one needing much more supportive research before any statement can be made regarding its relative effectiveness.

Contingency Management

The systematic use of contingency management procedures for the reduction of fears and phobias in children has its origins in the writings of Ivan Pavlov (e.g., Pavlov, 1927), B. F. Skinner (e.g., Skinner, 1938, 1953), and John B. Watson (e.g., Watson, 1913, 1919; Watson & Rayner, 1920). Each stressed the importance of the causal relationship between stimuli and behavior. In this section, we describe the most frequently used contingency management procedures for treating children's fears and phobias.

Positive Reinforcement

Positive reinforcement is typically defined as an event or activity that immediately follows a behavior and results in an increase in the frequency of performance of that behavior. Thus, a positive reinforcer is something that follows a particular behavior and strengthens the number of times that behavior occurs. A reinforcer is defined here in terms of its effects on a child's approach behavior toward the feared stimulus.

Positive reinforcement has been used alone and in combination with other behavioral therapy procedures to reduce various fears and fear-related behaviors in children in a variety of settings (see, for example, Conger & Keane, 1981; Hughes, 1993; King et al., 1988; Morris et al., 1988). For example, Leitenberg and Callahan (1973) used reinforcement to reduce children's fears of darkness. Fourteen children were each assigned to the experimental treatment and control (pretest and post test only) conditions with four girls and three boys in each group. The average age for the experimental group was 6 years, while for the control group it was 5 years, 4 months. The experimental group received a treatment procedure that Leitenberg called "reinforced practice." This procedure involved providing the children in the experimental group with feedback regarding the exact time they spent in the darkened room. In addition, praise reinforcement, repeated practice, and instructions were provided during each session. The results showed that the reinforced practice procedure produced significant improvement over the control condition in the length of time that the children remained in both the partially and completely darkened test rooms.

To increase the generalization of treatment effects, studies have also focused on the use of reinforcement by persons other than the therapist (Trueman, 1984). In this regard, parents and school personnel may be trained to provide the positive reinforcers. For example, a reinforcement contingency contracting system was used by Vaal (1973) to reduce the "school phobia" of a 13-year-old boy

who was absent from school on 94% of the school days over the first six months of the school year. After a meeting with the child, school personnel, and his parents, the following criteria/target behaviors were established for him as part of his contingency contract:

1. Coming to school on time without any tantrum behavior.
2. Attending all classes on the schedule.
3. Remaining in school until dismissed time that day (Vaal, 1973, p. 372).

If these criteria were met each day, he was allowed to engage in various privileges/activities of choice when he returned home (e.g., attending a professional basketball game, going bowling on Saturdays, playing basketball with friends after school). When he did not meet the criteria, these activities were withheld. The contingency contract started on the first school day of the seventh month of the school year and lasted 6 weeks. Vaal (1973) reported that for the next three months the boy "did not miss a single day of school … he came on time every day, came without any inappropriate tantrum behavior, attended all his classes, and was late for none" (p. 372). Following a 2-month summer vacation and over a 4-month period during the subsequent school year, the boy missed only one day of school.

Variations of Positive Reinforcement

Reinforcement has also been used with other contingency management procedures for reducing fears in children. For example, Ayllon, Smith, and Rogers, (1970) used positive reinforcement, shaping/prompting, and withdrawal of social consequences to reduce the "school phobia" of an 8-year-old girl. After conducting an extensive behavior analysis to determine the factors contributing to the child's school phobia, Ayllon et al., established a five-phase treatment procedure.

The first phase consisted of prompting and shaping the child's school attendance. This was accomplished by having an assistant take the child to school near the end of the school day and sit near her in the classroom until the school day was over.

She was also given candy to distribute to her siblings at the end of school and was encouraged to walk home with them. The amount of time that the child attended school in the afternoon gradually increased and the length of time that the assistant stayed with the child also decreased gradually. On the eighth day the child attended school by herself with her siblings, but this voluntary attendance behavior was not maintained the next day or for the next 6 school days. The second treatment phase was initiated when the child's mother was asked to leave for work at the same time that the child and her siblings were to leave for school. Ayllon et al., reasoned that this approach might remove the possibility of the child's receiving social rewards from the mother for staying home from school. This procedure did not result in any increase in the child's school attendance.

The third phase of treatment was then begun, involving a home-based contingent reinforcement and token-economy-like procedure for school attendance combined with the prompting/shaping procedure of phase one (this time involving the mother rather than an assistant). This procedure again resulted in the child's attending school with assistance, but it did not contribute to her voluntarily attending school. The final phase was then instituted. The mother met the child and her siblings at school and provided them with tangible reinforcers and social rewards. The home-based contingent reinforcement and token economy procedure for school attendance was also continued. If the child did not voluntarily go to the school with her siblings and meet her mother, her mother went home and on one occasion "firmly proceeded to take Val by the hand and with hardly any words between them, they rushed back to school." On another occasion, she "scolded Val and pushed her out of the house and literally all the way to school" (Ayllon et al., 1970, pp. 134-135). This procedure contributed to the child attending school voluntarily with her siblings.

During the fifth phase of treatment, the mother first withdrew from meeting the child and her siblings at school and subsequently withdrew the home-based positive reinforcement program. This fading procedure did not produce any disruption in the child's voluntary school attendance. Her voluntary attendance was also found to be maintained at the 6- and 9-month follow-up periods.

Other variations on the use of positive reinforcement for reducing fears in children have been discussed by Kellerman (1980); Lazarus, Davison, and Polefka (1965); Luiselli (1977); and Patterson (1965). However, too few controlled studies have been published on any one variation of positive reinforcement to suggest that any of these procedures is a viable fear-reduction technique.

Shaping

For various reasons, some children have difficulty approaching a feared stimulus even though they have received positive reinforcement for their approach behavior. In some cases, they do not respond to positive reinforcement because the approach behavior, or the series of responses that they emit, is too complex for them to master. That is, the approach behavior to the feared stimulus involves so many steps that the children are unresponsive to the reinforcement contingency.

In such cases, the therapist might consider the use of shaping, whereby the child is taught the desired behavior in successive steps, with each step gradually approximating the desired target behavior. For example, instead of reinforcing an 8-year-old boy who is afraid to leave his home to take short rides with his parents, the therapist might reinforce him for approaching the front of the house and then reinforce him for opening the door and looking outside. Then the child would be reinforced for standing on the porch, outside, and so forth, gradually prompting an increase in the time and distance the child was away from his house.

Other than the Allyon et al., (1970) study, only a few studies have been published using the shaping procedure. For example, Luiselli (1978) used a graduated exposure/shaping procedure with a 7-year-old boy diagnosed as autistic who was afraid to ride a school bus. Initially, the child was familiar with the bus by sitting in it with his mother while it was parked at the school. His mother also reinforced him for this behavior. The mother and the therapist then gradually removed themselves from the bus. The child was then reinforced for riding with the mother and therapist on the bus to school. This was followed by rides only with the therapist and then finally alone. Luiselli reports that the treatment took 7 days and that a year later, the boy continued to ride the bus alone. Tahmisian and McReynolds (1971) also used shaping to successfully reduce the "school phobia" (refusal to attend school) of a 13-year-old girl. This case was striking because the authors reported that they first tried systematic desensitization with this girl but found that it was not effective.

Stimulus Fading

In some instances, a fearful child can perform non-fearful behavior in *selected* settings or under certain conditions but not in other settings. When this occurs, some writers have proposed the use of a *stimulus-fading* procedure. This procedure involves teaching the child to perform the nonfearful response in the same manner and with the same frequency in the unsuccessful settings as she or he does in the successful settings. This fading process is accomplished by gradually shifting the characteristics of the successful setting to the unsuccessful one. For example, Neisworth, Madle, and Goeke (1975) used this procedure for the treatment of "separation anxiety" (crying, sobbing, screaming, withdrawal) in a 4-year-old, preschool girl. The mother was instructed to stay in the preschool for several sessions before being faded out and to reinforce the girl for nonanxious behavior. The child was also reinforced by staff for increased involvement in school activities. Treatment lasted for 18 hours over an 8-day period. Neisworth et al., report that the procedure produced almost an immediate cessation of anxious behavior on the part of the child, and that this behavior was maintained at the 2-, 4-, and 6-month follow-up periods. Only a few fear-related studies have been published using this method; consequently, any statements about its effectiveness must be made with caution.

Extinction

Some children may exhibit fears and/or fear-related responses because they are (or have been) reinforced for performing them. It is therefore possible to reduce this behavior by making certain that a child is not reinforced whenever she or he performs this behavior. *Extinction* refers to the removal of those reinforcing consequences that follow a child's avoidance response. For this procedure to be effective, the therapist *must* be able to identify those consequences that are reinforcing the child's fear response and be in a position to determine: (a) when those consequences will occur, (b) the relative contribution of those consequences to the frequency of the child's fear-related behavior, and (c) whether the therapist can modify the occurrence of the consequences. For example, one of the most common reinforcing consequences for a child's fear behavior is that of parents' attention. If, after a series of observations and discussions with parents, the therapist hypothesizes parental attention as a major contributing/causal factor to the child's fear behavior, she or he must determine the frequency and conditions under which that attention occurs and whether the parents are willing to modify their reactions to their child.

A number of studies have used the extinction procedure with children experiencing fears and related problems (e.g., Boer & Sipprelle, 1970; Hersen, 1970; Piersel & Kratochwill, 1981; Stableford, 1979; Waye, 1979). Many of these studies, however, have combined the extinction procedure with positive reinforcement for appropriate/ nonfearful behaviors. For example, Hersen (1970) worked with a 12-year-old boy who had a school phobia. The child's case was striking in that his five other siblings also had a history of school-phobic responses. Hersen also determined in the introductory (intake interview) sessions that the boy's parents inadvertently reinforced him each morning by coaxing and cajoling him for approximately 2 hours to go to school. A three-part procedure was therefore initiated over the 15 weeks of treatment. First, the child's mother was seen by the therapist and instructed, over a number of sessions, to: (a) be "deaf and dumb" to the child's crying and firm about him attending school; (b) reward the child with praise for his school-related coping behaviors, such as his success in extracurricular activities; and, (c) be aware that the child might show other school-related avoidant behaviors and that these also should be placed on extinction.

Next, Hersen speculated, from the initial intake interview, that a guidance counselor at school had also been a contributing reinforcing agent to the child's "phobia" by paying attention to the boy's crying and anxiety. The therapist then visited the counselor at school and instructed him to see the boy for only 5 minutes per visit and to insist firmly that the child return to classes. The third part of the treatment consisted of the therapist seeing the boy in therapy to: (a) give the therapist the opportunity to verbally reinforce him for demonstrating preschool coping responses, (b) extinguish through nonattention, inappropriate school-related responses, and (c) provide the child with an opportunity to express his views regarding such issues as the treatment program at home. Hersen reported that, following treatment, the boy was attending school normally and that his academic performance had returned to its prephobia level (above-average academic performance). A 6-month follow-up showed that the post treatment behavior was being maintained. Waye (1979) also reports the successful use of an extinction procedure as part of a treatment package for a 5-year-old girl who had a fear that her thumbs were shrinking.

Variations of Extinction

Many of the studies that have used the extinction procedure have also included the use of positive reinforcement for appropriate and/or nonfearful behaviors (e.g., Babbitt & Parrish, 1991; Boer & Sipprelle, 1970; Stableford, 1979). Combining the use of extinction and reinforcement in this manner is consistent with the general behavior modification approach to reducing those maladaptive behaviors that have been theorized or observed to be maintained by reinforcing consequences (see, for example, Kazdin, 1994; Kratochwill, 1981; Morris, 1985).

Another variation involving the use of extinction has been reported by Boer and Sipprelle (1970). They worked with a 4-year-old girl who avoided foods requiring chewing. Prior to treatment, she had lived on liquids for 6 months. The authors reported that her behavior apparently developed following a trip to a doctor's office for a sore throat, as well as

the earlier ingestion of an overdose of aspirin. Boer and Sipprelle concluded that she had developed a strong conditioned anxiety response to doctors. Treatment lasted for seven sessions and consisted of extinguishing her avoidance of doctors and reinforcing incompatible and appropriate behavior. The mother was also asked to stop paying attention to the child's noneating activities. In addition, shaping and positive reinforcement for appropriate eating took place, as well as generalization training to the home with her mother as therapy agent.

Boer and Sipprelle reported that after the fourth clinic session, the girl was eating solid foods in the clinic; after the fifth session, a "normal" eating pattern was found at home. At follow-up 13 months later, she ate solid foods at home without any restrictions.

An additional variation used by Stableford (1979) combined the use of extinction with *in vivo* deconditioning. The author worked with a 3-year-old girl who had a noise phobia. Treatment was carried out by her parents which involved (a) minimizing any parental attention to her fear reactions to noises and (b) exposing her to varying increasing levels of noise at home and in the car. Telephone contact with her parents revealed that, after 2 weeks, the child responded favorably to most noises; but after 5 weeks, she still could not tolerate sounds from the car radio. The parents were again asked to ignore the child's complaints/fear reactions and to distract her with toys. One month later, the child's behavior improved, and 6 months later, the child showed no signs of her noise phobia in any situation.

Supportive Research

The specific goal of contingency management treatment is to increase the rate or frequency of a child's or adolescent's approach behavior to the feared stimulus and to maintain it at that level over time. Treatment involves, first, an analysis of the factors that contribute to the low rate of approach behavior, followed by the manipulation of those factors to increase the frequency of the behavior and, finally, the provision of pleasant consequences to maintain the level of the approach behavior. Interestingly, few controlled experiments on contingency management procedures have been published that support the efficacy of this approach. The vast majority of studies are descriptive and uncontrolled case studies. In addition, most studies combine many contingency management procedures into one treatment package making it difficult to discern which procedures are responsible for the reduction of the client's fear response.

It also becomes clear that only a narrow range of children's fears and phobias have been investigated using the contingency management approach. The overriding majority of published studies involving contingency management have been limited to school phobia—with only 5 to 10 additional case studies investigating a few other fears or phobias. An immediate issue that arises here is the generalization of this approach to other clinical fears and phobias (see, for example, Ross, 1981). Given the restrictive nature of the literature in this nature, a therapist should proceed with caution in the use of any contingency management procedure of behaviors other than those related to school phobia.

In addition, no research has been reported in the contingency management literature on the relative contribution of therapist and/or client variables on the outcome of therapy. For example, would we find the same treatment outcome for a school-phobic child using positive reinforcement, whether the therapist was male or female, young or old, experienced or inexperienced in the use of the procedure? Does the ethnicity of the client or therapist matter? Would the treatment outcome be influenced by the age of the child receiving treatment, the gender of the client, the chronicity of the phobia, or the number of other fears that the client manifests?

Modeling

Behavior change that results from the observation of another person has been typically referred to as *modeling* (e.g., Bandura, 1969; Kazdin & Wilson, 1978; Morris, 1985). Although the concept of modeling or imitation has been studied for almost 100 years, active interest in its application to the treatment and understanding of children's fears and phobias has been investigated only over the past 30–35

years (see, for example, Bandura, 1969, 1971; Bandura & Walters, 1963).

Modeling Proper

Although there are two distinct categories of modeling, *live modeling* and *symbolic modeling*, we tend to find certain factors that are common to both categories. As Bandura (1969) states:

> [Through modeling] one can acquire intricate response patterns merely by observing the performance of appropriate models; emotional responses can be conditioned observationally by witnessing the affective reactions of others undergoing painful or pleasurable experiences; fearful and avoidant behavior can be extinguished vicariously through observation of modeled approach behavior toward feared objects without any adverse consequences accruing to the performer; ...and, finally, the expression of well-learned responses can be enhanced and socially regulated through the actions of influential models. (p. 118).

Modeling, therefore, involves learning through the observation of others and the imitative changes in a person's behaviors that may occur as a result of the observing activities. This procedure sets the occasion for the person to produce changes in his or her emotional and attitudinal responses and correlates of these behavior changes (Masters, Brush, Hollon, & Rimm, 1987).

The modeling procedure involves an individual called the model (e.g., a therapist, parent, teacher, peer, sibling) and a person called the *observer* (i.e., the fearful child). The observer typically observes the model engage in the behavior that the observer has a history of avoiding; this is done within a stimulus setting and focuses on a feared object, event, or stimulus familiar to the observer. Thus, if a child is fearful of very active, large dogs who are not chained or on a leash, it would not be appropriate to have a model touch and play with a small, quiet dog, unless, of course, the dog was only one in a series of gradually more active and larger dogs that the model was planning to touch and play with.

One aspect of the modeling situation that seems to be important for effecting positive behavior change in the observer is to have the child observe

the model experience positive and/or safe consequences with the feared situation, event, or object
(Perry & Furukawa, 1986). In addition, Bandura
(1969, 1977a) has delineated four component
processes that he theorizes govern modeling.
Although these four processes represent a theoretical statement by Bandura regarding the components
of modeling, they can, as Masters et al., (1987) suggest, relate to any direct application of the modeling
procedure to such areas as the treatment of children's fears and phobias. The therapist should be
certain that the child (a) can attend to the various
aspects of the modeling situation (e.g., the child can
sit and watch the modeling event throughout its
duration, the child can note the relevant contextual
aspects of the event, etc.); (b) can *retain* what has
been learned from observing the modeling situation;
(c) has the physical and cognitive ability *to motori-
cally reproduce* or match what was observed in the
modeling situation; and (d) when necessary, has the
motivation to perform the behavior that was
observed.

Finally, with respect to the nature of the model's
approach behavior toward the feared stimulus,
object, or event, most writers agree with Bandura
(1971) that the model should perform the approach
behavior in a graduated fashion. That is, as in the
case of the anxiety hierarchy in *in vivo* desensitization, the model should approach the feared stimulus
gradually in increasing steps, with each being perceived by the client as more and more threatening.

Live modeling. This involves the actual or live
demonstration of the graduated approach behavior
of the model toward the feared situation. For example, Bandura, Grusec, and Menlove (1967) studied
the effect of live modeling on the fear of dogs in 48
children ranging in age from 3 to 5 years. In addition
to live modeling, Bandura et al., studied the contribution of the modeling context (positive vs. neutral)
on the children's approach behavior. Specifically,
children were assigned to one of four groups: (a)
modeling, positive context—the children watched a
peer model fearlessly interact with a dog within the
context of a party atmosphere; (b) modeling, neutral
context—the children also observed the model
approach the dog, but they did so while seated at a

table; (c) exposure, positive context—the children
were having a party and the dog was present, but no
modeling with the dog was occurring; and, (d) positive context—the children were having a party with
no dog present. Each group of children was exposed
to eight 10-minute sessions held over 4 consecutive
days. Follow-up evaluation took place 1 month later.
The results showed that the live modeling conditions were superior to the other two. The children in
the two modeling groups demonstrated significantly
more approach behavior than the children in the
dog-exposure and/or positive-context-only conditions. In looking at the performance of the most
fearful children at pretest, Bandura et al., found that
55% of those in the modeling group performed the
terminal step in the behavior avoidance test, whereas only 13% from the remaining two groups did so.

White and Davis (1974) studied the relative
effectiveness of live modeling, observation/expo-
sure only, and a no-treatment control condition on
the dental-treatment-avoidance behavior of girls
ranging from 4 to 8 years of age. The live modeling
condition consisted of having each of the five participants sit behind a one-way screen with a dental
student and observe a patient/confederate (8-year-
old girl) undergo dental treatment. In the observa-
tion/exposure condition, the participants sat behind
the one-way screen and the dentist and his assistant
merely named and manipulated the equipment used
in the modeling condition. No model was present.
The children in both conditions were each exposed
to six sessions over a 3-week period. The results
showed that both the live modeling condition and
the exposure condition were significantly more
effective than the no-treatment condition in reducing the dental-treatment-avoidance behavior of the
children. In addition, White and Davis (1974) state,
"The behavior of the children under the modeling
condition was far more adaptive and mature. ...
These subjects never required direct support from a
significant other" (p. 31).

Mann and Rosenthal (1969) report a study involving seventh and eighth graders who were referred by
a counselor for test anxiety. They compared direct
systematic desensitization and modeled desensitization in individual and group situations. For example,
some children were desensitized individually while

being observed by a peer, while others were desensitized in a group and also being observed by a group of peers. There was also a condition in which a group of children observed a peer model being desensitized. The results showed that all of the treatment procedures produced significantly better self-report scores and performance on test-taking samples than did the no-treatment control condition.

Ritter (1968) compared the effects of live group modeling, contact desensitization (participant modeling), and a no-treatment control condition on the snake-avoidant behavior of 44 children who ranged from 5 to 11 years of age. Children in the live modeling condition observed several peers exhibit progressively more intimate interactions with a snake. The participant modeling group received Ritter's standard contact desensitization procedure. Children were seen for two 35-minute sessions over a 2-week period. The results showed that both live modeling and contact desensitization were more effective in reducing children's avoidance behavior than was the no-treatment condition. Further analyses revealed, however, that 53% of the children in the modeling condition completed the terminal item on the behavior avoidance test, whereas, 80% of those in the guided-participation group completed the terminal item. No follow-up information was provided.

Few controlled experiments have been published on live modeling with children. A few more have been published involving both children and adults (e.g., Bandura et al., 1969; Blanchard, 1970), but it is not clear what generalizations can be drawn from these latter studies. It should be noted further that the types of fears that have been studied with the live modeling procedure have been limited mostly to animals, test anxiety, and dental treatments. Consequently, any use of this procedure with other clinical fears and phobias in children should be viewed as speculative and the therapist should proceed with caution.

Symbolic modeling. This involves the presentation of the model through film, videotape, or imagination. For example, Bandura and Menlove (1968) studied the effects of filmed modeling on the dog-avoidant behavior of 48 children ranging in age from 3 to 5 years. One group observed a fearless 5-year-old boy

engage in increasingly fearful/fear-provoking contact with a dog. For example, the initial film sequences showed the model looking at the dog in the playpen and occasionally petting the dog, while subsequent sequences displayed the model inside the playpen with the dog, feeding and petting it.

The second experimental group observed several male and female models interacting , with a number of dogs of various sizes. The third group, a control condition, observed a film on Disneyland of equivalent length to the others (no dogs were depicted in the film). The children viewed eight different movies of 3 minutes each twice per day over four consecutive days. The results showed that children in both film modeling conditions significantly increased their approach scores at post test and follow-up on a behavior avoidance test over that of the control condition children. No significant differences were found between the approach scores of the two modeling groups. The authors report, however, that when the incidence of terminal performances (i.e., being alone with the dog in the playpen) of the two modeling groups were compared, the multiple model condition was slightly better at post test and significantly better at the 17-month follow-up than either the single model or control conditions. Other studies supporting the effectiveness of symbolic modeling include Hill, Liebert, and Mott (1988), Kornhaber and Schroeder (1974), and Faust and Melamed (1984).

A second illustrative experiment involving symbolic modeling was conducted by Melamed and Siegel (1975). They studied the relative effectiveness of symbolic modeling on reducing the anxiety level of children facing hospitalization and surgery. Sixty children ranging in age from 4 to 12 years were used in this study. They were hospitalized for the first time and scheduled to have elective surgery for either hernia, tonsil, or urinary-genital tract problems. Thirty children in the modeling condition arrived at the hospital 1 hour prior to admission and saw a 16-minute film called *Ethan Has an Operation.*

The 30 control children also arrived early at the hospital and saw a 12-minute film entitled *Living Things Are Everywhere* about a child on a nature walk. Following the films, all children were given the hospital's standard preoperative instructions. Six measures were used in the study: three indices of trait anxiety (the Anxiety Scale of the Personality Inventory for Children, Children's Manifest Anxiety Scale, and the Human Figure Drawing Test) and situational/state anxiety (Palmar Sweat Index, Hospital Fears Rating Scale, and an Observer Rating Scale of Anxiety). The trait measures were obtained prior to the children observing the films and at a 26-day postoperative follow-up period. The situational anxiety measures were taken prefilm, the evening before the surgery, and at the 26-day follow-up period.

The results showed that the filmed modeling condition significantly reduced all measures of situational anxiety compared to the control condition and that these significant differences were maintained at follow-up. No differences, however, were found between the modeling and control conditions on the trait anxiety measures.

Melamed and her colleagues have also shown symbolic modeling to be effective in reducing children's uncooperative behavior and fears during dental treatment (e.g., Melamed, Hawes, Heigy, & Glick, 1975; Melamed, Weinstein, Hawes, & Katin-Borland, 1975; Melamed, Yurcheson, Fleece, Hutcheson, & Hawes, 1978). Similarly, Vernon and Bailey (1974) studied the relative effectiveness of a modeling film on the induction of anesthesia in children. Geidel and Gulbrandsen (as cited in Melamed & Siegel, 1980) also investigated the use of a modeling videotape for preschool children coping with a physical examination.

Another form of modeling involved the combined use of filmed modeling and client participation. For example, Lewis (1974) examined the relative effectiveness of client participation plus filmed modeling with film modeling only, participation only, and a no-treatment control condition in children who had a fear of swimming. There were 10 African-American children in each group. They were between 5 and 12 years of age and were attending a boys' club summer camp. In the client-participation plus modeling condition, each child saw an 8-minute film, showing three children performing tasks in a swimming pool that were similar to the avoidance test items that each subject was exposed to during pretesting. Immediately following the

film, an experimenter spent 10 minutes in the pool with each subject. She encouraged the children to practice the items on the avoidance test and physically assisted each child, if necessary, in trying the steps. The experimenter also gave social reinforcement for each child's attempt at or completion of an item on the avoidance test. The children in the modeling condition viewed the 8-minute film and were exposed to a 10-minute game of checkers alongside the pool. There was no participation in the water. The children in the participation group were shown an 8-minute neutral film (three short cartoons) containing no elements of water activities; they also took part in the 10-minute checkers game. Lewis found that all three treatment procedures were more effective than the no-treatment control condition and that the filmed-modeling-plus client-participation condition was significantly better in reducing children's fears than were any of the other procedures. Similar findings regarding the relative effectiveness of client-participation plus modeling have been reported by Bandura, Jeffrey, and Wright (1974) and Ross, Ross, and Evans (1971).

An interesting alternative form of symbolic modeling involves reading stories to children on topics related to their particular fear (e.g., Fassler, 1985; Mikulas, Coffman, Dayton, Frayne, & Maier, 1985). For example, Fassler (1985) studied the effects of reading the story *Tommy Goes to the Doctor* (Wolpe, 1972), reading a poem about a child who wanted to give a doctor an injection, and engaging in play rehearsal on the reduction of children's fear of needles/injections. The results showed that the children in the experimental condition significantly reduced their fear of needles or injections in comparison to those in the no-treatment condition. Although there are some methodological problems with this study, it nevertheless represents an interesting alternative treatment to filmed modeling procedures for children undergoing dental or medical-related procedures.

Additional Considerations

As we mentioned earlier, Bandura (1969, 1977a, 1977b) maintains that for modeling to be effective the observer must be able to attend to the model, retain what she or he observes, be able to reproduce the modeled behavior, and be motivated, when necessary, to demonstrate the behavior. Perry and Furukawa (1986) point out that the therapist can do a great deal to ensure that conditions facilitate the modeling process by attending to his or her choice of the model and the modeled behaviors, the characteristics of the observer, and the structuring of the manner in which the model and his or her behaviors are represented.

Supportive Research

The vast majority of studies on the use of live and symbolic modeling to reduce children's fears and phobias have been controlled between-group experiments (see, for example, reviews by Bandura, 1969, 1977a, 1977b; Barrios & O'Dell, 1989; Bryan & Schwarz, 1971; Gelfand, 1978; Graziano et al., 1979; King et al., 1988; King et al., 1991; Melamed & Siegel, 1980; Morris & Kratochwill, 1983; Richards & Siegel, 1978). Generally, these studies *fall* into three categories: fear of animals, fear of impending dental or other medical treatment or elective surgery, and test anxiety. Little or no research has been conducted on children's other fears and phobias, such as speech anxiety, fear of the dark, using public toilets, loud noises, heights, school, nightmares, moving vehicles, and separation from parents. One might conclude, therefore, that any generalizability of the research findings on modeling to these other fears and phobias is quite limited (see, for example, Ross, 1981). In addition, as Graziano et al., (1979) suggest, we might question the extent to which the children typically used in the various modeling studies were, in fact, "severely fearful children." Graziano et al., acknowledge that some of the children in the Bandura and Menlove (1968) study and in the dental and medical fear studies were quite new, but they point out that most of the children included in the studies were not chosen because of their severe and intense levels of fear and anxiety or because of the long-standing duration of their fears and phobias.

Although a fair amount of research has been conducted on the relative contribution of model characteristics, client characteristics, and modeling setting factors on the outcome of modeling (see, for example,

reviews by Melamed & Siegel, 1980; Perry & Furukawa, 1986), additional research is needed on how such factors influence the outcome of the use of this procedure with children having fears and phobias. For example, one aspect of the modeling literature that has received a fair amount of attention is related to whether the model should engage in *coping versus mastery* performance (e.g., Bandura, 1969; Bruch, 1976; McMurray, Lucas, Arbes-Duprey, & Wright, 1985; Meichenbaum, 1971; Perry & Furukawa, 1986). The difference between these two performance styles has to do with whether the model should begin performing the approach behavior toward the feared situation at a level of proficiency that (a) is similar to that of the observer and then gradually move toward competent performances (coping style) or (b) reflects a competent performance to the observer from the very beginning of the modeling activity (mastery style). Although some writers (e.g., Perry & Furukawa, 1986) maintain that the empirical research is not completely "in favor" of the coping style, they feel that this approach should be considered, particularly for hesitant or anxious clients..." (p. 75). Some research (e.g., McMurray et al., 1985), however, suggests that both coping and mastery styles are comparably effective in reducing the "moderate to high" anxiety of dental-anxious children. Clearly, more research is needed in this area before any definitive statements can be made regarding advocating either model performance style to reduce fears and phobias.

Additional research is also needed on the contribution of such factors as the age of the client observer and the effect of the number and chronicity of client fears and phobias on the outcome of modeling. Moreover, data are needed on the contribution of the modeling facilitator (i.e., therapist, experimenter, parent, etc.) in these research studies. For example, to what extent does the modeling facilitator's behavior during treatment contribute to the outcome of these procedures?

Variations of the Modeling Procedure

In addition to live and symbolic modeling, a number of alternative procedures have been proposed (see, for example, reviews by Bandura, 1969; Barrios &

O'Dell, 1989; Mahoney, 1974; Masters et al., 1987; Perry & Furukawa, 1986) such as *covert modeling* (the child observes a model approaching and interacting with a feared stimulus), *participant modeling* (the child observes the model participating increasingly with the fear stimulus, followed by the child practicing what the model performed as well as receiving corrective feedback and verbal information about the feared stimulus from the therapist), and *graduated modeling* (the child observes the model perform components of a complicated behavior, and after each component is mastered the entire complicated behavior is reconstructed by the model for the child to perform). Although there is little research on covert and graduated modeling, there is a fair amount on participant modeling (e.g., Masters et al., 1987; Morris & Kratochwill, 1983). This procedure is very much like contact desensitization treatment; in fact, many writers use these two terms interchangeably (Masters et al., 1987). Both procedures, for example, make use of the following components: (a) gradually exposing the child in small steps to the feared object or situation after each step has first been modeled by the therapist, (b) physically assisting the child in performing the modeled step, (c) verbally encouraging the child to perform the step and providing him or her with corrective feedback, and (d) providing the child with realistic verbal information about the feared stimulus or situation. In addition, each procedure is administered within the framework of a good, positive relationship (Masters et al., 1987; Morris, 1985). The commonalities between these two procedures have led some writers (e.g., Masters et al., 1987) to state, "Since there is a tendency for one or the other [procedure] to be used consistently by a particular author, the divergence may indicate personal preference for a term rather than an actual difference in procedure" (p. 157).

Participant modeling has been found to be an effective procedure in reducing the fears and phobias in children with "normal intelligence" (e.g., Esveldt-Dawson, Wisner, Unis, Matson, & Kazdin, 1982) as well as those who have mentally retardation (e.g., Matson, 1981). What is not clear at this point is whether all of the above components and subcompo-

nents of this procedure are necessary for effecting positive behavioral change (see, for example, Klingman, Melamed, Cuthbert, & Hermecz, 1984).

Cognitive-Behavioral Interventions

The role of cognition and dysfunctional cognitive processes in the development of fears and related anxieties in children has been well-documented (e.g., Beck, 1976; Bernard & Joyce, 1993; Ellis & Bernard, 1983; Sarason, 1980). This has led to one of the most recent emphases in research and treatment to reduce fear: namely, cognitive-behavioral therapy. Cognitive-behavioral approaches encompass many techniques that, despite their differences, share the following assumptions:

1. Cognitive mediational processes are involved in human learning.
2. Thoughts, feelings, and behaviors are causally interrelated (the program, thus, has a cognitive-affective-behavioral, slant).
3. Cognitive activities, such as expectations, self-statements, and attributions, are important in understanding and predicting psychopathology and psychotherapeutical change.
4. Cognitions and behaviors are compatible: (a) cognitive processes can be integrated into behavioral paradigms, and (b) cognitive techniques can be combined with behavioral procedures.
5. The task of the cognitive behavioral therapist is to collaborate with the client to assess distorted or deficient cognitive processes and behaviors and to design new learning experiences to remediate the dysfunctional or deficient cognitions, behaviors, and affective patterns (Kendall & Braswell, 1985, p. 2).

Cognitive-behavioral interventions can be divided into various subcategories (see, for example, Haaga & Davison, 1986; Hughes, 1988, 1993; Mahoney & Arnkoff, 1978). In the area of children's fears and phobias, however, the subcategories appear at present to be self-control, self-instructional training, and rational-emotive therapy.

Self-Control

Self-control can be conceptualized as a process through which a person becomes the primary agent in directing and regulating those aspects of his or her behavior that lead to preplanned and specific behavioral outcomes and/or consequences (Goldfried & Merbaum, 1973; Kanfer & Gaelick, 1986; Richards & Siegel, 1978). Although the notions of self-control and related self-regulation processes have been included for almost 50 years in various theoretical discussions and in the empirical literature on learning and conditioning (e.g., Bandura, 1969; Homme, 1966; Kanfer & Phillips, 1970; Skinner, 1953), it was not until the early to mid-1970s that they gained some popularity and became integrated into the literature of behavior therapy (see, for example, Goldfried & Goldfried, 1980; Hughes, 1993 Mahoney, 1974; Meichenbaum, 1986; Morris, 1985).

Self-control encompasses several intervention methods, each of which acknowledge the contribution of cognitive processes and views the individual as capable of regulating his or her own behavior. According to Kanfer and his associates (e.g., Kanfer & Gaelick, 1986; Kanfer & Schefft, 1988), a common element between these self-control methods involves the therapist's role as the "instigator and motivator" in helping the client begin a behavior-change program. Self-control is thus a treatment strategy in which the therapist teaches the client how, when, and where to use various conditions to facilitate the learning of a new (and/or more personally satisfying) behavior pattern (Kanfer & Gaelick, 1986; Richards & Siegel, 1978). With regard to fear reduction, many writers maintain that an individual's self-statements may contribute significantly to his or her fear and anxiety (e.g., Goldfried & Davison, 1976; Kanfer & Gaelick, 1986). Self-control procedures focus on helping people develop specific thinking skills and to use these skills when confronted with a particular feared stimulus, event, or object.

In applying self-control procedures to the modification of childhood and adolescent fears and related anxieties, it must first be demonstrated that the child is aware of his or her fear or anxiety to the extent that he or she is able to identify the various components of the specific fear or anxiety and the conditions under which he or she became fearful or anxious (Kendall & Sessa, 1993; Morris & Kratochwill, 1983).

Prior to beginning a self-control program, the child's motivation for behavior change, as well as his or her willingness to accept responsibility for changing the behavior, must be addressed (Kanfer & Gaelick, 1986; Kanfer & Schefft, 1988). In this regard, Kanfer and Gaelick (1986) maintain that when a client is concerned about his or her behavior and can anticipate that the problem will be resolved, self-control may be used more easily and effectively.

Although a number of studies have been published on self-control treatment with adult fears and related anxieties (see, for example, Deffenbacher & Michaels, 1980; Goldfried & Davison, 1976; Morris, 1986), only a small number of studies have been published using this approach with fearful children (see, for example, Genshaft, 1982; Kanfer, Karoly, & Newman, 1975; King et al., 1991; Leal, Baxter, Martin, & Marx, 1981). Most of the studies that have been reported in the literature on the use of self-control procedures with fearful children have focused on the modifying of children's fear of the dark (e.g., Graziano, Mooney et al., 1979; Kanfer et al., 1975; Ollendick et al., 1991), medical fears (e.g., Peterson & Shigetomi, 1981), and dental fears (e.g., Siegel & Peterson, 1980). For example, Leal et al., (1981) compared cognitive modification, systematic desensitization, and a no-treatment control condition on reducing test anxiety in a group of tenth-grade students. The desensitization approach followed Wolpe; the cognitive modification procedure involved informing the students that their anxiety during exams was due to self-statements and thoughts that took place prior to the examination. Students were further instructed that an increasing awareness of these self-statements was necessary if they were to learn incompatible positive self-statements. The results showed that systematic desensitization was more effective than either the cognitive modification or no-treatment control condition on direct observation of test anxiety, whereas the cognitive modification procedure was more effective on the self-report measures. No follow-up assessment period or test for generalization was conducted.

In another study, Kanfer et al. (1975) compared the effectiveness of two types of verbal controlled responses on the reduction of children's fear of the dark. Forty-five children, 5 to 6 years of age, participated in the study. None of them could stay alone in the dark for more than 27 seconds. The children were assigned to one of three conditions: (a) competence group—the children heard and rehearsed sentences emphasizing their respective competence and active control in the fear situation (e.g., "I am a brave boy/girl: I can take care of myself in the dark."); (b) stimulus group—the children heard and rehearsed sentences emphasizing reduced aversive qualities of the fear situation (e.g., "The dark is a fun place to be. There are many good things in the dark."); (c) neutral group—the children rehearsed sentences related to "Mary Had a Little Lamb" (Kanfer et al., 1975, p. 253). Training took place in a well-lighted room and testing took place in a dark room. Pretest and post test measures consisted of duration of darkness tolerance and terminal light intensity (degree of illumination children needed to stay in room).

The results showed that from the pretest to first posttest period, the competence and stimulus groups remained in the darkened room significantly longer than the neutral group. At the second posttest period, the competence group remained in the room significantly longer than the stimulus or neutral groups—with no significant difference found between the stimulus and neutral groups at the second post test period. The competence group was superior to the other two groups with regard to illumination. Kanfer et al., (1975) concluded that training effectiveness was related to the content of the learned sentences in the three respective groups. Specifically, placing an emphasis on the child's competence in dealing with the dark may be the salient component in teaching children to cope with stressful/feared situations. An interesting extension of this study was conducted by Giebenhain and O'Dell (1984), who wrote a parent training manual designed to teach parents fear reducing skills that they could apply at home to help a child with fear

of the dark. The results showed that parents can implement a treatment package at home with a child having moderate to severe fear of the dark. The results were also found to be maintained at the 1-year follow-up.

In another study, Graziano et al., (1979) used self-control instructions plus relaxation training and pleasant imagery to reduce "severe, clinical-level" night-time fears of long duration in children. Five boys and two girls, ranging in age from 8.7 to 12.8 years, participated in the study. The children came from six families. The families were seen for 5 weeks (2 weeks for assessment and 3 weeks for instruction). The parents and children were seen in two groups. The children were instructed to practice relaxation, to imagine a pleasant scene, recite "brave" self-statements at night with their parents, and then to practice these exercises. A token-economy program for the children was also established. Many would receive tokens for doing the exercises at home and for going to bed and being brave throughout the night. The parents were instructed to initiate the children's exercises at night and to use tokens and praise. The measures included parent ratings of the number of child fears, strength of fears, and behavioral criteria (e.g., 10 consecutive fearless nights).

The results showed that it took from 3 to 19 weeks ($X = 8.7$ weeks) for all of the children to meet the behavioral criteria. Graziano et al., further report that each child's "fear strength" steadily decreased through post treatment and the 3-month, 6-month, and 1-year follow-up. Total number of fears also decreased, with only one of the children not completely free of fears, at the 1-year follow-up. Finally, both parents and children reported that the program improved the children's fear behavior and sleeping patterns. Graziano and Mooney (1980) used this treatment program with another set of families having children with "severe, nightly disruptive night-time fears," comparing the treatment outcome with a matched treatment control condition. They found, in comparison with the control condition, that the treatment package was significantly effective in reducing the strength of fears in the children, the frequency of their fears, and the duration of the fearful events. According to parent ratings, the experimental treatment children were also significantly less disruptive. Thus, it appears that the training package contributed greatly to the parent ratings of improvement in their children. Follow-up information via the telephone also confirmed the effectiveness of the treatment package. At 12-month follow-up, only one child in the experimental group did not meet the behavioral criterion discussed. Follow-up data on the "no-treatment" control group were not available, since the controls began receiving the treatment package after the experimental group completed the post test.

In a later study, Ollendick, Hagopian and Huntzinger (1991) used a self-control treatment package that was based on the one tested by Graziano and Mooney. Working with two girls, ages 8 and 10 years old, Ollendick et al., report that self-control training plus reinforcement for sleeping in one's own bed was "effective in reducing nighttime fears in these anxious girls experiencing separation anxiety" (p. 119). They further indicated that self-control training in the absence of reinforcement was only "moderately effective."

In another variation on the self-control approach, Peterson and Shigetomi (1981) conducted a study with children who were to receive elective tonsilectomies. The 66 children (35 girls and 31 boys) ages 2.5 to 10.5 years ($X = 5.47$ years), were assigned to one of four conditions:

1. preoperative information—children were invited to a "party" 4 days before their surgery, informed via a story and the use of a puppet of the "typical hospital stay from admission to discharge";
2. coping procedures—children received the preoperative information plus cue-controlled muscle relaxation (using the cue "calm"), distracting mental imagery training (imagining a scene that was "quiet and made them feel happy"), and comforting self-talk (the children were encouraged to think of and repeat the phrase "I will be all better in a little while");
3. filmed modeling—the children received the preoperative information and watched Melamed & Siegel's (1975) film *Ethan Has an Operation;*
4. coping plus filmed modeling—the children were given a 15-minute hospital tour, shown the

film, and spent another 15 to 20 minutes eating ice cream and cookies following the tour.

Six categories of dependent measures were used, encompassing the triple-mode response system discussed earlier. The results showed that children receiving the two coping conditions experienced less distress during their hospital stay than the children in the modeling-only or information-only groups. Furthermore, children receiving the coping-plus-modeling procedure were more calm and cooperative during invasive procedures than the coping or modeling-alone conditions. In another study, Siegel and Peterson (1980) conducted similar research with children undergoing dental treatment. They compared the coping-skills condition with a sensory-information condition (i.e., children were told what to expect and heard audiotape recordings of the dental equipment) and a no-treatment/attention condition. The results showed that there was no significant difference between the coping and sensory information conditions on any of the measures taken during or after restorative treatment and that both treatment groups faired better on the measures than the no-treatment control children. A self-control package was also used successfully by Chiodos and Maddux (1985) with a 16-year-old who was mentally retarded and had performance anxiety, and by Singer, Ambuel, Wade, and Jaffe (1992) with three boys who had food phobias.

Given the limited amount of controlled research self-control methods, we feel that no definitive statement can be made on the merits of this approach in reducing children's fears and phobias. It is certainly a promising area of treatment, but is in need of more well-controlled research like that of Kanfer et al., (1975).

Self-Instructional Training

This cognitive behavioral approach was initially developed by Meichenbaum and his colleagues (e.g., Meichenbaum & Goodman, 1971) in order to teach impulsive children a reflective problem-solving approach for improving academic performance. Treatment involves having the therapist model cognitive strategies for the child, such as: "What is my problem?" "What is my plan?" "Am I using my plan?" "How did I do?" The self-instructional training package involves the following:

1. An adult model performs a task while talking to him or herself out loud (cognitive training).
2. The child performs the same task under the direction of the model's instruction (overt, external guidance).
3. The child performs the task while instructing him or herself aloud (overt, self-guidance).
4. The child whispers the instructions to him or herself as she or he proceeds through the task (faded, overt self-guidance).
5. The child performs the task while guiding his or her performance via inaudible or private speech or nonverbal self-instructions (covert self-instruction) (Meichenbaum, 1986, p. 351).

The aim of this approach is to have the child apply his or her self-talk whenever the child is placed in a particular anxiety-provoking situation. In other words, this approach is designed to have the child:

1. Become aware of the habits of thought and thinking styles that impede performance and that lead to dysfunctional emotions that interfere with task-relevant activities.
2. Generate, in collaboration with the trainer, a set of incompatible, tasks-relevant specific behavioral and cognitive (self-statements) strategies and accompanying feelings of self-efficacy about implementing such skills.
3. Systematically implement the skills and learn from his or her mistakes (Meichenbaum, 1986, p. 359).

Several studies utilizing self-instructional training to treat children's fears have been reported in the literature (e.g., Foxx & Houston, 1981; Genshaft, 1982; Jones, Ollendick, McLaughlin, & Williams, 1989; Kelley, 1982). For example, Genshaft (1982) implemented a self-instructional training program in order to teach seventh-grade girls a strategy to control their anxiety regarding mathematics. Children were identified by their teachers as experiencing some degree of math anxiety and as lagging at least a year in math as compared with their reading achievement. The study compared self-instructional training plus tutoring, tutoring alone, and a no-treatment control condition in reducing math anxiety. The results showed a significant improvement in math computation for the group that had self-instructional training plus tutoring. It should be noted, however, that all three treatment groups were shown to improve on the test of math application. Unfortunately, no generalization or follow-up assessment data were provided.

As is the case with the self-control research, there is little well-controlled or case-study research on the application of self-instructional training to reduce children's fears and phobias. In addition, no information is presently available that suggests to which type of children with which types of fears or related anxieties—and under what environmental conditions—specific self-instructional procedures are appropriate.

Rational-Emotive Therapy

Rational-emotive therapy (RET) was developed about 30 years ago by Albert Ellis (e.g., Ellis, 1962, 1984) and extended to children on a systematic basis many years later (see, for example, Bernard & Joyce, 1984, 1993; Ellis & Bernard, 1983). Ellis has presented the view that psychological or emotional difficulties result from irrational thoughts and beliefs. Thus, an individual's thoughts or beliefs about particular events influence his or her feelings and behavior. The primary goal, therefore, of RET is to teach people to identify and change the irrational beliefs underlying their particular psychological difficulties—to train these people to the point where they can view themselves and others in a sensible and rational manner. Individuals are therefore taught to replace maladaptive thoughts such as "I can't stand it" with a more rational thought such as "It is unpleasant, but I can tolerate it."

Although at least two books on RET with children are available (e.g., Bernard & Joyce, 1984; Ellis & Bernard, 1983), supportive research for this procedure is quite sparse. In one study, Bernard, Kratochwill, and Keefauver (1983) applied RET and self-instructional training in order to reduce high-frequency chronic hair-pulling in a 17-year-old girl. From a cognitive-behavioral perspective, it was hypothesized that maladaptive thought patterns occasioned high levels of anxiety and worry during study periods and maintained the hair-pulling behavior. The results showed that RET led to a moderate reduction in hair-pulling behavior, while the introduction of self-instructional training in addition to RET produced a rapid cessation of all hair-pulling— with this behavior being maintained at a 2- and 3-week follow-up. In another study, Van der Ploeg-Stapert and Van der Ploeg (1986) evaluated a group treatment that incorporated various aspects of RET for reducing test anxiety in adolescents. The treatment program consisted of muscle relaxation exercises, instruction in study skills, self-monitoring procedures, hypnosis, and RET for "worry." The results showed a significant reduction in anxiety, as measured by the various self-report inventories, for adolescents who received the group treatment in comparison to those who had no treatment. In addition, a 3-month follow-up evaluation showed that the reduction in reported test anxiety was maintained.

Warren, Smith, and Velten (1984) studied the effectiveness of RET with and without imagery; they compared both groups to a relationship-oriented counseling group and a waiting-list control group. The participants in this study were 59 junior high school students who were experiencing interpersonal anxiety. The results showed that both of the RET groups were independently rated as significantly less anxious than was the waiting-list control group. Interestingly, no significant differences were found between the RET groups and the relationship-oriented counseling group; however, the levels of irrational thinking were significantly more reduced in the RET groups than in the relationship-oriented group.

Although RET has been shown to be effective in the reduction of fears and related anxieties in adults, its relative effectiveness with children has not been sufficiently demonstrated to permit any firm conclusions. In addition, no data are available regarding the types of fears and related anxieties that are amenable to this type of treatment. RET certainly appears to be a potentially useful procedure, but clearly more research is needed.

SUMMARY

In this chapter, we have reviewed assessment considerations regarding children's fears and phobias, as well as the five major behavior therapy approaches to fear reduction. In addition, variations of each major method were discussed, as was research supporting the relative effectiveness of these methods. Discussions concerning the use of each method with clinical populations were also presented, as were comments regarding procedural considerations for each method.

Without doubt, the most researched method of fear reduction is systematic desensitization and its variants, while the least researched method involves the use of cognitive-behavioral interventions. The next most heavily researched method is modeling and its variants. However, when one examines in detail the nature of the research supporting each method, it becomes clear that few well-controlled experimental studies have been published supporting the efficacy of any of these methods with clinically or severely fearful children.

Two of the most promising methods of fear reduction involve the use of positive reinforcement and cognitive-behavioral interventions. Since relatively few controlled studies have been published that use these methods either separately or in combination in the treatment of different clinical fears, no clear statement can presently be made concerning their relative effectiveness.

There are also major empirical questions regarding each of the five major procedures. First, researchers have not substantially verified the relative effectiveness of most of these procedures in a controlled experimental fashion, with both analogue and clinically relevant (in intensity chronicity, regularity, and disruptiveness of everyday life) fears.

Second, few researchers studying these methods have been concerned with assessing the outcome using the triple-mode response system. The literature on symbolic modeling comes closest to meeting these two criticisms favorably. Here, Bandura and his colleagues have examined the use of this approach with mostly nonclinical fears (of snakes or dogs), while Melamed and her colleagues have studied the application of this method with children who primarily have transitory and highly situation-specific clinical fears. In each set of studies, however, these have made some use of the triple-mode response system in their evaluation of the outcome of treatment.

A third question that has not yet been answered involves identifying those conditions in which the treatments are effective—for example, which procedures are effective for which age groups, for which fears and phobias, with which type of therapist, and in which type of setting.

Finally, the vast majority of supportive case studies and experiments reviewed in this chapter have involved working with a child who has only one fear or phobia. Most therapists realize very quickly that it is unusual to see such a child in either a clinic or school setting. The question then arises as to the applicability (i.e., external validity) of these research findings to clinical practice. Independent of these comments, however, there has been some very active research on these procedures, and they appear to be very promising fear-reduction methods.

REFERENCES

Anderson, J. C., Williams, S., McGee, R., & Silva, P. A. (1987). DSM-III disorders in preadolescent children. *Archives of General Psychiatry, 44,* 69–76.

Ayllon, T., Smith, D., & Rogers, M. (1970). Behavioral management of school phobia. *Journal of Behavior Therapy and Experimental Psychiatry, 1,* 125–138.

Babbitt, R. L., & Parrish, J. M. (1991). Phone phobia, phact or phantasy?: An operant approach to a child's disruptive behavior induced by telephone usage. *Journal of Behavior Therapy and Experimental Psychiatry, 22,* 123–129.

Baker, B. L., Cohen, D. C., & Saunders, J. T. (1973). Self-directed desensitization for acrophobic behavior. *Research Therapy, 11,* 79–89.

Bandura, A. (1969). *Principles of behavior modification.* New York: Holt, Rinehart & Winston.

Bandura, A. (1971). Psychotherapy based upon modeling principles. In A. E. Bergin & S.L. Garfield (Eds.), *Handbook of psychotherapy and behavior change* (pp. 653–708). New York: John Wiley & Sons.

Bandura, A. (1977a). *Social learning theory.* Englewood Cliffs, NJ: Prentice-Hall.

Bandura, A. (1977b). Seff-efficacy: Toward a unifying theory of behavior change. *Psychological Review, 84,* 191–215.

Bandura, A., Grusec, J., & Menlove, F. (1967). Vicarious extinction of avoidance behavior. *Journal of Personality and Social Psychology, 5,* 16–23.

Bandura, A., Jeffrey, R., & Wright, C. (1974). Efficacy of participant modeling as a function of response induction aids. *Journal of Abnormal Psychology, 83,* 56–64.

Bandura, A., & Menlove, F. (1968). Factors determining vicarious extinction of avoidance behavior through symbolic modeling. *Journal of Personality and Social Psychology, 8,* 99–108.

Bandura, A., & Walters, R. H. (1963). *Social learning and personality development.* New York: Holt, Rinehart & Winston.

Barabasz, A. (1973). Group desensitization of test anxiety in elementary schools. *Journal of Psychology, 83,* 295–301.

Barrios, B. A. (1988). On the changing nature of behavioral assessment. In A. Bellack & M. Hersen (Eds.), *Behavorial assessment* (pp. 3–41). Elmsford, NY: Pergamon Press.

Barrios, B. A., Hartmann, D. P., & Shigetomi, C. (1981). Fears and anxieties in children. In E. J. Mash & L. J. Terdal (Eds.), *Behavioral assessment in childhood disorders* (pp. 259–304). New York: Guilford Press.

Barrios, B. A., & Hartmann, D. P. (1988). Fears and anxieties. In E. J. Mash & L. J. Terdal (Eds.), *Behavioral assessment of disorders* (2nd ed., pp. 196–262). New York: Guilford Press.

Barrios, B. ., & O'Dell, S. L. (1989). Fears and anxieties. In E. J. Mash & R. A. Barkley (Eds.), *Treatment of childhood disorders* (pp. 167–221). New York: Guilford Press.

Beck, A. T. (1976). *Cognitive therapy and the emotional disorders.* New York: International Universities Press.

Bellack, A. S. & Hersen, M. (1977a). *Behavior modification: An introductory textbook.* Baltimore: Williams & Wilkins.

Bellack, A. S., & Hersen, M. (1977b). The use of self-report inventories in behavioral assessment. In J. D. Cone & R. P. Hawkins (Eds.), *Behavioral assessment: New directions in clinical psychology* (pp. 52–76). New York: Brunner/Mazel.

Bellack, A. S., & Hersen, M. (Eds.). (1988). Behavioral assessment (3rd ed.). Elmsford, NY: Pergamon Press.

Bentler, P. M. (1962). An infant's phobia treated with reciprocal inhibition therapy. *Journal of Child Psychology and Psychiatry, 3,* 185–189.

Bergland, B. W. & Chal, A. H. (1972). Relaxation training and a junior high behavior problem. *The School Counselor, 20,* 288–293.

Bernard, M. E., & Joyce, M. R. (1984). *Rational-emotive therapy with children and adolescents.* New York: John Wiley & Sons.

Bernard, M. E., & Joyce, M. R. (1993). Rational-emotive therapy with children and adolescents. In T. R. Kratochwill & R. J. Morris (Eds.), *Handbook of psychotherapy with children and adolescents* (pp. 221–246). Boston: Allyn and Bacon.

Bernard, M. E., Kratochwill, T. R., Keefauver, L. W. (1983). The effects of rational-emotive therapy and self-instructional training on chronic hair pulling. *Cognitive Therapy in Research, 7,* 273–280.

Blanchard, E. B. (1970). The relative contributions of modeling, information influences, and physical contact in the extinction of phobic behavior. *Journal of Abnormal Psychology, 76,* 55–61.

Boer, A. P., & Sipprelle, C. N. (1970). Examination of avoidance behavior in the clinic and its transfer to the normal environment. *Journal of Behavior Therapy and Experimental Psychiatry, 1,* 169–174.

Bornstein, P. H., & Knapp, M. (1981). *Journal of Behavior Therapy and Experimental Psychiatry, 12,* 218–285.

Boyd, L. T. (1980). Emotive imagery in the behavioral management of adolescent school phobia: A case approach. *School Psychology Review, 9,* 186–189.

Brady, J. B. (1966). Brevital relaxation treatment of frigidity. *Behavior Research and Therapy, 4,* 71–77.

Brady, J. P. (1972). Systematic desensitization. In W.S. Agras (Ed.), *Behavior modification: Principles and clinical applications* (pp. 127–150). Boston: Little, Brown.

Bruch, M. A. (1976). Coping model treatments: Unresolved issues and needed research. *Behavior Therapy, 7,* 711–713.

Bryan, J., & Schwarz, T., (1971). Effects of film material on children's behavior. *Psychological Bulletin, 75,* 50–59.

Cautela, J. R., & Groden, J. (1978). *Relaxation: A comprehensive manual for adults, children, and children with special needs.* Champaign, IL: Research Press.

Chiodos, J., & Maddux, J. E. (1985). A cognitive and behavioral approach to anxiety management of retarded individuals: Two case studies. *Journal of Child and Adolescent Psychotherapy, 2,* 16–20.

Chudy, J. F., Jones, G. E., & Dickson, A. L. (1983). Modified desensitization approach for the treatment of phobia behavior in children: A quasi-experimental case study. *Journal of Clinical Child Psychology, 12,* 198–201.

Cone, J.D. (1977). The relevance of reliability and validity for behavioral assessment. *Behavior Therapy, 8,* 411–426.

Cone, J. D. (1978). The behavioral assessment grid (BAG): A conceptual framework and a taxonomy. *Behavior Therapy, 9,* 882–888.

Cone, J. D. (1979). Confounded comparisons in triple response mode assessment research. *Behavioral Assessment, 1,* 85–95.

Conger, J. C., & Keane, S. P. (1981). Social skills intervention in the treatment of isolated or withdrawn children. *Psychological Bulletin, 90,* 478–495.

Costello, C. G. (1970). Dissimilarities conditioned avoidance responses and phobias. *Psychological Review, 77,* 250–254.

Craghan, L., & Musante, G. J. (1975). The elimination of a boy's high-building phobia by in vivo desensitization and game playing. *Journal of Behavior Therapy and Experimental Psychiatry, 6,* 87–88.

Deffenbacher, J. L., & Kemper, C. G. (1974a). Counseling test-anxious, sixth graders. *Elementary School Guidance & Counseling, 7,* 22–29.

Deffenbacher, J. L., & Kemper, C. G. (1974b). Systematic desensitization of test anxiety in junior high students. *The School Counselor, 22,* 216–222.

Deffenbacher, J. L., & Michaels, A. (1980). Two self-control procedures in the reduction of targeted and nontargeted anxieties. A year later. *Journal of Counseling Psychology, 27,* 9–15.

DiGiuseppe, R., & Miller, N. J. (1977). A review of outcome studies on rational-emotive therapy. In A. Ellis, and R. Grieger (Eds.), *Handbook of rational-emotive therapy* (pp. 72–95). New York: Springer.

DiNardo, P. A., & DiNardo, P. G. (1981). Self-control desensitization in the treatment of a childhood phobia. *The Behavior Therapist, 4,* 15–16.

Dong, Q., Xia, Y., Lei, L., Yang, B., & Ollendick, T. H. (1995). The stability and prediction of fears in Chinese children and adolescents: A one-year follow-up. *Journal of Child Psychology and Psychiatry, 36,* 819–831.

Dong, Q., Yang, B., & Ollendick, T. H. (1994). Fears in Chinese children and adolescents and their relations to anxiety and depression. *Journal of Child Psychology and Psychiatry, 35,* 351–363.

Eisenberg, L. (1958). School phobia: A study in the communication of anxiety. *American Journal of Psychiatry, 114,* 712–718.

Ellis, A. (1962). *Reason and emotion in psychotherapy.* New York: Stuart.

Ellis, A. (1984). *Rational-emotive therapy and cognitive behavior therapy.* New York: Springer.

Ellis A., & Bernard, M. (Eds.). (1983). *Rational emotive approaches to the problems of childhood.* New York: Plenum Press.

Eme, R., & Schmidt, D. (1978). The stability of children's fears. *Child Development, 49,* 1277–1279.

Erol, N., & Sahin, N. (1995). Fears of children and the cultural context: The Turkish norms. *European Child and Adolescent Psychiatry, 4,* 85–93.

Esveldt-Dawson, K., Wisner, K. L., Unis, A. S., Matson, J. L., & Kazdin, A. E (1982). Treatment of phobias in a hospitalized child. *Journal of Behavior Therapy and Experimental Psychiatry, 31,* 77–83.

Fassler, D. (1985). The fear of needles in children. *American Journal of Orthopsychiatry, 31,* 371–377.

Faust, J., & Melamed, B. G. (1984). Influence of arousal, previous experience, and age on surgery preparation of same day of surgery and in-hospital pediatric patients. *Journal of Consulting and Clinical Psychology, 52,* 359–365.

Foxx, J., & Houston, B. (1981). Efficacy of self-instructional training for reducing children's anxiety in an evaluative situation. *Behavior Research and Therapy, 19,* 509–515.

Frame, C. L., & Matson, J. L. (1987). (Eds.). *Handbook of assessment in childhood-Psychotherapy.* New York: Plenum Press.

Francis, G., & Ollendick, T. H. (1987). Anxiety disorders. In C.L. Frame & J.L. Matson (Eds.), *Handbook of assessment in childhood psychopathology* (pp. 373–400). New York: Plenum Press.

Freeman B. T., Roy, R. R., & Hemmick, S. (1976). Extinction of a phobia of physical examination in a 7-year-old mentally retarded boy: A case study. *Behavior Research and Therapy, 14,* 63–64.

Friedman, D. E. (1966). A new technique for the systematic desensitization of phobic symptoms. *Behavior Research and Therapy, 4,* 139–140.

Garvey, W., & Hegrenes, J. (1966). Desensitization technique in the treatment of school phobia. *American Journal of Orthopsychiatry, 36,* 147–152.

Gelfand, D. M. (1978). Behavioral treatment of avoidance, social withdrawal and negative emotional stress. In B.B. Wolman, J. Egan, & A.O. Ross (Eds.), *Handbook of treatment of mental disorders in childhood and adolescence* (pp. 330–353). Englewood Cliffs, NJ: Prentice-Hall.

Genshaft, J. L. (1982). The use of cognitive behavior therapy for reducing math anxiety. *School Psychology Review, 11,* 32–34.

Giebenhain, J. E., & O'Dell, S. L. (1984). Evaluation of a parent training manual for reducing children's fear of the dark. *Journal of Applied Behavior Analysis, 17,* 121–125.

Glasscock, S. G., & MacLean, W. E., Jr. (1990). Use of contact desensitization and shaping in the treatment of dog phobia and generalized fear of the outdoors. *Journal of Clinical Child Psychology, 19,* 169–172.

Goldfried, M. (1971). Systematic desensitization as training in self-control. *Journal of Consulting and Clinical Psychology, 37,* 228–234.

Goldfried, M., & Davison, G. (1976). *Clinical behavior therapy.* New York: Holt.

Goldfried, M., & Goldfried, A. P. (1977). Importance of hierarchy content in the self-control of anxiety. *Journal of Consulting and Clinical Psychology, 45,* 124–134.

Goldfried, M. R., & Goldfried, A. P. (1980). Cognitive change methods. In F. H. Kanfer & A. P. Goldstein (Eds.), *Helping people change* (2nd ed., pp. 917–130). Elmsford, NY: Pergamon Press.

Goldfried, M. R., & Merbaum, M. (1973). A perspective on self-control. In M. R. Goldfried & M. Merbaum (Eds.), *Behavior change through self-control* (pp. 3–36). New York: Holt.

Graziano, A., & DeGiovanni, I. S. (1979). The clinical significance of childhood phobias: A note on the proportion of child-clinical referrals for the treatment of children's fears. *Behavior Research and Therapy, 17,* 161–162.

Graziano, A. M., & DeGiovanni, I. S., & Garcia, K. A. (1979). Behavioral treatments of children's fears: A review. *Psychological Bulletin, 86,* 804–830.

Graziano, A. M., & Mooney, K. C. (1984). *Children and behavior therapy.* New York: Aldine.

Graziano, A. M., & Mooney, K. C. (1980). Family self-control instruction for children's nighttime fear reduction. *Journal of Consulting and Clinical Psychology, 48,* 206–213.

Graziano A. M., Mooney, K. C., Huber, C., & Igrasiak, D. (1979). Self-control instructions for children's fear reduction. *Journal of Behavior Therapy and Experimental Psychiatry, 10,* 221–227.

Haaga, D. A., & Davison, G. C. (1986). Cognitive change methods. In F. H. Kanfer & A. P. Goldstein (Eds.), *Helping people change* (3rd ed., pp. 236–282). Elmsford, NY: Pergamon Press.

Hampe, E., Noble, H., Miller, L. C., & Barrett, C. L. (1973). Phobic children 1 and 2 years posttreatment. *Journal of Abnormal Psychology, 82,* 446–453.

Hatzenbuehler, L. C., & Schroeder, H. E. (1978). Desensitization procedures in the treatment of childhood disorders. *Psychological Bulletin, 85,* 831–844.

Haynes, S. N. (1978). *Principles of behavioral assessment.* New York: Gardner Press.

Hersen, M. (1970). Behavior modification approach to a school-phobia case. *Journal of Clinical Psychology, 26,* 128–132.

Hill, J. H., Liebert, R. M., & Mott, D. E. W. (1968). Vicarious extinction of avoidance behavior through films: An initial test. *Psychological Reports, 22,* 192.

Hodgson, R., & Rachman, S. (1974). Desynchrony in measures of fear. *Behavior Research and Therapy, 12,* 319–326.

Homme, L. E. (1966). Contiguity theory and contingency management. *Psychological Record, 16,* 233–241.

Hugdahl, L. (1981). The three-system model of fear and emotion. A critical examination. *Behavior Research and Therapy, 19,* 75–85.

Hughes, J. (Ed.), (1988). *Cognitive behavior therapy with children in schools.* New York: Guilford Press.

Hughes, J. (1993). Behavior Therapy. In T. R. Kratochwill & R. J. Morris (Eds.), *Handbook of Psychotherapy with children and adolescents* (pp. 185–220). Boston: Allyn & Bacon.

Ilg, F. L., & Ames, L. B. (1955). *Child behavior.* New York: Dell.

Jackson, H. J., & King, N. J. (1981). The emotive imagery treatment of a child's trauma-induced phobia. *Journal of Behavior Therapy and Experimental Psychiatry, 12,* 325–328.

Jacobson, E. (1938). *Progressive relaxation.* Chicago: University of Chicago Press.

Javel, A. F., & Denholtz, M. A. (1975). Audible OSR feedback in systematic desensitization: A case report. *Behavior Therapy, 6,* 251–254.

Jersild, A. T. (1968). *Child psychology* (6th ed.). Englewood Cliffs, NJ: Prentice-Hall.

Jersild, A. T., & Holmes, F. B. (1935). *Children's fears. Child Development Monographs,* 1935, No. 20.

Johnson, S. B. (1979). Children's fears in the classroom setting. *School Psychology Digest, 8,* 382–396.

Jones, M. C. (1924a). The elimination of children's fears. *Journal of Experimental Psychology, 7,* 382–390.

Jones, M. C. (1924b). A laboratory study of fear: The case of Peter. *Journal of Genetic Psychology, 31,* 308–315.

Jones, R. T., Ollendick, T. H., McLaughlin, K. J., & Williams, C. E. (1989). Elaborative and behavioral rehearsal in the acquisition of fire emergency skills and the reduction of fear of fire. *Behavior Therapy, 20,* 93–101.

Kahn, J., & Nursten, J. (1962). School refusal: A comprehensive view of school phobia and other failures of school attendance. *American Journal of Orthopsychiatry, 32,* 707–718.

Kanfer, F. H., & Gaelick, L. (1986). Self-management methods. In F.H. Kanfer and A. P. Goldstein (Eds.), *Helping people change* (3rd ed., pp. 283–345). Elmsford, NY: Pergamon Press.

Kanfer, F. H., Karoly, P., & Newman, A. (1975). Reduction of children's fear of the dark by confidence-related and situational threat-related verbal cues. *Journal of Consulting and Clinical Psychology, 43,* 251–258.

Kanfer, F. H., & Phillips, J. S. (1970). *Learning foundations of behavior therapy.* New York: John Wiley & Sons.

Kanfer, F. H., & Schefft, B. K. (1988). *The basics of therapy.* Champaign, IL: Search Press.

Kazdin, A. E. (1994). *Behavior modification in applied settings* (rev. ed.). Homewood, IL: Dorsey Press.

Kazdin, A. E., & Hersen, M. (1980). The current status of behavior therapy. *Behavior Modification, 4,* 283–302.

Kazdin, A. E., & Wilson, G. T. (1978). *Evaluation of behavior therapy: Issues, evidence, and research strategies.* Cambridge, MA: Ballinger.

Kellerman, J. (1980). Rapid treatment of nocturnal anxiety in children. *Journal of Behavior Therapy and Experimental Psychiatry, 11,* 9–11.

Kellerman, J. (1981). *Helping the fearful child.* New York: W. W. Norton & Company.

Kelley, M.S. (1982). The effect of relaxation training and self-directed verbalizations on measures of anxiety and learning in learning-disabled children (United States International University). *Dissertation Abstracts International, 42,* 3806B–3807B.

Kendall, P. C., & Braswell, L. (1985). *Cognitive-behavioral therapy for impulsive children.* New York: Guilford Press.

Kendall, P. C., & Sessa, F. M. (1993). Cognitive assessment for intervention. In T. R. Kratochwill & R. J. Morris (Eds.), *Handbook of psychotherapy with children and adolescents* (pp. 58–74). Boston: Allyn & Bacon.

Kennedy, W. (1965). School phobia: Rapid treatment of fifty cases. *Journal of Abnormal Psychology, 70,* 285–289.

King, N. J., Gullone, E., & Tonge, B. J. (1991). Childhood fears and anxiety disorders. *Behaviour Change, 8,* 124–135.

King, N. J., Hamilton, D. I., & Ollendick, T. H. (1988). *Children's phobias: A behavioral perspective.* New York: John Wiley & Sons.

King, N. J., Ollendick, T. H., & Mattis, S. G. (1994). Panic in children and adolescents: Normative and clinical studies. *Australian Psychologist, 40,* 89–93.

King, N. J., Ollier, K., Iacuone, R., Schuster, S., Bays, K., Gullone, E., & Ollendick, T. H. (1989). Fears of children and adolescents. A cross-sectional Australian study using the revised Fear Survey for Children. *Journal of Child Psychology and Psychiatry, 30,* 775–784.

Kissel, S. (1972). Systematic desensitization therapy with children: A case study and some suggested modification. *Professional Psychology, 3,* 164–168.

Klingman, A., Melamed, B. G., Cuthbert, M. I., Hermecz, D. A. (1984). Effects of participant modeling on information acquisition and skill utilization. *Journal of Consulting and Clinical Psychology, 52,* 414–422.

Knoff, H. M., Batsche, G. M., & Carlyon, W. D. (1993). Projective techniques. In T.R. Kratochwill & R.J. Morris (Eds.), *Handbook of psychotherapy with children and adolescents* (pp. 9–37). Boston: Allyn & Bacon.

Koeppen, A. S. (1974). Relaxation training for children. *Journal of Elementary School Guidance and Counseling, 9,* 14–21.

Kondas, O. (1967). Reduction of examination anxiety and "stage fright" by group desensitization and relaxation. *Behavior Research and Therapy, 5,* 275–281.

Korchin, S. J., & Schuldberg, D. (1981). The future of clinical assessment. *American Psychol-ogist, 36,* 1147–1148.

Kornhaber, R. C., & Schroeder, H. E. (1974). Importance of model similarity on extinction of avoidance behavior in children. *Journal of Consulting and Clinical Psychology, 43,* 601–607.

Kozak, M. J., & Miller, G. A. (1982). Hypothetical constructs vs. intervening variables: A re-appraisal of the three-systems model of anxiety assessment. *Behavioral Assessment, 49,* 309–318.

Kratochwill, T. R. (1981). *Selective mutism: Implications for research and treatment.* New York: Lawrence Erlbaum.

Kratochwill, T. R., Accardi, A., & Morris, R. J. (1988). Anxieties and phobias: Psychological therapies. In J.L. Matson (Ed.), *Handbook of treatment approaches in childhood psychopathology* (pp. 249–278). New York: Plenum Press.

Kratochwill, T. R., & Morris, R. J. (1985). Conceptual and methodological issues in the behavioral assessment and treatment of children's fears and phobias. *School Psychology Review, 14,* 94–105.

Kuroda J. (1969). Elimination of children's fears of animals by the method of experimental desensitization—An application of theory to child psychology. *Psychologia, 12,* 161–165.

Kushner, M. (1965). Desensitization of a post-traumatic phobia. In L. P. Ullman & L. Krasner (Eds.), *Case studies in behavior modification* (pp. 193–195). New York: Holt, Rinehart & Winston.

Lang, P. J. (1968). Fear reduction and fear behavior: Problems in treating a construct. In J. M. Shlien (Ed.), *Research in psychotherapy* (Vol. 3, pp. 90–102). Washington, DC: American Psychological Association.

Lapouse, R., & Monk, M. A. (1959). Fears and worries in a representative sample of children. *American Journal of Orthopsychiatry, 29,* 803–818.

Laxer, R. M., Quarter, J., Kooman, A., & Walker, K. (1969). Systematic desensitization and relaxation of high test-anxious secondary school students. *Journal of Counseling Psychology, 16,* 446–451.

Lazarus, A. A. (1960). Elimination of children's phobias by deconditioning. In H. J. Eysenck (Ed.), *Behavior therapy and the neuroses* (pp. 114–122). Oxford: Pergamon Press.

Lazarus, A. A., & Abramovitz, A. (1962). The use of emotive imagery in the treatment of children's phobias. *Journal of Mental Science, 108,* 191–195.

Lazarus, A. A., Davison, G. C., & Polefka, D. A. (1965). Classical and operant factors in the treatment of phobia. *Journal of Abnormal Psychology, 70,* 225–229.

Leal, L. L., Baxter, E. G., Martin, J., & Marx, R. W. (1981). Cognitive modification and systematic desensitization with test anxious high school students. *Journal of Counseling Psychology, 28,* 525–528.

Leitenberg, H., & Callahan, E. J. (1973). Reinforcement practice and reductions of different kinds of fears in adults and children. *Behavior Research and Therapy, 11,* 19–30.

Lewis, S. A. (1974). A comparison of behavior therapy techniques in the reduction of fearful avoidant behavior. *Behavior Therapy, 5,* 648–655.

Luiselli, J. K. (1977). Case report: An attendant-administered contingency management program for the treatment of toileting phobia. *Journal of Mental Deficiency Research, 21,* 283-288.

Luiselli, J. K. (1978). Treatment of an autistic child's fear of riding a school bus through exposure and reinforcement. *Journal of Behavior Therapy and Experimental Psychiatry, 9,* 169–172.

Luiselli, J. K. (1980). Relaxation & training with the developmentally disabled: A reappraisal. *Behavior Research of Severe Developmental Disabilities, 1,* 191–213.

MacDonald, M. L. (1975). Multiply impact behavior therapy in a child's dog phobia. *Journal of Behavior Therapy and Experimental Psychiatry, 6,* 317–322.

Mahoney, M. J. (1974). *Cognition and behavior modification.* Cambridge, MA: Ballinger.

Mahoney, M. J., & Arnkoff, D. (1978). Cognitive and self-control theories. In S.J. Garfield & A.E. Bergin (Eds.), *Handbook of psychotherapy and behavior change* (2nd ed., pp. 689–722). New York: John Wiley & Sons.

Mann, J., & Rosenthal, T. L. (1969). Vicarious and direct counter-conditioning of test anxiety through individual and group desensitization. *Behavior Research and Therapy, 7,* 359–367.

Marks, I. M. (1969). *Fears and phobias.* New York: Academic Press.

Marshall, W. L., Gauthier, J., & Gordon, A. (1979). The current status of flooding as therapy. In M. Hersen, R.

E. Eister, & P. M. Miller (Eds.), *Progress in behavioral dedication* (Vol. 7). New York: Academic Press.

Mash, E. J., & Terdal, L. G. (Eds.). (1988). *Behavioral assessment of childhood disorders*. New York: Guilford Press.

Masters, J. C., Brush, T. G., Hollon, S. D., & Rimm, D. C. (1987). *Behavior therapy* (3rd ed.). New York: Harcourt Brace Jovanovich.

Matson, J. L. (1981). Assessment and treatment of clinical fears in mentally retarded children. *Journal of Applied Behavior Analysis, 14,* 287–294.

McMurray, N. E., Lucas, J. O., Arbes-Duprey, V., & Wright, F. A. C. (1985). The effects of mastery on dental stress in young children. *Australian Journal of Psychology, 37,* 65–70.

McReynolds, R. A., Morris, R. J., & Kratochwill, T. R. (1989). Cognitive-behavioral treatment of school-related fears and anxieties. In J. N. Hughes & R. J. Hall (Eds.), *Cognitive-behavioral psychology in the schools* (pp. 434–465). New York: Guilford Press.

Meichenbaum, D. (1971). Examination of model characteristics in reducing avoidance behavior. *Journal of Personality and Social Psychology, 17,* 298–307.

Meichenbaum, D. (1974). Self-instructional methods. In F. H. Kanfer & A. P. Goldstein (Eds.), *Helping people change* (pp. 357–392). Elmsford, NY: Pergamon Press.

Meichenbaum, D. (1986). Cognitive: behavior modification. In F.H. Kanfer & A.P. Goldstein (Eds.), *Helping people change* (3rd ed., pp. 346–380). Elmsford, NY: Pergamon Press.

Meichenbaum, D., & Genest, M. (1980). Cognitive behavior modification: An integration of cognitive and behavioral methods. In F. H. Kanfer & A. P. Goldstein (Eds.), *Helping people change* (2nd ed., pp. 390–422). Elmsford, NY: Pergamon Press.

Meichenbaum, D., & Goodman, J. (1971). Training impulsive children to talk to themselves: A means of developing self-control. *Journal of Abnormal Psychology, 77,* 115–126.

Melamed, B. G., Hawes, R. R., Heigy, E., & Glick, J. (1975). Use of filmed modeling to reduce uncooperative behavior of children during dental treatment. *Journal of Dental Research, 54,* 797–801.

Melamed, B. G., & Siegel, L. J. (1980). *Behavior Medicine*. New York: Springer.

Melamed, B. G., Weinstein, D., Hawes, R., & Katin-Borland, M. (1975). Reduction of fear related dental management problems using filmed modeling. *Journal of American Dental Association, 90,* 822–826.

Melamed, B. G., Yurcheson, R., Fleece, E. L., Hutcherson, S., & Hawes, R. (1978). Effects of film modeling on the reduction of anxiety related behaviors in individuals varying in level or previous experiment in the stress situation. *Journal of Consulting and Clinical Psychology, 46,* 1357–1367.

Melamed, B., & Siegel, L. (1975). Reduction of anxiety in children facing hospitalization and surgery by use of filmed modeling. *Journal of Consulting and Clinical Psychology, 43,* 511–521.

Mikulas, W. L., Coffman, M. G., Dayton, D., Frayne, C., & Maier, P. L. (1985). Behavioral bibliotherapy and games for treating fear of the dark. *Child and Family Behavior Therapy, 7,* 1–7.

Miller, L. C., Barrett, C. L., & Hampe, E. (1974). Phobias of childhood in a prescientific era. In A. Davids (Ed.), *Child personality and psychopathology: Current topics* (pp. 72–95). New York: John Wiley & Sons.

Miller, L. C., Barrett, C. L., Hampe, E., & Noble, H. (1972). Factor structure of childhood fears. *Journal of Consulting and Clinical Psychology, 39,* 264–268.

Miller, P. M. (1972). The use of visual imagery and muscle relaxation in the counterconditioning of a phobic child: A case study. *Journal of Nervous and Mental Disease, 154,* 457–460.

Morris, R. J. (1973). Shaping relaxation in the unrelaxed client. *Journal of Behavior Therapy and Experimental Psychiatry, 4,* 343–353.

Morris, R. J. (1985). *Behavior modification with exceptional children: Principles and practices*. Glenview, IL: Scott, Foresman & Company.

Morris, R. J. (1986). Fear reduction methods. In F. H. Kanfer & A. P. Goldstein (Eds.), *Helping people change* (3rd ed., pp. 145–190). Elmsford, NY: Pergamon Press.

Morris, R. J., & Kratochwill, T. R. (1983). *Treating children's fears and phobias: A behavioral approach*. Elmsford, NY: Pergamon Press.

Morris, R. J., & Kratochwill, T. R. (1985). Behavioral treatment of children's fears and phobias: A review. *School Psychology Review, 14,* 84.

Morris, R. J., Kratochwill, T. R., & Aldridge, K. (1988). Fear reduction methods in the school setting. In J.C. Witt, S.N. Elliott, & F.M. Gresham (Eds.), *Handbook of behavior-therapy in education* (pp. 679–717). New York: Plenum Press.

Morris, R. J., Kratochwill, T. R. & Dodson, C. L. (1986). Fears and phobias in adolescence: A behavioral perspective. In R. A. Feldman & A. R. Stiffman (Eds.), *Advances in adolescent mental health* (pp. 63–117). Santa Barbara, CA: JAI Press.

Morris, R. J., & Magrath, K. (1979). Contributions of therapist warmth to the contact desensitization treatment of acrophobia. *Journal of Consulting and Clinical Psychology, 47,* 786–788.

Morris, R. J., & Magrath, K. (1983). The therapeutic relationship in behavior therapy. in M. Lambert (Ed.), *Therapeutic relations in psychotherapy* (pp. 102–128). Homewood, IL: Dow-Jones-Irwin.

Morris, R. J., & Suckerman, K. R. (1974a). The importance of the therapeutic relationship in systematic desensitization. *Journal of Consulting and Clinical Psychology, 42,* 148.

Morris R. J., & Suckerman, K. R. (1974b). Therapist warmth as a factor in automated systematic desensitization. *Journal of Consulting and Clinical Psychology, 42,* 244–250.

Morris, R. J., & Suckerman, K. R. (1976). Studying therapist warmth in analogue systematic desensitization. *Journal of Consulting and Clinical Psychology, 44,* 285–289.

Murphy, C. M., & Bootzin, R. R. (1973). Active and passive participation in the contact desensitization of snake fear in children. *Behavior Therapy, 4,* 203–211.

Neisworth, J. T., Madle, R. A., & Goeke, K. E. (1975). Effortless elimination of separation anxiety: A case study. *Journal of Behavioral Therapy and Experimental Psychiatry, 6,* 79.

Nelson, R. O., & Hayes, S. C. (1979). The nature of behavioral assessment: A commentary. *Journal of Applied Behavior Analysis, 12,* 491–500.

Nietzel, M. T., & Bernstein, D. A. (1981). Assessment of anxiety and fear. In M. Hersen & A.S. Bellack (Eds.), *Behavioral assessment: A practical handbook* (2nd ed., pp. 215–245). Elmsford, NY: Pergamon Press.

Obler, M., & Terwilliger, R. F. (1970). Test effectiveness of systematic desensitization with neurologically impaired children with phobic disorders. *Journal of Consulting and Clinical Psychology, 34,* 314–318.

Ollendick, T. H. (1979a). Behavioral treatment of anorexia nervosa: A five year study. *Behavior Modification, 3,* 124–135.

Ollendick, T. H. (1979b). Fear reduction techniques with children. In M. Hersen, R. M. Eisler, & P. M. Miller (Eds.), *Progress in behavior modification* (Vol. 8). New York: Academic Press.

Ollendick, T. H. (1986). Child and adolescent behavior therapy. In S. L. Garfield & A. E. Bergin (Eds.), *Handbook of psychotherapy and behavior change* (3rd ed., pp. 525–564). New York: John Wiley & Sons.

Ollendick, T. H., Hagopian, L. P., & Huntzinger, R. M. (1991). Cognitive behavior therapy with nighttime fearful children. *Journal of Behavior Therapy and Experimental Psychiatry, 22,* 112– 121.

Ollendick, T. H., Yang, B., King, N. J., Dong, Q., & Akande, A. (1996). Fears in American, Australian, Chinese, and Nigerian children and adolescents.: A cross cultural study. *Journal of Child Psychology and Psychiatry, 37,* 213–220.

Ollendick, T. H., & King, N. J. (1994). Diagnosis, assessment, and treatment of internalizing problems in children: The role of longitudinal data. Journal of Consulting and Clinical Psychology, 19, 169–172.

Ollendick, T. H., Matson, J. L., & Helsel, W. J. (1985). Fears in children and adolescents: Normative data. *Behavior Research & Therapy, 23,* 465–467.

Ollendick, T. H., Yang, B., King, N. J., Dong, Q., & Akande, A. (1966). Fears in American, Australian, Chinese, and Nigerian children and adolescents: A cross cultural study. *Journal of Child Psychology and Psychiatry, 37,* 213–220.

Ollendick, T. H., Yule, W., & Ollier, K. (1991). Fears in British children and their relationship to manifest anxiety and depression. *Journal of Child Psychology and Psychiatry, 32,* 321–331.

O'Reilly, P. (1971). Desensitization of fire bell phobia. *Journal of School Psychology, 9,* 55–57.

Patterson, G. R. (1965). A learning theory approach to the treatment of the school phobic child. In L. P. Ullman & L. Krasner (Eds.), *Case studies in behavior modification* (pp. 279–294). New York: Holt, Rinehart & Winston.

Paul, G. L., & Bernstein, D. A. (1973). *Anxiety and clinical problems: Systematic desensitization and related techniques.* Morristown, NJ: General Press.

Pavlov, I. P. (1927). *Conditioned reflexes.* Trans. G.V. Anrep. London: Oxford University Press.

Perry, M. A., & Furukawa, M. J. (1986). Modeling methods. In F. H. Kanfer & A. P. Goldstein (Eds.), *Helping people change* (3rd ed., pp. 66–110). Elmsford, NY: Pergamon Press.

Peterson, L. & Shigetomi, C. (1981). The use of coping techniques in minimizing anxiety in hospitalized children. *Behavior Therapy, 12,* 1–14.

Piersel, W. C., & Kratochwill, T. R. (1981). A teacher-implemented contingency management package to assess and test selective mutism. *Behavioral Assessment, 3,* 371–382.

Rachman, S. J., & Hodgson, R. (1974). Synchrony and desynchrony in fear and avoidance. *Behavior Research and Therapy, 12,* 311–318.

Ramirez, S., Kratochwill, T. R., & Morris, R. J. (1977). Fears and phobias in school age children. In A. Thomas & J. Grimes (Eds.), *Children's needs: Psychological perspectives* (2nd ed., pp. 315–327). Washington, DC: National Association of School Psychologists.

Reeves, J. L., & Maelica, W. L. (1975). Biofeedback-assisted cue controlled relaxation for the treatment of flight phobias. *Journal of Behavior Therapy and Experimental Psychiatry, 6,* 106–109.

Richards, C. S., & Siegel, L. J. (1978). Behavioral treatment of anxiety states and avoidance behaviors in children. In D. Marholin (Ed.), *Child behavior therapy.* New York: Gardner Press.

Rimm, D. C., & Masters, J. C. (1974). *Behavior therapy: Techniques and empirical findings.* New York: Academic Press.

Ritter, B. (1968). The group desensitization of children's snake phobias using vicarious and contact desensitization procedures. *Behavior Research and Therapy, 6,* 1–6.

Ritter, B. (1969). The use of contact desensitization, demonstration-plus-participation and demonstration only in the treatment of acrophobia. *Behavior Research and Therapy, 7,* 41–45.

Rivenq, B. (1974). Behavior therapy of phobias: A case with gynecomastia with mental retardation. *Mental Retardation, 12,* 44–45.

Rosen, G. (1976). *Don't be afraid: A program for overcoming your fears and phobias.* Englewood Cliffs, NJ: Prentice-Hall.

Ross, A. O. (1981). Of rigor and relevance. *Professional Psychology, 12,* 273–279.

Ross, D. M., Ross, S. A., & Evans, T. A. (1971). The modification of extreme social withdrawal by modeling with guided participation. *Journal of Behavior Therapy and Experimental Psychiatry, 2,* 273–279.

Rutter, M., Tizard, J., & Whitmore, K. (1970). *Education, health and behavior.* New York: John Wiley & Sons.

Sarason, I. G. (1980). *Test anxiety: Theory, research and applications.* Hillsdale, NJ: Lawrence Erlbaum.

Saunders, D. G. (1976). A case of motion sickness treated by systematic desensitization and in vivo relaxation. *Journal of Behavior Therapy and Experimental Psychiatry, 7,* 381–382.

Scarr, S., & Salapatek, P. (1970). Patterns of fear development during infancy. Merrill-Palmer *Quarterly of Behavior and Development, 16,* 53–90.

Shapiro, E. S., & Skinner, C. H. (1993). Childhood behavioral assessment and diagnosis. In T. R. Kratochwill & R. J. Morris (Eds.), *Handbook of psychotherapy with children and adolescents* (pp. 75–107). Boston: Allyn & Bacon.

Sheslow, D. V., Bondy, A. S., & Nelson, R. O. (1983). A comparison of graduated exposure, verbal coping skills and their combination in the treatment of children's fear of the dark. *Child and Family Behavior Therapy, 4,* 33–45.

Siegel, L. J., & Peterson, L. (1980). Stress reduction in young dental patients through coping skills and sensory information. *Journal of Consulting and Clinical Psychology, 48,* 785–787.

Singer, L. T., Ambuel, B., Wade, S., & Jaffe, A. C. (1992). Cognitive-behavioral treatment of health-impairing food phobias in children. *Journal of the American Academy of Child and Adolescent Psychiatry, 31,* 847–852.

Skinner, B. F. (1938). *The behavior of organisms.* New York: Appleton-Century.

Skinner, B. F. (1953). *Science and human behavior.* New York: Macmillan.

Stableford, W. (1979). Parental treatment of a child's noise phobia. *Journal of Behavior Therapy and Experimental Psychiatry, 10,* 159–160.

Stedman, J. M., & Murphey, J. (1984). Dealing with specific child phobias during the course of family therapy: An alternative to systematic desensitization. *Family Therapy, 11,* 55–60.

Tahmisian, J., & McReynolds, W. (1971). The use of parents as behavioral engineers in the treatment of a school phobic girl. *Journal of Counseling Psychology, 18,* 225–228.

Tarler-Beniolo, L. (1978). The role of relaxation in biofeedback training. A critical review of literature. *Psychological Bulletin, 85,* 727–755.

Tasto, D. L. (1969). Systematic desensitization, muscle relaxation and visual imagery in the counterconditioning of a 4-year-old phobic child. *Behavior Research and Therapy, 7,* 409–411.

Taylor, D. W. (1972). Treatment of excessive frequency of urination by desensitization. *Journal of Behavior Therapy and Experimental Psychiatry, 3,* 311–313.

Trueman, D. (1984). What are the characteristics of school phobic children? *Psychological Reports, 54,* 191–202.

Ultee, C. A., Griffion, D., & Schellekens, J. (1982). The reduction of anxiety in children: A comparison of the effects of systematic desensitization in vitro and systematic desensitization in vivo. *Behaviour Research & Therapy, 20,* 61–67.

Vaal, J. J. (1973). Applying contingency contracting to a school phobic: A case study. *Journal of Behavior Therapy and Experimental Psychiatry, 4,* 371–373.

Van der Ploeg, H. M. (1975). Treatment of frequency of urination by stories competing with anxiety. *Journal of Behavior Therapy and Experimental Psychiatry, 6,* 165–166.

Van der Ploeg-Stapert, J. D., & Van der Ploeg, H. M. (1986). Behavioral group treatment of test-anxiety: An evaluation study. *Journal of Behavior Therapy and Experimental Psychiatry, 17,* 255-259.

Van Hassett, B. B., Hersen, M., Bellack, A. S., Rosenblum, N. D., & Lamparski, D. (1979). Tripartite assessment of the effects of systematic desensitization in a multi-phobic child: An experimental analysis. *Journal of Behavior Therapy and Experimental Psychiatry, 10,* 51–55.

Vernon, V. T., & Bailey, W. C. (1974). The use of motion pictures in the psychological preparation of children for induction of anesthesia. *Anesthesiology, 40,* 68–72.

Waranch, H. R., Iwata, B. A., Wohl, M. K., & Nidiffer, F. D. (1981). Treatment of a retarded adults mannequin phobia through in vivo desensitization and shaping approach responses. *Journal of Behavior Therapy and Experimental Psychiatry, 12,* 359–362.

Warren, R., Smith, G., & Velten, E. (1984). Rational-emotive therapy and the reduction of interpersonal anxiety in junior high school students. *Adolescence, 19,* 893–902.

Watson, J. B. (1913). Psychology as the behaviorist views it. Psychological Review, 20, 158–177.

Watson, J. B., (1919). *Psychology from the standpoint of a behaviorist.* Philadelphia: Lippincott.

Watson, J. B., & Rayner, R. (1920). Conditioned emotional reactions. *Journal of Experimental Psychology, 3,* 1–14.

Waye, M. F. (1979). Behavioral treatment of a child display comic-book mediated fear of hand shrinking: A case study. *Journal of Pediatric Psychology, 4,* 43–47.

White, W. C., & Davis, M. T. (1974). Vicarious extinction of phobic behavior in early childhood. *Journal of Abnormal Child Psychology, 2,* 25–37.

Wilson, B., & Jackson, H. J. (1980). An in vivo approach to the desensitization of a retarded child's, toilet phobia. *Australian Journal of Developmental Disabilities, 6,* 137–141.

Wish, P. A., Hasazi, J. E., & Jurgela, A. R. (1973). Automated direct deconditioning of a childhood phobia. *Journal of Behavior Therapy and Experimental Psychiatry, 4,* 279–283.

Wolpe, G. (1972). *Tommy goes to the doctor.* Boston: Houghton-Mifflin.

Wolpe, J. (1958). *Reciprocal inhibition therapy.* Stanford, CA: Stanford University Press.

Wolpe, J. (1962). The experimental foundations of some new psychotherapeutic methods. In A. J. Bachrach (Ed.), *Experimental foundations of clinical psychology* (pp. 554–575). New York: Basic Books.

Wolpe, J. (1969). *The practice of behavior therapy.* Elmsford, NY: Pergamon Press.

Wolpe, J. (1973). *The practice of behavior therapy* (2nd ed.). Elmsford, NY: Pergamon Press.

Wolpe, J., & Lazarus, A. A. (1966). *Behavior therapy techniques.* Elmsford, NY: Pergamon Press.

CHAPTER 5

ATTENTION-DEFICIT HYPERACTIVITY DISORDER

George J. DuPaul
Russell A. Barkley

Symptoms of attention-deficit hyperactivity disorder (ADHD; American Psychiatric Association, 1994) remain among the most frequent referral complaints to child guidance clinics in this country. Epidemiological studies indicate that this disorder occurs in 3% to 5% of the school-age population. As a result, ADHD continues to be one of the most heavily studied psychological disorders of childhood. Given its relatively high prevalence rate, it behooves clinicians and students of clinical child psychology to be able to assess this disorder competently and to design interventions that will effectively ameliorate both the core disorder and its associated deficits. The purpose of this chapter is to briefly review several treatment interventions that have demonstrated efficacy in the therapeutic management of ADHD and to provide an update regarding research into the salient parameters and outcomes associated with these interventions.

This chapter is not designed to be an exhaustive review of the literature on the treatment of children with ADHD, as this has already been accomplished (e.g., Barkley, 1990). Further, because there are many problems associated with ADHD, in addition to core deficits, it would be impossible to delineate all of the treatment interventions used with this population. The reader is directed to those chapters in this text that address these problems (aggressive behavior, academic problems, depression) in more detail. Alternatively, this chapter will focus on the core behavioral deficit felt to be central to ADHD; impaired delayed responding or impulsivity (Barkley, 1994). The emphasis previously given to problems with attention and/or excessive motor activity appear to be accounted for by a central impairment in delaying responding to the environment. It is this central deficit that accounts for the myriad problems that lead children with ADHD into chronic conflict with their social environment, cause them to be referred for treatment, and underlie their poor long-term adjustment (Weiss & Hechtman, 1993).

HISTORICAL PERSPECTIVES

Although Still (1902) is typically credited with first identifying the syndrome presently known as ADHD, he acknowledged references to these children dated in the 1860s. The serious student of the subject would be well-advised to review this classic paper not only for its historic value but also for its lucid discussion of the "defects in moral consciousness" characteristic of these children and its prophetic description of their usual symptoms, family patterns, and preponderance among males.

In subsequent years, researchers stressed the motor activity component of the disorder (Chess, 1960; Wender, 1971; Werry, 1968; Werry & Sprague, 1970), which resulted in the application of the label "hyperactivity" or " hyperkinesis" to it. At times, this emphasis on hyperactivity led to the exclusion of other identifying problems (e.g., impulsivity) now known to coexist with fidgetiness, restlessness, and gross motor overactivity. Others (e.g., Clements, 1966) attempted to describe symptoms so numerous that virtually any child might be felt to exhibit at least one of them at some time in his or her development. Because the disorder was defined in this fashion, it became difficult to distinguish it from any other psychological disorder of childhood. In 1972, Douglas emphasized the need to consider the child's inattention and impulsivity as the more pervasive and chronic problems associated with ADHD. Follow-up research (for review see Weiss & Hechtman, 1993) seems to have supported Douglas' contention. For this and related reasons, the label "hyperactivity" has been replaced by the term ADHD as espoused by the American Psychiatric Association (APA) in its recent DSM-IV (APA, 1994). During the 1980s, investigators began to consider deficits in behavioral self-regulation as a hallmark of ADHD. These have included hypothesized deficits in self-directed instruction (Kendall & Braswell, 1985), self-regulation of arousal to meet environmental demands (Douglas, 1983), and rule-governed behavior (Barkley, 1981, 1989).

More recently, Barkley (1994) has proposed a conceptualization of ADHD based on an adaptation of Bronowski's (1967) account of importance of delaying responding to the environment in the development of higher order cognitive skills. The impairment in delayed responding that is central to ADHD leads to important difficulties in: (a) separating informational from affective content in environmental stimuli, (b) prolonging the internal representation of a stimulus, (c) internalizing language, and (d) reconstitution (i.e., analysis and synthesis of environmental stimuli). Barkley posits that it is these effects of an impairment in delayed responding that lead to the myriad difficulties encountered by children with ADHD. Thus, the challenge for treatment programming is to arrange for prosthetic arrangements of the natural environments (e.g., home, school) of the child wherein he or she is provided with prompts, cues, and contingencies for inhibited behavior. Promoting a delay in responding to the environment thereby would allow the child to evidence growth in the four key cognitive skill areas delineated above.

It is clear from any historical review of this disorder that, until recently, there were few operational definitions that were useful, reliable, and valid for clinical or research purposes. Several commonalities (e.g., early onset of marked inattention, impulsivity, overactivity) among the various historical definitions were helpful in guiding the formulation of current diagnostic schemas. With these in mind, two definitions are currently available to aid the clinician or scientist in diagnosing ADHD. First, the APA (1994) has recently revised the diagnostic criteria for ADHD to include nine symptoms of inattention and nine symptoms of hyperactivity- impulsivity. This definition represents an advance over previous formulations as the diagnostic criteria are relatively objective, the breakdown of symptoms into two lists reflects factor analytic work, and the cutoff scores of six of nine symptoms in each category were established in a national clinical field trial.

Although these criteria are an improvement over those in previous DSM editions, they continue to have several limitations. First, no explicit guidelines are provided as to how the symptoms are established as deviant for the child's age. For instance, the use of behavior rating scales to establish developmental deviance are not dealt with in any detail. Second, the symptom cutoff scores are fixed, ignoring well-known age-related declines in these behaviors among both children with ADHD and their normal counterparts (e.g., Hart, Lahey, Loeber, Applegate, & Frick, 1995). Age-referenced cutoff scores would have been helpful because the score needed to show statistical deviance may be higher for younger children than for teenagers. Finally, no rationale has been established for the age-of-onset (i.e., prior to 7 years old) and duration (i.e., at least 6 months) criteria proposed.

Barkley (1990) has proposed a more stringent definition of the disorder that include diagnostic guidelines that require the child to: (a) obtain a score on a well-standardized behavior rating scale of attention and conduct problems completed by parents and teachers that places the child at or above the 93rd percentile for his or her age and sex; (b) exhibit problem behaviors that are pervasive across settings as evidenced by scores on the original Home and School Situations Questionnaires (Barkley, 1981) that place the child at or above the 93rd percentile for his or her age and sex; and (c) exhibit ADHD symptoms over a 12-month period, especially when the child is younger than 6 years old.

Several additional provisos should be kept in mind. First, the label "acquired ADHD secondary to _____" should be applied in cases where the child exhibits these symptoms after the age of 6 as a result of central nervous system trauma or disease. This will distinguish such children from the more common developmental, idiopathic form of ADHD typically encountered in clinical practice or research investigations. Second, when the child presents with significant noncompliance or conduct disturbance, quite common among children with ADHD, this does not preclude the diagnosis of ADHD. Rather, additional diagnoses (e.g., oppositional defiant disorder, conduct disorder) would need to be considered. Finally, the symptoms of ADHD may be viewed as lying on a continuum with normal development, wherein the diagnostic threshold has been established by using a somewhat arbitrary cutoff point (i.e., two standard deviations above the mean) along this continuum. One must be cognizant of the existence of borderline conditions lying near to but not beyond this cutoff point. Although ADHD is generally chronic, with a high degree of stability over development for most children (Weiss &

Hechtman, 1993), those placed in the borderline range of the continuum may move into or out of the ADHD category over development, because their individual scores may fluctuate as a function of situational or developmental variation.

Description and Developmental Course

In addition to the core diagnostic symptoms, children with ADHD may exhibit a variety of associated behavioral and emotional problems (e.g., conduct disturbance, poor peer relations, difficult temperament). Although these occur more frequently in children with ADHD than in their normal counterparts, there is a great deal of individual variability regarding symptom emergence and chronicity through the course of development. Despite these individual differences, a plethora of empirical data has been gathered suggesting that difficulties of temperament and behavior control begin in the child with ADHD's early years and continue throughout life.

Infants exhibiting difficult temperament who are excessively active, have poor sleeping and eating habits, and are prone to negative moods are at greater risk for eventual ADHD than are children with more normal temperaments (for reviews see Barkley, 1990; Ross & Ross, 1982). Those at risk also may have a higher rate of minor physical anomalies; however, these are not specific precursors of ADHD and may be associated with other behavior disorders (e.g., Pomeroy, Sprafkin, & Gadow, 1988).

The majority of children who will be identified as having ADHD will have begun to manifest significant overactivity, noncompliance, and short attention span by 3 years of age. Typically, complaints regarding these excessive behaviors are first brought to the parent's attention by other caretakers, such as teachers, day care personnel, or relatives. Toilet training may be difficult and may occur later than normal, presumably because of the child's frequent noncompliance (Hartsough & Lambert, 1985).

The stability of the child with ADHD's behavioral excesses from the preschool years to early elementary grades has been well-documented (see Campbell, 1990 for review). In fact, by the first grade (i.e., by age 6), more than 90% of children with ADHD will have been identified as problematic by their parents or teachers. The most significant difficulties during middle to late childhood (6 to 11 years old) include poor impulse control, short attention span, noncompliance with school and home rules, and excessive motor activity, particularly in structured situations (e.g., independent seatwork). Associated concerns may emerge, including poor relationships with peers (Pelham & Bender, 1982), chronic underachievement or specific learning disabilities (Cantwell & Baker, 1991), conduct problems (e.g., lying, stealing), disruptive behavior in group situations, and, in later years, feelings of low self-esteem.

At home, children with ADHD frequently evidence an inability to consistently complete routine chores and activities (e.g., preparing for school, completing homework, cleaning their rooms). In fact, this irresponsibility may cause parents to spend an inordinate amount of time supervising their children's activities. Stress in the parental role, as well as the risk for maternal depression, may increase at this time (e.g., Breen & Barkley, 1988; Cunningham, Benness, & Siegel, 1988).

Several distinct developmental patterns begin to emerge during adolescence. Many children with ADHD will continue to present with the core symptoms of the disorder, with estimates ranging from 30% (Gittelman, Manuzza, Shenkes, & Bonagura, 1985) to 71% (Barkley, Fischer, Edelbrock, & Smallish, 1990). Those children with "pure" ADHD who do not display significant aggressiveness or peer relationship problems are likely to exhibit continued difficulties with inattention and impulsivity, which lead primarily to poor performance at school (Weiss & Hechtman, 1993). Once out of school and working, these teenagers presumably experience less trouble with their behavior than they did at school. Alternatively, those adolescents exhibiting aggression and conduct problems apparently are at risk for more significant maladjustment. Not only are school performance problems evident, but difficulties with predelinquent or delinquent behavior in the community may emerge (Barkley, Fischer et al., 1990; Gittelman et al., 1985; Satterfield, Hoppe, & Schell, 1982) and problematic peer relationships may continue or become worse. There is some evidence to suggest that adolescents with ADHD are

more likely to abuse alcohol (Loney, Kramer, & Milich, 1981), although there are also contradictory findings (Barkley, Fisher et al., 1990). In fact, the risk for alcohol and drug use appears to be moderated by the comorbid presence of conduct problems with ADHD (Gittelman et al., 1985). In addition, these teenagers are at higher risk for automobile accidents, dropping out of school, experiencing feelings of low self-esteem, and poor social acceptance (Weiss & Hechtman, 1993).

In general, the behavior patterns described above may continue into adulthood, with most follow-up studies indicating that individuals with childhood ADHD function less adequately in a number of spheres (e.g., socially, psychologically, occupationally) relative to normal controls (see Weiss & Hechtman, 1993, for a review). Specifically, there is a greater than average risk for adult antisocial personality disorder, alcoholism, and complaints of interpersonal problems or psychological difficulties (Weiss, Hechtman, Milroy, & Perlman, 1985). These findings indicate that there are adult disorders that are equivalent to or are residual forms of ADHD.

This course is not evident for all children with ADHD and is apparently mediated by several factors. The research literature indicates that a number of significant variables are associated with poorer outcomes in this population, including low intelligence in childhood, aggressiveness and oppositional behavior, poor peer acceptance, emotional instability, and extent of parental psychopathology (Barkley, 1990; Weiss & Hechtman, 1993). Although extensive, long-term treatment through adolescence may reduce the risk of maladjustment (Satterfield, Satterfield, & Schell, 1987), less degrees of treatment, including stimulant medication in isolation, have not been found to have a significant impact on adult outcome (e.g., Hechtman, Weiss, & Perlman, 1984; Paternite & Loney, 1980). Thus, we have taken the approach that ADHD is a developmental disorder of self-control and social conduct that is chronic and without cure. An attitude of "coping" rather than "curing" is frequently communicated to the family by the clinician, intimating that treatment may lead to the reduction of problems, but not necessarily to their complete elimination.

Etiological Factors in Understanding ADHD

A wide variety of causative factors have been proposed to underlie ADHD, yet no single variable has been found to account fully for its genesis. In fact, it may be most prudent to view ADHD as the final common pathway of a number of possible etiological events, much as mental retardation or other developmental disabilities are conceptualized (Barkley, 1988). In general, the major causal variables that have been identified can be categorized as neurological factors, toxic reactions, genetic linkage, and environmental variables (Anastopoulos & Barkley, 1988).

The etiological role of neurological variables has been the most heavily investigated over the years. Initially, gross brain damage resulting from head trauma or neurologic illness was presumed to be the primary cause of ADHD (Strauss & Lehtinen, 1947). In fact, for a time it was assumed that all children with ADHD have some level of structural insult even in the absence of "hard" evidence. Hence, the terms "minimal brain damage" or "minimal brain dysfunction" (MBD) were used in labeling children who presented with ADHD symptomatology. More recent investigations have refuted this assumption by indicating that less than 5% of children with ADHD show evidence of neurological damage (Rutter, 1977), and most brain-injured children do not exhibit symptoms of ADHD (Rutter, Chadwick, & Shaffer, 1983). Despite the lack of evidence for structural damage, there is intriguing evidence that individuals with ADHD may have structural abnormalities in some brain structures (e.g., frontal lobes; Rapoport, 1996) and diminished levels of cerebral blood flow in the frontal white matter and frontal midbrain tracts relative to normal controls (Zametkin et al., 1990). Presumably, these findings suggest that children with ADHD exhibit decreased activity or stimulation in these regions (Fox & Raichle, 1985). In similar fashion, several studies have indicated potential neurotransmitter abnormalities in children with ADHD (e.g., Shaywitz, Shaywitz, Cohen, & Young, 1983), although their results are often equivocal.

Thus, there are strong indications that neurological dysfunction, perhaps related to neurotransmitter imbalances, is associated with ADHD; however, delineation of its causative role awaits more rigorous and specific investigation.

Food additives, sugar, and lead have been the most widely studied environmental toxins or allergens proposed to cause ADHD. In fact, Feingold (1975) hypothesized that the vast majority of children with ADHD contracted the disorder as a result of allergic reactions to food additives (e.g., artificial colorings). He and others presumed that removal of these additives from a child's diet would effectively reduce ADHD symptomatology. Many well-controlled studies have been conducted examining this issue; they indicate that dietary management is ineffective in most cases (see Conners, 1980 for review). The minority (i.e., 5%) of children with ADHD who do respond to such treatment evidence minimal behavior change and are typically under the age of 6. In similar fashion, ingestion of sugar has been proposed as causing ADHD (Smith, 1976). Once again, well-controlled studies, which include asparatame challenge conditions, have found no clinically significant increases in behaviors associated with ADHD following sucrose ingestion (Milich, Wolraich, & Lindgren, 1986). Finally, conflicting results have been obtained regarding the role of lead exposure in causing ADHD (see Barkley, 1990; Ross & Ross, 1982); the association between the two appears to be quite weak (Gittelman & Eskenazi, 1983).

Currently, the most fruitful line of etiological investigation is research into possible hereditary or genetic causes for ADHD. At a general level, it is well-documented that the incidence of psychiatric disorders (e.g., antisocial personality disorder, depression) among biological relatives of children with ADHD is significantly greater than in the general population (e.g., Biederman et al., 1986). More specifically, there is an increased incidence of ADHD among the biological parents and siblings of children with ADHD (Barkley, DuPaul, & McMurray, 1990). Further, studies of monozygotic twins have found a relatively high concordance rate for hyperactivity (e.g., Goodman & Stevenson,

1989). Taken together, these indicate the causative role of two possibly interrelated factors; the natural variation of biological characteristics (Kinsbourne, 1977) and some unspecified mode of inheritance of psychopathological symptomatology (Anastopoulos & Barkley, 1988).

Environmental or behavioral causes of ADHD have received minimal attention, yet the scant evidence available would indicate a limited etiological role for these factors. For example, Willis and Lovaas (1977) have surmised that ADHD is a result of poor stimulus control of behavior by parental commands, stemming from inconsistent child management techniques. Certainly, mothers of children with ADHD have been found to issue more commands and to use more negative statements relative to mothers of normal controls. These differences in disciplinary behaviors appear to be partly a function of the task required (Tallmadge & Barkley, 1983) and the age of the children (Barkley, Karlsson, & Pollard, 1985). Further, because these negative mother-child interactions are reduced when the children are treated with stimulant medication (e.g., Barkley, Karlsson, Strzelecki, & Murphy, 1984), maternal behavior is more likely a reaction to than a major cause of behavioral difficulties associated with ADHD.

Alternatively, environmental factors play an important role in modulating the severity of behavioral control difficulties, as will be discussed in subsequent sections reviewing behavioral interventions. Based on evidence gathered to date, ADHD appears to be related to multiple factors that may separately or in combination lead to the onset of symptoms. Biological factors (neurological and genetic) seem to account for the onset of symptoms in the vast majority of children. The interaction between these biologically based symptoms and the characteristics (e.g., availability of feedback, task demands, salience of reinforcers) of the environments that the child encounters determines the severity of the child's ADHD. Finally, it is best to view ADHD in similar fashion to mental retardation, in that the disorder represents the final common pathway of a number of etiological events (Anastopoulos & Barkley, 1988).

OVERVIEW OF TREATMENT METHODS FOR ADHD

Given the diversity, multiplicity, pervasiveness, and chronicity of behavior problems associated with ADHD, a variety of treatments implemented across settings and by different service providers often will be required. This necessitates the involvement of professionals from several different disciplines (e.g., physician, psychologist, social worker, special education teacher), each providing his or her own special expertise in dealing with specific problems. Thus, professional jealousies and antagonisms will have to be discarded to provide the services that will help both the child and family cope with the myriad problems likely to arise throughout the child's development.

As has been stated, there is no cure for ADHD. Even the most effective treatments available are typically short-term in nature and symptomatic in focus. Knowledge of the etiology of the disorder, which is minimal, provides little assistance in treatment selection. Although some evidence would suggest that long-term multimodal therapy reduces the risk for poor adolescent and adult outcome (Satterfield et al., 1987), the results of most outcome studies do not indicate significant long-term improvements. Alternatively, to the extent that a short-term reduction in problem severity is obtained, it also is likely to reduce the degree of censure, criticism, ostracism, disciplining, and potential for abuse of the child. That these interventions also can provide some relief to the families and teachers of these children further supports their use. Therefore, the goal of therapy is to cope with, not cure, the ADHD, and periodic intervention will almost certainly be needed to guide the child through his or her often stormy developmental years.

The major targets of intervention to be discussed in this chapter are the child's poor attention span, impulsivity or lack of self-control, noncompliance with authority figure directives, and inconsistent productivity and/or accuracy on academic tasks. Associated problems (e.g., aggression, poor peer relations, low self-esteem) may exist in any child with ADHD; however, their treatment is the subject of other chapters in this text and will not be addressed here. At the present time, the interventions that have shown the greatest effectiveness for treating ADHD are pharmacotherapy, parent counseling and training in child management skills, and modifications to classroom environments and/or instruction. The combination of these approaches is frequently necessary, owing to the severity and pervasiveness of the child with ADHD's difficulties. Alternative treatment methods with less well-demonstrated efficacies will be reviewed briefly as well. Given the variety and complexity of all these techniques, it is not possible to describe their implementation in great detail; however, references to more thorough discussions will be made throughout the remainder of this chapter. Even when these readings are pursued, the student should remember that none are intended as shortcuts to or substitutes for clinically supervised practicum experience. Finally, we will consider evidence for the generalization of treatment effects with this population, as well as practices that can promote maintenance and generalization.

SPECIFIC INTERVENTION METHODS

Pharmacotherapy

The use of stimulant medication for the treatment of ADHD and related disruptive behavior disorders is the most extensively studied intervention for childhood disorders. Over 70% of children with ADHD who take these medications evidence behavioral improvements based on parent/teacher judgments, laboratory task performance, and direct observations (Barkley, DuPaul, & Costello, 1993). Although a brief overview of the use of these drugs will be provided here, the reader is referred to the chapter on psychopharmacotherapy in this text for more detailed discussion of their clinical use and associated professional and ethical issues. It should be noted that although stimulant medications represent the drugs of choice in treating ADHD, several investigations have demonstrated the efficacy of antidepressant medications in ameliorating attention deficits while also modulating mood lability (Biederman, Baldessarini, Wright, Knee, & Harmatz, 1989). Further, other medications such as clonidine (Hunt, Mindera, & Cohen,

1985) have been found to exert positive effects on ADHD symptoms, at least in some subjects. Yet evidence continues to support stimulant medications as the first line of pharmacotherapy for ADHD, and nearly 90% of children treated for this disorder will respond positively to one or more of the stimulants (Elia & Rapoport, 1991).

The stimulant medications most commonly employed in the treatment of ADHD are listed in Table 5.1, along with their trade and generic names, tablet sizes, and typical dosage ranges. Traditionally, recommended dosages for stimulant medications have been based on a child's body weight, using a milligram per kilogram formula (American Academy of Pediatrics, 1987). Dose-response studies indicate, however, that the behavioral effects of methylphenidate (MPH) are highly idiosyncratic and not moderated by differences in body weight (e.g., Rapport, DuPaul, & Kelly, 1989). For this reason, Table 5.1 presents recommended dosages in terms of fixed doses, as they are typically prescribed.

Behavioral Effects of Stimulants

A great deal of evidence has been gathered indicating that MPH and other stimulants significantly enhance certain behavioral, cognitive, and academic processes. For example, MPH has been found to improve the performance of children with ADHD on laboratory tasks of sustained attention (Barkley, Fischer, Newby, & Breen, 1988; Rapport et al., 1987), impulsive-reflective responding (Brown & Sleator, 1979; Rapport et al., 1988), short-term recall (Barkley et al., 1988), and associative learning (Vyse & Rapport, 1989). Medication-induced enhancements of children's on-task and academic productivity rates in the classroom also have been obtained (Douglas et al., 1986; Pelham et al., 1993; Rapport et al., 1994), along with concomitant reductions in disruptive, out-of-seat behavior (Werry & Conners, 1979). Gains in academic productivity and learning are presumably due to a general enhancement of attentional processes. In a majority of cases, MPH can result in "normalized" classroom behavior at least with respect to observations of academic engagement and teacher ratings of social deport-

TABLE 5.1. Stimulant Medications, Tablet Sizes, and Dose Ranges

BRAND NAME[a]	TABLET SIZES	DOSAGE REGIMEN	DOSE RANGE[b]
Ritalin (methylphenidate)	5 mg 10 mg 20 mg SR 20 mg	Twice Daily Once Daily	2.5–25 mg 20–40 mg
Dexedrine (dextroamphetamine)	5 mg spansule 10 mg spansule 15 mg spansule 5 mg tablet	Once Daily	2.5–25 mg
	5 mg/5ml (elixir)	Twice Daily	2.5–25 mg
Cylert (pemoline)	18.75 mg 37.5 mg 75 mg	Once Daily	18.75–112.5

[a] Generic name in parentheses.

[b] Dose range for each administration is provided.

ment (DuPaul & Rapport, 1993). Finally, behavioral effects are found with respect to increased compliance, independent play, and responsiveness to social interactions with parents, teachers, and peers (e.g., Barkley et al., 1984; Cunningham, Siegel, & Offord, 1985). In response, the volume of commands, criticism, punishment, and censure directed at the children is often reduced.

In contrast to the above, the results of several long-term follow-up studies investigating stimulant medication effects have been quite disappointing (e.g., Hechtman et al., 1984). Children apparently remain on these medications from 2 to 10 years and then once treatment is discontinued there is little additional improvement seen beyond that obtained at the outset of treatment. It should be pointed out, however, that there are numerous methodological shortcomings (e.g., use of poor outcome measures) to these investigations, thus minimizing the likelihood of obtaining more positive findings. Nevertheless, the most prudent conclusion is that stimulant medication in isolation may be necessary for many children with ADHD but does not sufficiently address the multiple problems associated with this disorder, thus necessitating the combination of medication with other therapies.

Side Effects of Stimulants

The most frequent side effects associated with stimulant medications are relatively mild and include decreased appetite and insomnia (Barkley, McMurray, Edelbrock, & Robbins, 1990). In a minority of cases, several other side effects might occur including somatic symptoms (e.g., headaches, stomachaches), increased tension, growth inhibition, and benign increases in heart rate or blood pressure. In general, the frequency and severity of these side effects are dose-related and may diminish with reductions in dosage and/or the passage of time. In rare cases, symptoms of Tourette's Disorder may appear following treatment with stimulant medication. Although the research evidence documenting the validity of this side effect is equivocal, caution is advisable before prescribing these drugs for patients with a personal or family history of motor and/or vocal tics.

Guidelines for Pharmacotherapy

There are no set guidelines to determine when pharmacotherapy is necessary. The chief indications for medication are the severity of the child's problems, the degree of distress suffered by the child, parents, or teachers, as well as the success of psychosocial treatments. Several questions to consider have been proposed by Barkley (1981, 1990) as aids to this decision, as follows:

1. Has the child had an adequate physical and psychological evaluation? Medications should never be prescribed if the child has not been directly and thoroughly examined.
2. How old is the child? Drug treatment is often ineffective or leads to more severe side effects among children below the age of 4 years old. It is therefore not recommended for use in this age group.
3. What has been the success of other therapies? If this is the family's initial contact with the professional, prescription of medication might be postponed until the effects of alternative treatments (e.g., parent training in child management skills) have been assessed. Alternatively, when the child's behavior presents a severe problem and the family cannot participate in child management training, medication may be the only viable treatment option.
4. How severe is the child's current behavior? Where it is extremely unmanageable or distressing to the family, treatment with drugs may be the fastest and most effective way of dealing with the crisis until other forms of therapy can begin. Once progress with other therapies becomes evident, some effort can be made to reduce or discontinue medication.
5. Can the family afford the medication and associated costs (e.g., follow-up visits)? Long-term compliance rates are typically poor and may be particularly problematic among families of low socioeconomic status.
6. Are the parents sufficiently intelligent to adequately supervise the use of the medication and guard against its abuse?
7. What are the parents' attitudes toward pharmacotherapy? Some parents are simply "anti-drug" and should never be coerced into agreeing with this treatment.
8. Is there a delinquent sibling or drug-abusing parent in the household? If so, psychostimulant

medication should not be prescribed, because there is a high risk for its illicit use or sale.
9. Does the child have any history of tics, psychosis, or thought disorder? If so, stimulant medications are contraindicated.
10. Is the child highly anxious, fearful, or more likely to complain of psychosomatic disturbances? If so, psychostimulants may exacerbate these emotional difficulties.
11. Does the physician have time to monitor medication effects properly?
12. How does the child feel about medication and its alternatives? It is important that the use of medication be discussed with older children and adolescents. In cases where children oppose the use of medication, they may sabotage efforts to implement this treatment (e.g., by not swallowing their pills).

Treatment Generalization

Of all the interventions available in treating ADHD, pharmacotherapy produces effects across the widest variety of settings for the greatest length of time. It is typically effective for as long as the child requires it (e.g., several years or more), assuming minor dosage adjustments over the course of time. As would be expected, the effects of medication are limited to the active period of the drug (i.e., 3 to 7 hours, depending on the specific agent). Behaviors occurring outside of this time period may not be improved and, in fact, may be worsened because of a washout effect when the medication is wearing off.

Behavioral control is evident across home, school, and public situations during the time that the drug is active. Alternatively, medication effects differ to some extent across settings and appear to be most marked in situations that are highly structured or demand greater attention and self-control from the child. Further, there is a certain degree of behavioral specificity in the actions of psychostimulant medications. As summarized above, they primarily enhance sustained attention and impulse control, which indirectly leads to greater academic productivity and accuracy, diminished disruptive or noncompliant behavior, and the display of more appropriate interpersonal skills. The specific doses that optimize therapeutic changes may differ across behavioral realms.

PARENT COUNSELING AND TRAINING

Parent Counseling

As is the case with other forms of child psychopathology, one of the most important components to the overall treatment of the child with ADHD is the education and counseling of his or her parents on the nature, causes, course, prognosis, and treatment of this disorder. This treatment component does not directly address the management of child behavior but rather those issues pertaining to the parents' understanding of the disorder and the variety of practical life circumstances for which research gives us little guidance.

Parent education also may serve as an essential prerequisite to specialized training in behavior management because a number of procedures that parents will be asked to use are predicated on their understanding of the specific deficits that their children may display. The following list is not exhaustive but offers an overview of the types of information required to communicate to parents:

1. Copies of federal and state laws on mandated educational services for handicapped children (Individuals with Disabilities Education Act or equivalent). Also, awareness of laws governing the emergency placement of children in psychiatric hospitals, children's homes, or foster care. Along with these is the obvious need for an awareness of those social and educational agencies or community resources that deal with these subjects.
2. Copies of up-to-date reading material on ADHD or behavior management skills. Several recent books by Barkley (1995) as well as Ingersoll and Goldstein (1993) provide accurate and current information about ADHD for parents who can read at the high school level. Also, a series of videotapes by Barkley (1992) on ADHD are available.

3. The clinician should be prepared to give advice to parents, particularly those with young children, on how to childproof their home to diminish the likelihood of accidents, injuries, or the destruction of property. Similarly, the clinician should be ready to discuss practical issues raised by the parent of an adolescent with ADHD, such as frank discussions of sexual matters and whether the teenager will be allowed to obtain an automobile license.
4. Given the greater incidence of parental psychopathology in ADHD families, an awareness of community resources for marital, sexual, or substance abuse counseling is most useful.
5. Awareness of local support groups for parents of children with ADHD or learning disabilities will enable the clinician to provide parents with a social network that can offer the kind of help that is not provided by therapy alone.
6. The nonmedical professional must cultivate responsible medical referral sources when the total care of the child with ADHD calls for medication, neurologic and physical exams, or medical advice. The long-term treatment of this disorder calls for a multidisciplinary approach and well-developed ties with other professionals.

Parent Training

Parent training in child behavior management is an essential component in the overall treatment of most ADHD families. There are many programs on parent training, each differing in philosophy, method, and effectiveness. Barkley (1981, 1987; Anastopoulos & Barkley, 1990) has described a parent training program for use specifically with children with ADHD. Although it is similar to other parenting programs, it has several unique components that address the special needs of children with ADHD and their families. The program was built on several theoretical and empirical foundations, the earliest being the "two-stage program" developed by Hanf (1969) and later refined and extensively researched with noncompliant children by Forehand and McMahon (1981). The parent training program described here is unique in its emphasis on tailoring specific parenting methods to theoretically and empirically derived notions of ADHD. An especially prominent premise taught in the program is that ADHD is a largely biologically based predisposition to respond immediately to the environment (Barkley, 1994). This impairment in delayed responding accounts for the child's display of inattention, impulsivity, and overactivity. A variety of specialized parenting skills are emphasized to address these deficits.

Education in the management of child behavior is neither possible nor desirable for all parents of children with ADHD. An initial screening and the use of selection guidelines should be a matter of routine. In most cases, children between the ages of 3 to 11 years old will be responsive to the procedures that parents will learn to use. Along with age considerations, assessment should be made of other complicating diagnoses, such as severe language disorders, delays in cognitive skills, depression with suicidal ideation, and other medical or psychiatric disorders. Serious parental psychiatric disturbances such as substance abuse, depression, or severe marital problems will generally lead to a referral to appropriate mental health professionals before such parents can be enrolled in the parent training program. The presence of severe forms of aggressiveness, assaultiveness, violence, or antisocial behaviors (e.g., firesetting, chronic stealing) typically will preclude involvement in the program. Finally, those parents who are isolated from their community, engage in few social activities outside the home, or bear the burden of frequent unpleasant social contacts are a poor risk for parent training programs.

The parent training program, as described below, can be conducted with individual parents or in a group format. Usually the child does not participate in the training, except in cases where the therapist wants the parent to practice management skills *in vivo*. Training sessions last 1 to 1.5 hours for an individual family and 1.5 to 2 hours for groups of parents. Each training session follows a similar sequence of activities, including a review of the information covered the previous week, a brief assessment of whether any critical events occurred since the previous meeting, and a discussion of homework activities that were assigned at the end of

the last session. The therapist then provides instruction with respect to particular management methods that the parents are to practice during the subsequent week. Following didactic instruction, the therapist models the appropriate behavior(s). The parents rehearse the management strategies and receive feedback and further guidance from the therapist. At the end of the session, additional practice of management skills is assigned as homework for the coming week. Written handouts detailing the session's techniques and procedures are distributed for review.

Parent training is usually provided over the course of eight or nine weekly sessions. At the conclusion of the initial course of training, follow-up meetings are scheduled every several months to provide booster sessions in management techniques and to support maintenance of acquired skills. The content of the sessions is briefly described, below. For more detailed information regarding this parent training program, the reader should consult Barkley (1987, 1990).

Session 1: Overview of ADHD

The initial session is intended to provide parents with information regarding the characteristics, prevalence, possible etiologies, and effective treatment of ADHD. The emphasis is placed on coping with rather than curing the disorder through the creation of a therapeutic home environment.

Session 2: Understanding Parent-Child Relations and Principles of Behavior Management

Based on Bell and Harper's (1977) model of the reciprocal nature of parent-child interactions, four major factors are discussed as contributing to child misbehavior. These factors include characteristics of the child, characteristics of the parents, familial stressors, and situational antecedents and consequences. The rationale for parent training is thereby established as the need for parents to modify the way that they respond to their children's behavior. General principles of behavior management (e.g., positive and differential reinforcement) are outlined to set the stage for parents to practice these principles in subsequent weeks.

Session 3: Developing and Enhancing Parental Attention to Child Behavior

Patterson (1976) has demonstrated that the value of parental attention is diminished greatly in the families of children with behavior problems and is unlikely to be useful in reinforcing appropriate behavior. Thus, parents are instructed to employ a "special time" activity designed to increase both the amount and quality of parental attention to their children. The child chooses a one-to-one activity with the parent and the latter issues no commands or questions while praising any appropriate behavior that occurs.

Session 4: Attending to Appropriate Behavior

The parents are instructed to use positive attending skills to reinforce child behaviors occurring outside the context of the special time activity described above. Specifically, positive attention to compliance with parental commands as well as spontaneous adherence to household rules is emphasized. Finally, the parents receive information and the opportunity to practice the forms (e.g., stated request vs. asking a favor) and timing (e.g., after distractions have been reduced) of commands that increase the probability of child compliance.

Session 5: Establishing a Home Token Reinforcement System

The initiation of a structured, home token economy system is designed to augment parental attention to appropriate and compliant behavior, while introducing highly predictable, frequent, and immediate consequences for specific behaviors. This can be a useful procedure for impacting on school-related tasks such as homework completion and studying for tests. The use of privileges and rewards as back-up reinforcers increases the potency of reinforcement strategies.

Session 6: Using Response Cost and Time-Out From Positive Reinforcement

Until this point in training, the use of positive reinforcement has been emphasized with no instruction in punishment strategies. This session introduces two mild punishment techniques, response cost and time-out, that may be used as adjuncts to positive disciplinary methods. Response cost involves the removal of tokens and time-out is the withdrawal of attention from the child for short intervals contingent upon inappropriate behavior. Parents are instructed in the use of these two aversive procedures to reduce noncompliance with commands and household tasks.

Session 7: Managing Behavior in Public Settings

Most children with ADHD exhibit behavior control difficulties in public places such as stores, restaurants, churches, or the homes of others. If the parents have developed the skills necessary to implement behavior management procedures at home, then they are instructed in the use of similar strategies in public settings. First, parental anticipation of such problems is emphasized. Then, parents are encouraged to formulate a plan of action to address public displays of misbehavior. Specifically, parents are advised to increase their use of praise and positive reinforcement for appropriate behavior, and to use response cost and/or time-out from positive reinforcement for rule infractions. In addition, a home-school communication program (see below) can be designed such that home-based contingencies are used to enhance the child's performance at school.

Session 8: Managing Future Misbehavior

The final session of the parent training program is used to review the important principles of behavior management that were incorporated into each of the methods parents were taught to employ. Examples of anticipated or hypothetical problems are generated by the therapist and the parents are asked to develop a plan to handle such problems. Finally, the steps in gradually fading the use of the home token reinforcement system are discussed to discourage abrupt withdrawal of contingency management procedures.

At least one follow-up session is held approximately 4–6 weeks after the formal training is completed. This is to provide support for continued use of management procedures as well as to troubleshoot additional behavior problems that may have arisen. Parents are encouraged to contact the therapist for additional booster sessions, as necessary.

Despite its substantial research record in the treatment of noncompliance in children (Forehand & McMahon, 1981), the child management training program outlined above has begun only recently to receive empirical evaluation in the treatment of ADHD. Although there is preliminary evidence that this treatment approach is effective (e.g., Anastopoulos, Shelton, DuPaul, & Guevremont, 1993; Horn, Ialongo, Popovich, & Peradotto, 1987), many questions remain, given the relatively small number of empirical studies and the numerous differences in methodology that exist across investigations. In particular, future research will be necessary to examine the durability over time and the generalization across settings of obtained treatment effects with this population. Training programs to promote parent support in enhancing the academic and homework performance of their children also need to be developed (e.g., Olympia, Jenson, Clark, & Sheridan, 1992). Despite the need for further research, parent training in behavior modification strategies is an integral and, oftentimes, necessary component of a multimodal treatment program for ADHD.

INTERVENTIONS WITH ADOLESCENTS

Until recently, the prevailing clinical lore held that the symptoms of ADHD diminished significantly or disappeared during adolescence, presumably because of maturational processes. As summarized above, several independent prospective longitudinal investigations have refuted this belief while providing evidence for continued ADHD symptomatology into adolescence among a significant percentage of children diagnosed with this disorder (e.g., Barkley, Fischer et al., 1990; Gittelman et al., 1985).

Although teenagers with ADHD apparently exhibit a high rate of positive response to psychostimulant medications, similar to that of younger children (Klorman, Coons, & Borgstedt, 1987; Pelham, Vodde-Hamilton, Murphy, Greenstein, & Vallano, 1991), empirical investigations of the effects of psychosocial interventions with this age group are sorely lacking.

Application of the parent training program described above has generally been studied with children between the ages of 3 to 11 years old. Problems with attention span, impulse control, and restlessness may persist; however, by the time the typical child with ADHD reaches adolescence, most significant family issues center around acceptance of responsibilities (e.g., chores, homework), disagreements over rights and privileges, and permissible social activities. Thus, the target behaviors or goals included in such programs must be modified to account for these developmental differences. In addition, it is important to include adolescents in therapy sessions that will motivate them to participate in the negotiation of responsibilities and privileges.

In many cases, the normal striving for independence associated with adolescence may be complicated by more pronounced conduct problems and oppositional behavior, resulting in significant levels of family conflict. Robin and Foster (1989) have developed and evaluated a treatment program (Problem Solving Communication Training: PSCT) specifically addressing the conflicts encountered in distressed parent-adolescent relations. As in the parent training approach employed with preadolescents, family conflict is viewed in the context of bidirectional influences in which both parents and teenagers play prominent roles. Unlike child management training, however, the adolescent is asked to take part and his or her active participation is generally required.

PSCT entails a highly directive skill-oriented therapy that includes an integration of behavioral, cognitive, and family-systems models. Four components are used in the context of a relatively short-term approach generally involving 6 to 25 sessions: (a) teaching problem-solving skills, (b) modifying problematic communication patterns, (c) modifying faulty cognitions (e.g., irrational thoughts) that may precipitate or maintain problematic interactions, and (d) altering structural patterns (e.g., triangulation, nonparticipation of a parent) within the family. Integrated throughout therapy is the imparting of information pertaining to appropriate and effective behavior management strategies such as establishing incentives, clarifying and specifying household rules, and using contingency contracting as an adjunct to other, less formal methods. Underlying these methods is active shaping and instruction in negotiation and compromise, highlighting the bidirectional view of conflict and the developing role of the teenager as active in conflict resolution.

Although the use of PSCT in treating the families of adolescents with ADHD has not been studied extensively, the results of an initial investigation of its efficacy are promising. Barkley, Guevremont, Anastopoulos, and Fletcher (1992) found PSCT to be as effective as contingency management training and structural family therapy in reducing the number of conflicts and the intensity of anger during conflict discussions at home. In addition, PSCT significantly improved the quality of parent-adolescent communication according to the independent reports of 21 teenagers with ADHD and their mothers. Improvements also were reported by parents with respect to their adolescents' school adjustment and in the broad-band dimensions of both internalizing (e.g., depression) and externalizing (e.g., conduct problems) symptomatology. This treatment was rated positively by all family members on consumer satisfaction questionnaires and obtained improvements were maintained at a 3-month follow-up. Unfortunately, treatment effects were not obtained on direct observations of parent-adolescent conflict, did not result in clinically significant changes for most of the sample, and PSCT appeared to worsen the degree of irrational beliefs that some mothers held about their teenagers' conduct problems. The authors attributed the latter findings to the brevity of treatment (i.e., an average of nine sessions) and suggest that the course of PSCT should be lengthened with this population. It also is possible that greater treatment effects could be obtained if PSCT is combined with other treatment modalities (e.g., contingency contracting). Finally, the decision to use PSCT should be based on the moti-

vation of the adolescent and parents to enter family therapy, the level of verbal intelligence of family members, and the severity of conduct or oppositional problems.

Classroom Interventions

In general, empirical investigations have documented the effectiveness of behaviorally based interventions in the amelioration of ADHD-related behaviors (Barkley, 1990; DuPaul & Stoner, 1994). More specifically, contingent positive reinforcement and response cost techniques have been associated with clinically significant reductions in attention problems along with concomitant increases in academic productivity and accuracy (for review, see Fiore, Becker, & Nero, 1993). Presumably these interventions increase the stimulation value of an assigned task (i.e., lower the probability of escape behavior) and/or teach the child that the display of appropriate behavior will result in access to attention from teachers or peers. Although fewer studies have addressed the manipulation of antecedent events in enhancing attentive behaviors, certain academic interventions (e.g., peer tutoring) also have been associated with positive results (e.g., DuPaul & Henningson, 1993). Antecedent-based interventions may increase the stimulation value of academic tasks and/or provide more opportunities to gain attention from others in the environment.

Most of the research on behavioral interventions for attention problems has been conducted in special education settings. In fact, DuPaul and Eckert (1995) found that approximately 60% of the extant studies have been conducted in special education classrooms. Thus, when designing an intervention plan, the practitioner must not only be cognizant of the nature of problematic behavior but the practicality and acceptability of the proposed intervention for the person(s) who are implementing the plan. Unfortunately, what has been found to be effective in controlled investigations is not always acceptable to our consumers (i.e., teachers and parents).

In this section, we discuss the most effective antecedent-based and consequent-based interventions for reducing ADHD symptoms in the classroom (see Table 5.2 for a list of procedures in each

TABLE 5.2. School-based Interventions for ADHD

Manipulating Antecedent events (Proactive Interventions)

- Reduce workload and gradually increase expectations over time
- Provide a menu of choices for the completion of tasks
- Utilize peer tutoring or cooperative learning instead of independent seatwork
- Provide direct instruction in note-taking and study skills
- Post classroom rules and frequently prompt students to follow rules
- Provide access to computer-assisted instruction
- Train student to monitor on-task behavior and/or work completion
- Ongoing vocational guidance and counseling

Manipulating Consequent Events (Reactive Interventions)

- Praise on-task behavior and completion of classroom responsibilities
- Implement a token reinforcement system
- Develop a hierarchy of mild aversive contingencies for significant off-task behavior (i.e., prudent reprimands, response cost, removal from room)
- Develop a home-school communication system (daily report card) that includes home-based contingencies for school performance

category). Further, we will provide specific details of what we believe to be the best options in each category. It is our contention that ADHD-related behaviors are optimally addressed through the manipulation of both antecedent and consequent events over a long time period. Given the chronicity and complexity of these problem behaviors, a less intensive intervention plan is likely to fail.

Antecedent-Based Interventions

Over the years, a number of task-related and instructional modifications have been suggested for the prevention of significant ADHD symptoms (Barkley, 1990; DuPaul & Stoner, 1994). Suggested modifications have included: (a) reducing the amount of seatwork or homework, (b) ensuring student understanding prior to beginning a task, (c) providing extra time for the completion of tests and/or long-term assignments, (d) posting rules with frequent reminders of expectations for rule-following behavior, and (e) teaching study skills and note-taking strategies. Unfortunately, most of these strategies have not been subjected to empirical scrutiny, at least not in the context of helping students with ADHD.

Among the few antecedent-based interventions that have undergone empirical investigation are peer tutoring and allowing students to choose task activities. ClassWide Peer Tutoring (CWPT), as

described by Greenwood, Delquadri, and Carta (1988), has been found to enhance the mathematics, reading, and spelling skills of students of all achievement levels (see for review, Greenwood, Maheady, & Carta, 1991). CWPT includes the following steps: (a) dividing the class into two teams; (b) within each team, classmates form tutoring pairs; (c) students take turns tutoring each other; (d) tutors are provided with academic scripts (e.g., math problems with answers); (e) praise and points are contingent on correct answers; (f) errors are corrected immediately with an opportunity for practicing the correct answer; (g) teacher monitors tutoring pairs and provides bonus points for pairs that are following prescribed procedures; and (h) points are tallied for each individual student at the conclusion of each session. Each tutoring session typically lasts 20 minutes with an additional 5 minutes for charting progress and putting materials away. At the conclusion of each week, the team with the most points is applauded by the other team. Points are not usually exchanged for any back-up reinforcement.

Recently, the effects of CWPT on the attentional behavior and academic accuracy of students exhibiting significant ADHD-related behaviors have been investigated. DuPaul, Hook, Ervin, and Kyle (1995) found that the active engagement of 19 elementary school-aged children (16 boys, 3 girls; M age = 7.5) with ADHD increased from an average of 21.6% during baseline to an average of 82.3% when CWPT was implemented by their general education teachers. Observational data were collected in a continuous fashion for each student in the context of an ABAB reversal design. Data for three children are displayed in Figure 5.1 which clearly demonstrate the effectiveness of this intervention. In addition, children's weekly post-test scores increased from an average of 55.2% during baseline to 73% for CWPT conditions, thus indicating that this intervention affected both attentional behavior and academic performance. These results should not be surprising given that peer tutoring incorporates strategies (e.g., provision of immediate, frequent feedback about performance and the receipt of peer attention) known to optimize the performance of children with attention problems.

An advantage of some antecedent-based interventions is the ease with which they can be implemented in general education classrooms. For example, Dunlap and colleagues (1994) systematically varied whether independent tasks were teacher-assigned or chosen by students from a menu. Rates of task engagement and disruptive behavior were functionally related to the manipulation of teacher versus student choice with the latter leading to higher levels of engagement and lower levels of disruptive behavior. Results for an 11-year-old boy with ADHD in the context of an ABAB reversal design are presented in Figure 5.2. It should be noted that this boy was being treated with 75 mg, desipramine throughout this investigation, yet an environmental manipulation was necessary to elicit acceptable levels of task engagement.

Consequent-Based Interventions

There are two primary consequent-based approaches that are effective in addressing inattention and related behavior problems including positive reinforcement contingent on the display of appropriate levels of attention and the use of response cost contingent upon off-task behavior. Typically, the combination of the two approaches will be optimal.

As is the case for most target behaviors, token reinforcement programs that target task-related attention and productivity typically lead to increases in these behaviors. The development of a token reinforcement program involves several steps. First, specific target behaviors must be delineated. It is best to follow the "dead man's" rule (Lindsley, 1991) in deciding which behaviors to target. This rule states that if a dead man can perform a behavior, then it is not a good target for intervention. Thus, the program will ultimately be more effective if it targets active, appropriate responding (e.g., completion of assigned work) rather than the lack of problematic behavior (e.g., stay in seat). The second step is to develop a menu of back-up reinforcers that can be earned. Our experience is that it is best to include a variety of preferred activities as reinforcers rather than concrete rewards which many adults view as contrived attempts at "bribery." Also, the child should be involved in the selection of reinforcers. Finally, the specific time periods and/or situations for program implementation must be scheduled. To lessen the burdens on the teacher (and thereby increase the acceptability of intervention), it is best to initially implement the system for a short duration each day (e.g., during one academic period). As success is obtained, gradual implementation across settings and times could be accomplished. To achieve optimal treatment integrity, the practitioner must balance the comprehensiveness of treatment coverage with its acceptability by those who are implementing it.

Response cost, as it is typically implemented, involves providing an individual with a set number of token reinforcers at the outset of an activity whereby tokens are deducted contingent on the display of inappropriate behavior (Kazdin, 1989). A variant of this procedure has been found effective for classroom use with students who are exhibiting attentional difficulties (e.g., Rapport, Murphy, & Bailey, 1982). The response cost tactic employed by Rapport et al. (1982) includes a number of steps. As is the case for a token reinforcement system, target behaviors and back-up reinforcers must be specified. Also, specific situations (e.g., independent seatwork) where the response cost system will be implemented are delineated. The student starts the work period with 0 points and is able to earn points periodically (e.g., once per minute) so long as he or she is exhibiting the target behavior (e.g., attending to seatwork). The teacher must award points on an

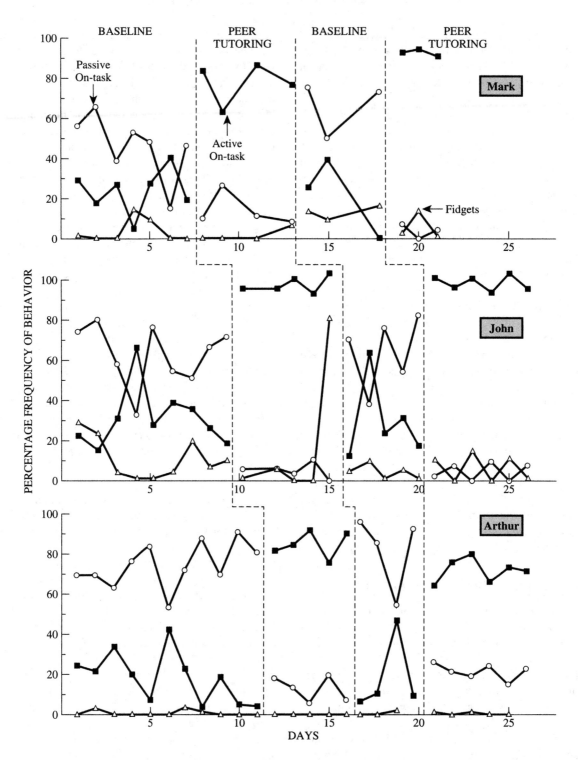

Figure 5.1. Rates of task engagement and off-task behavior for three children with ADHD as a function of baseline and ClassWide Peer Tutoring (CWPT) conditions. From DuPaul, Hook, Ervin, & Kyle, 1995.

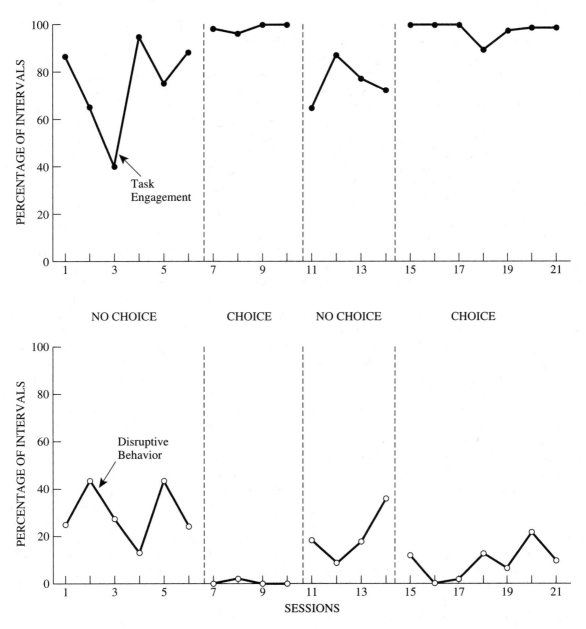

Figure 5.2. Percentage frequency of task engagement and disruptive behavior for a 12-old-boy with ADHD as a function of teacher choice and student choice conditions. From G. Dunlap et al. (1994). Reprinted by permission.

interval schedule, thus necessitating periodic monitoring of the child's behavior. If the child exhibits significant off-task behavior, a point is deducted by the teacher. At the end of the specified work period, the student is able to exchange his or her final net points for a certain amount of time of a preferred activity.

This response cost procedure has been found to elicit on-task behavior equivalent to that associated with stimulant medication (Rapport et al., 1982). In addition, response cost plus positive reinforcement has been found superior to positive reinforcement alone in the maintenance of on-task behavior

(Sullivan & O'Leary, 1990). Although under ideal circumstances practitioners would prefer to use positive reinforcement procedures in isolation, mild punishment strategies such as response cost appear necessary for many students with significant attentional problems. Further, response cost is acceptable to both students and teachers when it is delivered in the context of a management program weighted heavily in favor of positive reinforcement. In other words, the ratio of reinforcer delivery to response cost should be high (e.g., 3 or 4:1) and if a student consistently "zeroes out" in points then the program components should be modified.

Another alternative to the contingency-based approach is the use of a home-based reinforcement program. The child's behavior at school is evaluated over a specified time interval (e.g., one school day) and a report is sent home. Consequences at home are contingent upon the content of the daily report. This procedure can serve as an effective supplement to or substitute for classroom-based behavior modification systems (see Kelley, 1990 for details). Evaluation forms can vary with respect to target behaviors, frequency of evaluations, and complexity or detail of evaluation (see example of daily report card in Figure 5.3).

There are a number of features that enhance the likelihood that a home-school communication program will be successful (Barkley, 1990; DuPaul & Stoner, 1994). First, daily and/or weekly goals should be stated in a positive manner (i.e., in keeping with the "dead man's rule"). Approximately three to four goals should be identified that target both academic performance (e.g., completed 90% of assigned work) and social behavior (e.g., followed classroom rules). Second, rather than making subjective statements about performance, the teacher should provide quantitative feedback about student performance. For example, in the daily report card displayed in Figure 5.3, the teacher provides a rating from "1" (unacceptable) to "5" (excellent) for each goal area. Third, feedback is provided periodically throughout the day (e.g., after each academic period) rather than on a global basis for the entire day. Periodic feedback facilitates quick teacher decisions about ratings and can motivate the student to work on improving his or her performance throughout the day.

Another factor that definitely enhances the effectiveness of a home-school communication program is the regularity of teacher reports being sent home. Scheduled daily or weekly reports are preferred over periodic reports that are sent home only when the child has had a particularly bad or good day at school. Further, home-based contingencies must be linked to the quality of the child's school performance. Specifically, teacher ratings can be converted to points that are exchanged for both short- and long-term reinforcers in the home environment. This is the most critical aspect of the system because without back-up contingencies the child is unlikely to be motivated to work toward assigned goals.

One of the most common problems that can arise with a home-school communication program is a lack of adherence to treatment procedures by one or more participants (i.e., parent, teacher, student). Given that at least three individuals are active participants in this program, the probability of nonadherence occurring is high. One of the best ways to circumvent this problem is to ensure that all participants are actively involved in the planning of the program. An initial meeting should be held between the teacher(s) and parent(s) to jointly identify goals, outline a schedule of communication, and delineate the reinforcers to be used. Older children and adolescents should be included in this negotiation session. Further, all participants should realize that the initial implementation of the program may not be completely successful and that subsequent meetings will be necessary to make adjustments to goals and procedures. Scheduling additional meetings increases the likelihood that participants will feel accountable for following through on the agreed-on program.

Other Treatments

This chapter has reviewed numerous treatment modalities for children with ADHD which have proven efficacious through years of research. It is not within the purview of the present discussion to detail all of the interventions that have been proposed and/or studied with this population. The described interventions frequently are augmented by individualized academic instruction and/or social-skills training (Pelham & Bender, 1982). More empirical data

Daily Report Card

Name _____   Date _____

Please rate this student in each of the goal areas listed below as to how he or she performed in school today using ratings of "1" to "5". 1 = unsatisfactory, 2 = poor, 3 = fair, 4 = good, 5 = excellent.

CLASS PERIODS/SUBJECTS

BEHAVIOR	1	2	3	4	5	6	7	8
Paid Attention								
Completed Classwork								
Accurate Work								
Followed Rules								
Teacher's Initials								

COMMENTS:

Figure 5.3. Example of a daily report card for use in a home-based reinforcement program.

must be collected regarding the efficacy of these supplementary strategies before their value in treating children with ADHD can be determined.

The techniques of traditional psychotherapy applied at either an individual or family level have minimal effectiveness in treating children with ADHD. These strategies typically assume that behavioral difficulties are caused by emotional or family-system disturbances. Because these latter variables have not been shown to play a role in the etiology of ADHD, it stands to reason that treatments based on these assumptions would have limited success. More recently, certain "fad" therapies, such as EEG biofeedback training, have been proposed. Like traditional therapies, these treatments are based on questionable etiological assumptions and have not been proven to be effective.

Many laypeople have accepted the notion that food additives and sugars are a major cause of behavior problems in young children (e.g., Feingold, 1975). The removal of these substances from children's diets is therefore presumed to be therapeutic. As discussed in the section on etiological factors, a plethora of research studies have been conducted that refute a causative role for food additives (see Conners, 1980). In similar fashion, most of the well-controlled studies investigating the influence of

sugar (sucrose) on the behavior of children with ADHD and their normal counterparts have found only minor improvements associated with its removal from the diet (e.g., Rosen et al., 1988).

Given the number of treatments that have been touted over the years as helpful for ADHD, clinicians must help parents and teachers to consider several guidelines in evaluating the "newest" approach for helping children with this disorder (see Ingersoll & Goldstein, 1993). The most important factor in evaluating a prospective treatment is to examine the quality and quantity of empirical data that support its use. Moreover, the effects of the novel treatment in comparison with existing, efficacious interventions (e.g., stimulant medication) should be known. Above all, parents and teachers should be infused with a healthy dose of skepticism to avoid the squandering of precious time and resources on treatment approaches that will lead to minimal success.

TREATMENT PRESCRIPTIONS

Although it is clear that the optimal treatment approach for ADHD is the combination of stimulant medication and behavior modification implemented across home and school settings, there are minimal empirical data to guide the clinician in the choice of specific behavioral strategies for individual children. At present, the best way for clinicians to delineate the specific intervention techniques that should be used for a given child is through the consultative problem-solving approach described by Bergan and Kratochwill (1990). Four stages of consultation are followed including problem identification, problem analysis, plan implementation, and plan evaluation. The primary goal of consultative problem solving is to ascertain the function(s) of a student's ADHD-related difficulties. Information obtained through a parent and/or teacher interview combined with direct observation data is used to examine antecedent, sequential, and consequent conditions that may be associated with the behavior(s). Based on this analysis, alternative treatment strategies are generated to be implemented during the next stage. Given that ADHD-related behaviors typically are exhibited across school and home settings, it may be fruitful to conduct consultative problem solving jointly with the teacher and parent using conjoint behavior consultation procedures as described by Sheridan (1993).

In addition to the consultative problem-solving process described above, a technology has been developed in the field of applied behavior analysis that can help to pinpoint specific intervention strategies for an individual child. Functional analysis or functional assessment (Iwata, Dorsey, Slifer, Bauman, & Richman, 1982) involves the collection of data to determine the antecedent and consequent events maintaining problematic behavior as well as to determine the function of the problematic behavior. This technology has been applied with great success in developing specific, context-specific interventions for individuals with severe disabilities. Recent studies have demonstrated the success of functional assessment procedures in designing effective interventions for children with milder disabilities (e.g., Kern, Childs, Dunlap, Clarke, & Falk, 1994) including students with ADHD (e.g., Umbreit, 1995).

Through examination of antecedent and consequent events, hypotheses regarding the function(s) of ADHD-related behaviors can be developed. In our experience, we have found the following to be the most common hypothesized functions for inattentive and disruptive behaviors displayed in home or classroom settings. The most likely function for ADHD-related behavior is to *escape effortful tasks*, particularly those that involve independent writing activity (e.g., seatwork) or an extended sequence of chores. This is based on the assumption that presenting independent work or a chore is an antecedent for inattention, which is then followed by a lack of work completion. A second possible function is to *gain adult and/or peer attention*. A frequent consequent event for inattention and disruption is a verbal reprimand from the adult as well as nonverbal (e.g., smiles) and verbal reactions (e.g., laughter) from the student's classmates. An additional possible function is for the ADHD-related behavior to result in *sensory stimulation* that appears more reinforcing than the stimuli that the child is expected to attend to. For example, when presented with a set of written math problems to complete, the student begins playing with a toy that was kept in his pocket. It is important to note that developing hypotheses as to behavioral functions is an idiographic process, thus clinicians must determine these on an individual basis using interview and observation procedures as described by Bergan and Kratochwill (1990) and O'Neill, Horner, Albin, Storey, and Sprague (1990).

As an example of this approach to treatment prescription, Ervin, DuPaul, Kern, and Friman (in press) conducted descriptive and experimental functional analyses with four boys diagnosed as having ADHD and Oppositional Defiant Disorder (ODD). One of the boys, Joey (age 13) exhibited a variety of inattentive behaviors (e.g., looking out the window, playing with his pencil or other objects, sharpening his pencil excessively) that were hypothesized to be motivated by escape. Teacher interview and direct observation data indicated that these inattentive behaviors were reliably preceded by the teacher asking Joey to complete an independent writing task. During a student interview, Joey indicated that Writing and English were his least favorite subjects and that he disliked writing intensely. Further, he stated that he would prefer to talk about things rather than write about them and that he needed more time to think prior to beginning writing.

In Joey's case, there was a convergence among data gathered through direct observation as well as teacher and student interviews that provided several important pieces of information. First, the function of his inattentive behavior was to escape assigned tasks. Second, a reliable antecedent of this behavior was the presentation of written tasks in the areas of Reading and English. Finally, teacher and student interviews provided leads as to possible interventions that could reduce inattentiveness. More specifically, written tasks could be modified to be less aversive to Joey and he could be provided with a greater opportunity to think prior to writing. These ideas were used to formulate alternative hypotheses that were formally tested during the experimental functional analysis stage.

Given the information obtained through the descriptive analysis, two hypotheses were formulated regarding Joey's inattentive behaviors. First, it was hypothesized that, "Joey's off-task behavior will be reduced when he is given the opportunity to complete long (20 minutes or greater) writing tasks on the computer rather than by hand." An alternative writing method was posited to decrease the aversiveness of the task and thereby reduce the probability of escape behavior. The computer was chosen as the alternative writing method given the availability of a computer in the classroom and Joey's stated preference for this method. The direct observation data displayed in the top graph of Figure 5.4 are supportive of this hypothesis. The percentage of intervals in which Joey *did not* exhibit inattentive behaviors during long writing tasks was higher when he used the computer (M = 96.8%) versus when he was required to complete the task by hand (M = 64.8%).

A second hypothesis was that "Joey's inattentive behaviors will be reduced when he is able to brainstorm with a peer prior to a short (i.e., 5 to 7 minutes) written task vs. when he is not allowed to brainstorm." Joey's teacher believed that he was more likely to be actively engaged in a short writing task if he participated in a discussion about the topic prior to writing. This was corroborated by Joey's belief that he needed more time to think prior to writing. The most feasible way for the teacher to ensure that Joey would think about what he was going to write was to have him spend a few minutes discussing his topic with a peer prior to beginning the assignment. Direct observation data confirmed

this hypothesis (see bottom graph of Figure 5.4). The percentage of intervals where Joey *did not* exhibit inattentive behaviors was higher when he discussed the topic with a peer prior to writing (M = 91.4%) versus when no discussion was allowed (M = 63.2%).

Based on the data obtained during the problem analysis stage, an intervention was designed for writing class that involved the combination of brain-

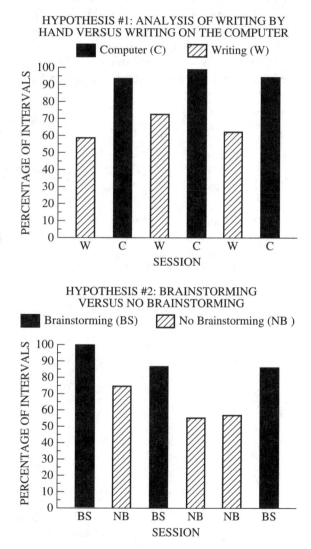

Figure 5.4. Results of an experimental functional analysis of two hypotheses for a 13-year-old boy diagnosed with ADHD. From Ervin, DuPaul, Kern, & Friman, in press.

storming ideas with a peer and completing written assignments on a computer. An ABAB reversal design was employed wherein baseline phases were alternated with intervention phases (see Figure 5.5). During the initial baseline phase, the percentage of intervals *without* off-task behaviors was variable and trending downward with a mean of 67.7% (range: 54.2% to 83.3%). When the intervention was implemented, there was an immediate and stable increase in the percentage of intervals in which Joey did not engage in off-task behavior ($M = 96\%$; range: 93.7% to 98.3%). When the intervention was withdrawn for one day, the percentage of intervals *without* off-task behavior decreased to 62.7%. Once the intervention was reimplemented, Joey's behav-

ior improved to a mean level of 95.4% (range: 90.7% to 98.7%). The percentage of nonoverlapping data points between baseline and intervention phases was 100%.

The combined use of the consultative problem-solving model and functional assessment procedures can facilitate the development of specific intervention strategies for children with ADHD. Although these procedures are relatively time intensive, presumably their use will lead to more effective treatments than the tactic of applying a set of generic treatment strategies to all children with this disorder. Of course, more empirical work is necessary to demonstrate the utility of a functional approach to the treatment of ADHD.

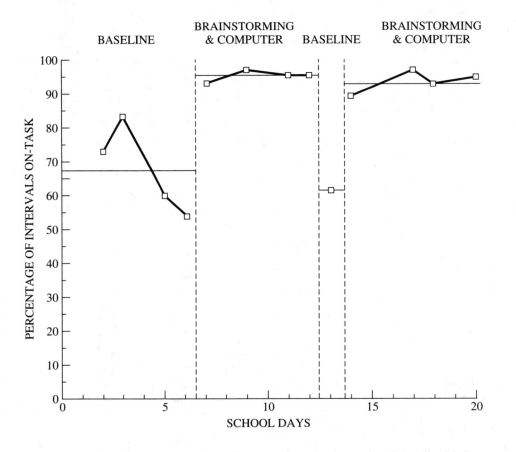

Figure 5.5. Results of intervention evaluation for Joey. Percentage of intervals without off-task behaviors are shown for writing class. Horizontal lines denote mean level of intervals without off-task behaviors during each condition. From Ervin, DuPaul, Kern, & Friman, in press.

GENERALIZATION OF TREATMENT METHODS

As is the case for the psychological intervention literature in general, very few intervention studies targeting children with ADHD have assessed or explicitly programmed for generalization. In fact, DuPaul and Eckert (1995) found that less than 20% of studies of school-based interventions for students with ADHD even included a follow-up assessment phase. Thus, beyond the recommendations offered in seminal articles by Stokes and Baer (1977) as well as Stokes and Osnes (1989), there is little in published literature to guide practitioners in generalization programming. Beyond these general guidelines, we discuss treatment methods that gradually transfer evaluation and reinforcement from an external agent (e.g., parent, teacher) to the individual with ADHD. In this section, we also discuss generalizability across client characteristics and behaviors as well as the relative costs and benefits associated with treatment.

Generalization Across Settings and Time

By definition, ADHD is a chronic disorder whose symptoms are pervasive across settings and over time. It is naive to assume that short-term intervention programs will address ADHD-related problems under all conditions and in a durable fashion. Thus, the success of what Stokes and Baer (1977) referred to as the "train and hope" strategy will be severely limited. This is why we have emphasized the need to involve parents, teachers, and children in treatment implementation and why treatment is simultaneously undertaken in both home and school settings. Treatment strategies such as contingency management are likely to be necessary over long time periods, thus requiring the clinician to provide periodic booster sessions to families and teachers. Of course, the ideal goal is for the child with ADHD to eventually exhibit greater self-control in the management of ADHD symptoms. Despite the initial promise of cognitive behavioral strategies for ADHD (e.g., Kendall & Braswell, 1985), empirical support for

cognitive strategies for this disorder has, thus far, been elusive to obtain (for review see, Abikoff, 1985). Alternatively, contingency-based self-management interventions, which include self-monitoring, self-evaluation, and self-reinforcement have received some empirical support with this population (e.g., Barkley, Copeland, & Savage, 1980; Hinshaw, Henker, & Whalen, 1984). In particular, contingency-based self-management programming may be helpful in weaning a child off of an externally managed token reinforcement program while maintaining behavioral improvements.

Hoff and DuPaul (1996) conducted a controlled case study of a contingency-based, self-management program for three children exhibiting significant ADHD-related behaviors in general education classrooms. These children participated in several treatment phases beginning with a teacher-managed token reinforcement program and proceeding through successive stages of self-evaluation and self-reinforcement (i.e., a modification of procedures first reported by Rhode, Morgan, & Young, 1983). Prior to the first stage of self-management, each student was trained by the teacher to recognize target behaviors associated with ratings from 0 to 5 (see Table 5.3). These behaviors were modeled for the child and the latter also role-played target behaviors while stating the rating associated with the behavior. During the first stage of self-management, the student and teacher independently rated the student's performance during one academic period. Ratings were compared wherein: (a) if student rating was within one point of teacher's, the student kept the points he gave himself; (b) if student rating matched teacher's exactly, he received the points he gave himself plus one bonus point; and (c) if student and teacher ratings deviated by more than one point, then no points were awarded. As in the token reinforcement phase, points were exchanged for preferred activities on a daily basis.

During successive stages of the treatment, the frequency of teacher-student matches was gradually reduced to 0%. For example, during the 50% match stage, a coin was flipped following each rating period wherein the student was required to match the teacher an average of 50% of the time. Given that

TABLE 5.3. Self-Management Rating Criteria

5 = Followed classroom rules (see below) entire interval
4 = Minor infraction of rules (e.g., talked out of turn); followed rules remainder of interval
3 = Did not follow all rules for entire time, but no serious offenses
2 = Broke one or more rules to extent behavior was unacceptable (e.g., physically aggressive with classmate), but followed rules remainder of interval
1 = Broke one or more rules almost entire interval or engaged in higher degree of inappropriate behavior most of the time
0 = Broke one or more rules entire interval

Classroom Rules:

1. Talking to classmates allowed only during group discussions.
2. Keep hands to self and own property unless you ask for teacher permission.
3. Follow teacher directives.

the outcome was random and unpredictable, the student could not assume prior to the coin flip that he didn't have to match the teacher's rating. On the occasions where he didn't have to match, the student automatically kept the points he gave himself. Figure 5.6 displays data for one of the students from Hoff and DuPaul (1996) across self-management phases.

Generalization across settings was programmed for and systematically evaluated. The data show that this student was able to maintain behavioral improvements initially elicited under token reinforcement despite the fading of teacher feedback. It is important to note that by the end of the study the student continued to provide written ratings of his performance and continued to receive back-up contingencies. The ideal outcome would be for written ratings to be faded to oral ratings while back-up contingencies are phased out.

For some students exhibiting ADHD-related behaviors, the process of teaching self-management (i.e., achieving generalization across time and settings) will take several months, while for others this will take several school years. Unfortunately, for some youngsters with more severe ADHD, this process may be a life-long affair. Nevertheless, a contingency-based, self-management protocol may be a viable option for promoting the generalization of behavior change obtained under adult-directed procedures.

Generalization Across Therapists/Service Providers

As is the case for generalization across settings and time, there is no evidence that treatment-induced improvements in ADHD symptoms will spontaneously transfer to service providers (e.g., therapists, teachers, parents) who were not directly involved in the original intervention program. Thus, explicit programming is necessary to elicit behavior change across service providers. Several examples of how to bring about this form of generalization have already been discussed. A home-school communication program or daily report card system can be used to bring about behavior change under the direction of a teacher through a linkage with ongoing programming at home supervised by the child's parents. That is, one can capitalize on the salutary effects of a home-based token economy by making some tokens contingent on behavior supervised by another person (i.e., teacher) in another setting. Another method for eliciting generalization across service providers is the use of conjoint behavior consultation (Sheridan, 1993) wherein the clinician conducts treatment planning and implementation simultaneously with more than one service provider, typically parents and teacher(s). Although these methods can tax limited time and resources, without such explicit programming generalization across service providers will not take place.

Generalization Across Behaviors

In general, minimal empirical data have been gathered to assess whether treatment effects obtained for one ADHD-related behavior (e.g., inattention) generalizes to other ADHD symptoms. There are at least two exceptions to this general conclusion. First, during the time period when stimulant medication effects are active, reliable changes are evidenced across a variety of behaviors including attention, impulse control, motor activity, academic productivity, and social interactions (for review see Barkley et al., 1993; Pelham, 1993; Rapport & Kelly, 1991). Thus, in addition to being the single most effective treatment for ADHD, stimulant med-

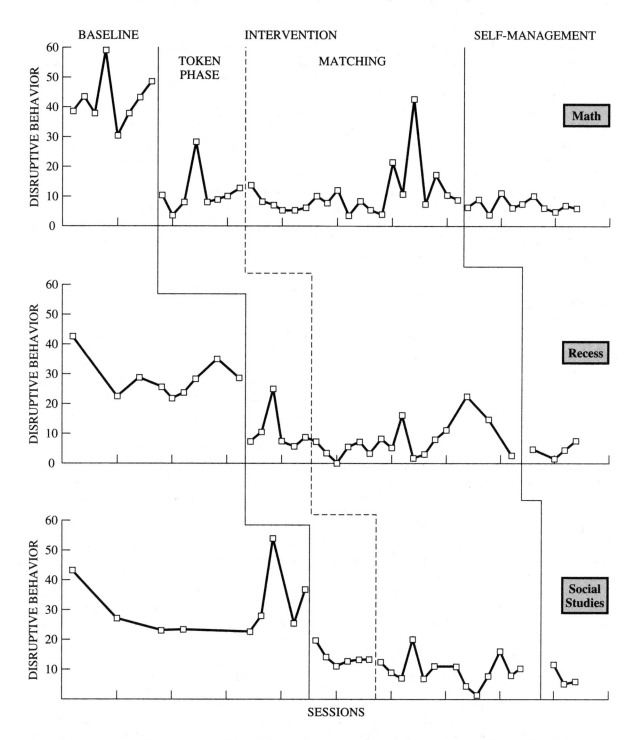

Figure 5.6. Percentage of disruptive behavior during a self-management intervention for an 8-year-old boy with ADHD across math, recess, and social studies periods. From Hoff & DuPaul, 1996.

ication affects a child's functioning in a number of key areas even though dosage is typically titrated by observing changes in one behavioral domain (e.g., reduction in disruptive behavior). Secondly, a number of research studies have demonstrated that when classroom interventions target increases in academic performance, improvements in disruptive behavior tend to occur as well. For example, Ayllon, Layman, and Kandel (1975) found that providing token reinforcement for completion of academic tasks was associated with improved academic performance and reductions in hyperactive behaviors. Similar findings have been obtained with interventions that provide academic instruction, such as peer tutoring. Alternatively, behavioral interventions that are focused on reducing problematic behavior typically have not been found to result in concomitant improvements in academic performance. Thus, school interventions for students with ADHD should primarily target academic behaviors to most efficiently address both scholastic performance and behavioral deportment.

Generalizability Across Client Characteristics

The differential effects of treatment for ADHD across various client variables (e.g., age, socioeconomic status, ethnic or cultural background) have been rarely studied. It is clear that stimulant medication improves the ADHD-related behaviors of individuals of all ages and backgrounds (Barkley et al., 1993). It also is evident that although behavioral interventions are effective for clients of varying backgrounds, modifications must be made on the basis of client age, ethnicity, cognitive status, and socioeconomic background. For instance, when treating adolescents with ADHD, clinicians must include the teenager in the development of the behavioral program and combine the more traditional behavioral approach with family therapy procedures such as PSCT. In similar fashion, modifications to treatment procedures must take into account differences in disciplinary practices (e.g., use of physical punishment) across cultural and ethnic groups. The bulk of the ADHD treatment outcome literature has been conducted with white male subjects from middle class backgrounds who were between the ages of 6 to

12 years old, thus research must be conducted with more diverse participants before clinicians are able to confidently apply the procedures discussed in this chapter in a universal fashion.

Costs and Benefits of Treatment

In delineating the costs and benefits of various treatment strategies for ADHD, one must consider these issues on both a short- and long-term basis. Over the short-term, treatment for ADHD (e.g., prescription of stimulant medication, outpatient parent training, implementation of school programs in general education classrooms) is relatively inexpensive compared to costs associated with inpatient hospitalization and/or residential treatment as might be the case for other childhood disorders. These costs are reduced even further when generic forms of psychotropic medication are used instead of the more expensive trade name varieties. Alternatively, treatment costs can be increased if special education placement is necessary. Further, the chronicity of ADHD requires the implementation of interventions over long time periods, which could tax a family's resources especially when insurance coverage for mental health benefits is depleted. In general, however, the costs associated with treating ADHD are outweighed by the presumed reduction in long-term costs that could result without treatment. Children with ADHD who have the most problematic outcomes will require some of society's most expensive resources including residential programming, unemployment and/or welfare benefits, and even incarceration in some cases. Although the long-term benefits of multimodal treatment for ADHD have yet to be definitively determined, it certainly appears to be quite risky to forego relatively inexpensive treatment procedures given the great costs to society that might be incurred over the long-term in the absence of intervention.

COMORBIDITY ISSUES

As discussed in the introduction to this chapter, there are a number of problem behaviors that typically are associated with ADHD. In fact, 35% or more of children with ADHD display the symptoms of Oppositional Defiant Disorder (ODD) or Conduct

Disorder (CD), with even higher rates of these disruptive disorders among adolescents with ADHD (Barkley, Fischer et al., 1990). The presence of one of these disorders increases the severity of ADHD symptoms, heightens the risk for poor outcome (e.g., Barkley, Fischer et al., 1990; Gittelman et al., 1985; Satterfield et al., 1982), and accentuates the need for long-term, intensive intervention. Further, the list of behaviors that must be targeted for intervention will need to be expanded beyond the core symptoms of ADHD to include noncompliance, verbal and physical aggression, temper control, and/or covert antisocial acts (e.g., lying, stealing). Interventions for conduct problems and aggression are delineated in other chapters in this text. It is clear that when clinicians encounter children with comorbid ADHD and ODD/CD, the emphasis must be on developing interventions that include intensive use of contingency management across home and school settings. These interventions must be implemented as early in the child's life as possible and must be applied consistently over many years in order to be effective in ameliorating symptoms of both ADHD and ODD/CD.

Another group of disorders that can be comorbid with ADHD are learning disabilities. In fact, about 30% to 40% of children with ADHD also have one or more learning disabilities (for review see DuPaul & Stoner, 1994; Semrud-Clikeman et al., 1992). Beyond those youngsters who evidence deficits in the acquisition of academic skills (i.e., have a learning disability), 80% or more of students with ADHD evidence problems with academic performance (i.e., showing what skills they possess) (Barkley, DuPaul, & McMurray, 1990; Cantwell & Baker, 1991). The determination of whether a student's academic difficulties are due to ADHD, a learning disability, or both has direct implications for treatment. The behaviors targeted for change, the treatment settings, and the specific interventions employed will vary as a function of assessment decisions. For example, the usual classroom target behaviors for a child with ADHD would include paying attention to instruction, following classroom rules, and getting along with others. To the extent that academic performance difficulties are present, certain scholastic behaviors will be targeted as well, including timely completion of seatwork and/or accuracy of written work. For those children who also have a learning disability, achievement-related behaviors and academic skill development will be the primary targets for intervention. This is due to the frequent finding that when academic performance is enhanced, classroom deportment often improves as well (Hinshaw, 1992; McGee & Share, 1988). It is not unusual, however, to find circumstances where both academic and deportment behaviors must be targeted for change to obtain consistent and durable effects. Further, for children who have both ADHD and a learning disability, extrinsic motivational programming must be combined with academic interventions regardless of the specific behaviors targeted for change (Hinshaw, 1992). Multiple professionals will be needed to successfully implement such programming, thus highlighting the need for effective communication and collaboration among treatment delivery agents (DuPaul & Stoner, 1994). Finally, although stimulant medications may enhance the attention and academic productivity of children with ADHD, pharmacotherapy has not been found to directly enhance skill acquisition and thus must be combined with academic interventions (Swanson, Cantwell, Lerner, McBurnett, & Hanna, 1991).

LIMITATIONS TO INTERVENTION STRATEGIES

In this section, the limitations of the three major treatment approaches discussed in this chapter (i.e., pharmacotherapy, parent counseling and training, and classroom interventions) will be delineated.

Limitations of Pharmacotherapy

The major limitation of drug treatment is that it must be carefully prescribed, titrated, monitored, and sometimes withdrawn under the supervision of a limited range of professionals (i.e., physicians). Thus, in certain rural areas where such medical care is scarce, pharmacotherapy may simply be unavailable. Several investigations have shown that the rate of compliance or adherence to regular administration of stimulant medications over long periods of time is alarmingly low (e.g., Firestone, 1982). Medication effects do not typically generalize to times or situations where the drug is not active; this limits long-term therapeutic benefits. Indeed, longitudinal outcome studies of stimulant treatment have failed to document significant effects beyond those associated with maturation (e.g., Hechtman et al., 1984). Further, psychostimulants may be ineffective or inappropriate in treating certain subgroups of children with ADHD (e.g., those with anxiety symptoms), some behavioral classes (e.g., academic skill acquisition), or behavior in certain settings. Thus, stimulant medication should never be used in isolation as it does not sufficiently address all of the problems associated with ADHD.

Limitations of Parent Counseling and Training

In the discussion of screening procedures to be conducted prior to initiating parent training, several parental and family characteristics (e.g., presence of severe psychiatric disorder, limited social support network) were identified that were predictive of limited success with this treatment. In addition, as is the case for stimulant medication, nonadherence with prescribed treatment procedures is a major problem. This should not be surprising given that the therapist is asking the parent to make time-consuming changes to his or her disciplinary style that may not lead to immediate behavioral effects. Thus, parents may abandon the treatment program after a few days of limited success. Even in cases where the parent continues to implement the program, there is no guarantee that he or she is following intervention procedures as designed. In the absence of treatment integrity checks, the clinician cannot be sure that the parent is accurately carrying out the intervention. Parent training also requires expenses (e.g., transportation, insurance co-payments, child care) that are prohibitive for some families. Unfortunately, these often are the families most in need of treatment.

Limitations of Classroom Interventions

Despite the generally positive outcome data obtained with both antecedent-based and consequent-based classroom interventions, several factors may limit their usefulness for individual children with ADHD. The primary limitation to a classroom program's successful implementation is teacher time and interest. For example, some teachers may hold philosophies of education that conflict with behavioral principles and methods—and, in some cases, this may require the parents to ask for a change to a new teacher. More often, the teacher finds it difficult to integrate program responsibilities into the classroom routine, particularly when he or she is charged with teaching a large group of heterogeneous students. In both cases, therapist sensitivity, skill, and diplomacy can go a long way toward persuading a recalcitrant teacher to try these programs. A second limiting factor is the severity of the child's behavioral control difficulties. The misbehaviors of some children will simply prove too disruptive to be treated within a regular classroom, thus necessitating placement in a more restrictive setting (e.g., special education classroom). Finally, the lack of parental interest or cooperation can limit program efficacy, particularly when home-based contingencies are involved. Obviously, a greater reliance on in-school consequences would be required in such cases.

CONCLUSIONS

The comprehensive treatment of children with ADHD is a long-term process that should not be undertaken by the uninitiated. These children typically present with a variety of problems (e.g., learning disabilities, social-skills deficits, conduct disorders) in addition to ADHD, which necessitate a working knowledge of the assessment and treatment of the most common psychological disorders of childhood. Therefore, a multimodal intervention approach must be adopted, wherein each component is designed to promote the common goal of coping with ADHD and associated difficulties.

The two treatment modalities that have proven efficacy in ameliorating the symptoms of ADHD are psychostimulant medications and behavior modification techniques applied at home and/or in the classroom. A number of investigations have demonstrated that their combination is superior to either treatment in isolation in producing short-term academic and behavioral improvement (e.g., Pelham et al., 1993). Alternatively, traditional individual or family psychotherapy, dietary management, EEG biofeedback, and removal of allergens have not proved useful in the management of this disorder. Frequently, the combination of stimulant medication and behavior modification is supplemented with special education instruction, social-skills training, and, to a lesser extent, residential placement to deal with associated behavioral or emotional difficulties. Surprisingly few (e.g,. Satterfield et al., 1987) well-controlled studies have examined the long-term results of treatment with a multimodal intervention approach. Fortunately, a large scale, multisite study is currently under way (Richters et al., 1995) to address this important gap in the literature.

It is apparent from the preceding discussion that ADHD is a common developmental disorder having an early onset, chronic course, and pervasive influence across many domains of adaptive functioning. No current treatment method can "cure" ADHD; however, significant improvements in child behavior can be attained when parents, teachers, and professionals consistently apply a combination of therapeutic techniques throughout the child's development. Future research needs to delineate the potential advantages of adopting a functional assessment approach to the design of interventions that are proactive rather than reactive in nature. Because of the chronicity of the disorder, strategies that can prevent or diminish the probability of future problems are likely to be more effective than techniques that involve reacting to behavior as it occurs. In sum, the optimal approach to coping with ADHD is to engineer and maintain a "best fit" between the characteristics of the child with ADHD and the demands of the social environment.

REFERENCES

Abikoff, H. (1985). Efficacy of cognitive training intervention in hyperactive children: A critical review. *Clinical Psychology Review, 5,* 479–512.

American Academy of Pediatrics. (1987). Medications for children with an attention deficit disorder. *Pediatrics, 80,* 758–760.

American Psychiatric Association (1994). *Diagnostic and statistical manual of mental disorders* (4th ed.). Washington, DC: Author.

Anastopoulos, A. D., & Barkley, R. A. (1988). Biological factors in attention-deficit hyperactivity disorder. *The Behavior Therapist, 11,* 47–53.

Anastopoulos, A. D., & Barkley, R. A. (1990). Counseling and training parents. In R. A. Barkley (Ed.), Attention deficit hyperactivity disorder: *A handbook for diagnosis and treatment* (pp. 397–431). New York: Guilford Press.

Anastopoulos, A. D., Shelton, T. L., DuPaul, G. J., & Guevremont, D.C. (1993). Parent training for attention deficit hyperactivity disorder: Its impact on parent functioning. *Journal of Abnormal Child Psychology, 21,* 581–596.

Ayllon, T., Layman, D., & Kandel, H. J. (1975). A behavioral-educational alternative to drug control of hyperactive children. *Journal of Applied Behavior Analysis, 8,* 137–146.

Barkley, R. A. (1981). *Hyperactive children: A handbook for diagnosis and treatment.* New York: Guilford Press.

Barkley, R. A. (1987). *Defiant children: A clinician's manual for parent training.* New York: Guilford Press.

Barkley, R. A. (1988). Attention-deficit hyperactivity disorder. In E. Mash & L. Terdal (Eds.), *Behavioral assessment of childhood disorders* (2nd ed., pp. 69–104). New York: Guilford Press.

Barkley, R. A. (1989). The problem of stimulus control and rule-governed behavior in children with attention deficit disorder with hyperactivity. In L. Bloomingdale & J. Swanson (Eds.), *Attention deficit disorders* (Vol. IV). Elmsford, NY: Pergamon Press.

Barkley, R. A. (1990). *Attention deficit hyperactivity disorder: A handbook for diagnosis and treatment.* New York: Guilford Press.

Barkley, R. A. (1992). *ADHD: What do we know?.* New York: Guilford Press.

Barkley, R. A. (1994). Impaired delayed responding: A unified theory of attention-deficit hyperactivity disorder. In D.K. Routh (Ed.), *Disruptive behavior disorders in childhood* (pp. 11–58). New York: Plenum Press.

Barkley, R. A. (1995). *Taking charge of ADHD: The complete, authoritative guide for parents.* New York: Guilford Press.

Barkley, R. A., Copeland, A., & Sivage, C. (1980). A self-control classroom for hyperactive children. *Journal of Autism and Developmental Disorders, 10,* 75–89.

Barkley, R. A., DuPaul, G. J., & Costello, A. J. (1993). Stimulants. In J. S. Werry & M. G. Aman (Eds.), *Practitioners guide to psychoactive drugs for children and adolescents* (pp. 205–237). New York: Plenum Press.

Barkley, R. A., DuPaul, G. J., & McMurray, M. B. (1990). A comprehensive evaluation of attention deficit disorder with and without hyperactivity as defined by research criteria. *Journal of Consulting and Clinical Psychology, 58,* 775–789.

Barkley, R. A., Fischer, M., Edelbrock, C. S., & Smallish, L. (1990). The adolescent outcome of hyperactive children diagnosed by research criteria: I. An 8-year prospective study. *Journal of the American Academy of Child and Adolescent Psychiatry, 29,* 546–557.

Barkley, R. A., Fischer, M., Newby, R., & Breen, M. (1988). Development of a multimethod clinical protocol for assessing stimulant drug responses in ADHD children. *Journal of Clinical Child Psychology, 17,* 14–24.

Barkley, R. A., Guevremont, D. C., Anastopoulos, A. D., & Fletcher, K. (1992). A comparison of three family therapy programs for treating family conflicts in adolescents with attention-deficit hyperactivity disorder. *Journal of Consulting and Clinical Psychology, 60,* 450–462.

Barkley, R. A., Karlsson, J., & Pollard, S. (1985). Effects of age on the mother-child interactions of hyperactive children. *Journal of Abnormal Child Psychology, 13,* 631–638.

Barkley, R. A., Karlsson, J., Strzelecki, E., & Murphy, J. (1984). Effects of age and Ritalin dosage on the mother-child interactions of hyperactive children. *Journal of Consulting and Clinical Psychology, 52,* 750–758.

Barkley, R. A., McMurray, M. B., Edelbrock, C. S., & Robbins, K. (1990). The side effects of Ritalin in ADHD children: A systematic placebo-controlled evaluation of two doses. *Pediatrics, 86,* 184–192.

Bell, R. Q., & Harper, L. V. (1977). *Child effects on adults.* Hillsdale, NJ: Lawrence Erlbaum. Associates.

Bergan, J. R., & Kratochwill, T. R. (1990). *Behavior consultation and therapy.* New York: Plenum Press.

Biederman, J., Baldessarini, R. J., Wright, V., Knee, D., & Harmatz, J.S. (1989). A double-blind placebo-controlled study of desipramine in the treatment of ADHD: I. Efficacy. *Journal of the American Academy of Child and Adolescent Psychiatry, 28,* 777–784.

Biederman, J., Munir, K., Knee, D., Habelow, W., Armentano, M., Autor, S., Hoge, S. K., & Waternaux, C. (1986). A family study of patients with attention deficit disorder and normal controls. *Journal of Psychiatric Research, 20,* 263–274.

Breen, M. J., & Barkley, R. A. (1988). Child psychopathology and parenting stress in girls and boys having attention deficit disorder with hyperactivity. *Journal of Pediatric Psychology, 13,* 265–280.

Bronowski, J. (1967). Human and animal languages. *To honor Roman Jacobson* (Vol. 1). The Hague, Netherlands: Morton & Co.

Brown, R. T., & Sleator, E. K. (1979). Methylphenidate in hyperkinetic children: Differences in dose effects on impulsive behavior. *Pediatrics, 64,* 408–411.

Campbell, S. B. (1990). *Behavior problems in preschool children: Clinical and developmental issues.* New York: Guilford Press.

Cantwell, D. P., & Baker, L. (1991). Association between attention-deficit hyperactivity disorder and learning disorders. *Journal of Learning Disabilities, 24,* 88–95.

Chess, S. (1960). Diagnosis and treatment of the hyperactive child. *New York State Journal of Medicine, 60,* 2379–2385.

Clements, S. D. (1966). *Task force one: Minimal brain dysfunction in children* (National Institute of Neurological Diseases and Blindness, Monograph No. 3). Washington, DC: U.S. Department of Health, Education, and Welfare.

Conners, C. K. (1980). *Food additives and hyperactive children.* New York: Plenum Press.

Cunningham, C. E., Benness, B. B., & Siegel, L. S. (1988). Family functioning, time allocation, and parental depression in the families of normal and ADDH children. *Journal of Clinical Child Psychology, 17,* 169–177.

Cunningham, C. E., Siegel, L. S., & Offord, D. R. (1985). A developmental dose response analysis of the effects of methylphenidate on the peer interactions of attention deficit disordered boys. *Journal of Child Psychology and Psychiatry, 26,* 955–971.

Douglas, V. I. (1972). Stop, look, and listen: The problem of sustained attention and impulse control in hyperactive and normal children. *Canadian Journal of Behavioural Science, 4,* 259–282.

Douglas, V. I. (1983). Attention and cognitive problems. In M. Rutter (Ed.), *Developmental neuropsychiatry* (pp. 280–329). New York: Guilford Press.

Dunlap, G., dePerczel, M., Clarke, S., Wilson, D., Wright, S., White, R., & Gomez, A. (1994). Choice making to promote adaptive behavior for students with emotional and behavioral challenges. *Journal of Applied Behavior Analysis, 27,* 505–518.

DuPaul, G. , & Eckert, T. L. (1995, August). *School-based interventions for students with ADHD: A meta-analysis.* Poster presented at the annual convention of the American Psychological Association, New York, NY.

DuPaul, G. J., & Henningson, P. N. (1993). Peer tutoring effects on the classroom performance of children with attention deficit hyperactivity disorder. *School Psychology Review, 22,* 134–143.

DuPaul, G. J., Hook, C. L., Ervin, R. A., & Kyle, K. (1995, August). *Effects of ClassWide Peer Tutoring on Students with Attention Deficit Hyperactivity Disorder.* Paper presented at the annual convention of the American Psychological Association, New York, NY.

DuPaul, G. J., & Rapport, M. D. (1993). Does methylphenidate normalize the classroom performance of children with attention deficit disorder? *Journal of the American Academy of Child and Adolescent Psychiatry, 32,* 190–198.

DuPaul, G. J., & Stoner, G. (1994). *ADHD in the schools: Assessment and intervention strategies.* New York: Guilford Press.

Elia, J., & Rapoport, J. L. (1991). Ritalin versus dextroamphetamine in ADHD: Both should be tried. In L. L. Greenhill & B. B. Osman (Eds.), *Ritalin: Theory and patient management* (pp. 69–74). New York: Mary Ann Liebert, Inc.

Ervin, R., DuPaul, G. J., Kern, L., & Friman, P. (in press). A functional assessment of the variables affecting classroom compliance for students with ADHD and ODD: Toward a proactive approach to classroom management. *Journal of Applied Behavior Analysis.*

Feingold, B. (1975). *Why your child is hyperactive.* New York: Random House.

Fiore, T. A., Becker, E. A., & Nero, R. C. (1993). Educational interventions for students with attention deficit disorder. *Exceptional Children, 60,* 163–173.

Firestone, P. (1982). Factors associated with children's adherence to stimulant medication. American Journal of Orthopsychiatry, 52, 447–457.

Forehand, R., & McMahon, R. (1981). *Helping the noncompliant child: A clinician's guide to parent training.* New York: Guilford Press.

Fox, P. T., & Raichle, M. E. (1985). Stimulus rate determines regional blood flow in striate cortex. *Annals of Neurology, 17,* 303–305.

Gittelman, R., & Eskanazi, B. (1983). Lead and hyperactivity revisited. *Archives of General Psychiatry, 42,* 827–833.

Gittelman, R., Mannuzza, S., Shenker, R., & Bonagura, N. (1985). Hyperactive boys almost grown up. *Archives of General Psychiatry, 42,* 937–947.

Goodman, R., & Stevenson, J. (1989). A twin study of hyperactivity: II. The etiological role of genes, family relationships, and perinatal adversity. *Journal of Child Psychology and Psychiatry, 30,* 691–709.

Greenwood, C. R., Delquadri, J., & Carta, J. J. (1988). *Classwide peer tutoring.* Seattle: Educational Achievement Systems.

Greenwood, C. R., Maheady, L., & Carta, J. J. (1991). Peer tutoring programs in the regular education classroom. In G. Stoner, M.R. Shinn, & H.M. Walker (Eds.), *Interventions for achievement and behavior problems* (pp. 179–200). Silver Spring, MD: National Association of School Psychologists.

Hanf, C. (1969). *A two stage program for modifying maternal controlling during mother-child interaction.* Paper presented at the Western Psychological Association meeting, Vancouver, British Columbia.

Hart, E. L., Lahey, B. B., Loeber, R., Applegate, B., & Frick, P. J. (1995). Developmental change in attention-deficit hyperactivity disorder in boys: A four-year longitudinal study. *Journal of Abnormal Child Psychology, 23,* 729–750.

Hartsough, C. S., & Lambert, N. M. (1985). Medical factors in hyperactive and normal children: Prenatal, developmental, and health history findings. American *Journal of Orthopsychiatry, 55,* 190–201.

Hechtman, L., Weiss, G., & Perlman, T. (1984). Young adult outcome of hyperactive children who received long-term stimulant treatment. *Journal of the American Academy of Child Psychiatry, 23,* 261–269.

Hinshaw, S. P. (1992). Academic underachievement, attention deficits, and aggression: Comorbidity and implications for intervention. *Journal of Consulting and Clinical Psychology, 60,* 893–903.

Hinshaw, S. P., Henker, B., & Whalen, C. K. (1984). Self-control in hyperactive boys in anger-inducing situations: Effects of cognitive-behavioral training and of methylphenidate. *Journal of Abnormal Child Psychology, 12,* 55–77.

Hoff, K. E., & DuPaul, G. J. (1996). *Reducing disruptive behavior in general education classrooms: The use of self-management strategies.* Unpublished manuscript, Lehigh University, Bethlehem, PA.

Horn, W. F., Ialongo, N., Popovich, S., & Peradotto, D. (1987). Behavioral parent training and cognitive-behavioral self-control therapy with ADD-H children: Comparative and combined effects. *Journal of Clinical Child Psychology, 16,* 57–68.

Hunt, R. D., Mindera, R. B., & Cohen, D. J. (1985). Clonidine benefits children with attention-deficit disorder and hyperactivity: Report of a double-blind placebo-crossover therapeutic trial. *Journal of the American Academy of Child and Adolescent Psychiatry, 24,* 617–629.

Ingersoll, B., & Goldstein, M. (1993). *Attention deficit disorder and learning disabilities: Realities, myths, and controversial treatments.* New York: Doubleday.

Iwata, B. A., Dorsey, M. F., Slifer, K. J., Bauman, K. E., & Richman, G. S. (1982). Toward a functional analysis of self-injury. *Analysis and Intervention in the Developmental Disabilities, 2,* 3–20.

Kazdin, A. E. (1989). *Behavior modification in applied settings* (4th ed.). Homewood IL: Dorsey Press.

Kelley, M. L. (1990). *School-home notes: Promoting children's classroom success.* New York: Guilford Press.

Kendall, P. C., & Braswell, L. (1985). *Cognitive-behavioral therapy for impulsive children.* New York: Guilford Press.

Kern, L., Childs, K. E., Dunlap, G., Clarke, S., & Falk, G. D. (1994). Using assessment-based curricular intervention to improve the classroom behavior of a student with emotional and behavioral challenges. *Journal of Applied Behavior Analysis, 27,* 7–19.

Kinsbourne, M. (1977). The mechanism of hyperactivity. In M. Blau, I. Rapin, & M. Kinsbourne (Eds.), *Topics in child neurology* (pp. 289–307). New York: Spectrum Publications.

Klorman, R., Coons, H. W., & Borgstedt, A. D. (1987). Effects of methylphenidate on adolescents with a childhood history of attention deficit disorder: I. Clinical findings. *Journal of the American Academy of Child and Adolescent Psychiatry, 26,* 363–367.

Lindsley, O. R. (1991). From technical jargon to plain English for application. *Journal of Applied Behavior Analysis, 24,* 449–458.

McGee, R., & Share, D. L. (1988). Attention deficit disorder-hyperactivity and academic failure: Which comes first and what should be treated? *Journal of the American Academy of Child and Adolescent Psychiatry, 27,* 318–325.

Milich, R., Wolraich, M., & Lindgren, S. (1986). Sugar and hyperactivity: A critical review of empirical findings. *Clinical Psychology Review, 6,* 493–513.

Olympia, D., Jenson, W. R., Clark, E., & Sheridan, S. (1992). Training parents to facilitate homework completion: A model of home-school collaboration. In S.L. Christenson & J.C. Conoley (Eds.), *Home-school collaboration: Building a fundamental educational resource* (pp. 309–331). Silver Spring, MD: National Association of School Psychologists.

O'Neill, R. E., Horner, R. H., Albin, R. W., Storey, K., & Sprague, J. R. (1990). *Functional analysis of problem behavior: A practical assessment guide.* Pacific Grove CA: Brooks Cole.

Paternite, C., & Loney, J. (1980). Childhood hyperkinesis: Relationships between symptomatology and home environment. In C.K. Whalen & B. Henker (Eds.), *Hyperactive children: The social ecology of identification and treatment* (pp. 105–141). New York: Academic Press.

Patterson, G. (1976). The aggressive child: Victim and architect of a coercive system. In E. Mash, L.

Hamerlynk, & L. Handy (Eds.), *Behavior modification and families* (pp. 267–316). New York: Brunner/Mazel.

Pelham, W. E. (1993). Pharmacotherapy of children with attention-deficit hyperactivity disorder. *School Psychology Review, 22,* 199–227.

Pelham, W. E., & Bender, M. E. (1982). Peer relationships in hyperactive children: Description and treatment. In K. Gadow & E. Bialer (Eds.), *Advances in learning and behavioral disabilities* (Vol. 1, pp. 365–436). Greenwich, CT: JAI Press.

Pelham, W. E., Carlson, C., Sams, S. E., Vallano, G., Dixon, M.J., & Hoza, B. (1993). Separate and combined effects of methylphenidate and behavior modification on boys with attention-deficit hyperactivity disorder in the classroom. *Journal of Consulting and Clinical Psychology, 61,* 506–515.

Pelham, W. E., Vodde-Hamilton, M., Murphy, D. A., Greenstein, J. L., & Vallano, G. (1991). The effects of methylphenidate on ADHD adolescents in recreational, peer group, and classroom settings. Journal of *Clinical Child Psychology, 20,* 293–300.

Pomeroy, J. C., Sprafkin, J., & Gadow, K. D. (1988). Minor physical anomalies as a biological marker for behavior disorders. *Journal of the American Academy of Child and Adolescent Psychiatry, 27,* 466–473.

Rapoport, J. (1996, January). *Anatomic magnetic resonance imaging in attention deficit/hyperactivity disordered boys.* Paper presented at the Seventh Scientific Meeting of the International Society for Research in Child and Adolescent Psychopathology, Santa Monica, CA.

Rapport, M. D., DuPaul, G. J., & Kelly, K. L. (1989). Attention-deficit hyperactivity disorder and methylphenidate: The relationship between gross body weight and drug response in children. *Psychopharmacology Bulletin, 25,* 285–290.

Rapport, M. D., Jones, J. T., DuPaul, G. J., Kelly, K. L., Gardner, M.J., Tucker, S.B., & Shea, M.S. (1987). Attention deficit disorder and methylphenidate: Group and single-subject analyses of dose effects on attention in clinic and classroom settings. *Journal of Clinical Child Psychology, 16,* 329–338.

Rapport, M. D., & Kelly, K. L. (1991). Psychostimulant effects on learning and cognitive function: Findings and implications for children with attention-deficit hyperactivity disorder. *Clinical Psychology Review, 11,* 61–92.

Rapport, M. D., Murphy, A., & Bailey, J. S. (1982). Ritalin vs. response cost in the control of hyperactive children: A within subject comparison. *Journal of Applied Behavior Analysis, 15,* 205–216.

Rapport, M. D., Stoner, G., DuPaul, G. J., Kelly, K. L., Tucker, S. B., & Schoeler, T. (1988). Attention deficit disorder and methylphenidate: A multi-level analysis of dose-response effects on children's impulsivity across settings. *Journal of the American Academy of Child and Adolescent Psychiatry, 27*, 60–69.

Rhode, G., Morgan, D. P., & Young, K. R. (1983). Generalization and maintenance of treatment gains of behaviorally handicapped students from resource rooms to regular classrooms using self-evaluation procedures. *Journal of Applied Behavior Analysis, 16*, 171–188.

Richters, J. E., Arnold, L. E., Jensen, P. S., Abikoff, H., Conners, C. K., Greenhill, L. L., Hechtman, L., Hinshaw, S. P., Pelham, W. E., & Swanson, J. M. (1995). NIMH collaborative multisite multimodal treatment study of children with ADHD: I. Background and rationale. *Journal of the American Academy of Child and Adolescent Psychiatry, 34*, 987–1000.

Robin, A. L., & Foster, S. L. (1989). *Negotiating parent-adolescent conflict: A behavioral-family systems approach.* New York: Guilford Press.

Rosen, L. A., Booth, S. R., Bender, M. E., McGrath, M. L., Sorrell, S., & Drabman, R. S. (1988). Effects of sugar (sucrose) on children's behavior. *Journal of Consulting and Clinical Psychology, 56*, 583–589.

Ross, D. M., & Ross, S. A. (1982). *Hyperactivity: Current issues, research, and theory* (2nd ed.). New York: John Wiley & Sons.

Rutter, M. (1977). Brain damage syndromes in childhood: Concepts and findings. *Journal of Child Psychology and Psychiatry, 18*, 1–21.

Rutter, M., Chadwick, O., & Schaffer, D. (1983). Head injury. In M. Rutter (Ed.), *Developmental neuropsychiatry* (pp. 83–111). New York: Guilford Press.

Satterfield, J. H., Hoppe, C. M., & Schell, A. M. (1982). A prospective study of delinquency in 110 adolescent boys with attention deficit disorder and 88 normal adolescent boys. *American Journal of Psychiatry, 139*, 795–798.

Satterfield, J. H., Satterfield, B. T., & Schell, A. M. (1987). Therapeutic interventions to prevent delinquency in hyperactive boys. *Journal of the American Academy of Child and Adolescent Psychiatry, 26*, 56–64.

Semrud-Clikeman, M., Biederman, J., Sprich-Buckminster, S., Lehman, B. K., Faraone, S. V., & Norman, D. (1992). Comorbidity between ADDH and learning disability: A review and report in a clinically referred sample. *Journal of the American Academy of Child and Adolescent Psychiatry, 31*, 439–448.

Shaywitz, S. E., Shaywitz, B. A., Cohen, D. J., & Young, J. G. (1983). Monoaminergic mechanisms in hyperactivity. In M. Rutter (Ed.), *Developmental Neuropsychiatry* (pp. 330–347). New York: Guilford Press.

Sheridan, S. M. (1993). Models for working with parents. In J. E. Zins, T. R. Kratochwill, & S. N. Elliott (Eds.), *Handbook of consultation services for children: Applications in educational and clinical settings* (pp. 110–136). San Francisco: Jossey-Bass.

Smith, L. (1976). *Your child's behavior chemistry.* New York: Random House.

Still, G. F. (1902). Some abnormal psychical conditions in children. *Lancet, I*, 1008–1012, 1077–1082, 1163–1168.

Stokes, T. F., & Baer, D. M. (1977). An implicit technology of generalization. *Journal of Applied Behavior Analysis, 10*, 349–367.

Stokes, T. F., & Osnes, P. G. (1989). An operant pursuit of generalization. *Behavior Therapy, 20*, 337–355.

Strauss, A. A., & Lehtinen, L. E. (1947). *Psychopathology and education of the brain-injured child.* New York: Grune & Stratton.

Sullivan, M. A., & O'Leary, S. G. (1990). Maintenance following reward and cost token programs. *Behavior Therapy, 21*, 139–151.

Swanson, J. M., Cantwell, D., Lerner, M., McBurnett, K., & Hanna, G. (1991). Effects of stimulant medication on learning in children with ADHD. *Journal of Learning Disabilities, 24*, 219–230.

Tallmadge, J., & Barkley, R. A. (1983). The interactions of hyperactive and normal boys with their mothers and fathers. *Journal of Abnormal Child Psychology, 11*, 565–579.

Umbreit, J. (1995). Functional assessment and intervention in a regular classroom setting for the disruptive behavior of a student with attention deficit hyperactivity disorder. *Behavioral Disorders, 20*, 267–278.

Vyse, S. A., & Rapport, M. D. (1989). The effects of methylphenidate on learning in children with ADDH: The stimulus equivalence paradigm. *Journal of Consulting and Clinical Psychology, 57*, 425–435.

Weiss, G., & Hechtman, L. (1993). *Hyperactive children grown up: ADHD in children, adolescents, and adults* (2nd ed.). New York: Guilford Press.

Weiss, G., Hechtman, L., Milroy, T., & Perlman, T. (1985). Psychiatric status of hyperactives as adults: A controlled prospective 15-year follow-up of 63 hyperactive children. *Journal of the American Academy of Child Psychiatry, 24*, 211–220.

Wender, P. H. (1971). *Minimal brain dysfunction in children.* New York: John Wiley & Sons.

Werry, J. S. (1968). Developmental hyperactivity. *Pediatric Clinics of North America, 19,* 9–16.

Werry, J. S., & Conners, C. K. (1979). Pharmacotherapy. In H. Quay & J. Werry (Eds.), *Psychopathological disorders of childhood* (2nd ed., pp. 336–386). New York: John Wiley & Sons.

Werry, J. S., & Sprague, R. L. (1970). Hyperactivity. In C.G. Costello (Ed.), *Symptoms of psychopathology* (pp. 397–417). New York: John Wiley & Sons.

Willis, T. J., & Lovaas, I. (1977). A behavioral approach to treating hyperactive children: The parent's role. In J.B. Millichap (Ed.), *Learning disabilities and related disorders* (pp. 119–140). Chicago: Yearbook Medical Publications.

Zametkin, A. J., Nordahl, T. E., Grass, M., King, A. C., Semple, W., Rumsey, J., Hamburger, M. S., & Cohen, R. M. (1990). Cerebral glucose metabolism in adults with hyperactivity of childhood onset. *The New England Journal of Medicine, 323,* 1361–1366.

CHAPTER 6

ACADEMIC PROBLEMS

John Wills Lloyd
Daniel P. Hallahan
James M. Kauffman
Clayton E. Keller

Academic problems are among the most frequent reasons that students are referred for special education (Anderson, Cronin, & Miller, 1986; Hutton, 1985; Lloyd, Kauffman, Landrum, & Roe, 1989). They characterize not only students with limited intellectual ability, but also other prevalent groups receiving special education—students identified as having learning disabilities and emotional or behavior disorders (Kauffman, 1997; Hallahan, Kauffman, & Lloyd, 1996). When one includes pupils receiving special services under Chapter 1 funding, as well as the many "slow learners" who fall between the officially sanctioned categories of learning disabilities and mental retardation, then the number of students with academic problems is indeed staggering.

Although the majority of referrals for special education evaluations identify problems in reading or written expression (Lloyd et al., 1989), problems also occur in mathematics. Lewis, Hitch, and Walker (1994) found that about 20% of the students with academic problems in their sample had difficulty with arithmetic alone and over 50% of those with problems had difficulties in both reading and arithmetic. In their study of students with learning disabilities, Norman and Zigmond (1980) reported that average mathematics achievement was 75% of what would be expected on the basis of the students' IQs.

In keeping with the enormous number of pupils with academic problems and the wide range of difficulties these youngsters exhibit, there has been considerable research directed at determining effective interventions for such students. Theories about how to address these problems most beneficially have abounded (see Hallahan et al., 1996). In this chapter we examine interventions that are based on several major models. In the immediately following section we describe four models: cognitive theory, instructional theory, cognitive-behavioral theory, and constructivist theory. In the next major section we address four areas in which pupils commonly experience difficulties in the academic learning situation—attention to task, reading, written expression, and arithmetic—and describe interventions for each based on the models. In the third and last major section, we discuss the integration of three of these models and their evidentiary bases into a comprehensive approach to treatment and prevention of learning problems.

MODELS

Earlier examinations of learning problems have described medical, process, and behavioral conceptual models as the basis for intervention (e.g., Bateman, 1967; Ysseldyke & Salvia, 1974). However, for at least four reasons, these classifications of models are no longer appropriate. First, the present review of school-based interventions reveals no need to adapt instruction based on biological status beyond such response requirements as are dictated by disabilities such as cerebral palsy or sensory deficits such as visual impairment (but, see Stevenson, 1992). Second, process training has been largely discredited as an approach to intervention in academic learning problems (e.g., Gersten & Carnine, 1984a; Hammill & Larsen, 1974; but, see Kavale, 1981). Third, newer findings have established much more sophisticated behavioral influences on learning problems than evidenced in earlier reviews. Fourth, more recent interventions, such as those described by Williams (1990), Pflaum and Pascarella (1980), or Bryant, Drabin, & Gettinger (1981), clearly do not fit into medical, process, or behavioral categories.

We have organized our discussion of conceptual models around cognitive, instructional, cognitive-behavioral, and constructivist theories because these categories seem to be a reasonable framework for brief exposition of the current state of affairs, not because the models themselves have clearly different origins or because distinctions among educational interventions based on these models are always clear and explicit. Descriptions of conceptual models require arbitrary decisions about how various theories and the interventions derived from them should be separated and grouped. The theoretical roots and emphases of various models overlap; the models are distinguished primarily by their *relative degree* of emphasis on such factors as how the student thinks about problems, the effects of setting events and consequences on academic performance, the student's sense of self-efficacy, or the nature of the task presented to the student. In practice, the differences blur, as we develop in the last section of this chapter. For each of the four models we discuss we shall briefly describe the theoretical roots of the basic concepts and the relative emphases in intervention strategies.

Cognitive Model

Cognitive approaches share an emphasis on the processes involved in human thinking, giving thought processes a role of greater importance than any of the other models. Advocates of cognitive approaches differ about what processes are considered important. Some emphasize the importance of metacognition (thinking about thinking), but others emphasize information processing factors such as memory or rehearsal.

The distinctions between this and the other models reveal the arbitrary nature of such divisions. The constructivist, cognitive-behavioral, and instructional models share the cognitive model's consideration of thinking. Although the cognitive model emphasizes thinking as the impetus for behavior, the cognitive-behavioral model reflects a greater interaction between overt behavior and covert thought processes. Similarly, although the cognitive model stresses traditional processes of thinking (e.g., memory), the instructional model stresses the formation of rules based on similarities and differences in the environment that are demonstrated during instructional presentations. The most distinctive feature of the cognitive model is its focus on mental operations and their primacy in determining overt behavior. Proponents of the cognitive model tend to downplay the importance of the acquisition of specific academic skills, preferring to focus on mentation leading to generalized competence in problem solving.

Theoretical Roots

Advocates of cognitive approaches base their ideas primarily on the work of cognitive psychologists, most notably Piaget and his interpreters (e.g., Inhelder, Sinclair, & Bovet, 1974; Piaget & Inhelder, 1969a, 1969b). Many other cognitive psychologists, particularly Flavell (Flavell, 1977) and Bruner, Goodnow, and Austin (1956) made significant contributions to the theoretical underpinnings of cognitive interventions. These roots are shared with the constructivist model.

The most important basic premise underlying cognitive approaches is that successful learners *actively* construct meaning from their prior experience *and* their thinking about new information. They use "executive" or "metacognitive" processes—reflective consideration of their own approaches to solving problems—to determine how new information is sought, perceived, related to stored information, stored, selected, and recalled. What distinguishes a skilled learner from an unskilled one is the inability of the unskilled learner to use executive processes effectively and efficiently. Unlike the skilled learner, the novice does not actively think about learning—metacognitive processes are not brought into play to guide perception, memory, and problem solving. The learner who has academic difficulties is "described as an inefficient learner—one who either lacks certain strategies or chooses inappropriate strategies and/or generally fails to engage in self-monitoring behavior" (Swanson, 1990, p. 35). Thus, basic research on the cognitive development of children and on the thought processes of successful and unsuccessful problem solvers provides the theoretical backdrop for cognitive interventions.

Emphases in Assessment and Intervention

Assessment of learner performance should be based on intensive observation and interview. Baroody and Ginsberg (1991) recommended that to be effective, assessment should include examination of formal and informal knowledge, examine strengths and weaknesses, evaluate skill accuracy and efficiency—that is, it should incorporate most usual features of assessment. However, they also emphasized examination of concepts, problem-solving skills, solution strategies, metacognitive beliefs, and affective factors—concerns that go beyond usual features. Often advocates of cognitive approaches recommend interview techniques that reveal close ties between assessment and intervention; for example, an assessor might use a stimulated recall technique in which the assessor has a student review actual academic work she has done and asks the student why she decided to perform the task in the way she did.

Cognitive interventions emphasize engaging students in activities that are meaningful, that are appropriately related to their prior learning, and that encourage them to acquire strategies for approaching and solving tasks. In an exemplary cognitive intervention, "reciprocal teaching," teacher and student engage in dialogue intended to result in the student's construction of the meaning of text or algorithms (e.g., Palinscar, 1986; Palinscar & Brown, 1984). The hallmarks of cognitive interventions are an emphasis on (a) the meaning of learning for the student, (b) relating instructional activities to prior experiences of the student, (c) active involvement of the student in learning and planning for learning, and (d) long-term as opposed to short-term memory.

Cognitive interventions organize material to be learned according to assumptions about hierarchical relationships among its constituent parts. If children normally develop some skills before other skills, advocates of a cognitive approach to academic learning would surely stress teaching activities of the earlier skills before the later skills. A good example in the area of reading would be the acquisition of phonemic awareness prior to basic decoding skills, which in turn, are requisite for reading comprehension (Adams, 1990).

Cognitive interventions share the emphasis of cognitive-behavioral approaches on metacognitive processes and the active engagement of the learner. Unlike cognitive-behavioral approaches, however, cognitive interventions de-emphasize detailed, direct measurement of student progress in acquiring the component skills of competent performance. For example, one would be less concerned with the rate at which students read stories or whether they could answer questions about the material and more concerned about whether the pupils' retelling of the story reflected an overall understanding of it.

Instructional Model

An instructional model draws heavily on behavior modification, which has had a major effect on interventions for academic problems. Early studies (e.g., Zimmerman & Zimmerman, 1962; Haring & Hauck, 1969) revealed that behavioral principles could be applied to learning problems outside the laboratory setting. More recently, researchers influenced by behavioral principles have conducted studies in each of the academic areas. Reviews by Lahey (1976), Rose, Koorland, and Epstein (1982), and Witt, Elliott, and Gresham (1988) describe this work. Components of a behavioral approach to human problems—particularly direct observation and measurement—that are essential to an instructional model are shared with the cognitive-behavioral model. In contrast, an instructional model does not assign attribution as much importance as does the cognitive-behavioral model.

Theoretical Roots

In part, an instructional model rests on the theory that behavior is a function of its consequences. Thus, an instructional model draws on the laboratory and applied work of behavioral psychologists, most notably the work of Skinner (e.g., Skinner, 1953, 1968). Applications of behavioral theory to academic learning grew rapidly with the contributions of other psychologists and educators such as Bijou (Bijou, 1970) and Haring (Haring, 1968; Haring, Lovitt, Eaton, & Hansen, 1978).

Although the instructional model draws from behavioral theory, contemporary versions do not completely eschew cognitive constructs. For example, Engelmann and Carnine (1982), perhaps the foremost advocates of an instructional perspective, make clear references to mental events such as

learners forming rules based on examples of concepts that teachers present. Indeed, they refer to Direct Instruction as a cognitive approach.

Direct Instruction is most closely associated with the work of Becker (e.g., Becker, Engelmann, & Thomas, 1975), Bereiter (e.g., Bereiter & Engelmann, 1966), Carnine (e.g., Carnine & Silbert, 1979), and Engelmann (e.g., Engelmann, 1969; Engelmann & Carnine, 1982). Observation of DI lessons would immediately reveal that the model owes a great deal to behavioral principles. Lessons are highly structured and rich with praise and rewards (e.g., points). Nevertheless, a closer examination of the content and structure of lessons reveals a debt to other literatures that are not directly in the behavioral tradition. For instance, one of the central features of the commercially available instructional programs authored by Engelmann and his colleagues is the extensive use of examples and not-examples and sequencing of them, as developed in the concept learning literature.

Although behavioral theory underscores the importance of consequences in shaping and maintaining behavior, instructional models expand on this emphasis. A behavioral analysis of learning difficulties looks first at the events that follow academic performance or approximations of academic responses; for example, a behavioral analysis of reading might examine the teacher's behavior after pupils have correctly answered a question (e.g., the frequency with which the teacher praises correct answers). An instructional analysis would look not only at the consequences of the behavior, but also at the instructions that preceded the behavior of concern (Engelmann, Granzin, & Severson, 1979); the analysis would assess whether the instruction could logically lead to a response other than the one the teacher expected.

Direct Instruction methods, which are perhaps the most widely known examples of an instructional model, have generated much research in academic learning. Although, the generic term "direct instruction" (e.g., Rosenshine & Stevens, 1986) gained currency in the late 1970s and early 1980s, Direct Instruction (DI) as used here differs from it in some specific ways. In both the Direct Instruction and the generic direct instruction approach, there is emphasis on specific control of typical behavioral variables (particularly in the form of correction, reinforcement, and provision of practice opportunities), but in the Direct Instruction model relatively greater emphasis is placed on the logical analysis of instructional communications (Engelmann & Carnine, 1982). Direct Instruction researchers have conducted many studies of these instructional programming principles, both with normally achieving students (e.g., Carnine, 1980) and handicapped learners (e.g., Gersten, White, Falco, & Carnine, 1982). A meta-analytic review of research with students with disabilities taught using DI revealed an average effect size of 0.81 for academic measures (White, 1988).

Emphases in Assessment and Intervention

Direct measurement of behavior—a hallmark of instructional approaches—involves frequent observation and recording of the target skills(s) for which instruction is offered. Words read correctly, words written correctly, or problems solved correctly per minute, for examples, might be target academic behaviors. The most immediately applicable version of this approach to assessment is often referred to as curriculum-based assessment (Deno & Fuchs, 1987; Fuchs & Deno, 1994; Howell, Fox, & Morehead, 1993).

Direct assessment of performance based on curricular materials often is coupled with analytic strategies for determining causal relations between instruction and behavior changes. The analysis of behavior and its controlling variables requires that the behavior be observed and recorded under conditions that are systematically altered, such that changes in the rate of behavior can be unambiguously attributed to specified, observable environmental events. Thus, for example, one would be expressly concerned with whether a reinforcement program caused improvement in the rate at which students complete arithmetic problems. Often, in fact, single-subject research methods (Kratochwill & Levin, 1992; Lloyd, Tankersley, & Talbott, 1994) are recommended for evaluating the utility of interventions.

Instructional models emphasize control of the details of the instructional interaction between teachers and students. For example, Direct Instruction lessons are presented by teachers according to carefully field-tested scripts. In a typical lesson, the teacher works with small groups of students, frequently asking questions that have specific answers. The students answer chorally and, based on the accuracy of the answer, the teacher provides praise or corrective feedback. Figure 6.1 shows one of a series of scripts for teaching students the structure and use of analogies.

The logical analysis of instruction proposed by Engelmann and Carnine (1982) is designed to admit to one and only one interpretation of a task. A central tenet of this approach is that if the instructional presentation admits to more than one interpretation, some students will learn the wrong interpretation and thus, will fail to learn the skill or concept being taught. Pupils with atypical learning characteristics are more likely than normals to adopt the "misrules" that faulty instruction provides. Engelmann and Carnine call instruction that prevents mislearning "faultless instruction."

Cognitive-Behavioral Model

The cognitive-behavioral model in education is an outgrowth of a larger movement in psychology, which retained the empirical base of a behavioral approach but accepted as useful or essential certain features of radical behaviorism's nemesis, mentalism (thoughts and affective states as causal variables). Advocates of an integrated cognitive and behavioral approach, often called cognitive-behavior modification (CBM), stress the role of metacognition (see previous discussion). Not only do cognitive-behaviorists contend that people's thoughts influence how they behave, but also they place additional emphasis on specific kinds of thoughts such as a sense of personal effectiveness, student involvement in instruction, and so forth.

For the most part, CBM interventions are designed to increase self-awareness and self-control and, therefore, to improve academic behavior. They often emphasize self-regulated learning; in this way, they share a concept that is central to cognitive approaches. Harris, Graham, and Pressley (1991), Gerber (1987), Kendall and Cummings (1988),

THINKING OPERATIONS

• Exercise 1   Analogies
  Task A
  The first Thinking Operation today is Analogies.
  1. **We're going to make up an analogy that tells how animals move. What is the analogy going to tell?**
     Signal. *How animals move.*
     Repeat until firm.
  2. **The animals we're going to use in the analogy are a hawk and a whale. Which animals?**
     Signal. *A hawk and a whale.*
  3. **Name the first animal.** Signal. *A hawk.*
     Yes, a hawk. How does that animal move?
     Signal. *It flies.* **Yes, it flies.**
  4. **So, here's the first part of the analogy.**
     A hawk is to flying.
     What's the first part of the analogy?
     Signal. *A hawk is to flying.*
     Yes, a hawk is to flying. Repeat until firm.
  5. **The first part of the analogy told how an animal moves. So, the next part of the analogy must tell how another animal moves.**
  6. **You told how a hawk moves. Now you're going to tell about a whale. What animal?** Signal.
     A whale. **How does that animal move?**
     Signal. It swims.
     Yes, it swims.
  7. **So, here's the second part of the analogy. A whale is to swimming. What's the second part of the analogy?** Signal.
     A whale is to swimming.
     Yes, a whale is to swimming.
  8. Repeat steps 2–7 until firm.
  9. **Now we're going to say the whole analogy. First, we're going to tell how a hawk moves and then we're going to tell how a whale moves. Say the analogy with me.** Signal.
     Respond with the students.
     A hawk is to flying as a whale is to swimming.
     Repeat until the students are responding with you.
  10. **All by yourselves. Say that analogy.** Signal.
      A hawk is to flying as a whale is to swimming.
      Repeat until firm.
  11. **That analogy tells how those animals move. What does that analogy tell?** Signal.
      How those animals move.
  12. Repeat steps 10 and 11 until firm.

  Individual test
  Call on individual students to do step 10 or 11.

• Exercise 12   Analogies opposites
  Now we're going to do some more analogies.
  1. **Here's an analogy about words.**
     Old is to young as asleep is to…
     Pause 2 seconds. **Get ready.**
     Signal. *Awake.*
     Everybody, say the analogy. Signal.
     Old is to young as asleep is to awake.
     Repeat until firm.
  2. **What are old and asleep?** Signal. *Words.*
     To correct students who say *Opposites:*
     a. **Old and asleep are words.**
     b. Repeat step 2.
     Old is to young as asleep is to awake. That analogy tells something about those words. Pause. **What does that analogy tell about those words?**
     Signal. *What opposites those words have.*
     Repeat until firm.
  3. **Say the analogy.** Signal.
     Old is to young as asleep is to awake.
     Repeat until firm.
  4. **And what does that analogy tell about those words?**
     Signal.
     What opposites those words have.
  5. Repeat steps 3 and 4 until firm.

• Exercise 13   Analogies
  Note: Praise all reasonable responses in this exercise, but have the group repeat the responses specified in the exercise.
  1. **Everybody, what class are a towel and a plate in?**
     Signal. *Objects.*
  2. **Finish this analogy.**
     A towel is to rectangular as a plate is to…
     Pause 2 seconds. **Get ready.** Signal. *Round.*
  3. **Everybody, say that analogy.** Signal.
     A towel is to rectangular as a plate is to round.
     Repeat until firm.
  4. **The analogy tells something about those objects.**
     Pause. **What does that analogy tell about those objects?** Signal.
     What shapes those objects are.
  5. Repeat steps 3 and 4 until firm.
  6. **A towel is to cloth as a plate is to…** Pause 2 seconds.
     Get ready.
     Signal. *Plastic.*
  7. **Everybody, say that analogy.** Signal.
     A towel is to cloth as a plate is to plastic.
     Repeat until firm.
  8. **The analogy tells something about those objects.**
     Pause. **What does that analogy tell about those objects?** Signal.
     What material those objects are made of.
  9. Repeat steps 7 and 8 until firm.

Figure 6.1 Sample teaching scripts from a Direct Instruction program. Note that the scripts come from two different lessons, the second of which would normally be taught about a month after the first. From the careful selection of multiple examples and systematic reduction of teacher assistance, pupils learn great facility with language skills such as understanding and using analogies. From *Thinking basics: Corrective reading comprehension A.* (pp. 121, 251) by S. Engelmann, P. Haddox, S. Hanner, and J. Osborn, 1978. Chicago: Science Research Associates. Copyright 1978 by Science Research Associates. Reprinted by permission of publisher.

Kneedler and Meese (1988), Loper and Murphy (1985), and Wong (1985a) have provided reviews of the literature in this area.

Theoretical Roots

The theory underlying cognitive-behavioral approaches is derived in part from principles of social learning, which melds cognitive and behavioral concepts. Principal among those whose ideas gave rise to cognitive-behavioral strategies are Bandura (e.g., Bandura, 1977, 1986), Mahoney (e.g., Mahoney, 1974), Meichenbaum (e.g., Meichenbaum, 1977), and Mischel (e.g., Mischel, 1973). In contrast to a strictly cognitive approach, cognitive-behavioral theory recognizes the considerable influence of contingencies of reinforcement on learning; in contrast to radical behaviorism, it views the self—including one's mental activities and affective states—as actively involved in determining behavior. A key concept in cognitive-behavioral theory is reciprocal determinism, the notion that behavior, environmental events, and internal variables (i.e., "self" or "person" variables such as thoughts and feelings) mutually affect one another. Thus management of external events, such as the consequences of behavior, is a legitimate intervention strategy. Likewise, a strategy designed to alter cognitive processing of information is legitimate. Indeed, cognitive-behavioral theory posits that the most effective strategies will combine behavioral and cognitive methods for overcoming learning and behavioral problems.

Emphases in Assessment and Intervention

Like the cognitive approach, cognitive-behavioral assessment emphasizes gaining access to learners' thoughts and feelings, but the emphasis is not limited to only those aspects. Assessment would also seek to develop an understanding of how the students approach tasks, particularly the strategies they use in solving problems and making decisions. Techniques would not only include interviewing students closely, but also having them think aloud as they perform tasks, recall their thinking while

reviewing their work, completing rating scales about their thoughts and feelings, and so forth (Keller, 1991).

Interventions emphasize actively involving the student in learning, particularly in learning to monitor and direct his or her own thought processes. This emphasis is combined, however, with concern for measuring directly the behavioral outcomes of intervention and for teaching the component skills involved in academic performance. Thus, a student might be taught word-attack skills in beginning reading, but these skills would likely be taught along with cognitive strategies for applying them. These and similar topics are discussed in greater detail by Braswell and Kendall (1988), Keogh and Hall (1984), and Whitman, Burgio, and Johnston (1984).

Considerable emphasis is placed in cognitive-behavioral interventions on self-control. Self-monitoring, self-assessment, self-recording, self-management of reinforcement, and so on are commonly used strategies. These are often effective, however, only if students are helped to become aware of their own thinking about their behavior and the strategies they are using (or not using) to approach problems. Thus metacognitive strategy training is often a critical part of these interventions. Self-control interventions are also dependent on prior learning of skills by a particular self-procedure. For example, for pupils to use a self-instructional strategy to guide their completion of a long-division task, they must learn not only the steps in the self-guiding strategy but also the steps in completing long division problems.

Constructivist Model

As a relatively more recent addition to the models of academic problems and, particularly, learning disabilities, constructivism has been presented largely as a reaction against other models. To be sure, there are many variations on constructivism (see Harris & Graham, 1994), but the strongest arguments in its favor have been an explicit rejection of those models we have described here as instructional and cognitive-behavioral. According to constructivist views, these models depend too much on isolating and teaching specific component skills. In contrast to these views of how students acquire academic competence, constructivist models contend that children must create their own understanding of such things as reading, social studies, and peer relations. For example, in one of the most impassioned pleas for a constructivist view, Poplin argued that

> constructivist theory, and holistic beliefs define the learning enterprise in opposition to reductionistic behavioral learning theory and suggest that the task of school is to help students develop new meanings in response to new experiences rather than to learn the meanings that others have created. (1988a, p. 401)

Theoretical Roots

In consort with its closest ally, the cognitive model, the constructivist model places great emphasis on thinking. In contrast to that model, though, the emphasis is less on components of thinking (e.g., memory) and more on processes and change in development (see Reid, 1991). These views clearly owe a lot to the later work of Piaget and Inhelder (1969b). The perspective has been advanced most strongly by Heshusius (1989, 1994), Iano (1986), Poplin (1988a,1988b), and Reid (1991). It is important to note that the perspective advanced by many advocates of constructivism is tied with political views about feminism, structuralism, and related perspectives; that is, constructivism is not simply a view of education, but a perspective that integrates education, political, and sociological concerns (Poplin, 1988a).

Emphases in Assessment and Intervention

Advocates of constructivism would stress many of the same assessment procedures recommended by advocates of cognitive and cognitive-behavioral models. In keeping with its loosely structured roots, the constructivist model recommends assessment that depends on "more reactive, free-wheeling responses to students' knowledge, perceptions, and behaviors" (Meltzer & Reid, 1994, p. 340) but does not completely reject some systematic assessment. Important emphases include considerations of the strategies stu-

dents use to solve problems and an insistence on a close relationship between assessment and instruction (Meltzer & Reid, 1994; Reid, 1991).

Along with each of the other models, constructivism considers strategies central to learning. As they base their views on the notion that students will learn best when they develop their own understanding of concepts and procedures, advocates of the constructivist approach de-emphasize explicit instruction in components of strategies, however. Instead, they argue that "effective instruction provides activities (in the broadest sense) to facilitate the *learner's ability to construct meaning* from experience" (Reid & Hresko, 1981, p. 49, emphasis in original). That is, the constructivist model is essentially one in which learners discover conceptual relationships or develop out of necessity means for resolving problems. Instruction creates a situation in which students are confronted with examples of concepts or with situations that require a solution and, by repeatedly working toward understanding or resolving them, the students gradually acquire a rich and deep set of strategies.

In part because of the loosely structured nature of such interventions and in part because of constructivism's dismissal of conventional research methods, there has been little empirical research on the effectiveness of these methods. Thus, it is difficult to provide detailed examples of effective practices that emanate from the constructivist view. Therefore, as we now turn to examining research-validated practices for handling specific academic problems, we shall focus our treatment on the models for which there is empirical evidence of effectiveness.

PROBLEM AREAS

According to some views of learning problems, these difficulties are reflections of more fundamental problems in other areas such as memory or the processing of stimuli, but the nature and extent of the relationship between such underlying capabilities and achievement problems is regularly a source of disagreement (for a more extensive treatment of these issues see Hallahan et al., 1996). At the very least, however, these difficulties are clearly manifested in performance deficits in the basic academic areas (reading, writing, and arithmetic) and related school areas (attention). We focus the remainder of this chapter on these problem areas. Thus, the following material is arranged according to problem area (attention to task, reading, handwriting, composition, and arithmetic) with a separate discussion of how each of the previously discussed models approaches each problem.

Attention to Task

One need only spend a few minutes in a teachers' lounge before hearing about problems in attention to task. Difficulties in securing pupils' attention to teacher presentations or individual assignments are regularly described in educational literature (e.g., Hallahan et al., 1996). Behaviorally, the problem is primarily one of what the pupil looks at during instruction. Looking at assigned work or the teacher is considered attending to task, while staring out the window, playing with objects during a lesson, and so forth are considered non-attending. Many are also concerned with whether the pupil is actually thinking about the assigned work or the teacher's presentation, but this aspect of the problem has not yet been successfully measured. Table 6.1 shows some interventions that have been used with attention problems. In the following subsections we discuss the evidence about interventions associated with the behavioral, cognitive-behavioral, and Direct Instruction models.

Instructional Model

There have been many demonstrations of reinforcement-based interventions for deficits in attention to task or study behavior. Indeed, the first article in the *Journal of Applied Behavior Analysis* described the beneficial effects of contingent praise on study behavior (Hall, Lund, & Jackson, 1968). Since that time there have been myriad similar studies demonstrating similar effects. However, one of the difficulties with simple reinforcement methods has been that manipulation of attending behavior has not uniformly lead to concomitant improvements in pupils'

academic performance. Ferritor, Buckholdt, Hamblin, and Smith (1972) reported that contingent reinforcement of attending behavior did not consistently affect the amount of work pupils accomplished, but contingent reinforcement of completing work affected levels of attending behavior.

Other variables influence attending, too, some of which Dunlap and his colleagues (Dunlap et al., 1993) have examined using functional analysis. For example, Dunlap et al. (1994) examined the effects of having students select from a list of options the academic activities in which they were to engage during independent work periods. Task engagement was clearly higher under the choice condition than it was when assignments were selected by teachers.

Another mediating factor is the pace of instruction. According to the Direct Instruction view, one of the requirements of teaching is to make the instruction so engaging that pupils attend at a very high level. To accomplish this, teachers should keep lessons moving at a lively pace. Carnine (1976) illustrated the effectiveness of this approach by manipulating the rate of teacher questions and recording the percentage of time pupils were attending to the teacher and the probability of correct answering. He found that at higher rates of teacher questions directed toward the entire group of pupils (approximately 12 questions per minute) students both attended better and were more likely to answer correctly than at lower rates of teacher questioning (approximately 6 questions per minute). The latter rate of questioning is still far more rapid than the rate of questioning in many classrooms where pupils may only be called on to answer one or two questions in an entire lesson. Of course, frequency of questioning must vary depending on the content of teacher presentations.

Cognitive-Behavioral Model

Self-recording is an example of a cognitive-behavioral intervention for deficits in attention to task. Self-recording of attending behavior has been extensively studied with atypical learners. Because theoretical opinions (see Hughes & Lloyd, 1993; Nelson & Hayes, 1981) differ about whether self-record-

TABLE 6.1. Selected Studies Illustrating Techniques for Treating Attention Problems

CITATION	INDEPENDENT VARIABLE
Bailey, Wolf, & Phillips, 1970	Home-based reinforcement
Carnine, 1976	Pacing of teacher questioning
Ferritor, Buckholt, Hamblin, & Smith, 1972	Token reinforcement of attending versus completing work
Hall, Lund, & Jackson, 1968	Teacher praise
Hallahan, Lloyd, Kneedler, & Marshall, 1982	Self-versus teacher-assessed self-recording
Hallahan, Lloyd, Kosiewicz, Kauffman, & Graves, 1979	Self-recording
Harris, 1986	Self-recording of attention versus productivity
Lloyd, Bateman, Landrum, & Hallahan, 1989	Self-recording of attention versus productivity
McLaughlin, 1984	Self-recording with and without consequences
Packard, 1970	Group contingency
Walker & Buckley, 1968	Token reinforcement

ing's beneficial effects are the result of its behavioral components (i.e., it makes environmental cues more salient) or its cognitive components (i.e., it makes the individual more aware of his or her behavior), it is difficult to achieve consensus about whether it is a behavioral or a cognitive intervention. We treat it as a cognitive-behavioral technique here because it seems to straddle the two camps.

In studies of self-recording of attention to task, teachers have provided their pupils with intermittent cues (via a preprogrammed audio-tape recording) that prompted the students to ask themselves whether they were paying attention to their assigned tasks. Students learned to record their answers to the question (either "yes" or "no") and then return to work. Box 6.1 illustrates (a) how a teacher might introduce self-recording of attention to a pupil and (b) how the pupil might implement it on subsequent days.

Overall, the results of these studies have indicated that the introduction of self-recording causes substantial and consistent improvements in attention to task as recorded by independent observers. Moreover, the studies have revealed (a) that the children benefit from having the cues and being required to perform the recording act during the period when they are learning to record their attention-to-task behavior, (b) that children can be weaned from reliance on the tape-recorded cues and the recording, (c) that these improvements often are accompanied by improvements in the rate of correct answering on assigned tasks, and (d) that self-recording has greater effects than a similar procedure in which the teacher makes the assessment and directs the pupil to record (Lloyd & Landrum, 1991). Research comparing self-recording of attention to task and self-recording of academic productivity has shown that both procedures have substantial effects on measures of both behaviors, that for most students neither procedure is consistently more effective than the other, and that pupils' preference for one or the other procedure is probably influenced by the ease with which they may be used.

Reading

Of the academic performance areas, reading is regularly judged to be of primary importance. In fact, reading problems occur in 6.2% to 7.5% of the elementary school population (Lewis et al., 1994; Shaywitz, Shaywitz, Fletcher, & Escobar, 1990), are the most common problem of students with learning disabilities (Norman & Zigmond, 1980), and are the focus of teachers' greatest efforts (Kirk & Elkins, 1975). Problems in reading range from difficulties with converting print into spoken equivalents to difficulties organizing the content of material being read. In this section we describe contributions from each of the models to the improvement of reading performance (see Table 6.2).

BOX 6.1   CASE STUDY: TRAINING AND IMPLEMENTATION OF A SELF-MONITORING PROGRAM

SCRIPT FOR TEACHER INTRODUCTION OF SELF-MONITORING

"Edwin, you know how paying attention to your work has been a problem for you. You've heard teachers tell you, 'Pay attention,' "Get to work,' 'What are you supposed to be doing?' and things like that. Well today we're going to start something that will help you help yourself pay attention better. First we need to make sure that you know what paying attention means. This is what I mean by paying attention." (Teacher models immediate and sustained attention to task.) "And this is what I mean by not paying attention." (Teacher models inattentive behaviors such as glancing around and playing with objects.) "Now you tell me if I was paying attention." (Teacher models attentive and inattentive behaviors and requires the student to categorize them.) "Okay, now let me show you what we're going to do. While you're working, this tape recorder will be turned on. Every once in awhile, you'll hear a little sound like this": (Teacher plays tone on tape.) " And when you hear that sound, quietly ask yourself, 'Was I paying attention?' If you answer yes, put a check in this box. If you answer no, put a check in this box. Then go right back to work. When you hear the sound again, ask the question, answer it, mark your answer, and go back to work. Now, let me shoe you how it works." (Teacher models entire procedure.) "Now, Edwin, I bet you can do this. Tell me what you're going to do every time you hear a tone. Let's try it. I'll start the tape and you work on these papers." (Teacher observes student's implementation of the entire procedure, praises its correct use, and gradually withdraws her presence.)

THE NEXT DAY

SCENE: A classroom of students engaged in various activities. One teacher is walking about the room, preparing for her next activity. Some students are sitting in a semicircle facing another teacher and answering questions he poses. Other students are sitting at their desks and writing on papers or in workbooks. Edwin is working at his own desk. The teacher picks up some work pages that have green strips of paper attached to their tops.

TEACHER: (Walking up to Edwin's desk.) "Edwin, here are your seat-work pages for today. I'm going to start the tape and I want you to self-record like you have been doing. What are you going to ask yourself when you hear the beep?"

EDWIN: (Taking papers.) "Was I paying attention?"

TEACHER: "Okay, that's it." (Turning away.) "Bobby, Jackie, and Anne: it's time for spelling group." (Starts a tape recorder and walks toward front of room where three students are gathering.)

EDWIN: (Begins working on his assignments: he is continuing to work when a tone comes from the tape recorder. Edwin's lips barely move as he almost inaudibly whispers.) "Was I paying attention? Yes." (He marks the green strip of paper and returns to work. Later, another tone comes from the tape recorder. Edwin whispers.) "Was I paying attention? Yes." (He marks the green strip of paper and returns to work. Later, as the students in one group laugh, Edwin looks up and watches them. While he is looking up, a tone occurs.) "Was I paying attention? No." (He marks the strip of paper and begins working again. He continues working, questioning himself when the tone occurs and recording his answers.)

Cognitive Model

In the area of reading, there is a great deal of overlap among the various models' approaches. For example, Brown, Campione, and Day (1980) call parts of their procedures "self-control" training, a term that evokes the cognitive-behavior modification model even though their work shares many characteristics with the cognitive model. For this reason it is hard to designate an intervention as rep-

TABLE 6.2. Selected Studies Illustrating Techniques for Treating Reading Problems

CITATION	INDEPENDENT VARIABLE
Brown, Campione, & Day, 1980	Self-control training
Carnine, Kameenui, & Coyle, 1984	Training pupils to use context with vocabulary words
Freeman & McLaughlin, 1984	Audiotaped modeling of reading words
Hendrickson, Roberts, & Shores, 1978	Modeling versus correction
Jenkins & Larson, 1979	Error-correction techniques
Knapczyk & Livingston, 1974	Encouraging students to ask questions
Levin, 1973	Imagery training
Lloyd, Epstein, & Cullinan, 1981	Direct instruction programs
Lovitt & Hansen, 1976	Skipping and drilling contingent on fluency and accuracy
Pascarella & Pflaum, 1981	Self-correction
Polloway, Epstein, Polloway, Patton, & Ball, 1986	Corrective Reading Program (DI)
Rose, 1985	Previewing of material to be studied
Schumaker, Deshler, Alley, Warner, & Denton, 1982	Study strategy instruction
Scruggs, Mastropieri, McLoone, Levin, & Morrison, 1987	Mnemonic strategy training
Swanson, 1981a	Self-recording and reinforcement contingencies

resentative of only one model. However, there are some studies of interventions that seem to fit better here than under the other categories.

A report by Williams (1980) provides an excellent illustration of the application of cognitive psychology to reading. Williams developed a program for teaching beginning reading which is based on extensive research about the component skills of pre-reading and reading. The program is very similar to other programs (e.g., those developed by Engelmann, 1969, and Wallach & Wallach, 1976), but was designed expressly for use with pupils identified or likely to be identified as having learning disabilities. The program taught the skills of phonemic analysis, sound blending, and basic decoding during the primary grades and Williams' carefully conducted field test of it indicated that it was effective in that pupils who were taught according to these principles were less likely to fail to acquire rudimentary reading skills.

Borkowski and his colleagues have studied the contribution of metacognitive processes and affective beliefs to reading performance (e.g., Borkowski, Weyhing, & Carr, 1988). Borkowski et al. tested an intervention for reading comprehension deficits that incorporated components focused on specific strategy knowledge, metacognitive routines, and attributions about effectiveness. Students in one group received the intervention described in Box 6.2; other groups participated in various control conditions. Pupils who received instruction that not only taught them how to perform reading comprehension tasks but also encouraged them to attribute their successes to use of the strategies and the effort they exerted, performed significantly better than pupils who only received training in reading strategies or attributions.

Palincsar and Brown's work on reciprocal teaching (Brown & Campione, 1984; Brown & Palinscar, 1982; Palinscar, 1986; Palinscar & Brown, 1984) is another example of programmatic research in reading developed from cognitive psychology. Based on Vygotsky's theory of the importance of a social context for learning, reciprocal teaching involves dialogues between teachers and students as they consider portions of text. Four strategies are used in the dialogues: summarizing, question generating, clarifying, and predicting

---

BOX 6.2   AN EXAMPLE OF A READING INTERVENTION THAT INCORPORATES ATTRIBUTION TRAINING

In a study by Borkowski and his colleagues (Borkowski et al., 1988) a group of pupils identified as having learning disabilities received and intensive training program. This was designed to remediate the pupils' reading comprehension deficits not only by teaching reading comprehension skills but also by encouraging the use of metacognitive routines and re-forming attributions about the value of using strategies in learning.

Pupils in the experimental group were taught memory strategies during the first sessions. For example, to help a student remember paired associates, the experimenter showed the pupil how to use an imagery strategy (i.e., the item pair *turtle-bus* might be imagined as a school bus with a turtle shell on it). To help them remember items in a free-recall task, pupils were taught a categorization strategy (sort items into categories of, for instance, clothes, vehicles animals). Also during thee sessions the trainers repeatedly told the pupils about the importance of exerting effort in making the strategies work effectively and of attributing failure and success to the appropriate use of strategies. For example, after making a mistake while modeling the procedure, the trainer might say, "I need to try and use the strategy" (Borkowski et al., 1988, p. 49).

In later sessions, the pupils were taught strategies for summarizing the content of written materials. For example, in summarizing what they had read, students were taught to (a) create titles for paragraphs, (b) located the main idea (topic sentence), and (c) find a rationale for the main idea. Again, the trainer emphasized the importance of attributing success and failure to the use of the strategies.

Thus, the experimenters gave pupils prior teaching in how to use strategies and how to link their success in completing tasks to the employment of strategies. They then taught the students how to use strategies and appropriate attributions when attacking reading tasks. The result was that pupils who received this sort of training had higher scores on certain follow-up tests.

(Palinscar & Klenk, 1992). Teachers and students (or, in some cases, just students) take turns leading the dialogues discussing the texts. At first the teachers provide more structure for the students as the students lead the dialogues; gradually the students take on more of the responsibility for leading the dialogues themselves. The reciprocal teaching technique has (a) been successful in both one-to-one situations and small groups, (b) led to improvements not only in reading comprehension but in other subjects requiring reading, and (c) shown durable effects (Palincsar & Brown, 1984).

Instructional Model

One of the most ubiquitous findings in the behavior modification literature is that behavior can be influenced by its consequences. When one conceives of reading—particularly oral reading or answering of questions about what was read—as behavior, it is easy to understand why there are so many studies demonstrating the influence of reinforcement in reading.

Haring and Hauck (1969) examined changes in four elementary-aged boys' reading performance. They compared the boys' skills under baseline conditions to their performance when programmed reading materials and token reinforcement were provided. Although their design was not frankly experimental, their results were consistent with much of the more recent research; when programmed learning materials, a more structured environment, and reinforcement were provided, the frequency of correct responding increased. Studies such as those by Lahey, McNees, and Brown (1973) and Jenkins, Barksdale, and Clinton (1978) have extended these findings in a systematic way. Similarly, clever arrangements of contingencies illustrate that the consequences controlling reading need not be tangible (e.g., tokens) or even social (praise). Lovitt and Hansen (1976) found that making rapid progress contingent on performance resulted in substantial improvements in the pupils' reading performance.

In contrast, instructional approaches such as Direct Instruction have produced substantial transfer. Direct Instruction reading programs have one of the most well-documented records for effects on reading performance (Abt Associates, 1976, 1977; Becker & Carnine, 1981; Engelmann, Becker, Carnine, & Gersten, 1988). Although this record primarily reflects work with children identified as disadvantaged, the programs have also been evaluated with atypical learners in several studies. In one study, Serwer, Shapiro, and Shapiro (1973) reported that pupils identified as at risk who received DISTAR reading performed the same as pupils receiving perceptual-motor remedial training or both conditions on most criterion measures. Although the DISTAR group lagged on two measures of motor skills and on measures of handwriting and arithmetic, it obtained a better score on the measure of wrong endings on words (as measured by the Gates-McKillop), the only significant difference on a measure of reading. Other studies are more supportive.

At the beginning reading level, a study by Stein and Goldman (1980) compared the DISTAR and Palo Alto reading programs with a sample identified as having "minimum brain dysfunction." The pupils given DISTAR reading instruction had significantly greater achievement as measured on the PIAT. At the remedial level, Lloyd, Epstein, and Cullinan (1981) and Lloyd, Cullinan, Heins, & Epstein (1980) reported the results of an intervention program based largely on Direct Instruction. Pupils with learning disabilities received reading instruction that included use of the Corrective Reading Program and their reading scores were compared to the reading scores of a randomly assigned comparison group after six months of instruction. The pupils in the Direct Instruction groups had significantly higher scores on (a) word reading, and (b) passage reading, (c) passage comprehension. Effect sizes for these measures were 0.71 or greater.

Other studies have investigated programmatic effects (e.g., Engelmann, 1997; Gregory, Hackney, & Gregory, 1982; Polloway, Epstein, Polloway, Patton, & Ball, 1986) and more specific aspects of DI programming in reading (e.g., Carnine, Prill, & Armstrong, 1978; Darch & Gersten, 1984; Dommes, Gersten, & Carnine, 1984; Kameenui, Carnine, & Maggs, 1980), often using low-performing pupils as subjects. These studies routinely reveal beneficial effects of application of the instructional model on reading, a result that was confirmed by White's (1988) meta-analysis of Direct Instruction effects on the performance of students with disabilities.

Cognitive-Behavioral Model

Swanson (1981a, 1981b) examined the effects of self-recording and reinforcement techniques on reading performance. In a series of studies (1981a), he found that these variables positively influenced oral reading accuracy, silent reading rate, and comprehension question accuracy. Malamuth (1979) evaluated a broad-based self-management program. Using assorted materials, the students were taught to scan materials during reading. Although conventional significance levels were not obtained, Malamuth interpreted the results as indicating the experimental program aided performance on reading tasks. However, Lloyd, Kneedler, and Cameron (1982) reported that requiring learning-disabled pupils to use a self-verbalized strategy for reading words did not facilitate word reading accuracy.

Research by Wong and others (see Wong, 1985a, 1985b, for reviews) has examined the efficacy of training another metacognitive process—self-questioning—to improve the reading comprehension- of learning-disabled students. In self-questioning interventions, pupils are trained to ask themselves the types of questions that monitor their understanding of what they are reading. For example, Wong and Jones (1982) trained learning-disabled and nonhandicapped students to use a five-step self-questioning procedure that focused on (a) determining the purpose of reading the passage, (b) finding the main ideas, (c) reformulating a main idea as a question, (d) learning the answers to the question, and (e) reviewing the sequence of previous questions and answers.

The intervention facilitated the learning-disabled students' reading comprehension and improved both their awareness of which parts of the passages were important the quality of the questions they generated. The training did not produce similar results in the nonhandicapped pupils however.

A technique that fits well with the cognitive, cognitive-behavioral, and instructional models is procedural facilitation. In procedural facilitation interventions, students learn to use a set of procedures that guide their application of a strategy. The self-recording intervention for improving attention described in an earlier section of this chapter is an example of procedural facilitation. In reading, an example of procedural facilitation is called story grammar. Students learn to follow a set of steps (often using a writing guide or diagram) that help them identify important parts of prose passages: Who is the protagonist, where the action takes place, what motivates the characters, what events transpired, and so forth. Although the evidence about effectiveness of story grammar is mixed, several studies of using story grammar with reading have reported benefits (e.g., Idol & Croll, 1987), particularly when combined with aspects of Direct Instruction (Carnine & Kinder, 1985; Diminio, Gersten, & Carnine, 1990). Procedural facilitation has a stronger record for benefits in written expression.

Handwriting

Handwriting has received considerably less study than some other areas of academic performance. Most of the studies that have been done in this area emanate from either the behavioral or the cognitive-behavioral model.

Instructional Model

Handwriting problems have been repeatedly studied by behaviorally oriented special educators. Despite the popular misconception that reversals of letters and numerals indicate neurological or perceptual problems (Fischer, Liberman, & Shankweiler, 1978; Holmes & Peper, 1977), they have developed what is nearly a "cure" for problems such as reversals despite having ignored psychological and physiological explanations of these problems. The procedure they have used is based on differential reinforcement contingencies: When the student writes a target letter, numeral, or word correctly, provide reinforcement (praise, for example); when the student writes an item incorrectly, require him or her to correct it. Studies of this type of procedure or one very similar to it have repeatedly shown its effectiveness (Fauke, Burnett, Powers, & Sulzer-Azaroff, 1973; Hasazi & Hasazi, 1972; Lahey, Busemeyer, O'Hara, & Beggs, 1977; Smith & Lovitt, 1973; Stromer, 1975, 1977). The procedure is illustrated in Box 6.3.

Cognitive-Behavioral Model

Advocates of the cognitive-behavioral model have encouraged teaching students to use self-verbalization to guide their behavior. In the area of handwriting it has been recommended that students guide themselves verbally while forming letters. For example, while writing the letter "b" the pupil might say, "First I make a tall stick: I start here and go all the way down. Then I make a ball: I start at the middle and go all the way around so it just touches the stick." Although two studies of such procedures (Hayes, 1982; Robin, Armel, & O'Leary, 1975) have shown that they produce small beneficial effects on handwriting, Graham (1983) did not find these benefits.

More extensive self-instruction procedures have been developed in order to affect handwriting performance. Kosiewicz, Hallahan, Lloyd, and Graves (1982) evaluated the effects of having a pupil use detailed self-guiding statements to help him copy handwriting materials more accurately and neatly. They found that these self-instructions—they had the boy repeat the word aloud, repeat it in syllables, repeat each letter in the syllable, and then repeat each letter as he wrote it—resulted in substantial improvements in the boy's handwriting. Similarly, Blandford and Lloyd (1987) found that having pupils consult a card that prompted self-questioning about handwriting performance (e.g., "Are all my letters sitting on the line?") produced improvement in handwriting quality. They were able to withdraw the task card while the effects were maintained.

BOX 6.3   A CASE ILLUSTRATION OF THE REMEDIATION OF HANDWRITING PROBLEMS

Benjamin B. Lahey and his colleagues (Lahey, Busmeyer, O'Hara, & Beggs, 1977) reported the results of two studies demonstrating the effects of a behavior modification program on handwriting problems. In the second of the these studies, they described a boy who was nearly 10 years old and had been identified as learning-disabled. They noted that the boy was considered untestable and that he usually looked at academic materials out of the side of his eye. In addition to his many other problems, the boy had very poor handwriting skills.

After obtaining baseline assessments of the boy's handwriting, Lahey and colleagues instituted a program of reinforcement and correction. When the boy wrote a word correctly, he was told that he had written it correctly and was given a token, which he could later exchange for raisins. When he wrote a word incorrectly, he was told that he erred and was given directions about how to write the word correctly; for example, the trainer said, " 'These letters are backwards. Watch me; they should go like this' "(p. 128). Later, the correction-and-reinforcement program was withdrawn and then reinstated; thus the program was evaluated across four phases: baseline, first treatment, second baseline, and second treatment.

Figures 6.2 and 6.3 illustrate the effects of this treatment on the boy's handwriting. Clearly, this program helped this pupil.

Written Expression

In written expression we have included both spelling and composition. These are substantial areas of deficit in atypical learners that have received considerable interest (see, e.g., Graham & Harris, 1988). Table 6.3 shows a selection of interventions. For reviews of interventions with students who have learning disabilities, see Gordon, Vaughn, and Schumm (1993) and McNaughton, Hughes, and Clark (1994).

Instructional Model

Bryant et al. (1981) and Gettinger, Bryant, and Fayne (1982) developed means of modifying usual spelling instructional programs to increase their effectiveness with learning-disabled children. Among the modifications they studied were (a) reductions in the number of words taught in any one lesson, (b) distribution of practice opportunities to increase retention, and (c) organization of spelling words to facilitate transfer from word to word. Their studies indicate that incorporation of these variables in spelling lessons improves spelling performance of elementary pupils with learning disabilities. Behavioral researchers have also studied the modifi-

cation of written expression. Reinforcing changes in particular parts of compositions have been examined repeatedly (Brigham, Graubard, & Stans, 1972; Maloney & Hopkins, 1973; Maloney, Jacobsen, & Hopkins, 1975) and leads to these conclusions: Reinforcement contingent on (a) writing more words increases the number of words written, (b) writing more action verbs (e.g., "hit," and "fly," but not "is" and "do") increases the number of action verbs in compositions, (c) using different words leads to wider vocabulary. However, reinforcing one aspect of writing usually does not influence other parts.

To obtain broader effects using reinforcement, it probably will be necessary to design a system that reinforces multiple different aspects of composing at the same time. Also, it is unlikely that reinforcement will induce new sentence structures (unless it is contingent on their use). This reemphasizes the theme that students must be shown how to write communicatively (Lloyd, 1988).

Cognitive-Behavioral Model

Studies from the cognitive-behavioral perspective have revealed that the type of instruction provided to pupils may interact with those pupils' characteris-

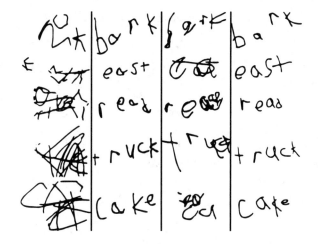

Figure 6.2 An example of one pupil's handwriting from the study by Lahey et al. (1977). The first panel shows the pupil's responses during the first baseline phase; the second, third, and fourth panels show the pupil's responses during the first treatment, second baseline, and second treatment phases. From B. B. Lahey, M. K. Busemeyer, C. O'Hara, and V. E. Beggs, "Treatment of severe perceptual-motor disorders in children diagnosed as Learning Disabled." *Behavior Modification 1* 1, pp. 135–136, copyright 1977 by Sage Publications. Reprinted by permission of Sage Publications, Inc.

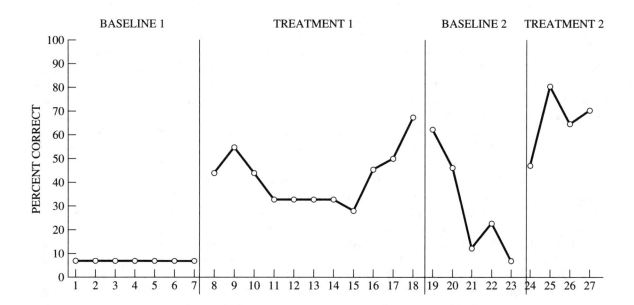

Figure 6.3 A graph showing the handwriting performance for the student in the Lahey et al. (1977) study. The graph reveals that the percent of correct responses in handwriting varied as a function of the reinforcement and correction treatment the authors implemented. From B. B. Lahey, M. K. Busemeyer, C. O'Hara, and V. E. Beggs, "Treatment of severe perceptual-motor disorders in children diagnosed as Learning Disabled." *Behavior Modification 1* 1, pp. 135–136, copyright 1977 by Sage Publications. Reprinted by permission of Sage Publications, Inc.

TABLE 6.3. Selected Studies Illustrating Techniques for Treating Writing Problems

CITATION	INDEPENDENT VARIABLE
Bendall, Tollefson, & Fine, 1980	Self-versus teacher-directed study conditions in spelling
Brigham, Graubard, & Stans, 1972	Reinforcement contingent on using certain types of words in compositions
Darch & Simpson, 1990	Morphenic analysis
Gettinger, Bryant, & Fayne, 1982	Lesson structure in spelling
Graves, Montague, & Wong, 1990	Story grammar
Harris & Graham, 1985	Self-control training in compositions
Karegianes, Pascarella, & Pflau, 1980	Peer editing effects on compositions
Kauffman, Hallahan, Haas, Brame, & Boren, 1978	Contingent imitation of errors in spelling
MacArthur & Graham, 1987	Mechanisms for producing compositions
Schumm, 1992	Story grammar
Stephens & Hudson, 1984	Direct instruction effects on spelling

tics. Bendall, Tollefson, and Fine (1980) identified an aptitude-by-treatment interaction: Students with relatively internal attributions learned more spelling words when they studied words in any way they wished than when their study methods were prescribed for them; however, students with relatively external attributions for success learned more words during the high-structure condition than the low-structure condition.

Peer-editing and self-evaluation are also techniques that have been found to be effective in teaching composition. Karegianes, Pascarella, and Pflaum (1980) taught students to use an editing and rating system for evaluating their peers' essays. They found that students in the peer-editing condition had higher scores on a post-test than others in a comparable condition in which teachers edited the essays. Also, third graders have been taught to check their own writing assignments according to guidelines (Ballard & Glynn, 1975). The self-evaluation procedure required that they count the number of sentences, words, and the various types of words used; also, they took other simple measures of writing. On the basis of their counts, students assigned themselves points in a reward system depending on how they had done in their essays. This combination of self-evaluation and self-reward had positive effects on the students' writing. Self-evaluation has been incorporated into writing programs, as well (Harris &

Graham, 1985; Moran, Schumaker, & Vetter, 1981).

Strong examples of cognitive and cognitive-behavioral interventions for composition have been developed by Graham and Harris (e.g., Graham, 1982; Harris, Graham, & Pressley, 1991), Montague, Graves, and Leavell (1991), and Englert and Raphael (1989). These methods share many of the features shown in Figure 6.4. In essence, students learn to plan their written products, execute the plan while monitoring their execution of it (particularly for conformation of the original plan), and edit their products according to some self-guiding principles. Given the complexity of written expression, these procuedres illustrate the strength and flexibility of cognitive-behavioral techniques.

Procedural facilitation helps the production of students' writing. In using procedural facilitation with written expression, the students would learn to identify the parts of a written product prior to writing and might also learn to monitor their execution of their plan for writing. For example, before students wrote a passage, Martin and Manno (1995) had 13- and 14-year olds complete a form on which they identified (a) main character, (b) other characters, (c) setting, (d) problem, (e) plan, and (f) ending for their passages. As the students wrote their essays, Martin and Manno had them check off whether they had included the parts indicated in their plans. Students' essays were improved in com-

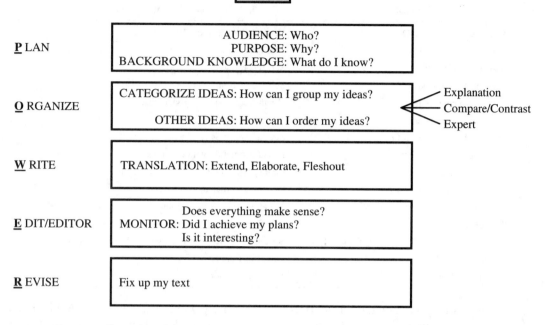

Figure 6.4 Illustration of the component steps in a strategy for generating written products.
Source: From Englert, C. S. (1991), p. 195.

pleteness (inclusion of elements) and quality (organization and coherence). Having students establish goals for editing (e.g., adding more details) enhances the benefits of procedural facilitation (Graham, McArthur, & Swartz, 1995).

Arithmetic

Arithmetic deficits have been extensively addressed and a wide range of interventions studied (see Table 6.4). Arithmetic difficulties range from deficits in simple computation to deficits in solving multi-step problems. The following paragraphs describe some interventions.

Cognitive Model

Recent work by cognitive psychologists and mathematics educators in the domain of mathematics has shown the importance of cognitive and metacognitive processes for understanding the nature, acquisition, and use of mathematics knowledge and skills. (For summaries of the work in this area, see: Baroody, 1987; Carpenter, Moser, & Romberg, 1982; Ginsburg, 1983; Hiebert, 1986; Lesh & Landau, 1983; Pellegrino & Goldman, 1987; Resnick & Ford, 1981; Romberg & Carpenter, 1986; Schoenfeld, 1987). By examining the cognitive demands of mathematics tasks, researchers in this area have determined (a) the procedural knowledge individuals need to accomplish different mathematics tasks, (b) the conceptual and factual knowledge they need for the tasks, and (c) how these types of knowledge interact during the tasks.

There are few interventions for arithmetic difficulties that reflect a strictly cognitive model despite the model's close connection to this developed body of research. It may be that the cognitive model's emphases, such as on a holistic presentation of content in a domain and the active involvement of the learner in constructing knowledge, may, in the case of mathematics, make interventions more amenable to presentation in the form of a curriculum than in a form such as a discrete series of procedural steps targeting a specific task, for instance, subtraction computation or two-step word problems.

TABLE 6.4. Selected Studies Illustrating Techniques for Treating Arithmetic Problems

CITATION	INDEPENDENT VARIABLE
Albion & Salzberg, 1982	General and specific self-instruction
Greenwood et al., 1984	Peer tutoring
Holman & Baer, 1979	Self-recording
Johnston & Whitman, 1987	Self-instruction
Kelly, Carnine, Gersten, & Grossen, 1986	Direct instruction using videodisc
Leon & Pepe, 1983	Self-instruction
Lloyd, Saltzman, & Kauffman, 1981	Strategy training
Perkins & Cullinan, 1984	Direct instruction with fractions
Schunk & Cox, 1986	Strategy training and attributional feedback
Seabaugh & Schumaker, 1994	General self-management
Smith & Lovitt, 1975	Modeling and demonstrations
Smith & Lovitt, 1976	Reinforcement contingencies
Thackwray, Meyers, Schlesser, & Cohen, 1985	Specificity of self-instructional strategies
Vreeland et al., 1994	Direct Instruction
Wellington, 1994	Direct Instruction

As an example of this last point, Reid and Hresko (1981) suggest that the Project MATH program developed by Cawley and his associates (Cawley et al., 1976) represents a more cognitively oriented approach to the instruction of mathematics for learning-disabled students. Project MATH emphasizes not only the acquisition of mathematics principles. Preliminary tests have supported the efficacy of Project MATH (Cawley, Fitzmaurice, Shaw, Kahn, & Bates, 1978), though more evaluations of the program should be conducted and reported.

Cognitive-Behavioral Model

Cognitive-behavioral interventions for students having difficulty in mathematics make use of the types of cognitive and metacognitive processes that are studied by cognitive psychologists and mathematics educators. These cognitive and metacognitive processes are used in cognitive-behavioral interventions in two general ways (Keller & Lloyd, 1989; Lloyd & Keller, 1989).

Some interventions have used procedures that facilitate access to the appropriate content knowledge for a task. For example, Parsons (1972) studied the effects on arithmetic accuracy of having pupils both circle and name the operation symbol before performing addition and subtraction computations.

Similarly, Lovitt and Curtiss (1968) required a student read each problem aloud before beginning to solve it. This procedure improved his arithmetic performance. The positive effects of these tactics have been interpreted as support for the idea that antecedent self-verbalization is a desirable component of CBM programs.

Other cognitive-behavioral approaches have trained students to use combinations of both metacognitive processes and content knowledge, usually in the form of an algorithm's procedures. The distinction between these two intervention components blur at times, however, for two reasons (Keller & Lloyd, 1989). Some steps in solving mathematical tasks—such as (a) identifying the pertinent information in a word problem, (b) identifying the question, and (c) planning how to solve the question—are identical to metacognitive processes in other situations. Also, it is not always clear from the descriptions of cognitive-behavioral interventions how the metacognitive components of the interventions are being used. Are the students trained to use the metacognitive processes to guide the other, more task-specific components of the intervention—more in line with the nature of metacognition—or are the metacognitive processes and content procedures trained as separate components?

As examples of interventions using metacognitive components, Johnston, Whitman, and Johnson (1981), Johnston and Whitman (1987), and Whitman and Johnston (1983) evaluated the effects of a self-instructional intervention for teaching arithmetic computation skills. In both studies, pupils were taught algorithms for solving specific types of arithmetic problems. The results indicated that this intervention had clear and substantial effects on the students' performance. One particular value of these studies is that they represent a systematic research effort with a clear theoretical basis and readily applicable results. Several other studies (Albion & Salzberg, 1982; Cameron & Robinson, 1980; Leon & Pepe, 1983; Thackwray, Meyers, Schleser, & Cohen, 1985) have also examined self-instructional interventions for students with difficulties in arithmetic. Johnston and Whitman (1987) though, found that a set of self-instructions focusing on both general and specific strategies, when taught through a self-instructional format, was more effective than (a) the same instructions taught through a didactic format and (b) a set of only specific self-instructions taught through either format. Follow-up analyses showed that these results held for those students who had less ability in math, too.

Instruction Model

Early examples of instruction models came from work in the behavioral literature. For example, Smith and Lovitt (1976) demonstrated an important relationship between reinforcement and academic performance. In two studies, they assessed the arithmetic computation performance of 10 elementary-aged boys (3 in one study and 7 in the other) identified as learning disabled. Their results indicated that reinforcement contingencies have little effect on rate or accuracy unless the pupils know how to perform the required operations. A similar finding is apparent in other studies (e.g., Grimm, Bijou, & Parsons, 1973). In a similar vein, Smith and Lovitt (1975) studied the effects of providing pupils with a demonstration of the steps in a solution algorithm and then leaving them a model of how to follow those steps. They found that the pupils' performance increased dramatically when they were taught by this procedure.

Direct Instruction studies of arithmetic have revealed that pupils likely to have problems acquiring arithmetic skills and knowledge can learn at a rate consistent with that of their nonhandicapped peers. Becker and Carnine (1981) and Gersten and Carnine (1984b) reported that among the nine major model sponsors in Project Follow Through, the Direct Instruction Model was one of only two to have positive effects on pupils' mathematics achievement. Furthermore, although the pupils participating in Follow Through were expected to perform at about the 20th percentile, the average Metropolitan Achievement Test (MAT) Total Math score for students receiving mathematics instruction under the Direct Instruction Model was at the 48th percentile; the average score for the other eight models was at the 17th percentile (see, also, Abt Associates, 1976, 1977). Although results on other measures on which more limited skills are required (e.g., the Wide Range Achievement Test) are consistent with these data, it is important to note that the Metropolitan scores are based on a combination of computation skill, problem solving, and conceptual knowledge. In addition, analyses of data for subjects who entered school with IQs of 80 or lower (Gersten, Becker, Heiry, & White, 1984) reveal that the effects with this subgroup are also instructive: "Those entering with low IQ scores tended to begin and end with lower MAT scores than their peers, *but they still maintained the same average growth grate of 1.0 grade-equivalent units a year*" (Gersten & Carnine, 1984b, emphasis in original).

Although much of the research on Direct Instruction has focused on nonhandicapped pupils, some studies have been conducted with students who have disabilities. For example, Perkins and Cullinan (1984) reported that upper-elementary aged students with learning disabilities learned to manipulate fractions when taught with a Direct Instruction program. Similarly, several studies have revealed that a technology-based Direct Instruction program for teaching fractions makes students with learning disabilities achieve the same level of mastery as their nondisabled peers (Grossen & Ewing, 1994; Kelly, Carnine, Gersten, & Grossen, 1986; Lubke, Rogers, & Evans, 1989).

In studies of some of the specific features of Direct Instruction, similar results have been obtained. Lloyd, Saltzman, and Kauffman (1981) examined the effects of "strategy training," an instructional procedure based on the Direct Instruction principle of teaching cognitive operations by isolating and teaching a series of steps that lead to solution of a type of problem (c.f., Cullinan, Lloyd, & Epstein, 1981; Lloyd, 1980). The authors found that transfer of training was predictable on the basis of the instruction provided learning-disabled pupils. The results are consistent with the findings of Carnine (1980) who reported that young nonhandicapped pupils provided instruction on the component skills of a multiplication strategy had more rapid acquisition of the strategy and greater transfer of it to untrained items than did young nonhandicapped pupils who were taught the component skills and the strategy at the same time.

INTEGRATION

Our review reveals that research has established the effectiveness of many interventions falling under each of the three models for which there is empirical support. For practitioners concerned with identifying interventions for specific academic problems, then, it is tempting to assume that teachers or consultants may select any model and implement it with reasonable hopes of success. As tempting as this may seem, we suspect that a different interpretation is more useful.

Early in our discussion of models, we argued that efforts to understand and improve the academic problems of students by discussing models was an arbitrary exercise. Models serve a heuristic value in that they help us to organize diverse material. But many interventions that have been successful—the focus of this treatment of academic problems—are only superficially associated with particular models. Not only can no particular model claim a corner on effectiveness, but many effective interventions appear consistent with features of different models.

Rather than assuming that one may adopt a model that suits his or her preference, we suspect that practitioners should examine the common features of the interventions that have been successful

and work from an integrated and synthetic model. We want to hasten to note that this should not be construed as an argument for the vacuous eclecticism—everything's good—that too often characterizes human services; instead, we are arguing that we can synthesize a general perspective on effective practice by inductive logic: If virtually every effective intervention has certain characteristics and few interventions that lack those features are effective, then probably those features are relevant to the effectiveness of the interventions. Assuming that effectiveness is an important consideration in choosing interventions, then *practitioners should choose those interventions that have the features of effective interventions, regardless of the model with which they are associated.*

Accordingly, in the remainder of this chapter, on the basis of atheoretical outcomes, we describe practices based on the commonalities in effective interventions for academic problems. These practices include (a) direct assessment and intervention, (b) strategy-based instruction, (c) provision of extensive practice opportunities (Lloyd, 1988).

Direct Assessment and Intervention

Many historic efforts to improve academic problems addressed what can be reasonably referred to as related or peripheral problems. For example, some important early efforts to treat learning disabilities focused on such skills as drawing, coordination, balance, and similar abilities (e.g., Barsch, 1967; Cratty, 1969; Kephart, 1971). More recently, despite disagreement about the causal relationship between self-concept and achievement (Helmke & van Aken, 1995; Marsh, 1990), one routinely finds recommendations (e.g., Lerner, 1997) for improving self-concept; given the limited evidence about the collateral benefits of programs to enhance self-concept or self-esteem, these seem like recommendations of little value for remedying academic problems. Contemporary treatments of academic problems place far greater emphasis on treating the specific academic problems themselves, rather than related skills. In our analysis, regardless of the model of intervention, the effective methods address the academic problems of concern. There is little evidence of, for example, improving self-concept as a means of improving achievement.

Thus, we conclude that people concerned with remedying problems in academic achievement should focus directly on performance in the academic areas. Not only should interventions be directed at academic performance, but so should assessment. Efforts to develop assessment practices that are genuinely or obviously related to the desired outcomes of therapy will yield better results than will those that are peripherally or indirectly related to outcomes of importance (Deno & Fuchs, 1987).

That is, if one is concerned about reading, one should assess reading performance and intervene on reading skills. Less direct assessments may be appropriate for purposes other than intervention (e.g., identification), but not for planning treatments nor for monitoring their effects. It will do less good to assess related performances (e.g., perceptual speed) and intervene on related skills (e.g., digit span). To be sure, digit span appears to be related to acquisition of facility with reading (Torgesen, 1988, 1991) but few would recommend that having students practice reciting digits—forward or backward—would be likely to accelerate acquisition of reading skills.

Not only should assessment practice measure performance on tasks of concern, but assessment should also provide information that directly informs instruction. Probably the most important application of assessment in this area is in monitoring the progress of students toward mastery of skills. Thus, a program of intervention for academic problems should have a formative evaluation component to assess the students' acquisition of both accuracy and fluency in the specific skill area being addressed.

Strategy-Based Instruction

Almost to a one, interventions that successfully teach a new skill to students who have academic problems (as opposed to a skill that they already have in their repertoires), provide students with instruction in how to perform a series of actions that lead to the correct solution of a task. Whether the intervention is championed by advocates who align themselves with a cognitive, cognitive-behavioral, or task-analytic perspective, there is usually some clear emphasis on teaching students an algorithm or a structured approach to doing something.

McKinney stressed the idea of strategies when he reviewed five years work by five research institutes that examined learning disabilities:

> The central concept that emerges from this research is that many LD students have not acquired efficient strategies for processing task information and they cannot use their abilities and experience to profit from conventional instruction. Most of this research, however, demonstrates that they are capable of acquiring the strategies that account for competent performance and that they can improve their academic skills and adaptive functioning when they are taught task-appropriate strategies. (1983, pp. 130-131)

These strategies usually correspond to the demands of the task that the students are learning. Thus, strategies for solving equations are likely to differ from strategies for understanding text. They may share some more fundamental skills (e.g., memory), but they are likely to have unique features. Some strategies (e.g., story grammar) may have analogs in related areas but those analogs are based on the shared features of the tasks (written passages often have structures that can be useful both in understanding and generating passages).

Provision of Extensive Practice Opportunities

For students to become facile with the application of strategies to academic tasks, interventions must provide copious numbers of practice opportunities. As introduced by LaBerge and Samuels (1974), the concept of automaticity is quite clearly relevant here; automaticity refers to the way in which the familiarity born of repetition frees the performer to focus attention on other aspects of a performance. Samuels described the concept of automaticity by drawing an analogy between reading and performance in other areas:

> Basketball players practice jump shots over and over again; musicians practice short musical selections repeatedly. Their goal is to develop skills to a level of fluid accuracy. With enough practice, they do not have to devote

much attention to the mechanics of their skills. With enough practice, readers will not have to devote much attention to the mechanics of decoding. (1981, pp. 23-24)

Similarly, it is only though repeated practice that students can acquire the fluency needed to use strategies automatically. Effective interventions must provide that amount of practice.

Those charged with designing, implementing, and evaluating interventions for academic problems probably should count on having some type of formative measurement that permits them to monitor progress toward automaticity. This idea brings us back to the argument we advanced at the beginning of this section: Intervening in academic problems requires direct, formative assessment of pupil performance (Fuchs, 1986; Howell et al., 1993). Through frequent evaluations of both speed and accuracy, one can ascertain whether students are acquiring automaticity in the use of the strategies that will help them to overcome their academic problems.

SUMMARY

Evidence about interventions for academic problems indicates that practitioners can select effective procedures with minimal reference to the various models discussed here. However, we do not believe that the breadth of possibilities implies that a person charged with designing or delivering interventions may choose among them eclectically. Rather than making decisions on the basis of consistency with the model they prefer, we recommend that practitioners use interventions that

- focus directly on the academic area of concern, both in assessment and intervention;
- teach students systematic means of approaching and solving the tasks posed in the academic area of concern; and
- provide sufficient practice opportunities for the students to acquire both accuracy and fluency with the strategies they are learning.

Such interventions require considerable sophistication on the part of those who are designing and implementing them. However, the data we have presented here make clear that the judicious and data-reactive application of interventions such as those described in this chapter will help relieve the academic problems experienced by many students for whom professionals must provide or design therapeutic programs.

REFERENCES

Abt Associates (1976). *Education as experimentation: A planned variation model* (Vol. 3A). Cambridge, MA: Author.

Abt Associates (1977). *Education as experimentation: A planned variation model* (Vol. 4). Cambridge, MA: Author.

Adams, M. J. (1990). *Beginning to read: Thinking and learning about print.* Cambridge, MA: MIT Press.

Albion, F. M., & Salzberg, C. (1982). The effect of self-instructions on the rate of correct addition problems with mentally retarded children. *Education and Treatment of Children, 5,* 121–131.

Anderson, P. L., Cronin, M. E., & Miller, J. H. (1986). Referral reasons for learning disabled students. *Psychology in the Schools, 23,* 388–395.

Bailey, J. W., Wolf, M. M., & Phillips, E. L. (1970). Home-based reinforcement and the modification of predelinquents' classroom behavior. *Journal of Applied Behavior Analysis, 3,* 223–233.

Ballard, K. D., & Glynn, T. L. (1975). Behavioral self-management in story writing with elementary school children. *Journal of Applied Behavior Analysis, 8,* 387–398.

Bandura, A. (1977). *Social learning theory.* Englewood Cliffs, NJ: Prentice-Hall.

Bandura, A. (1986). *Social foundations of thought and action.* Englewood Cliffs, NJ: Prentice-Hall.

Baroody, A. J. (1987). The case of Felicia: A young child's strategies for reducing memory demands during mental addition. *Cognition and Instruction, 1,* 109–116.

Baroody, A. J., & Ginsburg, H. P. (1991). A cognitive approach to assessing the mathematical difficulties of children labeled "learning disabled." In H. L. Swanson (Ed.), *Handbook on the assessment of learning disabilities: Theory, research, and practice* (pp. 177–227). Austin, TX: Pro-Ed.

Barsch, R. H. (1967). *Achieving perceptual-motor efficiency.* Seattle: Special Child.

Bateman, B. (1967). Three approaches to diagnosis and educational planning for children with learning disabilities. *Academic Therapy, 3,* 215–222.

Becker, W. C., & Carnine, D. (1981). Direct instruction: A behavior theory model for comprehensive educational intervention with the disadvantaged. In R. Ruiz & S. W. Bijou (Eds.), *Behavior modification: Contributions to education* (pp. 145–210). Hillsdale, NJ: Lawrence Erlbaum.

Becker, W. C., Engelmann, S., & Thomas, D. R. (1975). *Teaching 2: Cognitive learning and instruction.* Chicago: Science Research Associates.

Bendall, D., Tollefson, N., & Fine, M. (1980). Interaction of locus-of-control orientation and the performance of learning disabled adolescents. *Journal of Learning Disabilities, 13,* 83–86.

Bereiter, C., & Engelmann, S. (1966). *Teaching disadvantaged children in the preschool.* Englewood Cliffs, NJ: Prentice-Hall.

Bijou, S. W. (1970). What psychology has to offer education—now. *Journal of Applied Behavior Analysis, 3,* 65–71.

Blandford, B. J., & Lloyd, J. W. (1987). Effects of a self-instructional procedure on handwriting. *Journal of Learning Disabilities, 20,* 342–346.

Borkowski, J. G., Weyhing, R. S., & Carr, M. (1988). Effects of attributional retraining on strategy-based reading comprehension in learning-disabled students. *Journal of Educational Psychology, 80,* 46–53.

Braswell, L., & Kendall, P. C. (1988). Cognitive-behavioral methods with children. In K. S. Dobson (Ed.), *Handbook of cognitive-behavioral therapies* (pp. 167–213). New York: Guilford Press.

Brigham, T. A., Graubard, P. S., Stans, A. (1972). Analysis of the effects of sequential reinforcement contingencies on aspects of composition. *Journal of Applied Behavior Analysis, 5,* 421–429.

Brown, A. L., & Campione, J. C. (1984). Three faces of transfer: Implications for early competence, individual differences, and instruction. In M. E. Lamb, A. L. Brown, & B. Rogoff (Eds.), *Advances in developmental psychology* (Vol. 3, pp. 143–192). Hillsdale, NJ: Lawrence Erlbaum.

Brown, A. L., Campione, J. C., & Day, J. D. (1980). *Learning to learn: On training students to learn from texts.* Paper presented at the annual meeting of the American Educational Research Association meeting, Boston, April.

Brown, A. L., & Palincsar, A. S. (1982). Inducing strategic learning from text by means of informed, self-control training. *Topics in Learning and Learning Disabilities, 2,* 1–17.

Bruner, J. S., Goodnow, J. J., & Austin, G. A. (1956). *A study of thinking.* New York: Wiley.

Bryant, N. D., Drabin, I. R., & Gettinger, M. (1981). Effects of varying unit size on spelling achievement in learning disabled children. *Journal of Learning Disabilities, 14,* 200–203.

Cameron, M. I., & Robinson, J. J. (1980). Effects of cognitive training on academic and on-task behavior of hyperactive children. *Journal of Abnormal Child Psychology, 8,* 405–419.

Carnine, D., & Kinder, D. (1985). Teaching low-performing students to apply generative and schema strategies to narrative and expository material. *Remedial and Special Education, 6*(1), 20–30.

Carnine, D., & Silbert, J. (1979). Direct instruction reading. Columbus, OH: Charles E. Merrill.Carnine, D. W. (1976). Effects of two teacher-presentation rates on off-task behavior, answering correctly, and participation. *Journal of Applied Behavior Analysis, 9,* 199–206.

Carnine, D. W. (1980). Preteaching versus concurrent teaching on the component skills of a multiplication problem-solving strategy. *Journal for Research in Mathematic Education, 11,* 375–379.

Carnine, D. W., Kameenui, E., & Coyle, G. (1984). Utilization of contextual information in determining the meanings of unfamiliar words in context. *Reading Research Quarterly, 19,* 343–356.

Carnine, D. W., Prill, N., & Armstrong, J. (1978). *Teaching slower performing students general case strategies for solving comprehension items.* Eugene: University of Oregon Follow Through Project.

Carpenter, T. R., Moser, J. M., & Romberg, T. A. (Eds.). (1982). *Addition and subtraction: A cognitive approach.* Hillsdale, NJ: Lawrence Erlbaum.

Cawley, J. F., Fitzmaurice, A. M., Goodstein, H. A., Lepore, A. V., Sedlak, R., & Althaus, V. (1976). *Project MATH.* Tulsa, OK: Educational Development Corporation.

Cawley, J. F., Fitzmaurice, A. M., Shaw, R., Kahn, H., & Bates, H., III. (1978). Mathematics and learning disabled youth: The upper grade levels. *Learning Disability Quarterly, 1*(4), 37–52.

Cratty, B. (1969). *Perceptual-motor behavior and educational process.* Springfield, IL: Charles C. Thomas.

Cullinan, D., Epstein, M. H., & Lloyd, J. W. (1983). *Behavior disorders of children and adolescents.* Englewood Cliffs, NJ: Prentice-Hall.

Cullinan, D., Lloyd, J., & Epstein, M. H. (1981). Strategy training: A structured approach to arithmetic instruction. *Exceptional Education Quarterly, 2*(1), 41–49.

Darch, C., & Gersten, R. (1984). *Comparison of two direction setting activities to increase the comprehension of high school LD students.* Unpublished manuscript, University of Oregon, Eugene.

Darch, C., & Simpson, R. G. (1990). Effectiveness of visual imagery versus rule-based strategies in teaching spelling to learning disabled students. *Research in Rural Education, 7*(1), 61–70.

Deno, S. L., & Fuchs, L. S. (1987). Developing curriculum-based measurement systems for data-based special education problem solving. *Focus on Exceptional Children, 19*(2), 1–16.

Dimino, J., Gersten, R., & Carnine, D. (1990). Story grammar: An approach for promoting at-risk secondary students' comprehension of literature. *Elementary School Journal, 91,* 19–32.

Dommes, P., Gersten, R., & Carnine, D. (1984). Instructional procedures for increasing skill-deficient fourth graders' comprehension of syntactic structures. *Educational Psychology, 4,* 155–165.

Dunlap, G., dePerczel, M., Clarke, S., Wilson, D., Wright, S., White, R., & Gomez, A. (1994). Choice making to promote adaptive behavior for students with emotional and behavioral challenges. *Journal of Applied Behavior Analysis, 27,* 505–518.

Dunlap. G., Kern, L., dePerczel, M., Clarke, S., Wilson, D., Childs, K. E., White, R., & Falk, G. D. (1993). Functional analysis of classroom responding for students with emotional and behavioral disorders. *Behavioral Disorders, 18,* 275–291.

Engelmann, S. (1969). *Preventing failure in the primary grades.* Chicago: Science Research Associates.

Engelmann, S. (1997). Theory of mastery and acceleration. In J. W. Lloyd, E. J. Kameenui, & D. Chard (Eds.), *Issues in educating students with disabilities* (pp. 77–195). Hillsdale, NJ: Lawrence Erlbaum.

Engelmann, S., Becker, W. C., Carnine, D., & Gersten, R. (1988). The Direct Instruction Follow Through Model: Design and outcomes. *Education and Treatment of Children, 11,* 303–317.

Engelmann, S., & Carnine, D. (1982). *Theory of instruction.* New York: Irvington.

Engelmann, S., Granzin, A., & Severson, H. (1979). Diagnosing instruction. *Journal of Special Education, 13,* 355–263.

Englert, C. S. (1991). Unraveling the mysteries of writing through strategy instruction. In T. Scruggs & B. Y. L. Wong (Eds.), *Current intervention research in learning disabilities* (pp. 186–223). New York: Springer-Verlag.

Englert, C. S., & Raphael, T. E. (1989). Constructing well-formed prose: Process, structure, and metacognitive knowledge. *Exceptional Children, 54,* 513–520.

Fauke, J., Burnett, J., Powers, M. A., & Sulzer-Azaroff, B. (1973). Improvement of handwriting and letter recognition skills: A behavior modification procedure. *Journal of Learning Disabilities, 6,* 296–300.

Ferritor, D. C., Buckholdt, D., Hamblin, R. L., & Smith, L. (1972). The noneffects of contingent reinforcement for attending behavior on work accomplished. *Journal of Applied Behavior Analysis, 5,* 7–17.

Fisher, F. W., Liberman, I. Y., & Shankweiler, D. (1978). Reading reversals and developmental dyslexia: A further study. *Cortex, 14,* 496–510.

Flavell, J. H. (1977). *Cognitive development.* Englewood Cliffs, NJ: Prentice-Hall.

Freeman, T. J., & McLaughlin, T. F. (1984). Effects of taped-words treatment procedure on learning disabled students' sight-word oral reading. *Learning Disability Quarterly, 7,* 49–54.

Fuchs, L. S. (1986). Monitoring the performance of mildly handicapped students: Review of current practice and research. *Remedial and Special Education, 7,* 5–12.

Fuchs, L. S., & Deno, S. L. (1994). Must instructionally useful performance assessment be based in the curriculum? *Exceptional Children, 61,* 15–24.

Gerber, M. M. (1987). Application of cognitive-behavioral training methods to teaching basic skills to mildly handicapped elementary school students. In M. C. Wang, M. C. Reynolds, & H. J. Walberg (Eds.), *Handbook of special education: Research and practice. Vol. 1, Learner characteristics and adaptive education* (pp. 167–186). New York: Pergamon Press.

Gersten, R., & Carnine, D. (1984a). Auditory-perceptual skills and reading: A response to Kavale's meta-analysis. *Remedial and Special Education, 5*(1), 16–19.

Gersten, R., & Carnine, D. (1984b). Direct instruction mathematics: A longitudinal evaluation of low-income elementary school students. *The Elementary School Journal, 84*(4), 395–407.

Gersten, R. M., Becker, W. C., Heiry, T. J., & White, W. A. T. (1984). Entry IQ and yearly academic growth of children in Direct Instruction programs: A longitudinal study of low SES children. *Educational Evaluation and Policy Analysis, 6,* 109–121.

Gersten, R. M., White, W. A. T., Falco, R., & Carnine, D. (1982). Teaching basic discriminations to handicapped and non-handicapped individuals through a dynamic presentation of instructional stimuli. Analysis and *Intervention in Developmental Disabilities, 2,* 305–317.

Gettinger, M., Bryant, N. D., & Fayne, H. R. (1982). Designing spelling instruction for learning-disabled children: An emphasis on unit size, distributed practice, and training for transfer. *Journal of Special Education, 16,* 439–448.

Ginsburg, H. P. (Ed.). (1983). *The development of mathematical thinking.* New York: Academic Press.

Gordon, J., Vaughn, S., & Schumm, J. S. (1993). Spelling interventions: A review of literature and implications for instruction for students with learning disabilities. *Learning Disabilities Research and Practice, 8,* 175–181.

Graham, S. (1982). Composition research and practice: A unified approach. *Focus on Exceptional Children, 14*(8), 1–16.

Graham, S. (1983). The effect of self-instructional procedures on LD students' handwriting performance. *Learning Disability Quarterly, 6,* 231–234.

Graham, S., & Harris, K. R. (Eds.). (1988). Research and instruction in written language [Special issue]. *Exceptional Children, 54*(6).

Graham, S., McArthur, C., & Swartz, C. (1995). Effects of goal setting and procedural facilitation on the revising behavior and writing performance of students with writing and learning problems. *Journal of Educational Psychology, 87,* 230-240.

Graves, A., Montague, M., & Wong, Y. (1990). The effects of procedural facilitation on the story composition of learning disabled students. *Learning Disabilities Research, 5,* 88–93.

Greenwood, C. R., Dinwiddie, G., Terry, B., Wade, L., Stanley, S. O., Thibadeau, S., & Delquadri, J. C. (1984). Teacher-versus peer-mediated instruction: An ecobehavioral analysis of achievement outcomes. *Journal of Applied Behavior Analysis, 17,* 521–538.

Gregory, R. P., Hackney, C., & Gregory, N. M. (1982). Corrective reading programme: An evaluation. *British Journal of Education Psychology, 52,* 33–50.

Grimm, J. A., Bijou, S. W., & Parsons, J. A. (1973). A problem solving model for teaching remedial arithmetic to handicapped young children. *Journal of Abnormal Child Psychology, 1,* 26–39.

Grossen, B., & Ewing, S. (1994). Raising mathematical problem-solving performance: Do the NCTM teaching standards help? *Effective School Practices, 13*(2), 79–91.

Hall, R. V., Lund, D., & Jackson, D. (1968). Effects of teacher attention on study behavior. *Journal of Applied Behavior Analysis, 1,* 1–12.

Hallahan, D. P., Kauffman, J. M., & Lloyd, J. W. (1996). *Introduction to learning disabilities.* Boston: Allyn & Bacon.

Hallahan, D. P., Lloyd, J. W., Kneedler, R. D., & Marshall, K. J. (1982). A comparison of the effects of self- versus teacher-assessment of on-task behavior. *Behavior Therapy, 13,* 715–723.

Hallahan, D. P., Lloyd, J. W., Kosiewicz, M. M., Kauffman, J. M, & Graves, A. W. (1979). Self-monitoring of attention as a treatment for a learning disabled boy's off-task behavior. *Learning Disability Quarterly, 2*(3), 24–32.

Hallahan, D. P., Lloyd, J. W., & Stoller, L. (1981). *Improving attention with self-monitoring: A manual for teachers.* Charlottesville: University of Virginia Learning Disabilities Research Institute.

Hammill, D. D., & Larsen, S. C. (1974). The effectiveness of psycholinguistic training. *Exceptional Children, 41,* 5–14.

Haring, N. G. (1968). *Attending and responding.* San Rafael, CA: Dimensions.

Haring, N. G., & Hauck, M. (1969). Improved learning conditions in the establishment of reading skills with disabled readers. *Exceptional Children, 35,* 341–351.

Haring, N. G., Lovitt, T. C., Eaton, M. D., & Hansen, C. L. (1978). *The fourth R: Research in the classroom.* Columbus, OH: Merrill.

Harris, K. (1986). Self-monitoring of attentional behavior versus self-monitoring of productivity: Effects on on-task behavior and academic response rate among learning disabled children. *Journal of Applied Behavior Analysis, 19,* 417–423.

Harris, K. R., & Graham, S. (1985). Improving learning disabled students' composition skills: A self-control strategy training approach. *Learning Disability Quarterly, 8,* 27–36.

Harris, K. R., & Graham, S. (1994). Constructivism: Principles, paradigms, and integration. *Journal of Special Education, 28,* 233–247.

Harris, K. R., Grahan, S., & Pressley, M. (1991). Cognitive-behavioral approaches in reading and written language: Developing self-regulated learners. In. N. N. Singh & I. L. Beale (Eds.), *Learning disabilities: Nature, theory, and practice* (pp. 415–451). New York: Springer-Verlag.

Hasazi, J. E., & Hasazi, S. E. (1972). Effects of teacher attention on digit-reversal behavior in an elementary school child. *Journal of Applied Behavior Analysis, 5,* 157–162.

Hayes, D. (1982). Handwriting practice: The effects of perceptual prompts. *Journal of Educational Research, 75,* 169–172

Helmke, A., & van Aken, M. A. G. (1995). The causal ordering of academic achievement and self-concept of ability during elementary school: A longitudinal study. *Journal of Educational Psychology, 87,* 624–637.

Hendrickson, J., Roberts, M., & Shores, R. E. (1978). Antecedent and contingent modeling to teach basic sight vocabulary. *Journal of Learning Disabilities, 11,* 524–528.

Heshusius, K. (1989). The Newtonian mechanistic paradigm, special education, and contours of alternatives: An overview. *Journal of Learning Disabilities, 22,* 403–415.

Heshusius, K. (1994). Freeing ourselves from objectivity: Managing subjectivity or turning toward a participatory mode of consciousness?. *Educational Researcher, 23*(3), 15–22.

Hiebert, J. (Ed.). (1986). *Conceptual and procedural knowledge: The case of mathematics.* Hillsdale, NJ: Lawrence Erlbaum.

Holman, J., & Baer, D. M. (1979). Facilitating generalization of on-task behavior through self-monitoring of academic tasks. *Journal of Autism and Developmental Disabilities, 9,* 429–446.

Holmes, D. L., & Peper, R. J. (1977). An evaluation of the use of spelling error analysis in the diagnosis of reading disabilities. *Child Development, 48,* 1708–1711.

Howell, K. W., Fox, S. L., & Morehead, M. K. (1993). *Curriculum-based evaluation: Teaching and decision making* (2nd ed.). Pacific Grove, CA: Brooks/Cole.

Howell, K. W., & Morehead, M. K. (1987). *Curriculum-based evaluation for special and remedial education: A handbook for deciding what to teach.* Columbus, OH: Merrill.

Hughes, C., & Lloyd, J. W. (1993). An analysis of self-management. *Journal of Behavioral Education, 3,* 405–425.

Hutton, J. B. (1985). What reasons are given by teachers who refer problem behavior students? *Psychology in the Schools, 22,* 79–82.

Iano, R. (1986). The study and development of teaching: With implications for the advancement of special education. *Remedial and Special Education, 7*(5), 50–61.

Idol, L., & Croll, V. (1987). Story mapping training as a means of improving reading comprehension. *Learning Disability Quarterly, 10,* 214–230.

Inhelder, B., Sinclair, H., & Bovet, M. (1974). *Learning and the development of cognition.* Cambridge, MA: Harvard University Press.

Jenkins, J. R., Barksdale, A., & Clinton, L. (1978). Improving reading comprehension and oral reading: Generalization across behaviors, settings, and time. *Journal of Learning Disabilities, 11,* 607–617.

Jenkins, J. R., & Larson, K. (1979). Evaluating error-correction procedures for oral reading. Journal of Special Education, 13, 145–156.

Johnston, M. B., & Whitman, T. (1987). Enhancing math computation through variations in training format and instructional content. *Cognitive Therapy and Research, 11,* 381–397.

Johnston, M. B., Whitman, T. L., & Johnson, M. (1981). Teaching addition and subtraction to mentally retarded children: A self-instructional program. *Applied Research in Mental Retardation, 1,* 141–160.

Kameenui, E., Carnine, D. W., & Maggs, A. (1980). Instructional procedures for teaching reversible passive voice and clause constructions to three mildly handicapped children. *The Exceptional Child, 27*(1), 29–41.

Karegianes, M. L., Pascarella, E. T., & Pflaum, S. W. (1980). The effects of peer editing on the writing proficiency of low-achieving tenth grade students. *Journal of Educational Research, 73,* 203–207.

Kauffman, J. M. (1989). *Characteristics of children's behavior disorders* (4th ed.). Columbus, OH: Merrill.

Kauffman, J. M. (1997). *Characteristics of emotional and behavioral disorders of children and youth* (6th ed.) Upper Saddle River, NJ: Merrill.

Kauffman, J. M., Hallahan, D. P., Haas, K., Brame, T., & Boren, R. (1978). Imitating children's errors to improve their spelling performance. *Journal of Learning Disabilities, 11,* 217–222.

Kavale, K. (1981). Functions of the Illinois Test of Psycholinguistic Abilities (ITPA): Are they trainable? *Exceptional Children, 47,* 495–510.

Kavale, K. (1982). The efficacy of stimulant drug treatment for hyperactivity: A meta-analysis. *Journal of Learning Disabilities, 15,* 280–289.

Keller, C. E. (1991). Cognitive-behavioral assessment and intervention. In H. L. Swanson (Ed.), *Handbook on the assessment of learning disabilities: Theory, research, and practice* (pp. 331–349). Austin, TX: PRO-ED.

Keller, C. E., & Lloyd, J. W. (1989). Cognitive training: Implications for arithmetic instruction. In J. N. Hughes & R. J. Hall (Eds.), *Cognitive behavioral approaches in educational settings* (pp. 280–304). New York: Guilford Press.

Kelly, B., Carnine, D., Gersten, R., & Grossen, B. (1986). The effectiveness of videodisc instruction in teaching fractions to learning-disabled and remedial high school students. *Journal of Special Education Technology, 8*(2), 5–17.

Kendall, P. C., & Cummings, L. (1988). Thought and action in educational interventions: Cognitive-behavioral approaches. In J. C. Witt, S. N. Elliott, & F. M. Gresham (Eds.), *Handbook of behavior therapy in education* (pp. 403–418. New York: Plenum Press.

Keogh, B. K., & Hall, R. J. (1984). Cognitive training with learning-disabled pupils. In A. W. Meyers & W. E. Craighead (Eds.), *Cognitive behavior therapy with children* (pp. 163–191). New York: Plenum Press.

Kephart, N. C. (1971). *Slow learner in the classroom* (2nd ed.). Columbus, OH: Merrill.

Kirk, S. A., & Elkins, J. (1975). Characteristics of children enrolled in the child service demonstration centers. *Journal of Learning Disabilities, 8,* 630–637.

Knapczyk, D. R., & Livingston, G. (1974). The effects of prompting question-asking upon on-task and reading comprehension. *Journal of Applied Behavior Analysis, 7,* 115–121.

Kneedler, R. D., & Meese, R. L. (1988). Learning-disabled children. In J. C. Witt, S. N. Elliott, & F. M. Gresham (Eds.), *Handbook of behavior therapy in education* (pp. 601–629). New York: Plenum Press.

Kosiewicz, M. M., Hallahan, D. P., Lloyd, J., & Graves, A. W. (1982). Effects of self-instruction and self-correction procedures on handwriting performance. *Learning Disability Quarterly, 5,* 71–78.

Kratochwill, T. R., & Levin, J. R. (1992). S*ingle-case research design and analysis: New directions for psychology and education.* Hillsdale, NJ: Lawrence Erlbaum.

LaBerge, D., & Samuels, S. J. (1974). Toward a theory of automatic information processing in reading. *Cognitive Psychology, 6,* 293–323.

Lahey, B. B. (1976). Behavior modification with learning disabilities and related problems. In M. Hersen, R. M. Eisler, & P. M. Miller (Eds.), *Progress in behavior modification* (Vol. 3, pp. 173–205). New York: Academic Press.

Lahey, B. B., Busemeyer, M. K., O'Hara, C., & Beggs, V. E. (1977). Treatment of severe perceptual-motor disorders in children diagnosed as learning disabled. *Behavior Modification, 1,* 123–140.

Lahey, B. B., McNees, M. P., & Brown, C. C. (1973). Modification of deficits in reading for comprehension. *Journal of Applied Behavior Analysis, 6,* 475–480.

Leon, J. A., & Pepe, H. J. (1983). Self-instructional training: Cognitive-behavior modification for remediating arithmetic deficits. *Exceptional Children, 50,* 54–60.

Lerner, J. W. (1997). *Learning disabilities: Theories, diagnosis, and teaching strategies.* Boston: Houghton-Mifflin.

Lesh, R., & Landau, M. (Eds.). (1983). *Acquisition of mathematics concepts and processes.* New York: Academic Press.

Levin, J. R. (1973). Inducing comprehension in poor readers: A test of a recent model. *Journal of Education Psychology, 65,* 19–24.

Lewis, C., Hitch, G. J., & Walker, P. (1994). The prevalence of specific arithmetic difficulties and specific reading difficulties in 9- to 10-year-old boys and girls.

Journal of Child Psychology and Psychiatry and Allied Disciplines, 35, 283–292.

Lloyd, J. (1980). Academic instruction and cognitive-behavior modification: The need for attack strategy training. *Exceptional Education Quarterly, 1*(1), 53–63.

Lloyd, J. W. (1988). Direct academic interventions in learning disabilities. In M. C. Wang, M. C. Reynolds, & H. J. Walberg (Eds.), *The Handbook of Special Education: Research and Practice* (Vol. 2; pp. 345–366). Oxford, England: Pergamon Press.

Lloyd, J. W., Bateman, D. F., Landrum, T. J., & Hallahan, D. P. (1989). Self-recording of attention versus productivity. *Journal of Applied Behavior Analysis, 22,* 315–323.

Lloyd, J. W., Cullinan, D., Heins, E. D., & Epstein, M. H. (1980). Direct instruction: Effects on oral and written language comprehension. *Learning Disability Quarterly, 3*(4), 70–77.

Lloyd, J., Epstein, M. H., & Cullinan, D. (1981). Direct teaching for learning disabilities. In J. Gottlieb & S. S. Strichart (Eds.), *Developmental theory and research in learning disabilities* (pp. 278–309). Baltimore, MD: University Park Press.

Lloyd, J. W., Kauffman, J. M., Landrum, T. J., & Roe, D. L. (1991). Why do teachers refer pupils for special education? An analysis of referral records. *Exceptionality, 2,* 115–126.

Lloyd, J. W., Keller, C. E. (1989). Effective mathematics instruction. *Focus on Exceptional Children, 21*(7), 1–10.

Lloyd, J. W., Kneedler, R. D., & Cameron, N. A. (1982). Effects of verbal self-guidance on word reading accuracy. *Reading Improvement, 19,* 84–89.

Lloyd, J. W., & Landrum, T. J. (1991). Self-recording of attending to task: Treatment components and generalization of effects. In T. Scruggs & B. Y. L. Wong (Eds.), *Current intervention research in learning disabilities* (pp. 235–262). New York: Springer-Verlag.

Lloyd, J., Saltzman, N. J., & Kauffman, J. M. (1981). Predictable generalization in academic learning as a result of pre-skills and strategy training. *Learning Disability Quarterly, 4,* 203–216.

Lloyd, J. W., Tankersley, M., & Talbott, E. (1994). Using single-subject research methods to study learning disabilities. In S. Vaughn & C. Bos (Eds.), *Research issues in learning disabilities: Theory, methodology, assessment, and ethics* (pp. 163–177) New York: Springer-Verlag.

Loper, A. B., & Murphy, D. M. (1985). Cognitive self-regulatory training for underachieving children. In D.

Forrest-Pressley, G. E. MacKinnon, & T. G. Waller (Eds.), *Metacognition, cognition, and human performance* (Vol II, pp. 223–265). New York: Plenum Press.

Lovitt, T. C. (1973). *Applied behavior analysis techniques and curriculum research.* Report submitted to the National Institute of Education.

Lovitt, T. C., & Curtiss, K. A. (1968). Effects of manipulating an antecedent event on mathematics response rate. *Journal of Applied Behavior Analysis, 1,* 329–333.

Lovitt, T. C., & Hansen, C. L. (1976). The use of contingent skipping and drilling to improve oral reading and comprehension. *Journal of Learning Disabilities, 9,* 481–487.

Lovitt, T. C., & Hurlburt, M. (1974). Using behavior analysis techniques to assess the relationship between phonics instruction and oral reading. *Journal of Special Education, 8,* 57–72.

Lubke, M. M., Rogers, B., & Evans, K. T. (1989). Teaching fractions with videodiscs. *Teaching Exceptional Children, 21,* 55–56.

MacArthur, C. A., & Graham, S. (1987). Learning disabled students' composing under three methods of text production: Handwriting, word processing, and dictation. *Journal of Special Education, 21,* 22–42.

Mahoney, M. J. (1974) *Cognition and behavior modification.* Cambridge, MA: Ballinger.

Malamuth, Z. N. (1979). Self-management training for children with reading problems: Effects on reading performance and sustained attention. *Cognitive Therapy and Research, 3,* 279–289.

Maloney, K. B., & Hopkins, B. L. (1973). The modification of sentence structure and its relationship to subjective judgments of creativity in writing. *Journal of Applied Behavior Analysis, 6,* 425–433.

Maloney, K. B., Jacobson, C. R., & Hopkins, B. L. (1975). An analysis of the effects of lecture, requests, teacher praise, and free time on the creative writing behaviors of third-grade children. In E. Ramp & G. Semb (Eds.), *Behavior analysis: Areas of research and application* (pp. 244–260). Englewood Cliffs, NJ: Prentice-Hall.

Marsh, H. W. (1990). The structure of academic self-concept: The Marsh/Shavelson model. *Journal of Educational Psychology, 82,* 625–636.

Martin, K. F., & Manno, C. (1995). Use of a check-off system to improve story compositions by middle school students. *Journal of Learning Disabilities, 28,* 139–149.

McKinney, J. D. (1983). Contributions of the institutes for research on learning disabilities. *Exceptional Education Quarterly, 4*(1), 129–144.

McLaughlin, T. F. (1984). A comparison of self-recording plus consequences for on-task and assignment completion. *Contemporary Educational Psychology, 9,* 185–192.

McNaughton, D., Hughes, C. A., & Clark, K. (1994). Spelling instruction for students with learning disabilities: Implications for research and practice. *Learning Disability Quarterly, 17,* 169–185.

McNutt, G. (1984). A holistic approach to language arts instruction in the resource room. *Learning Disability Quarterly, 7,* 315–320.

Meichenbaum, D. (1977). *Cognitive-behavior modification: An integrative approach.* New York: Plenum Press.

Meltzer, L, & Reid, D. K. (1994). New direction in the assessment of students with special needs: The shift toward a constructivist perspective. *Journal of Special Education, 29,* 328–335.

Mischel, W. (1973). Toward a cognitive social learning reconceptualization of personality. *Psychological Review, 80,* 252–283.

Montague, J., Graves, A., & Leavell, A. (1991). Planning, procedural facilitation, and narrative composition of junior high students with learning disabilities. *Learning Disabilities Research and Practice, 6,* 219–224.

Moran, M. R., Schumaker, J. B., & Vetter, A. F. (1981). *Teaching a paragraph organization strategy to learning disabled adolescents* (Research Report No. 54). Lawrence, KS: University of Kansas Institute for Research in Learning Disabilities.

Nelson, R. O., & Hayes, S. N. (1981). Theoretical explanations for reactivity in self-monitoring. *Behavior Modification, 5,* 3–14.

Norman, C., & Zigmond, N. (1980). Characteristics of children labeled and served as learning disabled in school systems affiliated with child service and demonstration centers. *Journal of Learning Disabilities, 13,* 542–547.

Packard, R. G. (1970). The control of "classroom attention": A group contingency for complex behavior. *Journal of Applied Behavior Analysis, 3,* 13–28.

Palinscar, A. S. (1986). Metacognitive strategy instruction. *Exceptional Children, 53,* 118–124.

Palinscar, A. S., & Brown, A. L. (1984). The reciprocal teaching of comprehension fostering and comprehension monitoring activities. *Cognition and Instruction, 1,* 117–175.

Palinscar, A. S., & Klenk, L. (1993). Broader vision encompassing literacy, learners, and contexts. *Remedial and Special Education, 14,* 19–25.

Parsons, J. A. (1972). The reciprocal modification of arithmetic behavior and program development. In G. Semb (Ed.), *Behavior analysis and education—1972* (pp. 185–199). Lawrence: Kansas University Department of Human Development.

Pascarella, E. T., & Pflaum, S. W. (1981). The interaction of children's attribution and level of control over error correction in reading instruction. *Journal of Educational Psychology, 73,* 533–540.

Pellegrino, J. W., & Goldman, S. R. (1987). Information processing elementary mathematics. *Journal of Learning Disabilities, 20,* 23–32, 57.

Perkins, V. L., & Cullinan, D. (1984). Effects of direct instruction intervention for fraction skills. *Education and Treatment of Children, 7,* 109–117.

Pflaum, S. W., & Pascarella, E. T. (1980). Interactive effects of prior reading achievement and training in context on the reading of learning disabled children. *Reading Research Quarterly, 16,* 138–158.

Piaget, J., & Inhelder, B. (1969a). *Memory and intelligence.* New York: Basic Books.

Piaget, J., & Inhelder, B. (1969b). *The psychology of the child.* New York: Basic Books.

Polloway, E. J., Epstein, M. H., Polloway, C., Patton, J., & Ball, D. (1986). Corrective Reading Program: An analysis of effectiveness with learning disabled and mentally retarded students. *Remedial and Special Education, 7,* 41–47.

Poplin, M. S. (1988a). Holistic/constructivist principles of the teaching/learning process: Implications for the field of learning disabilities. *Journal of Learning Disabilities, 21*(7), 401–416.

Poplin, M. S. (1988b). The reductionistic fallacy in learning disabilities: Replicating the past by reducing the present. *Journal of Learning Disabilities, 21*(7), 389–400.

Reid, D. K. (1991). Assessment strategies inspired by genetic epistemology. In H. L. Swanson (Ed.), *Handbook on the assessment of learning disabilities: Theory, research, and practice* (pp. 249–263). Austin, TX: PRO-ED.

Reid, D. K., & Hresko, W. P. (1981). *A cognitive approach to learning disabilities.* New York: McGraw-Hill.

Resnick, L. B., & Ford, W. W. (1981). *The psychology of mathematics for instruction.* Hillsdale, NJ: Lawrence Erlbaum.

Robin, R. L., Armel, S., & O'Leary, K. D. (1975). The effects of self-instruction on writing deficiencies. *Behavior Therapy, 6,* 73–77.

Romberg, T. A., & Carpenter, T. P. (1986). Research on teaching and learning mathematics: Two disciplines of scientific inquiry. In M. C. Wittrock (Ed.), *Handbook of research on teaching* (3rd ed., pp. 850–873). New York: Macmillan.

Rose, T. L. (1985). The effects of two prepractice procedures on oral reading. *Journal of Learning Disabilities, 16,* 544–548.

Rose, T. L., Koorland, M.A., & Epstein, M. H. (1982). A review of applied behavior analysis with learning disabled children. *Education and Treatment of Children, 5,* 41–58.

Rosenshine, B., & Stevens, R. (1986). Teaching functions. In M. C. Wittrock (Ed.), *Handbook of research on teaching* (3rd ed., pp. 376–391). New York: Macmillan.

Samuels, S. J. (1981). Some essentials of decoding. *Exceptional Education Quarterly, 2*(1), 11–25.

Schoenfeld, A. H. (1987). *Mathematical problem solving.* Orlando, FL: Academic Press.

Schumaker, J. B., Deshler, D. D., Alley, G. R., Warner, M. M., & Denton, P. H. (1982). Multipass: A learning strategy for improving reading comprehension. *Learning Disability Quarterly, 5,* 295–304.

Schumm, J. S. (1992). Using story grammar with at-risk high school students. *Journal of Reading, 35,* 296.

Schunk, D. H., & Cox, P. D. (1986). Strategy training and attributional feedback with learning disabled students. *Journal of Educational Psychology, 78,* 201–209.

Scruggs, T. E., Mastropieri, M. A., McLoone, B. B., Levin, J. R., & Morrison, C. (1987). Mnemonic facilitation of text-embedded science facts with LD students. *Journal of Educational Psychology, 78,* 27–34.

Seabaugh, G. O., & Schumaker, J. B. (1993). The effects of self-regulation training on the academic productivity of secondary students with learning problems. *Journal of Behavioral Education, 4,* 109–133.

Serwer, B. L., Shapiro, B. J., & Shapiro, P. P. (1973). The comparative effectiveness of four methods of instruction of the achievement of children with specific learning disabilities. *Journal of Special Education, 7,* 241–249.

Shaywitz, S. E., Shaywitz, B. A., Fletcher, J. M., & Escobar, M. D. (1990). Prevalence of reading disability in boys and girls. *Journal of American Medical Association, 264,* 998–1002.

Skinner, B. F. (1953). *Science and human behavior.* New York: Macmillan.

Skinner, B. F. (1968). *The technology of teaching.* New York: Appleton-Century-Crofts (Prentice-Hall).

Smith, D. D., & Lovitt, T. C. (1973). The educational diagnosis and remediation of written b and d reversal problems: A case study. *Journal of Learning Disabilities, 6,* 356–363.

Smith, D. D., & Lovitt, T. C. (1975). The use of modeling techniques to influence the acquisition of computational arithmetic skills in learning-disabled children. In E. Ramp & G. Semb (Eds.), *Behavior analysis: Areas of research and application* (pp. 282–308). Englewood Cliffs, NJ: Prentice-Hall.

Smith D. D., & Lovitt, T. C. (1976). The differential effects of reinforcement contingencies on arithmetic performance. *Journal of Learning Disabilities, 9,* 21–29.

Stein, C. L'E., & Goldman, J. (1980). Beginning reading instruction for children with minimal brain dysfunction. *Journal of Learning Disabilities, 13,* 219–222.

Stephens, R., & Hudson, A. (1984). A comparison of the effects of direct instruction and remedial English classes on the spelling skills of secondary students. *Educational Psychology, 4,* 261–267.

Stevenson, J. (1992). Genetics. In N. N. Singh & I. L. Beale (Eds.), *Learning disabilities: Nature, theory, and practice* (pp. 327–351). New York: Springer-Verlag.

Stromer, R. (1975). Modifying letter and number reversals in elementary school children. *Journal of Applied Behavior Analysis, 8,* 211.

Stromer, R. (1977). Remediating academic deficiencies in learning disabled children. *Exceptional Children, 43,* 432–440.

Swanson, H. L. (1990). Instruction derived from the strategy deficit model: Overview of principles and procedures. In T. E. Scruggs & B. Y. L. Wong (Eds.), *Intervention research in learning disabilities* (pp. 34–65). New York: Springer-Verlag.

Swanson, L. (1981a). Modification of comprehension deficits in learning disabled children. *Learning Disability Quarterly, 4,* 189–202.

Swanson, L. (1981b). Self-monitoring effects on concurrently reinforced reading behavior of a learning disabled child. *Child Study Journal, 10,* 225–232.

Thackwray, D., Meyers, A., Schlesser, R., & Cohen, R. (1985). Achieving generalization with general versus specific self-instructions: Effects of academically deficient children. *Cognitive Therapy and Research, 9,* 291–308.

Torgesen, J. K. (1988). Studies of children with learning disabilities who perform poorly on memory span tasks. *Journal of Learning Disabilities, 21,* 605–611.

Torgesen, J. K. (1991). Subtypes as prototypes: Extended studies of rationally defined extreme groups. In L. V. Feagans, E. J. Short, & L. J. Meltzer (Eds.), *Subtypes of learning disabilities: Theoretical perspectives and research* (pp. 229–246). Hillsdale, NJ: Lawrence Erlbaum.

Vreeland, M., Vail, J., Bradley, L., Buetow, C., Cipriano, K., Green, C., Henshaw, P., & Huth, E. (1994). Accelerating cognitive growth: The Edison School math project. *Effective School Practices, 13*(2), 64–69.

Walker, H. M, & Buckley, N. K. (1968). The use of positive reinforcement in conditioning attending behavior. *Journal of Applied Behavior Analysis, 1,* 245–250.

Wallach, M. A., & Wallach, L. (1976). *Teaching all children to read.* Chicago: University of Chicago Press.

Weiss, M. P., & Lloyd, J. W. (in preparation). *Story grammar effects on reading and writing.* Unpublished manuscript, University of Virginia.

Wellington, J. (1994). Evaluating a mathematics program for adoption: Connecting Math Concepts. *Effective School Practices, 13*(2), 70–75.

White, W. A. T. (1988). A meta-analysis of the effects of direct instruction in special education. *Education and Treatment of Children, 11,* 364–374.

Whitman, T., & Johnston, M. B. (1983). Teaching addition and subtraction with regrouping to educable mentally retarded children: A group self-instructional training program. *Behavior Therapy, 14,* 127–143.

Whitman, T., Burgio, L., & Johnston, M. B. (1984). Cognitive behavioral interventions with mentally retarded children. In A. W. Meyers & W. E. Craighead (Eds.), *Cognitive behavior therapy with children* (pp. 193–227). New York: Plenum Press.

Williams, J. P. (1980). Teaching decoding with an emphasis on phoneme analysis and phoneme blending. *Journal of Educational Psychology, 72,* 1–15.

Williams, J. P. (1990). The use of schema in research on the problem-solving of learning-disabled adolescents. In T. E. Scruggs & B. Y. L. Wong (Eds.), *Intervention research in learning disabilities* (pp. 304–321). New York: Springer-Verlag.

Witt, J. C., Elliott, S. N., & Gresham, F. M. (Eds.). (1988). *Handbook of behavior therapy in education.* New York: Plenum Press.

Wong, B. Y. L. (1985a). Metacognition and learning disabilities. In D. L. Forrest-Pressley, G. E. MacKinnon, & T. G. Waller (Eds.), *Metacognition, cognition, and human performance* (Vol. 2, pp. 137–180). New York: Academic Press.

Wong, B. Y. L. (1985b). Issues in cognitive-behavioral interventions in academic skill areas. *Journal of Abnormal Child Psychology, 13,* 425–441.

Wong, B. Y. L., & Jones, W. (1982). Increasing metacomprehension in learning disabled and normally achieving students through self-question training. *Learning Disability Quarterly, 5,* 228–240.

Ysseldyke, J. E., & Salvia, J. (1974). Diagnostic-prescriptive teaching: Two models. *Exceptional Children, 41,* 181–186.

Zimmerman, E. H., & Zimmerman, J. (1962). The alteration of behavior in a special classroom situation. *Journal of Experimental Analysis of Behavior, 5,* 59–60.

CHAPTER 7

CONDUCT DISORDER

Alan E. Kazdin

Conduct disorder encompasses a broad range of anti-social behaviors such as aggressive acts, theft, vandalism, firesetting, lying, truancy, and running away. Although these behaviors are diverse, their common characteristic is that they tend to violate major social rules and expectations. Many of the behaviors often reflect actions against the environment, including both persons and property. Antisocial behaviors emerge in some form over the course of normal development. Fighting, lying, stealing, destruction of property, and noncompliance are relatively common at different points in childhood and adolescence. For the most part, these behaviors diminish over time, do not interfere with everyday functioning, and do not predict untoward consequences in adulthood.

The term conduct disorder is usually reserved for a pattern of antisocial behavior, that is associated with significant impairment in everyday functioning at home or school, and concerns of significant others that the child or adolescent is unmanageable. The extent to which antisocial behaviors are sufficiently severe to constitute conduct disorder depends on several characteristics of the behaviors including their frequency, intensity, and chronicity, whether they are isolated acts or part of a larger syndrome with other deviant behaviors, and whether they lead to significant impairment of the child, as judged by parents, teachers, or others.

Little in the way of effective treatment has been generated for the treatment of conduct disorder. This is unfortunate in light of the personal tragedy that conduct disorder can represent to children and their families and others who may be victims of aggressive and antisocial acts. From a social perspective,

Completion of this paper was supported by a Research Scientist Award (MH00353) and a grant (MH35408) from the National Institute of Mental Health. Support for this work is gratefully acknowledged. Correspondence should be directed to: Alan E. Kazdin, Department of Psychology, Yale University, P.O. Box 208205, New Haven, Connecticut, 06520-8205.

the absence of effective treatments is problematic as well. Conduct disorder is one of the most frequent bases of clinical referral in child and adolescent treatment services, has relatively poor long-term prognosis, and is transmitted across generations (see Kazdin, 1995b). Conduct disorder is likely to bring the youth into contact with various social agencies. Mental health services (clinics, hospitals) and the criminal justice system (police, courts) are the major sources of contact for youth whose behaviors are identified as severe. Within the educational system, special services, teachers, and classes are often provided to manage such children. Because children with conduct disorder often traverse multiple social services, the disorder is one of the most costly mental disorders in the United States (Robins, 1981).

There have been significant advances in treatment. This chapter reviews research for treatments that have shown considerable promise in the treatment of conduct disorder in children and adolescents.[1] The treatments were selected because they have been carefully evaluated in controlled clinical trials. This chapter describes and evaluates the underpinnings, techniques, and evidence in behalf of these treatments. Critical issues that are raised in providing treatment to conduct disorder children and their families also are examined. Evaluation of alternative treatments depends on clarifying the full range of characteristics of conduct disorder to convey the areas that treatment may need to address to be effective.

CHARACTERISTICS OF CONDUCT DISORDER

Descriptive Features: Diagnosis and Prevalence

The overriding feature of conduct disorder is a persistent pattern of behavior in which the rights of others and age-appropriate social norms are violated. Isolated acts of physical aggression, destruction of property, stealing, and firesetting are sufficiently severe to warrant concern and attention in their own right. Although these behaviors may occur in isolation, several of these are likely to appear together as a constellation or syndrome and form the basis of a clinical diagnosis. For example, in the *Diagnostic and Statistical Manual of Mental Disorders* (DSM-IV; American Psychiatric Association, 1994), the diagnosis of Conduct Disorder (CD) is reached if the child shows at least 3 of the 15 symptoms within in the past 12 months, with at least 1 symptom evident within the past 6 months. The symptoms include: bullying others, initiating fights, using a weapon, being physically cruel to others or to animals, stealing while confronting a victim, destroying property, breaking into others' property, stealing items of nontrivial value, staying out late, running away, lying, deliberate firesetting, and truancy.

Using these diagnostic criteria or prior versions of the DSM, the prevalence of the disorder among community samples of school-age youth is approximately 2–6% (see Zoccolillo, 1993). One of the most frequent findings is that boys show approximately 3–4 times higher rates of CD than girls. Rates of conduct disorder tend to be higher for adolescents (approximately 7% for youth ages 12–16) than for children (approximately 4% for children age 4–11) (Offord, Boyle, & Racine, 1991). The higher prevalence rate for boys is associated primarily with childhood-onset conduct disorder; the boy-to-girl ratio evens out in adolescence. Characteristic symptom patterns tend to differ as well. Child-onset conduct problems tend to reflect aggressive behavior, whereas adolescent-onset problems tend to reflect delinquent behavior (theft, vandalism).

The prevalence rates are only approximations of conduct disorder as a dysfunction among children and adolescents. The criteria for delineating individual symptoms as present and for delineating the diagnosis are somewhat arbitrary. Youth who approximate but fail to meet the diagnosis often are significantly impaired. Also, the symptom picture one obtains varies considerably as a function of source of information (e.g., parent, teacher, child).

---

[1]Children will be used to refer to both children and adolescents. When pertinent to the discussion, a distinction will be made and referred to accordingly.

For these reasons, it is useful to retain the distinction between conduct disorder as a general pattern of behavior and the diagnosis of CD. The general pattern of conduct disorder behavior has been studied extensively using varied populations (e.g., clinical referrals and delinquent samples) and defining criteria (Kazdin, 1995b). There is widespread agreement and evidence that a constellation of antisocial behaviors can be identified and has correlates related to child, parent, and family functioning. Moreover, antisocial behaviors included in the constellation extend beyond those recognized in diagnosis (e.g., substance abuse, associating with delinquent peers).

Causes and Long-Term Clinical Course

Conduct disorder is not the result of a single cause or simple set of antecedents. Current work tends to focus on characteristics, events, and experiences that influence the likelihood (increase the risk) of conduct disorder. The factors that predispose children and adolescents to conduct disorder have been studied extensively in the context of clinical referrals and adjudicated delinquents (see Kazdin, 1995b; Patterson, Reid, & Dishion, 1992; Robins & Rutter, 1990). Numerous factors have been implicated. Table 7.1 highlights several risk factors that have been studied along with a general statement of the relation that has been found.

Merely enumerating risk factors is misleading without conveying some of the complexities in how they operate. These complexities have direct implications for interpreting the findings, for understanding the disorder, and for identifying at-risk children for preventive interventions. First, risk factors tend to come in "packages." Thus, at a given point in time several factors may be present such as low income, large family size, overcrowding, poor housing, poor parental supervision, parent criminality, and marital discord, to mention a few (Kazdin, 1995b). Second, over time, several risk factors become interrelated, because the presence of one factor can augment the accumulation of other risk factors. For example, early academic dysfunction can lead to truancy and dropping out of school, which further increase risk for conduct disorder.

Third, risk factors may interact with (i.e., be moderated or influenced by) each other and with other variables (see Boyle & Offord, 1990). As one example, large family size has been repeatedly shown to be a risk factor for conduct disorder. However, the importance of family size as a predictor is moderated by income. If family income and living accommodations are adequate, family size is less likely to be a risk factor (West, 1982). As another example, risk factors often interact with age of the child (e.g., infancy, early or middle childhood). For example, marital discord or separation appear to serve as risk factors primarily when they occur early in the child's life (e.g., within the first 4 or 5 years) (Wadsworth, 1979). How risk factors exert impact in childhood and why some periods of development are sensitive to particular influences underscore the importance of understanding "normal" developmental processes.

There are important conclusions resulting from risk-factor research. First, no single characteristic or factor seems to be necessary or sufficient for the onset of the disorder. Second, even though some risk factors are more important than others, the accumulation of factors (i.e., number present) itself is important. One or two risk factors may not increase risk very much; with several risk factors, the likelihood of the outcome may increase sharply (e.g., Rutter, Tizard, & Whitmore, 1970; Sanson, Oberklaid, Pedlow, & Prior, 1991). Third, even with the presence of multiple risk factors, the outcome is not determined. Some individuals at high risk may not show the dysfunction (Werner & Smith, 1992). Many factors that contribute to reducing risk, referred to as protective factors, have been studied and identified (see Kazdin, 1995b).

Longitudinal studies have consistently shown that conduct disorder identified in childhood predicts a continued course of social dysfunction, problematic behavior, and poor school adjustment. For example, antisocial child behavior predicts multiple problems in adulthood 30 years later (Robins, 1966). Youth who are referred for their antisocial behavior, compared to youth with other clinical problems or matched normal controls, as adults suffer dysfunction in psychiatric symptoms, criminal behavior, physical health, and social adjustment. Even though conduct disorder in childhood portends a number of other significant problems in adulthood, not all antisocial children suffer impairment as adults.

TABLE 7.1. Factors that Place Youth at Risk for the Onset of Conduct Disorder

CHILD FACTORS

Child Temperament. A more difficult child temperament (on a dimension of "easy-to-difficult"), as characterized by more negative mood, lower levels of approach toward new stimuli, and less adaptability to change.

Neuropsychological Deficits and Difficulties. Deficits in diverse functions related to language (e.g., verbal learning, verbal fluency, verbal IQ), memory, motor coordination, integration of auditory and visual cues, and "executive" functions of the brain (e.g., abstract reasoning, concept formation, planning, control of attention).

Subclinical Levels of Conduct Disorder. Early signs (e.g., elementary school) of mild ("subclinical") levels of unmanageability and aggression, especially with early age of onset, multiple types of antisocial behaviors, and multiple situations in which they are evident (e.g., at home, school, the community).

Academic and Intellectual Performance. Academic deficiencies and lower levels of intellectual functioning.

PARENT AND FAMILY FACTORS

Prenatal and Perinatal Complications. Pregnancy and birth-related complications including maternal infection, prematurity and low birth weight, impaired respiration at birth, and minor birth injury.

Psychopathology and Criminal Behavior in the Family. Criminal behavior, antisocial personality disorder, and alcoholism of the parent.

Parent-Child Punishment. Harsh (e.g., severe corporal punishment) and inconsistent punishment increase risk.

Monitoring of the Child. Poor supervision, lack of monitoring of whereabouts, and few rules about where children can go and when they can return.

Quality of the Family Relationships. Less parental acceptance of their children, less warmth, affection, and emotional support, and less attachment.

Marital Discord. Unhappy marital relationships, interpersonal conflict, and aggression of the parents.

Family Size. Larger family size, that is, more children in the family.

Sibling With Antisocial Behavior. Presence of a sibling, especially an older brother, with antisocial behavior.

Socioeconomic Disadvantage. Poverty, overcrowding, unemployment, receipt of social assistance ("welfare"), and poor housing.

SCHOOL-RELATED FACTORS

Characteristics of the Setting. Attending schools where there is little emphasis on academic work, little teacher time spent on lessons, infrequent teacher use of praise and appreciation for school work, little emphasis on individual responsibility of the students, poor working conditions for pupils (e.g., furniture in poor repair), unavailability of the teacher to deal with children's problems, and low teacher expectancies.

Note: The list of risk factors highlights major influences. The number of factors and the relations of specific factors to risk are more complex than the summary statements noted here. For a more detailed discussion, other sources can be consulted (e.g., Kazdin, 1995b; Loeber, 1990; Mrazek & Haggerty, 1994).

Drawing from multiple samples, Robins (1978) noted that among the most severely antisocial children, less than 50% become antisocial adults. If diverse diagnoses are considered, rather than serious antisocial behavior alone, the picture of impairment in adulthood is much worse. Among children referred for antisocial behavior, 84% received a diagnosis of psychiatric disorder as adults (Robins, 1966). Similar patterns have been found in other follow-up studies of conduct disordered youth. In brief, the data suggest that the majority of children with clinically referred antisocial behavior will suffer from a significant degree of impairment over the course of their lives.

The Scope of Dysfunction

If one were to consider "only" the symptoms of conduct disorder and the persistence of impairment, the challenge of identifying effective treatments would be great enough. However, the presenting characteristics of children and their families usually raise a number of other considerations that are central to treatment.

Consider characteristics of children, families, and contexts that are associated with conduct disorder, as a backdrop for later comments on treatment.

Child Characteristics

Children who meet criteria for CD are likely to meet criteria for other disorders as well. The co-existence of more than one disorder is referred to as comorbidity. In general, diagnoses involving disruptive or externalizing behaviors (CD, Oppositional Defiant Disorder [ODD], and Attention Deficit/Hyperactivity Disorder [ADHD]) often go together. In studies of community and clinic samples, a large percentage of youth with CD or ADHD (e.g., 45–70%) also meet criteria for the other disorder (e.g., Fergusson, Horwood, & Lloyd, 1991; Offord et al., 1991). The co-occurrence of CD and ODD is common as well. Among clinic-referred youth who meet criteria for CD, 84–96% also meet concurrent diagnostic criteria for ODD (see Hinshaw, Lahey, & Hart, 1993). CD is sometimes comorbid with anxiety disorders and depression (Hinshaw et al., 1993; Walker et al., 1991).

Several other associated features of CD are relevant to treatment. For example, children with conduct disorder are also likely to show academic deficiencies, as reflected in achievement level, grades, being left behind in school, early termination from school, and deficiencies in specific skill areas such as reading. Youth with the disorder are likely to evince poor interpersonal relations, as reflected in diminished social skills in relation to peers and adults and higher levels of peer rejection. Conduct disorder youth also are likely to show deficits and distortions in cognitive problem-solving skills, attributions of hostile intent to others, and resentment and suspiciousness. Clearly, the disorder is pervasive in the scope of characteristics that are affected for the child with conduct disorder.

Parent and Family Characteristics

Several parent and family characteristics are associated with conduct disorder (see Kazdin, 1995b; Robins, 1991; Rutter & Giller, 1983). The prior comments on risk factors convey major characteristics that are likely to be evident among families with a conduct disorder child who is referred to treatment. Criminal behavior and alcoholism are two of the stronger and more consistently demonstrated parental characteristics. Parent disciplinary practices and attitudes, especially harsh, lax, erratic, and inconsistent discipline practices, often characterize the parents. Dysfunctional relations are also evident, as reflected in less acceptance of their children, less warmth, affection, emotional support, and less attachment, compared to parents of nonreferred youth. Less supportive and more defensive communications among family members, less participation in activities as a family, and more clear dominance of one family member are also evident. In addition, unhappy marital relations, interpersonal conflict, and aggression characterize the parental relations of antisocial children. Poor parental supervision and monitoring of the child and knowledge of the child's whereabouts also are associated with conduct disorder.

Contextual Conditions

Conduct disorder is associated with a variety of untoward living conditions such as large family size, overcrowding, poor housing, and disadvantaged school settings (see Kazdin, 1995b). Many of the untoward conditions in which families live place stress on the parents or diminish their threshold for coping with everyday stressors. The net effect can be evident in parent-child interactions in which parents inadvertently engage in patterns that sustain or accelerate antisocial and aggressive interactions (e.g., Dumas & Wahler, 1983; Patterson, Capaldi, & Bank, 1991).

Quite often the child's dysfunction is embedded is a larger context that cannot be neglected in conceptual views about the development, maintenance, and course of conduct disorder nor in the actual delivery of treatment. For example, at our outpatient clinical service (Yale Child Conduct Clinic), it is likely that a family referred for treatment will experience a subset of these characteristics: financial hardship (unemployment, significant debt, bankruptcy), untoward living conditions (dangerous neighborhood, small living quarters), transportation obstacles (no car or car in frequent repair, state provided taxi service), psychiatric impairment of one of the parents, stress related to significant others (former spouses, boyfriends, or girlfriends), and adversarial contact with an outside agency (schools, youth services, courts). Conduct disorder is conceived as a dysfunction of children and adolescents. The accumulated evidence regarding the symptom constellation, risk factors, and course over childhood, adolescence, and adulthood attests to the heuristic value of focusing on characteristics of the individual. At the same time, there is a child-parent-family-context *gestalt* that includes multiple and reciprocal influences that affect each participant (child and parent) and the systems in which they operate (family, school) (Kazdin, 1993). For treatment to be effective, it is likely that multiple domains will have to be addressed.

CURRENT TREATMENTS

The Challenges of Treatment

Many aspects of conduct disorder have major implications for the implementation and evaluation of alternative treatments. Key characteristics to bear in mind for effective intervention are the pervasiveness and stability of conduct disorder. Youth with conduct disorder are likely to show dysfunction in diverse areas of their lives. They are likely to function poorly at home and at school; and within a given setting multiple problems are likely to be evident. For example, at school, antisocial youth often perform poorly on academic tasks and have few prosocial relations with their peers. The core symptoms of the conduct disorder appear to begin a sequence of events that support continued dysfunction. Thus, failure to complete homework and possible truancy or lying are likely to portend further deterioration (expulsion, school transfer). In general, the associated features of conduct disorder convey the breadth of dysfunction in academic, cognitive, and interpersonal domains. Apart from pervasive dysfunction, parents and family correlates raise critical issues as well. Parents and the family may suffer significant dysfunction that is related to the child's problems. Parent psychopathology and

harsh child-rearing practices, already mentioned, may contribute directly to promote antisocial child behavior (see Kazdin, 1995b). In general, the challenge of antisocial behavior derives in part from the range of characteristics with which it is associated and the implications regarding where to intervene.

Overview of Current Treatments

Many different treatments have been applied to conduct disorder youth, including psychotherapy, pharmacotherapy, psychosurgery, home, school, and community-based programs, residential and hospital treatment, and social services (see Brandt & Zlotnick, 1988; Dumas, 1989; Kazdin, 1985, US Congress, 1991). A vast array of psychotherapies are available, extending to over 230 documented treatments for children and adolescents (Kazdin, 1988); the majority have not been studied. The treatments can be encompassed by broad classes; Table 7.2 highlights major classes of treatment and their therapeutic foci.

The majority of treatments focus on the individual by altering a particular facet of functioning or processes within the child. Diverse approaches that focus on changing the individual child include individual and group therapy, behavioral and cognitive therapies, and pharmacotherapies. A number of other treatments focus on the family. Treatment is aimed at altering interaction patterns or other family processes in the home; techniques such as family therapy and parent management training are examples. Other treatments are worth delineating on the basis of their use or incorporation of therapeutic influences in the context of the community. The influence of direct contact and involvement of youth with prosocial peers and community services is accorded major weight. Community-based techniques often rely on other treatments such as psychotherapy and behavior therapy. Yet these are integrated within a larger social, organizational, and peer-group context. Within a given class of treatment, several variations can be identified. For example, individual psychotherapy consists of psychodynamic, nondirective, play therapies, and others. Similarly, behavior therapy can include a range of techniques

TABLE 7.2. Therapeutic Focus and Processes of Major Classes of Treatment

TYPES OF TREATMENT	FOCUS	KEY PROCESSES
Child-Focused Treatments		
Individual Psychotherapy	Focus on intrapsychic bases of antisocial behavior, especially conflicts and psychological processes that were adversely over the course of development.	Relationship with the therapist is the primary medium through which change is achieved. Treatment provides a corrective emotional experience by providing insight and exploring new ways behaving.
Group Psychotherapy	Processes of individual therapy, as noted above. Additional processes are reassurance, feedback, and vicarious gains by peers. Group processes such as cohesion and leadership also serve as the focus.	Relationship with the therapist and peers as part of the group. Group processes emerge to provide children with experiences and feelings of others and opportunities to test their own views and behaviors.
Behavior Therapy	Problematic behaviors are presented as target symptoms. Prosocial behaviors are trained directly.	Learning of new behaviors through direct training, via modeling, reinforcement, practice and role playing. Training in the situations (e.g., at home, in the community) where the problematic behaviors occur.
Problem-Solving Skills Training	Cognitive processes and interpersonal cognitive problem-solving skills that underlie social behavior.	Teach problem-solving skills to children by engaging in a step-by-step approach to inter personal situations. Use of modeling, practice, rehearsal, and role play to develop problem-solving skills. Development of an internal dialogue or private speech that utilizes the processes of identifying prosocial solutions to problems.
Pharmacotherapy	Designed to affect the biological substrates of behavior, especially in light of laboratory-based findings on neuro humors, biological cycles, and other physiological correlates of aggressive and emotional behavior.	Administration of psychotropic agents to control antisocial behavior. Lithium carbonate and haloperidol have been used because of their antiaggressive effects.
Residential Treatments	Means of administering other techniques in day treatment or residential setting. Foci of other techniques apply.	Processes of other techniques apply. Also, separation of the child from parents or removal from the home situation may help reduce untoward processes or crises that contribute to the clinical problem.
Family-Focused Treatments		
Family Therapy	Family as a functioning system serves as focus rather than the identified patient. Interpersonal relationships, organization, roles, and dynamics of the family.	Communication, relationships, and structure within the family and such processes as developing autonomy, problem-solving skills, and the ability to negotiate.
Parent Management Training	Interactions in the home, especially those involving coercive exchanges.	Direct training of parents to develop prosocial behavior in their children. Explicit use of social learning techniques to influence the child.
Community-Based Treatments		
Community-Wide Interventions	Focus on activities and community programs to foster competence and prosocial peer relations.	Develop prosocial behavior and connections with peers. Activities are seen to promote prosocial behavior and to be incompatible with antisocial behavior.

Source: From *The Practice of Child Therapy* (2nd ed., p. 180) by T. R. Kratochwill and R. J. Morris (eds.), 1991, Boston: Allyn & Bacon. Copyright 1991 by Allyn & Bacon. Reprinted by permission.

such as social-skills training, contingency management, and token economies. At the level of specific techniques, rather than the more generic classes of treatment, the number of available procedures is great. Among those that have, none has been shown to controvert conduct disorder and its long-term course. Many treatments might seem reasonable to apply to conduct disorder. Conduct disorder is a dysfunction with pervasive features so that one can point to virtually any domain (e.g., psychodynamics, family interaction patterns, cognitive deficiencies) and find aberrations, deficits, and deficiencies.

A number of promising treatments have been identified. For present purposes, promising treatments are identified on the basis of multiple criteria. First, it is important for treatment to have some theoretical rationale that notes how the dysfunction, in this case conduct disorder, comes about and then how treatment redresses the dysfunction. Specification of the mechanisms leading to conduct disorder and leading to therapeutic change are required for this initial criterion. Second, basic research on these processes too would be very important to support the conceptualization. Basic research refers to studies that examine conduct problems and factors that lead to their onset, maintenance, exacerbation, amelioration, or attenuation. An example would be studies of the family that demonstrate specific interaction patterns among parents and children that exacerbate aggression within the home (Patterson et al., 1992). Third, outcome data that the treatment can achieve change are obviously central. In the present paper, randomized, controlled outcome research is used as the criterion for identifying treatments. Finally, evidence from outcome research that shows a relation between processes hypothesized to be critical to therapeutic change and actual change would be very persuasive. Assessment of processes might be reflected in cognitions, family interaction, or core conflicts and defenses. Therapeutic change would be shown to covary with the extent to which these processes

were altered in treatment. Very little research addresses this aspect of treatment and hence this criterion is important to note as an objective toward which research might strive.

No single treatment among those available adequately traverses all of these criteria. Yet, a number of promising treatments have been identified for conduct disorder. Four treatment approaches with evidence in their behalf are illustrated below. In highlighting the approaches, the purpose is not to convey that only four promising treatments exist. Yet, these four are clearly among the most well-developed in relation to the criteria highlighted here and the number of controlled clinical trials.[2]

PROMISING TREATMENT APPROACHES

Cognitive Problem-Solving Skills Training

Background and Underlying Rationale

Cognitive processes refer to a broad class of constructs that pertain to how the individual perceives, codes, and experiences the world. Individuals who engage in conduct disorder behaviors, particularly aggression, show distortions and deficiencies in various cognitive processes. These deficiencies are not merely reflections of intellectual functioning. Although selected processes (recall, information processing) are related to intellectual functioning, their impact has been delineated separately and shown to contribute to behavioral adjustment and social behavior. A variety of cognitive processes have been studied, such as generating alternative solutions to interpersonal problems (e.g., different ways of handling social situations), identifying the means to obtain particular ends (e.g., making friends), or consequences of one's actions (e.g., what could happen

---

[2] The rationale, empirical underpinnings, outcome research, and treatment procedures cannot be fully elaborated for each of the techniques. References will be made to reviews of the evidence and to treatment manuals that elaborate each of the treatments.

after a particular behavior); making attributions to others of the motivation of their actions; perceiving how others feel; expectations of the effects of one's own actions, and others (see Shirk, 1988; Spivack & Shure, 1982). Deficits and distortion among these processes relate to teacher ratings of disruptive behavior, peer evaluations, and direct assessment of overt behavior (e.g., Lochman & Dodge, 1994; Rubin, Bream, & Rose-Krasnor, 1991).

As an illustration, aggression is not merely triggered by environmental events, but rather through the way in which these events are perceived and processed. The processing refers to the child's appraisals of the situation, anticipated reactions of others, and self-statements in response to particular events. For example, attribution of intent to others represents a salient cognitive disposition critically important to understanding aggressive behavior. Aggressive youth tend to attribute hostile intent to others, especially in social situations where the cues of actual intent are ambiguous (see Crick & Dodge, 1994). Understandably, when situations are initially perceived as hostile, youth are more likely to react aggressively. In general, research on cognitive processes, as illustrated by this example, has served as an important heuristic base for conceptualizing treatment and for developing specific treatment strategies.

Characteristics of Treatment

Problem-solving skills training (PSST) consists of developing interpersonal cognitive problem-solving skills. Although many variations of PSST have been applied to conduct problem children, several characteristics usually are shared. First, the emphasis is on how children approach situations, that is, the thought processes in which the child engages to guide responses to interpersonal situations. The children are taught to engage in a step-by-step approach to solve interpersonal problems. They make statements to themselves that direct attention to certain aspects of the problem or tasks that lead to effective solutions. Second, behaviors that are selected (solutions) to the interpersonal situations are important as well. Prosocial behaviors are fostered through modeling and direct reinforcement as

part of the problem-solving process. Third, treatment utilizes structured tasks involving games, academic activities, and stories. Over the course of treatment, the cognitive problem-solving skills are increasingly applied to real-life situations in which oppositional, aggressive, and antisocial behavior have been evident for the child. Fourth, therapists usually play an active role in treatment. They model the cognitive processes by making verbal self-statements, applying the sequence of statements to particular problems, providing cues to prompt use of the skills, and deliver feedback and praise to develop correct use of the skills. Finally, treatment usually combines several different procedures including modeling and practice, role playing, and reinforcement and mild punishment (loss of points or tokens). These are deployed in systematic ways to develop increasingly complex response repertoires of the child.

Illustration

The application of PSST can be illustrated more concretely in a case application. Cory was a 10-year-old boy who was hospitalized on a short-term children's inpatient unit. He was hospitalized to begin a treatment regimen designed to control his aggressive and disruptive behavior at home and at school. At home, Cory constantly fought with his siblings, stole personal possessions of all family members, swore, disobeyed family rules, and refused to participate in family activities. He had been caught on three occasions playing with matches and setting fires in his room. At school, Cory had been in fights with several of his peers in class. He threatened peers, ran around the classroom throwing crayons and pencils as if they were darts, and hit the teacher with various toys and supplies. Before coming for treatment, he was suspended from school for assaulting a classmate and choking him to the point that the child almost passed out.

PSST was begun and completed while Cory was in the hospital because his parents said they could not bring him back for treatment on an outpatient basis once hospitalization had ended. Cory received 20 individual sessions of PSST with 2–3 sessions each week. The treatment was administered by a masters-degree level social worker with special training in PSST. The treatment sessions began by teaching Cory the problem-solving steps. These consist of specific self-statements, with each statement representing a step for solving a problem. The steps or self-statements include:

1. What am I supposed to do?
2. I have to look at all my possibilities.
3. I have to concentrate and focus in.
4. I need to make a choice and select a solution.
5. I need to find out how I did.

In the first session, Cory was taught the steps so they could be recalled without special reminders or cues from the therapist. In the next several sessions, the steps were applied to simple problems involving various academic tasks (e.g., arithmetic problems) and board games (e.g., checkers). In each of these sessions, Cory's task was to find out what the goal was (e.g., to move his checkers without being jumped), what the choices were and the consequences of each, what the best choice was, and so on. In the session, Cory and the therapist took turns using the steps to work on the task. In these early sessions, the focus was on teaching the steps and training Cory to become facile in applying them to diverse but relatively simple situations. After the eighth session, the games were withdrawn, and the focus was on applying the steps to problems that were related to interactions with parents, teachers, siblings, peers, and others.

Cory was also given assignments outside of treatment. The assignments initially were to identify "real" problems (e.g., with another child on the inpatient service) where he could use the steps. When he brought one of these situations to the session, he described how the steps could have been used. He earned points for bringing in such a situation and these points could be exchanged for small prizes. As the sessions progressed, he received points for not only thinking of situations outside of treatment but also for using the steps in the actual situations. His use of the steps was checked by asking him exactly what he did, role playing the situation within the session, and asking other staff on the ward if the events were accurate.

The majority of treatment consisted of applying the steps in the session to situations where Cory's aggressive and antisocial behaviors have emerged. To illustrate how this proceeds, portions of session 17 follow:

Therapist: Well, Cory today we are going to act out some more problem situations using the steps. You have been doing so well with this that I think we can use the steps today in a way that will make it even easier to use them in everyday life. When you use the steps today, I want you to think in your mind what the first steps are. When you get to step 4, say that one out loud before you do it. This will let us see what the solution is that you have chosen. Then, step 5, when you evaluate how you did, can also be thought in your mind. We are going to do the steps in our heads today like this so that it will be easier to use them in every day life without drawing attention to what we are doing. The same rules apply as in our other sessions. We still want to go slowly in using the steps and we want to select good solutions.

Okay, today I brought in a lot of difficult situations. I think it is going to be hard to use the steps. Let's see how each of us does. I have six stacks of cards here. You can see the stacks are numbered from 1 to 6. We will take turns rolling the die and take a card from the stack with the same number. As we did in the last session, we are going to solve the problem as we sit here, then we will get up and act it out as if it is really happening. Okay, why don't you go first and roll the die.

Cory: (rolls the die). I got a 4.

Therapist: Okay, read the top card in that stack (therapist points).

Cory: (reads the card) "The principal of your school is walking past you in the hall between classes when he notices some candy wrappers that someone has dropped on the floor. The principal turns to you and says in a pretty tough voice, 'Cory, we don't litter in the halls at this school! Now pick up the trash!'"

Therapist: This is a tough one—how are you going to handle this?

Cory: Well, here goes with the steps. (Cory holds his first finger up and appears to be saying step 1 to himself; he does this with steps 2 and 3 as well. When he gets to step 4 he says out loud,) I would say to him that I did not throw the wrappers down and I would keep walking.

Therapist: Well, it was great that you did not get mad and talk back to him. He was sort of accusing you and you hadn't really thrown the papers down. But, if you just say, "I didn't do it." and walk away, what might happen?

Cory: Nothing. Because I didn't do it.

Therapist: Yeah, but he may not believe youÑ maybe especially because you got into trouble before with him. Also, he asked you for a favor and you could help a lot by doing what he asked. Try going through the steps again and see if you can turn your pretty good solution into a great one.

Cory: (goes through steps 1, 2, and 3 again; at step 4 he says,) I would say to him that I did not throw the wrappers down but that I would gladly pick 'em up and toss them in the trash.

Therapist: (with great enthusiasm) That's greatÑthat's a wonderful solution! Okay, go to step 5, how do you think you did?

Cory: I did good because I used the steps.

Therapist: That's right but you did more than that. You nicely told the principal that you did not do it and you did the favor he asked. What do you think he will think of you in the future?

Very nicely done. Okay, now let's both get up and act this out. I am the principal. Why don't you stand over there (pointing to the opposite corner of the treatment room). Okay, let's start.

"Hey, Cory, pick up those wrappers on the floor, you are not supposed to litter in the halls, you now better than that."

Cory: (carries out steps 1, 2, and 3 in his head. At step 4 he acts out the step directly in face-to-face interaction with the principal [i.e., therapist] and says,) "Mr. Putnam, I didn't throw these on the floor but if you want I will pick them up and toss them in the trash."

Therapist: (acting as principal) Yeah, that would be great. Thanks for helping out; these kids make a mess of this place.

Therapist: (as herself). Well, Cory how do you think you did?

Cory: Pretty good because I used the steps and got a good solution.

Therapist: (as herself). I think you did great!

The treatment session continues like this with a variety of situations. When the child does especially well, the situation may be made a little more difficult or provocative to help him apply the steps under more challenging circumstances.

Overview of the Evidence

Several randomized clinical trials have been completed with impulsive, aggressive, and conduct disorder children and adolescents, as reviewed in meta-analyses (see Baer & Nietzel, 1991; Durlak, Furhman, & Lampman, 1991). Among the different studies, control and comparison conditions have included no-treatment, waiting list, and other treatments such as individual psychotherapy. Cognitively based treatments have significantly reduced aggressive and antisocial behavior at home, at school, and in the community and have surpassed the impact of these other control and comparison conditions. At follow-up, these gains have been evident up to one year later. Many early studies in the field (e.g., 1970s–80s) focused on impulsive children and nonpatient samples. Since that time, several studies have shown treatment effects with inpatient and outpatient samples (see Kazdin, 1993; Kendall, 1991; Pepler & Rubin, 1991).

There is only sparse evidence that addresses the child, parent, family, contextual, or treatment factors that influence treatment outcome. Some evidence suggests that older children profit more from treatment than younger children, perhaps due to their cognitive development (Durlak et al., 1991). However, the basis for differential responsiveness to treatment as a function of age has not been well tested. Conduct disorder children who show comorbid diagnoses, academic delays and dysfunction, and lower reading achievement and who come from families with high levels of impairment (parent psychopathology, stress, and family dysfunction) respond less well to treatment than children with less dysfunction in these domains (Kazdin, 1995a; Kazdin & Crowley, 1997). However, these child, parent, and family characteristics may influence the effectiveness of several different treatments for conduct disorder children rather than PSST in particular. Much further work is needed to evaluate factors that contribute to responsiveness to treatment.

Overall Evaluation

There are features of PSST that make it an extremely promising approach for clinical use. First, and perhaps most importantly, several controlled outcome studies with clinical samples have shown that cognitively based treatment leads to therapeutic change. Second, basic research in developmental psychology continues to elaborate the relation of maladaptive cognitive processes among children and adolescents and conduct problems that serve as underpinnings of treatment (Crick & Dodge, 1994; Shirk, 1988). Third, and on a more practical level, many versions of treatment are available in manual form (e.g., Feindler & Ecton, 1986; Finch, Nelson, & Ott, 1983; Shure, 1992) to facilitate further evaluation and refinement in research and application in clinical practice.

Fundamental questions remain regarding the effects of cognitively based treatment for conduct disorders. To begin, the role of cognitive processes in clinical dysfunction and treatment warrant further evaluation. Evidence is not entirely clear showing that a specific pattern of cognitive processes characterizes youth with conduct disorder, rather than adjustment problems more generally. Also, although evidence has shown that cognitive processes change with treatment, evidence has not established that change in these processes is correlated with improvements in treatment outcome. This means that the bases for therapeutic change has yet to be established. Also, characteristics of children and their families and parameters of treatment that may influence outcome have not been carefully explored in relation to treatment outcome. Clearly, central questions about treatment and its effects remain to be addressed. Even so, PSST is highly promising because treatment effects have been replicated in several controlled studies with conduct disorder youth.

Parent Management Training

Background and Underlying Rationale

Parent management training (PMT) refers to procedures in which parents are trained to alter their child's behavior in the home. The parents meet with a therapist or trainer who teaches them to use specific procedures to alter interactions with their child, to promote prosocial behavior, and to decrease deviant behavior. Training is based on the general view that conduct problem behavior is inadvertently developed and sustained in the home by maladaptive parent-child interactions. There are multiple facets of parent-child interaction that promote aggressive and antisocial behavior. These patterns include directly reinforcing deviant behavior, frequently and ineffectively using commands and harsh punishment, and failing to attend to appropriate behavior (Patterson, 1982; Patterson et al., 1992).

It would be misleading to imply that the parent generates and is solely responsible for the child-parent sequences of interactions. Influences are bidirectional, so that the child influences the parent as well (see Bell & Harper, 1977; Lytton, 1990). Indeed, in some cases, children engage in deviant behavior to help prompt the parent-child interaction sequences. For example, when parents behave inconsistently and unpredictably (e.g., not attending to the child in the usual ways), the child may engage in some deviant behavior (e.g., whining, throwing some object). The effect is to cause the parent to respond in more predictable ways (see Wahler & Dumas, 1986). Essentially, inconsistent and unpredictable parent behavior is an aversive condition for the child; the child's deviant behavior is negatively reinforced by terminating this condition. However, the result is also to increase parent punishment of the child.

Among the many interaction patterns, those involving coercion have received the greatest attention (Patterson et al., 1992). Coercion refers to deviant behavior on the part of one person (e.g., the child), which is rewarded by another person (e.g., the parent). Aggressive children are inadvertently rewarded for their aggressive interactions and their escalation of coercive behaviors, as part of the discipline practices that sustain aggressive behavior. The critical role of parent-child discipline practices has been supported by correlational research, relating specific discipline practices to child antisocial behavior, and by experimental research, showing that directly altering these practices reduces antisocial child behavior (see Dishion, Patterson, & Kavanagh, 1992).

The general purpose of PMT is to alter the pattern of interchanges between parent and child so that prosocial, rather than coercive, behavior is directly reinforced and supported within the family. This requires developing several different parenting behaviors, such as establishing the rules for the child to follow, providing positive reinforcement for appropriate behavior, delivering mild forms of punishment to suppress behavior, negotiating compromises, and other procedures. These parenting behaviors are systematically and progressively developed within the sessions in which the therapist shapes (develops through successive approximations) parenting skills. The programs that parents eventually implement in the home also serve as the basis for the focus of the sessions in which the procedures are modified and refined.

Characteristics of Treatment

Although many variations of PMT exist, several common characteristics can be identified. First, treatment is conducted primarily with the parents who implement several procedures in the home. The parents meet with a therapist who teaches them to use specific procedures to alter interactions with their child, to promote prosocial behavior and to decrease deviant behavior. There usually is little direct intervention of the therapist with the child. With young children, the child may be brought into the session to help train both parent and child how to interact and especially to show the parent precisely how to deliver antecedents (prompts) and consequences (reinforcement, time out from reinforcement). Older children may participate to negotiate and develop behavior-change programs in the home. Second, parents are trained to identify, define, and observe problem behaviors in new ways. Careful specification of the problem is essential for delivering reinforcing or punishing consequences and for evaluating if the program is achieving the desired goals. Third, the treatment sessions cover social learning principles and the procedures that follow from them including: positive reinforcement (e.g., the use of social praise and tokens or points for prosocial behavior), mild punishment (e.g., use of time out from reinforcement, loss of privileges),

negotiation, and contingency contracting. Fourth, the sessions provide opportunities for parents to see how the techniques are implemented, to practice using the techniques, and to review the behavior-change programs in the home. The immediate goal of the program is to develop specific skills in the parents. As the parents become more proficient, the program can address the child's most severely problematic behaviors and encompass other problem domains (e.g., school behavior). Over the course of treatment, more complex repertoires are developed, both in the parents and the child. Finally, child functioning at school is usually incorporated into the program. Parent-managed reinforcement programs for child deportment and performance at school, completion of homework, and activities on the playground often are integrated into the behavior-change programs. If available, teachers can play an important role in monitoring or providing consequences for behaviors at school.

Illustration

The application of PMT can be illustrated by a case of a 7-year-old boy, named Shawn, referred for treatment because of his aggressive outbursts toward his two younger sisters at home as well as his peers at school. He argued and had severe tantrums at home, stayed out late at night, and occasionally stole from his stepfather. At school, his behavior in class was difficult to control. He fought with peers, argued with the teacher, and disrupted the class. PMT was provided to the mother. The stepfather could not attend the meetings on a regular basis due to his work as a trucker and his extended periods away from home. Training began by discussing Shawn's behavior and discussing childrearing practices that might be useful in developing prosocial behavior as well as reducing or eliminating the problems for which he was referred.

A master-degree level clinician trained in PMT for over two years administered treatment. She agreed to meet with the parents once each week for approximately 16 sessions. The overall goals of treatment was to train the parents to behave differently in relation to Shawn and their other children. Specifically, they were to be trained to identify concrete behaviors to address their concerns, to observe these behaviors systematically, to implement positive reinforcement programs, to provide mild punishment as needed, and to negotiate such programs directly with Shawn.

The contents of the 16 sessions provided to the parents are highlighted in Table 7.3. In each session, the trainer reviewed the previous week's data collection and implementation of the program. The purpose was to identify the parents' behavior in relation to their children. Queries were made to review precisely what the parents did (e.g., praise, administer points or tokens, send Shawn to time out) in response to the Shawn's behavior. Although the parents would invariably focus on the behavior of the child and how well or poorly the child was doing, the trainer directed the conversation toward the behaviors that the parents performed in relation to the child. The trainer and parent(s) role-played situations at home where the parents might have responded more effectively. The parents practiced delivering the consequences and received feedback and reinforcement for this behavior from the trainer. Any problems in the programs, ambiguity of the observation procedures, or other facets were discussed. Thus, the initial portion of the session was used to review practical issues and applications for the previous week. After the program was reviewed, new material was taught (see Table 7.3).

Each session with Shawn's mother lasted about 2 hours. Between the weekly sessions, the trainer called the parents on two occasions to find out how the programs were working and to handle any problems. The calls between sessions were designed to correct problems immediately instead of waiting until one week had elapsed. Shawn's mother and the therapist developed a program to increase Shawn's compliance with requests. Simple chores were requested (e.g., cleaning his room, setting the table) in the first few weeks of the program to help the parents apply what they had learned. Time out from reinforcement was introduced to provide mild punishment for fighting. Any fights in the home resulted in Shawn going to an isolated place in the hall near the kitchen of his home for a period of 5 minutes. If he went to time out immediately on instructions from his mother or stepfather, the duration of

time out was automatically reduced to 2 minutes.

Over time, several behaviors were incorporated into a program where Shawn earned points that could purchase special privileges (e.g., staying up 15 minutes beyond bedtime, having a friend sleep over, small prizes, time to play his video game). About half way through treatment, a home-based reinforcement program was developed to alter behaviors at school. Two teachers at the school were contacted and asked to identify target behaviors. The program was explained in which they were asked to initial cards that Shawn carried to indicate how well he behaved in class and whether he completed his homework. Based on daily teacher evaluations, Shawn earned additional points at home.

After approximately 5 months, Shawn improved greatly in his behavior at home. He argued very little with his mother and sisters. His parents felt they were much better able to manage him. At school, Shawn's teachers reported that he could remain in class like other children. Occasionally, he would not listen to the teacher or get into heated arguments with peers on the playground. However, he was less physically aggressive than he had been prior to treatment.

Overview of the Evidence

Over the past 25 years, a large number of randomized, controlled studies of PMT have been completed with youth varying in age and degree of severity of dysfunction (e.g., oppositional, conduct disorder, delinquent youth) (see Kazdin, 1993; McMahon & Wells, 1989; Miller & Prinz, 1990; Patterson, Dishion, & Chamberlain, 1993). Treatment effects have been evident in marked improvements in child behavior on a wide range of measures including parent and teacher reports of deviant behavior, direct observation of behavior at home and at school, and institutional (e.g., school, police) records. The effects of treatment have also been shown to bring problematic behaviors of treated children within normative levels of their peers who are functioning adequately in the community. Follow-up assessment has shown that the gains are often maintained 1–2 years after treatment. Longer follow-up assessment is rarely assessed, although

TABLE 7.3. PARENT MANAGEMENT TRAINING SESSIONS FOR THE CASE OF SHAWN

SESSION, TOPIC, AND BRIEF DESCRIPTION

1. **Introduction and Overview**—This session provides the parents with an overview of the program and outlines the demands placed upon them and the focus of the intervention.

2. **Defining and Observing**—This session trains parents to pinpoint, define, and observe behavior. The parents and trainer define specific problems that can be observed, and develop a specific plan to begin observations.

3. **Positive Reinforcement**—This session focuses on learning the concept of positive reinforcement, factors that contribute to the effective application, and rehearsal of applications in relation to the target child. Specific programs are outlined where praise and points are to be provided for the behaviors observed during the week.

4. **Review of the Program and Data**—Observations of the previous week as well as application of the reinforcement program are reviewed. Details about the administration of praise, points, and back-up reinforcers are discussed and as needed enacted so the trainer can identify how to improve parent performance. Changes are made in the program as needed.

5. **Time Out from Reinforcement**—Parents learn about time out and the factors related to its effective application. The use of time out is planned for the next week for specific behaviors.

6. **Shaping**—Parents are trained to develop behaviors by reinforcement of successive approximations and to use prompts and fading of prompts to develop terminal behaviors.

7. **Review and Problem Solving**—In this session, the concepts discussed in all prior sessions are thoroughly reviewed. The parent is asked to apply these concepts to hypothetical situations presented within the session. Areas of weakness in understanding the concepts or their execution in practice serve as the focus.

8. Attending and Ignoring—In this session, parents learn about attending and ignoring and choose undesirable behavior that they will ignore and a positive opposite behavior to which they will attend. These procedures are practiced within the session.

9. **School Intervention**—In this session, plans are made to implement a home-based reinforcement program to develop school-related behaviors. Prior to this sessions, discussions with the teachers and parents have identified specific behaviors to focus on in class (e.g., deportment) and at home (e.g., homework completion). These behaviors are incorporated into the reinforcement system.

10. **Reprimands**—Parents are trained in effective use of reprimands.

11. **Family Meeting**—At this meeting, the child and parent(s) are bought into the session. The programs are discussed along with any problems. Revisions are made as needed to correct misunderstandings or to alter facets that may not be implemented in a way that is likely to be effective.

12. **Review of Skills**—Here the programs are reviewed along with all concepts about the principles. Parents are asked to develop programs for a variety of hypothetical everyday problems at home and at school. Feedback is provided regarding program options and applications.

13. **Negotiating and Contracting**—The child and parent meet together to negotiate new behavioral programs and to place these in contractual form.

14. **Low Rate Behaviors**—Parents are trained to deal with low rate behaviors such as firesetting, stealing, or truancy. Specific punishment programs are planned and presented to the child as needed for behaviors characteristic of the case.

15. and 16. **Review, Problem Solving, and Practice**—Material from other sessions is reviewed in theory and practice. Special emphasis is given to role playing application of individual principles as they are enacted with the trainer. Parents practice designing new programs, revising ailing programs, and responding to a complex array of situations in which principles and practices discussed in prior sessions are reviewed.

one program reported maintenance of gains 10–14 years later (Forehand & Long, 1988; Long, Forehand, Wierson, & Morgan, 1994).

The impact of PMT can be relatively broad. The effects of treatment are evident for child behaviors that have not been focused on directly as part of training. Also, siblings of children referred for treatment improve, even though they are not directly focused on in treatment. This is an important effect because siblings of conduct disorder youth are at risk for severe antisocial behavior. In addition, maternal psychopathology, particularly depression, decreases systematically following PMT (see Kazdin, 1985). These changes suggest that PMT alters multiple aspects of dysfunctional families.

Several characteristics of the treatment contribute to outcome. Duration of treatment appears to influence outcome. Brief and time-limited treatments (e.g., < 10 hrs..) are less likely to show benefits with clinical populations. More dramatic and durable effects have been achieved with protracted or time-unlimited programs extending up to 50 or 60 hours of treatment (see Kazdin, 1985). Second, specific training components, such as providing parents with in-depth knowledge of social learning principles and utilizing time out from reinforcement in the home, enhance treatment effects. Third, some evidence suggests that therapist training and skill are associated with the magnitude and durability of therapeutic changes, although this has yet to be carefully tested. Fourth, families characterized by many risk factors associated with childhood dysfunction (e.g., socioeconomic disadvantage, marital discord, parent psychopathology, poor social support) tend to show fewer gains in treatment than families without these characteristics and to maintain the gains less well (e.g., Dadds & McHugh, 1992; Dumas & Wahler, 1983; Webster-Stratton, 1985). Some efforts to address parent and family dysfunction during PMT have led to improved effects of treatment outcome for the child in some studies (e.g., Dadds, Schwartz, & Sanders, 1987; Griest et al., 1982), but not in others (Webster-Stratton, 1994). Much more work is needed on the matter given the prominent role of parent and family dysfunction among many youth referred for treatment.

One promising line of work has focused on implementation of PMT in community, rather than clinic settings. The net effect is to bring treatment to those persons least likely to come to, or remain in, treatment. In one study, for example, when PMT was delivered in small parent groups in the community, the effectiveness surpassed what was achieved with clinic-based PMT. Also, community-based treatment was considerably more cost effective (Cunningham, Bremner, & Boyle, 1995).

Conceptual development of processes underlying parent-child interaction and conduct disorder continues (e.g., Patterson et al., 1992). Also, recent research on processes in treatment represents a relat-ed and important advance. A series of studies on therapist-parent interaction within PMT sessions has identified factors that contribute to parent resistance (e.g., parent saying, "I can't," "I won't"). The significance of this work is in showing that parent reactions in therapy relate to their discipline practices at home, that changes in resistance during therapy predicts change in parent behavior, and that specific therapist ploys (e.g., reframing, confronting) can help overcome or contribute to resistance (Patterson & Chamberlain, 1994). This line of work advances our understanding of PMT greatly by relating in-session interactions of the therapist and parent to child functioning and treatment outcome.

Overall Evaluation

The extensive outcome evidence makes PMT one of the most promising treatments. The evidence is bolstered by related lines of work. First, the study of family interaction processes that contribute to antisocial behavior in the home and evidence that changing these processes alters child behavior provide a strong empirical base for treatment. Second, the procedures and practices that are used in PMT (e.g., various forms of reinforcement and punishment practices) have been widely and effectively applied outside the context of conduct disorder. For example, the procedures have been applied with parents of children with autism, language delays, developmental disabilities, medical disorders for which compliance with special treatment regimens is required, and with parents who physically abuse or neglect their children (see Kazdin, 1994a). Third, a great deal is known about the procedures and the parameters that influence the reinforcement and punishment practices that form the core of PMT. Consequently, very concrete recommendations can be provided to change behavior and to alter programs when behavior change has not occurred.

Treatment manuals and training materials for PMT are available for parents and therapists (e.g., Forehand & McMahon, 1981; Sanders & Dadds, 1993). Also noteworthy is the development of self-administered videotapes of treatment. In a programmatic series of studies with young conduct problem children (3–8 years), Webster-Stratton and her colleagues have developed and evaluated videotaped materials to present PMT to parents; treatment can be self-administered in individual or group format supplemented with discussion (e.g., Webster-Stratton, 1994; Webster-Stratton, Hollinsworth, & Kolpacoff, 1989). Controlled studies have shown clinically significant changes at post-treatment and follow-up assessments with variations of videotaped treatment. The potential for extension of PMT with readily available and empirically tested videotapes presents a unique feature in child treatment.

Several limitations of PMT can be identified as well. First, some families may not respond to treatment. PMT makes several demands on the parents, such as mastering educational materials that convey major principles underlying the program, systematically observing deviant child behavior and implementing specific procedures at home, attending weekly sessions, and responding to frequent telephone contacts made by the therapist. For some families, the demands may be too great to continue in treatment. Interestingly, within the approach several procedures (e.g., shaping parent behavior through reinforcement) provide guidelines for developing parent compliance and the desired response repertoire in relation to their children.

Second, perhaps the greatest limitation or obstacle in using PMT is that there are few training opportunities for professionals to learn the approach. Training programs in child psychiatry, clinical psychology, and social work are unlikely to provide exposure to the technique, much less opportunities for formal training. PMT requires mastery of social learning principles and multiple procedures that derive from them (Cooper, Heron, & Heward, 1987; Kazdin, 1994a). For example, the administration of reinforcement by the parent in the home (to alter child behavior) and by the therapist in the session (to change parent behavior) requires more than passing familiarity with the principle and the parametric variations that dictate its effectiveness (e.g., administration of reinforcement contingently, immediately, frequently, use of varied and high quality reinforcers; use of prompts, shaping). The requisite skills in administering these within the

treatment sessions can be readily trained but they are not trivial.

PMT has been applied primarily to parents of children and adolescents. Although treatment has been effective with delinquent adolescents (Bank, Marlow, Reid, Patterson, & Weinrott, 1991) and younger adolescents with conduct problems that have not yet been referred for treatment (Dishion & Andrews, 1995), some evidence suggests that treatment is more effective with preadolescent youth (see Dishion & Patterson, 1992). Parents of adolescents may less readily change their discipline practices and also have higher rates of dropping out of treatment. The importance and special role of peers in adolescence and greater time that adolescents spend outside the home suggest that the principles and procedures may need to be applied in novel ways. At this point, few PMT programs have been developed specifically for adolescents, and so conclusions about the effects for youth of different ages must be tempered. On balance, PMT is one of the most promising treatment modalities. No other intervention for conduct disorder has been investigated as thoroughly as PMT.

Functional Family Therapy

Background and Underlying Rationale

Functional family therapy (FFT) reflects an integrative approach to treatment that relies on systems, behavioral, and cognitive views of dysfunction (Alexander, Holtzworth-Munroe, & Jameson, 1994; Alexander & Parsons, 1982). Clinical problems are conceptualized from the standpoint of the functions they serve in the family as a system, as well as for individual family members. Problem behavior evident in the child is assumed to be the way in which some interpersonal functions (e.g., intimacy, distancing, support) are met among family members. Maladaptive processes within the family are considered to preclude a more direct means of fulfilling these functions. The goal of treatment is to alter interaction and communication patterns in such a way as to foster more adaptive functioning. Treatment is also based on learning theory and focuses on specific stimuli and responses that can be used to produce change. Social-learning concepts and procedures, such as identifying specific behaviors for change, reinforcing new adaptive ways of responding, and evaluating and monitoring change, are included in this perspective. Cognitive processes refer to the attributions, attitudes, assumptions, expectations, and emotions of the family. Family members may begin treatment with attributions that focus on blaming others or themselves. New perspectives may be needed to help serve as the basis for developing new ways of behaving.

The underlying rationale emphasizes a family-systems approach. Specific treatment strategies draw on findings that underlie PMT in relation to maladaptive and coercive parent-child interactions, discussed previously. FFT views interaction patterns from a broader systems view that focus also on communication patterns and their meaning. As an illustration of salient constructs, research underlying FFT has found that families of delinquents show higher rates of defensiveness in their communications, both in parent-child and parent-parent interactions, blaming, and negative attributions, and also lower rates of mutual support compared to families of nondelinquents (see Alexander & Parsons, 1982). Improving these communication and support functions is a goal of treatment.

Characteristics of Treatment

FFT requires that the family see the clinical problem from the relational functions it serves within the family. The therapist points out interdependencies and contingencies between family members in their day-to-day functioning and with specific reference to the problem that has served as the basis for seeking treatment. Once the family sees alternative ways of viewing the problem, the incentive for interacting more constructively is increased.

The main goals of treatment are to increase reciprocity and positive reinforcement among family members, to establish clear communication, to help specify behaviors that family members desire from each other, to negotiate constructively, and to help identify solutions to interpersonal problems. In therapy, family members identify behaviors they would like others to perform. Responses are incorporated into a reinforcement system in the home to promote adaptive behavior in exchange for privileges. However, the primary focus is within the treatment sessions where family communication patterns are altered directly. During the sessions, the therapist provides social reinforcement (verbal and nonverbal praise) for communications that suggest solutions to problems, clarify problems, or offer feedback.

Illustration

An illustration of the entire process of FFT is difficult to convey because of the complex set of techniques, their relation to the nature of family functioning, and their dependence on individual features of the family. The technique is well-illustrated elsewhere where guidelines are provided for therapists (Alexander & Parsons, 1982). Selected features of the techniques can be described and illustrated to convey the manner in which the technique operates.

The technique requires understanding of several types of functions that behaviors can serve within the family. These functions include behaviors that family members perform to sustain contact and closeness (merging), to decrease psychological intensity and dependence (separating), and to provide a mixture of merging and separating (midpointing). These processes are intricate because they usually involve the relations of all family members with each other. Also, the behaviors of a given family member may serve multiple and opposing functions in relation to different individuals within the family. Thus, a behavior that may draw one family member close may distance another member. Finally, several different behaviors (e.g., the fighting of a child with a sibling, getting into trouble at school, running away from home overnight) may serve quite similar functions (e.g., bring the mother and father together).

During the course of treatment all family members meet. The focus of treatment is to identify consistent patterns of behavior and the range of functions they serve and messages they send. A number of specific techniques that can be used to focus on relations in therapy are used. The specific techniques, goals, and illustrations are presented in Table 7.4.

TABLE 7.4. Selected Therapy Techniques in Functional Family Therapy

CHILD FACTORS	GOAL

Asking Questions—To help focus on the relationships raised by the issue or problem. Example: After a description of an event involving the child (named Ginger) and the mother, the therapist may ask the father, "How do you fit into all of this?"

Making Comments—To help identify and clarify relationships. Example: The therapist may say to the father, "So you are drawn into this argument when your wife gets upset."

Offering Interpretations—To go beyond the obvious observations by inferring possible motivational states, effects on others, and antecedents. Example: The therapist may say, "So when you have an argument, you believe that this is a message that you are needed. But at the same time, you feel pushed away."

Identifying Sequences—To point to the relations among sequences or patterns of behavior to see more complex effects of interactions, that is, several functional relations over time. Example: The therapist says, "It seems to me that the argument between Ginger and you (to the mother) make both you and your husband upset. This leads to everyone arguing for a while about who did what and what has to be done and no one agrees. But after the dust settles, you both (to mother and father) have something to talk about and to work on. This brings you both together at least for a little while. And this may help you a lot too Ginger because you don't get to see your mother and father talking together like this very often."

Using the Therapist as a Direct Tool—To have the therapist refer to his or her relation to the family within the session and what functions this could serve. Example: The therapist says, "I feel as if I am still being asked to choose sides here because it may serve a function similar to the one that Ginger serves. That is to help bring you two together. That's not good or bad. But we need to see how we can get you two together when there is no argument or battle with a third party."

Stopping and Starting Interaction—To intervene to alter interactions between or among family members. The purpose may be to induce new lines of communication, to develop relations between members not initiating contact, or to point out functions evident at the moment. Example: The therapist says to Ginger and the father, "What do you two have to say about the effect that this has on each of you?" (without the mother asked to comment here).

A number of other strategies are employed during the course of treatment. These include not blaming individuals; relabeling thoughts, feelings, and behaviors to take into account relational components; discussing the implications of symptom removal; changing the context of the symptom to help alter the functions it may have served; and shifting the focus from one problem or person to another. FFT is not designed merely to identify functional relations but also to build new and more adaptive ways of functioning. Communication patterns are altered and efforts are made to provide families with concrete ways of behaving differently both in the sessions and at home (see Alexander & Parsons, 1982).

Overview of the Evidence

Relatively few outcome studies have evaluated FFT (see Alexander et al., 1994). However, the available studies have focused on populations that are difficult to treat (e.g., adjudicated delinquent adolescents, multiple offender delinquents) and have produced relatively clear effects. In controlled studies, comparisons FFT has led to greater change than other treatment techniques (e.g., client-centered family groups, psychodynamically oriented family therapy) and various control conditions (e.g., group discussion and expression of feeling, no-treatment control groups). Treatment outcome is reflected in improved family communication and interactions and lower rates of referral to and contact of youth with the courts. Moreover gains have been evident in separate studies up to 2-1/2 years after treatment.

Research has examined processes in therapy to identify in-session behaviors of the therapist and how these influence responsiveness among family members (Alexander, Barton, Schiavo, & Parsons, 1976; Newberry, Alexander, & Turner, 1991). For example, providing support and structure and reframing (recasting the attributions and bases of a problem) influence family member responsiveness and blaming of others. The relations among such variables are complex insofar as the impact of various type of statements (e.g., supportive) can vary as a function of gender of the therapist and family member. Evidence of changes in processes proposed to be critical to FFT (e.g., improved communication in treatment, more spontaneous discussion) supports the conceptual view of treatment.

Overall Evaluation

Several noteworthy points can be made about FFT. First, the outcome studies indicate that FFT can alter conduct problems among delinquent youth who vary in severity and chronicity of antisocial behavior (e.g., youth with status offenses; others with multiple offenses and who have served in maximum security wards). The studies have produced consistent effects. Second, the evaluation of processes that contribute to family member responsiveness within the sessions, as well as to treatment outcome, represents a line of work rarely seen among treatment techniques for children and adolescents. Some of this process work has extended to laboratory (analogue) studies to examine more precisely how specific types of therapist statements (e.g., reframing) can reduce blaming among group members (e.g., Morris, Alexander, & Turner, 1991). Third, a treatment manual has been provided (Alexander & Parsons, 1982) to facilitate further evaluation and extension of treatment.

A number of limitations are worth mentioning. First, the primary focus of treatment has been with delinquent samples. Extensions to clinically referred youth to ensure that clinical applications to younger samples, youth with comorbid diagnoses, and families of such youth are important as well. Clinical samples are not necessarily any more recalcitrant to treatment. Yet, delinquency and conduct disorder are not the same designations and generalization of findings from one population to another is not assured. Second, the child, parent, and family characteristics that may moderate outcome have not been well studied. Third, further extensions are needed to replicate the treatment beyond the original program from which it emerged. One such effort demonstrated that delinquent youth who received FFT showed lower recidivism rates up to 2-1/2 years later than a comparison group of lower risk delinquent youth (Gordon, Arbuthnot, Gustafson, & McGreen, 1988). These results suggest that FFT can

be replicated. Further replication efforts in randomized controlled trials are needed.

Multisystemic Therapy

Background and Underlying Rationale

Multisystemic therapy (MST) is a family-systems based approach to treatment (Henggeler & Borduin, 1990). Family approaches maintain that clinical problems of the child emerge within the context of the family and focus on treatment at that level. MST expands on that view by considering the family as only one, albeit a very important, system. The child is embedded in multiple systems including the family (immediate and extended family members), peers, schools, neighborhood, and so on. Also, within a given system, different subsystem issues may be relevant. For example, within the context of the family, some tacit alliance between one parent and child may contribute to disagreement and conflict over discipline between the parents. Treatment may be required to address the alliance and sources of conflict in an effort to alter child behavior. Also, child functioning at school may involve limited and poor peer relations; treatment may address these areas as well. Finally, the systems approach entails a focus on the individual's own behavior insofar as it affects others. Individual treatment of the child or parents may be included in treatment.

Because multiple influences are entailed by the focus of the treatment, many different treatment techniques are used. Thus, MST can be viewed as a package of interventions that are deployed with children and their families. Treatment procedures are used "as needed" to address individual, family, and system issues that may contribute to problem behavior. The conceptual view focusing on multiple systems and their impact on the individual serves as a basis for selecting multiple and quite different treatment procedures.

Characteristics of Treatment

Central to MST is a family-based treatment approach. Several family therapy techniques (e.g., joining, reframing, enactment, paradox, assigning specific tasks) are used to identify problems, increase communication, build cohesion, and alter how family members interact. The goals of treatment are to help the parents develop behaviors of the adolescent, to overcome marital difficulties that impede the parents' ability to function as parents, to eliminate negative interactions between parent and adolescent, and to develop or build cohesion and emotional warmth among family members.

MST draws on many other techniques as needed, such as PSST, PMT, and marital therapy, to alter the response repertoire of the child, parent-child interactions at home, and marital communication, respectively. In some cases, practical advice and guidance are also given to address parenting issues (e.g., involving the adolescent in prosocial peer activities at school, restricting specific activities with a deviant peer group). Al-though MST includes distinct techniques of other approaches, it is not a mere amalgamation of them. The focus of treatment is on interrelated systems and how they affect each other. Domains are addressed in treatment (e.g., parent unemployment) if they raise issues for one or more systems (e.g., parent stress, increase alcohol consumption) and affect how the child is functioning (e.g., marital conflict, child-discipline practices).

In any given case, multiple interventions may be applied including those illustrated already. A difficulty is deciding what treatments to apply to whom, when, and for what problem domains. In general, the focus is on utilizing interventions with interventions on their behalf. Guidelines for applying treatments are provided in Table 7.5.

Overview of the Evidence

A number of randomized, outcome studies have evaluated MST, primarily with delinquent youth with arrest and incarceration histories including violent crime (e.g., manslaughter, aggravated assault with intent to kill). Thus, this is a group of extremely antisocial and aggressive youth. Results have shown MST to be superior in reducing delinquency, emotional and behavioral problems, and improving family functioning in comparison to other procedures including "usual services" provided to such youth (e.g., probation, court-ordered activities that

are monitored such as school attendance), individual counseling, and community-based eclectic treatment (e.g., Borduin et al., 1995; Henggeler et al., 1986; Henggeler, Melton, & Smith, 1992). Follow-up assessment up to 2, 4, and 5 years later, in separate samples, has shown that MST youth have lower arrest rates than youth who receive other services (see Henggeler et al., 1994).

Research has also shown that treatment affects critical processes proposed to contribute to deviant behavior (Mann, Borduin, Henggeler, & Blaske, 1990). Specifically, parents and teenage youth show a reduction in coalitions (e.g., less verbal activity, conflict and hostility) and increases in support, and the parents show increases in verbal communication and decreases in conflict. Moreover, decreases in adolescent symptoms are positively correlated with increases in supportiveness and decreases in conflict between the mother and father. This work provides an important link between theoretical underpinnings of treatment and outcome effects.

Overall Evaluation

Several controlled outcome studies are available for MST; they are consistent in showing that treatment leads to change in adolescents and that the changes are sustained. A strength of the studies is that many of the youth who are treated are severely impaired (delinquent adolescents with a history of arrest). Another strength is the conceptualization of conduct disorder as a problem involving multiple domains of dysfunction within and between individual, family, and extrafamilial systems. MST begins with the view that may different domains are likely to be relevant; they need to be evaluated and then addressed as needed in treatment.

A challenge of the approach is deciding what treatments to use in a given case, among the many interventions encompassed by MST. Although guidelines are available to direct the therapist, they are somewhat general (e.g., focus on developing positive sequences of behaviors between systems such as parent and adolescent, evaluate the interventions during treatment so that changes can be made; see Henggeler et al., 1994). Providing interventions as needed is very difficult without a consistent way to

TABLE 7.5. Principles for Designing Interventions in Multisystemic Therapy

1. The primary purpose of assessment is to understand the "fit" between the identified problems and their broader systemic context.
2. Therapeutic contacts should emphasize the positive and should use systemic strengths as levers for change.
3. Interventions should be designed to promote responsible behavior and decrease irresponsible behavior among family members.
4. Interventions should be present-focused and action-oriented, targeting specific and well-defined problems.
5. Interventions should target sequences of behavior within or between multiple systems.
6. Interventions should be developmentally appropriate and fit the developmental needs of the youth.
7. Interventions should be designed to require daily or weekly effort by family members.
8. Intervention efficacy is evaluated continuously from multiple perspectives.
9. Interventions should be designed to promote treatment generalization and long-term maintenance of therapeutic change.

Source: Adapted from Henggeler et al. (1994)

assess what is needed, given inherent limits of decision making and perception, even among trained professionals. Yet, there have been replications of MST beyond the original research program indicating that treatment can be extended across settings (Henggeler, Schoenwald, & Pickrel, 1995).

On balance, MST is quite promising given the quality of evidence and consistency in the effects that have been produced. The promise stems from a conceptual approach that examines multiple domains (systems) and their contribution to dysfunction, evidence on processes in therapy and their relation to outcome, and the outcome studies themselves. The outcome studies have extended to youth with different types of problems (e.g., sexual offenses, drug use) and to parents who engage in physical abuse or neglect (e.g., Borduin, Henggeler, Blaske, & Stein, 1990; Brunk, Henggeler, & Whelan, 1987). Thus, the model of providing treatment may have broad applicability across problem domains among seriously disturbed children. In passing, it may be worth noting that other literatures are relevant to MST. Some of the techniques included in treatment are variations of PSST and PMT, already discussed, and hence have evidence on their own behalf as effective interventions.

Limitations of Promising Treatments

Each of the above treatments has randomized, controlled trials in its behalf, includes replications of treatment effects in multiple studies, focuses on youth whose aggressive and antisocial behavior have led to impairment and referral to social services (e.g., clinics, hospitals, courts), and has assessed outcome over the course of follow-up, at least up to a year, but often longer. Even though these treatments have made remarkable gains, they also bear limitations worth highlighting.

Magnitude of Therapeutic Change

Promising treatments have achieved change, but is the change enough to make a difference in the lives of the youth who are treated? Clinical significance refers to the practical value or importance of the effect of an intervention, that is, whether it makes any "real" difference to the patients or to others with whom they interact (see Kazdin, 1998). Clinical significance is important because it is quite possible for treatment effects to be statistically significant, but not to have impact on most or any of the cases in a way that improves their functioning or adjustment in daily life.

There are several ways to evaluate clinical significance. As an example, one way is to consider the extent to which youth function at normative levels at the end of treatment (i.e., compared to same age and sex peers who are functioning well). This is particularly useful as a criterion in relation to children and adolescents because base rates of emotional and behavioral problems can vary greatly as a function of age. Promising treatments occasionally have shown that treatment returns individuals to normative levels in relation to behavioral problems and prosocial functioning at home and at school (see Kazdin, 1995b). Yet, the majority of studies, whether of promising or less well-evaluated treatments, have not examined whether youth have changed in ways that place them within normative range of functioning or have made gains that would reflect clinically significant changes (Kazdin, Bass et al., 1990).

Although the goal of treatment is to effect clinically significant change, other less dramatic goals are not trivial. For many conduct disorder youth, symptoms may escalate, comorbid diagnoses (e.g., substance abuse, depression) may emerge, and family dysfunction may increase. Also, such youth are at risk for teen marriage, dropping out of school, and running away. If treatment were to achieve stability in symptoms and family life and prevent or delimit future dysfunction, that would be a significant achievement. The reason evaluation is so critical to the therapeutic enterprise is to identify whether treatment makes a difference because "making a difference" can have many meanings that are important in the treatment of conduct disorder.

Maintenance of Change

Promising treatments have included follow-up assessment, usually up to a year after treatment. Yet, conduct disorder has a poor long-term prognosis, so it is especially important to identify whether treatment has enduring effects. Also, in evaluating the relative merit of different treatments, follow-up data play a critical role. When two (or more) treatments are compared, the treatment that is more (or most) effective immediately after treatment is not always the one that proves to be the most effective treatment in the long run (Kazdin, 1988). Consequently, the conclusions about treatment may be very different depending on the timing of outcome assessment. Apart from conclusions about treatment, follow-up may provide important information that permits differentiation among youth. Over time, youth who maintain the benefits of treatment may differ in important ways from those who do not. Understanding who responds and who responds more or less well to a particular treatment can be very helpful in understanding, treating, and preventing conduct disorder.

The study of long-term effects of treatment is difficult in general, but the usual problems are exacerbated by focusing on conduct disorder. Among clinic samples, families of conduct disorder youth have high rates of dropping out during treatment and during the follow-up assessment period due in part to the many parent and family factors (e.g., socioeconomic disadvantage, stress) often associated with the problem (Kazdin, 1996b). As the sample size decreases over time, conclusions about the impact of treatment become increasingly difficult to draw. Nevertheless, evaluation of the long-term effects of treatment remains a high priority for research.

Limited Assessment of Outcome Domains

In the majority of child therapy studies, child symptoms are the exclusive focus of outcome assessment (Kazdin, Bass et al., 1990). Other domains such as prosocial behavior and academic functioning are neglected, even though they relate to concurrent and long-term adjustment (e.g., Asher & Coie, 1990). A broader range of child functioning than symptoms is important to include in treatment evaluation. Beyond child functioning, parent and family functioning may also be relevant. Parents and family members of conduct disorder youth often experience dysfunction (e.g., psychiatric impairment, marital conflict). Parent and family functioning and the quality of life for family members are relevant outcomes and may be appropriate goals for treatment.

In general, there are many outcomes that are of interest in evaluating treatment. From existing research we already know that the conclusions reached about a given treatment can vary depending on the outcome criterion. Within a given study, one set of measures (e.g., child functioning) may show no differences between two treatments but another measure (e.g., family functioning) may show that one treatment is clearly better than the other (e.g., Kazdin et al., 1989; Kazdin, Siegel, & Bass, 1992; Szapocznik et al., 1989). Thus, in examining different outcomes of interest, we must be prepared for different conclusions that these outcomes may yield.

General Comments

In light of the above comments, clearly even the most promising treatments have several limitations. Yet, it is critical to place these in perspective. The most commonly used treatments in clinical practice consist of "traditional" approaches including psychodynamic, relationship, play, and family therapies (other than those mentioned above) (Kazdin, Siegel, & Bass, 1990). These treatments have rarely been tested in controlled outcome studies showing that they achieve therapeutic change in referred (or non-referred) samples of youth with conduct problems. Many forms of behavior therapy have a rather extensive literature showing that various techniques (e.g., reinforcement programs, social skills training) can alter aggressive and other antisocial behaviors (Kazdin, 1985; McMahon & Wells, 1989). Yet, the focus has tended to be on isolated behaviors, rather than a constellation of symptoms. Also, durable changes among clinical samples rarely have been shown.

Pharmacotherapy represents a line of work of some interest. For one reason, stimulant medication (e.g., methylphenidate), frequently used with children diagnosed with Attention-Deficit Hyperactivity Disorder, has some impact on aggressive and other antisocial behaviors (see Hinshaw, 1994). This is interesting in part because such children often have a comorbid diagnosis of Conduct Disorder. Still no strong evidence exists that stimulant medication can alter the constellation of symptoms (e.g., fighting, stealing) associated with conduct disorder. A review of various medications for aggression in children and adolescents has raised possible leads, but controlled studies on the treatment of aggressive behavior specifically or conduct disorder remain to be conducted (Stewart, Myers, Burket, & Lyles, 1990).

There is a genre of interventions that is worth mentioning in passing. Occasionally, interventions are advocated and implemented such as sending conduct disorder youth to a camp in the country where they learn how to "rough it," or how to take care of horses, or to experience military (e.g., basic training) regimens. The conceptual bases of such treatments and supportive research on the processes involved in the onset of conduct disorders are rarely provided. On the one hand, developing treatments that emerge outside of the mainstream of the mental health professions is to be encouraged precisely because traditional treatments have not resolved in the problem. On the other hand, this genre of intervention tends to eschew evaluation. Evaluation is key because well-intentioned and costly interventions can have little or no effect on the youth they treat (Weisz, Walter, Weiss, Fernandez, & Mikow, 1990) and may actually increase antisocial behavior (e.g., see Lundman, 1984).

DEVELOPING MORE EFFECTIVE TREATMENTS

There are a number of issues that emerge in the treatment of conduct disorder youth and decision making about what interventions to provide to whom. These issues reflect obstacles in delivering treatment, lacunae in our knowledge base, and limitations in the models of providing care. Addressing these issues in research are likely to increase the effectiveness of treatment, both in research and clinical applications.

What Treatments Do Not Work

With a few hundred or so treatments available for children, it would be quite helpful to know which among these do not work or do not work very well. Addressing the matter directly is not possible in light of the fact, noted previously, that the vast majority of treatment approaches have not been evaluated empirically. Thus, there is no accumulated body of evidence in which treatments have consistently emerged as weak or ineffective. Moreover, the nature of the dominant scientific research paradigm (inability to prove the null hypothesis) precludes firm demonstration of no effects of treatment. Treatments commonly used in clinical work (Kazdin, Siegel, & Bass, 1990), including psychodynamic therapy, relationship-based treatment, play therapy, and a plethora of eclectic combinations have not been carefully evaluated (Kazdin, Bass et al., 1990). Occasionally, variations of these treatments have been used as comparison or control conditions and have been shown to be less effective than one of the promising treatments noted previously (e.g., Borduin et al., 1995; Kazdin et al., 1987a, 1987b). From this limited research, it is premature to conclude that these latter treatments are ineffective. Yet, at best their benefits have yet to be demonstrated and more promising treatments with firmer empirical bases currently are the treatments of choice.

Although direct evidence on what does not work cannot be culled for a set of techniques, there are relevant literatures that one can bring to bear on the matter. First, conduct disorder youth usually show problems in multiple domains of functioning, including overt behavior, social relations (e.g., peers, teachers, family members), and academic performance. For a treatment to be effective, it is likely that several domains have to be addressed explicitly. Although one cannot say for certain what techniques will not work, it is much safer to say treatments that neglect multiple domains are likely to have limited effects.

Second, some evidence has emerged that is useful for selecting what treatments to avoid or to use with great caution. Often conduct disorder youth are treated in group therapy. Yet, placing youth together could impede improvement. For example, Feldman, Caplinger, and Wodarski (1983) randomly assigned youth (ages 8–17) to variations group therapy. In one type of group, all members were referred for conduct disorder; in another type of group, conduct disorder youth were placed with nonantisocial youth (without clinical problems). Those placed in a group of their deviant peers did not improve; those placed with nondeviant peers did improve. Interpretation of this is based on the likelihood that peer bonding to others can improve one's behavior, if those peers engage in more normative behavior; bonding to a deviant group can sustain deviant behavior.

Similarly, Dishion and Andrews (1995) evaluated several interventions for nonreferred youth (ages 10–14) with conduct problems. One of the treatment conditions included youth meeting in a group with a focus on self-regulation, monitoring, and developing behavior-change programs. This condition, whether alone or in combination with parent training, was associated with increases in behavioral problems and substance use (cigarette smoking). Again, it appeared that placing conduct problem teens in a group situation can exacerbate their problems. Other research has shown that individuals may become worse (e.g., increase in arrest rates) through association with deviant peers as part of treatment (O'Donnell, 1992).

Treatments for conduct disorder youth, in such settings as hospitals, schools, and correctional facilities, often are conducted in a group therapy format in which several conduct problem youth are together to talk about or work on their problems or go to the country for some fresh air experience to get better. There may be conditions under which this arrangement is beneficial. However, current research suggests that placing several such youth together can impede therapeutic change and have deleterious effects.

Who Responds Well to Treatment

We have known for many years that the critical question of psychotherapy is not what technique is effective, but rather what technique works for whom, under what conditions, as administered by what type of therapists, and so on (Kiesler, 1971). The adult psychotherapy literature has focused on a range of questions to identify factors (e.g., patient, therapist, treatment process) that contribute to outcome. The child and adolescent therapy research has neglected the role of child, parent, family, and therapist factors that may moderate outcome (Kazdin, Bass et al., 1990).

In the case of conduct disorder, a few studies have looked at who responds to treatment, mostly in the context of parent management training and problem-solving skills training. Although much more work is needed, current evidence suggests that risk factors for onset of conduct disorder and poor long-term prognosis (e.g., early onset, severe aggressive behavior, family adversity) are likely to influence responsiveness to treatment (Dumas & Wahler, 1983; Kazdin, 1995a, Kazdin & Crowley, 1997; Webster-Stratton, 1985). Our own work has shown that even those youth with multiple risk factors still improve with treatment, but the changes are not as great as those achieved for cases with fewer risk factors.

In current subtyping of conduct disorder youth, early (childhood) and later (adolescent) onset conduct disorder are distinguished (Hinshaw et al., 1993; Moffitt, 1993). Early-onset conduct disorder youth are characterized by aggressive behavior, neuropsychological dysfunction (in "executive" functions), a much higher ratio of boys to girls, and a poor long-term prognosis. Later-onset youth (onset at about age 15) are characterized more by delinquent activity (theft, vandalism), a more even distribution of boys and girls, and a more favorable prognosis. The subtype and associated characteristics are by no means firmly established, but reflect current conceptual and empirical work in the area (e.g., Patterson, DeBaryshe, & Ramsey, 1989; Moffitt, 1993). We can expect from this that youth with an early onset are more likely to be recalcitrant to treatment. At present and in the absence of very much treatment research on the matter, a useful guideline to predict responsiveness to treatment is to consider loading of the child, parent, and family on risk factors that portend a poor long-term prognosis (see Kazdin, 1995b; Robins, 1991).

A goal of research is to identify whether some children respond to one type of treatment more than another. At this point, the literature cannot speak to this issue. The characteristics that have been studied in relation to treatment outcome (e.g., comorbidity) have not be examined across different treatments. Consequently, we do not know whether these factors affect responsiveness to any treatment or to particular forms of treatment.

Combining Treatments

There is keen interest, both in clinical work and in research, in using combinations of treatment (see Kazdin, 1996a). In the case of conduct disorder, impetus stems from the scope of impairment evident in children (e.g., comorbidity, academic dysfunction) and families (e.g., stress, conflict), as well as limited effects of most treatments. The benefits of combined treatments can be identified in selected areas. For example, in the treatment of adult schizophrenia, combinations of treatment (e.g., medication and family counseling/therapy) surpasses the effects of the constituent components alone (e.g., Falloon, 1988).

In the case of child and adolescent therapy, combined treatments have not been well-studied. I have argued elsewhere that there are many reasons to expect combined treatments not to surpass the effects of any promising single treatment (Kazdin, 1996a). Among the reasons, we know very little about the parameters of a given treatment that influence its effectiveness and the cases to whom the treatment is most suitably applied. Combining techniques of which we know relatively little, particularly in time-limited treatment, is not a firm base to build more effective treatments. Also, there are many obstacles in combining treatment that materially affect their likely outcome, such as decision rules regarding what treatments to combine, how to combine them (e.g., when, in what order), how to evaluate their impact, and others.

An important assumption for combined treatments is that individual treatments are weak and, if combined, they would produce additive or synergistic effects. This is a reasonable, even if poorly tested, assumption. An alternative assumption is that the way in which treatment is usually administered, whether a single or a combined treatment, inherently limits the likelihood of positive outcome effects, a point discussed further below. As a general point, combining treatments itself is not likely to be an answer to developing effective treatment without more thought and evidence about the nature of these combinations.

Some of the promising treatments reviewed previously (MST, FFT) are combined treatments. For example, multisystemic therapy provides many different treatments for antisocial youth. Two points are worth noting. First, the constituent treatments that form a major part of treatment are those that have evidence on their behalf (e.g., PSST, PMT), so that not any combination is used. Second, we do not yet know that multisystemic therapy, as a combined treatment package, is more effective than the most effective constituent component administered for the same duration. The comparisons of multisystemic therapy have mostly included ordinary individual psychotherapy and counseling, important comparison groups to be sure. Although treatment has surpassed traditional therapy practices, this is not the same as showing that combinations of treatment per se are necessary to achieve therapeutic changes.

Combined treatments may be very useful and should be pursued. At the same time, a rash move to combine treatments is unwarranted. The effects of combined treatment obviously depend very much on the individual treatments that are included in the combination. For example, mentioned already was a study in which parent training and a teen-focused group were evaluated alone and in combination (Dishion & Andrews, 1995). Conditions that received the teen group component, whether alone or in combination with parent training, became worse. Obviously, one cannot assume that combined treatments will automatically be neutral or better than their constituent treatments. There is another more subtle and perhaps worrisome facet of combined treatments. A danger in promoting treatment combinations is to continue to use techniques with little evidence in their behalf as an ingredient in a larger set of techniques. Old wine in new bottles is not bad if the original wine has merit. However, without knowing if there is merit, the tendency is to view the wine as new and improved would be unfortunate. With promising treatments available, we have a comparative base to evaluate novel treatments, treatment combinations, and unevaluated treatments in current use. If a promising treatment is not used in clinical work, we would want evidence that it has clearly failed, that other promising treatments for whatever reason cannot be used, and that the treatment that is to be applied has a reasonable basis for addressing the scope of dysfunctions.

Models of Delivering Treatment

The model of treatment delivery in current research is to provide a relatively brief and time-limited intervention. For several clinical dysfunctions or for a number of children with a particular dysfunction such as conduct disorder, the course of maladjustment may be long term. In such cases, the notion of providing a brief, time-limited treatment may very much limit outcome effects. Even if a great combination of various psychotherapies were constructed,

administration in the time-limited fashion might have the usual, checkered yield. More extended and enduring treatment in some form may be needed to achieve clinically important effects with the greatest number of youth. Two ways of delivering extended treatment illustrate the point.

The first variation is referred to as a *continued-care model.* The model of treatment delivery that may be needed can be likened to the model used in the treatment of diabetes mellitus. With diabetes, ongoing treatment (insulin) is needed to ensure that the benefits of treatment are sustained. The benefits of treatment would end with discontinuation of treatment. Analogously, in the context of conduct disorder, a variation of ongoing treatment may be needed. Perhaps after the child is referred, treatment is provided to address the current crises and to have impact on functioning at home, at school, and in the community. After improvement is achieved, treatment is modified rather than terminated. At that point, the child could enter into maintenance therapy, that is, continued treatment perhaps in varying schedules ("doses"). Treatment would continue but perhaps on a more intermittent basis. Continued treatment in this fashion has been effective as a model for treating recurrent depression in adults (see Kupfer et al., 1992).

The second variation is referred to as a *dental-care model* to convey a different way of extending treatment. After initial treatment and demonstrated improvement in functioning in everyday life, treatment is suspended. At this point, the child's functioning begins to be monitored regularly (e.g., every 3 months) and systematically (with standardized measures). Treatment could be provided *pro re nata* (PRN) based on the assessment data or emergent issues raised by the family, teachers, or others. The approach might be likened to the more familiar model of dental care in the United States in which "check-ups" are recommended every 6 months; an intervention is provided if, and as needed based on these periodic checks.

Obviously, the use of ongoing treatment is not advocated in cases where there is evidence that short-term treatment is effective. A difficulty with most of the research on treatment of conduct disorder, whether promising, poorly investigated, or combined treatments, is that the conventional treatment model of brief, time-limited therapy has been adopted. Without considering alternative models of delivery, current treatments may be quite limited in the effects they can produce. Although more effective treatments are sorely needed, the way of delivering currently available treatments ought to be reconsidered.

CONCLUSIONS

Many different types of treatment have been applied to conduct disorder youth. Unfortunately, little outcome evidence exists for most of the techniques. Four treatments with the most promising evidence to date were highlighted: problem-solving skills training, parent management training, functional family therapy, and multisystemic therapy. Cognitive problem-solving skills training focuses on cognitive processes that underlie social behavior and response repertoires in interpersonal situations. Parent management training is directed at altering parent-child interactions in the home, particularly those interactions related to child-rearing practices and coercive interchanges. Functional family therapy utilizes principles of systems theory and behavior modification as the basis for altering interactions, communication, and problem solving among family members. Multisystemic therapy focus on the individual, family, and extrafamilial systems and their interrelations as a way to reduce symptoms and to promote prosocial behavior. Multiple treatments (e.g., PSST, PMT, family therapy) are used in combination to address domains that affect the child. Evidence in behalf of these four treatments was reviewed; each has multiple controlled outcome studies with follow-up data in its behalf.

We cannot yet say that one intervention can ameliorate conduct disorder and overcome the poor long-term prognosis. On the other hand, much can be said. Much of what is practiced in clinical settings is based on psychodynamically oriented treatment, general relationship counseling, various forms of family therapy (other than those in this chapter), and group therapy (with all antisocial youth as members). These and other procedures, alone and in various combinations in which they are often used, have not been evaluated carefully in controlled trials. Of course, absence of evidence is not tantamount to ineffectiveness. At the same time, promising treatments have advanced considerably and a very special argument might be needed to justify administration of treatments that have neither basic research on their conceptual underpinnings in relation to conduct disorder nor outcome evidence from controlled clinical trials on their behalf.

Promising treatments, at best, leave important questions unanswered. Further development of treatments clearly is needed. Apart from treatment studies, further progress in understanding the nature of conduct disorder is likely to have very important implications for improving treatment outcome. Improved triage of patients to treatments that are likely to work will require understanding of characteristics of children, parents, and families that will make them more or less amenable to current treatments.

REFERENCES

Alexander, J. F., Barton, C., Schiavo, R. S., & Parsons, B. V. (1976). Systems-behavioral intervention with families of delinquents: Therapist characteristics, family behavior, and outcome. *Journal of Consulting and Clinical Psychology, 44,* 656-664.

Alexander, J. F., Holtzworth-Munroe, A., & Jameson, P. B. (1994). The process and outcome of marital and family therapy research: review and evaluation. In A. E. Bergin & S. L. Garfield (Eds.), *Handbook of psychotherapy and behavior change* (4th ed., pp. 595–630). New York: John Wiley & Sons.

Alexander, J. F., & Parsons, B. V. (1982). *Functional family therapy.* Monterey, CA: Brooks/Cole.

American Psychiatric Association (1994). *Diagnostic and statistical manual of mental disorders* (4th ed.). Washington, DC: Author.

Asher, S. R., & Coie, J. D. (Eds.). (1990). *Peer rejection in childhood.* New York: Cambridge University Press.

Baer, R. A., & Nietzel, M. T. (1991). Cognitive and behavioral treatment of impulsivity in children: A meta-analytic review of the outcome literature. *Journal of Clinical Child Psychology, 20,* 400–412.

Bank, L., Marlowe, J. H., Reid, J. B., Patterson, G. R., & Weinrott, M. R. (1991). A comparative evaluation of parent-training interventions for families of chronic delinquents. *Journal of Abnormal Child Psychology, 19,* 15–33.

Bell, R. Q., & Harper, L. (1977). *Child effects on adults.* New York: John Wiley & Sons.

Bergin, A. E., & Garfield, S. L. (Eds.). (1994). *Handbook of psychotherapy and behavior change* (4th ed). New York: Wiley.

Borduin, C. M., Henggeler, S. W., Blaske, D. M., & Stein, R. (1990). Multisystemic treatment of adolescent sexual offenders. *International Journal of Offender Therapy and Comparative Criminology, 34,* 105–113.

Borduin, C. M., Mann, B. J., Cone, L. T., Henggeler, S. W., Fucci, B. R., Blaske, D. M., & Williams, R. A. (1995). Multisystemic treatment of serious juvenile offenders: Long-term prevention of criminality and violence. *Journal of Consulting and Clinical Psychology, 63,* 569–578.

Boyle, M. H., & Offord, D. R. (1990). Primary prevention of conduct disorder: Issues and prospects. *Journal of the American Academy of Child and Adolescent Psychiatry, 29,* 227–233.

Brandt, D. E., & Zlotnick, S. J. (1988). *The psychology and treatment of the youthful offender.* Springfield, IL: Charles C. Thomas.

Brunk, M., Henggeler, S. W., & Whelan, J. P. (1987). A comparison of multisystemic therapy and parent training in the brief treatment of child abuse and neglect. *Journal of Consulting and Clinical Psychology, 55,* 311–318.

Cooper, J. O., Heron, T. E., & Heward, W. L. (1987). *Applied behavior analysis.* Columbus, OH: Merrill.

Crick, N. R., & Dodge, K. A. (1994). A review and reformulation of social information processing mechanisms in children's social adjustment. *Psychological Bulletin, 115,* 74–101.

Cunningham, C. E., Bremner, R., & Boyle, M. (1995). Large group community-based parenting programs for families of preschoolers at risk for disruptive behaviour disorders: Utilization, cost effectiveness, and outcome. *Journal of Child Psychology and Psychiatry, 36,* 1141–1159.

Dadds, M. R., & McHugh, T. A. (1992). Social support and treatment outcome in behavioral family therapy for child conduct problems. *Journal of Consulting and Clinical Psychology, 60,* 252–259.

Dadds, M. R., Schwartz, S., & Sanders, M. R. (1987). Marital discord and treatment outcome in behavioral treatment of child conduct disorders. *Journal of Consulting and Clinical Psychology, 55,*396–403.

Dishion, T. J., & Andrews, D. W. (1995). Preventing escalation in problem behaviors with high-risk young adolescents: Immediate and 1-year outcomes. *Journal of Consulting and Clinical Psychology, 63,* 538–548.

Dishion, T. J., & Patterson, G. R. (1992). Age effects in parent training outcomes. *Behavior Therapy, 23,* 719–729.

Dishion, T. J., Patterson, G. R., & Kavanagh, K. A. (1992). An experimental test of the coercion model: Linking theory, measurement, and intervention. In J. McCord & R. E. Tremblay (Eds.), *Preventing antisocial behavior* (pp. 253–282). New York: Guilford Press.

Dumas, J. E. (1989). Treating antisocial behavior in children: Child and family approaches. *Clinical Psychology Review, 9,* 197–222.

Dumas, J. E., & Wahler, R. G. (1983). Predictors of treatment outcome in parent training: Mother insularity and socioeconomic disadvantage. *Behavioral Assessment, 5,* 301–313.

Durlak, J. A., Fuhrman, T., & Lampman, C. (1991). Effectiveness of cognitive-behavioral therapy for maladapting children: A meta-analysis. *Psychological Bulletin, 110,* 204–214.

Falloon, I. R. (1988). Expressed emotion: Current status. *Psychological Medicine, 18,* 269–274.

Feindler, E. L., & Ecton, R. B. (1986). *Adolescent anger control: Cognitive-behavioral techniques.* Elmsford, NY: Pergamon Press.

Feldman, R. A., Caplinger, T. E., & Wodarski, J. S. (1983). *The St. Louis conundrum: The effective treatment of antisocial youth.* Englewood Cliffs, NJ: Prentice-Hall.

Fergusson, D. M., Horwood, L. J., & Lloyd, M. (1991). Confirmatory factor models of attention deficit and conduct disorder. *Journal of Child Psychology and Psychiatry, 32,* 257–274.

Finch, A. J., Jr., Nelson, W. M., Ott, E. S. (1983). *Cognitive-behavioral procedures with children and adolescents: A practical guide.* Boston: Allyn & Bacon.

Forehand, R., & Long, N. (1988). Outpatient treatment of the acting out child: Procedures, long-term follow-up data, and clinical problems. *Advances in Behaviour Research and Therapy, 10,* 129–177.

Forehand, R., & McMahon, R. J. (1981). *Helping the non-compliant child: A clinician's guide to parent training.* New York: Guilford Press.

Gordon, D. A., Arbuthnot, J., Gustafson, K. E., & McGreen, P. (1988). Home-based behavioral-systems family therapy with disadvantaged juvenile delinquents. *American Journal of Family Therapy, 163,* 243–255.

Griest, D. L., Forehand, R., Rogers, T., Breiner, J., Furey, W., & Williams, C. A. (1982). Effects of parent enhancement therapy on the treatment outcome and generalization of a parent training program. *Behaviour Research and Therapy, 20,* 429–436.

Henggeler, S. W. & Borduin, C. M. (1990). *Family therapy and beyond: A multisystemic approach to teaching the behavior problems of children and adolescents.* Pacific Grove, CA: Brooks/Cole.

Henggeler, S. W., Melton, G. B., & Smith, L. A. (1992). Family preservation using multisystemic therapy: An effective alternative to incarcerating serious juvenile offenders. *Journal of Consulting and Clinical Psychology, 60,* 953–961.

Henggeler, S. W., Rodick, J. D., Borduin, C. M., Hanson, C. L., Watson, S. M., & Urey, J. R. (1986). Multisystemic treatment of juvenile offenders: Effects on adolescent behavior and family interaction. *Developmental Psychology, 22,* 132–141.

Henggeler, S. W., Schoenwald, S. K., & Pickrel, S. G. (1995). Multisystemic therapy: Bridging the gap between university- and community-based treatment. *Journal of Consulting and Clinical Psychology, 63,* 709–717.

Henggeler, S. W. Schoenwald, S. K., & Pickrel, S. G., Brondino, M. J., Borduin, C. M., & Hall, J. A. (1994). *Treatment manual for family preservation using multisystemic therapy.* Charleston, SC: Medical University of South Carolina, South Carolina Health and Human Services Finance Commission.

Hinshaw, S. P. (1994). *Attention deficits and hyperactivity in children.* Thousand Oaks, CA: Sage Publications.

Hinshaw, S. P., Lahey, B. B., & Hart, E. L. (1993). Issues of taxonomy and comorbidity in the development of conduct disorder. *Development and Psychopathology, 5,* 31–49.

Kazdin, A. E. (1985). *Treatment of antisocial behavior in children and adolescents.* Homewood, IL: Dorsey Press.

Kazdin, A. E. (1988). *Child psychotherapy: Developing and identifying effective treatments.* Boston: Allyn & Bacon.

Kazdin, A. E. (1993). Treatment of conduct disorder: Progress and directions in psychotherapy research. *Development and Psychopathology, 5,* 277–310.

Kazdin, A. E. (1994). Behavior modification in applied settings (5th ed.). Pacific Grove, CA: Brooks/Cole.

Kazdin, A. E. (1995a). Child, parent, and family dysfunction as predictors of outcome in cognitive-behavioral treatment of antisocial children. *Behaviour Research and Therapy, 33,* 271–281.

Kazdin, A. E. (1995b). *Conduct disorder in childhood and adolescence* (2nd ed.). Thousand Oaks, CA: Sage Publications.

Kazdin, A. E. (1996a). Combined and multimodal treatments in child and adolescent psychotherapy: Issues, challenges, and research directions. *Clinical Psychology: Science and Practice, 3,* 69–100.

Kazdin, A. E. (1996b). Dropping out of child psychotherapy: Issues for research and implications for practice. *Clinical Child Psychology and Psychiatry, 1,* 133–156.

Kazdin, A. E. (1998). *Research design in clinical psychology* (3rd ed.). Boston: Allyn & Bacon.

Kazdin, A. E., Bass, D., Ayers, W. A., & Rodgers, A. (1990). Empirical and clinical focus of child and adolescent psychotherapy research. *Journal of Consulting and Clinical Psychology, 58,* 729–740.

Kazdin, A. E., Bass, D., Siegel, T., & Thomas, C. (1989). Cognitive-behavioral treatment and relationship therapy in the treatment of children referred for antisocial behavior. *Journal of Consulting and Clinical Psychology, 57,* 522–535.

Kazdin, A. E., & Crowley, M. (1997). Moderators of treatment outcome in cognitively based treatment of antisocial children. *Cognitive Therapy and Research, 2,* 185–207.

Kazdin, A. E., Esveldt-Dawson, K., French, N. H., & Unis, A. S. (1987a). Problem-solving skills training and relationship therapy in the treatment of antisocial child behavior. *Journal of Consulting and Clinical Psychology, 55,* 76–85.

Kazdin, A. E., Esveldt-Dawson, K., French, N. H., & Unis, A. S. (1987b). The effects of parent management training and problem-solving skills training combined in the treatment of antisocial child behavior. *Journal of the American Academy of Child and Adolescent Psychiatry, 26,* 416–424.

Kazdin, A. E., Siegel, T. C., & Bass, D. (1990). Drawing upon clinical practice to inform research on child and adolescent psychotherapy: A survey of practitioners. *Professional Psychology: Research and Practice, 21,* 189–198.

Kazdin, A. E., Siegel, T., & Bass, D. (1992). Cognitive problem-solving skills training and parent management training in the treatment of antisocial behavior in children. *Journal of Consulting and Clinical Psychology, 60,* 733–747.

Kendall, P. C. (Ed.). (1991). *Child and adolescent therapy: Cognitive-behavioral procedures.* New York: Guilford Press.

Kiesler, D. J. (1971). Experimental designs in psychotherapy research. In A.E. Bergin & S.L. Garfield (Eds.), *Handbook of psychotherapy and behavior change: An empirical analysis* (pp. 36–74). New York: Wiley.

Kupfer, D. J., Frank, E., Perel, J. M., Cornes, C., Mallinger, A. G., Thase, M. E., McEachran, A. B., &

Grochocinski, V. J. (1992). Five-year outcome for maintenance therapies in recurrent depression. *Archives of General Psychiatry, 49,* 769–773.

Lochman, J. E., & Dodge, K. A. (1994). Social-cognitive processes of severely violent, moderately aggressive, and nonaggressive boys. *Journal of Consulting and Clinical Psychology, 62,* 366–374.

Loeber, R. (1990). Development and risk factors of juvenile antisocial behavior and delinquency. *Clinical Psychology Review, 10,* 1–41.

Long, P., Forehand, R., Wierson, M., & Morgan, A. (1994). Does parent training with young noncompliant children have long-term effects? *Behaviour Research and Therapy, 32,* 101–107.

Lundman, R. J. (1984). *Prevention and control of juvenile delinquency.* New York: Oxford University Press.

Lytton, H. (1990). Child and parent effects in boys' conduct disorder: A reinterpretation. Developmental *Psychology, 26,* 683–697.

Mann, B. J., Borduin, C. M., Henggeler, S. W., & Blaske, D. M. (1990). An investigation of systemic conceptualizations of parent-child coalitions and symptom change. *Journal of Consulting and Clinical Psychology, 58,* 336–344.

McMahon, R. J., & Wells, K. C. (1989). Conduct disorders. In E. J. Mash & R. A. Barkley (Eds.), *Treatment of childhood disorders* (pp. 73–132). New York: Guilford Press.

Miller, G. E., & Prinz, R. J. (1990). Enhancement of social learning family interventions for child conduct disorder. *Psychological Bulletin, 108,* 291–307.

Moffitt, T. E. (1993). The neuropsychology of conduct problems. *Development and Psychopathology, 5,* 135–151.

Morris, S. M., Alexander, J. F., & Turner, C. W. (1991). Do reattributions reduce blame? *Journal of Family Psychology, 5,* 192–203.

Mrazek, P. J., & Haggerty, R. J. (Eds.). (1994). *Reducing risks for mental disorders: Frontiers of preventive intervention research.* Washington, DC: National Academy Press.

Newberry, A. M., Alexander, J. F., & Turner, C. W. (1991). Gender as a process variable in family therapy. *Journal of Family Psychology, 5,* 158–175.

O'Donnell, C.R. (1992). The interplay of theory and practice in delinquency prevention: From behavior modification to activity settings. In J. McCord & R.E. Tremblay (Eds.), *Preventing antisocial behavior* (pp. 209–232). New York: Guilford Press.

Offord, D.R., Boyle, M.H., & Racine, Y.A. (1991). The epidemiology of antisocial behavior. In D.J. Pepler & K.H. Rubin (Eds.), *The development and treatment of childhood aggression* (pp. 31–54). Hillsdale, NJ:

Lawrence Erlbaum.

Patterson, G. R. (1982). *Coercive family process.* Eugene, OR: Castalia.

Patterson, G. R., Capaldi, D., & Bank, L. (1991). An early starter model for predicting delinquency. In D. J. Pepler & K. H. Rubin (Eds.), *The development and treatment of childhood aggression* (pp. 139–168). Hillsdale, NJ: Lawrence Erlbaum.

Patterson, G. R., & Chamberlain, P. (1994). A functional analysis of resistance during parent training therapy. *Clinical Psychology: Science and Practice, 1,* 53–70.

Patterson, G. R., DeBaryshe, B. D., & Ramsey, E. (1989). A developmental perspective on antisocial behavior. *American Psychologist, 44,* 329–335.

Patterson, G. R., Dishion, T. J., & Chamberlain, P. (1993). Outcomes and methodological issues relating to treatment of antisocial children. In T.R. Giles (Ed.), *Handbook of effective psychotherapy* (pp. 43–87). New York: Plenum Press.

Patterson, G. R., Reid, J. B., & Dishion, T. J. (1992). *Antisocial boys.* Eugene, OR: Castalia.

Pepler, D. J., & Rubin, K. H. (Eds.). (1991). *The development and treatment of childhood aggression.* Hillsdale, NJ: Erlbaum.

Robins, L. N. (1966). *Deviant children grown up.* Baltimore: Williams & Wilkins.

Robins, L. N. (1978). Sturdy childhood predictors of adult antisocial behavior: Replications from longitudinal studies. *Psychological Medicine, 8,* 611–622.

Robins, L. N. (1981). Epidemiological approaches to natural history research: Antisocial disorders in children. *Journal of the American Academy of Child Psychiatry, 20,* 566–680.

Robins, L. N. (1991). Conduct disorder. *Journal of Child Psychology and Psychiatry, 32,* 193–212.

Robins, L., & Rutter, M. (Eds.). (1990). *Straight and devious pathways from childhood to adulthood.* Cambridge, MA: Cambridge University Press.

Rubin, K.H., Bream, L.A., Rose-Krasnor, L. (1991). Social problem solving and aggression in childhood. In D.J. Pepler & K.H. Rubin (Eds.). *The development and treatment of childhood aggression* (pp. 219–248). Hillsdale, NJ: Lawrence Erlbaum.

Rutter, M., & Giller, H. (1983). *Juvenile delinquency: Trends and perspectives.* New York: Penguin Books.

Rutter, M., Tizard, J., & Whitmore, K. (Eds.). (1970). *Education, health and behaviour.* London: Longmans.

Sanders, M. R., & Dadds, M. R. (1993). *Behavioral family intervention.* Boston: Allyn & Bacon.

Sanson, A., Oberklaid, F., Pedlow, R., & Prior, M. (1991). Risk indicators: Assessment of infancy predictors of pre-school behavioural maladjustment. *Journal of Child Psychology and Psychiatry, 32,* 609–626.

Shirk, S. R. (Ed.). (1988). *Cognitive development and child psychotherapy.* New York: Plenum Press.

Shure, M. B. (1992). *I can problem solve (ICPS): An interpersonal cognitive problem solving program.* Champaign, IL: Research Press.

Spivack, G., & Shure, M. B. (1982). The cognition of social adjustment: Interpersonal cognitive problem solving thinking. In B.B. Lahey & A.E. Kazdin (Eds.), *Advances in clinical child psychology* (Vol. 5, pp. 323–372). New York: Plenum Press.

Stewart, J. T., Myers, W. C., Burket, R. C., & Lyles, W. B. (1990). A review of the psychopharmacology of aggression in children and adolescents. *Journal of the American Academy of Child and Adolescent Psychiatry, 29,* 269–277.

Szapocznik, J., Rio, A., Murray, E., Cohen, R., Scopetta, M., Rivas-Vasquez, A., Hervis, O., Posada, V., & Kurtines, W. (1989). Structural family versus psychodynamic child therapy for problematic Hispanic boys. *Journal of Consulting and Clinical Psychology, 57,* 571–578.

United States Congress, Office of Technology Assessment (1991). *Adolescent health.* (OTA-H-468). Washington, DC: US Government Printing Office.

Wadsworth, M. (1979). *Roots of delinquency: Infancy, adolescence and crime.* New York: Barnes & Noble.

Wahler, R. G., & Dumas, J. E. (1986). Maintenance factors in coercive mother-child interactions: The compliance and predictability hypotheses. *Journal of Applied Behavior Analysis, 19,* 13–22.

Walker, J. L., Lahey, B. B., Russo, M. F., Christ, M. A. G., McBurnett, K., Loeber, R., Stouthamer-Loeber, M., & Green, S. M. (1991). Anxiety, inhibition, and conduct disorder in children: I. Relation to social impairment. *Journal of the American Academy of Child and Adolescent Psychiatry, 30,* 187–191.

Webster-Stratton, C. (1985). Predictors of treatment outcome in parent training for conduct disordered children. *Behavior Therapy, 16,* 223–243.

Webster-Stratton, C. (1994). Advancing videotape parent training: A comparison study. *Journal of Consulting and Clinical Psychology, 62,* 583–593.

Webster-Stratton, C., Hollinsworth, T., & Kolpacoff, M. (1989). The long-term effectiveness and clinical significance of three cost-effective training programs for families with conduct-problem children. *Journal of Consulting and Clinical Psychology, 57,* 550–553.

Weisz, J. R., Walter, B. R., Weiss, B., Fernandez, G. A., & Mikow, V. A. (1990). Arrests among emotionally disturbed violent and assaultive individuals following minimal versus lengthy intervention through North Carolina's Willie M. Program. *Journal of Consulting and Clinical Psychology, 58,* 720–728.

Werner, E. E., & Smith, R. S. (1992). *Overcoming the odds: High risk children from birth to adulthood.* Ithaca, NY: Cornell University Press.

West, D. J. (1982). *Delinquency: Its roots, careers and prospects.* Cambridge, MA; Harvard University Press.

Zoccolillo, M. (1993). Gender and the development of conduct disorder. *Development and Psychopathology, 5,* 65–78.

CHAPTER 8

SOMATIC DISORDERS

Lawrence J. Siegel

INTRODUCTION

Western culture before the 17th century saw our bodily health as inextricably linked to our mental and spiritual health, even though no one could have provided proof of the importance of this linkage as modern researchers would demand (Weil, 1988; Dienstfrey, 1991). Psychological factors have been viewed as important in medicine since the time of Hippocrates. Beginning early in the 17th century, modern scientific empiricism began to grow out of the analytical and unemotional thinking of Bacon, Descartes, and Newton. They were all mathematical, methodological, mechanistic thinkers who drew a short distinction among body, mind, and soul (Gatchel, 1993).

In contrast, the Chinese approach to medicine has always emphasized the mind-body connection (Beinfield & Korngold, 1991). It has always been considered that complete health represents a harmonious balance among all of our basic elements.

However, as Western medicine became occupied with the mechanistic aspects of illness and health, our scientific research became more refined and more focused on individual cellular and subcellular mechanisms, without regard to the whole system (Weil, 1988).

During the 20th century, there has been a reawakening throughout Western society to the concept of ourselves as whole systems, who do not develop illness or dysfunction independently of other human beings or of our environment. This integrational approach to health and illness has given way to a new approach to medicine referred to as "holistic" (Lipowski, 1986). The mind-body model of health and illness is finding increasing research support. It has attracted the attention not only of biological scientists but also of the lay public with the emergence of many forms of treatment for medical ailments, sometimes in the face of opposition from mainstream medicine (Ornstein & Sobel, 1987; Poole, 1993).

The influence of the fields of psychiatry and psychology in this century, to debates over a mind-body dichotomy led to a distinction between disorders caused by "physical" factors and disorders caused by "emotional" or "psychological" factors.

This conceptual approach to disease gave rise in the early 1900s to the field generally referred to as psychosomatic medicine. In more recent times, the term "psychophysiological" was applied to disorders that have traditionally been called psychosomatic illnesses (American Psychiatric Association (APA), 1968). Psychosomatic or psychophysiological disorders have been defined as disorders in which:

> There is a significant interaction between somatic and psychological components, with varying degrees of weighting in each component. Psychophysiological disorders may be precipitated and perpetuated by psychological or social stimuli of a stressful nature. Such disorders ordinarily involve those organ systems that are innervated by the autonomic or involuntary portion of the central nervous system....Structural change occurs..., continuing to a point that may be irreversible and that may threaten life in some cases (Group for the Advancement of Psychiatry, 1966, p. 258)

Beginning with the third edition of the *Diagnostic and Statistical Manual of Mental Disorders* (DSM-III-R) (American Psychiatric Association, 1987), the diagnostic category of psychophysiological disorders was no longer included. Instead, DSM-III-R had several diagnostic categories that subsumed the disorders previously referred to as psychophysiological. These new categories included: (a) "Psychological Factors Affecting Physical Condition" pertaining to disorders in which psychological factors are presumed to cause or exacerbate a physical condition; and (b) "Somatoform Disorders" defined as physical symptoms with "no demonstrable organic findings or known physiological mechanisms and for which there is positive evidence, or a strong presumption, that the symptoms are linked to psychological factors or conflicts" (American Psychiatric Association, 1987, p. 255). Among the disorders included in this diagnostic category are Conversion Disorder, Somatization Disorder, Psychogenic Pain Disorder, and Hypochondriasis.

In the most recent revision of the *Diagnostic and Statistical Manual of Mental Disorders* (DSM-IV) (American Psychiatric Association, 1994), several similar diagnostic categories were retained including (a) "Psychological Factors Affecting Medical Condition" defined as "one or more specific psychological or behavioral factors that adversely affect a medical condition" (p. 675), and "Somatoform Disorders" defined as "the presence of physical symptoms that suggest a general medical condition. ...and are not fully explained by a general medical condition, by the direct effects of a substance, or by another mental disorder" (p. 445). In contrast to the former diagnostic category, Somatoform Disorders involve psychological factors that can have an adverse impact on a *diagnosable medical condition*.

Regarding a diagnosis of Psychological Factors Affecting Medical Condition, DSM-IV further elaborates on the specific factors that can affect a medical condition and the mechanisms by which these factors can impact on the medical condition. The specific factors that can affect a medical condition include a mental disorder, psychological symptoms, personality traits or coping styles, maladaptive health behaviors, and stress-related physiological responses. These various factors can affect a medical condition by influencing the course of the condition, interfering with the treatment of the condition, providing an additional health risk, and/or precipitating or exacerbating symptoms of a medical condition through stress-related physiological responses.

A final relevant diagnostic category, that appears for the first time in DSM-IV (APA, 1994), is "Mental Disorders Due to a General Medical Condition." Disorders included in this category involve the "presence of mental symptoms that are judged to be the direct physiological consequence of a general medical condition" (p. 165). Such a diagnosis is warranted when the psychological disturbance "is etiologically related to the general medical condition through a physiological mechanism" (p. 166).

At the present time, it is the general consensus that the concepts "psychosomatic," "psychophysiological," or "somatopsychic" are of limited usefulness and lead to a simplistic notion about the relationship between psychological factors and a *distinct* group of physical or somatic disorders. The prevailing view is that an interaction of multiple, complex factors (i.e., biological, environmental, psychological, and social) contributes to the development and maintenance of most physical disorders (Kimball, 1970; Lipton, Sternschneider, & Richmond, 1966; Schwab, McGinnis, Morris, & Schwab, 1970). This view is expressed by Lipowski (1977):

The concept of psychogenisis of organic disease…is no longer tenable and has given way to the multiplicity of all disease.…The relative contributions of these factors [social and psychological] varies from disease to disease, from person to person, and from one episode of the same disease in the same person to another episode.…If the foregoing arguments are accepted then it becomes clear that to distinguish a class of disorders as "psychosomatic disorders" and to propound generalizations about psychosomatic patients is misleading and redundant. Concepts of single causes and unilinear causal sequences for example from psyche to soma and vise versa are simplistic and obsolete (p. 234)

Davison and Neale (1974) similarly have noted that:

> Many diseases are viewed as being partially caused by emotional or psychological factors. The list, a long one, includes multiple sclerosis, pneumonia, cancer, tuberculosis, and the common cold. In fact, the emotional state of the patient is now recognized as playing an important role in the precipitation or exacerbation of many illnesses. (p. 152)

To avoid this arbitrary distinction between "psychosomatic disorders" and other health-related problems, Siegel and Richards (1978) have proposed that the term "somatic disorder" be used to refer to any bodily dysfunction irrespective of the presumed etiology as psychological or behavioral factors likely have a potential role in the development or treatment of almost every medical condition. Therefore, this chapter will use the more generic term "somatic" disorder to refer to a diverse array of problems associated with dysfunctions of various organ systems of the body.

THEORETICAL MODELS OF SOMATIC DISORDERS

During the past several decades, numerous theories have been put forth to account for the etiology of somatic disorders in which psychological or emotional factors are presumed to play a significant role. There are four major theoretical models that dominate the field at the present time: the stress model, the family-systems model, the cognitive-perceptual model, and the behavioral model. Each of these models will be briefly reviewed.

Stress Model

Psychological stress has been implicated as an important factor in the development and maintenance of many somatic problems. A number of theories have been proposed to account for the relationship between stress and disease. One of the earliest theories to link stress to illness was the general adaptation syndrome proposed by Selye (1956). According to Seyle, a noxious or stressful stimulus results in increased physiological activity which, if prolonged, can lead to lowered resistance of the body systems and eventually to disease.

A major research focus in recent years has been the effects of stressful life events on a host of health-related problems. It has been proposed that life changes, whether positive or negative, require some readjustment by the person affected. A consequence of frequent life-change events is an enhanced susceptibility to disease (Holmes & Rahe, 1967). A large body of literature has demonstrated a significant relationship between measures of life change and the occurrence of a wide range of somatic disorders (Johnson & Bradlyn, 1988), although the etiological link between stressful life events and physical problems remains open to debate. The complexity of this relationship is further illustrated by a number of factors that serve as moderator variables, such as the role of appraisal of life events as stressful or not stressful and the availability of personal resources (e.g., coping behaviors, social support) (Lazarus, 1966). Similar findings with health-related outcomes have also been reported with the occurrence of daily hassles, which represent common, daily events that are irritating, frustrating, and annoying (Kanner, Coyne, Schaefer, & Lazarus, 1980).

The field of psychoneuroimmunology, which has proliferated during the past decade, is concerned with the study of biological mechanisms that serve to link stress-related factors and the onset and exacerbation of disease processes. Research suggests that the body's immune system, in interaction with the neuroendocrine system, is responsive to a variety of psychological events (Siegel & Graham-Pole, 1995). In particular, acute and chronic stress can suppress different aspects of the immune system (Ader, Felton, & Cohen, 1991; Herbert & Cohen, 1993; Rogers, Dubey, & Reich, 1979). While conclusive evidence remains to be empirically demonstrated, it has been suggested that the resulting immune suppression can result in disease onset and maintenance (Keicolt-Glaser & Glaser, 1988; Siegel & Graham-Pole, 1991).

Family-Systems Model

Various theories have addressed the role that the family plays in the etiology and maintenance of physical symptoms among its members (Kazak, Segal-Andrews, & Johnson, 1995; Mullins, Olson, & Chaney, 1992; Payne & Norfleet, 1986; Turk & Kerns, 1985). The literature in this area is represented by a preponderance of theorists who subscribe to a family-systems model. Family-systems theorists are particularly concerned with the nature of the family's interaction patterns and regard the somatic symptoms as having a functional significance in stabilizing and maintaining the status quo of the family system (Haggerty, 1983; Meisner, 1974).

Minuchin and his colleagues (Minuchin, Baker, Liebman, Milman, & Todd, 1975; Minuchin, Rosman, & Baker, 1978) have developed one of the most comprehensive and influential theories pertaining to family relationships and somatic symptoms such as asthma, diabetes, and anorexia nervosa. These researchers observed that families of children diagnosed as having severe "psychosomatic" symptoms demonstrated a number of consistent characteristics, particularly when threatened by stresses. These families were found to be rigid in their rules and expectations at times when flexibility and change were important; they lacked appropriate conflict-resolution skills, so that the somatic symptoms served to distract the family from solving significant family problems; and there was excessive and inappropriate overprotectiveness. Support for this theory is limited primarily to reports from Minuchin and his colleagues; these indicate the successful treatment of somatic symptoms in children by means of intervention programs designed to change dysfunctional patterns of family organization and interaction.

Cognitive-Perceptual Model

A number of diverse theories examine the role that cognitive-perceptual processes play in the development of physical symptoms. A common theme of these theoretical approaches is that the preoccupation with or heightened sensitivity to bodily states contributes to symptom development.

Pennebaker & Skelton (1978) argue that attending to one's internal states serves to enhance the perceived intensity of physical symptoms. Using the concept of private body consciousness, investigators have shown that persons who tend to focus on normal bodily sensations also report more somatic symptoms (Ahles, Cassens, & Stallings, 1983). Similarly, Mechanic (1983) refers to the notion of introspectiveness, which he defines as a learned focus on inner thoughts and feelings that can lead to a greater sensitivity to bodily changes. He suggests that an increased reporting of somatic symptoms during adolescence can be attributed to a greater degree of introspectiveness and self-monitoring during this period of rapid bodily changes. Finally, Barsky and his colleagues (Barsky & Klerman, 1983; Barsky, Goodson, Lane, & Cleary, 1988) propose the concept of an "amplifying somatic style" to account for persons who report frequent somatic complaints. Such individuals exhibit a tendency to experience normal physiological sensations as disturbing and respond to such sensations with hypervigilance. As a result, these sensations are amplified and misinterpreted.

While the theories included under the cognitive-perceptual model are relatively new, cognitive-behavioral intervention techniques that focus on a person's cognitions and appraisals can easily incorporate this perspective. Hypervigilance and misinterpretation of bodily sensations, once identified as part of the problem, can become targets for change using cognitive-behavioral approaches.

Behavioral Model

There is considerable research evidence that learning mechanisms can play a significant role in a variety of somatic disorders regardless of the specific etiology involved. Research has shown that the body's physiological responses can be influenced and modified by specific learning experiences. Autonomic or visceral responses can be affected or altered by both respondent (classical) conditioning or operant (instrumental) conditioning (cf. Blanchard & Young, 1974; Miller, 1969; Schwartz, 1973; Shapiro & Surwit, 1976). It was presumed until very recently that autonomic responses were "involuntary" and as such could be modified only through the process of respondent conditioning. However, there is now substantial clinical and research evidence, accumulated over the past several decades, indicating that many autonomic or visceral responses such as heart rate (Brener, 1974; Engle, 1972), blood pressure (Elder, Ruiz, Deabler, & Dillenkoffer, 1973; Shapiro, Tursky, & Schwartz, 1970), skin temperature (Roberts, Kewan, & Macdonald, 1973; Sargent, Greene & Walters, 1973), brain wave activity (Beatty, 1977), and muscular activity (Basmajian, 1977) are in fact subject to voluntary control through operant conditioning mechanisms. These findings have led to significant developments in our basic understanding of the etiology and treatment of numerous somatic disorders. However, Davison and Neale (1974) have proposed that the primary role of operant and respondent conditioning mechanisms in physical disorders "is probably best viewed as a factor that can exacerbate an already existing illness rather than cause it" (p. 157).

In another, more detailed conceptualization of physical illnesses within a behavioral framework described by Whitehead, Fedoravicius, Blackwell, and Wooley (1979), somatic symptoms are regarded as the result of interactions between stress reactions and operant and respondent conditioning. This

behavioral model of somatic disorders is illustrated in a case described by Siegel and Richards (1978). An 8-year-old child had experienced severe abdominal pains for several days as a result of gastrointestinal problems that developed during a viral infection. When the child drank milk during this illness, the stomach pains worsened, becoming more intense. As a result of this repeated, learned association between the stomachaches and the milk, the act of drinking milk alone was sufficient to elicit the stomach pains, despite the fact that the child no longer had the virus. Therefore, each time the child subsequently attempted to drink milk, stomach pains occurred for a short time. This learned association between the abdominal pains and the drinking of milk can be accounted for by the process of respondent conditioning, in which involuntary or reflexive behaviors (i.e., contractions of the gastrointestinal tract) can be made to occur in the presence of a previously neutral stimulus (i.e., milk) which does not naturally elicit the physiological response. It is also possible for physical symptoms to be shaped and maintained by operant conditioning mechanisms. "Operant conditioning" refers to a learning process that involves the occurrence of a response (e.g., stomach pains) and the consequences that contingently and systematically follow it. The response is more or less likely to occur in the future depending on whether the consequences that follow it are reinforcing, punishing, or neutral. For example, in the case of the child with stomach pains, it is possible that upon exhibiting verbal and/or nonverbal pain behaviors, a number of positive events or benefits (sometimes referred to as secondary gains) may follow in a contiguous manner. The child, for instance, may receive considerable adult attention and comfort for the reported pain. In addition, as a result of the stomach pains, the parents may permit the child to remain home from school or to avoid unpleasant activities, such as completing household chores or doing homework assignments. These reinforcing consequences can then perpetuate the symptomatic behaviors even when the illness, which may have initially precipitated the abdominal pains, no longer exists. Other learning-based intervention procedures, such as modeling, have received little attention in the treatment of somatic disorders in children, although more comprehensive behavioral models of treatment have been proposed (Mullins, et al., 1992; Wooley, Blackwell, & Winget, 1978). It is within this conceptual model that behavioral procedures have developed as an effective treatment approach for many somatic disorders in children.

INTERVENTION STRATEGIES WITH SOMATIC DISORDERS

An understanding of the etiology of a particular somatic disorder is important primarily to the extent that organic or physical factors, if present, need to be identified for appropriate medical intervention. Where any physical or somatic complaints are presented as a problem, a thorough medical examination is imperative to evaluate the need for medical treatment prior to any treatment by psychological methods. Furthermore, many somatic disorders, despite their etiology, can result in extensive tissue damage or physical changes in a particular organ system so that a combination of medical and psychological interventions may be required. For example, while enuresis typically has a nonorganic etiology, in some instances it can be caused by such organic factors as a urinary-tract infection, a neurological disorder, or a defect in the urogenital tract. Therefore, while less than 10% of the cases of childhood enuresis can be attributed to organic causes (Walker, 1995), the effectiveness of any psychological treatment might be impeded should any of these conditions exist. In addition, the disorder may even worsen if psychological treatment is pursued in the context of an inadequate medical evaluation.

It should be emphasized, however, that the need for medical treatment does not preclude the simultaneous use of empirically derived psychological interventions. Behavioral procedures have served a useful and highly effective adjunctive role in the direct treatment of somatic disorders and indirectly through patient management (Melamed & Siegel, 1980). The concurrent application of behavioral methods and medical procedures has been effective in preventing the exacerbation of symptomatic behaviors and in alleviating discomfort in a variety of somatic disorders. Because it is generally recognized

that psychological, environmental and physiological factors contribute to the development of many health problems, treatment strategies beyond traditional medical approaches are clearly warranted in many cases. Our knowledge of the multiple determinants of problems of health and illness underscores the need for a multifaceted treatment approach that integrates behavioral as well as medical methods of treatment for somatic disorders. In this regard, Katz and Zlutnick (1975) have noted that:

> In conjunction with already established medical technology, behavioral techniques allow for a more comprehensive approach to patient care. In contrast, lack of attention to the environmental, behavioral, and social components of health problems may result in a less than satisfactory outcome. Clearly, the patient profits from the collaboration between medical practitioners and behavioral scientists. (p. XV)

The merits of this interdisciplinary approach to the treatment of health problems have been recognized in recent years (Drotar, 1995). This new orientation to health and illness has given rise to several fields or disciplines variously referred to as behavioral medicine, psychosomatic medicine, and health psychology.

The remainder of this chapter presents various behavioral intervention methods that have been demonstrated to be effective or show considerable promise in the treatment of several somatic disorders in children. This chapter presents an overview of some of the psychological treatment approaches that have been used either alone or in combination with medical procedures to alleviate or reduce the symptomatic behaviors associated with various somatic disorders in children. In some cases, these psychological approaches have been used successfully to treat somatic disorders when medical interventions have failed to affect any changes in the bodily dysfunction. Furthermore, various psychological interventions have shown considerable promise in the treatment of physical disorders that have potentially debilitating or life-threatening consequences for the child.

The past several decades have witnessed a proliferation of the literature in this area (cf. Magrab,

1978; Melamed & Siegel, 1980; Olson Mullins, Gillman, & Chaney, 1994; Roberts, 1995; Schaefer, Millman, & Levine, 1979; Siegel & Richards, 1978; Varni, 1983). It is, therefore, not possible in a single chapter to present a comprehensive review of all somatic problems in children that have been treated by psychological approaches. This chapter will focus on the treatment of several bodily dysfunctions that occur with a sufficient frequency to be of particular interest to practitioners from various disciplines who work with children. Included in this review is a discussion of intervention methods for eating disorders, elimination disorders, and headaches. An emphasis is placed on treatment strategies that are consistent with learning-based behavioral approaches to modifying disordered behavior. Behavioral procedures have shown considerable promise in this area and many innovative treatment programs have been developed by behavioral practitioners. Most impressively, research has demonstrated that behavioral methods, in contrast to other medical and nonmedical approaches, have been the most effective therapeutic strategies with several somatic disorders in children. While other intervention strategies, such as family therapy approaches, may also be clinically useful, less empirical data are available to document their efficacy.

Eating Disorders

Diagnostic categories within the DSM-IV eating disorders subclass include Anorexia Nervosa, Bulimia Nervosa, Pica, Rumination Disorder, and Feeding Disorder of Infancy or Early Childhood (American Psychiatric Association, 1994). Eating Disorder Not Otherwise Specified is also included and applicable when a person does not meet all the criteria for either anorexia or bulimia. Other eating-related problems that are not included in DSM-IV but are of importance psychologically are obesity, food refusal, and restricted eating patterns. Obesity is a significant somatic problem in which treatment components often involve psychological techniques. Food refusal and restricted eating patterns may present during the early ages of childhood when food preferences typically develop. Treatment

issues related to obesity and anorexia will be reviewed in this section because clinically, these disorders are found more often in childhood or adolescence than pica, rumination, or food refusal and have received more empirical attention in the literature. While bulimia nervosa is seen during adolescence (Garner & Garner, 1992; Howatt & Saxton, 1988), it is beyond the scope of this chapter to review all areas. The reader is referred to reviews of treatment approaches to bulimia by Johnson, Conners, and Tobin (1987) and Wilson & Fairburn, (1993). Linscheid (1992) and Siegel (1983) have reviewed the treatment of food refusal, restricted eating patterns, rumination, and vomiting.

OBESITY

Obesity is usually defined as a weight that is 20% above the ideal, which, for children, is based on height, age, and gender (Epstein & Wing, 1987). While the problem of obesity in adults has been extensively investigated (Brownell & Jeffrey, 1987), only in the past decade has greater emphasis been placed on this problem in children and adolescents. The increased interest may be due in part to the fact that weight reduction with obese adults has resulted in little long-term success (Brownell, 1982; Brownell & Jeffrey, 1987; Brownell & O'Neil, 1993) and that being overweight as a child places a person at greater risk for obesity during adulthood, increasing morbidity and mortality (Nieto, Szklo, & Comstock, 1992). The risk factor increases from approximately 2 during infancy to 6.5 by the preadolescent years (e.g., Epstein, 1986). In addition, the prevalence of obesity in children appears to be increasing. While one recent study has estimated it at only about 9%, among adolescents this represents a substantial increase (39% for obesity; 64% for superobesity) from the previous results of the National Health and Examination Survey, Cycle 1 (Gortmaker, Dietz, Sobol, & Wehler, 1987). A similar trend has been noted in younger children, with greater increases noted in boys 6 to 11 years of age and adolescent girls (Gortmaker et al., 1987).

As with adults, childhood obesity can have significant medical impact including increased risk for hypertension, hypercholesterolemia, carbohydrate intolerance, increased insulin secretion, and decreased growth hormone release (Chiumello, del Guercio, Carnelutti, & Bidone, 1969; Gillum et al., 1983; Lauer, Conner, Leaverton, Reiter, & Clarke, 1975; Laskarzewski et al., 1979; Londe, Bourgoignie, Robson, & Goldring, 1972). The psychological impact of being overweight, while intuitively appealing, has not been consistently documented (Friedman & Brownell, 1995). Some studies have found lower self-esteem in obese children relative to normal-weight peers (Sallade, 1973), while others have found no significant differences (Wadden, Foster, Brownell, & Finley, 1984). Given society's emphasis on thinness, being overweight can have social repercussions (e.g., Millman, 1980). Studies have indicated that, given a choice of several visible physical disabilities, a child is least likely to select an overweight person as a friend (Staffieri, 1967). Further investigation in this area is warranted, as children seeking treatment for their obesity may do so as a result of teasing by peers or concerns about acceptance by peers. These children may look different on standardized measures of psychological adjustments (Wadden et al., 1984). It would be interesting to know if emotional discomfort results in greater motivation both to seek and to follow through with treatment.

Etiological factors. Simply stated, obesity is the result of an energy imbalance; that is, a person consumes more calories than are expended in the output of energy (Garrow, 1986). While this etiology seems simple enough, the attempt to understand why some children have more difficulty maintaining an optimum energy balance than others becomes very complex because so many factors are related to energy balance (e.g., metabolic rate, responsive of metabolism to food and exercise) (Garrow, 1986; Keesey, 1986). Research on the etiology of obesity has been plagued with the problem inherent in trying to untangle genetic and environmental influences. Only a cursory overview of this debate and biological theories of obesity will be presented.

On the side of genetics, children of obese parents are more likely to be overweight than children of thin parents, and this risk increases when both parents are overweight (Epstein, 1986). In addition, researchers have suggested that it is easier for obese children of thin parents to lose and maintain their weight loss than it is for children with obese parents (Epstein, Wing, Koeske, & Valoski, 1987; Epstein, Wing, Valoski, & Gooding, 1987). Twin studies have revealed an increased concordance of obesity in monozygotic twins relative to other sibling pairs (Foch & McClearn, 1980). Yet the most convincing evidence for a genetic component has been provided by Stunkard and his colleagues (Stunkard et al., 1986) in an adoption study, which showed greater correlations between the weight of adopted children and their biological parents than the children and their adopted parents. Other studies have suggested that genetics differentially affects different types of body fat (i.e., internal vs. subcutaneous) (Bouchard, Perusse, LeBlanc, Tremblay, & Theriault, 1988). These studies would certainly argue for some degree of genetic involvement in the development of obesity.

If genetics plays a role, then what is inherited? Current theories regarding obesity suggest that weight is physiologically regulated so that attempts to reduce weight through restricted diet may lower the metabolic rate and thus, the required number of calories to maintain the original weight (Keesey, 1986). That is, some obese individuals may have a higher set-point for their body weight. The reader is referred to Keesey (1986) for a more detailed discussion of the set-point theory of obesity. Other researchers have focused on the number and size of fat cells (Sjostrom, 1980) as being at least in part genetically determined.

On the side of environmental influences, studies suggest that parents can influence their children's preferences for particular types of foods, as well as the amounts of food they consume through exposure, prompting, reinforcement, and modeling (e.g., Birch & Marlin, 1982; Duncker, 1938; Epstein, Masek, & Marshall, 1978; Harper & Sanders, 1975; Klesges et al., 1983). These behavioral principles have been noted to apply to the amount of physical activity in which children engage as well (Epstein, Woodall, Goreczny, Wing, & Robertson, 1984;

Klesges, Malott, Boschee, & Weber, 1986). In addition, parental expectations regarding food consumption and amount of physical activity may play a role, as it has been shown that parents feel their obese children need more to eat and will be less active relative to their thinner siblings (Waxman & Stunkard, 1980). These studies would suggest that behavioral factors such as exposure to and availability of foods (e.g., stimulus control), reinforcement principles, and cognitive variables such as expectations and modeling are also involved in the development of obesity in childhood.

While behavioral factors have been shown to influence food consumption and activity level, the data are less consistent as to whether obese children actually differ from thin children in these ways (O'Brien, Walley, Anderson-Smith, & Drabman, 1982; Woodall & Epstein, 1983). There is evidence that obese and thin children differ in their perception of different types of physical activities and foods, but it is unclear if these perceptions preceded the obesity (Worsley, Coonan, Leitch, & Crawford, 1984; Worsley, Peters, Worsley, Coonan, & Baghurst, 1984). Other studies have suggested that obese children differ in their eating styles (Geller, Keane, & Scheirer, 1981) and have more difficulty delaying gratification when food is involved (Bonato & Boland, 1983; Sobhany & Rogers, 1985).

Though not a comprehensive review, these studies suggest that genetic, behavioral, and environmental factors can all contribute to obesity in children. The degree to which each factor is involved will likely vary between children. For example, a genetic component that may predispose children to gain weight more easily may be a major factor in some children, while obesity in others may be due primarily to self-regulatory difficulties with regard to food and activity. Certainly further investigations are needed in order to individualize treatment programs for children with different reasons for being overweight (Brownell & Wadden, 1991). In particular, continued evaluation of differences between obese and nonobese children with regard to eating and activity behaviors is needed to clarify what behavioral treatment components are needed. In the future particular attention should be paid to whether behaviors are a cause or result of increased weight.

Overview of treatment approaches. Treatment approaches for childhood obesity have been patterned primarily after those used with adults, with behavioral techniques as the major treatment components. One important difference between adult and child weight reduction is that since children are still growing both in height and weight, and any methods used, especially dietary, must consider the child's nutritional needs to promote optimal growth (Epstein & Wing, 1987). Therefore, it is important to ensure that children receive recommended daily allowances of nutrients and to monitor changes in height carefully during treatment. In addition, it is usually best to base treatment success on decreases in percent overweight rather than actual pounds lost. For example, a child may maintain baseline weight and still decrease percent overweight with an increase in height. Finally, developmental differences that can affect understanding of the rationale for treatment as well as adherence to various treatment components should be considered (Wolfle, Farrier, & Rogers, 1987).

In general, treatment should include two phases; the initial weight loss or decrease in percent overweight and the maintenance of gains made during the initial period (Brownell & Wadden, 1991; Epstein & Wing, 1987). Studies with adults have suggested that duration of initial treatment is correlated with amount of weight lost (Brownell & Jeffrey, 1987). While it is relatively easy to achieve some initial weight loss, the success of a program is best judged by long-term maintenance (e.g., 1 to 5 years) (Brownell & Jeffrey, 1987).

A typical program for children and adolescents usually includes behavioral techniques such as self-monitoring, stimulus control, and reinforcement of behavior change. Most programs include dietary modifications and exercise components as well. A typical program and factors related to successful initial "losers" and "maintainers" will be reviewed in greater depth. Other approaches used with adults—such as pharmacotherapy (e.g., appetite suppressants) and surgical techniques that have not been a primary clinical or research focus with children—are not reviewed. Readers are referred to other sources for information regarding these types of interventions (Cohen & Stunkard, 1983; Kral & Kissileff, 1987).

A typical program involves having the child and/or parent self-monitor or keep records of various treatment components, which may include type and amount of food consumed, type and duration of exercise, actual weight, and reinforcements earned. The child's age and the complexity of the record keeping are usually determinants of who maintains the records, though even younger children can be involved in some way (e.g., "helping" parent record the data). Most programs include education on the role of stimulus control, diet, activity, and use of reinforcements. Stimulus control involves reducing the number of cues associated with eating. For example, rather than eating in front of the television or while studying, the child consumes all foods at the dinner table. High caloric foods are either not kept at home or are stored in opaque containers or on shelves out of children's reach. Low-calorie foods, such as carrots or celery, are prepared and placed in a prominent location in the refrigerator for easy access. Specific eating behaviors; such as using smaller plates with smaller portions of food, putting the fork down between bites, and chewing food a specified number of times may be taught as well.

As food intake is one major part of the energy-balance equation, most programs include detailed education about the nutritional and caloric value of various foods. Epstein and his colleagues (Epstein, et al., 1978) have developed the "Traffic Light Diet," which is easily understood by younger children because foods are divided into green—eat all you want, low calorie foods; yellow;—alright to eat but use caution as to amount consumed; and red—high-caloric, low-nutritional-value foods that should be limited. Successful weight reduction using this diet has been correlated with limiting the number of foods rated red eaten each week (Epstein, Wing, Koeske, Andrasik, & Ossip, 1981).

One of the difficulties with most typical weight-loss programs is that despite decreases in percent overweight, most children do not achieve a non -obese status, especially if they are markedly obese. The use of very low calorie protein-sparing diets has gained considerable attention with adults as one means of achieving even greater initial weight loss, with behavioral components being used to facilitate maintenance (Blackburn, Lynch, & Wong, 1986; Kirschner, Schneider, Ertel, & Gorman, 1988). These diets require close medical supervision, but there is some evidence that this approach can be used with children and adolescents without adverse effects (Blackburn et al., 1986; Merrit, 1978). Further collaborative investigations with physician colleagues will be important to carefully explore the safe application of this type of diet with children.

Activity level, the other major component in the equation, has gained more attention and is now included in most programs. Exercise not only increases energy expenditure but also decreases the loss of lean body mass during a diet, improves psychological functioning, and may act to suppress appetite and offset the decline in basal metabolic rate associated with dieting (Brownell & Stunkard, 1980). Low intensity activity (e.g., walking) that is equivalent in energy expenditure to a high intensity, programmed activity (e.g., aerobics) is more likely to result in adherence to the program and to be associated with greater maintenance of fitness and weight loss (Epstein, Wing, Koeske, & Valoski, 1985; Epstein, Wing, Koeske, Ossip, & Beck, 1982). Shaping of the desired exercise behavior may be needed for children who are moderately obese and/or sedentary; this can be accomplished by setting a short-term goal that is increased each week until the desired endpoint is attained.

The use of reinforcements by other family members such as praise contingent on changes in eating or activity levels, is another component included in most programs (e.g., Epstein et al., 1981). For some children a point system, where achieving daily or weekly treatment goals or adhering to specific behaviors can earn points that can be used to "buy" backup reinforcers, can be an additional motivator. Like reinforcement, contingency contracting is often used where monetary deposits are made prior to treatment and a specified amount is returned contingent on either attendance or weight loss (Epstein et al., 1987; Kirschenbaum, Harris, & Tomarken, 1984). There is some suggestion that contracts contingent on weight loss as opposed to adherence results in greater weight loss (Epstein et al., 1987; Coates, Jeffrey, Slinkard, Killen, & Danaher, 1982). No investigations have compared the utility of contracting contingent on weight loss with no contracting in children, though it has resulted in greater weight loss in adults (Brownell & Jeffrey, 1987).

While many programs are provided through medical or psychological clinics, there is evidence that weight-reduction programs can be implemented within the school setting (Brownell & Kaye, 1982; Foster, Wadden, & Brownell, 1985; Lansky & Brownell, 1982). Generally, school-based programs have resulted in smaller weight losses than clinic-based programs; evidence of maintenance of losses or behavioral changes that may stabilize weight are needed (Foster et al., 1985).

Factors related to weight loss and maintenance. In assessing factors related to weight loss, the issue of how and when to include parents has been a focus of research. There is some evidence that adolescents are best treated in groups separate from the parents, though both receive the same information (Brownell, Kelman, & Stunkard, 1983). In treating children 9 to 13 years of age, no differences were found in weight lost between children treated with parents in the same group or children treated alone with parents receiving detailed written information (Kirschenbaum, et al., 1984). Attrition was lower in the group that included the parents. As adolescence is a time for developing independence, separate treatment may be more important for adolescents than for younger children.

Epstein et al. (1987) have found that targeting both parent and child for weight loss results in greater maintenance for the child at 5-year follow-up, despite the fact that parents regained their weight. While parent modeling and support can account for changes during treatment, modeling is unlikely to be related to maintenance, though continued support may be of importance. Israel, Stolmaker, and Andrian (1985) have noted that adding a general behavioral-management training component to the weight-reduction program resulted in greater maintenance of weight loss at 1-year follow-up. These parents may have been able to

generalize their additional training to other problem situations that may have occurred during the follow-up year; absence of such generalization may have contributed to relapse in the standard treatment group (Epstein, & Wing, 1987).

In addition to parental involvement, greater weight loss at post treatment has been predicted by children's perceptions of greater personal control over their weight, that weight loss would be difficult, and that their excess weight is not due to family problems. Parental perception that the child was less likely to be overweight in the future was also a significant predictor (Uzark, Becker, Dielman, Rocchini, & Katch, 1988). Similarly, Flanery, and Kirschenbaum (1986) found that flexible problem solving and attributions of ability and lack of effort predicted greater maintenance of weight loss, though keeping a weight chart was predictive as well. Cohen, Gelfand, Dodd, Jensen, and Turner (1980) found that greater self-regulation and physical exercise distinguished "maintainers" from "regainers" and normal-weight peers. Regainers also reported greater parental regulation of weight management relative to normal-weight peers. Though few in number, these studies suggest that children's self-efficacy (Bandura, 1977), attributions about the ability to lose weight, thoughts regarding relapse events, and ability to continue to self-monitor are important variables during the maintenance phase of weight loss (Israel, Guile, Baker, & Silverman, 1994). Parental support and expectations regarding success are probably important factors during this phase as well.

Though investigations with adults have focused on factors related to maintenance, such as continued therapist contact and the inclusion of a relapse component in the program (Perri, Shapiro, Ludwig, Twentyman, & McAdoo, 1984) these factors have not been empirically assessed in younger samples. Given that obesity may well be a chronic condition requiring continuous application of behavioral techniques and self-restraint, continued therapist contact may be one means of solidifying important behavioral changes and providing external motivation during periods of relapse.

In the longest follow-up study to date of the behavioral treatment of childhood obesity (10 years post treatment) (Epstein, Valoski, Wing, & McCurley, 1994), 34% of the children had decreased their percent overweight (20% or more) while as many as 30% were no longer in the obese weight range. These findings are impressive and a significant improvement in the long-term maintenance of weight loss as compared with obese adults. This study provided further support for the use of family-based behavioral treatment of childhood obesity and demonstrated the importance of exercise, in addition to diet, and the presence of support from the child's family and friends for diet and activity change.

As Wilson (1994) notes that the importance of the Epstein et al. (1994) study lies in identifying the factors contributing to the long-term effective of their treatment program. Wilson (1994) speculates that one of the reasons for these highly positive findings was that the treatment program focused on young children. As a result, it was easier to control the child's environment associated with food management and activity level than is typically possible with adults.

Anorexia Nervosa

One of the most serious eating disorders is anorexia nervosa. This disorder is characterized by excessive weight loss without organic causes. Current DSM-IV (American Psychiatric Association, 1994) criteria for weight loss is 15% of original body weight. For children and adolescents, weight gain attributable to growth should be included in the 15% figure as well. Anorexia can pose a grave danger to the patient, with estimates of mortality as high as 15% (Dally, 1969; Palla & Litt, 1988). This disorder typically begins during adolescence, with most cases occurring by young adulthood, however, cases have been diagnosed in 7 to 14-year-olds (Fosson, Knibbs, Bryant-Waugh, & Lask, 1987). Anorexia occurs most frequently in females (Halmi, 1974) and in middle and upper socioeconomic classes (Garfinkel & Garner, 1982). Estimates of the prevalence of anorexia have ranged from 0.5% to 2.1% and epidemiological studies have suggested that the incidence of this disorder is increasing (Nussbaum,

1992; Strober, 1986). In addition to profound weight loss, anorexia nervosa is typically associated with cessation of menstruation, serious electrolyte imbalances, and other medical abnormalities (Palla & Litt, 1988). Other common features of this disorder include distorted perceptions of body image, preoccupation with food preparation, unrealistic fears of being overweight, and lack of sensitivity to internal cues of hunger. The anorexic may also engage in compulsive overeating, followed by self-induced vomiting, laxative use, or high activity levels to avoid the intense fear of weight gain (Crisp, Hsu, Harding, & Hartshorn, 1980).

While the diagnostic criteria for this disorder is quite similar for DSM-IV and its predecessor, DSM-III-R, there is a major change in the newest edition. DSM-IV delineates two subtypes of anorexia nervosa. The "restricting" type does not engage in binge-eating or purging behaviors (self-induced vomiting or excessive use of laxatives, diuretics, or enemas). Persons who are categorized as "binge-eating/purging" type, however, engage in recurrent episodes of binge eating but lose weight through the excessive use of these various purging behaviors.

Etiological factors. The etiology of anorexia nervosa is unknown, although numerous theories have been suggested to account for it (Bemis, 1978). Given the multiple physiological abnormalities found in these patients and the fact that in some patients amenorrhea precedes weight loss, some have suggested a hypothalamic dysfunction (Garfinkel & Kaplan, 1986). Yet studies have found that the majority of physiological abnormalities are the result of weight loss and caloric restriction. Studies of semistarved samples have reported obsessive food-related thoughts and behaviors similar to those in anorexic patients (Keys, Brozek, Henschel, Mickelsen, & Taylor, 1950). A genetic component has been hypothesized, based on evidence that eating disorders are more prevalent in relatives of anorexic patients (Strober, Morrell, Burroughs, Salkin, & Jacobs, 1985), and twin studies have documented greater concordance in monozygotic than dizygotic twins for anorexia (Holland, Hall, Murray, Russell, & Crisp, 1984). In addition, an increased prevalence of affective disorders has been found in first-degree relatives of anorexics although the reverse is not true (e.g., there is not a higher prevalence of anorexia in relatives of depressed patients) (Gershon, et al., 1983). Sociocultural values have been implicated in the onset of anorexia, as the high value society places on thinness may interact with personality variables (Childress, Brewerton, Hodges, & Jarrell, 1993; Garner, Garfinkel, & Olmstead, 1983).

Psychological studies have suggested that, as a group, anorexics tend to be perfectionistic, to feel more personally ineffective, to exhibit greater interpersonal distrust, and to lack awareness of or exhibit confusion over internal emotional and physiological states (Bruch, 1977; Crisp, 1980; Garner et al., 1983; Strober, 1980). Crisp (1980) has described anorexics as having a "weight phobia," which results from a fear of maturation and sexuality. This fits well with behavioral conceptualizations that anorexic behavior is an example of a conditioned avoidance response to real or perceived fears related to weight, development, and performance (Garner, 1986; Williamson, Davis, Duchman, McKenzie, Watkins, 1990). In addition, in a context of feeling ineffective, the ability to master a specific part of one's life can be highly reinforcing and may account for the perpetuation of the behaviors despite an emaciated condition (Garner, 1986). Cognitive-behavioral theorists have pointed to misperceptions regarding self-concept, separation, perfectionism, and relationships (Garner, 1986), issues that seem consistent with the view of psychodynamic theorists. Family interactional patterns have also been hypothesized as contributing to the onset and perpetuation of the disorder through patterns such as overprotection, enmeshment, inability to express and resolve conflict openly, detachment, and lack of empathy and affection (Garner, 1993; Minuchin et al., 1975; Strober & Humphrey, 1987). In a review of family contributions to both anorexia and bulimia, Strober and Humphrey (1987) interpret the available literature as suggesting that a family environment characterized by the above interactional patterns may interfere with the development of a stable identity and feelings of independence and self-efficacy. These authors call for more sophisticated investiga-

tions of family interactional patterns to support this hypothesis.

Overview of treatment approaches. Given that anorexia is probably the result of a complex interaction of social, familial, biological, and personality factors, careful assessment is needed to develop an appropriate treatment plan.

A detailed discussion of the assessment of eating disorders is beyond the scope of this chapter. The reader is referred to Garner and Garner (1992) and Williamson et al. (1990) for a comprehensive presentation of various approaches to the assessment of anorexia nervosa and other eating disorders.

A team approach that includes close collaboration between physician and therapist is imperative in the treatment of these patients. Most clinicians would agree that anorexia is a very difficult disorder to treat. A majority of patients require inpatient hospital treatment, especially in the early phases of intervention. The primary purpose of hospitalization is to promote refeeding and weight gain (Garner & Garner, 1992; Williamson, Davis, & Duchman, 1992). Once this has been accomplished, further treatment typically occurs in outpatient settings. Many patients with anorexia are reluctant to seek treatment as their symptoms are not perceived as a problem. Therefore, the initial phases of any treatment approach will be to engage the patient in the therapeutic relationship in a collaborative manner. Garner, Rocket, Olmstead, Johnson, and Coscina (1985) have suggested that education material on anorexia, the effects of starvation, medical complications, nutrition, physiology of weight regulation, and consequences of dieting can be helpful in this context.

Attention to eating habits and physical condition are an important part of the treatment and likely to be the initial focus (Li, 1994). Depending on the degree of weight loss and medical condition, treatment may be instituted in a hospital or in an outpatient setting (Anderson, 1986; Palla & Litt, 1988). Contracts regarding a minimal acceptable weight and contingencies related to hospitalization are a part of many outpatient treatments. Behavioral approaches to treatment have helped patients to increase their weight through control of factors associated with the maladaptive eating patterns. Typically, the focus of treatment is on weight gain rather than eating per se. This approach places greater responsibility for eating on the patient and avoids problems of the patient engaging in vomiting after eating. The most frequently used procedure has been the manipulation of environmental contingencies in order to maximize calorie intake, food consumption, and weight gain. This has been accomplished by making activities, privileges, and reinforcers contingent on eating behavior or weight gain (Bemis, 1987). These procedures have been effective in cases where other treatment approaches (such as tube feeding, insulin, tranquilizers, and traditional psychotherapy) have failed to modify the symptomatic behavior (Walen, Hauserman, & Lavin, 1977).

With some resolution of the patient's semistarved state, the therapeutic focus can shift to other issues regarding the misperceptions and fears noted previously. Yet attention to weight should be given throughout treatment in order to deal quickly with relapses. Several treatment programs for anorexia have been reported in which behavioral techniques have been combined with drug therapy (Munford, 1980) or family therapy (Lagos, 1981). Other behavioral approaches have focused primarily on the fear component of the disorder, using systematic desensitization to reduce fears of weight gain, criticism, and rejection; concerns about appearance; and fears of specific foods. Cognitive-behavioral techniques have been useful in changing misperceptions and distortions in thinking, symptoms that persist even after weight is gained (Garner, 1986). Various approaches to the treatment of anorexia nervosa have been reviewed by Bemis (1987) and Murray (1986). As the majority of the empirical literature has focused on behavioral techniques, several of these approaches will be described. Unfortunately relatively few empirical studies are available regarding psychodynamic and family approaches to treatment.

Premack principle. Based on their observation that many anorexic patients exhibit a high level of activity, Blinder, Freeman, and Stunkard (1970) used access to physical activity as a reinforcer for weight gain in several adolescent girls diagnosed as having anorexia nervosa. Previous research has demonstrated that access to high-frequency behaviors can be used to reinforce contingently low-frequency behaviors (Premack, 1965). Therefore, physical activity, a high-frequency behavior in these patients, was used as a positive reinforcer for weight gain. Previous treatment with medication and traditional psychotherapy had failed to result in any improvements in these girls' physical condition. In the behavioral treatment program, each patient was permitted 6 hours outside the hospital on days when her morning weight check indicated that she was at least 1/2 pound above the previous day's weight. This treatment approach provided a rapid weight gain for all the girls. There was an increase of approximately 4 pounds each week for all patients over a 6-week period. These weight gains were maintained or increased after discharge from the hospital, as revealed by an 8- to 10-month follow-up assessment. Similar results with adolescent anorexic patients using a variety of reinforcers for food consumption and weight gain are reported by Garfinkel, Kline, and Stancer (1973); Halmi, Powers, and Cunningham (1975); Leitenberg, Agras, and Thompson (1968); and Werry and Bull (1975).

Systematic desensitization. Hallsten (1965) treated a 12-year-old anorexic girl by systematic desensitization. Several years prior to treatment, the patient had been teased for being overweight; she then went on a diet and lost an excessive amount of weight. She expressed a fear of being fat and periodically induced vomiting. After training in deep-muscle relaxation, a hierarchy of items was constructed that related to her fears of becoming fat and of being teased by her peers for being overweight. Hierarchy items included visualizing herself being called to the table, eating at the table, eating fattening foods, standing in front of the mirror observing that she was gaining weight and so on. Treatment was conducted over 12 sessions, during which she began to eat complete meals. There was a concomitant increase in her weight. These improvements in her eating pattern and weight were maintained at a 5-month follow-up.

Reinforcement, feedback, and meal size. In a series of single case studies, Agras, Barlow, Chapin, Abel, and Lietenberg (1974) systematically investigated several variables to determine their relative importance in the behavioral treatment of anorexia nervosa. The first study investigated the effects of reinforcing weight gain on several children 10 and 17 years old. The patients recorded the number of mouthfuls eaten and calories consumed at each meal. They were also informed of their daily weight and asked to keep records of their progress through self-monitoring. Daily weight gain of a specified amount was reinforced with access to serious activities in the hospital. These procedures resulted in a rapid increase in weight. Using a reversal procedure in which contingent reinforcement was discontinued, the patients continued to show a weight gain. While only suggestive, these results indicated that reinforcement was instrumental in establishing weight gain, but that the maintenance and additional increase in weight were the result of other factors.

In a second experiment, reinforcement, without self-monitoring was delivered contingent on weight gain. This produced an increase in daily caloric intake and weight. However, when reinforcement was provided noncontingently, there was a decline in the rate of weight gain and a marked decrease in caloric intake. When reinforcement was again made contingent on weight gain, there was a significant increase in both caloric intake and weight.

In the third series of experiments, Agras et al. (1974) systematically evaluated the effects of reinforcement and information feedback. The reinforcement contingencies, like those in early experiments, remained in effect during this investigation. Information feedback in which the patient received information about the number of calories and mouthfuls eaten and about daily weight was introduced for several days, discontinued, and reintroduced. The results of this experiment revealed that maximum increases in caloric intake and weight gain were obtained only when the information-feedback condition was in effect. The investigators suggested that information regarding caloric intake and weight may enhance the effectiveness of

reinforcement because it provides a cue for the patient that reinforcement is forthcoming.

The final experiment reported by Agras et al. (1974) demonstrated that the size of the meal given to an anorexic patient may affect the quantity of food eaten. When a large meal was provided, the patient's caloric intake increased, even when all of the meal was not eaten. However, when the size of the meal was decreased, there was a concomitant decrease in the number of calories consumed.

Operant reinforcement and family therapy. Minuchin and his colleagues (Liebman, Minuchin, & Baker, 1974; Minuchin, et al., 1978) have described a comprehensive treatment program for anorexic patients in which behavioral procedures in the hospital and at home are combined with family therapy. They propose that weight gain alone should not be the primary goal of treatment but should also include a restructuring of dysfunctional patterns of family interaction; this is intended to prevent relapses and promote weight gain once the patient is discharged from the hospital. It is assumed that these maladaptive relationship patterns within the family serve to maintain the child's anorexic behaviors. If hospitalization is warranted for medical reasons, the child is admitted to the hospital to facilitate weight gain and to engage the family in treatment. In operant reinforcement programs, family lunch sessions in the hospital are used to initiate weight gain. Weight gain, (as assessed each morning) of at least a 1/2 pound enables the patient to remain out of bed, watch television, have visitors, and have 4 hours of unrestricted hospital activity. Family therapy sessions continue on an outpatient basis when the child is discharged from the hospital. In this program, the patient is typically hospitalized for several weeks and weekly family therapy sessions occur over a period of 5 to 12 months.

Minuchin et al. (1978) have reported on 53 anorexic patients (ages 9 to 21) who were treated with this intervention program. Based on their criteria for treatment effectiveness (i.e., no evidence of eating disturbances and good adjustment at home and at school), they report a success rate of approximately 86% after a follow-up period ranging from 4 months to 4 years.

Cognitive-behavioral therapy. In recent years cognitive-behavioral therapy has received increased attention in the treatment of anorexia nervosa and other eating disorders (Garner & Garner, 1992; Vitousek, 1996). A cognitive-behavioral approach to the treatment of anorexia nervosa is based on the premise that distorted cognitions and faulty assumptions related to beliefs and feelings about food, weight, body images, and control over one's environment are central to the onset and maintenance of this disorder (Bowers, Evans, & Van Cleve, 1996). The maladaptive cognitions associated with weight and weight gain that are "held by individuals with anorexia serve an adaptive function for them, providing them with a sense of identity, self-worth, and personal control" (Bowers et al., 1996, p. 234).

Within this framework, treatment involves the use of *cognitive restructuring* strategies. In this approach to therapy, the patient is taught to identify and self-monitor their thoughts and feelings concerning their weight, body size, and issues of self-esteem. They are then taught to challenge their maladaptive thought process by using more rational and appropriate interpretations of events in their environment. Patients also are taught cognitive problem-solving skills and behavioral coping strategies to use when confronting stressful situations in their lives.

Factors related to treatment outcome. As noted, anorexia is a very difficult, often recalcitrant disorder to treat. While prognostic indicators have been difficult to determine, anorexic patients who also exhibit bulimic symptoms appear to have a more chronic course than patients who do not engage in vomiting or purging (Casper, Eckert, Halmi, Goldberg, & Davis, 1980; Garfinkel, Moldofsky, & Garner, 1977). Bulimic anorexics are more likely to have a history of childhood maladjustment and obesity; they are also more likely to experience depression and to have impulse-control problems such as alcoholism. Families of bulimic anorexics are characterized as more conflictual and negative in their interactions, and a family history of obesity is more likely (Casper, et al., 1980; Garfinkel, et al., 1980; Strober, 1981). Other factors that have been associated with a poorer prognosis in anorexics as a group include older age of onset, longer duration of illness, lower body weight, poorer childhood adjustment, disturbed family relationships, and a history of previous psychiatric treatment (Szmuckler & Russell, 1986).

In a review of studies that provide long-term results, Szmuckler and Russell (1986) conclude that outcome is quite variable even within the same treatment centers. Some patients make complete recoveries, others appear to have more chronic courses, and some die. There is evidence that the percentage of patients who recover continues to increase up to about 4 years after treatment (Szmuckler & Russell, 1986) although it was not clear whether patients continued to receive treatment during the follow-up period. Szmuckler and Russell (1986) thoughtfully reflect on what constitutes a cure in these patients: successful maintenance of a specific body weight and menses, change in eating habits, and/or change in psychological disturbance or misperceptions.

At present, though behavioral approaches appear to be effective in producing initial weight gain, there are few comparative studies suggesting that one approach is superior to another (Szmuckler & Russell, 1986). While Bruch (1974) has argued that behavior modification can result in further psychological damage to the anorexic patient (because the therapist takes control), empirical data supporting this hypothesis are lacking. Several recent studies that compared family therapy with individual therapy in treating anorexia and bulimia suggested that, after 1 year of treatment, family therapy was more effective than individual therapy for patients who had developed their condition before age 19 and who had their symptoms for a shorter period of time prior to treatment (Dare, Eisler, Russell, & Szmukler, 1990; Russell, Szmukler, Dare, & Eisler, 1987). In the description of both therapies, it was clear that a variety of techniques were used under the headings of "family therapy" and "individual therapy." This points out one of the research challenges to a therapist: the need to define what specific therapies are being used and to determine what components of a multicomponent treatment approach are effective for different patients. Different types of interventions may impact the various characteristics of anorexia differentially or different interventions may work better with certain as yet unidentified subgroups of patients. Some treatment approaches have integrated a variety of behavioral, family, and psychodynamic components in an attempt to address the complexity involved in this disorder (e.g., Anderson, 1986; Geller, 1975; Liebman et al., 1974).

Discussion

While some eating disorders (such as pica, vomiting, and rumination) continue to have relatively low base rates, other eating-related problems, such as obesity and anorexia appear to be increasing. Factors related to these increases are not well-understood, though television has been suggested as one culprit in the increase in obesity (Dietz & Gortmaker, 1985). Certainly, society continues to value thinness highly, particularly in women, often equating a slim physique with power and attractiveness. At present, dieting appears to be a normative behavior (Polivy & Herman, 1987; Rosen & Gross, 1987) that has prompted investigators to consider the relationship between normal eating behavior (e.g., dieters) and disordered eating. Polivy and Herman (1987) offer a conceptualization of "reordered" eating behaviors where obese, anorexic, and bulimic patients use other than physiological boundaries (e.g, hunger and satiety) to govern their eating behavior; boundaries that are similar to those used by dieters, though more extreme. Differences between dieters and eating-disorder patients become more apparent when in comparison of personality traits such as self-esteem, interpersonal trust and relationships, ability to recognize feeling states accurately, and family relationships (Polivy & Herman, 1987; Humphrey, 1988). As previously noted, there appears to be some overlap between anorexic and bulimic behaviors. Other studies have provided evidence that a significant proportion of obese patients engage in bingeing behavior, which may be related to higher levels of dietary restraint and ability to control urges to eat (Marcus & Wing, 1987). This suggests a possible overlap between these two eating-related disorders. Further investigations regarding the similarities and differences between these disorders will be important, particularly if a preventive approach is to be utilized in the future.

Numerous intervention approaches have been applied to the treatment of inappropriate food preferences; including anorexia nervosa, the most serious condition; with varying degrees of success. Many children who exhibit these disorders are in imminent physical danger because of extreme weight loss and biochemical imbalances in bodily functioning; therefore, an immediate goal of treatment is to bring their weight up to safe levels as quickly as possible. Taken together, the available evidence suggests that in the most extreme cases of food refusal, behavioral techniques can provide a useful strategy for rapidly restoring children's eating behavior and weight. The most frequently used technique in the behavioral treatment of food refusal has been the contingent reinforcement of food consumption, caloric intake, and weight gain. A critical factor in the success of these treatment programs has been the selection of potent reinforcers that can supersede the strong avoidance-of-eating behaviors exhibited by children with eating disorders. The observation that high-frequency behaviors can be used as reinforcers for low-frequency behaviors (Premack, 1965) provides an effective and efficient means for selecting appropriate reinforcers to reinstate normal eating and accelerate weight gain in a relatively short time.

With older adolescents, the reinforcement of weight gain per se, rather than food consumption, seems to be an effective strategy. This approach appears to avoid many manipulative and undesirable behaviors, such as self-induced vomiting, that sometimes occur when the target response is amount of food eaten. However, with younger children, reinforcing responses that are temporally and topographically as close as possible to the target response may be more effective than a strategy involving a longer delay between the response and reinforcement, as is the case with reinforcing weight gain. Thus, food consumption with younger children would be a much closer target response than is weight gain. Some research efforts (such as those reported by Agras et al. (1974), have attempted to isolate the essential treatment variables in the behavioral treatment of Anorexia Nervosa through controlled investigations. They appear to be the most fruitful in providing empirical documentation of treatment efficacy, but such a detailed analysis of eating habits may inadvertently foster the development of other abnormal eating behaviors (Bemis, 1987). Certainly future investigations of treatment approaches will have to consider the impact of treatment on eating behavior over the long term.

It appears that for the disorders reviewed here, that treatment approaches must include several phases. Van Buskirk (1977) has noted that the efficacy of treatment techniques for anorexia nervosa must be evaluated from two perspectives: their effects on facilitating rapid weight gain to restore the patient to a safe level of physical functioning and their effects on long-term maintenance of appropriate weight and adequate psychological adjustment. While behavioral techniques have shown particular effectiveness in the initiation of rapid weight gain in children in critical physical condition who require immediate intervention in the acute phase of the disorder, their long-term results have been disappointing (Bemis, 1978; Herzog et al., 1993; Hsu, 1990). Similar comments can be made regarding obesity, as treatment for this involves initial weight reduction and then long-term maintenance of weight loss or return to age-appropriate weight gain for height (Epstein, 1986). While behavioral techniques have proven effective, other techniques to facilitate initial weight loss in extremely obese children (such as the very low calorie diet) warrant further investigation. With regard to maintenance of weight loss, more emphasis on including relapse techniques and/or continued therapist contact in some manner would appear to be useful (Perri et al., 1984). These strategies in children, however, await further empirical evidence.

Enuresis

A common problem of childhood, which may continue into adolescence, is enuresis. Specifically, functional enuresis is defined by DSM-IV (American Psychiatric Association, 1994) as: (a) repeated voiding of urine during the day or night into bed or clothes, whether involuntary or intentional; (b) at least 3 consecutive months of two or more weekly wetting incidents or accompanying

distress or impairment in social, academic, or other important areas of function; (c) a chronological age or developmentally equivalent age of 5 years; and (d) the absence of a causative medical condition such as diabetes or a seizure disorder, or the direct physiological effects of a substance, such as a diuretic. Childhood enuresis may take the form of wetting during the day (diurnal) and/or at night (nocturnal), the latter being more frequent. Enuresis has also been classified as primary or secondary. In primary enuresis the child has never attained daytime or nighttime bladder control. Secondary enuresis, on the other hand, refers to the loss of previously acquired bladder control after at least a year of continence (American Psychiatric Association, 1987; Forsythiea, Merrett, & Redmond, 1972).

Estimates of incidence vary; however, enuresis appears to be a common problem, with more than 3 million children in this country exhibiting some form of it (Baller, 1975; Foxman, Valdez, & Brook, 1986). Approximately 20% of 5-year olds continue to wet their beds. Half of these children remain enuretic at 10 years of age. Nocturnal enuresis also occurs twice as often in boys as in girls, and it diminishes with age (Lovibond & Coote, 1970; Oppel, Harper, & Rowland, 1968). Approximately 30% of children who are nocturnally enuretic also exhibit diurnal enuresis (Forsythe & Redmond, 1974). Untreated enuresis is reported to remit spontaneously in approximately 15% of the remaining cases between ages 5 to 19 each year (Forsythe & Redmond, 1974). Houts (1991) reports that there is no evidence that children outgrow nocturnal enuresis. If no systematic intervention occurs, only 1 out of 8 children with enuresis are symptom-free after 1 year, and of those who continue to be enuretic, it takes on average, more than 3 years for the bed-wetting to remit spontaneously.

While less than 10% of childhood enuresis is attributed to an organic etiology (Pierce, 1967), a medical examination should be conducted to determine whether organic factors are present. Among the organic or physical causes of enuresis are bladder or urinary tract infections, neurological problems such as central nervous system impairment, and anatomical problems in the genitourinary system (Novello & Novello, 1987).

Micturition, or the process of urination, is a complex act requiring the child to establish cognitive control over the bladder reflex. The child must be able to (a) inhibit bladder contractions until the bladder is full, (b) demonstrate an awareness of bladder distention as a need to void, and (c) postpone or initiate micturition at varying degrees of bladder fullness (Muellner, 1960; Yeates, 1973). Numerous theories have been suggested for a delay in control over micturition. A common assumption that enuresis is a symptom of psychological or emotional disturbance has not received support in the research literature (Ferguson, Horwood, & Shannon, 1986; Schaefer, 1979; Werry, 1967). Wagner, Smith, and Norris (1988) report, however, that while enuretic children exhibited no overall adjustment problems relative to nonenuretic children, there was evidence that children who had both diurnal and nocturnal enuresis reported lower self-esteem than children with only nocturnal enuresis. This finding is further supported by a study by Moffat, Kato, and Pless (1987), who found improvements in self-concept in children and adolescents following successful conditioning treatment of nocturnal enuresis. Further studies are needed to clarify the direction of causality in this area (e.g., do psychological factors such as lower self-esteem contribute to enuresis or do repeated enuretic episodes lead to lower self-esteem?). Research findings pertaining to the notion that depth of sleep is associated with enuresis are also equivocal (Doleys, 1979; Norgaard et al., 1989). Finally, it has been suggested that the volume of urine that enuretic children can retain before voiding is smaller than that of nonenuretic children; this could also account for their more frequent micturition (Muellner, 1960). While there is some evidence for this latter view (Esperanca & Gerrard, 1969; Starfield, 1967), research has not found all enuretic children to have smaller bladder capacities (Doleys, 1977; Houts, 1991).

Overview of Treatment Approaches

It is generally recognized that learning plays a significant role in the process of bringing the bladder reflex under cognitive control (Lovibond & Coote, 1970; Mowrer & Mowrer, 1938). From this perspective, enuresis is regarded as a behavioral deficit that results from faulty learning. The acquisition of bladder control is regarded as a high-level skill that may not develop because the particular behaviors necessary for initiating and inhibiting micturition were not learned. An enuretic child has not learned to exercise adequate control of the bladder's sphincter muscles and, therefore, when the bladder is distended, fails to inhibit the bladder reflex controlling urination. Both classical and instrumental conditioning mechanisms are presumed to play a role in this learning process.

A wide variety of approaches to the treatment of childhood enuresis have been reported, including special diets, fluid restrictions, nighttime awakening, psychotherapy, and medication (Doleys & Ciminero, 1976; Johnson, 1980). However, there is little or no evidence for the efficacy of these methods (Johnson, 1980; Walker, Milling, & Bonner, 1988).

Behavioral approaches to childhood enuresis have received the most systematic research attention. Both operant and respondent conditioning procedures have been employed with varying degrees of success. The most frequently used procedures have included the urine-alarm or bell-and-pad procedure, techniques to directly increase functional bladder capacity, and approaches involving a combination of procedures.

Bell-and-pad procedure. To date, the most effective and frequently used behavioral method for treating enuresis in children is the bell-and-pad or urine-alarm conditioning procedure. This device was first used in the treatment of enuresis by Mowrer and Mowrer (1938) to help children learn nighttime bladder control. Although the bell-and-pad procedure was originally based on a respondent conditioning paradigm, the exact mechanism of its operation remains to be clearly determined (Lovibond, 1963). The systematic use of this procedure in the treatment of enuresis did not occur until 30 years after it was initially developed.

In the bell-and-pad procedure, the child sleeps on a specially constructed pad. It is made of two foil outer sheets, the top one having holes, which are separated by an absorbent paper connected to a buzzer. As soon as the child begins to urinate, the paper sheet becomes wet, completing an electric circuit that activates a bell or buzzer. The noise from the buzzer is presumed to inhibit further urination in bed by causing the bladder muscles to contract reflexively (automatically). The noise awakens the child at the time when his or her bladder is full. After a number of pairings of the noise with the full bladder, the child learns to wake up to the cues for bladder fullness and the need to urinate. Eventually the child learns to respond to the bladder cues without the help of the bell and pad so that bladder distension automatically elicits contraction of the sphincter muscles and wakes up the child. More recently, a modification of the bell-and-pad device was introduced; it comprises a sensor electrode that reacts to only a few drops of urine and is attached directly to the child's underwear (Walker et al., 1988).

Despite misconceptions that drinking before bedtime should be curtailed, in this procedure the child is *encouraged* to drink fluids before bedtime to ensure that sufficient pairings of the bell and the act of micturition will occur. The child and parents should be informed that the alarm will most likely sound at least several times in the first several nights of treatment (it is often incorrectly assumed that if treatment is working appropriately, the child will not be wetting the bed so frequently).

The child is asked to sleep without pajama bottoms or in light underclothing so that the alarm is triggered at the exact moment that urination begins. When the alarm is activated, the child is instructed to turn it off and to go immediately to the bathroom to finish urinating. If the child has difficulty awakening, the parents are asked to rouse him or her, making sure the child is completely awake before going to the bathroom by washing his or her face with cold water. After returning to the bedroom, the device is reset, the pad is washed off, and a dry sheet is placed on the pad. The child typically is given primary responsibility to remake the bed before going back to sleep.

The parents are asked to keep a record of the number of times that the bell rings each night and the diameter of the wet spot on the sheet. As the procedure begins to take effect, the size of the spot and the number of times that the bell rings should decrease. The child is rewarded with praise and sometimes with tangible reinforcers for each dry night, and parents are instructed not to make negative comments about any wetting incidents.

To maintain parental motivation and make sure that the procedure is being followed correctly, weekly contact with the parents and child is essential, particularly during the first several weeks of treatment. It should be explained to the parents and child that within 3 weeks after starting treatment, some reduction in wetting patterns should be noted. Use of the bell and pad is typically discontinued following 2 weeks of consecutive dry nights. Parents are told that relapses (typically defined as two or more wet nights in a week) may occur and are asked to reinstate the bell-and-pad procedure if this happens. Most enuretic children require 4 to 8 weeks with the bell-and-pad method before treatment can be terminated. More detailed descriptions of the bell-and-pad procedure are presented by Lovibond and Coote (1970), Walker (1978), and Werry (1967).

The bell-and-pad device can be purchased at several national catalogue stores at a modest price or it can be rented from several commercial firms (Mountjoy, Ruben, & Bradford, 1984; Walker, 1995). Instructions for constructing this equipment are also available (Fried, 1974; Kashinsky, 1974). Despite the ready availability of this apparatus to nonprofessionals, it should not be used without professional consultation, as it is likely to be used incorrectly and result unnecessarily in treatment failure.

Research has revealed a high degree of effectiveness for the bell-and-pad procedure for children who remain in treatment (Walker, 1995). The bell-and-pad conditioning procedure has been found superior to traditional psychotherapy (DeLeon & Mandell, 1966; Werry & Cohressen, 1965) and drug therapy (Forrester, Stein, & Susser, 1964; Wille, 1986; Young & Turner, 1965) for the treatment of childhood enuresis. This procedure has demonstrated an initial success of between 75% and 80% (Doleys, 1977; Lovibond & Coote, 1970).

One problem in the use of this procedure has been the relapse rate, which has ranged from 20% to 30% (Doleys, 1977; O'Leary & Wilson, 1975). Several procedural modifications of the bell and pad have been found to effectively reduce the relapse rate. One of these procedures involves the reintroduction of the bell and pad immediately after a relapse occurs. An overlearning procedure (whereby the child increases fluid intake before bedtime and uses the bell-and-pad apparatus beyond the criterion point where it is normally withdrawn) has been effective in reducing the relapse rate (Houts, Peterson, & Whelan, 1986; Jehu, Morgan, Turner, & Jones, 1977; Young & Morgan, 1972). Doleys (1979a) has cautioned that excessive fluid intake prior to bedtime might result in renewed bedwetting and therefore discourage the parents and child. He suggests that some children may benefit from a delay in the use of the overlearning technique for several weeks after the initial training period and suggests a gradual increase in the quantity of liquids given.

A final method for reducing the rate of relapse is the use of intermittent reinforcement. In this method the alarm is activated during a variable number of wetting incidents (usually 50% to 70%) rather than after each wetting has occurred. According to learning theory this procedure should be effective in reducing relapse rate because an intermittent schedule of reinforcement should make the trained response (i.e., bladder control) more resistant to extinction. Use of an intermittent reinforcement schedule has shown promise as a technique for reducing the relapse rate with the bell and pad (Finley, Besserman, Bennett, Clapp, & Finley, 1973; Finley & Wansley, 1976).

Bladder retention control training. Based on the observation that enuretic children tend to urinate more frequently during the day and with a smaller volume of urine than nonenuretic children (Starfield & Mellitis, 1968; Zaleski, Gerrard, & Shokier, 1973), Muellner (1960) suggested a treatment program to increase bladder capacity and to reduce frequency of urination to weak bladder cues. Zaleski et al. (1973) have outlined several simple methods for assessing functional bladder capacity in children. In one method, the child drinks 30 milliliters of water for each kilogram of body weight. The child then inhibits urination until uncomfortable and two consecutive voids are measured with the larger specimen regarded as the maximum functional bladder

capacity. In the second method, the parent is instructed to measure the volume of urine each time the child voids over the course of a week. The largest volume during the week is recorded as the maximum functional capacity of the child.

Kimmel and Kimmel (1970) have developed a systematic treatment program based on the method proposed by Muellner (1960) in which the child is taught to increase his bladder capacity through a daytime shaping procedure. At the point where bladder tension is sufficiently strong to stimulate urination, the child is taught to delay urination voluntarily for increasingly longer periods of time. It is assumed in this procedure that increased bladder control during the waking hours will generalize to nighttime retention of urine.

In the bladder retention training procedure, the child is encouraged to drink as many liquids as he or she wants during the day. When the child experiences the need to urinate, he or she is asked to "hold it" for an initial 5-minute period and then is permitted to go to the bathroom. This period of refraining from voiding is gradually increased several minutes each day until the child is able to delay urination for 30 to 45 minutes. Kimmel and Kimmel (1970) report that most children are able to reach this criterion in 3 weeks or less. Following each withholding period, parents are instructed to reinforce the child with praise and tangible reinforcers. Parents are also instructed to keep a record of the child's frequency of daytime urinations, the volume of urine, and the number of dry nights.

Paschalis, Kimmel, and Kimmel (1972) investigated the use of the daytime retention control procedure with 31 children between 6 and 11 years of age who had never experienced a dry night. At the end of treatment, 15 of the children were no longer wetting their beds at night and 8 showed significant reductions in their nighttime bedwetting. These improvements were maintained at a 3-month follow-up assessment. This procedure also receives support from a case study in the treatment of a 13-year-old girl who had been enuretic all her life (Paschalis et al., 1972). Noteworthy in this case is the fact that parental involvement was not required in any aspect of the treatment. The adolescent was able to follow the procedure and keep records of her frequency of urination during the day and the number of times she wet the bed at night. By the end of 3 months, she was no longer wetting the bed. A 3-month follow-up indicated that she had had only four wetting incidents.

Using the retention training procedure, Miller (1973) was able to eliminate bedwetting completely in two adolescents with secondary enuresis. During a 3-week baseline period, the adolescents kept a record of the number of times they wet their beds each week and the frequency of daytime urination. Retention control training was initiated subsequent to the baseline condition. The adolescents were instructed to delay urination an additional 10 minutes each week, so that by the third week of treatment they had held back urination for 30 minutes. Fluid intake was also increased during this treatment period. Following 3 weeks of treatment, the baseline condition was reinstated (i.e., the urination-delay procedure was discontinued). During the final phase of the program, the adolescents returned to the retention control training, which continued until they achieved 3 consecutive weeks of dry nights. A 7-month follow-up evaluation revealed that both adolescents had remained dry at night, with no relapses reported. There was a concomitant decrease in both the frequency of enuretic episodes and daily urinations when retention control training was in effect. These results suggest that this procedure also increased bladder capacity, since little urination occurred during the waking hours. Despite these positive results, there are some data to suggest that this procedure may not be effective with all children (Doleys, 1977; Hunsaker, 1976).

Combination of procedures. Azrin, Sneed, and Foxx (1974) have recently presented a treatment procedure for enuresis referred to as "dry-bed training." This method is a multicomponent, complex treatment program that includes the use of both the bell-and-pad and retention-control training procedures. In addition, a number of other techniques, primarily operant procedures, are incorporated into the treatment program including hourly wakenings, positive practice in going to the toilet, punishment for wetting the bed, and positive reinforcement for going to the bathroom at night. The treatment program as originally outlined by Azrin et al. (1974) involves one night of intensive training by a therapist-trainer who comes to the child's home. Dramatic results using this program were reported by Azrin et al. (1974), with all of the 24 children achieving the criterion of 7 consecutive dry nights. A relapse rate of 29% was noted, necessitating a brief reinstatement of the treatment program. Furthermore, they found dry-bed training to be more effective in eliminating enuresis than the bell-and-pad procedure alone.

Similar results are reported by Bollard and Woodroffe (1977) using the dry-bed training procedure. They achieved a 100% initial success rate with a 17% relapse rate. In this study, parents instead of professional trainers, administered the intensive training program. In contrast, Doleys, Ciminero, Tollison, Williams, and Wells (1977) found that only 38% of the children achieved criterion for success within a 6-week period. In addition, one third of these children relapsed. However, they did find that the dry-bed training procedure was more effective than retention training alone.

Azrin and his colleagues (Azrin, Hontos, & Besalel-Azrin, 1979; Azrin & Theines, 1978) reported modification of the dry-bed training program in which the bell-and-pad conditioning apparatus was eliminated from the procedure. Ninety-four children 3 to 15 years old were treated using a procedure that was less complicated to implement than the program initially developed by Azrin et al. (1974). These investigators reported that all the children who received this training were successfully treated using a 2-week criterion of consecutive dry nights despite the elimination of the bell-and-pad procedure. Less than 20% of the children evidenced relapses, and these were reversed by a second training session. This reduction in bed-wetting was greater than that in children in the group receiving the bell-and-pad procedure alone. Despite these very positive results, Ross (1981) suggests that the dry-bed training procedure appears to be less effective when the bell and pad is removed from treatment. He notes that more relapses were reported with the modified dry-bed procedure in the follow-up period than were reported in the Azrin et al. (1974) study in which the bell-and-pad training method was included in the treatment program. Bollard and Woodroffe (1977) and Bollard, Nettelbeck, and Roxbee (1982) also found that dry-bed training without the bell-and-pad procedure was less effective, suggesting that the bell and pad may be an essential component in the treatment of some children with enuresis.

Finally, Houts, Liebert, and Padawer (1983) examined the efficacy of the bell-and-pad procedure combined with cleanliness training, retention training, and overlearning in the treatment of 60 children with primary enuresis. These investigators found that 81% of the children responded to the treatment program by achieving the initial criterion of 14 consecutive dry nights. At a 1-year follow-up assessment, 24% of the sample had relapsed. This treatment program was carried out with a limited amount of professional time per each child and family. Additional studies by Houts and his colleagues (Houts, 1996) have investigated this multicomponent treatment program for nocturnal enuresis which they call "Full Spectrum Treatment". In these latter studies, they have utilized a modified form of an overlearning procedure in order to address the problem of relapse. This consists of the child drinking larger and larger quantities of fluids before going to bed while continuing the use of the urine alarm until 14 consecutive dry nights have been achieved. Using this procedure, only 10% of the children have been found to relapse at a 1-year follow-up.

Discussion

Several procedures have been shown to be effective in decreasing the frequency of bedwetting. There are, however, no definitive guidelines to assist the therapist in choosing a particular method for a given child. Ciminero and Doleys (1976) have noted several factors that should be considered in selecting an appropriate treatment method for enuresis. One of the most important factors to consider is the degree of motivation and cooperation that can be expected from the parents and child, since the success of any treatment procedure depends on how accurately and consistently it is applied. For example, retention training places fewer demands on the parents or child, and it might, therefore, be considered for use where cooperation of the participants is judged to be less than optimal. In contrast, dry-bed training is considerably more complex to implement and requires a great deal of parental time and involvement.

The child's age should also be considered in choosing a treatment strategy. Younger children may have more difficulty understanding the retention-training procedure than the other approaches, which depend to a greater extent on parental management. For older children and adolescents who can monitor their own voiding behavior and for whom parental involvement can be minimal, retention training or the bell-and-pad procedure may be preferable. Finally, where motivation is assessed to be high and where severity of the problem seems to warrant it, multiple procedures might effectively be used.

Because parental cooperation is essential to treatment success, especially in the bell-and-pad and dry-bed training procedures, the motivation and capabilities of the parents and child should be assessed in the early phases of treatment. To assist in this endeavor, Morgan and Young (1975) have developed the Tolerance Scale for Enuresis, which measures parental attitudes and tolerance toward bedwetting. Morgan and Young (1975) found that parents who were more intolerant were more likely to discontinue treatment with the bell-and-pad procedure prematurely. A measure like the Tolerance Scale might be useful in identifying families in need of greater support and supervision throughout the treatment program.

Another method for evaluating the family's capabilities for complying with the treatment program is to use an extended baseline period in which the parents and child are asked to keep records of the volume and frequency of urination during the day and the number of dry nights. If the family is unable to comply with these simple requests, it is unlikely that they will be able to adhere to the demands of a multifaceted treatment approach such as dry-bed training.

To date, few therapeutic interventions, including other behavioral methods, can claim as dramatically positive results as the bell-and-pad procedure (Sorotzkin, 1984). In fact, this procedure is the best researched and most well-documented approach for the treatment of enuresis. While the dry-bed training and the retention-control training procedures show considerable promise, there are significantly fewer studies evaluating their treatment efficacy compared to the bell-and-pad method.

Johnson (1980) has aptly noted that children with enuresis represent a heterogenous group and that therefore one method is unlikely to prove equally effective with every child. She has also pointed to the almost complete lack of integration between the assessment of factors contributing to enuresis in a particular child and the choice of a treatment procedure. In this regard, there has been little research attention to individual differences that might lead to a more systematic set of guidelines for selecting the most effective method of intervention for each child. For example, there has been little attempt to document before treatment is initiated, whether children have appropriate functional bladder capacity. Children who exhibit deficient bladder capacity might benefit from retention-control training in addition to the bell-and-pad procedure. On the other hand, where functional bladder-capacity is within normal limits, the focus of the treatment program might be on training in bladder control or appropriate toileting skills rather than on bladder capacity training (Doleys, 1979a). These issues have yet to be systematically investigated.

Another area that has received limited attention is the treatment of children who exhibit daytime wetting. The major focus in the literature has been on the treatment of nocturnal enuresis. To date, only a few studies have examined methods of treatment for children with daytime enuresis (Fielding, 1980; Halliday, Meadow, & Berg, 1987).

Finally, the treatment program should include plans for treating relapses after formal contact with the therapist has terminated. It is inevitable that bedwetting will recur in some children after initial treatment. Parents and children need to be informed of this possibility so that they do not become discouraged when it happens. They need to be reassured that relapses can be managed effectively by reinstating the treatment program for a brief period of time as soon as the problem recurs. Encouraging results recently have been reported in the use of overlearning procedures to effectively reduce the relapse rate in children undergoing behavioral treatment of nocturnal enuresis (Houts, 1996).

Headaches

A common complaint during childhood is the occurrence of headache pain (Duckro & Cantwell-Simmons, 1989). While it is not a life-threatening disorder, chronic headache is associated with a number of physiological, psychological, and social consequences (Blanchard & Andrasik, 1985). Extensive epidemiological studies indicate that almost 40% of children have had headaches by age 7 and that this rate increasing to 75% by age 15 (Billie, 1962; Sillanpaa, 1983). Girls have been found to develop migraine headaches at a later age than boys. The incidence of migraine headaches peaks between 5 and 11 years for boys, whereas for girls, they peak between 12 and 17 years of age (Stewart Linet, Celentano, Van Natta, & Zieglea, 1991). The preventive implications of focusing on the management of headaches in children and adolescents is underscored by research that demonstrates that as many as 60% continue to experience chronic headaches into adulthood (Billie, 1981; Sillanpaa, 1983).

While over 100 different types of headaches have been described, the 2 most frequently diagnosed headaches are the muscle-contraction or tension headache and the vascular or migraine headache. A third type, the mixed or combined headache, includes features of both migraine and muscle-contraction headaches (International Headache Society, 1988). As the names suggest, each type of headache is presumed to originate from a different pathophysiological source. Muscle-contraction headaches are assumed to result from sustained contraction of muscles of the face, scalp, and neck. Migraine headaches, on the other hand, are thought to result from an excessive response (vasoconstriction and vasodilation) of the cranial and cerebral arteries (Bakal, 1975).

In the most recent attempt to provide nomenclature for headaches with specific diagnostic criteria (International Headache Society, 1988), the term tension headache replaces the former diagnosis of muscle-contraction headache. Tension-type headaches are further defined as chronic when the headache occurs, on average, 15 or more days per month, and episodic if the headache is present fewer than 15 days per month. Recent evidence from psychophysiological investigations of headache patients suggests that there are little data to support the distinction between muscle-contraction and vascular headaches (Hatch, 1993). More specifically, the literature indicates that high levels of tension in the head and neck and vasoconstriction of the scalp arteries have been observed in both types of headaches. Interestingly, a wide range of muscle tension in the head and neck has been found in some patients suffering from tension headaches, whereas others show normal levels of muscle activity (Cohen, 1978; Philips, 1978). Further research is needed to determine what, if any, differences exist between tension and migraine headaches. The etiology of both types of headaches appears to be varied and often difficult to specify (Feuerstein & Garner, 1982). Because the specific etiology for headache pain has not been identified, the focus of treatment is primarily on the pain symptoms themselves (Hatch, 1993).

Overview of Treatment Approaches

Treatment should begin with a comprehensive evaluation of the headaches including a thorough medical and neurological examination to ensure that neurological problems such as tumors, hematomas, and seizures are not present. This step is necessary despite the fact that less than 5% of headaches in children represent underlying organic problems (Shinnar & D'Souza, 1981). Once the physical examination has ruled out potential organic factors, further assessment is needed to ascertain the characteristics of the headache and environmental events that may precipitate or maintain headache episodes. Such an assessment is typically accomplished with the help of a headache diary in which the patient is instructed to monitor the daily frequency, duration, and intensity of headache pain as well as the quantity and type of medication used. In addition, information regarding when and where the headache occurred and who was present at the time is recorded (Diamond, 1991; Diamond & Dalessio, 1992). The assessment information is subsequently used to develop appropriate treatment plans and provides an ongoing record regarding the effectiveness of the treatment program.

At present, there is no truly adequate treatment for chronic headaches, particularly the migraine type. The clinical approach to chronic headache is, therefore, directed at the *management* of the acute headache episodes rather than the elimination of headaches per se (Blanchard & Andrasik, 1985). The most common treatment for both migraine and muscle-contraction headaches is medication (Turner & Stone, 1979). However, aggressive treatment of headaches in children and adolescents is discouraged because of potential problems and risks, such as the occurrence of side effects, problems with patient compliance, and the potential for drug dependence and drug abuse (Hatch, 1993). The issues of drug dependence and abuse are particularly important, given the evidence for the continued occurrence of headaches into adulthood (Medina & Diamond, 1977; Shinnar & D'Souza, 1981). Because of these problems, there is a strong impetus for the development of effective nonpharmacological treatment approaches for headaches in children.

Specific psychological treatment approaches. Several psychological approaches to the treatment of headaches in children and adolescents have been reported. The most widely used nonpharmacological treatment strategies for vascular and muscle-contraction headaches have been relaxation techniques, biofeedback, and various combinations of these strategies (Andrasik, Blake, & McCarren, 1986).

A variety of relaxation techniques have been used in the management of headaches, ranging from more passive forms of relaxation (such as meditation and autogenic phrases) to more active forms (such as progressive muscle relaxation) (Feuerstein & Garner, 1982). Autogenic training is a relaxation technique involving a passive, suggestive type of relaxation in which the individual covertly repeats phrases involving suggestions of warmth and body heaviness (Schultz & Luthe, 1969). The primary goal of each of these relaxation techniques is the modification of the overreactive sympathetic nervous system and a reduction in skeletal muscle activity. Following treatment, it is presumed that the individual has learned to elicit a relaxation response simply through recall. The relaxation response is practiced daily and is used as an active coping skill in situations that might increase autonomic arousal. In addition, it is suggested that the relaxation response can serve to reduce the severity of a headache when it is elicited during an attack.

While relaxation techniques have a more global effect on the body, biofeedback techniques are directed at more specific physiological responses. In biofeedback training, the individual is taught a physiological response that is incompatible with the pathophysiological response presumed to underlie the headache (Finley & Jones, 1992; Melamed & Siegel, 1980). Given the widely held assumption that sustained muscle contraction of the head and neck is the major component of tension headaches, a primary goal of treatment is to reduce muscle activity through relaxation and thereby reduce headache pain. Electromyographic (EMG) biofeedback to assist the person to achieve deep levels of muscle relaxation has been used as the primary non-pharmacological treatment for muscle-contraction headaches. Typically, the individual receives feedback from muscles of the forehead area (frontalis muscle) and is trained to voluntarily reduce the frontalis EMG to increasingly lower levels.

Despite this accepted practice, research indicates that there is no consistent relationship between frontalis EMG levels and self-reports of frequency and intensity of headache pain (Blanchard & Andrasik, 1985). These findings suggest that for some headache patients, factors other than muscle tension may account for subjective reports of pain. In particular, environmental and social factors may be important in influencing headache pain behaviors such as verbal complaints, avoidance of usual activities, medication use, and so on (Fordyce, 1976). Therefore, the treatment procedures may differentially affect the physiological, subjective, and behavioral components of the headache pain, resulting in different rates of change in these three response systems (Melamed & Siegel, 1980).

While the specific pathophysiology of migraine headaches is unknown, a disturbance of the circulation in the cranial arteries is most often implicated as the cause of the debilitating pain accompanying this type of headache (Bakal, 1975). To modify this presumed abnormal response of the cranial arteries, a thermal biofeedback procedure has been used. In this procedure, the individual is trained to exercise voluntary control over the blood flow in a specific area of the periphery of the body (usually the hands), producing a concomitant increase in the skin temperature of that area. It is thought that since migraine headaches are a result of excessive dilation of cranial arteries, temperature biofeedback functions to increase blood flow away from the forehead, thereby decreasing arterial dilation (Feuerstein & Garner, 1982). By teaching patients to increase the temperature of their hands, migraine attacks might then be reduced or prevented. At the present time, the mechanisms for the clinical effectiveness of thermal biofeedback in the treatment of migraine headaches remains highly speculative (Shapiro & Surwit, 1976). More recently, a more direct approach to modifying arterial blood flow has been introduced in the form of blood-volume pulse (BVP) biofeedback. In this form of biofeedback, the individual learns to decrease bloodflow directly in the temporal artery as a means of aborting a headache (Blanchard & Andrasik, 1985).

One of the earliest treatment studies is reported by Diamond and Franklin (1975). Thirty-two children and adolescents (9 to 18 years old) with migraine headaches were treated by a combination of thermal biofeedback using autogenic phrases, frontalis EMG biofeedback, and home practice of muscle relaxation and hand warming. Twenty-six of the patients were reported to show a good response to this treatment program (defined as a decrease in the frequency and severity of migraine). Only 2 patients were found to be completely nonresponsive to treatment. These findings are particularly impressive considering that all of these children had not responded to medication.

A more methodologically adequate study of treatment outcome of 7-to16-year-old children with migraines is reported by Labbe and Williamson (1984). Twenty-eight children were randomly assigned to thermal biofeedback combined with autogenic training or a waiting-list control group. At the end of a 7-week period and at a 1-month follow-up, 88% of the subjects were either symptom-free or considerably improved. At a 6-month follow-up, 62% maintained significant improvement.

The efficacy of EMG biofeedback combined with meditative relaxation training and meditative relaxation training alone in the treatment of pediatric migraine was investigated with 18 children between 8 and 12 years of age (Fentress, Masek, Mehegan, & Benson, 1986). Subjects were randomly assigned to either of the two treatment groups or to a waiting-list control group. The results indicated that both treatment groups exhibited a significant reduction in headache symptoms and were significantly improved compared to the control group. There were no differences in effectiveness between the two treatment conditions. These findings were maintained 1 year following treatment.

In a study by McGrath et al. (1988), 99 children and adolescents between 9 and 17 years of age, who had been diagnosed with frequent migraine headaches were randomly assigned to one of three groups: progressive muscle relaxation, attention-placebo control (recognizing and discussing feelings), or a control group consisting of a single-session contract by a therapist who helped each patient identify factors that might trigger migraine attacks. The findings indicated that all three groups showed a significant reduction in headaches following treatment. These improvements were maintained at a 1-year follow-up. The investigators conclude from these data that the important ingredient in effective treatment programs for migraine headaches in this population may be suggestions of techniques for self-control of headaches.

Burke and Andrasik (1989) evaluated the efficacy and cost-effectiveness of home-based thermal biofeedback training compared with the clinic-based treatment of 9 children 10 to 14 years of age who presented with migraine headache. A multiple-baseline research design was used in which the children were randomly assigned to one of three treatment conditions: (a) clinic-based; therapist administered, (b) home-based; child-administered, and (c) home-based; parent administered. Each group received 10, 1-hour biofeedback sessions; however, therapist contact time was 10 hours for the clinic group and only 3 hours for the home-based treatment groups. While all treatment conditions were found to produce improvement in headache activity and reductions in medication usage, the two home-based programs were three times more efficient (relative to therapist contact time) than the clinic based procedure. Feuerstien and Adams

(1977) report the use of BVP biofeedback of the temporal artery in a 15 year old with migraine headaches. Using a single-subject research design, EMG biofeedback was found to increase measures of headache activity whereas BVP biofeedback significantly reduced headache activity. At a 9-week follow-up, headache frequency decreased 85%, duration decreased 68%, and intensity decreased 53% from baseline levels.

In an interesting study by Olness, MacDonald, and Uden (1987), the effectiveness of a psychological treatment program (self-hypnosis) was compared to the effectiveness of medication (propranolol) in the treatment of migraine headache. The children were randomly assigned to a propranolol or placebo condition for 3 months and then crossed over for 3 months to the other condition. Following this phase of the study, all children were taught a self-hypnosis procedure that involved progressive muscle relaxation exercises combined with pleasant imagery. The self-hypnosis treatment was found to reduce significantly the number of headaches reported by the children compared to the medication and placebo conditions. No significant changes in subjective or objective measures of headache severity were obtained with either treatment condition.

High school students were treated for either tension headaches or headaches of the mixed type (tension and migraine) in their school setting in a study reported by Larson, Melin, Lamminen, and Ullstedt (1987). Thirty-six adolescents were randomly assigned to one of three conditions: self-help relaxation (audiotaped progressive muscle relaxation), a problem-discussion group in which students discussed common problems that they were experiencing and possible solutions to these problems, or a self-monitoring condition in which the adolescents simply kept a headache diary throughout the course of the study. The self-help relaxation treatment resulted in significant improvements in all dimensions of headache activity following the 5-week treatment period. In addition, the relaxation treatment was found to be more effective than the problem-discussion group in reducing headache activity. These treatment effects were maintained at a 5-month follow-up.

Discussion

While the research on psychological approaches to the treatment of headaches in children is limited compared to the studies with adult populations, the findings are highly encouraging. Most of the research has focused on the treatment of childhood migraine. Only a few studies have been reported in the treatment of muscle-contraction headaches in this group. Both biofeedback and relaxation techniques are emerging as promising alternatives to the pharmacological treatment of chronic headaches in children. The relative safety of these psychological approaches and their avoidance of the problems associated with long-term medication use makes these strategies a particularly appealing alternative.

In an extensive review of the research findings on the behavioral treatment of headaches, Blanchard (1992) reports that behavioral therapy was found to be more effective in the management of headache pain when compared to patients in untreated control groups, patients receiving medication placebo, and patients exposed to credible behavioral placebo. These findings were consistent for tension-type headache but not for migraine headache. Finally, Blanchard (1992) concluded that the use of cognitive stress coping-skills training in addition to relaxation procedures increased treatment effectiveness with tension headaches; however, the former intervention techniques did not contribute to enhancing the effectiveness of thermal biofeedback for migraine headache.

A meta-analysis by Holroyd and Penzian (1990) was conducted on 25 studies comparing pharmacological treatments with relaxation training combined with thermal biofeedback in the treatment of migraine headache. The meta-analysis demonstrated that both the behavioral and pharmacological treatment approaches were more effective than a medication placebo. However, both treatments were equally effective in the management of migraine headaches.

A number of methodological shortcomings in research in this area must be addressed before more definitive conclusions can be drawn regarding the efficacy of relaxation techniques, biofeedback, and other behavioral techniques (Hoelscher & Lichstein, 1984). Most of the reports in the literature with child

and adolescent patients represent anecdotal or systematic case reports, single-subject experimental designs, and single-group outcome studies. Definitive outcome studies are needed that compare the treatment techniques with waiting-list and attention-placebo control groups. In addition, the ultimate effectiveness of a treatment program for chronic headaches can only be judged over an extended period of time. To date, most investigations in this area have reported relatively short follow-up evaluations.

The treatment programs reported in the literature typically have used a variety of techniques simultaneously, making it difficult to isolate the components most responsible for the treatment effects. In addition, there is a need to identify those patient characteristics that are predictive of response to a particular treatment program; this would enhance the effectiveness of the intervention techniques. The lack of convincing evidence for the superiority of one technique over another provides little guidance to the clinician as to which treatment approach to use. At the present time, factors such as practicality and the personal bias of the therapist play a major role in the decision process for selecting a treatment method.

Another fruitful area of research that has received almost no attention with children is the monitoring of the physiological responses that are the focus of the intervention. For example, studies using thermal biofeedback have rarely reported changes in skin temperature over the course of the treatment program, so that there is no evidence that blood flow was in fact modified. Similarly, Blanchard and Andrasik (1985) have discussed the importance of evaluating psychophysiological responses both during a headache-free period as well as during a headache episode. Such information will provide useful data regarding some of the etiological factors associated with chronic headache in children.

SUMMARY AND CONCLUSIONS

The somatic disorders presented in this chapter are only a sample of many that could have been included. In treating these disorders, it is important to reiterate that collaboration between physician and men-tal-health professional is necessary to provide opti-mal care for the child (Drotar, 1995). As can be surmised, individual cases will differ in the degree to which there is identifiable organic pathology that can be treated medically, but this must always be assessed. Though medical evaluation is imperative when a somatic disorder is suspected, it is also advisable to schedule a psychological assessment early in the diagnostic process. This can help the child and family begin to understand that psycho-logical factors may play a role in somatic sympto-matology and that treatment may have to include psychological intervention. This is an important point, as all too often psychological assessment and intervention are included "as a last resort" after other treatment approaches have failed to alleviate the problem behavior.

As an alternative intervention strategy or as an adjunctive procedure to augment medical treatment, behavioral techniques offer several advantages for individuals who provide health-care services to chil-dren. First, behavioral methods of treatment can eliminate or avoid the use of other procedures that may have serious drawbacks or that can be highly aversive for the child. For example, tube feeding, which is often required in cases of anorexia nervosa to ensure nutritional intake, carries with it the risk of infection and the potential for aspiration of food into the lungs (Browning & Miller, 1968). In addition, behavioral treatment programs have effectively reduced or eliminated symptomatic behaviors that had previously necessitated pharmacological inter-vention. As a result, it has been possible to reduce significantly or to discontinue the use of medication that the child was taking. These findings have con-siderable implications for the child, because many problems may result from repeated, long-term use of certain medications. For instance, several drugs that are often used in treating the disorders present-ed in this chapter can result in undesirable physical side effects that may, in some instances, be perma-nent. Furthermore, there is some evidence to suggest that the learning process may be affected adversely by certain drugs. That is, research findings have indicated that learning that occurs while the child is taking the drug may not transfer to the nondrug state

(Overton, 1966; Turner & Young, 1966). These sug-gestive findings are of particular concern when the goal of the treatment program is to help the child with somatic problems to learn more appropriate and adaptive behaviors. That is, behaviors acquired during a behavioral treatment program while a child is on certain medications may not persist following the withdrawal of the medication.

One of the significant features of behavioral treatment programs for somatic problems in chil-dren has been the extent to which parents and other significant persons in the child's environment, such as teachers, have been enlisted as primary change agents. With professional guidance and support, these individuals were trained to modify a variety of somatic disorders while the child was in its natural environment. Since it was clearly demonstrated in some cases that social contingencies were contribut-ing to the maintenance of the symptomatic behav-iors, the success of the behavioral procedures was dependent, to a considerable degree, on the partici-pation and cooperation of significant persons in the child's world. Such individuals have been trained to use a wide variety of behavioral techniques for treat-ing many somatic disturbances and to ensure that newly acquired adaptive behaviors would be main-tained following treatment. Because behavioral pro-cedures provide a systematic and explicit approach to treatment, many intervention programs can be effectively implemented by persons with little train-ing and experience under professional supervision (Gordon & Davidson, 1981; McBurnett, Hobbs, & Lahey; O'Dell, 1974). Finally, this model of treat-ment has important implications for *preventing* the development of other somatic problems by training significant members of the child's environment in behavioral techniques.

The efficacy of any treatment approach must be judged not only for its ability to initiate behavior change but also for its potential to promote the maintenance of the behavior change after treatment (O'Leary & Wilson, 1975). The research evidence presented in this chapter supports the efficacy of psychological interventions for producing short-term changes in a number of somatic disorders in children. However, once desired changes in behav-ior have been achieved, these gains are often not maintained over longer periods of time. As Marholin, Siegel, and Phillips (1976) note in this regard, "research directed at providing techniques to assure transfer and maintenance [of treatment effects] has lagged significantly behind efforts to demonstrate the functional relationships between behavior change and the manipulation of pertinent variables in the treatment setting" (p. 331). In addition, long-term follow-up studies in the psychological treatment of somatic disorders are at present clearly an exception. Since somatic disorders present in childhood are often carried into adulthood, methods for achieving long-term changes in behavior remains a research priority in this area.

While a number of effective psychological interventions are now available to modify dysfunctional somatic behaviors in children, until recently this area has lacked empirically validated assessment strategies. Children present a unique challenge in the assessment process as their participation in this process is often limited by developmental factors, particularly cognitive and language development. Given these constraints, mental health professionals working with children in health-related settings have made considerable progress in the development of reliable and valid instruments for assessing a variety of somatic problems (Karoly, 1988). Multiple sources of information (e.g., child, parent, teacher) are often helpful in providing a detailed picture of factors contributing to the child's somatic disorder, which can then be used to develop an effective treatment approach.

Progress in the development of effective methods for changing dysfunctional somatic behaviors in children rests on the accumulation of rigorous research. However, notably lacking at this time are systematic, well-controlled investigations directed at isolating the critical variables in the psychological treatment of childhood somatic disorders. Many interventions include multicomponent approaches, and it is not always known which of these components account for the changes found. Unfortunately, many somatic disorders are not readily amenable to group research designs, and only these can assess the comparative effects of various approaches. Furthermore, several disorders are highly disruptive or present serious, life-threatening dangers to the

child. As a result, many of these disorders require immediate and complete intervention, often at the expense of an adequate experimental design. However, well-controlled single-subject experimental designs can still enable the investigator to tell whether a change in the child's behavior can be attributed to the treatment program or to some other events that might have occurred at the same time (cf. Hersen & Barlow, 1976; Kratochwill, 1978).

Despite these problems, the preliminary results are sufficiently encouraging to warrant continued efforts in the psychological treatment of somatic disorders. The integration of behavioral scientists into health-care settings and the collaborative efforts of these individuals with various health-related disciplines, represents one of the significant developments in the field of health care. This collaboration between medicine and behavioral science has led to the development of many innovative treatment approaches with a wide array of somatic problems in children. In addition to the disorders presented in this chapter, other somatic problems that have been the focus of behavioral methods of intervention include sleep disorders, asthma, seizure disorders, chronic pain, recurrent abdominal pain, and cardiovascular problems, to name just a few. There are many exciting opportunities in developing new and effective approaches to the treatment of somatic problems in children. It is anticipated that in the future, we shall see a systematic expansion of theory, research, and practice in this area.

REFERENCES

Ader, R., Felton, D. L., & Cohen, N. (1991). *Psychoneuroimmunology,* New York: Academic Press.

Agras, W. S., Barlow, D. H., Chapin, H. N., Abel, G. G., & Leitenberg, H. (1974). Behavior modification of anorexia. *Archives of General Psychiatry, 30,* 279–285.

Ahles, T. A., Cassens, H. L., & Stallings, R. B. (1983). Private body consciousness, anxiety, and the perception of pain. *Journal of Behavior Therapy and Experimental Psychiatry, 18,* 215–222.

American Psychiatric Association (1968). *Diagnostic and statistical manual of mental disorders* (2nd ed.). Washington, DC: Author.

American Psychiatric Association (1987). *Diagnostic and statistical manual of Mental disorders* (3rd ed. rev.). Washington, DC: Author.

American Psychiatric Association (1994). *Diagnostic and statistical manual of mental disorders* (4th ed.). Washington, DC: Author.

Anderson, A. E. (1986). Inpatient and outpatient treatment of anorexia nervosa. In K. D. Brownell & J. P. Foreyt (Eds.), *Handbook of eating disorders* (pp. 331–350). New York: Basic Books.

Andrasik, F., Blake, D., & McCarren, M. S. (1986). A biobehavioral analysis of pediatric headache. In N. A. Krasnegor, J. D. Arasteh, & M. F. Cataldo (Eds.), *Child health behavior: A behavioral pediatrics perspective* (pp. 394–434). New York: John Wiley & Sons.

Azrin, N. H., Hontos, P. T., & Besalel-Azrin, V. (1979) Elimination of enuresis without a conditioning apparatus: An extention by office instruction of the child and parents. *Behavior Therapy, 10,* 14–19.

Azrin, N. H., Sneed, T. J., & Foxx, R. M. (1974). Dry-bed: Rapid elimination of childhood enuresis. *Behavior Research and Therapy, 12,* 147–156.

Azrin, N. H., & Thienes, P. M. (1978). Rapid elimination of enuresis by intensive learning without a conditioning apparatus. *Behavior Therapy, 9,* 342–354.

Bakal, D. A. (1975). Headache: A biopsychological perspective. *Psychological Bulletin, 82,* 369–382.

Baller, W. R. (1975). *Bedwetting: Origins and treatment.* Elmsford, NY: Pergamon Press.

Bandura, A. (1977). Self-efficacy: Toward a unifying theory of behavioral change. *Psychological Review, 83,* 191–215.

Barsky, A. J., Goodson, J. D., Lane, R. S., & Cleary, P. D. (1988). The amplification of somatic symptoms. *Psychosomatic Medicine, 50,* 510–519.

Barsky, A. J., & Klerman, G. L. (1983). Overview: Hypochondriasis, bodily complaints, and somatic styles. *American Journal of Psychiatry, 140,* 273–283.

Basmajian, J. V. (1977). Learned control of single motor units. In G. E. Schwartz & J. Beatty (Eds.), *Biofeedback: Theory and Research* (pp. 176–195). New York: Academic Press.

Beatty, J. (1977). Learned regulation of alpha and theta frequency activity in the human electroencephalogram. In G. E. Schwartz & J. Beatty (Eds.), *Biofeedback: Theory and research* (pp. 142–156). New York: Academic Press.

Beinfield, H., & Korngold., E. (1991). *Between heaven and earth: A guide to Chinese medicine.* New York: Ballantine Books.

Bemis, K. (1978). Current approaches to the etiology and treatment of anorexia nervosa. *Psychological Bulletin, 85,* 593–617.

Bemis, K. (1987). The present status of operant conditioning for the treatment of anorexia nervosa. *Behavior Modification, 11,* 432–463.

Billie, B. (1962). Migraine in school children. *Acta Paediatrac, 51,* 1–51.

Billie, B. (1981). Migraine in childhood and its prognosis. *Cephalalgia, 1,* 71–75.

Birch, L. L., & Marlin, D. W. (1982). I don't like it; I never tried it: Effects of exposure on two-year-old children's food preferences. *Appetite: Journal of Intake Research, 3,* 353–360.

Blackburn, G. L., Lynch, M. E., & Wong, S. L. (1986). The very low-calorie diet: A weight-reduction technique. In K. D. Brownell & J. P. Foreyt (Eds.), *Handbook of eating disorders* (pp. 198–212). New York: Basic Books.

Blanchard, E. B. (1992). Psychological treatment of benign headache disorders. *Journal of Consulting and Clinical Psychology, 60,* 537–551.

Blanchard, E. B., & Andrasik, F. (1985). *Management of headaches: A psychological approach.* Elmsford, NY: Pergamon Press.

Blanchard, E. B., & Young, L. D. (1974). Clinical applications of biofeedback training: A review of evidence. *Archives of General Psychiatry, 30,* 573–589.

Blinder, B. J., Freeman, D. M., & Stunkard, A. J. (1970). Behavior therapy of anorexia nervosa: Effectiveness of activity as a reinforcer of weight gain. *American Journal of Psychiatry, 126,* 1093–1098.

Bollard, J., Nettlebeck, T., & Roxbee, L. (1982). Dry-bed training for childhood bedwetting: A comparison of group with individually administered parent instruction. *Behavior Research and Therapy, 20,* 209–217.

Bollard, R., & Woodroffe, P. (1977). The effect of parent-administered dry-bed training on nocturnal enuresis in children. *Behavior Research and Therapy, 15,* 159–165.

Bonato, D. P., & Boland, F. J. (1983). Delay of gratification in obese children. *Addictive Behavior, 8,* 71–74.

Bouchard, C., Perusse, L., LeBlanc, C., Tremblay, A., & Theriault, G. (1988). Inheritance of the amount and distribution of human body fat. *International Journal of Obesity, 12,* 205–215.

Bowers, W. A., Evans, K., & Van Cleve, L. (1996). Treatment of adolescent eating disorders. In M. A. Reinecke, F. M. Dattilio, & A. Freeman (Eds.), *Cognitive therapy with children and adolescents* (pp. 227–250). New York: Guilford Press.

Brener, J. A. (1974). A general model of voluntary control applied to the phenomena of learned cardiovascular change. In P. A. Obrist, A. H. Black, J. Brener, & L. V. DiCara (Eds.), *Cardiovascular psychophysiology* (pp. 206–239). Chicago: Aldine.

Brownell, K. D. (1982). Obesity: Understanding and treating a serious, prevalent, and refractory disorder. *Journal of Consulting and Clinical Psychology, 50,* 820–840.

Brownell, K. D., & Jeffrey, R. W. (1987). Improving long-term weight loss: Pushing the limits of treatment. *Behavior Therapy, 18,* 353–374.

Brownell, K. D., & Kaye, F. S. (1982). A school-based behavior modification, nutrition education, and physical activity program for obese children. *The American Journal of Clinical Nutrition, 35,* 277–283.

Brownell, K. D., Kelman, M. S., & Stunkard, A. J. (1983). Treatment of obese children with and without their mothers: Changes in weight and blood pressure. *Pediatrics, 71,* 515–523.

Brownell, K. D., & O'Neil, P. M. (1993). Obesity. In D. H. Barlow (Ed.), *Clinical handbook of psychological disorders.* (pp. 318–361). New York: Guilford Press.

Brownell, K. D., & Stunkard, A. J. (1980). Physical activity in the development and control of obesity. In A. J. Stunkard (Ed.), *Obesity* (pp. 300–324). Philadelphia: Saunders.

Brownell, K. D., & Wadden, T. A. (1991). The heterogeneity of obesity: Fitting treatments to individuals. *Behavior Therapy, 22,* 153–177.

Browning, C. H., & Miller, S. I. (1968). Anorexia nervosa: A study in prognosis and management. *American Journal of Psychiatry, 124,* 1128–1132.

Bruch, H. (1974). Perils of behavior modification in treatment of anorexia nervosa. *Journal of the American Medical Association, 230,* 1419–1422.

Bruch, H. (1977). Psychological antecedents of anorexia nervosa. In R. A. Vigersky (Ed.), *Anorexia nervosa* (pp. 1–10). New York: Raven Press.

Burke, E. J., & Andrasik, F. (1989). Home- versus clinic-based biofeedback treatment for pediatric migraine: Results of treatment through one-year follow-up. *Headache, 29,* 434–440.

Casper, R. C., Eckert, E. D., Halmi, K. A., Goldberg, S. C., & Davis J. M. (1980). Bulimia: Its incidence and clinical importance in patients with anorexia nervosa. *Archives of General Psychiatry, 37,* 1030–1034.

Childress, A. C., Brewerton, T. D., Hodges, E. K., & Jarrell, M. P. (1993). The Kids' Eating Disorder Survey (KEDS): A survey of middle school students. *Journal of the American Academy of Child and Adolescent Psychiatry, 32,* 843–850.

Chiumello, G., del Guercio, M. J., Carnelutti, M., & Bidone, G. (1969). Relationship between obesity, chemical diabetes, and beta pancreatic function in children. *Diabetes, 18,* 238–243.

Ciminero, A. R., & Doleys, D. M. (1976). Childhood enuresis: Considerations in assessment. *Journal of Pediatric Psychology, 4,* 17–20.

Coates, T. J., Jeffrey, R. W., Slinkard, L. A., Killen, J. D., & Danaher, B. G. (1982). Frequency of contact and monetary reward in weight loss, lipid change, and blood pressure reduction with adolescents. *Behavior Therapy, 13,* 175–185.

Cohen, E. A., Gelfand, D. M., Dodd, D. K., Jensen, J., & Turner, C. (1980). Self-control practices associated with weight loss maintenance in children and adolescents. *Behavior Therapy, 11,* 26–37.

Cohen, M. J. (1978). Psychophysiological studies of headache: Is there similarity between migraine and muscle contraction headache? *Headache, 18,* 189–196.

Cohen, R. Y., & Stunkard, A. J. (1983.) Behavior therapy and pharmacotherapy of obesity: A review of the literature. *Behavior Medicine Update, 4,* 7–12.

Crisp, A. H. (1980). *Anorexia nervosa: Let me be.* New York: Grune & Stratton.

Crisp, A. H., Hsu, L. K., Harding, B., & Hartshorn, J. (1980). Clinical features of anorexia nervosa: A study of a consecutive series of 120 female patients. *Journal of Psychosomatic Research, 24,* 171–191.

Dally, P. (1969). *Anorexia nervosa.* New York: Grune & Stratton.

Dare, C., Eisler, I., Russell, M. R., & Szmukler, G. I. (1990). The clinical and theoretical impact of a controlled trial of family therapy in anorexia nervosa. *Journal of Marital and Family Therapy, 16,* 39–57.

Davison, G. C., & Neal, J. M. (1974). *Abnormal Psychology: An experimental clinical approach.* New York: John Wiley & Sons.

DeLeon, G., & Mandell, W. A. (1966). A comparison of conditioning and psychotherapy in the treatment of functional enuresis. *Journal of Clinical Psychology, 22,* 326–330.

Diamond, S. (1991). Migraine headaches. *Medical Clinics of North America, 75,* 545–566.

Diamond, S., & Dalessio, D. J. (1992). Taking a headache history. In S. Diamond & D. J. Dalessio (Eds.), *The practicing physician's approach to headache.* (pp. 11–24). Baltimore: William and Wilkins.

Diamond, S., & Franklin, M. (1975). Biofeedback: Choice of treatment in childhood migraine. In W. Luthe & F. Antonelli (Eds.), *Therapy in psychosomat-*

ic medicine (Vol. 4), (pp. 118–123). Rome: Autogenic Therapy.

Dienstfrey, H. (1991). *Where the mind meets the body.* New York: Harper Collins.

Dietz, W. H., & Gortmaker, S. L. (1985). Do we fatten our children at the TV set? Obesity and television viewing in children and adolescents. *Pediatrics, 75,* 807–812.

Doleys, D. M. (1977). Behavioral treatment of nocturnal enuresis in children: A review of the recent literature. *Psychological Bulletin, 84,* 30–54.

Doleys, D. M. (1979). Assessment and treatment of childhood enuresis. In A. J. Finch & P. C. Kendall (Eds.), *Treatment and research in child psychopathology* (pp. 207–233). New York: Spectrum Publications.

Doleys, D. M., & Ciminero, A. R. (1976). Childhood enuresis: Considerations in treatment. *Journal of Pediatric Psychology, 4,* 21–23.

Doleys, D., Ciminero, A., Tollison, J. W., Williams, C. L., & Wells, K. C. (1977). Dry-bed training and retention control training: A comparison. *Behavior Therapy, 8,* 541–548.

Drotar, D. (1995). *Consulting with pediatricians: Psychological perspectives.* New York: Plenum Press.

Duckro, P. N., & Cantwell-Simmons, E. (1989). A review of studies evaluating biofeedback and relaxation training in the management of pediatric headache. *Headache, 29,* 428–433.

Duncker, K. (1938). Experimental modification of children's food preferences through social suggestion. *Journal of Abnormal and Social Psychology, 33,* 489–507.

Elder, S. T., Ruiz, Z. R., Deabler, H. L., & Dillenkoffer, R. L. (1973). Instrumental conditioning of diastolic blood pressure in essential hypertensive patients. *Journal of Applied Behavior Analysis, 6,* 377–382.

Engle, B. T. (1972). Operant conditioning of cardiac functioning: A status report. *Psychophysiology, 9,* 161–177.

Epstein, L. H. (1986). Treatment of childhood obesity. In K. D. Brownell & J. P. Foreyt (Eds.), *Handbook of Eating Disorders* (pp. 159–179). New York: Basic Books.

Epstein, L. H., Masek, B. J., & Marshall, W. R. (1978). A nutritionally based school program for control of eating in obese children. *Behavior Therapy, 9,* 766–788.

Epstein, L. H., & Wing, R. R. (1987). Behavioral treatment of childhood obesity. *Psychology Bulletin, 101,* 331–342.

Epstein, L. H., Valoski, A., Wing, R. R., & McCurley, J. (1994). Ten-year outcome of behavioral family-based treatment for childhood obesity. *Health Psychology, 13,* 373–383.

Epstein, L. H., Wing, R. R., Koeske, R., Andrasik, F., & Ossip, D. J. (1981). Child and parent weight loss in family-based behavior modification programs. *Journal of Consulting and Clinical Psychology, 49,* 674–685.

Epstein, L. H., Wing, R. R., Koeske, R., Ossip, D., & Beck, S. (1982). A comparison of lifestyle change and programmed exercise on weight and fitness changes in obese children. *Behavior Therapy, 13,* 651–665.

Epstein, L. H., Wing, R. R., Koeske, R., & Valoski, A. (1985). A comparison of lifestyle exercise, aerobic exercise, and calisthenics on weight loss in obese children. *Behavior Therapy, 16,* 345–356.

Epstein, L. H., Wing, R. R., Koeske, R., & Valoski, A. (1987). Long-term effects of family-based treatment of childhood obesity. *Journal of Consulting and Clinical Psychology, 55,* 91–95.

Epstein, L. H., Wing, R. R., Valoski, A., & Gooding, W. (1987). Long-term effects of parent weight on child weight loss. *Behavior Therapy, 18,* 219–226.

Epstein, L. H., Woodall, K., Goreczny, A. J., Wing, R. R., & Robertson, R. J. (1984). The modification of activity patterns and energy expenditure in obese young girls. *Behavior Therapy, 15,* 101–108.

Esperanca, M., & Gerrard, J. (1969). A comparison of the effect of imipramine and dietary restriction on bladder capacity. *Canadian Medical Association Journal, 101,* 324–327.

Fentress, D. W., Masek, B. J., Mehegan, J. E., & Benson, H. (1986). Biofeedback and relaxation-response training in the treatment of pediatric migraine. *Developmental Medicine and Child Neurology, 28,* 139–146.

Ferguson, D. M., Horwood, L. J., & Shannon, F. T. (1986). Factors related to the age of attainment of nocturnal bladder control: An 8 year-longitudinal study. *Pediatrics, 78,* 884–890.

Feuerstein, M., & Adams, H. E. (1977). Cephalic vaso motor feedback in the modification of migraine headaches. *Biofeedback and self-regulation, 2,* 241–254.

Feuerstein, M., & Garner, J. (1982). Chronic headache: Etiology and management. In D. M. Doleys, R. L. Meredith, & A. R. Ciminero (Eds.), *Behavioral medicine: Assessment and treatment strategies* (pp. 199–249). New York: Plenum Press.

Fielding, D. (1980). The response of day and night wetting in children and adolescents who only wet at night to retention control training and the enuresis alarm. *Behavior Research and Therapy, 18,* 305–317.

Finley, W. W., Besserman, R. L., Bennett, L. F., Clapp, R. K., & Finley, P. M. (1973). The effect of continuous intermittent, and "placebo" reinforcement on the effectiveness of the conditioning treatment of enuresis nocturnal. *Behavior Research and Therapy, 11,* 289–297.

Finley, W. W., & Jones, L. (1992). Biofeedback with children. In C. E. Walker & M. C. Roberts (Eds.), *Handbook of clinical child psychology* (2nd ed. pp. 809–827). New York: John Wiley & Sons.

Finley, W. W., & Wansley, R. A. (1976). Use of intermittent reinforcement in a clinical-research program for the treatment of enuresis nocturnal. *Journal of Pediatric Psychology, 4,* 24–27.

Flanery, R. C., & Kirschenbaum, D. S. (1986). Dispositional and situational correlates of long-term weight reduction in obese children. *Addictive Behaviors, 11,* 249–261.

Foch, T. T., & McClearn, G. E. (1980). Genetics, body weight, and obesity. In A. J. Stunkard (Ed.), *Obesity* (pp. 48–71). Philadelphia: Saunders.

Fordyce, W. (1976). *Behavioral methods for chronic pain and illness.* St. Louis: Mosby.

Forrester, R., Stein, Z., & Susser, M. A. (1964). A trial of conditioning therapy in nocturnal enuresis. *Developmental Medicine and Child Neurology, 6,* 158–166.

Forsythe, W., Merrett, J., & Redmond, A. A. (1972). A controlled study of trimipramine and placebo in the treatment of enuresis. *British Journal of Clinical Practice, 26,* 119–121.

Forsythe, W. I., & Redmond, A. (1974). Enuresis and spontaneous cure rate: Study of 1129 enuretics. *Archives of Diseases of Childhood, 49,* 259–276.

Fosson, A., Knibbs, J., Bryant-Waugh, R., & Lask, B. (1987). Early onset anorexia nervosa. *Archives of Disease in Childhood, 62,* 114–118.

Foster, G. D., Wadden, T. A., & Brownell, K. D. (1985). Peer-led program for the treatment and prevention of obesity in the schools. *Journal of Consulting and Clinical Psychology, 53,* 538–540.

Foxman, B., Valdez, R. B., & Brook, R. H. (1986). Childhood enuresis: Prevalence, perceived impact, and prescribed treatments. *Pediatrics, 77,* 482–487.

Fried, R. (1974). A device for enuresis control. *Behavior Therapy, 5,* 682–684.

Friedman, M. A., & Brownell, K. D. (1995). Psychological correlates of obesity: Moving to the next research generation. *Psychological Bulletin, 117,* 3–20.

Garfinkel, P. E., & Garner, D. M. (1982). *Anorexia nervosa: A multidimensional perspective.* New York: Brunner/Mazel.

Garfinkel, P. E., & Kaplan, A. S. (1986). Anorexia nervosa: diagnostic conceptualizations. In K. D. Brownell & J. P. Foreyt (Eds.), *Handbook of eating disorders* (pp. 266–282). New York: Basic Books.

Garfinkel, P. E., Kline, S. A., & Stancer, H. C. (1973). Treatment of anorexia nervosa using operant conditioning techniques. *Journal of Nervous and Mental Disease, 157,* 428–433.

Garfinkel, P. E., Moldofsky, H., & Garner, D. M. (1977). The outcome of anorexia nervosa: Significance of clinical features, body image, and behavior modification. In R. Vigersky (Ed.), *Anorexia nervosa* (pp. 315–329). New York: Raven Press.

Garner, D. M. (1986). Cognitive therapy for anorexia nervosa. In K. D. Brownell & J. P. Foreyt (Eds.), *Handbook of eating disorders* (pp. 301–327). New York: Basic Books.

Garner, D. M. (1993). Pathogenesis of anorexia nervosa. *Lancet, 341,* 1631–1640.

Garner, D. M., Garfinkel, P. E., & Olmstead, M. (1983). An overview of sociocultural factors in the development of anorexia nervosa. In P. L. Darby, P. E. Garfinkel, D. M. Garner, & D. V. Coscina (Eds.), *Anorexia nervosa: Recent developments in research* (pp. 65–82). New York: Alan R. Liss.

Garner, D. M., & Garner, M. V. (1992). Testing of eating disorders in adolescents: Research and recommendations. In C. E. Walker & M. C. Roberts (Eds.), *Handbook of clinical child psychology* (2nd ed. pp. 623-641). New York: John Wiley & Sons.

Garner, D. M., Rocket, W., Olmstead, M. P., Johnson, C., & Coscina, D. V. (1985). Psychoeducational principles in the treatment of bulimia and anorexia nervosa. In D. M. Garner & P. E. Garfinkel (Eds.), *A handbook of psychotherapy for anorexia and bulimia* (pp. 513–572). New York: Guilford Press.

Garrow, J. S. (1986). Physiological aspects of obesity. In K. D. Brownell & J. P. Foreyt (Eds.), *Handbook of eating disorders* (pp. 45–62). New York: Basic Books.

Gatchel, R. J. (1993). Psychophysiological disorders: Past and present perspectives. In R. J. Gatchel & E. B. Blanchard (Eds.), *Psychophysiological disorders: Research and clinical applications* (pp. 1–21). Washington, DC: American Psychological Association.

Geller, J. L. (1975). Treatment of anorexia nervosa by the integration of behavior and psychotherapy. *Psychotherapy and Psychosomatics, 26,* 167–177.

Geller, S. E., Keane, T. M., & Scheirer, C. J. (1981). Delay of gratification, locus of control, and eating patterns in obese and nonobese children. *Addictive Behavior, 6,* 9–14.

Gershon, E. S., Schreiber, J. L., Hamovit, J. R., Dibble, E. D., Kaye, W. H., Nurnberger, J. I., Anderson, A., & Ebert, M. H. (1983). Anorexia nervosa and major affective disorders associated in families: A preliminary report. In S. B. Guze, F. J. Earls, & J. E. Barrett (Eds.), *Childhood psychopathology and development* (pp. 279–284). New York: Raven Press.

Gillum, R. F., Prineas, R. J., Sopko, G., Koga, Y., Kubicek, W., Robitarlle, N. M., Bass, J., Sinaiko, A. (1983): Elevated blood pressure in school children—prevalence, persistence, and hemodynamics: The Minneapolis children's blood pressure study. *American Heart Journal, 105,* 316–322.

Gordon, S. B., & Davidson, N. P. (1981). Behavioral parent training. In A. Gurman & D. Kniskern (Eds.), *Handbook of family therapy* (pp. 326-387). New York: Brunner/Mazel.

Gortmaker, S. L., Dietz W. H., Jr., Sobol, A. M., & Wehler, C. A. (1987). Increasing pediatric obesity in the United States. *American Journal of Diseases of Children, 141,* 535–540.

Group for the Advancement of Psychiatry (1966). *Psychopathological disorders in childhood: Theoretical considerations and a proposed classification* (Vol. 6) (Report No. 62).

Haggerty, J. J. (1983). The psychosomatic family: An overview. *Psychosomatics, 24,* 615–623.

Halliday, S., Meadow, S. R., & Berg, I. (1987). Successful management of daytime enuresis using alarm procedures: A randomly controlled trial. *Archives of Disease in Childhood, 62,* 132–137.

Hallsten, E. A. (1965). Adolescent anorexia nervosa treated by desensitization. *Behavior Research and Therapy, 32,* 87–91.

Halmi, K. A. (1974). Anorexia nervosa: Demographic and clinical features in 94 cases. *Psychosomatic Medicine, 36,* 18–25.

Halmi, K. A., Powers, P., & Cunningham, S. (1975). Treatment of anorexia nervosa with behavior modification. *Archives of General Psychiatry, 32,* 93–96.

Harper, L. V., & Sanders, K. M. (1975). The effects of adults eating on young children's acceptance of unfamiliar food. *Journal of Experimental Child Psychology, 20,* 206–214.

Hatch, J. P. (1993). Headache. In R. J. Gatchel & E. B. Blanchard (Eds.), *Psychophysiological disorders: research and clinical applications.* (pp. 111–149). Washington, DC: American Psychological Association.

Herbert, T. B., & Cohen, S. (1993). Stress and immunity in humans: A meta-analytic review. *Psychosomatic Medicine, 55,* 364–379.

Hersen, M. H., & Barlow, D. H. (1976). *Single case experimental designs: Strategies for studying behavior change.* Elmsford, NY: Pergamon Press.

Herzog, D. B., Sachs, N. R., Keller, M. B., Lavori, P. W., von Ranson, K. B., & Gray, H. M. (1993). Patterns and predictors of recovery in anorexia nervosa and bulimia nervosa. *Journal of the American Academy of Child and Adolescent Psychiatry, 32,* 835–842.

Hoelscher, T. J., & Lichstein, K. L. (1984). Behavioral assessment and treatment of child migraine: Implications for clinical research and practice. *Headache, 24,* 94–103.

Holland, A. J., Hall, A., Murray, R., Russell, G. F.,M., & Crisp, A. H. (1984). Anorexia nervosa: A study of 34 twin pairs. *British Journal of Psychiatry, 145,* 414–419.

Holmes, T. H., & Rahe, R. A. (1967). The Social Readjustment Rating Scale. *Journal of Psychosomatic Research, 11,* 213–218.

Holroyd, K. A., & Penzien, D. B. (1990). Pharmacological versus nonpharmacological prophylasix of recurrent migraine headache: A meta-analytic review of clinical trials. *Pain, 42,* 1–13.

Houts, A. C. (1991). Nocturnal enuresis as a biobehavioral problem. *Behavior Therapy, 22,* 133–151.

Houts, A. C. (1996). Behavioral treatment of enuresis. *The Clinical Psychologist, 49,* 5–6.

Houts, A. C., Liebert, R. M., & Padawer, W. (1983). A delivery system for the treatment of enuresis. *Journal of Abnormal Child Psychology, 11,* 513–520.

Houts, A. C., Peterson, J. K., & Whelan, J. P. (1986). Prevention of relapse in full-spectrum home training for primary enuresis: A components analysis. *Behavior Therapy, 17,* 462–469.

Howat, P. M., & Saxton, A. M. (1988). The incidence of bulimic behavior in a secondary and university school population. *Journal of Youth and Adolescence, 17,* 221–231.

Hsu, L. K. G. (1990). *Eating Disorders.* New York: Guilford Press.

Humphrey, L. L. (1988). Relationships within subtypes of anorexic, bulimic, and normal families. *Journal of the American Academy of Child and Adolescent Psychiatry, 27,* 544–551.

Hunsaker, J. H. (1976). A two-process approach to nocturnal enuresis: Preliminary results. *Behavior Therapy, 6,* 560–561.

International Headache Society (1988). Classification and diagnostic criteria for headache disorders, cranial neuralgias and facial pain. *Cephalalgia, 8* (Suppl. 7), 1–96.

Israel, A. C., Guile, C. A., Baker, J. E., & Silverman, W. (1994). An evaluation of enhanced self-regulation training in the treatment of childhood obesity. *Journal of Pediatric Psychology, 19,* 737–749.

Israel, A. C., Stolmaker, L., & Andrian, C. A. (1985). The effects of training parents in general child management skills on a behavioral weight loss program for children. *Behavior Therapy, 16,* 169–180.

Jehu, D., Morgan, R. T. T., Turner, A., & Jones, A. (1977). A controlled trial of the treatment of nocturnal enuresis in residential homes for children. *Behavior Research and Therapy, 15,* 1–16.

Johnson, S. B. (1980). Enuresis. In R. Daitzman (Ed.), *Clinical behavior therapy and behavior modification* (pp. 81–142). New York: Garland Press.

Johnson, C., Conners, M., & Tobin, D. L. (1987). Symptom management of bulimia. *Journal of Consulting and Clinical Psychology, 55,* 668–676.

Johnson, J. H., & Bradlyn, A. S. (1988). Assessing stressful life events in children and adolescents. In P. Karoly (Ed.), *Handbook of child health assessment: Biopsychosocial assessment* (pp. 303–331). New York: John Wiley & Sons.

Kanner, A. D., Coyne, J. C., Schaefer, C., & Lazarus, R. S. (1980). Comparison of two modes of stress measurement: Daily hassles and uplifts versus major life events. *Journal of Behavioral Medicine, 4,* 1–39.

Karoly, P. (1988). *Handbook of child health assessment: Biopsychosocial perspectives.* New York: John Wiley & Sons.

Kashinsky, W. (1974). Two low cost micturition alarms. *Behavior Therapy, 5,* 698–700.

Katz, R. C., & Zlutnick, S. (Eds.). (1975). *Behavior therapy and health care: Principles and applications.* Elmsford, NY: Pergamon Press.

Kazak, A. E., Segal-Andrews, A. M., & Johnson, K. (1995). Pediatric psychology research and practice: A family/systems approach. In M. C. Roberts (Ed.), *Handbook of pediatric psychology* (2nd ed., pp. 84–104). New York: Guilford Press.

Keesey, R. E. (1986). A set-point theory of obesity. In K. D. Brownell & J. P. Foreyt (Eds.), *Handbook of eating disorders* (pp. 61–87). New York: Basic Books.

Keicolt-Glaser, J. K., & Glaser, R. (1988). Behavioral influences on immune function: Evidence for the interplay between stress and health. In T. M. Field, P. M. McCabe, & N. Schneidman (Eds.), *Stress and coping across development* (pp. 189–205). Hillsdale, NJ: Lawrence Erlbaum.

Keys, A., Brozek, J., Henschel, A., Mickelsen, O., & Taylor, H. L. (1950). *The biology of human starvation.* Minneapolis: University of Minnesota Press.

Kimball, C. P. (1970). Conceptual developments in psychosomatic medicine: 1939–1969. *Annals of Internal Medicine, 73,* 307–316.

Kimmel, H. D., & Kimmel, E. (1970). An instrumental conditioning method for the treatment of enuresis. *Journal of Behavior Therapy and Experimental Psychiatry, 1,* 21–123.

Kirschenbaum, D. S., Harris, E. S., & Tomarken, A. J. (1984). Effects of parental involvement in behavioral weight loss therapy for preadolescents. *Behavior Therapy, 15,* 485–500.

Kirschner, M. A., Schneider, G., Ertel, N. H., & Gorman, J. (1988). An eight-year experience with a very low calorie formula diet for control of major obesity. *International Journal of Obesity, 12,* 69–80.

Klesges, R. C., Coates, T. J., Brown, G., Sturgeon-Tillisch, J., Moldenhauer-Klesges, L. M., Holzer, B., Woolfrey, J., & Vollmer, J. (1983). Parental influences on children's eating behavior and relative weight. *Journal of Applied Behavioral Analysis, 16,* 371–378.

Klesges, R. C., Malott, J. M., Boschee, P. F., & Weber, J. M. (1986). Parental influences on children's food intake, physical activity, and relative weight: An extension and replication. *International Journal of Eating Disorders, 5,* 335–346.

Kral, J. G., & Kissileff, H. R. (1987). Surgical approaches to the treatment of obesity. *Annals of Behavioral Medicine, 9,* 15–19.

Kratochwill, T. R. (1978). *Single subject research.* New York: Academic Press.

Labbe, E. L., & Williamson, D. A. (1984). Treatment of childhood migraine using autogenic feedback training. *Journal of Consulting and Clinical Psychology, 52,* 968–976.

Lagos, J. M. (1981). Family therapy in the treatment of anorexia nervosa: Theory and technique. International *Journal of Psychiatry in Medicine, 11,* 291–302.

Lansky, D., & Brownell, K. D. (1982). Comparison of school-based treatments for adolescent obesity. *The Journal of School Health, 52,* 384–387.

Larson, B., Melin, L., Lamminen, M., & Ullstedt, F. (1987). A school-based treatment of chronic headaches in adolescents. *Journal of Pediatric Psychology, 12,* 553–566.

Laskarzewski, P., Morrison, J. A., deGroot, I., Kelly, K. A., Mellies, M. J., Khoury, P., & Glueck, C. J. (1979). Lipid and lipoprotein tracking in 108 children over a four-year period. *Pediatrics, 64,* 584–591.

Lauer, R. M., Conner, W. E., Leaverton, P. E., Reiter, M. A., & Clarke, W. R. (1975). Coronary heart disease risk factors in school children. *Journal of Pediatrics, 86,* 697–706.

Lazarus, R. S. (1966). *Psychological stress and the coping process.* New York: McGraw-Hill.

Leitenberg, H., Agras, W. S., & Thomson, L. E. (1968). A sequential analysis of the effect of selective positive reinforcement in modifying anorexia nervosa. *Behaviour Research and Therapy, 6,* 211–218.

Li, B. U. K. (1994). Anorexia nervosa: Medical issues. In R. A. Olson, L. L. Mullins, J. B. Gillman, & J. M. Chaney (Eds.), *The sourcebook of pediatric psychology.* (pp. 322–345). Boston: Allyn & Bacon.

Liebman, R., Minuchin, S., & Baker, L. (1974). An integrated treatment program for anorexia nervosa. *American Journal of Psychiatry, 131,* 432–436.

Linscheid, T. R. (1992). Eating problems in children. In C. E. Walker & M. C. Roberts (Eds.), *Handbook of clinical child psychology* (2nd ed., pp. 451–473). New York: John Wiley & Sons.

Lipowski, Z. J. (1977). Psychosomatic medicine in the seventies: An overview. *American Journal of Psychiatry, 134,* 233–244.

Lipowski, Z. J. (1986). Psychosomatic medicine: Past and present, Part 1. Historical background. *Canadian Journal of Psychiatry, 31,* 2–7.

Lipton, E. L., Sternschneider, A., & Richmond, J. B. (1966). Psychophysiological disorders in children. In L. W. Hoff & M. L. Hoffman (Eds.), *Review of child development research,* Vol. 2, (pp. 132–146). New York: Russell Sage.

Londe, S., Bourgoignie, J. J., Robson, A. M., & Goldring, D. (1972). Hypertension in apparently normal children. *Journal of Pediatrics, 78,* 569–575.

Lovibond, S. H. (1963). The mechanism of conditioning treatment of enuresis. *Behaviour Research and Therapy, 1,* 17–21.

Lovibond, S. H., & Coote, M. A. (1970). Enuresis. In C. G. Costello (Ed.), *Symptoms of psychopathology* (pp. 373–390). New York: John Wiley & Sons.

Magrab, P. R. (Ed.). (1978). *Psychological management of pediatric problems* Vol. 1. Baltimore: University Park Press.

Marcus, M. D., & Wing, R. R. (1987). Binge eating among the obese. *Annals of Behavioral Medicine, 9,* 23–27.

Marholin, D., Siegel, L. J., & Phillips, D. (1976). Treatment and transfer: A search for empirical procedures. In M. Hersen, R. M. Eisler, & P. M. Miller (Eds.), *Progress in behavior modification* (Vol. 3, pp. 293–342). New York: Academic Press.

McBurnett, K., Hobbs, S. A., & Lahey, B. B. (1989). Behavioral treatment. In T. H. Ollendick & M. Hersen (Eds.), *Handbook of child psychopathology* (2nd ed.) New York: Plenum Press.

McGrath, P. J., Humphrey, P., Goodman, J. T., Keene, D., Fireston, P., Jacob, P., & Cunningham, S. J. (1988).

Relaxation prophylaxis for childhood migraine: A randomized placebo-controlled trial. *Developmental Medicine and Child Neurology, 30,* 626–631.

Mechanic, D. (1983). Adolescent health and illness behavior: A review of the literature and a new hypothesis for the study of stress. *Journal of Human Stress, 9,* 4–13.

Medina, J. L., & Diamond, S. (1977). Drug dependency in patients with chronic headache. *Headache, 17,* 12–14.

Meisner, W. W. (1974). Family process and psychosomatic disease. *International Journal of Psychiatry in Medicine, 5,* 411–430.

Melamed, B. G., & Siegel, L. J. (1980). *Behavioral medicine: Practical applications in health care.* New York: Springer.

Merrit, R. J. (1978). Treatment of pediatric and adolescent obesity. *International Journal of Obesity, 2,* 207–214.

Miller, N. E. (1969). Learning of visceral and glandular responses. *Science, 163,* 434–445.

Miller, P. M. (1973). An experimental analysis of retention control training in the treatment of nocturnal enuresis in two institutionalized adolescents. *Behavior Therapy, 4,* 288–294.

Millman, M. (1980). *Such a pretty face: Being fat in America.* New York: W. W. Norton & Company.

Minuchin, S., Baker, L., Liebman, R., Milman, L., & Todd, T. C. (1975). A conceptual model of psychosomatic illness in children. *Archives of General Psychiatry, 32,* 1031–1038.

Minuchin, S., Rosman, B. L., & Baker, L. (1978). *Psychosomatic families: Anorexia nervosa in context.* Cambridge, MA: Harvard University Press.

Moffatt, M. E., Kato, C., & Pless, I. B. (1987). Improvements in self-concept after treatment of nocturnal enuresis: Randomized controlled trial. *Journal of Pediatrics, 110,* 647–652.

Morgan, R., & Young, G. (1975). Parental attitudes and the conditioning treatment of childhood enuresis. *Behaviour Research and Therapy, 13,* 197–199.

Mountjoy, P. T., Ruben, D. H., & Bradford, T. S. (1984). Recent technological advances in the treatment of enuresis: Theory and commercial devices. *Behavior Modification, 8,* 291–315.

Mowrer, O. H., & Mowrer, W. M. (1938). Enuresis: A method for its study and treatment. *American Journal of Orthopsychiatry, 8,* 436–459.

Muellner, S. R. (1960). The development of urinary control in children: A new concept in cause, prevention and treatment of primary enuresis. *Journal of Urology, 84,* 714–716.

Mullins, L. L., Olson, R. A., & Chaney, J. M. (1992). A social learning/family systems approach to the treatment of somatoform disorders in children and adolescents. *Family Systems Medicine, 10,* 201–212.

Munford, P. R. (1980). Haloperidol and contingency management in a case of anorexia nervosa. *Journal of Behavior Therapy and Experimental Psychiatry, 11,* 67–71.

Murray, J. B. (1986). Psychological aspects of anorexia nervosa. *Genetic Psychological Monographs, 112,* 7–40.

Nieto, F. J., Szklo, M., & Comstock, G. W. (1992). Childhood weight and growth rate as predictors of adult mortality. *American Journal of Epidemiology, 136,* 201–213.

Norgaard, J. P., Hansen, J. H., Wildschiotz, G., Sorensen, S., Rittig, S., & Djurhuus, J. C. (1989). Sleep cystometrics in children with nocturnal enuresis. *Journal of Urology, 141,* 1156–1159.

Novello, A. C., & Novello, J. R. (1987). Enuresis. *Pediatric Clinics of North America, 34,* 719–733.

Nussbaum, M. P. (1992). Anorexia nervosa. In E. R. McAnainey, R. E. Kreipe, D. P. Orr, & G. D. Comerci (Eds.), *Textbook of adolescent medicine* (pp. 536–541). Philadelphia: Saunders.

O'Brien, T. P., Walley, P. B., Anderson-Smith, S., & Drabman, R. S. (1982). Naturalistic observation of the snack selecting behavior of obese and non-obese children. *Addictive Behavior, 7,* 75–77.

O'Dell. S. (1974). Training parents in behavior modification: A review. *Psychological Bulletin, 81,* 418–433.

O'Leary, K. D., & Wilson, G. T. (1975). *Behavior therapy: Application and outcome.* Englewood Cliffs, NJ: Prentice-Hall.

Olness, K. O., MacDonald, J. T., & Uden, D. I. (1987). Comparison of self-hypnosis and propranolol in the treatment of juvenile classic migraine. *Pediatrics, 79,* 593-597.

Olson, R. A., Mullins, L. L., Gillman, J. B., & Chaney, J. M. (Eds.). (1994). *The sourcebook of pediatric psychology.* Boston: Allyn & Bacon.

Oppel, W., Harper, P., & Rowland, V. (1968). The age of attaining bladder control. *Journal of Pediatrics, 42,* 614-626.

Ornstein, R., & Sobel, D. (1987). *The healing brain.* New York: Simon & Schuster.

Overton, D. A. (1966). State-dependent learning produced by depressant and atropineline drugs. *Psychopharmacologia, 10,* 6-31.

Palla, B., & Litt, I. (1988). Medical complications of eating disorders in adolescents. *Pediatrics, 81,* 613–623.

Paschalis, A., Kimmel, H. D., & Kimmel, E. (1972). Further study of diurnal instrumental conditioning in the treatment of enuresis nocturnal. *Journal of Behavior*

Therapy and Experimental Psychiatry, 3, 253–256.

Payne, B., & Norfleet, M. A. C. (1986). Chronic pain and the family: A review. *Pain, 26,* 1–22.

Pennebaker, J. W., & Skelton, J. A. (1978). Psychological parameters of physical symptoms. *Personality and Social Psychology Bulletin, 4,* 524–530.

Perri, M. G., Shapiro, R. M., Ludwig, W. W., Twentyman, C. T., & McAdoo, W. G. (1984). Maintenance strategies for the treatment of obesity: An evaluation of relapse prevention training and post treatment contact by mail and telephone. *Journal of Consulting and Clinical Psychology, 52,* 404–413.

Philips, C. (1978). Tension headache: Theoretical problems. *Behavior Research and Therapy, 16,* 249–261.

Pierce, C. M. (1967). Enuresis. In A. M. Freedman & H. I. Kaplan (Eds.), *Comprehensive textbook of psychiatry* (pp. 2780–2788). Baltimore: Williams and Wilkins.

Polivy, J., & Herman, C. P. (1987). Diagnosis and treatment of normal eating. *Journal of Consulting and Clinical Psychology, 55,* 635–644.

Poole, W. (1993). *The heart of healing: The institute of noetic sciences.* Atlanta: Turner.

Premack, D. (1965). Reinforcement theory. In D. Levine (Ed.), *Nebraska symposium on motivation* (pp. 224–256). Lincoln: University of Nebraska Press.

Roberts, A., Kewan, D. G., & Macdonald, H. (1973). Voluntary control of skin temperature: Unilateral changes using hypnosis and feedback. *Journal of Abnormal Psychology, 82,* 163–168.

Roberts, M. C. (1995). *Handbook of pediatric psychology* (2nd ed.), New York: Guilford Press.

Rogers, M. P., Dubey, D., & Reich, P. (1979). The influence of the psyche and the brain on immunity and disease susceptibility: A critical review. *Psychosomatic Medicine, 41,* 147-164.

Rosen, J. C., & Gross, J. (1987). Prevalence of weight reducing and weight gaining in adolescent girls and boys. *Health Psychology, 6,* 131–147.

Ross, A. O. (1981). *Child behavior therapy: Principles, procedures and empirical basis.* New York: John Wiley & Sons.

Russell, G. F., Szmukler, G. I., Dare, C., & Eisler, I. (1987). An evaluation of family therapy in anorexia nervosa and bulimia nervosa. *Archives of General Psychiatry, 44,* 1047–1056.

Sallade, J. (1973). A comparison of psychological adjustment of obese vs. non-obese children. *Journal of Psychosomatic Research, 17,* 89–96.

Sargent, J. D., Greene, E. E., & Walters, E. D. (1973). Preliminary report on the use of autogenic feedback training in the treatment of migraine and tension headaches. *Psychosomatic Medicine, 35,* 129–135.

Schaefer, C. E. (1979). *Childhood enuresis and encopresis: Causes and therapy.* New York: Van Nostrand.

Schaefer, C. E., Millman, H. L., & Levine, G. F. (1979). *Therapies for psychosomatic disorders in children.* San Francisco: Jossey-Bass.

Schultz, J. H., & Luthe, U. (1969). *Autogenic training.* New York: Grune & Stratton.

Schwab, J. J., McGinnis, N. H., Morris, L. B., & Schwab, R. B. (1970). Psychosomatic medicine and the contemporary social scene. *American Journal of Psychiatry, 126,* 1632–1642.

Schwartz, G. E. (1973). Biofeedback as therapy: Some theoretical and practical issues. *American Psychologist, 28,* 666–673.

Seyle, H. (1956). *The stress of life.* New York: McGraw-Hill.

Shapiro, D., & Surwit, R. S. (1976). Learned control of psychological function and disease. In H. Leitenberg (Ed.), *Handbook of behavior modification and behavior therapy* (pp. 442–485). Englewood Cliffs, NJ: Prentice-Hall.

Shapiro, D., Tursky, B., & Schwartz, G. E. (1970). Control of blood pressure in man by operant conditioning. *Circulation Research* (Suppl. 1), 27, 27–32.

Shinnar, S., & D'Souza, B. J. (1981). Diagnosis and management of headaches in childhood. *Pediatric Clinics of North America, 29,* 79–94.

Siegel, L. J., (1983). Psychosomatic and psychophysiological disorders. In R. J. Morris & T. R. Kratochwill (Eds.), *The practice of child therapy* (pp. 253–286). Elmsford, NY: Pergamon Press.

Siegel, L. J., & Graham-Pole, J. (1991). Stress, immunity, and disease outcome in children undergoing cancer chemotherapy. In J. H. Johnson & S. B. Johnson (Eds.), *Advances in child health psychology* (pp 28–41). Gainesville: University Press of Florida.

Siegel, L. J., & Graham-Pole, J. (1995). Psychoneuroimmunology. In M. C. Roberts (Ed.), *Handbook of pediatric psychology* (2nd ed. pp. 759–773). New York: Guilford Press.

Siegel, L. J., & Richards, C. S. (1978). Behavioral interventions with somatic disorders in children. In D. Marholin (Ed.), *Child behavior therapy* (pp. 339–394). New York: Gardner Press.

Sillanpaa, M. (1983). Changes in the prevalence of migraines and other headaches during the first seven school years. *Headache, 23,* 15–19.

Sjostrom, L. (1980). Fat cells and body weight. In A. J. Stunkard (Ed.), *Obesity* (pp. 72–100). Philadelphia: Saunders.

Sobhany, M. S., & Rogers, C. S. (1985). External responsiveness to food and non-food cues among obese and non-obese children. *International Journal of Obesity, 9,* 99–106.

Sorotzkin, B. (1984). Nocturnal enuresis: Current perspectives. *Clinical Psychology Review, 4,* 293–316.

Staffieri, J. R. (1967). A study of social stereotype of body image in children. *Journal of Personality and Social Psychology, 7,* 101–104.

Starfield, B. (1967). Functional bladder capacity in enuretic and non-enuretic children. *Journal of Pediatrics, 70,* 777–782.

Starfield, B., & Mellitis, E. D. (1968). Increase in functional bladder capacity and improvements in enuresis. *Journal of Pediatrics, 72,* 483–487.

Stewart, W. F., Linet, M. S., Celentano, D. D., Van Natta, M., & Zieglea, D. (1991. Age- and sex-specific incidence rates of migraine with and without visual aura. *American Journal of Epidemiology, 134,* 1111–1120.

Strober, M. (1980). A cross-sectional and longitudinal analysis of personality and symptomological features in young non-chronic anorexia nervosa patients. *Journal of Psychosomatic Research, 24,* 353–359.

Strober, M. (1981). The significance of bulimia in juvenile anorexia nervosa: An exploration of possible etiologic factors. *International Journal of Eating Disorders, 1,* 28–43.

Strober, M. (1986). Anorexia nervosa: History and psychological concepts. In K. D. Brownell & J. P. Foreyt (Eds.), *Handbook of eating disorders* (pp. 231–246). New York: Basic Books.

Strober, M., & Humphrey, L. L. (1987). Familial contributions to the etiology and course of anorexia nervosa and bulimia. *Journal of Consulting and Clinical Psychology, 55,* 654–659.

Strober, M., Morrell, W., Burroughs, J., Salkin, B., & Jacobs, C. (1985). A controlled family study of anorexia nervosa. *Journal of Psychiatric Research, 19,* 239–246.

Stunkard, A. J., Sorensen, T. I. A., Hanis, C., Teasdale, T. W., Chakraborty, R., Schull, W. J., & Schulsinger, F. (1986). An adoption study of human obesity. *New England Journal of Medicine, 314,* 193–198.

Szmuckler, G. I., & Russell, G. F. M. (1986). Outcome and prognosis of anorexia nervosa. In K. D. Brownell & J. P. Foreyt (Eds.), *Handbook of eating disorders* (pp. 283-300). New York: Basic Books.

Turk, D. C., & Kerns, R. D. (Eds.). (1985). *Health, illness, and families: A life-span perspective.* New York: Wiley.

Turner, D. B., & Stone, A. J. (1979). Headache and its treatment: A random survey. *Headache, 19,* 74–77.

Turner, R. K., & Young, G. C. (1966). CNS stimulant drugs and conditioning treatment of nocturnal enuresis: A long term follow-up study. *Behavior Research and Therapy, 4,* 225–228.

Uzark, K. C., Becker, M. H., Dielman, T. E., Rocchini, A. P., & Katch, V. (1988). Perceptions held by obese children and their parents: Implications for weight control intervention. *Health Education Quarterly, 15,* 185–198.

Van Buskirk, S. S. (1977). A two-phase perspective in the treatment of anorexia nervosa. *Psychological Bulletin, 84,* 529–538.

Varni, J. W. (1983). *Clinical behavioral pediatrics: An interdisciplinary biobehavioral approach.* New York: Pergamon Press.

Vitousek, K. M. (1996). The current status of cognitive-behavioral models of anorexia nervosa and bulimia nervosa. In P. M. Salkovskis (Ed.), *Frontiers of cognitive therapy.* New York: Guilford Press.

Wadden, T. A., Foster, G. D., Brownell, K. D., & Finley, E. (1984). Self-concept in obese and normal-weight children. *Journal of Consulting and Clinical Psychology, 52,* 1104–1105.

Walen, S., Hauserman, N. M., & Lavin, P. J. (1977). *Clinical Guide to Behavior Therapy.* Baltimore: Williams and Wilkins.

Wagner, W. G., Smith, D., & Norris, W. R. (1988). The psychological adjustment of enuretic children: A comparison of two types. *Journal of Pediatric Psychology, 13,* 33–58.

Walker, C. E. (1978). Toilet training, enuresis, encopresis. In P. R. Magrab (Ed.), *Psychological management of pediatric problems* (Vol. 1, pp. 129–189). Baltimore: University Park Press.

Walker, C. E. (1995). Elimination disorders: Enuresis and encopresis. In M. C. Roberts (Ed.), *Handbook of pediatric psychology* (2nd ed., pp. 537-557). New York: Guilford Press.

Walker, C. E., Milling, L. S., & Bonner, B. L. (1988). Incontinence disorders: Enuresis and encopresis. In D. Routh (Ed.), *Handbook of pediatric psychology* (pp. 363–397). New York: Guilford Press.

Waxman, M., & Stunkard, A. J. (1980). Caloric intake and expenditure of obese boys. *Journal of Pediatrics, 96,* 187–193.

Weil, K. (1988). *Health and healing.* Boston: Houghton-Mifflin.

Werry, J. (1967). Enuresis nocturnal. *Medical Times, 95,* 985–991.

Werry, J., & Cohressen, J. (1965). Enuresis—An etiologic and therapeutic study. *Journal of Pediatrics, 67,* 423–431.

Werry, J. S., & Bull, D. (1975). Anorexia nervosa—A case study using behavior therapy. *Journal of the American Academy of Child Psychiatry, 14,* 646–651.

Whitehead, W. E., Fedoravicius, A. S., Blackwell, B., & Wooley, S. (1979). A behavioral conceptualization of psychosomatic illness: Psychosomatic symptoms as learned responses. In J. R. McNamara (Ed.), *Behavioral approaches to medicine: Application and analysis* (pp. 65–99). New York: Plenum Press.

Wille, S. (1986). Comparison of desmopressin and enuresis alarm for nocturnal enuresis. *Archives of Disease in Childhood, 61,* 30–33.

Williamson, D. A., Davis, C. J., Duchmann, E. G., McKenzie, S. M., & Watkins, P. C. (1990). *Assessment of eating disorders.* New York: Pergamon Press.

Williamson, D. A., Davis, C. J., Duchmann, E. G. (1992). Anorexia and bulimia nervosa. In V. B. Van Hassel & D. J. Kolko (Eds.), *Inpatient behavior therapy for children and adolescents.* (pp. 341–364). New York: Plenum Press.

Wilson, G. T. (1994). Behavioral treatment of childhood obesity: Theoretical and practical implications. *Health Psychology, 13,* 371–372.

Wilson, G. T., & Fairburn, C. G. (1993). Cognitive treatments for eating disorders. *Journal of Consulting and Clinical Psychology, 61,* 261–269.

Wolfle, J. A., Farrier, S. C., & Rogers, C. S. (1987). Children's cognitive concepts of obesity: A developmental study. *International Journal of Obesity, 11,* 73–83.

Woodall, K., & Epstein, L. H. (1983). The prevention of obesity. *Behavioral Medicine Update, 5,* 15–21.

Wooley, S. C., Blackwell, B., & Winget, C. (1978). The learning theory model of chronic illness behaviors: Theory, treatment, and research. *Psychosomatic Medicine, 40,* 379–401.

Worsley, A., Coonan, W., Leitch, D., & Crawford, D. (1984). Slim and obese children's perceptions of physical activities. *International Journal of Obesity, 8,* 201–211.

Worsley, A., Peters, M., Worsley, A. J., Coonan, W., & Baghurst, P. A. (1984). Australian 10-year-olds' perceptions of food. III. The influence of obesity status. *International Journal of Obesity, 8,* 327–340.

Yeates, W. K. (1973). Bladder function in normal micturition. In I. Kolvin, R. C. MacKeith, & S. R. Meadow (Eds.), *Bladder control and enuresis* (pp. 28–36). Philadelphia: Saunders.

Young, G., & Turner, R. (1965). CNS stimulant drugs and conditioning treatment of nocturnal enuresis. *Behaviour Research and Therapy, 3,* 93–101.

Young, G. C., & Morgan, R. T. T. (1972). Overlearning in the conditioning treatment of enuresis: A long-term follow-up study. *Behaviour Research and Therapy, 10,* 419–420.

Zaleski, A., Gerrard, J. W., & Shokier, M. H. K. (1973). Nocturnal enuresis: The importance of a small bladder capacity. In I. Kolvin, R. C. MacKeith, & S. R. Meadow (Eds.), *Bladder control and enuresis.* Philadelphia: Saunders.

CHAPTER 9

CHILDHOOD AUTISM

Marjorie H. Charlop-Christy
Laura Schreibman
Karen Pierce
Patricia F. Kurtz

In 1943, Leo Kanner described a group of 11 children who displayed a strikingly similar pattern of specific symptoms while differing from children with other childhood disorders. Kanner identified this severe form of child psychopathology as "early infantile autism" (Kanner, 1943, 1944). The children he described were, from early in life, markedly withdrawn and aloof. As infants, these children were not cuddly, disliked being held, and did not mold to their parents' bodies. They much preferred to be alone. These children were unresponsive to people as well as to their environment. They often manipulated objects in a rigid, stereotyped manner and lacked appropriate play. Kanner also noted that these children failed to acquire normal speech; in addition, many of the children displayed delayed echolalia and had difficulties with pronoun use. The children described also demonstrated an anxious insistence upon sameness in their environment, excellent rote memories, a normal physical appearance, and good cognitive potential. In a subsequent paper, Eisenberg

and Kanner (1956) reduced the essential symptoms for diagnosis to two primary characteristics: (a) extreme aloneness and (b) an obsessive insistence on the preservation of sameness. Thus, the language abnormalities that had previously been considered major symptoms of the syndrome were excluded.

More than five decades have passed since Kanner's (1943) identification of autism; much more is now known about the syndrome. Autism occurs in approximately 2–5 per 10,000 live births (American Psychiatric Association, 1994). Among children with autism, boys outnumber girls 3 or 4 to 1 (Dunlap, Koegel, & O'Neill, 1985; Kanner, 1944). Autism is characterized by extreme withdrawal, pervasive deficits in language, social behavior and attention; and the presence of bizarre and/or repetitive behaviors. Typically, autism is diagnosed between the ages of 2 and 5. Presently there is no dominant theory of etiology, however, most researchers agree that autism is caused by organic factors and is present from birth.

BEHAVIORAL CHARACTERISTICS OF AUTISM

The diagnosis of autism is based on the manifestation of the behaviors (symptoms) characteristic of the syndrome. A child must display the majority but not necessarily all of the following characteristics in order to be diagnosed as autistic. While Eisenberg and Kanner (1956) reduced the essential symptoms to extreme aloneness and preservation of sameness, Rutter (1978) brought back the emphasis on language and defined autism in terms of four essential criteria: onset before the age of 30 months, impaired social development, delayed and deviant language development, and insistence on sameness. The behaviors discussed below have been described by Kanner (1943) and Rutter (1978) as well as other researchers (e.g., Schreibman, 1988; Volkmar & Cohen, 1994) and are those characteristics typically displayed by most children with autism.

Social Behavior

Children with autism display profound deficits in social behavior (Kanner, 1943; Rimland, 1964; Rutter, 1978). These children generally have difficulties developing relationships with other people and rarely initiate interactions with others; they often do not express affection (Charlop & Walsh, 1986) and may actively resist physical contact (Kanner, 1943). Children with autism also tend to avoid eye contact (Rimland, 1964). As infants, they may not reach out in anticipation of being picked up or mold to their parents' bodies when held; rather, they may remain quite rigid when picked up or may "go limp." When older, children with autism typically will not seek out attention or comfort from parents, preferring instead to be alone. Indeed, they may appear to be quite indifferent to the arrival or departure of a parent (Kanner, 1943). This detachment contrasts sharply with the children's intense attachments to inanimate objects such as credit cards or pieces of string. Overall, these children generally do not play appropriately with toys or with other children (e.g., Charlop, Owen, Tan, & Milstein, 1988).

Children with autism also display difficulties understanding the intentions, motivations and beliefs of others. In short, it is extremely challenging for these children to take the perspective of people in their environment. Many modern theorists consider deficits in the ability to interpret the beliefs and intentions of others as one of the core deficits of autism. In a series of studies, (Baron-Cohen, 1988, 1989a, 1989b, Baron-Cohen, Leslie, & Frith, 1985, Leslie & Frith, 1988) investigators presented evidence that children with autism have deficits in a specific aspect of social cognition—that of attributing beliefs, intentions and other mental states to others—a deficit they describe as an impairment in the autistic child's "theory of mind." In a classic theory of mind task, children with autism are presented with a story such as "Jamie is eating a chocolate bar. Because it is time to go to school, Jamie puts her chocolate on top of her bed to save for when she returns. While at school, Jamie's mother takes the chocolate bar and puts it in her dresser drawer. When Jamie returns home from school, where will she look for the chocolate?" Children with autism will typically respond to where they know it is (i.e., in the drawer) rather than where Jamie thinks it is (i.e., on her bed). It has been argued that this deficit accounts for the impairments in communication and social behavior noted in this population (e.g., Frith, 1989). In addition, children with autism have been shown to use significantly less language referring to cognitive mental states than Down syndrome language matched control subjects (Tager-Flusberg, 1992).

The ability to understand the emotions of self and others (i.e., emotion perception) is an area of social competence that has also been shown to be deficient in children with autism. Specifically, children with autism have difficulties comprehending facial, vocal, or bodily expressions of affect (e.g., Hobson & Lee, 1989; Ozonoff, Pennington & Rogers, 1990), interpreting faces (e.g., Tantam, Monaghan, Nicholson & Stirling, 1989) and coordinating faces and voices (Hobson, Ouston, & Lee, 1988), and understanding complex emotions, such as pride or embarrassment (e.g., Capps, Yirmiya, & Sigman, 1992).

Deficits in social competency, especially theory of mind and emotion perception, seem to be related to age and degree of mental retardation with older nonretarded children with autism performing better on social perception tasks than younger, more retarded children with autism. Even in these high-functioning groups, however, deficits in social understanding and interactions still persist.

Speech and Language

Approximately 50% of children with autism fail to acquire functional speech (Rimland, 1964; Rutter, 1978). Although the structural or physiological components necessary for language are intact, some children may emit only a few sounds. These children who do not speak may resort to gestures as a means to communicate in a very limited manner (e.g., Rutter, 1978). For example, an autistic child may point with his or her hand or lead a person by the hand to the desired object.

Additionally, of the children who do acquire speech (50%), particular speech abnormalities characteristic of autism are typical. The verbal children with autism tend to display echolalia, the repetition of words or phrases spoken by others (Carr, Schreibman, & Lovaas, 1975; Tager-Flusberg et al., 1990). There are two broad categories of echolalia. Immediate echolalia occurs when the child repeats something he or she has just heard; for example, an autistic child may repeat in a parrotlike manner, "How was school today?" when asked this question, rather than answering appropriately. Immediate echolalia often interferes with learning and communication, as demonstrated by the child who echoes the task instructions rather than performing the task. Autistic children's immediate echolalia will likely increase in unfamiliar learning settings with unfamiliar task stimuli (Carr et al., 1975; Charlop, 1986) as well as when difficult or incomprehensible questions are presented (Schreibman & Carr, 1978). With delayed echolalia, the child echoes words or phrases he or she has heard in the past, a few hours, days, or months ago. Such echolalic speech is generally non-communicative and contextually inappropriate. For example, an autistic child might sing a jingle from a TV commercial he or she heard a few hours earlier or repeat part of a conversation from a few days before. It has been suggested that the occurrence of delayed echolalia may increase in the presence of aversive or fearful stimuli (Miller, 1969) or during high-arousal situations (Charlop, Gonzalez, & Cugliari, 1987).

For example, when one child was verbally reprimanded by his therapist for grabbing a cookie, the child shook a finger at the therapist and shouted, "Don't poke that dog!"—something his teacher had said a week before.

Children with autism who do use speech to communicate commonly display pronominal reversal (Kanner, 1943; Rutter, 1978). These children often use I-you pronouns incorrectly, as by saying, "Can you have a cookie?" when requesting a cookie. Or the child may simply refer to himself by name (e.g., "Johnny wants a drink, please."). This phenomenon appears to be closely related to echolalia (Bartak & Rutter, 1974).Also, comprehension of language is severely impaired (Kanner, 1943; Rutter, 1978). The children may interpret language quite literally (Kanner, 1943). For example, when one autistic child was instructed by a sibling to finish a sentence by a request to "Spit it out," the child then spit across the room. Children with autism may also have great difficulty following instructions. Additionally, these children may use language in a self-stimulatory manner, repeating sounds or words over and over again (e.g., "Strawberries, strawberries, strawberries!"). Typically, children with autism do not engage in the to-and-fro interaction characteristic of conversational speech (Charlop & Milstein, 1989). The prosodic features of their speech are often abnormal and characterized by unusual intonation and inaccurate rhythm, inflection, pitch, and articulation (e.g., Baltaxe, 1981; Tager-Flusberg et al., 1990; Schreibman, Kohlenberg, & Britten, 1986). In summary, these deficits in speech and language profoundly affect the child's ability to learn, to communicate, and to develop relationships with others.

Ritualistic Behavior and the Insistence on Sameness

This category is delineated into four common behaviors (Rutter, 1978). First, children with autism may display limited or rigid play. That is, they may repeatedly line up blocks or other household objects (e.g., bottles of salad dressing on the floor in order of size) or collect objects of a particular texture or shape. Second, children with autism frequently develop intense attachments to specific objects. They may be "obsessed" with such unusual things as business cards, vacuum cleaners, Honda cars, specific toys, pine cones, or particular letters of the alphabet. The child may talk repetitively about the object or insist on carrying it everywhere; if the object is lost or taken away, the child may become extremely upset. Such obsessions with objects may change suddenly or may last for years. Third, children with autism may also develop preoccupations with concepts such as colors, bus routes, numbers, and geometric patterns. Fourth, many children with autism develop rigid routines that must be followed exactly. For example, one child would sleep only in the family room in front of the television set, surrounded by a semicircle of plastic pegs sorted by color and with all the television sets in the house turned on all night. Any slight deviation from an established routine, such as rearranging the furniture or changing a regularly scheduled therapy appointment, may be extremely agitating to the child with autism.

Abnormalities in Response to the Physical Environment

Children with autism exhibit an unusual responsiveness to environmental events or stimuli (Kanner, 1943; Ritvo & Freeman, 1978; Wing, 1976). Typically, these children are described by their parents as "living in a shell" or "lost in their own world." They may not seem to hear their names being called or see a person standing right before their eyes (Schreibman, 1988). Indeed, children with autism are often incorrectly suspected of being deaf or blind. They may not react when a door is slammed, yet they can hear a crinkling candy wrapper across the room. Thus, they are said to exhibit an "apparent" sensory deficit. Additionally, some children may overreact to certain stimuli, as by covering their ears when the rustling of a newspaper is heard.

Children with autism also display what has been termed "stimulus overselectivity." This is defined as the failure to respond to the simultaneous presentation of multiple cues (Koegel & Wilhelm, 1973; Lovaas, Koegel, & Schreibman, 1979; Lovaas, Schreibman, Koegel, & Rehm, 1971; Schreibman, Charlop, & Koegel, 1982). For example, to learn to

discriminate the letters "E" and "F," a normal child will note that the letters are identical except for the bottom horizontal line (the relevant feature or cue). In contrast, a child with autism may "overselect," or attend only to, an irrelevant cue of the stimulus (such as the top horizontal line) or respond to a very restricted number of cues, thereby failing to learn to discriminate the letters. Because of this failure to attend to multiple cues, the use of extrastimulus prompts (e.g., finger prompts) typically used to aid learning will be unsuccessful (Schreibman, 1975; Schreibman et al., 1982). The children's consistent failure to respond to complex multiple cues in the environment may account in part for the children's difficulty in learning speech (Lovaas, Litrownik, & Mann, 1971) and appropriate social behavior (Schreibman & Lovaas, 1973) as well as for their poor generalization of newly acquired skills (Rincover & Koegel, 1975).

Self-stimulatory Behavior

Children with autism frequently display bizarre, repetitive behaviors (Kanner, 1943; Rutter, 1978). These stereotyped movements appear to serve no other purpose than to provide sensory input and are thus deemed self-stimulatory (Lovaas, Litrownik, & Mann 1971; Lovaas, Newsom, & Hickman, 1987; Wing, 1972). Self-stimulatory behaviors may involve motor movements, such as rhythmic body rocking, arm or hand flapping, body arching or posturing, darting, toe walking, and spinning the body around; or these may involve objects, such as tapping, mouthing, or twirling objects, or flapping an object in front of the eyes. More subtle forms of the behavior may be exhibited, including rubbing hands on surfaces, squinting eyes, gazing at lights, or sniffing objects. Generally, each child will have his or her own repertoire of self-stimulatory behaviors.

Self-stimulatory behavior is a highly preferred activity of children with autism; indeed, if permitted, children with autism may engage in such bizarre behaviors for hours at a time, to the exclusion of all other activities. The occurrence of self-stimulation is highest when they are alone in an unstructured setting (i.e., free play) (Runco, Charlop, & Schreibman, 1986). During structured learning situations, self-stimulatory behaviors occur significantly more often in the presence of an unfamiliar rather than a familiar therapist (Runco et al., 1986). Importantly, when engaging in self-stimulation, children with autism are particularly unresponsive to their environment. Self-stimulatory behaviors have been demonstrated to interfere with learning discrimination tasks (Koegel & Covert, 1972) and with engaging in appropriate play (Koegel, Firestone, Kramme, & Dunlap, 1974) and social behavior (Wing, 1972). Unfortunately, generalized, durable elimination of these bizarre interfering behaviors has not yet been achieved.

Self-injurious Behavior

Self-injurious behavior (SIB) may be the most dangerous behavior exhibited by children with autism. SIB is the infliction of physical damage by the child on his or her own body. The most common forms of SIB are head banging and self-biting (Rutter & Lockyer, 1967); other examples include hair pulling, eye gouging, face or head slapping, and arm and leg banging. Some children may run head-first into walls, repeatedly scratch their faces, or progressively bite their fingertips. The intensity of self-injury may vary, ranging from slight (where bruises, redness, or calluses result) to severe injury (in which broken bones, skull fractures, or removal of portions of skin may occur). In cases where there is risk of physical injury to the child, physical restraint (e.g., camisole) or protective equipment (e.g., padded gloves or helmet) may be necessary. However, extended use of restraints may lead to structural changes, such as arrested motor development, shortening of tendons, and demineralization of bones (Lovaas & Simmons, 1969) as well as the restriction of opportunities to learn and to engage in appropriate behaviors.

Intellectual Functioning

It was originally thought that children with autism possessed normal intelligence, due to their excellent rote memory, clever and manipulative behavior, serious facial expression, and absence of physical abnormalities (Kanner, 1943). Later research, however, has not supported this hypothesis. The majority of children with autism are functionally mentally retarded (Ritvo & Freeman, 1978). It is estimated that 60% of children with autism have IQs below 50, 20% measure between 5O and 70, and 20% have IQs of 70 or more (Ritvo & Freeman, 1978).

Intellectual assessment of children with autism is often difficult (e.g., Schreibman & Charlop, 1987). First, the children display many inappropriate behaviors, which interfere with test taking (e.g., SIB, self-stimulation). Second, due to their language impairment, these children tend to perform poorly on tests of abstract thought and symbolic or sequential logic; they tend to do best on tests assessing manipulative or visual-spatial skills and rote memory (Ritvo & Freeman, 1978). Thus, IQ test performances for children with autism tend to be variable.

Rutter (1978) suggested that IQ scores have the same properties in children with autism as they do in other children. Studies have consistently found that the IQ scores of children with autism remain quite stable throughout middle childhood and adolescence (e.g., Lockyer & Rutter, 1969). As with normal or retarded children, IQ also tends to be predictive of educational performance for children with autism (Rutter & Bartak, 1973). Thus, evidence suggests that children with autism are frequently functionally retarded.

Additional Characteristics

In addition to the above characteristics, some children with autism also display islets of superior ability, most commonly in the areas of music, mathematics, or mechanical skill (Rimland, 1978). One child may be able to dismantle and assemble complex machinery; another may remember and repeat complex musical melodies (Schreibman, 1988). Some children with autism can calculate on what day of the week a particular calendar date will fall. Such isolated "savant" skills often appear in children who concomitantly display low levels of functioning in other areas. One child, for example, could read a college-level psychology textbook but was not toilet trained.

Autistic children also commonly display behavior problems, including feeding, toileting, and sleeping problems; pica (ingestion of inedible objects, such as rocks or buttons); noncompliance; tantrums; and aggression. Because of the behavior problems and cognitive deficits noted above, some parents of children with autism report feeling overwhelmed, as well as high levels of stress (e.g., Bristol, Gallagher, & Schopler, 1988)

ETIOLOGY AND TREATMENT PARADIGMS

Although there has been a recent emphasis on exploring neurological and biochemical etiologies of autism (e.g., Freeman & Ritvo, 1984; Ornitz, 1985), the focus of this chapter is on treatment and therefore only the etiological theories that have led to a treatment protocol will be discussed. For a detailed discussion of additional theories of etiology, the reader is referred to Schreibman (1988).

Neurological Dysfunction Model and Treatment

Findings from several areas of research suggest the role of neurological factors in the etiology of autism (e.g., Courchesne et al., 1994a, 1994b; Mesibov & Dawson, 1986). One of the most consistent findings in the neuropathology of autism is a decrease in cerebellar volume (i.e., cerebellar hypoplasia) compared to normal individuals (e.g., Bauman & Kemper, 1990; Courchesne, Yeung-Courchesne, Press, Hesselink, & Jernigan, 1988, Courchesne et al., 1994a). Traditionally, the cerebellum is thought of as the center for motor control and coordination. In a series of papers (e.g., Courchesne, 1987, 1989, 1991; Courchesne et al., 1988, 1994b), Courchesne and his colleagues hypothesized that in addition to its traditional role, the cerebellum might be involved in the ability to coordinate and shift attention to social and environmental stimuli. The authors thus hypothesized that the cerebellar abnormalities found in children with autism may be responsible for their difficulties in following the rapidly changing verbal, gestural, and facial cues present during social interactions. Several behavioral studies support the notion that individuals with autism have deficits in shifting attention between object and interactant dur-

ing social situations, known as "joint attention" (e.g., Kasari, Sigman, Mundy, & Yirmiya, 1990; Mundy, Sigman, & Kasari, 1990; Lewy & Dawson, 1992).

As a result of these findings and others, several researchers have investigated the mechanisms that might "normalize" the attentional patterns in children with autism including increasing social stimulation (e.g., Lewy & Dawson, 1992), requiring attention during play activities (e.g., Pierce & Schreibman, 1995) and reinforcing attention to multiple object cues (e.g., Burke & Cerniglia, 1990).

Biochemical Model and Pharmacotherapy

Most research in biochemical processes in the etiology of autism has focused on the neurotransmitter serotonin. Serotonin is used by the body's arousal system. High levels of blood serotonin that are measured in normal infants have been found to decrease throughout childhood and stabilize in adulthood (Mesibov & Dawson, 1986; Ritvo et al., 1970). However, approximately 30% to 40% of autistic individuals show hyperserotonemia, an elevated level of blood serotonin, throughout life (Freeman & Ritvo, 1984). This failure to show the expected maturational decrease suggests immaturity in the neurological system. Additionally, Campbell and her colleagues (Campbell et al., 1976) have provided some evidence of a relationship between hyperserotonemia and poor intellectual functioning.

Based on the serotonin theory, Ritvo and his colleagues treated children with autism by administering fenfluramine (an anorectic agent) to reduce the levels of blood serotonin (e.g., Geller, Ritvo, Freeman, & Yuwiler, 1982). Improvements following administration of fenfluramine were reported. These included increased eye contact, social awareness, and attention to schoolwork; improved IQ scores; decreased hyperactivity and repetitive behaviors (e.g., hand flapping); and improved sleep patterns (e.g., August, Raz, & Baird, 1985; Ritvo, Freeman, Geller, & Yuwiler, 1983; Ritvo et al., 1984, 1986). However, a recent investigation suggests that fenfluramine use may be associated with several adverse side effects including weight loss, excessive sedation, loose stools and irritability (Campbell et al, 1988). Further, fenfluramine intake had a retarding effect on discrimination learning. Additional research has also suggested that fenfluramine has negative side effects, such as confusion, increased social isolation and self-stimulatory behavior (Piggott, Gdowski, Villanueva, Fischhoff, & Frohman, 1986). In addition to adverse side effects, some reports suggest that fenfluramine is not an effective drug treatment for most autistic patients. In a study by Ekman, Miranda-Linne, Gilberg, and Garle (1989), 20 children with autism were given two daily doses of fenfluramine for 16 weeks. Although serotonin levels decreased by 53% during drug administration, no significant improvement in social relatedness, affectual response, language, or IQ was found. Additional studies have replicated these negative findings (e.g., Duker, Welles, Seys et al., 1991; Sherman, Factor, Swinson et al., 1989). Although initial research reports were encouraging, adverse side effects and recent evidence suggesting minimal or no treatment gains for children who take fenfluramine suggest that this may not be an appropriate treatment approach for many children with autism.

Generally, drug therapy has been criticized for improper usage (e.g., high dosages over long periods of time; no drug holidays), poor drug monitoring, and side effects (e.g., excessive sedation) that interfere with learning. Importantly, when drug treatment is withdrawn, behavioral symptoms often reappear. Finally there is a lack of methodologically sound studies that demonstrate the efficacy of pharmacological treatment, particularly when used in combination with other behavioral treatments (Schreibman, 1988).

The pharmacological treatment of children with autism has had limited success. As no specific cause for autism has been identified, drug treatments have focused on alleviating some of the more disruptive symptoms. A wide variety of drugs have been used to treat these children, including antipsychotics and major tranquilizers such as haloperidol (Haldol) (e.g., Anderson et al., 1984), chlorpromazine (Thorazine) (e.g., Korein, Fish, Shapiro, Gerner, & Levidow, 1971), trifluoperazine (Stelazine) (e.g., Campbell, Green, & Deutsch, 1985), L-dopa (e.g., Ritvo et al.,

1971), and megavitamins (Rimland, Callaway, & Dreyfus, 1978). However, many studies have yielded conflicting findings. Ampheta-mines, for example, may reduce overactivity and improve the attention span of children with autism, but a worsening of other symptoms often occurs (Mesibov & Dawson, 1986). Thus, drugs are not commonly administered to children with autism.

BEHAVIORAL APPROACH TO AUTISM

Behavioral Model

The behavioral approach views the syndrome of autism as a cluster of specific behaviors and has promoted measurable and observable changes in such behaviors. This model suggests that child development consists primarily of the acquisition of behaviors and of stimulus functions, or aspects of the environment that acquire "meanings" for the child (Lovaas & Newsom, 1976; Lovaas, Schreibman, & Koegel, 1974). The behavioral perspective therefore suggests that manipulation of antecedents and consequences to make aspects of the environment meaningful to children with autism. In general, behavioral *deficits* are increased by teaching and systematically reinforcing occurrences, while behavioral *excesses* are the targets of reduction and elimination. The behavioral view of autism thus differs from the traditional conceptualization of the disorder as a "disease." Historically, autism (and other forms of psychopathology) has been viewed as a diagnostic entity. However, this traditional view has not proved useful in that a diagnosis of autism per se does not (a) lead to a specific treatment, (b) facilitate communication between professionals, or (c) predict a specific prognosis.

The failure of the diagnosis to suggest a specific treatment is primarily due to the tremendous heterogeneity in the population labeled as autistic. Because the syndrome, by any definition, comprises several behaviors, children referred to as "autistic" may individually appear quite different. For example, both a verbal echolalic child and a mute, self-injurious child may have a diagnosis of autism, although they manifest quite different levels of functioning. Thus, there is substantial variability in the meaning of autism, and this diagnosis communicates little about any particular child. Consequently, there may be agreement regarding treatment techniques for particular behaviors (e.g., removal of attention for tantrums), but there is a lack of consensus among professionals as to how to treat the *syndrome* of autism as a whole. Finally, the diagnosis of autism does not suggest a differential prognosis. It is known that without treatment most children with autism will not improve (Rutter, 1968) and the general prognosis for these children is very poor. However, some research has demonstrated that many children with autism will improve greatly with treatment (e.g., Lovaas, 1987). Therefore, a diagnosis of autism does not suggest which children will improve and which ones will not. The following section discusses current research in the treatment of children with autism.

Treatment

The literature suggests that the behavioral approach is the only treatment model empirically demonstrated to be effective with children with autism (cf. Egel, Koegel, & Schreibman, 1980; Lovaas et al., 1974; Schreibman & Koegel, 1981). Indeed, a recent study by Lovaas (1987) reported optimistic findings regarding the progress of children with autism as a result of intensive behavioral treatment. In this study, two groups of very young (less than 46 months of age) children with autism were provided with either more than 40 hours weekly (experimental group) or less than 10 hours weekly (control group) of intensive one-to-one behavioral intervention. Both groups received a minimum of 2 years of treatment; a second control group which, did not receive treatment was also included in the study to guard against a sampling or referral bias. Results of this study indicated that 47% of the children receiving the long-term intensive treatment achieved normal intellectual and educational functioning, with normal-range IQ scores and successful first-grade performance in regular public schools. Another 42% of the subjects in this group were placed in aphasia classes and scored in the mildly retarded range. In contrast, subjects in the control

groups fared rather poorly. Only 2% of these children achieved normal functioning, 45% scored in the mildly retarded range and were assigned to aphasia classes, and 53% scored in the severely retarded range and were placed in classes for the autistic/retarded. While these results are promising in that they suggest that some children with autism may become "normal" through comprehensive behavior therapy, they must be interpreted with caution. These findings need to be replicated; additionally, certain methodological problems (e.g., use of contingent aversives in the experimental group but not in the control group) must be addressed. However, these findings clearly demonstrated that children with autism may make significant progress with behavioral-oriented treatment.

Behavioral techniques have a broad basis in the literature, and many have been studied extensively. Because of this strong empirical evidence documenting the effectiveness of the behavioral model, the remainder of this chapter will be devoted to a description and discussion of behavioral intervention with children with autism.

BEHAVIORAL EXCESSES

A great deal of research over the past 50 years has focused on the treatment of behavioral excesses common in autism: aggression, tantrums, self-stimulatory and self-injurious behaviors. Although successful treatment of these problems has been obtained using reinforcement and punishment procedures, these behaviors remain difficult to treat, and a treatment strategy that is effective with one child, may not be effective with another. In addition, ethics considerations have justifiably steered practitioners away from the more restrictive punishment techniques, such as the use of aversives (e.g., forced ingestion of lemon juice following a disruptive act). Researchers and therapists are now faced with the challenge of developing treatment strategies that are minimally intrusive to the child.

Identifying and understanding the variables maintaining maladaptive behavior is the first step toward effective treatment. The approach that focuses on identifying and analyzing environmental variables has come to be known as the "functional analysis model" of assessment and treatment, and is a widely used strategy for the treatment of an array of maladaptive behaviors including, self-injury, aggression, and tantrums. Although this technique has been utilized with both children with and without autism, it has been instrumental in the advancement of nonaversive treatment strategies for children with autism due to the high rates of maladaptive behavior typically found in this population.

Functional Analysis

The primary goal of any functional analysis is to identify the function of maladaptive behavior. Is the child engaging in self-injury to get attention, to escape from a difficult task, or because he or she wants to be left alone? The list of potential answers to explain behavior is endless. Gathering information to answer these questions and others via a functional analysis is typically implemented in three ways: (a) interview, (b) direct observation, and (3) systematic manipulations.

Interview

The simplest approach to learning about behavior occurs through an indirect method of assessment; the interview. In essence, the therapist asks questions to relevant persons (e.g., parent, teacher, caregiver) regarding the nature of the behavior problem as well as surrounding events. An assessment interview focusing on behavioral function should attempt to provide a clear description of (a) the behavior, (b) the situations in which the behavior does and does not occur, (c) antecedent events that may precipitate the behavior, and (d) the typical reactions of others (Iwata, Vollmer, & Zarcone, 1990). This information can be gathered informally or by the use of a formal questionnaire, such as the Functional Analysis Interview (O'Neill, Homer, Albin, Storey, & Sprague, 1990) or Motivation Assessment Scale (Durand & Crimmins, 1988). While interview techniques can be quickly implemented, are inexpensive, and may yield valuable information regarding the functions of maladaptive behavior, some researchers question the validity of information obtained. Unless careful attention is given to the manner in which

questions are posed, the relationship between the informant and child, and the relationship between the informant and interviewer, information can sometimes be misleading. For example, because a child engages in repeated tantrums while in the home, parents may infer that their child engages in tantrums in every environment (when they in fact do not) and thus report inaccurate information during the interview. Nonetheless, interviews are a valuable information-gathering tool and are typically the first form of assessment used when attempting to identify patterns of maladaptive behavior. Many therapists, however, elect to complement this strategy with either a direct observation and/or experimental manipulation to be discussed in the following sections.

Direct Observation

During direct observation, the child is observed at various times of the day while engaging in typical activities. Depending on the amount of time available for assessment, the child may be observed for some or all waking hours of the day. Touchette, MacDonald, and Langer (1985) introduced the "scatterplot" assessment, which utilizes a grid box with time and day on each axis of the box to aid in the collection of information. This technique allows the implementor to chart the frequency of maladaptive behavior during time intervals that coincide with changes in the child's schedule. After several days of scatterplot use, a therapist, parent, or teacher can visually inspect patterns of behavior over time. The goal of this technique is to identify a relationship between the maladaptive behavior and local variables (e.g., settings, time, activities, people present). This assessment places emphasis on antecedents (i.e., what happened immediately prior to a behavior) and setting events (e.g., what general environmental events were present, such as illness) to help determine patterns associated with maladaptive behavior. For example, if after 2 weeks of scatterplot use, it was determined that a particular child exhibited problem behaviors predominantly from 4–6 PM, Monday through Friday (i.e., after school), then additional assessments would focus on trying to figure out what was operating during those times for the child (e.g., what people were present? was the child hungry? bored?). Adaptations of the scatterplot technique have also been used, such as the Functional Analysis Observational Form (FAOF; O'Neill et al., 1990), which require more in depth recording of antecedent events as well as consequent events. Although these techniques are extremely useful, some parents and teachers find that they do not have enough time to implement an extensive observation over long periods.

Systematic Manipulations

If sufficient information was not obtained via the interview and/or observation, a treatment provider may elect to implement a formal manipulation of the environment in order to determine the maintaining variables of maladaptive behavior. Some researchers suggest that implementing a systematic manipulation is not required in every case, if sufficient information can be obtained otherwise (O'Neill et al., 1990), while others would insist that this step is necessary to provide accurate information regarding maladaptive behavior (e.g., Iwata et al., 1990). All would agree, however, that systematic manipulations are a valuable assessment tool and can only enhance subsequent treatment efforts. In order to illustrate this procedure, two seminal research papers (i.e., Carr & Durand, 1985; Iwata, Dorsey, Slifer, Bauman, & Richman, 1982) will serve as references.

In a landmark paper in the area of functional analysis, Iwata et al., (1982) implemented a comprehensive assessment package in order to determine the functional relationships between self-injurious behavior and environmental events. Nine participants were exposed to four experimental conditions in a multi-element experimental design: (a) social disapproval in which the experimenter applied verbal attention contingent upon self-injury to assess attention motivated behavior; (b) academic demand in which the experimenter terminated teaching trials contingent upon self-injury to assess escape motivated behavior; (c) unstructured play was used as a control condition in which the experimenter was present, but demands were absent; and (d) alone in which the individual was placed in a therapy room alone, without access to toys to assess a sensory stimulation motivation. For

six out of the nine subjects, a consistent pattern emerged in which they engaged in higher levels of self-injurious behavior during one of the four conditions. This paper prompted much research interest in the area of functional analysis and gave valuable insights as to how to treat maladaptive behavior.

To demonstrate the importance of environmental variables for the maintenence of behavior problems with children with developmental disabilities, Carr and Durand (1985) manipulated two specific environmental variables: adult attention and task difficulty. Based on parental and teacher report, these two variables were hypothesized to play a critical role in the maintenance of behavior problems for the children in the study. Children were placed in experimental conditions where they received either high (100%) or low (33%) adult attention and high (difficult) or low (easy) task demands. By comparing behavior during the easy task + 100% adult attention to easy task + 33% adult attention conditions, attention-seeking behavior could be identified. That is, the only environmental variable that changed during these two conditions was adult attention, and if child behaviors consistently differ during the two conditions, it is reasonable to assert that attention is an important variable maintaining that behavior. Similarly, by comparing behavior during the easy task + 100% adult attention to difficult task + 100% adult attention, escape motivated behavior could be identified. That is, the only environmental variable that changed during the two conditions was task difficulty, and if child behaviors differ consistently during the two conditions, it is reasonable to assert that task demands is an important variable maintaining that behavior. Children who engaged in problem behaviors during the low adult-attention conditions only, were likely doing so in order to receive adult attention and children who were engaging in high levels of behavior problems during the difficult tasks were likely doing so in order to escape the task. We know this because once attention was reinstated during the high-attention conditions for the attention seeking children, behavior problems were virtually eliminated. Similarly, once task demands were lowered for the escape-motivated children, problem behavior also decreased.

Although the use of functional analysis techniques are extremely helpful to the treatment provider, it is important to note, however, that some child behaviors may have multiple functions (e.g., to escape task demands and to get attention) and/or unclear functions (i.e., a functional analysis does not reveal behavior function).

Treatment Programs Based on Functional Analysis Assessment

As the above discussion suggests, maladaptive behavior can be learned in a variety of ways. Thus, attempting to treat all behaviors of a similar type (e.g., all tantrums) with the same intervention (e.g., time-out) may not always be effective. Once maintaining contingencies and associated variables for maladaptive behavior have been identified through a functional analysis, then the treatment provider is ready to develop a intervention program that is individualized for a specific child. The goal of this intervention is to develop techniques that will eliminate, reverse, or alter the variables that are currently maintaining the maladaptive behavior. Although there are myriad reasons that may explain maladaptive behavior in children with autism, research indicates three major recurring themes: attention-motivated behavior, escape-motivated behavior, and self-stimulatory–motivated behavior hereafter called "automatic reinforcement." What follows are examples of treatment strategies that have been adapted from functional analysis findings and can be applied to behaviors motivated by attention, escape and automatic reinforcement.

Functional Communication Training

Once the "function" of a behavior problem is identified, then it becomes possible to replace that behavior problem with a communicative equivalent. For example, teaching a child to tap adults on the shoulder when she wants attention to replace her tantrum behavior would be considered a functional communication-training technique only if the child engaged in tantrums to get attention. If the child engaged in tantrum behavior to get out of a task or

because she was bored, then teaching her to tap adults on the shoulder would not be an appropriate treatment approach because this behavior would not be a functionally equivalent response for her. This technique has been used successfully by many researchers to alleviate and/or eliminate severe behavior problems including self-injurious behavior, self-stimulatory behaviors, tantrums, and aggression (e.g., Carr & Durand, 1985; Durand & Carr, 1991; Horner & Day, 1991). An important consideration for the success of functional communication training appears to be finding the most effective "response match." That is, the newly trained behavior should elicit the same environmental response as the maladaptive behavior. In addition, the communicative act should be mastered easily by the child and be highly effective at eliciting the necessary response from the environment. The following vignette will illustrate the importance of finding appropriate response matches:

Lisa is a ten-year-old girl with autism possessing some verbal skills who throws herself on the floor, kicks and screams during difficult tasks. After functional analysis assessments, it was hypothesized that Lisa engaged in maladaptive behavior in order to escape from task demands. It was decided that Lisa would be taught to ask for a different assignment when the task was too difficult by saying "I don't want to do this, can I do something else?" After several months, however, Lisa did not utilize the communicated phrase at the appropriate times. Additional observations suggested that this phrase was too long and labor intensive for Lisa to use and thus she was taught a different phrase "finished." Lisa quickly began to use the communicative phrase and her maladaptive behavior decreased. Note that it was initially faster and easier for Lisa to engage in maladaptive behavior than to use the taught phrase. However, once Lisa was taught a communicative strategy that would allow her to get what she wanted from the environment as easily (and probably easier) as her tantrum, she elected to engage in that behavior instead.

The individual also need not be verbal; actions, such as tapping someone on the shoulder, the use of signs, and assistive devices have also been shown to be effective techniques (e.g., Bird, Dores, Moniz, &

Robinson, 1989; Durand & Kishi, 1987; Horner & Budd, 1985). In addition, this strategy works well to replace the function of attention- seeking (Durand & Carr, 1992), escape seeking (Horner & Day, 1991), and self-stimulatory-seeking behaviors (e.g., Durand & Carr, 1987).

Extinction and Time Out

If adult attention is determined to be the maintaining variable for maladaptive behavior, then a typically effective strategy for eliminating such behavior is the use of procedures that break the behavior-environmental response relationship. The planned ignoring or "extinction" of the maladaptive behavior may be achieved by discontinuing attention to the target behaviors (e.g., Lovaas & Simmons, 1969). This strategy introduces nothing into the environment that may inadvertently reinforce maladaptive behavior. Completely ignoring a child, however, may be difficult for some parents and teachers. If the use of planned ignoring is too difficult, then caregivers may elect to implement a time-out procedure where the child is placed in exclusion for a brief period of time, usually no more than 20 minutes (White, Nielsen, & Johnson, 1972). The philosophy is still the same: adult attention (or anything else in the environment that affects the child's behavior) is removed and thus not maintaining the behavior problem. Notice that if a treatment provider applied this technique with a child who is engaging in maladaptive behavior in order to escape from a difficult task, ignoring the child (and thus not requiring him/her to do work) and/or time-out will serve to increase the rate of the problem behavior.

Differential Reinforcement of Other Behavior (DRO)

Differential reinforcement of alternative replacement behaviors becomes possible when the function of a maladaptive behavior is known and again is typically an effective treatment when attention is determined to be the maintaining variable. Treatment strategies are designed to keep this function for the individual, but to replace it with a behav-

ior that is more socially acceptable and adaptive. To illustrate, assume a child is engaging in maladaptive behavior in order to receive adult attention. Using a DRO procedure, an adult applies attention to the child contingent on an interval with no instances of the target behavior. If the child's behavior problems are motivated by attempts to gain adult attention, he or she will learn that maladaptive behavior delays adult attention. Essentially, DRO procedures involve systematically providing reinforcement when the child is not engaging in maladaptive behavior (e.g., Favell, McGimsey, & Jones, 1978).

Relaxation Training

When a functional analysis suggests that frustration induced by a difficult task may be the causative stimulus for inappropriate behavior, teaching children with autism responses that are incompatible with their frustration (i.e., relaxation) may serve to reduce that frustration. In a recent study, Charlop-Christy and Greenberg (1996) taught a child with autism to engage in a variety of relaxation behaviors such as deep breathing and relaxing shoulders during times of high anxiety for the child. Results indicated that relaxation training was an effective technique for reducing the behavior problems of this child.

Sensory Extinction and Differential Reinforcement of Incompatible Behavior (DRI)

Identification of auto reinforcement as the maintaining variable for a behavior problem leaves the treatment provider with one of the most difficult behaviors to reduce. Because sensory consequences can not be eliminated if the individual engages in the preferred behavior, techniques have centered around preventing the behavior from occurring and/or masking or attenuating the sensations produced by the behavior. For example, Rincover, Cook, Peoples, and Packer (1979) carpeted tabletops to reduce auditory stimulation of object-spinning and placed gloves on a child's hands to reduce stimulation from hand rubbing. These types of sensory extinction procedures have been used in conjunction with DRI procedures that teach the child behaviors that are incompatible with their stimulatory behavior followed by reinforcement for engagement in that behavior. For example, assume a child's preferred stimulatory behavior is hand-flapping. An appropriate DRI procedure might be to teach the child to draw with markers, use a yo-yo or play with a ball, behaviors that would eliminate the opportunity for hand-flapping. In addition, the caregiver might apply reinforcement to this new behavior with preferred items, such as food or praise.

BEHAVIORAL DEFICITS

The general categories of behavioral deficits are speech and language, attention, motivation, and social behavior and play. A voluminous amount of research addressing these areas has been conducted in the past decade, and a variety of prompting procedures and other methods of aiding acquisition have been developed and have greatly improved our effectiveness in remediating these deficits.

Speech and Language

The failure of children with autism to acquire language and to use speech in a communicative manner is one of the most debilitating aspects of autism. As mentioned earlier, approximately 50% of children with autism are functionally mute (Rimland, 1964). These children lack receptive as well as expressive speech. Because research has indicated that the acquisition of speech prior to age 5 suggests a more favorable clinical prognosis for the autistic child (e.g., Eisenberg & Kanner, 1956; Lovaas, 1987; Rutter, 1968), most therapy time is often spent on language acquisition. Detailed descriptions of behavioral techniques for teaching functionally mute children with autism have been provided by Fay and Schuler (1980) and Lovaas (1977). The reader is referred to these references for more detailed information, as a comprehensive discussion of language training is beyond the scope of this chapter. Following is a brief description of the initial steps of such language training.

An early procedure that continues to be used to teach speech is based on imitation. The child is taught to imitate vocalizations until a verbal imitative repertoire is acquired. Initially, the speech-training program consists of a series of steps in which finer discriminations are required of the child. For example, during initial stages, any vocalizations made by the child are reinforced so as to increase the frequency of vocalizations. When vocalizations are occurring at a high rate, the child's vocalizations are reinforced only if emitted within 5 seconds of the therapist's vocalization. For example, the therapist might say "ah" to which the child must emit any sound within 5 seconds. This establishes a temporal discrimination and for the first time the child's vocal behavior is under the control of the therapist's vocal behavior. Through shaping, the child is required to imitate the therapist's vocalization more and more closely until the child repeats the therapist's vocalization exactly. Initially, any sound that resembles the verbal stimulus is reinforced. Across progressive trials, only sounds that more closely approximate the therapist's model are reinforced.

Once such a repertoire is acquired, it is then necessary to transfer stimulus control of the imitated vocalization from the therapist's model to the appropriate object. That is, rather than imitate the therapist's model "ball," the child is taught to say "ball" when the appropriate referent (ball) is presented. Thus, the meaning of the verbal response is taught. The child is taught to label objects both receptively and expressively. With receptive labeling, the child must provide a nonverbal response but is not required to verbalize the label (i.e., "Give me the ball"). Expressive labeling requires the child to actually say the label (i.e., "What is this?" "Ball"). Initially, prompting procedures are used. Prompting procedures for receptive labeling tasks usually consist of a therapist pointing at or manually guiding the child's hand to the requested object; the prompt is gradually faded out over successive trials. For expressive labeling tasks prompts typically consist of providing the child with the correct answer (the therapist's model) and allowing him or her to imitate the vocalization in the presence of the object. This prompt is gradually faded until the presence of the object elicits the vocalization. For example, the therapist would provide the answer to the question (e.g., "What is this?" "Ball") and then gradually fade out the presentation of the prompt "ball" to the presentation of the /b/ sound. The therapist may then whisper the /b/ sound until it is no longer necessary. This prompting technique is also used to teach the child to speak in full sentences (e.g., "What is this?" "This is a ball."). Prompts may be similarly faded out until the child can answer "This is a ball" when asked, "What is this?"

Despite the success of these procedures, many children with autism remain without vocal speech. Researchers have explored the use of sign language as an alternative communication system for these children. The interested reader is referred to a series of studies by Carr and his colleagues (e.g., Carr 1979; Carr & Kologinsky, 1983; Carr, Kologinsky, & Leff-Simon, 1987).

Another language intervention program for children with autism is the natural language paradigm (NLP) developed by Koegel and his colleagues (e.g., Koegel, O'Dell, & Koegel, 1987). NLP is conducted during short play sessions in which the therapist and child play together with a variety of toys and activities. During a session, the therapist models a variety of appropriate responses and provides numerous opportunities for the child to imitate. All attempts to communicate verbally are reinforced with access to a toy and with praise. Thus, this program incorporates specific variables that closely approximate normal language interactions (e.g., turn taking, sharing, natural consequences) and increase autistic children's motivation to respond (e.g., novel stimuli, task variation, direct reinforcers). Koegel et al. (1987) report that while the traditional discrete-trial language-training procedure, similar to the one previously described resulted in a low level of imitative and spontaneous speech in two nonverbal children with autism, NLP training led to rapid increases in imitation and spontaneous speech. Importantly, generalization to settings outside the clinic occurred following NLP training.

An extension of these findings has been reported by Laski, Charlop, and Schreibman (1988). As a means to further enhance generalization, parents of verbal and nonverbal children with autism were trained to use NLP during play sessions at home. Specifically, parents were trained to criterion on four dimensions of NLP: (a) reinforcing the child's attempts (i.e., praising child's vocal attempts and providing contingent access to toys), (b) turn taking (i.e., exchanging toys back and forth), (c) task variation (i.e., frequently changing toys or words/phrases), and (d) shared control (permitting child to choose toy and or words to be used). Parents were instructed to conduct daily 15-minute sessions of NLP at home. Following training in a clinic (experimental) setting, generalization probes were conducted in three nontraining settings: structured free-play settings at the clinic and at home, and in a less structured setting in the clinic waiting room. The results of this investigation indicated that parents readily learned to use NLP to teach their children speech. Additionally, following NLP training, both nonverbal and verbal children increased the frequency of their imitations, answers, and spontaneous speech. Importantly, generalization of speech gains across nontraining settings was observed. These findings are important in that they demonstrate the efficacy of NLP as a speech and language training program and the feasibility of teaching parents to use the program to teach their children speech and improve generalization.

As mentioned earlier, many children with autism do speak. However, their speech is predominantly echolalic, the meaningless repetition of words previously heard. Because of the presence of such speech, the procedures for teaching speech to echolalic children differ from those described for teaching mute children. In the case of the echolalic child, the goal of speech training is to teach the child to discriminate between appropriate and inappropriate echolalic utterances and to use speech in a communicative fashion (Fay & Schuler, 1980).

Several prompting procedures have been designed to eliminate echolalic speech (e.g., Lovaas, Varni, Koegel, & Lorsch, 1977). For example, the therapist can present a picture of a ball, say "That's a ball," and wait until the child echoes, "That's a ball." Over successive trials the prompt would gradually be faded out (e.g., "That's a b__") until stimulus control was transferred from the verbal prompt to the picture of the ball; thus, upon presentation of the picture, the child says, "That's a ball." In another procedure, Freeman, Ritvo, and Miller (1975) provided an answer-first/question-last paradigm to take advantage of the child's echolalia while teaching appropriate speech. For example, the therapist would present a picture and say, "Sitting. What is the boy doing?" When the child started to echo he or she would be presented with reinforcers immediately after saying "Sitting," but before he or she had a chance to continue and echo the question.

Carr and his colleagues (1975) determined that one factor that influenced the occurrence of echolalia was the "comprehensibility" of the verbal stimulus. In this study, when verbal children with autism were presented with nonsense phrases, they would echo the verbal stimulus; however, when presented with a stimulus for which they had a response (discriminative stimulus), the child would respond appropriately. Additionally, when the children were taught the appropriate responses to verbal stimuli their echolalia ceased. As it would be impossible to teach responses to every novel verbal stimulus, Schreibman and Carr (1978) taught the children a generalized verbal response to previously echoed questions. When asked such a question, the children were taught to say, "I don't know," an appropriate verbal response common in nonhandicapped children.

Although the above procedures are designed to decrease the echolalic speech of children with autism, one study has demonstrated how echolalia may be used as an advantage to teach children with autism appropriate speech. Instead of eliminating echolalia, Charlop (1983) designed a procedure that utilized echolalia to teach receptive labeling. In this procedure, the therapist verbally labeled one of two objects. The child was then allowed the opportunity to echo this verbalization. The experimenter then placed the objects before the child and labeled the object again, and the child handed the experimenter an object. For example, the therapist would say, "boat," wait for the child to echo "boat," then present the toy boat and car and again say "boat" and allow the child to select the correct object. Charlop (1983) suggests that by echoing the word "boat," the children provided their own discriminative stimulus before responding manually, thus facilitating acquisition and generalization of object labels. These findings suggest that echolalia may be a useful tool in the treatment of children with autism.

The techniques for language acquisition and remediation described above are typically employed in a highly structured therapeutic environment. Although these techniques have been successful, speech remains an extremely difficult and complex behavior to teach. Language responses acquired in therapeutic training settings are often used in a rote, mechanical manner, and may be nonfunctional in more natural environments (Halle, 1982). Additionally, language use often fails to occur outside of the training environment. Therefore, an important and promising area of research has focused on teaching language under more natural conditions to promote spontaneous, generalized language use. Importantly, these procedures are designed to refine and naturalize the children's speech. Thus, these procedures focus not only on the natural environment per se but also on the use of the natural environment to facilitate more sophisticated and generalized use of speech.

One such procedure that has been very effective in teaching spontaneous speech is time delay (e.g., Halle, Baer, & Spradlin, 1981; Halle, Marshall, & Spradlin, 1979). This procedure consists of transferring stimulus control of an appropriate response from the therapist's prompt (e.g., saying "cookie") to the presentation of a stimulus (i.e., a cookie). Generally, this is accomplished by presenting the stimulus and modeling the correct verbal response; gradually, the presentation of the prompt is delayed (e.g., in 2-second increments) until the child anticipates the prompt and speaks spontaneously.

The effectiveness of this procedure was demonstrated by Charlop, Schreibman, and Thibodeau (1985), who taught seven children with autism to request desired items spontaneously. In this study, the experimenter presented a highly preferred object (e.g., held up a cookie) and immediately said, "I want a cookie." If the child correctly imitated this model, the object was provided as a reinforcer. After three consecutive trials of correct imitation, a graduated time-delay procedure was implemented. Specifically, after the presentation of the object, a 2-second delay occurred before the experimenter modeled the appropriate request. Child requests made prior to the model and imitative responses were considered correct and were reinforced by providing the preferred object. Contingent upon three correct responses, the delay was increased by 2-second increments until a 10-second delay had been reached. Following time delay, generalization probes were presented. Results of this investigation indicated that all of the children learned to request items spontaneously using the time-delay procedure. Also, generalization of spontaneous speech was demonstrated across unfamiliar settings, persons, situations, and untrained objects, thus providing additional support for the efficacy of this procedure. A series of studies by Charlop and Schreibman and their colleagues have assessed the transfer of stimulus control using more obvious physical referents (e.g., cookie) to less obvious cues such as certain actions, settings, or temporal cues. In one such study, the time-delay procedure was also successfully used to teach children with autism to provide verbal expressions of affection spontaneously (e.g., "I love you") in the presence of an action (a hug) (e.g., Charlop & Walsh, 1986).

This procedure has also been effective in promoting setting-cued speech. For example, children with autism were successfully taught to make spontaneous requests in appropriate environments, such as "I want to swing" at the playground, or requesting a cookie in the kitchen (Schreibman, Charlop, & Tryon, 1981). In another study, Charlop and Trasowech (1991) taught parents of children with autism to implement the time-delay procedure at home so as to increase their children's spontaneous speech. In this study, children with autism were taught to speak spontaneously in response to temporal cues. That is, parents implemented the time-delay procedure at specific times throughout the day to teach contextually appropriate speech. For example, the children were taught to say "Good morning, Mom" upon waking; "May I have a snack please?" after school; and "Goodnight, Mom" at bedtime. Results indicated that parents effectively employed the procedure to increase their children's spontaneous speech. Importantly, the children's spontaneous speech occurred at the appropriate times of day but in a variety of settings, suggesting that the children's behavior was not dependent upon a specific location.

Another promising line of research has investigated the effects of modeling in facilitating the speech and language skills of children with autism.

While conflicting findings regarding the efficacy of modeling have been reported (e.g., Charlop & Walsh, 1986; Varni, Lovaas, Koegel, & Everett, 1979), a few studies (e.g., Charlop, Schreibman, & Tryon, 1983; Coleman & Stedman, 1974; Egel, Richman, & Koegel, 1981) have demonstrated that children with autism can benefit from observation of peer models. In one study, four low-functioning children with autism learned to receptively label objects through observation of an autistic peer model (Charlop et al., 1983). Results indicated that peer modeling was an effective procedure; additionally, as compared to a traditional discrete-trial approach, generalization and maintenance of correct responding were superior in the peer-modeling condition. This line of research has recently been extended by Charlop and Milstein (1989), who assessed the efficacy of using video modeling to increase the conversational speech of children with autism. In this study, verbal children with autism observed a videotape of two adult models engaging in conversations about specific toys. Results indicated that the children learned appropriate conversations through video modeling and generalized these skills to other topics of conversation other than those that were modeled. In general, the results of these studies suggest that modeling may be an effective procedure for improving the speech of children with autism.

Attention

One of the most serious problems displayed by children with autism is their lack of responsiveness to the environment. These children may not appear to notice salient features of their environment, such as comings and goings of people; indeed, as discussed earlier, these children often have early histories of suspected blindness or deafness. Conversely, children with autism may be overly sensitive to low-level stimulation (e.g., shadows from sunlight, turning of a book page). The failure of these children to effectively utilize environmental stimulation plus their great difficulty in learning new behaviors has led to extensive research in the area of attentional deficits; it is hoped that effective treatment procedures will ultimately be developed.

As previously discussed, when children with autism are presented with a learning situation in which response to multiple cues is required, they characteristically respond to a very restricted number of the available cues. This unique pattern of responding, deemed "stimulus overselectivity" was first identified by Lovaas and his colleagues (Lovaas, Schreibman, Koegel, & Rehm, 1971). In this study, autistic, retarded, and nonhandicapped children were trained to respond to a complex stimulus comprising a visual, an auditory, and a tactile component. Following this training, each component was presented separately to determine how much control it had acquired over the children's responses. Surprisingly, results indicated that while the non-handicapped children responded equally to all three component cues, the children with autism responded to only one (either auditory or visual). The retarded children responded between these two extremes. Furthermore, subsequent training demonstrated that the children with autism could learn to respond to previously nonfunctional cues, thus suggesting that the problem lay in responding to the cues in the context of other cues rather than in a particular sensory modality. The phenomenon of stimulus overselectivity has been demonstrated to occur across different sensory modalities (e.g., Lovaas, Litrownik, & Mann, 1971; Lovaas & Schreibman, 1971) and within a single modality (e.g., Koegel & Wilhelm, 1973; Reynolds, Newsom, & Lovaas, 1974). Additionally, the presence of overselectivity may be more a function of low mental age than of autism per se (Schreibman, Kohlenberg, & Britten, 1986).

The implications of overselective responding are serious. Consider, for example, the fact that most learning situations require a response to multiple cues. The inability of children with autism to respond accurately in these situations severely interferes with learning. Overselectivity has been implicated as a variable influencing language acquisition (Lovaas, Schreibman, Koegel, & Rehm, 1971; Reynolds et al., 1974; Schreibman et al., 1986), social behavior (Schreibman & Lovaas, 1973), observational learning (Varni et al., 1979), prompting (Koegel & Rincover, 1976; Schreibman, 1975), and generalization (Rincover & Koegel, 1975).

Having identified the existence and parameters of stimulus overselectivity, researchers have focused on ameliorating the effects of this attentional deficit. One approach has involved attempting to directly remediate the overselectivity by teaching the children to respond to multiple cues. A second approach has involved developing teaching strategies that allow the children to learn despite the overselective attention. Both of these approaches will be discussed in turn.

As research suggested that, under some conditions, the overselectivity effect disappeared (e.g., Schreibman, Koegel, & Craig, 1977), it thus appeared likely that overselective responding could be changed. Indeed, studies by Koegel and Schreibman (1977) and Schreibman, Charlop, and Koegel (1982) demonstrated that overselective children with autism could learn to respond to multiple cues if trained on a conditional discrimination. For example, Schreibman, Charlop, and Koegel (1982) demonstrated that overselective children with autism failed to learn difficult discrimination tasks when provided with a pointing prompt; however, after the children were trained to respond to multiple cues on several consecutive conditional discriminations, they could learn from such a prompt. The conditional discriminations used in this investigation are presented in Figure 9.1. Upon failure to use a pointing prompt, each child was presented with a training stimulus set until criterion was reached. Testing stimuli were then introduced to determine whether the training discrimination had been learned on the basis of only one cue (i.e., overselective responding). If this was the case, training on the test discrimination continued until the child was responding on the basis of multiple cues. Training then began on the next set of training stimuli until the child learned two consecutive training discriminations without demonstrating overselective responding. Results indicated that although the children had previously "overselected" to the pointing prompt and failed to attend to the stimulus materials, they were able, after multiple-cue training, to benefit from the prompting procedure. Importantly, these findings suggested that children with autism could learn from a more traditional teaching technique, and may be generally able to respond to their

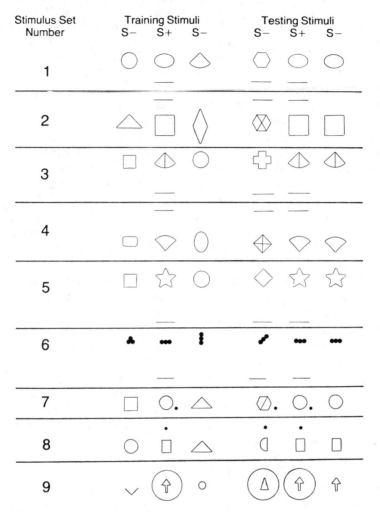

Figure 9.1. Examples of training and testing stimulus sets to teach response to multiple cues.

Source: "Teaching autistic children to use extra-stimulus prompts" by L. Schreibman, M. H. Charlop, and R. L. Koegel, 1982, *Journal of Experimental Child Psychology, 33,* pp. 475–491. Copyright 1982 by Academic Press. Reprinted by permission.

environment in a manner more similar to that of nonhandicapped children.

Although the above approach is encouraging in that it suggests a treatment for overselectivity, this procedure has not been successful with all children with autism. Thus, special techniques have been developed for these children so that they may learn despite their overselective responding. As mentioned, one frequently used teaching technique is prompting. This involves adding an extra cue to guide the child to the correct response. Examples of such "extra-stimulus" prompts (Schreibman, 1975) include pointing to the correct answer, underlining, or using different colors. These prompts are commonly used and then gradually faded out until the child responds correctly without the prompt. Unfortunately, in the case of overselective children with autism, the total removal of an extra-stimulus prompt can be problematic in that the child may overselect to the prompt and fail to respond to the training stimulus.

Schreibman (1975) developed a "within-stimulus" prompting procedure, a prompting strategy that essentially took advantage of the children's tendency toward overselective responding. A within-stimulus prompt involves exaggerating a relevant feature of the S+ (correct) choice in a discrimination; this exaggeration is then gradually faded until the feature is again in the normal form (Schreibman, 1975). Thus, the child need only attend to the relevant component and not to multiple cues. For example, a within-stimulus prompting procedure for teaching the discrimination of " X versus X" is presented in Figure 9.2. The relevant cue for the discrimination of these two stimuli is the vertical versus horizontal dots. The "X" is redundant. Thus, the first step in within-stimulus prompting is to pretrain using an exaggerated presentation of the S+, the horizontal dots (Part A, Step 1). Only the horizontal dots are presented in this step to ensure that the child responds only on the basis of this cue. Once the child learns this step, the vertical dots (S–) are slowly faded (Steps 2 through 5). The child is now reliably discriminating S+ from S–. The exaggerated size of the dots is then gradually faded to their normal size (Part B). Finally, the redundant component of the discrimination ("X") is slowly faded (Part C).

There has been a good deal of research on improving the attentional deficits found in this population. Although results of these studies are encouraging, the procedures described are tedious and limited in potential use. Additional research in this area is needed to effect widespread changes in the children's functioning by eliminating overselective responding to the environment.

Motivation

One of the major obstacles in the treatment of children with autism is their pervasive lack of motivation to learn. These children seem to be motivated only by the most primary of reinforcers, such as food or avoidance of pain. As these children rarely respond to reinforcers such as praise or achievement, teachers and therapists have typically resorted to the use of primary reinforcers to increase motivation. There are several limitations to this approach, however.

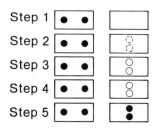

Figure 9.2. An example of a within-stimulus prompt fading progression to teach the discrimination "X versus X." (A) Fade in S–. (B) Fade out size and position prompts. (C) Fade in redundant components.

Source: Adapted from "Effects of within-stimulus and extra-stimulus prompting on discrimination learning in autistic children by L. Schreibman, 1975, *Journal of Applied Behavior Analysis, 8,* pp. 91–112. Copyright 1975 by the Society for the Experimental Analysis of Behavior, Inc. Reprinted by permission.

Importantly, reinforcers such as food or drink may become artificial for some older children, since they may be only used in certain settings (e.g., a clinic environment). Also, generalization of treatment effects may be limited because these reinforcers are not available in settings outside of therapy (generalization). Finally, a common problem is that the children may quickly become satiated and cease to work.

As a result of these problems, one area of research has focused on identifying ways to enhance the effectiveness of available food reinforcers.

One approach, suggested by Egel (1981), is to prevent or delay satiation by presenting a variety of food reinforcers, rather than the same reinforcer, during learning of new tasks. Egel (1981) demonstrated that children with autism satiated more rapidly when constant reinforcers were presented for correct responding than when reinforcers were varied. Further, the children responded more rapidly when varied reinforcers were presented. Litt and Schreibman (1981) found that in addition to varying reinforcers, reinforcer effectiveness was further enhanced by pairing a particular reinforcer to a particular training stimulus. For example, during a receptive labeling task, correct responses to "Point to the ball" were always reinforced with a piece of cookie, while correct responses to "Point to the car" were always reinforced with a raisin. Compared to a varied condition (e.g., Egel, 1981) this stimulus-specific reinforcement led to faster learning (as measured by trials to criterion).

Another method designed to increase food reinforcer effectiveness was suggested by Koegel and Williams (1980). These investigators demonstrated that if a reinforcer was obtained as a natural part of the correct response sequence, it was more effective than if it was presented in an independent manner. For example, when the concepts "in" and "under" were being taught, the reinforcers were placed in the box and under the box, respectively, thus leading directly to acquisition of the reinforcer. This direct response-reinforcer relationship resulted in faster learning than an indirect response-reinforcer relationship, where the child was handed a food reinforcer following a correct response. Thus, a number of efficient methods for enhancing the effectiveness of available food reinforcers have been devised.

An alternative approach to increasing the motivation of children with autism has been to develop new, salient reinforcers. As previously discussed, the sensory or perceptual reinforcers provided by self-stimulation have been demonstrated to be highly salient reinforcers (e.g., Lovaas et al., 1987; Rincover, Newsom, Lovaas, & Koegel, 1977). Rincover and his colleagues (1977) studied the properties of sensory stimulation for these children. The preferred sensory stimulus for each child was identified and then used as a reinforcer for correct responding on a learning task. For example, contingent on correct response, brief presentations of the child's preferred sensory event (e.g., music) were presented. Results indicated that the use of sensory reinforcers produced high levels of responding that were durable over time. Importantly, if some satiation to a specific sensory event (e.g., a certain song) occurred, a minor change in that event (e.g., a different song) led to the recovery of a high rate of responding.

In another strategy for increasing motivation, Charlop, Kurtz, and Casey, (1990) assessed the efficacy of using the self-stimulatory and aberrant behavior (e.g., echolalia) of children with autism as reinforcing events. In a series of three experiments, reinforcer conditions of self-stimulation, delayed echolalia and obsessive behavior were compared with food reinforcer and varied (food/aberrant behavior) reinforcer conditions. Interestingly, sessions in which self-stimulation was briefly permitted contingent on correct response were associated with the highest task performance. Poorest task performance occurred during sessions of the food condition. Importantly, ancillary measures of the occurrence of aberrant and off-task behaviors demonstrated that there were no negative side effects of using self-stimulation as a reinforcer.

Another approach to the motivation problem has focused on the effects of repeated failure experiences. That is, frequent incorrect responding when attempting a learning task may be a significant factor in deficient levels of motivation. To assess this effect, Koegel and Egel (1979) investigated the influence of correct versus incorrect task completion on the motivation of children with autism to respond. Importantly, they found that children with autism responded in a manner similar to normal children. When children with autism worked on tasks at which they were typically unsuccessful, their attempts to respond (i.e., motivation) generally decreased. However, when procedures designed to maximize correct responding (and the receipt of reinforcers) were implemented, the children's attempts to respond on these tasks increased. This study demonstrated the importance of success-induced motivation.

In a desire to further increase motivation levels of children with autism to learn new tasks, subsequent studies have carefully analyzed and manipulated various features of the learning situation. Dunlap and Koegel (1980), for example, demonstrated that the presentation of new tasks interspersed with the presentation of previously learned (maintenance) tasks resulted in better performance than when the traditional format of massed trials of a single new task was used. Dunlap (1984) further demonstrated that learning of a new task was facilitated by the interspersal of maintenance tasks only—not by acquisition tasks. Although these studies manipulated antecedent variables as a means of improving the children's motivation to respond, Charlop, Kurtz, and Milstein (1993) assessed the effects of reinforcement contingencies in conjunction with task interspersal procedures on the acquisition of new tasks. These researchers suggested that when food reinforcers were presented for interspersed maintenance tasks (a typical motivation-enhancing procedure), the density of reinforcement favored the maintenance tasks rather than the new one. Thus, children presented with many more food reinforcers for previously acquired tasks may not be motivated to learn a new, more difficult task. In a comparison of various reinforcement contingencies for interspersed tasks, these researchers demonstrated that the learning of new tasks occurred more rapidly when either praise or no reinforcers were presented for interspersed maintenance tasks. Thus, performance was further enhanced by providing schedules of reinforcement that favored the acquisition task.

An additional means of enhancing the motivation of children with autism is to allow them to have some control over the learning situation. Specifically, by giving children with autism some choice as to topic of conversation, stimulus materials to be used, or activities to be engaged in, interest and motivation may be increased. For example, Koegel et al. (1987) demonstrated that allowing children with autism to select instructional stimuli and share materials and tasks with the therapist resulted in more spontaneous communication by the children and decreased avoidance. Similarly, inci-dental teaching procedures (e.g., Hart & Risley, 1974), which consist of arranging the natural environment to attract children to desired materials and activities, rely on child-initiated interactions to obtain access to desired reinforcers. When modified for children with autism, these procedures have been successful in teaching the children sign language (Carr & Kologinsky, 1983), receptive object labels (McGee, Krantz, Mason, & McClannahan, 1983), preposition use (McGee, Krantz, & McClannahan, 1985), and reading skills (McGee, Krantz, & McClannahan, 1986). Thus, these studies suggest that the sharing of control, topics, and materials in learning situations may serve to increase the motivation of children with autism to respond or partici-pate in various activities.

Social Behavior and Play

One of the hallmark features of autism is the children's severe withdrawal from the social environment. Characteristically, these children avoid eye contact, affection, and interaction with others; they also engage in solitary, stereotyped play. Many researchers (e.g., Ferster, 1961; Lovaas & Newsom, 1976) have noted the difficulty involved in establishing meaningful social reinforcers for many children with autism. The focus of recent research has been on structuring the natural environment to teach children with autism behaviors that may lead to more social responsiveness and the establishment of social reinforcers. Generally, treatment strategies for the social deficits found in autism can be broken down into three main approaches.

Integration and Peer Initiation Training

Many researchers have focused on integrating children with autism with handicapped and nonhandi-capped peers in natural settings. A series of studies by Strain and his colleagues (e.g., Odom, Hoyson, Jamieson, & Strain, 1985; Odom & Strain, 1984, 1986; Strain, 1983; Strain, Kerr, & Ragland, 1979) have demonstrated the efficacy of this approach as a means of increasing the initiations and social inter-actions of children with autism. Typically, socially competent peers are taught to initiate interactions by saying, for example, "Let's go play," and handing the autistic child a toy. Using such forms of peer-mediated social initiations, large increases in positive social behavior have been observed. Additionally, methods of increasing the social behavior of children with autism in integrated settings have been facilitated by teacher prompts (Odom & Strain, 1986).

Prompting/Modeling Procedures

Procedures that focus on providing prompts to the child with autism as a cue to initiate or maintain interactions have had success in both the classroom and home environment. In a recent study, Krantz, McDuff, and McClannahan (1993) taught four children with autism to initiate social interactions using a script-fading procedure. Initially, participants in this study relied on written prompts (e.g., "What did you do today?") to initiate conversations with peers during an art project. Eventually prompts were faded (e.g., "What did") until only a blank piece of paper was used as a prompt. Scripts have also been used successfully in the improvement of other complex social behaviors, such as socio-dramatic play (e.g., Goldstein & Cisar, 1992).

In another prompting procedure, self-management, children with autism are taught to self-monitor their own behavior and administer their own reward. In a study by Koegel and Frea (1993), two children with autism were taught to increase their positive social behaviors (e.g., eye contact, appropriate conversation topics) via a self-management procedure. During self-management training, participants were taught to identify the presence or absence of a particular target behavior (e.g., eye contact). Correct independent identification of the presence of the target behavior afforded the child access to a reinforcer (e.g., toy). Results of this study indicated that this procedure is effective at producing generalized, durable social behavior change and may be an appropriate technique to use in school settings.

Video-modeling techniques have also shown to be efficacious for increasing the social and play behaviors of children with autism. Charlop and colleagues taught children with autism cooperative

play skills (Charlop, Milstein, & Moore, 1989) and independent play (Charlop, Spitzer, & Kurtz, 1990) via video modeling. In these studies, adult models demonstrated various examples of the target behavior (e.g., playing a board game). Following the presentation of video modeling tapes, all children with autism who participated in these studies showed increased levels of play competency. In addition, acquisition of new skills learned via video modeling typically occurred quickly (e.g., after watching the videotape two or three times), and generalized to new settings and new training stimuli.

Naturalistic Strategies

A naturalistic strategy can be loosely defined as any technique that can be conducted in loosely controlled environments (e.g., a playground), utilizes shared control (e.g., turn taking), and multiple exemplars (e.g., many toy materials). Recently, naturalistic interventions, such as NLP described earlier, have been utilized to enhance complex play skills (e.g., symbolic and socio-dramatic) in children with autism. Current research examining symbolic play and autism has found that these children perform fewer symbolic play actions and less complex actions than do typical children matched for language ability (e.g., Lewis & Boucher, 1988). Briefly, symbolic play can be defined as a child using one object as if it were another (e.g., using a block as an airplane), attributing attributes to an object that it does not possess (e.g., describing a toy stove as 'hot'), or pretending an absent object is present (e.g., pantomime). Deficits in this type of creative play could severely impact a child's ability to interact with other children. In a recent study (Stahmer, 1995), seven children with autism were taught to engage in symbolic play actions using a variation of the NLP procedure described earlier, a procedure called Pivotal Response Training (PRT). Results indicated that after PRT training, all seven children increased their ability to play symbolically, and that this ability generalized to different toys and different settings. That is, children with autism did not simply learn how to play symbolically with a specific set of toys in a specific location, rather, they were able to generalize their new play skills to new environments and new play materials. One of the most important components of this treatment approach was it's focus on increasing the *motivation* of the child to perform the difficult task. If a child with autism can be motivated to engage in a behavior (e.g., symbolic play), the likelihood of that child performing the behavior is greater than if the child was told directly to engage in that behavior. Consider the following example using a naturalistic technique, such as the one utilized by Stahmer (1995)

A child is given the choice between playing with a toy stove or cash register. The child chooses the toy stove. Next the child is given the choice of what activity to perform either directly (e.g., "Do you want to cook some eggs or bake a cake?") or indirectly ("What do you want to do?"). After the child takes his or her turn the therapist then takes his or her turn and models appropriate play behavior (e.g., therapist "bakes cookies"). The child with autism looks away from the stove and starts to play with the cash register. The therapist quickly asks "Do you want $5.00 or $10.00 for your cash register? (as the therapist holds out play money)." The child receives the money and the interaction continues. It is easy to imagine that if the therapist simply told the child "Okay, now we are going to practice our play skills." and proceeded to drill certain skills, the child might not be as motivated to learn the skill.

In addition to having sophisticated toy play skills, a child with autism needs to be able to initiate play and conversation, as well as maintain interactions in order to successfully socialize with their peers. In a recent study, Pierce and Schreibman (1995) taught two children with autism complex social interaction skills via a naturalistic procedure adapted from PRT principles. As with the symbolic-play training mentioned above, this training focused on increasing the child's motivation to play and socially interact. Interestingly, this study utilized peers as behavior change agents, a strategy that has been used with much success in the past (e.g., McGee, Almeida, Sulzer-Azaroff, & Feldman, 1992; Odom et al., 1985). After several months of peer training, the children with autism engaged in many complex social behaviors (e.g., initiating conversations) and these behaviors generalized to new environments and new play materials.

Although deficits in social behaviors are among the most difficult to treat, research in this area is promising and suggests that some children with autism can acquire the social skills necessary to interact with peers.

GENERALIZATION

The previous section described treatment procedures that have been successful in teaching children with autism appropriate behaviors and decreasing inappropriate behaviors. However, treatment gains do not always generalize to settings other than the treatment environment or to untreated behaviors. Often, improvement is setting- and task-specific (Schreibman, 1988). Clearly, treatment is of only limited value if behavioral gains do not generalize. Because generalization does not tend to occur automatically, many treatment procedures now being explored incorporate provisions to promote generalization. A number of strategies discussed by Stokes and Baer (1977) have been added to the treatment of children with autism to facilitate generalization.

One approach to promoting generalized treatment gains is to implement procedures that directly occasion generalization. Sequential modification is a procedure in which generalization is programmed in every condition (e.g., across persons, settings, stimuli) where generalization has not occurred. For example, if an autistic child learned speech in a clinic setting but did not use speech at home, parents would be taught to teach speech to their child in the home (see section on parent training below).

Sequential modification can often be a tedious process, especially in situations where generalization must occur across many stimuli (e.g., each time the child sees a different printed version of the letter "A" when learning the alphabet) or across many settings (e.g., home, school, peer's home, day care). In this situation, a more feasible approach would be to train sufficient exemplars (Stokes & Baer, 1977). For example, Stokes, Baer, and Jackson (1974) demonstrated that when greeting responses were being taught to mentally retarded children, the children did not generalize such behavior to any other persons besides the experimenter. However, when 2 persons (exemplars) served as experimenters, generalization occurred and the children greeted more than 20 other persons.

Another strategy for promoting generalization is to make the treatment setting more similar to the natural environment (Stokes & Baer, 1977). The use of intermittent schedules of reinforcement during treatment provides an atmosphere that is more similar to the natural environment, where behaviors are seldom reinforced on a continuous (CRF) basis. Results from several studies (e.g., Koegel & Rincover, 1974, 1977) have suggested that intermittent schedules have increased the durability of treatment gains by reducing the discriminability of the reinforcement schedules used in therapy settings and settings outside of therapy. Additionally, intermittent schedules have served to maintain treatment gains, allowing naturally occurring intermittent reinforcers to "take over" easily in natural environments.

The use of naturally maintaining contingencies (natural reinforcers) during treatment will also liken the treatment setting with other, more natural environments. Reinforcers should be similar to those that could be encountered in natural settings; additionally, specific behaviors that are more likely to acquire such reinforcers should be taught. Several studies have provided encouraging results with children with autism. For example, Carr (1979) taught children with autism to use sign language to request items that are easily found outside the treatment setting. The children were taught to spontaneously request their most preferred foods and toys as opposed to common but nonfunctional items (e.g., pictures of farm animals). Thus, when the children signed for a favorite food they were likely to receive that food at home or school. In another study, Charlop and her colleagues (1985) taught verbal children with autism through time-delay procedures to spontaneously request their preferred food item. The children not only acquired the target behavior (spontaneous requests for preferred foods) but generalized such requests to environments other than the training setting. Additionally, this approach incorporates the use of common stimuli, those found in both treatment settings and extratherapy environments (Stokes & Baer, 1977).

Finally, a technique that has also proved useful is mediated generalization. This is the use of behaviors that are likely to occur in both treatment and non-treatment settings that occasion the occurrence of the target response. The most common mediator is language. Mediated generalization is advantageous over other procedures such as sequential modification and training sufficient exemplars, as those procedures can often be tedious when many examples are needed. Also, it is difficult to determine a priori how many exemplars will be necessary. Mediated generalization, then, is a more parsimonious approach to facilitating generalization.

Although few studies have addressed mediated generalization with children with autism, there is some indication that this may be a promising avenue to pursue. Charlop (1983) used the immediate echolalia of children with autism as a verbal mediator. Recall that in this study, the verbal children with autism who were permitted to echo the experimenter's request (the object's label) before handing the experimenter the object learned the receptive labeling tasks faster and displayed generalized treatment gains. Charlop (1983) suggested that mediated generalization occurred for the echolalic children because, unlike the nonverbal children, they provided their own self-imposed discriminative stimulus (echo of the object's label), which was easily transported to the generalization setting. Self-management procedures may also be considered mediated generalization because the target behavior (self-management) can be transported easily to multiple settings. Recent research suggests that this procedure is effective for teaching myriad behaviors to children with autism including daily living skills (Pierce & Schreibman, 1994), appropriate play skills (Stahmer & Schreibman, 1992), and social skills (Koegel, Koegel, Hurley, & Frea, 1992), and that newly acquired behaviors generalize across non-treatment settings. Generally, the child is taught to self-record the occurrence of a specific target behavior, then to self-evaluate after a predetermined time period and self administer reinforcers. After the child correctly self-monitors in a training setting, the program is introduced in a natural setting (e.g., classroom). In the final step, self-management materials are gradually faded out.

Recently, in an attempt to incorporate many of the above procedures, researchers have explored the use of the natural environment for treatment. As a result, several promising techniques have emerged. These include time delay (previously described), NLP, and incidental teaching. Recall that the time-delay procedure uses natural stimuli in natural settings. Additionally, this procedure incorporates a natural prompt (a time period) that can easily be transferred in a variety of settings and can be used for a variety of behaviors (Charlop & Walsh, 1986; Charlop et al., 1985; Touchette, 1971).

Incidental-teaching procedures embed teaching trials with the child's daily activities. In one study, for example, children with autism were taught receptive labels of objects used in meal preparation (McGee et al., 1983). The training took place in the kitchen of the children's residential group home, when they were preparing the day's lunch with their care provider. In addition to enhancing motivation (see previous section), incidental teaching provides several techniques that enhance generalization. The "loose structure" in the teaching situation helps promote generalization (Stokes & Baer, 1977). Additionally, the behaviors taught are maintained by naturally occurring daily events in the individual's environment. Incidental teaching has been effective in facilitating generalization of a variety of behaviors such as sign language (Carr & Kologinsky, 1983), preposition use (McGee et al., 1985), and reading skills (McGee et al., 1986).

A third promising procedure, used specifically to teach speech, is the natural language paradigm (NLP). NLP has been designed to incorporate procedures to increase motivation (e.g., child-initiated episodes, turn taking, reinforcing attempts) with procedures for promoting generalization (loose structure, common stimuli, natural environment). During NLP, child and therapist interact in a play setting with a variety of toys. The child initially selects the toy he or she would like to "talk about" and play with. The therapist then models an appropriate verbalization for the child to imitate (e.g., "I want ball."). When the child makes any communicative attempt (e.g., imitates phrase or part of phrase, gestures toward the toy), the toy is given to the child as a reinforcer. After a short interval, it is the therapist's "turn" to play with the toy; the therapist then either models a different verbalization (e.g., "Catch the

ball.") or provides a new referent for the initial verbalization. NLP has been shown to facilitate acquisition and generalization as compared to traditional speech protocols (Koegel et al., 1987). Recently, the efficacy of this procedure has been demonstrated with parents using NLP in their homes (Laski et al., 1988). Thus, in summary, the inclusion of strategies that promote generalization into the development of treatment procedures for children with autism may lead to a better understanding and more efficacious treatment of this most complex disorder.

CONCLUDING COMMENTS

Treatment research and application in the area of autism has evolved substantially over the past decade as researchers, clinicians, parents, and teachers move away from rigid prompting procedures to more naturalistic interventions. These interventions are based on the premise that children with autism *can* engage in many behaviors that were once thought too challenging to teach (e.g., social competence) and thus emphasizes increasing the motivation of the child to engage (or not engage) in a particular behavior. In addition, with the help of functional analysis technology, treatment packages are typically individualized for each child with autism, so that the "one size fits all" strategy often used in the past is obsolete. While as yet there is no cure for autism, we believe that the future outlook is bright in that we will continue to improve the quality of care and, ultimately, the quality of life for these children.

REFERENCES

American Psychiatric Association (1994). Diagnostic and statistical manual of mental disorders (4th ed.). Washington DC: Author.

Anderson, L. T., Campbell, M., Grega, D. M., Perry, R., Small, A. M., & Green, W. H. (1984). Haloperidol in infantile autism: Effects on learning and behavioral symptoms. *American Journal of Psychiatry, 141,* 1195–1202.

August, G. J., Raz, N., & Baird, T. D. (1985). Brief report: Effects of fenfluramine on behavioral, cognitive, and affective disturbances in autistic children. *Journal of Autism and Developmental Disorders, 15,* 97–107.

Baltaxe, C. A. (1981). Acoustic characteristics of prosody in autism. In P. Mittler (Ed.), *Frontiers of knowledge in mental retardation* (pp. 223–233). Baltimore: University Park Press.

Baron-Cohen, S. (1988). Social and pragmatic deficits in autism: Cognitive or affective? *Journal of Autism and Developmental Disorders, 18,* 379–402.

Baron-Cohen, S. (1989a). Are children with autism "behaviorists"? An examination of their mental-physical and appearance-reality distinctions. *Journal of Autism and Developmental Disorders, 19,* 579–600.

Baron-Cohen, S. (1989b). The autistic child's theory of mind: A case of specific developmental delay. *Journal of Child Psychology and Psychiatry, 30,* 285–298.

Baron-Cohen, S., Leslie, A. M., & Frith, U. (1985). Does the autistic child have a theory of mind? *Cognition, 21,* 37–46.

Bartak, L., & Rutter, M. (1974). The use of personal pronouns by autistic children. *Journal of Autism and Childhood Schizophrenia, 4,* 217–222.

Bauman, M. L. & Kemper, T. L. (1990). Limbic and cerebellar abnormalities are also present in an autistic child of normal intelligence. *Neurology, 40,* 359.

Bird, F., Dores, P. A., Moniz, D., & Robinson, J. (1989). Reducing severe aggressive and self-injurious behaviors with functional communication training: Direct, collateral and generalized results. *American Journal of Mental Retardation, 94,* 37–48.

Bristol, M. M., Gallagher, J. J., & Schopler, E. (1988). Mothers and fathers of young developmentally disabled and non-disabled boys: Adaptation and spousal support. *Developmental Psychology, 24,* 441–451.

Burke, J. C., & Cerniglia, L. (1990). Stimulus complexity and autistic children's responsivity: Assessing and training a pivotal behavior. *Journal of Autism and Developmental Disorders, 20,* 233–253.

Campbell, M., Adams P., Small, A. M., & Curren, E. L. (1988): Efficacy and safety of fenfluramine in autistic children. *Journal of the American Academy of Child and Adolescent Psychiatry, 27,* 434–439.

Campbell, M., Green, W., & Deutsch, S. (1985). *Child and adolescent psychopharmacology.* Beverly Hills, CA: Sage Publications.

Campbell, M., Small, A., Collins, P., Friedman, E., David, R., & Genieser, N. (1976). Levodopa and levoamphetamine: A crossover study in young schizophrenic children. *Current Therapeutic Research, 19,* 70–86.

Capps, L, Yirmiya, N., & Sigman, M. (1992). Understanding of simple and complex emotions in non-retarded children with autism. *Journal of Child Psychology and Psychiatry, 33,* 1169–1182.

Carr, E. G. (1979), Teaching autistic children to use sign language: Some research issues. *Journal of Autism & Developmental Disorders, 9,* 345–359.

Carr, E. G., & Durand, V. M. (1985). Reducing behavior problems through functional communication training. *Journal of Applied Behavior Analysis, 18,* 111–126.

Carr, E. G., & Kologinsky, E. (1983). Acquisition of sign language by autistic children. II. Spontaneity and generalization effects. *Journal of Applied Behavior Analysis, 16,* 297–314.

Carr, E. G., Kologinsky, E., Leff-Simon, S. (1987). Acquisition of sign language by autistic children, III: Generalized descriptive phrases. *Journal of Autism & Developmental Disorders, 17,* 217–229.

Carr, E. G., Schreibman, L., & Lovaas, O. I. (1975). Control of echolalic speech in psychotic children. *Journal of Abnormal Child Psychology, 3,* 331–351.

Charlop, M. H. (1983). The effects of echolalia on acquisition and generalization of receptive labeling in autistic children. *Journal of Applied Behavior Analysis, 16,* 111–126.

Charlop, M. H. (1986). Setting effects on the occurrence of autistic children's immediate echolalia. *Journal of Autism and Developmental Disorders, 16,* 473–483.

Charlop, M. H., Gonzalez, J., & Cugliari, C. P. (1987). Environmental effects on the functional aspects of the delayed echolalia of autistic children. Unpublished manuscript.

Charlop, M. H., Kurtz, P. F., & Casey, F. G. (1990). Using aberrant behaviors as reinforcers for autistic children. *Journal of Applied Behavior Analysis, 22,* 275–285.

Charlop, M. H., Kurtz, P. F., & Milstein, J. P. (1993). Too much reinforcement, too little behavior: Assessing different reinforcement schedules in conjunction with task variation with autistic children. *Journal of Applied Behavior Analysis, 26,* 225–239.

Charlop, M. H., & Milstein, J. P. (1989). Teaching autistic children conversational speech using video modeling. *Journal of Applied Behavior Analysis, 22,* 275–285.

Charlop, M. H., Milstein, J. P., & Moore, M. (1989, May). Teaching autistic children cooperative play. Paper presented at the Annual Convention for the Association of Behavior Analysis, Milwaukee, WI.

Charlop, M. H., Owen, G., Tan, N., & Milstein, J. P. (1988, November). *Teaching autistic children cooperative play.* Paper presented at the annual meeting of the Association for the Advancement of Behavior Therapy, New York.

Charlop, M. H., Schreibman, L., & Thibodeau, M. G. (1985). Increasing spontaneous verbal responding in autistic children using a time delay procedure. *Journal of Applied Behavior Analysis, 18,* 155–166.

Charlop, M. H., Schreibman, L., & Tryon, A. S. (1983). Learning through observation: The effects of peer modeling on acquisition and generalization in autistic children. *Journal of Abnormal Child Psychology, 11,* 355–366.

Charlop, M. H., Spitzer, S., & Kurtz, P. F. (1990, May). Teaching autistic children independent play through video modeling. Paper presented at the Annual Convention for the Association for Behavior Analysis, Nashville, TN.

Charlop, M. H., & Trasowech, J. B. (1991). Increasing autistic children's daily spontaneous speech. *Journal of Applied Behavior Analysis, 24,* 247–261.

Charlop, M. H., & Walsh, M. E. (1986). Increasing autistic children's spontaneous verbalizations of affection: An assessment of time delay and peer modeling procedures. *Journal of Applied Behavior Analysis, 19,* 307–314.

Charlop-Christy, M.H., & Greenberg, M. (1996). Relaxation training as a stress management technique for use with children with autism. Paper to be presented at the annual meeting of the Association for Behavior Analysis, San Francisco.

Coleman, S. G., & Stedman, J. M. (1974). Use of a peer model in language training in an echolalic child. *Journal of Behavior Therapy and Experimental Psychiatry, 5,* 275–279.

Courchesne, E. (1987). A neurophysiological view of autism. In E. Schopler and G. B. Mesibov (Eds.), *Neurobiological issues in autism* (pp. 285–324) New York: Plenum Press Corporation.

Courchesne, E. (1989). Neuroanatomical systems involved in infantile autism: The implications of cerebellar abnormalities. In G. Dawson (Ed.), Autism: *New perspectives on diagnosis, nature and treatment,* (pp. 119–143) Guildford Press.

Courchesne, E. (1991). Neuroanatomic imagining in autism. *Pediatrics, 87,* 781–790.

Courchesne, E., Saitho, O., Yeung-Courchesne, R., Press, G. A., Lincoln, A. J., Haas, R. H., & Schreibman, L. (1994a). Abnormality of cerebellar vermian lobules VI and VII in patients with infantile autism: Identification of hypoplastic and hyperplastic subgroups by MR imaging. *American Journal of Roentgenology, 162,* 123–130.

Courchesne, E., Towsend, J., Akshoomoff, N. A., Saitoh, O., Yeung-Courchesne, R., Lincoln, A. J., James, H. E., Haas, R. H., Schreibman, L. & Lau, L. (1996). Impairment in shifting attention in autistic and cerebellar patients, *Behavioral Neuroscience, 108,* 1–17.

Courchesne, E., Yeung-Courchesne, R., Press, G. A., Hesselink, J. R., & Jernigan, T. L. (1988). Hypoplasia of cerebellar vermal lobes VI and VII in autism. *New England Journal of Medicine, 318,* 1349–1354.

Duker, P. C., Welles, K., Seys, D., Rensen, H., Vis, A. & van der Berg, G. (1991). Brief report: Effects of fenfluramine on communicative, stereotypic and inappropriate behaviors of autistic-type mentally handicapped individuals. *Journal of Autism and Developmental Disorders, 21,* 355–363.

Dunlap, G. (1984). The influence of task variation and maintenance tasks on the learning and affect of autistic children. *Journal of Experimental Child Psychology, 37,* 41–64.

Dunlap, G., & Koegel, R. L. (1980). Motivating autistic children through stimulus variation. *Journal of Applied Behavior Analysis, 13,* 619–627.

Dunlap, G., Koegel, R. L., & O'Neill, R. O. (1985). Pervasive developmental disorders. In P. H. Bornstein & A. E. Kazdin (Eds.), *Handbook of clinical behavior therapy with children* (pp. 499–540). Homewood, IL: Dorsey Press.

Durand, V. M., & Carr, E. G. (1987). Social influences on self-stimulatory behavior: Analysis and treatment application. *Journal of Applied Behavior Analysis, 20,* 119–132.

Durand, V. M., & Carr, E. G. (1991). Functional communication training to reduce challenging behavior: Maintenance and application in new settings. *Journal of Applied Behavior Analysis, 25,* 251–264.

Durand V. M., & Carr, E. G. (1992). An analysis of maintenance following functional communication training. *Journal of Applied Behavior Analysis, 25,* 777–794.

Durand, V. M., & Crimmins, D. B. (1988). Identifying the variables maintaining self-injurious behavior. *Journal of Autism and Developmental Disorders, 18,* 99–117.

Durand, V. M. & Kishi, G. (1987). Reducing severe behavior problems among persons with dual sensory impairments: An evaluation of a technical assistance model. *Journal of the Association for Persons with Severe Handicaps, 10,* 79–86.

Egel, A. L. (1981). Reinforcer variation: Implications for motivating developmentally disabled children. *Journal of Applied Behavior Analysis, 14,* 345–350.

Egel, A. L., Koegel, R. L., & Schreibman, L. (1980). A review of educational treatment procedures for autistic children. In L. Mann & D. Sabatino (Eds.), *Fourth review of special education* (pp. 109–149). New York: Grune & Stratton.

Egel, A. L., Richman, G., & Koegel, R. L. (1981). Normal peer models and autistic children's learning. *Journal of Applied Behavior Analysis, 14,* 3–12.

Eisenberg, L., & Kanner, L. (1956). Early infantile autism. *American Journal of Orthopsychiatry, 26,* 556–566.

Ekman, G., Miranda-Linne, F., Gillberg, C., & Garle, M. (1989). Fenfluramine treatment of twenty children with autism. *Journal of Autism & Developmental Disorders, 19,* 511–532.

Favell, J. E., McGimsey, J. G., & Jones, M. L. (1978). The use of physical restraint in the treatment of self-injury and as positive reinforcement. *Journal of Applied Behavior Analysis, 11,* 225–241.

Fay, W. H., & Schuler, A. L. (1980). Emerging language in autistic children. Baltimore: University Park Press.

Ferster, C. B. (1961). Positive reinforcement and behavioral deficits of autistic children. *Child Development, 32,* 437–456.

Freeman, B. J., & Ritvo, E. R. (1984). The syndrome of autism: Establishing the diagnosis and principles of management. *Pediatric Analysis, 13,* 284–305.

Freeman, B. J., Ritvo, E. R., & Miller, R. (1975). An operant procedure to teach an echolalic, autistic child to answer questions appropriately. *Journal of Autism and Childhood Schizophrenia, 5,* 169–176.

Frith, U. (1989). *Autism: Explaining the enigma.* Oxford: Basil Blackwell.

Geller, E., Ritvo, E. R., Freeman, B. J., & Yuwiler, A. (1982). Preliminary observations on the effects of fenfluramine on blood serotonin and symptoms in three autistic boys. *New England Journal of Medicine, 307,* 165.

Goldstein, H., & Cisar, C. L. (1992). Promoting interaction during sociodramatic play: Teaching scripts to typical preschoolers and classmates with disabilities. *Journal of Applied Behavior Analysis, 25,* 265–280.

Halle, J. W. (1982). Teaching functional language to the handicapped: An integrative model of the natural environment teaching techniques. *Journal of the Association for the Severely Handicapped, 7,* 29–36.

Halle, J. W., Baer, D. M., & Spradlin, J. E. (1981). Teachers' generalized use of delay as a stimulus control procedure to increase language use in handicapped children. *Journal of Applied Behavior Analysis, 14,* 389–409.

Halle, J. W., Marshall, A. M., & Spradlin, J. E. (1979). Time delay: A technique to increase language use and facilitate generalization in retarded children. *Journal of Applied Behavior Analysis, 12,* 431–439.

Hart, B., & Risley, T. R. (1974). Using preschool materials to modify the language of disadvantaged children. *Journal of Applied Behavior Analysis, 7,* 243–256.

Hobson, R., P. & Lee, A. (1989). Emotion-related and abstract concepts in autistic people: Evidence from the British Picture Vocabulary Scale. *Journal of Autism and Developmental Disorders, 19,* 601–623.

Hobson, R.P., Ouston, J., & Lee, A. (1988). Emotion recognition in autism: Coordinating faces and voices. *Psychological Medicine, 18,* 911–923.

Horner, R. H., & Budd, C. M., (1985). Acquisition of manual sign use: Collateral reduction of maladaptive behavior, and factors limiting generalization. *Education and Training of the Mentally Retarded, 20,* 39–47.

Horner, R. H., & Day, H. M. (1991). The effects of response efficiency on functionally equivalent competing behaviors. *Journal of Applied Behavior Analysis, 24,* 719–732.

Iwata, B. A., Dorsey, M. F., Slifer, K. J., Bauman, K. E., & Richman, G. S. (1982). Toward a functional analysis of self-injury. *Analysis and Interaction in Developmental Disabilities, 2,* 3–20.

Iwata, B. A., Vollmer, T. R. & Zarcone, J. R. (1990). The experimental (functional) analysis of behavior disorders: Methodology, applications and limitations. In A. C. Repp & N. N. Singh (Eds.), *Perspectives on the use of nonaversive and aversive interventions for persons with developmental disabilities* (pp. 301–330). Sycamore, IL: Sycamore Publishing.

Kanner, L. (1943). Autistic disturbances of affective contact. *Nervous Child, 2,* 217–250.

Kanner, L. (1944). Early infantile autism. *Journal of Pediatrics, 25,* 211–217.

Kasari, C., Sigman, M., Mundy, P., & Yirmiya, N. (1990). Affective sharing in the context of joint interactions of normal, autistic and mentally retarded children. *Journal of Autism and Developmental Disorders, 20,* 87–99.

Koegel, L. K, Koegel, R. L., Hurley, C., & Frea, W. D. (1992). Improving social skills and disruptive behavior in children with autism through self-management. *Journal of Applied Behavior Analysis, 25,* 341–354.

Koegel, R. L., & Covert, A. (1972). The relationship of self-stimulation to learning in autistic children. *Journal of Applied Behavior Analysis, 5,* 381–387.

Koegel, R. L., & Egel, A. L. (1979). Motivating autistic children. *Journal of Abnormal Psychology, 88,* 418–426.

Koegel, R. L., Firestone, P. B., Kramme, K. W., & Dunlap, G. (1974). Increasing spontaneous play by suppressing self-stimulation in autistic children. *Journal of Applied Behavior Analysis, 7,* 521–528.

Koegel, R. L., & Frea, W. D. (1993). Treatment of social behavior in autism through the modification of pivotal skills. *Journal of Applied Behavior Analysis, 26,* 369–377.

Koegel, R. L., O'Dell, M. C., & Koegel, L. K. (1987). A natural language teaching paradigm for nonverbal autistic children. *Journal of Autism and Developmental Disorders, 17,* 187–200.

Koegel, R. L., & Rincover, A. (1974). Treatment of psychotic children in a classroom environment: I. Learning in a large group. *Journal of Applied Behavior Analysis, 7,* 45–59.

Koegel, R. L., & Rincover, A. (1976). Some detrimental effects of using extra stimuli to guide learning in normal and autistic children. *Journal of Abnormal Child Psychology, 4,* 59–71.

Koegel, R. L., & Schreibman, L. (1977). Teaching autistic children to respond to simultaneous multiple cues. *Journal of Experimental Child Psychology, 24,* 299–311.

Koegel, R. L., & Wilhelm, H. (1973). Selective responding to the components of multiple visual cues by autistic children. *Journal of Abnormal Child Psychology, 4,* 536–547.

Koegel, R. L., & Williams, J. (1980). Direct vs. indirect response-reinforcer relationships in teaching autistic children. *Journal of Abnormal Psychology, 4,* 337–347.

Korein, J., Fish, B., Shapiro, T., Gerner, E. W., & Levidow, L. (1971). EEG and behavioral effects of drug therapy in children: Chlorpromazine and diphenhydramine. *Archives of General Psychiatry, 24,* 552–563.

Krantz, P. J., MacDuff, M. T. and McClannahan, L. E. (1993). Teaching children with autism to initiate to peers: Effects of a script fading procedure. *Journal of Applied Behavior Analysis, 26,* 121–132.

Laski, K. E., Charlop, M. H., & Schreibman, L. (1988). Training parents to use the natural language paradigm to increase their autistic children's speech. *Journal of Applied Behavior Analysis, 21,* 391–400.

Leslie, A. M., & Frith, U. (1988). Autistic children's understanding of seeing, knowing and believing. *British Journal of Developmental Psychology, 4,* 315–324.

Lewis, V., & Boucher, J. (1988). Spontaneous, instructed and elicited play in relatively able autistic children. *British Journal of Developmental Psychology, 6,* 325–339.

Lewy, A. L., & Dawson, G. (1992). Social stimulation and joint attention in young children with autism. *Journal of Abnormal Child Psychology, 20,* 555–566.

Litt, M. D., & Schreibman, L. (1981). Stimulus specific reinforcement in the acquisition of receptive labels by autistic children. *Analysis and Intervention in Developmental Disabilities, 1,* 171–186.

Lockyer, L., & Rutter, M. (1969). A five to fifteen year follow-up study of infantile psychosis. III.

Psychological aspects. British Journal of Psychology, 115, 865–882.

Lovaas, O. I. (1977). *The autistic child.* New York: Irvington.

Lovaas, O. I. (1987). Behavioral treatment and normal educational and intellectual functioning in young autistic children. *Journal of Consulting and Clinical Psychology, 55,* 3–9.

Lovaas, O. I., Koegel, R. L., & Schreibman, L. (1979). Stimulus overselectivity in autism: A review of research. *Psychological Bulletin, 86,* 1236–1254.

Lovaas, O. I., Litrownik, A., & Mann, R. (1971). Response latencies to auditory stimuli in autistic children engaged in self-stimulatory behavior. *Behavior Research and Therapy, 9,* 39–49.

Lovaas, O. I., & Newsom, C. D. (1976). Behavior modification with psychosis children. In H. Leitenberg (Ed.), *Handbook of behavior modification and behavior therapy* (pp. 303–360). Englewood Cliffs, NJ: Prentice-Hall.

Lovaas, O. I., Newsom, C., & Hickman, C. (1987). Self-stimulatory behavior and perceptual reinforcement. *Journal of Applied Behavior Analysis, 20,* 45–68.

Lovaas, O. I., & Schreibman, L. (1971). Stimulus overselectivity of autistic children in a two stimulus situation. *Behavior Research and Therapy, 9,* 305–310.

Lovaas, O. I., Schreibman, L., & Koegel, R. L. (1974). A behavior modification approach to the treatment of autism. *Journal of Autism and Childhood Schizophrenia, 4,* 111–129.

Lovaas, O. I., Schreibman, L., Koegel, R. L., & Rehm, R. (1971). Selective responding by autistic children to multiple sensory input. *Journal of Abnormal Psychology, 77,* 211–222.

Lovaas, O. I., & Simmons, J. Q. (1969). Manipulation of self-destruction in three retarded children. *Journal of Applied Behavior Analysis, 2,* 143–157.

Lovaas, O. I., Varni, J., Koegel, R. L., & Lorsch, N. L. (1977). Some observations on the non-extinguishability of children's speech. *Child Development, 48,* 1121–1127.

McGee, G. G., Almeida, C., Sulzer-Azaroff, B., & Feldman, R. (1992). Promoting reciprocal interactions via peer incidental teaching. *Journal of Applied Behavior Analysis, 25,* 117–126.

McGee, G. G., Krantz, P. J., Mason, D., & McClannahan, L. E. (1983). A modified incidental-teaching procedure for autistic youth: Acquisition and generalization of receptive object labels. *Journal of Applied Behavior Analysis, 16,* 329–338.

McGee, G. G., Krantz, P. J., & McClannahan, L. E. (1985). The facilitative effects of incidental teaching on preposition use by autistic children. *Journal of Applied Behavior Analysis, 18,* 17–31.

McGee, G. G., Krantz, P. J., & McClannahan, L. E. (1986). An extension of incidental teaching procedures to reading instruction for autistic children. *Journal of Applied Behavior Analysis, 19,* 147–157.

Mesibov, G. B., & Dawson, G. (1986). Pervasive developmental disorders and schizophrenia. In J. M. Reisman (Ed.), *Behavior disorders in infants, children, and adolescents* (pp. 117–152). New York: Random House.

Miller, L. N. (1969). *A preliminary report: The effect of fear on echolalic speech in autistic children.* Unpublished manuscript.

Mundy, P., Sigman, M., & Kasari, C. (1990). A longitudinal study of joint and language development in children with autism. *Journal of Autism and Developmental Disorders, 20,* 115–128.

Odom, S. L., Hoyson, M., Jamieson, B., & Strain, P. S. (1985). Increasing handicapped preschoolers' peer social interactions: Cross-setting and component analysis. *Journal of Applied Behavior Analysis, 18,* 3–16.

Odom, S. L., & Strain, P. S. (1984). Classroom-based social skills instruction for severely handicapped preschool children. *Topics in Early Childhood Special Education, 4,* 97–116.

Odom, S. L., & Strain, P. S. (1986). A comparison of peer-initiation and teacher-antecedent interventions for promoting reciprocal social interaction of autistic preschoolers. *Journal of Applied Behavior Analysis, 19,* 59–71.

O'Gorman, G. (1970). *The nature of childhood autism.* London: Butterworths.

O'Neill, R. E., Horner, R. H., Albin, R. W., Storey, K., & Sprague, J. R. (1989). The functional analysis interview. In R. H. Horner, J. L., Anderson, E.G. Carr, G. Dunlap, R. L. Koegel, & W. Sailor (Eds.), *Functional analysis: A practical assessment guide* (pp. 10–23). Eugene: University of Oregon Press.

O'Neill, R. E., Horner, R. H., Albin, R.W., Storey, K., & Sprague, J. R. (1990). *Functional analysis: A practical assessment guide.* Sycamore, IL: Sycamore Publishing.

Ornitz, M. (1985). Neurophysiology of infantile autism. *Journal of the American Academy of Child Psychiatry, 24,* 251–262.

Ozonoff, S., Pennington, B. F., & Rogers, S. J. (1990). Are there emotion perception deficits in young children with autism? *Journal of Child Psychology and Psychiatry, 31,* 343–361.

Pierce, K., & Schreibman, L. (1994). Teaching children with autism daily living skills in unsupervised settings through pictorial self-management. *Journal of Applied Behavior Analysis, 28,* 285–295.

Pierce, K., & Schreibman, L. (1995). Increasing complex social behaviors in children with autism via peer-implemented pivotal response training. *Journal of Applied Behavior Analysis, 28,* 285–295.

Piggott, L., Gdowski, C., Villanueva, D., Fischhoff, J., & Frohman, C. (1986). Side effects of fenfluramine in autistic children. *Journal of the American Academy of Child Psychiatry, 25,* 287–289.

Reynolds, B. S., Newsom, C. D., & Lovaas, O. I. (1974). Auditory overselectivity in autistic children. *Journal of Abnormal Child Psychology, 2,* 253–263.

Rimland, B. (1964). *Infantile autism.* New York: Appleton-Century-Crofts.

Rimland, B. (1978). Inside the mind of an autistic savant. *Psychology Today, 12,* 68–80.

Rimland, B., Callaway, E., & Dreyfus, P. (1978). The effect of high doses of vitamin B-6 on autistic children: A double-blind crossover study. *American Journal of Psychiatry, 135,* 472–475.

Rincover, A., Cook, R., Peoples, A., & Packard, D. (1979). Sensory extinction and sensory reinforcement principles for programming multiple behavior change. *Journal of Applied Behavior Analysis, 12,* 221–233.

Rincover, A., & Koegel, R. L. (1975). Setting generality and stimulus control in autistic children. *Journal of Applied Behavior Analysis, 8,* 235–246.

Rincover, A., Newsom, C. D., Lovaas, O. I., & Koegel, R. L. (1977). Some motivational properties of sensory stimulation in psychotic children. *Journal of Experimental Child Psychology, 24,* 312–323.

Ritvo, E. R., & Freeman, B. J. (1978). National Society for Autistic Children definition of the syndrome of autism. *Journal of Autism and Childhood Schizophrenia, 8,* 162–167.

Ritvo, E. R., Freeman, B. J., Geller, E., & Yuwiler, A. (1983). Effects of fenfluramine on 14 outpatients with the syndrome of autism. *Journal of the American Academy of Child Psychiatry, 22,* 549–558.

Ritvo, E. R., Freeman, B. J., Sheibel, A. B., Duong, T., Robinson, R., Guthrie, D., & Ritvo, A. (1986). Lower Purkinje cell counts in the cerebella of four autistic subjects: Initial findings of the UCLA-NSAC autopsy research report. *American Journal of Psychiatry, 143,* 862–866.

Ritvo, E. R., Freeman, B. J., Yuwiler, A., Geller, E., Yokota, A., Schroth, P., & Novak, P. (1984). Study of fenfluramine in outpatients with the syndrome of autism. *Journal of Pediatrics, 105,* 823–828.

Ritvo, E. R., Yuwiler, A., Geller, E., Kales, A., Rashkis, S.,

Schicor, A., Plotkin, A., Axelrod, R., & Howard, C. (1971). Effects of L-dopa on autism. *Journal of Autism and Childhood Schizophrenia, 1,* 190–205.

Ritvo, E. R., Yuwiler, A., Geller, E., Ornitz, E. M., Saeger, K., & Plotkin, S. (1970). Increasing blood serotonin and platelets in early infantile autism. *Archives of General Psychiatry, 23,* 566–572.

Runco, M. A., Charlop, M. H., & Schreibman, L. (1986). The occurrence of autistic children's self-stimulation as a function of familiar versus unfamiliar stimulus conditions. *Journal of Autism and Developmental Disorders, 16,* 31–44.

Rutter, M. (1968). Concepts of autism: A review of research. *Journal of Child Psychology and Psychiatry, 9,* 1–25.

Rutter, M. (1978). Diagnosis and definition of childhood autism. *Journal . of Autism and Childhood Schizophrenia, 8,* 139–161.

Rutter, M., & Bartak, L. (1973). Special educational treatment of autistic children: A comparative study. II. Follow-up findings and implications for services. *Journal of Child Psychology and Psychiatry, 14,* 241–270.

Rutter, M., & Lockyer, L. (1967). A five to fifteen year follow-up study of infantile psychosis. I. Description of sample. *British Journal of Psychiatry, 113,* 1169–1182.

Schreibman, L. (1975). Effects of within-stimulus and extra-stimulus prompting on discrimination learning in autistic children. *Journal of Applied Behavior Analysis, 8,* 91–112.

Schreibman, L. (1988). *Autism.* Newbury Park, CA: Sage Publications.

Schreibman, L., & Carr, E. G. (1978). Elimination of echolalic responding to questions through the training of a generalized verbal response. *Journal of Applied Behavior Analysis, 11,* 453–463.

Schreibman, L., & Charlop, M. H. (1987). Autism. In V. B. Van Hasselt & M. Hersen (Eds.), *Psychological evaluation of the developmentally and physically disabled* (pp. 155–177). New York: Plenum Press.

Schreibman, L., Charlop, M. H., & Koegel, R. L. (1982). Teaching autistic children to use extra-stimulus prompts. *Journal of Experimental Child Psychology, 33,* 475–491.

Schreibman, L., Charlop, M. H., & Tryon, A. S. (1981, August). *The acquisition and generalization of appropriate spontaneous speech in autistic children.* Paper presented at the American Psychological Association Annual Convention, Los Angeles, CA.

Schreibman, L., & Koegel, R. L. (1981). A guideline for planning behavior modification programs for autistic

children. In S. M. Turner, K. S. Calhoun, & H. E. Adams (Eds.), *Handbook of clinical behavior therapy* (pp. 500–526). New York: John Wiley & Sons.

Schreibman, L., Koegel, R. L., & Craig, M. S. (1977). Reducing stimulus overselectivity in autistic children. *Journal of Abnormal Child Psychology, 5,* 425–436.

Schreibman, L., Kohlenberg, B. S., & Britten, K. R. (1986). Differential responding to content and intonation components of a complex auditory stimulus by non-verbal and echolalic autistic children. *Analysis and Intervention in Developmental Disabilities, 6,* 109–125.

Schreibman, L., & Lovaas, O. I. (1973). Overselective response to social stimuli by autistic children. *Journal of Abnormal Child Psychology, 1,* 152–168.

Sherman, J., Factor, D. C., Swinson, R., & Darjes, R. W. (1989). The effects of fenfluramine (hydrochloride) on the behaviors of fifteen autistic children. *Journal of Autism and Developmental Disorders, 19,* 533-543.

Stahmer, A. (1995). Teaching symbolic play skills to children with autism using Pivotal Response Training. *Journal of Autism and Developmental Disorders, 25,* 123–141.

Stokes, T. F., & Baer, D. M. (1977). An implicit technology of generalization. *Journal of Applied Behavior Analysis, 10,* 349–368.

Stokes, T. F., Baer, D. M., & Jackson, R. L. (1974). Programming the generalization of a greeting response in four retarded children. *Journal of Applied Behavior Analysis, 1,* 599–610.

Strain, P. S., Kerr, M. M., & Ragland, E. U. (1979). Effects of peer-mediated social initiations and prompting/reinforcement procedures on the social behavior of autistic children. *Journal of Autism and Developmental Disorders, 9,* 41–54.

Tager-Flusberg, H. (1992). Autistic children's talk about psychological states: Deficits in the early acquisition of a theory of mind. *Child Development, 63,* 161–172.

Tager-Flusberg, H., Calkins, S., Nolin, T., Baumberger, T., Anderson, M., & Chadwick-Dias, A. (1990). A longitudinal study of language acquisition in autistic and down syndrome children. *Journal of Autism and Developmental Disorders, 20,* 1–21.

Tantam, D., Monaghan, L., Nicholson, H., & Sterling, J. (1989). Autistic children's ability to interpret faces: A research note. *Journal of Child Psychology and Psychiatry, 4,* 623–630.

Touchette, P. (1971). Transfer of stimulus control: Measuring the moment of transfer. *Journal of Experimental Analysis of Behavior, 15,* 347-354.

Touchette, P. E., MacDonald, R. F., & Langer, S. N. (1985). A scatterplot for identifying stimulus control of problem behavior. *Journal of Applied Behavior Analysis, 18,* 343-351.

Varni, J., Lovaas, O. I., Koegel, R. L., & Everett, N. L. (1979). An analysis of observational learning in autistic and normal children. *Journal of Abnormal Child Psychology, 7,* 31-43.

Volkmar, F. R., & Cohen, D. J. (1994). Autism. Current concepts. *Child and Adolescent Psychiatric Clinics of North America, 3,* 43-52.

White, G. D., Nielson, G., & Johnson, S. M. (1972). Time-out duration and the suppression of deviant behavior in children. *Journal of Applied Behavior Analysis, 5,* 111–120.

Wing, L. (1972). *Autistic children: A guide for parents.* New York: Brunner/Mazel.

Wing, L. (1976). Diagnosis, clinical description and prognosis. In L. Wing (Ed.), *Early childhood autism: Clinical, educational and social aspects* (2nd ed., pp. 15–64). Elmsford, NY: Pergamon Press.

CHAPTER 10

MENTALLY RETARDED CHILDREN

Johnny L. Matson
Heather Applegate
Brandi Smiroldo
Sydney Stallings

HISTORICAL PERSPECTIVES

In ancient Greece and Rome, mentally retarded persons were objects of scorn and persecution. They were considered a burden to society, and it was not uncommon for parents to kill their mentally retarded children for "the betterment of society." Attitudes toward mentally retarded persons began to change with the dawn of Christianity. During this period, limited attempts were made to provide comfort and support. By the time of the Middle Ages, however, the concept of these persons as fools, hardly worthy of society's care, had reemerged. This orientation persisted over hundreds of years in both Europe and the Orient as well as among American Indians (Rosen, Clark, & Kivitz, 1976). While mentally retarded persons were not intentionally killed during this period, no attempts were made to educate or care for them (Kanner, 1967).

With the Renaissance and the Reformation came the renewed interest in scientific inquiry, education, and humanitarianism that eventually brought about new approaches to the care of mentally retarded persons. In one of the earliest sustained and systematic programs on record, Itard, an eighteenth century French physician, educated Victor, the "wild boy of Aveyron" (Rosen et al., 1976). Testing and placement considerations provided impetus for much of the early work done with mentally retarded individuals. In the early 1900s, Binet developed the first standardized intellectual assessment tests to identify and separate "feeble-minded" people from the general populace.

Interest in the care and habilitation of developmentally disabled individuals has grown. The most substantial amount of change has occurred in the last 20 years, fueled by the growth of deinstitutionalization and advances in medical and behavior modification technology. A voluminous and ever-expanding literature on treatment, classification, etiology, and epidemiology stands as a testament to the progress made in recent years. Most of what will be discussed in this chapter will be based on recent historical developments.

CLASSIFICATION, ETIOLOGY, AND INCIDENCE AND PREVALENCE

Classification

Traditionally the American Association on Mental Retardation (AAMR) has been the leader in defining and classifying the construct of mental retardation. During the late nineteenth and early twentieth centuries, mental retardation was defined solely by deficits in intellectual functioning noted during the developmental period—prior to age 18 (Scheerenberger, 1987). Labels such as idiot, imbecile, and moron were initially used to classify individuals into specific categories (Matson & Marchetti, 1988; Scheerenberger, 1987). Later categories based on intellectual test scores were used to delineate distinct groups (Heber, 1961). These categories included borderline, mild, moderate, severe and profound. In 1936 Doll added deficits in adaptive behavior, or social inadequacy, to the requirements for a diagnosis of mental retardation (Matson & Marchetti, 1988; Scheerenberger, 1987). The additional focus on adaptive behavior deficits sparked the development of numerous measures to assess such deficits including the Vineland Adaptive Behavior Scale (Sparrow, Balla, & Cicchetti, 1984) and the AAMD Adaptive Behavior Scale (Nihira, Foster, Schellhaas, & Leland, 1974). These measures focus on identifying strengths and weaknesses in the individual's functioning in areas such as communication, social behaviors, motor skills, and self-help skills (Leland, 1991).

The person would have to score in the mentally retarded range on adaptive functioning. Whichever score, intellectual test, or adaptive behavior score, was highest would determine the person's classification. Therefore, a person with an IQ score in the moderate range and an adaptive behavior score in the mild range would be categorized as mildly mentally retarded. In 1992 the AAMR redefined mental retardation again (AAMR, 1992). Unlike previous definitions, this one has produced a great deal of controversy. It is a dramatic departure from previous definitions and requires different dimensions of behavior to be sampled. As required by the new definition, a person must display deficiencies in 2 of 10 adaptive skill areas: communication, self-care, home living, social skills, community use, self-direction, health and safety, functional academics, leisure, and work. Additionally, the four levels of mental retardation (mild, moderate, severe, and profound) have been omitted. Instead, the current definition uses four levels of support (intermittent, limited, extensive, and pervasive). Furthermore, the IQ cutoff has been raised to 75 from a previous cutoff of 70.

Because of these changes, concerns have been voiced regarding the new definition (MacMillan, Gresham, & Siperstein, 1993). Psychologists in particular are concerned with the practicality of making an adequate, reliable, and valid diagnosis given these new criteria. Several specific concerns have been cited. First, in reference to the increased IQ cutoff score, the American Psychological Association has stated that the number of people diagnosed as mentally retarded will dramatically increase. This situation is especially true regarding minorities. There is a disproportionate representation of minorities in the mild range of mental retardation (Reschly & Ward, 1989). Persons in the severe/profound ranges are relatively proportionate to the general population. Second, the 10 areas of adaptive functioning were not empirically derived. Additionally, there are currently no standardized tests specifically designed to assess functioning in these areas. Therefore, deficits in these adaptive areas cannot be evaluated reliably. Finally, it has been noted that there are no normative measures to assess the support levels (MacMillan, et al., 1993).

The American Psychiatric Association has adopted portions of the new definition for it's fourth edition of the *Diagnostic and Statistical Manual of Mental Disorders,* while retaining portions of the 1993 definition (APA, 1994). Previous editions had followed AAMR criteria almost exactly; therefore, this discrepancy between DSM-IV and the AAMR definition represents a significant departure in policy. DSM-IV requires subaverage intellectual functioning as evinced by an IQ of approximately 70 (two standard deviations below the mean) or below on standardized intelligence tests. The 10 areas of adaptive functioning delineated in the 1992 AAMR definition are utilized in DSM-IV as is the requirement of deficits in 2 of these areas. However, unlike the new AAMR definition, DSM-IV continues to classify subgroups of individuals with mental retardation by the levels traditionally used.

It will be of interest to see how these differences in definitions are reconciled. Both of these organizations exert a great deal of influence on the field of developmental disabilities. Although it is likely that one of these definitions will eventually become the accepted approach, it is unlikely that this will occur in the near future.

Etiology

Classification of individuals diagnosed as mentally retarded may tell the clinician something about the individual's level of functioning, but it does not provide insight into the etiology of the disorder. Etiology of mental retardation is unknown in a majority of those receiving a diagnosis, particularly in those with mild or moderate mental retardation who account for approximately 95% of the group (APA, 1994). Of those cases in which etiologies are not identified, social deprivation is thought to be a primary factor in the development of mental retardation. It has been suggested that these individuals do not receive adequate environmental stimulation. It is, therefore, possible that environment is a factor in the cause of delayed development in many mild and moderately mentally retarded persons.

As inferred above, organic disorders are more often identified as etiologies of mental retardation in the severe and profound ranges (Abuelo, 1991). It is estimated that genetic causes of mental retardation occur in half of individuals with IQs below 50. Phenylketonuria (PKU), Tay-Sachs, Tuberous Sclerosis, and Lesch-Nyhan syndrome are examples of genetic disorders that often result in mental retardation with Down's syndrome being the most common (Abuelo, 1991). Other possible etiological factors include infections and traumas both prenatally and postnatally. With tremendous advancements in the technology of prenatal care and early detection of such disorders, more accurate prognosis and plans for immediate treatment are possible.

One issue complicating the ability to link specific causes to the occurrence of mental retardation is the frequent co-occurrence of potential etiological factors in the same individual. An interaction between several factors such as genetic disorders, medical complications, and environmental conditions may result in mental retardation (Matson & Mulick, 1991).

Incidence and Prevalence

Due to difficulties in diagnosing and identifying cases of mental retardation, prevalence and incidence of the disorder are often difficult to establish. Two methods exist for calculating incidence and prevalence. One is statistical, the other epidemiological.

The statistical approach involves plotting intellectual functioning along a normal curve. Individuals who are two or more standard deviations below the mean are classified as mentally retarded. The statistical approach was used in the 1960s by the President's Panel on Mental Retardation. The panel reported a 3% prevalence rate, stating that 5.4 million Americans were identified as mentally retarded (Scheerenberger, 1987).

Epidemiological studies provide more precise data on frequency and types of mental retardation. Although such studies are infrequently utilized in the United States, European countries employ them often. Among studies with children 5–14 years of age, prevalence of persons with IQs below 50 range from 3.45–5.8 per thousand. These studies include England (Goodman & Tizard, 1962; Kushlick, 1961, 1964), America (Lemkau, Tietze, & Cooper, 1943), Sweden (Akesson, 1959), Scotland (Birch, Richardson, Baird, Harobin, & Illsby, 1970), and Northern Ireland (Drillien, Jameson, & Wilkinson, 1966).

CHAPTER OUTLINE

In a single review chapter it would be impossible to consider the entire gamut of behavior change procedures employed with mentally retarded children. The basic procedures of reinforcement, punishment, and social learning have been used over the years to develop an extensive array of programs for mentally retarded children. The present chapter, therefore, provides only a brief overview of empirically validated techniques. Apart from the addition of studies that have appeared since the second edition of this book, the present chapter also includes sections on topic areas that have received increasing attention from researchers and clinicians recently. Our coverage begins with a brief discussion of behavioral assessment. While the focus of this chapter is on treatment, assessment has assumed greater importance in the behavior therapy literature in recent years (Matson & Frame, 1987). This belated attention has come with the realization that assessment is an integral part of any intervention program. Successful treatment relies not only on identifying variables that may foster and maintain desirable behavior, but also on identifying conditions that presently control behavioral excesses and deficiencies. The basic paradigms of reinforcement (positive and negative) and punishment (physical aversives, time out, and overcorrection) are considered next. Two additional classes of procedures receiving increasing attention here are social learning and self-control methods. Our coverage concludes with a look at several of the more important concerns and developments in intervention of technology of late, including (a) communication skills training, (b) social skills training, (c) independent functioning in community settings, (d) functional analysis, (e) dual diagnosis, (f) behavioral psychopharmacology, and (g) generalization and maintenance.

ASSESSMENT

While a complete discussion of assessment issues is beyond the scope of this chapter, a brief overview will be presented. Accurate assessment and diagnosis are essential in ensuring effective treatment. A thorough assessment will include gathering of information regarding life and medical history, environmental factors, standardized intellectual, adaptive and achievement testing, and behavioral observations (Matson & Mulick, 1991). Intellectual assessments are generally conducted using the Stanford-Binet Intelligence Scale or the Wechsler Scales, while adaptive functioning is assessed with such measures as the Vineland Adaptive Behavior Scale or the AAMD Adaptive Behavior Scales (Leland, 1991; Sattler, 1992). Assessment should be directly

linked with treatment. Once the clinician has the results of the assessment, he or she should be able to devise a treatment based on these results and evaluate the efficacy of the treatment using the assessment procedure. The most recent advances in assessment of problems and skills deficits in individuals presenting with mental retardation have been made in the areas of self-injury and psychopathology. The development of functional analysis for the assessment of problem behaviors in this population has received much attention (Cooper, Wacker, Sasson, Reimers, & Donn, 1990; Durand & Crimmins, 1988; Northup, Wacker, Sasso, Steege, Cigrand, Cook, & DeRaad, 1991; Vollmer & Matson, 1995). The bulk of this work has been conducted with individuals presenting with self-injurious behavior. With regard to psychopathology in the mentally retarded, recent advancements have focused on developing instruments specifically for assessing mental health problems in this population (Matson, 1995; Matson, Kazdin, & Senatore, 1984). Both functional analysis and psychopathology in the mentally retarded will be discussed in greater detail later in the chapter.

Conducting a thorough assessment should be a stepping stone toward development of an effective treatment program. The following sections will describe various techniques used in the treatment of mentally retarded children.

REINFORCEMENT

Reinforcement refers to any event or object that increases the likelihood of a response (Bijou, 1993). Reinforcement methods are typically less intrusive and well-accepted by professionals and family members. There are two types of reinforcement typically employed in the treatment of individuals with mental retardation: positive reinforcement and negative reinforcement.

Positive Reinforcement

When positive-reinforcement methods are used, the likelihood of a response is increased based on the presentation of a preferred object or event (Bijou, 1993).

Generally, such procedures are employed to increase and strengthen positive behaviors such as social, language, and adaptive skills in individuals with mental retardation. Positive-reinforcement procedures may involve the use of primary reinforcers (e.g., edibles or social rein-forcement), the use of secondary reinforcers (e.g., tokens), and/or reinforcing behaviors that are incompatible with a maladaptive behavior.

Primary reinforcers such as edibles strengthen a response as a result of intrinsic reinforcing properties, while secondary reinforcers strengthen responses based on their association with primary reinforcers. Secondary reinforcers must be paired with primary reinforcers in order to effectively reinforce behavior. Thus, primary reinforcers are most frequently used with young children and those with mental retardation (Foxx, 1982).

Prescription

Positive-reinforcement procedures are often utilized to increase adaptive behaviors such as compliance, social skills, and communication skills. Procedure 1 is used to establish a response, and procedure 2 is a means of maintaining the response once an appropriate behavior has been established.

Procedure 1

Cataldo, Ward, Russo, Riordan, and Bennett (1988) compared the frequency of compliance and the frequency of inappropriate behaviors during conditions of contingent reinforcement and noncontingent reinforcement of compliance. Inappropriate behaviors included aggression, crying, destructiveness, climbing, lying on the floor, mouthing, opening the door, and playing with light switches. During the contingent-reinforcement condition, small edibles, praise, and physical contact were given to each child only when the child complied with a request (i.e., "come here," "sit down or stand up," "go there," "give me the (toy)," or "put the (toy) in the box"). All requests were presented with the child's name and an appropriate gesture. In the noncontingent-reinforcement condition each child was presented with the reinforcement on a variable time schedule with 15 rein-

forcers per session never within 5 seconds of a command. Compliance increased 100% in all subjects and remained high only in the contingent-reinforcement condition. In addition, many inappropriate behaviors decreased during the contingent-reinforcement phase, but not during the noncontingent reinforcement phase.

Procedure 2

The example mentioned in Procedure 1 illustrates the efficacy of reinforcement procedures in skill training for individuals with mental retardation. In addition to the procedures noted above generalization and maintenance techniques should be employed. Training should occur across settings and in the natural environment in order to aid in generalization, while reinforcement contingencies should gradually be increased to aid in the maintenance of treatment effects. For example, in order to ensure maintenance of appropriate responses in the example given in Procedure 1, several trainers could have been used, as well as incidental training in the child's natural environment. Furthermore, reinforcement contingencies could have been increased so that compliance must occur within a specified time period in order to receive reinforcement.

Negative Reinforcement

Negative-reinforcement methods increase the likelihood of a response by removing an aversive object or ending an aversive event (Bijou, 1993). A typical example of the use of negative reinforcement to increase or strengthen a response in individuals with mental retardation involves removal of a demand or task situation for a brief amount of time.

Prescription

Negative-reinforcement procedures are most often utilized in training communication skills during demand situations. The procedure described is a means of establishing the communication response. Generalization and maintenance techniques are similar to those used with positive reinforcement.

Procedure

Steege and colleagues (1990) utilized negative-reinforcement procedures to treat self-injurious behavior (SIB) and increase appropriate communication skills in two children with profound mental retardation. Results of a functional analysis indicated that the SIB occurred primarily during demand situations. A treatment package was devised consisting of negative reinforcement and guided compliance to teach a more appropriate means of requesting a break from task demands. The children were given a 10-second break from a grooming activity when a microswitch that said "stop" was pressed. The rates of SIB were consistently reduced and appropriate communication increased for both children.

Examples of both positive and negative reinforcement are outlined in Table 10.1.

PUNISHMENT

Punishment refers to any event or object that decreases the likelihood of a response (Bijou, 1993). These events or objects are aversive to the individual. There has been much controversy surrounding the use of aversive procedures to decrease maladaptive behaviors (Axelrod, 1990; Donnellan & LaVigna, 1990; Matson & Taras, 1989). Proponents of the use of aversives point to the effectiveness of such methods and the aversive, dangerous, and restrictive nature of many maladaptive behaviors exhibited by individuals with mental retardation. These individuals also endorse the use of a combination of procedures including reinforcement and aversives. Opponents of the use of aversives purport that the aversive procedures are not effective, are inhumane, and have negative side effects. There has been little support for these contentions in the literature.

Due to the intrusiveness of such procedures it is recommended that the use of aversives be conducted in a systematic manner and only with extreme problem behaviors (Foxx, 1982). Those procedures that are least intrusive should be attempted first, and more intrusive procedures should be implemented if the preceding treatment is not effective. Thus, extinction and differential-reinforcement procedures should be employed before time-out or contingent electric shock.

Aversive procedures include numerous treatment techniques. Some of the most widely used and effective procedures are (a) physical punishment, (b) overcorrection, and (c) time-out. The following is a review of these procedures and examples of their application. Additional studies utilizing punishment procedures are outlined in Table 10.2.

Physical Punishment

Physical punishment includes procedures such as contingent electric shock, loud noises, restraint, noxious odors, hair pulling, slapping, and tickling

TABLE 10.1. Sample Treatment Studies with Reinforcement

AUTHORS	TYPES OF PERSONS	BEHAVIOR	TREATMENT
Bird, Dores, Moniz, & Robinson (1989)	Two mentally retarded adults	Lack of functional communicatoin & self-injury	FCT—secondary & negative
Matson & Francis (1994)	Two developmentally delayed children	Limited verbal communication	Positive reinforcement
Combs & Jansma (1990)	Five mentally retarded adults	Lack of fitness	Positive reinforcement
Mason & Newson (1990)	Three adolescents with mental retardation, autism, or schizophrenia	Stereoptypes	Sensory reinforcement
Kennedy & Haring (1993)	Three mentally retarded adolescents	Destructive behavior	Reward & escape

TABLE 10.2. Sample Treatment Studies Using Punishment

AUTHORS	TYPES OF PERSONS	BEHAVIOR	TREATMENT
Iwata, Pace, Kalsher, Cowdery, & Cataldo (1990)	Mentally retarded children	SIB	Escape extinction
Jordan, Singh, & Repp (1989)	Mentally retarded adults and children	Stereoptypes	Gentle teaching vs. visual screening
Zarcone, Iwata, Vollmer, Jagtiani, Smith, & Mazaleski	Mentally retarded women	DIB	Escape extinction
Figueroa, Thyer, & Thyer (1992)	Mentally retarded boys	Aggression	Escape extinction & DRO
Fisher, Piazza, Bowman Hagopian, & Langdon (1994)	Mentally retarded children	SIB, Pica, aggression, & disruption	Facial screen, escape extinction, & DRO

(DiLorenzo & Land, 1988; Paniagua, Braverman, & Capriotti, 1986; Koegel & Covert, 1972; Bailey, Pikrzywinski, & Bryant, 1983; Tanner & Zeiler, 1975; Griffin, Locke, & Landers, 1975). There is a trend in the literature to utilize less extreme procedures such as face washing, brief arm restraints, and similar procedures. These procedures should only be administered by a highly trained behavior therapist who has taken all necessary steps to ensure the client's safety during the procedures. A one-to-one treatment setting is generally the best for implementing physical punishment.

Prescription

Physical punishment procedures are typically employed to reduce only the most aberrant behaviors including severe self-injury, aggression, rumination, and pica. Most treatment packages involving physical punishment also incorporate reinforcement. The application of physical punishment consists of presenting the stimuli immediately after the occurrence of the maladaptive behavior. In most cases, a warning is given in conjunction with the aversive stimuli. The warning is gradually faded so that the warning takes on the properties of the aversive stimuli. Generally, the procedure is most effective when a considerable amount of the aversive stimulus is presented from the onset of treatment. If the intensity of the stimulus is gradually

increased, the client will become accustomed to the aversive and be able to withstand high levels of the stimulus.

Procedure

Johnson, Hunt, and Siebert (1994) treated two profoundly retarded adolescents for pica, the ingestion of inedible objects, with physical punishment and reinforcement. During treatment the individuals were allowed to eat edible substances situated on a mat in front of them. Inedible substances were placed on the outside of the mat. If the subjects moved an inedible item toward their mouths, the therapists instructed them to stand up and remove the object. For one subject, either physical restraint (holding his arms down for 15 seconds) or face washing was also employed following attempts to ingest inedibles. Only face washing was utilized with the second subject. Pica significantly decreased for both subjects, although greater decreases were noted with the second subject.

Prescription

One means of physical punishment that has received attention recently, but sparks controversy is the use of contingent electric shock to control maladaptive behaviors (Iwata & Rodgers, 1992; Linscheid, Iwata, Ricketts, Williams, & Griffin, 1990). The procedure has been shown to be effective in reducing the most severe forms of SIB, but should be utilized with extreme caution.

Procedure

In a study examining the effectiveness of the Self-Injurious Behavior Inhibiting System (SIBIS), one of the most recently introduced devices for administering contingent electric shock, Linscheid and colleagues (1994) employed the device to reduce severe head hitting in a severely mentally retarded boy with cerebral palsy. The boy had a ventricular peritoneal shunt placed as a result of hydrocephalus. There was concern about damage to the shunt due to his frequent episodes of head hitting. Injury to the brain and death were plausible results of such damage. Use of SIBIS was compared to normal parental consequences and solely wearing the SIBIS head gear. SIBIS was effective in reducing the head hitting from rates as high as 120 incidences per 10-minute interval.

Overcorrection

Foxx and Azrin (1973) first described the use of overcorrection procedures. Overcorrection involves having the child correct some aspect of the environment following the behavior- and/or practice-appropriate related behaviors. The latter is often referred to as restitution correction, while the former is called positive practice. Additionally, manual guidance may be used in noncompliant subjects or those with severe physical and sensory impairments. Mackenzie-Keating and McDonald (1990) suggest that due to the numerous methods of implementing procedures, overcorrection is not a simple treatment approach, but a complex combination of techniques.

Prescription

Overcorrection procedures are typically utilized to treat eating problems and toilet training. With some modifications overcorrection is applicable for all ages and levels of intellectual ability. In general, graduated guidance and modeling are useful

for compliant individuals, while more stringent overcorrection procedures may be necessary with noncompliant individuals

Procedure

In a study investigating the efficacy of overcorrection, Sisson, Van Hasselt, and Hersen (1993) treated two individuals presenting with multiple problem behaviors. The individuals engaged in stereotypic movements, property destruction, and aggression. A treatment program was instituted using a combination of differential reinforcement of adaptive behaviors and overcorrection. The individuals were trained to engage in sorting and packaging tasks. Compliance with the task was reinforced, while exhibition of the maladaptive behaviors resulted in overcorrection using manual guidance through the appropriate behaviors. Compliance increased and rates of the maladaptive behaviors decreased.

Time-Out

Time-out is a frequently employed procedure in this population. It includes removing the child from a preferred situation or removing a preferred reinforcer. Time-out may be exclusionary or nonexclusionary. Exclusionary time-out would involve having the child removed from the room containing the preferred object or in which the preferred situation was occurring. In contrast, nonexclusionary time-out refers to a procedure in which the child remains in the room, but is not allowed to partake in the preferred situation or have the preferred object. Of the two variations exclusionary time-out is considered more aversive and should be employed in more severe cases.

Prescription

Time-out procedures are utilized to decrease numerous problem behaviors. Any time-out procedure should be implemented immediately following the inappropriate behavior. A brief reprimand conveying disapproval should accompany the time-out, and the individual should be guided to the time-out seat or room with little or no attention given.

Procedure

Rortvedt and Miltenberger (1994) investigated the effectiveness of time-out as compared to high-probability requests on the rate of compliance of two children. The authors developed a list of 12 high-probability commands and 12 low-probability commands based on interviews and observations of interaction between the mothers and children participating in the study. The high-probability phase consisted of the mothers presenting a sequence of 3 high-probability commands followed by a low-probability command. Compliance was praised and noncompliance was ignored. If the child did not comply with the last high-probability command, additional high-probability commands were given until the child complied. In contrast, the time-out phase consisted of the mothers delivering a low-probability request. If the child did not comply, he or she was guided to a chair in another room for 1 minute and required to sit quietly for 10 seconds.

The high-probability sequence increased compliance to low-probability requests for only one child, and the increase was only 61%. Time-out increased compliance to 81% for both children. Effects were maintained at 2-, 4-, and 6-week follow-up.

SOCIAL LEARNING METHODS

Social-learning methods include some common techniques such as modeling, imitation, role-playing, social reinforcement, and performance feedback. These procedures are typically used to train communication, social, and self-help skills in mildly to severely mentally retarded individuals. The effectiveness of social-learning methods in the mentally retarded population has been demonstrated by several researchers. For instance, Kelly, Furman, Phillips, Hathorn, and Wilson (1979) demonstrated the efficacy of using a modeling/coaching procedure with two moderately mentally retarded adolescents to teach conversational skills. Both of the subjects were reported to have severe deficiencies in interactions with their peers. The researchers were interested in improving the subjects' conversational skills in the following ways: increasing the amount of information provided by the subject when asked a direct question by a peer, increasing the number of questions the subject asked a peer, and increasing the number of social invitations extended to a peer.

During the training phase, the subject watched a modeling videotape of two people engaging in conversation. In the tape, the partner made 13 standard comments, and the model replied appropriately. After watching the tape, the subject received brief coaching in which he was offered the opportunity to rehearse his responses to the 13 standard comments before talking with a nonretarded peer (cohort). Once the subject was finished rehearsing, a nonretarded peer entered the room and made the 13 standard comments. Modeling and coaching improved the conversational skills of the two subjects. More importantly, the results generalized to 3 weeks later when the subjects were approached by a novel peer who made the 13 comments without benefit of coaching. Furthermore, the researchers found that both of the subjects' nonverbal and verbal behavior in free-play situations had improved following conversation-skills training.

Prescription

Social-learning approaches differ considerably, but all are aimed primarily at the acquisition of new responses. The level of cognitive functioning dictates the variety of methods that are applicable. In the next section, a procedure is describe using social-learning methods to train self-help skills.

Procedure

Taras, Matson, and Felps (1993) demonstrated that independence training improving the independent-living skills of three children and four young men. Independence training combines social-learning methods (e.g., modeling, performance feedback, social reinforcement) and operant procedures (e.g., shaping) with instructions, self-monitoring, and evaluation (Matson, 1981, 1982a). All of the subjects were visually impaired, and five of the seven were mentally retarded. The children composed the first group, and the young men composed the second. Both groups were taught independent-living skills. The first group was taught how to dial 911, fold a shirt, and spread soft foods on crackers. The second group was taught three leather-work tasks because it was functional and the young men did not engage in many leisure activities. The training occurred in small groups of two to four subjects, and involved a modified modeling procedure because the subjects were visually impaired. For example, the trainer physically guided the hands of the subject to fold a shirt while giving a narrative of the correct procedure. Following modeling, the trainer asked the subject to perform the task while the other subjects listened. When an error was made in one of the steps toward task completion, the trainer stopped the procedure, explained the last step that was completed correctly, and then had one of the other subjects describe what the next step should be to complete the behavior correctly. If the performing subject could not follow the peer's or trainer's verbal prompt, then the trainer physically guided the subject through the task.

After the subject completed the task, the trainer asked him or her to rate his or her performance and the reason behind the rating. The trainer and peers then gave feedback on performance and the accuracy of the self-evaluation. Furthermore, social reinforcement in the form of praise was given by the trainer and peers for performing well on the tasks.

Training was effective for teaching mentally retarded children and young men with visual impairments self-help skills. Specifically, the children learned how to fold a shirt, dial 911, and spread soft foods on crackers. The young men learned how to use leather to make coin purses, belts, and bolo ties. Furthermore, the results were maintained 10 months later.

The cognitive abilities of the client should be taken into consideration when choosing a social-learning technique. Typically, individuals with lower cognitive functioning benefit from simpler procedures such as modeling (Goldstein & Mousetis, 1989; Matson, Manikam, Coe, Raymond, Toras, & Long 1988), social reinforcement (Matson, et al., 1988), and feedback (Matson, 1980).

Individuals with higher cognitive abilities can benefit from more complex procedures, such as vicarious conditioning or role playing, which are more cost effective and less time-constrictive than the others. Many other uses of social learning procedures have been made, some of which are outlined in Table 10.3.

SELF-CONTROL PROCEDURES

Self-control procedures with mentally retarded individuals have become more popular in recent years as shown by the increasing number of studies using these techniques to train a variety of behaviors (Cavalier, Murphy, & Murphy, 1993). In Shapiro's (1981) review of self-control procedures, he states

TABLE 10.3. Sample Treatment Studies Using Social Learning

AUTHORS	TYPES OF PERSONS	BEHAVIOR	TREATMENT
O'Connor (1969)	Socially withdrawn children	Social skills	Modeling
Goldstein & Mousetis (1989)	Mentally retarded children	Generalized expressive language	Modeling
Matson, Sevin, Box, Francis, & Sevin (1993)	Autistic and mentally retarded children	Self-initiated speech	Treatment package (modeling)
Whitman, Mercurio, & Caponigri (1970)	Mentally retarded boys	Ball-playing	Instructions & feedback
Ralph & Birnbrauer (1986)	Mentally retarded men	Social skills	Reinforcement, feedback, & modeling

that the ultimate goal of self-control procedures is to increase independence. Considering the fact that most mentally retarded individuals are deficient in areas of independent functioning, self-control procedures are essential provided they are effective and generalizable from training situations to natural settings. For example, Koegel and Frea (1993) demonstrated the efficacy of self-monitoring in two autistic adolescents. Target behaviors for the first subject were eye contact and nonverbal gestures. Eye contact was operationally defined as looking in the direction of the trainer of the object of conversation. Inappropriate behavior was looking away from the trainer for longer than 3 seconds. Nonverbal gestures were considered appropriate if they were relevant to the topic of conversation. Inappropriate gestures included body rubbing, excessive limb movement, or overexaggerated gestures. Target behaviors for the second subject were perseveration of topic. Perseveration of topic was appropriate if the child followed the topic of conversation throughout the trial. If the child talked about a topic previously discussed, or did not follow conversational cues to change topics, the verbalizations were considered inappropriate.

Each subject was taught through modeling and imitation to discriminate between appropriate and inappropriate instances of the target behaviors. Once each child was able to correctly identify the target behaviors, self-monitoring began. Treatment took place in a community setting in which the opportunity to play video games was used for reinforcement. Each subject was given a digital watch with a preset alarm. When the alarm sounded, the subjects recorded the instances of appropriate target behaviors. If an instance was recorded, then the subjects were allowed to play a video game. During the self-monitoring sessions, intervals of time increased from 1 to 9 minutes for one subject, and from 1 to 7 minutes for the other. After a 5-minute interval was reached, the number of instances of appropriate target behaviors increased before reinforcement could be earned. The results indicated that both of the subjects' appropriate target behaviors increased to either 100% or close to 100%. Furthermore, the researchers demonstrated that social behaviors not targeted for treatment also improved. For the first

subject, perseveration of topic increased to nearly 100% even though it was not a target behavior. Likewise, appropriate eye gaze and nonverbal gestures reached nearly 100% for the second subject.

Prescription

Training self-control is most effective if the target behaviors are those that the child already performs, but on a variable basis. Obviously, it is easier to focus training on self-control if the target behaviors are already in the child's repertoire. However, it is important that the target behavior occur on a variable basis so that monitoring and adjusting of behavior can be practiced. For example, a mentally retarded child who is capable of independently brushing his or her teeth, but does so on an inconsistent basis, may be a good candidate for self-control training. Initially, the trainer should model tooth-brushing while narrating the entire sequence (e.g., "First I brush my front teeth, then I brush the teeth on one side, then I brush the teeth on the other side, etc."). The trainer then requests that the child imitate the entire sequence. Gradually, modeling, imitation, and feedback are withdrawn so that the child is exhibiting the behavior on his or her own. Periodic checks are recommended to ensure that the child continues to use self-control procedures to monitor target behaviors. Examples of self-control procedures are provided in Table 10.4.

GENERAL TRENDS AND RECENT DEVELOPMENTS

Communication-Skills Training

Deficiencies in communication skills in mentally retarded individuals has received a great deal of attention in recent literature (Goldstein & Hockenberger, 1991). Severely and profoundly mentally retarded individuals often do not develop basic communication skills due to cognitive and/or physical deficits (Matson & Coe, 1991). Research on verbal communication training has focused on three types of procedures in recent years; mand-model, incidental teaching, and delayed prompting.

TABLE 10.4. Treatment Studies Using Self-Control Procedures

AUTHORS	TYPES OF PERSONS	BEHAVIOR	TREATMENT
Coleman & Whitman (1984)	Mentally retarded adolescents	Exercise	Self-monitor, & self-reinforce
Irvine, Singer, Erikson, & Stahlberg (1992)	Mentally retarded students	Chores	Self-management
Wheeler, Bates, Marshall, & Miller (1988)	Mentally retarded man	Social skills	Social-skills training & self-monitor

The first procedure, mand-modeling, was originally described by Bruner in 1978. It involves placing the child in a natural setting containing many stimulating materials. A typical example is a classroom in which there are several toys, books, puzzles, and other fun objects placed throughout the room. When the child approaches an object and shows interest, the trainer says, "Tell me what you want." If the child responds inappropriately (e.g., grabs the object, throws a temper tantrum), then the trainer models the appropriate response and encourages the child to imitate the behavior. The child receives the object once an attempt is made to appropriately request the item. The obvious advantages of this training procedure is that it involves training in natural settings, and it allows parents and teachers to become active participants in teaching the child appropriate skill acquisition. Furthermore, several researchers have demonstrated that the mand-model of communication training is generalizable to other settings (Warren, McQuarter, & Rogers-Warren, 1984) and that it increases the rates of verbalizations, vocabulary, and complexity of vocalizations (Rogers-Warren & Warren, 1980).

The second procedure to receive a great deal of attention in recent years is incidental teaching. Incidental teaching is very similar to the mand-model approach of language acquisition. Training takes place in a natural setting and when the child approaches a desired object the trainer prompts verbal communication in order to receive the object. If the child doesn't respond appropriately, the behavior is modeled by the trainer and then imitated by the child. Finally, the trainer verbally acknowledges the correct response and the child receives the object. The major difference between the mand-model approach and incidental teaching lies in the fact that the former involves placing reinforcing materials in the room with the child, whereas the latter relies on the child finding reinforcing materials on his or her own.

The third procedure is delayed prompting, which is designed to promote transference of language acquisition in an experimental setting to a naturalistic one. This procedure involves prompting the child to make the correct response at the same time the desired object is presented. For example, the trainer would place a reinforcing toy in front of the child while simultaneously asking, "Do you want the toy?" The amount of time between object presentation and prompting gradually increases so that the child has ample opportunity to make the correct response before prompting occurs. Matson, Sevin, Fridley, and Love (1990) used a procedure similar to a delayed prompting to teach three autistic children with little or no spontaneous speech to say "please" and "thank you" as well as "your welcome." The authors found that the spontaneous speech of all three children increased dramatically across all treatment phases. The "please" and "thank you" response increased to 100% in all three children and was maintained at high levels at 1, 2, and 6 months post-treatment.

Unfortunately, mentally retarded individuals who lack appropriate communication skills typically resort to maladaptive behaviors as a means of communication. In such cases, a functional analysis is conducted to determine the function of the targeted behaviors. Functional-communication training is often used to teach individuals appropriate verbal or nonverbal communication that serves the same function as the problem behavior (Durand, 1993). For example, if a child typically becomes aggressive in order to receive a tangible item, he or she would be trained to make appropriate requests for tangible items. By teaching communicative responses that serve the same function as the maladaptive behavior, the frequency of the target behavior usually declines and the use of appropriate responses increases (Durand & Carr, 1991; Durand & Carr, 1992). Examples of communication skills training are listed in Table 5.

Social Skills

By definition, individuals with mental retardation have deficits or excesses in social skills (AAMR, 1992; APA, 1994). Additionally, researchers have consistently documented the presence of such deficits in this population (Bellack, Morrison, Wixted, & Muser, 1990; Marchetti & Campbell, 1990). Social skills affect numerous areas of an individual's life including leisure and vocational and school functioning (Coe, Matson, Craigie, & Gossen, 1991; Factor & Schilmoeller, 1983; Greenwood, Todd, Hops, & Walker, 1982; Kolstoe & Shafter, 1961; Raymond & Matson, 1989; Wheeler, Bates, Marshall, & Miller, 1988). Thus, research and understanding in this area are important for those who work with these individuals.

Numerous factors may contribute to the social-skills problems inherent in this population. First, individuals with mental retardation lack appropriate peer models (Guralnick, 1986; Kelly, Furman, Phillips, Hathorn, & Wilson, 1979). One important form of learning is through modeling and imitation. These individuals are not often given the opportuni-

ty to witness appropriate social interactions. Second, for individuals with normal intelligence, one important means of social interaction is verbal communication. Individuals with mental retardation are oftentimes delayed in the acquisition of verbal skills or are nonverbal (Whitman, Sciback, & Reid, 1983).

Despite these difficulties, researchers have consistently documented that individuals with mental retardation can acquire appropriate social skills (Matson et al., 1988; Matson, Fee, Coe, & Smith, 1991). Matson and colleagues (1991) utilized a training package consisting of modeling, role playing, instructions, and reinforcement to train positive social behaviors to 28 preschoolers with mild or moderate mental retardation. The target behaviors included greeting, asking to see a toy, initiating play, and showing a toy. The behaviors were introduced one at a time over several sessions with the final sessions containing training on all behaviors. Reinforcement included edibles and social praise. The participants showed marked improvement in the target behaviors, as well as a decrease in inappropriate social behaviors. Additional studies employing social-skills training are outlined in Table 10.6.

Independent Living

Independent-living skills refer to those skills necessary for an individual to function independently in the community. This skills include self-help skills (toileting, dressing, personal hygiene), as well as skills required to utilize community services (bus riding, pedestrian skills). Training of such skills is an important area of focus due to the growing trend

TABLE 10.5. Sample Treatment Studies Using Communication-Skills Training

AUTHORS	TYPES OF PERSONS	BEHAVIOR	TREATMENT
Charlop & Walsh (1986)	Autistic children	Self-initiated speech	Modeling
Whitehurst, Ironsmith, & Goldfein (1974)	Preschool children	Receptive & expressive language	Modeling reinforcement & graduated time delay
Kratzer, Spooner, Test, & Koorland (1993)	Severe multiple disabilities	Requesting skils	Constant time delay
Halle, Marshall, & Spradlin (1979)	Mentally retarded individuals	Requesting meals appropriately	Time delay

TABLE 10.6. Sample Treatment Studies Targeting Social Skills

AUTHORS	TYPES OF PERSONS	BEHAVIOR	TREATMENT
Matson, Fee, Coe, & Smith (1991)	Developmentally delayed preschoolers	Greetings, asking for a toy, showing a toy, & initiating play	Peer modeling, role playing, instructions, & reinforcement
Farmer-Dougan (1994)	Mentally retarded males	Appropriate requests	Peer-delivered incidental teaching & verbalization
Coe, Matson, Craigie, & Gossen (1991)	Two boys with autism & mental retardation	Play skils	Verbal & tangible reinforcers, prompts, & sibling trainers
Haseltine & Miltenberger (1990	Eight adults with mental retardation	Self-protection skills	Modeling, feedback, & praise

of community integration (Kelly et al., 1979; Guralnick, 1986; Marchetti & Campbell, 1990). Public Law 94-142 mandates placement for all children in the "least restrictive environment." This idea of the least restrictive environment along with the normalization movement has led to a growing number of mentally handicapped individuals being moved out of institutions (Gottlieb, Alter, & Gottlieb, 1991). Thus, training these individuals in independent-living skills will better prepare them for functioning and interacting in the community. A sample of treatment studies is listed in Table 10.7.

Numerous researchers have investigated the acquisition of independent-living skills in individuals with mental retardation (Vollmer, Iwata, Smith, & Rodgers, 1992). Vollmer and colleagues (1992) trained toothbrushing skills in a 29-year-old blind man with profound mental retardation. Toothbrush-ing was chosen because he engaged in multiple aberrant behaviors during self-care skills. Treatment involved the differential reinforcement of the appropriate toothbrushing behavior. Compliance with the task increased and rates of inappropriate behaviors decreased.

Functional Analysis

Functional analysis refers to an assessment technique for evaluating the maintaining factors for maladaptive behaviors (Carr, 1977; Iwata, Dorsey, Slifer, Bauman, & Richman, 1982; Iwata, Pace, Kalsher, Cowdery, & Cataldo, 1990; Northup et al., 1991; Vollmer, Iwata, Zarcone, Smith, & Mazaleski, 1993;

Wacker et al., 1990). During a functional analysis procedure the individual is exposed to various conditions manipulated by the examiner including an attention condition, an escape condition, an access-to-tangibles condition, a play condition (control), and an alone condition. Occurrence of the target behavior is documented and compared across conditions. Those conditions in which occurrence is high are considered to contain the maintaining factors.

The results of a functional analysis provide valuable treatment information. For example, if a particular maladaptive behavior is maintained by attention, then treatment will likely focus on training adaptive methods of communicating a desire for attention and extinguishing the maladaptive method. Likewise if a behavior occurs for nonsocial reasons (in the alone condition), emphasis may be placed on training social and interactive skills.

Wacker and colleagues (1990) utilized a functional analysis procedure to investigate the maintaining factors of severe behavior problems in two children and one adult with severe to profound mental retardation. Subject 1 exhibited hand biting, subject 2 exhibited body rocking, and subject 3 engaged in aggressive behavior (slapping or biting others). A functional analysis consisting of four conditions (attention, tangible, escape, and alone) was conducted for each participant. Subject 1's hand biting was maintained by access to tangibles, subject 2's body rocking occurred for nonsocial reasons (in the alone condition), and subject 3's aggression was primarily maintained by escape-from-task demands. Funct-

TABLE 10.7. Sample Treatment Studies Targeting Independent Living Skills

AUTHORS	TYPES OF PERSONS	BEHAVIOR	TREATMENT
Taras, Matson, & Felps (1993)	Seven students with mental retardation & visual impairment	Self-help skills	Self-evaluation, peer evaluation modleing, & prompting
Cuvo, Davis, O'Reilly, Mooney & Crowley (1992)	Eleven adults with mental retardation	Self-care skills	Task analyses, prompting, feedback

ional communication training was implemented for all participants to replace the maladaptive behavior. Thus, subject 1 was trained to communicate a desire for tangibles and so on. For all subjects a decrease in the maladaptive behavior was noted along with an increase in the communicative response. The increase in communication skills was greater for subjects 1 and 3 in which a particular maintaining factor could be detected.

Numerous variations of the functional-analysis procedure have been developed. Some examples include brief functional analysis (Northup et al., 1991), use of parents as therapists (Cooper et al., 1990), within-session functional analysis (Vollmer et al., 1993), and functional-analysis rating scales (Durand & Crimmins, 1988; Vollmer & Matson, 1995).

Dual Diagnosis

The presence of psychopathology in individuals with mental retardation was long overlooked (Reiss, 1982; Reiss, Levitan, & Szyszko, 1982; Reiss & Szyszko, 1983). However, researchers have consistently documented the presence of mental disorders in this population (Borthwick-Duffy, 1994). Further an emphasis on adequate assessment and treatment for such individuals is evident.

Few instruments exist for adequately assessing psychopathology in this population. However, a few promising developments have been made. Matson, Kazdin, & Senatore, 1984; Matson, 1995) have developed two instruments specifically for use in assessing psychopathology in individuals with mental retardation. *The Psychopathology Instrument for Mentally Retarded Adults (PIMRA)* is a 57-item screening instrument for use with individuals with mild or moderate mental retardation, while the *Diagnostic Assessment for the Severely Handicapped-II (DASH-II)* is an 84-item screening instrument for use with individuals with severe and profound mental retardation. Both scales have acceptable reliability and validity studies are currently being conducted.

The presence of psychopathology in an individual with mental retardation will greatly impact treatment decisions. For instance, treatment for the psychopathological symptoms will likely be interwoven with any additional treatment considerations and may dictate certain aspects of the treatment. There are some situations in which it may be possible to train acceptable replacement behaviors for the symptoms. Additionally, depending on the severity of the symptoms, aversive procedures or a DRO schedule may be put into place to extinguish them.

Behavioral Psychopharmacology

Traditionally, individuals with mental retardation have commonly been prescribed a wide array of psychotropic medications for behavioral problems. The immense body of psychopharmacology literature with mentally retarded individuals does not permit a complete review of all drugs used in this chapter; however, Aman and Singh (1991) provide an excellent review of drugs used with the mentally retarded population.

Because mentally retarded children often exhibit behavior and learning problems, psychotropic and/or stimulant medication is commonly prescribed to treat the existing problems. Psychotropic medications include thioridazine, chlorpromazine, and haloperidol. These types of drugs are most often prescribed for aggression, self-injury, hyperactivity, and other behavior disorders (Aman & Singh, 1991; Handen, 1993). Aman, Teehan, White, Turbot, and

Vaithianathan (1989) reported dramatic reductions in stereotypies of severely and profoundly mentally retarded adolescents and adults treated with haloperidol. Williams and colleagues (Williams, Kirkpatrick-Sanchez, & Crocker, 1994) documented significant decreases in aggression and tantrums of a severely mentally retarded women with schizophrenia treated with clozapine combined with behavioral interventions (differential reinforcement and time-out). Naltrexone, a relatively new drug frequently used to treat SIB, was effective in eliminating self-injury and stereotypy in two women with developmental disabilities (Smith, Gupta, & Smith, 1995). The authors also noted that the women increased smiling, eye contact, and tolerance to touch while taking Naltrexone.

Estimates of the number of mentally retarded individuals taking psychotropic medications differ depending on whether the individual lives in an institution or in the community. The estimate of individuals receiving psychotropics who live in institutions ranges from 50% to 75% (Aman & Singh). For those who live in the community, the estimate ranges from 7% to 74% (Aman, Field, & Bridgman, 1985; Davis, Cullari, & Breuning, 1982; Gadow & Kalachnik, 1981; Hill, Balow, & Bruininks, 1985; Intagliata & Rinck, 1985; Martin & Agran, 1985). It is important for the therapist to remember that correct diagnosis of the problem is imperative before recommending a psychotropic medication be prescribed.

Traditionally, psychotropic medications have been prescribed in the mentally retarded population in the absence of any clear theoretical rationale. Before the prescription of any psychotropic medication is recommended, it is important that the therapist understand the underlying biological mechanism involved in the problem, and whether or not it is treatable through behavior strategies. In all but extreme cases, behavior strategies should be implemented first, with reliance on psychotropic medications avoided if at all possible.

Generalization and Maintenance Procedures

Generalization and maintenance of treatment effects are important considerations in developing any treatment program for individuals with mental retardation. Although there is still much room for improvement, researchers are making progress in determining the conditions in which skills will generalize and remain stable after treatment. A sample of studies that investigate generalization and/or maintenance are listed in Table 10.8.

Foxx and McEvoy (1993) and Brown and Odom (1994) reviewed the efficacy of numerous studies employing social-skills training packages. Both review articles suggest specific strategies to aid in generalizing and maintaining treatment effects. First, multiple exemplars, such as several peer trainers, settings, scenarios, and skills, should be included in training. Second, trainers should use naturally occurring contingencies. Third, reinforcement should be applied indiscriminantly. Fourth, conduct training in the natural environment. Finally, the use of self-control techniques that are easily transferable from one behavior or setting to another may aid in generalization and maintenance of treatment effects.

In addition to the above-mentioned guidelines for increasing generalization, Stokes and Baer (1977) provide a taxonomy of types of generalization procedures that may be used. The "train-and-hope" method consists of simply documenting generalizability with no attempts to ensure it. The sequential-modification technique is an extension of the train-and-hope method that if generalization is absent or weak, attempts are the made to train in each nongeneralized environment. The third method involves actually using contingencies in the training setting that are likely to occur in the natural environment. The next two methods include training with multiple exemplars (e.g., multiple trainers) or exerting loose control over stimuli in the training session hoping to sample enough relevant domains. It is also possible to increase generalizability by using intermittent reinforcement schedules. Additionally, using stimuli present in the natural environment is a passive method for attaining generalization. Using a mediating variable such as language may aid in generalization of training. This method is tantamount to expecting action to follow expression (e.g., the individual says he does it, and eventually he does). Finally, reinforcement of generalization responses can be utilized. Stokes and Baer (1977) recommend a combination of these procedures to maximize generalization effects.

TABLE 10.8. Sample Generalization and Maintenance Studies

AUTHORS	TYPES OF PERSONS	BEHAVIOR	TREATMENT
Laski, Charlop, & Schreibman (1988)	Four echolalic & four non-verbal children	Lack of appropriate speech	Natural paradigm & parents as trainers
Moran & Whitman (1991)	Eight mentally retarded children	Compliance task-oriented behavior, & affect	Parent trained as therapist
Martella, Marchand-Martella, Young, & Macfarlane (1995)	One adolescent with mental retardation	Compliance & motor activity	Multiple peer tutors
Hughes, Harmer, Killian, & Niarhos (1995)	Four mentally retarded students	Conversational skills	Peer modeling, self-instruction, & multiple exemplars
Hunt, Alwell, Goetz, & Sailor (1990)	Three severely disabled students	Conversational skills	Multiple exemplars

Davis and colleagues (Davis, Bredy, Williams, & Hamilton, 1992) demonstrate successful generalization of responses trained to two boys exhibiting behavior problems. Compliance was trained using behavioral-momentum techniques. They utilized several trainers and training in the natural environment to promote generalization of treatment effects. Compliance to requests by adults not used in the training paradigm increased.

Koegel and Rincover (1977) noted the importance of distinguishing between generalization and maintenance problems. They pointed out that failure to "generalize" to a new setting may truly represent failure to maintain treatment effect, if generalization probes are only employed following acquisition of skills in the treatment setting. To address such problems, two strategies for improving maintenance are identified. First, thin schedules of reinforcement should be used. The authors demonstrated that maintenance was greater under partial reinforcement schedules versus continuous. Second, infrequent, periodic noncontingent rewards should be given. Those participants receiving noncontingent rewards throughout the follow-up phases maintained treatment gains longer than those not receiving rewards.

CONCLUSION

The use of behavior-analytic techniques in diagnosing and treating individuals with mental retardation is widespread. Such techniques have proven to be effective in (a) decreasing maladaptive behaviors, (b) treating psychopathological symptoms, (c) increasing functional communication skills, (d) social-skills training, and (e) improving independent-living skills for community placement.

The most effective procedures tend to be a combination of various techniques mentioned throughout this chapter. For example, it is recommended that aversives be used in conjunction with reinforcement procedures. Combining these procedures is likely to result in a greater decrease in the maladaptive behavior as it includes training of adaptive skills to replace such behaviors. Additionally, training packages that incorporate social-learning methods, reinforcement, self-management techniques, and feedback have been successful in training social skills and independent-living skills. Finally, the use of pharmacologic techniques should be utilized along with behavioral techniques and should be employed only in those cases where (a) the behavior being treated is severe enough to warrant medication, (b) behavioral techniques alone will not suffice, and/or (c) the medication is designed for the treatment of the behavior/symptom causing a problem.

This chapter also highlights the importance of a thorough assessment of the individual's problem behaviors, psychological symptoms, and skills in order to appropriately devise an effective and individualized treatment plan. Two important issues to consider when conducting this assessment are use of scales specifically designed for use with this population and the completion of a functional analysis of the problem behavior(s).

All of the issues mentioned are particularly salient in light of the growing trend toward deinstitutionalization and normalization, as well as increased independence and personal choice. As more individuals with mental retardation begin to reside in community settings, the importance of communication, independent-living skills, and social-skills training, as well as, controlling problematic behaviors is highlighted. Adaptive skills are necessary to effectively and safely function in society, and exhibition of maladaptive behaviors may lead to isolation and social stigma.

REFERENCES

Abuelo, D. N. (1991). Genetic Disorder. In J. L. Matson & J. A. Mulick (Eds.), *Handbook of mental retardation.* New York: Pergamon Press.

Akesson, H. (1959). *Epidemiology and genetics of mental deficiency in a southern Swedish population.* Sweden: University of Uppsala.

Aman, M. G., Field, C. J., & Bridgemena, G. O. (1985). City-wide survey of drug patterns among non-institutionalized mentally retarded person. *Applied Research in Mental Retardation, 6,* 159–171.

Aman, M. G., & Singh, N. N. (1991). Pharmacological intervention. In J. L. Matson and J. A. Mulick (Eds.), *Handbook of mental retardation* (2nd ed., pp. 347–372). New York: Pergamon Press.

Aman, M. G., Teehan, C. J., White, A. J., Turbot, S. H., & Vaithianathan, C. (1989). Haloperidol treatment with chronically medicated residents: Dose effects on clinical behavior and reinforcement contingencies. *American Journal on Mental Retardation, 93,* 452–460.

American Association on Mental Retardation (1992). *Mental retardation: Definition, classification, and systems of support.* Washington DC: American Association on Mental Retardation.

American Psychiatric Association (1994). *Diagnostic and statistical manual of mental disorders,* (4th ed.) Washington DC: American Psychiatric Association.

Axelrod, S. (1990). Myths that (mis)guide our profession. In A. C. Repp & N. N. Singh (Eds.), *Perspective on the use of nonaversive and aversive interventions for persons with developmental disabilities.* Sycamore, IL: Sycamore Publishing.

Bailey, S. L., Pikrzywinski, J. & Bryant, L. E. (1983). Using water mist to reduce self-injurious and stereotypic behavior. *Applied Research in Mental Retardation, 4,* 229–241.

Bijou, S. W. (1993). *Behavior analysis of child development.* Reno, NV: Context Press.

Birch, H. G., Richardson, S. A., Baird, D., Harobin, G., & Illsby, R. (1970). *Mental subnormality in the community: A clinical and epidemiological study.* Baltimore: Williams and Wilkins.

Bird, F., Dores, P. A., Moniz, D., & Robinson, J. (1989). Reducing severe aggressive and self-injurious behaviors with functional communication training. *American Journal on Mental Retardation, 94,* 37–48.

Borthwick-Duffy, S. (1994). Epidemiology and prevalence of psychopathology in people with mental retardation. *Journal of Consulting and Clinical Psychology, 62,* 17–27.

Brown, W. H., & Odom, S. L. (1994). Strategies and tactics for promoting generalization and maintenance of young children's social behavior. *Research in Developmental Disabilities, 15,* 99–118.

Bruner, J. (1978). Prelinguistic prerequisites of speech. In R. N. Campbell & P. T. Smith (Eds.), *Recent advances in the psychology of language: Language development and mother-child interaction.* New York: Plenum Press.

Carr, E. G. (1977). The motivation of self-injurious behavior: A review of some hypotheses. *Psychological Bulletin, 84,* 800–816.

Cataldo, M. F., Ward, E. M., Russo, D. C., Riordan, M., & Bennett, D. (1986). Compliance and correlated behavior in children: Effects of contingent and noncontingent reinforcement. *Analysis and Intervention in Developmental Disabilities, 6,* 265–282.

Charlop, M. H., & Walsh, M. E. (1986). Increasing autistic childrens' spontaneous verbalizations of affection: An assessment of time delay and peer modeling procedures. *Journal of Applied Behavior Analysis, 19,* 307–314.

Coe, D. A., Matson, J. L., Craigie, C. J., & Gossen, M. A. (1991). Play skills of autistic children: Assessment and instruction. *Child and Family Behavior Therapy, 13,* 13-40.

Coleman, R. S., & Whitman, T. L. (1984). Developing, generalizing, and maintaining physical fitness in mentally retarded adults: Toward a self-directed program. *Analysis and Intervention in Developmental Disabilities, 5,* 109–127.

Combs, C. S., & Jansma, P. (1990). The effects of reinforcement-based fitness training on adults who are institutionalized and dually diagnosed. *Adaptive Physical Activity Quarterly, 7,* 156–169.

Cooper, L. J., Wacker, D. P., Sasso, G. M, Reimers, T. M., & Donn, L. K. (1990). Using parents as therapists to evaluate appropriate behavior of their children: Application to a tertiary diagnostic clinic. *Journal of Applied Behavior Analysis, 23,* 285-296.

Cuvo, A. J., Davis, P. K., O'Reilly, M. F., Mooney, B. M., & Crowley, R. (1992). Promoting stimulus control with textual prompts and performance feedback for persons with mild disabilities. *Journal of Applied Behavior Analysis, 25,* 477–489.

Davis, C. A., Brady, M. P., Williams, R. E., & Hamilton, R. (1992). Effects of high-probability requests on the acquisition and generalization of responses to requests in young children with behavior disorders. *Journal of Applied Behavior Analysis, 25,* 905–916.

DiLorenzo, T. M. & Land, J. S. (1988). Later childhood. In J. L. Matson & A. Marchetti (Eds.), *Developmental disabilities: A life-span perspective.* Philadelphia: Grune & Stratton.

Donnellan, A. M. & LaVigna, G. W. (1990). Myths about punishment. In A. C. Repp & N. N. Singh (Eds.), *Perspectives on the use of nonaversive and aversive interventions for persons with developmental disabilities.* Sycamore, IL: Sycamore Publishing.

Drillien, C. M. , Jameson, S., & Wilkinson, E. M. (1966). Studies in mental handicap. Part I: Prevalence and distribution of clinical type and severity of defect. *Archives of Disturbed Children, 41,* 528–538.

Durand, V. M. (1993). Problem behavior as communication. *Behaviour Change, 10,* 197–207.

Durand, V. M., & Carr, E. G. (1991). Functional communication training to reduce challenging behavior: Maintenance and application in new settings. Special issue: Social validity: Multiple perspectives. Journal of *Applied Behavior Analysis, 24,* 251–264.

Durand, V. M., & Carr, E. G. (1992). An analysis of maintenance following functional communication training. *Journal of Applied Behavior Analysis, 25,* 777–794.

Durand, V.M. & Crimmins, D.B. (1988). Identifying the variables maintaining self-injury. *Journal of Autism and Developmental Disabilities, 18,* 99–117.

Factor, D. C., & Schilmoeller, G. L. (1983). Social skill training of preschool children. *Child Study Journal, 13,* 41–55.

Farmer-Dougan, V. (1994). Increasing requests by adults with developmental disabilities using incidental teaching by peers. *Journal of Applied Behavior Analysis, 27,* 533–544.

Figueroa, R. G., Thyer, B. A., & Thyer, K. B. (1992). Extinction and DRO in the treatment of aggression in a boy with severe mental retardation. *Journal of Behavior Therapy and Experimental Psychiatry, 23,* 133–140.

Fisher, W., Piazza, C. C., Bowman, L. G., Hagopian, L. P., & Langdon, N. A. (1994). Empirically derived consequences: A data-based method for prescribing treatments for destructive behavior. *Research in Developmental Disabilities, 15,* 133–149.

Foxx, J. J., McEvoy, M. A. (1993). Assessing and enhancing generalization and social validity of social skills interventions with children and adolescents. *Behavior Modification, 17,* 339–366.

Foxx, R. M. (1982). *Decreasing behaviors of persons with severe retardation and autism.* Champaign, IL: Research Press.

Foxx, R. M., & Azrin, N. H. (1973). The elimination of self-stimulatory behavior by overcorrection. *Journal of Applied Behavior Analysis, 6,* 1-14.

Frame, C. L., & Matson, J. L. (Eds.). (1987). *Handbook of assessment in child psychopathology.* New York & London: Plenum Press.

Gadow, K. D., & Kalachnik, J. (1981). Prevalence and pattern of drug treatment for behavior and seizure disorders of TMR students. *American Journal on Mental Deficiency, 85,* 588–595.

Goldstein, H., & Hockenberger, E. H. (1991). Significant progress in child language intervention: An 11-year retrospective. *Research in Developmental Disabilities, 12,* 401–424.

Goldstein, H. & Mousetics, L. (1989). Generalized language learning by children with severe mental retardation: Effects of peers' expressive modeling. *Journal of Applied Behavior Analysis, 22,* 245–259.

Goodman, N., & Tizard, J. (1962). Prevalence of imbecility and idiocy among children. *British Medical Journal, 1,* 216–219.

Gottlieb, J., Alter, M., & Gottlieb, B. W. (1991). Mainstreaming mentally retarded children. In J. L. Matson & J. A. Mulick (Eds.), *Handbook of mental retardation* (2nd ed.). New York: Pergamon Press.

Greenwood, C. R., Todd, N. M., Hops, H., & Walker, H. M. (1982). Behavior change targets in the assessment of socially withdrawn preschool children. *Behavioral Assessment, 4,* 273-297.

Griffin, J. C., Locke, B. J., & Landers, W. F. (1975). Manipulation of potential punishment parameters in the treatment of self-injury. *Journal of Applied Behavior Analysis, 8,* 458-464.

Grossman, H.J. (Ed.). (1983). *Classification in mental retardation.* Washington D.C.: American Association on Mental Deficiency.

Guralnick, M. J. (1986). *Children's social behavior: Development, assessment, and modification.* Orlando, FL: Academic Press.

Halle, J., Marshall, A., & Spradlin, J. (1979). Time delay: A technique to increase language use and facilitate generalization in retarded children. *Journal of Applied Behavior Analysis, 12,* 431–439.

Handen, B. L. (1993). Pharmacotherapy in mental retardation and autism. *School Psychology Review, 22,* 162–183.

Haseltine, B., & Miltenberger, R. G. (1990). Teaching self-protection skills to persons with mental retardation. *American Journal on Mental Retardation. 95,* 188–197.

Heber, R. (1961). Modification in the manual on terminology and classification in mental retardation. *American Journal on Mental Deficiency, 66,* 499-500.

Hughes, C., Harmer, M. L. , Killian, D. J., & Niarhos, F. (1995). The effects of multiple-examplar self-instructional training on high school students' generalized conversational interactions. *Journal of Applied Behavior Analysis, 28,* 201–218.

Hunt, P., Alwell, M., Goetz, L., & Sailor, W. (1990). Generalized effects of conversation skill training. *Journal of the Association for Severe Handicaps, 15,* 250–260.

Irvine, A. B., Singer, G. H., Erikson, A. M., & Stahlberg, D. (1992). A coordinated program to transfer self-management skills from school to home. *Education and training in Mental Retardation, 27,* 241–254.

Iwata, B. A., Dorsey, M. F., Slifer, K. J., Bauman, K. E., & Richman, G. S. (1982). Toward a function analysis of self-injury. *Analysis and Intervention in Developmental Disabilities, 3,* 1–20.

Iwata, B. A., Pace, G. M., Kalsher, M. J., Cowdery, G. E., & Cataldo, M. F. (1990). Experimental analysis and extinction of self-injurious escape behavior. *Journal of Applied Behavior Analysis, 23,* 11–27.

Iwata, B. A., & Rodgers, T. A. (1992). Self-injurious behavior. In. E. A. Konarski, Jr. and J. E. Favell (Eds.), *Manual for the assessment and treatment of the behavior disorders of people with mental retardation.* Morgantown, NC: Western Carolina Center Foundation.

Johnson, C. R., Hunt, F. M., & Siebert, M. J. (1994). Discrimination training in the treatment of pica and food scavenging. *Behavior Modification, 18,* 214–229.

Jordan, J., Singh, N. H., & Repp, A. C. (1989). An evaluation of gentle teaching and visual screening in the reduction of stereotypy. *Journal of Applied Behavior Analysis, 22,* 9–22.

Kanner, L. (1967). A history of the care and study of the mentally retarded. Springfield, IL: Charles C. Thomas.

Kelly, J.A., Furman, W., Phillips, J., Hathorn, S., & Wilson, T. (1979). Teaching conversational skills to retarded adolescents. *Child Behavior Therapy, 1,* 85-97.

Kennedy, C. H., & Haring, T. G. (19913). Combining reward and escape DRO to reduce the problem behavior of students with severe disabilities. *Journal of the Association of Severe Handicaps, 18,* 85–92.

Koegel, R., & Covert, A. (1972). The relationship of self-stimulation to learning in autistic children. *Journal of Applied Behavior Analysis, 5,* 381-387.

Koegel, R., & Frea, W. D. (1993). Treatment of social behavior in autism through modification of pivotal social skills. *Journal of Applied Behavior Analysis, 26,* 369–377.

Koegel, R. L., & Rincover, A. (1977). Research on the difference between generalization and maintenance in extra-therapy responding. *Journal of Applied Behavior Analysis, 10,* 1–12.

Kolstoe, O.P. & Shafter, A.J. (1961). Employability prediction for mentally retarded adults: A methodological note. *American Journal on Mental Deficiency, 66,* 287-289.

Kratzer, D. A., Spooner, F., Test, D. W., & Koorland, M. A. (1993). Extending the application of constant time delay: Teaching a requesting skill to students with severe multiple disabilities. *Education and Treatment of Children, 16,* 235–253.

Kushlick, A. (1961). Subnormality in Salford. In M. w. Susser & A. Kushlick (Eds.), *A report on the mental health services of the city of Salford for the year 1960.* United Kingdom: Salford Health Department.

Kushlick, A. (1964). *The prevalence of recognized mental subnormality of I.Q. under 50 among children in the South of England, with reference to the demund for places for residential care.* Paper presented at the International Copenhagen Conference on the Scientific Study of Mental Retardation, Copenhagen.

Laski, K. E., Charlop, M. H., & Schreibman, L. (1988). Training parents to use the natural language paradigm to increase their autistic children's speech. *Journal of Applied Behavior Analysis, 21,* 391–400.

Leland, H. (1991). Adaptive Behavior Scales. In J. L. Matson & J. A. Mulick (Eds.), *Handbook of mental retardation.* New York: Pergamon Press.

Levitan, G.W. & Reiss, S. (1983). Generality of diagnostic overshadowing across disciplines. *Applied Research in Mental Retardation, 4,* 59-64.

Lemkau, P., Tietze, L., & Cooper, M. (1943). Mental-hygiene problems in an urban district. Fourth paper. *Mental Hygiene, 27,* 279–295.

Linscheid, T. R., Iwata, B. A., Rickets, R. W., Williams, D. E., & Griffin, J. C. (1990). Clinical evaluation of the self-injurious behavior inhibiting system. *Journal of Applied Behavior Analysis, 23,* 53–78.

Linscheid, T. R., Pejeau, C., Cohen, S., & Footo-Lenz, M. (1994). Positive side effects using the Self-Injurious Behavior Inhibiting System (SIBIS): Implications for operant and biochemical explanations of SIB. *Research in Developmental Disabilities, 15,* 81–90.

MacMillan, D. L., Gresham, F. M., & Siperstein, G. N. (1993). Conceptual and psychometric concerns about the 1992 AAMR definition of mental retardation. *American Journal on Mental Retardation, 98,* 325-335.

Marchetti, A. G. & Campbell, V. A. (1990). Social skills. In J.L. Matson (Ed.) Handbook of behavior modification with the mentally retarded. New York: Pergamon Press.

Martella, R. C., Marchand-Martella, N. E., Young, K. R., & Macfarlane, C. A. (1995). Determining the collateral effects of peer tutor training on a student with severe disabilities. *Behavior Modification, 19,* 170–191.

Martin, J. E., & Agran, M. (1985). Psychotropic and anticonvulsant drug use by mentally retarded adults community residential vocational placement. *Applied Research in Mental Retardation, 6,* 33–49.

Mason, S. A., & Newsom, C. D. (1990). The application of sensory change to reduce sterotyped behavior. *Research in Developmental Disabilities, 11,* 257–271.

Matson, J. L. (1980). A controlled group study of pedestrian-skill training for the mentally retarded. *Behaviour Research and Therapy, 18,* 99–106.

Matson, J. L. (1981a). Use of independent training to teach shopping skills to mildly mentally retarded adults. *American Journal on Mental Deficiency, 86,* 178–183.

Matson, J. L. (1981b). Assessment and treatment of clinical phobias in mentally retarded children. *Journal of Applied Behavior Analysis, 14,* 141–152.

Matson, J. L. (1982a). Independence training vs. modeling procedures for teaching conversation skills to the mentally retarded. *Behavior Research and Therapy, 20,* 505–511.

Matson, J. L. (1982b). Treatment of obsessive-compulsive behavior in mentally retarded adults. *Behavior Modification, 6,* 551–567.

Matson, J. L. (1995). *Diagnostic assessment for the severely handicapped.* Baton Rouge, LA: Scientific Publishers.

Matson, J. L., Kazdin, A.E., & Senatore, V. (1984). Psychometric properties of the psychopathology instrument for mentally retarded adults. *Applied Research in Mental Retardation, 5*(1), 81-89.

Matson, J. L., Manikam, R., Coe, D., Raymond, K., Taras,

M., & Long, N. (1988). Training social skills to severely mentally retarded multiply handicapped adolescents. *Research in Developmental Disabilities, 9,* 195-208.

Matson, J. L. & Marchetti, A. (1988). *Developmental Disabilities: A life-span perspective.* Philadelphia: Grune & Stratton.

Matson, J.L. & Taras, M. (1989). A 20-year review of punishment and alternative methods to treat problem behaviors in developmentally delayed persons. *Research in Developmental Disabilities, 10,* 85-104.

Moran, D. R., & Whitman, T. L. (1991). Developing generalized teaching skills I mothers of autistic children. *Child and Family Behavior Therapy, 13,* 13–37.

Nihira, K., Foster, R., Schelhaas, N., & Leland, H. (1974). *AAMR Adaptive Behavior Scale manual.* Austin, TX: PRO-ED.

Northup, J., Wacker, D., Sasso, G., Steege, M., Cigrand, D., Cook, J., & DeRaad, A. (1991). A brief functional analysis of aggressive and alternative behavior in an outpatient clinic setting. *Journal of Applied Behavior Analysis, 24,* 509-522.

O'Connor, R. D. (1969). Modification of social withdrawal through symbolic modeling. *Journal of Applied Behavior Analysis, 2,* 15-22.

Paniagua, F. A., Braverman, C., & Capriotti, R. M. (1986). Use of a treatment package in the management of a profoundly mentally retarded girl's pica and self-stimulation. *American Journal on Mental Deficiency, 90,* 550-557.

Ralph, A., & Birnbrauer, J. S. (1986). The potential of correspondence training for facilitating generalization of social skills. *Applied Research in Mental Retardation, 7,* 415–430.

Raymond, K. L., & Matson, J. L. (1989). Social skills in the hearing impaired. *Journal of Clinical Child Psychology, 18,* 247-258.

Reiss, S. (1982). Psychopathology and mental retardation: Survey of a developmental disabilities mental health program. *Mental Retardation, 20,* 128–132.

Reiss, S., Levitan, G. W., & Szyszko, J. (1982). Emotional disturbance and mental retardation: Diagnostic overshadowing. *American Journal on Mental Deficiency, 86,* 567-574.

Reiss, S. & Szyszko, J. (1983). Diagnostic overshadowing and professional experience with mentally retarded persons. *American Journal on Mental Deficiency, 87,* 396-402.

Reschly, D. J., & Ward, S. M. (1991). Use of adaptive behavior measures and overrepresentation of black students in programs for students with mild mental retardation. *American Journal on Mental Retardation, 96,* 257–268.

Rogers-Warren, A., & Warren, S. F. (1980). Mands for verbalizations: Facilitating the display of newly trained language in children. *Behavior Modification, 4,* 361–381.

Rortvedt, A. K., & Miltenberger, R. G. (1994). Analysis of a high-probability instructional sequence and time-out in the treatment of child noncompliance. *Journal of Applied Behavior Analysis, 27,* 327–330.

Rosen, M., Clark, G. R., & Kivitz, M. S. (1976). *The history of mental retardation* (Vol. 1). Baltimore: University Park Press.

Sattler, J. (1992). *Assessment of children.* San Diego: author.

Scheerenberger, R. C. (1987). *A history of mental retardation.* Baltimore: Brookes Publishing.

Shapiro, E. S. (1981). Self-control procedures with the mentally retarded. In M. Hersen, R. M. eisler, & P. Miller (Eds.), *Progress in behavior modification,* (Vol. 2, pp. 265–297) New York: Academic Press.

Sisson, L. A., VanHasselt, V. B., & Hersen, M. (1993). Behavioral interventions to reduce maladaptive responding in youth with dual sensory impairment: An analysis of direct and concurrent effects. *Behavior Modification, 17,* 164–188.

Smith, S. G., Gupta, K. K., & Smith, S. H. (1995). Effects of naltrexone on self-injury, stereotypy, and social behavior of adults with developmental disabilities. *Journal of Developmental and Physical Disabilities, 7,* 137–146.

Sparrow, S. S., Balla, D. A., & Cicchetti, D. V. (1984). *Vineland Adaptive Behavior Scale.* Circle Pines, MN: American Guidance Service.

Steege, M. W., Wacker, D. P., Cigrand, K. C., Berg, W. K., Novak, C. G., Reimers, T. M., Sasso, G. M., & DeRaad, A. (1990). Use of negative reinforcement in the treatment of self-injurious behavior. *Journal of Applied Behavior Analysis, 23,* 459–467.

Stokes, T. F. & Baer, D. M. (1977). An implicit technology of generalization. *Journal of Applied Behavior Analysis, 10,* 349–368.

Tanner, B. A., & Zeiler, M. (1975). Punishment of self-injurious behavior using aromatic ammonia as the aversive stimulus. *Journal of Applied Behavior Analysis, 8,* 53-57.

Taras, M. E., Matson, J. L., & Felps, J. N. (1993). Using independence training to teach independent living skills to children and young men with visual impair-

ments. *Behavior Modification, 17,* 189–208.

Vollmer, T. R. & Matson, J. L. (1995). *Questions about behavioral function.* Baton Rouge, LA: Scientific Publishers.

Vollmer, T. R., Iwata, B. A., Smith, R. G., & Rodgers, T. A. (1992). Reduction of multiple aberrant behaviors and concurrent development of self-care skills with differential reinforcement. *Research in Developmental Disabilities, 13,* 287–299.

Vollmer, T. R., Iwata, B. A., Zarcone, J. R., Smith, R. G., & Mazaleski, J. L. (1993). Within-session patterns of self-injury as indicators of behavioral function. *Research in Developmental Disabilities, 14,* 479-492.

Wacker, D. P., Steege, M. W., Northup, J., Sasso, G., Berg, W., Reimers, T., Cooper, L., Cigrand, K., & Donn, L. (1990). A component analysis of functional communication training across three topographies of severe behavior problems. *Journal of Applied Behavior Analysis, 23,* 417-429.

Warren, S. F., McQuarter, R. J., & Rogers-Warren, A. K. (1984). The effects of mands and model s on the speech of unresponsive socially isolated children. *Journal of Speech and Hearing Disorders, 47,* 42–52.

Wheeler, J. J., Bates, P., Marshall, K. J., & Miller, S. R. (1988). Teaching appropriate social behaviors to a young man with moderate mental retardation in a supportive competitive environment. *Education and Training in Mental Retardation, 23,* 105-116.

Whitehurst, G., Ironsmith, M., & Goldfein, M. (1974). Selective imitation of the passive construction through modeling. *Journal of Experimental Child Psychology, 17,* 288–302.

Whitman, T. L., Mercurio, J. R., & Caponigri, V. (1970). Development of social responses in 2 severely retarded children. *Journal of Applied Behavior Analysis, 3,* 133–138.

Whitman, T. L., Sciback, J. W., & Reid, D. H. (1983). *Behavior modification with the severely and profoundly retarded.* New York: Academic Press.

Williams, D. E., Kirkpatrick-Sanchez, S., & Crocker, W. T. (1994). A long-term follow-up of treatment for severe self-injury. *Research in Developmental Disabilities, 15,* 187–501.

Zarcone, J. r., Iwata, B. A., Vollmer, T. R., Jagtiani, S., Smith, R. G., & Mazaleski, J. L. (1993). Extinction of self-injurious escape behavior with and without instructional fading. *Journal of Applied Behavior Analysis, 26,* 353–360.

CHAPTER 11

CHILDREN MEDICALLY AT RISK

Lawrence J. Siegel

Children who would have died a number of years ago are now reaching adolescence and/or young adulthood as a result of advances in biomedical science and medical technology. These children live with chronic medical conditions. Current data indicate that over 80% of children who have chronic medical conditions now survive into adulthood (Blum & Gerber, 1992). Mattsson (1972) has defined a chronic illness as "a disorder with a protracted course which can be fatal or associated with a relatively normal life span despite impaired physical or mental functioning. Such a disease frequently shows a period of acute exacerbations requiring intensive medical attention" (p. 801). Similarly, Pless and Pinkerton (1975) describe a chronic medical condition as one that interferes with daily functioning for more than 3 months in a year or results in hospitalization for more than 1 month during a year. Chronic medical conditions of childhood are diverse and include many disease categories such as juvenile rheumatoid arthritis, diabetes, asthma, phenyl-ketonuria, sickle cell disease, leukemia, cystic fibrosis, congenital heart disease, hemophilia, and chronic kidney disease.

Many pediatric chronic diseases individually have a low incidence. However, taken together, they represent disproportionate numbers in terms of their use of the health-care system. It is estimated that 10% to 15% of children in the United States will experience one or more chronic medical conditions by 18 years of age (Gortmaker, 1985; Pless & Roghmann, 1971). Medically, most chronic medical conditions are mild in terms of functional limitations. Yet approximately one-third of these children have conditions of moderate severity resulting in some distress or limitations in their activities and, approximately 10% of children with chronic diseases are so severely affected by their medical condition that they exhibit major functional limitations and disruptions in their daily activities (Haggerty, Roghmann, & Pless, 1975; Hobbs, Perrin, & Ireys, 1985; Newacheck & Taylor, 1992).

A chronic medical condition in childhood is generally assumed to be a major life stressor. These diseases and the various approaches used in their medical management place systematic and unpredictable stresses on the lives of the children and their families. Among other things, these individuals must cope with frequent and painful invasive medical procedures, repeated hospitalizations and clinic visits, surgery, periodic and unpredictable exacerbation of symptoms, physical discomfort, bodily disfigurement, side effects of medication, and the potential for a shortened life expectancy (Eiser, 1990; Mattsson, 1977; Travis, 1976).

A chronic disease can seriously disrupt a family's routines and lifestyle. In many conditions, children and their families must adhere to complex, long-term regimens that may involve dietary and activity modifications, medication taking, and other daily-care routines and medical treatments such as dialysis for children with chronic kidney disease. Such regimens contribute to a child's feeling of being "different" and can interfere with his or her autonomy needs. This can present a particular problem for adolescents who want to maintain some degree of independence from their families (Magrab & Calcagno, 1978).

Another factor that contributes to this experience of "feeling different" from one's healthy peers is the physical changes that often occur as a result of the disease process and/or medical treatment. For example, growth failure, facial hair and weight gain from steroids, loss of hair from chemotherapy and radiation treatment, amputations, and crippling of joints in arthritis and hemophilia can all result in reduced self-esteem and can deter normal peer socialization. Peer relationships are also affected by the frequent school absences that these children may experience as a result of numerous hospitalizations and exacerbations of their disease symptoms. Problems associated with academic achievement often are an additional consequence of numerous disruptions in school attendance.

In addition to the impact of the chronic medical condition on the affected child, the condition also imposes a potential strain on other family members and can disrupt family roles and relationships. Conflicts may arise over competing demands imposed by the child's medical condition and the needs of other family members. Each family member shares in the child's suffering and may be affected by the redirecting of physical, emotional, and financial resources necessary for the care of the ill child (Hobbs, Perrin, & Ireys, 1985). Siblings may be particularly vulnerable to the stresses that result from the burdens of caring for a child with a chronic medical condition.

Because of the pervasive stressors to which these children are exposed throughout their lives, it is intuitively appealing to assume that this population is at greater risk for developing considerable problems in psychological adjustment. Early researchers in this area generally concluded that children with chronic diseases were seriously maladjusted compared to their healthy peers and that their families tended to cope poorly (Pless & Pinkerton, 1975). However, the research on which these findings are based had a number of serious methodological problems including retrospective reports, subjective evaluations and clinical case material, the use of measures with questionable reliability and validity, and a lack of appropriate control groups. Recent, better-designed investigations tend to suggest that children with chronic medical conditions are considerably less deviant when compared with normative groups than was initially noted (Drotor, Owens, & Gotthold, 1980; Gayton, Friedman, Tavormina, & Tucker, 1977; Kellerman, Zeltzer, Ellenberg, Dash, & Rigler, 1980; Kupst & Schulman, 1988; Lask, 1992; Tavormina, Kastner, Slater, & Watt, 1976; Wysocki, Hough, Ward, & Green, 1992).

Current research suggests that although a chronic medical condition can be a life stressor for children and place them at greater risk for adjustment problems than physically healthy children, the disease itself does not appear to be the primary cause of more serious emotional and behavioral problems. Rather, it has been suggested that the adjustment problems that these children face (including feelings of anxiety, depression, and anger) are best regarded as normal responses to stressful experiences associated with long-term illness and/or treatment regimens; that is, they cannot be seen as psychiatric disorders (Drotar, 1981; Varni, 1983). In their recent summary of the research on children's adjustment to chronic medical conditions, Wallander and Thompson (1995) conclude: "It is clear that a simple or direct universal relationship between chronic physical condition and psychosocial adjustment does not exist. Rather a wide range of responses to this source of life stress is to be expected. However, although major psychiatric disturbance is not common among children with chronic conditions, this population is increased risk for mental health and adjustment problems" (pp. 127–128). A meta-analysis of research in this area suggests that these children may be at risk particularly for internalizing behavior disorders such as anxiety and depression (Lavigne & Faier-Routman, 1993).

Research has not demonstrated a consistent relationship between objective measures of severity of illness and the occurrence of adjustment problems. Instead, there are many potential determinants of the impact of the child's chronic medical condition on his or her overall adjustment including age of disease onset, degree of disability, the course of the illness (i.e., progressive, stable, relapsing), life-threatening nature of the disease, visibility of the disease, family dysfunction, level of social support, family resources, and the coping skills of the child and family (Drotar & Bush, 1985, Hobbs et al., 1985; Lavigne & Faier-Routman, 1993; Perrin & Gerrity, 1984; Pless & Pinkerton, 1975). These factors can influence a child's reaction to a chronic medical condition regardless of the specific disease. As a result, researchers have proposed that there are many common aspects of having a chronic condition that cut across diverse physical disease processes. These commonalities have led to a general agreement among researchers to view the psychosocial aspects of chronic medical conditions in children within a noncategorical framework (Hobbs et al., 1985; Pless & Perrin, 1985; Stein & Jessop, 1982, 1984).

The purpose of this chapter is to present an overview of a wide range of psychological approaches used to manage various problem areas that are common to children with chronic medical conditions. As noted earlier, the child who exhibits serious adjustment problems is the exception rather than the rule. Most of these children show considerable resilience in face of the stressful experiences associated with their illness and require minimal psychological intervention (Drotar & Bush, 1985). On the other hand, Fritz (1992) appropriately has cautioned that mental health practitioners should not accept as inevitable major emotional distress and poor psychological and social functioning in children and adolescents with chronic medical conditions. He lists a number of symptoms that clearly warrant a referral for psychological intervention with these children including (a) suicidal threats and ideation, (b) significant noncompliance with medical regimens following attempts to improve it, (c) developmentally inappropriate behaviors which persist for more than several weeks, (d) significant social withdrawal, and (5) longstanding depressive symptoms. Most of the problems presented by the child with a chronic medical condition pertain to coping with their disease and medical treatments—problems that affect the tasks of daily living and age-appropriate developmental tasks. The focus of this chapter is on interventions that address these developmental and disease-related tasks.

OVERVIEW OF ASSESSMENT ISSUES

The reasons for assessing children who are medically at risk, are generally multifaceted and can be prompted by general as well as specific, acute concerns. An assessment can be used to provide diagnostic information regarding the child's current medical status, level of psychosocial functioning, and how these factors may interact so that appropriate interventions can be initiated. A second purpose could be to document the impact of medical and psychological interventions. Similarly, assessment information may be used to determine the effect of the medical condition over time, irrespective of interventions. Evaluations may be needed to address very specific concerns raised by health-care providers, the child, and/or parents. Finally, assessments can be an important tool in terms of prevention by helping to identify strengths and vulnerabilities that may shake the child's overall adjustments.

There are particular times during the treatment of a medical condition that may be more stressful or anxiety-provoking than others. These include the period of initial diagnosis as well as transition points in the medical treatment and the child's own development. Therefore, the context in which the evaluation is made and the timing with regard to duration of illness, stage of medical treatment, and general physical and emotional growth and development should be considered in collecting data and interpreting results. Given the many complex issues that must be addressed in evaluating children's and their family's adjustment to a chronic medical condition, the use of multiple methods of assessment and multiple informants is necessary in order to develop a comprehensive understanding of the child's and family's level of functioning. (Wallander & Thompson, 1995).

Assessment must cover both medical and psychosocial areas, with particular attention as to how they influence each other. The scope of areas assessed will depend on whether a question has been raised about a specific area of functioning or whether a more general picture of the child's adjustment is needed. Leventhal (1984) has posed six questions that can be used to guide a global clinical assessment:

1. What is the extent of the disease and its complications in the child?
2. What are the physical effects of the illness on the child?
3. How has the illness affected the child's performance at home, with peers, and at school?
4. How has the child adjusted to the illness, including an understanding of the disease, a view of self, and relationships with important people in the child's life?
5. What impact does the child's illness have on the family and its members?
6. How has the family adjusted to the special impact or burden of the illness? (pp. 71–72).

These questions outline the importance of understanding the impact of a medical condition on the child, his or her family system, and his or her functioning in other important systems like school. In addition, answers to these questions depend, in part, on a comparison with the child's previous level of psychological adjustment and development. Given that a child's understanding of his or her medical condition is often essential to adjustment and, in some cases, to medical management, a careful evaluation of a child's cognitive-developmental level is essential (Elkind, 1985). Although intellectual functioning as assessed by standardized intellectual tests is one means to ascertain cognitive-developmental level, an assessment using a Piagetian framework may be more useful in this regard. If the child is reasonably intelligent, one may first want to know how he or she is making sense of the world; then one can try to offer help by explaining his or her medical condition and its treatment. This will be particularly important if the child is expected to participate in the ongoing medical management of the condition as with insulin-dependent diabetes (Ingersoll, Orr, Herrold, & Golden, 1986). Age is often inappropriately used as a measure of cognitive development: tools are available for a more individualized assessment (Burbach & Peterson, 1986).

In adjusting to the diagnosis of a chronic medical condition, both child and parents bring to this situation coping behaviors learned through various life experiences (Lazarus & Folkman, 1984; Siegel & Smith, 1989). Therefore, it may be helpful to ask children and their parents directly how they have coped with previous stressful situations, so as to gain some idea of their experience with prior stressful events, types of coping strategies used, and their perceived success. (Melamed, Siegel, & Ridley-Johnson, 1988). This offers the health-care provider an opportunity to reinforce coping behaviors that are likely to facilitate successful adjustment to the current medical condition and all that it involves. In addition, strategies that might have a negative effect on adjustment can be identified and discussed.

Just as knowledge of previous stressful situations can help identify and anticipate the use of various coping strategies by the child and parent, a careful assessment of parenting style can aid in the identification of families who may be at risk for parent-child problems or health-care provider—child problems. For example, is this a child whose parents have been inconsistent in their expectations for responsibilities and limitsetting when appropriate?

Are these parents who, prior to the medical diagnosis, typically were more protective of the child, being reluctant to let him or her engage in age-appropriate activities away from home?

A variety of paper-and-pencil measures are available to assess a number of psychological constructs that may be relevant to the child with a chronic medical condition. These include anxiety, depression, self-esteem, behavior problems, hospital-related fears, impact of illness on family, family adaptability and cohesion, parenting stress, and coping strategies (Karoly, 1988). The majority of these measures include some normative references as to how children of different ages and/or gender typically respond to the questionnaire. Yet with few exceptions, the normative samples comprise children without any significant medical conditions. Questions have been raised as to the appropriateness of these norms for children with significant medical conditions (Beck & Smith, 1988; Perrin, Stein, & Drotar, 1991). In particular, concerns have been noted regarding the problems in interpreting scores from instruments which contain items pertaining to physical symptoms.

Instruments for intellectual and academic assessment can be used to address specific concerns regarding changes in cognitive functioning and/or academic progress. These tools are often used to determine the impact of a chronic medical condition (Franceschi et al., 1984; Ryan, 1988) or a medical treatment (Copeland, et al., 1985; Stehbens, Kisker, & Wilson, 1983) on cognitive abilities. As can be surmised, assessment of the child who is medically at risk can be complex, requiring expertise in a variety of areas. Therefore, it is important that the assessment process involve an interdisciplinary team (Varni & Babani, 1986). Children with medical conditions receive periodic evaluation of the condition itself; some level of ongoing psychosocial assessment should be included to facilitate optimal total health care (Drotar & Bush, 1985). Assessments for specific, acute problems may be handled quickly and intervention initiated promptly. An evaluation of current psychological functioning and the impact a medical condition may have on the child and family will require more time and can become very complex.

AN INTERDISCIPLINARY APPROACH TO TREATMENT

Given the diversity of physical, psychological, and social issues that may be involved in the treatment of children and adolescents with medical conditions, the experts involved in the health care of this population must reflect this same diversity (Hobbs et al, 1985; Klerman, 1985; Magrab & Calcagno, 1978; Varni & Babani, 1986). The ideal approach to total health- care in this population calls for an interdisciplinary team composed of a physician, mental-health professional, and other allied health care professionals. The advantage to this system is the collaboration that can occur in the assessment of children with medical conditions and in the development of treatment plans that are sensitive to both medical and psychosocial needs. An additional advantage for the mental-health professional in working within a team framework is that his or her involvement in the child's treatment may be more readily accepted. If the mental-health professional is perceived by the child and family as "another team member," there is often less resistance to needed psychological intervention. Families or individual family members do not have to feel "singled out" when a psychological intervention is suggested, as this type of intervention is "routine." In this vein, Cameron (1978) has suggested that simultaneous medical and psychological assessment and treatment, as opposed to a sequential one, may help minimize patient's negative reactions to a psychological referral. Since coping with a medical condition is an ongoing, dynamic process, the continuity of having a psychological expert on the team (one who is known to the family) can facilitate the therapeutic relationship when psychological interventions are needed.

Drotar, Crawford, and Ganofsky (1984) provide a model for an interdisciplinary, collaborative approach or preventive interventions with children with chronic medical conditions. They propose that this interdisciplinary model of intervention should include the following foci with the child and family: "(1) mastery of potentially disruptive anxiety related to the disease and its physical management; (2) a reasonable understanding of and adherence to necessary medical regimens; (3) integration of illness into family life, especially the reconciliation of family needs with those of the ill child; and (4) adaptation to hospitals, school and peers" (Drotar, 1995, p. 79).

The concept of an interdisciplinary team must include the child and family as active, participating members. This philosophy is crucial for medical conditions such as insulin-dependent diabetes mellitus, cystic fibrosis, and others, where the child and family are actively involved in medical management of the condition on a daily basis. As will be noted later, the inclusion of patients in the development of a treatment plan will contribute to greater adherence and feelings of personal responsibility for self-care (Meichenbaum & Turk, 1987). Involvement in decision making may promote a greater sense of perceived control in parents and older children and enhance feelings of self-efficacy in managing what oftentimes can be a rigorous treatment plan.

Problems Associated With the Medical Condition and Treatment Acquisition of Information

Education of medically at-risk children and families regarding the medical condition and necessary treatment is important for a variety of practical and psychological reasons. Informed consent by the parent and/or child, if of legal age, is necessary to provide appropriate medical assessment and treatment as with chemotherapy for cancer patients or a kidney biopsy in a child with end-stage renal disease. With some medical conditions, (such as insulin-dependent diabetes mellitus, cystic fibrosis, or spina bifida), active participation in medical management is required of the child and parent. Without accurate knowledge, such participation is not possible. Psychologically, providing information can facilitate adjustment to the medical condition and treatment by decreasing anxiety (Melamed, 1982; Shaw, Stephens, & Holmes, 1986) and in some instances by increasing perceptions of control (Jamison, Lewis, & Burish,1986; Nannis, Susman, Strope & Woodruff, 1982). Given that the patient's knowledge is related to obtaining informed consent, to increasing active participation in medical care or

adherence, and to facilitating psychological adjustment, it is important to consider factors that may affect how children and their parents acquire information. Cognitive-developmental level, coping style, and timing are all variables that can affect the acquisition of information.

A number of investigations have documented the relationship between cognitive-developmental level and conception of illness in children both with and without a significant medical condition (Bibace & Walsh, 1979; Brewster, 1982; Perrin & Gerrity, 1981; Shagena, Sandler, & Perrin, 1988; Susman, Dorn, & Fletcher, 1987). In general these studies indicate that the child's conception of illness becomes more sophisticated as his or her cognitive abilities mature through the preoperational, concrete operational, and formal operational levels of development (Piaget, 1929). Through systematic investigations, Bibace and Walsh (1979) have identified six levels of understanding of illness: phenomenism, contagion (preoperational), contamination, internalization (concrete operational), physiological, and psychophysiological (formal operational), which are briefly summarized in Table 11.1.

The documented relationship between children's cognitive reasoning abilities and their ability to understand the concept of illness has direct clinical implications when one is trying to teach children about their own medical conditions and management. As noted by Brewster (1982), providing accurate information to children does not necessarily result in accurate knowledge for several reasons: "...children have their own conceptions of what has happened to them, their ability to assimilate the information is limited and they often distort what they are told, and other factors, unrelated to cognition, may have a greater bearing on their responses to treatment." (p. 355). At the very minimum, educational programs must be developmentally based. They should incorporate instruction geared to the child's developmental level or one stage above as it has been suggested that children can understand explanations one level beyond their current level of cognitive reasoning (Kohlberg,1963; Turiel, 1969). Educational programs should routinely elicit the child's current understanding about how he or she came to have the medical condition and what he or

TABLE 11.1. Developmental Stages of Children's Conceptualizations of Illness

APPROXIMATE AGE RANGE	PIAGETIAN STAGE	CAUSAL UNDERSTANDING OF ILLNESS
3 to 7	Preoperational	**Phenomenism:** Illness due to magical process or an event that happened at same time as symptom occurred.
		Contagion: Illness the result of some event that was linked spatially or temporally; direct contact not required.
8 to 12	Concrete operational	**Contamination:** Illness the results of contact through germs, dirt, or misbehavior.
		Internalization: Illness due to an external contaminant that has entered the body in some observable manner.
13 and older	Formal operational	**Physiological:** Illness due to the malfunctioning of internal body parts or processes.
		Psychophysiological: Illness can have psychological causes and symptoms in addition to physiological.

Adapted from Bibace and Walsh (1979)

she thinks will need to be done to manage it. Attempts to correct any misperceptions or distortions in the child's thinking should again be geared toward his or her current level of reasoning or one stage beyond. An understanding of the child's level of cognitive reasoning will also allow the healthcare provider to respond more effectively to fears and concerns related to the medical condition and treatment (Bibace & Walsh, 1979). For example, a child at the preoperational level may feel that the bone marrow biopsy she has to undergo is a punishment for some imagined or real misdeed, resulting in even greater pretreatment anxiety. The healthcare provider can listen empathetically and reassure her that the bone marrow is not intended to punish her but to see if the "special medicine" (chemotherapy) is doing its job. Concerns regarding the long-term implications of having a medical condition are unlikely to be reported until the child has achieved the formal operational reasoning level. At this point, concerns regarding how the medical condition or treatment may affect relationships with others (as well as plans for the future) should be expected (Allen, Affleck, Tennen, McGrade, & Ratzan, 1984).

Understanding something about cognitive reasoning can help clinicians in developing appropriate expectations for adherence to a prescribed treatment regimen. For children at the preoperational stage, incorporating the necessary behaviors into the cur-

rent daily routine (with appropriate praise and rewards from parents when the behavior is performed) is likely to result in greater adherence than discussing the benefits of such behavior with the child. Informational statements about how certain adherence behaviors, like taking medication, will make the child feel better are more likely to have a beneficial effect on children as they reach the concrete operational stage of internalization.

Using a cognitive-developmental framework to foster adherence during adolescence can be of particular importance. Yet it should be remembered that even though an adolescent may be capable of more complex cognitive reasoning, this skill may not always be used. Since the child is "older," healthcare providers and parents may automatically raise their expectations regarding independent adherence behaviors; a step that may not always be appropriate. For example, with more complicated treatment programs, such as those required of a child with diabetes, the ability to make adjustments in insulin dose has been associated with cognitive maturity (Ingersoll, Orr, Herrold, & Golden, 1986), which does not necessarily correlate with age. In addition, greater cognitive maturity, which theoretically should enable greater independent adherence, comes at a time when other concerns, such as peer relationships and social activities, may take priority over caring for one's medical condition. Therefore, a decrease in adherence may actually be observed, especially when the behavior must be performed in a social setting (e.g., for an adolescent with diabetes following a meal plan, or for an adolescent with spina bifida excusing oneself to catheterize). In addition, greater cognitive sophistication enables the adolescent to think about his or her medical condition and the impact it has had on his or her life in a more complex manner. The adolescent can begin to think about what life would have been like without the condition and treatment. As a result, an adolescent who previously appeared to have adjusted well to having a chronic medical condition may experience feelings of depression, anger, or other psychological reactions to these cognitions (Elkind, 1985).

Acquisition of information may also be affected by the child's style of coping with medical procedures and the medical condition. The assessment of preferred coping style is a relatively new area of investigation that has taken several approaches (Rudolph, Denning, & Weisz, 1995). One of these has been to identify specific behavioral coping strategies that children use when confronted with medical procedures or other stressful events (Siegel, 1983). Another approach has been to investigate children's preferences for obtaining or avoiding information related to required medical procedures and disease states (Peterson & Toler, 1986; Levenson, Pfefferbaum, Copeland & Silberberg, 1982; Smith Ackerson, & Blotcky, 1989). These initial investigations suggest that children, like adults, differ, even after controlling for age, in how much information they prefer (Peterson & Toler, 1986). For children with cancer, the preferred coping style regarding information appears to be related to duration of illness (Smith, et al., 1989; Levenson et al., 1982). Children who have had their disease for a shorter period of time are less likely to want additional information regarding it or detailed information during the invasive medical procedures necessary for treatment. For these patients, an avoidant coping style may be the means of dealing with this potentially life-threatening disease.

If children have preferred coping styles regarding the level of information they receive about their medical condition and treatment, an important question is raised. Should health-care providers attempt to offer detailed information to those children who would prefer not to have that level of information? For medical conditions that require life style changes and active participation by the child in medical management, it would be difficult to honor the child's desire not to have detailed information. For medical conditions where these factors are not an issue, the question posed must be addressed empirically, as one may hypothesize that providing information to a child who prefers an avoidant coping style may result in negative repercussions such as adjustment difficulties. One study has addressed this question in pediatric cancer patients undergoing invasive medical procedures (Smith, et al., 1989). Children who preferred to avoid information but were given detailed information about what was happening and what they might think and feel during the medical procedures actually gave lower subjective reports of experienced pain than did those who were offered verbal distraction during the procedures. Therefore it may not always be detrimental to provide an intervention that seems inconsistent with a child's preferred coping style. Certainly further information is needed across a variety of medical conditions and settings before definitive statements can be made.

When patient education is necessary to facilitate adherence, it is important to remember that the timing of that education in relation to the diagnosis is important. Patients and their families typically react emotionally on hearing a diagnosis of a chronic medical condition, and this may well interfere with their ability to process additional information (Meichenbaum & Turk, 1987). It may be prudent to provide basic skills initially, with the timing of further education dependent on when the family has had an opportunity to work through emotions generated by the diagnosis.

In summary, there are multiple factors that health-care providers need to consider in developing educational approaches to enhance parents' and children's knowledge about medical conditions and treatment. These factors should also be considered when professionals involved in medical care speculate about what children "should" or "need to know." In those situations where children need information to participate in their own care, it is extremely important to remember that adequate knowledge does not necessarily translate into adequate adherence or performance of necessary self-care. The application of knowledge may be inhibited by a variety of factors, including the child's emotional adjustment, level of self-control, and perceptions of self-efficacy.

Management of Pain and Discomfort

Pain is a special source of stress for a number of children with diseases such as arthritis, hemophilia, sickle cell disease, kidney disease, and cancer (Travis, 1976; Walco, Siegel, Dolgin, & Varni, 1992). Many children with chronic medical conditions must endure chronic pain associated with the disease process. Much of the stress that occurs with chronic pain results from the unpredictability of painful episodes and their degree of severity. Chronic pain not only results in considerable discomfort for these children but can interfere with the activities of daily living. It can cause social isolation and lead to dependence on analgesic medications as well as on the medical care system (Anderson, Fanurik D., & Zeltzer, 1992; Varni & Gilbert, 1982; Walco & Dampier, 1987).

Chronic pain, longstanding and intractable, is caused by severe injury or progressive disease (Bonica, 1977). Fordyce (1976) has noted that although pain may result from underlying organic pathology, environmental consequences can modify and further maintain various aspects of chronic pain behaviors. These include a number of observable pain responses such as complaining, grimacing, restricted body movement, inactivity, and medication use. They may, in turn, be affected by socioenvironmental consequences. Thus, the patient's family and medical staff may actually help him or her to learn chronic pain behaviors by inadvertently reinforcing overt manifestations of pain. Consequences such as attention and sympathy from others, rest, and the avoidance of unpleasant duties and responsibilities, for example, can eventually maintain the pain behaviors independent of disease-related factors (Bonica, 1977).

Because pain is a private, subjective experience, it is important to evaluate factors that may affect individual differences in pain perception and pain behavior (Varni, 1983). For children, these factors include the child's cognitive-developmental level, attitude toward the pain, previous experiences with pain events, perceived ability to handle pain (i.e., self-efficacy), and repertoire of coping skills, as well as family influences that may provide reinforcement and models for pain behavior (Siegel & Smith, 1989; Siegel & Smith, 1991). Given the complex nature of pain in children, an adequate assessment of pain problems in this population calls for an interdisciplinary approach that includes an evaluation of self-report, cognitive, behavioral, social-environmental, and medical factors (Lavigne, Schulein, & Hahn, 1986a, 1986b; Thompson & Varni, 1986; Varni, 1983). A detailed discussion of pain assessment in children is presented by Varni, Blount, Waldron, and Smith (1995).

A variety of behavioral intervention strategies have been used in the management of chronic pain in children (Masek, Russo, & Varni, 1984). Varni (1983) has noted that behavioral techniques used in the management of pain can be classified as being methods that regulate either pain perception or pain behavior. In the former approaches, the child is taught to regulate or modify his or her perception of pain through self-regulatory methods such as hypnosis, guided imagery, relaxation, and biofeedback training. Techniques to regulate pain behavior involve the manipulation and modification of environmental events that are seen as maintaining pain behaviors. In this latter approach, environmental events such as social attention, entertainment, and special activities are systematically controlled and made to occur contingent on age-appropriate, adaptive behaviors. Family members are taught to respond to the child in ways that reduce pain-related disability and to maximize healthy behaviors.

Zeltzer, Dash, and Holland (1979) describe a treatment program for helping adolescents with sickle cell disease to deal with painful vasoocclusive crises that occur when misshapen sickle cells block the flow of blood in small blood vessels. These adolescents were taught to use a self-hypnosis procedure that involved eye fixation and progressive muscle relaxation. Following this induction procedure, the subjects were instructed in guided imagery involving a pleasant scene and given suggestions for body warmth and dilation of their blood vessels. After learning these techniques, the adolescents were told to use these procedures at the onset of a painful crisis. Using thermal biofeedback equipment, this intervention was found to increase peripheral skin temperature significantly (indicating that they had learned to produce vasodilation) and to reduce the frequency and intensity of pain crises and analgesics used over an 8-month period. Reductions in outpatient visits and total number of days of hospitalization were also noted.

Varni and his associates (Varni, 1981; Varni & Gilbert, 1982) have investigated the use self-regulation techniques in the control of chronic arthritic pain in children with hemophilia. This pain typically results from repeated bleeding episodes in the joints. The treatment program involved progressive muscle relaxation training, meditative breathing and guided imagery. The patients were instructed to imagine themselves in a scene associated with warmth and pain relief. These techniques were effective in reducing the number of days of perceived chronic pain and analgesic medication use. Improvements were also noted in the patients' mobility and sleep. Monitoring by means of thermal biofeedback equipment indicated that skin temperature increased over the targeted joints. Similar findings have been reported using the same treatment approach with children experiencing chronic and recurrent pain from juvenile rheumatoid arthritis (Walco, Varni, and Ilowite, 1992).

Adherence to Therapeutic Regimens

No discussion of medically at-risk children would be complete without specific attention to the issue of adherence to medical and/or behavioral therapeutic regimens. While advances in medicine have resulted in more effective treatments for children with chronic medical conditions, they have also placed greater demands on children and their families to follow more complex and intensive treatment regimens (Christophersen, 1993; LaGreca & Schuman, 1995). Therapeutic regimens vary depending on the medical condition in the specific components involved (e.g., taking medication, dietary changes, exercise,

etc.), the complexity of the regimen, and the duration of treatment. Typically, the purpose of the regimen is to facilitate optimal physiological functioning in the child via management of the medical condition, though with some diseases, such as leukemia and other cancers, the purpose of treatment is curative. More often than not, the regimen must be adhered to over a longer period of time, often years, whereas more acute problems such as infections may call for briefer treatments.

In keeping with current nomenclature, the term "adherence" rather than "compliance" is being used. Often these terms have been used interchangeably, though recent discussions in the literature have argued for consistent use of "adherence" (Kasl, 1975; Varni & Wallender, 1984), as this term connotes a more active, collaborative patient role. "Compliance," on the other hand, connotes a passive, obedient, "do what the doctor says" role that no longer seems to apply to patient/physician relationships. In addition, the term "noncompliance" has a negative connotation often implying that the patient alone is to blame for not following a therapeutic regimen (Meichenbaum & Turk, 1987; Rapoff & Barnard, 1991). In fact, some treatment prescriptions may be too vague, too complex, or misunderstood due to poor communication between patient and physician. Therefore, the term "adherence" is recommended and is used throughout this chapter.

Studies of adherence to medical regimens indicate that a significant number of patients do not adhere, with estimates ranging from 10% to 60% in pediatric practice (LaGreca, 1988). Typically, adherence to treatment for chronic medical conditions is lower than that for acute problems (Haynes, 1976). In general, studies that attempt to assess adherence are faced with several methodological issues that can affect the results. Adherence is often difficult to operationalize (e.g., at what point is a person classified as nonadherent? La Greca, 1988). It is a difficult concept to assess adequately (Rudd, 1979; La Greca, 1988) and results obtained may be biased in that people who are not adherent are less likely to participate in these studies (Cluss & Epstein, 1985).

Of particular concern to the clinician is the ability to assess adherence. A variety of methods have been used, including or parent- or self-monitoring, interviews and 24-hour recall, biochemical markers, pill counts, and clinical outcome or health status (Johnson, Silverstein, Rosenbloom, Carter, & Cunningham, 1986; LaGreca & Schuman, 1995; Meichenbaum & Turk, 1987; Parrish, 1986). Each method has its disadvantages though Parrish (1986) has noted that while parent or self-report may overestimate adherence, it may be the most efficient means of obtaining the data. Good interviewing skills can enhance the accuracy of reporting nonadherent behaviors. Interviews can be advantageous in that information regarding obstacles to adherence can often be gleaned from parents' and patients' responses (Parrish, 1986). Interviews that focus on recent periods of time and ask specifically what the patient did or did not do will enhance the accuracy of patient or parent report (Johnson et al., 1986; Kovacs, Goldston, Obrosky, & Iyengar, 1992).

Czajkowski and Koocher (1986) have developed an instrument that predicts nonadherence in patients with cystic fibrosis. The Medical Compliance Incomplete Stories Test is composed of five stories where the main character is faced with the decision of whether or not to follow medical recommendations. The patient is required to complete the story and note what the outcome for the character will be. Responses to the story are scored for compliance/ coping, optimism, and self-efficacy. This innovative approach to predicting adherence seems easily adaptable to other situations and may be another means of identifying patients at risk for nonadherence.

The use of clinical outcome or health status as a measure of adherence represents a significant tautological problem and requires the assumption that the most effective treatment for that individual has been prescribed (Johnson, 1988; Pickering, 1979). For example, Johnson (1994) found that one third of children with diabetes were rated as having "good" levels of adherence to their medical and dietary regimen had poor metabolic control whereas one third of the children rated as showing "poor" compliance had good metabolic control. Therefore, until more is known regarding the relationship between clinical outcome and adherence, the use of the former to assess the latter is discouraged (Johnson, 1988). Moreover, in future investigations, it will be more helpful to include both adherence and health-status

measures to facilitate a greater understanding of the relationship among these measures and variables that may affect one or both of them (La Greca, 1988; Johnson, 1988).

A variety of factors have been correlated with adherence, including duration and complexity of treatment, health beliefs regarding the medical condition and treatment, patient's level of knowledge and skill, presence of symptoms and effect of treatment on symptoms, and patient satisfaction with medical treatment and relationship with the healthcare provider. A comprehensive review of this extensive literature is beyond the scope of this chapter; the reader is referred to other sources for a more thorough discussion (Haynes, 1976; Janis, 1984; La Greca, 1988; LaGreca & Schuman, 1995; Meichenbaum & Turk, 1987). It is important to conceptualize adherence as a dynamic rather than a static process, as adherence is apt to change over time particularly for chronic conditions (Meichenbaum & Turk, 1987). In addition, adherence is not an "all or none" situation in that, with more complex regimens, adherence to one aspect of the treatment is not necessarily related to adherence to others (Johnson et al., 1986; Schafer, Glasgow, McCaul, & Dreher, 1983). For example, an adolescent may almost always take his insulin injections at the appropriate time, although he may rarely follow an appropriate meal plan. Therefore, adherence must be assessed periodically over time and adherence to different treatment components should be assessed separately.

A number of techniques have been identified as useful in enhancing adherence with a diverse range of treatment programs. Some of these procedures are summarized in Table 11.2.

The complexity of a regimen and the specificity of recommendations made by the health-care provider are two factors, related to the treatment regimen itself, which have been associated with adherence (Haynes, 1976; Meichenbaum & Turk, 1987). One practical guideline is to keep treatment demands that are placed on patients and their families as simple as possible. Therefore, if a medication can be administered in one dose each day versus two or three, then the simpler regimen is more likely to facilitate adherence. Yet some treatment regimens, such as those typically prescribed for diabetes or

TABLE 11.2. Methods of Improving Patient's Compliance with Medical Regimens

1. Involve the patient and family in treatment planning.
2. Ensure the patient understands the procedures associated with the medical regimen.
3. Keep the treatment simple and consistent with the daily routine of the family.
4. Obtain the patient's commitment to follow the treatment program.
5. Ensure the patient's family supports and encourages adherence to the treatment program.
6. Use patient self-monitoring of specific behaviors related to treatment adherence.
7. Use reminders to prompt behaviors consistent with the treatment program.
8. Reinforce adherence to the treatment program on a regular basis.

cystic fibrosis, are quite complex and/or require multiple steps that can interfere with day-to-day functioning. In these cases in particular, adherence may be enhanced by trying to fit the regimen into the patient's lifestyle rather than the reverse (Meichenbaum & Turk, 1987).

Specific guidelines as to the particular behaviors a patient should follow and when these should be performed is another practical step that can improve adherence. While this is a seemingly simple guideline, in some instances health-care providers may be unaware that their recommendations lack specificity. Zola (1981) provides multiple examples of treatment prescriptions that may sound clear to the health-care provider yet can be confusing to the patient. For example, 'Take the drug 4 times a day.' Does this mean every 6 hours? That is, must the patient wake up in the middle of the night? What if the patient forgets; should he or she take twice the dose when he or she remembers?" (p. 247).

Obviously patients and their families must possess knowledge about the disease and be able to perform the behaviors necessary to follow the appropriate treatment plan. Although issues related to patient education were reviewed in a previous section, it should be remembered that knowledge and skill are necessary but not sufficient conditions to promote adherence (LaGreca & Skyler, 1995; Lorenz, Christensen, & Pichert, 1985; McCaul, Glasglow, & Schafer, 1987). Varni and Babani (1986) provide a cogent review of behavioral methods used to facilitate education and implementation of treatment regimens, with specific attention to antecedents and consequences that may interfere with adherence. Reduction of symptoms has been associated with greater adherence to health-care

provider recommendations (Arnhold et al., 1970; Shope, 1981). Yet with some chronic medical conditions, following a prescribed treatment regimen may have no obvious, immediate effect (as when a child with diabetes does not check his or her blood sugar). In some situations adherence may result in aversive symptoms, such as nausea or hair loss with chemotherapy or increased weight due to prednisone therapy in children with renal transplants. Therefore the immediate consequence of adherent behavior may be unnoticeable or aversive (Lemanek, 1990: Tamaroff, Festa, Adesman, & Walco, 1992). For example, Dolgin, Katz, Doctors, and Siegel (1986) found greater nonadherence associated with more treatment side effects and visible physical changes in one sample of children and adolescents with cancer. Moreover, some health care providers and/or parents may feel that maintaining good health or preventing future complications should be sufficient motivators to ensure adherence in children and adolescents. Cognitive-developmental level and concerns about feeling different are often not taken into consideration when this perception is held (LaGreca & Schuman, 1995). To facilitate adherence over longer periods of time, Varni and Babani (1986) suggest that external positive reinforcers may be necessary to increase motivation to engage in adherent behaviors.

One of the primary means of promoting adherence is to foster a collaborative relationship between the health-care provider, the patient, and his or her family (Korsch, Gozzi, & Francis, 1968; Korsch & Negrete, 1972; Meichenbaum & Turk, 1987). In dealing with chronic medical problems over time, the relationship between the family and the medical-care system is particularly important if obstacles to adherence or dissatisfaction with treatment are to be uncovered and if the health-care provider is to be an effective motivator for adherent behaviors. Good communication skills and rapport as well as continuity of care appear to be important ingredients to fostering such a relationship (Meichenbaum & Turk, 1987). The Health Belief Model (Becker & Rosenstock, 1984; Rosenstock, 1985) may be a useful heuristic device to aid the health-care provider in understanding current adherence or nonadherence (DiMatteo & DiNicola, 1982). A patient's perceived susceptibility to such things as future complications, availability of reminders to engage in the necessary adherent behaviors, perceived obstacles and costs/benefits ratio of engaging in the required behaviors, and beliefs regarding one's ability to perform the required behaviors (e.g., self-efficacy) should all be assessed to more clearly understand why a patient may not adhere to a prescribed treatment regimen (Becker & Rosenstock, 1984; Rosenstock, 1985). In addition, the patient's beliefs regarding the treatment's effectiveness should be addressed.

Several studies with children and adolescents with chronic medical conditions highlight the importance of these factors. McCaul and colleagues (1987) found that self-efficacy beliefs were the strongest predictors across adherence behaviors in adolescents with diabetes. Brownlee-Duffeck et al., (1987) found that perceived costs were significantly predictive of adherent behaviors in adolescents with IDDM. Yet Czajkowski and Koocher (1986) sensitively note that some patients may not express their beliefs regarding the medical condition and or treatment in a direct manner. Using the Medical Compliance Incomplete Stories described earlier, patients' responses revealed negative and depressing feelings regarding the future that had not been directly expressed.

The role of the family and other sources of social support in facilitating adherence has been addressed (see reviews by La Greca, 1988; LaGreca & Schuman, 1995: Meichenbaum & Turk, 1987; Parrish, 1986). Specific examples include the finding that in adolescents with diabetes, negative interactions with parents were associated with less adherence to diet and less frequent blood sugar

monitoring (Schafer et al., 1983). Beck et al. (1980) noted that "family instability" (e.g., parents divorced, parent did not accompany child to clinic, child responsible for medication) was associated with less adherence in children who had kidney transplants.

Though current studies are limited by the complex methodology required to investigate interactional patterns (La Greca, 1988), an additional guideline for the clinician is to assess not only the patient's beliefs regarding the medical condition and treatment but those of all significant family members as well. Some family interactional patterns such as overprotection may inadvertently reinforce unnecessary sick-role behavior. In addition, parents (out of care and concern) may do too much for the child and decrease the child's opportunity to gain experience and develop feelings of mastery in dealing with his or her medical condition.

In reviewing different factors that may facilitate or impede adherence to treatment, the health-care provider should not lose sight of the fact that nonadherence may be the end result of a decisional process. Deaton (1985) is one of the few to study the adaptability of nonadherence in pediatric patients with a chronic medical condition: asthma. Others have suggested that a decision to not adhere to a prescribed treatment regimen is a means by which patients may exert control (Donovan & Blake, 1992; Hayes-Bautista, 1976; Koocher, McGrath, & Gudas, 1990) or, even less adaptive, that it is a form of indirect self-destructive behavior (Faberow, 1986).

Adjustment to Hospitalization and Medical Procedures

Children with chronic medical conditions often require numerous hospitalizations for diagnostic procedures, surgery, medical treatments, and the management of exacerbations of their disease process. Hospitalization, for example, may be necessary to treat a diabetic child in ketoacidosis, to manage joint pain in a child with sickle cell disease, to give highly toxic drugs to children with leukemia, or to manage joint bleeding in a child with hemophilia. For some of these children, extended periods of hospitalization will occur throughout their lives.

While children with chronic medical conditions encounter many experiences in the hospital similar to those of acutely ill children or children admitted for elective treatment, the stresses of a chronic diagnosis present special problems and challenges in adjustment. Long-term and/or repeated hospitalizations have significant consequences for the development of children and adolescents (Hobbs et al., 1985). School absences, separation from family members and peers, isolation from normal childhood activities and experiences, immobility, and loss of control over daily events are among these consequences. In addition, frequent medical procedures that are often distressing and painful have to be endured (Siegel, 1983; Siegel & Hudson, 1992). Given these experiences, there are numerous opportunities for clinicians to provide preventive interventions for children with chronic medical conditions in order to promote adaptive coping (Harbeck-Weber & McKee, 1995).

For those children with potentially life-threatening, chronic medical conditions, admission to the hospital may have a considerably different meaning than it does for children who are hospitalized with less serious illnesses or for elective surgeries. Thus, while all hospitalized children may encounter similar experiences while in the hospital, the nature of their medical problems and the purpose of the admission can present different challenges to the child's adaptation (Siegel, 1988).

There is substantial literature documenting the stressful effects of hospitalization and surgery in normal children (Thompson, 1985; Vernon, Foley, Sipowicz, & Schulman, 1965). Short- and long-term emotional and behavioral problems have been reported in as many as 30% of children both during and following the period of hospitalization (Siegel, 1976). There is evidence that repeated and prolonged hospitalizations are risk factors for the development of behavioral disturbances in children and adolescents. (Thompson, 1985); a common situation for many children with chronic medical diagnoses.

In one of the few studies in this area, Wells and Schwebel (1987) investigated the effects of hospitalization and surgery on children from infancy through 13 years of age who had chronic medical conditions. They found that children with chronic conditions were no more likely to exhibit behavioral disturbances than children without chronic diagnoses. Approximately 44% of the medically at-risk children showed some signs of posthospitalization adjustment problems.

A child's response to the hospital experience is influenced by a number of factors. One of the most important is the child's cognitive-developmental level (Siegel, 1983, 1988). In general, the literature consistently supports the finding that younger children tend to be at greater risk for developing emotional and behavioral problems both during and following hospitalization (Melamed & Siegel, 1980). These findings are consistent with the developmental literature, which indicates that younger children have a lower level of conceptual understanding of illness and medical procedures which, in turn, contributes to their higher level of anxiety and fearful behavior.

While there is some disagreement about the ideal timing for the preparation of children for the hospital experience, particularly when this is accompanied by surgery or other medical procedures, there is almost universal agreement in the literature about the necessity for some form of preparation to reduce the stress associated with hospitalization (Peterson & Brownlee-Duffeck, 1984; Siegel, 1976). Most of the work in this area has been in the preparation of children for surgery or invasive diagnostic procedures. There is considerable evidence for the effectiveness of various preparation programs in reducing anxiety before, during, and after hospitalization, in minimizing posthospitalization behavioral disturbance, and in facilitating adaptive coping during hospitalization (Siegel, 1976; Thompson, 1985; Vernon & Thompson, 1993).

There are five major components that are the focus of most preparation programs with children, including giving information, encouraging emotional expression, establishing a trusting relationship between the child and hospital staff, providing the parents with information, and providing coping strategies to the child and/or parents (Elkins & Roberts, 1983; Vernon et al., 1965). Several interventions that include one or more of these components have received empirical support. One has been the use of filmed models. In this method, the child is exposed to various aspects of the hospital experience through the perspective of another child. During various medical procedures, the model typically responds in a manner that demonstrates relatively nonanxious and cooperative behaviors. Various types of information are also provided in filmed modeling. In this regard, Cohen and Lazarus (1980) have identified four specific types of information that can be provided in the context of medical treatment, including the reasons for medical treatment, the actual medical procedures that will be used, the sensations that will be experienced, and specific coping strategies that the patient might use. Filmed modeling has been shown to be effective in reducing anxiety and facilitating cooperative behavior in impending surgery (Ferguson, 1979; Melamed & Siegel, 1975) and specifically in anesthesia induction (Vernon & Bailey, 1974).

Another method of preparing children for hospitalization and surgery involves training children in specific coping skills. For example, Peterson and Shigetomi (1981) taught children to use several cognitive-behavioral coping strategies comprising cue-controlled relaxation; they paired deep muscle relaxation with the cue word "calm." In addition, the subjects were instructed to use distracting imagery (i.e., imagining a pleasant scene) and calming self-instructional phrases. The children were encouraged to use these techniques during particularly stressful or painful experiences in the hospital. This intervention was effective in reducing distress and increasing cooperative behaviors in children 2 to 10 years of age who were hospitalized for elective surgery.

Some investigators have focused on the parents of hospitalized children, usually the mother, as the primary point of intervention in facilitating adjustment to the hospital. This is based on the assumption that parents who are anxious might communicate their anxiety to their child and would therefore be less effective in supporting the child during the hospitalization (Siegel, 1976). Skipper and his colleagues (Skipper & Leonard, 1968; Skipper, Leonard, & Rhymes, 1968) found a reduction in stress responses by mothers and less emotional distress for their children when a supportive nurse provided mothers with information about hospital routines and medical procedures and informed the mothers of their role in caring for their child in the hospital. Wolfer and Visintainer (1975) developed a preparation program that focused on both the child and the parents. In the experimental condition, the mother and child received preparation and supportive care at six "stress points" throughout the hospitalization. The child's preparation included procedural and sensory information, rehearsal of appropriate behaviors, and emotional support. Mothers were provided with support by a nurse, including individual attention at stress points, an opportunity to clarify their feelings and thoughts, accurate information, and an explanation regarding ways in which they could help care for their children. This comprehensive program was found to reduce distress-related behaviors and to facilitate cooperation in the children, decrease self-reported maternal anxiety, and increase satisfaction with the care the children received.

Campbell and associates (1992) investigated the effects of four different preparation programs on mothers of preschool children undergoing cardiac catheterization. The mothers were assigned to one of five groups: education orientation, orientation plus stress-management training, orientation plus brief supportive psychotherapy, a combination of the first three components, or a nonintervention control group. These researchers found that children whose mothers received stress-management training were significantly less upset and more cooperative at venipuncture and during the catheterization than were children in the other group. Mothers who received stress-management training also reported a more favorable posthospital adjustment for their children than mothers in the other intervention group.

Children with chronic medical conditions must sometimes receive medical care in unusually stressful settings within the hospital, such as intensive care units and protected environments. A child in a pediatric intensive care unit (PICU) is typically immobilized and confronted with periods of overstimulation alternating with periods of sensory deprivation (Rothstein, 1980). Cataldo, Bessman, Parker, Pearson, and Rogers (1979) describe an intervention program designed to improve patient's overall psychosocial functioning in the PICU.

Children were given the opportunity to interact with a child-life worker while playing with age-appropriate toys. This brief and relatively simple intervention resulted in an increase in the children's interactions, attention to activities, and positive affect and a reduction in inappropriate and nonadaptive behaviors.

Where the risk of infections must be minimized, some children need to be confined, often for extended periods of time, to a room where the air is continuously cleaned. The use of such protected environments is particularly common with pediatric cancer patients undergoing chemotherapy or bone marrow transplants, where the medication they receive significantly increases the risk of infection by affecting the child's immune system. Prolonged isolation can have a potentially deleterious effect on the child's adjustment because of potential sensory deprivation as a result of confinement and exposure to a limited number of persons.

Kellerman and his colleagues (Kellerman et al.,1976; Kellerman, Rigler, & Siegel, 1979) developed a comprehensive intervention program designed to mitigate the effects of prolonged isolation for children in protected environments. This approach included the provision of access to window views and clocks, the establishment of daily schedules, regular visits from family members, the services of a play therapist and school teacher, and counseling for the family. These investigators found that while some children experienced transitory periods of depression, this comprehensive psychosocial program was effective in preventing significant or prolonged psychological adjustment problems.

As noted earlier, these children must often endure painful and highly aversive medical procedures. A number of intervention programs have been developed to help them cope with this more effectively. For example, pediatric cancer patients experience frequent diagnostic and treatment procedures such as bone marrow aspirations and lumbar punctures. Children, particularly younger ones, can become so distressed during these procedures that they require physical restraint to permit the procedures to be performed (Jay, Ozolins, Elliott, & Caldwell, 1983). Hypnosis (involving progressive

muscle relaxation, focused attention, and imagery) has been used to help these children manage the acute distress they often experience. (Kellerman, Zeltzer, Ellenberg, & Dash, 1983; Zeltzer & LeBaron, 1982).

Jay, Elliott, Ozolins, Olson, and Pruitt (1985) describe a multicomponent treatment program for reducing behavioral distress in preadolescent cancer patients undergoing bone marrow aspirations and lumbar punctures. This program involved a number of cognitive-behavioral techniques including filmed modeling, breathing exercises, emotive imagery (fantasies in which superhero figures are used to help the child cope), behavioral rehearsal, and positive reinforcement of cooperative behavior. After each child practiced these techniques, the therapist accompanied the child into the treatment room and "coached" him or her in the use of these coping techniques. The results indicated that this program was effective in reducing behavioral distress and self-reported pain.

In a more recent study, Jay and her colleagues (Jay, Elliott, Woody, & Siegel, 1991) compared this same cognitive-behavioral treatment program alone with a combination of this program plus 0.15 mg/kg of oral Valium (diazepam) administered 30 minutes prior to the medical procedures. They found that both interventions resulted in lower distress-related behaviors, self-reported pain, and heart rate. Because there were no differences found between the two treatment conditions, it was concluded that small dosages of oral Valium provided no therapeutic benefits to the children undergoing these diagnostic medical procedures beyond that of the cognitive-behavioral intervention alone.

Cardiac catheterization is a highly invasive and stressful diagnostic procedure used to evaluate the cardiac status of children with congenital heart disease. Naylor, Coates, and Kan (1984) examined the efficacy of a preparation program in reducing the distress experienced by 40 children 3 to 6 years of age undergoing cardiac catheterization. The intervention included behavioral rehearsal in the catheterization lab (including distraction techniques) and the provision of procedural and sensory information. Children who received this intervention cried less, had fewer pain complaints, and exhibited less motor activity than did children who were not exposed to this intervention. The experimental-group children also exhibited fewer behavior problems at home following the catheterization.

A major source of distress for children with cancer is the side effects of the chemotherapy agents typically used in the treatment of these diseases. Toxic anticancer medications often cause nausea and vomiting, which typically occur within hours of the drugs' administration. In addition to this, some patients develop nausea and vomiting prior to the administration of the drugs. Research with pediatric populations suggests that anticipatory nausea and vomiting (ANV) occurs in approximately 20% to 30% of these patients (Dolgin, Katz, McGinty, & Siegel, 1985).

There is a general consensus that ANV is a conditioned response whose etiology can be attributed to a classical conditioning paradigm (Carey & Burish, 1988). According to this learning model, chemotherapy serves as an unconditioned stimulus that elicits drug-induced nausea and vomiting (the unconditioned response). Previously neutral stimuli preceding the chemotherapy and associated with the treatment environment (i.e., clinic odors, sights of the hospital, tastes, and thoughts), through pairing with the unconditioned response, may become conditioned stimuli capable of eliciting ANV.

Anticipatory and post-treatment nausea and vomiting have been particularly refractory to treatment with antiemetic drugs (Oliver, Simon, & Aisner, 1986). A number of behavioral treatment approaches have been investigated as alternative methods for reducing these side effects. Zeltzer and her colleagues (LeBaron & Zeltzer, 1984; Zeltzer, LeBaron, & Zeltzer, 1984) found that compared to a supportive counseling group, hypnosis helped to reduce nausea and vomiting (as well as anxiety associated with chemotherapy) in children 6 to 17 years of age. The hypnosis procedure consisted of helping the children to become as intensely involved as possible in imagery and fantasy. Another intervention used with children involves attention-diversion/cognitive-distraction techniques. In a multiple-baseline design with three adolescent cancer patients, Kolko and Richard-Figueroa (1985) investigated the use of video games as a means of diverting attention away from the chemotherapy experience and potential conditioned stimuli in the treatment environment. This procedure resulted in a reduction in the number of anticipatory symptoms and a decrease in the aversiveness of the post-chemotherapy side effects. Similar findings are reported by Redd et al. (1987) using the same treatment approach. While the effectiveness of interventions such as progressive muscle relaxation training, systematic desensitization, and biofeedback in ameliorating the stress-related side effects of chemotherapy with adult cancer patients has been demonstrated, the use of these procedures has not been reported with children (Carey & Burish, 1988; Morrow & Dobkin, 1988).

Terminal Illness and the Dying Child

Despite the improved outlook for the medical treatment of children with life-threatening diseases such as cancer and cystic fibrosis, many of them die from their disease. Few experiences are more challenging and require greater emotional sensitivity on the part of health-care professionals than working with children and their families during the terminal stage of illness. Meeting the needs of these individuals requires not only special professional and interpersonal skills but also self-awareness on the part of the caregivers with regard to their own values and attitudes toward death and dying (Wiener, 1970).

One of the most difficult situations that the families of children with life-threatening illnesses face is the emotional "roller coaster" that results from episodes of relapse and critical illness that are interspersed with periods of improvement and a temporary return of normal functioning (Bronheim, 1978; Travis, 1976). Multiple medical crises contribute to the family's "anticipatory mourning." While this anticipatory process can help family members prepare for the child's impending death, it can also have a negative effect by causing the family to withdraw from the child emotionally long before the child's actual death. As a result, the child may experience a profound sense of abandonment and isolation at a time when he or she most needs support (Bronheim, 1978; Koocher & Sallan, 1978; Martinson & Papadatou, 1994).

Children with life-threatening illnesses and their families require emotional support throughout the course of illness. This should begin at the time of diagnosis and continue through the terminal phase of illness (Koocher, 1977; Stehbens, 1988). Repeated supportive contacts with the family by various members of the health-care team help to establish these individuals as a supportive resource for the family during the crisis period of the child's impending death. It is a difficult task, at best, for caregivers to build an effective supportive relationship during the terminal phase of a child's illness when a prior relationship with the family has not been established.

In addition to the medical management of the child's illness, there are several major tasks that health-care professionals must confront in their work with the terminally ill child and his or her family. One of the most basic therapeutic goals is to help to normalize the life of the child and family as much as may be possible within the constraints of the child's illness (Blake & Paulsen, 1981). Another basic goal is to facilitate effective coping with stressful events that are associated with the disease and its treatment (Stehbens, 1988). The methods for achieving these goals include facilitating communication among family members, encouraging the expression of feelings and concerns, and fostering a sense of mastery and control (Koocher & Sallan, 1978).

One of the most important and difficult tasks facing caregivers who work with critically ill children involves the process and content of informing children about their disease and communicating about the issue of death (Bearison, 1991; Koocher & Gudas, 1992). It is the general consensus among clinicians that children should receive an honest, factual, and age-appropriate explanation of their disease and the seriousness of their illness (Koocher & Sallan, 1978; Reynolds, Miller, Jelalian, & Spirito, 1995: Spinetta, 1980; Stehbens, 1988). This information can be provided to the child in a sensitive and supportive manner and in a way that does not deprive the child of hope for the future. Specifically, Koocher and his colleagues (Koocher & O'Malley, 1981; Koocher & Sallan, 1978) recommend that a child with a life-threatening illness be told the name

of the disease, given accurate information about the nature of the illness within the child's level of conceptual understanding, and be told that it is a serious illness from which children sometimes die.

It is important for those professionals who work with critically ill children to be familiar with the development of children's concepts of death. Research in this area suggests that children's abilities to conceptualize death and to comprehend its irreversibility are related to Piagetian stages of cognitive development similar to those presented earlier in this chapter in a discussion of children's concepts of illness (Koocher, 1973; Lazar & Torney-Purta, 1991; Spinetta, 1974).

In general, research with physically healthy children has shown that children under 5 years of age do not understand either the permanence or the universality of death. Children between 6 and 9 years of age tend to view death as a process of physical harm that may result from some wrongdoing. Older children and adolescents attain an idea of death as a gradual cessation of bodily functioning that is permanent and irreversible (White, Elsom, & Prawat, 1978). Some authors, based on clinical observations, have suggested that the development of a more advanced understanding of death can be accelerated in younger children who personally experience a life-threatening illness (Bluebond-Langer, 1974; Spinetta, 1974). A study by Jay, Green, Johnson, Caldwell, and Nitschke (1987), however, found no evidence that children with cancer demonstrated more mature concepts of death than did physically well children.

Communication with children about illness or death should be determined by the child's needs and desire for information. Health-care professionals need to be sensitive to the child's need to communicate when he or she is ready to do so. In order to facilitate communication with terminally ill children, it is important to accept their feelings, avoid putting off questions, and provide honest, simple explanations.

Koocher and Sallan (1978) note that children's failure to ask questions about their illness should not be interpreted as an indication that they do not want to "know." Often children will not ask questions because they perceive barriers that interfere with attempts at open communication. These perceptions may stem from the actions of parents and health-care workers, who unwittingly provide verbal and nonverbal hints that they feel uncomfortable discussing this subject (Koocher, 1977; Stehbens, 1988). Typically, children need to feel that they have "permission to talk about these difficult topics" (Spinetta, 1980).

Support for this open approach to communication with terminally ill children comes from a number of different sources. Clinical observations indicate that even when children are not directly informed about the seriousness of their illness, they obtain information from others (e.g., medical staff and parents who are overheard talking, other patients, and from nonverbal communication). Thus, despite the intentions of adults to "protect" children from knowledge of their illness, even young children are often well-informed about the nature of their disease and their impending death (Bluebond-Langer, 1974; Spinetta & Maloney, 1975; Vernick & Karon, 1965).

Spinetta (1980) offers several practical considerations that the clinician must address when communicating with children about the possibility of death. In addition to developmental factors, he notes that it is important to understand the parents' own philosophy of death so that death can be discussed with the child within this context. One must also assess the family's emotional responses and personal experiences with death, since each family expresses its fears and grieves differently. The child's views of death can best be understood in relation to the family's patterns of coping with death and other stressful situations. Finally, Spinetta (1980) suggests that the child's emotional response to a serious illness depends more on *how* information is provided than on the *content* of the information.

In addition, Spinetta (1980) has provided practical advice on how to talk with children about their own impending death in a sensitive and reassuring manner. He suggests that the basic messages to communicate to the child include the following: (a) the child will not be alone at death or after death; (b) children should know that they have done all that they could do with their lives; (c) it is all right to cry and feel sad and angry and not want to talk at times about the illness or death; (d) when it comes, death

will not hurt, and their will be no pain after death; (e) they will be able to say good-bye to friends and family if they want to; (f) adults do not always understand why children die, and they too sometimes cry because they do not want to lose their child; and (g) the parents will always remember the child after he or she dies and will be happy for the good times that they shared together.

Several studies indicate that the level of adjustment of terminally ill children, survivors of life-threatening disease, and family members following a child's death is related to their level of communication regarding the child's illness. There is evidence that failure to communicate honestly with children about their disease can lead to a sense of isolation, depression, and mistrust (Spinetta, 1974; Spinetta & Maloney, 1975; 1978). Families who are able to communicate openly about the child's illness have consistently been found to achieve a better adjustment, whether they are surviving patients or families of children who have died from their disease. In a study of childhood cancer survivors, children who had been told about their diagnosis early in the course of their illness were found to be better adjusted than children from whom such information was deliberately withheld (Slavin, O'Malley, Koocher & Foster, 1981). Similarly, parents who were able to communicate openly with their child tended to exhibit better adaptation to his or her eventual death than parents who were unable to talk honestly with their child (Spinetta, Swarner, & Sheposh, 1981).

Following a child's death, continued contact with the family is essential in order to monitor parental and sibling reactions and to assess their adjustment. The hospital where the child has been treated and a familiar caregiver can serve as a supportive resource during the period of mourning and periodically thereafter (Koocher & Sallan, 1978). If ongoing support has been provided to the family while the child was alive, it is likely that the extent of psychological intervention required after the child's death will be minimal (Bronheim, 1978; Koocher & O'Malley, 1981; Worden, 1991).

Over the past decade, as a means of assisting parents in their efforts to cope with the stresses of their child's life-threatening illness and/or the death of their child, numerous self-help groups have developed. The primary purpose of these groups is to enhance the social support available to parents by providing a network of people who are experiencing similar stresses in their lives (Borman, 1985). The Candlelighters Foundation is an international network of parent groups who have experienced childhood cancer and other life-threatening illnesses. This group was founded in order to help parents to deal with their fears and frustrations through the sharing of feelings and experiences, thus reducing their sense of isolation. The group also provides educational information regarding the illness, treatment approaches, and side effects. Compassionate Friends is a group for parents whose child has died irrespective of the cause. The focus of the group is on preventing family dysfunction and maladaptive grieving responses. Group discussions include methods for maintaining relationships with friends and relatives who often withdraw from the bereaved parents (Borman, 1985).

A recent trend in the treatment of terminally ill children has been home or hospice care during the terminal stage. Home care of the dying child maximizes the quality of the child's life during his or her final days and has a number of psychological advantages compared with hospitalization. Children do not have to be separated from parents, siblings, and friends and they can participate in family activities until they die. Parents can be trained to provide care at home, which can help to reduce the sense of helplessness that parents often feel when they relinquish their parental role in the hospital setting. Nurses are available on a 24-hour basis at the parents' request. Advocates of home care for the terminally ill child acknowledge that this approach is not appropriate for all families, since some may not have the necessary emotional or physical resources (Armstrong & Martinson, 1980; Twycross, 1990). Such families require the security of the hospital, and hospitalization is always available even for families that elect to use home care.

An alternative to home care for the terminally ill is the hospice. The hospice concept includes both home care or inpatient care in a health-care facility that is more like a home environment and is staffed by specially trained medical and mental-health personnel (Beck & Strang, 1993; Davidson, 1985; National Hospice Organization, 1984).

Martinson, Nesbit, and Kersey (1984) investigated the adaptation of 68 families who cared for their children at home during the terminal stage of cancer, following them for more than 5 years after their child's death. The findings from this study indicate a high level of satisfaction and good adjustment among family members. Families of 37 children who had died of cancer were studied by Mulhern, Lauer, and Hoffman (1983). The investigators found that the parents of 13 children who had died in the hospital were more anxious and had more somatic problems than were the parents whose children had received terminal care at home. Siblings of children who had died in the hospital were also found to be more emotionally inhibited, withdrawn, and fearful than siblings who had participated in the home-care program.

The emotional impact of a child's life-threatening illness is not limited to the child and his or her family. Members of the health-care team must also cope with the painful reality of the dying child (Martin & Mauer, 1982; Vernick & Karon, 1965). Koocher and Sallan (1978) refer to the difficulties experienced by professionals who provide care for children with life-threatening illnesses over extended periods of time, develop close personal relationships with these children and their families, and then must face the eventual death of some of these children. "Burnout" is, therefore, a risk for these caregivers (Kolotkin, 1981). Various approaches to facilitating adaptive coping among health-care professionals who work with these children have been described, including professional support groups (Stuetzer, 1980) and course work for training caregivers to cope with death and dying (Barton, 1972; Woolsey, 1985).

PROBLEMS ASSOCIATED WITH TASKS OF DAILY LIVING

Education Management

Since schooling is the main occupation of children, the interruption of the educational process by illness and its treatment should be minimized (Perrin, Ireys, Shayne, & Moynihan, 1984). The importance of integrating the child with a chronic medical condition into the regular school program has implications for the social development of the child, the quality of education received by the child, and the child's later integration into the adult workforce and the community. The continuum-of-services model as proposed by Deno (1973) includes four levels of regular classroom placement, including the regular classroom plus consultation, itinerant teaching and resource-room services. More restrictive settings include hospital or homebound instruction, self-contained classrooms, and special-day or residential schools. In keeping with the requirement of Public Law 94-142, the Mandatory Education of the Handicapped Act, the child must be educated in the least restrictive environment (LRE). Therefore, every effort should be made to place children in the least intensive/most integrated setting possible. If a child must be placed in a more intensive/less integrated program, consideration for a more integrated placement should occur at the earliest possible date.

Children with chronic medical conditions often have special educational needs that can be met if the child qualifies for special education placement under one of three labels: orthopedically handicapped, other health-impaired, or multiply handicapped. In some cases, certain related services such as occupational and physical therapy and transportation must also be provided, as required by Public Law 94-142. In 1986, this law was extended to children ages 3 to 5; and was implemented in all states by the 1990–91 school year. In addition, funding incentives have been made available to states to develop early intervention programs for handicapped and medically at-risk children under the age of 36 months. However, if a child's impairment does not interfere with his or her ability to function in the regular classroom setting, he or she may not qualify for special education services. In order to provide the related services (e.g., transportation, physical therapy, etc.) special education placement is a prerequisite.

A number of service delivery options are utilized to provide educational services to children with chronic medical conditions or physical handicaps. For some children, no special administrative arrangements are needed aside from providing time and a place to take care of daily treatment needs such as monitoring blood sugars (for children with diabetes) or self-catheterization (in minimally affected children with spina bifida). Other medical conditions may be so severe or hospitalizations so frequent that a homebound program is required. With this program, the special teacher provides all the instruction the child needs at home until the child is able to return to school. If hospitalized for long periods of time, the child may receive instruction through a hospital school. Home and hospital programs, while often the only educational option for students with chronic medical conditions, may vary in quality and instructional time allotted. For example, some states require only 3 hours per week (Perrin et al., (1984).

In addition to the traditional academic areas, children who are medically at risk may have specialized educational needs such as vocational and career preparation, disease management, nutrition, use of leisure time, care of medical equipment, and adaptive physical education. Supportive services needed may involve transportation and physical therapy for children with physical disabilities (e.g., juvenile rheumatoid arthritis, spina bifida, muscular dystrophy), special diets for children with endocrine disorders (diabetes, cystic fibrosis), in-school administration of medications, special treatments such as catheterization, counseling, and liaison services (Baird & Ashcroft, 1984). The individualized educational program (IEP) is the planning and management tool utilized to deliver special education and related services to handicapped children under Public Law 94-142. Although there is no clear role for physicians and health professionals in the development of an IEP, their participation may be critical for children with certain chronic conditions who require related services. Though provision of related services, when necessary, is required by Public Law 94-142, some school systems have tended to avoid listing all of a child's needs and the necessary services on an IEP fearing that they may ultimately be responsible for the cost of these services. If parents feel that their child`s educational rights have been violated, they may appeal to their state's department of education for a "due process hearing." Parents have the right to an independent evaluation if they have reason to believe that their child's needs have not been accurately diagnosed by the school system.

In addition, each state has an advocacy office for children with special needs.

Some children with chronic medical conditions may be considered "temporarily handicapped" and have a need for special education services for brief periods only while out of school. These children also have a right to a free and appropriate public school while they are temporarily impaired. Their right to educational access is protected by Section 504 of the Rehabilitation Act of 1973 (National Association of State Directors of Special Education and National Association of State Boards of Education, 1979).

A number of approaches have been suggested to help school systems meet the needs of children with chronic medical conditions. Nader and Parcel (1978) recommend that schools develop health education programs that will meet the needs of certain target groups, such as asthmatic children. Certain disease-oriented voluntary associations (American Cancer Society, Arthritis Foundation, National Association for Sickle Cell Disease) have developed educational materials that may be helpful to school programs. Baird and Ashcroft (1984) have suggested that the itinerant-teacher, resource-room, and consultant-teacher models frequently utilized to provide educational services to handicapped children could be expanded to provide programs for those with chronic medical needs. Grandstaff (1981) suggested a model that would allow for flexible arrangements for children; it included both full- and part-time teachers to provide services to hospitalized and homebound children. In addition, he suggested hourly employees for very specialized curricular areas.

A few programs across the country have developed innovative practices to serve school-age children with chronic illnesses. The Chronic Health Impaired Project (CHIP) of the Baltimore City Schools has full-time teachers who visit chronically ill children every day they are out of school, beginning with the first day of absence. CHIP personnel also provide additional services, including child and family counseling, career guidance, and peer-tutoring programs (Baird & Ashcroft, 1984). The School Health Corporation developed by the Robert Wood Johnson Foundation in Commerce City, Colorado offers a program designed to provide health-care services within the school system. As a separate entity, the corporation protects the school district from liability, allows for third-party reimbursement, and maintains separation between educational and medical dollars (Clark, 1982).

Technological models have also been utilized in meeting the educational needs of chronically ill children at home or in the hospital, for example, telephone devices that, even though costly, provide two-way communication between the child and the classroom (Grandstaff, 1981). Computer technology will undoubtedly allow for sophisticated teaching models for these children in the near future.

An innovative social-skills training program for children newly diagnosed with cancer was developed by Varni, Katz, Colgrove, and Dogin (1992) to facilitate their psychological adjustment and social support in school. Children who received an intervention program that included social cognitive problem solving, assertive training, and handling teasing and name calling were found to have fewer behavioral problems and greater classmate and teacher support at a 9-month follow-up evaluation than children who received a school reintegration intervention without the social-skills training component.

The efficacy of a comprehensive program for facilitating the school and social reintegration of newly diagnosed children and adolescents with cancer was investigated by Katz, Rubinstein, Hubert, and Bleu (1989). Specific components of the School Reintegration Project included: preparing the child and parents for a return to school as soon as possible after diagnosis and maintaining contact with the school and teachers until the child returned to school; inservice training for school personnel to provide information about the child's medical diagnosis, treatment, and plans for school absences; providing classmates (with the child present) with age-appropriate information about the child's diagnosis and treatment; maintaining continued contact with the school to facilitate communication between the family, medical staff, and school; and keeping the school informed of the child's medical status. Compared to a control group, children in the School Reintegration Project exhibited fewer behavior problems, were less depressed, and showed higher levels of social competence and self-esteem. There were no differences between groups on school grades or absenteeism. A comprehensive discussion of school re-entry programs for children with chronic medical conditions is provided by Sexson and Madan-Swain (1993).

This project highlights ways to overcome many of the barriers that can be met in trying to reintegrate the child at school. Parental concerns regarding the child's safety can be a problem, particularly in the case of younger children, another is finding someone who can help the child with daily care needs. The teacher's attitude about educating the child with a chronic medical condition in a regular classroom setting can pose another dilemma. Teachers may not know enough about chronic medical conditions (Eiser & Town, 1987) or they may feel ill-equipped to handle medical emergencies (Bradbury & Smith, 1983). Teachers may believe that children with serious illnesses will create emotional difficulties for healthy children; few may perceive it as their responsibility to inform all the children about the sick child's medical condition. Some teachers may even isolate a child in the belief that his or her illness might be contagious (Eiser & Town, 1987).

Within the classroom, teachers may have mistaken ideas about the academic skills and capacities of children with chronic medical diagnoses. For example, a teacher may be too willing or too reluctant to excuse poor achievement because a child has been frequently absent for medical treatment or was unusually tired as a result of a particular treatment (Baird & Ashcroft, 1984). Teachers may also have goals that differ or are incompatible with those of health-care professionals working with the child. For example, the physician of an asthmatic child may request limited exercise while the school is interested in helping the child to achieve certain goals in physical education.

A study by Deasy-Spinetta and Spinetta (1980) investigated how regular classroom teachers view the school functioning of children with cancer. Teachers of 42 children in grades K–12 responded to a questionnaire comparing children with cancer to their peers in the same classroom. The results indicated significantly different views of certain behaviors in the children with cancer as opposed to the controls. Children with cancer were seen as having more difficulty concentrating, being underactive, and lacking in energy. They were also viewed as more inhibited and less willing to try new things. Children with cancer were also seen as less able to express positive or negative emotions.

A number of studies have suggested that some chronic medical conditions and medical treatments have a negative effect on cognitive functioning in children (DeMaso, Beardslee, Silbert, & Fyler, 1990; Fowler et al., 1988; Fennell, Rasbury, Fennel, & Morris, 1984; Peckman, Meadows, Bastil, & Marrero, 1988; Stewart, Campbell, McCallon, Walter, & Andrews, 1992). These findings have important implications for a child's academic achievement as well as parental and teacher expectations. At present, these results should be interpreted cautiously, as important variables such as parental occupation, social class and disease severity have not always been considered (Brown et al., 1993; Trantman et al., 1988). Moreover, frequent school absences and a learned adaptation style secondary to having a chronic medical condition are potential confounding variables that are not typically considered. For the clinician trying to reintegrate the child into school, it may be helpful to obtain a baseline of cognitive functioning early in the diagnosis and prior to treatments (e.g., chemotherapy, radiation) so as to determine whether the medical condition and/or treatment has a significant impact on cognitive functioning in each given instance.

Aside from the impact on academic achievement, frequent school absences can significantly affect the child's socialization experiences and the development of normal peer relationships. Embarrassment over their disease may further increase the social isolation of these children. As a result, maladaptive social behaviors and social-skills deficits may appear. Absenteeism may be directly related to the chronic illness, or it may be related to adjustment problems that lead to school avoidance (Pless & Roghmann, 1971). A recent study of children with cardiac conditions hypothesized that school absence would be related to the severity of the cardiac disease, psychosocial factors, and family functioning (Fowler, Johnson, Welshimer, Atkinson, & Loda, 1987). Results indicated that absenteeism was indeed related to medical factors such as necessary clinic visits, hospitalization, limitations imposed by a physician, or keeping a child out of school due to a minor illness. However, in comparison to the control group who were not ill, no significant differences related to psychosocial factors or family functioning were found. While these findings are encouraging, investigations of other types of medical conditions are needed to answer the question of how psychological factors and family functioning affect school attendance in children with chronic medical diagnoses.

Effect of Child's Illness on Family Functioning

For all children, whether ill or well, the family is the most important social milieu and a major focus of experience. Although previously, the primary focus of care for chronically ill children was the hospital, such children now receive much of their treatment in the community with the family as the primary provider.

The impact of a chronic illness on the family is best understood through a systematic and developmental perspective. The family is conceptualized as a semiclosed system in which all members interact and events affecting one member will touch all the others within the system (Kazak, Segal-Andrews, and Johnson, 1995). A chronic medical condition will, therefore, not only change the life of the affected child, parents, and siblings but also impair the development of intrafamily relationships. The onset of a chronic condition can create a crisis for the family and disrupt the stability of the family system.

It is also important to consider the stages of the family life cycle in seeking to understand the impact of a chronic medical condition. For example, those families unto which a child is born with a chronic medical condition will need to cope with the grief of not having the "ideal" child. For the family with a toddler, a chronic medical condition may present difficulties in trying to obtain day care. The usual stress related to transition periods such as school entrance, adolescence, and school exit may be intensified by the presence of a chronic medical condition.

A family may react to the initial diagnosis of a chronic illness in a variety of ways. The reaction of some families may follow a series of stages such as those suggested by Drotar, Baskiewicz, Irvin, Kennel, and Klaus (1975). These stages include initial shock (at time of birth/diagnosis), denial, sadness, anger, and anxiety. In dealing with these families, stage theory should be applied with caution, since all families may not experience each stage or go through them in a systematic manner. Also, since some medical conditions may intensify at certain intervals, families may reexperience various stressors and reactions at either periodic or unpredictable times. For example, each time a child with cancer relapses, the family may experience a new shock or grief reaction.

The impact of a chronic medical diagnosis on a particular family member depends on a number of factors that include the limitations imposed by the medical condition and its treatment, tangible family resources (e.g., financial resources, transportation, job stability), the social support system both within and outside the family itself, coping resources, and the general psychological functioning of the family prior to the onset of the illness. For example the severity of a certain illness may require more frequent physician visits, intermittent or prolonged hospital stays, and greater demands on the child's primary caregivers. In addition, a family may not have insurance or sufficient funds to cover medical expenses or the cost of specialized equipment. In a study of chronic medical conditions in families, Pless and Satterwhite (1975) reported that 66% of the families mentioned financial difficulty as a major concern. So called "middle class" families may already be overextended, and even families on public assistance may lack basic resources such as transportation.

In today's society, where the single-parent and dual-career nuclear family are more common and increased mobility has resulted in greater distances from extended family, a social support system that will help in caring for siblings or provide respite care for the medically at-risk child is not always available. Moreover, a family's current support network may be affected when care demands interfere with previous social opportunities. Parents may have little or no time to participate in community activities. The parents, and in particular a nonworking mother, may feel extremely isolated (Krahn, 1993).

The effects of having a child with a chronic medical condition on the parent's marital relationship have been investigated. A number of studies suggest that either the marital relationship faces a greater risk of divorce or that intact relationships are brought closer together by the experience (McAndrew, 1976). Friedrich and Friedrich (1981) conducted a study with families of 34 handicapped children. When their responses were compared to those of a control group, the parents of the handicapped children reported a less satisfactory marriage, less social support, less religiousness, and less psychological well-being. The handicapped parents' group not only appeared to be under greater stress but also had fewer psychological assets to cope with the stress. Conversely, Markova, MacDonald, and Forbes (1979) stated that half of the 16 families they studied felt the child's illness had brought them closer together. In a study of terminally ill children, Obetz, Swenson, McCarthy, Gilchrist, and Burgert, (1980) found that many parents had altered their values and priorities and experienced personal growth as a result of having a child with leukemia in the family. A more recent study by Wood, Siegel, and Scott (1989) compared the effects of stress and marital satisfaction in families of chronically ill, handicapped, and well/nonhandicapped children. While families of chronically ill and handicapped children reported greater stress, parents of chronically ill children indicated greater marital satisfaction than either parents of handicapped or well/nonhandicapped children. Sabbath and Leventhal (1984) suggest that couples with a chronically ill child are no more likely to divorce than couples with healthy children but are more likely to be dissatisfied and argumentative than parents of healthy children. A chronic illness that has a high probability of genetic recurrence may indirectly threaten a marriage through a rational decision to have no more children. However, in a review of the literature on families attending genetic counseling clinics, Begleiter, Burry, and Harris (1976) found that the divorce rate for these families was lower than the overall national average.

The evidence regarding the impact on siblings' adjustment is mixed as well. Several reviews of this area suggest that the presence of a child with a chronic medical condition is not consistently associated with adjustment problems in healthy siblings (Drotar & Crawford, 1985; Lobato, Faust, & Spirito, 1988). Some studies have found more adjustment problems in siblings of a child with a chronic medical condition than in the siblings of healthy children (Breslau, Weitzman, & Messenger, 1981; Lavigne & Ryan, 1979; Spinetta & Deasy-Spinetta, 1981; Tew & Lawrence, 1975). These adjustment problems may be related to lack of personal attention from parents, increased demands for siblings to assume adult responsibilities, and from extreme feelings of repressed anger and guilt. Research with siblings of handicapped and chronically ill children has consistently shown significant interaction effects with birth order and gender (Breslau, 1982; Tew & Lawrence, 1975). Although younger children may assume roles that contradict birth order and older children may take on the responsibilities of teacher and caregiver (Brody & Stoneman, 1986), the greatest impact seems to be on younger brothers and older sisters.

Conversely, some studies have shown that having a sibling with a chronic medical condition can have a positive impact on peer relationships, social competence, interpersonal qualities such as compassion and sensitivity, and appreciation for one's own good health (Ferrari, 1984; Grossman, 1972). Siblings of chronically ill children have often attributed their own adjustment or reaction to their parents communication pattern regarding the disease as well as their parents acceptance of the disease (Gogan & Slavin, 1981). Simensson and McHale (1981) have stated that the comprehensibility of the disease will affect the siblings reactions and adjustment. The mother's mental and physical health has also been mentioned as a factor having an impact on sibling adjustment (Tew & Lawrence, 1975).

Mothers have been and continue to be viewed as the primary caregivers to the child with a chronic medical condition; consequently they have been the subject of a number of investigations, which suggest a negative impact on the mother's emotional and physical functioning (Breslau, Staruch, & Mortimer, 1982; Tew & Lawrence, 1975; Wallander et al., 1989). Very little research attention has been directed toward the fathers of these children or to comparisons between mothers and fathers. In a study of emotional well-being and communication styles, Shapiro and Shumaker (1987) found that fathers perceived the overall family environment more negatively than did their wives. Fathers communicated less openly and frequently with their ill child and generally rated their child's adjustment lower than did their wives. On the other hand, Wood, Siegel and Scott (1989) obtained no significant differences in stress or marital satisfaction scores between fathers and mothers of children with chronic medical conditions.

Much of the difficulty encountered by families coping with chronic illness may be related to perceived stress and coping resources. Nevin and McCubbin (1979) found that those families of children with spina bifida who were perceived to be under low levels of stress were more cohesive, better organized and lower in conflict than more highly stressed families. Shulman (1983) studied children with leukemia and found that 85% of their families coped well. Factors associated with good family adjustment included a history of prior good coping, good quality of marital and familial relationships, good support system, religious faith, and a trusting relationship with a physician.

More recently, research has focused on identifying the specific nature of the stresses experienced by families with a child having a chronic medical condition. For example, Quittner and her colleagues (Quittner, Opipari, Regoli, Jacobsen, & Eigen, 1992) found that mothers of children with cystic fibrosis spent significantly more time involved with medical care and less time in recreation and play activities than mothers of healthy children. Furthermore, role strain and marital satisfaction was found to correlate with depressive symptomatology in mothers with children with cystic fibrosis. The researchers concluded that daily stresses, particularly those associated with following the medical regimens, were a significant source of distress for the parents.

Holiday (1984) has discussed three major coping strategies successfully utilized by parents of a child with a chronic medical diagnosis: (a) gaining as much information about the child's illness in order to understand it and assign meaning to the illness; (b) integrating the child into the mainstream of society to the maximum extent possible and thereby achieving normalization; and (c) establishing a social support system to share the burden of the illness. One of the most effective support systems cited by Holiday is the parent-to-parent support group. Parents who have had experience with chronic medical conditions in their own children can help other parents gain insight into their own situations. Mattsson (1977) outlined a number of suggestions to assist these families in the development of coping skills. These included parental attitudes and behaviors related to child discipline, utilizing cognitive techniques to maintain control, and becoming better informed about the child's condition. Parents were also urged to encourage their children in self-care, reasonable physical activities, and regular school attendance.

Support groups of various types have been of benefit to families of children with chronic medical conditions. Providing mutual support is often related to the members' stage of coping and integration. Toseland and Hacker (1982) conducted an investigation of self-help groups and emphasized that leadership, direction, and participation should come from within the target population. Frequently a group can serve as a forum for problem identification and solution, information sharing, and discussions related to medical treatment. The value of support groups for siblings of chronically ill children has not been thoroughly investigated; however, sibling groups may have particular value for adolescents (McKeever, 1983). Although support groups can be beneficial, families that appear to be dysfunctional because of the additional stress stemming from their child's illness may be candidates for a referral to family therapy.

Educational programs that provide information and/or skills training may also be beneficial to these families. Kirkham, Schilling, Norelius, and Schinke (1986) reported positive results of a training program designed to reduce stress, develop coping skills, and enhance social support in mothers of handicapped children. An educational program developed for parents of children with cancer was evaluated in six pediatric oncology centers (Wallace, Bakke, Hubbard, & Pendergrass, 1984). Gaining more knowledge about their child's disease promoted greater parental understanding toward the child and the overall effect of cancer on the family. An additional benefit of the program was decreased parental feelings of isolation and greater opportunity for staff to interact with family members.

Minimizing "Sick Role" Behavior

Becoming or being sick has been recognized as a social-psychological as well as a physical process (Mechanic & Volkart, 1961; Parsons, 1951, 1958). Behaviors ascribed to the sick role are in part socially determined, as once the label of "sick" or "disabled" is applied, others' exceptions for the sick person change. In addition, the expectations the person holds about his or her own behavior change as well. Changes in behavioral expectations by self and others are sanctioned by societal norms and often involve special privileges and reduction in day-to-day obligations such as work and/or school (Twaddle & Hessler, 1977). Furthermore, it is assumed that professional assistance is needed to recover from whatever condition has made the person sick. This places the sick person in a dependent and helpless role with respect to others. In short, the person behaves differently and others respond differently to the person who has been labeled sick (Melamed & Siegel, 1980).

The above conceptualization was developed during a time when acute, infectious illnesses were the primary source of illness. Today, chronic medical conditions have become more prominent and a question is raised as to whether these persons should be considered sick or healthy (Rosenstock & Kirscht, 1979). Individuals with a chronic medical condition such as diabetes or asthma typically have periods where they do not feel ill, yet a medical diagnosis still applies. When does or should the sick role apply for these children? What criteria should be used to legitimize periods of ill health and wellness? Such is the dilemma that faces children with a medical condition, their parents, and those who provide their health care.

Helping the child maintain a normal routine with respect to day-to-day functioning (e.g., attending school, doing chores, etc), as discussed earlier in this chapter, is one means of minimizing the sick role in children with a chronic medical condition.

Modifying expectations to match the child's physical state of health may be necessary from time to time. What complicates this seemingly simple picture is that these children, may later, as adults, continue to perceive themselves as ill during periods of relatively good health and therefore may be more likely to try to remove themselves from routine activities and responsibilities associated with daily living (Twaddle, 1969). Moreover, receiving preferential treatment from others because of a medical condition can result in a greater display of sick-role behaviors. Such preferential treatment and removal of typical daily responsibilities can be highly reinforcing and result in significant secondary gain or benefit to the child. As a result of such powerful reinforcers, the child may continue to display behaviors or symptoms of being ill, and cooperation with treatments to improve the medical condition may be less than optimum (Melamed & Siegel, 1980).

For many children this sequence is a learned behavior that parents, friends, and health-care providers may inadvertently teach out of care and concern for the child's health and emotional adjustment. Creer and Christian (1976) have noted that family members and health-care providers are often caught in what is referred to as an "illness trap" when interacting with an individual who has a chronic medical condition or disability. Greater attention is paid to physical complaints, requests for assistance, and noncompliance with treatment than to more adaptive, independent behaviors, which may be overlooked. Yet, continued adoption of the sick role can also become a deliberate manipulation, particularly during the adolescent years (Elkind, 1985).

Aside from the above-mentioned learning model, very little empirical evidence is currently available to document factors that may contribute to the persistence of sick-role behavior. Family interactional styles and cognitive-perceptual styles are factors that have received some empirical attention.

Certain types of family interactional styles may promote and maintain sick-role behavior. Minuchin and his colleagues (Minuchin et al., 1975) have noted interactional styles between family members that appear to exacerbate symptoms in some types of chronic medical conditions such as asthma and diabetes. Interactional styles that appear problematic include those where family members are enmeshed, overprotective, and rigid and where conflict-resolution skills are poor. In addition to citing maladaptive interactional styles, Minuchin and his colleagues (1975) propose that by maintaining a sick role the child may serve a homeostatic function for the family. Focus on the sick child may help the family to avoid dealing with other areas of conflict, such as marital difficulties between the parents.

Research that has involved either direct observation of parent-child interactions or questionnaires regarding family interactional styles lend support to this hypothesis. Several studies with adolescents who have diabetes indicate that poorer metabolic control is associated with greater family conflict (Anderson, Miller, Auslander, & Santiago, 1981) and greater difficulty in negotiating areas of conflict (Bobrow, AvRuskin, & Siller, 1985). Yet typically these studies are based on cross-sectional data so it is impossible to discern cause and effect. Longitudinal studies that can map interactional patterns across time and status of medical condition, such as that by Hauser and his colleagues (cf. Hauser et al., 1986), are needed to more fully investigate these hypotheses regarding family interactional patterns and to guide the development of effective, family-based interventions.

Unfortunately, interactional styles with other systems (e.g., health-care providers, school system) with which the child and family interact have received even less empirical attention. It is conceivable that health-care providers may interact with patients and their families in similar ways to promote and maintain sick-role behavior, such as encouraging excessive dependency. Teachers may also promote excessive sick-role behavior by limiting activities unnecessarily (e.g., overprotectiveness). Future research focusing on interactional styles must expand to include other systems besides the family to further our understanding of how interactions within larger systems contribute to or minimize the occurrence of sick-role behavior.

Differences in perception and interpretation of bodily states is another factor that may contribute to sick-role behavior. Studies of the development of physical symptoms in generally healthy samples have shown that some children and adolescents have a heightened awareness of or preoccupation with bodily states which contributes to the development and persistence of physical symptoms (see Siegel, Somatic Disorders, Chapter 8 of this book). While the concepts of "introspection" (Mechanic, 1983) and "amplifying somatic style" (Barsky, Goodson, Lane, & Cleary, 1988; Barsky & Klerman, 1983) have not been studied in the context of a chronic medical condition, this may be a population at risk for such learned behavior. Most medical conditions involve some fluctuation in physical symptoms that requires attention so that appropriate medical treatment can be instituted. Yet this may result in heightened sensitivity to all bodily states and to the identification of benign physical sensations as signs of not feeling well. Family members may inadvertently reinforce the report of these symptoms due to their own sensitivity to the fact that, at times, medical action is necessary, resulting in maintenance of the sick role.

Though specifics may vary depending upon medical diagnosis, several basic guidelines can help in minimizing sick-role behaviors in children with chronic medical conditions. Normalize the child's life by maintaining a regular routine and expectations regarding school and chores when medically possible (Perrin et al., 1984). This would apply to scheduled hospitalizations as well where, when physically possible, the child should maintain a regular schedule (e.g., sleep/wake cycle, personal grooming, school, etc.) Guidelines regarding maintenance of a normal routine have been discussed at length in a previous section of this chapter.

Use of the term medical "condition" versus "illness" by health-care providers in conjunction with anticipatory guidance on how to discriminate illness episodes that need treatment or medical attention are two practical suggestions to help minimize sick-role behavior. The term "medical illness" has obvious connotations that may not always apply to many children with a chronic medical condition. Even children with life-threatening diseases, such as leukemia and cystic fibrosis, are likely to experience some episodes of health. For other children with diagnoses such as diabetes or sickle cell anemia, periods of good health may be the norm, with only episodic illnesses. By using the term "medical condition," health-care providers can encourage an identification with health.

Given that the sick role may be reinforcing due to greater attention and decrease in responsibilities during illness episodes, it can be helpful for the health-care provider to work with the family in setting concrete guidelines as to when "sick day" rules apply. A particular problem may arise in trying to decide when a child should or should not go to school. The child may complain of not feeling well and the parent is faced with the task of trying to discern if the complaints are due to the medical condition, an acute illness, avoidance of school, wanting to remain home with the parent (separation issues), or some combination of these factors. In addition, for those days where it is deemed necessary that the child remain at home, adherence to bed rest the entire day as opposed to just school hours is recommended. Caretakers should carefully weigh the amount of increased attention given to the child when he or she has to remain at home, particularly if there is a question regarding whether the child is trying to avoid school or is concerned with separating from the parent. If health-care providers have helped the family anticipate what to do when this situation arises, then the possibility of inadvertently reinforcing inappropriate sick-role behavior may be minimized. Of course, these general guidelines will need to be used flexibly, as, for example, a child who is required to remain home due to low white cell counts may benefit from extra attention to help structure the day at home. Yet extra attention for a child with sickle cell anemia who has had to remain home because of a painful crisis may result in an increase in pain complaints and/or increased duration of the crisis.

CONCLUSIONS

The methodological sophistication of psychosocial research with children diagnosed with chronic health problems has improved considerably over the past several decades. The majority of these investigations have focused on identifying risk factors for problems of adjustment in the child and his or her family. As such, the preponderance of data in these predictive studies is correlational in nature. In con-

trast, there are considerably fewer intervention studies addressing the numerous tasks and stressful experiences with which these children and their families must cope over extended periods of time. Yet, the effects of the interventions that have been studied with this population have generally been limited to several problems areas. For example, there is a comparatively large body of literature pertaining to treatment approaches for reducing the stresses associated with hospitalization and medical treatment and in helping children to manage pain associated with their disease or various diagnostic and medical procedures. On the other hand, there are a limited number of intervention studies in the areas of adherence to medical regimens, school programs for children with chronic health problems, and programs for facilitating the adjustment of family members. It is anticipated that treatment studies in these latter areas will increase in the future as research provides useful data on those factors that are predictive of adaptive behavior in these various situations.

Most of the research in this area has relied on single assessment, cross-sectional designs. There is a greater need for longitudinal evaluations to examine the course of psychosocial and medical adaptation over time as a function of developmental changes. Longitudinal studies with children with chronic medical conditions are particularly important since their physical status is likely to vary over time. Many of the issues that affect children with chronic medical conditions are not single-episode events and as such repeated evaluations of the child and/or family over the course of a given period is needed to significantly advance our understanding of this area. This longitudinal approach takes on even greater importance given the multitude of ongoing developmental influences that must be taken into consideration (Siegel, 1995).

Most intervention programs are presented to all children with a given medical condition in a similar manner with the assumption that they will benefit equally from a particular treatment (Siegel & Hudson, 1992). In addition, research has tended to evaluate whether one intervention is superior to another. Future research needs to move beyond merely demonstrating the efficacy of a given intervention to attempting to identify criteria for matching interventions to specific patient characteristics (e.g., coping dispositions, developmental factors, previous experiences) in order to determine which children respond most favorably to a particular treatment strategy.

One area that warrants further study is specific coping behaviors that differentiate children and families who experience few adjustment problems from those individuals who exhibit serious maladjustment in relation to the chronic medical condition and disease-related tasks and experiences. The coping skills that children and family members use in their attempts to manage the potential stresses imposed by the illness have received little research attention. It is suggested that specific coping skills are an important focus of study in order to understand the individual differences observed in children's and families' response to the disease in the face of comparable degrees of severity and type of illness (Melamed, Siegel, & Ridley-Johnson, 1988; Rudolph et al., 1995). In this regard, Drotar (1981) has noted that coping behavior in chronically ill children and their families is "best studied from an ipsative and/or developmental perspective...over time...measures which link coping processes to adaptive outcome in life situations" (p. 219).

Coping strategies in children with chronic medical conditions need to be evaluated from two perspectives. First, one must study how children negotiate the normal tasks of childhood and adolescence. Whether or not a child is physically ill, adaptation and coping must be assessed within the context of age-appropriate developmental tasks that must be accomplished by all children. A long-term health problem may or may not increase the difficulty faced by a child in seeking to master the various developmental tasks.

The second level of assessment of coping in children with chronic medical conditions must also focus on disease-related tasks that are unique to a child's particular illness, such as adherence to a specific medication regimen or tolerating invasive medical procedures. This would permit the identification of specific behaviors associated with the child's attempts to meet the demands imposed by the various disease-related tasks.

Using this approach, it would be possible to determine whether these children differ from their physically healthy peers both in terms of accomplishing appropriate developmental tasks and using coping strategies. In addition, research in this area would permit investigators to assess whether children with different disease-related tasks show different levels of adjustment based on their use of particular coping strategies. By systematically identifying adaptive coping strategies, it will be possible to develop more effective intervention programs for children with chronic health problems. Building on the coping skills that are already in a child's repertoire will permit researchers to develop interventions that can be tailored to a particular child's specific needs to assist him or her in their efforts to negotiate key developmental and disease-related tasks.

Children with chronic medical conditions and their families are confronted with multiple demands on a daily basis to follow complex medical, dietary, and other disease-related prescribed treatment regimens. Given the importance of daily disease management for children with chronic medical conditions, researchers need to place greater emphasis on studies that evaluate the efficacy of various strategies for teaching self-management skills to these children.

Health-care providers play a central role in all aspects of the diagnosis and medical management of a child with a chronic medical condition. Despite their important influence on these children and their families, health-care providers have rarely been the focus of study in this area. For example, research data is needed on the effects of communications between health-care providers and the children and their families on such issues as adherence to medical regimens and cooperation with potentially distressing medical procedures.

Given that a chronic medical condition has the potential to disrupt a child's normal growth and development and to interfere with a family's relationships and tasks, all of these children and their families should be followed periodically to monitor their ongoing psychological adjustment and adaptation. An interdisciplinary and comprehensive approach to the care of children with chronic health problems is recognized as essential for maximizing their physical, emotional, intellectual, and social potential (Magrab & Calcagno, 1978; Mullins, Gillman, & Harbeck, 1992). This includes the provision of ongoing psychosocial support and educational interventions (Drotar & Bush, 1985; Hobbs et al., 1985). Psychosocial services offered during the early stages of a child's illness provide an opportunity to prevent major psychological crises from occurring and enables the mental-health professional to assist the child and family in their adjustment to particularly difficult developmental and disease-related transition periods. In addition, the introduction of such services early in the course of a child's illness reduces the likelihood that the child and family will feel "singled out" for seeing a mental-health professional during periods of crisis or when experiencing severe adjustment problems.

A report by the Surgeon General of the United States (Koop, 1987) has advocated a "family-centered, community-based approach" to the comprehensive care of children with special health-care needs. This report strongly recommends that parents and professionals collaborate at all levels of the child's care. In addition, community-based services are encouraged. Here children would receive the majority of medical, mental health, educational, and other supportive services in their local communities rather than going to tertiary care facilities that are often considerable distances from their homes. Recently, Stein and Jessop (1991) have provided evidence for the effectiveness of a family-centered, home-based approach to comprehensive care on the long-term psychological adjustment of children with chronic medical conditions. This approach would appear to have a profound impact on normalizing the lives of children with chronic medical conditions and minimizing the pervasive disruptions experienced by their families.

As this chapter has indicated, there are numerous instances throughout the life of a child with a chronic medical condition in which access to the services of mental-health professionals is essential. Unfortunately, there are many barriers that interfere with the ability of children with chronic medical conditions and their families to receive this appropriate comprehensive care. Sabbeth and Stein (1990) have

noted, for example, that even where physicians recognize the need for psychological services for these children, such services may not be available to a particular child because of financial considerations and/or a lack of available services or trained professionals in the child's community. Furthermore, recent changes following from health-care reform and the managed care movement, with an emphasis on cost-effective care, is likely to have a significant impact on comprehensive care programs for children with chronic medical conditions. Kaplan (1990) has cogently argued that there are only two health outcomes that are of primary importance. These outcomes are extending life expectancy and improving an individual's quality of life. Only recently have practitioners and researchers begun to focus on issues pertaining to the impact of disease and medical treatment on the quality of life of children with chronic medical conditions (Aaronson & Beckman, 1993; Goodwin, Boggs, & Graham-Pole, 1994; Mulhern et al., 1989). Complex and often difficult issues must be taken into consideration in balancing treatment-related decisions, particularly pertaining to medical treatments that may or may not prolong a child's life, with decisions that affect the degree of quality of life for a child and his or her family (Tovian, 1991; Weithorn & McCabe, 1988). Research that addresses these important factors in the medical management of children with chronic medical conditions is clearly needed.

REFERENCES

Aaronson, N. K., & Beckman, J. (Eds.). (1993). *The quality of life of cancer patients.* New York: Raven Press.

Allen, D. A., Affleck, G., Tennen, H., McGrade B. J., & Ratzan, S. (1984). Concerns of children with a chronic illness: A cognitive-developmental study of juvenile diabetes. *Child: Care, Health, and Development, 10,* 211–218.

Anderson, C. T., Fanurik, D., & Zeltzer, K. K. (1992). Pain in adolescence, In. E. R. McAnarney, R. E. Kreipe, D. P. Orr, & G. D. Comerci (Eds.), *Textbook of Adolescent Medicine.* (pp. 140–145). Philadelphia: Saunders.

Anderson, B. J., Miller, J. P., Auslander, W. F., & Santiago, J.V. (1981). Family characteristics of diabetic adolescents: Relationship to metabolic control. *Diabetes Care, 4,* 586–594.

Armstrong, G. D., & Martinson, I. M. (1980). Death, dying, and terminal care: Dying at home. In J. Kellerman (Ed.), *Psychological aspects of cancer in children.* (pp. 295–311). Springfield, Il: Charles C. Thomas.

Arnhold, R. G., Adebonojo, F. O., Callas, E. R., Callas, J., Carte, E., & Stein, R. C. (1970). Patients and prescriptions: Comprehension and compliance with medical instructions in a suburban pediatric practice. *Clinical Pediatrics, 9,* 648–651.

Baird, S. M., & Ashcroft, S. C. (1984). Education and chronically ill children: A need-based policy orientation. *Peabody Journal of Education, 61,* 91–129.

Barsky, A. J., Goodson, J. D., Lane, R. S., & Cleary, P. D. (1988). The amplification of somatic symptoms. *Psychosomatic Medicine, 50,* 510–519.

Barsky, A. J., & Klerman, G. L. (1983). Overview: Hypochondriasis, bodily complaints, and somatic styles. *American Journal of Psychiatry, 140,* 273–283.

Barton, D. (1972). Death and dying: A course for medical students. *Journal of Medical Education, 47,* 945–951.

Bearison, D. J. (1991), *"They never want to tell you." Children talk about cancer.* Cambridge, MA: Harvard University Press.

Beck, D. E., Fennell, R. S., Yost, R. L., Robinson, J. D., Geary, D., & Richards, G. A. (1980). Evaluation of an educational program on compliance with medical regimens in pediatric patients with renal transplants. *Journal of Pediatrics, 96,* 1094–1097.

Beck, S., & Smith, L. K. (1988). Personality and social skills assessment of children with special reference to somatic disorders. In P. Karoly (Ed.), *Handbook of child health assessment: Biopsychosocial perspectives* (pp. 149–172). New York: John Wiley & Sons.

Beck, B., & Strang, P. (1993). The family in hospital-based home care with special reference to terminally ill cancer patients. *Journal of Palliative Care, 9,* 5–13.

Becker, M. H., & Rosenstock, I. M. (1984). Compliance with medical advice. In A. Steptoe & A. Mathews (Eds.) *Health care and human behavior* (pp. 175–208). New York: Academic Press.

Begleiter, M. L., Burry, V. F., & Harris, D. J. (1976). Prevalence of divorce among parents of children with cystic fibrosis and other chronic diseases. *Social Biology, 23,* 260–264.

Bibace, R., & Walsh, M. E. (1979). Developmental stages in children's conceptions of illness. In G. C. Stone, F. Cohen, & N. E. Adler (Eds.), *Health psychology* (pp. 285–301). San Francisco: Jossey-Bass.

Blake, S., & Paulsen, K. (1981). Therapeutic interventions with terminally ill children: A review. *Professional Psychology, 12,* 655–663.

Bluebond-Langer, M. (1974). I know, do you? A study of awareness, communication and coping in terminally ill children. In B. Schoenberg, A. C. Curr, A. H. Kutscher, D. Perets, & I. Goldenberg (Eds.), *Anticipatory grief* (pp. 171–181). New York: Columbia University Press.

Blum, R. W., & Geber, G. (1992). Chronically ill youth. In E. R. McAnarney, R. E. Kreipe, D. P. Orr & G.D. Comerci (Eds.), *Textbook of adolescent medicine* (pp. 222–228). Philadelphia: Saunders.

Bobrow, E. S., AvRuskin, T. W., & Siller, J. (1985). Mother-daughter interaction and adherence to diabetes regimens. *Diabetes Care, 8,* 146–151.

Bonica, J. J. (1977). Neurophysiologic and pathologic aspects of acute and chronic pain. *Archives of Surgery, 112,* 750–761.

Borman, L. D. (1985). Self-help and mutual aid groups. In N. Hobbs & J. M. Perrin (Eds.), *Issues in the care of children with chronic illnesses* (pp. 771–789). San Francisco: Jossey-Bass.

Bradbury, A.J., & Smith, C.S. (1983). An assessment of the diabetic knowledge of school teachers. *Archives of Disease in Childhood, 58,* 692–696.

Breslau, N. (1982). Siblings of disabled children: Birth order and age-spacing effects. *Journal of Abnormal Child Psychology, 10,* 85–96.

Breslau, N., Staruch, K., & Mortimer, E. (1982). Psychological distress in mothers of disabled children. *American Journal of Diseases of Children, 136,* 682–686.

Breslau, N., Weitzman, M., & Messenger, K. (1981). Psychological functioning of siblings of disabled children. *Pediatrics, 67,* 344–353.

Brewster, A. B. (1982). Chronically ill hospitalized children's concepts of their illness. *Pediatrics, 69,* 355–362.

Brody, G., & Stoneman, L. (1986). Contextual issues in the study of sibling socialization. In J. J. Gallagher & P. M. Vietze (Eds.), *Families of handicapped persons: Research, programs, and policy issues* (pp. 122–136). Baltimore: Paul H. Brooks.

Bronheim, S. P. (1978). Pulmonary disorders: Asthma and cystic fibrosis. In P. Magrab (Ed.). *Psychological management of pediatric problems: Vol.1. Early life conditions and chronic diseases* (pp. 309–344). Baltimore: University Park Press.

Brown, R. T., Buchanan, J., Doepke, K., Eckman, J. Baldwin, K., & Schoenherr, S. (1993). Cognitive and academic functioning in children with sickle-cell disease. *Journal of Consulting and Clinical Psychology, 22,* 207–218.

Brownlee-Duffeck, M., Peterson, L., Simonds, J. F., Goldstein, D., Kilo, C., & Hoette, S. (1987). The role of health beliefs in the regimen adherence and metabolic control of adolescents and adults with diabetes mellitus. *Journal of Consulting and Clinical Psychology, 55,* 139–144.

Burbach, D. J., & Peterson, L. (1986). Children's concepts of physical illness: A review and critique of the cognitive-developmental literature. *Health Psychology, 5,* 307–325.

Cameron, R. (1978). The clinical implementation of behavior change techniques: A cognitively oriented conceptualization of therapeutic "compliance" and "resistance." In J. P. Foreyt & D. P. Rathjen (Eds.), *Cognitive behavior therapy: Research and application* (pp. 233–250). New York: Plenum Press.

Campbell, L. A., Kirkpatrick, S. E.,Berry, C. C., Penn, N. E., Waldman, J. D. & Mathewson, J. W. (1992). Psychological preparation of mothers of preschool children undergoing cardiac catheterization. *Psychology and Health, 7,* 175–185.

Carey, M. P., & Burish, T. G. (1988). Etiology and treatment of the psychological side effects associated with cancer chemotherapy: A critical review and discussion. *Psychological Bulletin, 104,* 307–325.

Cataldo, M. F., Bessman, C. A., Parker, L. H., Pearson, J. E., & Rogers, M. C. (1979). Behavioral assessment for pediatric intensive care units. *Journal of Applied Behavior Analysis, 12,* 83–97.

Christophersen, E. R. (1993). *Pediatric compliance: A guide for the primary care physician.* New York: Plenum Press.

Clark, D., (1982). *Colorado school health program.* Unpublished manuscript, Vanderbilt University, Chronically Ill Child Project, Nashville, TN.

Cluss, P. A., & Epstein, L. H. (1985). The measurement of medical compliance in the treatment of disease. In P. Karoly (Ed.), *Measurement strategies in health psychology.* New York: Wiley.

Cohen, F., & Lazarus, R. S. (1980). Coping with the stress of illness. In G. C. Stone, F. Cohen, & N. E. Adler (Eds.), *Health psychology: A handbook* (pp. 217–254). San Francisco: Jossey-Bass.

Copeland, D. R., Fletcher, J. M., Pfefferbaum-Levine, B., Jaffe, N., Ried, H., & Maor, M. (1985). Neuropsychological sequelae of childhood cancer in long-term survivors. *Pediatrics, 75,* 745–753.

Creer, T. L., & Christian, W. P. (1976). *Chronically ill and handicapped children: Their management and rehabilitation.* Champaign, IL: Research Press.

Czajkowski, D. R., & Koocher, G. P. (1986). Predicting medical compliance among adolescents with cystic fibrosis. *Health Psychology, 5,* 297–305.

Davidson, G. W. (Ed.). (1985). *The hospice: Development and administration* (2nd ed.). Washington, DC: Hemisphere.

Deasy-Spinetta, P., & Spinetta, J. J. (1980). The child with cancer in school. *American Journal of Pediatric Hematology/Oncology, 2,* 89–94.

Deaton, A. V. (1985). Adaptive noncompliance in pediatric asthma. The parent as expert. *Journal of Pediatric Psychology, 10,* 1–14.

DeMaso, D. R., Beardslee, W. R., Silbert, A. R., & Fyler, D. C. (1990). Psychological functioning in children with cyanotic heart defects. *Journal of Developmental and Behavioral Pediatrics, 11,* 289–293.

Deno, E. (1973). *Instructional alternatives for exceptional children.* Reston, VA: Council for Exceptional Children.

DiMatteo, M.R., & DiNicola, D.D. (1982). *Achieving patient compliance: The psychology of the medical practitioner's role.* New York; Pergamon Press.

Dolgin, M. J., Katz, E. R., McGinty, K., & Siegel, S. E. (1985). Anticipatory nausea and vomiting in pediatric cancer patients. *Pediatrics, 75,* 547–552.

Dolgin, M. J., Katz, E. R., Doctors, S. R., & Siegel, S. (1986). Caregivers' perceptions of medical compliance in adolescents with cancer. *Journal of Adolescent Health Care, 7,* 22–27.

Donovan, J. L. & Blake, D. R. (1992). Patient non-compliance: Deviance or reasoned decision making? *Social Science and Medicine, 34,* 507–513.

Drotar, D. (1981). Psychological perspectives in chronic childhood illness. *Journal of Pediatric Psychology, 6,* 211–228.

Drotar, D. (1995). *Consulting with pediatricians: Psychological perspectives.* New York: Plenum Press.

Drotar, D., Baskiewicz, A., Irvin, N., Kennell, J., & Klaus, M. (1975). The adaptation of parents to the birth of an infant with a congenital malformation: A hypothetical model. *Pediatrics, 56,* 710–717.

Drotar, D., & Bush, M., (1985). Mental health issues and services. In N. Hobbs & J. M. Perrin (Eds.). *Issues in the care of children with chronic illnesses: A sourcebook on problems, services, and politics* (pp. 514–550). San Francisco: Jossey-Bass.

Drotar, D., & Crawford, P. (1985). Psychological adaptation of siblings of chronically ill children: Research and practice implications. *Journal of Developmental and Behavioral Pediatrics, 6,* 355–362.

Drotar, D., Crawford, P., & Ganofsky, M. A. (1984). Prevention with chronically ill children. In M. C. Roberts & L. Peterson (Eds.), *Prevention of problems in childhood: Psychological research and applications* (pp. 232–265). New York: John Wiley & Sons.

Drotar, D., Owens, R., & Gotthold, J. (1980). Personality adjustment of children and adolescents with hypopituitarism. *Child Psychiatry and Human Development, 11,* 59–66.

Eiser, C. (1990). *Chronic childhood disease: An introduction to psychological theory and research.* Cambridge, England: Cambridge University Press.

Eiser, C., & Town, C. (1987). Teacher's concern about chronically sick children: Implications for pediatricians. *Developmental Medicine and Child Neurology, 29,* 56–63.

Elkind, D. (1985). Cognitive development and adolescent disability. *Journal of Adolescent Health Care, 6,* 84–89.

Elkins, P. D., & Roberts, M. C. (1983). Psychological preparation for pediatric hospitalization. *Clinical Psychology Review, 3,* 1–21.

Faberow, N. L. (1986). Noncompliance as indirect self-destructive behavior. In K. E. Gerber & A. A. Nehemkis (Eds.), *Compliance: The dilemma of the chronically ill* (pp. 24–43). New York: Springer.

Fennell, R. S., Rasbury, W. C., Fennell, E. B., & Morris, M. K. (1984). The effects of kidney transplantation on cognitive performance in a pediatric population. *Pediatrics, 74,* 273–278.

Ferguson, B. F. (1979). Preparing young children for hospitalization: A comparison of two methods. *Pediatrics, 64,* 656–664.

Ferrari, M. (1984). Chronic illness: Psychosocial effects on siblings: I. Chronically ill boys. *Journal of Child Psychology and Psychiatry, 25,* 459–476.

Fordyce, W. E. (1976). *Behavioral methods for chronic pain and illness.* St. Louis: C. V. Mosby.

Fowler, M. G., Johnson, M. P., Welshimer, K. J., Atkinson, S. S., & Loda, F. A. (1987). Factors related to school absence in children with cardiac factors. *American Journal of Diseases in Children, 141,* 1317–1320.

Fowler, M.G., Whitt, J.K., Lallinger, R.R., Nash, K.B., Atkinson, S.S., Wells, R.J., & McMillan, C. (1988). Neuropsychologic and academic functioning of children with sickle cell anemia. *Developmental and Behavioral Pediatrics, 9,* 213–220.

Franceschi, M., Cecchetto, R., Minicucci, F., Smizne, S., Baio, G., & Canal, N. (1984). Cognitive processes in insulin-dependent diabetes mellitus. *Diabetes Care, 7,* 228–231.

Friedrich, W. N., & Friedrich, W. L. (1981). Psychosocial assets of parents of handicapped and nonhandicapped children. *American Journal of Mental Deficiency, 85,* 551–553.

Fritz, G. K. (1992). Chronic illness and psychological health. In E. R. McAnarney, R. E. Kreipe, D. P. Orr, & G. D. Comerci (Eds.), *Textbook of adolescent medicine* (pp. 1133–1137). Philadelphia: Saunders.

Gayton, W. F., Friedman, S. B., Tavormina, J. F., & Tucker, F. (1977). Children with cystic fibrosis: 1. Psychological test findings of patients, siblings, and parents. *Pediatrics, 59,* 888–894.

Gogan, J. L., & Slavin, L. (1981). Interviews with brothers and sisters. In G. P. Koocher & J. E. O'Malley (Eds.), *The Damocles syndrome: Psychosocial consequences of surviving childhood cancer* (pp. 101–111). New York: McGraw-Hill.

Goodwin, D. A. J., Boggs, S. R., & Graham-Pole, J. (1994). Development and validation of the Pediatric Oncology Quality of Life Scale. *Psychological Assessment, 6,* 321–328.

Gortmaker, S.L. (1985). Demography of chronic childhood diseases. In N. Hobbs & J.M. Perrin (Eds.), *Issues in the care of children with chronic illness: A sourcebook on problems, services, and policies* (pp. 135–154). San Francisco: Jossey-Bass.

Grandstaff, C. L. (1981). Creative approaches to compliance with P.L. 94–142 and home/hospital programs. *Journal of the Division of the Physically Handicapped, Council for Exceptional Children, 5,* 37–44.

Grossman, F. K. (1972). *Brothers and sisters of retarded children: An exploratory study.* New York: Syracuse University Press.

Haggerty, R. J., Roghmann, K. J., & Pless, I. B. (1975). *Child health and the community.* New York: John Wiley & Sons.

Harbeck-Weber, C., & McKee, D. H. (1995). Prevention of emotional and behavioral distress in children experiencing hospitalization and chronic illness. In M. C. Roberts (Ed.), *Handbook of pediatric psychology* (2nd ed., pp. 167–184). New York: Guilford Press.

Hauser, S. T., Jacobson, A. M., Wertlieb, D., Weiss-Perry, B., Follansbee, D., Wolfsdorf, J. I., Herskowitz, R. D., Houlihan, J., & Rajapark, D. C. (1986). Children with recently diagnosed diabetes: Interactions within their families. *Health Psychology, 5,* 273–296.

Hayes-Bautista, D. E. (1976). Modifying the treatment: Patient compliance, patient control, and medical care. *Social Science & Medicine, 10,* 233–238.

Haynes, R. B. (1976). A critical review of the "determinants" of patient compliance with therapeutic regimens. In D. L. Sackett & R. B. Haynes (Eds.), *Compliance with therapeutic regimens* (pp. 26–39). Baltimore: John Hopkins University Press.

Hobbs, N., Perrin, J.M., & Ireys, H.T. (1985). *Chronically ill children and their families.* San Francisco: Jossey-Bass.

Holiday, B. (1984). Challenges of rearing a chronically ill child: Caring and coping. *Nursing Clinics of North America, 19,* 361–368.

Ingersoll, G. M., Orr, D. P., Herrold, A. J., & Golden, M. P. (1986). Cognitive maturity and self-management among adolescents with insulin-dependent diabetes mellitus. *Journal of Pediatrics, 108,* 620–623.

Jamison, R. N., Lewis, S., & Burish, T. (1986). Psychological impact of cancer on adolescents: Self-image, locus of control, perception of illness, and knowledge of cancer. *Journal of Chronic Disease, 39,* 609–617.

Janis, I.L. (1984). Improving adherence to medical recommendations: Prescriptive hypotheses derived from recent research in social psychology. In A. Baum, S. E. Taylor, & J. E. Singer (Eds.), *Handbook of psychology and health: Vol 4. Social psychology of aspects of health* (pp 113–148). Hillsdale, NJ: Lawrence Erlbaum.

Jay, S. M., Elliott, C. H., Ozolins, M., Olson, R. A., & Pruitt, S. D. (1985). Behavioral management of children's distress during painful medical procedures. *Behavioral Research and Therapy, 23,* 513–520.

Jay, S. M., Elliott, C. H., Woody, P.D., & Siegel, S. (1991) An investigation of cognitive-behavior therapy combined with oral Valium for children undergoing painful medical procedures. *Health Psychology, 10,* 317–322.

Jay, S. M., Green, V., Johnson, S., Caldwell, S., & Nitschke, R. (1987). Differences in death concepts between children with cancers and physically healthy children. *Journal of Clinical Child Psychology, 16,* 301–306.

Jay, S. M., Ozolins, M., Elliott, C. H., & Caldwell, S. (1983). Assessment of children's distress during painful medical procedures. *Health Psychology, 2,* 133–147.

Johnson, S. B. (1988, April). *Compliance in pediatric psychology.* Paper presented at the Florida Conference on Child Health Psychology, Gainesville, FL.

Johnson, S. B. (1994). Health behavior and health status: Concepts, methods, and applications. *Journal of Pediatric Psychology, 19,* 129–141.

Johnson, S. B., Silverstein, J., Rosenbloom, A., Carter, R., & Cunningham, W. (1986). Assessing daily management in childhood diabetes. *Health Psychology, 5,* 545–564.

Kaplan, R. M. (1990). Behavior as the central outcome in healthcare. *American Psychologist, 45,* 1211–1220.

Karoly, P. (Ed.). (1988). *Handbook of child health assessment: Biosocial perspectives.* New York: John Wiley & Sons.

Kasl, S. V. (1975). Issues in patient adherence to health care regimens. *Journal of Human Stress, 1,* 5–18.

Katz, E. R., Rubinstein, C. L., Hubert, N. C., & Bleu, A. (1989). School and social reintegration of children with cancer. *Journal of Psychosocial Oncology, 6,* 123–140.

Kazak, A. E., Segal-Andrews, A. M., & Johnson, K. (1995). Pediatric psychology research and practice: A family-systems approach. In M. C. Roberts (Ed.), *Handbook of pediatric psychology* (2nd ed., pp. 84–104). New York: Guilford Press.

Kellerman, J., Rigler, D., & Siegel, S. E. (1979). Psychological responses of children to isolation in a protected environment. *Journal of Behavioral Medicine, 2,* 263–274.

Kellerman, J., Rigler, D., Siegel, S. E., McCue, K., Pospisil, J., & Uno, R. (1976). Pediatric cancer patients in reverse isolation utilizing protected environments. *Journal of Pediatric Psychology, 1,* 21–25.

Kellerman, J., Zeltzer, L., Ellenberg, L., & Dash, J. (1983). Adolescents with cancer: Hypnosis for the reduction of the acute pain and anxiety associated with medical procedures. *Journal of Adolescent Health Care, 4,* 85–90.

Kellerman, J., Zeltzer, L., Ellenberg, L., Dash, J., & Rigler, D., (1980). Psychological effects of illness in adolescence: Anxiety, self-esteem and the perception of control. *Journal of Pediatrics, 97,* 126–131.

Kirkham, M. A., Schilling, R. F., Norelius, K., & Schinke, S. P. (1986). Developing coping styles and social networks: An intervention. *Child Care Health and Development, 12,* 313–323.

Klerman, L. V. (1985). Interprofessional issues in delivering services to chronically ill children and their families. In N. Hobbs & J. M. Perrin (Eds.), *Issues in the care of children with chronic illness* (pp. 420–440). San Francisco: Jossey-Bass.

Kohlberg, L. (1963). Development of children's orientations toward a moral order. I. Sequence in development of moral thought. *Vita Hum, 6,* 11–33.

Kolko, D. J., & Richard-Figueroa, J. L. (1985). Effects of video games on the adverse corollaries of chemotherapy in pediatric oncology patients: A single-case analysis. *Journal of Consulting and Clinical Psychology, 53,* 223–228.

Kolotkin, R. A. (1981). Preventing burn-out and reducing stress in terminal care: The role of assertiveness training. In H. J. Sobel (Ed.), *Behavioral therapy in terminal care: A humanistic approach* (229–252). Cambridge, MA: Ballinger.

Koocher, G. P. (1973). Childhood, death, and cognitive development. *Developmental Psychology, 9,* 369–374.

Koocher, G. P. (Ed.). (1977). Death and the child. *Journal of Pediatric Psychology* 2(2).

Koocher, G. P. & Gudas, L. J. (1992). Grief and loss in childhood. In C.E. Walker & M.C. Roberts (Eds.), *Handbook of Clinical Child Psychology* (2nd ed.) (pp. 1025–1034). New York: John Wiley & Sons.

Koocher, G. P., McGrath, M. L., & Gudas, L. J. (1990). Typologies of nonadherence in cystic fibrosis. *Journal of Developmental and Behavioral Pediatrics, 11,* 353–358.

Koocher, G. P., & O'Malley, J. E. (1981). *The Damocles syndrome: Psychological consequences of surviving childhood cancer.* New York: McGraw-Hill.

Koocher, G. P., & Sallan, S.E. (1978). Pediatric oncology. In P. Magrab (Ed.), *Psychological management of pediatric problems: Vol. 1. Early life conditions and chronic diseases* (pp. 283–307). Baltimore: University Park Press.

Koop, C. E. (1987). *Surgeon General's Report: Children with special health care needs.* Washington, DC: United States Public Health Service.

Korsch, B., Gozzi, E., & Francis, V. (1968). Gaps in doctor-patient interaction and patient satisfaction. *Pediatrics, 42,* 855–871.

Korsch, B., & Negrete, V. (1972). Doctor-patient communication, *Scientific American, 227,* 66–74.

Kovacs, M., Goldstein, D., Obrosky, D. S., & Iyengar, S. (1992). Prevalence and predictors of pervasive noncompliance with medical treatment among youths with insulin-dependent diabetes mellitus. *Journal of the American Academy of Child and Adolescent Psychiatry, 31,* 1112–1119.

Krahn, G. (1993). Conceptualizing social support in families of children with special health care needs. *Family Process, 32,* 235–248.

Kupst, M. J., & Schulman, J. L. (1988). Long-term coping with pediatric leukemia: A six-year follow-up study. *Journal of Pediatric Psychology, 13,* 7–22.

LaGreca, A. M. (1988). Adherence to prescribed medical regimens. In D. K. Routh (Ed.), *Handbook of pediatric psychology* (pp. 229–320). New York: Guilford Press.

LaGreca. A. M. & Schuman, W. B. (1995). Adherence to prescribed medical regimens. In M.C. Roberts (Ed.) *Handbook of Pediatric Psychology* (2nd ed.) (pp. 55–83).

LaGreca, A. M., & Skyler, J. S. (1995). Psychological management of diabetes. In C. J. H. Kelnar (Ed.), *Childhood diabetes* (pp. 295–310). London: Chapman & Hall.

Lask, B. (1992). The need for psychological interventions: How to convince the skeptic. *Pediatric Pulmonology, 14*(Suppl. 8), 232–233 (Abstract).

Lavigne, J. V., & Faier-Routman, J. (1993). Correlates of psychosocial adjustment to pediatric physical disorders: A meta-analytic review and comparison with existing models. *Journal of Developmental and Behavioral Pediatrics, 14,* 117–123.

Lavigne, J. V., & Ryan, M. (1979). Psychological adjustment of siblings of children with chronic illness. *Pediatrics, 63,* 616–627.

Lavigne, J. V., Schulein, M. J., & Hahn, Y. S. (1986a). Psychological aspects of painful medical conditions in children. I. Developmental aspects and assessment. *Pain, 27,* 133–146.

Lavigne, J. V., Schulein, M. J., & Hahn, Y. S. (1986b). Psychological aspects of painful medical conditions in children. II. Personality factors, family characteristics and treatment. *Pain, 27,* 147–169.

Lazar, A., & Torney-Purta, J. (1991). The development of the subconcepts of death in young children: A short-term longitudinal study. *Child Development, 62,* 1321–1333.

Lazarus, R. S., & Folkman, S. (1984). *Stress, appraisal, and coping.* New York: Springer.

LeBaron, S., & Zeltzer, L. (1984). Behavioral intervention for reducing chemotherapy related nausea and vomiting in adolescents with cancer. *Journal of Adolescent Health Care, 5,* 178–182.

Lemanek, K. (1990). Adherence issues in the medical management of asthma. *Journal of Pediatric Psychology, 15,* 437–458.

Levenson, P. M., Pfefferbaum, B. J., Copeland, D., & Silberberg, Y. (1982). Information preferences of cancer patients ages 11–20 years. *Journal of Adolescent Health Care, 3,* 9–13.

Leventhal, J. M. (1984). Psychosocial assessment of children with chronic physical disease. *Pediatric Clinics of North America, 31,* 71–86.

Lobato, D., Faust, D., & Spirito, A. (1988). Examining the effects of chronic disease and disability on children's sibling relationships. *Journal of Pediatric Psychology, 13,* 389–407.

Lorenz, R. A., Christensen, N. K., & Pichert, J. W. (1985). Diet-related knowledge, skill, and adherence among children with insulin dependent diabetes mellitus. *Pediatrics, 75,* 872–876.

Magrab, P. R., & Calcagno, P. L. (1978). Psychological impact of chronic pediatric conditions. In P.R. Magrab (Ed.). *Psychological management of pediatric problems. Vol. 1. Early life conditions and chronic diseases* (pp. 3–14). Baltimore: University Park Press.

Markova, I., MacDonald, K., & Forbes, C. (1979). Impact of haemophilia on child-rearing practices and parental cooperation. *Journal of Child Psychology and Psychiatry, 21,* 153–161.

Martin, G. W., & Mauer, A. M. (1982). Interactions of health-care professionals with critically ill children and their parents. *Clinical Pediatrics, 21,* 540-544.

Martinson, I. M., Nesbit, M., & Kersey, J. (1984). Home care for the child with cancer. In A. E. Christ & K. Flomenhaft (Eds.), *Childhood cancer: Impact on the family* (pp. 177–198). New York: Plenum Press.

Martinson, I., & Papadatou, D. (1994). Care of the dying child and the bereaved. In D. Bearison & R. Mulhern (Eds.), *Pediatric psychooncology: Psychological research on children with cancer* (pp. 193–214). New York: Oxford University Press.

Masek, B. J., Russo, D. C., & Varni, J. W. (1984). Behavioral approaches to the management of chronic pain in children. *Pediatric Clinics of North America, 31,* 1113–1131.

Mattsson, A. (1972). Long-term physical illness in childhood: A challenge to psychosocial adjustment. *Pediatrics, 50,* 801–810.

Mattsson, A. (1977). Long term physical illness in childhood: A challenge to psychosocial adaptation. In R.J. Moos (Ed.), *Coping with physical illness* (pp. 183–199). New York: Plenum Press.

McAndrew, I. (1976). Children with a handicap and their families. *Child Care, Health, and Development, 2,* 213–218.

McCaul, K. D., Glasgow, R. E., & Schafer, L. C. (1987). Diabetes regimen behaviors: Predicting adherence. *Medical Care, 25,* 868–881.

McKeever, P. (1983). Siblings of chronically ill children: A literature review with implications for research and practice. *American Journal of Orthopsychiatry, 53,* 209–218.

Mechanic, D. (1983). Adolescent health and illness behavior: A review of the literature and a new hypothesis for the study of stress. *Journal of Human Stress, 9,* 4–13.

Mechanic, D., & Volkart, E. H. (1961). Stress, illness behavior, and the sick role. *American Sociological Review, 26,* 51–58.

Meichenbaum, D., & Turk, D. C. (1987). *Facilitating treatment adherence: A practitioner's guidebook.* New York: Plenum Press.

Melamed, B. G. (1982). Reduction of medical fears: An information processing analysis. In J. Boulougouris (Ed.), *Learning theory approaches to psychiatry* (pp. 205–218). New York: John Wiley & Sons.

Melamed, B. G., & Siegel, L. J. (1975). Reduction of anxiety in children facing hospitalization and surgery by use of filmed modeling. *Journal of Consulting and Clinical Psychology, 43,* 411–521.

Melamed, B. G., & Siegel, L. J. (1980). *Behavioral medicine: Practical applications in health care.* New York: Springer.

Melamed, B.G., Siegel, L.J., & Ridley-Johnson, R. R. (1988). Coping behaviors in children facing medical stress. In T. Fields, P. McCabe, & N. Schneiderman (Eds.), *Stress and coping across development* (pp. 109–137). Hillsdale, NJ: Lawrence Erlbaum.

Minuchin, S., Baker, L., Rosman, B. L., Liebman, R., Milman, L., & Todd, T. C. (1975). A conceptual model of psychosomatic illness in children. *Archives of General Psychiatry, 32,* 1031–1038.

Morrow, G. R., & Dobkin, P. L. (1988). Anticipatory nausea and vomiting in cancer patients undergoing chemotherapy treatment: Prevalence, etiology, and behavioral interventions. *Clinical Psychology Review, 8,* 517–556.

Mulhern, R. K., Horowitz, M. E., Ochs, J., Friedman, A. G. Armstrong, F. D., Copeland, D., & Kuhn, L. E. (1989). Assessment of quality of life among pediatric patients with cancer. Psychological Assessment: A *Journal of Consulting and Clinical Psychology, 1,* 130–138.

Mulhern, R., Lauer, M. E., & Hoffman, R. G. (1983). Death of a child at home or in the hospital: Subsequent psychological adjustment of the family. *Pediatrics, 71,* 743–747.

Mullins, L. D., Gillman, J., & Harbeck, C. (1992). Multiple-level interventions in pediatric psychology settings: A behavioral systems perspective. In A. M. LaGreca, L. J. Siegel, J. L. Wallander, & C. E. Walker (Eds.), *Stress and coping in child health.* (pp. 371–399). New York: Guilford Press.

Nader, P. R., & Parcel, G. S. (1978). Competence: The outcome of health and education. In P.R. Nader (Ed.), *Options for school health: Meeting community needs* (pp. 1–17), Germantown, MD: Aspen Systems Corporation.

Nannis, E., Susman, E. J., Strope, B. E., & Woodruff, P. J. (1982). Correlates of control in pediatric cancer patients and their families. *Journal of Pediatric Psychology, 7,* 75–84.

National Association of State Directors of Special Education and National Association of State Boards of Education (1979). *Answering your questions about Public Law 94–142 and Section 504.* Washington, DC: Authors.

National Hospice Organization (1984). *Fact sheet.* Arlington, VA: National Hospice Organization.

Naylor, D., Coates, T. J., & Kan, J. (1984). Reducing distress in pediatric cardiac catheterization. *American Journal of Diseases of Children, 138,* 726–729.

Nevin, R.S., & McCubbin, H. (1979). Parental coping with physical handicaps: Social policy implications, *Spina Bifida Therapy, 2,* 151–164.

Newacheck, P. W. & Taylor, W. R. (1992). Childhood chronic illness: Prevalence, severity, and impact. *American Journal of Public Health, 82,* 364–371.

Obetz, S. W., Swenson, W. M., McCarthy, C. A., Gilchrist, G. S., & Burgert, E. O. (1980). Children who survive malignant disease: Emotional adaptation of the children and their families. In J. L. Schulman & M. J. Kupst (Eds.), *The child with cancer: Clinical approaches to psychosocial care-research in psychosocial aspects* (pp. 194–210). Springfield, IL: Charles C. Thomas.

Oliver, I. N., Simon, R. M., & Aisner, J. (1986). Antiemetic studies: A methodological discussion. *Cancer Treatment Reports, 20,* 555–563.

Parrish, J. M. (1986). Parent compliance with medical and behavioral recommendations. In N. A. Krasnegor, J. D. Arasteh, & M. F. Cataldo (Eds.), *Child health behavior: A behavioral pediatrics perspective* (pp. 453–501). New York: John Wiley & Sons.

Parsons, T. (1951). *The social system.* Glencoe, IL: Free Press.

Parsons, T. (1958). Definitions of health and illness in light of American values and social structure. In E. Jaco (Ed.), *Patients, physicians, and illness* (pp. 165–187). New York: Free Press.

Peckman, V. C., Meadows, A. T., Bastil, N., & Marrero, O. (1988). Educational late effects in long-term survivors of childhood acute lymphocytic leukemia. *Pediatrics, 81,* 127–133.

Perrin, E., & Gerrity, P. S. (1981). There's a demon in your belly: Children's understanding of illness. *Pediatrics, 67,* 841–849.

Perrin, E. C., & Gerrity, P. S. (1984). Development of children with a chronic illness. *Pediatric Clinics of North America, 31,* 19–31.

Perrin, E. C., Stein, R. E. K., & Drotar, D. C. (1991). Cautions in using the child behavior checklist: Observations based on research about children with chronic illness. *Journal of Pediatric Psychology, 16,* 411–421.

Perrin, J. M., Ireys, H. T., Shayne, M. W. & Moynihan, L.C. (1984). Children and schools: The special issues of chronically ill children. In S. C. Ashcraft (Ed.), *Education and chronically ill children: A need-based policy orientation. Peabody Journal of Education, 61,* 10–15.

Peterson, L., & Brownlee-Duffeck, M. (1984). Prevention of anxiety and pain due to medical and dental procedures. In M. . Roberts & L. Peterson (Eds.), *Prevention of problems in childhood: Psychological research and applications* (pp. 266–308). New York: John Wiley & Sons.

Peterson, L., & Shigetomi, C. (1981). The use of coping techniques to minimize anxiety in hospitalized children. *Behavior Therapy, 12,* 1–14.

Peterson, L., & Toler, S. M. (1986). An information seeking disposition in child surgery patients. *Health Psychology, 4,* 343–358.

Piaget, J. (1929). *The child's conception of the world.* New York: Harcourt Brace Jovanovich.

Pickering, G. (1979). Therapeutics: Art or science. *Journal of the American Medical Association, 242,* 649–653.

Pless, I. B., & Perrin, J. M. (1985). Issues common to a variety of illnesses. In N. Hobbs & J. M. Perrin (Eds.), *Issues in the care of children with chronic illness: A sourcebook on problems, services, and policies* (pp. 41–60). San Francisco: Jossey-Bass.

Pless, I. B., & Pinkerton, P. (1975). *Chronic childhood disorder: Promoting patterns of adjustment.* Chicago: Year Book Medical Publishers.

Pless, I. B., & Roghmann, K. J. (1971). Chronic illness and its consequences: Some observations based on three epidemiological surveys. *Journal of Pediatrics, 79,* 351–359.

Pless, I. B., & Satterwhite, B. B. (1975). Chronic illness. In R. Haggerty, K. Roghmann, & I. B. Pless (Eds.), *Child health and the community* (pp. 78–94). New York: John Wiley & Sons.

Quittner, A. L., Opipari, L. C., Regoli, M. J., Jacobsen, J., & Eigen, H. (1992). The impact of caregiver and role strain on family life: Comparisons between mothers of children with cystic fibrosis and matched controls. *Rehabilitation Psychology, 37,* 275–290

Rapoff, M. A., & Barnard, M. U. (1991) Compliance with pediatric medical regimens. In J. A. Cramer & B. Spiker (Eds.), *Patient compliance in medical practice and clinical trials* (pp. 73–98). New York: Raven Press.

Redd, W. H., Jacobsen, P. B., Die-Trill, M., Dermatis,H., McEvoy, M., & Holland, J. C. (1987). Cognitive/attentional distraction in the control of conditioned nausea in pediatric cancer patients receiving chemotherapy. *Journal of Consulting and Clinical Psychology, 55,* 391–395.

Reynolds, L. A., Miller, D. L., Jelalian, E., & Spirito, A. (1995). Anticipatory grief and bereavement. In M. C. Roberts (Ed.), *Handbook of pediatric psychology* (2nd ed., pp. 142–164). New York: Guilford Press.

Rosenstock, I. M. (1985). Understanding and enhancing patient compliance with diabetic regimens. *Diabetes Care, 8,* 610–616.

Rosenstock, I. M., & Kirscht, J. P. (1979). Why people seek health care. In G. C. Stone, F. Cohen, & N. Adler (Eds.), *Health psychology* (pp. 161–188). San Francisco: Jossey-Bass.

Rothstein, R. (1980). Psychological stress in families of children in a pediatric intensive care unit. *Pediatric Clinics of North America, 27,* 613–620.

Rudd, P. (1979). In search of the gold standard for compliance measurement. *Archives of Internal Medicine, 139,* 627–628.

Rudolph, K. D., Denning, M. D., & Weisz, J. R. (1995). Determinants and consequences of children's coping in the medical setting: Conceptualization, review, and critique. *Psychological Bulletin, 118,* 328–357.

Ryan, C. M. (1988). Neurobehavioral complications of Type 1 diabetes: Examination of possible risk factors. *Diabetes Care, 11,* 86–93.

Sabbeth, B. F., & Leventhal, J. M. (1984). Marital adjustment to chronic childhood illness: A critique of the literature. *Pediatrics, 73,* 762–768.

Sabbeth, B. F., & Stein, R. E. K. (1990). Mental health referral: A weak link in the comprehensive care of children and chronic physical illness. *Journal of Development and Behavioral Pediatrics, 11,* 73–78.

Schafer, L. C., Glasgow, R. E. McCaul, K. D., & Dreher, M. (1983). Adherence to IDDM regimens: Relationship to psychosocial variables and metabolic control. *Diabetes Care, 6,* 493–498.

Sexson, S. B., & Madan-Swain, A. (1993). School reentry for the child with chronic illness. *Journal of Learning Disabilities, 26,* 115–125.

Shagena, M. M., Sandler, H. K., & Perrin, E. C. (1988). Concepts of illness and perception of control in healthy children and in children with chronic illnesses. *Developmental and Behavioral Pediatrics, 9,* 252–256.

Shapiro, J., & Shumaker, S. (1987). Differences in emotional well-being and communication styles between mothers and fathers of pediatric cancer patients. *Journal of Psychosocial Oncology, 5,* 121–131.

Shaw, S. N., Stephens, L. R., & Holmes, S. S. (1986). Knowledge about medical instruments and reported anxiety in pediatric surgery patients. *Children's Health Care, 14,* 134–141.

Shope, J. T. (1981). Medication compliance. *Pediatric Clinics of North America, 28,* 5–21.

Shulman, J. L. (1983). Coping with major disease—child, family, and pediatrician. *Pediatrics, 102,* 988–991.

Siegel, L. J. (1976). Preparation of children for hospitalization: A selected review of the research literature. *Journal of Pediatric Psychology, 1,* 26–30.

Siegel, L. J. (1983). Hospitalization and medical care of children. In E. Walker & M. Roberts (Eds.), *Handbook of clinical child psychology* (pp. 1089–1108). New York: John Wiley & Sons.

Siegel, L. J. (1988). Measuring children's adjustment to hospitalization and to medical procedures. In P. Karoly (Ed.), *Handbook of child health assessment: Biosocial perspectives* (pp. 265–302). New York: John Wiley & Sons.

Siegel, L. J. (1995). Commentary: Children's reactions to aversive medical procedures. *Journal of Pediatric Psychology, 20,* 429–433.

Siegel, L. J., & Hudson, B. O. (1992). Hospitalization and medical care of children. In C. E. Walker & M. C. Roberts (Eds.), *Handbook of clinical child psychology* (2nd ed., pp. 845–858). New York: John Wiley & Sons.

Siegel, L. J., & Smith, K. E. (1989). Children's strategies for coping with pain. *Pediatrician: International Journal of Child and Adolescent Health, 16,* 110–118.

Siegel, L. J., & Smith, K. E. (1991). Coping and adaptation in children's pain. In J. P. Bush & S.W. Hawking (Eds.), *Children in pain: Clinical and research issues from a developmental perspective* (pp. 149–170). New York: Springer-Verlag.

Simensson, R. J., & McHale, S. M. (1981). Review: Research on handicapped children: Sibling relationships. *Child Care Health and Development, 7,* 153–171.

Skipper, J. K., & Leonard, R. C. (1968). Children, stress, and hospitalization: A field experiment. *Journal of Health and Social Behavior, 9,* 275–287.

Skipper, J. K., Leonard, R. C., & Rhymes, J. (1968). Child hospitalization and social interaction: An experimental study of mother's feelings of stress, adaptation, and satisfaction. *Medical Care, 6,* 496–506.

Slavin, L., O'Malley, J. E., Koocher, G. P., & Foster, D. J. (1981). Communication of the cancer diagnoses to pediatric patients: Impact on long-term adjustment. *American Journal of Psychiatry, 139,* 179–183.

Smith, K. E., Ackerson, J. D., & Blotcky, A. D. (1989). Reducing distress during invasive medical procedures: Relating behavioral interventions to preferred coping style in pediatric cancer patients. *Journal of Pediatric Psychology, 14,* 405–419.

Spinetta, J. J. (1974). The dying child's awareness of death: A review. *Psychological Bulletin, 81,* 256–260.

Spinetta, J. J. (1980). Disease-related communication: How to tell. In J. Kellerman (Ed.), *Psychological aspects of childhood cancer* (pp. 257–269). Springfield, IL: Charles C. Thomas.

Spinetta, J. J., & Deasy-Spinetta, P. (Eds.). (1981). *Living with childhood cancer.* St. Louis: C. V. Mosby.

Spinetta, J.J., & Maloney, L.J. (1975). Death anxiety in the outpatient leukemic child. *Pediatrics, 65,* 1034–1037.

Spinetta, J. J., & Maloney, L. J. (1978). The child with cancer: Patterns of communication and denial. *Journal of Consulting and Clinical Psychology, 46,* 1540–1541.

Spinetta, J. J., Swarner, J. A., & Sheposh, J. P. (1981). Effective parental coping following the death of a child from cancer. *Journal of Pediatric Psychology, 6,* 251–263.

Stehbens, J. A. (1988). Childhood cancer. In D. K. Routh (Ed.), *Handbook of pediatric psychology* (pp. 135–161). New York: Guilford Press.

Stehbens, J. A., Kisker, C. T., & Wilson, B. K. (1983). Achievement and intelligence test-retest performance in pediatric cancer patients at diagnosis and one year later. *Journal of Pediatric Psychology, 8,* 47–56.

Stein, R. E. K., & Jessop, D. J. (1982). A noncategorical approach to chronic childhood illness. *Public Health Reports, 97,* 354–362.

Stein, R. E. K., & Jessop, D. J. (1984). Relationship between health status and psychological adjustment among children with chronic conditions. *Pediatrics, 73,* 169–174.

Stein, R.E. K. & Jessop, D.J. (1991). Long-term mental health effects of a pediatric home care program. *Pediatrics, 88,* 490–496.

Stewart, S. M., Campbell, R. A., McCallon, D., Waller, D. A., & Andrews, W. S. (1992). Cognitive patterns in school-age children with end-stage liver disease. *Journal of Developmental and Behavioral Pediatrics, 13,* 331–338.

Stuetzer, C. (1980). Support systems for professionals. In J. L. Schulman & M. J. Kupst (Eds.), *The child with cancer: Clinical approaches to psychosocial care research in psychosocial aspects* (pp. 63–71). Springfield, IL: Charles C. Thomas.

Susman, E. J., Dorn, L. D., & Fletcher, J. C. (1987). Reasoning about illness in ill and healthy children and adolescents: Cognitive and emotional developmental aspects. *Developmental and Behavioral Pediatrics, 8,* 266–273.

Tamaroff, M. H., Festa, R. S., Adesman, A. R., & Walco, G. A. (1992). Therapeutic adherence to oral medication regimens by adolescents with cancer. II. Clinical and psychological correlates. *Journal of Pediatrics, 120,* 812–817.

Tavormina, J., Kastner, L. S., Slater, P. M., & Watt, S. L. (1976). Chronically ill children: A psychologically and emotionally deviant population? *Journal of Abnormal Child Psychology, 4,* 99.

Tew, B., & Lawrence, K. M. (1975). Some sources of stress in mothers of spina bifida children. *British Journal of Prevention and Social Medicine, 29,* 27–30.

Thompson, K. L., & Varni, J. W. (1986). A developmental cognitive-biobehavioral approach to pediatric pain assessment. *Pain, 25,* 283–296.

Thompson, R. H. (1985). *Psychosocial research on pediatric hospitalization and health care: A review of the literature.* Springfield, IL: Charles C. Thomas.

Toseland, R., & Hacker, L. (1982). Self-help groups and professional development. *Social Work, 27,* 341–347.

Tovian, S. M. (1991). Integration of clinical psychology into adult and pediatric oncology programs. In J. J. Sweet, R. H. Rozensky, & S. M. Tovian (Eds.), *Handbook of clinical psychology in medical settings* (pp. 331–352). New York: Plenum Press.

Trantman, P. D., Erickson, C., Shaffer, D., O'Conner, P. A., Sitarz, A., Correra, A., & Schonfeld, I. S. (1988). Prediction of intellectual deficits in children with acute lymphoblastic leukemia. *Journal of Developmental and Behavioral Pediatrics, 9,* 122–128.

Travis, G. (1976). *Chronic illness in children: Its impact on child and family.* Stanford, CA: Stanford University Press.

Turiel, E. (1969). Developmental processes in the child's moral thinking. In P. Mussen, J. Langer, & M. Covington (Eds.), *New directions in developmental psychology* (pp. 92–133). New York: Holt, Rinehart & Winston.

Twaddle, A. C. (1969). Health decisions and sick role variations: An exploration. *Journal of Health and Social Behavior, 10,* 105–115.

Twaddle, A. C., & Hessler, R. M. (1977). *A sociology of health.* St. Louis: C. V. Mosby.

Twycross, R. G. (1990). Terminal care of cancer patients and home care. In J. J. Bonica (Ed.), *The management of pain* (2nd ed., pp. 445–460). Philadelphia: Lea & Febigar.

Varni, J. W. (1981). Self-regulation techniques in the management of chronic arthritic pain in hemophilia. *Behavior Therapy, 12,* 185–194.

Varni, J. W. (1983). *Clinical behavioral pediatrics: An interdisciplinary biobehavioral approach.* Elmsford, NY: Pergamon Press.

Varni, J. W., & Babani, L. (1986). Long-term adherence to health care regimens in pediatric chronic disorders. In N. A. Krashegor, J. D. Arasteh, & M. F. Cataldo (Eds.),

Child health behavior: A behavioral pediatrics perspective (pp. 502–520). New York: John Wiley & Sons.

Varni, J. W., Blount, R. L., Waldron, S. A., & Smith, A. J. (1995). Management of pain and distress. In M.C. Roberts (Ed.), *Handbook of pediatric psychology* (2nd ed., pp. 105–123). New York: Guilford Press.

Varni, J. W., & Gilbert, A. (1982). Self-regulation of chronic arthritic pain and long-term analgesic dependence in a hemophiliac. *Rheumatology and Rehabilitation, 21,* 171–174.

Varni, J. W., Katz, E. P., Colgrove, R., & Dolgin, M. (1992). The impact of social skills training on the adjustment of children with newly diagnosed cancer. *Journal of Pediatric Psychology, 18,* 751–767.

Varni, J. W., & Wallender, J. L. (1984). Adherence to health-related regimens in pediatric chronic disorders. *Clinical Psychology Review, 4,* 585–596.

Vernick, J., & Karon, M. (1965). Who's afraid of death on a leukemia ward? *American Journal of Diseases of Children, 109,* 393–397.

Vernon, D. T. A., & Bailey, W. C. (1974). The use of motion pictures in the psychological preparation of children for induction of anesthesia. *Anesthesiology, 40,* 68–74.

Vernon, D. T. A., Foley, J. M., Sipowicz, R. R., & Schulman, J. L. (1965). *The psychological responses of children to hospitalization and illness.* Springfield, IL: Charles C. Thomas.

Vernon, D. T. A., & Thompson, R. H. (1993). Research on the effect of experimental interventions on children's behavior after hospitalization: A review and synthesis. *Journal of Developmental and Behavioral Pediatrics, 14,* 36–44.

Walco, G. A., & Dampier, C. D. (1987). Chronic pain in adolescent patients. *Journal of Pediatric Psychology, 12,* 215–225.

Walco, G. A., Siegel, L. J., Dolgin, M. J., & Varni, J. W. (1992). Pediatric pain. In V. B. Van Hasselt & D. J. Kolko (Eds.), *Inpatient behavior therapy for children and adolescents* (pp. 183–203). New York: Plenum Press.

Walco, G. A., Varni, J. W., & Ilowite, N. T. (1992). Cognitive-behavioral pain management in children with juvenile rheumatoid arthritis. *Pediatrics, 89,* 1075–1079.

Wallace, M. H., Bakke, K., Hubbard, A., & Pendergrass, T. W. (1984). Coping with childhood cancer: An educational program for parents of children with cancer. *Oncology Nursing Forum, 11,* 30–35.

Wallander, J. L., & Thompson, R. J. (1995). Psychosocial adjustment of children with chronic physical conditions. In M. C. Roberts (Ed.), *Handbook of pediatric psychology* (2nd ed., pp. 124–141). New York: Guilford Press.

Wallander, J. L., Varni, J. W., Babani, L., Banis, H. T., Dehaan, C. B., & Wilcox, K. T. (1989). Disability parameters, chronic strain, and adaptation of physically handicapped children and their mothers. *Journal of Pediatric Psychology, 14,* 23–42.

Weithorn, L. A., & McCabe, M. A. (1988). Emerging ethical and legal issues in pediatric psychology. In D. K. Routh (Ed.), *Handbook of Pediatric Psychology* (pp. 567–606). New York: Guilford Press.

Wells, R. D., & Schwebel, A. I. (1987). Chronically ill children and their mothers: Predictors of resilience and vulnerability to hospitalization and surgery stress. *Developmental and Behavioral Pediatrics, 8,* 83–89.

White, E., Elsom, B., & Prawat, R. (1978). Children's conceptions of death. *Child Development, 49,* 307–310.

Wiener, J. M. (1970). Response of medical personnel to the fatal illness of a child. In B. Schoenberg, A. Carr, D. Perets, & A. Kutscher (Eds.), *Loss and grief: Psychological management in medical practice.* New York: Columbia University Press.

Wolfer, J. A., & Visintainer, M. A. (1975). Pediatric surgical patients' and parents' stress responses and adjustment. *Nursing Research, 24,* 244–255.

Wood, T. A., Siegel, L. J., & Scott, R. L. (April, 1989). *A comparison of marital adjustment and stress with parents of chronically ill, handicapped, and non-handicapped children.* Paper presented at the Second Florida Conference on Child Health Psychology, Gainesville, FL.

Woolsey, S. (1985). A medical school course in coping with death: An opportunity to consider some basic health care issues. *Developmental and Behavioral Pediatrics, 6,* 91–99.

Worden, J. W. (1991). *Grief counseling and grief therapy: A handbook for the mental health practitioner.* New York: Springer.

Wysocki, T., Hough, B., Ward, K., & Green, L. (1992). Diabetes mellitus in the transition to adulthood: Adjustment, self-care, and health status. *Developmental and Behavioral Pediatrics, 13,* 194–201.

Zeltzer, L. K., Dash, J., & Holland, J. P. (1979). Hypnotically induced pain control in sickle cell anemia. *Pediatrics, 64,* 533–536.

Zeltzer, L., & LeBaron, S. (1982). Hypnoses and nonhypnotic techniques for reduction of pain and anxiety during painful procedures in children and adolescents with cancer. *Journal of Pediatrics, 101,* 1032–1035.

Zeltzer, L., LeBaron, S., & Zeltzer, P.M. (1984). The effectiveness of behavioral intervention for reduction of nausea and vomiting in children and adolescents receiving chemotherapy. *Journal of Clinical Oncology, 2,* 683–690.

Zola, I. K. (1981). Structural constraints on the doctor-patient relationship: The case of non-compliance. In L. Eisenberg & A. Kleinman (Eds.), *The relevance of social science for medicine* (pp. 241–252). New York: D. Reidel.

CHAPTER 12

SEXUAL AND OTHER ABUSE OF CHILDREN

Judith V. Becker
Barbara Bonner

INTRODUCTION AND HISTORICAL PERSPECTIVES REGARDING SEXUAL AND PHYSICAL ABUSE

Children and adolescents in our society are more likely to be victims of sexual and other forms of abuse than are adults. Finkelhor and Dziuba-Leatherman (1994) cite data from the 1990 National Crime Survey indicating that other than for homicide, children are victims of rape, assault, and robbery at a rate of double to triple that of the population of adults.

In an attempt to illustrate the spectrum of child victimization, Finkelhor and Dziuba-Leatherman (1994) examined national statistics from multiple sources. Interestingly they found that some forms of abuse that children are subject to have not been subject to criminal sanctions, including sibling assaults and forms of corporal punishment. These authors go on to define three broad categories of victimization experiences children may be subject to: *Category 1*—assaults by siblings, assaults or robbery by peers, physical punishment by parents; *Category 2*—neglect, family abductions and physical and sexual abuse; and *Category 3*—child homicides and non- family abductions. More children experience Category 1 victimizations than categories 2 or 3 and yet less attention is paid to category one victimizations.

Finkelhor and Dziuba-Leatherman (1994) provide the following statistics on rates of abuse per 1,000 children. While .035 children per 1,000 were the victims of homicide, 3 per 1,000 were psychologically maltreated, 6.3 per 1,000 sexually abused, 20 per 1,000 neglected, 23.5 per 1,000 physically abused, 118 per 1,000 raped, 246 per 1,000 robbed, 311 per 1,000 assaulted, 499 per 1,000 physically punished and 800 per 1,000 were assaulted by their siblings.

Given that there is a dearth of scientific literature on Category 1 forms of victimization and that fortunately Category 3 forms of victimization are infrequent, this chapter will focus on two forms of child victimization, sexual and physical abuse, noting that there is a considerably larger data base on the sexual abuse of children than on physical abuse.

More children are abused in intrafamilial circumstances and by acquaintances than by people not known to them. A legitimate question to raise is, why are children victimized at a rate considerably greater than adults? Although there is no simple answer to this question, there are many variables to consider including the size of children, and in many cases, their inability to defend themselves and their dependency on others. In cases of intrafamilial violence the children are "captive" victims. They are dependent on their parents to meet their needs, some are too young to leave home, others who run away may face juvenile court sanctions themselves. Children must attend school and consequently if they are victimized at school (e.g., robbed, bullied, assaulted) they cannot elect not to attend school. Children do not have the resources that adults have and they do not have the "voice" to influence legislation that directly bears on their health and well-being. All of these factors, in part, play a part in describing why children are at increased risk for victimization, since they are in many circumstances powerless.

Fortunately, society and professional organizations have begun to take the maltreatment of children seriously. The American Psychological Association (APA) recently published work-group reports on child abuse prevention, treatment, legal issues in the area of child abuse and neglect, and issues for the field relative to educating and training students who are obtaining degrees in the mental-health field (APA, 1995). Specialty organizations have also been formed over the past two decades to address issues of the maltreatment of children and treatment of perpetrators of sexual abuse of children. The American Professional Society on the Abuse of Children (APSAC) is one such organization that holds national training conferences, has established guidelines for the assessment of maltreated children and recently has published a comprehensive handbook on child maltreatment (Briere, Berliner, Bulkley, Jenny, & Reid, 1996). Another organization, The Association for the Treatment of Sexual Abusers (ATSA) has established guidelines for working with adult offenders. This organization also holds national conferences in which individuals within the mental-health field can receive training and be brought up to date on the latest research advances in working with adult and juvenile sexual offenders.

While a considerable amount of research has been conducted to date on both the incidence and impact of child physical and sexual abuse, many gaps remain. Psychologists, psychiatrists, social workers, and other mental-health professionals have an important role to play in developing prevention strategies, assessment methods, and treatment. It is particularly important that mental-health professionals receive training at the postgraduate level as well as undergraduate and graduate levels on issues of child abuse. Haugaard, Bonner, Linares, Tharinger, Weisz, and Wolfe (1995) present recommendations made by the American Psychological Association Working Group relative to education and training in child abuse and neglect.

An important area to consider in reviewing published studies to date are definitional issues. Prevalence and incidents rates may vary based on how a specific behavior is defined. As Kolko (1996) notes, "A fine distinction exists between child physical abuse and some of the more extreme forms of parent to child discipline (e.g. beating vs. spanking or slapping)" (p. 22). Rates of physical abuse may vary based on definitions as well as reporting laws. A number of models and theories have been proposed to explain child physical abuse and some of these will be described in this chapter. In determining etiology and risk it is important to take into consideration characteristics of the child, the parent, and the family system. Child physical abuse can impact on a child's medical and physical functioning, developmental functioning, cognitive and attributional style, academic and social behavior, as well as attachment. Treatments that are multifaceted and multimodel are likely to have the most impact.

As with child physical abuse, studies on the incidence and prevalence of child sexual abuse also vary depending on the data source and the definition of the behavior. Research to date indicates that children who have been sexually abused can present with a wide range of psychological and interpersonal problems. As Berliner and Elliott (1996) note,

"Unlike studies of adults that have been conducted with non-clinical as well as with clinical samples, most information on children is derived from clinical samples, virtually all of which have some involvement with child protection or criminal justice authorities" (p. 55). While sexually abused children are usually recommended for treatment, there is relatively little data available empirically evaluating treatment effectiveness.

This chapter will focus on what published literature has indicated to date on etiological factors, assessment and treatment of both victims and perpetrators of child sexual and physical abuse.

ETIOLOGICAL FACTORS

Victims of Sexual or Physical Abuse

In considering the etiological basis of psychological problems in victims of sexual or physical abuse, it is important to understand that abuse is an experience, rather than a disorder or a syndrome in itself (e.g., Finkelhor & Berliner, 1995). Children who have been physically or sexually abused can present with a wide range of affective and behavioral disorders, from asymptomatic to severely disturbed (Conte & Berliner, 1988). The short- and long-term negative effects of abuse on children, adolescents, and adults have been clearly documented in the literature (Beitchman, Zucker, Hood, daCosta, & Akman, 1991; Kendall-Tackett, Williams, & Finkelhor, 1993; Milner & Crouch, 1993; Widom, 1989).

The symptoms presented by these children can differ by the form of abuse; the child's developmental age, gender, and adjustment prior to the abuse; the severity and chronicity of the abuse; the relationship of the child to the perpetrator; and factors related to family conflict, cohesion, and support of the child (Becker et al., 1995). While these factors have a significant effect on the child's behavior and affective functioning, recent research indicates that sociocultural factors and the family climate may have more influence on the child's developmental outcome than the abusive incidents. A 1995 study by Herrenkohl, Herrenkohl, Rupert, Egolf, and Lutz found that socioeconomic status, maternal interaction with the child (e.g., rejection, control, affection, support), child health problems, and the absence of a male head of the household are more predictive of behavioral functioning than abuse or neglect.

Physical abuse represents an act of commission on the part of a parent or caretaker and can involve beatings or some other form of physical assault that results in injuries to a child, including fractures, burns, internal injuries, bruises, head trauma, lacerations, and death. Theories in the area of physical abuse have attempted to explain the behavior of the parent from various perspectives, including intrapsychic, sociological, and interactive (e.g., Walker, Bonner, & Kaufman, 1988). Significantly less attention has been focused on developing theories related to the impact of physical abuse or the treatment of physically abused children.

The effects of physical abuse on children have been well-described in the literature (e.g., Becker et al., 1995; Kolko, 1992, 1996; Milner & Crouch, 1993) and they are often manifested differently depending on the age of the child. Infants and preschoolers display problems with attachment (Crittenden & Ainsworth, 1989) and show aggressive behavior toward their peers (Hoffman-Plotkin & Twentyman, 1984). Older children who are attending school show decreased self-esteem and social withdrawal (Fantuzzo, 1990), depression (Blumberg, 1981), anxiety (Wolfe & Mosk, 1983), academic difficulties (Salzinger, Kaplan, Pelcovitz, Samit, & Kreiger, 1984), and aggressive behavior (Wodarski, Kurtz, Gaudin, & Howing, 1990). Adolescents with a history of physical abuse can demonstrate alcoholism, mental illness, or premature death (McCord, 1983). Widom's (1989) study documented that abused and neglected children are more likely to be arrested for delinquency, adult crimes, and violent criminal behavior than matched controls. A surprising finding that has recently emerged in the literature is that victims of physical abuse are at greater risk to be involved in sexually assaultive behavior than youth with a history of sexual abuse or a nonabused group (Widom, 1995; Browne, 1996).

One behavioral sequela that continues to be cited in the literature as an effect of physical abuse on children is high levels of externalizing behavior problems, such as conduct problems, serious aggressiveness, hyperactivity, and delinquency (e.g., Milner & Crouch, 1993; Kolko, 1996; Williamson, Borduin, & Howe, 1991). Physically abused children are described as having more external locus of control, a poor grasp of social roles (Barahal, Waterman, & Martin, 1981), hostile attributional styles, and aggressive approaches to solving problems (Dodge, Bates, & Peltit, 1990).

Over the past 10 years, research in child maltreatment has primarily focused on sexual abuse and its effects on children. This form of abuse is broadly defined as involving dependent, developmentally immature children and adolescents in sexual activities they do not fully understand and to which they are unable to give informed consent (Krugman & Jones, 1987). It includes various forms of sexual exploitation such as voyeurism, fondling, masturbation, oral sex, genital and anal intercourse, and involving children in pornography and prostitution.

A recent comprehensive review indicates that sexually abused children are more symptomatic than nonabused children and the abuse accounts for 14% to 45% of the variance (Finkelhor & Berliner, 1995). A 1993 review of 45 studies of child victims of sexual abuse documented several interesting findings, including (a) one third of the children had no symptoms, (b) approximately two thirds of the children recovered in the first 12 to 18 months, and (c) there was no specific syndrome in sexually abused children and no single traumatizing process (Kendall-Tackett et al., 1993).

The short and long-term effects of sexual abuse on children, adolescents, and adults have been well-documented in the literature (Beitchman et al., 1991; Berliner & Elliott, 1996; Browne & Finkelhor, 1986; Kendall-Tackett et al., 1993). Finkelhor and Berliner's (1995) review indicated that although no one symptom was found in a majority of the children, they frequently presented with fearfulness, posttraumatic stress disorder, behavior problems, poor self-esteem, and sexualized behaviors. Preschool and school-age children referred for treatment due to sexual abuse are more likely to engage in increased or unusual sexualized behaviors (Friedrich, 1993) and sexually abused adolescents may be more likely to show sexual frustration (Johnson & Shrier, 1985). As noted earlier, the effects of sexual abuse often vary as a function of several mediating factors that have been described in the literature, including age (Black, Dubowitz, & Harrington, 1994) and gender of the child (Faller, 1989), invasiveness and the degree of force in the assault (Elwell & Ephross, 1987), frequency and duration of the abuse (Nash, Zivney, & Hulsey, 1993; Burgess, Hartman, McCausland, & Powers, 1984), the number of perpetrators (Nash et al., 1993), the amount of time since the abuse (Friedrich, Urquiza, & Beilke, 1986), and the relationship between the child and the perpetrator (Adams-Tucker, 1982; Herman 1981).

In summary, the negative psychological effects of physical and sexual abuse on children and adolescents is well-described in both the clinical and empirical literature. Based on these affective and behavioral effects, clinicians can conduct an assessment and develop an initial treatment plan (for a comprehensive review on assessment, see Bonner, Kaufman, Harbeck, & Brassard, 1992).

Offenders of Sexual and Physical Abuse

Until somewhat recently, most of what was known about perpetrators of child sexual abuse was based on incarcerated offenders. While those studies have added to our knowledge base about offenders, they do not necessarily represent accurately the population of nonincarcerated offenders, which may be substantially larger. Abel, Mittelman, Becker, Rathner, and Rouleau (1988), from 1977 to 1985, interviewed a sample ($n = 561$) of nonincarcerated male sexual offenders under a certificate of confidentiality. This sample included intrafamilial as well as extrafamilial child molesters, rapists, and individuals who had other forms of paraphilia. These individuals ranged in age from 13-79 years old with an average age of 31.5 years old. Eighty percent of them were 20-49 years of age. This was one of the first studies to evaluate a large group of sexual offenders under a certificate of confidentiality and consequently yielded some important information. This study indicated that offenders committed many more offenses than they had ever been arrested for, and that many of the sex offenders had multiple paraphilias. For example, some of the child molesters engaged in incestuous as well as nonincestuous abuse and targeted male as well as female children. Fifty-eight percent of the adult offenders reported the onset of their deviant sexual interest prior to age 18.

While a number of theories have been proposed in an attempt to explain why some individuals are attracted to children, we are lacking a theory that has been empirically derived, universally agreed on, and that addresses the heterogeneity of the offender population. In all likelihood, there is not one causative factor, but rather, multiple pathways by which a person develops a sexual attraction to minors.

Psychoanalytic and psychodynamic theories have related the cause of deviant sexual behaviors to conflicts or trauma experienced in early childhood. Learning theorists propose that sexual arousal develops when an individual engages in a sexual behavior that is subsequently reinforced through sexual fantasies and masturbation. Biological factors have been postulated as perhaps being causative in the development of deviant sexual interest patterns. It has also been suggested that abnormal levels of androgens may contribute to inappropriate sexual behavior. It is important to note, however, that the majority of studies of androgen treatment have dealt only with violent sex offenders and have yielded inconclusive results (Bradford, 1990). Finkelhor has proposed a four-factor model (Finkelhor, 1984). These factors include (a) emotional congruence (i.e., the nonsexual and emotional needs met through molesting a child), (b) sexual arousal (the degree of sexual attraction an individual has to a child), (c) blockage (those factors that may interfere with the development of appropriate adult relationships), and (d) disinhibitions (those factors that allow an individual to overcome the internal and societal inhibitions against molesting children).

While there are numerous theories that address the etiology of sexual offending behavior against children, what is needed is a comprehensive, integrated theory that is empirically derived. Marshall and Barbaree (1990) describe such an integrated theory, which brings together psychological, biological, and sociological factors. What existing literature on sex offenders does reveal is that the population of child molesters is heterogenous as to the offender's motivations and the types of sexual behaviors they engage in with children.

Knight, Carter, and Prentky (1989) have developed and tested a typology utilizing cases of 177 nonincestuous child molesters who were civilly committed to a treatment center for sexually dangerous persons. It is important to note that this typology is based on a selected population of child molesters who had been apprehended and convicted and consequently may not be applicable to those offenders in the community who have not been apprehended. These authors found that nonincestuous child molesters could be classified by both the offender's degree of fixation on children and the offender's behavior during the molestation. Histories allowed Knight and colleagues to divide offenders into six types representing a range of behaviors.

Historically, it was believed that those responsible for sexual abuse and assault in our society were adult males. Recent data indicate that sexual abuse and assault are perpetrated by adult females as well as males and by female adolescents as well as juvenile males.

As noted previously, Abel et al. (1988) found that of more than 400 adult sex offenders interviewed, 58% reported the onset of their deviant sexual interest pattern prior to age 18. Reports indicate that juveniles are responsible for 20% of reported rapes and that as many as 30% of cases of child sexual abuse may be perpetrated by juveniles. Over the past decade and a half there has been a tremendous growth in programs to treat juvenile offenders in the United States. While in 1982 only 20 programs had been identified nationally that treated juvenile offenders, by 1993 there were more than 800 specialized treatment programs for juvenile sex offenders in the United States (National Task Force on Juvenile Sex Offending, 1993). In 1986, a National Task Force on Juvenile Sex Offenders was created. That task force issued its first report in 1988 and a revised report was published in 1993 (National Task Force, 1993).

While there has been a tremendous increase in available clinical services for juvenile sex offenders, there has not been much in the way of controlled research on this population. Research indicates however that juvenile sex offenders show many of the same types of sexually abusive behaviors as do adults. As with adult offenders, a number of theories have been proposed to explain the etiology of sexually inappropriate behavior. There is however no generally accepted theory regarding juvenile sexual offending. A number of factors that have received empirical and clinical attention in the literature include maltreatment experiences, exposure to pornography, substance abuse, and exposure to aggressive role models (Hunter & Becker, 1994).

Very few scientific articles have addressed the topic of juvenile female sexual offenders. Fehrenbach & Monastersky (1988) reported on a sample of 28 juvenile female sexual offenders. They reported that 50% of this population had a history of having been sexually abused themselves and 20% had been physically abused. Hunter, Lexler, Goodwin, Browne, and Dennis (1993) reported on 10 severely psychosexually and emotionally disturbed female offenders in residential treatment. They report that the majority of these girls also had a history of maltreatment and sexual abuse. Recently, Matthews, Hunter, and Vuz (in press) compared 67 juvenile female sexual offenders with a sample of 70 juvenile male sexual offenders. These authors report that more of the female offenders than the males had been sexually abused (77.6% vs. 44.3%). Female offenders were abused at younger ages than male offenders. Female offenders had more perpetrators and physical abuse was more prevalent in the histories of female offenders than male offenders (60% vs. 44.9%).

Given the heterogeneity of both the adult as well as the juvenile sex offender population, more research is needed in the development of classification and typologies both for adult and juvenile offenders as well as those who are in residential and community-based settings.

There exists an extensive literature on parental or perpetrator characteristics of those who physically abuse children and the reader is referred to Milner (1991) and Milner & Chilamkurti (1991). In general, parental characteristics reflect heightened levels of dysfunction including depression and physical symptoms as well as distress. These families are also marked by inappropriate parenting strategies. The literature indicates that it has been estimated that about 30% of abused children become abusive parents (Kolko, 1996). Other factors that have been implicated include psychological or contextual factors associated with general aggressivity, gender, maternal depression, poverty, poor parenting skills, and stress (Kolko, 1996). Certain personality and psychiatric disturbances including hostile personality, depression, and substance abuse have been implicated in cases of child physical abuse. Famularo, Fenton, and Kinscherff (1992) report that current and past affective disorder, substance abuse, and posttraumatic stress are more common in abusive families than in control parents. Parents' cognitive style has also been implicated in that physical abusers evidence more negative cognitive attributional styles and see their children in a more negative light than nonabusive parents (Azar & Siegel, 1990). Kolko (1996) notes that "the psychological characteristics of abusive parents do not conform consistently to any specific traits or diagnostic profile beyond concerns related to their parenting role in stressful family circumstances.... The broad characteristics attributed to abusive families underscore the multidimensional nature of aggressive interactions" (p. 28).

Overview and Treatment/Intervention

Treatment for families in which physical abuse has occurred has typically focused on the abusive parents and failed to address the significant treatment needs of the children (Cohn & Daro, 1987; Graziano & Mills, 1992). Two comprehensive reviews of the literature on treatment intervention with abusive parents and their children documented that (a) the most typical treatment for children is therapeutic day care, and (b) more rigorous research designs and longer term follow-up of families are necessary (Oates & Bross, 1995; Wolfe & Wekerle, 1993). These reviews illustrate the significant lack of literature on treatment of school-age children and adolescents who have been physically abused.

Therapeutic interventions for children that are described in the literature are almost exclusively on abused infants and preschool children. Treatment for abused infants has focused on increasing the parents' or caretakers' knowledge about child development, improving the parent-child relationship, and promoting the child's progress and overall development. Studies have documented the effectiveness of visual prompts for increasing mother-baby stimulation in at-risk and abusive single mothers (Lutzker, Lutzker, Braunling-McMarrow, & Eddleman, 1987). Abused preschoolers are typically involved in therapeutic day care programs (Oates & Bross, 1995). In some programs, the therapeutic day care is one component of a family preservation program providing comprehensive, family-centered services to prevent out-of-home placement or to facilitate reunification (Ayoub, 1991). These programs focus on providing a safe, nurturing environment to improve psychosocial development (Ayoub, 1991) and on increasing stimulation to facilitate the child's language, motor, social-emotional, and cognitive development (Culp, Little, Letts, & Lawrence, 1991). Research indicates that therapeutic day care programs have resulted in positive development outcomes (e.g., Wolfe & Wekerle, 1993).

Other approaches with infants and young children emphasize the importance of addressing insecure attachment relationships in abused children (Cicchetti, Toth, & Bush, 1988). Programs addressing attachment help parents develop more positive parent-child interactions and address the relationships that the parent had with their own parents and the ways in which they were reared (Guidano & Liotti, 1983; Hunter & Kilstrom, 1979).

Abused toddlers and preschool children, as with infants, may show developmental delays and disturbed parent-child relationships. Treatment with these young children focuses on direct interventions with the child for behavioral or affective difficulties and on the parent-child relationship. Parent-Child Interaction Therapy (PCIT), a program designed to treat behavioral problems in young children and modify dysfunctional parent-child interactions, has documented significant improvements in children's oppositional behavior, parental stress, parent report of activity level, child internalizing problems, and child self-esteem in a sample of families with a high proportion of single mothers (55%) and families on welfare (35%) (Eisenstadt [Hembree-Kigin], Eyberg, McNeil, Newcomb, & Funderburk, 1993). Although few empirical treatment outcome studies with predominantly physically abused children can be found in the literature, techniques such as cognitive-control therapy (Santostefano, 1985), modeling (Howes & Espinosa, 1985), cognitive-behavioral approaches (Leahy, 1988), play therapy (e.g., Gil, 1991), social-skills training (Kelly & Hansen, 1987), and treatment from an object-relations approach (Seinfeld, 1989) have been utilized with this population for a comprehensive review, see Bonner et al., 1992).

A recent study randomly assigned physically abused school-age children and their parents to either individual child and parent cognitive-behavioral treatment (CBT) or family therapy (FT) and assessed high-risk indicators and treatment progress from the participants' perspective on a weekly basis over 12 sessions (Kolko, 1996). Utilizing treatment manuals and sessions conducted both in the clinic and at home, the results indicated wide variation in response to treatment, with continuing high levels of physical discipline, parental anger, and family problems. However, CBT children and parents reported lower levels of parental anger and less use of physical discipline/force than FT parents. The study emphasizes the importance of regular monitoring of progress during treatment and suggests that results may be improved by increasing the duration and comprehensiveness of the treatment interventions (Kolko, 1996).

To date, there is a significant amount of literature regarding the effects of physical abuse on children and adolescents. However, the literature on effective interventions to ameliorate these effects in children of different ages is markedly lacking. Effective therapeutic interventions with physically abused school-age children and adolescents are areas in particular need of additional research.

Treatment of Sexually Abused Children

Treatment interventions for sexually abused children have received significantly more attention over the past 10 years than those for physically abused children. Numerous books and articles describing treatment models and approaches with sexually abused children have been published (e.g., Berliner, 1991; Friedrich, 1990, 1991; Gagliano, 1987; Keller, Cicchinelli, & Gardner, 1989). These include the use of play therapy (Gil, 1991; Jones, 1986; Kelly, 1995), self-esteem exercises (Corder, Haizlip, & DeBoer, 1990), drama therapy (McCay, Gold, & Gold, 1987), guided written disclosure exercises (DeYoung & Corbin, 1994), family therapy, (e.g., Monck et al., 1994), pharmacological interventions (Famularo, Kinscherff, & Fenton, 1988), and cognitive-behavioral techniques (Deblinger, McLeer, & Henry, 1990) among others. In contrast to treatment for physically abused children, research studies on treatment outcome with sexually abused children of different ages have been conducted.

A 1995 comprehensive review of 29 research studies on treatment outcome documented that sexually abused children improve with treatment (Finkelhor & Berliner, 1995). The review had several other interesting findings including (a) only 5 of 29 studies could document that the child's recovery was not due simply to the passage of time or some other variable outside of therapy; (b) certain behaviors, such as aggressiveness and sexualized behaviors are quite resistant to change; and (c) the possible existence of significant "sleeper" effects (symptoms that may not emerge until many years later). Longitudinal studies have shown that as a group, sexually abused children improve over time whether they are in treatment or not (Gomes-Schwartz, Horowitz, Cardarelli, & Sauzier, 1990; Runyan, Everson, Edelsohn, Hunter, & Coulter, 1988). Finkelhor & Berliner (1995) noted the need for more outcome research based on the increasing requirements for accountability by the health-care system.

The current literature on child sexual abuse victims indicates that many children and adolescents are receiving treatment (Friedrich, 1991; Friedrich, Jaworski, Berliner, & James, 1994). A survey of treatment practices in child sexual abuse found that most therapists have a master's degree (MSW/MA); agree that family reunification should not be a routine goal of treatment; and think that clinicians should have broad-based clinical skills, training in child development, an understanding of offender treatment, and a goal-oriented approach to treat-

ment (Friedrich et al., 1994). The respondents did not reach consensus on such issues as the degree to which the abuse needs to be focused on in treatment; whether individual or group therapy was the preferred modality for treatment; or a preferred treatment approach, even though the literature has indicated the effectiveness of cognitive-behavioral therapy for treating PTSD and other symptoms in school-age children and adolescents (e.g., Cohen & Mannarino, 1996; Deblinger et al., 1990; Stauffer & Deblinger, 1996). As the survey utilized an available rather than a randomly selected sample, the authors clearly stated its limitations and made recommendation for future research. In spite of these caveats, the results indicated the professional interest in and current lack of consensus in treating victims of sexual abuse. It is also interesting to note that no such surveys have been conducted in other areas of child maltreatment.

Although it may appear that there is adequate literature on treating sexually abused children, a more careful review indicates that the empirical evaluation of treatment effectiveness is in the beginning stages. While few studies have sound methodology, (i.e., random assignment, outcome measures, and control groups), there are some studies with adequate methodology utilizing group treatment approaches and a few well-designed case studies and reports of individual treatment with larger groups of children. However, few of these studies utilize control groups, most likely due to the ethical considerations of withholding or delaying treatment for these children.

Currently, studies using abuse-specific treatment have shown their effectiveness when compared to no-treatment control groups (Finkelhor & Berliner, 1995) and nondirective supportive therapy (Cohen & Mannarino, 1996) (see following section on treatment prescriptions for additional information on abuse-specific treatment). It is important to note that studies conducted from 1986 to 1995 utilizing psychodynamic approaches; nondirective supportive therapy; family therapy only; drama therapy; or mixed unspecified interventions, have not shown significant improvements in children's symptomatology (Finkelhor & Berliner, 1995).

In an early case study, Becker, Skinner, and Abel (1982) trained a 4-year-old girl's mother to utilize behavior modification techniques to reduce the child's symptoms of decreased eating, phobic behavior, self-injurious behavior, and statements about her father and paternal grandfather. Techniques used were positive reinforcement for eating, ignoring the phobic and self-injurious behaviors unless serious injury resulted, and ignoring the child's statements about her father and grandfather. The family members responded and listened to her when she commented about the abuse but did not initiate conversations with her. Improvements were shown in the target behaviors, although an upcoming visitation with the paternal grandmother resulted in a worsening of symptoms for a period of time.

A case study reported by Kolko 91989) documented the effective use of social-cognitive—skills training with an 11-year-old boy with an extensive history of sexual abuse and neglect. The boy was hospitalized after he had inappropriate sexual contact with a 6-year-old girl. The target behaviors for treatment were clear voice quality, consistent eye contact, conversation skills, and expressive physical gestures. The boy practiced his responses through role playing several social situations with confederates and received feedback about his performance. He was rated in individual therapy sessions, on the hospital unit twice a day, and a 1-year follow-up was conducted. The initial and 1-year results indicated acquisition and maintenance across all target behaviors.

A more recent study provided individual therapy to children age 3 to 16 and their nonoffending caretakers, utilizing cognitive-behavioral techniques to reduce the children's Post-Traumatic Stress Disorder (PTSD) symptoms (Debliner et al., 1990). Objective assessments were administered to the child at baseline, just before therapy, and post-treatment. Over the 12 child sessions, the therapists employed gradual exposure to abuse-related memories, thoughts, and discussion; training in coping skills (e.g., relaxation and anger management); sexual abuse education; and prevention-skills training. An educational approach was used with the caretakers, providing information on the consequences of

sexual abuse, training in behavior-management skills, and instruction in parent-child communication and in modeling adaptive coping behavior for the child. The results at post-treatment showed significant reductions in the children's symptoms of PTSD, depression, and general anxiety.

Two approaches to individual treatment for preschool-age children and their parents, abuse-specific/cognitive-behavioral therapy (CBT) and nondirective supportive treatment (NST), were assessed by Cohen and Mannarino (1996). Sixty-seven children and parents were randomly assigned to treatment that consisted of 12 individual sessions for both the child and parent. The study utilized standardized instruments, treatment manuals, and intensive training and supervision. At the end of treatment, the abuse-specific CBT group showed highly significant improvement of symptoms on most outcome measures, whereas the NST group had no significant changes in symptomatology. The authors concluded that the findings offered strong preliminary evidence that a specific cognitive-behavioral treatment model is effective with sexually abused children and their parents.

Group therapy is the most frequently described approach to treatment in the literature (e.g., Berman, 1990; Corder, Haizlip, & DeBoer, 1990; Friedrich, Luecke, Beilke, & Place, 1992; Hiebert-Murphy, DeLuca, & Runtz, 1992; Kweller, & Ray, 1992; Steward, Farguar, Dichary, Glick, & Martin, 1986). The groups typically are described as providing education and support, and are time limited.

The group addresses topics such as sex education; prevention of reabuse; the child's feelings about the abuse, the offender, and other family members; information to correct the child's views of the abuse; and court preparation. In more recent descriptions, concurrent parent groups addressing similar topics are utilized (e.g., Cohen & Mannarino, 1996).

The majority of treatment outcome studies with sexually abused children and adolescents are of group treatment approaches comparing pre- and post-treatment measures of symptoms. Some of the studies have used a control group (e.g., Oates, Bross, 1995) while others have not (e.g., Lindon &

Nourse, 1994). In a study that combined group treatments, individual therapy, family therapy, and parent training with 33 4- to 16-year-old sexually abused boys, the results indicated a decrease in behavior problems, maternal depression, sibling behavior problems, and improvement in maternal social support and family functioning (Friedrich, Luecke, Bielke, & Place, 1992). The group therapy utilized structured activities focusing on personal safety, social interactions, disclosure of feelings, and sharing of sexual abuse experiences, followed by a period of play and informal discussion. However, the forms of treatment varied from child to child making it difficult to assess the relative effectiveness of each intervention.

A more rigorously designed study assessed the effectiveness of cognitive-behavioral groups for nonoffending mothers and their sexually abused children ages 2 to 6 (Stauffer & Deblinger, 1996). The study utilized standardized assessment of parents' distress level and parental reports of children's behavioral functioning at initial contact, pre-treatment, post-treatment, and a 3-month follow-up. The parents' sessions focused on assisting the parents to cope with their reactions to their children's abuse, teaching them behavior-management skills, and educating them to communicate with the children about the abuse and healthy sexuality issues. The children's group intervention used cognitive-behavioral techniques to manage the children's behavior and develop their skills in communicating, body safety, and coping with their feelings. The results indicated significant decreases in the children's sexual behaviors and in parental distress that were maintained at follow-up.

In summary, some promising approaches to treat the sequelae of child physical and sexual abuse are being developed and empirically evaluated for treatment effectiveness, particularly in the area of child sexual abuse. As this is a developing field of clinical interventions, it is recommended that clinicians (a) utilize as wide a variety of techniques as are necessary to address a child's treatment needs, (b) select approaches that are appropriate for the child's level of developmental and cognitive functioning, and (c) employ techniques that have been found effective in alleviating the child's symptoms (Bonner et al.,

1992; for additional reading on treatment, see Chaffin, Bonner, Worley, & Lawson, 1996; Friedrich, 1996).

Treatment of Perpetrators of Sexual or Physical Abuse

Ideally in evaluating the efficacy of treatment for sex offenders, one would like to employ methodology that involves random assignment to experimental and control conditions. However, given that these individuals represent a risk to the community, ethically it is questionable to assign sex offenders who are being treated in a community setting to treatment or no treatment control conditions. Consequently, the review of the literature reveals a paucity of control therapy outcome studies on the effectiveness of treatment for both adult and juvenile sex offenders. Some have argued that there is insufficient evidence to prove the effectiveness of treatment for child molesters (Furby, Weinrott, & Blackshaw, 1989), while others report that the situation is much more optimistic (Marshall & Pithers, 1994; Hall, 1995).

The majority of individuals who molest children come to treatment because they have been referred to treatment by the criminal or juvenile justice system. Only a small number of child molesters voluntarily seek treatment. Child molesters may be referred as part of a pretrial diversion program that includes treatment or following a finding of guilty at a trial or through a plea bargain. Some offenders may receive treatment while incarcerated, others might receive treatment while placed on probation in the community. Treatment of adolescent and adult sexual offenders should be highly structured. Given that the safety of the community needs to be taken into consideration, it is important that treatment be coordinated and that good relationships exist between the treatment provider and those individuals who will be providing monitoring of the perpetrator if he or she is being treated within the community.

It is critical that comprehensive assessments be conducted and that a treatment plan be based on the needs of each offender as determined by the assessment. Treatment modalities that have been described in the literature include individual and group cognitive-behavior therapies, psychoeducational interventions, family therapy, psychopharmacologic therapies and relapse prevention.

A treatment model that has gained in popularity over the years is a relapse-prevention model. Relapse prevention is a treatment model based on the premise that precursors to sexual abuse can be identified and used in treatment to enhance an abuser's self-management skills and supervision. Relapse prevention involves two dimensions. The first is an internal self-management dimension that is used to enhance the client's self-control, and the second is an external supervisory dimension employed by the therapist and community members who monitor the abuser's behavior. This model can be employed with children who have sexual behavior problems, adolescent sexual abusers, and adult offenders (Pithers, Becker, Kafka, Morenz, Schlank, & Leombruno, 1995). The relapse-prevention model involves teaching the patient or client to recognize the chain of precursive events involved in the relapse process. Patients are taught to identify "warning signals." They are then taught how to cope with these elements. Specific modalities that are used can include stimulus-control procedures, for example, removing from the person's environment stimuli that may serve as a precursor, teaching avoidance strategies and teaching escape strategies. It is also important to teach specific coping skills to the client or patient.

SPECIFIC INTERVENTION METHODS

Physical Abuse

There have been numerous types of interventions utilized to address the problems in physically abusive families and to reduce the chances that reabuse will occur. These include child-focused approaches (e.g., Mannarino & Cohen, 1990); home-based treatment services (e.g., Amundson, 1989; Whittaker, Kinney, Tracy, & Booth, 1990); parent-focused behavioral treatment programs (e.g., Wolfe, 1994); and comprehensive, multiservice programs (e.g., Ayoub & Willett, 1992; Brunk, Henggeler, & Whelan, 1987). A review of the current literature indicates that parent-focused behavioral programs are one of the most common interventions with physically abusive families (Kolko, 1996; Wolfe & Wekerie, 1993).

An approach that focuses on improving the parent-child relationship, Parent-Child Interaction Therapy (PCIT), is currently being implemented with physically abusive families. The PCT program has an intensive positive training component, involves both the parent and child in the treatment sessions, utilizes live coaching by the therapist, and provides a means to change the dysfunctional parent-child relationship (Eyberg & Robinson, 1982). In an excellent conceptual article, Urquiza and McNeil (1996) describe PCIT and its potential application with this population. While noting the limitations of PCIT with physically abusive families, the authors assert that by increasing the positive parent-child interaction through PCIT, several aspects of the relationship can be effected, that is, reducing negative parental affect, increasing the child's positive affect and compliance, reducing parental stress, and reducing parental physical aggression. The effectiveness of PCIT in improving the parent-child relationship and in decreasing children's disruptive and noncompliant behavior is well documented (Hembree-Kigin & McNeil, 1995).

PCIT is conducted in two major phases, with pre- and post-treatment assessment sessions. Phase 1 is the Child-Directed Interaction (CDI) and focuses on enhancing the parent-child relationship. Phase 2 is the Parent-Directed Interaction (PDI) and focuses on discipline. The typical course of treatment takes from 8 to 12 sessions. Each of the treatment phases begins with initial didactic training followed by the therapist coaching the parent in sessions with the child. The parent wears a "bug-in-the-ear" device and the therapist coaches from an observation room. During each phase the parents are taught and then practice specific ways to communicate with and manage their child's behavior. The following list is a typical course of treatment

• Pretreatment assessment of child and family functioning and feedback (1–2 sessions)
• Child-Directed Interaction
  Teaching behavioral play therapy skills (1 session)

Conducting behavioral play therapy skills (2–4 sessions)
- Parent Directed Interaction
Teaching discipline skills (1 session)
Coaching discipline skills (4 6 sessions)
- Post-treatment assessment of child and family functioning and feedback (1–2 sessions)
- Booster sessions (as needed)

Child Directed Interaction (CDI) is usually conducted for seven sessions in which the parents are instructed to play with their child while being coached. During this phase parents are taught to follow their child's lead in play and to avoid criticizing or directing the child. They are told to describe and imitate the child's play, praise the child for appropriate behavior, and reflect the child's communication. The therapist prompts and gives the parent specific statements to make to the child during the play sessions through the ear device. The primary objective of the CDI phase is to establish or strengthen a warm, positive, rewarding relationship between the parent and child (Eyberg, 1988; Hembree-Kigin & McNeil, 1995). This relationship must be established before moving to Phase 2 of the treatment program.

The Parent Directed Interaction (PDI) follows the CDI phase and usually lasts seven sessions. The major objective of this phase is to teach the parents specific and effective skills for managing their child's behavior. During this phase the parents learn and practice the use of clear, positively stated, direct instructions and consistent consequences for behavior (i.e., the child is consistently praised for complying with the instructions or placed in a time out chair for not complying). The parents practice implementing the consequences under the therapist's direction in the sessions with their child (for complete, step-by-step directions on implementing PCIT, see Hembree-Kigin & McNeil, 1995).

Case Example

PCIT was utilized with a parent and her child referred for physical abuse. Donald S., a 4-year-old boy, was observed in day care to have numerous bruises and welts on his lower legs. When questioned, he stated, "Mama hits me with the belt, I hit her back." The day care staff had previously discussed Donald's repeated aggressive behavior with his mother. A report of suspected abuse was made by the day care staff to Child Protective Services (CPS).

Donald and his mother were referred by CPS to a child guidance clinic that utilized PCIT. During the pre-treatment assessment, Ms. S. said her son was highly aggressive, active, and noncompliant. She reported that Donald had not had contact with his father since he was 3 months old. She described Donald as a quiet, lovable baby who slept well and rarely cried. She reported that he was frequently ill during his first year with 10 trips to the emergency room due to vomiting, diarrhea, and colds. while his physical development appeared within normal limits, his language development was described as "slow." His current vocabulary was limited and he did not comprehend conversation as well as his peers. These observations were verified by the day care personnel.

Ms. S. stated that Donald would not mind her and often hit and threw things at her. She reported that she spanked him with "a belt or whatever was handy," frequently using a belt, fly swatter, or cord from a coffee pot. On "good days," Donald would have up to three spankings and on "bad days," he could be spanked up to five times. Ms. S. appeared unconcerned about the bruises and stated that the spankings were necessary even though she stated that ignoring Donald "worked best."

During the assessment session in which Donald was to lead the play, he was unable to engage his mother in playing a game with him. He then had a tantrum, cried, threw objects at his mother, and refused to follow her instructions to clean up the playroom. Ms. S. eventually picked up a stick from play set and tapped and poked Donald on the shoulders, buttocks, and legs to get him to pick up the toys.

Ms. S. and Donald were seen for 16 sessions followed by monthly booster sessions for 6 months. The four extra CDI sessions were utilized to strengthen the parent-child relationship before moving to the discipline phase of treatment and the booster sessions were added to monitor progress and recidivism. Although Ms. S. was initially resistant to the treatment approach, stating, "This stuff won't work with Donald," she eventually became quite interested in the program and reported that it also worked well with her two-year-old daughter.

Based on pre- and post-testing, the following results were noted at the end of treatment: (a) Donald's compliance had significantly increased; (b) his aggressive and tantrum behavior had decreased significantly at home and in day care; and (c) Donald showed increases in self-esteem, attention span, and expressive language over the course of treatment. Ms. S. replaced spanking with the time out chair, stating, "Well, it takes more time than a spanking, but Donald minds me better because he doesn't want to go to time out." Child Protective Services monitored Ms. S. and Donald's progress in the program. Due to Donald"s progress and the lack of further physical abuse, the case was closed at the end of one year.

Sexual Behavior Problems

One of the documented sequelae of child sexual abuse is increased sexual behavior. Studies have consistently found higher rates of sexual behavior in children who have been sexually abused than in nonabused, neglected, physically abused, or psychiatrically disturbed.children (e.g., Friedrich et al., 1992; Kolko, Moser, & Weldy, 1988). The Child Sexual Behavior Inventory (CSBI) was developed by Friedrich and his colleagues to assess the degree of sexual behavior evidenced by children. Data from the general population indicate that some sexual behaviors, such as children touching their private parts at home and undressing in front of others, are common in children. More explicit sexual behaviors, however, are quite rare. For example, inserting objects into the anus or vagina and oral-genital contact were reported by only 1% of the parents.

Various treatment approaches for children with sexual behavior problems have been described in the literature (e.g., Ballester & Pierre, 1995; Cunningham & MacFarlane, 1991, 1996; Gil & Johnson, 1993; Johnson, 1991). The treatment generally focuses on issues such as reducing the child's inappropriate sexual behavior, dealing with the child's own abuse issues, and family problems. Specific topics may include sex education, impulse

control, social skills, empathy, and factors related to the inappropriate sexual behavior such as denial, taking responsibility, and identifying risk factors. The necessity of focusing specifically on the inappropriate sexual behavior is indicated by research showing that sexualized behaviors do not decrease when children are seen in conventional abuse-focused therapy (Finkelhor & Berliner, 1995).

Currently, there are no empirical studies to document the effectiveness of different interventions with this population of children, although two federally funded studies are nearing completion (Bonner, Walker, & Berliner, 1995; Gray & Pithers, 1995). Each of these studies is comparing two approaches to treatment, is utilizing standardized assessment instruments, and will have 2-year follow-up data on the participants. The studies are particularly noteworthy in that they are federally funded (National Center on Child Abuse and Neglect, U.S. Department of Health and Human Services) and that they were initiated very early in the development of clinical interventions for this particular behavior problem with children. As a comparison, no such studies have been conducted on treatment for adolescent sex offenders, for whom treatment has been provided for the past 15 to 20 years.

One method of intervention for children with sexual behavior problems that is currently being empirically evaluated is a cognitive-behavioral group-therapy approach for children ages 6 to 12, and their caretakers (Bonner et al., 1995). The treatment program consists of 12 1-hour group sessions for both the children and their parents or caregivers. The primary focus of treatment is to reduce the children's inappropriate sexual behavior. It is a highly structured approach in which the therapists are active and directive. Boys and girls from ages 6 to 12 participate in groups together. In this approach, the children's inappropriate sexual behavior is addressed immediately in the first session. After initial introductions and rapport building, the children are told they are in the group because they broke a Sexual Behavior Rule and that they will learn how not to break the rules in the future.

The components of the program include learning and applying the Sexual Behavioral Rule (see Table 12.1), sex education, improving impulse control

TABLE 12.1.

CHILDREN'S GROUP	PARENT'S GROUP
Session 1 Introductions	Introductions
Introduce: Group Process 　　　　　Describe Activities 　　　　　Group Rules Assessment	Introduce: Group Rules 　　　　　Group Purpose 　　　　　Group Format
Session 2 Introductions	Introductions
Review:　Purpose of Group Introduce: Sexual Behavior Rules (SBR) 　　　　　Private Parts 　　　　　Applying SBR Assessment	Introduce: Sexual Behavior 　　　　　Parental Expectations 　　　　　Discussing Feelings
Session 3 Review:　Group Purpose 　　　　Private Parts 　　　　SBR Introduce: Discussing Feelings Assessment	Introduce: Rules in Your House 　　　　　Supervision Guidelines
Session 4 Review:　SBR 　　　　Group Purpose 　　　　Discussing Feelings Introduce: Disclosure Assessment	Introduce: Turtle Techniques 　　　　　Expected Sexual Behavior in Children
Session 5 Review:　SBR 　　　　Turtle Technique 　　　　Disclosure Assessment	Introduce: Developmentally Expected Sexual 　　　　　Behavior
Session 6 Review:　SBR 　　　　Turtle Technique 　　　　Disclosure Assessment	Introduce: Behavior Management 　　　　　Techniques
Session 7 Review:　Turtle Technique Assessment	Introduce: Managing Sexual Misbehavior
Session 8 Introduce: Sex Education 　　　　　Talking about Sex Review:　Private Parts Assessment	Introduce: Sex Education 　　　　　Abuse Prevention
Session 9 Review:　Turtle Technique Assessment	Introduce: Talking with your Child about Sex
Session 10 Review:　Private Parts Introduce: Abuse Prevention Assessment	Review:　Materials from Previous Sessions Introduce: Open Discussion

TABLE 12.1., continued

CHILDREN'S GROUP	PARENT'S GROUP
Session 10	
Review: Private Parts	Review: Materials from Previous Sessions
Introduce: Abuse Prevention	Introduce: Open Discussion
Assessment	
Session 11	
Review: Private Parts	Individual Meetings with Therapists to Receive
SBR	Information on Child's Progress and Make
Turtle Technique	Recommendations
Session 12	
Saying Goodbye	Post-Assessment Session for Parents to
	Complete Instructions

(Turtle Technique), discussing feelings, and prevention of abuse. Due to the time-limited treatment (12 sessions), the most relevant concepts were selected to be introduced, repeated, and reinforced. At the end of each session, a five-item assessment of knowledge is administered to determine if the children are learning the didactic content.

The parents' sessions also use a cognitive-behavioral approach in which the therapists take an active role. The topics from the children's group are generally introduced a week earlier to the parents in order to prepare them to assist their children. The parents are introduced to the Sexual Behavior Rules (SBR), the Turtle Technique (used to increase impulse control), sex education materials, and ways to prevent abuse. In addition, the sessions include discussions of developmentally expected sexual behavior in children, family rules regarding sexual behavior, supervision of children with sexual behavior problems, behavior management, and talking with children about sexuality.

Assessment

Mrs. L. was referred by Child Protective Services to the Children with Sexual Behavior Problems Program with Jennifer, her 11-year-old foster child. Jennifer had been removed from her mother's custody after she was physically and sexually abused by her stepfather. He pled guilty and was currently in prison. Jennifer had evidenced numerous inappropriate sexual behaviors at home and at school. These included touching classmates on the buttocks

frequently; exposing her genitals at school one to two times a week; sexually stimulating herself daily by rubbing Mrs. L.'s cat against her genitals; attempting to have a dog copulate with her; masturbating frequently and actively, causing her bed to rock and make noise during the night; and going through Mrs. L.'s cabinets and other people's trash looking for feminine hygiene materials. Jennifer had been suspended from school for her inappropriate sexual behavior and was attending a specialized Day Treatment program.

Jennifer's assessment revealed that she was in the average range of intelligence, had significant externalizing behavior problems, and was creating a great deal of stress for her foster mother. She demonstrated inappropriate sexual behavior during the assessment, one of only a few children who did so. She was observed putting her hand down the front of her pants and stimulating herself and lying on her stomach on a divan with her hand in the genital area and moving her hips up and down. Her initial diagnoses were Separation Anxiety, Functional Enuresis and Encopresis, Oppositional Disorder, and PTSD. Jennifer reported being afraid that "my mother will die before I get to live with her again."

Mrs. L. further reported that Jennifer appeared unable to control her inappropriate behavior and that she gained attention from others in a very negative manner. Numerous problems were reported in the Day Treatment setting, including lying, not paying attention, disobeying the teacher, not completing her work, being noisy in class, and being aggressive with other students. Due to the nature and extent of

Jennifer's problems, she was referred for individual therapy, and for an evaluation for attention deficit disorder. ADHD was diagnosed and Jennifer was placed on Ritalin. Her ability to attend and concentrate improved and her aggressive behavior decreased over time.

Jennifer and Mrs. L. attended all 12 treatment sessions. Jennifer participated in the group but continued to have problems with distracting behavior, not waiting her turn to speak, and making inappropriate noises. However, by the seventh session, Jennifer's behavior had improved significantly. Over the course of treatment, she learned the Sexual Behavior Rules, acknowledged the rules that she had broken, demonstrated the steps of the Turtle Technique, and understood the steps to prevent further abuse.

At the end of treatment, Mrs. L. reported a significant decrease in Jennifer's inappropriate sexual behavior. There had been no reports of sexual behavior problems at school for 10 weeks and her masturbatory behavior was less frequent and confined to her room. Jennifer continued to be seen individually for issues related to her abuse and other behavioral problems, which also improved over time. Approximately 10 months after she completed treatment, Jennifer was returned to her mother's custody in a city two hours away. She has since been lost to follow-up.

Case Example of an Adolescent

Billy is a 15-year-old Caucasian male who was referred for an evaluation by the juvenile court. Billy had been arrested for sexually abusing four children for whom he was babysitting. Two of the victims were female, two of the victims were male. They ranged from 5 to 7 years of age. The sexual behavior consisted of Billy rubbing his penis against their genitals and having them perform oral sex on him. Billy is residing in a single family home. His mother is employed at a local telephone company. His parents divorced when he was 7 years of age. His father moved out of state and has remarried and other than receiving a birthday and Christmas card from his father, he has not seen him since the divorce. Billy is an only child. His mother reported

that she had no difficulty when she was pregnant with Billy, that he was a normal birth and met the appropriate developmental milestones. His mother did report that he was molested by an older male when he was approximately 6 years of age. Billy's mother reported that apparently the abuse had been going on for a period of 1 year and Billy had not disclosed the abuse because his perpetrator had threatened that he would harm both Billy and his mother were he to report it to anyone. The abuse became known to the mother when Billy experienced a change in his behavior. He became enuretic and encopretic and became quite "clingy" and did not want to be out of sight of his mother.

Billy was described by his mother as being a somewhat shy child who found making friends difficult and who in general could be considered a loner. She reported that rarely did other children invite him to come play with them or did he invite children to come to his home. She reported that he was an average student and other than having molested children, he had not engaged in any other behavior that would be considered illegal or for which he was arrested.

During the initial interview, Billy sat with his head down and appeared to be quite ashamed and embarrassed about the behavior that he had been arrested for. He acknowledged that he first developed fantasies about molesting little children when he entered puberty. He reported that his fantasies involved both little boys and little girls and that he would masturbate to these fantasies. He reported that while on occasion he had fantasies about girls his own age, that he found it difficult to initiate conversation with a female peer and that in general he was shunned by his peers at school. A comprehensive sexual history was taken and Billy denied ever having fantasies or engaging in any other form of paraphiliac behavior. He reported that he liked being in the company of younger children because they seemed to accept him and it was easy for him to communicate with them. He stated that he enjoyed babysitting because he liked being around little children and they looked up to him. While Billy knew that the behavior that he engaged in was inappropriate, he reported that he had difficulty stopping himself from engaging in the behavior. when he was asked if he felt that he was at risk to engage in the behavior in the future, he reluctantly acknowledged that he would have difficulty not being sexual with children if he was left alone in their presence.

Billy reported that he was an average student, that he liked school, but that sometimes he had difficulty concentrating. He reported that he was angry that his peers taunted him and that he did not have any friends in school. He reported that when he was not baby sitting he spent most of his time watching television. He indicated that the four children that he had molested he had engaged in sexual activity with each one of them over 30 times each. He reported that he was able to engage the children in sexual behavior with him initially by telling them that it was a game. He also told the children to keep them silent that if they were to tell anybody about the behavior that they would get in trouble for going along with it.

Billy reported that on occasion he had flashbacks of his own victimization and on occasion also had "bad dreams" about somebody harming him. He acknowledged that he felt badly about what he had done because "he had been caught" and that his mother was upset with him because of what he had done. Further evaluation indicated that Billy had some of the signs and symptoms of PTSD in relation to his own victimization. It was also apparent that he had a sexual arousal pattern not only to female peers but also to prepubescent male and female children. Billy acknowledged that this behavior was a problem and indicated that he would be willing to enter into treatment.

The results of the assessment indicated that Billy had an early history of having been sexually abused himself and because he had been threatened not to disclose the abuse, did not reveal his own abuse until he had been apprehended for sexually molesting young boys and girls. The evaluation also indicated that he was sexually aroused by prepubescent children. Because Billy had been bullied and taunted by his peers, he tended to avoid interacting with his peers and appeared to lack the necessary age-appropriate peer interactional skills. While Billy knew that the behavior he had engaged in was inappropriate, he really did not have an appreciation for why the behavior was inappropriate and appeared to

be lacking in empathy for his victims. Billy's mom was supportive of him receiving therapy and agreed with the treatment staff that Billy would benefit from placement in a residential treatment center where he could receive intensive treatment with other youth who had similar sexual behavior problems. Billy was admitted to a residential treatment center for youthful sexual offenders where he received both individual therapy, specialty group therapy, and family therapy. The following is a description of the treatment that he received.

The residential treatment program consisted of three phases of treatment. Before progressing from Phase I to Phase II the adolescent had to have successfully completed the specialty treatment groups and made progress in individual and family therapy. Phase I of treatment consisted of individual therapy, family therapy, and the youth participated in a social skills group, a sex education group, and a values clarification group. He also met as part of a process group on the unit. Billy was in the residential treatment school during the morning and until 2:30 in the afternoon, at which time he then received his individual therapy and participated in other groups. Upon completion of Phase I of treatment he moved on to Phase II of treatment. During Phase II he continued his individual and family therapy and continued to participate in the process group. He also participated in a specialty group in which his beliefs (cognitive distortions) about his behavior were explored and confronted. Also during Phase II of treatment he participated in a group that taught him the precursors and consequences to engaging in sexually inappropriate behavior. Upon successful completion of Phase II, he moved into the third phase of treatment while continuing in his individual and family therapy. During Phase III of treatment, Billy participated in an empathy group and a relapse prevention group. Pre- and post-tests, either written or behavioral, were given prior to Billy's moving from one phase of treatment to another. During Phase III of his treatment Billy was given passes to go home, initially to spend a day at home, then a day and an evening, and finally a weekend at home. This "stepping down" process enabled his mother to report back to the treatment staff about how he was doing and also allowed Billy to discuss with the treatment staff any issues or difficulties that he had encountered while in the community.

Billy was discharged from the treatment program, returned to his home and to his community. He continued to receive outpatient therapy and to be monitored by the probation department. His adjustment back to the community went well and to our knowledge there have been no further reports of inappropriate sexual behavior. Billy has been able to develop relationships with his peers and is becoming in his words, "just one of the guys."

CONCLUSION

This chapter has reviewed the studies and clinical reports conducted to date on both child victims of physical and sexual abuse as well as intervention for perpetrators. While a considerable amount of knowledge has been accrued, many questions remain to be answered. In the area of child physical abuse, Kolko (1996) lists the following salient issues to be addressed in future research. (1) Researchers need to investigate other related aspects of family and community violence in an attempt to understand the context of child physical abuse. (2) Those mental-health professionals who specialize in the area of child physical abuse need to know how to best deal with and confront perpetrator's denial of abuse allegations and their "disdain for the system." Longitudinal studies are needed to determine the long term effects of child physical maltreatment as may impact on children differently across developmental stages. Also, how does child physical maltreatment relate to the development of PTSD? (3) Obstacles to families involving themselves in therapy need to be addressed and solutions found to overcome those obstacles. (4) Clinical researchers need to evaluate the general impact of interventions and duration of gains made over time. (5) More research is needed on the development and evaluation of rigorous assessment instruments. (6) Further research should also focus on what role psychopharmacology may play in treating perpetrators of child maltreatment, as well as assisting victims in reducing the sequelae of child physical maltreatment.

Regarding the sexual abuse of children, Berliner and Elliott (1996) have noted that child sexual abuse

experiences not only can produce immediate difficulties but may constitute a significant risk factor for subsequent psychological, health, and life-functioning difficulties. Longitudinal perspective studies are needed so that child sexual abuse victims can be followed into adulthood in order to ascertain what life experiences may reduce sequelae and what life experiences may exacerbate the sequelae.

Major strides have been made in the treatment of both adult and adolescent sexual offenders. While there is no one treatment intervention or combination of interventions with proven 100% efficacy, treatment utilizing cognitive-behavioral interventions along with, in some cases, the use of psychopharmacologic intervention has proven effective. Further research is needed, however, to determine which interventions are most effective with which category of sexual offender. Also, long-term follow-up studies are needed to ascertain what factors increase the risk for recidivism and which diminish that risk.

Future research also needs to focus on identifying those youth at risk and those parents at risk for engaging in the abuse and maltreatment of children. Finally, as Haugaard et al. (1995) have noted, "One important way of reducing the number of children who experience abuse and neglect, and diminishing the harm caused by abuse and neglect is through education and training" (p. 78). These authors note that nonprofessionals and preprofessionals should be educated about child abuse and neglect issues.

Training should be provided both at an undergraduate and graduate level for psychologists about child abuse and neglect issues. Further work is needed on expanding interdisciplinary education and training on issues of abuse and neglect.

REFERENCES

Abel, G. G., Mittelman, M., Becker, J. V., Rathner, J., & Rouleau, J. L. (1988). Predicting child molesters' response to treatment. *Annals of the New York Academy of Science* (pp. 223–235). New York: New York Academy of Science.

Adams-Tucker, C. (1982). Proximate effects of sexual abuse in childhood: A report on 28 children. *American Journal of Psychiatry, 139,* 1252-1256.

American Psychological Association (1995). Psychological issues related to child maltreatment: Working group reports of the American Psychological Association coordinating committee on child abuse and neglect. *Journal of Clinical Child Psychology, 24,* 2–83.

Amundson, J. J. (1989). Family crisis care: A home-based intervention program for child abuse. *Issues in Mental Health Nursing, 10,* 285–296.

Ayoub, C. (1991). Physical violence and preschoolers: The use of therapeutic day care in the treatment of physically abused children and children from violent families. The *APSAC Advisor, 4*(4), 1–16.

Azar, S. T., & Seigel, B. R. (1990). Behavioral treatment of child abuse: A developmental perspective. *Behavior Modification, 14,* 279–300.

Ballester, S., & Pierre, F. (1995). Monster Therapy: The use of a metaphor in psychotherapy with abuse reactive children. In M. Hunter (Ed.), *Child survivors and perpetrators of sexual abuse* (pp. 125–146). Thousand Oaks, CA: Sage Publications.

Barahal, R. M., Waterman, J., & Martin, H. P. (1981). The social cognitive development of abused children. *Journal of Consulting and Clinical Psychology, 49,* 508–516.

Becker, J. V., Skinner, L. J., & Abel, G. G. (1982). Treatment of a four-year-old victim of incest. *American Journal of Family Therapy, 10,* 41–46.

Beitchman, J. H., Zucker, K. J., Hood, J. E., da Costa, G. A., & Akman, D. (1991). A review of the short-term effects of child sexual abuse. *Child Abuse and Neglect, 15,* 537–556.

Berliner, L. (1991). Therapy with victimized children and their families. *New Directions for Mental Health Services, 51,* 29–45.

Berliner, L., & Elliott, D. M. (1996). Sexual abuse of children. In J. Briere, L. Berliner, J. Bulkley, C. Jenny, & T. Reid (Eds.), *APSAC handbook of child maltreatment* (pp. 51–71). Thousand Oaks, CA: Sage Publications.

Berman, P. (1990). Group therapy techniques for sexually abused preteen girls. *Child Welfare, 69,* 239–252.

Black, M., Dubowitz, H., & Harrington, D. (1994). Sexual abuse: Developmental differences in children's behavior and self-perception. *Child Abuse and Neglect, 18,* 85–95.

Blumberg, J. (1981). Depression in abused and neglected children. *American Journal of Psychotherapy, 35,* 342–355.

Bonner, B., Kaufman, K., Harbeck, C., & Brassard, M. (1992). Child maltreatment. In C. E. Walker & M. C. Roberts (Eds.), *Handbook of clinical child psychology* (2nd ed., pp. 967- 1008). Mew York: Wiley.

Bonner, B. L., Walker, C. E., & Berliner, L. (1995). *Aggressive sexual behavior problems in young chil-*

dren. Presented at the 103rd Annual Convention of the American Psychological Association, New York, NY.

Bradford, J. (1990). The antiandrogen and hormonal treatment of sex offenders. In W. Marshall, D. Laws, & H. Barbaree (Eds.), *Handbook of sexual assault* (pp. 297–327). New York: Plenum Press.

Briere, J., Berliner, L., Bulkley, J. A., Jenny, C., & Reid, T. (1966). *The APSAC handbook on child maltreatment.* Thousand Oaks, CA: Sage Publications.

Browne, A., & Finkelhor, D. (1986). Impact of child sexual abuse: A review of the research. *Psychological Bulletin, 99,* 66–77.

Browne, K. D. (1996). The characteristics of young persons at the Glen Thorne Centre. *Youth Treatment Service Journal, 1,* 53–71.

Burgess, A. W., Hartman, C. R., McCausland, M. P. & Powers, P. (1984). Response patterns in children and adolescents exploited through sex rings and pornography. *American Journal of Psychiatry, 141,* 656–662.

Chaffin, J., Bonner, B. L., Worley, K. B., & Lawson, L. (1996). Treating abused adolescents. In J. Briere, L. Berliner, J. Bulkley, C. Jenny, & T. Reid (Eds.), *APSAC handbook of child maltreatment* (pp. 21–50). Newbury Park, CA: Sage Publications

Cohen, J. A., & Mannarino, A. P. (1966). A treatment outcome study for sexually abused preschool children. Initial findings *Journal of the American Academy of Child and Adolescent Psychiatry, 35,* 42–50.

Cicchetti, D., Toth, S., & Bush, M. (1988). Developmental psychopathology and incompetence in childhood: Suggestions for intervention. In B. B. Lahey & A. E. Kazdin (Eds.), *Advances in clinical child psychology* (pp. 1–71). New York: Plenum Press.

Cohn, A. H., & Daro, D. (1987). Is treatment too late? What ten years of evaluative research tell us. *Child Abuse and Neglect, 11,* 433–442.

Conte, J. R., & Berliner, L. (1988). The impact of sexual abuse on children: Empirical findings. In L. E. Walker (Ed.), *Handbook of sexual abuse of children* (pp. 72–93). New York: Springer.

Corder, B. F., Haizlip, T., & DeBoer, P. (1990). A pilot study for a structured, time-limited therapy group for sexually abused preadolescent children. *Child Abuse and Neglect, 14,* 243–251.

Crittenden, P. M., & Ainsworth, N. D. S. (1989). Child maltreatment and attachment theory. In D. Cicchetti & V. Carlson (Eds.), *Child maltreatment* (pp. 432-463). New York: Cambridge University Press.

Crouch, J. L., & Milner, J. S. (1993). Effects of child neglect on children. *Criminal Justice and Behavior, 20,* 49–65.

Culp, R. E., Little, V., Letts, D., & Lawrence, H. (1991). Maltreated children's self-concept: Effects of a comprehensive treatment program. *American Journal of Orthopsychiatry, 61,* 114–121.

Cunningham, C., & MacFarlane, K. (1991). *When children molest children.* Orwell, VT: Safer Society Press.

Deblinger, E., McLeer, S. V., & Henry, D. (1990). Cognitive behavioral treatment for sexually abused children suffering posttraumatic stress: Preliminary findings. *Journal of the American Academy of Child and Adolescent Psychiatry, 29,* 747–752.

DeYoung, J., & Corbin, B. (1994). Helping early adolescents tell: A guided exercise for trauma-focused sexual abuse treatment groups. *Child Welfare, 73,* 141–154.

Dodge, K. A., Bates, J. E., & Peltit, G. S. (1990). Mechanisms in the cycle of violence. *Science, 250,* 1678–1682.

Eisenstadt [Hembree-Kigin], T. H., Eyberg, S. M., McNeil, C. B., Newcomb, K., & Funderburk, B. (1993). Parent child interaction therapy with behavior problem children: Relative effectiveness of two stages and overall treatment outcome. *Journal of Clinical Child Psychology, 22,* 42–51.

Elwell, M. E., & Ephross, P. H. (1987). Initial reactions of sexually abused children. *Social Coursework, 68,* 109-116.

Eyberg, S. M. (1988). Parent-child interaction therapy: Integration of traditional and behavioral concerns. *Child and Family Behavior Therapy, 10,* 33–38.

Eyberg, S. M. (1982). Parent-child interaction training. Effects on family functioning. *Journal of Clinical Child Psychology, 11,* 130–137.

Faller, K. C. (1989). Characteristics of a clinical sample of sexually abused children: How boy and girl victims differ. *Child Abuse and Neglect, 13,* 281–291.

Famularo, R. A., Fenton, T., & Kinscherff, R. T. (1992). Medical and developmental histories of maltreated children. *Clinical Pediatrics, 31,* 536–541.

Famularo, R. A., Kinscherff, R. T., & Fenton, T. (1988). Post traumatic stress disorder among children clinically diagnosed as borderline disorder. *Journal of Nervous and Mental Diseases, 179,* 428–431.

Fantuzzo, J. W. (1990). Behavioral treatment of the victims of child abuse and neglect. *Behavior Modification, 14,* 316–339.

Fehrenbach, P. A., & Monastersky, C. (1988). Characteristics of female adolescent sexual offenders. *American Journal of Orthopsychiatry, 58,* 148–151.

Finkelhor, D. (1984). *Child sexual abuse: New theory and research.* New York: Free Press.

Finkelhor, D., & Berliner, L. (1995). Research on the treatment of sexually abused children: A review and recommendations. *Journal of the American Academy of Child and Adolescent Psychiatry, 34,* 1408 1423.

Finkelhor, D., & Dziuba-Leatherman, J. (1994). Victimization of Children. *American Psychologist, 49*(3), 173–183.

Friedrich, W. N. (1990). *Psychotherapy of sexually abused children and their families.* New York: Norton.

Friedrich, W. N. (1991). *Casebook of sexual abuse treatment.* New York: W. W. Norton, & Company.

Friedrich, W.N. (1993). Sexual victimization and sexual behavior in children: A review of recent literature. *Child Abuse and Neglect, 17,* 59-66.

Friedrich, W. N., Jaworski, T. M., Berliner, L., & James, B. (1994). Sexual abuse treatment practices. A survey. *The APSAC Advisor, 7*(2), 17, 18–24.

Friedrich, W. N., Luecke, W. J., Bielke, R. L., & Place, U. (1992). Psychotherapy outcome of sexually abused boys: An agency study. *Journal of Interpersonal Violence, 7,* 396–409.

Friedrich, W. N., Urquiza, A. J., & Beilke, R. L. (1986). Behavior problems in sexually abused young children. *Journal of Pediatric Psychology, 11,* 47–57.

Furby, L., Weinrott, M. R., & Blackshaw, L. (1989). Sex offender recidivism: A review. *Psychological Bulletin, 105*(1), 3–30.

Gagliano, C. K. (1987, February). Group treatment for sexually abused girls. *Social Course work: The Journal of Contemporary Social Work,* 102–108.

Gil, E. (1991). *The healing power of 'Play: Working with abused children.* New York: Guilford Press.

Gil, E., & Johnson, T. C. (1993). *Sexualized children: Assessment and treatment of sexualized children and children who molest.* Rockville, MD: Launch Press.

Gomes-Schwartz, B., Horowitz, J. M., Cardarelli, A. P., & Sauzier, M. (1990). *The aftermath of child sexual abuse: Eighteen months later.* In B. Gomes-Schwartz, J. M. Horowitz, A. P. Cardarelli (Eds.), *Child sexual abuse: The initial effects.* (pp. 132–151). Newbury Park, CA: Sage Publications.

Gray, A., & Pithers, W. (1995, October). *Children in treatment for sexual behavior problems: Current trends in descriptive analysis and classification data from two national center on child abuse and neglect studies.* Presented at the 14th Annual Association for the Treatment of Sexual Abusers Research and Treatment Conference, New Orleans, LA.

Graziano, A. M., & Mills, J. R. (1992). Treatment for

abused children: When is a partial solution acceptable? *Child Abuse and Neglect, 16,* 217–228.

Guidano, V. F., & Liotti, G. (1983). *Cognitive processes and emotional disorders: A structural approach to psychotherapy.* New York: Guilford Press.

Hall, G. C. (1995). Sexual offender recidivism revisited: A meta-analysis of recent treatment studies. *Journal of Consulting and Clinical Psychology, 63*(5), 802–809.

Haugaard, J., Bonner, B. L., Linares, O., Tharinger, D., Weisz, V., & Wolfe, D. A. (1995). Recommendations for education and training in child abuse and neglect: Issues from high school through postdoctoral levels. *Journal of Clinical Child Psychology, 24,* 78–83.

Hiebert-Murphy, D., DeLuca, R., & Runtz, J. (1992). Group treatment for sexually abused girls: Evaluating outcome. *Families in Society, 73,* 205–213.

Hembree-Kigin, T., & McNeil, C. B. (1995). *Parent-Child Interaction Therapy,* New York: Plenum.

Herman, J. (1981). Father-daughter incest. *Professional Psychology, 12,* 76–80.

Herrenkohl, E. C., Herrenkohl, R. C., Rupert, L. J., Egolf, B. P., & Lutz, J. G. (1995). Risk factors for behavioral dysfunction: The relative impact of maltreatment, SES, physical health problems, cognitive ability, and quality of parent-child interaction. *Child Abuse and Neglect, 19,* 191–203.

Hoffman-Plotkin, D., & Twentyman, C. T. (1984). A multimodel assessment of behavioral and cognitive deficits in abused and neglected preschoolers. *Child Development, 55,* 794–802.

Howes, C., & Espinosa, M. (1985). The consequences of child abuse for the formation of relationships with peers. *Child Abuse and Neglect, 9,* 397–404.

Hunter, J. A., Jr., & Becker, J. V. (1994). The role of deviant sexual arousal in juvenile sexual offending: Etiology, evaluation and treatment. *Criminal Justice and Behavior, 21*(1), 132–149.

Hunter, J. A., Jr., Lexler, L. J., Goodwin, D. W., Browne, P.A., & Dennis, C. (1993). Psychosexual, attitudinal, and developmental characteristics of juvenile female sexual perpetrators in a residential treatment setting. *Journal of Child and Family Studies, 4,* 317–326.

Hunter, R.S., & Kilstrom, N. (1979). Breaking the cycle in abusive families. *American Journal of Psychiatry, 136,* 1320-1322.

Johnson, R. L., & Shrier, D. K. (1985). sexual victimization of boys. *Journal of Adolescent Health Care, 6,* 372–376.

Johnson, T. C. (1991). Children who molest children: Identification and treatment approaches for children who molest other children. *APSAC Advisor, 4,* 9–23.

Jones, D. P. H. (1986). Individual psychotherapy for the sexually abused child. *Child Abuse and Neglect, 10,* 377–385.

Keller, R. A., Cicchinelli, L. F., & Gardner, D. M. (1989). Characteristics of child sexual abuse programs. *Child Abuse and Neglect, 13,* 316–368.

Kelly, M. M. (1995). Play therapy with sexually traumatized children: Factors that promote healing. *Journal of Child Sexual Abuse, 4*(3), 1–12.

Kelly, R. J., & Hansen, D. J. (1987). Social interactions and adjustments in V. B. Van Hasselt & M. Hersen (Eds.), *Handbook of adolescent psychology* (pp. 131–146). New York: Pergamon Press.

Kendall-Tackett, K. A., Williams, L. M., & Finkelhor, D. (1993). Impact of sexual abuse on children: A review and synthesis of recent empirical studies. *Psychological Bulletin, 113,* 164–180.

Knight, R., Carter, D., & Prentky, R. (1989). A system for classification of child molesters. *Journal of Interpersonal Violence, 4*(1), 3–23.

Kolko, D.J. (1986). Social-cognitive skills training with a sexually abused and abusive child psychiatric inpatient: Training, generalization, and follow-up. J*ournal of Family Violence, 1,* 149-165.

Kolko, D. J. (1992). Characteristics of child victims of physical violence: Research findings and clinical implications. *Journal of Interpersonal Violence, 7,* 244–276.

Kolko, D. J. (1996). Child physical abuse. In J. Briere, L. Berliner, J. Bulkley, C. Jenny, & T. Reid (Eds.), *APSAC handbook of child maltreatment* (pp. 21–50). Thousand Oaks, CA: Sage Publications.

Kolko, D. J., Moser, J. T., & Weldy, S. R. (1988). Behavioral/emotional indicators of child sexual abuse among child psychiatric inpatients: A comparison with physical abuse. *Child Abuse & Neglect, 12,* 529–541.

Krugman, R., & Jones, D. P., II, (1987). Incest and other forms of sexual abuse. In R. E. Helfer & R. S. Kempe (Eds.), *The battered child* (4th ed., pp. 286–300). Chicago: University of Chicago Press.

Kweller, R. B., & Ray, S. A. (1992). Group treatment of latency-age male victims of sexual abuse. *Journal of Child Sexual Abuse, 1*(4), 1–18.

Leahy, R. L. (1988). Cognitive therapy of childhood depression: Developmental consideration. In S. R. Shirk (Ed.), *Cognitive development and child psychotherapy* (pp. 187–206). New York: Plenum Press.

Lindon, J., & Nourse, C. A. (1994). A multi-dimensional model of group work for adolescent girls who have been sexually abused. *Child Abuse and Neglect, 18,* 341–348.

Lutzker, S. Z., Lutzker, J. R., Braunling-McMarrow, D., & Eddleman, J. (1987). Prompting to stimulate mother–baby-stimulation with single mothers. *Journal of Child and Adolescent Psychotherapy, 4,* 2–12.

Mannarino, A. P., & Cohen, J. A. (1990). Treating the abused child. In R. T. Ammerman & M. Hersen (Eds.), *Children at risk: An evaluation of factors contributing to child abuse and neglect* (pp. 249–266). New York: Plenum Press.

Marshall, W., & Barbaree, H. (1990). An integrated theory of the etiology of sex offending. In W. Marshall, D. Laws, & H. Barbaree (Eds.), *Handbook of sexual assault: Issues, theories and treatment of the offender* (pp. 257–275). New York: Plenum Press.

Marshall, W., & Pithers, W. (1994). A reconsideration of treatment outcome with sex offenders. *Criminal Justice and Behavior, 21,* 10–27.

Matthews, R., Hunter, J. A., Jr., & Vuz, J. (in press) Juvenile female sexual offenders: Clinical characteristics and treatment issues. *Sexual Abuse: A Journal of Research and Treatment.*

McCay, B., Gold, M., & Gold, E. (1987). A pilot study in drama therapy with adolescent girls who have been abused. *Arts in Psychotherapy, 14,* 77–84.

McCord, J. (1983). A forty-year perspective on effects of child abuse and neglect. *Child Abuse and Neglect, 7,* 265–270.

Milner, J. S. (1991). Physical child abuse perpetrator's screening and evaluation. *Criminal Justice and Behavior, 18,* 47–63.

Milner, J. S., & Chilamkurti, C. (1991). Physical child abuse perpetrator characteristics: A review of the literature. *Journal of Interpersonal Violence, 6,* 345–366.

Milner, J. S., & Crouch J. L. (1993). Physical child abuse. In R. L. Hampton, T. P. Gullotta, G. R. Adams, E. H. Potter, & R. P.Weissberg (Eds.). *Family violence* (pp. 25–55). Newbury Park, CA: Sage Publications.

Monck, E., Shailand, E., Bentovin, A., Goodall, G., Hyde, C., & Lewin, B. (1994). *Child sexual abuse: A descriptive and treatment outcome study.* London: HMSO.

Nash, M. R., Zivney, O. A., & Hulsey, T. (1993). Characteristics of sexual abuse associated with greater psychological impairment among children. *Child Abuse and Neglect, 17,* 401–408.

The National Adolescent Perpetrator Network (1993). The revised report from the National Task Force on Juvenile Sex Offending. *Juvenile and Family Court Journal, 4*(4), 1–120.

Oates, R. K., & Bross, D. C. (1995). What have we learned about treating child physical abuse? A literature review of the last decade. *Child Abuse and Neglect, 19,* 463–473.

Pithers, W. D., Becker, O. V., Kafka, M., Morenz, B., Schlank, A., & Leombruno, T. (1995). Children with sexual behavior problems, adolescent sexual abusers, and adult sex offenders: Assessment and treatment. In J. M. Oldham & M. Riba (Eds.), *Review of Psychiatry* (pp. 779–818). Washington, DC: American Psychiatric Press.

Runyan, D. K., Everson, J. D., Edelsohn, G. A., Hunter, W. M., & Coulter, M. L. (1988). Impact of intervention on sexually abused children. *Journal of Pediatrics, 113,* 657–653.

Salzinger, S., Kaplan, S., Pelcovitz, D., Samit, C., & Krieger, R. (1984). Parent and teacher assessment of children's behavior in child maltreating families. *Journal of the American Academy of Child Psychiatry, 23,* 458–464.

Santostefano, S. (1985). *Cognitive control therapy with children and adolescents.* New York: Pergamon Press.

Seinfeld, J. (1989). Therapy with a severely abused child: An object relations perspective. *Clinical Social Work Journal, 17,* 40–49.

Urquiza, A. J., & McNeil, C. B. (1966). Parent-child interaction therapy. An intensive dyadic intervention for physically abusive families. *Child Maltreatment 1,* 134–144.

Walker, C. E., Bonner, B. L., & Kaufman, K. L. (1988). *The physically and sexually abused child: Evaluation and treatment.* New York: Pergamon Press.

Widom, C. S. (1989). Does violence beget violence? A critical examination of the literature. *Psychological Bulletin, 106,* 3–28.

Widom, C. S. (1995, March). *Victims of childhood sexual abuse: Later criminal consequences.* Research in Brief, National Institute of Justice, 1–8.

Williamson, J. M., Borduim, C. M., & Howe, B. A. (1991). The ecology of adolescent maltreatment: A multilevel examination of adolescent physical abuse, sexual abuse, and neglect. *Journal of Consulting and Clinical Psychology, 59,* 449–457.

Wodarski, J. S., Kurtz, P. D., Gaudin, J. M., & Howing, P. T. (1990). Maltreatment and the school-aged child: Major academic, socioeconomic and adaptive outcomes. *Social Work, 35,* 506–513.

Wolfe, D. A., & Mosk, M. D. (1983). Behavioral comparisons of children from abusive and distressed families. *Journal of Consulting and Clinical Psychology, 51,* 702–708.

Wolfe, D. A., & Wekerle, C. (1993). Treatment strategies for child physical abuse and neglect: A critical progress report. *Clinical Psychology Review, 13,* 473–500.

Wolfe, D. A. (1994). The role of intervention and treatment services in the prevention of child abuse and neglect. In G. B. Melton and F. D. Barry (Eds.). *Protecting children from abuse and neglect: Foundations for a new national strategy.* New York: Guilford Press.

CHAPTER 13

POSTTRAUMATIC STRESS DISORDER

Philip A. Saigh

HISTORY

The psychological effects of traumatic stress have been chronicled for hundreds of years. A vivid example is evident in the 1666 diary of Samuel Pepys. Writing six months after he witnessed the Great Fire of London, Pepys observed that "it is strange to think how to this very day I cannot sleep a night without great terrors of the fire; and this very night could not sleep to almost two in the morning through great terrors of the fire" (quoted in Daly, 1983, p. 66). During the nineteenth century, Emil Kraepelin used the term *schrecneurose* (i.e., fright neuroses) to describe a clinical disorder made up of "multiple nervous and psychic phenomena arising as a result of severe emotional upheaval or sudden fright which would build up sudden anxiety: it can therefore be observed after serious accidents and injuries, particularly fires, railway derailments or

collisions" (Kraepelin, 1896, translated by Jablensky, 1985, p. 737).

More recent descriptions of individuals who were exposed to war-related stressors during World War I (Mott, 1919; Southard, 1919) and World War II (e.g., Eitinger, 1962; Grinker & Spiegel, 1945; Raines & Kolb, 1943) as well as disasters (e.g., Adler, 1943; Prasard, 1934), and criminal victimization (e.g., Bender & Blau, 1937) underscored the unique psychiatric morbidity of individuals who were exposed to extreme stress. For example, Bender and Blau (1937) described the psychiatric morbidity of child sexual abuse victims who were in treatment at Bellevue Hospital. It is of interest to note that the authors made distinct reference to the patient's feelings of fear, avoidance, irritability, nightmares, trauma-reminiscent re-enactments, and hypervigilance. In a similar vein, Bradner (1943) described how Finnish families were forcefully

The editorial assistance of Anastasia E. Yasik, B.A. is deeply appreciated.

evacuated from their homes during the Russio-Finnish War, crowded into unheated railroad cars, moved to unspecified locations at night, and repeatedly strafed by Soviet aircraft. Bradner's report also made reference to the children's posttraumatic fears, blunted affect, nightmares, avoidance, and psychological arousal to war-related material. He also observed that "even a year after the war, the sight of ruins had a profoundly depressing effect upon the children...war films, saddening war pictures in illustrated magazines, reports of war of any kind, still caused such symptoms of wartime to return at any given moment" (Bradner, 1943, p. 319).

Following World War II, Carey-Trefzer (1949) examined 1,203 British children who had been exposed to a number of war-related events (e.g., the London blitz) and determined that 212 children (17.62% of the sample) "showed disturbances caused or aggravated by war experiences" (p. 556). These disturbances consisted of war-related nightmares and fears, avoidance behaviors, academic difficulties, irritability, concentration and memory impairment, and sleep impairment. Analogously, Friedman (1948) described the "Buchenwald Syndrome" of Jewish children who survived the Nazi death camps. According to medical and psychiatric examinations that were performed at a detention center, it was determined that 50% to 60% of the children presented with physical complaints for which no organic causes could be found. Friedman also reported that these children suffered from subjective fears, sleep disorders, hypervigilance, and "affective anesthesia."

Given the excessive rate of war-related psychiatric morbidity following World War II (Glass, 1954; Glass, Ryan, Lubin, Reddy, & Tucker, 1956), the American Psychiatric Association's (APA) Committee on Nomenclature and Statistics listed *gross stress reaction* as a psychiatric category in the *Diagnostic and Statistical Manual of Mental Disorders* (DSM-I) of 1952. According to the DSM-1, gross stress reaction was indicated in situations involving exposure to "severe physical demands or extreme stress, such as in combat or civilian catastrophe (fire, earthquake, explosion, etc.)" (APA, 1952, p. 40). The DSM-I also indicated (contrary to the prevailing psychodynamic view) that "in many

instances this diagnosis applies to previously more or less 'normal' persons who experience intolerable stress" (APA, 1952, p. 40). While the classification achieved a measure of recognition by the mental-health community (Anderson, 1985), it was not included in the DSM-II (APA, 1968). In its place, *transient situational disturbance* was substituted. The classification involved "transient disorders of any severity (including those of psychotic proportions) that occur in individuals without any underlying mental disorders and that represent an acute reaction to overwhelming environmental stress" (APA, 1968, p. 48).

In view of the DSM-II's limited operational criteria, poor reliability, and narrow coverage (Feighner, Robins, Guze, Woodruff, Winokur, & Munoz, 1972; Morey, Skinner, & Blashfield, 1986; Saigh, 1992a), the APA appointed a task force to update the manual. Under the stewardship of Robert Spitzer, psychiatrists, psychologists, and social workers collaborated in preparing detailed symptomological descriptions for 265 classifications. In the finest sense of the Kraepelinian tradition, different committees collaborated and provided information as to age of onset, associated features, course, predisposing factors, prevalence, gender ratio, and differential diagnosis. Acting on the basis of the extant literature and independent clinical observations, the APA's Reactive Disorders Committee formulated the diagnostic criteria for what came to be known as *posttraumatic stress disorder* (DSM-III, APA, 1980). According to the DSM-III, PTSD was evident by the "development of characteristic symptoms following a psychiatrically traumatic event that is generally beyond the realm of normal human experience" (APA, 1980, p. 236). The DSM-III also specified that the "stressor producing this syndrome would evoke significant symptoms of distress in most people and is generally outside the range of such common experiences as simple bereavement, chronic illness, business losses or marital conflict" (APA, 1980, p. 236). In a departure from its predecessors, the DSM-III provided a detailed set of criteria for diagnosing cases. In addition to mandatory exposure to extreme stress (Criterion A), polymorphic symptom clusters were used to formulate a diagnoses. Viewed in this context, Criterion B required the presence of one of three reexperiencing symptoms (recurrent trauma-related thoughts, nightmares, and a sudden feeling that the traumatic event was reoccurring). Criterion C required the presence of at least one of three psychic numbing symptoms (diminished interest, detachment, and constricted affect). Criterion D required the presence of at least two of six symptoms that were not apparent before the trauma (sleep disturbance, hypervigilance, guilt, memory/concentration impairment, avoidance, and exasperation of symptoms on exposure to traumatic stimuli). It is of some significance to observe that the DSM-III text did not include age-specific information involving PTSD. Moreover, the actual criteria for PTSD in the DSM-III did not provide for expression of symptoms by children or adolescents.

Despite wide-range acceptance of the DSM-III in the United States, revisionary efforts were initiated in 1983 and the DSM-III-R was published in 1987. As in the case of the DSM-III PTSD classification, the 1987 nosology indicated that PTSD may occur after a "psychologically distressing event that is outside the range of normal human experience" (APA, 1987, p. 247) (Criterion A). On the other hand, Criterion B was revised to include a minimum of one of five reexperiencing symptoms (recurrent dreams about the trauma, recurrent thoughts of the trauma, sudden acting or feeling that the traumatic event was reoccurring, and intense psychological distress at exposure to trauma reminiscent stimuli). Criterion C was also expanded to include at least three of seven avoidance or numbing symptoms (avoidance of behaviors that induce traumatic recollections, efforts to avoid thinking about the trauma, inability to recall traumatic material, diminished interest, detachment, constricted affect, and a sense of foreshortened future). Criterion D was modified to exclude feelings of guilt and required at least two of six increased arousal symptoms (sleep impairment, irritability, concentration impairment, hypervigilance, exaggerated startle response, and physiological reactivity on exposure to trauma-related stimuli). In a departure from the DSM-III, the DSM-III-R text provided information on age-specific features of PTSD (e.g., "young children may not have the sense that they are reliving the past; reliving the trauma occurs in action, through repetitive

play," APA, DSM-III-R, 1987, p. 249). On the other hand, the diagnostic criteria did not make provisions for the developmental variations in the expression of the disorder.

In 1988, the APA initiated a systematic series of efforts to develop a fourth edition of the DSM. With regard to PTSD, this process drew on the results of field trials (Kilpatrick, Resnick, & Freedy, 1993) and comprehensive literature reviews (Davison & Foa, 1994). As earlier studies demonstrated that the stressors that could induce PTSD (e.g., rape, motor vehicle accidents) were relatively common in the United States (Breslau, Davis, Andreski, & Peterson, 1991: Kilpatrick, Saunders, & Best, 1993), the DSM-IV PTSD committee withdrew the provision that the stressor must have been "outside the range of normal human experience" (APA, 1987, p. 247). In its place, Criterion A was revised to require that an individual must have "experienced, witnessed, or been confronted with an event or events that involve actual or threatened death or serious injury, or a threat to the physical integrity to oneself or others" (APA, 1994, p. 428). Criterion A was further revised to specify that responses must have "involved intense fear, helplessness, or horror" (APA, p. 428).

The DSM-IV also rearranged a number of the symptom clusters and modified diagnostic thresholds. Physiological reactivity on exposure to traumatic stimuli was deleted from the arousal cluster (Criterion D) and inserted in the reexperiencing cluster (Criterion B). Criterion B now requires the presence of a minimum of one of five reexperiencing symptoms (recurrent thoughts of the traumatic event, recurrent dreams about the traumatic event, intense psychological discomfort at exposure to trauma-reminiscent stimuli, sudden acting or feeling that the traumatic event was reoccurring, and physiological reactivity on exposure). As in the case of the DSM-III-R, Criterion C requires the presence of at least three of seven avoidance or numbing symptoms (avoidance of behaviors that induce traumatic recollections, efforts to avoid thinking about the trauma, diminished interest, detachment, inability to recall traumatic material, constricted affect, and a sense of foreshortened future). With the exception of removing physiological reactivity, the symptoms that make up Criterion D in the DSM-IV are identical to the symptoms that were specified in the DSM-III-R. In effect, Criterion D requires the presence of two of five increased arousal symptoms (irritability, hypervigilance, concentration impairment, sleep impairment, and exaggerated startle response). The DSM-IV also added the provision that the disturbance causes "clinically significant distress or impairment in social, occupational, or other important areas of functioning" (APA, 1994, p. 429). Finally, in a significant departure from its predecessors, the DSM-IV diagnostic criteria include age-specific provisions for the expression of PTSD symptoms by youth. Table 13.1 presents the DSM-IV PTSD diagnostic criteria.

EPIDEMIOLOGY OF CHILD-ADOLESCENT EXPOSURE TO TRAUMATIC EVENTS

With reference to general exposure to traumatic events, government statistics and general population surveys have examined the prevalence of child-adolescent exposure to traumatic events (e.g., criminal victimization, motor vehicle accidents, various disasters) in the United States. Hernandez (1992) surveyed ninth graders who were randomly selected from 94% of the school districts in the Minnesota public school system. Of the 3,178 students that were sampled (1,643 males and 1,535 females), 10% reported having experienced some type of sexual abuse, 3% reported having been sexually abused within and outside their family, 2% reported only having experienced incest, and 6% reported only having experienced extrafamilial sexual abuse. It was also reported that sexually abused adolescents were more likely to report drinking and drug use than nonabused youth. In a similar vein, Bell and Jenkins (1993) surveyed 536 black elementary school students (289 males and 247 females) who were attending the second, fourth, sixth, or eighth grades at three inner-city Chicago schools. One in four elementary school students (25%) reported that they had seen someone being shot and 30% reported having witnessed a stabbing. In the same study, Bell and Jenkins surveyed 1,035 students (age range

10–19 years old, gender ratio not reported) who were attending four high schools and two middle schools in Chicago's east side. The Bell and Jenkins data interviews revealed that approximately 75% of the students had observed one or more violent crimes. More specifically, 35% witnessed a stabbing, 39% witnessed a shooting, and 24% witnessed a murder (23%). In terms of direct victimization experiences, 11% reported having been shot at and 3% reported that they had been shot. Another 3% said that they had been stabbed and 4% acknowledged that they had been sexually assaulted.

Also within the context of adolescent exposure to crime in America, Singer, Anglin, Song and Lunghofer (1995) administered an anonymous self-report questionnaire to 3,735 randomly selected students (age range 14–19 years old 52% female; 35% African American, 33% white, and 23% Hispanic) who were attending six schools in Ohio and Colorado. As based on reports across survey sites, Singer et al. (1995) reported that 33% to 44% (exposure estimates varied across schools) of the male youth reported being slapped, hit, or punched at school. Three to 22% reported that they had been beaten or mugged in their neighborhoods. Moreover, 3% to 33% of the male youth indicated that they were shot at or shot within the preceding year and 6% to 16% reported being assaulted or stabbed by a knife. Male adolescents also reported high rates of witnessing violent events. Nine to 21% reported seeing someone being sexually abused or assaulted, 32% to 82% said they saw others being beaten or mugged at school, 11% to 72% reported seeing someone being beaten or mugged in their neighborhood, 11 % to 72% reported seeing someone attacked or stabbed with a knife, and 5% to 62% said they saw others shot at or actually shot.

In a similar vein, 34% to 56% of the female adolescents indicated that they had been slapped, hit, or punched at home; 34% to 56% reported that they were attacked or actually stabbed with a knife; 0% to 9% reported that they were shot at or actually shot; and 12% to 17% reported being sexually abused or assaulted. It was also reported that 15% to 20% of the adolescent females said that they saw others being sexually abused or assaulted, 15% to 20% reported witnessing a beating or mugging in her neighborhood (incidence of witnessed neighborhood assault was not reported), 24% to 82% reported seeing others attacked or stabbed with a knife, and 5% to 49% reported that they saw others being shot at or actually shot. Singer et al. (1995) also reported that with the exceptions of physical victimization at home and sexual assault/abuse, the self-reported victimization rates of female adolescents were lower than the rates of males.

While the aforementioned surveys do not represent a systematic analysis of child-adolescent criminal victimization rates across the United States, the reported findings are in synchrony with the United States Department of Justice's national crime statistics (1994). These data indicate that approximately one and a half million youth (ages 12–17) were assaulted, robbed, or raped in 1992. Although juveniles accounted for one tenth of the U.S. population, 1 in 4 violent crimes involved a juvenile victim in 1992. In terms of probability, 1 juvenile in 13 was the victim of a violent crime.

While the prevalence of child-adolescent exposure to accidents and disasters has received less study, the United States Department of Transportation (1993) reported that 894,000 American youth (ages birth–20 years old) were injured in motor vehicle accidents in 1992. In a similar vein, the United States Centers for Disease Control and Prevention reported that 8,714,000 youth under the age of 15 made injury-related visits to hospital emergency departments in 1992 (Burt, 1995).

With respect to the prevalence of PTSD resulting from such events, Breslau et al. (1991) administered the Diagnostic Interview Schedule (DIS; Robins, Helzer, Croughan, & Ratcliff, 1981) to 1,007 young adults (age range 21–30 years old) in the Detroit area. Breslau and her colleagues reported that seeing others killed or injured and experiencing actual life threat produced a lifetime PTSD rate of approximately 25%. Rape induced PTSD among 80% of the victims, and accidental injury induced PTSD in 12% of the exposed subjects. Breslau et al. (1991) estimated that the lifetime rate of PTSD in the general population of young adults was approximately 9%. Other studies have also estimated the prevalence of

PTSD in more specialized populations. For example, Kulka et al. (1990) observed lifetime PTSD rates of 31% male and 27% female among a representative national sample of Vietnam veterans. In a similar vein, Resnick et al. (1993) used a random digit-dial procedure to sample 4,008 adult women. They reported that 12.3% of the subjects had PTSD at one time in their lives (i.e., lifetime prevalence). They also reported that 4.6% currently met criteria for PTSD.

EPIDEMIOLOGY OF CHILD-ADOLESCENT PTSD

Even though community surveys involving the prevalence of PTSD among school-age populations have not been conducted, information involving at risk (i.e., traumatized) youth is available. The majority of this information involves school-age samples who were exposed to war-related stressors, criminal victimization, or disasters.

War-Related PTSD

Kinzie and his colleagues (Kinzie, Sack, Angell, Clark, & Ben, 1989; Kinzie, Sack, Angell, & Mason, 1986) examined the psychiatric morbidity of a sample of Cambodian adolescents who emigrated to America following the fall of the violent Poll Pot regime (1975–1979). Between the ages of 8 to 12 years old, the subjects suffered "catastrophic trauma caused by separation from their families, forced labor, starvation, personal injuries, and the witnessing of many deaths and executions" (Kinzie et al., 1986, p. 501). Kinzie et al. (1986) administered the Diagnostic Interview Schedule (Robins et al., 1981) to 40 subjects (25 males and 15 females; mean age 17 years) approximately 2.5 years after their immigration to the United States and observed that 50% met criteria for PTSD. Three years later, Kinzie et al. (1989) located and re-examined 27 of the Cambodian subjects (gender not reported; mean age 20 years). Of these, 8 (29.6%) met criteria for PTSD as measured by the Diagnostic Interview Schedule. Eleven (40.8%)

TABLE 13.1   DSM-IV Criteria for Posttraumatic Stress Disorder

A. The person has been exposed to a traumatic event in which both of the following have been present:

   1. the person has experienced, witnessed, or been confronted with an event or events that involve actual or threatened death or serious injury, or a threat to the physical integrity to oneself or others.

   2. the person's responses involved intense fear, helplessness, or horror. Note: in children it may be expressed by disorganized or agitated behavior.

B. The traumatic event is reexperienced in at least two of the following ways:

   1. recurrent and intrusive distressing recollections of the event including images, thoughts, or perceptions. Note: in young children, repetitive play may occur in which themes or aspects of the trauma are expressed.

   2. recurrent distressing dreams of the event. Note: In young children, there may be frightening dreams without recognizable content.

   3. acting or feeling as if the traumatic event were recurring (includes sense of reliving the experience, illusions, hallucinations, and dissociative flashback episodes, including those that occur on awakening or when intoxicated). Note: in young children, trauma-specific reenactment may occur.

   4. intense psychological distress at exposure to internal or external cues that resemble an aspect of the traumatic event.

   5. physiological reactivity upon exposure to internal or external cues that symbolize or resemble an aspect of the traumatic event.

C. Persistent avoidance of stimuli associated with the trauma and numbing of general responsiveness (not present before the trauma), as indicated by at least three of the following:

   1. efforts to avoid thoughts, feelings, or conversations associated with the trauma.

   2. efforts to avoid activities, places, or people that arouse recollections of the trauma.

   3. inability to recall an important aspect of the trauma.

   4. markedly diminished interest or participation in significant activities.

   5. feeling of detachment or estrangement from others.

   6. restricted range of affect.

   7. sense of foreshortened future (e.g., does not expect to have a career, marriage, children, or a normal life span).

D. Persistent symptoms of increased arousal (not present before the trauma), as indicated by at least two of the following:

   1. difficulty in falling or staying asleep.

   2. irritability or anger outbursts.

   3. difficulty concentrating.

   4. hypervigilance.

   5. exaggerated startle response.

E. Duration of the disturbance (symptoms in B, C, and D) is more than one month.

F. The disturbance causes clinically significant distress or impairments in social, occupational, or other important areas of functioning.

Specify if:

   Acute: if duration of symptoms is less than three months.

   Chronic: if duration of symptoms is three months or more.

   With Delayed Onset: onset of symptoms at least three months or more.

Source: Criteria from the American Psychiatric Association (1994). *Diagnostic and Statistical Manual of Mental Disorders*, Fourth Edition. Washington, DC: Author. Reproduced by permission.

subjects never met criteria, and 8 (29.6%) evidenced a variable course.

Working against the background of the Lebanese conflict, Saigh (1988) carried out a prospective study involving 12 undergraduates at the American University of Beirut (age range 18–22 years old). The course PTSD (as measured by an author-devised DSM-III-based structured interview) was assessed 63 days before the subjects were exposed devastating artillery bombardment, as well as 37 and 316 days later. Although none of the subjects had PTSD before the incident, 9 (75% of the subjects) warranted an acute PTSD diagnosis 37 days after the bombardment. Interestingly, only 1 student (or 8.3% of the sample) remained symptomatic 316 days after the incident. Saigh (1989a) administered the Children's PTSD Inventory (Saigh, 1989b) to 840 Lebanese children (397 males and 443 females; age range 8–12 years old) who were referred for assessment by physicians, Red Cross personnel, mental-health practitioners, and teachers after they were exposed to extreme forms of war-related stress. Although the data were collected from 1 to 2 years after the subjects' stressful experiences, 230 subjects (104 males and 126 females), or 27.38% of the sample, met diagnostic criteria for PTSD. Clearly, the gender ratios were not significantly different in a related study.

Five months following the departure of Iraqi forces from Ku Nader, Pynoos, Fairbanks, Frederick, Al-Ajeel, and Al-Asfour (1993) administered the Reaction Index (Fredrick, 1985) to 51 subjects (16 males and 35 females; age range 8–21 years old) who were attending a Kuwait summer school. They reported that 70% of the subjects had PTSD. Nonsignificant differences were apparent in the distribution of PTSD by gender. Also within the context of the Gulf War, Wiesenberg, Schwarzwald, Waysman, Solomon, and Klingman (1993) administered a version of the Reaction Index to 492 Israeli children (227 males and 265 females) who were enrolled in grades 5 through 10. The subjects had remained with their families in hermetically sealed rooms and had worn gas masks during Iraqi missile attacks. Based on the assessments that occurred 3 weeks after the war, it was estimated that 25.6% of the children had PTSD. Information involving gender and age effects for PTSD were not reported.

Sack, McSharry, Kinney, Seeley, and Lewinson (1994) administered the DICA and K-SADS to 209 Khmer survivors of the Poll Pot (104 males and 105 females with a mean age 19.5 years). After repeated exposures to traumatic stressors in Cambodia, the subjects resided in the United States from 3 to 9 years. In this instance, the point prevalence (18.2%) was closely associated with lifetime prevalence (21.5%). While gender was not predictive of PTSD, older subjects had a significantly higher prevalence of the disorder. Comorbidity in the form of major depression was also observed with a point prevalence of 11.0% and a lifetime prevalence of 34.9%. Additional DSM-III-R diagnoses indicated extremely low prevalence rates (e.g., 1.0% and 1.9% for current and lifetime prevalence of conduct disorder and no cases of psychoactive substance use were identified). In a similar vein, Saigh, Mroweh, Zimmerman, and Fairbank (1995) administered the Children's PTSD Inventory to 85 nonreferred students (48 males and 37 females; mean age 13.0 years) at four Lebanese schools. Although 20 subjects had histories denoting exposure to stressful war-related events (mean interval between exposure and assessment was 1.8 years), only 10 met criteria for PTSD (11.8% of the overall sample or 50.0% of the subjects who were exposed to extreme stress). With respect to gender, 10.4% of the males and 13.5% of the females that were sampled met criteria for PTSD.

In an effort to estimate the incidence of war-related PTSD and associated psychopathology of Cambodian refugees without the confounding effects of resettlement stress, Savin, Sack, Clarke, Nee, and Richart (in press) administered a Khmer version of the DICA and the Kiddie Schedule for Affective Disorders and Schizophrenia for School Age Children (K-SADS; Puig-Antich, Orvaschel, Tabrinzi, & Chambers, 1980) to 99 Khmer youth (age range 18–25 years old). The subjects had fled Cambodia after experiencing the horrors of the Poll Pot regime as children. Although they resided in the relative safety of a refugee camp (i.e., the Site Two Camp) located in Thailand for 10 years, 26.3% of the subjects met diagnostic criteria for war-related PTSD and 31.3% had a lifetime prevalence of the disorder. It is, of considerable interest to note that Savin and his colleagues reported that the prevalence rates of the Site Two Poll Pot survivors were comparable to the prevalence rates among a matched cohort in the United States (Sack, in press). Savin and his colleagues went on to conclude that the diagnosis of war-related PTSD is a direct product of the original trauma and not a byproduct of contextual or resettlement stress.

As may be noted from Table 13.2, war-related PTSD point prevalence estimates ranged from

TABLE 13.2. Prevalence of War-Related PTSD in Children and Adolescents

INVESTIGATION	INSTRUMENT	SUBJECTS	EXPOSURE ASSESSMENT INTERVAL	PREVALENCE (%)
Kinzie et al., 1986	Diagnostic Interview Schedule	40 Cambodian adolescents; 25 males and 15 females; mean age 17 years	2.5 years	50.00 overall
Saigh, 1988	Author-devised DSM-III structured interview	12 female Lebanese undergraduates; age range 18–22 years old	37 and 316 days	75.0 at 37 days 8.3 at 316 days
Kinzie et al., 1989	Diagnostic Interview Schedule	27 Cambodian young adults, gender not reported; mean age 20 years	5.5 years	26.60 overall
Saigh, 1989b	Children's PTSD Inventory	840 clinically referred Lebanese children; 397 males and 443 females; age range 8–12 years old	1–2 years	27.38 overall 26.19 males 28.44 females
Nader et al., 1993	Reaction Index	51 Kuwati children; 16 males and 35 females; age range 8–21 years old	5 months	70.00 overall Nonsignificant gender effect
Wiesenberg et al., 1993	Reaction Index	492 Israeli children; 227 males and 265 females; grades 5–10	3 weeks after the end of the Gulf War	25.6 overall
Sack et al., 1994	DICA and K-SADS	209 Cambodian adolescents; 104 males and 105 females; mean age 19.5 years	3–9 years	18.2 current 21.5 lifetime (overall)
Saigh et al., 1995	Children's PTSD Inventory	85 Lebanese adolescents; 48 males and 37 females; mean age 13.0 years	1.8 years	11.76 overall 10.41 males 13.51 females
Savin, et al., in press	DICA and K-SADS	99 Cambodian adolescents; x males and y females; age range 18–25 years old	10 years	26.3 current 31.3 lifetime

10.41% (Saigh et al., 1995) to 75.00% (Saigh, 1988). It is also apparent from the longitudinal studies that were reviewed (Kinzie et al., 1989; Saigh, 1988) that the prevalence of PTSD in youth decreased over time. Whereas two of the nine studies that were reviewed (Nader et al., 1993; Saigh, et al., 1995) reported prevalence estimates by gender, these studies did not reflect significant differences by gender.

Criminal Victimization-Related PTSD

Given the inordinate rates of exposure to criminal violence in America, investigators have sought to estimate the prevalence of PTSD among child and adolescent crime victims. One month after a sniper assault on a Los Angeles elementary-school playground (one youth was killed and 13 were injured),

Pynoos et al. (1987) administered the DSM-III-based version of the Reaction Index to 159 children (79 females and 80 males; age range 5–13 years old). Pynoos and his colleagues determined that 60.4% of the subjects had PTSD. They also reported that PTSD symptoms increased as a function of the level of stress exposure. Children who were in the playground had a higher prevalence of PTSD than youth who were at home or in the neighborhood. Age, gender, and ethnicity were not predictive of PTSD. In a follow-up study, Nader, Pynoos, Fairbanks, and Frederick (1990) conducted a 14-month follow-up involving 100 of the 159 Los Angeles youth (age and gender were not reported) that were initially examined by Pynoos et al. (1987). Although Pynoos and his colleagues reported that 60.4% of the school children had PTSD 1 month after the assault, Nader and associates (1990) observed a 19.0% point prevalence 14 months after the incident. Interestingly, the Nader et al. (1990) report failed to denote significant differences in the distribution of children across exposure levels relative to gender, age, prior acquaintance with the victims, previous trauma, level of stress exposure during the attack, secondary stress exposure following the attack, or the provision of psychological services after the incident.

Examined from a different perspective, McLeer, Deblinger, Atkins, Foa, and Ralphe (1988) examined 31 sexually abused children (25 females and 6 males with a mean age of 8.4 years) at a university-based outpatient child psychiatry clinic. Although the interval between stress exposure and assessment was not reported, McLeer and associates (1988) determined that 48.4% of the subjects met criteria for PTSD as indicated by an author-constructed DSM-III-R PTSD checklist. It was reported that 75% of the youth that were abused by natural fathers and 25% of those abused by a trusted adult developed PTSD. In considerable contrast, none (0.0%) of the children who were abused by an older youth met diagnostic criteria.

In an attempt to determine if different types of abuse are associated with divergent PTSD estimates, Livingston, Lawson, and Jones (1993) administered the DSM-III-R version of the Diagnostic Interview for Children and Adolescents (DICA-R; Reich,

Shayka, & Taibleson, 1991) to 41 children (23 males and 18 females; mean age 10.2 years). Twenty-six had been sexually abused and 15 had been physically abused. All of the subjects were the victims of repeated parental abuse that occurred within a year of the assessment. Livingston and his coauthors determined that 51.7% of the sexually abused and 33.3% of the physically abused subjects met criteria for PTSD. The type of stressor (sexual vs. physical abuse), age, and gender were not predictive of PTSD. On the other hand, the intensity of the stressor was significantly associated with the development of the disorder. Pelcovitz et al. (1994) administered the DSM-III-R PTSD module of the Structure Clinical Interview (SCID; Spitzer, Endicott, & Robins, 1987) to 27 court-referred adolescents (12 males and 15 females with a mean age of 15.1 years; interval between exposure and assessment not reported) and with legally documented histories of intrafamilial physical abuse. The SCID was also administered to 27 demographically matched randomly selected controls (16 females and 11 males with a mean age of 15.1 years). Although 3 (11.1 %) of the physically abused subjects met criteria for PTSD, their condition was attributed to incidents other than intrafamilial abuse (all 3 developed PTSD following extrafamilial sexual assaults). None of the controls evidenced PTSD, despite the fact that 3 of the individuals had been exposed to extreme stress (i.e., 1 was assaulted by a gang, a second saw the body of her brother following his suicide, and a third was sexually assaulted).

Merry and Andrews (1994) conducted a methodologically rigorous assessment of sexually abused children in New Zealand. The DSM-III-R version of the Diagnostic Interview for Children-2 (DISC-2; Shaffer, Fisher, Piacenti, Schwab-Stone, & Wicks, 1989) was administered to 66 children (11 males and 55 females; mean age 8 years). The subjects were recruited from child welfare agencies and examined 3 to 6 months after stress exposure. Data analysis revealed that 63.5% of the sexually abused children had at least one psychiatric disorder relative to a base rate of 17.6%. In terms of PTSD prevalence, Merry and Andrews reported that 18.2% of their sample met criteria. Interestingly, 10 girls (18.2% of the female cohort) and 2 boys (18.2% of the male cohort) received a PTSD diagnosis. Also within the context of sexual abuse, McLeer, Callaghan, Henry, and Wallen (1994) administered the epidemiological version of the K-SADS (Orvaschel, Puig-Antich, Chambers, & Abrizi, 1982) to 26 sexually abused children (17 males and 9 females; mean age 9.0 years; interval between last exposure and assessment not reported) and 23 psychiatric controls (10 males and 13 females with a mean age of 10.4 years). Both groups were receiving outpatient services at university-based psychiatry clinics. McLeer et al. (1994) reported that 42.3% of the sexually abused subjects and 8.7% of the psychiatric controls met DSM-III-R criteria for PTSD. Of interest among the sexually abused cohorts was the finding that co-occurred PTSD with ADHD and conduct disorder (CD). More specifically, 23.1% of the sexually abused youth had PTSD and ADHD; 15.4% had PTSD and CD; and 11.5% had PTSD, ADHD, and CD. Similar clusters were not observed among the psychiatric comparison group. It is also of interest to note that PTSD was not the most frequently diagnosed disorder among the sexually abused subjects as 46.0% met diagnostic criteria for ADHD.

In a similar vein, Wolfe, Sas, and Wekerle (1994) administered an author-devised DSM-III-R checklist to 90 Canadian children with documented histories of sexually abuse (21 males and 69 females; mean age 12.4 years; interval between stress exposure and assessment not reported). Data analysis revealed a point prevalence of 48.9%. PTSD was significantly associated with female gender (55.1% vs. 28.5%) and older youth. Youth with PTSD were more likely to have been abused for longer intervals (more than one year) and stress-exposed PTSD negatives tended to have experienced singular episodes of abuse.

Examined from the perspective of gang-related violence and PTSD, Burton, Foy, Bwanausi, Johnson, and Moore (1994) used the Foy Symptom Checklist (Foy, Sipprelle, Rueger, & Carroll, 1984) to formulate DSM-III PTSD diagnoses among 91 male juvenile offenders who were incarcerated in Los Angeles. All of the subjects (mean age 16 years; interval between exposure and assessment was not reported) had exhibited a pattern of serious and repeated criminal activities. Burton et al. reported that 22 (24.2%) of the subjects had PTSD. They also reported a significant relation between family functioning and PTSD.

In the only study involving PTSD in preschool youth, Diamond, Saigh, and Fairbank (in press) administered the DSM-III-based Children's PTSD Inventory and the DICA-R-P to 24 preschool children (14 males and 10 females) with documented or suspected histories involving physical abuse as denoted by the New York Social Services Law. Approximately 71% of the sample (8 females and 9 males; mean age 4.5 years; mean interval between exposure and assessment 6 months) met criteria for PTSD.

As may be noted from Table 13.3, the overall point prevalence of the disorder among sexually abused youth ranged from 18.2% (Merry & Andrews, 1994) to 51.7% (Livingston et al., 1993). Rates for physical abuse-related PTSD ranged from between 11.1 % (Pelcovitz et al., 1994) to 70.83% (Diamond et al., in press). Examined across the 10 criminal victimization studies that were reviewed, 4 investigations were associated with nonsignificant gender differences (Pynoos et al., 1987; Livingston et al., 1993; Merry & Andrews, 1994; Nader et al., 1990). Two studies evidenced appreciably higher proportions of PTSD among females (Diamond et al., in press; Wolfe et al., 1994). As in the case of the war-related studies, longitudinal criminal victimization research suggests that the rate of the disorder decreases over time (Nader et al., 1990).

Accident-Disaster–Related PTSD

With respect to accident and disaster-related PTSD, Handford et al. (1986) developed and administered an author devised PTSD questionnaire to 35 children (16 males and 19 females; age range 6–19 years) approximately one and a half years after the Three Mile Island (TMI) nuclear accident. While it was indicated that 11.4% of the sample had psychiatric disorders (e.g., conduct disorder or dysthymia), none of the children met criteria for PTSD. Likewise, Earls, Smith, Reich, and Jung (1988) administered the DSM-III version of the DICA (Reich, Herjanic, Welner, & Gandhy, 1982) to 32 youth (16 males and 16 females; age range 6–17

TABLE 13.3. Prevalence of Victimization-Related PTSD in Children and Adolescents

INVESTIGATION	INSTRUMENT	SUBJECTS	EXPOSURE ASSESSMENT INTERVAL	PREVALENCE (%)
Pynoos et al., 1987	Reaction Index	79 male and 80 female victims of a school shooting; age range 5–13 years old	30 days	66.4 overall Nonsignificant age, age, gender, and ethnicity differences
McLeer et al., 1988	Author-devised DSM-III-R checklist	25 female and 6 male sexual abuse victims; mean age 8.4 years	Not reported	48.4 overall 75.0 abused by natural fathers, 25 by a trusted adult, and 0% by and older youth
Nader et al., 1990	Reaction Index	100 elementary school victims of a school-based shooting; gender and age not reported	14 months	19.0 overall Nonsignificant age and gender differences
Burton et al., 1994	Foy Symptom Checklist	91 male juvenile offenders; mean age 16 years	Not reported	24.2 overall
Livingston et al., 1993	DICA	23 male and 18 female sexual and physical abuse victims; mean age 10.2 years	1 year	51.7 sexual abuse 33.3 physical abuse Gender, age, and type of abuse not predictive of PTSD
McLeer et al., 1994	K-SADS	17 male and 9 female sexual abuse victims; mean age 9.0 years	Not reported	42.3 overall
Merry & Andrews, 1994	DISC-2	11 male and 55 female sexual abuse victims; mean age 8 years	3–6 months	18.2 overall 18.2 males 18.2 females
Pelcovitz et al., 1995	SCID	12 male and 15 female victims of intrafamilial physical abuse; mean age 15.1 years	Not reported	11.1 overall
Wolfe et al., 1994	DSM-III-R author-devised checklist	21 male and 69 female sexual abuse victims; mean age 12.4 years	Not reported	48.9 overall 28.5 males 55.1 females
Diamond et al., in press	Children's PTSD Inventory	14 male and 10 female physical abuse victims; mean age 4.5 years	6 months	70.83 overall 64.3 males 80.0 females

years old) who were exposed to a flood and dioxin contamination. Based on assessments conducted 1 year following exposure, it was determined that none of the subjects met diagnostic criteria for PTSD. On the other hand, 10% met criteria for adjustment disorder that was associated with stress exposures. In a similar vein, Korol (1990) administered an abbreviated version of the Reaction Index to 120 youths (gender not reported, age range 7–15 years old) who resided within 5 miles of a weapons facility that exposed the community of Fernald, Ohio to nuclear contamination. Assessments were conducted approximately 5 years after the residents were told that the area had been contaminated. Korol reported that 5.0% of the sample met DSM-III-R criteria for PTSD. She also reported that the behavioral and emotional symptoms of the exposed subjects were not significantly different from those of a nonexposed cohort.

One and a half years after the 1988 Armenian earthquake, Pynoos et al. (1993) administered the Reaction Index and clinical interviews to 111 youth (gender not reported; age range 8–16 years old) who resided in three cities that were at increasing distances from the epicenter of the earthquake. The first cohort resided in a city near the epicenter of earthquake and was virtually destroyed. According to Pynoos and his colleagues, "nearly all the schools were demolished, and in some schools more than half of the children were killed" (1993, p. 290). The second cohort lived 35 km from the epicenter and experienced "less total destruction of homes and schools and lower rates of injury and loss" (Pynoos et al., 1993, p. 240). The third cohort resided 75 km from the epicenter and experienced "mild damage and no significant loss of life" (Pynoos et al., 1993, p. 290). Of the 111 youth who underwent clinical interviews, 70.3% met DSM-III-R criteria for PTSD. Given the respective cohorts, 91.4%, 90.9%, and 37.2% met criteria for PTSD. Although the point prevalence by gender was not reported, females had a significantly higher prevalence of PTSD. Pynoos and his colleagues also observed a nonsignificant effect for age.

Three months after Hurricane Hugo struck Berkeley County, South Carolina, Shannon, Lonigan, Finch, and Taylor (1994) administered a DSM-III-R version of the Reaction Index to 5,686 school age children (2,786 males and 2,900 females, mean age 14.0 years). Shannon and her colleagues reported a 5.4% overall PTSD point prevalence. It was also reported that females had significantly higher rates (6.9%) than males (3.8%). In addition,

younger children were at significantly greater risk for PTSD (preadolescents, 9.2%; early adolescents, 4.2%; and late adolescents, 3.1%). Nonsignificant effects for age and ethnicity were reported. Also within the context of Hurricane Hugo, Garrison, Weinrich, Hardin, Weinrich, and Wang (1993) administered an author-developed DSM-III-R PTSD inventory to 1,264 adolescent students (265 white males, 306 white females, 335 black males, and 358 black females, age range 11 to 17 years old). Assessments occurred 1 year after the storm devastated the South Carolina coastal plane. Garrison and her colleagues determined that: 11% of the subjects were not with their parents during the hurricane, 12% had to move out of their homes for at least a week, 4% had someone close to them injured during the storm, 10% were physically injured, and 71% experienced fear of injury during the hurricane. Despite these levels of exposure, Garrison et al. reported an overall PTSD prevalence rate of 5% (6.2% white females, 4.7% black females, 3.8% white males, and 1.5% black males). In contrast to the Shannon et al. (1994) report, the authors also indicated that PTSD was significantly associated with female gender, a history of earlier exposure to extreme stress (i.e., abuse or assault), and Caucasian ethnicity.

As may be seen in Table 13.4, the point prevalence of the PTSD among the victims of accidents and disasters ranged from 0.0% (Earls et al., 1988; Handford et al., 1986) to 70.3% (Pynoos et al., 1993). With the exception of the Pynoos et al. (1993) study, the remaining disaster-accident studies denote very low prevalence estimates among the youth that were sampled (i.e., 0.0%–5.4%). Whereas the majority of accident-disaster studies did not report prevalence information involving gender, the Garrison et al. (1993) report determined that the PTSD point prevalence was significantly greater among females.

Although it is apparent that exposure to a severe and psychologically distressing event usually was not sufficient to induce PTSD in most of the subjects sampled, it is also apparent that the overriding majority of stressors described were capable of inducing PTSD among a subset of children and adolescents. Clearly, children and adolescents (much

TABLE 13.4. Prevalence of Accident/Disaster-Related PTSD in Children and Adolescents

INVESTIGATION	INSTRUMENT	SUBJECTS	EXPOSURE ASSESSMENT INTERVAL	PREVALENCE (%)
Handford et al., 1986	Author-devised PTSD	16 male and 19 female survivors of nuclear accident; age range 6–19 years old	18 months	0.0 overall
Earls et al., 1988	DICA	16 male and 16 female flood and dioxin contamination victims; age range 6–17 years old	1 year	0.0 overall
Korol, 1990	Reaction Index	120 residents of an area exposed to nuclear contamination; age range 7–15 years old; gender not reported	5 years	5.0 overall
Pynoos et al., 1993	Reaction Index	111 Armenian earthquake victims; age range 8–16 years old; gender not reported	18 months	70.3 overall
Garrison et al., 1993	Author-devised PTSD inventory	265 white male, 306 white female, 335 black male, and 358 black female hurricane victims; age range 11–17 years old	1 year	5.0 overall 3.8 white males 1.5 black males 6.2 white females 4.7 black females Significantly higher prevalence among females and Caucasians
Shannon et al., 1994	Reaction Index	2,786 male and 2,900 female hurricane victims; mean age 14.0 years	3 months	5.4 overall 3.8 males 6.9 females 9.2% preadolescents; 4.2% early adolescents; 3.1% adolescents
Diamond et al., in press	Children's PTSD Inventory	14 male and 10 female physical abuse victims; mean age 4.5 years	6 months	70.83 overall 64.3 males 80.0 females

like adults) experience differential levels of psychiatric morbidity after exposure to extremely stressful events. It is also readily apparent that PTSD point prevalence estimates among children and adolescents have been associated with a good deal of variability within and between stressor categories. Despite these variations, war-related events and criminal victimization have been associated with higher estimates of PTSD than less deliberate acts or events. Indeed, the research clearly indicates that less discernable or "silent" stressors such as exposure to nuclear or chemical contamination were associated with very low levels of psychiatric morbidity.

Of the 26 studies that were reviewed, 11 tested for proportional differences between genders or actually reported point prevalence estimates by sex. Seven of these studies were associated with nonsignificant findings (Livingston et al., 1993; Merry

& Andrews, 1994; Nader et al., 1990; Nader et al., 1993; Pynoos et al., 1987; Saigh, 1989a; Saigh et al., 1995). Four others denoted significantly higher estimates among females (Diamond et al., in press; Garrison et al., 1993; Shannon et al., 1994; Wolfe et al., 1994). Findings with regard to age are more limited as only four studies tested for variations by age. Three reports failed to denote significant differences as a function of subject age (Livingston et al., 1993; Nader et al., 1990; Pynoos et al., 1987). On the other hand, Shannon et al. (1994) reported significantly higher rates of PTSD among older youth. Clearly more systematic inquiry into the correlates of PTSD among children and adolescents is necessary. Research designed to examine the influence of pre-trauma factors (e.g., psychopathology, traits such as inhibition, and intellectual ability) may be of value in determining variables that are associated with increased risk. In a similar vein, a systematic analysis of the qualitative aspects of posttrauma parental support and secondary stressors may facilitate our understanding of additional risk factors that are associated with the development of PTSD in youth.

BEHAVIORAL TREATMENT OF PTSD IN CHILDREN AND ADOLESCENTS

Whereas exposure-based paradigms have gained recognition as effective treatments for fears and phobias in recent years, different forms of these procedures have been used for hundreds of years (Saigh, 1992b). Goethe's autobiography provides a description of a successful self-initiated treatment of acrophobia (Boudewyns & Shipley, 1983). More recently, Malleson (1959) described an *in vitro* or imaginal flooding technique that he employed to reduce the emotional anxiety of a test-phobic graduate student. The student was described as"...classically panic stricken...sobbing and fearful, bewailing his fate, and terrified of the impending examination..." (p. 225). Malleson advised the student to "tell of the awful consequences that he felt would follow his failure—derision from his colleagues... disappointment from his family and financial loss" (p. 225). The student was also advised that whenever he "felt a little wave of spontaneous alarm, he was not to push it aside, but was to augment it, to try to experience it more profoundly and more vividly" (p. 225). Although the procedure was marked by a degree of discomfort, the student complied with Malleson's instructions and reported that he was virtually unable to feel anxious as the examination date approached. As it were, he was able to pass the test with ease.

Stampfl (1961) subsequently coined the term *implosive therapy* to characterize a regimen that "may be regarded as a synthesis between Freudian-oriented and Mowerian approaches to psychotherapy" (p. 1). Stampfl and Levis (1967) developed an elaborate description of the procedure as well as a theoretical rationale to account for its efficacy. They reported that the primary objective of implosive therapy involves the identification of the exteroceptive and interoceptive conditioned stimuli or cues that are being avoided. It was hypothesized that fear-inducing cues occur in a variety of forms (e.g., auditory, tactile, cognitive). It was also proposed that these stimuli are interdependent and ordered in a serial hierarchy according to the degree of avoidance. Cues were said to be selected from subjective experiences wherein "objects or situations are known to have high-anxiety eliciting value, as in specific traumatic situations, material produced by dreams or symbolism of a psychoanalytic nature" (Stampfl & Levis, 1967, p. 502). Once recognized, cues are presented in a sequential order by instructing patients to repeatedly imagine and verbalize significant symptom-contingent cues until extinction takes place.

Rachman (1966) went on to introduce the term *flooding* to the clinical literature. Rachman attributed the description to Pollin (1959) who initially used it to describe the aversive component of an infrahuman laboratory extinction experiment. Although Rachman (1966) initially concluded that systematic desensitization was more successful than flooding in reducing the symptoms of phobic individuals, he acknowledged that the subjects that were flooded had received less than 2 minutes of anxiety-inducing stimulation at a time and that it was "possible therefore that the crucial element omitted in the present technique is prolonged exposure" (p. 6). Following the initial reports by Stampfl (1961), Stampfl and Levis (1967), and Rachman (1966), a number of reports involving longer intervals of therapeutic exposure (i.e., 40–60 minutes of stimulation) were conducted (e.g., Hogan & Kirchner, 1967; Levis & Carrera, 1967). Unlike the Rachman (1966) investigation, these reports denoted efficacy across a variety of simple and social phobics.

By 1972, a considerable number of flooding experiments had been carried out by different investigators across a wide-range of subjects and treatment sites. Following a review of the flooding literature, Marks (1972) developed an important definition of the flooding process. According to this definition,

> Flooding is at one end of a continuum of approach to distressing situations, at the opposite end of which is desensitization. The difference between the two is largely one of degree. The more sudden the confrontation, the more it is prolonged, and the greater the emotion that accompanies it, the more apt is the label *flooding* for that procedure. (Marks, 1972, p. 154)

From the 1970s to date, a number of flooding studies had been published with child (Sellick & Peck, 1981; Yule, Sacks, & Hersov, 1974), and adult (Jacobson, 1991) simple or social phobia cases. Although it is well beyond the scope of this chapter to review this literature base, it may be said that flooding, in one form or another, has been effectively used to treat a wide range of phobic individuals.

The Use of Flooding with Traumatized Individuals

Given the extent exposure-based anxiety disorder therapeutic literature, Fairbank, DeGood, and Jenkins (1981) employed a multi-faceted flooding package in the treatment of an accident victim. Their investigation involved a 32-year-old female survivor of a motor vehicle collision. The patient and two of her daughters incurred multiple physical injuries (i.e., one child was rendered unconscious following a head injury and the patient sustained severe lacerations). Although the woman recovered from her injuries and was able to drive, she experienced acute anxiety attacks whenever she attempted

to drive a motor vehicle. She also reported a shortness of breath and a proclivity to tug the steering wheel to the right whenever she saw an oncoming vehicle. Using a treatment package comprising directed relaxation, self-monitoring, and *in vivo* exposures, Fairbank and his associates (1981) eliminated the startle reaction and appreciably reduced the women's self-rated anxiety estimates following five treatment sessions. These impressive improvements continued to be seen at 1, 4, and 6-month follow-up assessments.

Keane and Kaloupek (1982) subsequently published a frequently cited article involving "imaginal flooding in the treatment of posttraumatic stress disorder" (p. 321). Their paper described the treatment of a 36-year-old male Vietnam veteran who developed PTSD following a series of war-related incidents. Keane and Kaloupek identified traumatic experiences that presented in the form of intrusive and highly arousing thoughts and nightmares. Nineteen flooding sessions were used wherein the patient was instructed to imagine the traumatic events for approximately 40 minutes. Keane and Kaloupek were able to observe significant reductions in self-reported anxiety as well as significant reductions in heart rate reactivity during traumatic simulations. The veteran also reported that his sleep and work-related efficacy significantly improved. Follow-up assessments denoted continued efficacy at 3- and 12-month follow-ups.

Rychtarik, Silverman, and Van Landingham (1984) subsequently described the use of imaginal flooding with a 22-year-old female incest victim. The patient reported that between the ages of 12 and 15 years old, her father had repeatedly forced her to experience a number of incestuous activities. She presented with anxiety-evoking incest-related thoughts, isolation, sleep disturbance, and alcohol abuse. Treatment consisted of nine sessions that involved 10 minutes of therapist-directed relaxation exercises and 80–90 minutes of imaginal exposure to incestuous scenes. Rychtarik and his colleagues reported that the incidence of self-monitored incest-related thoughts and nightmares that were fairly prominent before treatment were virtually nonexistent after therapy. Similar results were observed at a 6-month follow-up. Clinically significant reductions in self-reported anxiety as measured by the State Trait Anxiety Inventory (STAI; Spielberger, Gorsuch, & Lushane, 1968) were observed at 6 and 8-week follow-ups. Follow-up assessments also evidenced clinically significant reductions on skin conductance levels that were recorded during the imaginal exposures to incest-reminiscent material.

McCaffrey and Fairbank (1985) went on to describe the treatment of a 31-year-old male witness to a fatal helicopter crash and a 28-year-old female motor vehicle accident victim. Eighteen to 20 months after their respective experiences, the subjects met DSM-III criteria for PTSD. The first subject received four 2-hour treatment sessions that involved relaxation training, as well as imaginal exposure and an unspecified number of *in vivo* exposure sessions to trauma-reminiscent stimulus cues. The second subject received a comparable regimen involving eight imaginal and *in vivo* exposure sessions.

In order to assess the efficacy of the therapeutic package, the subjects self-monitored the frequency of nightmares as well as the amount of sleep that they experienced before and after therapy. The total number of self-monitored, trauma-related dreams decreased from two to zero for the first subject and from six to two for the second. It is of considerable interest to observe that the second subject "reported for the first time that she neither awakened in a cold sweat nor avoided returning to sleep following a nightmare" (McCaffrey & Fairbank, 1985, p. 412). Clinically significant post-treatment gains involving decreased self-reported anxiety and increased sleep were reported. Pre- and post-treatment heart rate (HR) and skin resistance levels (SRL) were monitored as the subjects observed video taped simulations involving trauma-reminiscent scenarios. While the first subject's pre- and post-treatment HR and SRL were similar, the second subject's basal level of cardiovascular reactivity markedly decreased after therapy.

Given the absence of information involving the effects of flooding with traumatized youth and a pressing need to provide services for traumatized youth during the Lebanese crisis, Saigh carried out a number of single-case flooding trials at the American University of Beirut Medical Center. Saigh (1987a) initially described the treatment of a 14-year-old Lebanese boy who had been abducted and tortured.

Six months after the incident, the boy met diagnostic criteria for PTSD as measured by the Children's PTSD Inventory (Saigh, 1989a). Before treatment, the WISC-R Coding and Digit Span subtests were administered, as PTSD is indicated in part by deficits in short-term memory and concentration. The boy also marked the STAI, the Rathus Assertiveness Schedule (RAS; Rathus, 1973), and the Beck Depression Inventory (BDI; Beck, Ward, Mandelson, Mock, & Erbaugh, 1961). A 12-item Behavioral Avoidance Test (BAT) was developed in order to measure the quantitative aspects of his trauma-related avoidance behaviors. In effect, the BAT involved a 10-minute behavioral walk wherein the boy left his home and proceeded along the route that he had taken to the place where the abduction occurred.

Four anxiety-evoking scenes were identified through a series of clinical interviews. These scenes reflected the chronological sequence of traumatic events that the youth had experienced (i.e., being stopped, forced into a car at gun point, blindfolded, and driven away). The imaginal flooding process involved 10 minutes of therapist-directed deep muscle relaxation exercises that were followed by 60 minutes of therapeutic stimulation wherein the youth was instructed to imagine the particular details of the anxiety-evoking scenes according to a multiple baseline across traumatic scenes design (Fairbank & Keane, 1982). Emotional distress relative to the traumatic scenes that were presented during the imaginal stimulations was measured through subjective units of disturbance (SUDS) ratings. In so doing, subjective levels of anxiety relative to each scene were rated according to a 0–10-point scale with 0 denoting "no discomfort" and 10 denoting "maximum discomfort." SUDS ratings were elicited at 2-minute intervals during each of the aversive scene presentations. The boy's SUDS levels appreciably decreased after seven flooding sessions. As may be noted from Figure 13.1, his multiple-baseline across traumatic scenes SUDS ratings markedly decreased over time. A 4-month follow-up revealed that the youth experienced almost no distress as measured by trauma-specific SUDS ratings.

Clinically significant pre- and post-treatment gains were observed on the WISC-R Coding and Digit Span subtests. Post-treatment and 4-month fol-

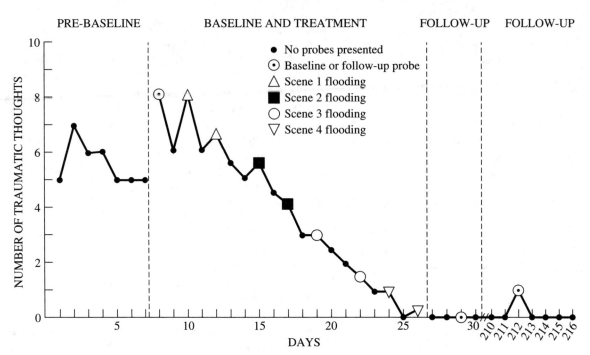

Figure 13.1. Multiple Baseline across traumatic scenes SUDS ratings.

Source: Saigh, P. A. (1987a). *In vitro* flooding of an adolescent posttraumatic stress disorder. *Journal of Clinical Child Psychology, 16,* 147–150. Reprinted by permission.

low-up assessments also reflected clinically significant treatment gains with respect to self-reported anxiety, depression, and misconduct. While the boy only completed one third of the BAT items before the treatment, 100% of the BAT activities were completed after the final treatment session. These gains continued to be observed at a 4-month follow-up evaluation.

Saigh (1987b, 1987c, 1987d, 1989d) went on to conduct four single-case replications wherein flooding was used in the treatment of traumatized youth. In each instance, traumatic scenes were identified and verbally presented according to a multiple-baseline across traumatic scenes design. Viewed in this context, Table 13.5 presents the transcript of a flooding session involving a 10-year-old Lebanese female who developed PTSD after being exposed to an artillery barrage (Saigh, 1987b). As may be noted from the table, stimulus and response imagery cues (Levis, 1980) were employed during the flooding process. Stimulus cues involved the visual, auditory, olfactory, and tactile components of each scene. Response cues involved the behavioral and cognitive aspects of the scene.

The frequency of intrusive trauma-related thoughts (excluding the ones that were induced in therapy) were self-monitored on pocket frequency counters (i.e., the Knit Tally, Boyle Needle Company) in two of the Lebanese reports (Saigh, 1987b, 1987c). Figure 13.2 presents the frequency of spontaneous trauma-specific thoughts that were self-monitored by the youth who experienced the artillery barrage (Saigh, 1987b). As may be noted from the figure, treatment seemingly induced a brief exacerbation of intrusive trauma-related thoughts. It may also be seen that the frequency of these traumatic memories markedly decreased over time. Similar patterns of arousal and habituation were observed in a follow-up study involving three Lebanese children with war-related PTSD (Saigh, 1987c).

Clinically significant pre- and post-treatment gains were apparent on the WISC-R Digit Span and Coding subtests in Saigh's single-case studies. Likewise, significant reductions in self-reported reactivity to the traumatic scenes were evident on the SUDS ratings that were monitored before ther-apy, during therapy, at post-treatment, and follow-up assessments.

TABLE 13.5. Imaginal Flooding Process with a 10-Year-Old Female

Therapist 1:	Imagine that you are playing in a neighborhood garden in the afternoon. Imagine the color of the grass and the plants. Imagine the people slowly walking by. Can you picture this?
Mariam 1:	Yes.
Therapist 2:	Imagine running after the ball that your mother threw. Now, imagine that you are looking at the shrubs. Imagine how you are separating the shrubs in search of the ball. Can you imagine yourself doing this?
Mariam 2:	Yes.
Therapist 3:	Now I want you to keep on imagining that you are leafing through the shrubs. Imagine the texture of the shrubs against your hands. Imagine the color of the underside of the leaves. Can you imagine this?
Mariam 3:	Yes.
Therapist 4:	According to the scale that we discussed, how much does this bother you?
Mariam 4:	7.
Therapist 5:	Very good. Keep on picturing this. (Ten-second pause). Now imagine that you can hear loud noises that sound like thunder in the distance as you are looking for the ball. Can you imagine these noises?
Mariam 5:	Yes.
Therapist 6:	Good. Now I want you to imagine that you are still looking for the ball in the shrubs. (Ten second pause). Suddenly, you hear a very loud explosion nearby. Imagine that you are looking up. People are running away. Imagine how everyone is running. Can you do this?
Mariam 6:	Yes.
Therapist 7:	How much does it bother you?
Mariam 7:	10.
Therapist 8:	Keep on imagining how people are running away. Imagine that you are turning away from the shrub. You want to find your mother. Imagine looking at the place where your mother had been. She is not there. Imagine that you suddenly hear a very loud explosion. Imagine that you are starting to run to the place where your mother had been. Can you picture this?
Mariam 8:	Yes. It's very bad.
Therapist 9:	How disturbing is it?
Mariam 9:	10.

Source: Saigh, P. A. (1987b). *In vitro* flooding of a childhood posttraumatic stress disorder. *School Psychology Review, 16,* 203–211. Reprinted by permission.

Appreciable improvements were observed across a number of self-report measures of anxiety and depression. Four of the Lebanese child-adolescent reports (Saigh, 1987b, 1987c, 1987d, 1989d) included performance measures. In each of these instances appreciably less avoidance was evident as measured by BAT performance at posttreatment and follow-up assessments. Finally, the subject's anecdotal comments supported the social validity (Schwartz & Bear, 1991; Wolf, 1978) of the interventions as they represented that the treatment outcome was worth the temporary discomfort that they experienced.

More recently, Saigh (1995) conducted a quasi-experimental analysis of the research involving Lebanese youth (see above). The subject pool involved eight patients (5 males and 3 females) with a mean age of 11 years. All subjects met DSM-III criteria for PTSD as measured by the Children's PTSD Inventory. The mean duration between stress exposure and treatment was approximately 2 years. Although different outcome measures were employed in a number of these trials (e.g., RCMAS, STAI, and CDI), all of the subjects received administrations of the WISC-R Digit Span and Coding subtests. In addition, SUDS ratings were recorded during all of the simulations. All of the Lebanese single-case trials used treatment packages that involved relaxation (10–15 min.), imaginal exposure to traumatic scenes (24–60 min.), and additional relaxation (5–10 min.). Data analysis determined that imaginal flooding was associated with statistically sig-

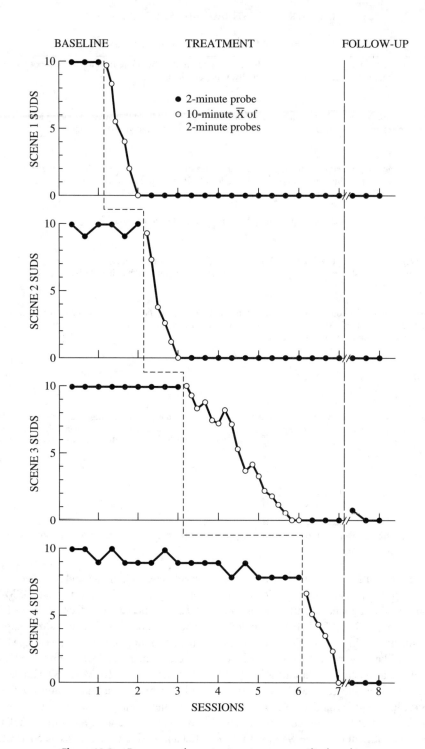

Figure 13.2. Frequency of spontaneous trauma-specific thoughts.

Source: Saigh, P. A. (1987b). *In vitro* flooding of a childhood posttraumatic stress disorder. *School Psychology Review, 16,* 203–211. Reprinted by permission.

nificant gains on the Digit Span and Coding subtests. Significant post-treatment reductions were also noted on the trauma-specific indicators of emotional distress. Four- to 6-month follow-up assessments were associated with statistically significant Digit Span and Coding gains and significant SUDs reductions.

Although the single-case and quasi-experimental reports denote efficacy, these designs do not provide the same quality of external validity that is associated with experimental designs (Saigh, 1992b; Saigh, Yule, & lnamdar, in press). With this in mind, it is of interest to note that three experimental studies involving adult veterans of the Vietnam conflict have been conducted (Boudewyns & Hyer, 1990; Cooper & Clum, 1989; Keane, Fairbank, Caddel, & Zimmering, 1989). Imaginal flooding in these studies was associated with significantly decreased startle reactions. The investigations that measured self-reported state anxiety reported that the flooding groups had significantly lower post-treatment scores (Cooper & Clum, 1989; Keane et al., 1989). Moreover, flooding was associated with significantly lower estimates of avoidance (Cooper & Clum, 1989), guilt (Keane et al., 1989), and alienation (Boudewyns & Hyer, 1990). In addition, the experimental flooding studies reported significantly greater post-treatment estimates of memory (Keane et al., 1989), physical vigor, and self-efficacy (Boudewyns & Hyer, 1990). Whereas Keane and his colleagues and Boudewyns and Hyer reported that flooding was associated with significantly lower estimates of trait anxiety and depression, nonsignificant differences were reported by Cooper and Clum. The investigations that used psychophysiological measures (Boudewyns & Hyer, 1990; Cooper & Clum, 1989) also failed to observe significant variations.

Examined *in toto,* it may be said that the child-adolescent single-case and quasi-experimental flooding trials as well as the adult investigations speak well for the efficacy of therapeutic exposure in the treatment of PTSD. Indeed, flooding may effectively reduce PTSD symptoms and a number of the associated features of the disorder. On the other hand, it may also be said that additional research (particularly with children and adolescents) must be conducted before a stronger conclusion can be reached.

CLINICAL AND ETHICAL CONCERNS

While this chapter is not intended to serve as a clinical guide[1], a number of applied and ethical concerns warrant consideration. As flooding is an aversive technique, efforts should be made to protect the rights of children and adolescents. Therapists should inform child-adolescent PTSD patients and their parents about the procedures that are employed throughout the flooding process. They should candidly answer questions that may arise. Without a doubt, the informed consent of children-adolescents and their parents or guardians should be obtained before flooding is attempted. Families, mental-health practitioners, and medical personnel should be informed that PTSD symptoms usually increase during the early stages of therapy (cf. Saigh, 1987a, 1992b; Saigh, Yule, & Inamdar, in press).

The Association for the Advancement of Behavior Therapy's (AABT, 1977) ethical guidelines should serve as a working guide as they provide operational recommendations for clinical practice and address concerns that are relevant to the needs of children and adolescents. The AABT guidelines indicate that therapists should determine if a patient's participation is voluntary by considering possible sources of coercion and by ensuring that they can withdraw from the treatment without penalty. Likewise, when the competence of a subordinate client (e.g., a child or adolescent) is limited, it is recommended that efforts should be made to ensure that the "client as well as the guardian participate in treatment discussions to the extent that the client's ability permits" (AABT, 1977, p. vi). The AABT also advocates that the patient's understanding of the treatment goals should be verified by asking the patient to restate the goals either verbally (a highly recommended procedure with young children) or in writing. The AABT guidelines fur-

---

[1] Those interested in a description of actual flooding procedures are referred to Saigh (1992b).

TABLE 13.6. Single-Case, Quasi-Experimental, and Experimental PTSD Flooding Studies

INVESTIGATION	TYPE OF STUDY	SUBJECT CHARACTERISTICS	TREATMENT	OUTCOMES
Fairbank, DeGood, & Jenkins, 1981	1	32-year-old female motor vehicle accident victim. Presented 3 months post-trauma.	Five sessions involving self-monitoring, relaxation training, behavioral rehearsal, and *in vivo* flooding (duration (duration unspecified).	Eliminated startle reaction and lower SUDS ratings.
Keane & Kaloupek, 1982	1	36-year-old male Vietnam veteran. Presented 14 years posttrauma.	Nineteen sessions involving 10 min. of relaxation followed by 40 min. of imaginal flooding.	Fewer nightmares, lower STAI scores, increased sleep, and heart rate during simulations.
Rychtarik, Silverman, & Van Landingham, 1984	1	22-year-old female incest victim. Presented 7 years posttrauma.	Nine sessions involving 10 min. of relaxation followed by 80–90 min. of imaginal flooding.	Fewer and less aversive traumatic recollections, nightmares, lower STAI scores.
McCaffery & Fairbank, 1985	1	31-year-old male witness of helicopter crash. Presented 20 months posttrauma.	Four 2-hour imaginal flooding sessions involving relaxation followed by exposure and unspecified number of *in vivo* exposures.	Fewer and less aversive traumatic recollections, fewer nightmares, lower self-reported anxiety, heart rate, and skin resistance during simulations unchanged.
		28-year-old female motor vehicle accident survivor. Presented 18 months posttrauma.	Seven 2-hour imaginal flooding sessions involving relaxation followed by exposure and un-specified number of *in vivo* exposures.	Fewer and less aversive traumatic recollections, fewer nightmares, lower self-reported anxiety, lower heart rate, and skin resistance during simula-tions. Appreciably lower at post-treatment.
Saigh, 1987a	1	14-year-old Lebanese male. Presented 6 months posttrauma.	Seven flooding sessions (10 min. relaxation, 60 min. imaginal flooding, and 10 min. relaxation).	Post-treatment gains on the WISC-R Digit Span and Coding subtests. Lower SUDs ratings during simulations, lower STAI, and RAS scores. Improved BAT perfor-mance
Saigh, 1987b	1	10-year-old Lebanese female. Presented 38 months posttrauma.	Nine flooding sessions (10 min. relaxation, 60 min. imaginal flooding, and 5 min. relaxation between scenes)	Post-treatment gains on the WISC-R Digit Span and Coding subtests. Lower SUDs ratings during simulations, RCMAS, CDI, and CTRS scores, self-moni-tored and trauma-related ideation. Improved BAT performance.

INVESTIGATION	TYPE OF STUDY	SUBJECT CHARACTERISTICS	TREATMENT	OUTCOMES
Saigh, 1987c	1	11-year-old Lebanese female. Presented 32 months posttrauma.	Ten flooding sessions (10 min. relaxation, 60 min. imaginal flooding, and 5 min. relaxation between scenes.	Post-treatment gains on the WISC-R Digit Span and Coding subtests. Lower SUDs ratings during simulations, self-monitored trauma-related ideation, RCMAS, CTI, and CTRS score. Improved BAT performance
	1	11-year-old Lebanese female. Presented 36 months posttrauma.	Nine flooding sessions as described above.	Same as above.
	1	12-year-old Lebanese male. Presented 28 months posttrauma.	Ten flooding sessions as described above.	Same as above.
Saigh, 1987d	1	6.5-year-old Lebanese male. Presented 25 months posttrauma.	Eleven flooding sessions (15 min. relaxation, 24 min. imaginal flooding, and 10 min. relaxation).	Post-treatment gains on the WISC-R Digit Span and Coding subtests. Lower SUDs ratings during simulations, RCMAS, CDI, and CTRS score.
Saigh, 1989d	1	13-year-old Lebanese female. Presented 14 months posttrauma.	Thirteen flooding sessions (10 min. relaxation, 60 min. imaginal flooding, and 10 min. relaxation).	Post-treatment gains on the WISC-R Digit Span and Coding subtests. Lower SUDs ratings during simulations, self-monitored trauma-related ideation, RCMAS, CDI, and CTRS score. Improved BAT performance.
	1	14-year-old Lebanese male. Presented 16 months posttrauma.	Twelve flooding sessions as described above.	Post-treatment gains on the WISC-R Digit Span and Coding subtests. Lower SUDs ratings during simulations, self monitored trauma-related ideation, RCMAS, CDI, and CTRS score. Improved BAT performance.
Saigh, 1995	2	3 females and 5 males; mean age 11 years; 2 year mean exposure-treatment interval.	Six to 13 sessions (10–15 min. relaxation, 24–60 min. imaginal exposure, and 5–10 min. relaxation).	Significant gains on the WISC-R Digit Span and Coding subtests. Significantly lower SUDs ratings during simulations.

INVESTIGATION	TYPE OF STUDY	SUBJECT CHARACTERISTICS	TREATMENT	OUTCOMES
Cooper & Clum, 1989	3	8 male Vietnam veteran (mean age 39.6 years) experimental subjects.	Ten to 12 sessions involving 50 min. imaginal simulation.	Flooding group had significantly fewer nightmares, significantly lower STAI State Scores, self-reported startle response and enhanced BAT performance. No significant group differences were evident on STAI Trait, BDI, or heart rates during simulations.
		8 male Vietnam veteran (mean age 39.3 years) control subjects.	Ten to 12 sessions of "standard VA treatment" unreported duration. Exposure-treatment interval not specified.	
Keane, Fairbank, Caddell, & Zimmering, 1989	3	11 male Vietnam veteran (mean age 34.7 years) experimental subjects.	Fourteen imaginal flooding sessions. 9 (15-min. discussions, 10 min. relaxation, 45 min. imaginal flooding, 10 min. relaxation, and 10 min. debriefing).	Flooding group had significantly fewer trauma-reexperiencing symptoms, startle reactions, self-reported guilt, and less memory impairment. Flooding group had significantly lower STAI State and Trait, BDI, and Fear Survey Schedule scores. Nonsignificant group differences on therapist ratings of sleep disturbance, social adjustment, and MMPI PTSD subscale.
		13 male Vietnam veteran (mean age 34.5 years) control subjects.	Ten of the 13 controls received anxiolytic medications. Exposure-treatment interval not specified.	
Bouedewyns & Hyer, 1990	3	12 male Vietnam veteran (mean age 39.3 years) experimental subjects.	Ten to 12, 50 min. of imaginal flooding.	Flooding group had significantly fewer startle reactions, self-reported anxiety, depression, and feelings of alienation.
		12 male Vietnam veteran (mean age 39.6 years) control subjects.	Ten to 12, of "conventional therapy or counseling" (duration unspecified). Exposure-treatment interval not specified.	Improved physical vigor and self efficacy. Nonsignificant differences on measures of heart rate, EMG, & skin conductance during simulation.

1 = Single-Case, 1 = Quasi-Experimental, and 3 = Experimental Designs

ther recommend that the choice of treatment methods should be thoroughly considered. Given that PTSD may spontaneously remit over time (Saigh & Fairbank, in press; Saigh, Green, & Korol, in press), therapists may wish to consider the time-limited use of supportive counseling (Scott & Stradling, 1992) or anxiolytic medications with youth who meet criteria for PTSD shortly after stress exposure.

Examined from a more clinical perspective, investigators and practitioners would be well-advised to recognize that exposure-based paradigms for PTSD should be delivered within the context of a supportive therapeutic relationship (Fairbank & Nicholson, 1987; Resick & Schnicke, 1993). It should also be realized that PTSD flooding regimens have occurred within comprehensive treatment plans that targeted the multiple dimensions of PTSD (Saigh, 1992b). Whereas flooding has been associated with favorable outcomes, supportive counseling and educational interventions may serve to offset pathological self-efficacy expectations (Saigh, Mroweh et al., 1995) and academic impairments (Saigh & Mroweh, 1993). In a similar vein, the use of behavioral anger-management techniques (Feindier & Ecton, 1987) and assertion training (Wolpe, 1990) may be of value in addressing associated symptoms of anger and irritability.

Very young children may not be able to imagine traumatic material, follow detailed relaxation procedures, or tolerate extended *in vitro* presentations (Morris & Kratochwill, 1983). In these instances, asking traumatized youth to draw pictures of their stressful experience and verbally describe the content of their drawings may present a useful adjunct to more traditional forms of exposure. Likewise, the use of trauma-reminiscent prompts may facilitate the ability to imagine stressful material in therapeutic settings. For example, Saigh (1987c) reported that a 12-year-old Lebanese boy, whose home had been destroyed when it was hit by an artillery round, was not able to imagine the components of a scene involving the shelling incident that eventually led to the destruction of his home. In this case, the sounds of progressively closer and louder shell and rocket explosions that occurred during a particularly violent

episode of the Lebanese crisis were audio taped. The sound track was amplified by two 50 watt speakers and played in session as the therapist asked the boy to imagine the shelling incident. As it were, the youth reported that the sound track was very "real." This, coupled with the therapist's instructions to imagine the traumatic material, was associated with a positive therapeutic outcome.

While the flooding literature has been associated with favorable outcomes, flooding may not always be the treatment of choice. Flooding may be contraindicated when child-adolescent PTSD cases present with comorbid conditions (e.g., psychosis, limited mental ability, depression, conduct disorder, oppositional defiant disorder, attention deficit hyperactive disorder, or substance abuse). A history of noncompliance, inability to establish and/or maintain mental images, reduced reexperiencing symptoms, and directed compensation-seeking efforts were listed by Litz, Blake, Gerardi, and Keane (1990) as reasons for not prescribing flooding. It is of some interest to observe that all of the subjects in the Lebanese trials were carefully screened before treatment to ensure that they could establish and maintain both positive and aversive mental images and follow instructions. Efforts were also consistently made to ensure that the parents of the participating youth were sufficiently motivated to attend to the psychological needs of their children throughout the flooding process. Moreover, their mental ability was within or above normal limits. In instances where flooding is not advisable, alternative procedures such as supportive counseling, family therapy, or psychopharmacological regimens are recommended.

RECOMMENDATIONS FOR FUTURE TREATMENT RESEARCH

Given the apparent success of the singe-case trials and experimental trials, experimental-flooding studies involving traumatized youth would be of exceptional relevance as the child-clinical literature is currently limited to a modicum of single-case and quasi-experimental trials. As the assignment of traumatized youth to no treatment, waiting list, or nonspecific control conditions may not be feasible or ethically defensible, the use or randomized active treatment designs (Kazdin, 1992) is regarded as the preferred manner in which to proceed. Given these points, it would also be of interest to explore the comparative effects of flooding and *in vitro* participant modeling (Bandura, Jeffery, Wright, 1974) as this approach does not involve imaginal exposure and as young children who are unable to imagine traumatic scenes may benefit from this form of exposure.

Research designed to identify child-adolescent PTSD patient, therapist, treatment, and family factors that are associated with successful outcomes is clearly in order. Viewed in this context, Morris and Kratochwill's (1983) analysis of the systematic desensitization and flooding literature concluded that researchers should identify child-adolescent factors that are associated with treatment efficacy (i.e., age, ability to imagine, the quality of visual imagery, the ability to follow verbal instruction, threshold for fatigue, and the ability to relax). There is also a need to identify comorbid conditions that occur during the developmental period (e.g., oppositional defiant disorder, conduct disorder, attention deficit hyperactive disorder) that may influence therapeutic outcomes. Likewise, the influence of moderator variables such as the quality of therapeutic relationships and the qualitative aspects of parental support warrant systematic examination. Clinical investigators should also attempt to demonstrate the integrity of these treatments as the experimental studies that were reviewed did not control for this form of variance. It is relevant to recall that the Lebanese youth who responded to flooding regimens were the victims of war-related events. Although these subjects met diagnostic criteria for PTSD, they did not present with associated feelings of shame, guilt, and diminished trust. Given that child sexual and physical abuse victims frequently report these symptoms (Wolfe, 1991), it would be of interest to test the efficacy of regimens that combine therapeutic exposure and cognitive interventions as described in recent studies involving adult rape victims (cf. Resick & Schnicke, 1993; Rothbaum & Foa, 1992).

REFERENCES

Adler, A. (1943). Neuropsychiatric complications in victims of Boston's Coconut Grove disaster. *Journal of the American Medical Association, 123,* 1098–1101.

American Psychiatric Association (1952). *Diagnostic and statistical manual of mental disorders.* Washington, DC: Author.

American Psychiatric Association (1968). *Diagnostic and statistical manual of mental disorders* (2nd ed.). Washington, DC: Author.

American Psychiatric Association (1980). *Diagnostic and statistical manual of mental disorders* (3rd ed.). Washington, DC: Author.

American Psychiatric Association (1987). *Diagnostic and statistical manual of mental disorders* (3rd ed., rev.). Washington, DC: Author.

American Psychiatric Association (1994). *Diagnostic and statistical manual of mental disorders* (4th ed.). Washington, DC: Author.

Anderson, N. C. (1985). Posttraumatic stress disorder. In H. I. Kaplan & B. J. Sadock (Eds.), *Comprehensive textbook in psychiatry* (4th ed., pp. 918–924). Baltimore: William and Wilkins.

Association for the Advancement of Behavior Therapy. (1977). Ethical issues for human services. *Behavior Therapy, 8,* v–vi.

Bandura, A., Jeffery, R. W., & Wright, E. (1974). Efficacy of participant modeling as a response to instructional aids. *Journal of Abnormal Psychology, 83,* 56–64.

Beck, A. T., Ward, C. H., Mandelson, M., Mock, J., & Erbaugh, J. (1961). An inventory for measuring depression. *Archives of General Psychiatry, 4,* 561–571.

Bell, C. B., & Jenkins, E. (1993). Community violence and children on Chicago's south side. *Psychiatry, 56,* 46–54.

Bender, L., & Blau, A. (1937). The reaction of children to sexual relations with adults. *The American Journal of Orthopsychiatry, 7,* 500–518.

Boudewyns, P. A., & Hyer, I. (1990). Physiological response to combat memories and preliminary treatment outcome in Vietnam veteran PTSD patients treated with direct therapeutic exposure. *Behavior Therapy, 21,* 63–87.

Boudewyns, P. A., & Shipley, R. H. (1983). *Flooding and implosive therapy.* New York: Plenum Press.

Bradner, T. (1943). Psychiatric observations among Finnish children during the Russio-Finnish War of 1939–1940. *Nervous Child, 2,* 313–319.

Breslau, N., Davis, G. C., Andreski, P., & Peterson, E. (1991). Traumatic events and posttraumatic stress disorder in an urban population of young adults. *Archives of General Psychiatry, 48,* 216–222.

Burt, C. W. (1995). *Injury related visits to hospital emergency departments: United States, 1992.* Vital and Health Statistics of the Centers for Disease Control and Prevention/National Center for Health Statistics. Number 261. Hayatsville, MD: United States Department of Health and Human Services.

Burton, D., Foy, D., Bwanausi, C., Johnson, J., Moore, L. (1994). The relationship between traumatic exposure, family dysfunction, and posttraumatic stress symptoms in male juvenile offenders. *Journal of Traumatic Stress, 7,* 83–92.

Carey-Trefzer, C. J. (1949). The results of a clinical study of war-damaged children who attended a child guidance clinic. *Journal of Mental Science, 95,* 535–559.

Cooper, N. A., & Clum, G. A. (1989). Imaginal flooding as a supplementary treatment for PTSD in combat veterans: A controlled evaluation. *Behavior Therapy, 20,* 381–391.

Daly, R. J. (1983). Samuel Pepys and posttraumatic stress disorder. *British Journal of Psychiatry, 143,* 64–68.

Davidson, J. R. T., & Foa, E. B. (Eds.). (1994). *Posttraumatic stress disorder: DSM-IV and beyond.* Washington, DC: American Psychiatric Press.

Diamond, R., Saigh, P. A., & Fairbank, J. A. (in press). An analysis of internalizing and externalizing problems in preschool children with PTSD or ADHD. *Journal of Traumatic Stress.*

Earls, F., Smith, E., Reich, W., & Jung, K. G. (1988). Investigating psychopathological consequences of a disaster in children: A pilot study incorporating a structured diagnostic interview. *Journal of the American Academy of Child and Adolescent Psychiatry, 27,* 90–95.

Eitinger, L. (1962). Concentration camp survivors in the postwar world. *American Journal of Orthopsychiatry, 32,* 367–375.

Fairbank, J. A., DeGood, D. D., & Jenkins, C. W. (1981). Behavioral treatment of a persistent post-traumatic startle response. *Journal of Behavior Therapy and Experimental Psychiatry, 12,* 321–324.

Fairbank, J. A., & Keane, T. M. (1982). Flooding for combat-related stress disorders: Assessment of anxiety reduction across traumatic memories. *Behavior Therapy, 13,* 499–510.

Fairbank, J. A., & Nicholson, R. A. (1987). Theoretical and empirical issues in the treatment of posttraumatic stress disorder in Vietnam veterans. *Journal of Clinical Psychology, 43,* 44–55.

Feighner, J. P., Robins, E., Guze, S. B., Woodruff, P. F., Winokur, G. W., & Munoz, R. (1972). Diagnostic criteria for use in psychiatry. *Archives of General Psychiatry, 26,* 57–63.

Feindler, E. L., & Ecton, R. B. (1987). *Adolescent anger control training: Cognitive-behavioral techniques.* New York: Pergamon Press.

Foy, D. W., Sipprelle, R. C., Rueger, D. B., & Carroll, E. M. (1984). Etiology of posttraumatic stress disorder in Vietnam veterans: Analysis of premilitary, military, and combat exposure influences. *Journal of Consulting and Clinical Psychology, 52,* 79-87.

Fredrick, C. J. (1985). Posttraumatic stress disorder and child molestation. In A. Burgess & C. Hartman (Eds.), *Sexual exploitation of clients by mental health professionals* (pp. 133–142). New York: Praeger.

Friedman, P. (1948). The effects of imprisonment. *Acta Medica Orientalia, 7,* 163–167.

Garrison, C. Z., Weinrich, M. W., Hardin, S. B., Weinrich, S., & Wang, L. (1993). Posttraumatic stress disorder in adolescents after a hurricane. *American Journal of Epidemiology, 138,* 522–530.

Glass, A. J. (1954). Psychotherapy in the combat zone. *American Journal of Psychiatry, 110,* 725–731.

Glass, A. J., Ryan, F. J., Lubin, A., Reddy, C. V., & Tucker, A. C. (1956). *Psychiatric prediction and military effectiveness.* Walter Reed Army Institute of Research, Walter Reed Army Medical Center, Washington, DC.

Grinker, R. R., & Spiegel, J. P. (1945). *Men under stress.* Philadelphia: Blakiston.

Handford, H., Mayes, S., Mattison, R., Humphrey, F., Bagnato, S., Bixler, E., & Kales, J. (1986). Child and parent reactions to the Three Mile Island nuclear accident. *Journal of the American Academy of Child and Adolescent Psychiatry, 25,* 346–356.

Hernandez, J. T. (1992). Substance abuse among sexually abused adolescents and their families. *Journal of Adolescent Health, 13,* 658–662.

Hogan, R. A., & Kirchner, J. H. (1967). Preliminary report on the extinction of learned fears via short term therapy. *Journal of Abnormal Psychology, 72,* 106–109.

Jablensky, A. (1985). Approaches to the definition and classification of anxiety and related disorders in European psychiatry. In A. H. Tuma & J. D. Masser (Eds.), *Anxiety and the anxiety disorders* (pp. 223–254). Hillsdale, NJ: Lawrence Erlbaum.

Jacobson, P. B. (1991). Treating a man with a needle phobia who requires daily injections of medication. *Hospital and Community Psychiatry, 42,* 877–879.

Kazdin, A. (1992). *Research designs in clinical psychology* (2nd ed). New York: Macmillan.

Keane, T. M., Fairbank, J. A., Caddell, J. M., & Zimmering, R. T. (1989). Implosive (flooding) therapy reduces symptoms of PTSD in Vietnam combat veterans. *Behavior Therapy. 20,* 245–260.

Keane, T. M., & Kaloupek, D. G. (1982). Imaginal flooding in the treatment of post-traumatic stress disorder. *Journal of Consulting and Clinical Psychology, 50,* 138–140.

Kilpatrick, D. G., Resnick, H. S., & Freedy, J. R. (1993). *DSM-IV posttraumatic stress disorder field trial: Criterion A and other stressor event histories associated with PTSD in clinical and community samples.* Crime Victims Center, Medical University of South Carolina, Charleston, SC.

Kilpatrick, D. G., Saunders, B. E., Vernon, L. J., Best, C. L., & Von, J. M. (1987). Criminal victimization: Lifetime prevalence, reporting to police, and psychological impact. *Crime and Delinquency, 33,* 479–489.

Kinzie, J. D., Sack, W. H., Angell, R. H., Clarke, G., & Ben, R. (I 989). A three year follow-up of Cambodian young people traumatized as children. *Journal of the American Academy of Child and Adolescent Psychiatry, 28,* 501–504.

Kinzie, J.D., Sack, W.H., Angell, R.H., & Mason, S.M. (1986). The psychiatric effects of massive trauma on Cambodian children. *Journal of the American Academy of Child and Adolescent Psychiatry, 25,* 370– 376.

Korol, M. (1990). *Childrens psychological responses to a nuclear waste disaster in Fernald, Ohio.* Unpublished doctoral dissertation, University of Cincinnati, Cincinnati, OH.

Kulka, R. C., Schlenger, W. E., Fairbank, J. A., Hough, R. L., Jordan, B. K., Marmar, C. R., & Weiss, D. S. (1990). *Trauma and the Vietnam generation: Report of findings from the national Vietnam veterans readjustment study.* New York: Brunner Mazel.

Levis, D. J. (1980). Implementing the technique of implosive therapy. In A. Goldstein & E. Foa (Eds.), *Handbook of behavioral interventions: A clinical guide* (pp. 92–51). New York: Wiley.

Levis, D. J., & Carrera, R. N. (1967). Effects of ten hours of implosive therapy in the treatment of outpatients: A preliminary report. *Journal of Abnormal Psychology, 72,* 504–508.

Litz, B.T., Blake, D.D., Gerardi, R.G., & Keane, T.M. (1990). Decision making guidelines for the use of direct therapeutic exposure in the treatment of post-traumatic stress disorder. *The Behavior Therapist, 13,* 91–93.

Livingston, R., Lawson, L., & Jones, J. G. (1993). Predictors of self-reported psychopathology in children abused repeatedly by a parent. *Journal of the American Academy of Child and Adolescent Psychiatry, 32,* 948–953.

Malleson, N. (1959). Panic and phobia: A possible method of treatment. *Lancet, 1,* 225– 227.

Marks, I. A. (1972). Flooding (implosion) and allied treatments. In S. Argas (Ed.), *Behavior modification: Principles and clinical applications* (pp. 151–211). Boston: Little, Brown.

McCaffrey, R. J., & Fairbank J. A. (1985). Behavioral assessment and treatment of accident-related posttraumatic stress disorder: Two case studies. *Behavior Therapy, 16,* 406–416.

McLeer, S. V., Callaghan, M., Henry, D., & Wallen, J. (1994). Psychiatric disorders in sexually abused youth. *Journal of the American Academy of Child and Adolescent Psychiatry, 33,* 313–319.

McLeer, S. V., Deblinger, E., Atkins, M. S., Foa, E. B., & Ralphe, D. L. (1988). Post-traumatic stress disorder in sexually abused children. *Journal of the American Academy of Child and Adolescent Psychiatry, 27,* 650–654.

Merry, S., & Andrews, L. K. (1994). Psychiatric status of sexually abused children 12 months after disclosure of abuse. *Journal of the American Academy of Child and Adolescent Psychiatry, 33,* 939–944.

Morey, L. C., Skinner, H. A., & Blashfield, R.K. (1986). Trends in the classification of abnormal behavior. In A. R. Cimenaro, K. S. Kalhoun, & H. E. Adams (Eds.), *Handbook of behavioral assessment* (2nd ed., pp. 47–78). New York: Wiley.

Morris, R. J., & Kratochwill, T. R. (1983). *Treating children's fears: A behavioral approach.* New York: Pergamon Press.

Mott, F.W. (1919). *War neuroses and shell shock.* London: Oxford University Press.

Nader, K., Pynoos, R., Fairbanks, L., & Frederick, C. (1990). Children's PTSD reactions one year after a sniper attack at their school. *American Journal of Psychiatry, 147,* 1526–1530.

Nader, K., Pynoos, R., Fairbanks, L., Frederick, C., Al-Ajeel, M., & Al-Asfour, A. (1993). A preliminary study of PTSD and grief among the children of Kuwait following the Gulf crisis. *British Journal of Clinical Psychology, 32,* 407–416.

Orvaschel, H., Puig-Antich, P., Chambers, W., & Abrizi, M. (1982). Retrospective assessment of prepubertal major depression with the Kiddie SADS. *Journal of the American Academy of Child and Adolescent Psychiatry, 21,* 392–397.

Pelcovitz, D., Kaplan, S., Goldenberg, B., Mendel, F., Lehane, J., & Guarrera, J. (1994). Post-traumatic stress disorder in physically abused adolescents. *Journal of the American Academy of Child and Adolescent Psychiatry, 33,* 305–312.

Polin, A. T. (1959). The effects of flooding and physical suppression as extinction techniques on an anxiety motivated avoidance locomotor response. *Journal of Psychology, 47,* 235–245.

Prasard, J. (1934). Psychology of rumors: A study of the great Indian earthquake of 1934. *British Journal of Psychology, 26,* 1–15.

Puig-Antich, J., Orvaschel, H., Tabrinzi, M. H., & Chambers, W. (1980). *The Schedule for Affective Disorders and Schizophrenia for School Age Children (Kiddie SADS).* New York Psychiatric Institute and Yale University School of Medicine.

Pynoos, R. S., Frederick, C., Nader, K., Arroyo, W., Steinberg, A., Eth, S., Nunez, F., & Fairbanks, L. (1987). Life threat and posttraumatic stress in school-age children. *Archives of General Psychiatry, 44,* 1057–1063.

Pynoos, R. S., Goenjian, A., Tashjain, M., Karakashian, M., Manjikian, R., Manoukian, G., Steinberg, A. M., & Fairbanks, L. A. (1993). Post-traumatic stress reactions in children after the 1988 Armenian earthquake. *British Journal of Psychiatry, 163,* 239–247.

Rachman, S. J. (1966). Studies in desensitization:II. Flooding. *Behaviour Research and Therarpy, 4,* 1–6.

Raines, G. N., & Kolb, L. C. (1943 July). Combat fatigue and war neurosis. *U.S. Navy Medical Bulletin,* 923–926, 1299–1309.

Rathus, S. A. (1973). A 30-item schedule for assessing assertive behavior. *Behavior Therapy, 4,* 398–406.

Reich, W., Herjanic, B., Weiner, Z., & Gandhy, P. R. (1982). Development of a structured interview for children: Agreement on diagnosis comparing child and parent interviews. *Journal of Abnormal Child Psychiatry, 10,* 325–336.

Reich, W., Shayka, J. J., & Taibleson, C. (1991). *Diagnostic Interview for Children and Adolescents-Revised-Parent Version (DICA-R-P).* Washington University Division of Child Psychiatry.

Resick, P. A., & Schnicke, M. K. (1993). *Cognitive processing therapy for rape victims. A treatment manual.* Newbury Park, CA: Sage Publications.

Resnick, H. S., Kilpatrick, D. G., Dansky, B. S., Saunders, B. E., & Best, C. L. (1993). Prevalence of civilian trauma and posttraumatic stress disorder in a representative national sample of women. *Journal of Consulting and Clinical Psychology, 61,* 984–991.

Robins, L. N., Helzer, J. E., Croughan, J., & Ratcliff, K. (1981). National Institute of Mental Health Interview Schedule. *Archives of General Psychiatry, 38,* 381–389.

Rothbaum, B. O., & Foa, E. B. (1992). Cognitive-behavioral treatment of posttraumatic stress disorder. In P.A. Saigh (Ed.), *Posttraumatic stress disorder: Theory research and treatment* (pp. 85–110). Boston: Allyn & Bacon.

Rychtarik, R. G., Silverman, W. K., & Van Landingham, W.P. (1984). Treatment of an incest victim with implosive therapy: A case study. *Behavior Therapy, 15,* 410–420.

Sack, W. H. (in press). The Khmer adolescent project: III. A study of trauma from Thailand's Site II Refugee Camp. *Journal of the American Academy of Child and Adolescent Psychiatry.*

Sack, W. H., McSharry, S., Kinney, R., Seeley, J., & Lewinson, P. (1994). The Khmer adolescent project: II. Functional capacities in two generations of Cambodian refugees. *Journal of Nervous and Mental Diseases, 182,* 387–395.

Saigh, P. A. (1987a). *In vitro* flooding of an adolescent's posttraumatic stress disorder. *Journal of Clinical Child Psychology, 16,* 147–150.

Saigh, P. A. (1987b). *In vitro* flooding of a childhood posttraumatic stress disorder. *School Psychology Review, 16,* 203–211.

Saigh, P. A. (1987c). *In vitro* flooding of childhood posttraumatic stress disorder: A systematic replication. *Professional School Psychology, 2,* 133–145.

Saigh, P. A. (1987d). *In vitro* flooding of a 6-year-old boy's posttraumatic stress disorder. *Behaviour Research and Therapy, 24,* 685–689.

Saigh, P. A. (1988). Anxiety, depression, and assertion across alternating intervals of stress. *Journal of Abnormal Psychology, 97,* 338–342.

Saigh, P. A. (1989a). The validity of the DSM-III posttraumatic stress disorder classification as applied to children. *Journal of Abnormal Psychology, 98,* 189–192.

Saigh, P. A. (1989b). The development and validation of the Children's Posttraumatic Stress Disorder Inventory. *International Journal of Special Education, 4,* 75–84.

Saigh, P. A. (1989d). The use of *in vitro* flooding in the treatment of traumatized adolescents. *Journal of Behavioral and Developmental Pediatrics, 10,* 17–21.

Saigh, P. A. (1992a). History, current nosology, and epidemiology. In P.A. Saigh (Ed.), *Posttraumatic stress disorder: A behavioral approach to assessment and treatment* (pp. 1–27). Boston: Allyn & Bacon.

Saigh, P. A. (1992b). The behavioral treatment of child and adolescent posttraumatic stress disorder. *Advances in Behaviour Research and Therapy, 14,* 247–275.

Saigh, P. A. (1995, November). The effects of therapeutic flooding on the memories of child-adolescent PTSD patients. In D. J. Bremner (Chair), *Memory and cognition in PTSD.* Symposium conducted at the annual meeting of the International Society of Traumatic Stress Studies, Boston, MA.

Saigh, P. A., & Fairbank, J. A. (in press). War-related posttraumatic stress disorder among children and adolescents. In T. Miller (Ed.), *Stressful life events* (2nd ed.). Madison, CT: International Universities Press.

Saigh, P. A., Green, B., & Korol, M. (1996). The history and prevalence of posttraumatic stress disorder in children and adolescents. *Journal of School Psychology, 34,* 107–132.

Saigh, P. A., & Mroweh, A. (1993, January). Scholastic impairments among traumatized adolescents. In P. A. Saigh (Chair), *Current research on child and adolescent posttraumatic stress disorder.* Symposium presented at the Lake George Research Conference on Posttraumatic Stress Disorder, Bolton Landing, NY.

Saigh, P. A., Mroweh, A., Zimmerman, B., & Fairbank, J. A. (1995). Self-efficacy expectations among traumatized adolescents. *Behaviour Research and Therapy, 33,* 701–705.

Saigh, P. A., Yule, W., & Inamdar, S. (1996). Imaginal flooding in the treatment of traumatized children and adolescents. *Journal of School Psychology, 34,* 163–184.

Savin, D., Sack, W. H., Clarke, G. N., Nee, M., & Richart, I. (in press). The Khmer Adolescent Project: II. A study of trauma from Thailand's Site Two refugee camp. *Journal of the American Academy of Child and Adolescent Psychiatry.*

Schwartz, I. S., & Bear, D. M. (1991). Social validity assessments: Is current practice the state of the art? *Journal of Applied Behavior Analysis, 24,* 189–204.

Scott, M. J., & Stradling, S. G. (1992). *Counseling for posttraumatic stress disorder.* London: Sage Publications.

Sellick, K. J., & Peck, C. L. (1981). Behavioral treatment of fear in a child with cerebral palsy using a flooding procedure. *Archives of Physical Medicine and Rehabilitation, 62,* 398–400.

Shaffer, D., Fisher, P., Piacenti, J., Schwab-Stone, M., & Wicks, J. (1989). *DISC-2 parent version.* New York: Division of Child and Adolescent Psychiatry, New York State Psychiatric Institute.

Shannon, M. T., Lonigan, C., Finch, A. J., & Taylor, C. (1994). Children exposed to disaster: I. Epidemiology of posttraumatic symptoms and symptom profiles.

Journal of the American Academy of Child and Adolescent Psychiatry, 33, 80–93.

Singer, M. I., Anglin, T. M., Song, L., & Lunghofer, L. (1995). Adolescents' exposure to violence and associated symptoms of psychological trauma. *Journal of the American Medical Association, 8*(276), 477–482.

Southard, E. (1919). *Shell shock and neuropsychiatric problems.* Boston: Leonard.

Spielberger, C. D., Gorsuch, R. L., & Lushane, R. E. (1968). *Manual for the State Trait Anxiety Inventory.* Palo Alto, CA: Consulting Psychologist Press.

Spitzer, R. L., Endicott, J., & Robins, E. (1978). Research diagnostic criteria: Rationale and reliability. *Archives of General Psychiatry, 23,* 41–55.

Stampfl, T. G. (1961). *Implosive therapy: A learning theory derived psychodynamic technique.* Unpublished manuscript. John Carroll University, Cleveland, OH.

Stampfl, T. G., & Levis, D. J. (1967). Essentials of implosive therapy: A learning-based psychodynamic behavioral therapy. *Journal of Abnormal Psychology, 72,* 496–503.

United States Department of Justice (1994). *Juvenile victimization: 1987–1992.* Office of Juvenile Justice and Delinquency Prevention. Fact sheet 17. Washington, DC: Author.

United States Department of Transportation (1993). *Traffic safety facts.* National Highway Traffic Safety Administration. Report DOT HS 808 022. Washington, DC: Author.

Wiesenberg, M., Schwarzwald, J., Waysman, M., Solomon, Z., & Klingman, A. (1993). Coping of school-age children in the sealed room during Scud missile bombardment and postwar stress reactions. *Journal of Consulting and Clinical Psychology, 61,* 462–467.

Wolf, M. M. (1978). Social validity: The case of subjective measurement or how applied behavior analysis is finding its heart. *Journal of Applied Behavior Analysis, 11,* 315–329.

Wolfe, D. A. (1991). *Preventing physical and emotional abuse of children.* New York: Guilford Press.

Wolfe, D. A., Sas, L., & Wekerle, C. (1994). Factors associated with the development of posttraumatic stress disorder among child victims of sexual abuse. *Child Abuse and Neglect, 18,* 37–50.

Wolpe, J. (1990). *The practice of behavior therapy* (4th ed.). Elmsford: Pergamon Press.

Yule, W., Sacks, B., & Hersov, L. (1974). Successful flooding treatment of a noise phobia in an 11-year-old boy. *Journal of Behaviour Therapy and Experimental Psychiatry, 5,* 209–211.

CHAPTER 14

AN OVERVIEW OF PSYCHOPHARMACOTHERAPY FOR CHILDREN AND ADOLESCENTS

John C. Pomeroy
Kenneth D. Gadow

INTRODUCTION

Drug therapy for emotional and behavioral problems is a contentious issue that produces widely divergent opinions on its appropriate applications. Child and adolescent disorders commonly have an intermingling of developmental, biological, and environmental factors, which necessitates a broad orientation to assessment and intervention. Psychopharmacotherapy is but one part of the full armamentarium of effective treatments available, but it is apparent that the increasingly sophisticated scientific investigation of this treatment has been one of the major advances for child psychiatrists. Earlier in this century, relatively few psychotropic drugs were available for clinical application (see Darrow, 1929; Meyer, 1922), but this situation began to change in the late 1930s with the discovery that amphetamine was a useful intervention for the management of behavior disorders.

When we wrote the chapter for the first edition of this book, we commented on the fact that the most commonly prescribed psychotherapeutic medica-tions were actually discovered in the era between the late 1930s to the late 1950s. However, in five years there has been a dramatic growth in the literature regarding pharmacologic treatments for child psychiatric disorders, plus the introduction of many new drugs, notably new anti-depressants and antipsychotic medications. Also, several drugs that were originally marketed for other medical purposes have recently been shown to have psychotropic properties, and they are being assessed for their value in ameliorating or treating the emotional problems of childhood. Pediatric psychopharmacotherapy has moved from being characterized as "islands of understanding in a sea of ignorance" (Taylor, 1983, p. 322) and as lagging behind adult psychopharmacology (Werry, 1982) to showing the signs of significant progress. However, it continues to be evident that there has been much less advance in the development and evaluation of practical treatment procedures for application in typical clinical settings (Gadow, 1988a) or in the formulation and critical examination of rationales for treatment.

Numerous reviews (e.g. Campbell & Cueva, 1995a, 1995b; Gadow, 1992; Kaplan & Hussain, 1995) and texts (e.g., Rosenberg, Holttum, & Gershon, 1994) on pediatric psychopharmacotherapy have recently been published, and the *Journal of Child and Adolescent Psychopharmacology* was inaugurated in 1990. There is growing evidence of more aggressive use of psychotropic medication in North America, including combinations of more than one drug (Wilens, Spencer, Biederman, Wozniak, & Connor, 1995) for the treatment of severe and complex behavioral and emotional problems of childhood. This probably reflects improved diagnostic procedures and the awareness that many children seen in child psychiatric clinics suffer from combinations of disorders (comorbidity). Furthermore, it is now more commonly assumed that for many disorders a biological explanation can or will be derived for the manifestation of symptoms and thus a physical intervention (medication) is warranted, which may require augmentation, such as a second medication, if no or limited response is observed. We suggest caution in adopting a narrow view in conceptualizing the nature of child psychiatric disorders and their appropriate treatment, an opinion that has been endorsed by seasoned practitioners in the United States, such as Rabinowitz and Wiener (1990). Elsewhere in the world there is some antipathy toward the comparatively high rate of psychotropic prescriptions for American children (Bramble, 1995; Kaplan & Hussain, 1995; Kayser, 1991; Rochet, Revol, Maillet, & deVillard, 1993; Taylor, 1988).

In reviewing the latest literature there appears to be two different approaches taken by most psychopharmacologic researchers. The first is to take drugs that have been shown to be effective in adult psychiatric disorders and apply them to childhood disorders where clinical symptoms resemble the adult disorder. The second is to use drugs that are thought to counteract neurochemical dysfunctions that are hypothesized to be a cause for the manifestation of particular symptoms. This means that many of the new drugs being assessed may not have FDA approval for use in children or for the disorder for which they are being prescribed. Under these circumstances a high degree of scientific rigor is required before adopting a treatment as valuable and/or worth the potential risks that it may present.

Unfortunately, much of our present knowledge about newer drug products rests on case reports or small studies. Many of the larger, better controlled, studies have not had time to be replicated.

This chapter presents an overview of pharmacotherapy for mood, thought, and behavior disorders in children and adolescents. The specific disorders that are covered (and the drugs that are characteristically used to treat them) are presented in alphabetical order in Table 14.1. In keeping with the organization of this text, drug therapy is discussed by diagnostic category instead of drug class. This organization plan, unfortunately, creates some redundancy because many psychoactive agents have multiple therapeutic applications, often at comparable doses. It was therefore decided to limit more detailed discussions of therapeutic and untoward effects to a particular diagnostic category, generally the one for which the drug is most commonly prescribed. Information about general clinical management is also presented, but space limitations preclude a thorough discussion of this topic. Little attention is given to diagnostic procedures or alternative treatments because they are addressed in other chapters in this book. Specific drugs are referred to by trade names, because professionals from nonmedical backgrounds are generally more familiar with these than with generic names. For readers more accustomed to the latter, the generic name appears in parentheses following the first mention of each trade name product. A list of many psychotherapeutic drugs in current use is presented in the Appendix at the end of this chapter. Deciding upon the most appropriate label for each disorder is also a problem, because diagnostic nomenclature has changed repeatedly over the years. So as not to imply uniformity in subject-selection criteria in drug studies conducted over the past several decades, we use more general terms to refer to the various childhood and adolescent disorders discussed in this chapter. However, the American Psychiatric Association's (1994) categorical label appears in parentheses following the subheading for each disorder. The material presented in this chapter was originally based on the two-volume series Children On Medication (Gadow, 1986a, 1986b) and has been updated to reflect current developments in psychopharmacology.

TABLE 14.1. Psychoactive Drugs Currently Being Used (or Under Investigation) for the Treatment of Childhood and Adolescent Disorders

DISORDER	DRUG CLASS	REPRESENTATIVE TRADE PRODUCTS[a]
Academic underachievement and learning disabilities[b]	Stimulants	Ritalin, Dexedrine, Cylert
Affective		
Bipolar	Antimanics	Eskalith, Lithane, Lithobid
	Neuroleptics	Mellaril, Haldol, Thorazine
	Antiepileptics	Tegretol, Depakote, Depakene
Depression	Antidepressants	
	Tricyclics	Tofranil, Elavil, Norpramin
	MAOIs	Nardil, Parnate
	SSRIs	Prozac, Zoloft, Paxil, Luvox
Anxiety		
Anxiety states	Antianxiety agents	Valium, Ativan, Xanax, Buspar
	Beta blockers	Inderal
	SSRIs	Prozac
Obsessive compulsive/	Antidepressants	
Panic disorder	Tricyclics	Anafranil, Tofranil, Norpramin
	MAOIs	Nardil, Parnate
	SSRIs	Prozac, Zoloft, Luvox
Separation anxiety	Tricyclic antidepressants	Tofranil
Autism	Neuroleptics	Haldol, Risperdal
	Stimulants	Ritalin
	Anorectics	Pondimin
	Opioid antagonists	ReVia
	SSRIs	Prozac, Luvox
Conduct problems		
Aggression	Neuroleptics	Mellaril, Thorazine, Haldol
	Stimulants	Ritalin, Dexedrine
	Antimanics	Eskalith, Lithane, Lithobid
	Beta blockers	Inderal
	Antiepileptics	Tegretol
Oppositional behavior	Stimulants	Ritalin, Dexedine, Cylert
Enuresis	Tricyclic antidepressants	Tofranil, Norpramin, Elavil
	Desmopressin	DDAVP
	Stimulants	Ritalin
Hyperactivity	Stimulants	Ritalin, Dexedrine, Cylert
	Neuroleptics	Mellaril, Haldol
	Tricyclics	Tofranil, Norpramin, Elavil
	Other antidepressants	Wellbutrin, Prozac
	Antihypertensives	Catapres, Tenex
Schizophrenia	Neuroleptics	Mellaril, Navane, Haldol, Loxitane, Clozaril, Risperdal
Self-injurious behavior	Neuroleptics	Mellaril, Haldol, Thorazine
	Opioid antagonists	Narcan, ReVia
	Antimanics	Eskalith, Lithane, Lithobid
Speech and language	Stimulants	Benzedrine, Dexedrine, Ritalin
	Neuroleptics	Haldol

continued

TABLE 14.1. Psychoactive Drugs Currently Being Used (or Under Investigation) for the Treatment of Childhood and Adolescent Disorders, continued

DISORDER	DRUG CLASS	REPRESENTATIVE TRADE PRODUCTS[a]
Stereotypies	Neuroleptics	Mellaril, Haldol, Thorazine
	Antidepressants	Prozac, Anafranil
Tourette syndrome	Neuroleptics	Haldol, Prolixin, Orap, Risperdal
	Antihypertensives	Catapres, Tenex

[a]Only trade-name products marketed in the United States are listed. In the case of drugs no longer protected by patent laws, the inclusion of trade names other than the original was arbitrary.

[b]At the present time, academic underachievement is not a recognized indication for any approved psychoactive drug.

ACADEMIC UNDERACHIEVEMENT (LEARNING DISORDERS)

Although no drug in therapeutic use in the United States is approved specifically for enhancing academic performance, many psychotropic agents can affect academic functioning, and underachievement is a pervasive problem in children referred for psychiatric evaluation. When academic performance is enhanced, this is generally considered to be a good thing, particularly for children and adolescents who are underachieving prior to drug exposure. There are, of course many disorders for which academic underachievement is a commonly associated problem. In some cases underachievement is expected, because the child is of below-average mental ability. For other youngsters, the symptoms of their behavioral disability are an impediment to learning. When academic performance (measured by a standardized achievement test) is significantly below what would be predicted on the basis of innate ability (determined by an individually administered IQ test) and not the consequence of another educationally recognized disorder (e.g., mental retardation), the condition is referred to as a learning disability.

Caregiver and peer reactions to academic performance are hypothesized to play an important role in the formation of self-concept and personal happiness; hence underachievement is believed to have important psychosocial sequelae. Academic achievement is also believed to be an extremely important contributor to success and happiness in adult life (particularly for people from middle- and upper-class backgrounds), in spite of a truly compelling literature to the contrary. This is even true for children with learning disabilities, whose primary disability is academic underachievement. When evaluating the effect of a psychotropic drug on academic functioning and its potential role in treatment, it is important for the clinician to be cognizant of patient characteristics, the exact nature of the academic performance problem, and the personal and social implications of underachievement.

The adverse effects of medication on academic progress is a primary clinical concern. Although many psychoactive drugs are known to induce behavior and cognitive changes that would likely result in impaired school performance (reviewed by Aman & Rojahn, 1991; Gadow, 1986a; Judd, Squire, Butters, Salmon, & Paller, 1987), academic productivity and achievement are rarely used in research or clinical settings to assess behavioral toxicity. In spite of the logistical problems that one often encounters in trying to obtain such information, an effort should be made to elicit reports from caregivers about changes in schoolwork.

In his seminal paper on Benzedrine (amphetamine) in children with behavior disorders, Bradley (1937) observed that treatment with stimulant medication led to improvement in schoolwork as demonstrated by increased productivity, comprehension, and accuracy, which was attributed to a " 'drive' to accomplish as much work as possible during the school period" (p. 578). Bradley conducted additional research and concluded that the drug did accelerate academic progress by increasing the number of pages of arithmetic "thoroughly learned" during a 1-month period (Bradley & Bowen, 1940).

However, the effect on the number of lists of spelling words thoroughly learned was less dramatic. Another important finding from this study was the fact that response to stimulants is variable. Some children showed vast improvement with medication, whereas others actually became worse.

Molitch and Sullivan's (1937) investigation into the effects of a single dose of Benzedrine on juvenile delinquents who were housed in a state-operated residential facility was the first stimulant drug study to employ a standardized achievement test. Although their data were not analyzed statistically, Molitch and Sullivan concluded that the medication group clearly outperformed the placebo group in enhancing academic achievement test performance. Nevertheless, the magnitude of the drug effect was modest.

It is a curious fact, but nevertheless true, that our understanding of stimulant drug effects on academic performance has progressed very little since these early efforts. Academic productivity (e.g., amount of correct work completed) is still the most popular measure of academic performance, and the size of the treatment effect is relatively large, at least for some types of academic skills. Standardized achievement tests are also occasionally used; but because they are generally more suitable for longer periods of drug exposure, their value for understanding treatment effects in short-term studies (which dominate the literature) is limited. Collectively, the findings from a number of investigations suggest that the academic achievement test gains associated with stimulant drug treatment are not particularly robust, long-lasting, or cumulative, which is not to say that they are nonexistent.

Reading

The research findings on stimulants and reading performance in children with attention-deficit hyperactivity disorder (ADHD) are mixed. Medication does enhance the amount of accurate reading-related seat work that is completed during the school day (e.g., Pelham, Bender, Caddell, Booth, & Moorer, 1985; Pelham, Swanson, Bender, & Wilson, 1980; Rapport, Stoner, DuPaul, Birmingham, & Tucker, 1985), but the mechanism of action is entirely unknown. Standardized achievement test perfor-

mance, however, is affected much less dramatically. This is not to suggest that everyone shares this interpretation of the research literature or that the findings from all studies are equally discouraging. For example, Richardson, Kupietz, Winsberg, Maitinsky, and Mendell (1988) reported a study of Ritalin (methylphenidate) in children with ADD-H who were underachievers in reading and who were participating in a special after-school reading program. Although the size of the drug effect was very small after 6 months of treatment, a subgroup of "good" responders (determined on the basis of teacher ratings of classroom behavior) were said to have benefited much more. Methodological and other considerations aside, the clinical implications of these findings for children with both ADHD and learning disability is unclear.

Three studies have been published on stimulant medication for children with learning disabilities (Aman & Werry, 1982; Gittelman-Klein & Klein, 1976; Gittelman, Klein, & Feingold, 1983). In their first study, Gittelman-Klein and Klein (1976) randomly assigned children to either Ritalin or placebo conditions. All subjects were selected on the basis of being 2 years below reading grade level despite average intelligence, and most were receiving academic remediation in school. At the end of 12 weeks, differences in achievement test scores for arithmetic and spelling were trivial, but the difference in reading scores approached statistical significance. Teachers' global ratings of reading and arithmetic performance did not discriminate between the two treatment groups. On the basis of these and other findings, Gittelman-Klein and Klein concluded that Ritalin was not an effective agent for the remediation of reading deficits in children with learning disabilities who did not have ADHD. They also noted, however, that medication effects may be manifested only in the presence of a specialized academic intervention.

To test this hypothesis, Gittelman et al. (1983) conducted a second study in which children with marked reading disability (but not ADHD) were randomly assigned to one of three groups: (a) reading remediation (phonics program) and placebo, (b) academic tutoring (without reading instruction) and placebo, and (c) reading remediation and Ritalin. The results indicated that although medication did enhance cognitive task performance, it did not facilitate academic achievement. Some reading achievement measures, however, did show drug effects or trends favoring the medication-treated group, suggesting that the impact of Ritalin on reading instruction was not a strong one. Quite unexpectedly, medication markedly enhanced other areas of academic performance (e.g., social studies) that were not part of the reading program. However, a retest of these academic skills 8 months after the termination of pharmacotherapy failed to show residual benefits. In other words, gains in achievement test scores appeared to fade over time after medication was stopped.

Aman and Werry (1982) administered Ritalin, Valium (diazepam), and placebo for 1 week each to 15 children diagnosed as being severely reading-retarded (but with normal IQ). Medication was not found to improve cognitive functions presumed to be associated with reading disability.

In sum, although stimulant medication does not appear markedly to improve reading achievement in children with hyperactivity (Barkley & Cunningham, 1978) or learning disability (Gittelman-Klein & Klein, 1976; Gittelman et al., 1983) or to correct the underlying problem that is causing the reading disability (Aman & Werry, 1982), it does increase the amount of reading-related workbook assignments in underachieving children with hyperactivity. One would predict that if medication helped students to pay attention and complete more schoolwork, their reading levels would improve. At the present time, however, it is difficult to say with certainty whether this conclusion is true or false. Furthermore, our increased knowledge of the underlying deficits in phonologic coding and the genetic transmission (Pennington, 1990) of reading disabilities is likely to lead to different intervention strategies that may or may not include the additional use of appropriate pharmacologic agents.

Arithmetic

Since Bradley's (1937; Bradley & Bowen, 1940) early studies were published, a number of other investigators have also shown that stimulant medication enhances academic productivity on classroom and laboratory arithmetic tasks (e.g., Douglas,

Barr, O'Neill, & Britton, 1986; Pelham et al., 1985; Rapport et al., 1985; see also Sprague's study in Gadow & Swanson, 1985). In spite of these encouraging reports, improvement in academic achievement test performance is less dramatic. For example, of the 11 short-term studies in Barkley and Cunningham's (1978) review that employed measures of arithmetic achievement, statistically significant drug effects were reported in only one instance (Conners, Rothschild, Eisenberg, Stone, & Robinson, 1969). Interestingly, the Gittelman et al. (1983) study found significant Ritalin-induced gains on the arithmetic subtests of the Stanford Achievement Test in children with learning disability, even though arithmetic skill development was not part of the intervention program.

The findings from studies of stimulant medication and arithmetic productivity are fairly consistent. Drug therapy appears to increase work output without sacrificing accuracy; however, there are only a few reports of improved performance on standardized achievement tests (Conners et al., 1969; Gittelman et al., 1983). Nothing is known about the effects of stimulants on children who have a specific arithmetic disability with or without a concurrent behavior or learning disorder.

Spelling

There were 11 short-term drug studies included in the review by Barkley and Cunningham (1978) that employed either measures of spelling achievement (*n* = 10) or productivity (*n* = 1); significant drug effects were demonstrated in only two instances (Conners, Taylor, Meo, Kurz, & Fournier, 1972; Weiss, Minde, Douglas, Werry, & Sykes, 1971). Pelham et al. (1985) reported a modest Ritalin-related increase in the proportion of words correct on weekly spelling tests, which consisted of words that the children with ADD could not spell correctly. In a similar study, however, Cylert (pemoline) failed to enhance spelling performance (Pelham et al., 1980). Another investigation (Stephens, Pelham, & Skinner, 1984) of Ritalin, Cylert, and placebo revealed that stimulant drugs produced a 25% reduction in spelling errors (nonsense words) compared with placebo. In view of these conflicting findings, no definite conclusions can be drawn about stimulant medication and spelling. Furthermore, there is no drug research on spelling disability per se.

Handwriting

A number of investigators have reported that stimulant drugs can enhance handwriting ability in children and adolescents with ADHD. Moreover, there are a number of published handwriting samples (e.g., Levy, 1973; Schain & Reynard, 1975; Taylor, 1979) that compellingly demonstrate the magnitude of this effect. Nevertheless, poor handwriting is rarely the basis for medical referral, nor is it a clinical indication for treatment. The only published study that selected children (diagnosed as having minimal brain dysfunction) on the basis of poor handwriting was conducted by Lerer, Lerer, and Artner (1977). They found that handwriting improved in 52% of those initially receiving Ritalin and in only 4% of those initially receiving placebo. In general, handwriting deteriorated subsequent to drug withdrawal, but improvement was maintained for months in those children who remained on medication.

Although these findings seem exciting, neatness is only one small component of what people generally refer to as written communication skills. The latter includes spelling, sentence structure, grammar, the ability to express and organize ideas, and so forth. It is important not to underestimate neatness and legibility, but we must also realize that little is known about the effect of stimulant drugs on more serious forms of written communication disorders.

General Cognitive Measures

The use of psychostimulants in the classroom setting generally supports some overall nonspecific beneficial effects on cognitive performance. However, concern has been expressed that, particularly at higher doses, stimulants could impair flexible thinking leading to "overfocusing" or cognitive perseveration. The findings from two recent studies (Douglas, Barr, Desilets, & Sherman, 1995; Tannock & Schachar, 1992) that assessed the effects of different doses of Ritalin on tasks requiring cognitive flexibility tend to be relatively encouraging, suggesting that the drug has a positive rather than deleterious effect in most situations, actually improving task persistence. There

were a number of children, however, who showed the classic U-shaped dose-response function (e.g., Sprague & Sleator, 1977) for perseverative errors, in which cognitive performance is improved on low doses of Ritalin and seriously impaired at high doses. Thus, both research groups suggest caution in using doses above 0.6 mg/kg.

An interesting study by Malone, Couitis, Kershner, and Logan (1994) examined the effects of Ritalin on subtle right-hemisphere deficits detected in 17 children with ADHD. The partial neglect of stimuli in the children's left side of vision, an assumed marker of right-hemisphere dysfunction, was found mainly in children with both ADHD and learning disability. Ritalin was found to "correct" this deficit. Obviously requiring further replication and evaluation, this type of finding suggests that specific underlying defects related to learning difficulties might prove to be responsive to particular drugs.

The only other drug that has been assessed for its benefit in improving overall cognitive performance, and its potential role in treatment of children with reading disability, is piracetam, which belongs to a class of drugs known as nootropics. There was some initial enthusiasm for its ability to enhance reading skills (DiIanni et al., 1985), but this has not been replicated in a subsequent study (Ackerman, Dykman, Holloway, Paal, & Gocio, 1991). The early findings, anyway, seemed only to suggest improved reading rate. There appears to be no indication for the use of piracetam in the treatment of childhood learning disabilities at this time.

Clinical Considerations

Stimulant drugs do increase academic productivity in children with ADHD (and, in all probability, children with learning disabilities). Moreover, treated children are aware of this change in their academic behavior (see Gadow, 1988b), which may lead to less stress in their lives. As Bradley (1957) noted, "medication is at best a crutch, but if in the long run it enables the child to experience success and a sense of being loved and appreciated, it is well justified" (p. 1051). It seems plausible that for some children a dramatic improvement in productivity and proficiency may even be more clinically meaningful than a modest increase in standardized achievement test performance. In addition, one of the commonly associated reasons for treatment in the first place is that the child does not complete his or her school-work and consequently may not make satisfactory academic progress. Some clinicians, therefore, believe that if medication makes a child more responsive to educational instruction, then it is clinically useful. After all, the education literature is replete with scientific studies that document how various strategies designed to increase task motivation improve academic productivity. Nevertheless, careful consideration must be given to the seriousness of academic underachievement, the magnitude of the treatment effect, and the safety of the drug.

If one were to seriously consider the clinical implications of learning disabilities, the clear focus is on reading. The other areas of skill performance are simply not that essential to satisfactory adjustment in a typical employment setting (Chandler, 1978). Snyder (1979, 1983) even makes a compelling case for the questionable necessity of reading skills in most areas of employment because, when they are necessary, there is usually some way to compensate. The real problem with learning disabilities is that they are handicaps with regard to obtaining most traditional post-secondary education (e.g., college, trade school). The tragedy is that most jobs require very little academic ability; however, in order to get them, one must run the gauntlet of traditional academic instruction. Fortunately, follow-up studies of children with learning disabilities generally show a favorable adult outcome (Horn, O'Donnell, & Vitulano, 1983). The same can be said for many clinically diagnosed and treated cases of ADHD, but there is some disagreement on this point.

With regard to nonpharmacological interventions, research indicates that certain academically-oriented behavioral interventions are clearly superior to stimulant medication in facilitating academic performance in children with hyperactivity or learning disabilities (Gadow, 1985). Moreover, although stimulant drugs enhance a variety of learning-related behaviors (e.g., attention span) and have been shown to increase academic productivity, they do not appear markedly to facilitate academically oriented behavioral interventions unless the latter are ineffective. These findings are fairly consistent across a number of studies that vary greatly, which suggests that if a clinically significant combination treatment effect does exist, it is not particularly robust.

AFFECTIVE DISORDERS (MOOD DISORDERS)

The primary disorders of affect are an abnormally lowered (depression) or elevated (mania) mood. Although mania is considerably less common, it does occur in adolescents (and possibly, but less clearly, in children) and is part of a special type of mood disorder known as bipolar affective disorder (or manic-depressive illness). In such cases, phases or cycles of illness are seen in which either mania or depression are manifested. Bipolar and some unipolar depressive disorders have characteristics that suggest that the individual is genetically or, in some way, biologically predisposed.

In preadolescents there is little doubt that the full range of depressive syndromes can be observed, but the relationship between the depressive symptoms in children and disorders observed in adults is not fully understood. For example, biological characteristics and treatment response appear to be different in the two age groups. There is a rapid increase in the rate and discreteness of affective disorders following puberty. Adolescents who experience these problems suffer recurring, intermittent disturbances that may or may not be related to external precipitants (e.g., death in the family, poor school grades); but the disorder itself is believed to have a physiological component. Diagnosis is complicated by the fact that the associated symptoms of mood disorders vary so greatly in children and teenagers and include such behaviors as refusal to go to school, social withdrawal, deteriorating academic performance, unexplained conduct disturbance, and antisocial activities.

Depression (Depressive Disorders)

Depression in prepubertal children has generated much interest, and most of the research on this disorder has appeared within the past 15 years. Once considered a vary rare condition, more recent surveys show that the prevalence of major depressive disorder in prepubertal children in the United States is approximately 1.8% (Kashani & Simonds, 1979).

Many of the children who fit the criteria for depression are not taken for psychological or psychiatric help, and few are currently treated with medication (Kovacs, Feinberg, Crouse-Novak, Paulaukas, & Finkelstein, 1984). Children with major depressive disorder are unlikely to recover within the first 3 months of the depressive episode, but remission generally occurs within 6 to 18 months. If the child does not recover by that time, the illness is likely to be protracted. The more early the age of onset of the disorder, the longer the recovery period.

Until 1990, antidepressant medication consisted largely of two major groups of drugs: the tricyclics and MAOls (monoamine oxidase inhibitors). Newer antidepressants have now been developed, and there is evidence to suggest that they may replace the tricyclics as the primary agents for the management of mood disorders.

Children

There are several placebo-controlled studies of tricyclic antidepressants for the treatment of major depressive disorder in children. Unfortunately, the findings of these studies fail to show that tricyclics are superior to placebo in diminishing depressive symptoms (reviewed by Ambrosini, 1987; also Puig-Antich, Perel, & Lupatkin, 1987). The major difficulty in detecting pharmacologic effects in children with depression has been the high rate of placebo response, suggesting that many children with depression have spontaneous remission of their symptoms. Efforts to relate drug response to evidence of severity and chronicity of symptoms, or adequate serum levels of the drugs have only had limited support in regard to the tricyclic antidepressants (e.g., Geller, Cooper, Graham, Fetner, Marsteller & Wells, 1992; Puig-Antich et al., 1987). Despite these observations, clinical experience still supports the use of anti-depressants in selected cases (Harrington, 1992), even though there are reports of the effectiveness of psychological therapies (Fine, Forth, Gilbert, & Haley, 1991).

Until very recently, it would have been reasonable to conclude that antidepressants have a very limited role in the treatment of prepubertal depression. In the late 1980s considerable excitement was raised by the introduction of a new class of antidepressants, the selective serotonin re-uptake inhibitor or SSRIs. Prozac (fluoxetine) emerged as a powerful treatment for both severe and mild, acute and chronic depressive disorders in adults. Although not approved by the FDA for use in children, there have been numerous studies and obvious clinical use of these drugs for a number of childhood disorders. In 1995, the first double-blind controlled trial to report the efficacy of antidepressant therapy for children was presented. Using Prozac, and with careful screening out of early placebo responses by a prolonged period of observation prior to treatment, Elmslie (Elmslie, Kowatch, Costello, Travis, & Pierce, 1995; Elmslie, Rush, Weinberg, Kowatch, Hughes, & Rintelmann, 1995) showed a significant antidepressant response in children and adolescents with depression (8–17 years of age). Zoloft (sertraline), another SSRI, may also be an effective antidepressant for children and adolescents (Tierney, Joshi, Llinas, Rosenberg, & Riddle, 1995).

Children who meet the diagnostic criteria for major depressive disorder may also experience other psychiatric problems. Many have conduct disorders (Carlson & Cantwell, 1980; Puig-Antich, 1982) or exhibit antisocial behavior (Geller, Chestnut, Miller, Price, & Yates, 1985), anxiety disorder (Kovacs et al., 1984), separation anxiety (Geller et al., 1985), school phobia (Kolvin, Berney, & Bhate, 1984), or psychotic symptoms such as hallucinations or delusions (Freeman, Poznanski, Grossman, Buchsbaum, & Banesas, 1985). For these children, the total treatment plan is complicated by the presence of multiple target behaviors, some of which may become the reason for pharmacotherapy.

Adolescents

Until recently, the most common pharmacological treatment of adolescent depression has also been the tricyclic medications, particularly Tofranil. In adolescents, the therapeutic dose of Tofranil, Elavil (amitriptyline), and Norpramin (desipramine) ranges up to 5 mg/kg per day, whereas the average dose of Pamelor (nortriptyline) is 1 mg/kg to 2 mg/kg per day (Ryan & Puig-Antich, 1987). Tofranil can safely be administered as a single dose at night, particularly once a steady state has been achieved (Ryan et al., 1987). It is possible to measure the amount of tricyclic medication in the blood, if required, to ensure a therapeutic level (see Table 14.2). This can be particularly helpful in ruling out the possibility that individual variation in medication causes (a) drug failure at high doses because of a subtherapeutic level of medication in the blood or (b) side effects at low doses due to an unexpectedly high level of drug in the blood (Preskorn, Bupp, Weller, & Weller, 1989). Because there is a delay in the onset of the antidepressant effect, it may take from 4 to 7 weeks before the response to medication can be adequately evaluated. The best indicators that an adolescent with depression will respond to antidepressant medication are the presence of so-called vegetative (biological) symptoms such as sleep disturbance, change in eating patterns, and lack of drive, particularly if there is also a family history of depression.

Many of our present assumptions about the use of tricyclics in adolescents with depression are based on an extrapolation of information from adult studies and clinical experience. Strangely, the controlled studies of drug treatment in adolescents have not been compelling. Kramer and Feiguine (1981) showed no advantage for Elavil 200 mg per day over placebo in 10 adolescent inpatients with major depression, nor did Norpramin used at the same dose for 60 adolescents prove to have benefit over placebo (Kutcher et al., 1994). Ryan et al. (1986) found that less than half of their sample of 34 adolescents with depression had a complete recovery within 4 weeks of a final weight-adjusted dose of Tofranil (mean = 234 mg per day), but all had at least a partial response. No relationship was found between plasma level and clinical response in these studies, but the findings of non blind evaluation of clinical response to Pamelor in adolescents with depression suggest that plasma drug levels and length of treatment are related to clinical recovery (Ambrosini, Bianchi, Metz, & Rabinovich, 1994).

Tricyclic antidepressants often produce unwanted side effects that are troublesome but rarely dangerous. These include dry mouth, drowsiness, lethargy, nausea, blurred vision, constipation, and—very rarely—an inability to pass urine (urinary retention). Another major complication is its effect on electrochemical conduction within the heart muscle (Biederman et al., 1989). Therapeutic levels of the tricyclics can produce changes in heart function that register on EKG records, and susceptible individuals may develop unusual heart rhythms or a "racing" of the heart (tachycardia). During treatment, therefore, it is imperative for the physician to assess heart function thoroughly. It is recommended that an EKG be obtained prior to the beginning of treatment, to determine whether there is a preexisting heart disorder, and after each increase in dosage (Ryan & Puig-

TABLE 14.2. Tricyclic Antidepressants Used in Children and Adolescents

DRUG	TRADE NAME	PLASMA LEVEL	ANTICHOLINERGIC SYMPTOMS	DEGREE OF SEDATION
Imipramine	Tofranil	150–240 ng/mL [b]	4+	2+
Desipramine[a]	Norpramin	115 ng/mL	1+	1+
Amitriptyline[a]	Elavil	100–300 ng/mL	4+	4+
Nortriptyline[a]	Pamelor[c]	50–100 ng/mL	3+	2+

[a]Not currently approved by the Food and Drug Administration for use with children under 12 years of age.

[b]Based on studies conducted with children.

[c]Available in liquid form.

Source: From "Depression: Pharmacotherapies" by C. A. Carlson in Handbook of treatment approaches in childhood psychopathology (p. 355) edited by J. L. Matson, 1988, New York: Plenum Press. Copyright 1988 by Plenum Press. Reprinted by permission.

Antich, 1987). The effect on the heart is one of the main reasons why these drugs can be lethal in overdose (accidental or not), which is an important consideration when treating children or adolescents, particularly those with suicidal ideas. The risk to the heart is also the reason why a single nighttime dose may be ill advised in preadolescent children, because they are more likely than adolescents to develop toxic blood levels. Particular concern has been raised by reports of sudden deaths occurring in three children receiving Norpramin (among other medications). Although there is some contention regarding the role Norpramin played in these deaths, it would seem that this drug could be more likely than other tricyclic medications to cause cardiac changes and therefore might be either avoided for use in children or monitored closely (Biederman, Baldessarini, Goldblatt, Lapey, Doyle, & Hesslein, 1993; Popper & Elliott, 1990). A rare adverse reaction to tricyclics is the development of epileptic seizures, which appears to be associated with higher doses of medication.

The effects of tricyclic medication on cognitive and academic performance have not been studied extensively, but most reports with children are encouraging. The tricyclics have some actions that are similar to those of the stimulants, which probably accounts for their beneficial effect, such as increasing attention span and decreasing impulsivity, on some children with hyperactivity (Rapoport, Quinn, Bradbard, Riddle, & Brooks, 1974; Yepes, Balka, Winsberg, & Bialer, 1977). There is also evidence that long-term tricyclic treatment does not cause deterioration in academic performance (Quinn & Rapoport, 1975). Nevertheless, some children with depression treated with tricyclics appear forgetful, perplexed, or confused.

When adolescents respond to tricyclic antidepressants, there is a need to consider how long treatment should be continued. Mood disorders carry a risk of recurrence; the evidence from studies of adults with depression suggests that treatment should be maintained for 3 to 6 months after full recovery. This policy also seems practical for adolescents. Reduction of the medication should be gradual because withdrawal symptoms (sleep disturbance, nightmares, nausea, headache, and other

physical complaints) may occur if medication is stopped abruptly. Occasionally, adolescents predisposed to bipolar disorder "switch" to mania or even a rapid cycling process (continuous bouts of mania and depression; Wehr & Goodwin, 1979, 1987) during the course of treatment with an antidepressant (Strober & Carlson, 1982; Van Scheyen & Van Kamman, 1979). This is an indication to withdraw the antidepressant medication and use an antimanic drug. At the present time there is some controversy as to whether the "switch" is due to the pharmacologic properties of the antidepressant drug or purely a part of the illness process (Geller, Fox, & Fletcher, 1993). Because the tricyclics are among the more commonly used drugs for attempted suicide in this age group (Fazen, Lovejoy, & Crone, 1986), medication should be administered and safely stored by the parent.

Adolescents who do not respond favorably to an adequate trial of tricyclic medication may show improvement with the addition of lithium carbonate to the treatment regimen. Research on this practice is limited but nevertheless encouraging (Ryan, Meyer, Dachille, Mazzie, & Puig-Antich, 1988a; Strober, Freeman, Rigali, Schmidt, & Diamond, 1992).

Several MAOIs are available for medical use, of which Nardil (phenelzine) is one of the more commonly prescribed. They are considered to act as antidepressants because they inhibit an enzyme that breaks down certain chemical transmitters within the nervous system. The MAOIs are more commonly used in adults as the drug of second choice for depression, and there are few, if any, indications for their use in adolescents except in intractable (difficult to control) depressions (Ryan et al., 1988b) and severe emotional disorders.

The side effects of the MAOIs are usually few but include nausea, dizziness, and sleep disturbance, particularly if given later in the day. The main concern is the potential for life-threatening reactions when treated individuals eat food containing tyramine (e.g., matured cheeses, yeast products) or are given a number of different medications. The combination of MAOIs and these substances can produce a rapid rise in blood pressure because the normal biochemical mechanism for breaking down these chemicals has been inhibited by the drug. It is therefore important that the adolescent who is given an MAOI (a) takes medication in the prescribed manner; (b) follows all dietary restrictions; and (c) avoids illicit drugs, particularly cocaine and amphetamine (speed).

As already discussed in the previous section, recent progress in treatment of adolescent depression has been due to the introduction of the SSRIs. The early nonblind studies suggesting that adolescent depression might respond to Prozac (Boulos, Kutcher, Gardner, & Young, 1992; Colle, Bélair, DiFeo, Weiss, & LaRoche, 1994) have been supported by Elmslie and colleagues' (Elmslie, Kowatch et al., 1995; Elmslie, Rush, et al., 1995) work. Not only do these drugs appear to be more efficacious, but their side-effect profile is also more benign. In child and adolescent studies the most common side effects are tremor, nausea, sweating, and decreased appetite. Opinions vary as to the degree to which these side effects are likely to prevent continued use. Effects on the heart are much less significant than with the tricyclics. Because of the way these drugs are metabolized by the body, some caution should be given when they are used in conjunction with other medications since this can result in large changes in drug blood levels. The most serious limiting factor in the use of SSRIs is the emergence of behavioral changes that can range from transient behavioral activation (silliness and disruptiveness, including possible increase in self-destructive behavior) to mania (Colle et al., 1994; King et al., 1991; Venkataraman, Naylor, & King, 1992). The studies to date suggest that introduction and use of low doses of these drugs may be both effective and better tolerated. Response time varies from between 7 and 28 days, meaning that stable, acceptable doses of medication should be maintained for a number of weeks before deciding that the drug is either ineffective or that higher doses are required. The actual dose range shows wide variation in adult studies and has not yet been correlated with any biologic measures (e.g., serum levels) that can assist the clinician in selecting the appropriate dose. For children and adolescents an initial dose of 5 mg or 10 mg daily of Prozac or 25 mg to 50 mg of Zoloft is common practice, and the dose may be increased up to 20mg to 40 mg of Prozac and 100 mg to 150 mg of Zoloft if it appears clinically warranted.

Mania and Bipolar Affective Disorder (Bipolar Disorders)

Children

Bipolar affective disorder is considered to be a rare condition in prepubertal children, and there is no consensus of opinion about its diagnostic features. It has been described by DeLong (1978) as a condition characterized by "cyclic or periodic hostile aggressiveness; extremes of mood including manic excitement, depression, and angry irritability; distractibility; neurovegetative disorders (hyperdipsia, hyperphagia, encopresis, salt or sugar craving, excess sweating); and a family history of affective disorder" (DeLong & Aldershof, 1987, p. 389). Children exhibiting such symptoms may be responsive to treatment with lithium, implying but not confirming a continuity with adult bipolar disorder. Weller, Weller, and Fristad (1986) provide guidelines for adjusting lithium dose in prepubertal children (see Table 14.3). Many young patients with bipolar disorder show both manic and depressive symptoms simultaneously, which is referred to as mixed bipolar disorder.

Adolescents

The existence and treatment of mania is somewhat better documented in adolescents (Carlson, 1983, 1986). Antimanic agents that are most commonly used are of three major types, the neuroleptics, lithium salts (e.g., Eskalith, Lithane, Lithobid), and antiepileptics (Tegretol, Depakote). All the drugs are efficacious in treatment of the acute state of mania, although the neuroleptics and antiepileptics generally have a more rapid calming effect. Lithium and, probably, the antiepileptics are also effective in reducing the recurrence of mood disorder in individuals prone to bipolar affective disorder.

The increasing use of lithium in adolescent psychiatry is attested to by a number of recent review articles on this topic (e.g., Alessi, Naylor, Ghaziuddin, & Zubieta, 1994; Campbell, Perry, & Green, 1984b; Steinberg, 1980). Although noted in the 1940s to be a possible treatment for manic excitement (Cade, 1949), it was not until the 1960s

TABLE 14.3. Lithium Carbonate Dosage Guide for Prepubertal School-Aged Children[a]

WEIGHT (mg)	DOSAGE (mg)			
	8 AM	12 NOON	6 PM	TOTAL DAILY DOSE
<25	150	150	300	600
25–40	300	300	300	900
40–50	300	300	600	1,200
50–60	600	300	600	1,500

[a]Dose specified in schedule should be maintained at least 5 days with serum lithium levels drawn every other day 12 hours after ingestion of the last lithium dose until two consecutive levels appear in the therapeutic range (0.6–1.2 mEq/L). Dose may then be adjusted based on serum level, side effects, or clinical response. Do not exceed 1.4 mEq/L serum level. With mentally retarded children, lower doses are recommended.

Source: From E. B. Weller, R. A. Weller, & M. A. Fristad, "Lithium dosage guide for prepubertal children: A preliminary report," *Journal of the American Academy of Child Psychiatry, 25* (p. 93), 1986. Copyright 1986 by the American Academy of Child and Adolescent Psychiatry. Reprinted by permission.

in Scandinavia that the beneficial effects of lithium were really tested. One of the difficulties of using the drug is that there is a narrow range between therapeutic and toxic drug blood levels; consequently regular measurements of the level of lithium in the blood are necessary.

Lithium is effective in treating mania. In the initial phase of the illness, however, it is commonly given in combination with a neuroleptic, because the latter helps the adolescent calm down. Haldol (haloperidol) is not recommended by some clinicians for use in combination with lithium, because there are a few older reports of brain damage in patients taking both these drugs (Tyrer & Shopsin, 1980). Long-term pharmacotherapy with lithium is considered appropriate when (a) there is clear evidence of frequently recurring episodes of mood disorder, and (b) the manic episodes are disruptive enough to warrant the risks of such treatment. Dosage is generally in the range of 1,000 mg to 1,600 mg per day, but the true measure of dose is the amount of lithium necessary to keep the level in the blood within the known therapeutic range (0.6 mg/mL to 1.2 mg/mL). Adolescents reportedly tolerate larger doses of lithium than older adults because they tend to excrete lithium through their kidneys more rapidly.

The side effects of lithium include nausea, headache, fine tremor (slight trembling or shaking, usually of the hands), thirst, excessive need to urinate (polyuria), and loose stools. Signs of toxicity are vomiting, diarrhea, shaking, sleepiness, slurred speech, and dizziness. Concerns about long-term adverse reactions include potentially irreversible effects on the kidney and thyroid, as well as possible effects on bone structure (Birch, 1980). None of these problems has proven to be common, and all can be easily watched for by regular testing of chemical and hormonal levels in the blood. Because there is a risk of birth defects with lithium treatment (Weinstein, 1980), it should be used with caution for females who may become pregnant.

The effects of lithium on cognitive function are unclear. In normal volunteers, lithium can induce apathy, impair word learning, and reduce performance on visual-motor tasks, but studies of patients on long-term lithium therapy have found no gross impairment on standardized intelligence test performance (Judd et al., 1987). One study of children with conduct disorder treated with lithium found no adverse effects on cognition at optimal doses (Platt, Campbell, Green, & Grega, 1984). It seems reasonable, therefore, to conclude that for adolescents with severe recurrent mood disorder, neither side effects nor fear of cognitive deterioration are sufficient reasons not to use lithium in appropriate cases. In regard to young children (6 years and under) the use of lithium is associated with frequent side effects, mostly benign, but also potentially serious (e.g., neurotoxic effects) although not preventing the reintroduction of lithium after a withdrawal period (Hagino, Weller, Weller, Washing, Fristrad, & Koutras, 1995). Higher lithium levels and doses, the introductory period of treatment, and concurrent infection were factors associated with increased side effects in young children.

Initial reports of an antimanic effect of Tegretol (carbamazepine) (Ballenger & Post, 1978) have been followed by more rigorous studies that confirm that the drug is useful in the treatment of mania and rapid-cycling mood disorders (prolonged mood disturbance with rapid switches between mania and depression) as well as for long-term treatment to prevent mood disorder (Kishimoto, Ogura, Hazama, & Inoue, 1983; Roy-Byrne, Joffe, Uhde, & Post, 1984a). In the study by Kishimoto et al. (1983) there was evidence that Tegretol was more effective in patients with an onset of bipolar affective disorder before the age of 20.

At present Tegretol is used largely for lithium-resistant patients (Post, 1987). Therapeutic doses are similar to those for the treatment of seizure disorders and are usually based on measurement of drug level in the blood. Combination therapy with lithium and Tegretol has been reported as beneficial. In adult studies of the rapid stabilization of acute mania, Depakote (valproic acid) has become the most actively researched drug, suggesting that it may be the first line of treatment for acute mania. The finding of nonblind studies in adolescents (Papatheodorou & Kutcher, 1993; West et al., 1994; West, Keck, & McElroy, 1995) suggest that it may be useful, for this age group. Kutcher and Robertson (1995) have also shown that use of electroconvulsive therapy should be considered for treatment-resistant bipolar disorders in adolescence, and the new atypical antipsychotics (e.g., Clozaril) may prove to have a role to play in chronic bipolar disorder that is unresponsive to treatment (Fuchs, 1994). All of these newer treatments have significant side effects or limitations to consider, suggesting that, for a while, they will remain alternative treatments.

Clinical Considerations

It is important to realize that depressive (and occasionally manic) symptoms are often observed in association with environmental stress (e.g., death of a loved one), drug and alcohol abuse, physical illness, and other psychiatric disorders. Focusing treatment on the depressive symptoms instead of a patient's life problems may be ineffective or even detrimental. Medical treatment for serious mood disorders is recommended for all age groups. Although these disorders are self-limiting, appropriate medical management significantly reduces the length and severity of disturbance and the risk of harm either through self-neglect or suicide. Management consists of both therapy for the acute illness and long-term treatment for prevention of recurrence.

ANXIETY DISORDERS

Children

The diagnostic classification of the anxiety disorders has gone through many changes. In 1987, the American Psychiatric Association recognized three childhood anxiety disorders (separation anxiety disorder, avoidant disorder, overanxious disorder) and several adult anxiety disorders that could occur in prepubertal children (simple phobia, social phobia, obsessive compulsive disorder, and posttraumatic stress disorder), but there had been very little research on the validity of these diagnostic constructs as separate entities in children (Gittelman & Koplewicz, 1986), and the position of obsessive compulsive disorder within the group of anxiety disorders was controversial (Elkins, Rapoport, & Lipsky, 1980). Nevertheless, there was some evidence that separation anxiety disorder and overanxious disorder represented distinct conditions in children. For example, one investigation found that of children referred for evaluation on the basis of anxiety symptoms, those who were diagnosed as having overanxious disorder were older (pubertal) and more likely to have concurrent anxiety disorders (simple phobia, panic disorder) than patients with separation anxiety (Last, Hersen, Kazdin, Finkelstein, & Strauss, 1987). The most recent diagnostic system (American Psychiatric Association, 1994) deleted overanxious disorder and avoidant disorder, replacing these with generalized anxiety disorder (with childhood onset) and (childhood onset) social phobia, respectively. The only specific childhood anxiety disorder that was retained was separation anxiety disorder. The trend is therefore to accentuate continuity between anxiety disorders in children and adults, except where developmental issues seem to play a significant part. Thus, reviews of pharmacologic treatment of anxiety disorders are hampered by changing diagnostic approaches.

One common symptomatic manifestation of separation anxiety disorder is school refusal, and Gittelman-Klein and Klein (1971; Gittelman-Klein, 1975) showed that Tofranil was superior to placebo in facilitating school attendance. Treatment with medication resulted in a considerable reduction in depression, severity of phobia, maternal dependence, physical complaints, and fear of going to school. British workers are less enthusiastic about this type of medication and have shown that behavioral treatments can be as effective for the treatment of this disorder (Berney et al., 1981). Further, Klein, Koplewicz, and Kanner (1992) were unable to replicate the benefits of Tofranil in 20 children with separation anxiety disorder. Given that school refusal may encompass a wider range of disorders than the diagnosis of separation anxiety disorder, it is possible that the differing diagnostic criteria for the older and newer studies could be a significant factor in the contradictory findings. Thus, the true benefit of tricyclic medication for separation anxiety is uncertain.

The average dose of Tofranil given for separation anxiety is 75 to 100 mg per day with a maximal upper limit of 200 mg per day. Although behavioral improvement may be evident immediately after the onset of treatment, it is more characteristically manifested sometime within the first 2 weeks. Unfortunately, many children who have a complete remission of symptoms with Tofranil later suffer relapses. Medication is often given before bed to avoid side effects (e.g., drowsiness, dry mouth). Total duration of treatment, including a gradual withdrawal period, lasts about 3 months. To be truly effective, treatment must include psychotherapy as well as the cooperation of the school, family, and child. Behavioral intervention strategies should be considered before a trial of medication. Interestingly, the evidence of additional depressive disorder in accompaniment with separation anxiety disorder

has not proven to be associated with a better response to imipramine (see Allen, Leonard, & Swedo, 1995, for review).

The other childhood anxiety disorder shown to be responsive to medication is obsessive compulsive disorder (OCD). All the drugs that have been found to be effective treating OCD, enhance the action of the neurotransmitter serotonin. In children, symptoms commonly take the form of repetitive thoughts of violence, contamination, or doubt and ritualistic actions involving handwashing, counting, checking, or touching. Flament et al. (1985) found that Anafranil (clomipramine) was effective for controlling these symptoms in children and adolescents. Unfortunately, most drug responders did not recover fully, and there was a relapse in symptoms after drug withdrawal. Patients with compulsions responded better than those with obsessions only. Doses ranged from 100 mg to 200 mg per day, and untoward reactions included tremor, dry mouth, dizziness, constipation, and acute dyskinesia. One patient experienced a tonic-clonic seizure. The positive effects of Anafranil have been confirmed in other studies (e.g., DeVeagh-Geiss et al., 1992) and switching responders to another antidepressant, Norpramin, caused 90% of them to relapse, showing that Anafranil, rather than all tricyclics, is a specifically effective agent for OCD (Leonard et al., 1991).

The findings from an uncontrolled study suggest that Prozac, may be effective for the control of OCD in children and adolescents (Riddle, Hardin, King, Scahill, & Woolston, 1990). Study doses ranged from 10 mg to 40 mg per day. A follow-up double-blind crossover trial (Riddle et al., 1992) showed a marked but not significant trend for Prozac to improve OCD symptoms in children compared with placebo. The results of a nonblind trial of another SSRI, Luvox (fluvoxamine), suggest that this drug also may be beneficial for childhood OCD (Apter et al., 1994).

Many children experience appropriate anxiety about strange events and people as well as a natural development of certain types of fears (e.g., animals, abandonment, parents' health). However, by adolescence, continuing anxiety reactions are often related to familial, constitutional, and environmental factors and begin to differentiate into the more classical group of anxiety disorders described in adult psychiatry: phobic disorders (agoraphobia, social phobia, specific phobia), anxiety states (panic disorder, generalized anxiety disorder, obsessive compulsive disorder), and posttraumatic stress disorder.

Adolescents

Panic disorder, obsessive compulsive disorder, and social phobias commonly have their onset in adolescence. Unfortunately, the anxiety disorders of adolescents, unlike those of younger children, tend to be more chronic in nature. There is undoubtedly some overlap between anxiety disorders and depression in certain patients, and milder depressed states may have a predominance of anxiety symptoms. Early adolescent school refusers with severe anxiety symptoms often report depressive symptoms (dysphoria, low self-esteem, anhedonia, suicidal ideation); and it has been suggested that the co-occurrence of the two disorders may be a type of depression (Bernstein & Garfinkel, 1986).

Because adolescent anxiety disorders are similar to adult states, it is reasonable to apply the experience of adult psychiatrists to their management (reviewed by Brown, Mulrow, & Stoudemire, 1984). This is helpful because there have been few significant adolescent studies on the value of drug treatment. Some of the major advances in the treatment of anxiety and phobias have been in the area of cognitive behavioral therapy, which challenges the thinking patterns of the patient and incorporates relaxation techniques with internal imagery of fears and/or direct exposure to fears (reviewed by Hersov, 1985).

Inderal (propranolol) has been known to reduce the physical symptoms of anxiety since the 1960s, but controlled studies of the different anxiety disorders have produced discrepant results. Some clinicians suggest that Inderal is comparable to the benzodiazepines (given fears about the dependency and abuse of the latter) and may be a useful adjunct therapy (Hallstrom, Treasaden, Edwards, & Lader, 1981). Clinical experience suggests that although Inderal may block the physical aspects of anxiety, it,

unlike most benzodiazepines, does not alter the perception of fear. Most benzodiazepines also have a central calming effect.

The benzodiazepines (e.g., Valium, Librium) have dominated the market for the management of anxiety symptoms, and by the late 1970s the level of drug prescribing had reached staggering proportions. Until then, these drugs were considered safe (even in very large doses), the major complications being related to sedation and reduced coordination. Occasionally, a "paradoxical reaction" occurs when susceptible individuals become aggressive and hostile (Lion, Azcarate, & Koepke, 1975). However, concerns about the level of prescribing, the tendency to use the drugs to avoid more active psychological therapies, and reports of abuse and even physiological addiction has led to a reappraisal of their use.

At this time, short-term drug therapy (2 to 3 months) for anxiety states while at the same time also initiating psychological treatments seems to be the most common clinical practice. Many practitioners are using the more rapidly eliminated benzodiazepines, such as Ativan (lorazepam), or Xanax (alprazolam), but it is uncertain that this is of significant advantage. In situations where recurrent stress related to medical procedures leads to marked anticipatory or situational anxiety, Xanax has been shown to be an effective agent for children and adolescents (Pfefferbaum et al., 1987). Inderal and the benzodiazepines have been indicated for most anxiety states except obsessive compulsive disorder.

The antidepressant drugs, tricyclics, MAOIs, and SSRIs, have shown some specific benefits for agoraphobia, panic disorder, and obsessive compulsive disorder. One particular researcher has been interested in the usefulness of tricyclic antidepressants for the treatment of panic attacks in agoraphobic patients (Klein, 1981).

As previously noted, the tricyclic Anafranil is of interest in the treatment of anxiety states because it has been shown to be an effective agent in some adolescents with obsessive compulsive disorder (reviewed by Elkins et al., 1980; Flament et al., 1985). Other drugs, including the MAOIs, have also been reported in uncontrolled studies to benefit patients with obsessional states. The MAOIs are useful for the treatment of panic attacks and may even be superior to tricyclics (Sheehan, Ballenger, & Jacobsen, 1980), but concerns about their safety prevent general acceptance as the drug of first choice. Recent studies suggest that Prozac (Birmaher et al., 1994) and Buspar (Buspirone), a nonbenzodiazepine antianxiety drug (Simeon et al., 1994), may be useful for a wide range of child and adolescent anxiety states, even more beneficial than the benzodiazepines (Simeon et al., 1992; Graae, Milner, Rizzotto, & Klein, 1994).

AUTISM (AUTISTIC DISORDER)

Because autism can be extremely debilitating and difficult to treat, it is not an exaggeration to say that over the years investigators have examined the clinical efficacy of almost every psychotropic and antiepileptic drug for this condition (reviewed by Campbell & Deutsch, 1985; Campbell, Anderson, Deutsch, & Green, 1984a; Fish, 1976). Owing to the early onset of symptoms, pharmacotherapy may be initiated during the early childhood period. No drugs cure this disorder, but symptom suppression is achieved in some cases.

Children

Neuroleptics

Neuroleptics are often considered to be the drugs of first choice for symptomatic improvement in children with autism. For some patients, they reduce withdrawal, hyperactivity, stereotypies, fidgetiness, emotional lability, and abnormal object relations. Haldol is superior to the phenothiazines (e.g., Mellaril, Thorazine, Stelazine) because it is less likely to cause sedation at optimal dosages. Haldol has also been shown to increase the effectiveness of a language-based behavioral therapy program (Campbell et al., 1978) and appears to facilitate discrimination learning (Anderson et al., 1984). The optimal dose for most preschoolers ranges between 0.5 mg to 1.0 mg per day. Hypo-

active children with autism are not helped by treatment with Haldol; their symptoms may even become worse.

Campbell et al. (1984a) report the following adverse drug reactions to Haldol in children with autism:

> Unlike in adults, affectomotor side effects (e.g., irritability, alterations in level of motor activity) occur commonly with neuroleptic administration to children. On the other hand, parkinsonian side effects appear to be a function of age; the younger the child, the less frequent their occurrence. These side effects in children are best treated by dosage reduction. Antiparkinsonian medication is avoided because there is some evidence that they may reduce serum neuroleptic levels (Rivera-Calimlin et al., 1976) and contribute to worsening of behavioral symptoms and cognition due to central anticholinergic properties. Acute dystonic reactions are less frequent if drug is begun with very low doses and increases are gradual. However, should they occur, they are usually rapidly responsive to diphenhydramine (Benadryl), either orally or intramuscularly (25 mg). These dystonic reactions result from involuntary contractions of skeletal muscle groups and may be manifest as painful stiffening or arching of the back, neck, or tongue, and oculogyric casts. (p. 313)

Apart from acute dystonic reaction, preschoolers are also at risk for the development of other extrapyramidal symptoms. One long-term treatment study of Haldol found that 22% of the children developed dyskinesias (like those associated with tardive dyskinesia) either during treatment or when switched to placebo (Campbell et al., 1983). In a few cases the dyskinesias were manifested as an aggravation of preexisting stereotypies. The dyskinesias appeared anywhere from 5 weeks to 16 months after the initiation of medication. The dyskinesias stopped within 16 days to 9 months after they first began. In some cases they ceased while the child was on medication, and in others after the child had been switched to a placebo or medication was discontinued.

Dosage guidelines for the neuroleptics are difficult to set because there is a great deal of variability across children. Titration is the recommended procedure, and the optimal dose in milligrams per kilogram may be higher than for adults. This can be explained in part by the fact that children metabolize many types of drugs at a faster rate than do adults. A Haldol dosing schedule of 5 days on medication and 2 days off was found to be just as effective as a 7-day on medication schedule (Perry et al., 1989).

The duration of treatment is determined in part by the degree to which the drug continues to produce a clinically meaningful therapeutic response. This can only be assessed with systematic dose reductions and drug-free periods. One study has shown that Haldol remained clinically effective even after 2-1/2 years of drug administration (Campbell et al., 1983). Nevertheless, other children in that same investigation no longer required drug therapy after several months of medication.

The clinical management of maladaptive behaviors in children with autism can be a difficult process. Children who respond favorably to one type of drug at an early age may do much better on a different medication when older. Also, the search for an effective agent may be a long and tedious process of gradually adjusting the dose and assessing therapeutic benefits. It may also require trials of several different drugs. The duration of treatment varies depending upon the magnitude of the therapeutic response. Because relatively little is known about the use of neuroleptics with young children, careful monitoring is in order for this age group, and drug-free periods should be scheduled regularly to assess the continued need for treatment. The side effects associated with the use of neuroleptics make many clinicians wary about their use in children with autism. The emergence of new atypical antipsychotics (Clozaril, Risperdal) that do not have the same degree of neurologic side effects may prove to be of interest. Early case reports of use of Risperdal (Purdon, Lit, Labelle, & Jones, 1994; Horrigan & Barnhill, 1995) suggest that it may be useful for control of disruptive, aggressive, and stereotypic behavior in older individuals with autism.

Stimulants

The usefulness of stimulants for the treatment of learning and behavioral disorders in children with

autism is controversial. Campbell, Fish, Shapiro, Collins, and Koh (1972), for example, found that Dexedrine (dextroamphetamine) often exacerbated the symptoms of autism by increasing social withdrawal and stereotypies. Many youngsters also became more hyperactive and irritable. Their subject sample, however, was confined to preschoolers, who are known to be overly sensitive to these types of reactions (see Ounsted, 1955). Other investigators, however, report favorable treatment outcomes (reduction of hyperactivity symptoms and aggression) for elementary school-aged children with autism receiving Dexedrine (Geller, Guttmacher, & Bleeg, 1981) and Ritalin (Birmaher, Quintana, & Greenhill, 1988; Strayhorn, Rapp, Donina, & Strain, 1988; Vitriol & Farber, 1981). Our own experience in evaluating Ritalin response in hyperactive and/or inattentive children with autism has been favorable, and we encourage clinicians to consider this drug in appropriate cases. A small study of Ritalin given under double-blind placebo-controlled conditions to 10 children aged 7 to 11 years confirmed that treatment with this drug produced positive effects (Quintana et al., 1995).

Pondimin

For a period of time, during the 1980s, there was considerable enthusiasm for the treatment of autism with Pondimin (fenfluramine). It is approved by the Food and Drug Administrator for the treatment of obesity and is pharmacologically similar to the amphetamines. Pondimin was reported to decrease hyperactivity, distractibility, and stereotypies and to increase eye contact, social responsiveness, and language performance (reviewed by Aman & Kern, 1989; Campbell, 1988). The daily dose employed in studies with children ranges from 1.2 to 2.1 mg/kg per day, which is divided into a morning and an afternoon dose. Side effects are generally mild and include decreased appetite, lethargy, and irritability, which may respond to dose reduction (see also Piggott, Gdowski, Villaneuva, Fischhoff, & Frohman, 1986). Many children appear to experience a rebound effect (irritability, restlessness, aggressivity) upon drug withdrawal. For preschool-aged children with autism in a hospital setting, therapeutic benefits are much less noteworthy, and there is a risk of impairment of learning ability (Campbell et al., 1988). Furthermore, some investigators have found that Pondimin has little effect on reducing maladaptive behavior in older (9 to 28 years of age) individuals with autism in a residential treatment program and that side effects (tension, agitation, insomnia, sweating) can be troublesome (Yarbrough, Santat, Perel, Webster, & Lombardi, 1987). Opinions vary but some researchers suggest that there does appear to be a group of children with autism who show positive change related to use of Pondimin (Stern, Walker, Sawyer, Oades, Badcock, & Spence, 1989).

ReVia

There was some encouraging preliminary research on the opiate antagonist ReVia (naltrexone) as a treatment for autism. Clinicians were interested in the opioid antagonists because some autistic children with autism appeared to have abnormal levels of endogenous opioids, which may be related to elevated pain thresholds and self-injurious behavior. For example, Campbell et al. (1989) found that 0.5 mg/kg to 2.0 mg/kg per day doses of ReVia reduced stereotypies, hyperactivity, and social withdrawal and increased verbal production in several preschool-aged children with autism. The findings from two placebo-controlled studies of 13 (Kolmen, Feldman, Handen, & Janosky, 1995) and 41 (Campbell, Anderson, Small, Adams, Gonzalez, & Ernst, 1993) children receiving ReVia indicated modest improvements in hyperactivity and, possibly, self-injurious behavior with minimal side effects. Further study is required.

Adolescents

Because compulsive-like ritualistic behaviors are often observed in individuals with autism, the drugs that have shown promise for the treatment of OCD have been investigated in people with autism. Early reports suggest that Anafranil (McDougle et al., 1992) and Prozac (Cook, Rowlett, Jaselskis, & Leventhal, 1992) might improve symptoms in children with autism such as social withdrawal, ritualism, and aggressive and impulsive behavior. Over the years, some symptoms of autism may change and new problems may arise.

Those children who appear hyperactive may have a reduction in their extreme activity level in adolescence. However, new problems in adolescence are common. Seizures begin to occur in a third of the autistic population, and between 10% and 30% of adolescents with autism show a significant deterioration in performance and behavior (reviewed by Paul, 1987). This may include loss of verbal, social, and self-help skills, increased aloofness, and the development of stereotypic and self-injurious behaviors. Many of these children also show cyclic behavioral disturbance, with hyperactive and aggressive or more withdrawn, apathetic periods. It has been proposed that there is increased risk for this change in female patients and in the presence of a family history of affective disorder. Other problems that may be related to pubescence itself include adjustment to sexual development (which can lead to inappropriate public sexual behavior) and, for many higher-functioning adolescents with autism, increasing insight into their difference from nonautistic peers (which can lead to marked depression).

Therefore, in the adolescent years, pharmacotherapy may become more crucial, particularly for patients who show deterioration. Neuroleptics may be required for the control of behavior disorders; antidepressant treatment may help mood-related symptoms; and for periodic disorders, lithium or Tegretol may be considered. Inderal has reduced severe aggressive behavior disorders in some adolescents with autism.

Clinical Consideration

Children with autism require intense educational intervention to facilitate the acquisition of language and social skills and to suppress maladaptive behaviors (reviewed by Rutter, 1985). There exists a truly impressive literature on the effectiveness of behavioral therapy techniques with this population; and they are routinely employed in exemplary intervention programs. As was previously noted, drug researchers have been emphatic about the adjunctive status of medication in the treatment of children and adolescents with autism. Although there are some data to suggest that neuroleptic medication may make educational interventions more effective (Campbell et al., 1978), the magnitude of the therapeutic benefit from medication is in general modest. In short, even on medication these children remain seriously disabled. Because children with autism typically receive special education and other services, medication should be used only when it leads to more rapid cognitive, academic, or social development.

CONDUCT PROBLEMS (DISRUPTIVE BEHAVIOR DISORDERS)

Conduct problems involve a variety of aggressive (fighting), oppositional (noncompliant, defiant), antisocial (lying, stealing), and delinquent (status offenses, drug abuse) behaviors. They are commonly found in children with ADHD, especially those who are referred to special diagnostic and treatment facilities, youngsters in special education programs for the emotionally disturbed/behavior disordered, patients in psychiatric hospitals and residential community mental-health facilities, and people with mental retardation in institutions and community placements. Two DSM-IV diagnostic constructs that are defined in terms of conduct problems are oppositional defiant disorder and conduct disorder. Under the current diagnostic plan, a child who has both oppositional defiant disorder and conduct disorder receives only one diagnosis, namely, conduct disorder. However, a child who exhibits both ADHD and conduct disorder (or oppositional defiant disorder) is diagnosed as having both conditions.

Aggression (Conduct Disorder)

Aggression is manifest in a variety of ways: verbal aggression (cursing, threatening, malicious teasing), object aggression (breaking toys, destroying property), symbolic aggression (feigning physical attack, making offensive gestures), and physical aggression (striking, shoving, or tripping other people). Individuals can also aggress against or hurt themselves (self-injurious behavior), but this disorder is present primarily in children and adolescents who have moderate to profound mental retardation or autism and is treated as a separate topic in this chapter. Aggression is a poorly developed concept, at least in terms of its behavioral referents in the child psychopathology literature. It includes oppositional behavior, emotional lability, and norm-violating behaviors. This unwieldy use of the term is also evident in the items constituting "aggression" factors in some behavior rating scales. The popularity of these instruments in medication evaluation studies has resulted in a lack of precision in documenting and describing treatment effects. Aggressive behavior is a relatively common characteristic of many childhood and adolescent psychiatric disorders, and it is currently believed that the treatment of aggressive behavior in the absence of a thorough diagnostic evaluation can lead to inappropriate drug selection, or, equally disconcerting, divert attention away from the primary cause of the behavioral disturbance. Aggressive behavior is generally managed with a neuroleptic drug; however, recent interest has focused on tricyclic antidepressants and stimulants. In the case of intermittent outbursts of violence, three medications (Inderal, lithium, and Tegretol) have shown some early promise of efficacy.

Neuroleptics

When aggression is the primary target behavior, clinicians are most likely to prescribe a neuroleptic drug. This is particularly true for children and adolescents in residential treatment settings. Numerous studies have shown that neuroleptic drugs can suppress aggressive behavior in youngsters diagnosed as having mental retardation (reviewed by Gadow & Poling, 1988), hyperactivity (e.g., Gittelman-Klein, Klein, Katz, Saraf, & Pollack, 1976; Werry & Aman, 1975), autism (see Campbell et al., 1978), and conduct disorder (e.g., Campbell et al., 1984c). The three most commonly prescribed neuroleptic drugs for severe conduct problems (especially children who are also hyperactive and/or impulsive) are Mellaril (thioridazine), Haldol (haloperidol), and Thorazine (chlorpromazine). In general, neuroleptics are prescribed only when necessary because they are associated with a greater risk of side effects than are the stimulants. Because Mellaril has been reported to have a favorable effect on seizure reduction, this drug can be used with some confidence in the treatment of behavior disorders in children with seizure disorder (Kamm & Mandel, 1967).

There is a considerable range in the reported doses of neuroleptics across studies with children

TABLE 14.4. Neuroleptic Drug Dosages for Children Under 12 Years of Age[a]

		ORAL DOSE
GENERIC NAME	TRADE NAME	(mg/day)
chlorpromazine	Thorazine	10–200
clozapine[b]	Clozaril	50–800
fluphenazine[b]	Prolixin	0.25–16
haloperidol	Haldol	0.25–16
molindone[b]	Moban	1–40
pimozide[c]	Orap	1–7
risperidone[b]	Risperdal	1–6
thioridazine	Mellaril	10–200
thiothixene[b]	Navane	1–40
trifluoperazine[d]	Stelazine	1–15

[a]The most current issue of the *Physician's Desk Reference* should he consulted for dosage information.

[b]Not approved by the Food and Drug Administration for use with children under 12 years of age.

[c]Approved for use in the pediatric age range only for the treatment of Tourette syndrome.

[d]Recommended for use only with children who are hospitalized or under close supervision.

(see Table 14.4). The average daily dose of Mellaril and Thorazine ranges from 75 mg to 150 mg. Some clinicians prescribe one large dose at night to prevent daytime drowsiness, whereas others divide the total amount into two or three doses during the day (Katz, Saraf, Gittelman-Klein, & Klein, 1975; Winsberg & Yepes, 1978). Relative to body weight, the average dose is 3 mg/kg to 6 mg/kg per day. The effective dose of haloperidol ranges from 2 mg to 5 mg per day, which is divided into three daily doses. It is noteworthy that, in boys with hyperactivity, significant improvements in cognitive performance have been reported with low (0.025 mg/ kg) doses of Haldol (Werry & Aman, 1975).

The side effects of neuroleptics in children are similar to those reported in adults. Sedative effects (drowsiness, lethargy, and apathy) are common with Thorazine, but children usually develop a tolerance for this reaction within several days to a few weeks. Dose reduction may be necessary in some cases. It is noteworthy that irritability and excitability are also possible. Skin reactions are infrequent. Also reported are diarrhea, upset stomach, dry mouth, blurred vision, constipation, urinary retention, and abdominal pain. A number of studies report increased appetite, weight gain, or both, during drug treatment.

Katz et al. (1975) stated that in their experience the side effects of Mellaril in children with hyperactivity were frequent and severe. Drowsiness was the most common adverse reaction and was difficult to manage. If the dose was reduced, the drowsiness was less severe, but the therapeutic response was weaker. Many children developed enuresis and had to be taken off medication. Increased appetite was also common, as was puffiness around the eyes and dry mouth. Stomachache, nausea, and vomiting necessitated dosage reduction in a number of children. Other side effects included nose bleed, mild tremor, and orthostatic hypotension. Some children who reacted well to Mellaril later developed changes in temperament. They became irritable, moody, and belligerent and due to this, medication eventually had to be stopped.

Extrapyramidal syndromes are frequently reported in studies using Haldol to control behavior disorders in children. Clinicians manage these side effects by administering an anticholinergic agent either at the beginning of drug treatment (a practice that is controversial) or after symptoms appear. The possibility of more severe and persistent neurologic abnormalities (i.e., tardive dyskinesia, tardive dystonia, or tardive Tourette's Syndrome) also limit the use of neuroleptics. Children seem to be at similar risk as adults to develop these syndromes (see review by Wolf & Wagner, 1993). Although Haldol is usually not associated with sedative effects, drowsiness has sometimes been reported in studies of children. Other side effects include nausea, ataxia, slurred speech, and weight gain. A rare but potentially life-threatening side effect, neuroleptic malignant syndrome, which is characterized by fever, rigidity, altered mental status, and tachycardia has been reported and requires clinicians to be sensitive to the early clinical signs, so that intervention can be rapidly instituted (Steingard, Khan, Gonzalez, & Herzog, 1992).

Perhaps the most controversial side effect of the neuroleptics is cognitive and academic impairment. This issue is controversial because the studies in this area have not been particularly well-designed and are few in number (see Winsberg & Yepes, 1978). Nevertheless, there are good examples of research on the use of neuroleptics for individuals with hyperactivity (e.g., Sprague, Barnes, & Werry, 1970; Werry & Aman, 1975) and mental retardation (e.g., Wysocki, Fuqua, Davis, & Breuning, 1981), which strongly suggest that mental impairment is a definite possibility, but not necessarily significant (Aman, Marks, Turbott, Wilsher, & Merry, 1991). It is important, therefore, to monitor adaptive behavior during dosage adjustment and to assess the extent to which desirable behaviors may be adversely affected.

Stimulants

Given the relative safety and pervasive use of stimulant medication, it is noteworthy that little is known about its effect on child and adolescent aggression. An aggression suppression effect is often inferred from rating-scale data (e.g., Campbell, Cohen, & Small, 1982); but, as previously noted, "aggression" factor scores typically represent an amalgam of conduct problems. Allen, Safer, and Covi (1975) commented that a post hoc analysis of specific rating-scale items showed that stimulant drug treatment led to lower teacher ratings of aggressive behavior (fights; defiant). Similarly, Amery, Minichiello, and Brown (1984) reported that the administration of Dexedrine resulted in lower parent and teacher ratings of aggressiveness as well as decreased levels of fantasy and object aggression in a clinic playroom setting. Others have observed a reduction in the rate of negative verbal statements in the classroom for hyperactive children taking Ritalin (e.g., Abikoff & Gittelman, 1985; Whalen, Henker, Collins, Finck, & Dotemoto, 1979). Be-

cause acts of physical aggression are infrequent, particularly in classrooms and laboratory playrooms, less is known about drug effects on this behavior. An in-depth examination of the effect of Ritalin on aggressive children in public school settings (classroom, lunchroom, playground) using direct observation procedures was conducted by Gadow, Nolan, Sverd, and Paolicelli (1990). They found that medication did, in fact, suppress physical aggression during school recess periods. Moreover, some of these same children also showed concurrently increased rates of appropriate social interaction. Cylert might be a consideration for children with mixed conduct and hyperactive disorders that do not respond satisfactorily to Ritalin (Shah, Seese, Abikoff, & Klein, 1994). Catapres (clonidine), a antihypertensive agent that has also been used for hyperactivity, reduced aggression in 15 of 17 children aged 5–15 years in one nonblind study (Kemph, DeVane, Levin, Jarecke, & Miller, 1993).

Lithium

There are a growing number of reports on the efficacy of lithium treatment for aggressive behavior in prepubertal children. Campbell et al. (1984c), for example, conducted a thorough and well-controlled investigation into the effects of Haldol and lithium on hospitalized, conduct disordered, undersocialized, aggressive children between 5 and 13 years of age. The optimal dose of Haldol ranged from 1.0 mg to 6.0 mg per day (0.04 mg/kg to 0.21 mg/kg per day), and the optimal dose of lithium was 500 mg to 2,000 mg per day (or serum levels of 0.32 mEq/L to 1.51 mEq/L). Both Haldol and lithium were highly effective in reducing aggressive behavior. Qualitatively, whereas Haldol rendered the children more manageable, lithium reduced the explosive nature of their aggressive behavior, which enabled other positive changes to take place. Subjectively, the children receiving Haldol felt "slowed down," and the youngsters receiving lithium thought that medication "helped to control" them. It appeared that the optimal dose of Haldol interfered with daily functioning more than lithium.

Lithium has shown some effectiveness as an anti-aggression agent for some people with mental retardation (reviewed by Gadow & Poling, 1988), patients with seizure disorder, and male delinquents (reviewed by Sheard, 1978). Among the latter group, certain characteristics seem to be associated with the effectiveness of lithium treatment: mood lability (rapid changes between euphoria and depression), irritability, hostility, restlessness, impulsivity, distractibility, pressured speech (excessive, rapid talking), and a loud and provocative manner. Other workers have described a similar personality profile among adolescent girls, which they have called the emotionally unstable character disorder (Rifkin, Quitkin, Carillo, Blumberg, & Klein, 1972). Individuals with this disorder are also purported to show a response to lithium therapy. The doses of lithium recommended in these studies are the same as those used to control mania in adolescents. A recent review of the studies of lithium for the treatment of aggression in children and adolescents (Campbell, Kafantaris, & Cueva, 1995) concluded that the efficacy of lithium is not proven. However the marked variation in treatment outcome between the studies was thought to be due to differences in length of treatment, size and type of population, and degree of "explosiveness" seen in subjects selected.

Beta Blockers

A relatively new drug for the treatment of aggression and explosive aggressive outbursts is Inderal (propranolol), a beta-adrenergic blocking agent or "beta blocker" (Silver & Yudofsky, 1985). This drug is used primarily for the treatment of hypertension (high blood pressure), angina (intense chest pains), and cardiac arrhythmias (irregular heartbeat). An increasing number of studies (reviewed by Gualtieri, Golden, & Fahs, 1983) indicate that Inderal may be effective for a variety of psychiatric disorders; however, it is not yet approved by the Food and Drug Administration for use in the treatment of these conditions. Reports of Inderal's effectiveness for childhood behavior disorders have focused on children with some form of organic brain damage or brain dysfunction (e.g., Williams, Mehl, & Yudofsky, 1982). The average dose for children and adolescents is 160 mg per day, but the optimal range is 50

to 960 mg/day. (Maximal doses are considerably higher than for other medical uses.) Side effects include a reduction in blood pressure and pulse rate and, rarely, breathing difficulties, nightmares, and decreased motor coordination. When Inderal is used with the "right" children and dosage is gradually increased, side effects are not a major problem. A key point here is use with the right children. Inderal should be employed only in cases where conventional pharmacological and behavioral treatments have failed. The use of this drug is contraindicated for children and youths with a history of cardiac or respiratory disease (e.g., asthma), who have hypoglycemia, or who are taking MAOIs (Gualtieri et al., 1983). Connor (1993), in a review of the use of beta blockers in children notes that there are no double-blind placebo-controlled studies, and beta-blockers can only be recommended as adjunctive treatment. However, if used, beta-blockers should be administered for a minimum of 12 weeks to adequately assess possible response.

A study of Inderal for the treatment of aggression and self-injurious behavior in adults with severe and profound mental retardation was conducted by Ratey et al. (1986). Over half the patients made pronounced therapeutic gains on Inderal, which was an especially important outcome because all "had undergone numerous trials of varying drug, educational, and behavioral regimens without benefit" (p. 103). The investigators employed doses (40 mg to 240 mg per day) lower than those used by others and cautioned that because the onset of therapeutic response may be gradual in some patients, there is a risk of increasing the dose prematurely. The primary side effects were hypotension and bradycardia (abnormally slow heart rate).

Tegretol

A number of reports show that Tegretol is helpful in reducing aggressive and impulsive behavior occurring in patients with various different diagnoses, including schizophrenia, personality disorder, and brain disorders such as trauma or seizures (reviewed by Roy-Byrne, Uhde, & Post, 1984b, 1984c), and this drug is currently receiving increasing application in child psychiatry (reviewed by Evans, Clay, &

Gualtieri, 1987). The enthusiasm for Tegretol was tempered by early reports that it might worsen aggression in some children and adolescents, but Roy-Byrne et al. (1984b) have stated that the therapeutic effects of Tegretol are in many ways similar to those of lithium. This is particularly noticeable in one controlled study, which showed that Tegretol significantly reduced self-destructive behavior (overdosing, wrist cutting, and cigarette burning) in 13 girls who exhibited symptoms similar to those of the emotionally unstable character disorder.

The side effects of Tegretol include drowsiness, ataxia, nausea, anorexia, and visual disturbances. Although there is also a risk of blood and bone disorders, these adverse reactions are rare. Nevertheless, they could be fatal and therefore blood monitoring is mandatory. Tegretol has been reported to induce tics (Evans et al., 1987) and seizures (e.g., Lerman, 1986) in some children. Clinicians who prescribe Tegretol for the control of aggression and other behavior disorders should also conscientiously monitor for behavioral toxicity, the signs of which include irritability, hyperactivity, agitation, aggression, impulsivity, and manic symptoms (e.g., euphoria, pressured speech, grandiose ideas; Pleak, Birmaker, Gavrilescu, Abichandani, & Williams, 1988). The doses of Tegretol used for the control of aggression are generally the same as those used for the treatment of seizure disorders. However, Evans et al. (1987) note that little is known about the length of adequate drug trials, significance of blood levels, and degree of negative cognitive effects in psychiatric patients.

Oppositional Behavior (Oppositional Defiant Disorder)

DSM-IV defines oppositional defiant disorder as a pattern of behavior characterized by "negativistic, defiant, disobedient and hostile behavior" with specific symptoms such as "loses temper, argues with adults, actively defies or refuses adult requests or rules, deliberately does things to annoy other people, blames others for...own mistakes" (American Psychiatric Association, 1994, p. 91). To the best of our knowledge, there are no psychotropic drug studies of children or adolescents who were diagnosed as having "pure" oppositional defiant disorder. Nevertheless, these negativistic behaviors are common in children

with ADHD or conduct disorder and their responsiveness to stimulant and neuroleptic medication has been commented on for many years (e.g., Bradley, 1937). More recently, psychopharmacologists have employed direct observation techniques in natural settings to examine changes in specific behaviors more precisely. The results of these investigations show that children with ADD/ADHD who are oppositional do become more compliant with regard to adult directives when receiving stimulant medication (e.g., Gadow, Nolan et al., 1990, 1995). Parents, in particular, see the treated child as being more manageable. Dramatic reductions in emotional liability (temper tantrums, irritability, argumentativeness) are also observed in children for whom this is a major clinical concern (e.g., Speltz, Varley, Peterson, & Beilke, 1988).

Antisocial Behavior (Conduct Disorder)

There is really no well-controlled research on drug therapy for nonconfrontational forms of antisocial behavior such as lying, stealing, illicit substance use, and so forth. Although it is certainly plausible that in some cases (particularly when impulsivity is a major factor) decreases in such behaviors might be expected consequent to effective pharmacotherapy, these often low frequency and sometimes secretive behaviors are difficult to study.

ENURESIS (FUNCTIONAL ENURESIS)

In an excellent review of the literature, Blackwell and Currah (1973) stated that the tricyclic antidepressants were the only drugs that have consistently proved to be more effective than placebo for the treatment of nocturnal enuresis (bed-wetting). Several different tricyclics are presently available, but Tofranil is the one most commonly used to treat this disorder. It was first reported effective for the treatment of enuresis by MacLean in 1960 and 13 years later was approved by the FDA for use with this disorder. Other tricyclics used for enuresis include Norpramin and Elavil.

When Tofranil works, the response is immediate, usually during the first week of treatment. A complete cure (total remission of symptoms), however, is reported for less than half of the children treated with tricyclic medication. It should be noted that if a less stringent criterion is used (e.g., 50% fewer wet nights), the "success" rate is much higher. Unfortunately, "relapse tends to occur immediately following withdrawal after short periods of treatment, and long-term follow-up studies suggest that total remission (no wet nights) occurs in only a minority of patients" (Blackwell & Currah, 1973, p. 253).

The total daily dose of Tofranil commonly reported in the literature is 25 mg to 50 mg given in one oral dose at bedtime. For children over 12 years of age, the dose may be increased to 75 mg if the smaller amount is unsuccessful. The FDA recommends that the dose of Tofranil not exceed 2.5 mg/kg per day because there is a risk of severe side effects at higher doses (Robinson & Barker, 1976). Fritz, Rockney, and Yeung (1994) found that measuring serum levels of imipramine could assist in improving treatment response and there was marked (700%) variation between individuals in their serum level at a range of different doses up to 2.5 mg/kg.

Daytime wetting is referred to as diurnal enuresis. This condition is more common in girls and is often associated with behavior problems at home and at school (Meadow & Berg, 1982). It is a difficult disorder to treat successfully (i.e., no relapses). In one study that examined the utility of two different doses of Tofranil (25 mg and 50 mg administered in the morning) for diurnal enuresis, Meadow and Berg (1982) found that medication was not more effective than placebo.

Although stimulant drugs are not generally prescribed for nocturnal enuresis, there have been numerous reports over the years of how children with hyperactivity with nocturnal enuresis became dry after taking stimulant medication for hyperactivity. Research on stimulants for enuresis has a long history (e.g., Molitch & Poliakoff, 1937), and it has recently been suggested that Ritalin may be an effective treatment for some enuretic patients who become dry and later relapse (Diamond & Stein, 1983).

DDAVP (desmopressin), an antidiuretic hormone used for the treatment of diabetes insipidus, has also been shown to diminish nocturnal enuresis in several placebo-controlled studies (reviewed by Klauber, 1989). It has a rapid onset of action and negligible side effects for most, but case reports of fluid reten-

tion leading to metabolic problems and seizures have started to appear (Thompson & Rey, 1995). Child patients are generally treated with doses ranging from 20 to 40 micrograms administered intranasally at bedtime. DDAVP's efficacy in nocturnal enuresis is related to its ability to increase water reabsorption in the kidneys, which reduces the volume of water entering the bladder. The drawbacks of DDAVP treatment are the relatively high cost of the medication and the likelihood of relapse when medication is discontinued (Miller, Goldberg, & Atkin, 1989). Gradual tapering of the dose during the withdrawal period (which may last several months) reduces the probability of relapse.

The treatment of first choice for nocturnal enuresis is use of the pad-and-buzzer device, which may or may not be incorporated into a more elaborate behavioral therapy program (Shaffer, 1985). Medication should be considered only when proven behavioral interventions have failed or are not practical or when special circumstances warrant, such as vacations or highly stressful home settings. Studies comparing psychological and pharmacological treatments for enuresis have resulted in mixed findings. For example, Kolvin et al. (1972) examined the relative efficacy of Tofranil, conditioning, and placebo. Children in the study were separated into three groups, each receiving one of the aforementioned treatments. Therapy for each group lasted 2 months, with the results being evaluated 2 months later. Treatment was considered successful if there was an 80% decrease in wet nights. Using this criterion, 42% of the placebo group, 30% of the medication group, and 50% of the pad-and-buzzer group were considered improved. Conversely, Wagner, Johnson, Walker, Carter, and Wittner (1982) found tricyclic antidepressants to be superior to the pad and buzzer in a short-term study.

ATTENTION-DEFICIT HYPERACTIVITY DISORDER

The most common reason for psychiatric referral and for the prescription of psychotropic medication to children is for ADHD, a disorder that is now saddled with legion of labels (e.g., minimal brain dysfunction, hyperkinesis, hyperkinetic syndrome, hyperkinetic reaction of childhood, attention-deficit disorder with hyperactivity, attention-deficit hyperactivity disorder). The traditionally recognized symptoms of the disorder have been motor restlessness, short attention span, and impulsivity. However, the use of the term "hyperactivity" as a diagnostic construct is currently undergoing change. This is due in part to the idea that poor attending skills rather than excessive motor restlessness may be the essence of the problem (Douglas, 1972; Douglas & Peters, 1979), a notion that has been discussed for a number of years (e.g., Ounsted, 1955) and is now somewhat controversial (see, for example, Porrino et al., 1983). One consequence of the controversy concerning the "right" label, the primary symptoms, and the diagnostic criteria has been the obfuscation of target symptoms. Taylor (1985), for example, noted that it is unclear from the drug research literature exactly what is being treated: hyperactivity, aggression, or both. The fact that aggression is poorly operationalized also complicates matters. For some researchers and clinicians in the ADHD area, the primary reason for treatment is to render the child more manageable. Morever, the behavior problem is attributed to the child's abnormal activity level, attention deficits, impulsivity, or some combination of these problems. Because academic underachievement was considered to be "almost a hallmark of this syndrome" (Wender, 1973, p. 16), drug-induced improvement in academic productivity and associated cognitive deficits was widely embraced as a justification and a reason for treatment (Gadow, 1983). So as not to belabor the point, suffice it to say that with the notable exception of Charles Bradley (Bradley, 1957; Bradley & Bowen, 1941), few investigators in this area have either formulated or critically examined theories of (or rationales for) treatment.

The associated features of ADHD are several and include oppositional behavior (defiance of authority figures, emotional lability), peer aggression (verbal, physical), conduct problems (delinquency, lying, stealing, physical violence), affective symptoms (anxiety, depression), and learning disabilities. Because these symptomatic concomitants of ADHD are also recognized as being distinct disorders (in the presence or absence of ADHD) and are addressed separately in this chapter, the present discussion focuses primarily but not exclusively on ADHD symptoms and interpersonal relations.

Stimulants

The stimulants (Ritalin, Dexedrine, and Cylert) are the most commonly prescribed drugs for hyperactivity, and Ritalin is by far the preferred drug and the most extensively studied. Because a number of comprehensive reviews of stimulant drug therapy are available (Barkley, 1990; Conners, 1971; Eisenberg & Conners, 1971; Gadow, 1986a, 1992; Schachar & Tannock, 1993; Sprague & Werry, 1974; see also the chapter by DuPaul, Guerremont, & Barkley in this volume), only a few representative studies are noted here.

The effect of stimulant drugs on activity level is greatly influenced by task and setting variables. For example, Ellis, Witt, Reynolds, and Sprague (1974) found little effect of Ritalin on motor movement in the playroom, yet these same children were perceived by their teacher to be less active in school (Sleator & von Neumann, 1974) and to wiggle less in their chair while performing a laboratory task (Sprague & Sleator, 1973) when taking medication compared with placebo. Others have found that stimulants reduce activity during highly structured, task-oriented classroom situations (e.g., Gadow, Nolan et al., 1990, 1995; Whalen et al., 1979).

Stimulant drugs improve performance on a variety of cognitive tasks including measures of sustained attention (e.g., Conners & Rothschild, 1968; Sykes, Douglas, Weiss, & Minde, 1971), impulsivity (e.g., Brown & Sleator, 1979), short-term memory (e.g., Sprague & Sleator, 1977; Weingartner et al., 1980), and paired-associate learning (e.g., Conners & Rothschild, 1968; Swanson & Kinsbourne, 1976). There is also research to suggest that problem-solving behaviors may be enhanced, as evidenced by studies of search strategies (Dykman, Ackerman, & McCray, 1980), flexible thinking (Dyme, Sahakian, Golinko, & Rabe, 1982), information processing (Reid & Borkowski, 1984), visual scanning patterns (Flintoff, Barron, Swanson, Ledlow, & Kinsbourne, 1982), and inspection strategy (Sprague, 1984). In spite of years of research on stimulant drugs and their effect on cognitive performance, the exact mechanism(s) by which these performance gains are achieved is poorly understood.

There are at least several ways in which stimulant-induced changes in the behavior of a child with

ADHD result in modifications of parent, teacher, and peer behavior. As children with ADHD become less disruptive and more compliant, others around them begin to react differently. For example, mothers become less controlling and less negative in response to the improvement in their child's behavior (e.g., Barkley & Cunningham, 1979; Humphries, Kinsbourne, & Swanson, 1978). Moreover, changes in the mother's behavior appear to be dose-related (Barkley, Karlsson, Strezlecki, & Murphy, 1984); that is, they are more evident at moderate (0.5 mg/kg twice a day) than low (0.15 mg/kg twice a day) doses. Teachers also may react to children with ADHD much differently depending on whether they are receiving medication or placebo. Whalen, Henker, and Dotemoto (1980) found that when the child is receiving Ritalin, the teacher is less controlling (i.e., guidance, commands, and admonitions), less intense (i.e., vigor, loudness, rapidity, and emotionality), and less likely to call out the child's name. There are few studies of how the behavior of peers changes in response to stimulant-induced improvement in the behavior of the child with ADHD. In one laboratory study, Cunningham, Siegel, and Offord (1985) found that Ritalin treatment resulted in decreased levels of controlling behavior in children with ADD, and peers responded to this change by reacting to the child in a less controlling manner. Another study by Gadow, Paolicelli et al. (1992) in public school classrooms found that peers engaged in less nonphysical aggression when an aggressive boy with ADD was receiving Ritalin than when he was taking placebo.

At moderate doses, stimulant drugs produce few serious side effects and are generally considered to be safe. At the onset of drug treatment, two of the more common adverse reactions are insomnia and anorexia (loss of appetite). Insomnia is typically not a problem if medication is administered only in the morning, but many children receive a dose at noon and some even get medication late in the day. If such a schedule is necessary, an additional drug may be prescribed to induce sleep. Anorexia can usually be managed by taking the pill just before or with meals. Other minor side effects include headache, stomachache, nausea, and increased talkativeness. Stimulant drugs can also produce mood changes such as dysphoria (withdrawal, lethargy, apathy,

serious facial expression, unusual inactivity, weepiness), fearfulness, irritability, and euphoria (rare). Younger children appear to be more susceptible to mood changes. Children typically develop a tolerance for these side effects, but the dose may have to be reduced and gradually increased to lessen the degree of discomfort.

There are other possible side effects of stimulant medication that do not occur very often but should be monitored nevertheless. One such reaction is involuntary movement of muscles. This would include a variety of actions such as protrusion of the tongue, grimacing, facial tics (spasm or twitching of the facial muscles), choreoathetoid (jerking and writhing) movements of arms or legs, and twisting of the head and neck (e.g., Denkla, Bemporad, & McKay, 1976; Husain, Chapel, & Malek-Ahmadl, 1980; Mattson & Calvery, 1968; Robbins & Sahakian, 1979). These drugs can also induce or exacerbate stereotypies such as nail biting (e.g., Robbins & Sahakian, 1979). In some cases, these side effects will abate by simple reduction of the dosage. In others, treatment may have to be discontinued or the child switched to a different drug.

There have been reports of stimulant-induced hallucinations (Lucas & Weiss, 1971) and psychosis (Greenberg, Deem, & McMahon, 1972), but this is considered a rare phenomenon. A child who experiences such a reaction may complain about "hearing things" or talk in a strange or bizzarre manner. Discontinuation of medication is recommended.

The only long-term side effects of Ritalin or Dexedrine that have been reported so far are small changes in height and weight (e.g., Mattes & Gittelman, 1983; Safer & Allen, 1973). However, when drug treatment is stopped, children show a growth rebound, an increase in growth rate that compensates for the slower rate while on medication (Safer, Allen, & Barr, 1975). The Pediatric Advisory Panel of the FDA reviewed the available literature about stimulants and growth suppression (Roche, Lipman, Overall, & Hung, 1979) and concluded that "stimulant drugs, particularly in the 'high normal' dose range, moderately suppress growth in weight. . .[but] early growth suppression during treatment is no longer evident in adulthood" (p. 849). However, Zeiner (1995) suggests there may be a small number of more susceptible children who show significant reduction in weight gain, and they may need to be identified for closer monitoring. At present there is no evidence that long-term treatment with Ritalin (approximately 0.25 mg/kg given twice a day) adversely affects the functioning of the liver, the endocrine system, or the cardiovascular system (Satterfield, Schell, & Barb, 1980). Children with both ADHD and anxiety disorder may show a slightly exaggerated cardiovascular response (increased blood pressure) to a dose of Ritalin (Urman, Ickowicz, Fulford & Tannock, 1995). There is also evidence that children who have both ADHD and internalizing disorders (e.g., anxiety, depression) have a less robust or even negative reaction to use of Ritalin (Tannock, Ickowicz, & Schachar, 1995; DuPaul, Barkley, & McMurray, 1994).

Stimulants are relatively short-acting drugs. Their behavioral effects can be observed within a half hour after being administered orally. A 10-mg tablet of Ritalin produces a therapeutic effect for approximately 3 to 4 hours, and a 20-mg tablet lasts for at least an hour longer (Carter, 1956; Safer & Allen, 1976). Dexedrine Spansules, a timed-release product, produce a longer lasting effect (approximately 12 hours) than do Dexedrine tablets. Also, a long-lasting (approximately 8 hours) form of Ritalin called Ritalin-SR is now available. The SR stands for "sustained-release." According to one report, one 20-mg tablet of Ritalin-SR administered at breakfast produces a therapeutic effect equivalent to a 10-mg tablet of regular Ritalin given twice a day (Whitehouse, Shah, & Palmer, 1980). The findings from another study, however, indicate that standard Ritalin (10 mg twice a day) is superior to Ritalin-SR (20 mg) in suppressing certain forms of disruptive behavior (Pelham et al., 1987), but this difference may not have any clinical relevance over a more prolonged treatment period (Fitzpatrick, Klorman, Brumaghim, & Borgstedt, 1992).

Children differ greatly in terms of optimal dose. Some do well on a low dose (0.1 mg/kg), whereas others appear unchanged unless the dose is very high (e.g., 1.0 mg/kg). For this reason, most clinicians start out with a small dose that is gradually increased until the desired effect is achieved. (The figures for milligrams per kilogram given here refer to individual doses of medication, which may or

may not be administered more than once per day.) The average daily dose of Ritalin is usually 20 mg to 30 mg, with a morning dose of 10 mg to 20 mg and a noon dose of 10 mg (Safer & Allen, 1976). It is not unusual, however, to find reports stating that the average daily dose of Ritalin is 55 mg or that some children are receiving as much as 120 mg to 140 mg per day (Gittelman-Klein & Klein, 1976; Renshaw, 1974).

It is common clinical lore that Dexedrine is twice as potent as Ritalin (Safer & Allen, 1976). However, in actual practice, the daily doses of these drugs prescribed by physicians appear to be comparable (Gadow, 1981).

The beginning dose of Cylert (pemoline) is usually 37.5 mg, which may be increased to 75 mg per day (Safer & Allen, 1976). The dosage ratio of Ritalin to Cylert ranges from 1:4 to 1:6 (Pelham, 1983; Stephens et al., 1984). In other words, the behavioral effect produced by 0.3 mg/kg of Ritalin administered twice a day is similar to the effect produced by 1.2 mg/kg to 1.8 mg/kg of Cylert given once a day. Pelham, Swanson, Furman, and Schwindt (1995) found that, contrary to some opinion, Cylert was as efficacious and immediately responsive as the other stimulants, but commonly used doses may be too low and can be increased up to 112.5 mg per day.

Nonstimulant Drugs

Not all children with ADHD can be effectively managed with stimulant medication, particularly those who exhibit severe behavior disorders or who are multiply disabled. For such children clinicians are more likely to prescribe a neuroleptic (see the discussion of conduct problems), such as Mellaril (e.g., Gittelman-Klein et al., 1976) or Haldol (e.g., Werry & Aman, 1975), or a tricyclic antidepressant, such as Tofranil, which was once considered the drug of second choice for the treatment of hyperactivity on the basis of findings from several studies (e.g., Rapoport et al., 1974; Werry, Aman, & Diamond, 1980). Unfortunately, many children appear to develop a tolerance for the therapeutic response (Quinn & Rapoport, 1975). There are some data to suggest that children with ADHD who (a) are more difficult to manage in the evening hours, (b) have mood-disturbance symptoms, or (c) are highly anxious may be more responsive to Tofranil than to stimulant drugs (Pliszka, 1987). The total daily dose of Tofranil ranges from 50 mg to 200 mg, usually administered in divided doses. The primary side effects are drowsiness, dizziness, dry mouth, profuse sweating, nausea, increased appetite, weight gain, and weight loss. Tofranil may also lower the seizure threshold, especially in children with brain damage (Brown, Winsberg, Bialer, & Press, 1973).

Another tricyclic antidepressant, desipramine, which is marketed as Norpramin, was also found to be effective for children and adolescents with ADD, many of whom were poor responders to stimulants (Biederman, Baldessarini, Wright, Knee, & Harmatz, 1989). The average daily dose used by Biederman et al. was 4.6 mg/kg, but they note that in clinical practice the average daily dose should be increased gradually with concurrent assessment of therapeutic and untoward effects. Other antidepressants, such as Pamelor (Wilens, Biederman, Geist, Steingard, & Spencer, 1993), Wellbutrin (Barrickman et al., 1995) and Prozac (Barrickman, Noyes, Kuperman, Schumacher, & Verda, 1991) have shown some evidence of reducing symptoms of ADHD.

Tourette Syndrome

In addition to motor and vocal tics, approximately half of all diagnosed cases of Tourette syndrome also experience the behavioral symptoms of ADD/ADHD (e.g., Comings & Comings, 1984; Sverd, Curley, Jandorf, & Volkersz, 1988). Our own research with stimulants in children with both ADHD and Tourette syndrome indicate that Ritalin is effective for ADHD symptoms (Gadow, Nolan, Sprafkin, & Sverd, 1995; Gadow, Sverd, Sprafkin, Nolan, & Ezor, 1995). Furthermore, for most children there is little or no worsening of tics at moderate doses. Because stimulant drugs can induce tics and exacerbate the symptoms of Tourette syndrome in some individuals, they should be carefully monitored in patients with Tourette syndrome; the risks of treatment must be carefully explained to caregivers and, when appropriate, the child patient. Unfortunately, all of the commonly prescribed drugs

for ADHD and for Tourette syndrome can induce or exacerbate tics (Gadow & Sverd, 1990). It is controversial whether stimulants can cause Tourette syndrome in children who would not otherwise develop it. For this reason, some clinicians have cautioned against the use of stimulants for ADHD with children who have a first-degree relative (parent, brother, or sister) with Tourette syndrome and recommend drug withdrawal for children who experience drug-induced tics but were tic-free before treatment. The latter is also controversial because tics may abate with dose reduction. Alternative treatments that have been proposed for children with comorbid tic disorder and ADHD include the tricyclic antidepressants (Spencer, Biederman, & Wilens, 1994), Catapres (Steingard, Biederman, Spencer, Wilens, & Gonzalez, 1993) and Tenex (guanfacine), which is a similar drug to Catapres but longer acting and less sedating (Chappell et al., 1995). Tenex has also been assessed in non blind studies as a primary treatment for ADHD (Horrigan & Barnhill, 1995; Hunt, Arnsten, & Asbell, 1995).

Clinical Considerations

Although one can never overemphasize the idiosyncratic nature of stimulant drug response in terms of behavioral effects, dose, and dose response relationships, the general pattern of treatment with Ritalin is as follows: The typical dose for elementary school-aged children is 10 mg to 15 mg administered in the morning and at noon. Many (but certainly not all) clinicians believe that individual doses greater than 0.6 mg/kg are generally not necessary for adequate therapeutic response and clinical management. When possible, it is recommended that medication not be given at times when it is unnecessary (e.g., on weekends and during summer vacations). However, such breaks from medication are not in the best interests of some patients. In good responders, treatment typically lasts for several (2 to 4) years, but periodic drug-free periods (at least once a year) are recommended to ascertain the need for continued treatment. Multiple-drug regimens are almost always ill advised. Drug therapy is typically terminated before the child enters junior high, but this does not mean that medication is no longer effective. Quite the contrary; stimulants appear to be efficacious for symptom suppression in patients with ADHD of all ages (infancy to adulthood). The probability of success when withdrawing medication can be greatly increased by the concurrent or subsequent implementation of alternative interventions (e.g., behavior therapy).

Stimulant drug therapy is a palliative; to the best of our knowledge, no one has yet demonstrated that medication leads to the permanent alteration of neurological structures, imparts new learning, or is even instrumental in the acquisition of skills that would not develop had treatment been withheld. Serious, thoughtful consideration must therefore be given to all the patient's clinical needs and to those of his or her caregivers if the latter bear on the patient's well-being, and they often do.

SCHIZOPHRENIA

Children

Childhood schizophrenia is a rare disorder, and it does appear to be a separate diagnostic entity from infantile autism. Follow-up studies show that even during the elementary school years, children with infantile autism remain distinguishable from youngsters with schizophrenia (Green et al., 1984; McClellan & Werry, 1992). One important difference between the two groups is that children with autism, on clinical examination, do not have auditory or visual hallucinations or delusions, whereas these are diagnostic characteristics for children with schizophrenia.

There has been relatively little psychotropic drug research on prepubertal children with schizophrenia. Although they were no doubt included in early investigations of autism or psychosis, drug response has rarely been examined separately for this diagnostic entity. Based on the adolescent and adult literature, neuroleptics would be the drugs of choice. Neuroleptics that are more "stimulating" (e.g., Navane, Haldol) have generally been preferred. Whether these drugs actually suppress hallucinations, delusions, and disordered thought in prepubertal children with schizophrenia is not well-

documented, and cases of drug failure have been reported (e.g., Green et al., 1984). Spencer et al. (1992) suggest that, in a controlled study, Haldol does benefit most children with childhood onset schizophrenia, but as many as one third of these children may be candidates for alternative, newer, treatments (Rapoport, 1994).

Considerable excitement has been generated by the introduction of atypical antipsychotics such as Clozaril (clozapine) and Risperdal (risperidone). These drugs differ from the previous generation of antipsychotics in that they have more specific and broader effects on neurotransmitters (dopamine and serotonin). These differences have been important for adult patients with chronic schizophrenia because the treatment effects seem not only to improve the florid symptoms of schizophrenia (e.g., hallucinations and delusions) but also the more treatment-resistant, negative symptoms (e.g. apathy, withdrawal). Furthermore, these drugs have a decreased likelihood of causing extrapyramidal symptoms (Clozaril more than Risperdal) and may be less likely to induce tardive dyskinesia than traditional antipsychotics.

A number of case reports have been published showing that Clozaril may be helpful in reducing schizophrenic symptoms in children (Mozes et al., 1994; Towbin, Dykens, & Pugliese, 1994) and adolescents (Frazier, Gordon, McKenna, Lenane, Jih, & Rapoport, 1994; Remschmidt, Schulz, & Martin, 1994). Risperdal may also be effective for this patient population (Quintana & Keshavan, 1995: Simeon, Carrey, Wiggins, Milin, & Hosenbocus, 1995). Unfortunately, the benefits of these drugs are counteracted by serious and limiting side effects. With Clozaril there is a high risk of seizures, excessive weight gain, and, most concerning, a potentially life-threatening reduction of white blood cells (agranulocytosis). The latter has necessitated firm rules of monitoring that require weekly sampling of blood. In reality many people tolerate Clozaril well but reports of its use in children suggest that the risk of serious side effects, including akathisia (extreme restlessness), are worryingly high and comparable to findings in adult studies (Rapoport, 1994). Although Risperdal does not have such serious concerns, sedation, weight gain, and extrapyramidal symptoms can occur with its use, and it seems to be somewhat less effective than Clozaril for the treatment-resistant adults with chronic schizophrenia.

Adolescents

There are few methodologically sound studies of the efficacy of neuroleptic medication for the treatment of schizophrenia in adolescents. One of the better studies, conducted by Pool, Bloom, Mielke, Roniger, and Gallant (1976), showed that Haldol and Loxitane (loxapine) were superior to placebo in controlling psychotic symptoms. Similarly, Realmuto, Erickson, Yellin, Hopwood, and Greenberg (1984) studied adolescents receiving Mellaril and Navane (thiothixene) and found that (compared with baseline) treatment with either medication was associated with decreased anxiety, tension, excitement, and hallucinations, and, to a modest extent, cognitive disorganization. The optimal doses of Mellaril and Navane were 3.3 mg/kg per day and 0.30 mg/kg per day, respectively. Unfortunately, despite the diminution of symptoms, the youths "continued to be quite impaired" (p. 441) and, by the end of the study, only half were considered to be improved. Particularly troubling was the finding that drug-induced drowsiness was a common side effect, not only for Mellaril (75%) but also for Navane (54%), which is a less sedating neuroleptic, at least for adults.

In adolescence, the unwanted effects of neuroleptic medication have to be weighed against the severity of psychiatric disturbance. For example, a minor deterioration in intellectual performance is much less clinically relevant in a patient who is experiencing hallucinations and delusions and who will be institutionalized unless treated with neuroleptic medication. The management of acute (short-term) psychosis raises few concerns about the use of neuroleptics. Most side effects are self-limiting and reversible or, in the case of the acute extrapyramidal syndromes, treatable with anticholinergic drugs. The major clinical problem is for adolescents who require chronic or long-term treatment. Unfortunately, the findings from one study suggest that adolescents with schizophrenia have a poor response to neuroleptics (Welner, Welner, & Fishman, 1979). More-

over, long-term neuroleptic treatment may cause tardive dyskinesia in some patients (Gualtieri, Barnhill, McGinsey, & Schell, 1980; Gualtieri, Quade, Hicks, Mayo, & Schroeder, 1984) and also produce changes in hormone secretions (Apter et al., 1983) and deterioration in cognitive performance (Erickson, Yellin, Hopwood, Realmuto, & Greenberg, 1984). Clozaril and Risperdal are important drugs for use in adolescents who are unresponsive to the traditional neuroleptics, but it is to be hoped that newer and safer antipsychotics with similar clinical profiles will be produced.

At present, the use of long-term neuroleptic treatment should be carefully considered. If the adolescent disorder is significantly improved with medication, it may only be a matter of trying to maintain the lowest dose and using the low-dose high-potency drugs (e.g., Haldol, Navane, Loxitane) when possible. The development of serious side effects (e.g., tardive dyskinesia) usually necessitates a withdrawal of medication and a review of other approaches to treatment. In the case of schizophrenia, social and vocational intervention are crucial aspects of treatment, and the sole reliance on medication is not likely to be effective.

SELF-INJURIOUS BEHAVIOR (STEREOTYPIC MOVEMENT DISORDER WITH SELF-INJURIOUS BEHAVIOR)

Studies of people with mental retardation in institutions (e.g., Griffin, Williams, Stark, Altmeyer, & Mason, 1986; Schroeder, Schroeder, Smith, & Dalldorf, 1978) suggest that approximately 10% to 15% exhibit self-injurious behavior (generally referred to as SIB). The extent of this problem is often unappreciated. Schroeder, Bickel, and Richmond (1986), for example, estimated that as many as 34,000 persons with severe and profound mental retardation exhibit serious SIB, which may result in tissue damage, permanent impairment, and even death. Despite the seriousness of this disorder and our heartfelt reactions to it, there are few well-conducted studies that have examined the effectiveness of neuroleptics, even though these drugs are generally considered to be therapeutic (reviewed by Farber, 1987; Singh & Millichamp, 1985). Both the phenothiazines (e.g., Mellaril, Thorazine) and Haldol have been reported to reduce SIB.

The opiate antagonist Narcan (naloxone), which is used to treat respiratory depression resulting from narcotic overdose, has recently been shown to be effective for the control of SIB (Davidson, Kleene, Carroll, & Rockowitz, 1983; Richardson & Zaleski, 1983; Sandman et al., 1983). Narcan can be administered intravenously, intramuscularly, or subcutaneously, but not orally. Unfortunately, Narcan is not effective for all individuals with mental retardation (Beckwith, Conk, & Schumacher, 1986), and the necessity of administration by injection also limits the clinical utility of the drug. ReVia (naltrexone), however, is an opiate antagonist that can be administered orally, and it was shown to be effective for SIB in at least one controlled case study (Bernstein, Hughes, Mitchell, & Thompson, 1987).

Lithium may also be of some value in the treatment of SIB (reviewed by Farber, 1987). However, this suggestion is based primarily on uncontrolled studies. Case reports also exist that propose use of Prozac (Bass & Beltis, 1991: King, 1991) or Clozaril (Hammock, Schroeder, & Levine, 1995) for control of SIB.

Because SIB has multiple etiologies, both psychological (Durand, 1986) and biological (Schroeder et al., 1986), careful consideration should be given in formulating a treatment plan to the possibility that specific environmental events are maintaining this behavior. A variety of behavioral techniques can be used to suppress SIB (see Romanczyk, 1986). Durand (1982) showed that Haldol in combination with mild punishment was more effective than either treatment used alone in reducing SIB in an adolescent with profound mental retardation.

SPEECH, LANGUAGE, AND COMMUNICATION DISORDERS (COMMUNICATION DISORDERS)

Although it is true that relatively little psychopharmacotherapy research has been conducted on speech, language, and communication disorders, there are a surprising number of case studies or anecdotes about how various psychotropic drugs affect the speech or language of specific children. Bender and Cottington (1942), for example, described a case of elective mutism that appeared to respond to Benzedrine. However, there were other children with developmental aphasia or organic brain damage for whom stimulant medication had no beneficial effect. Ginn and Hohman (1953) described the treatment of a 4-year-old boy with hyperactivity with 7.5 mg of Dexedrine in the morning. The boy "jabbered only a few words" and stuttered. Medication presumably made him talk more slowly.

Most of the research on the effects of drugs on verbal behavior pertains to children with hyperactivity; the nature of whatever speech and language problems they may have is generally not specified. Creager and VanRiper (1967), for example, administered Ritalin (20 mg twice a day) and placebo to 30 children with "cerebral dysfunction." The children were referred to a psychiatric clinic for a variety of reasons, including "hyperactivity, scholastic difficulty, unmanageable behavior, withdrawal, short attention span, and maturational delay" (p. 624). An analysis of their verbal behavior indicated that medication caused the children to talk more. The authors believed that this was important for children undergoing speech therapy, because the child must talk if therapy is going to work. Similarly, Ludlow, Rapoport, Brown, and Mikkelson (1979) found that Dexedrine increased verbal productivity and language complexity in boys with hyperactivity.

The observed effects of stimulant drugs on verbal behavior are determined to a considerable degree by the characteristics of the task and setting. This is obvious from the findings from two additional studies. In one of these, Barkley, Cunningham, and Karlsson (1983) administered Ritalin and placebo to children with hyperactivity who did not exhibit deficits in language complexity and found that medication reduced the number of vocalizations in both free and structured settings with no concurrent change in complexity. Whalen et al. (1978) also found that Ritalin significantly reduced task-irrelevant speech and verbal productivity to a more normal level.

Collectively, although these studies provide us with information about stimulants and children with hyperactivity, they tell us relatively little about the usefulness of stimulant medication for the treatment of communication disorders. Nevertheless, Cantwell and Baker's studies on speech and language impaired children clearly show that such children exhibit a variety of psychiatric disorders, most notably hyperactivity (Baker & Cantwell, 1985; Cantwell & Baker, 1985). Therefore, the successful management of behavior disorders may have direct bearing on the efficacy of speech and language therapy and possibly on language development.

There are several published reports on the effect of Haldol on stuttering (e.g., Burns, Brady, & Kuruvilla, 1978; Tapia, 1969). In general, the findings from these studies and case reports indicate that Haldol can suppress or diminish stuttering in some individuals. Why Haldol should have this effect on stutterers is unclear, and, as for all disorders for which this drug is prescribed, careful consideration must be given to the risks of treatment versus the benefits. Interestingly, in an uncontrolled study, Fisher, Kerbeshian, and Burd (1986) found that Haldol also had a marked effect on facilitating language development in nonautistic children with pervasive developmental disorder.

STEREOTYPIES (STEREOTYPIC MOVEMENT DISORDER)

Stereotypic behaviors are of concern to caregivers because they interfere with educational and habilitative efforts. Moreover, they can be an impediment to normalization in that bizarre behaviors are generally perceived in a negative way by others. Surveys (e.g., Eyman & Call, 1977) show that approximately half of children with mental retardation under 13 years of age in institutions have stereotypies (repetitive, often bizarre motor activity). In general, the figures are lower for those in community placements and for older residents with moderate mental retardation. Examples of such behavior are rhythmic rocking, head weaving, mouthing, hand or arm flapping, and rubbing parts of the body (see Baumeister & Forehand, 1973). There is now substantial evidence that Mellaril reduces levels of stereotypic

behavior in people with mental retardation (e.g., Aman & White, 1988; Davis, 1971; Davis, Sprague, & Werry, 1969; Singh & Aman, 1981; Zimmerman & Heistad, 1982). Whether drug-induced reductions in stereotypies lead to performance gains in other areas is unknown. Singh and Aman (1981) found that a low dose (2.5 mg/kg) of Mellaril was as effective as higher therapeutic doses in controlling stereotypies. Interestingly, although Zimmermann and Heistad (1982) found that withdrawal from Mellaril led to a marked increase in stereotypic behavior (e.g., rocking, undirected repetitive vocalizations, masturbation, arm swinging, repetitive behaviors) in adults with severe mental retardation housed in a large state institution, stereotypies were rarely targeted as the reason for prescribing medication in the first place. Early reports suggest that antidepressant drugs that enhance serotonergic mechanisms (Anafranil, Prozac) might be a useful adjunct therapy (Garber, McGonigle, Slomka, & Monteverde, 1992; Rickets et al., 1993).

TOURETTE SYNDROME (TOURETTE'S DISORDER)

Because the symptoms of Tourette syndrome can produce a considerable degree of emotional anguish for a child, the benefits of treatment must be carefully weighed against the associated risks (e.g., adverse drug reactions, psychosocial aspects of taking medication). Several different drugs are currently being used in the pharmacological management of this disorder; each is briefly discussed. More detailed presentations of this disorder and its pharmacological treatment are available elsewhere (e.g., Cohen, Bruun, & Leckman, 1988; Shapiro, Shapiro, Young, & Feinberg, 1988).

Since the 1960s, the drug of first choice for the treatment of Tourette syndrome has been Haldol. Approximately 80% of all people show some initial benefit from medication, but owing primarily to side effects—far less (approximately 20% to 30%) take the drug for extended periods. Haldol is very effective at low doses. Children are generally started on a dose of 0.25 mg to 0.5 mg per day (administered at bedtime), which is increased every 4 or 5 days (at no more than 0.5 mg increments) to an average daily dose of 3 mg to 4 mg. At low doses, many patients experience a complete remission of symptoms and few adverse reactions.

The withdrawal of Haldol may lead to an exacerbation of symptoms to a level far worse than before, and this exacerbation can last up to 2 to 3 months. Conversely, some children may show improvement following drug discontinuation, only to get worse later and gradually improve again. The withdrawal of medication may also be greeted with some relief, because side effects such as cognitive blunting dissipate. For these reasons, evaluating the need to continue treatment is a complex process, and the patient and his or her family should be prepared for these possible outcomes. Drug-free periods or dosage reductions should be scheduled to assess the need to continue medication.

Although the results of early uncontrolled investigations (e.g., Cohen, Detlor, Young, & Shaywitz, 1980) indicated that Catapres, an antihypertensive drug, was an effective agent for the treatment of Tourette syndrome, more recent studies indicate that it is less effective than Haldol (e.g., Shapiro, Shapiro, & Eisenkraft, 1983) and no better than placebo for controlling tics (Goetz et al., 1987). It may, however, be useful in controlling the associated symptoms, such as hyperactivity and inattentiveness. Catapres is initiated at a small daily dose (0.05 mg) that is gradually increased over several weeks to 0.15 mg to 0.30 mg. Because Catapres has a short half-life, it is administered in small doses three to four times per day. Catapres has a slower onset of action than Haldol and may take 3 weeks or more to produce a therapeutic response. Tolerance to beneficial effects is a problem in some children.

The major side effect of Catapres is sedation, but this generally goes away after several weeks. Nevertheless even transient sedation can have significant consequences, as evidenced by one patient who was involved in a serious auto accident because of this reaction (Shapiro et al., 1983). Teenagers who drive (and their parents) must be warned of the risks associated with drug-induced sedation. Other reported side effects include impaired cognition, dry mouth, sensitivity of eyes to light, bradycardia, hypotension, dizziness, irritability, nightmares, and insomnia. As noted in an earlier section, there is interest in the longer acting antihypertensive, Tenex, as an alternative to clonidine, and we await further study of the possible advantages.

Orap is a powerful neuroleptic shown to be effective for the treatment of Tourette syndrome (e.g., Shapiro & Shapiro, 1984); uncontrolled studies suggest that it may be as effective as Haldol and less sedating. Treatment is typically initiated with a dose of 1 mg per day, which is gradually increased to 6 mg to 10 mg per day (0.2 mg/kg per day). Because Orap has a relatively long half-life, it is possible to administer medication once a day. The side effects of Orap are similar to those of Haldol. Because Orap can have an adverse effect on heart function, an EKG should be administered prior to treatment. The possibility that Risperdal may be an alternative treatment has received support in a small nonblind study (Lombroso et al., 1995).

The behavioral concomitants of Tourette syndrome (e.g., hyperactivity, obsessions, compulsions) and its psychological sequelae (e.g., embarrassment, social rejection, anxiety from not being in control of one's own body) and associated academic impediments (both drug-induced and preexisting) relegate drug therapy to an adjunctive role in the treatment process. An effort should be made to ensure that the child is receiving an adequate educational program and that his or her emotional needs are being attended to (see Bauer & Shea, 1984).

SUMMARY

The discovery and empirical verification of clinically effective psychoactive drugs is one of the most significant developments in child and adolescent psychiatry. Many of the commonly prescribed agents in current use have been noted in the literature for over three decades. In prepubertal children, by far the most researched pharmacological treatments are for the management of hyperactivity, oppositional behavior, and aggression. Collectively, research findings show that stimulant treatment can produce profound symptomatic improvement in ADHD behaviors. Other drugs, such as the neuroleptics and the tricyclic antidepressants, are also effective, but concerns about untoward reactions relegate them to the status of alternative agents.

Much less is know about effective pharmacological interventions for affective and anxiety disorders in this age group. With the exception of serotonin enhancing antidepressants for obsessive-compulsive disorder, drug therapy for these disorders remains tentative. Medication can provide symptomatic relief for some individuals with developmental disabilities (e.g., autism, mental retardation), but prudence dictates that the benefits of treatment must clearly outweigh the risks. Programmatic pharmacological research on these disorders is currently limited to an extremely small number of clinics, and early studies in this area were not particularly laudatory with regard to methodological rigor. At the present time, neuroleptics, particularly Haldol, may be of some benefit for children with autism. Individuals with mild to moderate mental retardation appear to show the full spectrum of psychiatric disorders, and their response to medication is generally similar to that of nonretarded peers. However, the incidence of drug failure is reportedly higher in this population; diagnostic features may differ; and the evaluation of clinical response can be greatly complicated by the presence of multiple disabilities (see Gadow & Poling, 1988).

There are relatively few well-controlled drug studies of adolescent psychiatric disorders; consequently, evidence for drug efficacy and guidelines for clinical management must often be extrapolated from research on adults. Briefly, ADHD in adolescence is responsive to both the stimulants and the tricyclics, with child psychiatrists favoring the latter. Although antidepressant and antimanic drugs are routinely prescribed for adolescent affective disorders, evidence for their effficacy from rigorous clinical trials is somewhat discouraging. Neuroleptics are an important adjunctive treatment for adolescent schizophrenia, but even with medication, many patients are still seriously disabled.

One of the more important advances in the past 5 years has been the introduction of totally new types of antidepressants (SSRIs) and antipsychotics (Clozaril and Risperidone). The rather broad effects of these medications on mood, behavioral, psychotic, anxiety, and movement disorders represents an extremely exciting era for childhood psychopharmacology. However, the enthusiasm should be tempered by lack of controlled studies of efficacy and reliance on case reports, plus potentially significant and serious side effects of some of these treatments. It seems likely that this early experience will lead to more specific and safer interventions for many children with severe dysfunction.

This chapter has addressed the classical syndromes seen in child and adolescent psychiatry and the drugs that are generally used in their management. This does not, however, exhaust all the clinical psychiatric situations in which drug therapy or drug interactions may be of importance (e.g., sleep disorders, encopresis, drug and alcohol abuse, eating disorders). Although space constraints have precluded detailed discussion of the psychosocial aspects of these disorders and their management (e.g., patient-clinician interaction), it bears repeating that our intent is not to suggest that pharmacotherapy is necessarily appropriate or desirable for all or even most young patients with mood, thought, or behavior disorders. Child and adolescent psychiatric disorders can be extreme and volatile, and many different elements (biological, psychological, and environmental) interact to produce them. For this reason, different types of intervention might result in some improvement for the patient, but the social and personal pressures on the psychiatrist to successfully and rapidly "treat" the condition can lead to the use of medication before other therapeutic approaches have been tried.

Ideally, psychopharmacotherapy would be used only for those child and adolescent psychiatric disorders in which a biological disturbance is being specifically improved by the action of the drug itself. Many of the descriptions of drug use in this chapter have shown that although medication may improve target symptoms, it does not necessarily alter the overall course of illness. It is important, therefore, that the risks of drug therapy be clearly weighed against the benefits. It is not unusual for the side effects of a particular drug to lead to the use of additional medications to manage the side effects (e.g., the concomitant use of anticholinergic and neuroleptic drugs), or an introduction of two or more drugs to treat pieces of the clinical picture. For the patient with severe disturbance, such treatment may be appropriate, but it is salutory to realize that child psychiatry has had to address concerns about drugs being a factor in sudden deaths in children (Popper & Elliott, 1990; Popper, 1995), and there are increasing reports of use of polypharmacy. It is to be hoped that clinicians using these powerful new drugs are both well-versed in the potential pharmacologic interactions that might be expected and careful in their decision to apply such treatments.

Perhaps the most difficult challenge lies in helping adolescents who have both physical illnesses and psychological problems. The importance of physical appearance and peer acceptance during adolescence can make physical illness a very traumatic and, at times, self-destructive experience. The psychiatrist's role is in helping the adolescent adjust to the effects and demands of managing the illness. Depressive reactions, often expressed as anger and hostility, can be common in these situations, but the psychiatrist must also be aware of the potential psychological reactions to the treatment itself or stemming directly from it. For example, steroid drug treatment (hormone therapy), commonly used in the management of immunological disorders, can cause severe psychological change, usually mimicking depression or mania.

In summary, therefore, it is important to realize the limitations of pharmacotherapy as well as the benefits. Medication can, at times, be crucial to recovery, but even in these situations, secondary social handicaps may remain after recovery that will require more intensive psychological therapies. Most child and adolescent psychiatric disorders respond to psychological interventions without medication and—except in rare circumstances, such as acute psychosis—these interventions are generally recommended as the first approach. However, when behavioral treatments are ineffective, impractical, or unavailable, drug therapy may produce marked symptomatic improvement, much to the relief of patient and caregiver.

APPENDIX

AN OVERVIEW OF PSYCHOPHARMACOTHERAPY FOR CHILDREN AND ADOLESCENTS—SELECTED PSYCHOTHERAPEUTIC DRUGS

GENERIC NAME	TRADE NAME

ANTIANXIETY AGENTS

Propanediols

meprobamate	Equanil, Miltown

Diphenylmethane

hydroxyzine	Atarax, Vistaril

Benzodiazepines

alprazolam	Xanax
chlordiazepoxide	Librium
clonazepam	Klonopin
clorazepate	Valium
flurazepam	Dalmane
lorazepam	Ativan
oxazepam	Serax
temazepam	Restoril
traizolam	Halcion

Azaspirodecanediones

buspirone	BuSpar

ANTIDEPRESSANTS

Tricyclic

amitriptyline	Elavil, Endep
clomipramine	Anafranil
desipramine	Norpramin
doxepin	Sinequan
imipramine	Toranil
nortriptyline	Pamelor
trimipramine	Surmontil

Tetracyclic

maprotiline	Ludiomil

Atypical

trazodone	Desyrel
amoxapine	Asendin
bupropion	Wellbutrin

Monoamine Oxidase Inhibitors

isocarboxazid	Marplan
phenelzine	Nardil
tranylcypromine	Parnate

SSRIs

fluoxetine	Prozac
fluvoxamine	Luvox
paroxetine	Paxil
sertraline	Zoloft
venlafaxine	Effexor

ANTIMANIA AGENTS

lithium carbonate	Eskalith, Lithane, Lithobid

NEUROLEPTICS (ANTIPSYCHOTICS)

Phenothiazine
Aliphatic

chlorpromazine	Thorazine

Piperdine

mesoridazine	Serentil
thioridazine	Mellaril

GENERIC NAME	TRADE NAME
NEUROLEPTICS (ANTIPSYCHOTICS), continued	
Piperazine	
fluphenazine	Prolixin
perphenazine	Trilafon
prochlorperazine	Compazine
trifluoperazine	Stelazine
Thioxanthenes	
chlorprothixene	Taractan
thiothixene	Navane
Butyrophenone	
haloperidol	Haldol
Dihydroindolone	
molindone	Moban
Benzisoxazole	
risperidone	Risperdal
Dibenzazepine	
clozapine	Clozaril
Dibenzoxazepines	
loxapine	Loxitane
Diphenylbutylpiperidine	
pimozide	Orap
SEDATIVE-HYPNOTICS	
Barbituates	
amobarbital	Amytal
butabarbital	Butisol
mephobarbital	Mebaral
pentobarbital	Nembutal
phenobarbital	Luminal
secobarbital	Seconal
Nonbarbituates	
chloral hydrate	
ethchlorvynol	Placidyl
glutethimide	Doriden
STIMULANTS	
dextroamphetamine	Dexedrine
methamphetamine	Desoxyn
methylphenidate	Ritalin
pemoline	Cylert
MISCELLANEOUS	
carbamazepine	Tegretol
clonidine	Catapres
guanfacine	Tenex
fenfluramine	Pondimin
naloxone	Narcan
naltrexone	ReVia
propranolol	Inderal
valproic acid	Depakene, Depakote

*Only tradename products marketed in the United States are listed. In the case of drugs no longer protected by patent laws, the inclusion of trade names other than the original was arbitrary.

REFERENCES

Abikoff, H., & Gittelman, R. (1985). The normalizing effects of methylphenidate on the classroom behavior of ADDH children. *Journal of Abnormal Child Psychology, 13,* 3344.

Ackerman, P. T., Dykman, R. A., Holloway, C., Paal, N. P., & Gocio, M. Y. (1991). A trial of piracetam in two subgroups of students with dyslexia enrolled in summer tutoring. *Journal of Learning Disabilities, 24,* 542–549.

Alessi, N., Naylor, M. W., Ghaziuddin, M., & Zubieta, J. K. (1994). Update on lithium carbonate therapy in children and adolescents. *Journal of the American Academy of Child and Adolescent Psychiatry, 33,* 291–304.

Allen, A. J., Leonard, H., & Swedo, S. E. (1995). Current knowledge of medication for the treatment of childhood anxiety disorder. *Journal of the American Academy of Child and Adolescent Psychiatry, 34,* 976–986.

Allen, R. P., Safer, D., & Covi, L. (1975). Effects of psychostimulants on aggression. *Journal of Nervous and Mental Disease, 160,* 138–145.

Aman, M. G., & Kern, R. A. (1989). Review of fenfluramine in the treatment of the developmental disabilities. *Journal of the American Academy of Child and Adolescent Psychiatry, 28,* 549–565.

Aman, M. G., Marks, R. E., Turbott, S. H., Wilsher, C. P., & Merry, S. N. (1991). Methylphenidate and thioridazine in the treatment of intellectually sub-average children: Effects on cognitive-motor performance. *Journal of the American Academy of Child and Adolescent Psychiatry, 30,* 816–824.

Aman, M. G. & Rojahn, J. (1991). Pharmacologic intervention. In N. N. Singh and I. L. Beale (eds), *Current perspectives in learning disabilities: Nature, theory and treatment.* New York: Springer.

Aman, M. G., & Werry, J. S. (1982). Methylphenidate and diazepam in severe reading retardation. *Journal of the American Academy of Child Psychiatry, 1,* 31–37.

Aman, M. G., & White, A. J. (1988). Thioridazine dose effects with reference to stereotypic behavior in mentally retarded residents. *Journal of Autism and Developmental Disorders, 18,* 355–366.

Ambrosini, P. J. (1987). Pharmacotherapy in child and adolescent major depressive disorder. In H. Y. Meltzer (Ed.), *Psychopharmacology: The third generation of progress* (pp. 1247–1254). New York: Raven Press.

Ambrosini, P. J., Bianchi, M. D., Metz, C., & Rabinovich, H. (1994). Evaluating clinical response of open nortriptyline pharmacotherapy in adolescent major depression. *Journal of Child and Adolescent Psychopharmacology, 4,* 233-244.

American Psychiatric Association (1994). *Diagnostic and statistical manual of mental disorders* (4th ed.). Washington, DC: Author.

Amery, B., Minichiello, M. D., & Brown, G. L. (1984). Aggression in hyperactive boys: Response to d-amphetamine. *Journal of the American Academy of Child Psychiatry, 23,* 291–294.

Anderson, L. T., Campbell, M., Grega, D. M., Perry, R., Small, A. M., & Green, W. H. (1984). Haloperidol in the treatment of infantile autism: Effects on learning and behavioral symptoms. *American Journal of Psychiatry, 141,* 1195–1202.

Apter, A., Dickerman, Z., Gonen, N., Assa, S., Prager-Lewin, R., Kaufman, H., Tyano, S., & Laroy, Z. (1983). The effect of chlorpromazine on hypothalamic-pituitary-gonadal function in 10 adolescent schizophrenic boys. *American Journal of Psychiatry, 140,* 1588–1591.

Apter, A., Ratzoni, G., King, R. A., Weizman, A., Iancu, I., Binder, M., & Riddle, M. A. (1994). Fluvoxamine open-label treatment of adolescent inpatients with obsessive-compulsive disorder or depression. *Journal of the American Academy of Child and Adolescent Psychiatry, 33,* 342–348.

Baker, L., & Cantwell, D. P. (1985). Psychiatric and learning disorders in children with speech and language disorders: A critical review. In K. D. Gadow (Ed.), *Advances in learning and behavioral disabilities* (Vol. 4, pp. 1–27). Greenwich, CT: JAI Press.

Ballenger, J. C., & Post, R. M. (1978). Therapeutic effects of carbamazepine in affective illness: A preliminary report. *Communication in Psychopharmacology, 2,* 159–175.

Barkley, R. A. (1990). *Hyperactive children: A handbook for diagnosis and treatment.* New York: Guilford Press.

Barkley, R. A., & Cunningham, C. E. (1978). Do stimulant drugs improve the academic performance of hyperkinetic children? *Clinical Pediatrics, 17,* 85–92.

Barkley, R. A., & Cunningham, C. E. (1979). The effects of methylphenidate on the mother-child interactions of hyperactive children. *Archives of General Psychiatry, 36,* 201–208.

Barkley, R. A., Cunningham, C. E., & Karlsson, J. (1983). The speech of hyperactive children and their mothers: Comparison with normal children and stimulant drug effects. *Journal of Learning Disabilities, 16,* 105–110.

Barkley, R. A., Karlsson, J., Strzelecki, E., & Murphy, J. V. (1984). Effects of age and Ritalin dosage on the mother-child interactions of hyperactive children. *Journal of Consulting and Clinical Psychology, 52,* 750–758.

Barrickman, L., Noyes, R., Kuperman, S., Schumacher, E., & Verda, M. (1991). Treatment of ADHD with fluoxetine: A preliminary trial. *Journal of the American Academy of Child and Adolescent Psychiatry, 30,* 762–767.

Barrickman, L. L., Perry, P. J., Allen, A. J., Kuperman, S., Arndt, S. V., Herrmann, K. J., & Schumacher, E. (1995). Bupropion versus methylphenidate in the treatment of attention deficit hyperactivity disorder. *Journal of the American Academy of Child and Adolescent Psychiatry, 34,* 649–657.

Bass, J. N., & Beltis, J. (1991). Therapeutic effect of fluoxetine on naltrexone-resistant self-injurious behavior in an adolescent with mental retardation. *Journal of Child and Adolescent Psychopharmacology, 1,* 331–340.

Bauer, A. M., & Shea, T. M. (1984). Tourette syndrome: A review and educational implications. *Journal of Autism and Developmental Disorders, 14,* 69–80.

Baumeister, A. A., & Forehand, R. (1973). Stereotyped acts. In N. R. Ellis (Ed.), International review of research in mental retardation (Vol. 6, pp. 55–96). Orlando, FL: Academic Press.

Beckwith, B. E., Conk, D. I., & Schumacher, K. (1986). Failure of naloxone to reduce self-injurious behavior in two developmentally disabled females. *Applied Research in Mental Retardation, 7,* 183–188.

Bender, L., & Cottington, F. (1942). The use of amphetamine sulfate (Benzedrine) in child psychiatry. *American Journal of Psychiatry, 99,* 116–121.

Berney, T. B., Kolvin, 1., Bhate, S. R., Garside, R. F., Jeans, J., Kay, B., & Scarth, L. (1981). School phobia: A therapeutic trial with clomipramine and outcome. *British Journal of Psychiatry, 138*(1) 10–18.

Bernstein, G. A., & Garfinkel, B. D. (1986). School phobia: The overlap of affective and anxiety disorders. *Journal of the American Academy of Child Psychiatry, 25,* 235–241.

Bernstein, G. A., Hughes, J. R., Mitchell, J. E., & Thompson, T. (1987). Effects of narcotic antagonists on self-injurious behavior: A single case study. *Journal of the American Academy of Child and Adolescent Psychiatry, 26,* 886–889.

Biederman, J., Baldessarini, R. J., Goldblatt, A., Lapey, R. A., Doyle, A., & Hesslein, P. S. (1993). A naturalistic study of 24-hour electrocardiographic recordings and electrocardiographic findings in children and adolescents treated with desipramine. *Journal of the American Academy of Child and Adolescent Psychiatry, 32,* 805–813.

Biederman, J., Baldessarini, R. J., Wright, V., Knee, D., & Harmatz, J. S. (1989). A doubleblind placebo controlled study of desipramine in the treatment of ADD: I. Efficacy. *Journal of the American Academy of Child and Adolescent Psychiatry, 28,* 777–784.

Biederman, J., Baldessarini, R. J., Wright, V., Knee, D., Harmatz, J. S., & Goldblatt, A. (1989). A double-blind placebo controlled study of desipramine in the treatment of ADD: II. Serum drug levels and cardiovascular findings. *Journal of the American Academy of Child and Adolescent Psychiatry, 28,* 903–911.

Birch, N. J. (1980). Bone side-effects of lithium. In F. N. Johnson (Ed.), *Handbook of lithium therapy* (pp. 365–371). Lancaster, England: MTP Press.

Birmaher, B., Quintana, H., & Greenhill, L. L. (1988). Methylphenidate treatment of hyperactive autistic children. *Journal of the American Academy of Child and Adolescent Psychiatry, 27,* 248–251.

Birmaher, B., Waterman, G. S., Ryan, N., Cully, M., Balach, L., Ingram, J., & Brodsky, M. (1994). Fluoxetine for childhood anxiety disorder. *Journal of the American Academy of Child and Adolescent Psychiatry, 33,* 993–999.

Blackwell, B., & Currah, J. (1973). The psychopharmacology of nocturnal enuresis. In I. Kolvin, R. C. MacKeith, & S. R. Meadow (Eds.), *Bladder control and enuresis* (pp. 231–257). London: Heinemann.

Boulos, C., Kutcher, S., Gardner, D., & Young, E. (1992). An open naturalistic trial of fluoxetine in adolescents and young adults with treatment-resistant major depression. *Journal of Child and Adolescent Psychopharmacology, 2,* 103–111.

Bradley, C. (1937). The behavior of children receiving Benzedrine. *American Journal of Psychiatry, 94,* 577–585.

Bradley, C. (1957). Characteristics and management of children with behavior problems associated with organic brain damage. *Pediatric Clinics of North America, 4,* 1049–1060.

Bradley, C., & Bowen, M. (1940). School performance of children receiving amphetamine (Benzedrine) sulfate. *American Journal of Orthopsychiatry, 10,* 782–788.

Bradley, C., & Bowen, M. (1941). Amphetamine (Benzedrine) therapy of children's behavior disorders. *American Journal of Orthopsychiatry, 11,* 92–103.

Bramble, D. J. (1995). Antidepressant prescription by British child psychiatrists: Practice and safety issues. *Journal of the American Academy of Child and Adolescent Psychiatry, 34,* 327–331.

Brown, D., Winsberg, B. G., Bialer, I., & Press, M. (1973). Imipramine therapy and seizures: Three children treated for hyperactive behavior disorders. *American Journal of Psychiatry, 130,* 210–212.

Brown, J. T., Mulrow. C. D., & Stoudemire. G. A. (1984). The anxiety disorders. *Annals of Internal Medicine, 100,* 55B–564.

Brown, R. T., & Sleator, E. K. (1979). Methylphenidate in hyperkinetic children: Differences in dose effects on impulsive behavior. *Pediatrics, 64,* 408–411.

Burns, D., Brady, J. P., & Kuruvilla, K. (1978). The acute effect of haloperidol and apomorphine on the severity of stuttering. *Biological Psychiatry, 13,* 255–264.

Cade, J. F. J. (1949). Lithium salts in the treatment of psychotic excitement, *Medical Journal of Australia, 36,* 349–352.

Campbell, M. (1988). Fenfluramine treatment of autism. Annotation. *Journal of Child Psychology and Psychiatry, 29,* 1–10.

Campbell, M., Adams, P., Small, A. M., Curren, E. L., Overall, J. E., Anderson, L. T., Lynch, N., & Perry, R. (1988). Efficacy and safety of fenfluramine in autistic children. *Journal of the American Academy of Child and Adolescent Psychiatry, 27,* 434–439.

Campbell, M., Anderson, L. T., Deutsch, S. I., & Green, W. H. (1984a). Psychopharmacological treatment of children with the syndrome of autism. *Pediatric Annals, 13,* 309–316.

Campbell, M., Anderson, L. T., Meier, M., Cohen, I. L., Small, A. M., Samit, C., & Sachar, E. J. (1978). A comparison of haloperidol and behavior therapy and their interaction in autistic children. *Journal of the American Academy of Child Psychiatry, 17,* 640–655.

Campbell, M., Cohen, I. L., & Small, A. M. (1982). Drugs and aggressive behavior. *Journal of the American Academy of Child Psychiatry, 21,* 107–117.

Campbell, M., & Deutsch, S. I. (1985). Neuroleptics in children. In G. D. Burrows, T. Norman, & B. Davies (Eds.), *Drugs in psychiatry: Vol. 3. Antipsychotics* (pp. 213–238). New York: Elsevier Biomedical.

Campbell, M., Fish, B., Shapiro, T., Collins, P., & Koh, C. (1972). Response to triiodothyronine and dextroamphetamine: A study of preschool schizophrenic children. *Journal of Autism and Childhood Schizophrenia, 2,* 343-358.

Campbell, M., Anderson, L. T., Small, A. M., Adams, P., Gonzalez, N. M., & Ernst, M. (1993). Naltrexone in autistic children: Behavioral symptoms and attentional learning. *Journal of the American Academy of Child and Adolescent Psychiatry, 32,* 1283–1291.

Campbell, M. & Cueva, J. E. (1995a). Psychopharmacology in child and adolescent psychiatry: A review of the past seven years. Part I. *Journal of the American Academy of Child and Adolescent Psychiatry, 34,* 1124–1132.

Campbell, M. & Cueva, J. E. (1995b). Psychopharmacology in child and adolescent psychiatry: A review of the past seven years. Part II. Journal of the American Academy of Child and Adolescent Psychiatry, 34, 1262-1272.

Campbell, M., Kafantaris, V., & Cueva, J. E. (1995). An update on the use of lithium carbonate in aggressive children and adolescents with conduct disorder. *Psychopharmacology Bulletin, 31,* 93-102.

Campbell, M., Overall, J. E., Small, A. M. Sokol, M. S., Spencer, E. K., Adams, P., Foltz, R. L., Monti, K. M., Perry, R., Nobler, M., & Roberts, E. (1989). Naltrexone in autistic children: An acute open dose range tolerance trial. *Journal of the American Academy of Child and Adolescent Psychiatry, 28,* 200–206.

Campbell, M., Perry, R., Bennett, W. G., Small, A. M., Green, W. H., Grega, D., Schwartz, V., & Anderson, L. (1983). Long-term therapeutic efficacy and drug-related abnormal movements: A prospective study of haloperidol in autistic children. *Psychopharmacology Bulletin, 19,* 80–83.

Campbell, M., Perry, R., & Green, W. H. (1984b). Use of lithium in children and adolescents. *Psychosomatics, 2,* 95–106.

Campbell, M., Small, A. M., Green, W. H., Jennings, S. J., Perry, R., Bennett, W. G., & Anderson, L. (1984c). Behavioral efficacy of haloperidol and lithium carbonate: A comparison in hospitalized aggressive children with conduct disorder. *Archives of General Psychiatry, 120,* 650–656.

Cantwell, D. P., & Baker, L. (1985). Psychiatric and learning disorders in children with speech and language disorders: A descriptive analysis. In K. D. Gadow (Ed.), *Advances in learning and behavioral disabilities* (Vol. 4, pp. 27–47). Greenwich, CT: JAI Press.

Carlson, G. A. (1983). Bipolar affective disorders in childhood and adolescence. In D. P. Cantwell & G. A. Carlson (Eds.), *Affective disorder in childhood and adolescence: An update* (pp. 61–83). New York: Spectrum.

Carlson, G. A. (1986). Classification issues of bipolar disorder in childhood. *Psychiatric Development, 6,* 273–285.

Carlson, G. A. (1988). Depression: Pharmacotherapies. In J. L. Matson (Ed.), *Handbook of treatment approaches in childhood psychopathology* (pp. 345–363). New York: Plenum Press.

Carlson, G. A., & Cantwell, D. P. (1980). Unmasking masked depression in children and adolescents. *American Journal of Psychiatry, 137,* 445–449.

Carter, C. H. (1956). The effects of reserpine and methylphenidate (Ritalin) in mental defectives, spastics, and epileptics. *Psychiatric Research Reports, 4,* 44–48.

Chandler, H. N. (1978). Confusion compounded: A teacher tries to use research results to teach math. *Journal of Learning Disabilities, 11,* 361–369.

Chappell, P. B., Riddle, M. A., Scahill, L., Lynch, K. A., Schutz, R., Arnsten, A., Leckman, J. F., & Cohen, D. J. (1995). Guanfacine treatment of comorbid attention-deficit hyperactivity disorder and Tourette's syndrome: Preliminary clinical experience. *Journal of the American Academy of Child and Adolescent Psychiatry, 34,* 1140–1146.

Cohen, D. J., Bruun, R. D., & Leckman, J. F. (Eds.). (1988). *Tourette's syndrome and tic disorders.* New York: John Wiley & Sons.

Cohen, D. J., Detlor, J., Young, J. G., & Shaywitz, B. A. (1980). Clonidine ameliorates Gilles de la Tourette syndrome. *Archives of General Psychiatry, 37,* 1350–1357.

Colle, L. M., Bélair, J. F., DiFeo, M., Weiss, J., & LaRoche, C. (1994). Extended open-label fluoxetine treatment of adolescents with major depression. *Journal of Child and Adolescent Psychopharmacology, 4,* 225–232.

Comings, D. E., & Comings, B. G. (1984). Tourette's syndrome and attention deficit disorder with hyperactivity: Are they genetically related? *Journal of the American Academy of Child Psychiatry, 23,* 138–146.

Conners, C. K. (1971). Drugs in the management of children with learning disabilities. In L. Tarnopol (Ed.), *Learning disorders in children: Diagnosis, medication, education* (pp. 253–301). Boston: Little, Brown.

Conners, C. K., & Rothschild, G. H. (1968). Drugs and learning in children. In J. Hellmuth (Ed.), *Learning disorders* (Vol. 3, pp. 191–223). Seattle, WA: Special Child.

Conners, C., Rothschild, G., Eisenberg, L., Stone, L., & Robinson, E. (1969). Dextroamphetamine in children with learning disorders. *Archives of General Psychiatry, 21,* 182–190.

Conners, C. K., Taylor, E., Meo, G., Kurz, .M. A., & Fournier, M. (1972). Magnesium pemoline and dextroamphetamine: A controlled study in children with minimal brain dysfunction. *Psychopharmacologia, 26,* 321–336.

Connor, D. F. (1993). Beta blockers for aggression: A review of the pediatric experience. *Journal of Child and Adolescent Psychopharmacology, 3,* 99–114.

Cook, E. H., Rowlett, R., Jaselskis, C., & Leventhal, B. L. (1992). Fluoxetine treatment of children and adults with autistic disorder and mental retardation. *Journal of the American Academy of Child and Adolescent Psychiatry, 31,* 739–745.

Creager, R. O., & VanRiper, C. (1967). The effect of methylphenidate on the verbal productivity of children with cerebral dysfunction. *Journal of Speech and Hearing Research, 10,* 623-628.

Cunningham, C. E., Siegel, L. S., & Offord, D. R. (1985). A developmental dose-response analysis of the effects of methylphenidate on the peer interactions of attention deficit disordered boys. *Journal of Child Psychology and Psychiatry, 26,* 955-971.

Darrow, C. W. (1929). Psychological effects of drugs. *Psychological Bulletin, 26,* 527-545.

Davidson, P. W., Kleene, B. W., Carroll, M., & Rockowitz, R. J. (1983). Effects of naloxone on self-injurious behavior: A case study. *Applied Research in Mental Retardation, 4,* 1–4.

Davis, K. V. (1971). The effect of drugs on stereotyped and nonstereotyped operant behavior in retardates. *Psychopharmacology, 22,* 195–213.

Davis, K. V., Sprague, R. L., & Werry, J. S. (1969). Stereotyped behavior and activity level in severe retardates: The effect of drugs. *American Journal of Mental Deficiency, 73,* 721–727.

DeLong, G. R. (1978). Lithium carbonate treatment of select behavior disorders in children suggesting manic-depressive illness. *Journal of Pediatrics, 93,* 689–694.

DeLong, G. R., & Aldershof, A. L. (1987) Long-term experience with lithium treatment in childhood: Correlation with clinical diagnosis. *Journal of the American Academy of Child and Adolescent Psychiatry, 26,* 389–394.

Denkla, M. B., Bemporad, J. R., & McKay, M. D. (1976). Tics following methylphenidate administration. *Journal of the American Medical Association, 235,* 1349–1351.

DeVeaugh-Geiss, J., Moroz, G., Biederman, J., Cantwell, D., Fontaine, R., Greist, J. H., Reichler, R., Katz, R., & Landau, P. (1992). Clomipramine hydrochloride in childhood and adolescent obsessive-compulsive disorder—a multicenter trial. *Journal of the American Academy of Child and Adolescent Psychiatry, 31,* 45–49.

Diamond, J. M., & Stein, J. M. (1983). Enuresis: A new look at stimulant therapy. *Canadian Journal of Psychiatry, 28,* 395-397.

DiIanni, M., Wilsher, C. R., Blank, M.S., Conners, C. K., Chase, C. H., Funkenstein, H. H., Helfgott, F., Holmes, J. M., Lougee, L., Maletta, G. J., Milewski, J., Pirozzolo, F. J., Rudel, R. G., & Tallal, P. (1985). The effects of piracetam in children with dyslexia. *Journal of Clinical Psychopharmacology, 5,* 272–278.

Douglas, V. I. (1972). Stop, look, and listen: The problem of sustained attention and impulse control in hyperactive and normal children. *Canadian Journal of Behaviour Science, 4,* 259–282.

Douglas, V. I., Barr, R. G., Desilets, J., & Sherman, E. (1995). Do high doses of stimulants impair flexible thinking in attention-deficit hyperactivity disorder? *Journal of the American Academy of Child and Adolescent Psychiatry, 34,* 877–885.

Douglas, V. I., Barr, R. G., O'Neill, M. E., & Britton, B. G. (1986). Short term effects of methylphenidate on the cognitive, learning and academic performance of children with attention deficit disorder in the laboratory and the classroom. *Journal of Child Psychology and Psychiatry, 27,* 191–211.

Douglas, V. I., & Peters, K. G. (1979). Toward a clearer definition of the attention deficit of hyperactive children. In G. A. Hale & M. Lewis (Eds.), *Attention and cognitive development* (pp. 173–247). New York: Plenum Press.

DuPaul, G. J., Barkley, R. A., & McMurray, M. B. (1994). Response of children with ADHD to methylphenidate: Interaction with internalizing symptoms. *Journal of the American Academy of Child and Adolescent Psychiatry, 33,* 894–903.

Durand, V. M. (1982). A behavioral/pharmacological intervention for the treatment of severe self-injurious behavior. *Journal of Autism and Developmental Disorders, 12,* 243–251.

Durand, V. M. (1986). Self-injurious behavior as intentional communication. In K. D. Gadow (Ed.), *Advances in learning and behavioral disabilities* (Vol. 5, pp. 141–155). Greenwich, CT: JAI Press.

Dykman, R. A., Ackerman, P. T., & McCray, D. S. (1980). Effects of methylphenidate on selective and sustained attention in hyperactive, reading-disabled, and presumably attention-disordered boys. *Journal of Nervous and Mental Disease, 168,* 745–752.

Dyme, I. Z., Sahakian, B. J., Golinko, B. E., & Rabe, E. F. (1982). Perseveration induced by methylphenidate in children: Preliminary findings. *Progress in Neuropsychopharmacology & Biological Psychiatry, 6,* 269–273.

Eisenberg, L., & Conners, C. K. (1971). Psychopharmacology in childhood. In N. B. Talbot, J. Kagan, & L. Eisenberg (Eds.), *Behavioral science in pediatric medicine* (pp. 397-423). Philadelphia: Saunders.

Elkins, R, Rapoport, J. L., & Lipsky, A. (1980). Obsessive-compulsive disorder of childhood and adolescence: A neurobiologic viewpoint. *Journal of the American Academy of Child Psychiatry, 19,* 511–524.

Ellis, M. J., Witt, P. A., Reynolds, R., & Sprague, R. L. (1974). Methylphenidate and the activity of hyperactives in the informal setting. *Child Development, 45,* 217–220.

Elmslie, G., Rush, H. A., Weinberg, W., Kowatch, R., Hughes, C., & Rintelmann, J. (1995). *Efficacy of fluoxetine in depressed children and adolescents.* Paper presented at the Annual Meeting of the American Academy of Child and Adolescent Psychiatry, New Orleans, LA.

Elmslie, G. J., Kowatch, R., Costello, L., Travis, G., & Pierce, L. (1995). *Double-blind study of fluoxetine in depressed children and adolescents.* Paper presented at the annual meeting of the American Academy of Child and Adolescent Psychiatry, New Orleans, LA.

Erickson, W. D., Yellin, A. M., Hopwood, J. H., Realmuto, G. M., & Greenberg, L. M. (1984). The effects of neuroleptics on attention in adolescent schizophrenics. *Biological Psychiatry, 19,* 745–753.

Evans, R. W., Clay, T. H., & Gualtieri, C. T. (1987). Carbamazepine in pediatric psychiatry. *Journal of the American Academy of Child and Adolescent Psychiatry, 26,* 2–8.

Eyman, R. K., & Call, T. (1977). Maladaptive behavior and community placement of mentally retarded persons. *American Journal of Mental Deficiency, 82,* 137–144.

Farber, J. M. (1987). Psychopharmacology of self-injurious behavior in the mentally retarded. *Journal of the American Academy of Child and Adolescent Psychiatry, 26,* 296–302.

Fazen, L. E., Lovejoy, F. H., & Crone, R. K. (1986). Acute poisoning in a children's hospital. A 2-year experience. *Pediatrics, 77,* 144–151.

Fine, S., Forth, A., Gilbert, M., & Haley, G. (1991). Group therapy for adolescent depression disorder: A comparison of social skills and therapeutic support. *Journal of the American Academy of Child and Adolescent Psychiatry, 30,* 79–85.

Fish, B. (1976). Pharmacotherapy for autistic and schizophrenic children. In E. R. Ritvo, B. J. Freeman, E. M. Ornitz, & P. E. Tanguay (Eds.), *Autism: Diagnosis, current research and treatment* (pp. 107–119). New York: Spectrum Publications.

Fisher, W., Kerbeshian, J., & Burd, L. (1986). A treatable language disorder: Pharmacological treatment of pervasive developmental disorder. *Developmental and Behavioral Pediatrics, 7,* 73–76.

Fitzpatrick, P., Klorman, R., Brumaghim, J. T., & Borgstedt, A. D. (1992). Effects of sustained-release and standard preparations of methylphenidate on attention-deficit disorder. *Journal of the American Academy of Child and Adolescent Psychiatry, 31,* 226–234.

Flament, M. F., Rapoport, J. L., Berg, C. J., Sceery, W., Kilts, L., Mellstrom, B., & Linnoila, M. (1985). Clomipramine treatment of childhood obsessive-compulsive disorders. *Archives of General Psychiatry, 42,* 977-983.

Flintoff, M. M., Barron, R. W., Swanson, J. M., Ledlow, A., & Kinsbourne, M. (1982). Methylphenidate increases selectivity of visual scanning in children referred for hyperactivity. *Journal of Abnormal Child Psychology, 10,* 145-161.

Frazier, J. A., Gordon, C. T., McKenna, K., Lenane, M. C., Jih, D., & Rapoport, J. L. (1994). An open trial of clozapine in 11 adolescents with childhood-onset schizophrenia. *Journal of the American Academy of Child and Adolescent Psychiatry, 33,* 658–663.

Freeman, L. N., Poznanski, E. O., Grossman, J. A., Buchsbaum, Y. Y., & Banesas, M. E. (1985). Psychotic

and depressed children: A new entity. *Journal of the American Academy of Child Psychiatry, 24,* 95–102.

Fritz, G. K., Rockney, R. M. & Yeung, A. S. (1994). Plasma level and efficacy of imipramine treatment for enuresis. *Journal of the American Academy of Child and Adolescent Psychiatry, 33,* 60–64.

Fuchs, D. C. (1994). Clozapine treatment of bipolar disorder in a young adolescent. *Journal of the American Academy of Child and Adolescent Psychiatry, 33,* 1299–1302.

Gadow, K. D. (1981). Drug therapy for hyperactivity: Treatment procedures in natural settings. In K. D. Gadow & J. Loney (Eds.), *Psychosocial aspects of drug treatment for hyperactivity* (pp. 13–76). Boulder, CO: Westview Press.

Gadow, K. D. (1983). Effects of stimulant drugs on academic performance in hyperactive and learning disabled children. *Journal of Learning Disabilities, 16,* 290–299.

Gadow, K. D. (1985). Relative efficacy of pharmacological, behavioral, and combination treatments for enhancing academic performance. *Clinical Psychology Review, 5,* 513–533.

Gadow, K. D. (1986a). *Children on medication: Vol. 1. Hyperactivity, learning disabilities, and mental retardation.* Austin, TX: PRO-ED.

Gadow, K. D. (1986b). *Children on medication: Vol 2. Epilepsy, emotional disturbance, and adolescent disorders.* Austin, TX: PRO-ED.

Gadow, K. D. (1988a). Attention deficit disorder and hyperactivity: Pharmacotherapies. In J L. Matson (Ed.), *Handbook of treatment approaches in childhood psychopathology* (pp. 215–247). New York: Plenum Press.

Gadow, K. D. (1988b). Pharmacotherapy. In K. A. Kavale, S. R. Forness, & M. Bender (Eds.), *Handbook of learning disabilities: Vol. 2. Methods and interventions* (pp. 195–214). Boston: College-Hill Press.

Gadow, K. D. (1992). Pediatric psychopharmacotherapy: A review of recent research. *Journal of Child Psychology and Psychiatry, 33,* 153–195.

Gadow, K. D., Nolan, E. E., Sprafkin, J., & Sverd, J. (1995). School observations of children with attention-deficit hyperactivity disorder and comorbid tic disorder: Effects of methylphenidate treatment. *Journal of Developmental and Behavioral Pediatrics, 16,* 167–176.

Gadow, K. D., Nolan, E. E., Sverd, J., & Sprafkin, J., Paolicelli, L. M. (1990). Methylphenidate in aggressive-hyperactive boys: I. Effects on peer aggression in public school settings. *Journal of the American Academy of Child and Adolescent Psychiatry, 29,* 710–718.

Gadow, K. D., Paolicelli, L. M., Nolan, E. E., Schwartz. J., Sprafkin, J., & Sverd, J. (1992). Methylphenidate in aggressive-hyperactive boys: II. Indirect effects of medication treatment on peer behavior. *Journal of Child and Adolescent Psychopharmacology, 2,* 49–61.

Gadow, K. D., & Poling, E. (1988). *Pharmacotherapy and mental retardation.* Austin. TX: PRO-ED.

Gadow, K. D., & Sverd, J. (1990). Stimulants for ADHD in child patients with Tourette's syndrome: The issue of relative risk. *Journal of Developmental and Behavioral Pediatrics,* 11, 269–271.

Gadow, K. D., Sverd, J., Sprafkin, J., Nolan, E. E., & Ezor, S. N. (1995). Efficacy of methylphenidate for attention-deficit hyperactivity disorder in children with tic disorder. *Archives of General Psychiatry, 52,* 444–455.

Gadow, K. D., & Swanson, H. L. (1985). Assessing drug effects on academic performance. *Psychopharmacology Bulletin, 21,* 877–886.

Garber, H. J., McGonigle, J. J., Slomka, G. T., & Monteverde, E. (1992). Clomipramine treatment of stereotypic behaviors and self-injury in patients with developmental disabilities. *Journal of the American Academy of Child and Adolescent Psychiatry, 31,* 1157–1160.

Geller, B., Chestnut, E. C., Miller, M. D., Price, D. T., & Yates, E. (1985). Preliminary data on DSM III associated features of major depressive disorder in children and adolescents. *American Journal of Psychiatry, 142,* 643–644.

Geller, B., Cooper, T. B., Graham, D. L., Fetner, H. H., Marsteller, F. A., & Wells, J. M. (1992). Pharmaco-kinetically designed double-blind placebo-controlled study of nortriptyline in 6–12 year olds with major depressive disorder. *Journal of the American Academy of Child and Adolescent Psychiatry, 31,* 34–44.

Geller, B., Fox, L. W., & Fletcher, M. (1993). Effect of tricyclic antidepressants on switching to mania and on the onset of bipolarity in depressed 6- to 12-year olds. *Journal of the American Academy of Child and Adolescent Psychiatry, 32,* 43-50.

Geller, B., Guttmacher, L., & Bleeg, M. (1981). Coexistence of childhood onset pervasive developmental disorder and attention deficit disorder with hyperactivity. *American Journal of Psychiatry, 138,* 388–389.

Ginn, S. A., & Hohman, L. B. (1953). The use of dextroamphetamine in severe behavior problems of children. *Southern Medical Journal, 46,* 1124–1127.

Gittelman, R., Klein, D. F., & Feingold, I. (1983). Children with reading disorders: II. Effects of methylphenidate in combination with reading remediation. *Journal of Child Psychology and Psychiatry, 24,* 193–212.

Gittelman. R.. & Koplewicz, H. S. (1986). Pharmacotherapy of childhood anxiety disorders. In R. Gittelman (Ed.), *Anxiety disorders of childhood* (pp. 188-203). New York: Guilford Press.

Gittelman-Klein, R. (1975). Pharmacotherapy and management of pathological separation anxiety. *International Journal of Mental Health, 4,* 255–271.

Gittelman-Klein, R., & Klein, D. F. (1971). Controlled imipramine treatment of school phobia. *Archives of General Psychiatry, 25,* 204–207.

Gittelman-Klein, R., & Klein, D. F. (1976). Methylphenidate effects in learning disabilities. *Archives of General Psychiatry, 33,* 655–664.

Gittelman-Klein, R., Klein, D. F., Kartz, S., Saraf, K., & Pollack, E. (1976). Comparative effects of methylphenidate and thioridazine in hyperactive children. *Archives of General Psychiatry, 33,* 1217–1231.

Goetz, C. G., Tanner, C. M., Wilson, R. S., Carroll, S., Como, P. G., & Shannon, K. M. (1987). Clonidine and Gilles de la Tourette's syndrome: Double-blind study using objective rating methods. *Annals of Neurology, 21,* 307–310.

Graae, F., Milner, J., Rizzotto, L., & Klein, R. G. (1994). Clonazepam in childhood anxiety disorder. *Journal of the American Academy of Child and Adolescent Psychiatry, 33,* 372-376.

Green, W. H., Campbell, M., Hardesty, A. S., Grega, D. M., Padron-Gayol, M., Shell, J., & Erlenmeyer-Kimling, L. (1984). A comparison of schizophrenic and autistic children. *Journal of the American Academy of Child Psychiatry, 23,* 399–409.

Greenberg, L. M., Deem, M. A., & McMahon, S. (1972). Effects of dextroamphetamine, chlorpromazine, and hydroxyzine on behavior and performance in hyperactive children. *American Journal of Psychiatry, 129,* 532–539.

Griffin, J. C., Williams, D. E., Stark, M. T., Altmeyer, B. K., & Mason, M. (1986). Self-injurious behavior: A state-wide prevalence survey of the extent and circumstances. *Applied Research in Mental Retardation, 7,* 105–116.

Gualtieri, C. T., Barnhill, J., McGinsey, J., & Schell, D. (1980). Tardive dyskinesia and other movement disorders in children treated with psychotropic drugs. *Journal of the American Academy of Child Psychiatry, 19,* 491–510.

Gualtieri, C. T., Golden, R. N., & Fahs, J. J. (1983). New developments in pediatric psychopharmacology. *Developmental and Behavioral Pediatrics, 4,* 202–209.

Gualtieri, C. T., Quade, D., Hicks, R. E., Mayo, J. P., & Schroeder, S. R. (1984). Tardive dyskinesia and other clinical consequences of neuroleptic treatment in children and adolescents. *American Journal of Psychiatry, 141,* 20–23.

Hagino, O. R., Weller, E. G., Weller, R. A., Washing, D., Fristad, M. A., & Koutras, S. B. (1995). Untoward effects of lithium treatment in children aged four through six years. *Journal of the American Academy of Child and Adolescent Psychiatry, 34,* 1584–1590.

Hallstrom, C., Treasaden, I., Edwards J. G., & Lader, M. (1981). Diazepam, propranolol and their combination in the management of chronic anxiety. *British Journal of Psychiatry, 139,* 417–421.

Hammock, R. G., Schroeder, S. R., & Levine, W. R. (1995). The effect of clozapine on self-injurious behavior. *Journal of Autism and Developmental Disorders, 25,* 611–626.

Harrington, R. (1992). Annotation: The natural history and treatment of child and adolescent affective disorders. *Journal of Child Psychology and Psychiatry, 33,* 1287–1302.

Hersov, L. (1985). Emotional disorders. In M. Rutter & L. Hersov (Eds.), *Child and adolescent psychiatry: Modern approaches* (rev. ed., pp. 368–381). Oxford: Blackwell.

Horn, W. F., O'Donnell, J. P., & Vitulano, L. A. (1983). Long-term follow-up studies of learning disabled persons. *Journal of Learning Disabilities, 16,* 542–555.

Horrigan, J. P., & Barnhill, L. J. (1995). Guanfacine for treatment of attention-deficit hyperactivity disorder in boys. *Journal of Child and Adolescent Psychopharmacology, 5,* 215–223.

Horrigan, J. P., & Barnhill, L. J. (1995). *Risperidone and explosive, aggressive autism.* Paper presented at the Annual Meeting of the American Academy of Child and Adolescent Psychiatry, New Orleans, LA.

Humphries, T., Kinsbourne, M., & Swanson, J. (1978). Stimulant effects on cooperation and social interaction between hyperactive children and their mothers. *Journal of Child Psychology and Psychiatry, 19,* 13–22.

Hunt, R. D., Arnsten, A. F. T., & Asbell, M. D. (1995). An open trial of guanfacine in the treatment of attention-deficit hyperactivity disorder. *Journal of the American Academy of Child and Adolescent Psychiatry, 34,* 50–54.

Husain, A., Chapel, J., & Malek-Ahmadl, P. (1980). Methylphenidate, neuroleptics and dyskinesia-dystonia. *Canadian Journal of Psychiatry, 25,* 254–258.

Judd, L. L., Squire, L. R., Butters, W., Salmon, D. P., & Paller, K. A. (1987). Effects of psychotropic drugs on cognition and memory in normal humans and animals. In H. Y. Meltzer (Ed.), *Psychopharmacology: The third generation of progress* (pp. 1467–1476). New York: Raven Press.

Kamm, I., & Mandel, A. (1967). Thioridazine in the treatment of behavior disorders in epileptics. *Diseases of the Nervous System, 28,* 46–48.

Kaplan, C. A., & Hussain, S. (1995). Use of drugs in child and adolescent psychiatry. *British Journal of Psychiatry, 166,* 291–298.

Kashani, J., & Simonds, J. F. (1979). The incidence of depression in children. *American Journal of Psychiatry, 136,* 1203–1205.

Katz, S., Saraf, K., Gittelman-Klein, R., & Klein, D. F. (1975). Clinical pharmacological management of hyperkinetic children. *International Journal of Mental Health, 4,* 157181.

Kayser, H. G. (1991). Omsetning av sentralstimulereude medikamenter i Norge 1980–89. *Tidsskrift for Den Norske Laegeforening, 111,* 863–864.

Kemph, J. P., DeVane, C. L., Levin, G. M., Jarecke, R., & Miller, R. L. (1993). Treatment of aggressive children with clonidine: Results of an open pilot study. *Journal of the American Academy of Child and Adolescent Psychiatry, 32,* 577–581.

King, B. H. (1991). Fluoxetine reduced self-injurious behavior in an adolescent with mental retardation. *Journal of Child and Adolescent Psychopharmacology, 1,* 321–329.

King, R. A., Riddle, M. A., Chappell, P. B., Hardin, M. T., Anderson, G. M., Lombroso, P., & Scahill, L. (1991). Emergence of self-destructive phenomena in children and adolescents during fluoxetine treatment. *Journal of the American Academy of Child and Adolescent Psychiatry, 30,* 179–186.

Kishimoto, A., Ogura, C., Hazama, H., & Inoue, K. (1983). Long-term prophylactic effects of carbamazepine in affective disorder. *British Journal of Psychiatry, 143,* 327–331.

Klauber, G. T. (1989). Clinical efficacy and safety of desmopressin in the treatment of nocturnal enuresis. *Journal of Pediatrics, 114,* 719–722.

Klein, D. F. (1981). Anxiety reconceptualized. In D. F. Klein & J. G. Rabkin (Eds.), *Anxiety: New research and current concepts.* New York: Raven Press.

Klein, R. G., Koplewicz, H. S., & Kanner, A. (1992). Imipramine treatment of children with separation anxiety disorder. *Journal of the American Academy of Child and Adolescent Psychiatry, 31,* 21–28.

Kolmen, B. K., Feldman, H. M., Handen, B. L., & Janosky, J. E. (1995). Naltrexone in young autistic children: A double-blind placebo-controlled crossover study. *Journal of the American Academy of Child and Adolescent Psychiatry, 34,* 223–231.

Kolvin, I., Berney, T. P., & Bhate, S. R. (1984). Classification and diagnosis of depression in school phobia. *British Journal of Psychiatry, 145,* 347–357.

Kolvin, I., Taunch, J., Currah, J., Garside, R. F., Nolan, J., & Shaw, W. B. (1972). Enuresis—a descriptive analysis and a controlled trial. *Developmental Medicine and Child Neurology, 14,* 715–726.

Kovacs, M., Feinberg, T. L., Crouse-Novak, M. A., Paulauskas, S. L., & Finkelstein, R. (1984). Depressive disorders in childhood: I. A longitudinal prospective study of characteristics and recovery. *Archives of General Psychiatry, 41,* 229–237.

Kramer, A. D., & Feiguine, R. J. (1981). Clinical effects of amitriptyline in adolescent depression: A pilot study. *Journal of the American Academy of Child and Adolescent Psychiatry, 20,* 636–644.

Kutcher, S., Boulos, C., Ward, B., Marton, P., Simeon, J., Ferguson, H. B., Szalai, J., Katic, M., Roberts, N., Dubois, C., & Reed, K. (1994). Response to desipramine treatment in adolescent depression: A fixed-dose, placebo-controlled trial. *Journal of the American Academy of Child and Adolescent Psychiatry, 33,* 686–694.

Kutcher, S. & Robertson, H. A. (1995). Electroconvulsive therapy in treatment-resistant bipolar youth. *Journal of Child and Adolescent Psychopharmacology, 5,* 167–175.

Last, C. G., Hersen, M., Kazdin, A. E., Finkelstein, R., & Strauss, C. C. (1987). Comparison of DSM-III separation anxiety and overanxious disorders: Demographic characteristics and patterns of comorbidity. *Journal of the American Academy of Child and Adolescent Psychiatry, 26,* 527–531.

Leonard, H. L., Swedo, S. E., Lenane, M. C., Rettew, D. C., Cheslow, D. L., Hamburger, S. D., & Rapoport, J. L. (1991). A double-blind desipramine substitution during long-term clomipramine treatment in children and adolescents with obsessive-compulsive disorder. *Archives of General Psychiatry, 48,* 922–927.

Lerer, R. J., Lerer, M. P., & Artner, J. (1977). The effects of methylphenidate on the handwriting of children with minimal brain dysfunction. *Journal of Pediatrics, 91,* 127–132.

Lerman, P. (1986). Seizures induced or aggravated by anticonvulsants. *Epilepsia, 27,* 708710.

Levy, H. B. (1973). Square pegs, round holes: The learning-disabled child in the classroom and the home. Boston: Little, Brown.

Lion, J. R., Azcarate, C. L., & Koepke, H. H. (1975). "Paradoxical rage reactions" during psychotropic medication. Diseases of the Nervous System, 36, 557–558.

Lombroso, P. J., Scahill, L., King, R. A., Lynch, K. A., Chappell, P. B., Peterson, B. S., McDougle, C. J., & Leckman, J. F. (1995). Risperidone treatment of children and adolescents with chronic tic disorder: A preliminary report. *Journal of the American Academy of Child and Adolescent Psychiatry, 34,* 1147–1152.

Lucas, A., & Weiss, M. (1971). Methylphenidate hallucinosis. *Journal of the American Medical Association, 217,* 1079–1081.

Ludlow, C., Rapoport, J., Brown, G., & Mikkelson, E. (1979). The differential effects of dextroamphetamine on the language and communicative skills of hyperactive and normal children. In R. Knights & D. Bakker (Eds.), *Rehabilitation, treatment, and management of learning disorders.* Baltimore: University Park Press.

MacLean, R. E. G. (1960). Imipramine hydrochloride and enuresis. *American Journal of Psychiatry, 117,* 551.

Malone, M. A., Couitis, J., Kershner, J. R., & Logan, W. J. (1994). Right hemisphere dysfunction and methylphenidate effects in children with attention-deficit/hyperactivity disorder. *Journal of Child and Adolescent Psychopharmacology, 4,* 245–253.

Mattes, J. A., & Gittelman, R. (1983). Growth of hyperactive children on maintenance regimen of methylphenidate. *Archives of General Psychiatry, 40,* 317–321.

Mattson, R. H., & Calverly, J. R. (1968). Dextroamphetamine-sulfate-induced dyskinesias. *Journal of the American Medical Association, 204,* 400–402.

McClellan, J. M., & Werry, J. S. (1992). Schizophrenia. *Psychiatric Clinics of North America, 15,* 131–147.

McDougle, C. J., Price, L. H., Volkmar, F. R., Goodman, W. K., Ward-O'Brien, D., Nielsen, J., Bregman, J., & Cohen, D. J. (1992). Clomipramine in autism: Preliminary evidence of efficacy. *Journal of the American Academy of Child and Adolescent Psychiatry, 31,* 746–750.

Meadow, R., & Berg, I. (1982). Controlled trial of imipramine in diurnal enuresis. *Archives of Disease in Childhood, 57,* 714–716.

Meyer, M. F. (1922). The psychological effects of drugs. *Psychological Bulletin, 19,* 173–182.

Miller, K., Goldberg, S., & Atkin, B. (1989). Nocturnal enuresis: Experience with long term use of intranasally administered desmopressin. *Journal of Pediatrics, 114,* 723–726.

Molitch, M., & Poliakoff, S. (1937). Effect of benzedrine sulfate on enuresis. *Archives of Pediatrics, 54,* 499–501.

Molitch, M., & Sullivan, J. P. (1937). Effect of benzedrine sulfate on children taking the New Stanford Achievement Test. *American Journal of Orthopsychiatry, 7,* 519–522.

Mozes, T., Toren, P., Chernauzau, N., Mester, R., Yoran-Hegesh, R., Blumensohn, R., & Weizman, A. (1994). Clozapine treatment in very early onset schizophrenia. *Journal of the American Academy of Child and Adolescent Psychiatry, 33,* 65–70.

Ounsted, C. (1955). The hyperkinetic syndrome in epileptic children. *Lancet, 2,* 303–311.

Papatheodorou, G., & Kutcher, S. P. (1993). Divalproex sodium treatment in late adolescent and young adult acute mania. *Psychopharmacology Bulletin, 29,* 213–219.

Paul, R. (1987). Natural history. In D. J. Cohen, A. M. Donnellan, & R. Paul (Eds.), *Handbook of autism and pervasive developmental disorders* (pp. 121–130). New York: John Wiley & Sons.

Pelham, W. E. (1983). The effects of psychostimulants on academic achievement in hyperactive and learning-disabled children. *Thalamus, 3,* 1–49.

Pelham, W. E., Bender, M. E., Caddell, J., Booth, S., & Moorer, S. H. (1985). Methylphenidate and children with attention deficit disorder: Dose effects on classroom academic and social behavior. *Archives of General Psychiatry, 42,* 948–952.

Pelham, W. E., Sturges, J., Hoza, J., Schmidt, C., Bijlsma, J. J., Milich R., & Moorer, S. (1987). The effects of Sustained Release 20 and 10 mg Ritalin b.i.d. on cognitive and social behavior in children with attention deficit disorder. *Pediatrics, 80,* 491–501.

Pelham, W. E., Swanson, J., Bender, M., & Wilson, J. (1980, September). *Effects of pemoline on hyperactivity: Laboratory and classroom measures.* Paper presented at the annual meeting of the American Psychological Association, Montreal, Canada

Pelham, W. E., Swanson, J. M., Furman, M. B., & Schwindt, H. (1995). Pemoline effects on children with ADHD: A time-response by dose-response analysis on classroom measures. *Journal of the American Academy of Child and Adolescent Psychiatry, 34,* 1504–1513.

Pennington, B. F. (1990). The genetics of dyslexia. *Journal of Child Psychology and Psychiatry, 31,* 193–201.

Perry, R., Campbell, M., Adams, P., Lynch, N., Spencer, E. K., Curren, E. L., & Overall, J. E. (1989). Long-term efficacy of haloperidol in autistic children: Continuous versus discontinuous drug administration. *Journal of the American Academy of Child and Adolescent Psychiatry, 28,* 87–92.

Pfefferbaum, B., Overall, J. E., Boren, H. A., Frankel, L. S., Sullivan, M. P., & Johnson, K. (1987). Alprazolam in the treatment of anticipatory and acute situational anxiety in children with cancer. *Journal of the American Academy of Child and Adolescent Psychiatry, 26,* 532–535.

Piggott, L. R., Gdowski, C. L., Villanueva, D., Fischhoff, J., & Frohman, C. F. (1986). Side effects of fenfluramine in autistic children. *Journal of the American Academy of Child and Adolescent Psychiatry, 25,* 287–289.

Platt, J. E., Campbell, M., Green, W. H., & Grega, D. M. (1984). Cognitive effects of lithium carbonate and haloperidol in treatment-resistant aggressive children. *Archives of General Psychiatry, 120,* 657–662.

Pleak, R. R., Birmaker, B., Gavrilescu, A. Abichandani, C., & Williams, D. T. (1988). Mania and neuropsychiatric excitation following carbamazepine. *Journal of the American Academy of Child and Adolescent Psychiatry, 27,* 500–503.

Pliszka, S. R. (1987). Tricyclic antidepressants in the treatment of children with attention deficit disorder. *Journal of the American Academy of Child and Adolescent Psychiatry, 26,* 127–132.

Pool, D., Bloom, W., Mielke, D. H., Roniger, J. J., & Gallant, D. M. (1976). A controlled evaluation of Loxitane in seventy-five adolescent schizophrenic patients. *Current Therapeutic Research, 19,* 99–104.

Popper, C. W. (1995). Combining methylphenidate and clonidine: Pharmacologic questions and news reports about sudden death. *Journal of Child and Adolescent Psychopharmacology, 5,* 157–166.

Popper, C. W., & Elliott, G. R. (1990). Sudden death and tricyclic antidepressants: Clinical considerations for children. *Journal of Child and Adolescent Psychopharmacology, 1,* 125–132.

Porrino, L. J., Rapoport, J. C., Behar, D., Sceery, W., Ismond, D. R., & Bunney, E. E. (1983). A naturalistic assessment of the motor activity of hyperactive boys. *Archives of General Psychiatry, 40,* 681–687.

Post, R. M. (1987). Mechanisms of action of carbamazepine and related anticonvulsants in affective illness. In H. Y. Meltzer (Ed.), *Psychopharmacology: The third generation of progress* (pp. 567–576). NY: Raven Press.

Preskorn, S. H., Bupp, S. J., Weller, E. B., & Weller, R. A. (1989). Plasma levels of imipramine and metabolites in 68 hospitalized children. *Journal of the American Academy of Child and Adolescent Psychiatry, 28,* 373–375.

Puig-Antich, J. (1982). Major depression and conduct disorder in puberty. *Journal of the American Academy of Child Psychiatry, 18,* 616–627.

Puig-Antich, J., Perel, J. M., & Lupatkin, W. (1987). Imipramine in prepubertal major depressive disorders. *Archives of General Psychiatry, 44,* 81–89.

Purdon, S. E., Lit, W., Labelle, A., & Jones, B. D. W. (1994). Risperidone in the treatment of pervasive developmental disorder. *Canadian Journal of Psychiatry, 39,* 400–405.

Quinn, P. O., & Rapoport, J. L. (1975). One year follow-up of hyperactive boys treated with imipramine or methylphenidate. *American Journal of Psychiatry, 132,* 241–245.

Quintana, H., Birmaher, B., Stedge, D., Lennon, S. Freed, J., Bridge, J., & Greenhill, L. (1995). Use of methylphenidate in the treatment of children with autistic disorder. *Journal of Autism and Developmental Disorders, 25,* 283–294.

Quintana, H. & Keshavan, M. (1995). Case study: Risperidone in children and adolescents with schizophrenia. *Journal of the American Academy of Child and Adolescent Psychiatry, 34,* 1292–1296.

Rabinowitz, C. B., & Wiener, J. (1990). Learning about innovations in clinical treatment. Journal of Child and Adolescent Psychopharmacology, 1, 165–168.

Rapoport, J. L. (1994). Clozapine and child psychiatry. *Journal of Child and Adolescent Psychopharmacology, 4,* 1–3.

Rapoport, J. L., Quinn, P. O., Bradbard, G.. Riddle, K. D., & Brooks, E. (1974). Imipramine and methylphenidate treatments of hyperactive boys. *Archives of General Psychiatry, 30,* 789–793.

Rapport, M. D., Stoner, G., DuPaul, G. J., Birmingham, B. K., & Tucker, S. (1985). Methylphenidate in hyperactive children: Differential effects of dose on academic, learning, and social behavior. *Journal of Abnormal Child Psychology, 13,* 227–244.

Ratey, J. J., Mikkelsen, E. J., Smith, G. B., Upadhyaya, A., Zuckerman, H. S., Martell, D., Sorgi, P., Polakoff, S., & Bemporad, J. (1986). β blockers in the severely and profoundly mentally retarded. *Journal of Clinical Psychopharmacology, 6,* 103–107.

Realmuto, G. M., Erickson, W. D., Yellin, A. M., Hopwood, J. H., & Greenberg, L. M. (1984). Clinical comparison of thiothixene and thioridazine in schizophrenic adolescents. *American Journal of Psychiatry, 141,* 440–442.

Reid, M. K., & Borkowski, J. G. (1984). Effects of methylphenidate (Ritalin) on information processing in hyperactive children. *Journal of Abnormal Child Psychology, 12,* 169–185.

Remschmidt, H., Schulz, E., & Martin, P. D. M. (1994). An open trial of clozapine in thirty-six adolescents with schizophrenia. *Journal of Child and Adolescent Psychopharmacology, 4,* 31–41.

Renshaw, D. C. (1974). *The hyperactive child.* Chicago: Nelson-Hall.

Richardson, E., Kupietz, S. A., Winsberg, B. G., Maitinsky, S., & Mendell, N. (1988). Effects of methylphenidate dosage in hyperactive reading-disabled children: II. Reading achievement. *Journal of the American Academy of Child and Adolescent Psychiatry, 27,* 78–87.

Richardson, J. S., & Zaleski, W. A. (1983). Naloxone and self-mutilation. *Biological Psychiatry, 18,* 99–101.

Ricketts, R. W., Goza, A. B., Ellis, C. R., Singh, Y. N., Singh, N. N., & Cooke, J. C. (1993). Fluoxetine treatment of severe self-injury in young adults with mental retardation. *Journal of the American Academy of Child and Adolescent Psychiatry, 32,* 865–869.

Riddle, M. A., Hardin, M. T., King, R., Scahill, L., & Woolston, J. L. (1990). Fluoxetine treatment of children and adolescents with Tourette's and obsessive compulsive disorders: Preliminary clinical experience. *Journal of the American Academy of Child and Adolescent Psychiatry, 29,* 45–48.

Riddle, M. A., Scahill, L., King, R. A., Hardin, M. T., Anderson, G. M., Ort, S. I., Smith, J. C., Leckman, J. F., & Cohen, D. J. (1992). Double-blind, crossover trial of fluoxetine and placebo in children with obsessive-compulsive disorder. *Journal of the American Academy of Child and Adolescent Psychiatry, 31,* 1062–1069.

Rifkin, A., Quitkin, F., Carillo, C., Blumberg, A. G., & Klein, D. F. (1972). Lithium carbonate in emotionally unstable character disorder. *Archives of General Psychiatry, 27,* 519–523.

Robbins, T. W., & Sahakian, B. J. (1979). "Paradoxical" effects of psychomotor stimulant drugs in hyperactive children from the standpoint of behavioral pharmacology. *Neuropharmacology, 18,* 931–950.

Robinson, D. S., & Barker, E. (1976). Tricyclic antidepressant cardiotoxicity. *Journal of the American Medical Association, 236,* 2089–2090.

Roche, A. F., Lipman, R. S., Overall, J. E., & Hung, W. (1979). The effects of stimulant medication on the growth of hyperkinetic children. *Pediatrics, 63,* 847–850.

Rochet, T., Revol, O., Maillet, J., & deVillard, R. (1993). Les psychotropes en psychiatrie de l'enfant et de l'adolescent. *Annales de Pediatrie, 40,* 555–563.

Romanczyk, R. G. (1986). Self-injurious behavior: Conceptualization, assessment, and treatment. In K. D. Gadow (Ed.), *Advances in learning and behavioral disabilities* (Vol. 5, pp. 29–56). Greenwich, CT: JAI Press.

Rosenberg, D. R., Holttum, J., & Gershon, S. (1994). *Textbook of pharmacotherapy for child and adolescent psychiatric disorders.* New York: Brunner/Mazel.

Roy-Byrne, P. P., Joffe, R. T., Uhde, T. W., & Post, R. M. (1984a). Approaches to the evaluation and treatment of rapid-cycling affective illness. *British Journal of Psychiatry, 145,* 543–550.

Roy-Byrne, P. P., Uhde, T. W., & Post, R. M. (1984b). Carbamazepine for aggression, schizophrenia and non-effective syndromes. *International Drug Therapy Newsletter, 19,* 9–12.

Roy-Byrne, P. P., Uhde, T. W., & Post, R. M. (1984c). Carbamazepine for hyperactivity, anxiety and withdrawal syndromes. *International Drug Therapy Newsletter, 19,* 25–26.

Rutter, M. (1985). The treatment of autistic children. *Journal of Child Psychology and Psychiatry, 26,* 193–214.

Ryan, N. D., Meyer, V., Dachille, S., Mazzie, D., & Puig-Antich, J. (1988a). Lithium antidepressant augmentation of TCA-refractory depression in adolescents. *Journal of the American Academy of Child and Adolescent Psychiatry, 27,* 371–376.

Ryan, N. D., & Puig-Antich, J. (1987). Pharmacological treatment of adolescent psychiatric disorders. *Journal of Adolescent Health Care, 8,* 137–142.

Ryan, N. D., Puig-Antich, J., Cooper, T. B., Rabinovich, H., Ambrosini, P., Davies, M., King, J., Torres, D., & Fried, J. (1986). Imipramine in adolescent major depression: Plasma level and clinical response. *Acta Psychiatrica Scandinavica, 73,* 275–288.

Ryan, N. D., Puig-Antich, J., Cooper, T. B., Rabinovich, H., Ambrosini, P., Fried, J., Davies, M., Torres, D., & Suckow, R. F. (1987). Relative safety of single versus divided dose imipramine in adolescent major depression. *Journal of the American Academy of Child and Adolescent Psychiatry, 26,* 400–406.

Ryan, N. D., Puig-Antich, J. Rabinovich, H., Fried, J., Ambrosini, P., Meyer, V., Torres, D., Dachille, S., & Mazzie, D. (1988b). MAOIs in adolescent major depression unresponsive to tricyclic antidepressants. *Journal of the American Academy of Child and Adolescent Psychiatry, 27,* 755–758.

Safer, D. J., & Allen, R. P. (1973). Factors influencing the suppressant effects of two stimulant drugs on the growth of hyperactive children. *Pediatrics, 51,* 660–667.

Safer, D. J., & Allen, R. P. (1976). *Hyperactive children: Diagnosis and management.* Baltimore: University Park Press.

Safer, D., Allen, R., & Barr, E. (1975). Growth rebound after termination of stimulant drugs. *Pediatrics, 86,* 113–116.

Sandman, C. A., Datta, P. C., Barron, J., Hoehler, F. K., Williams, C., & Swanson, J. M. (1983). Naloxone attenuates self-abusive behavior in developmentally disabled clients. *Applied Research in Mental Retardation, 4,* 5–11.

Satterfield, J. H., Schell, A. M., & Barb, S. D. (1980). Potential risk of prolonged administration of stimulant medication for hyperactive children. *Journal of Developmental and Behavioral Pediatrics, 1,* 102–107.

Schachar, R., & Tannock, R. (1993). Childhood hyperactivity and psychostimulants: A review of extended treatment studies. *Journal of Child and Adolescent Psychopharmacology, 3,* 81–97.

Schain, R. J., & Reynard, C. L. (1975). Observations on effects of central stimulant drug (methylphenidate) in children with hyperactive behavior. *Pediatrics, 55,* 709–716.

Schroeder, S. R., Bickel, W. K., & Richmond, G. (1986). Primary and secondary prevention of self-injurious behaviors: A lifelong problem. In K. D. Gadow (Ed.), *Advances in learning and behavioral disabilities* (Vol. 5, pp. 63–85). Greenwich, CT: JAI Press.

Schroeder, S. R., Schroeder, C. S., Smith, B., & Dalldorf, J. (1978). Prevalence of self-injurious behaviors in a large state facility for the retarded: A three-year follow-up study. *Journal of Autism and Childhood Schizophrenia, 8,* 261–269.

Shaffer, D. (1985). Enuresis. In M. Rutter & L. Hersov (Eds.), *Child and adolescent psychiatry* (2nd ed., pp. 465–481). London: Blackwell Scientific.

Shah, M. R., Seese, L. M., Abikoff, H., & Klein, R. G. (1994). Pemoline for children and adolescents with conduct disorder: A pilot investigation. *Journal of Child and Adolescent Psychopharmacology, 4,* 255–261.

Shapiro, A. K., & Shapiro, E. (1984). Controlled study of pimozide vs. placebo in Tourette's syndrome. *Journal of the American Academy of Child Psychiatry, 2,* 161–173.

Shapiro, A. K., Shapiro, E., & Eisenkraft, G. J. (1983). Treatment of Gilles de la Tourette's syndrome with clonidine and neuroleptics. *Archives of General Psychiatry, 40,* 1235–1240.

Shapiro, A. K., Shapiro, E. S., Young, J. G., & Feinberg, T. E. (1988). *Gilles de la Tourette syndrome* (2nd ed.). New York: Raven Press.

Sheard, M. H. (1978). The effects of lithium and other ions on aggressive behavior. In L. Valzelli (Ed.), *Modern problems of pharmacopsychiatry* (Vol. 13, pp. 53–68). New York: Karger.

Sheehan, D. V., Ballenger, J., & Jacobsen, G. (1980). Treatment of endogenous anxiety with phobic, hysterical and hypochondrial symptoms. *Archives of General Psychiatry, 37,* 51–59.

Silver, J. M., & Yudofsky, S. (1985). Propranolol for aggression: Literature review and clinical guidelines. *International Drug Therapy Newsletter, 20,* 9–12.

Simeon, J. G., Carrey, N. J., Wiggins, D. M., Milin, R. P., & Hosenbocus, S. N. (1995). Risperidone effects in treatment-resistant adolescents: Preliminary case reports. *Journal of Child and Adolescent Psychophar-macology, 5,* 69–79.

Simeon, J. G., Ferguson, B., Knott, V., Roberts, N., Gauthier, B., Dubois, C., & Wiggins, D. (1992). Clinical, cognitive and neurophysiologic effects of alprazolam in children and adolescents with overanxious and avoidant disorders. *Journal of the American Academy of Child and Adolescent Psychiatry, 31,* 29–33.

Simeon, J. G., Knott, V. J., Dubois, C., Wiggins, D., Geraets, I., Thatte, S., & Miller, W. (1994). Buspirone therapy of mixed anxiety disorders in childhood and adolescence: A pilot study. *Journal of Child and Adolescent Psychopharmacology, 4,* 159–170.

Singh, N. N., & Aman, M. G. (1981). Effects of thioridazine dosage on the behavior of severely mentally retarded persons. *American Journal of Mental Deficiency, 85,* 580–587.

Singh, N. N., & Millichamp, C. J. (1985). Pharmacological treatment of self-injurious behavior in mentally retarded persons. *Journal of Autism and Developmental Disorders, 15,* 257–267.

Sleator, E. K., & von Neumann, A. (1974). Methylphenidate in the treatment of hyperkinetic children. *Clinical Pediatrics, 13,* 19–24.

Snyder, R. D. (1979). The right not to read. *Pediatrics, 63,* 791–794.

Snyder, R. D. (1983). Coping strategies for inefficient readers. *Journal of Learning Disabilities, 5,* 261–263.

Speltz, M. L., Varley, C. K., Peterson, K., & Beilke, R. L. (1988). Effects of dextroamphetamine and contingency management on a preschooler with ADHD and oppositional defiant disorder. *Journal of the American Academy of Child and Adolescent Psychiatry, 27,* 175–178.

Spencer, E. K., Kafantaris, V., Padron, G., Gayol, M. V., Rosenberg, C. R., & Campbell, M. (1992). Haloperidol in schizophrenic children: Early findings from a study in progress. *Psychopharmacology Bulletin, 28,* 183–186.

Spencer, T., Biederman, J., & Wilens, T. (1994). Tricyclic antidepressant treatment of children with ADHD and tic disorders. *Journal of the American Academy of Child and Adolescent Psychiatry, 33,* 1203–1204.

Sprague, R. L. (1984). Preliminary report of cross-cultural study and cognitive strategies of ADD children. In L. M. Bloomingdale (Ed.), *Attention deficit disorder: Diagnostic, cognitive, and therapeutic understanding* (pp. 211–219). New York: Spectrum Publications.

Sprague, R. L., Barnes, K. R., & Werry, J. S. (1970). Methylphenidate and thioridazine: Learning, reaction time, activity, and classroom behavior in emotionally disturbed children. *American Journal of Orthopsychiatry, 40,* 615–628.

Sprague, R. L., & Sleator, E. K. (1973). Effects of psychopharmacologic agents on learning disorders. *Pediatric Clinics of North America, 20,* 719–735.

Sprague, R. L., & Sleator, E. K. (1977). Methylphenidate in hyperkinetic children: Differences in dose effects on learning and social behavior. *Science, 198,* 1274–1276.

Sprague, R. L., & Werry, J. S. (1974). Psychotropic drugs and handicapped children. In L. Mann & D. A. Sabatino (Eds.), *The second review of special education* (pp. 1–50). Philadelphia: JSE Press.

Steinberg, D. (1980). The use of lithium carbonate in adolescence. *Journal of Child Psychology and Psychiatry, 21,* 263–271.

Steingard, R., Biederman, J., Spencer, T., Wilens, T., & Gonzalez, A. (1993). Comparison of clonidine response in the treatment of attention-deficit hyperactivity disorder with and without comorbid tic disorder. *Journal of the American Academy of Child and Adolescent Psychiatry, 32,* 350–353.

Steingard, R., Khan, A., Gonzalez, A., & Herzog, D. B. (1992). Neuroleptic malignant syndrome: Review of experience with children and adolescents. *Journal of child and Adolescent Psychopharmacology, 2,* 183–198.

Stephens, R. S., Pelham, W. E., & Skinner, R. (1984). The state-dependent and main effects of methylphenidate and pemoline on pairedassociates learning and spelling in hyperactive children. *Journal of Consulting and Clinical Psychology, 523,* 104–113.

Stern, L. M., Walker, M. K., Sawyer, M. G., Oades, R. D., Badcock, N. R., & Spence, J. G. (1990). A controlled crossover trial of fenfluramine in autism. *Journal of Child Psychology and Psychiatry, 31,* 569–585.

Strayhorn, J. M., Rapp, N., Donina, W., & Strain, P. (1988). Randomized trial of methylphenidate for an autistic child. *Journal of the American Academy of Child and Adolescent Psychiatry, 27,* 244–247.

Strober, M., & Carlson, G. A. (1982). Bipolar illness in adolescents with major depression. *Archives of General Psychiatry, 39,* 549–555.

Strober, M., Freeman, R., Rigali, J., Schmidt, S., & Diamond, R. (1992). The pharmacotherapy of depressive illness in adolescence: II. Effects of lithium augmentation in nonresponders to imipramine. *Journal of the American Academy of Child and Adolescent Psychiatry, 31,* 16–20.

Sverd, J., Curley, A. D., Jandorf, L., & Volkersz, L. (1988). Behavior disorder and attention deficits in boys with Tourette syndrome. *Journal of the American Academy of Child and Adolescent Psychiatry, 27,* 413–417.

Swanson, J. M., & Kinsbourne, M. (1976). Stimulant-related state-dependent learning in hyperactive children. *Science, 192,* 1354–1357.

Sykes, D. H., Douglas, V. I., Weiss, G., & Minde, K. K. (1971). Attention in hyperactive children and the effect of methylphenidate (Ritalin). *Journal of Child Psychology and Psychiatry, 2,* 129–139.

Tannock, R., Ickowicz, A., & Schachar, R. (1995). Differential effects of methylphenidate on work-ing memory in ADHD children with and without comorbid anxiety. *Journal of the American Academy of Child and Adolescent Psychiatry, 34,* 886–896.

Tannock, R., & Schachar, R. (1992). Methylphenidate and cognitive perseveration in hyperactive children. *Journal of Child Psychology and Psychiatry, 33,* 1217–1228.

Tapia, F. (1969). Haldol in the treatment of children with tics and stutterers—and an incidental finding. *Psychiatric Quarterly, 43,* 647–649.

Taylor, E. (1979). The use of drugs in hyperkinetic states: Clinical issues. *Neuropharmacology, 18,* 951–958.

Taylor, E. (1983). Critical notice: From romance to ritual: The development of pediatric psychopharmacology. *Journal of Child Psychology and Psychiatry, 24,* 321–323.

Taylor, E. (1985). Drug treatment, In M. Rutter & L. Hersov (Eds.), *Child and adolescent psychiatry* (pp. 781–793). London: Blackwell Scientific.

Taylor, E. (1988). Commissioned review - psychopharmacology in childhood. *Newsletter of the Association for Child Psychology and Psychiatry, 10,* 3–6.

Thompson, S., & Rey, J. M. (1995). Functional enuresis: Is desmopressin the answer? *Journal of the American Academy of Child and Adolescent Psychiatry, 34,* 266–271.

Tierney, E., Joshi, P. T., Llinas, J. F., Rosenberg, L. A., & Riddle, M. A. (1995). Sertraline for major depression in children and adolescents: Preliminary clinical experience. *Journal of Child and Adolescent Psychopharmacology, 5,* 13–27.

Towbin, K. E., Dykens, E. M., & Pugliese, R. G. (1994). Clozapine for early developmental delays with childhood-onset schizophrenia: Protocol and 15-month outcome. *Journal of the American Academy of Child and Adolescent Psychiatry, 33,* 651–657.

Tyrer, S. P., & Shopsin, B. (1980). Neural and neurotransmitter effects of lithium. In F. N. Johnson (Ed.), *Handbook of lithium therapy* (pp. 289–309). Lancaster, England: MTP Press.

Urman, R., Ickowicz, A., Fulford, P., & Tannock, R. (1995). An exaggerated cardiovascular response to methylphenidate in ADHD children with anxiety. *Journal of Child and Adolescent Psychopharmacol-ogy, 5,* 29–37.

Van Scheyen, J. D., & Van Kamman, D. P. (1979). Clomipramine induced mania in unipolar depression. *Archives of General Psychiatry, 36,* 560—565.

Veakataraman, S., Naylor, M. W., & King, C. A. (1992).

Mania associated with fluoxetine treatment in adolescents. *Journal of the American Academy of Child and Adolescent Psychiatry, 31,* 276–281.

Vitriol, C., & Farber, B. (1981). Stimulant medication in certain childhood disorders. *American Journal of Psychiatry, 138,* 1517–1518.

Wagner, W., Johnson, S. B., Walker, D., Carter, R., & Wittner, J. (1982). A controlled comparison of two treatments for nocturnal enuresis. *Journal of Pediatrics, 101,* 302–307.

Wehr, T. A., & Goodwin, F. K. (1979). Rapid cycling in manic-depressives induced by tricyclic antidepressants. *Archives of General Psychiatry, 36,* 555–559.

Wehr, T. A., & Goodwin, F. K. (1987). Can antidepressants cause mania and worsen the course of affective illness? *American Journal of Psychiatry, 144,* 1403–1411.

Weingartner, H., Rapoport, J. L., Buchsbaum, M. S., Bunney, W. E., Ebert, M. H., Mikkelsen, E. J., & Caine, E. D. (1980). Cognitive processes in normal and hyper-active-children and their response to amphetamine treatment. *Journal of Abnormal Psychology, 89,* 25–37.

Weinstein, M. R. (1980). Lithium treatment of women during pregnancy and in the postdelivery period. In F. N. Johnson (Ed.), *Handbook of lithium therapy* (pp. 421–432). Lancaster, England: MTP Press.

Weiss, G., Minde, K., Douglas, V., Werry, J., & Sykes, D. (1971). Comparison of the effects of chlorpromazine, dextroamphetamine and methylphenidate on the behavior and intellectual functioning of hyperactive children. *Canadian Medical Association Journal, 104,* 20–25.

Weller, E. B., Weller, R. A., & Fristad, M. A. (1986). Lithium dosage guide for prepubertal children: A preliminary report. *Journal of the American Academy of Child Psychiatry, 25,* 92–95.

Welner, A., Welner, Z., & Fishman, R. (1979). Psychiatric adolescent inpatients: Eight to ten year follow-up. *Archives of General Psychiatry, 36,* 698–700.

Wender, P. (1973). Minimal brain dysfunction in children. New York: John Wiley & Sons.

Werry, J. S. (1982). An overview of pediatric psychopharmacology. *Journal of the American Academy of Child and Adolescent Psychiatry, 21,* 3–9.

Werry, J. S., & Aman, M. G. (1975). Methylphenidate and haloperidol in children. *Archives of General Psychiatry, 32,* 790–795.

Werry, J. S., Aman, M. G., & Diamond, E. (1980). Imipramine and methylphenidate in hyperactive children. *Journal of Child Psychology and Psychiatry, 21,* 27–35.

West, S. A., Keck, P. E., & McElroy, S. L. (1995). Oral loading doses in the valproate treatment of adolescents with mixed bipolar disorder. *Journal of Child and Adolescent Psychopharmacology, 5,* 225–231.

West, S. A., Keck, P. E., McElroy, S. L., Strakowski, S. M., Minnery, K. L., McConville, B. J., & Sorter, M. T. (1994). Open trial of valproate in the treatment of adolescent mania. *Journal of Child and Adolescent Psychopharmacology, 4,* 263–267.

Whalen, C., Collins, B., Henker, B., Alkus, S., Adams, D., & Stapp, J. (1978). Behavior observations of hyperactive children and methylphenidate effects in systematically structured classroom environments: Now you see them, now you don't. *Journal of Pediatric Psychology, 3,* 177–187.

Whalen, C. K., Henker, B., Collins, B. E., Finck, D., & Dotemoto, S. (1979). A social ecology of hyperactive boys: Medication effects in structured classroom environments. *Journal of Applied Behavior Analysis, 12,* 65–81.

Whalen, C. K., Henker, B., & Dotemoto, S. (1980). Methylphenidate and hyperactivity: Effects on teacher behaviors. *Science, 208,* 1280–1282.

Whitehouse, D., Shah, U., & Palmer, F. B. (1980). Comparison of sustained release and standard methylphenidate in the treatment of minimal brain dysfunction. *Journal of Clinical Psychiatry, 41,* 282–285.

Wilens, T. E., Biederman, J., Geist, D. E., Steingard, R., & Spencer, T. (1993). Nortriptyline in the treatment of ADHD: A chart review of 58 cases. *Journal of the American Academy of Child and Adolescent Psychiatry, 32,* 343–349.

Wilens, T. E., Spencer, T., Biederman, J., Wozniak, J., & Connor, D. (1995). Combined pharmacotherapy: An emerging trend in pediatric psychopharmacology, *Journal of the American Academy of Child and Adolescent Psychiatry, 34,* 110–112.

Williams, D. T., Mehl, R., & Yudofsky, S. (1982). The effect of propranolol on uncontrolled rage outbursts in children and adolescents with organic brain dysfunction. *Journal of the American Academy of Child and Adolescent Psychiatry, 21,* 129–135.

Winsberg, B. G., & Yepes, L. E. (1978). Antipsychotics (major tranquilizers, neuroleptics). In J. S. Werry (Ed.), *Pediatric psychopharmacology: The use of behavior modifying drugs in children* (pp. 234–273). New York: Brunner/Mazel.

Wolf, D. V,. & Wagner, K. D. (1993). Tardive dyskinesia, tardive dystonia, and tardive Tourette's syndrome in children and adolescents. *Journal of Child and Adolescent Psychopharmacology, 3,* 175–198.

Wysocki, T., Fuqua, W., Davis, V. J., & Breuning, S. E. (1981). Effects of thioridazine (Mellaril) on titrating delayed matching-to-sample performance of mentally retarded adults. *American Journal of Mental Deficiency, 85,* 539–547.

Yarbrough, E., Santat, U., Perel, I., Webster, C., & Lombardi, R. (1987). Effects of fenfluramine on autistic individuals residing in a state developmental center. *Journal of Autism and Developmental Disorders, 17,* 303–314.

Yepes, L., Balka, E., Winsberg, B., & Bialer, I. (1977). Amitriptyline and methylphenidate treatment of behaviorally disordered children. *Journal of Child Psychology and Psychiatry, 18,* 39–52, 409.

Zeiner, P. (1995). Body growth and cardiovascular function after extended treatment (1.75 years) with methylphenidate in boys with attention-deficit hyperactivity disorder. *Journal of Child and Adolescent Psychopharmacology, 5,* 129–138.

Zimmermann, R. L., & Heistad, G. T. (1982). Studies of the long term efficacy of antipsychotic drugs in controlling the behavior of institutionalized retardates. *Journal of the American Academy of Child and Adolescent Psychiatry, 21,* 136–143.

CHAPTER 15

INTEGRATING BEHAVIORAL INFORMATICS INTO THE PRACTICE OF CHILD THERAPY

Ron L. Meredith
Steven L. Bair
Greg R. Ford
Richard J. Morris

BEHAVIORAL INFORMATICS

Behavioral informatics refers to various applications of computer technology to clinical practice. Although the concept may be unfamiliar, extremely useful information and technological resources will soon be available to assist the clinician in delivering high quality child clinical services. While many clinicians are aware of early attempts to simulate psychotherapy using computer technology (DeMuth, 1984) and the use of computers for automated scoring and interpretation of psychological assessment instruments (Fowler, 1985), they may be largely unaware of the changes in information technology that have accompanied the onset of the "information age." Computerized administration, scoring, and reporting of various assessment instruments, financial management, computer-assisted therapy, sophisticated computerized patient records, and electronic connectivity to various accountability centers and payors are available (Meredith & Bair,

1995). Clinical skill and sensitivity is being augmented by finger tip access to clinical information and products associated with this emerging computer technology. In fact, clinical practice has advanced to the point where ignoring the available computer technology actually contributes to inefficiency in our work with children and adolescents.

A survey by Rosen (1995a) suggests that psychologists have been more receptive to technological advances than the average citizen (see Table 15.1) and are probably fairly similar to other behavioral health professionals in their level of computer sophistication. According to this survey about 72% of psychologists are using a computer in some capacity in their practices compared to about 55% utilization six years previously (Farrell, 1989). Most psychologists use computers primarily for word processing, although 69% reported having modems and hence the capability for on-line connectivity. Only about 50% use computers to handle financial records while less than 25% have used computers to

TABLE 15.1.   Use of Computers by Psychologists

	PERCENTAGE
PSYCHOLOGISTS USING COMPUTERS IN CLINICAL PRACTICE	72%
Hardware	
IBM Computers	66%
Lazer Printers	50%
Modems	60%
Connectivity to On-Line Service	24%
Clerical/Administrative Tasks	
Word Processing	69%
Financial Records	50%
Printing Insurance Forms	33%
Electronic Billing	3%
Clinical Applications	
Test Administration	25%
Test Scoring	11%
Printing Psychological Profiles	22%

Source: Adapted from Rosen, L. (1995a). Cruising the info-ban: Psychologists relish computer opportunities. *The National Psychologist, 4*(14), 14–15.

administer, score, or interpret psychological test results. Computers were used more by younger psychologists and those engaged in various types of psychological assessment. The general conclusion reached by Rosen (1995a) was that psychologists as a group are not yet taking full advantage of the available technology.

Cagney and Woods (1994), note that "To many providers, the term clinical information systems evoke...images of machines and numbers, frustration and fear." Rosen and Weil (1995) identify three types of attitudes displayed by computer users. These include "The Eager Adopters" (10%), the "Hesitant Prove-Its" (50%) and the "Technology Resisters" (40%). With specific respect to psychologists, about 30% rated themselves as moderately to highly technophobic, while 36% indicated that they would rather not use the emerging technology unless they must. Rosen and Weil also found that 54% wanted to wait until the new technology was proven before they decided to use it. These responses suggest that behavioral health professionals may be at risk for "technological antiquation" as various computerized systems become the core of administrative and clinical operations in emerging behavioral health-care systems.

The evolution of behavioral informatics evolved gradually. Early applications focused on the use of computers in psychological testing (Fowler, 1985), computer interviews (Erdman, Klein, & Griest, 1985), triage screening (Chang, 1987), the development of rudimentary psychiatric records (Van Vort & Mattson, 1987), and computer generated electronic charts (Meredith & Bair, 1990). These applications were relatively simple in terms of functionality and clinical sophistication. Financial management systems, specifically billing systems, soon followed as more offices became computerized and behavioral clinicians became aware of the cost and time savings realized from such tools. In 1984, Griest wrote:

> "We need a generation of clinicians who will take the powerful tools presently available and apply them with care, ingenuity, diligence, and patience to difficult mental health problems, which will gradually yield to our steady efforts. Over time, this basically conservative approach can produce radically beneficial changes in our professions and in patient outcomes" (Farrell, 1991, p. 175).

With emerging technology and with the impetus of increased accountability resulting from a more complex payor system, computerized clinical applications erupted onto the scene in the late 1980s. Farrell (1989) observed that three different psychware publications each listed at least 150 different computer applications available for behavioral health professionals. Systems exist that process billing information electronically and electronically handle transfer of funds from the payor to the bank account of the provider. Expert systems built on clinical logic and those which derive from complex algorithms now are available to predict the need for hospitalization, the appropriate level of triage for a given client and the optimal time for discharge from outpatient care (Gray & Glazer, 1994). Child therapists can also store client information in computerized patient records and transmit via modem both clinical and financial data to third party payors for on-line review and claims adjudication (MCO's Select Software: Providers Come On-Line, 1995).

While many child behavioral health-care providers have been busily involved with their practices and embroiled in trying to cope with "the managed care movement", a major information revolution has quietly occurred around them. This movement comes with tremendous promise to aid and assist the provider, and ultimately, the client, but also brings with it many ethical issues and concerns associated with the safekeeping and care of computerized patient information (Freedman, 1994).

THE COMPUTERIZED OFFICE

As computers become more integrated into child therapy practices, the typical provider office will change from "cottage industry" to a high tech center for the provision of therapeutic services. If the leading prognosticators (Cummings, 1995) are accurate, most child behavioral health-care providers will practice in organized groups or in integrated health-care settings. This trend away from the child therapist in a solo practice to a group practice setting will necessitate an administrative structure that manages the finances of health care and controls the flow of clients. This structure, in turn, also produces pressure for accountability as well as a need for a communication system that permits child behavioral health-care workers to communicate with each other, the administrative structure,

and the payor system. Central to this approach is also the need for an office information system which schedules clients for appointments, compiles both assessment and treatment data, automatically prepares client chart notes, processes financial information, and collects various types of outcome measurement. These computerized systems also have the advanced capability to analyze stored data to generate cost information, select level and type of care needed, down-load electronic treatment plans, evaluate client improvement, examine provider and organizational effectiveness, collect fees, and connect to other provider systems (e.g., hospitals, residential treatment facilities). This type of system also follows a client-server model where one primary computer loaded with all necessary programs is networked to "work stations" for individual child therapist users.

The computerized office also changes various aspects of the intake process. Intake questionnaires and screening inventories can easily be administered at computer intake stations. This permits the availability of an appreciable amount of clinical and diagnostic information when a child or adolescent is seen for the first visit. Treatment plans can then be electronically generated and/or modified based on ratings of problems and issues from the intake process and the first session. Outcome measures can be selected and tracked using these systems.

Information sharing with children and their families can also take place in the computerized office. For example, CD-ROM technology permits the transmission of unlimited information to parents and clients about childhood behavior disorders, treatment, and so on. In addition, interactive learning modules can guide children and parents through educational materials designed to facilitate treatment. Parents can also interact with parent educational programs to address specific problems.

The addition of computer technology to the child therapist's office also permits access to the prescriptive treatment literature in any on-line library database. It also permits information sharing between providers (e.g., pediatrician, behavioral health provider) via secure internet domains. On-line forums with "expert" professionals can assist the child therapist in refining existing skills. Immediate access to pharmacological data bases can also alert the clinician to medication side-effects and to possible drug interactions. Virtual reality can simulate social interactions, parent-child interactions, classroom situations, and exposure to phobic stimuli (e.g., different elevations), to facilitate assessment and treatment.

BEHAVIORAL INFORMATICS IN THE DIAGNOSIS AND ASSESSMENT OF CHILDREN'S BEHAVIORAL DISORDERS

Tables 15.2 lists the general types of assessment instruments and programs available for clinical use. These include intake evaluations, diagnostic instruments, software for assessment of specific problems, problem behavior/symptom rating scales, cognitive evaluation, personality evaluation, and various utility programs.

On Line with DSM-IV

The Diagnostic and Statistical Manual of Mental Disorders (4th edition), DSM-IV, (American Psychiatric Association, 1994) is the recognized standard in this country for classification of psychological and psychiatric disorders. This system uses a multiaxial schema that allows the clinician to classify client characteristics across the following dimensions: Primary Clinical Disorders, Personality Disorders/Mental Retardation, General Medical Conditions, Psychosocial and Environmental Problems, and Assessment of Global Functioning. Thus, the diagnostic system is a formal categorization system and it also defines parameters relevant to assessment and treatment.

Various on-line products (see Table 15.3) are available to facilitate the process of making an accurate and meaningful diagnosis. A diagnostic software product (DICA-R) is available for assessment of children that presents the Diagnostic Interview for Children and Adolescents on-line for completion by either the child (ages 6–12 and 13–18 years of age) or a parent (Relch, Welner, & Herjanic, 1996). The program examines 22 different diagnostic entities and produces a number of clinical reports including a summary report, positive and negative symptoms, and a complete interview summary.

A second diagnostic aid developed by First, Williams, and Spitzer (1996) is the DTREE: The DSM-IV Expert. The clinician follows screen prompts consisting of simple "yes" or "no" responses about the client's presentation. The system uses a branching technology that reviews (or rules out) psychotic disorders, medical disorders, mood disorders, anxiety disorders, somatoform disorders and substance use disorders compiling a clinical diagnostic report.

Several additional computerized instruments are available that have applications in diagnostic screening. These diagnostic screening programs support parent-report interviews (both on-line and off-line) for children as well as self-report interviews for adolescents. Both of the Child and Adolescent Diagnostic Screening Batteries (1996) feature self-report and clinician-report (or parent-report) questionnaires which are completed off-line and then entered at the keyboard. In contrast, several instruments (Child and Adolescent Diagnostic Screening Inventory, 1996; Children's Diagnostic Scale, 1996; Children's Psychiatric Rating Scale, 1996) support on-line administration. The American Psychiatric Association has released an Electronic DSM-IV (1996) for use with either IBM or Macintosh formats. The system includes the entire DSM-IV, word for word, and is fully searchable by diagnostic code, term, phrase, and number. It is hyperlinked to allow rapid movement through the system. Using this system the clinician can quickly review diagnostic information and criteria thus facilitating the assessment process.

One other software product (OPTAIO Practice Manager, 1997) for the DSM-IV that allows the user to easily navigate the system using electronic menus and hyperlinked text references. This system is integrated with a billing module to link diagnoses to current procedural terminology (i.e., CPT codes) for processing billing information. The SMI system also integrates these components into a comprehensive computerized patient record which incorporates relational data bases to produce robust data analysis and report capabilities. The user is thus able to select diagnoses on-line, track outcome electronically and examine various types of financial, clinical, demographic, and administrative information to assist in providing cost effective care.

TABLE 15.2.   Computerized Assessment Instruments for Children and Adolescents

TYPES OF INSTRUMENTS	ON-LINE ADMINISTRATION	ELECTRONIC SCORING	NARRATIVE REPORTS
Intake			
Telephone Intake Histories	Yes	No	Yes
Psychosocial Histories	Yes	No	Yes
Screening Inventories	Yes	Yes	Yes
Mental Status Evaluations	Yes	Yes	Yes
Symptom Checklists	Yes	Yes	Yes
Diagnostic Systems			
DSM-IV	Yes	NA	NA
Diagnostic Formulations	Yes	Yes	Yes
Assessment of Specific Problems			
Anxiety	Yes	Yes	Yes
ADHD	Yes	Yes	Yes
Chemical Dependency	Yes	Yes	Yes
Depression	Yes	Yes	Yes
Development Assessment	Yes	Yes	Yes
Domestic Violence	Yes	Yes	Yes
Eating Disorders	Yes	Yes	Yes
Self-Concept Scales	Yes	Yes	Yes
Stress Assessment	Yes	Yes	Yes
Suicidality	Yes	Yes	Yes
Problem Behavior/Symptom Rating Scales			
General	Yes	Yes	Yes
School	Yes	Yes	Yes
Institutional	Yes	Yes	Yes
Cognitive Evaluation			
Intellectual Assessment	No	Yes	Yes
Neuropsychological Screening	Yes	Yes	Yes
Neuropsychological Norms	No	Yes	Yes
Academic Achievement	Yes	Yes	Yes
Personality Evaluation			
Projective	No	Yes	Yes
Objective	Yes	Yes	Yes
Screening	Yes	Yes	Yes
Outcome Measurement			
Patient Satisfaction	Yes	Yes	Yes
Clinician Rating Scales	Yes	Yes	Yes
Psychometric Scales	Yes	Yes	Yes
Behavioral Tracking	Yes	Yes	Yes
Utility Programs			
Report Writing Programs	No	No	Yes
Scale Conversion Programs	Yes	Yes	Yes
Norm Development Programs	Yes	Yes	Yes

Computerized Assessment of Child and Adolescent Problems

The use of computers for scoring and interpreting psychological assessment instruments represents an early application of computer technology to the practice of psychology (Fowler, 1985). The early programs, however, were relatively limited in terms of functionality. For example, many allowed only the entry of data from previously scored paper-and-pencil instruments but did not administer protocols or score tests on-line.

This situation, however, has changed greatly. For example, Psychware Sourcebook (Krug, 1993)

TABLE 15.3. Intake Instruments: Psychosocial History and Screening

PRODUCT NAME	PUBLISHER	COMPUTER	PRICING	COST BASIS	ON-LINE ADMINISTRATION	ELECTRONIC SCORING	PROPERTIES
Psychosocial History							
Automated Child/Adolescent Social History (ACASH)	NCS/Professional Assessment Services	IBM	On-Site	Per Test	Yes	Yes	C, A, PRF, NR
Development History Checklist: Computer Report	Psychological Assessment Resources	IBM	On-Site	Unlimited			C, PRF or CRF, NR
Developmental History Report	MHS	IBM & Apple	On-Site	Unlimited	Yes	Yes	C, PRF, NR
Giannetti On-Line Psychosocial History	NCS/Professional Assessment Services	IBM	On-Site	Per Test	Yes	Yes	A, SRF, NR
Intake Evaluation Report (IER)	MHS	IBM & Apple	On-Site	Unlimited		Yes	A, CRF, NR
Pediatric Intake (PEDI)	Integrated Professional Systems	IBM	Mail-In; On-Site	Per test or Unlimited	Yes	Yes	C, PRF, NR, PP
Personal History Checklist Adolescent: Computer Report	Psychological Assessment Resources	IBM	On-Site	Unlimited			A, NR
Psychological/Social History Report	MHS	IBM	On-Site	Unlimited	Yes		A, NR
Psychological/Psychiatric Status Interview 2.0	MHS	IBM	On-Site	Unlimited	Yes		A, PRF, NR
Quickview Social History	NCS/Professional Assessment Services	IBM	On-Site	Per Test	Yes	Yes	A, SRF, NR
Screening							
Adolescent Diagnostic Screening Battery	Behavior Data Systems	IBM & Apple	On-Site	Unlimited			A, CRF, SRF, NR
Child and Adolescent Diagnostic Screening Inventory	Psychologists, Inc.	IBM	On-Site	Unlimited	Yes		C, A, PRF, or CRF
Child Diagnostic Screening	Reason House	IBM & Apple	On-Site	Unlimited			C, SRF or PRF, CRF
Children Diagnostic Scale	Integrated Professional Systems	IBM	Mail-in; On-Site	Per Test or Unlimited	Yes		C, A, CRF
Children Psychiatric Rating Scale	Integrated Professional Systems	IBM	Mail-in; On-Site	Per Test or Unlimited	Yes		C, A, CRF
Diagnostic Interview for Children/Adolescents-Revised	MHS	IBM	On-Site	Unlimited	Yes	Yes	C, A, PRF, SRF, NR, M
(RISK) Rating Inventory for Screening Kindergartners	PRO-ED	IBM & Apple	On-Site	Unlimited	Yes		C, TRF,
Screening Children for Related Early Educational Needs	PRO-ED	IBM & Apple	On-Site	Unlimited	Yes		C, TRF, NR

Properties: C = Child; A = Adolescent; CRF = Clinician-Report Form; PRF = Parent-Report-Form; SRF = Self-Report Form; TRF = Teacher-Report Form; NR = Narrative Report; M = Manual; PP = Psychometric Properties; IX = Interactive.

offers a comprehensive listing and analysis of available software for behavioral health. Additionally, it includes sample interpretative reports for many of these computerized instruments. Available to the clinician are numerous instruments allowing for the automation of many facets of child assessment, with on-line assessment capabilities including administration, scoring, and interpretation. Utility software is also reviewed which transforms paper-and-pencil inventories to on-line products along with software which produces comprehensive reports for virtually all categories of psychometric instruments including those administered on-line and off-line. Products are differentiated on the basis of features/functionality: on-line administration/off-line administration, scoring (on-site, mail-in, or teleprocessing), cost (unlimited or finite number of administrations), automated interpretation, production of narrative reports, editing from word processing files, and so on. Given that most children and adolescents are growing up with computers as an integral component of their education, the application of computer technology to the practice of child and adolescent assessment offers the clinician a powerful tool to streamline his or her practice, while engaging the child in a way that paper-and-pencil instruments simply cannot.

Most of the computerized instruments are available for IBM-compatible computers and some are also available for Apple computers. A few instruments are available only for Apple computers. In addition, many of these instruments have good psychometric properties associated with them, including separate child and adolescent normative data, however, before utilizing these instruments, the practitioner should examine the psychometric properties of these instruments in relation to the intended population. Computerized evaluative instruments can be very impressive in function and form but may lack strong empirical support.

These computerized assessment products offer rapid scoring, interpretation of test results and report-generation, and reduce professional time and effort. Many of these programs permit the user to send the finished document to a word processing file so that it can be modified or incorporated into other documents. Clerical time and expense is also reduced, especially with systems which use sophis-

ticated report writing technology. Turnaround time for delivery of the product (e.g., report-out to parents) can also be reduced significantly.

Overview of Computerized Assessment Products

A number of different types of products are available to the child therapist for use at different points along the assessment continuum.

Intake Instruments

Included in this category are instruments (see Tables 15.3 and 15.4) assessing psychosocial history, general mental status and specific behavioral and/or physical health symptoms, as well as screening instruments that may aid in diagnostic formulations and in the identification of early educational needs, such as speech and language difficulties.

Several software publishers offer a range of age-appropriate psychosocial history instruments, including instruments allowing on-line developmental history-taking via parent input as well as self-report instruments for use with adolescents (see Table 15.3). For example, the Automated Child/Adolescent Social History (Rhode, 1996) is a parent-report form whereas the Giannetti On-line Psychosocial History (Giannetti, 1996) and the Quickview Social History (Giannetti, 1996) each assess psychosocial history via adolescent self-report. All three instruments utilize sophisticated "branching" technology thus tailoring the interview based on the previous response given, thereby truncating the interview considerably. In addition, each produces a detailed narrative report. Structured interviews have also been developed for children (e.g., Developmental History Report 4.0 by Rainwater & Slade, 1996) and for adolescents (e.g., Psychological/Social History Report 4.0 by Rainwater & Coe, 1996; Psychological/Psychiatric Status Interview 2.0 by Honaker & Harrell, 1996). In addition to the latter two instruments completed by the adolescent, the Intake Evaluation Report (Harrell & Honaker, 1996), is a program that is completed by the clinician following his or her initial evaluation of a client. Report-writing programs for

TABLE 15.4. Intake Instruments: Mental Status Evaluations and Symptom Checklists

PRODUCT NAME	PUBLISHER	COMPUTER	PRICING	COST BASIS	ON-LINE ADMINISTRATION	ELECTRONIC SCORING	PROPERTIES
Mental Status Evaluations							
Mental Status Checklist-Adolescent: Computer Report	Psychological Assessment Resources	IBM	On-Site	Unlimited			A, NR
Mental Status Checklist-Adolescent: Computer Report	Psychological Assessment Resources	IBM	On-Site	Unlimited			C, NR
Symptom Checklists							
Brief Symptom Checklist (BSI)	NCS/Professional Assessment Services	IBM	On-Site	Per Test	Yes	Yes	A, SRF, NR, M, PP
Comprehensive Survey of Symptoms 77 (SS-77)	The Psychological Corporation	IBM	On-Site	Unlimited	Yes	Yes	A, SRF, M
Health Status Questionnaire Compute Scoring and Report	The Psychological Corporation	IBM	On-Site	Unlimited	Yes	Yes	A, SRF, M. NR
Symptom Checklist-90-Revised (SCL-90-R)	NCS/Professional Assessment Services	IBM	On-Site	Per Test	Yes	Yes	A, SRF, M, NR, PP

Properties: C = Child; A = Adolescent; CRF = Clinician-Report Form; PRF = Parent-Report-Form; SRF = Self-Report Form; TRF = Teacher-Report Form; NR = Narrative Report; M = Manual; PP = Psychometric Properties; IX = Interactive.

the Developmental History Checklist (Dougherty & Schinka, 1996) and for the Personal History Checklist—Adolescent (Dougherty & Schinka, 1996) are also available although neither program allows for on-line administration; however, the Pediatric Intake (1993) software program gathers basic social and demographic information about a child and his or her family via clinician-report on- or off-line.

Screening instruments for early educational needs are also available such as the RISK (1996) and the SCREEN (1996). The RISK is designed to predict future school difficulties with kindergarten children via screening of such areas as social, behavioral, and motor functioning. The SCREEN is an academic screening test for children ages 3–7 sampling abilities in such areas as reading, writing, and arithmetic. SCREEN also produces a detailed narrative report.

Table 15.4 lists mental status evaluations and symptom checklists available to the clinician, for example, the Mental Status Checklist-Children (Dougherty & Schinka, 1996) and the Mental Status Checklist-Adolescent (Dougherty & Schinka, 1996). Each produce a comprehensive report following paper-and-pencil administration. In addition, when combined with the corresponding intake checklist report (e.g., Personal History Checklist-Adolescent by Dougherty & Schinka, 1996), each provides the clinician with a comprehensive overall report.

Finally, several computerized behavioral and/or physical health symptom checklists are available for on-line administration, scoring, and report generation with adolescents. These include three behavioral symptom checklists: the Symptom Checklist-90-Revised (SCL-90-R, by Derogatis, 1996), the Brief Symptom Inventory (BSI) (Derogatis, 1996), and the Comprehensive Survey of Symptoms 77 (Johnson, 1995). Both the SCL-90-R and the BSI offer separate norms for nonpatient adolescents, as well as psychiatric outpatients and inpatients. The Health Status Questionnaire Computer Scoring and Report (HSQ) (1996) is a brief questionnaire assessing broad-based health, including physical and social functioning and emotional well-being. The HSQ supports off-line administration only but produces a brief report.

Assessment of Specific Problems

Available to the clinician are a number of software programs (see Tables 15.5 and 15.6) to assess client problems in specialized areas. These instruments are listed alphabetically by problem area. They include programs appropriate for assessing anxiety and depression in children and adolescents (see Table 15.5), including computerized versions of well-known tests such as the Children's State-Trait Anxiety Inventory (1996) and the State-Trait Anxiety Inventory (1996), suitable for older adolescents (>17), as well as the Children's Depression Inventory (1996).

Two other on-line self-report depression questionnaires are available for older adolescents, the Multiscore Depression Inventory for Children (1996) and the Multiscore Depression Inventory (1996) suitable for older adolescents. Two other instruments, the Reynolds Child Depression Scale (1996) and the Reynolds Adolescent Depression Scale (1996) have computer programs that score and interpret the responses following off-line administration. For use with older adolescents (>17) are several of Beck's scales including the Beck Depression Inventory (1996), the Beck Scale for Suicide Ideation (1996), the Beck Hopelessness Scale (1996), and the Beck Anxiety Inventory (1996). A second computerized instrument to assess suicidality is the Inventory of Suicide Orientation-30 (ISO-30) (King & Lowalchuk, 1996). Designed to help identify adolescents at risk for suicide, the ISO-30 utilizes scores in two areas: hopelessness and suicide ideation, to help classify overall suicidal risk.

Perhaps the most innovative computerized instruments are in the area of Attention Deficit Hyperactivity Disorder (see Table 15.5). Two programs, the ADD-H Comprehensive Teacher's Rating Scale-2 (1996) and the Conners' Rating Scale Computer Program (1996), facilitate on-line assessment of ADHD behaviors, by teachers and/or parents, and thereby offer the clinician direct observation data to supplement paper-and-pencil data. Both systems feature strong psychometric properties and offer the ability to confirm a suspected diagnosis of ADHD, as well as to monitor the effect of stimulant medication.

TABLE 15.5. Assessment of Specific Problems: Anxiety, ADHD, Chemical Dependency, and Depression

PRODUCT NAME	PUBLISHER	COMPUTER	PRICING	COST BASIS	ON-LINE ADMINISTRATION	ELECTRONIC SCORING	PROPERTIES
Anxiety							
Beck Anxiety Inventory	The Psychological Corporation	IBM	On-Site	Per Test	Yes	Yes	A, SRF, NR, M, PP
Children's State-Trait Anxiety Inventory Computer Program	MHS	IBM & Apple	On-Site	Per Test	Yes	Yes	C, SRF, PP
Coping With Tests	Consulting Psychologists Press	IBM & Apple	On-Site	Unlimited		Yes	A, SRF, IX
Endler Multidimensional Anxiety Scales (EMAS)	Western Psychological Services	IBM	Mail-In; On-Site; Teleprocessing	Per Test	Yes	Yes	A, SRF, NR, M, PP
State-Trait Anxiety Inventory Computer Program	MHS	IBM & Apple	On-Site	Per Test	Yes	Yes	A, SRF, PP
ADHD							
ADD-H Comprehensive Teacher's Rating Scale-2	Metric Tech	IBM	On-Site	Unlimited	Yes	Yes	C, TRF, PP
Captain's Log: Cognitive Training System	Braintrain	IBM & Apple	On-Site	Unlimited	Yes	Yes	C, A, SRF, IX
Conners' Rating Scales Computer	MHS	IBM	On-Site	Per Test	Yes	Yes	C, A, PRF, TRF, NR, M, PP
Conners' Continuous Performance Test (CPT 3.0)	MHS	IBM	On-Site	Unlimited	Yes	Yes	C, A, SRF, NR, M, PP, IX
Gordon Diagnostic System	Gordon Systems	IBM	On-Site	Unlimited	Yes	Yes	C, A, SRF, M, IX
IVA Computerized Visual and Auditory CPT	Braintrain	IBM	On-Site	Per Test	Yes	Yes	C, A, SRF, NR, M, PP, IX
Test of Variables of Attention (TOVA)	Universal Attention Disorders	IBM & Apple	On-Site	Per Test or Unlimited	Yes	Yes	C, A, SRF, NR, M, FP, IX
Vigil	ForThought	IBM	On-Site	Unlimited	Yes	Yes	C, A, SRF,IX

Properties: C = Child; A = Adolescent; CRF = Clinician-Report Form; PRF = Parent-Report-Form; SRF = Self-Report Form; NR = Narrative Report; M = Manual; PP = Psychometric Properties; IX = Interactive.

continued

480

TABLE 15.5. Assessment of Specific Problems: Anxiety, ADHD, Chemical Dependency, and Depression, continued

PRODUCT NAME	PUBLISHER	COMPUTER	PRICING	COST BASIS	ON-LINE ADMINISTRATION	ELECTRONIC SCORING	PROPERTIES
Chemical Dependency							
Adolescent Chemical Dependency Inventory	Behavior Data Systems, Ltd.	IBM	On-Site	Per Test		Yes	A, SRF, NR, M, PP
Alcohol Use Inventory	NCS/Professional Assessment Services	IBM	Mail-In; On-Site; Teleprocessing	Per Test	Yes	Yes	A, SRF, NR, M, PP
Assessment of Chemical Health Inventory	Recovery Software, Inc.	IBM	On-Site	Per Test	Yes	Yes	A, SRF, NR, PP
Chemical Dependency Assessment Profile	Psychologists, Inc.	IBM & Apple	On-Site	Unlimited	Yes		A, SRF, NR
If You Drink	MHS	IBM	On-Site	Unlimited	Yes	Yes	A, SRF, IX
Minnesota Assessment of Chemical Health (MACH)	IPS International Professional Services, Inc.	IBM	On-Site	Per Test or Unlimited	Yes	Yes	A, SRF, PP, IX
Personal Experience Inventory	Western Psychological Services	IBM	Mail-In; On-Site	Per Test	Yes	Yes	A, SRF, NR, M, PP
Depression							
Beck Depression Inventory	The Psychological Corporation	IBM	On-Site	Per Test	Yes	Yes	A, SRF, NR, M, PP
Beck Hopelessness Scale	The Psychological Corporation	IBM	On-Site	Per Test	Yes	Yes	A, SRF, NR, M, PP
Children's Depression Inventory (CDI)	MHS	IBM	On-Site	Per Test	Yes	Yes	C, A, SRF, NR, M, PP
Multi-Score Depression Inventory (MDI)	Western Psychological Services	IBM	Mail-In; On-Site	Per Test	Yes	Yes	A, SRF, NR, M, PP
Multi-Score Depression Inventory Children (MDIC)	Western Psychological Services	IBM	Mail-In; On-Site	Per Test	Yes	Yes	C, A, SRF, NR, M, PP
Reynolds Adolescent Depression Scale (RADS)	Psychological Assessment Resources, Inc.	IBM	Mail-In	Per Test		Yes	A, NR, PP
Reynolds Child Depression Scale (CDS)	Psychological Assessment Resources, Inc.	IBM	Mail-In	Per Test		Yes	A, NR, PP

Properties: C = Child; A = Adolescent; CRF = Clinician-Report Form; PRF = Parent-Report-Form; SRF = Self-Report Form; TRF = Teacher-Report Form; NR = Narrative Report; M = Manual; PP = Psychometric Properties; IX = Interactive.

TABLE 15.6. Assessment of Specific Problems: Development, Domestic Violence, Eating Disorders, Self-Concept, Stress, and Suicidality

PRODUCT NAME	PUBLISHER	COMPUTER	PRICING	COST BASIS	ON-LINE ADMINISTRATION	ELECTRONIC SCORING	PROPERTIES
Developmental Abilities/Disabilities							
Arlin Test of Formal Reasoning-Computer Report (ATFR-CR)	Slosson Educational Publications	IBM & Apple	On-Site	Unlimited			C, A, NR
ASIEP Computerized Scoring and Interpretation Program	PRO-ED	Apple	On-Site	Unlimited		Yes	C, A, NR
California Adaptive Behavior Scale (CABS)	Planet Press	IBM & Apple	On-Site	Unlimited	Yes	Yes	C, A, PRF, NR, PP
Compuscore for the Scales of Independent Behavior	The Riverside Publishing Company	IBM & Apple	On-Site	Unlimited		Yes	C, A, NR, PP
Developmental Profile II	Western Psychological Services	IBM	Mail-In;	Per Test	Yes	Yes	C, PRF, NR, PP
Emotional Problems Scales Computer Report	Psychological Assessment Resources	IBM	On-Site	Unlimited	Yes	Yes	A, NR, PP
Functional Skills Screening Inventory	Functional Assessment and Training Consultants	IBM & Apple	On-Site	Unlimited		Yes	C, A, NR
Test of Adolescent Language-2 (TOAL-2)	PRO-ED	Apple	On-Site	Unlimited		Yes	A, NR, PP
Vineland Adaptive Behavior Scales-ASSIST	American Guidance Service	IBM & Apple	On-Site	Unlimited		Yes	C, A, NR, PP
Domestic Violence							
CAPSCORE 1.04 (Child Abuse Potential Inventory)	Psytek	IBM & Apple	On-Site	Per Test		Yes	PRF, PP
Domestic Violence Inventory (DVI)	Risk & Needs Assessment	IBM	On-Site	Per Test		Yes	PRF, NR, PP

Properties: C = Child; A = Adolescent; CRF = Clinician-Report Form; PRF = Parent-Report-Form; SRF = Self-Report Form; TRF = Teacher-Report Form; NR = Narrative Report; M = Manual; PP = Psychometric Properties; IX = Interactive.

TABLE 15.6. Assessment of Specific Problems: Development, Domestic Violence, Eating Disorders, Self-Concept, Stress, and Suicidality, continued

PRODUCT NAME	PUBLISHER	COMPUTER	PRICING	COST BASIS	ON-LINE ADMINISTRATION	ELECTRONIC SCORING	PROPERTIES
Eating Disorders							
Eating Disorder Inventory-2 (EDI-2): Computer Version	Psychological Assessment Resources	IBM	On-Site	Per Test	Yes	Yes	A, SRF, NR, M, PP
Self-Concept Scales							
Dimensions of Self-Concept	Educational and Industrial Testing	IBM	Mail-In	Per Test		Yes	C, A, SRF, M, PP
Perception of Ability Scale for Students (PASS)	Western Psychological Services	IBM	Mail-In	Per Test		Yes	C, SRF, NR, M, PP
Piers-Harris Children's Self-Concept Scale	Western Psychological Services	IBM	Mail-In; On-Site; Teleprocessing	Per Test	Yes	Yes	C, A, SRF, NR, M, PP
Tennessee Self-Concept Scale	Western Psychological Services	IBM	Mail-In; On-Site; Teleprocessing	Per Test	Yes	Yes	A, SRF, NR, M, PP
Stress Assessment							
Coping Inventory for Stressful Situations (CISS)	MHS	IBM	On-Site	Per Test	Yes	Yes	A, SRF, NR, M, PP
Parenting Stress Index (PSI) Software System	Psychological Assessment Resources	IBM	On-Site	Per Test	Yes	Yes	PRF, M, PP
PSI Professional Report Service	Psychological Assessment Resources	IBM	Mail-In	Per Test	Yes	Yes	NR, PP
Suicidality							
Beck Hopelessness Scale	The Psychological Corporation	IBM	On-Site	Per Test	Yes	Yes	A, SRF, NR, M, PP
Beck Scale for Suicide Ideation	The Psychological Corporation	IBM	On-Site	Per Test	Yes	Yes	A, SRF, NR, M, PP
Inventory of Suicide Orientation	NCS/Professional Assessment Services	IBM	On-Site	Per Test	Yes	Yes	A, SRF, NR, M, PP

Properties: C = Child; A = Adolescent; CRF = Clinician-Report Form; PRF = Parent-Report-Form; SRF = Self-Report Form; TRF = Teacher-Report Form; NR = Narrative Report; M = Manual; PP = Psychometric Properties; IX = Interactive.

A second category of these instruments includes a new generation of interactive tests of sustained attention. These instruments, listed in Table 15.5, allow for *in-vivo* assessment of inattention and impulsivity, in some cases distinguishing between visual and auditory inattention, and in other cases allowing for differential diagnosis of an attentional deficit versus other learning disabilities. Many of these instruments offer the ability to diagnose an attentional deficit, as well as to monitor symptoms and/or response to medication over time. These interactive instruments include the Conners' Continuous Performance Test (CPT 3.0) (1996), the Gordon Diagnostic System (1996), the IVA Computerized Visual and Auditory Continuous Performance Test (CPT) (1996), the Test of Variables of Attention CPT (TOVA) (1996), and Vigil (1996). These tools are all variants of the continuous performance test (CPT), which require a keyboard response when target stimuli are presented. Stimuli may be language- or nonlanguage-based and may additionally be presented visually or auditorially. Each monitors several outcome variables, including response times and errors of commission (responding when there is no target) and omission (failing to respond when a target is presented). A final instrument, the Captainís Log: Cognitive Training System (1996), was developed for the training of multiple cognitive skills, including attention and concentration, with learning disabled and other cognitively disabled populations, but has been used recently in the diagnosis and treatment of ADHD. Most germane to ADHD is an attentional module which involves a visual tracking task.

Several of these instruments (IVA, TOVA, and Conners' CPT) were reviewed by Rosen (1995b), who summarized the important features of each. As pointed out by Rosen, both the IVA and TOVA provide immediate feedback and produce extensive narrative reports of results. Additionally, the IVA allows for a differential assessment of visual and auditory inattention. All three have extensive manuals and demonstrate high validity and reliability. As a group, these instruments are very versatile and offer the clinician rapid on-line assessment. Of note is the potential value of these instruments in monitoring the effects of medication in reducing ADHD symptoms.

Computerized programs are also available for assessing such problems as chemical abuse/dependency (see Table 15.5) and eating disorders (see Table 15.6). For example, the Eating Disorder Inventory-2 (1996) is suitable for ages 12 and older and assesses a range of psychological symptoms associated with the development and maintenance of eating disorders. All facets of administration are computerized. Several computerized products designed specifically to detect adolescent alcohol and chemical abuse are also available. These include the Adolescent Chemical Dependency Inventory (1996), the Assessment of Chemical Health Inventory (1996), the Personal Experience Inventory (1996), and the Chemical Dependency Assessment Profile (Honaker, Harrell, & Ciminero, 1996). The latter instrument assesses drinking history, patterns of reinforcement, beliefs about chemical dependency, and self-concept and relationships. Horn, Wanberg, and Foster (1996) have developed the Alcohol Use Inventory, which measures a broad spectrum of factors related to problem drinking including benefits, styles, consequences, concerns, and subtle drinking attitudes. This instrument is normed on 1,200 individuals treated in residential programs. As a group, these instruments are useful in the detection, referral, and treatment of alcohol and chemical abuse and related problems with adolescents.

Several other chemical dependency instruments are interactive. The Minnesota Assessment of Chemical Health (1996) features an interactive interview that "branches" to substantially reduce administration time. It includes a database with multiple criteria for establishing problem drinking and is normed on an adolescent sample. "If You Drink" (Meier, 1996) is an interactive tool designed for adolescents and adults with several modules to assess attitudes and knowledge about drinking and provide education in these areas.

Specialty scales are also available for assessment of self-concept (see Table 15.6), including computerized versions of such well-known and well-validated instruments as the Piers-Harris Children's Self-Concept Scale (1996), appropriate for use with children and adolescents, and the Tennessee Self-Concept Scale (1996) for ages 12 and older. Both feature on-line administration and detailed narrative reports. Also available is the Perception of Ability Scale for Students (1996), a well-validated instrument that assesses academic self-concept specifically related to the identification and remediation of high-risk children in grades 3-6. The Dimensions of Self-Concept (1996) also assesses academic self-concept with separate forms for elementary, secondary, and college-level students.

Several programs are available for the identification and evaluation of stress (Table 15.6). The Coping Inventory for Stressful Situations (1996) examines different coping styles and provides extensive normative data and a narrative report. The Parenting Stress Index Software System (PSI3 Plus) (1996), is a computerized version of the PSI featuring on-line administration, scoring, and narrative report generation. The PSI3 Plus identifies parent-child stress in two domains, Child and Parent, and is appropriate for use with parents with children 12 years of age or younger.

Numerous computerized instruments are available in the area of developmental abilities/disabilities (see Table 15.6). The majority of these instruments offer computerized scoring and report generation following assessment of functional skills and/or problem behaviors off-line. Instruments are available for individuals with disabilities including: Pervasive Developmental Disorder (Autism Screening Instrument for Educational Planning (ASIEP) Computerized Scoring and Interpretation Program, 1996), mental retardation and other developmental disabilities (California Adaptive Behavior Scale, 1996; Compuscore for the Scales of Independent Living, 1996; Emotional Problem Scales Computer Report, 1996; Vineland Adaptive Behavior Scales-ASSIST, 1996), and multiple disabilities, including physical disability (Functional Skills Screening Inventory, 1996). The Arlin Test of Formal Reasoning-Computer Report (ATFR-CR) (1996) offers computerized scoring and narrative report generation for the ATFR, which assesses cognitive abilities according to Piaget's five stages of cognitive development. The Test of Adolescent Language-2 (TOAL-2) (1996) is a computerized scoring system and report generation device for the TOAL-2, a multi-component language assessment device for children experiencing language problems.

Problem Behavior/Symptom Scales

Computerized scales which assess problem behaviors/symptoms (see Table 15.7) in children or adolescents are listed alphabetically under one of three headings: General, School-Based, and Institutional. Among scales with more general usefulness are several well-known instruments with sound psychometric properties, including the Louisville Behavior Checklist (1996) and Parent Questionnaire (Conners, 1996). Both of these instruments feature computerized assessment of behaviors associated with psychopathology via parent-report form, along with scoring and report generation. The Children's Behavior Inventory (1996) similarly is a computerized instrument completed on-line by the clinician. BASC Plus (Behavior Assessment for Children-BASC Plus, 1996) offers a comprehensive assessment of a child's personality and behavior through multiple sources of assessment, including self-report, parent report, teacher report, classroom observation, and a psychosocial history. BASC Plus software supports on-line administration and scoring and additionally performs validity checks and graphically displays all scaled scores in a narrative report. Several instruments are designed specifically to assess behavioral, emotional, and personality characteristics of adolescents and are geared toward identifying adolescents at risk for delinquent behavior. These include the Hilson Adolescent Profile (1996), the Jesness Behavior Checklist Computer Program (1996) and the Jesness Inventory Computer Program (1996).

Among instruments for school and institutional use, several are designed for evaluation of mental retardation, autism, and severe behavioral/emotional disorders in school-age children (Table 15.7). These scales include the Adaptive Behavior Inventory (1996), the Adaptive Behavior Scale-School, Second Edition (1996), and the Adaptive Behavior Scale-Residential and Community, Second Edition (1996). These scales assist in screening and placement by assessing adaptive behaviors which are central to personal responsibility and independent living. The Teacher Questionnaire (Conners, 1996) is the school-based version of the Conner's Parent Questionnaire, off-

TABLE 15.7. Problem Behavior/Symptom Scales

PRODUCT NAME	PUBLISHER	COMPUTER	PRICING	COST BASIS	ON-LINE ADMINISTRATION	ELECTRONIC SCORING	PROPERTIES
General							
Behavior Assessment System for Children-BASC PLUS	American Guidance Service	IBM	On-Site	Per Test or Unlimited	Yes	Yes	C, A, PRF, TRF, SRF, NR, M, PP
Children Behavior Inventory	Integrated Professional Systems	IBM	Mail-In; On-Site	Per Test or Unlimited	Yes	Yes	C, A, CRF
Hilson Adolescent Profile (HAP)	Hilson Research	IBM	Mail-In Teleprocessing	Per Test	Yes	Yes	A, SRF, NR, PP
Jesness Behavior Check List Computer Program	MHS	IBM	On-Site	Per Test			A, CRF, SRF, M
Jesness Inventory Computer Program	MHS	IBM	On-Site	Per Test	Yes	Yes	C, A, SRF, NR,M
Louisville Behavior Checklist	Western Pyschological Services	IBM & Apple	Mail-In; On-Site	Per Test	Yes	Yes	C, A, PRF, NR,M, PP
Parent Questionnaire	Integrated Professional Systems	IBM	Mail-In; On-Site	Per-Test or Unlimited	Yes	Yes	C, A, PRF
Psychological Examination Behavior Profile	Integrated Professional Systems	IBM	Mail-In; On-Site	Per-Test or Unlimited	Yes	Yes	C, A, CR
School-Based							
Adaptive Behavior Inventory	PRO-ED	Apple	On-Site	Unlimited		Yes	C, TRF, NR
Adaptive Behavior Scale-School, 2nd Edition	MHS	IBM	On-Site	Per Test		Yes	C, A, TRF, NR
Teacher Questionnaire	Integrated Professional Systems	IBM	Mail-In; On-Site	Per Test or Unlimited	Yes	Yes	C, A, TRF
Institutional							
Adaptive Behavior Scale-Residential and Community Edition	MHS	IBM	On-Site	Per Test		Yes	A, CRF, NR,M, PP
Children Psychiatric Rating Scale	Integrated Professional Systems	IBM	Mail-In; On-Site	Per Test or Unlimited	Yes	Yes	C, A, CRF
Psychiatric Rating Scale A (PRS-A)	Integrated Professional Systems	IBM	Mail-In; On-Site	Per Test or Unlimited	Yes	Yes	A, CRF

Properties: C = Child; A = Adolescent; CRF = Clinician-Report Form; PRF = Parent-Report-Form; SRF = Self-Report Form; TRF = Teacher-Report Form; NR = Narrative Report; M = Manual; PP = Psychometric Properties; IX = Interactive.

ering on-line teacher ratings of symptoms typically associated with behavioral disorders of children.

Two instruments allow on-line observer ratings in inpatient psychiatric settings. The first, the Children's Psychiatric Rating Scale (1996), is appropriate for children 15 years of age and younger, while the Psychiatric Rating Scale A (PRS-A) (1996), is appropriate for assessing treatment response in older adolescents. Additional computerized assessment products that might be of value to the clinician include symptom inventories such as the Brief Symptom Inventory (Derogatis, 1996) and the SCL-90-R (Derogatis, 1996), both of which produce computerized narrative reports describing presenting symptomology.

An interesting development is the Computerized Assessment System for Psychotherapy Evaluation and Research (CASPER) (McCullough, Farrell, & Longabaugh, 1986). CASPER is used to identify presenting problems, track these problems over time, and evaluate treatment outcome. Once particular problems have been identified, then additional questions which further define the problem are presented for response. During subsequent interviews, the client's problem list is accessed and additional ratings can be entered to reflect changes over time. This system has been subjected to psychometric evaluation and meets basic requirements for internal consistency, convergent validity, and discriminant validity.

Cognitive Evaluation

Available to the clinician are numerous instruments (see Table 15.8) for use with the Wechsler scales (WPPSI-R, WISC-III, WAIS-R). Most of these programs produce narrative reports for one or more of these scales following entry of standard scale scores and IQ scores. For example, the Report Writer: Children's Intellectual and Achievement Tests—4.0 (1996) provides comprehensive psychoeducational reports for most intellectual and achievement tests suitable for children and adolescents, including the Wechsler Scales, the Stanford-Binet Intelligence Scale, the Kaufman Test of Educational Achievement, the Kaufman Assessment Battery for Children, the Peabody Individual Achievement Test-Revised, and the Woodcock-Johnson Achievement

Tests. Following entry of demographic data, standard test scores for one or more tests, along with behavioral observations, Report Writer provides most of the report, including behavioral observations, statistical comparisons, pattern analysis, and educational recommendations. In addition, the Scoring Assistant for the Wechsler Scales (1996), the WISC-III Writer: Interpretative Software System (1996), the WPPSI-R Writer: Interpretive Software System (1996), and the WAIS-R Microcomputer-Assisted Interpretive Report (1996) combine narrative report generation with all phases of scoring, including norm table conversions, ability/achievement discrepancies, and score difference analyses. The WISC-III Writer allows the user to choose among three report formats; an extensive clinical report, a parent report, and a report solely composed of tables and graphs.

Halstead-Reitan normative programs are also available (e.g., HRB Norms Program, 1996; Comprehensive Norms for an Expanded Halstead-Reitan Battery, 1996). Another program uses the Russell, Neuringer, and Sparks scoring system to generate ratings, calculate test findings and summarize various hypotheses in a narrative report (Halstead-Reitan Neuropsychological Test Battery, 1996). The Halstead-Reitan Hypothesis Generator (1996) is also available to automatically provide data interpretation based on keyboard entry of test scores. On-line administration and scoring of the Halstead Category Test (Category Test Computer Program, 1996; Halstead Category Test-A Computer Version, 1996) is also available. In addition, on-line administration and scoring of the Wisconsin Card Sort Test (WCST) is available Wisconsin Card Sort Test Computer Version-2 Research Edition, 1996). There is also a program available for use with children and adults that scores and provides interpretation of the Luria-Nebraska Neurological Test Battery (1996), as well as an on-line version of the MicroCog: Assessment of Cognitive Functioning (1996) which measures a variety of cognitive skills including attention, memory, reasoning, spatial processing, reaction time, and other measures of cognitive efficiency. Two different aphasia screening instruments (Western Aphasia Battery Scoring Assistant, 1996; Boston Diagnostic Aphasia Examination, 1996) are available.

TABLE 15.8. Intellectual Assessment, Neuropsychological/Norms, Neuropsychological Screening, and Academic Achievement Assessment

PRODUCT NAME	PUBLISHER	COMPUTER	PRICING	COST BASIS	ON-LINE ADMINISTRATION	ELECTRONIC SCORING	PROPERTIES
Intellectual Assessment							
Report Writer: Children's Intellectual and Achievement Tests-4.0	MHS	IBM	On-Site	Unlimited			C, A, NR, PP
Report Writer: WISC-III/WISC-R/WPPSI-R	Psychological Assessment Resources	IBM	On-Site	Unlimited			C, NR, PP
Scoring Assistant for the Wechsler Scales	The Psychological Corporation	IBM & Apple	On-Site	Unlimited		Yes	C, A, M, PP
WAIS-R Microcomputer-Assisted Interpretive Report	The Psychological Corporation	IBM & Apple	On-Site	Unlimited		Yes	A, M, PP
WAIS-R Narrative Report Program	Psychological Testing Service	IBM	On-Site; Teleprocessing	Per Test or Unlimited			A, NR, PP
WAIS-R Report Version 3.0	Psychologists, Inc.	IBM & Apple	On-Site	Unlimited			A, NR, PP
Wechsler Interpretation System	AI Software	IBM & Apple	On-Site	Unlimited			C, A, NR, PP
WISC-III Report	Psychologists, Inc.	IBM & Apple	On-Site	Unlimited			C, A, NR, PP
WISC-III Report 3.0	MHS	IBM & Apple	On-Site	Unlimited			C, A, NR, PP
WISC-III Writer: Interpretive Software System	The Psychological Corporation	IBM & Apple	On-Site	Unlimited		Yes	C, A, NR, M, PP
WPPSI-R Writer: The Interpretive Software System	The Psychological Corporation	IBM	On-Site	Unlimited		Yes	C, A, NR,M. PP
WPPSI Report Version 2.0	Psychologists, Inc.	IBM & Apple	On-Site	Unlimited			A, NR, PP
Neuropsychological/Norms							
Category Test Computer Program 6.0	MHDS	IBM	On-Site	Unlimited	Yes	Yes	C, A, NR,M, PP
Halstead Category Test-A Computer Version	Precision People	IBM	On-Site	Unlimited	Yes	Yes	C, A, NR,M, PP
Halstead Reitan Battery (HRB Norms Program	MHS	IBM	On-Site	Unlimited		Yes	A, PP
HRB Norms Program	Psychological Assessment Resources	IBM	On-Site	Unlimited		Yes	A. PP
Halstead-Reitan Hypothesis Generator	Precision People	IBM	On-Site	Unlimited			A, PP

Properties: C = Child; A = Adolescent; CRF = Clinician-Report Form; NR = Narrative Report; M = Manual; PP = Psychometric Properties; IX = Interactive.

SRF = Self-Report Form; TRF = Teacher-Report Form; PRF = Parent-Report-Form;

continued

TABLE 15.8. Intellectual Assessment, Neuropsychological/Norms, Neuropsychological Screening, and Academic Achievement Assessment, continued

PRODUCT NAME	PUBLISHER	COMPUTER	PRICING	COST BASIS	ON-LINE ADMINISTRATION	ELECTRONIC SCORING	PROPERTIES
Luria-Nebraska Neuropsychological Battery	Western Psychological Services	IBM & Apple	Mail-In; On-Site	Per Test	Yes	Yes	C, A, NR, PP
MicroCog: Assessment of Cognitive Functioning	The Psychological Corporation	IBM	On-Site	Per Test	Yes	Yes	C, NR, PP
The Computerized Boston	The Psychological Corporation	IBM	On-Site	Unlimited		Yes	C, A, NR, M, PP
Western Aphasia Battery Scoring Assistant	The Psychological Corporation	IBM	On-Site	Unlimited		Yes	C, A, NR, M, PP
Wisconsin Card Sort Test Computer Version-2 Research Edition	MHS	IBM	On-Site	Unlimited	Yes	Yes	C, A, NR, M, PP
Neuropsychological Screening							
Bender Clinical Report	Precision People	IBM & Apple	On-Site	Unlimited			C, NR, PP
Bender Report 4.0	MHS	IBM	On-Site	Unlimited			C, NR, PP
Bender Report	Psychometric Software	IBM	On-Site	Unlimited			C, NR, PP
Academic Achievement Assessment							
Compuscore for the Woodcock-Johnson Battery-Revised	The Riverside Publishing Co.	IBM & Apple	On-Site	Unlimited		Yes	C, A, PP
Detroit Tests of Learning Aptitude (DTLA-3)	PRO-ED	IBM & Apple	On-Site	Unlimited		Yes	C, A, NR, PP
Diagnostic Achievement Battery-2 Second Edition	MHS	IBM & Apple	On-Site	Unlimited		Yes	C, NR, PP
DTLA-3 Software Scoring and Report	MHS	IBM & Apple	On-Site	Unlimited		Yes	C, A, NR, PP
Kaufman Assessment Battery for Children-ASSIST	American Guidance Service	IBM & Apple	On-Site	Unlimited		Yes	C, NR, M, PP
Oral nd Written Language Scales (OWLS)-ASSIST	American Guidance Service	IBM & Apple	On-Site	Unlimited		Yes	C, A, NR, M, PP
Tests of Language Development-2 Primary and Intermediate	MHS	IBM & Apple	On-Site	Unlimited		Yes	C, A, NR, M, PP

Properties: C = Child; A = Adolescent; CRF = Clinician-Report Form; PRF = Parent-Report-Form; SRF = Self-Report Form; TRF = Teacher-Report-Form; NR = Narrative Report; M = Manual; PP = Psychometric Properties; IX = Interactive.

Several software programs (see Table 15.6) to assist with neuropsychological screening are available. These include the Bender Report (1996), the Bender Clinical Report (1996) and the Bender Report 4.0 (1996). In addition, the Memory Assessment Scale (1996) allows for comparison of memory functions with Wechsler scores, while the Wechsler Memory Scale Report (1996) provides a scale by scale narrative for the Wechsler Memory Scale Report (WMS).

Electronic scoring and narrative report generation programs are available for such well-known and well-validated academic achievement batteries as the Detroit Tests of Learning Aptitude (DTLA) (DTLA-3, 1996; DTLA-P: 2, 1996), the Woodcock Johnson Psychoeducational Battery-Revised (Compuscore for WJB-Revised, 1996), the Kaufman Assessment Battery for Children (K-ABC-ASSIST) (1996), and the Oral and Written Language Scales (OWLS-ASSIST) (1996).

Broad-Based Personality Evaluation

Computerized versions of a number of popular broad-based assessment instruments (see Table 15.9) are also available. For example, software to score, interpret, and report projective test results (e.g., Rorschach Technique, 1996; Rorschach Interpretation Assistance Program, 1996; Exner's Rorschach Scoring Program, 1996; Hermann: The Rorschach Assistant, 1996; Rorschach Interpretation Program Version 3.1, 1996; Rorschach Scoring and Interpretation, 1996). There is also available scoring and interpretive programs for the House-Tree-Person Drawing Test and for the Human Figure Drawing Test (e.g., Projective Drawing Tests: Computer Analysis, 1996), and conversion norms for adolescent populations and an adolescent interpretative system.

For the Minnesota Multiphasic Personality Inventory-Adolescent (MMPI-A) Interpretative System Version 2 (1996) provides a structured summary of scored protocols, whereas the MMPI-A Interpretation System (1996) provides a detailed summary derived from scored protocols that includes profile validity, presenting problems, probable symptoms, treatment issues and suggestions, diagnostic

considerations, and configural interpretations. On-line administration, scoring, and report generation are also available (MMPI-A, 1996). A narrative report based on actuarial data derived from the Marks system for both children and adolescents (Marks MMPI Adolescent Report, 1996) is also available.

Software scoring and report packages have been developed for the Million Adolescent Clinical Inventory (1996), the Million Adolescent Personality Inventory (1996) and for adolescents 16 years and older the Sixteen Personality Factor Questionnaire (1996). There is also a computer software program for on-line administration, scoring, and interpretation of the Personality Inventory for Children (1996). Virtually all broad-based personality inventories for children are available for on-line administration, scoring, and report generation, including the following, presented with salient features in Table 15.7: the Adolescent Multiphasic Personality Inventory (1996), AUTOPACL (Adjective Checklist, 1996), the Basic Personality Inventory (1996), the Eysenck Personality Inventory Junior (1996), the Interpersonal Style Inventory (1996), and the Jesness Inventory Computer Program (1996).

Utility Programs

Several utility programs (see Table 5.10) are available that allow the practitioner to create computerized assessment instruments from paper-and-pencil forms. These allow the clinician to convert intake information, screening information, psychosocial historical information, and a virtually unlimited range of questionnaires and rating scales to computer accessible instruments. Other utility tools produce detailed reports for most of the major psychological and/or educational psychometric instruments (e.g., WISC-III, 1996). Of the various utility tools allowing for the creation of computerized instruments, The Interactive Tester (1996) facilitates this process through "interactive information input" to produce an instrument that is computer driven in all facets (e.g., administration, scoring, profiling, and interpretation). A second tool, Q-Fast (1996), allows for the computerization of questionnaires, surveys, and interviews. Questionnaire entry

TABLE 15.9. Personality Evaluation: Projective and Objective Instruments

PRODUCT NAME	PUBLISHER	COMPUTER	PRICING	COST BASIS	ON-LINE ADMINISTRATION	ELECTRONIC SCORING	PROPERTIES
Projective							
Exner's Rorschach Scoring Program	The Psychological Corporation	IBM	On-Site	Unlimited		Yes	C, A, PP
Hermann: The Rorschach Assistant	MHS	IBM	On-Site	Unlimited		Yes	C, A, NR
Projective Drawing Test: Computer Analysis	Reason House	IBM & Apple	On-Site	Unlimited		Yes	C, A, NR
Rorschach Interpretation Assistance Program (RIAP3)	The Psychological Corporation	IBM	On-Site	Unlimited		Yes	C, A, NR, M, PP
Rorschach Interpretation Assistance Program (RIAP3 PLUS)	Psychological Assessment Resources	IBM	On-Site	Unlimited		Yes	C, A, NR, M, PP
Rorschach Scoring and Interpretation	Reason House	IBM & Apple	On-Site	Unlimited			C, A, NR, M, PP
Objective							
Adolescent Multiphasic Personality Inventory	Precision People	IBM & Apple	On-Site	Unlimited	Yes	Yes	A, SRF, NR PP
AUTOPACL (Personality Adjective Check List	21st Century Assessment	IBM	On-Site	Unlimited	Yes	Yes	A, SRF, NR PP
Basic Personality Inventory (BPI)	Sigma Assessment Systems	IBM	Mail-In; On-Site	Per Test	Yes	Yes	A, SRF, NR PP
Children's Personality Questionnaire Narrative Report	Institute for Personality and Ability Testing	IBM	Mail-In; Teleprocessing	Per Test		Yes	C, SRF, NR PP
CPQ Narrative Report	Psychological Testing Services	IBM	On-Site; Teleprocessing	Per Test			C, A, SRF, NR PP
Eysenck Personality Questionnaire	Educational and Industrial Testing Service	IBM	On-Site	Per Test	Yes	Yes	C, A, SRF
High School Personality Questionnaire Report	Institute for Personality and Ability Testing	IBM	Mail-In; Teleprocessing	Per Test		Yes	A, SRF
HSPQ Narrative Report	Psychological Testing Services	IBM	On-Site;	Per Test		Yes	A, SRF, NR
Hilson Adolescent Profile (HAP)	Hilson Research	IBM	Mail-In; Teleprocessing	Per Test		Yes	A, SRF, NR, PP
Interpersonal Style Inventory	Western Psychological Services	IBM	Mail-In; On-Site	Per Test	Yes	Yes	A, SRF, PP
Jesness Inventory Computer Program	MHS	IBM	On-Site	Per Test	Yes	Yes	A, SRF, NR, , M, PP

Properties: C = Child; A = Adolescent; CRF = Clinician-Report Form; PRF = Parent-Report-Form; SRF = Self-Report Form; TRF = Teacher-Report Form; NR = Narrative Report; M = Manual; PP = Psychometric Properties; IX = Interactive.

continued

TABLE 15.9. Personality Evaluation: Projective and Objective Instruments, continued

PRODUCT NAME	PUBLISHER	COMPUTER	PRICING	COST BASIS	ON-LINE ADMINISTRATION	ELECTRONIC SCORING	PROPERTIES
Milton Adolescent Clinical Inventory	NCS/Professional Assessment Services	IBM	Mail-In; On-Site Teleprocessing	Per Test	Yes	Yes	A, SRF, NR, M, PP
Milton Adolescent Personality Inventory (MAPI)	NCS/Professional Assessment Services	IBM	Mail-In; On-Site Teleprocessing	Per Test	Yes	Yes	A, SRF, NR, M, PP
Marks MMPI Adolescent Clinical Report	Western Psychological Services	IBM	On-Site	Per Test			A, NR, PP
Marks MMPI Adolescent Feedback and Treatment Report	Western Psychological Services	IBM	On-Site	Per Test			A, NR, PP
Minnesota Multiphasic Personality Inventory-Adolescent (MMPI-A)	NCS/Professional Assessment Services	IBM	Mail-In; On-Site Teleprocessing	Per Test	Yes	Yes	A, SRF, NR, M, PP
MMPI-A Interpretative System	MHS	IBM	On-Site	Unlimited			A, NR, PP
MMPI Adolescent Interpretative System Version 2	Psychological Assessment Resources	IBM & Apple	On-Site	Unlimited			A, NR, PP
MMPI Clinical Report (MMPI-CR)	Integrated Professional Systems	IBM & Apple	On-Site	Per Test	Yes	Yes	A, NR, PP
MMPI-83 Version 2.1 Scoring and Interpretation System	Precision People	IBM & Apple	On-Site	Unlimited			A, NR, M, PP
Narrative Score Report (NSR)-16PF	Institute for Personality and Ability Testing	IBM	Mail-In; On-Site; Teleprocessing	Per Test		Yes	A, SRF, NR PP
Personality Inventory for Children (PIC)	Western Psychological Services	IBM	Mail-In; On-Site	Per Test	Yes	Yes	C, SRF, NR PP
PIC-Revised Narrative Report	Psychological Testing Services	IBM	On-Site Teleprocessing	Per Test or Unlimited		Yes	C, NR PP
Sixteen Personality Factor Questionnaire	NCS/Professional Assessment Services	IBM	Mail-In; On-Site; Teleprocessing	Per Test	Yes	Yes	A, SR, NR, M, PP

Properties: C = Child; A = Adolescent; CRF = Clinician-Report Form; PRF = Parent-Report-Form; SRF = Self-Report Form; TRF = Teacher-Report Form; NR = Narrative Report; M = Manual; PP = Psychometric Properties; IX = Interactive.

TABLE 15.10. Utility Programs—Report Writing and Scale Conversion

PRODUCT NAME	PUBLISHER	COMPUTER	PRICING	COST BASIS	ON-LINE ADMINISTRATION	ELECTRONIC SCORING	PROPERTIES
Report Writing Programs							
Psycho-Educational Report Writing System	Planet Press	IBM	Mail-In; On-Site	Per Test or Unlimited			C, A, NR
RADAR PLUS	Computerized Psychological Diagnostics	IBM	On-Site	Per Test	Yes	Yes	C, A, NR
Report Builder-Screentest	NFER-Nelson Publishing	IBM	On-Site	Unlimited	Yes	Yes	C, A, NR
Report Writer: Children's Intellectual and Achievement Tests	Psychological Assessment Resources	IBM	On-Site	Unlimited			C, A, NR, PP
Report Writer: WISC-R/WPPSI-R	Psychological Assessment Resources	IBM & Apple	On-Site	Unlimited			C, A, NR, PP
Session Summary	Psychologists, Inc.	IBM & Apple	On-Site	Unlimited	Yes		C, A, NR
Termination/Discharge Summary	Psychologists, Inc.	IBM & Apple	On-Site	Unlimited	Yes		C, A, NR
Scale Conversion Programs							
Interactive Tester	PSYTEK Services	IBM	On-Site	Unlimited	Yes	Yes	C, A, NR
MicroCAT Testing System	Assessment Systems Corporation	IBM	On-Site	Unlimited	Yes	Yes	C, A, PP
Q-Fast	StatSoft	IBM & Apple	On-Site;	Unlimited	Yes	Yes	C, A,

Properties: C = Child; A = Adolescent; Narrative Report; M = Manual; PP = Psychometric Properties; IX = Interactive.

is similarly menu-driven, producing an instrument which can be administered on-line, scored, and stored in a form compatible with other software. The MicroCAT Testing System (1996) contains subsystems which are sold separately or as a package. It features one subsystem that incorporates graphic or scanned images in test construction; a separate subsystem controlling on-line administration, scoring, and report generation; a subsystem capable of performing test development functions such as item analysis; and a subsystem allowing the user to build his or her own conventional test.

The second type of utility programs facilitate report generation and also differ in terms of sophistication. The Psycho-Educational Report Writing System (1996) was designed for school psychologists. It generates comprehensive narrative reports according to school specifications for such widely used psychometric instruments as the WPPSI and WRAT-R. In addition, it is capable of producing two types of reports: one detailed and extensive and the second shorter and more concise. A second report-generation utility tool, RADAR PLUS (1996), represents an on-line psychological software library and delivery system connecting the provider with over 70 psychometric instruments, including tests, history-gathering devices, and checklists. RADAR PLUS guides the clinician through demographic information entry and then selection of instruments to be administered from a test menu. It then guides the client through all phases of assessment, including instructions and administration. Finally, RADAR PLUS scores all instruments interactively at a separate site through modem connection and produces printable results. A final report generation utility device is the Report Builder-Screentest (1996). The Report Builder-Screentest, which runs in conjunction with the Screentest Assessment and Data Manager (1996), allows the user to build customized narrative report formats for questionnaires, attitude surveys, and performance appraisal forms. It creates the overall definitions for individual reports, which can then be printed, displayed on screen, or sent to a word processing program for further editing. Attention should be paid to avoid copyright violation and to be aware of the psychometric properties of the various instruments which are

employed. Two report writing programs, Session Summary (1996) and Termination/Discharge Summary (1996) produce brief reports at the conclusion of each session and at termination/discharge, respectively.

Although additional software assessment packages are available commercially, this overview provides some sense of the range and diversity of products available. The fact that the major publishing houses have moved into this area further documents the emerging trend of computer-based assessment. Clinicians now have available sophisticated assessment software tools that provide a cost-effective, rapid and efficient means to examine a variety of client data. Clearly the movement will be toward computer systems loaded with a variety of commonly used instruments that will become standard fare in the provider's office.

Observational Data

Computers have been used to collect both self-monitoring data and observational data. Two interesting systems are presented by Farrell (1991), one showing the application of computers (Tombari, Fitzpatrick, & Childress, 1985) in monitoring behavior and rewards for compliance with "in seat" behavior at school and a second, an obesity training program, which uses hand-held computers to monitor caloric intake and exercise (Agras, Taylor, Feldman, Losch, and Burnett, 1990). Repp, Harman, Felce, Acker & Karsh (1989) also developed a software program for a portable computer that recorded observational data on 43 different target behaviors and automatically prepared summary statistics. Similarly, a direct observation software package, Empiricist (1996), permits on-line entry of observed behaviors. Designed for both clinical and research settings, EMPIRICIST is versatile in terms of both data entry and data reduction, supporting data entry under one of several coding systems, and providing simple summary statistics along with the capacity for data down-load for more complex statistical analyses. These representational software packages clearly demonstrate how child therapists can use technology to monitor treatment through accurate and reliable assessment of child behavior patterns.

On-Line Analysis of Psychophysiological Data

Psychophysiological measures, including electroencephalography (EEG), electrodermal activity (EDA), and cardiovascular activity (CVA), have been applied in a variety of clinical settings since the early 1980s. EEG technology, for example, has been used to identify early cortical abnormalities in low birth-weight infants that places them at increased risk of manifesting speech and language disorders (Cone-Wesson, Kurtzberg, & Vaughan, 1983). On-line EEG measurement is also critical in the diagnosis and monitoring of clients with epilepsy (Novelly, 1992), and in the diagnosis and treatment of sleep disorders. Measures of electrodermal activity, including Skin Conductance Levels (SCLs), have been utilized in the treatment of anxiety disorders (Lader & Noble, 1975), as well as learning disability (Mangina & Beuzeron-Mangina, 1988). In addition, on-line measurement of cardiovascular activity, including the ambulatory monitoring of heart rate (HR) and blood pressure (BP) has proven a useful tool in the clinical management of clients with panic disorder (Taylor, Telch, & Havvik, 1983), in the diagnosis and management of individuals with essential hypertension (Perloff, Sokolow, & Cowan, 1983), and in stimulant drug monitoring of children with attention deficit hyperactivity disorder (Solanto & Conners, 1982). With the recent availability of software allowing for the reduction and/or on-line use of these measures, what was once assessed primarily in the laboratory is now assessed by the clinician in the office setting, offering a powerful and immediate source of direct data for various child behavior disorders and medical conditions such as epilepsy and hypertension.

BEHAVIORAL INFORMATICS IN THE PROVISION OF PSYCHOTHERAPY SERVICES TO CHILDREN AND ADOLESCENTS

Electronic Treatment Plans

Effective treatment starts with an organized conceptualization of the presenting problems, identification of treatment goals/targets, and a choice of intervention method. Currently, several automated treatment plans are available for use with personal computers. One such product, TP Write, (Reason House, 1996) allows the user to make selections from menu screens that produce narrative text which can be edited by a word processor program. The system covers both client and provider data, as well as diagnostic information, reason for treatment, description of treatment, functional impairment, mental status, psychological test results, previous treatment information, treatment modalities, and goals and treatment progress. It produces a number of reports including Initial Treatment Plans, Treatment Plan Updates, Clinical Progress Notes, Mental Status Reports and generates reports for Referral Sources. Importantly, the user can customize report formats for their unique purposes.

A second approach to treatment planning is the OPTAIO Provider Desktop (1997), one of two clinical platforms presented by The Psychological Corporation. Provider Desktop incorporates a treatment planner and automated note writer with a system that administers, scores, and prepares automated narrative reports for a variety of psychometric instruments. The system tracks and displays outcome data, identifies issues impacting treatment effectiveness, and provides inforamtion for risk assessment.

The OPTAIO Practice Manager (1997) is a fully integrated office management system. This more robust system includes a scheduler, a billing system, automated narrative and management reports, outcome measurement, connectivity between providers and administrative systems, and rich extract capabilities for data analysis. It includes an electronic treatment plan and an electronic treatment plan formulary. This system allows users to develop step-by-step treatment plans specifying relevant treatment parameters (e.g., type of provider, diagnosis, type of treatment, target behaviors to be treated, type of medication, type of assessment, number of authorized sessions, review cycle, outcome measures to be employed). The electronic treatment plan is integrated into a comprehensive computerized patient record and assists the practitioner in monitoring and directing the treatment process. Treatment plans can be down-loaded automatically from an administrative server and reviewed by the clinician at a remote site or can be developed by the practitioner and uploaded to a host site for review.

The treatment plan formulary electronically filters session data according to user-defined rules. The formulary sorting process automates various care decisions, that is, dispositions such as referral of an identified case for utilization review, provider collection of additional clinical or psychometric data, medical review, and so on. Electronic mail allows an ongoing dialogue between the practitioner and the case reviewer to establish the parameters of treatment for a given case. Electronic prompts advise the clinician activities they record are inconsistent with the parameters of the electronic treatment plan. In this fashion, practitioners can reduce clerical time while also facilitating the reporting process required by various payors.

Computerized Clinical Treatment Tools

The use of computer systems by skilled and sensitive practitioners offers great promise for the child therapist. Computers can be useful in teaching specific cognitive, interpersonal, and behavioral skills to children and adolescents, as well as in helping parents develop new information, attitudes, and parenting behaviors. The provision of computer-assisted treatment information to facilitate the implementation of various types of child therapy is becoming increasingly a routine feature in provider clinics, offices, and school settings. This technology utilizes prepackaged multimedia information modules, CD-ROM technology, and Virtual Reality.

Computer-Assisted Treatment for Attention Problems

Research on the characteristics and etiology of ADHD have increasingly suggested that this childhood behavior problems is largely a motivational disorder. Children with ADHD frequently can maintain attentional focus under conditions in which they are highly motivated to do so, such as when playing a video game. Because of this characteristic of ADHD, interactive computerized programs offer great potential for treatment. Of the interactive

ADHD assessment instruments reviewed, Vigil (1996) and the Captain's Log: Cognitive Training System (1996) offer a treatment component. Vigil is a continuous performance task which also contains a sequencing component. It is primarily used for assessment of sustained attentional abilities in ADHD and Head Injury. However, it is also useful in the treatment of ADHD due to its employment of "ramping" technology, whereby the rate of stimulus presentation speeds up or slows down based on the success or failure at the preceding level. With success, therefore, the child is both further engaged due to the changing stimulus parameters and gradually gains mastery at a successively more difficult task. While ADHD treatment is not the primary purpose of Vigil, it is easy to see how "ramping" facilitates such treatment. A second instrument useful in the treatment of ADHD is the Captain's Log. Like Vigil, it was not originally designed for the treatment of ADHD, but has been adopted for this purpose due to its flexibility of features. Captain's Log is particularly useful since it is designed to train basic abilities to learn (e.g., attention, memory, etc.) with modules sold separately for each of these purposes, in a manner similar to a video game. That is, it is a multilevel instrument with the flexibility to program the degree of difficulty. Thus, a relatively low degree of difficulty can be chosen at first to engage the child and build self-esteem, evolving into a more difficult standard of performance in a step-wise fashion. Although software development in this treatment area is in its "infancy," these programs are examples from which future systems will doubtlessly evolve.

Computerized Approaches to Behavioral Management

Tombari, Fitzpatrick, and Childress (1985) used a software program to promote positive behaviors in school by making the playing of a computerized game contingent on performance of the desirable target behavior. Based on basic behavior modification principles, menus can now be used to define target behaviors, select specific intervals for evaluation, define anchors for goal attainment, and identify potential reinforcers (including computer games or activities) that the child can earn with performance of target behaviors. These systems can also be enriched with animation and graphics to add a dimension of fun and interactive technology for the child and parent or teacher. Progress can also be automatically plotted for each target behavior across time.

Computer Technology in Child Psychotherapy Sessions

Several early attempts at incorporating computer systems into therapy with children and adolescents are reported by Schwartz (1984). The first example Allen (1984), reviews the use of action-oriented computer games in play therapy. He notes that some commercially available games provide an opportunity to expose the child to challenging situations which require positive coping skills for success. Clarke and Schoech (1996) report on the development of an action-oriented game that was designed to teach impulse control and positive coping strategies. Integrated into a "Dungeons and Dragons" type of scenario, the user receives prompts concerning self-control statements that actually facilitate performance in the game. These are especially interesting applications, because they successfully use the computer to involve the child in the therapy process in a fashion that is not intrusive. Learning about psychotherapeutic concepts and techniques becomes part of a recreational activity which is intrinsically interesting to the child. This approach allows the child to operate in a familiar venue while integrating psychotherapeutic concepts into their play.

Cognitive therapy also provides an example where computer technology can be used to present information and teach specific skills. Unlike the use of "therapeutic computer games," these types of applications would be more direct and problem-focused, while also designed to be stimulating and entertaining. For example, computerized training aids can be fairly easily developed to facilitate treatment programs for anger control problems (Finch, Nelson, & Moss, 1993), social-skills development (Polyson & Kimball, 1993), impulse control problems (Finch, Spirito, Imm, & Ott, 1993), anxiety reduction (Grace, Spirito, Finch, & Ott, 1993), and the reduction of depressed feelings (Carey, 1993). In each case, the treatment process involves the acquisition of fairly specific information and cognitive skills that can be transmitted using interactive learning units.

For illustrative purposes, the treatment of aggressive behavior as outlined by Finch, Nelson, and Moss (1993) will serve as a model of this type of application. Treatment starts with a detailed assessment. One assessment method described is the "run a movie" technique where the child describes in detail the last occasion of aggressive behavior. In this scenario, the therapist typically guides the child through a careful examination of relevant variables associated with the child's performance of aggressive behavior. The therapist then notes the variables which the child details as they cognitively review their reactions. This information is then used in the treatment process.

Computer-assisted, this might take the form of a software program that provides specific instructions to the child to help her or him select relevant details from menus reflecting generic items that are common to aggressive children. For example, the program might access menus to define behavior/reactions across the following dimensions: internal speech, physiological sensations, behavior of others, or other relevant contextual information. Once compiled, this information could generate descriptive scenes to be presented visually and auditorily for use in Stress Inoculation Training or an Anger Reduction Training package.

In addition to generating descriptive scenes, computer interactive materials can be used to guide a child through various types of cognitive coping responses required at each step of the treatment process that Finch, Nelson, and Moss (1993) outline. For example, the computer can guide the child through coping-skills training, in an interactive fashion, during which the child is presented with a scene by the computer, prompted to make a response (e.g., a verbal coping response, a physiological response such as relaxation), view a modeling scene, and/or view a mini-tutorial about the required response. Level of success by the child can also be automatically plotted in order to provide the child with a choice of reinforcers available through the computer terminal.

Client-administered treatment modules have been developed for teaching clients cognitive skills (HELP-Think, 1996), assertive skills (HELP-Assert, 1996), self esteem (HELP-Esteem, 1996) and stress reduction techniques (HELP-Stress, 1996). In addition, a computerized assessment and treatment program for test-taking anxiety has been developed (Coping with Tests, 1996). This system is an interactive tool that assesses the level of client anxiety and then offers several procedures for intervention (e.g., systematic desensitization, relaxation training, concentration training, success rehearsal). The system can be used with individuals or with groups. The use of computer tools are in most cases adjunctive to ongoing child therapy. Generally, within the computerized setting the therapist is present and continues to have a positive and interactive relationship with the child. Not only does the therapist continue to relate to the child in a therapeutic manner but she or he also assists the child in using the computer and in understanding concepts and techniques presented using this technology. As there is no substitute for the interaction between the child and the therapist, the therapist continues to support the child as the technology supports the treatment process. The computer, therefore, becomes a tool to assist the therapist in addressing a variety of child and adolescent difficulties. Applications will find their way into various types of child psychotherapy adding an interactive dimension to more formal treatment methods.

Computer-Assisted Parent Evaluation/Training

Some attention has been focused on the development of computerized assessment instruments to evaluate parenting difficulties. For example, one company has developed a computerized assessment instrument that evaluates the potential for child abuse (CAPSCORE 1.04, 1996). This scale assesses distress, rigidity, unhappiness, problems with a child, problems within the family, and problems with others. Moreover, another software publisher has developed a computerized scale that assesses dimensions relevant to domestic violence (Domestic Violence Inventory, 1996). This scale examines

truthfulness, use of alcohol and drugs, aggressivity, violence, stress-coping abilities, and so on. Other scales of family function and distress include the Parenting Stress Index Software System (1996), which examines level and type of stress within the family and the Comprehensive Computerized Stress Inventory (1996), which looks at stress across a number of different situations.

Given an accurate evaluation, parent training materials can rather easily be displayed with user-developed or prepackaged information modules. Such skills as "listening," behavior-management skills, anger-control techniques, conflict-resolution skills, limit setting, and so on lend themselves readily to the emerging technology. Multimedia presentations prepackaged on CD-ROM discs are increasingly becoming available to help parents develop more effective parenting behavior. Examples include units on developing assertive behavior (Assertiveness training, 1996), self-esteem (Self-Esteem and Values, 1996) and stress-management training (Total Stress Management System, 1996).

Virtual Reality as a Clinical Aid

The virtual reality technology is increasingly coming into its own in applications affordable to the practitioner (Lanier & Biocca, 1992). The potential use of this technology is enormous for developing training programs which utilize psychological principles, teach new skills, or involve exposure to specific stimuli. Child behavior problems which require exposure treatments, modeling, or behavioral rehearsal lend themselves very well to the use of virtual reality techniques. Treatment of childhood fears and phobias has been exhaustively reviewed by Morris and Kratochwill (1983). Treatment techniques which have proven effective include variations of systematic desensitization, combinations of positive reinforcement, shaping and stimulus fading, extinction techniques, and various modeling techniques as well as cognitive behavioral interventions.

Virtual reality offers a controlled but very vivid method to expose the child or adolescent to fear-evoking stimulus situations. Using a multimedia format with sound and realistic visual images, hierarchies of phobic stimuli can be prepackaged to assist the clinician in promoting positive behavioral change in the client. School avoidance, fears of specific stimuli or events (e.g., animals, heights, thunderstorms), fears of school performance (test-taking anxiety), or fears of public scrutiny (public speaking, etc.), as examples, may prove to be very amenable to computer-assisted assessment and intervention.

Standardized stimulus presentations can also be developed that will allow for the hierarchical assessment of fears. A child, therefore, who is frightened of thunderstorms could be exposed to different "virtual thunderstorms" using realistic images and sound to construct hierarchies for various imaginal or exposure treatments. These types of "virtual assessment instruments" can then be used to assess outcome throughout the treatment process. Of particular relevance to young children is the use of animation to depict various exercises or models successfully confronting the phobic stimuli. Treatment follows similar prescriptions like those depicted by Morris and Kratochwill (1991) with the added advantage of an intermediate step between imaginal work and actual exposure. In one example, Rothman (1995) presents a clinical case study employing virtual reality in treatment of acrophobia and discusses clinical and practical considerations.

The value of virtual reality in social skills training also appears to be significant due to the ability to configure mock social situations and to provide rich modeling experiences. Leroy (1994), for example, lists 11 different social-skill targets for children and adolescents which can be modularized as virtual reality assessment and treatment units. These include: Creating Positive Interactions, Getting to Know Others, Making Requests, Expressing Your Feelings Directly, How to Say "No," Asserting Your Rights, The Art of Empathy, Dealing With Those in Authority, Responsible Decision Making, Learning to Negotiate, and Asking for Help. Each of these units lends itself to a computerized assessment process where the child is asked to respond to a series of "Virtual Interactions." The therapist can also guide, encourage and develop the appropriate scenarios "on the fly" from standardized menus of stimulus situations and modeling examples.

Prescriptive Treatments and Therapy Research

Due to increased demands for accountability, a growing trend (Barlow, 1994) has been the development of standardized treatment protocols that are designed as specific interventions for specific clinical problems (i.e., prescriptive treatments). These protocols typically detail the treatment process in a step-by-step fashion. Deriving from the clinical laboratory, these techniques are often the most well-researched and empirically supported interventions for a given problem (Chambless, 1995).

The tradition of research on psychotherapy has focused on either highly controlled experimental conditions that lend themselves to little or no generalizability (Persons, 1991) or more loosely defined studies of generic approaches that are relatively vague in definition and description of subject variables, therapeutic variables, and experimental conditions. It is not surprising, therefore, that initial developments in prescriptive treatments and treatment guidelines have originated more from the clinical laboratory than from the field (Sanderson, 1995). While almost all psychotherapy is performed by clinicians in the field, almost all clinical research is conducted in the laboratory or other controlled conditions. The results of these studies do not, however, necessarily impact the day to day behavior of the provider community. Critics point out that such treatments often do not reflect the moment to moment decision points of "actual therapy" nor do they provide the clinician with the flexibility to change goals or interventions based on client issues or idiosyncratic response to the intervention (Kendall & Morris, 1991).

Consistent with Seligman (1995) and his advocacy of clinical field studies, the role of computer technology in prescriptive treatment will be increasingly important. The availability of sophisticated computerized patient records will allow clinicians in diverse settings to utilize standardized assessment and outcome measures to evaluate the effectiveness and costs associated with more standardized treatments for specifically defined diagnoses, problems, or target behaviors. Here to fore practitioners have not had access to a readily available mechanism for collection of clinical outcome data. With the advent of powerful personal computer systems with relational databases, clinicians have the tools for generating a strong empirical base for commonly employed interventions. These systems also make it possible for clinicians in the field to participate in large scale field trials and to connect on-line to various research-oriented data banks to share standardized data. Once large data bases have been established, specific questions can be asked of the anonymous data which can be used to define more effective treatment approaches.

Leroy (1994) recently edited a very impressive series of treatment manuals for children and adolescents. Included are manuals in areas such as Rational Emotive Therapy with Children (Linscott & DiGiuseppe, 1994), Social Skills Training (LeRoy, 1994), Cognitive-Behavioral Anger Control Training (Feindler & Guttman, 1994), A Treatment Program for Adolescent Bulimics and Binge Eaters (Weiss, Wolchik, & Katzman, 1994), and The Treatment of Depressed Children: A Skills Training Approach to Working with Children and Families (Stark, Raffaelle, &Reysa, 1994). These types of treatment manuals promise to provide practitioners with valuable, organized information in a structured format to allow for more specified and replicable treatments. The next logical step is the computerization of these protocols and the testing of these treatment programs by clinicians in the field. The technology is available for large relatively well controlled field studies to be performed to convert these "Empirically Validated Treatments" into a consumer sensitive context as "Clinically Effective Treatments."

NATIONAL CLEARING HOUSE FOR CHILD BEHAVIORAL HEALTH

Office computer systems will interface with multiple administrative structures allowing the provider to be credentialed and to communicate electronically with any payor or network they are formally affiliated with. Herein lies the possibility of an integrated national database from which to develop treatment guidelines based on "Clinical Effectiveness.". Initially, each major payor will create their own proprietary outcome measures and decision formulas to operate their particular businesses. A step beyond the present proprietary developments, however, will be a national clearing house for behavioral health data. Data will be stored from diverse client groups which can be aggregated for analysis and disseminated through databased reports for government, business and industry, various payors, professional associations, networks, and providers. Industry-wide collaboration regarding large scale studies of outcome in behavioral health will address the cost/quality issues which characterize the current behavioral health industry. Addressing such issues as employee productivity and medical cost offset on a large scale will bolster arguments for parity with medicine in terms of benefit design and structure. The creation of generic, psychometrically sophisticated measurement instruments that can be added to proprietary protocols and that can be distributed to practitioners and clients for large-scale outcome studies will greatly facilitate this development. Such instruments will have to be "child sensitive" to assess level of functioning in the child's world (e.g., home, family, peer group, school, general health, etc.).

ETHICAL AND LEGAL ISSUES IN THE UTILIZATION OF BEHAVIORAL INFORMATICS

A number of ethical issues arise in the general area of behavioral informatics. Specifically, these issues include: confidentiality of data, system security, transmission security, informed consent, provider/payor interfaces, and the use of computerized psychological assessment and scoring interpretation services. None of these issues is more critical than the issue of client confidentiality. For example, Freedman (1994) has suggested that "The most controversial and emotionally-charged issue related to health care information systems is the privacy of individual patient data" (p. 32). A 1993 Harris-Equifax poll (Turek-Brezina & Kozloff, 1994) reported that 80% of respondents expressed concern about threats to privacy in general, and many believed that consumers have lost control over how their personal information is used. Interestingly, 87% of the respondents felt they could trust their providers of direct care to preserve their confidentiality. However, 75% were concerned specifically about the use of computerized health information for non-health related purposes.

Four related concepts are important in looking at the issue of confidentiality. The first is informational privacy, that restricts the child therapist from revealing any form of client information to others without prior authorization. This form of therapist-client confidentiality is legally mandated in most states for certain types of therapists (e.g., psychologists, psychiatrists, behavioral health counselors, etc.) and is specifically cited in the ethics codes of various behavioral health professions. The second concept involves "conditional confidentiality," which is the assurance from the child therapist or health-care organization that client information will only be revealed for purposes of obtaining third-party reimbursement and/or authorization from an insurance company or managed-care company for initial or continuing psychological services.

The third concept involves "legally mandated restrictions to confidentiality," where the therapist is mandated by a particular state's statutes to report all instances of situations in which (a) a child has been physically or sexually abused and/or neglected, (b) situations in which the child intends to harm herself/himself or others, (c) court cases in which the child's records have been court-ordered to be brought to a judge, and (d) regulatory board and related administrative law proceedings where a child's records have been requested by the board as part of a complaint filed against the licensed therapist. The fourth concept involves "data security" which is the assurance from a child therapist or health-care organization that a reasonable series of technical and procedural policies have been implemented to protect a client's records from theft, fire or unwanted destruction or disclosure.

Turek-Brezina and Kozloff (1994) state, "Individuals have the right to expect, and the system has the obligation to provide assurances that personal records are accurate, timely and complete, and that all records will be kept confidential and secure from inquiry and observation" (p. 36). There are, however, limitations to such confidentiality and a client should be informed about such limitations.

One method to inform a client is to provide them with an "informed consent statement" which she/he would be asked to sign. Such a form is presented in Table 15.11.

When computerized records go on-line, all four of the above issues of privacy are confronted. Informational privacy means that records may be viewed or handled only by certain individuals who have prior consent or authorization to view such records. Consequently, computer systems must have security features which assign "security clearance" to individuals which limit or define their relative responsibilities for the safe keeping of clinical data. As Webman (1994) has suggested: "The facility must be held accountable for the training and supervision of paraprofessionals (and Professionals) with regard to privacy, confidentiality and the electronic record" (p. 37). In this sense facility might refer to a private practitioner's office, a multidisciplinary clinic, a network, an integrated health-care delivery system, and various payors and/or host entities that could end up storing clinical data. With the advent of computerized information systems linking providers to various treatment facilities and to various payors or networks additional responsibilities accrue to ensure that the information provided is accurate, detailed, and safe for review by "secured" individuals. This also means that clients should be informed initially that if they agree to having their therapist or behavioral health agency release records to payors through computer linking then every effort will be made to keep the information secure when it is transmitted, but that following transmission no assurances can be made by the therapist or agency as to who views the records when they are received.

In an interesting article by Brannigan (1994) on legal standards regarding the collection and storage of client information using computer systems, he notes that the Federal Privacy Act "...provides no specific technical measures which must be taken to protect privacy" (p. 57). He further indicates that there are three standards for clinical records. The first standard involves the security measures found in most hospital information retrieval systems. For this level of security, the use of passwords to enter the system and the availability of audit trails is recommended. The second level of security protects

TABLE 15.11. Informed Consent

INFORMED CONSENT REGARDING CONFIDENTIALITY

I understand that the issues discussed during my (my child's) course of therapy are confidential, meaning that information I (my child) reveal will not be discussed or shared in any format with others without my knowledge and written consent. My (my child's) records will not be discussed or sent to others without a signed release from me. There are several important exceptions to this confidentiality. They include the following:

> Situations of potential harm to myself (my child) or others.
>
> Child abuse, sexual abuse, or neglect.
>
> Court cases where my (my child's) records are court-ordered.
>
> Insurance companies or managed-care companies seeking information about my (my child's) treatment to determine eligibility/continued eligibility for psychological services.
>
> Revealing my (my child's) name to office staff for routine scheduling of appointments, telephone messages, office billing, and correspondence.
>
> Revealing my (my child's) name to a collection agency or attorney for purposes of collecting unpaid balances on my (my child's) account with this office.

I further understand that should I agree in writing to have my (my child's) case records, reports, and/or financial statements transmitted by electronic mail or by surface mail to my insurance company or managed-care company that my therapist or behavioral health agency can not make any assurances to me (or my child) as to who will view the records once they are received.

I have read, understood, and agree to all of the typed material in this informed consent document.

_____   _____
Signature of client (or legally responsible   Date
person if client is a minor).

_____   _____
Witness   Date

against sophisticated assault on data. Recommendations include encryption of data, read/write limitations for different personnel, and physical keys required to access the data system. The third level of security relates to specific litigation (Whalen v. Roe, 1977). This case involved a centralized record of clients who were lawfully prescribed certain drugs which also had unlawful uses and the misuse of this information by those who were privy to the information. The standards accepted in this case were very specific: (a) tapes of the prescription database were kept in a locked cabinet, (b) when tapes were in use the computer was to be off-line, (c) access was restricted to a limited number of users, and (d) plans were in place to destroy the data base at some point. In the Whalen case, Justice Brennan concluded:

"What is more troubling about this scheme, however, is the central computer storage of data thus collected....The Constitution puts limits not only on the type of information the State may gather, but also on the means it may use to gather it. The central storage and easy accessibility of computerized data vastly increase the potential for abuse of that information, and I am not prepared to say that future developments will not demonstrate the necessity of some curb on such technology" (Brannigan, 1994, p. 60).

There is, in fact, existing technology that can provide safe and secure storage and transmission of behavioral health records electronically. Most information systems establish multiple levels of security to limit who sees different types of information, who can perform various chart functions (change data vs. enter data), and who can review highly confidential information. Data must be handled carefully. Only encrypted raw data, not text, should be sent upstream. Modems and telephone transfer of information must also be secure. There is a general agreement that the most highly personal and sensitive information is not the focus of outcome effectiveness data. Other questions arise, however, about what happens to data once they are collected and stored by a payor or by a data bank.

What if data are sent to a national behavioral health care clearinghouse for review and analysis? A number of international guidelines have been formulated since the 1970s to protect the rights of clients (Gulbinat, 1994). Most discussions consider "the client as an individual and autonomous subject who provides information which belongs to him or her, and who is entitled to derive benefits for himself or herself from the health care system" (Gulbinat, 1994; p. 39). This viewpoint has been referred to as "radical individualism" (Gulbinat, 1994). Thus, use of client data for research purposes requires voluntary client consent, by a legally competent, informed, and comprehending client. This standard, however, raises particular problems for children who are unable to legally provide consent. In this case parental consent or ethical review by an appropriate human subjects committee would be indicated. Also indicated are limitations on who can access what type of data, as well as policies on secure storage of records and backup files.

It should also be noted that computerized patient record systems not only contain information about clients, but also contain extensive information about providers and payors, including policies and procedures about business contracts. To what extent should these types of data be subject to similar types of authorized control over dissemination? Do providers, for example, give up ipso facto their right to control over data concerning their performance or the financial aspects of their practices? This question remains unanswered.

With regard to assessment, the American Psychological Association (APA) (1992) has developed standards concerning the appropriate use of computerized testing. These recommendations include provisions that the psychologist assume responsibility for any "test factors," conditions, or characteristics of the client that might limit or modify interpretation of test data. Furthermore, the psychologist is held responsible for all aspects of collecting, scoring, interpreting, and reporting test data. The fact that data may in some fashion be computer-related does nothing to lessen the ethical responsibilities of the psychologist. Lastly, psychologists must assume full responsibility for the use of test results and the reporting of test results to others. What the APA (1992) is proposing is one standard of practice, which is not in any fashion diluted by changes in technology or the way that practitioners gather and disperse data.

THE TECHNOLOGY INFRASTRUCTURE

The technology to improve the practice of child behavioral health care is becoming increasingly available. Child practitioners can now use computers to assist with diagnosis, assessment, and various psychotherapy activities. The technology also provides a new infrastructure that allows for connectivity of providers to various administrative and clinical entities (e.g., networks, managed care organizations, integrated health care systems, on-line consultation, etc.). Child practitioners also have, as a function of computer systems, more clinical and financial data for decision-making than ever before. The challenge for child therapists is to learn to use these databases that are available to develop more efficient and responsive service delivery systems. The opportunity also exists for practitioners to participate in National Data Clearing House Enterprises in order to build empirical support for services and techniques that are "field tested" and empirically validated. New responsibilities also accompany the use of these systems as child therapists and other practitioners grope with the ethical issues associated with this technology.

REFERENCES

Abidin, R. R. (1996). Parenting Stress Index Software System (PSI3 Plus) [Computer software]. Odessa, FL: Psychological Assessment Resources.

Adaptive Behavior Inventory [Computer software]. (1996). Austin, TX: PRO-ED.

Adaptive Behavior Scale-School (2nd ed.) [Computer software]. (1996). North Tonawanda, NY: MHS.

Adaptive Behavior Scale-Residential and Community, (2nd ed.) [Computer software]. (1996). North Tonawanda, NY: MHS.

Adolescent Chemical Dependency Inventory [Computer software]. (1996). Phoenix, AZ: Behavior Data Systems.

Adolescent Multiphasic Personality Inventory [Computer software]. (1996). Jacksonville, FL: Precision People

ADD-H Comprehensive Teacher's Rating Scale-2 [Computer software]. (1996). Champaign, IL: MetriTech.

Agras, W. S., Taylor, C. B., Feldman, D. E., Losch, M., & Burnett, K. F. (1990). Developing computer-assisted therapy in the treatment of obesity. *Behavior Therapy, 21,* 99–109.

Allen, D. H. (1984). The use of computer fantasy games in child therapy. In M. D. Schwartz (Ed.), *Using computers in clinical practice: Psychotherapy and mental health applications* (pp. 321–327). New York: Haworth Press.

American Psychiatric Association (1994). *Diagnostic and statistical manual of mental disorders* (4th ed.). Washington, DC: Author.

American Psychological Association (1992). *Guidelines for computerized testing.* Washington, DC: Author.

Arlin Test of Formal Reasoning-Computer report [Computer software]. (1996). East Aurora, NY: Slosson Educational Publications.

Autism Screening Instrument for Educational Planning [Computer software]. (1996). Austin, TX: PRO-ED.

Assessment of Chemical Health Inventory [Computer software]. (1996). Minneapolis, MN: Recovery Software.

Assertiveness Training [Computer software]. (1996). San Diego: Psychological Psoftware.

AUTOPACL (Personality Adjective Checklist) [Computer software]. (1996). South Pasadena, CA: 21st Century Assessment.

Barlow, D. H. (1994). Psychological interventions in the era of managed competition. *Clinical Psychology: Science and Practice, 1 ,* 109–122.

Basic Personality Inventory [Computer software]. (1996). Port Huron, MI: Sigma Assessment Systems.

Behavior Assessment System for Children-BASC Plus [Computer software]. (1996). Circle Pines, MN: American Guidance Service.

Beck Anxiety Inventory [Computer software]. (1996). San Antonio, TX: The Psychological Corporation.

Beck Depression Inventory [Computer software]. (1996). San Antonio, TX: The Psychological Corporation.

Beck Hopelessness Scale [Computer software]. (1996). San Antonio, TX: The Psychological Corporation.

Beck Scale for Suicide Ideation [Computer software]. (1996). San Antonio, TX: The Psychological Corporation.

Bender clinical report [Computer software]. (1996). Jacksonville, FL: Precision People.

Bender report [Computer software]. (1996). North Tonawanda, NY: MHS

Bender report 4.0 [Computer software]. (1996). Melborne, FL: Psychometric Software.

Boston Diagnostic Aphasia Examination [Computer software]. (1996). San Antonio, TX: The Psychological Corporation.

Brannigan, V. M. (1994). Behavioral healthcare computer systems and the law: the problem of privacy. *Behavioral Healthcare Tomorrow, 3*(1), 57–61.

Brief Symptom Inventory [Computer software]. (1966). Minneapolis, MN: NCS.

Captain's Log: Cognitive Training System [Computer software]. (1996). Richmond, VA: Braintrain.

Cagney, T., & Woods, D. R. (1994). Clinician update: clinical MIS. *Behavioral Healthcare Tomorrow, 3*(1), 43–45.

California Adaptive Behavior Scale [Computer software]. (1996). Newport Beach, CA: Planet Press.

CAPSCORE 1.04 [Computer software]. (1996). Los Angeles, CA: PSYTECK.

Carey, M. P. (1993). Child and adolescent depression: Cognitive-behavioral strategies and interventions. In A. J. Finch, M. Nelson, & E. Ott (Eds.), *Cognitive-behavioral procedures with children and adolescents: A practical guide* (pp. 289–311). Boston: Allyn & Bacon.

Category Test Computer Program [Computer software]. (1996). North Tonawanda, NY: MHS.

Chambless, D. L. (1995). Training in and dissemination of empirically-validated psychological treatments. The Clinical Psychologist, 48, 3–24.

Chang, M. (1987). Clinician-entered computerized psychiatric triage records. Hospital and Community Psychiatry, 38 , 652-656.

Child and Adolescent Diagnostic Screening Inventory [Computer software]. (1996). Indialantic, FL: Psychologistics, Inc.

Children's Behavior Inventory [Computer software]. (1996). Youngstown, OH: Integrated Professional Systems.

Children's Diagnostic Scale [Computer software]. (1996). Youngstown, OH: Integrated Professional Systems.

Children's Depression Inventory [Computer software]. (1996). North Tonawanda, NY: MHS.

Children's Psychiatric Rating Scale [Computer software]. (1996). Youngstown, OH: Integrated Professional Systems.

Children's State-Trait Anxiety Inventory [Computer software]. (1996). North Tonawanda, NY: MHS.

Clarke, B., & Schoech, D. (1984). A computer-assisted therapeutic game for adolescents: Initial development and comments. In M. D. Schwartz (Ed.), *Using computers in clinical practice: Psychotherapy and mental health applications* (pp. 321–327). New York: Haworth Press.

Comprehensive norms for an expanded Halstead-Reitan battery: Demographic corrections, research findings, and clinical applications [Computer software]. (1996). North Tonawanda, NY: MHS.

Comprehensive Computerized Stress Inventory [Computer software]. (1996). Lawrence, KS: Preventive Measures.

Compuscore for the Scales of Independent Living [Computer software]. (1996). Chicago, IL: The Riverside Publishing Company.

Compuscore for WJB-Revised [Computer software]. (1996). Chicago, IL: The Riverside Publishing Company.

Cone-Wesson, B., Kurtzberg, D., & Vaughan, H. G., Jr. (1983). *Detection of auditory system dysfunction in very low birthweight infants.* Paper presented at the meeting of the Society for Ear, Nose, & Throat Advance in Children, San Diego, CA.

Conners, K. (1996). Parent Questionnaire [Computer software]. Youngstown, OH: Integrated Professional Systems.

Conners, K. (1996). Teacher Questionnaire [Computer software]. Youngstown, OH: Integrated Professional Systems.

Conners' Continuous Performance Test [Computer software]. (1996). North Tonawanda, NY: MHS.

Conners' Rating Scales Computer Program [Computer software]. (1996). North Tonawanda, NY: MHS.

Coping Inventory for Stressful Situations [Computer software]. (1996). North Tonawanda, NY: MHS.

Coping with Tests [Computer software]. (1996). Palo Alto, CA: Consulting Psychologists Press.

Cummings, N. A. (1995). Impact of managed care on employment and training: A primer for survival. *Professional Psychology: Research and Practice, 26,* 10–15.

Demuth, P. (1984). Eliza and her offspring. In M. D. Schwartz (Ed.), *Using computers in clinical practice: Psychotherapy and mental health applications* (pp. 321–327). New York: Haworth Press.

Detroit Tests of Learning Aptitude-Primary: 2 Software Scoring and Report System [Computer software]. (1996). North Tonawanda, NY: MHS.

Detroit Tests of Learning Aptitude-3 Software Scoring and Report System [Computer software]. (1996). North Tonawanda, NY: MHS.

Dimensions of Self-Concept [Computer software]. (1996). San Diego, CA: Educational and Industrial Testing Service.

Derogatis, L. R. (1996). SCL-90-R [Computer software]. Minneapolis, MN: NCS.

Domestic Violence Inventory [Computer software]. (1996). Phoenix, AZ: Risk & Need Assessment.

Dougherty, E. H., & Schinka, J. A. (1996). Mental Status Checklist-Adolescent: Computer report [Computer software]. Odessa, FL: Psychological Assessment Resources.

Dougherty, E. H., & Schinka, J. A. (1996). Developmental History Checklist: Computer report [Computer software]. Odessa, FL: Psychological Assessment Resources.

Dougherty, E. H., & Schinka, J. A. (1996). Mental Status Checklist-Children: Computer Report [Computer software]. Odessa, FL: Psychological Assessment Resources.

Dougherty, E. H., & Schinka, J. A. (1996). Personal History Checklist-Adolescent: Computer Report [Computer software]. Odessa, FL: Psychological Assessment Resources.

Eating Disorder Inventory-2 [Computer software]. (1996). Odessa, FL: Psychological Assessment Resources, Inc.

Electronic DSM-IV [Computer software]. (1996). Washington DC: American Psychiatric Association.

Emotional Problem Scales: Computer report [Computer software]. (1996). Odessa, FL: Psychological Assessment Resources.

EMPIRICIST [Computer software]. (1996). Brookline, MA: Ironwood Development Systems.

Erdman, H. P., Klein, M. H., & Griest, J. H. (1985). Direct patient computer interviewing. *Journal of Consulting and Clinical Psychology, 53,* 760–773.

Exner's Rorschach Scoring Program [Computer software]. (1996). San Antonio, TX: The Psychological Corporation.

Eysenck Personality Inventory (Junior) [Computer software]. (1996). San Diego, CA: Educational and Industrial Testing Service.

Farrell, A. D. (1989). Impact of computers on professional practice: a survey of current practices and attitudes. *Professional Psychology: Research and Practice, 20,* 172–178.

Farrell, A. D. (1991). Computers and behavioral assessment: Current applications, future possibilities, and obstacles to routine use. *Behavioral Assessment, 13,* 159–179.

Feindler, E. L., & Guttman, J. (1994). Cognitive-behavioral anger control training. In C. W. Leroy (Ed.), *Handbook of child and adolescent treatment manuals,* (pp. 170–199). New York: Lexington.

Finch, A. J., Nelson, M., & Moss, J. H. (1993). Childhood aggression: Cognitive-behavioral therapy strategies and interventions. In A. J. Finch, M. Nelson, & E. Ott (Eds.), *Cognitive-behavioral procedures with children and adolescents: A practical guide* (pp. 148–201). Boston: Allyn & Bacon.

Finch A. J., Spirito, A., Imm, P. S., & Ott, E. S. (1993). Cognitive self-instruction for Impulse control in Children. In A. J. Finch, M. Nelson, & E. Ott (Eds.), *Cognitive-behavioral procedures with children and adolescents: A practical guide* (pp. 233–254). Boston: Allyn & Bacon.

First, M. B., Williams, J. B., & Spitzer, R. L. (1996). DTREE: The DSM-IV Expert [Computer software]. North Tonawanda, NY: MHS.

Fowler, R. D. (1985). Landmarks in computer-assisted psychological assessment. *Journal of Consulting and Clinical Psychology, 53,* 748–759.

Freedman, M. A. (1994). Editorial. *Behavioral Healthcare Tomorrow, 3*(1), p. 32.

Functional Skills Screening Inventory [Computer software]. (1996). Austin, TX: Functional Assessment & Training Consultants.

Giannetti, R. A. (1996). Giannetti On-line Psychosocial History [Computer software]. Minneapolis, MN: NCS/Professional Assessment Services.

Giannetti, R. A. (1996). Quickview Social History [Computer software]. Minneapolis, MN: NCS/Professional Assessment Services.

Gordon Diagnostic System [Computer software]. (1996). DeWitt, NY: Gordon Systems.

Grace, N., Spirito, A., Finch, A. J., & Ott, E. S. (1993). Coping skills for anxiety control in children. In A. J. Finch, M. Nelson, & E. Ott (Eds.), *Cognitive-behavioral procedures with children and adolescents: A practical guide* (pp. 257–284). Boston: Allyn & Bacon.

Gray, G., & Glazer, W. (1994). Psychiatric decision making in the 90s. *Behavioral Healthcare Tomorrow, 3*(1), 47–54.

Gulbinat, W. (1994). Balancing individual and societal needs: Micro- vs. macro-ethics. *Behavioral Healthcare Tomorrow, 3*(1), 33, 39–41.

Halstead Category Test-A Computer Version [Computer software]. (1996). Jacksonville, FL: Precision People.

Halstead-Reitan Hypothesis Generator [Computer software]. (1996 Jacksonville, FL: Precision People.

Halstead-Reitan Neuropsychological Test Battery [Computer software]. (1996). Youngstown, OH: Integrated Professional Systems.

Harrell, T., & Honaker, L. M. (1996). Intake Evaluation report [Computer software]. North Tonawanda, NY: MHS.

HRB Norms Program [Computer software]. (1996). Odessa, FL: Psychological Assessment Resources.

HELP-Assert [Computer software]. (1996). North Tonawanda, NY: MHS.

HELP-Esteem [Computer software]. (1996). North Tonawanda, NY: MHS.

HELP-Stress [Computer software]. (1996). North Tonawanda, NY: MHS.

HELP-Think [Computer software]. (1996). North Tonawanda, NY: MHS.

Health Status Questionnaire Computer Scoring and report [Computer software]. (1996). San Antonio, TX: The Psychological Corporation.

Hermann: The Rorschach Assistant [Computer software]. (1966). North Tonawanda, NY: MHS.

Hilson Adolescent Profile [Computer software]. (1996). Kew Garden, NY: Hilson Research.

Honaker, L. M., & Harrell, T. (1996). Psychological/Psychiatric Status Interview 2.0 [Computer software]. North Tonawanda, NY: MHS.

Honaker L. M., Harrell, T., & Ciminero, A. (1966). Chemical Dependency Assessment Profile [Computer software]. North Tonawanda, NY: MHS.

Horn, J. L., Wanberg, K. W., & Foster, F. M. (1996). Alcohol Use Inventory [Computer software]. Minneapolis, MN: NCS.

Interactive Tester [Computer software]. (1996). Los Angeles, CA: PSYTEK.

Interpersonal Style Inventory [Computer software]. (1996). Los Angeles, CA: Western Psychological Services.

IVA Computerized Visual and Auditory Continuous Performance Test (Computer software]. (1996). Richmond, VA: Braintrain.

Jesness Behavior Checklist Computer Program [Computer software]. (1996). North Tonawanda, NY: MHS.

Jesness Inventory Computer Program [Computer software]. (1996). North Tonawanda, NY: MHS.

Johnson, J. L. (1995). Comprehensive Survey of Symptoms 77 [Computer software]. San Antonio, TX: The Psychological Corporation.

Kaufman Assessment Battery for Children [Computer software]. (1996). Circle Pines, MN: American Guidance Service.

Kendall, P., & Morris, R. J. (1991). Child therapy: Issues and recommendations. *Journal of Consulting and Clinical Psychology, 59,* 777–789.

King, J. D., & Lowalchuk, B. (1996). Inventory of Suicide Orientation-30 [Computer software]. Minneapolis, MN: NCS.

Krug, S. (1993). *Psychware sourcebook: A reference guide to computer-based products for assessment in psychology, education, and business.* Champaign, IL: Metritech.

Lader, M., & Noble, P. (1975). The affective disorders. In P. H. Venables & M. J. Christie (Eds.), *Research in psychophysiology* (pp. 259–281). New York: Wiley.

Lanier, J., & Biocca, F. (1992). An insider's view of the future of virtual reality. *Journal of Communication, 42*(4), 150–172.

Leroy, C. W. (1994). Handbook of child and adolescent treatment manuals. New York: Lexington.

Leroy, C. W. (1994). Social skills training. In C. W. Leroy (Ed.), *Handbook of child and adolescent treatment manuals* (pp. 126–169). New York: Lexington.

Linscott, J., & DiGiuseppe, R. (1994). Rational emotive therapy with children. In C. W. Leroy (Ed.), *Handbook of child and adolescent treatment manuals* (pp. 5–40). New York: Lexington.

Louisville Behavior Checklist [Computer software]. (1996). Los Angeles, CA: Western Psychological Services.

Luria-Nebraska Neurological Battery [Computer software] (1996). Los Angeles, CA: Western Psychological Services.

Mangina, C. A., & Beuzeron-Mangina, J. H. (1988). Learning abilities and disabilities: Effective diagnosis and treatment. *International Journal of Psychophysiology, 6,* 79–90.

Marks MMPI Adolescent report [Computer Software]. (1996). Los Angeles, CA: Western Psychological Services.

MCO's select software: Providers come on-line (1995). *Practice Strategies, 1,* 1–2.

McCullough, L., Farrell, A., & Longabaugh, R. (1986). The development of a microcomputer-based mental health information system: A potential tool for bridging the scientist-practitioner gap. *American Psychologist, 41,* 207–214.

Meier, S. (1996). If You Drink [Computer software]. North Tonawanda, NY: MHS.

Memory Assessment Scale [Computer software]. (1996). Odessa, FL: Psychological Assessment Resources.

Meredith, R. L., & Bair, S. L. (1990). Computer generated client record keeping. *Register Report, 16*(3), 15–19.

Meredith, R. L., & Bair, S. L. (1995). Myrt rides the superhighway. (1995). *Register Report, 21*(2), 1, 14–17.

MicroCAT Testing System [Computer software]. (1996). St. Paul, MN: Assessment Systems Corporation.

MicroCog: Assessment of Cognitive Functioning [Computer software]. (1996). San Antonio, TX: The Psychological Corporation.

Millon Adolescent Clinical Inventory [Computer software]. (1996). San Antonio, TX: The Psychological Corporation.

Millon Adolescent Personality Inventory [Computer software]. (1996). San Antonio, TX: The Psychological Corporation.

Minnesota Assessment of Chemical Health [Computer software]. (1996). Chaska, MN: International Professional Services.

MMPI-A Interpretive System [Computer software]. (1966). North Tonawanda, NY: MHS.

MMPI-A [Computer software]. (1996). Minneapolis, MN.: NCS.

MMPI-A Interpretive System Version 2 [Computer software] (1996). Odessa, FL: Psychological Assessment Resources.

Morris, R. J., & Kratochwill, T. R. (1991). Childhood fears and phobias. In T. R. Kratochwill, & R. J. Morris, R. J. (Eds.), *The practice of child therapy* (pp. 76–114). New York: Plenum Press.

Morris, R. J., & Kratochwill, T. R. (1983). *Treating children's fears and phobias: A behavioral approach.* New York: Pergamon Press.

Multi-Score Depression Inventory [Computer software]. (1996). Los Angeles, CA: Western Psychological Services.

Multi-Score Depression Inventory for Children [Computer software]. (1996). Los Angeles, CA: Western Psychological Services.

Novelly, R. A. (1992). The debt of neuropsychology to the epilepsies. *American Psychologist, 47,* 1126–1129.

OPTAIO Practice Manager [Computer software]. (1997). San Antonio, TX: The Psychological Corporation.

OPTAIO Provider Desktop [Computer software]. (1997) San Antonio, TX: The Psychological Corporation.

Oral and Written Language Scales [Computer software]. (1996). Circle Pines, MN: American Guidance Service.

Pediatric Intake [Computer software]. (1996). Youngstown, OH: Integrated Professional Systems.

Perception of Ability Scale for Students [Computer software]. (1996). Los Angeles, CA: Western Psychological Services.

Perloff, D., Sokolow, M., & Cowan, R. (1983). The prognostic value of ambulatory blood pressures. *Journal of the American Medical Association, 249,* 2792–2798.

Personal Experience Inventory [Computer software]. (1996). Los Angeles, CA: Western Psychological Services.

Personality Inventory for Children [Computer software]. (1996). Los Angeles, CA: Western Psychological Services.

Persons, J. P. (1991). Psychotherapy outcome studies do not accurately represent current models of psychotherapy. *American Psychologist, 46,* 99–106.

Piers-Harris Children's Self-Concept Scale [Computer software]. (1996). Los Angeles, CA: Western Psychological Services.

Polyson, J., & Kimball, W. (1993). Social skills training with physically aggressive children. In A. J. Finch, M. Nelson, & E. Ott (Eds.), *Cognitive-behavioral procedures with children and adolescents: A practical guide* (pp. 206–228). Boston: Allyn & Bacon.

Projective Drawing Tests: Computer Analysis [Computer software]. (1996). Towson, MD: Reason House.

Psychiatric Rating Scale A [Computer software]. (1996). Youngstown, OH: Integrated Professional Systems.

Psycho-educational Report Writing system [Computer software]. (1996). Newport Beach, CA: Planet Press.

Q-Fast [Computer software]. (1996). Tulsa, OK: Statsoft.

RADAR PLUS [Computer software]. (1996). Newport Beach, CA: Computerized Psychological Diagnostics.

Rainwater, G., & Coe, D.S. (1996). Psychological/Social History Report 4.0 [Computer software]. North Tonawanda, NY: MHS.

Rainwater, G., & Slade, B. (1996). Developmental History Report 4.0 [Computer software]. North Tonawanda, NY: MHS.

Reason House (1996) *TP Write* [Brochure]. Towson, MD: Corporate Author.

Relch, W., Welner, Z., & Herjanic, B. (1996). Diagnostic Interview for Children and Adolescents -Revised (for DSM IV) Computer Program: Child/Adolescent Version and Parent Version [Computer software]. North Tonawanda, NY: MHS.

Report Builder-Screentest [Computer software]. (1996). Berkshire, England: Nelson Publishing.

Report Writer: Children's Intellectual and Achievement Tests-4.0 [Computer software]. (1996). Odessa, FL: Psychological Assessment Resources.

Repp, A. C., Harman, M. L., Felce, D., Acker, R. V., & Karsh, K. G. (1989). Conducting behavioral assessments on computer-collected data. *Behavioral Assessment, 11,* 249–268.

Reynolds Adolescent Depression Scale [Computer software]. (1996). Odessa, FL: Psychological Assessment Resources.

Reynolds Child Depression Scale [Computer software]. (1996). Odessa, FL: Psychological Assessment Resources.

Rhode, M. (1996). Automated Child/Adolescent Social History. [Computer software]. Minneapolis, MN: NCS.

RISK [Computer software]. (1996). Austin, TX: PRO-ED.

Rorschach Interpretation Assistance Program [Computer software]. (1996). San Antonio, TX: The Psychological Corporation.

Rorschach Interpretation Program (Version 3.1) [Computer software]. (1996). Odessa, FL: Psychological Assessment Resources.

Rorschach Scoring and Interpretation [Computer software]. (1996). Towson, MD: Reason House.

Rorschach Technique [Computer software]. (1996). San Antonio, TX: The Psychological Corporation.

Rosen, L. (1995a). Cruising the info-ban: Psychologists relish computer opportunities. *The National Psychologist, 4*(14), 14–15.

Rosen, L. (1995b). Three ADHD tests prove computerized technology vital tool for clinicians. *The National Psychologist, 4*(6), 20–21.

Rosen, L., & Weil, M. (1995). Tips for mental health professionals to merge on-line. Treatment Today, Fall, 48–49.

Rothman, B. O. (1995) Virtual reality graded exposure in the treatment of acrophobia: A case report. *Behavior Therapy, 26,* 547–554.

Sanderson, W. C. (1995). Which therapies are proven effective? *American Psychological Association Monitor, 26,* 4.

Schwartz, M. D. (1984). *Using computers in clinical practice: Psychotherapy and mental health applications.* New York: Haworth Press.

Scoring Assistant for the Wechsler Scales [Computer software]. (1996). San Antonio, TX: The Psychological Corporation.

SCREEN [Computer software]. (1996). Austin, TX: PRO-ED.

Screentest Assessment and Data Manager [computer software]. (1996). Berkshire, England: Nelson Publishing Company.

Self-Esteem and Values [Computer software]. (1996). San Diego, CA: Psychological Psoftware.

Seligman, M. E. P. (1995). The effectiveness of psychotherapy. *American Psychologist, 50,* 965–974.

Session Summary [Computer software]. (1996). Indialantic, FL: Psychologistics, Inc.

Sixteen Personality Factor Questionnaire [Computer software]. (1996). Minneapolis, MN: NCS.

Solanto, M. V., & Conners, C. K. (1982). A dose-response and time action analysis of autonomic and behavioral effects of methylphenidate in attention deficit disorder with hyperactivity. *Psychophysiology, 19,* 658–667.

Stark, K. D., Raffaelle, L., & Reysa, A. (1994). The treatment of depressed children: a skills training approach to working with children and families. In C. W. Leroy (Ed.), *Handbook of child and adolescent treatment manuals* (pp. 343–397). New York: Lexington

State-Trait Anxiety Inventory [Computer software]. (1966). North Tonawanda, NY: MHS.

Taylor, C. B., Telch, M. J., & Havvik, D. (1983). Ambulatory heart rate changes during panic attacks. *Journal of Psychiatric Research, 17,* 261–266.

Tennessee Self-Concept Scale [Computer software]. (1996). Los Angeles, CA: Western Psychological Services.

Termination/Discharge Summary [Computer software]. (1996). Indialantic, FL: Psychologistics, Inc.

Test of Adolescent Language-2 [Computer software]. (1996). Austin, TX: PRO-ED.

Test of Variables of Attention [Computer software]. (1996). Los Alamitos, CA: Universal Attention Disorders.

Tombari, M. L., Fitzpatrick, S. J., & Childress, W. (1985). Using computers as contingency managers in self-monitoring interventions: A case study. *Computers in Human Behavior, 1,* 75–82.

Total Stress Management [Computer software]. (1996). San Diego, CA: Psychological Psoftware.

Turek-Brezina, J., and Kozloff, R. (1994). Protecting data privacy under federal healthcare reform. *Behavioral Healthcare Tomorrow, 3*(1), 32–36.

Van Vort, W., & Mattson, M. (1987). A strategy for enhancing the clinical utility of the psychiatric record. *Hospital and Community Psychiatry, 40,* 407–409.

Vigil [Computer software]. (1996). Nashua, NH: ForThought.

Vineland Adaptive Behavior Scales-ASSIST [Computer software]. (1996). Circle Pines, MN: American Guidance Service.

WAIS-R Microcomputer-Assisted Interpretive Report [Computer software]. (1996). San Antonio, TX: The Psychological Corporation.

Webman, D. (1994). Integration of information systems lowering standards for patient confidentiality and data privacy? *Behavioral Healthcare Tomorrow, 3*(1), 33 & 37–38.

Wechsler Memory Scale report [Computer software]. (1996). Melbourne, FL: Psychometric Software.

Weiss, L., Wolchik, S., & Katzman, M. (1994). A treatment program for bulimics and binge eaters. In C. W. Leroy (Ed.) *Handbook of child and adolescent treatment manuals* (pp. 278–342). New York: Lexington

Western Aphasia Battery Scoring Assistant [Computer software]. (1996). San Antonio, TX: The Psychological Corporation.

Whalen v. Roe, Supreme Court of the United States, 429 U.S. 589; 97 S.Ct. 869; 1977 U.S. Lexis 42; 51L. Ed. 2d 64; February 22, 1977.

WISC-III Writer: Interpretive Software System [Computer software]. (1966). San Antonio, TX: The Psychological Corporation.

Wisconsin Card Sort Test Computer Version-2 Research Edition [Computer software]. (1996). North Tonawanda, NY: MHS.

WPPSI-R Writer: The Interpretive Software System [Computer software]. (1996). San Antonio, TX: The Psychological Corporation.

CHAPTER 16

PREVENTION

Jeffery P. Braden
A. Dirk Hightower

This chapter shifts the focus from treatment of childhood disorders to prevention of childhood disorders. Previous chapters review therapeutic methods and techniques designed for specific disorders; in some cases, sections on the prevention of these disorders is also included. However, the practice of psychology is still dominated by treatment of existing disorders. The goals of treatment are "neither unworthy nor unneeded; they simply are not prevention" (Cowen, 1983, p. 11). This chapter is intended to complement other chapters in this book by providing a historical context for prevention, explaining the basic principles of prevention, by illustrating prevention methods, and by discussing the forces that encourage and discourage prevention of children's mental disorders.

HISTORICAL CONTEXT

Because detailed developmental and historical analyses of the prevention movement are available in other sources (e.g., Albee, 1982; Albee & Joffe,

1977; Cowen, 1986; Felner et al., 1983; Joffe, Albee, & Kelly 1984; Kessler & Goldston, 1986; Price, Cowen, Lorion, & Ramos-McKay, 1988; Roberts & Peterson, 1984; Spaulding & Balch, 1983) only a brief summary is provided here. Prevention in mental health for children has, like child therapy, roots that go back to Clifford Beers's writings about the early mental hygiene movement and the establishment of child guidance clinics. Mental-health prevention's formal history was triggered by the passage of the Mental Health Study Act in the 1950s. That act created the Joint Commission on Mental Health and Mental Illness. The Commission was charged to review prevention practices and make recommendations designed to reduce the number of new cases, and the duration/impact, of mental illness. Using the Joint Commission Report as a foundation, President Kennedy (1963) cited the social, economic, and prognostic advantages of prevention.

Later in 1963, the Mental Retardation Facilities and Community Mental Health Centers Construction

Act (PL 88-164) provided for five essential services. One of the specified services (i.e., consultation and education) specified prevention as a service that Community Mental Health Centers (CMHCs) must provide. Unfortunately, CMHCs have historically neglected prevention; instead, CMHCs concentrate on direct fee for service models based on traditional treatment approaches (Roberts & Peterson, 1984).

At about this time, Caplan (1964) translated the public-health concepts of primary, secondary, and tertiary prevention into the mental-health arena. Caplan's effort provided a conceptual base for prevention in mental health. Caplan also pioneered the provision of psychological consultation (called "mental-health consultation") to further prevention goals among mental-health providers. Caplan also recognized the need to include paraprofessionals (e.g., clergy) and lay people in prevention efforts via consultation services.

Community psychology was born at the Swampscott Conference (Anderson et al., 1966; Iscoe & Spielberger, 1970). Prevention, as a major focus of community psychology, is reflected by the many articles published in its associated journals: *American Journal of Community Psychology, Journal of Community Psychology, Community Mental Health Journal,* and *Prevention in Human Services.* Since 1974, the Vermont Conference on the Primary Prevention of Psychopathology (VCPPP) has met annually, and has produced a series of volumes reporting current prevention issues, research on programming, interventions, and training. This group has also maintained publication of the *Journal of Primary Prevention.*

The Federal role in developing prevention concepts and priorities stimulated important expansion of prevention. The President's Commission on Mental Health (1978) established two task panels. One panel addressed Prevention, and the other addressed Learning Failure and Unused Learning Potential. Together, these panels documented prevention needs, rationales, definitions, targets, and barriers/priorities for children. As direct outgrowths of the President's Commission, the National Institute of Mental Health created an Office of Prevention, developed a network of Preventive Intervention Research Centers, and developed the Prevention Publication Series to disseminate, stimulate, and promote prevention activities in mental health.

In 1981, the American Psychological Association (APA) appointed a Task Force on Prevention Alternatives. The goal of the Task Force was to identify exemplary prevention programs that addressed mental-health issues. Over the course of six years, this panel contacted 900 professionals knowledgeable about prevention, received 300 replies describing prevention efforts, evaluated 52 programs with reasonable evidence of effectiveness, and chose 14 model promotion, prevention, or intervention alternatives worthy of dissemination (Price et al., 1988). Of the 14 programs described, 5 were designed and targeted toward infancy and early childhood, an additional 5 targeted school-aged children and adolescents, and 4 targeted adults.

In 1997, APA appointed a second task force to address prevention. Its charges are to encourage and feature prevention-related research in the 1998 APA Annual Convention, develop a special issue of the *American Psychologist* on prevention, update and provide a listing of "best practices" on prevention programs and prevention training for psychologists, and to institutionalize APA's commitment to prevention via creating a formal division of APA addressing prevention and establish a journal to feature prevention-related research. These activities update and extend APA's prior commitments to prevention work, and enhance the development of prevention programs in professional psychology.

Although prevention in mental health for children has a history of several decades, it is still in its infancy. The growth of this field has been slow but steady. Many of its early efforts were relatively ineffective—not an uncommon situation in a discipline's infancy. But, as the field matures (i.e., as it gets past the "terrible twos"), it will present a stronger challenge to past practices and the status quo, both of which emphasize treatment of existing conditions over prevention.

DEFINING PREVENTION

Psychologists define prevention as reducing either the *prevalence* or *incidence* of some form of psychopathology. *Prevalence* refers to problem severity in those individuals who express the problem. *Incidence* refers to the number of individuals who exhibit a particular problem at any given point in time. Therefore, a prevention program that reduces the number of children who experiment with illegal substances would reduce drug abuse incidence, whereas a program to help children reduce drug abusing behaviors (e.g., smoking cessation) would primarily reduce the drug abuse prevalence. In this framework, most traditional therapies seek to reduce the prevalence or severity of childhood disorders, but do relatively little to reduce their incidence, or frequency of occurrence in the population.

Prevention programs can be described by three distinct facets or features (Rappaport, 1978; Winett, Riley, King, & Altman, 1989). These facets are: (a) timing, (b) conceptual basis, and (c) service delivery. We describe each of these facets in the following sections.

Timing

Prevention programs target three different points in the development of a disorder: *primary, secondary,* and *tertiary.* These points generally relate to the stages of intervening before there is any manifest evidence of a disorder (*primary*), intervening when indications of risk or early signs of the disorder are shown (*secondary*), and intervening after the disorder is evident (*tertiary*).

Primary prevention programs deliver services to individuals to prevent early signs of problems and/or to promote well-being in individuals. Generally, primary prevention programs target the population at large. For example, putting fluoride in drinking water reduces tooth decay in all individuals, and does so before any symptoms of tooth decay are evident.

Defining primary prevention has proven to be difficult. Indeed, there is still substantial disagreement over the definition of primary prevention among authors in the field (e.g., Bloom, 1977, 1979; Bower, 1977; Caplan, 1964; Cowen, 1980, 1983; Felner, Jason, Moritsugu & Farber, 1983; Goldston, 1987; Kessler & Albee, 1975; Klein & Goldston, 1977; Rappaport, 1977; Roberts & Peterson, 1984).

However, one defining characteristic of primary prevention efforts is that they seek to *change the incidence* of new cases by intervening proactively; that is, before disorders occur.

Examples of primary prevention programs include the following: (a) improving social, academic, or vocational competencies through education; (b) training/debriefing to improve coping strategies in people who experience stressful life events and crises; (c) modification of environments to reduce, or counteract, harmful circumstances, and (d) increasing support systems for individuals at social, medical, and other levels. In sum, primary prevention efforts do not attempt to reduce existing problems; rather they call for proactive preemptive efforts.

Secondary prevention programs deliver services to individuals who are at risk of developing disorders. Generally, secondary prevention programs target individuals who express early symptomatology, or who share conditions associated with the disorder. For example, dropout prevention programs may target children with unexcused absences or low grades (i.e., those who exhibit early symptomatology) or minority children from low SES households (i.e., those who share conditions associated with dropping out).

Others (e.g., Felner et al., 1983; Zax & Spector, 1974) have described secondary prevention as the application of treatment methodologies, similar to those described in earlier chapters, to target populations. For example, some would argue that posttrauma counseling (e.g., meeting with child survivors of a hurricane) is primary prevention, because the service is delivered prior to symptom presentation (i.e., before the children exhibit posttraumatic stress syndrome). Others would argue the same program is a good example of secondary prevention, as it illustrates the delivery of services (i.e., group counseling) to an at-risk population (i.e., children who were exposed to life-threatening trauma). Thus, experts in the field often differ with respect to the distinctions between primary and secondary prevention.

Psychological practices also make it difficult, if not impossible, to differentiate among treatment or primary and secondary prevention efforts by their activities. For example, children from divorced families are "at risk" for developing more serious dysfunction. If such children are brought together as a group to: (a) share common experiences, thoughts, and feelings in a warm, empathetic, supportive atmosphere; (b) observe and rehearse various behaviors through modeling and role playing; and (c) learn new ways of handling anger or anxiety, these activities may be effective in reducing the potential for stress or actual stress along the prevention-treatment spectrum. Given that the majority of children in the United States will experience parental separation, death, or divorce at some point in their childhood, such a group might be reasonably defined as a primary prevention effort (i.e., targeting a common group to prevent symptom expression). It could also be defined as a secondary prevention approach, in that the delivery of services targets a group at risk of later mental-health disorders. Finally, one could conceptualize this group as a form of treatment for children who have a condition (parental divorce or a situational stressor).

Tertiary prevention programs deliver services to individuals after they exhibit chronic and/or severe evidence of a disorder. Generally, these programs are rehabilitative (i.e., they help individuals who have a disorder overcome it) or adaptive/compensatory (i.e., they reduce the negative effects of the disorder). For example, a program to reduce recidivism in juvenile offenders is rehabilitative because it seeks to overcome the problems associated with juvenile arrest. In contrast, a program to help mentally retarded adolescents transition to community and work settings is adaptive or compensatory, because it alleviates some of the difficulties associated with mental retardation, but it does not alleviate the condition of mental retardation. Although such clinical treatments are called "tertiary prevention" within a public-health model, using the term *prevention* to describe rehabilitation or treatment of individuals with established disorders can be confusing.

An alternative framework for prevention identifies four, not three, prevention targets or levels (Tannahill, 1985; cited in Fodor, 1996). These targets are:

1. preventing the first occurrence of a disease or problem;
2. preventing the avoidable consequences of a disease or problem;
3. preventing the avoidable complications of an irreversible disease; and
4. preventing recurrence of a disease.

In this framework, primary prevention encompasses efforts addressed at the first level (i.e., preventing a disease or problem from occurring). Secondary prevention might address the second target—that is, secondary prevention would identify early symptoms of a problem (e.g., "at-risk" status) and prevent the avoidable consequences of the problem. Tertiary prevention would address the third and fourth targets in this approach.

To help reduce confusion throughout the rest of this chapter, we use the term *prevention* to mean secondary and primary prevention in mental health. We consider tertiary prevention activities to be best described as *treatment*. This in no way minimizes the value of effective treatments, nor should it minimize the long-term value of early treatments for preventing later problems. For example, treatment of children's academic or social difficulties may have "preventive" effects for their later development (e.g., such treatments may reduce the probability of school dropout or drug abuse). However, we consider efforts to alleviate problems in children who have a diagnosed disorder to be treatment, not prevention, if they are aimed at reducing the problems associated with the disorder and/or preventing recurrence of the disorder.

Finally, we want to emphasize that prevention generally works best when a program includes and coordinates all prevention timing elements. For example, a program to reduce school violence should coordinate discipline policies and affective curricula (primary prevention programs), corrective/punitive consequences for violent behavior episodes (secondary prevention programs), and intensive programming for individuals who exhibit severe and/or chronic violence (treatment programs). Thus, an ideal prevention program would incorporate primary, secondary, and treatment elements to reduce the prevalence and incidence of a disorder.

Conceptual Basis

Prevention programs are driven by their conceptual bases. Conceptual bases provide the assumptions underlying the program, and in so doing, dictate the content and method of the program. Some of the major conceptual bases for prevention programs include biogenetic, behavioral, rational, coping, ecological, and developmental frameworks. The selection and articulation of conceptual bases (what Cowen 1980, 1986, refers to as the "generative knowledge base") should determine the content and methods of prevention programs. For example, a drug abuse prevention program that assumes individuals act in a largely rational way may assume drug abuse is a function of poor information. In this model, the prevention program attempts to disseminate accurate information about drugs and the consequences of drug abuse so that children will make appropriate choices (i.e., they won't use drugs). In contrast, a different drug abuse prevention program might assume individuals use drugs because they are socially unsuccessful. Therefore, the program would enhance interpersonal efficacy and social skills to reduce the prevalence of drug abuse. These examples illustrate the ways in which assumptions about the nature of the disorder drive the content and methods of prevention. Ultimately, the scientific knowledge base of psychology should create the generative knowledge, or conceptual, basis for prevention programs.

Although different disorders may be best described by different models, some common elements span all efforts to understand and prevent mental-health disorders. These common elements address the cause of the problem, and the factors that modulate whether an individual succumbs to or resists a particular disorder.

Environmental/Experiential Adversity

The degree to which environments or experiences affect the expression of mental-health disorders is termed *adversity*. That is, some environments or experiences are low in adversity, meaning they are unlikely to induce children to express a disorder. Other environments or experiences are high in adversity, meaning they are more likely to induce children to express a disorder.

Vulnerability and Resilience

Why do some child witnesses to fatal or life-threatening events develop posttraumatic stress disorder (PTSD), and other child witnesses do not? Why do some children develop drug abuse problems, whereas their peers do not? These questions derive from the observation that there are substantial individual differences in the degree to which children (and adults) succumb to (or resist) disorders despite similar environmental circumstances.

Vulnerability is the degree to which individuals are more likely to express a disorder; resilience is the degree to which individuals are less likely to express a disorder. Many factors enter into vulnerability and resilience, including the child's physical environment, life experiences, and genetic predisposition. These factors combine to predispose an individual toward a disorder (i.e., the individual is vulnerable), or to predispose an individual to resist a disorder (i.e., the individual is resilient). Thus, children who share similar environments may be vulnerable—or resilient—to expression of a disorder.

Risk and Protective Factors

Factors that increase the incidence or prevalence of a disorder are termed *risk factors*. Research on mental disorders identifies many factors that increase the likelihood that a child will experience a disorder. Although many of these risk factors are associated with environmental or experiential adversity (e.g., single-parent household, poverty), some risk factors are clearly genetic. For example, phenylketonuria (PKU) is a genetic disease that can cause mental retardation. A child who inherits the recessive PKU genes cannot metabolize phenylaline; the excess phenylaline acts as a toxin, resulting in poisoning and mental retardation. If the condition can be identified early, and the child can be given a special diet free from phenylaline, mental retardation can be prevented. Thus, inheritance of the PKU gene is a risk factor for mental retardation.

However, many risk factors are not clearly separated into environmental or genetic influences. One example is the link between household poverty and children's school and criminal behavior. Although low income is a risk factor for school failure and criminal behavior, it is also true that low parental income is associated with low parental intelligence (Lynn, 1995). Intelligence is substantially—but not exclusively—heritable in contemporary Western societies (Brody & Crowley, 1995; Neisser, 1996). Children from low-income families are therefore likely to be less intelligent. Separating the relative risk of being less intelligent versus poor is a complex and controversial process (see Herrnstein & Murray, 1994; cf. Neisser et al., 1996). However, research demonstrates genetic risk factors for many childhood disorders, including alcoholism, criminal behavior, low intelligence (and its relationship to many social and academic difficulties), mental retardation, schizophrenia, learning disabilities, and other mental and behavioral problems (see Rose, 1994; Whitney, 1995).

It is important to note that classification of a risk factor as being primarily (or even exclusively) genetic does not connote "genetic determinism," nor does it mean prevention of the disorder should be medical in nature. For example, PKU is entirely a genetic risk factor, but it is treated entirely via environmental intervention (diet). Likewise, finding alcoholism is a largely inherited trait should not lead psychologists to abandon environmental interventions (e.g., access to alcohol is needed to express the disorder). It is also important to note that showing substantial environmental influences for a disorder does not necessarily lead to environmental treatments or prevention. For example, most of the environmental effects on intelligence are unique influences, meaning they are not shared by other family members (Brody & Crowley, 1995). Unique environmental influences include factors such as birth order, position in the family hierarchy, and availability of older/younger siblings, which are not directly amenable through environmental intervention. Although genetic and unique environmental factors are obviously important in certain adverse outcomes, research has documented repeatedly the effects of socioeconomic status (SES), community

conditions such as poverty, the influence of schools and their staff, as well as various parental and familial characteristics on the incidence and prevalence of conditions (Bloom, 1977; Botvin & Tortu, 1988; Davidson & Redner, 1988; Gump, 1980; Insel & Moos, 1974; Kellam, Branch, Agrawal, & Ensminger, 1975; Task Panel Report: Learning Failure and Unused Learning Potential, 1978; Lorion, Tolan, & Wahler, 1987; Moos, 1974; Prevention Task Panel Report, 1978).

Factors that decrease the incidence or prevalence of a disorder are termed *protective factors*. Research on mental disorders identifies many factors that decrease the likelihood that a child will experience a disorder. Protective factors include environmental factors, such as interpersonal and domestic stability, and genetic factors, such as temperament. For example, individuals with an extroverted/relaxed temperament are less susceptible to social difficulties and depression than individuals with an introverted/anxious temperament. Such temperamental differences are demonstrated early in infancy, and appear to be largely genetic (Kagan, 1994). As is true for risk factors, separating protective factors into genetic and environmental influences is a difficult task that is made more difficult over the child's developmental span. For example, children with extroverted/relaxed temperaments generally elicit positive social reactions from adults and peers, thus creating an environmental and experiential base to complement their genetic predisposition.

Risk and Protective Mechanisms

The identification of a risk factor is not the same as understanding the mechanisms by which the risk factor encourages expression of the problem. For example, noting household poverty is a risk factor for school failure leaves open myriad risk mechanisms (e.g., lack of appropriate nutrition, poor health, lack of parental support for home study, attendance at underfunded schools), all of which indicate somewhat different foci for prevention efforts. Therefore, research seeks to understand the mechanisms by which risk and protective factors affect vulnerability and resilience for particular disorders (Rutter, 1987). When the mechanisms by which factors such as parental divorce, poverty, or temperament affect disorders are understood, psychologists will be better able to plan and execute effective prevention programs.

Conceptual Bases and Prevention Efforts

We stated prevention efforts are driven by the scientific or generative knowledge base regarding a disorder. We lied. Many prevention efforts are not clearly linked to a conceptual knowledge base. In some cases, it is because the knowledge base does not yet exist. Psychologists have not yet identified all of the risk factors, nor do they fully understand the functional mechanisms that cause many disorders. In other cases, it is because prevention programs are designed to meet political or social needs independent of the generative knowledge base. Program leaders may be ignorant of the knowledge base, or they may choose to ignore it, when designing prevention programs. For example, lawmakers may respond to juvenile crime by recriminalizing juvenile offenses (e.g., trying juveniles as adults in court), despite evidence of more effective (but less politically appealing) alternatives (e.g., U.S. Department of Justice, 1995).

As we bemoan the foolishness of nonpsychologists for their willful or unintentional ignorance, we should note that psychologists also succumb to selection biases. Some psychologists adamantly insist that problems must be solely understood as learning or environmental influences, whereas others may assume a biogenetic framework. Rigid allegiance to particular psychological ideologies can also impair prevention efforts, and so psychologists must be careful not to assume a narrow or exclusive framework for developing the generative knowledge base for prevention efforts.

Assuming one wants to use the generative knowledge base to drive an intervention, one must consider two issues. The first issue is the "weight" of the evidence supporting the conceptual basis. That is, what models have the most empirical support? The answer to this question may change rapidly and radically with research advances. For example, many disorders previously thought to be acquired through environmental experiences are now being reconceived as biogenetic disorders (e.g., learning disabilities; Light & DeFries, 1995). The second issue is the degree to which practicality should influence model selection. On one hand, a model with terrific empirical support might not be selected because the model is unworkable or incompatible in a given program context. For example, schools would avoid a prevention program that emphasized genetic counseling, because it would be incompatible with their mission and service activities. On the other hand, psychologists must discourage systems from squandering prevention resources on demonstrably weak, unproven, naive, or poorly defined conceptual prevention models. For example, psychologists should discourage schools from spending resources (including class time) on drug prevention programs that use only scare tactics or otherwise emphasize the negative legal and health consequences of drug use.

Ironically, the interest in competing models to account for childhood disorders often overshadows the more important aspects of timing and service delivery in prevention. Psychologists tend to define themselves by their conceptual bases (e.g., behavioral, cognitive-behavioral, psychodynamic) and/or their methods (e.g., art therapist, brief therapy). In contrast, few psychologists define themselves by the timing (e.g., tertiary) or delivery (see next section) of their services.

Service Delivery

The way in which professionals deliver prevention services is defined by two distinct concepts: *stance* and *level*. The *stance* of a program characterizes the degree to which service delivery is proactive or reactive. A proactive delivery stance is characterized by seeking out or initiating opportunities to provide services. In contrast, a reactive delivery stance is characterized by waiting for individuals to seek services, and then to respond to those efforts. Prevention is generally associated with a proactive stance, in that psychologists seek out opportunities to prevent disorders before they occur.

The second concept defining service delivery is the level where services are focused. There are three levels at which services are delivered: (a) individual, (b) interpersonal, and (c) organizational. Prevention at the individual level seeks to change individual characteristics, such as knowledge, competencies, thought processes, coping mechanisms, and the like. Prevention at the interpersonal level seeks to change relationships between individuals, such as family dynamics or interpersonal communication patterns. Prevention at the organizational level seeks to change organizational patterns and structures, such as reward/punishment systems, allocation of system resources, hierarchical versus collaborative work structures, and the like.

It is important to distinguish levels of service delivery from timing. There is a tendency to equate individual-level services with tertiary prevention, and organizational-level services with primary prevention. The level of service delivery is independent of program timing. For example, individual-level programs may be primary (e.g., teaching all children anger-management strategies), secondary (e.g., using in-school-suspension for children with severe or repeated violent behaviors), or tertiary (e.g., using intensive individual therapy or aggression-replacement training for incarcerated juvenile offenders).

Different levels of service delivery are associated with the breadth and depth of program effects. Individual-level services often have less breadth than interpersonal-level services, which have less breadth than organizational- or systems-level services. That is, programs that target interpersonal relationships or systems affect more people than individual-level programs. They are also more likely to be sustained, because relationships and organizations have mechanisms for sustaining changes (e.g., patterns of behavior, policies) that outlive individual membership in the unit or organization. However, interventions at the interpersonal and organizational levels often have less direct effects on individuals. Consequently, the depth of program effects is often higher with individual-level services. Rather than choose between depth or breadth of impact, prevention programs may coordinate multiple service levels to generate the greatest benefit for the most people.

The public health model defines prevention programs according to timing, conceptual basis, and service delivery aspects. Although there is some controversy in the field regarding these characteristics (e.g., some argue "tertiary prevention" is not prevention at all), there is substantial consensus that effective prevention programs incorporate multiple levels of timing and service delivery aspects, rather than adopting a singular focus.

PREVENTION VERSUS PROMOTION

Recently, medicine has explored changing from a disease model to a health model for service delivery. Indeed, the first international conference on promotion of health (rather than prevention of disease) occurred in 1986 under the auspices of the World Health Organization. There are substantial differences in the implications of this shift with respect to prevention. Essentially, "prevention" is a disease model concept. In other words, one prevents something bad (e.g., a disease) from happening. This is not the same as encouraging something good to happen (i.e., promoting health). As the medical field explores the relative benefits of health promotion versus disease prevention, so too the mental-health field has begun to explore the relative benefits of mental-health promotion versus mental illness prevention.

Mental Illness Versus Mental Health

Tudor (1996) argues that mental illness and mental health are related, but conceptually distinct, concepts. Disease models tend to describe health as the absence of disease. Therefore, disease-oriented approaches define "mental health" as the absence of mental disorder or illness; this places mental health and mental illness on opposite ends of a single continuum. Health models describe health as the presence of certain characteristics, such as behaviors or states that enable and sustain the physical, psychological, and social well-being of the person. Therefore, it is possible to consider the mental health of a person with a mental illness (e.g., To what degree does a child with attention deficit disorder engage in behaviors that enable and sustain well-being?). By separating mental illness on a continuum of "present" to "absent," and by considering mental health to be a separate continuum represented by "functional" and "dysfunctional" ends, psychologists can consider the promotion of mental health as a worthy objective independent of mental illness prevention.

Mental illness prevention programs have been largely predicated on a medical model. That medical model assumes three key features influence prevention: (a) a causative agent (e.g., a virus or toxin), (b) a susceptible host (i.e., a vulnerable person), and (c) an environment that brings the causative agent and the susceptible host together (Tudor, 1996, p. 42). Thus, prevention programs oriented to reducing mental disorders in children emphasize reducing exposure to potentially threatening things or events, and enhancing host resistance to threats. Table 16.1 presents some examples of how prevention programs emphasize reduced exposure to and enhanced resistance to psychological problems.

In contrast, mental-health promotion efforts seek to promote environments and behaviors that encourage well-being. In some cases (e.g., encouraging positive, prosocial relationships among peers), promotion efforts may also be preventive (e.g., such prosocial relationships may reduce violent conflict). However, the link between promotion efforts and prevention targets often is not—and cannot—be clearly defined. Advocates of mental-health promotion argue promotion efforts are worthy and valuable in and of themselves, and do not require demonstrated reductions in mental illness for justification.

Characteristics of Mental-Health Promotion

Whereas mental illness prevention typically focuses on reducing exposure to risks and increasing resistance in the host (person), mental-health prevention focuses on eight characteristics. These characteristics are presented in Figure 16.1.

Mental-health prevention efforts focus primarily on personal attributes—that is, those things that the person can control. This does not imply that mental-health promotion does not also value environmental foci for interventions. Indeed, some proponents of mental-health promotion argue that radical social and physical changes are necessary for mental health (Tudor, 1996). However, mental-health promotion largely encourages intrapersonal strategies for promoting health. These strategies include factors that mediate between the person and the environment (e.g., coping, stress management), a sense of well-being (e.g., self-esteem), and adaptation and growth (e.g., change, social mobility).

Most industrialized nations have some form of mental illness prevention policy, but none of them have a genuine mental-health promotion policy (Tudor, 1996). This is less true for children than for adults. Indeed, it could be argued that universal public education is one of the largest, most evident societal efforts to promote mental health in children. Although mental health is not the primary focus of schooling, children nonetheless acquire knowledge, skills, and abilities that will promote their mental health by enhancing their social and economic competence. The question of whether, and to what degree, schools should focus on mental-health promotion is controversial. Some advocate instruction to enhance self-esteem, coping, stress management, and the like, whereas others (e.g., Seligman, 1995) argue that emphasis on such nonacademic aspects of development may actually undermine mental health by reducing opportunities to acquire academic skills and accurate self-appraisal.

Linking Promotion and Prevention

Mental-health promotion may be conceptually distinct from mental illness prevention, and it may be intrinsically worthwhile (i.e., promoting mental health may be good even if it does not lead to reduced mental illness). There are, however, links between mental-health promotion and mental illness prevention.

- Coping
- Tension and stress management
- Self-concept and identity
- Self-esteem
- Self development
- Autonomy
- Interpersonal change/adaptation
- Interpersonal change/adaptation
- Social support and movement

Figure 16.1. The eight components of mental-health promotion.

TABLE 16.1.   Examples of How Prevention Programs Reduce Exposure and Enhance Resistance

PROBLEM	REDUCTION OF EXPOSURE	ENHANCED RESISTANCE
Drug abuse	Zero tolerance; drug-free schools; discipline policies that prohibit drugs in schools and other areas with high juvenile populations; reduction of advertising in media outlets targeting children; providing supervised areas/activities for social interaction.	Just say "no;" peer refusal skills; assertiveness skills; knowledge of drug effects; knowledge of legal and social consequences of drug use; prosocial attachment to anti-drug activities and philosophies.
Smoking	Active enforcement of laws prohibiting sales to minors, banning advertisements aimed at children; increased tax on tobacco products.	Just say "no;" peer refusal skills; assertiveness skills; knowledge of tobacco effects; inculcation of anti-smoking values.
Academic failure	Reduction/elimination of inappropriate curricula (e.g., developmentally, culturally, socially irrelevant, or inappropriate materials & methods).	Study skills; self-talk scripts to enhance problem-solving; note-taking strategies; increase prior knowledge base.
Social dysfunction	Remove/eliminate dysfunctional role models; reduce authoritarian discipline.	Social-skills training for initiating and maintaining peer relationships.
Violence	Discipline policies prohibiting weapons and violent acts; punishment/removal of violent offenders.	Peace-making skills; conflict resolution skills; personal safety knowledge/skills.

Albee (1994) proposed that the incidence of mental disorders is directly affected by the incidence and severity of risk factors, and by the availability and strength of protective factors. The incidence of risk factors and the availability of protective factors form a reciprocal relationship to determine the incidence of mental disorders. This relationship is illustrated in Figure 16.2.

Because prevention programs generally focus on reducing risk factors, whereas mental-health promotion programs generally focus on increasing protective factors, one could argue that mental illness prevention and mental-health promotion are conceptually linked. The actual relationships between these factors, and their relative weights, vary according to the disorder. That is, some disorders may be better addressed through risk reduction programs, whereas other disorders may be more amenable to enhancing protective factors and mental-health promotion.

PREVENTION VERSUS TREATMENT

The essence of secondary prevention is early identification of problems and intervention before they become severe psychological disorders. Identifying and dealing with problems in their earliest stages, to shorten their duration and minimize the intensity,

reduces the prevalence of disorders. Children are often targets of secondary prevention approaches because of their psychological malleability and flexibility. The younger the child, the less likely problems or disorders will be developed and entrenched and the more favorable the prognosis for intervention.

The Nature of the Problem

In the last analysis, of course, the key issue both for treatment and prevention programs is how well they meet their desired goals. But most treatments have not reduced the prevalence of various disorders. Likewise, health disorders (mental or otherwise) have never been eliminated or controlled through treatment, but only as a result of successful prevention (Albee, 1982, 1986; Kessler & Albee, 1975). Consequently, we make the argument for prevention (and mental-health promotion).

Approximately 15–20% of the U.S.A.'s population need mental-health services (Price et al., 1988). At present, that figure represents five times the size of the present mental health services delivery system. The gap between demand and services has been stable since the 1950s (Albee, 1959), although recent figures suggest the gap may be increasing (Albee, 1994; Tudor, 1996). Contemporary trends toward reduced mental-health services in managed-

$$\text{Incidence of Disorder} = \frac{\Sigma\ (\text{Biogenetics, Environmental Stressors, Gene/Environment Interaction})}{\Sigma\ (\text{Social/Coping Skills, Self-esteem, Social Supports})}$$

Figure 16.2. The hypothesized relationship between problem incidence, protective factors, and risk factors. *Source:* Adapted from Albee, 1994, and Tudor, 1996.

care systems suggest that the supply of mental-health services may be stagnant at best, or decreasing, in the face of increasing need.

The Solution

Essentially, there are two ways to close the gap between the supply of and the demand for mental-health services. The first is to dramatically increase the supply of mental-health services and service providers. This alternative has always been unlikely, in part because of the gap between current and needed supply, and in part because of the cost for human and financial resources. Albee's dictum that "There will never be enough mental health professionals to provide help for such widespread distress" (Price et al., 1988) is as true today as it was 50 years ago.

The second way to solve the problem is to reduce the demand or need for mental-health services. To accomplish this, mental-health professionals must change their focus from individual diagnosis treatment of clients to "at-risk" or population-oriented approaches. This implies a shift in service stance (i.e., from reactive to proactive) and in the level of service delivery (i.e., from individuals to groups). Although rational arguments for prevention are well developed, the resources, manpower, and research base for such programs are insufficient (Albee, 1982; Albee & Joffe, 1977; Cowen, 1982a, 1982b, 1986; Lorion, 1983; Price et al., 1988). Moreover, this problem is international, in that no country has clearly recognized and adequately funded mental-health promotion/mental illness prevention policies (Tudor, 1996).

The challenge of working with children before they experience problems can be put within the framework of this book. What if some of the techniques designed for treating individuals were inten-

tionally modified, adapted, and evaluated for children before they struggled with substance use, parental divorce, delinquency, or school transitions? Those same techniques might also be effective with those individuals just starting to show signs of disturbances, or who have a propensity to develop such conditions.

In sum, the paradigm shift from treatment to prevention can be a relatively small yet a logical change for many mental-health professionals. Whereas many intervention technologies are surprisingly similar, conceptual and philosophical distinctions between treatment and prevention are real. In essence, treatment and prevention differ primarily in terms of the "time" of intervention in relation to the period of onset of difficulties and the "target" of such interventions. That is, individuals experiencing problems to the population at large or "at-risk" groups. The distinction among types of "prevention" may be less important than the demonstrated effectiveness of the interventions. The ever-present need for mental-health services, the continuing shortage of professionals and funding, and the relatively small gains made in treating or eliminating various behavioral conditions or mental disorders, all point to the need for further development of prevention programs.

FACTORS THAT INFLUENCE PREVENTION PROGRAM DEVELOPMENT

Several factors, in combination, facilitate the development, evaluation, and dissemination of prevention programs. These include: educating prevention professionals, understanding the needs of constituent groups, establishing baselines for problems or competencies, clarifying important interactions between personal and environmental dimensions, and developing a generative knowledge-base of health-associated variables. Several of these factors are discussed in this section. Barriers to implementing prevention programs are reviewed later in the chapter.

Prevention Professionals

Until very recently, prevention professionals have been self-educated, rather than formally trained (Price, 1986). Specifically, Price (1986) noted that many participants in the Vermont Conference of Primary Prevention of Psychopathology,

> did not initially identify themselves as prevention researchers. They were experts on specific problems and content areas, some of whom for the first time discovered that the knowledge they were developing could actually be applied to primary prevention efforts. (p. 292).

Indeed, the four roles Price (1983, 1986) specifically proposed for prevention professionals, that is, problem analyst, innovation designer, field evaluator, and diffusion researcher, all have parallels in traditional graduate programs for preparing mental-health professionals.

Problem Analyst

The problem-analyst role, for example, requires defining the issue, developing an understanding of the problem's etiology, and determining the needs of various populations (Price, 1983). These activities are no less important within traditional treatment paradigms. One distinguishing function of a prevention professional is to clarify risk factors associated with problem or competence development.

Innovative designers

Price (1983, 1986) defines innovative designers as, "people with a broad knowledge of change methods" (p. 292). Existing graduate training program standards from organizations such as the American Psychological Association, the National Association of School Psychologists, and the National Association of Social Workers and many state licensing boards, include provisions to insure that qualified professionals have a broad knowledge base. Although competent mental health practitioners and researchers qualify as innovative designers, their focus has not typically been directed to prevention activities.

Field Evaluators

Professionals involved in prevention use many program evaluation competencies and skills already taught in current graduate training programs (Lorion, 1983; Lorion & Lounsbury, 1981). Program evaluation methods, experimental designs and statistics generalize across conceptual frames of a problem. "True" experimental designs (where researchers control selection, assignment, and treatment of participants), and quasi-experimental large group designs (where researchers have less control over selection, assignment, and/or treatments) may be used to evaluate a variety of prevention programs. Single-case designs using alternating treatments (e.g., ABAB) or multiple-baseline designs may also be used for prevention research and practice. In either case, traditional graduate training in research and statistics should provide a conceptual and functional basis for prevention program evaluation.

Prevention Program Components

Prevention programs typically have four components, or parts. These include a theoretical orientation, a generative knowledge base, a treatment component, and an evaluation plan. Effective programs generally demonstrate a tight, coherent link between these major prevention program features.

Theoretical Orientations

Theoretical orientations explain behaviors guide prevention program development from its inception. There are behavioral, psychodynamic, humanistic, developmental, ecological, and eclectically based preventive interventions. Characteristics or variables deemed important enough to attend to and manipulate may differ by theoretical persuasion, but working with people before significant problems become established is consistent across all prevention efforts. We have discussed the issue of theoretical orientation previously in this chapter (see "Conceptual Bases"), and so we will move on to discussion of the next program element—generative knowledge base.

Generative Knowledge Base

Sound generative knowledge bases are the foundation for effective prevention programs (Cowen, 1980, 1986; Lorion, 1983; Lorion, Tolan, & Wahler, 1987). Knowledge about the etiology of competencies and problems offers one source of valuable information on the timing and development of relevant interventions. Such information must come from "core" areas of psychology (e.g., social, developmental, organizational, clinical, school), social work, sociology, education, and medicine, and must be integrated to avoid past mistakes and to develop realistic future plans (Cowen, 1980, 1986; Lorion, 1983; Price, 1983; Munoz, Snowden, & Kelly, 1979; Zins, Conyne, & Ponti, 1988). However, it is important to note that the theoretical orientation to the problem guides the selection of the knowledge base. Behavioral prevention professionals will use a different knowledge base to drive juvenile delinquency prevention than psychodynamically-oriented professionals. Regardless of orientation, however, prevention specialists must identify and carefully define and consider the generative knowledge base if they want to build effective prevention programs.

One important body of generative information for prevention program development and evaluation is knowledge about base rates for certain types of outcome conditions. Because most definitions of prevention are anchored by the reduction of problems or the increase of competencies, establishing the efficacy of primary prevention interventions is tied to changes in the incidence of these conditions. This is also important for determining the effectiveness of other types of mental-health interventions (e.g., Cronbach & Meehl, 1955) and is no less important today in determining the validity of preventive interventions (Lorion et al., 1987).

In sum, the generative knowledge base that informs prevention programs comes from diverse fields and orientations, from work with individuals, environments and their interactions, and from basic and applied research. This meaningful body of knowledge is available to all creative, innovative, competent mental-health professionals. For it to be applied to prevention, however, a paradigm shift (Kuhn, 1970), away from treatment and toward preventive interventions is needed. Prevention by definition is an applied endeavor. Neither the prevalence nor the incidence of dysfunctional conditions can be changed toward greater health anywhere but in the real world. As such, all preventive work is subject both to the benefits and risks inherent to applied, *in vivo* program efforts.

Treatment

Prevention programs vary widely in the types of treatments they deliver. Later in this chapter, we will provide examples of prevention program treatments. At this juncture, it is important to realize that the treatment regimen or plan should be congruent with the theoretical orientation and the generative knowledge base. That is, there should be an obvious link between what prevention researchers do and the body of knowledge available to them. However, the content and implementation of prevention treatments is often influenced by available resources and political/social processes (see Kelly, 1988). Effective prevention programs successfully resolve these contextual issues, resulting in a program that adheres to scientific theory and knowledge while capitalizing on and remaining congruent with contextual resources and norms. Effective prevention programs target individual and environmental factors, and the interactions and transactions among them. A significant change in any of these factors can cause shifts in incidence or prevalence rates (Albee, 1982; Lorion et al., 1987; Sameroff & Chandler, 1975).

Evaluation Plans

Other chapters in this volume describe evaluation findings for treatment and reports of treatment effectiveness across settings, providers, times, and behaviors. Those types of evaluation yardsticks are just as important for prevention efforts (Cowen,

1980, 1983, 1986; Lorion, 1983; Lorion & Lounsbury, 1981; Price & Smith, 1985). Understanding the differential effectiveness, and generalization, of treatment approaches can provide insights for innovative development of prevention programs (Lorion et al., 1987). Knowledge of specific prevention models with associated steps and processes can be used to *transfer, execute,* and *develop* preventive interventions (cf., Cowen, 1982a, 1986; Price, 1983, 1986). Thus, evaluation contributes to the generative knowledge base for future prevention efforts, and modification of ongoing prevention work.

Two types of evaluation are essential for prevention programs. The first is formative evaluation, and the second is summative evaluation. Formative evaluation focuses on insuring the program is successfully implemented. This is akin to treatment integrity in the clinical literature (i.e., the degree to which a particular treatment was actually implemented according to plan) (see Gresham, Gansel, Noell, Cohen, & Rosenblum, 1993). In contrast, summative evaluation focuses on treatment outcomes (i.e., to what degree has the clients' status changed as a consequence of the treatment?). Effective prevention programs plan both types of evaluation before starting preventive treatments. Formative evaluation plans must clearly define goals for treatment implementation, and mechanisms for monitoring and modifying treatment implementation to meet the dual needs of treatment integrity (appropriate adherence to the generative knowledge base) and treatment acceptability (appropriate modification to be accepted and supported in the context for service delivery) (see Paget, 1991).

Summative or outcome evaluation plans must include some means for addressing the question "Has the prevention program improved (or changed) things?" Researchers can use two types of designs to answer this question. The first is a between-groups design, in which researchers compare one ore more groups receiving a treatment to one or more groups receiving no treatment (i.e., a control or comparison group), or a different form of treatment (i.e., an alternate treatment group). These designs generally fall under the rubric of experimental or quasi experimental designs. The second type of research design for evaluating prevention programs is the single-case design. Single-case designs are popular with clinicians because they allow treatment evaluation for the client being served (hence they are often called "*N*=1" or "single-subject" designs). Prevention researchers often use single-case designs in the same way as practitioners, but the "case" is often the group or population (not individual) served in the program. That is, researchers may monitor base rates of problems in a setting or group over time, rather than the behavior of a single individual. These may also be termed *longitudinal* studies, because they require researchers to monitor a group over a period of time.

Prevention researchers who use single-case designs may select either an alternating treatments design (ABAB), or a multiple-baseline design. Alternating treatments are simple in a conceptual framework, but are rarely appropriate for evaluating prevention programs. The reason they are rarely appropriate is that the treatments in most prevention programs are intended to be irreversible (i.e., once treated, a group should not regress back to pretreatment levels when treatment is withdrawn). Therefore, most prevention programs use multiple-baseline designs, in which treatments are staggered across settings, groups, or target behaviors. Multiple baseline designs have the added benefit of not requiring a system to arbitrarily implement and withdraw a treatment. Although between-groups and single-case designs are quite different in concept, effective evaluation designs often combine between-groups and single-case elements (e.g., the Stanford Heart Disease Prevention Program; Maccoby & Altman, 1988).

Summary

The most important characteristic of effective prevention programs is that the elements or components of prevention (i.e., conceptual basis, generative knowledge base, treatment, and evaluation) are clearly and consistently coordinated. Prevention programs must be implemented in real-world contexts, and those contexts contain resources, limitations, and forces that affect all prevention program components. Many prevention programs fail to successfully resolve these challenges (Zins et al., 1988); effective programs coordinate the conceptual, generative knowledge, treatment, and evaluation components to form a coherent prevention program.

SPECIFIC PREVENTIVE INTERVENTIONS

We will describe three prevention programs in detail to exemplify prevention programming possibilities for children and adolescents. The first example is the Primary Mental Health Project (PMHP), which is a secondary prevention effort. PMHP targets the reduction of school adjustment problems in young children. The second program we will review is the School Transitional Environment Project (STEP), which is a primary prevention program that assists middle- and high school entrants to make the transition from less to more complex school environments. We conclude our examples with the Life Skills Training (LST) program, which prevents substance use and abuse by targeting junior-high students. Each example provides a brief overview, followed by Background, Program Description, and Evaluation Results sections. Because all of these programs have existed for at least one decade, more comprehensive information is available in the literature citations.

Primary Mental Health Project (PMHP)

The PMPH is a secondary prevention program targeted at primary-age children (K–third grade) who are at risk for developing school adjustment problems. By means of an early detection and screening process involving multiple sources of information and multiple methods, children at risk are identified and provided with helping services individually or in small groups by para-professional child associates. Because direct services to children are being provided by the child associates, the role of the professional mental-health worker (e.g., psychologist, social worker) changes to that of providing indirect student services, such as child-associate training and supervision and consultation with parents and

school staff. Detailed descriptions of PMHP are provided elsewhere (e.g., Cowen & Hightower, 1989, 1990; Cowen, Trost, Izzo, Lorion, Dorr, & Isaacson, 1975, 1996).

Background

PMHP began in one Rochester, New York city school in 1957 following two clinical observations: (a) teachers reported that relatively few students, 2-4, required approximately 50% of their disciplinary efforts, and (b) children referred for mental-health services in later elementary- and high school years typically experienced school adjustment difficulties in the primary grades. In fact, initial studies showed that at-risk students presented more school adjustment difficulties over time (Cowen et al., 1975; Cowen, Zax, Izzo, & Trost, 1966). Cowen and his colleagues recognized, as did others working the area of early identification (e.g., Bower, 1977, 1978; Keogh & Becker, 1973), that identification without effective interventions may do more harm than good.

PMHP explored alternatives to providing services to children at-risk, a historically under-served population (e.g., Glidewell & Swallow, 1969; Namir & Weinstein, 1982; Prevention Task Panel Report, 1978). Consultation was provided to teachers by the mental-health team. Children's needs and associated individual plans were discussed, developed, and implemented. Other school personnel became involved as children's needs dictated. After-school activity groups were run by teachers, selected for their natural care-giving characteristics of warmth, empathy and genuineness. Mental health professionals provided discussion groups for teachers and parents. Although these earlier attempts did not significantly reduce school adjustment difficulties, they were seeds from which PMHP developed.

Program Description

PMHP programs have four basic structural consistencies, although specific program practices vary. A description of these consistencies is followed by a brief program description.

PMHP programs involve an early detection and screening component. Specifically, screening is an ongoing process that continues throughout the school year. As such, there are no rigid procedures or criteria established for student entry into the project. However, recommended practices include: (a) using multiple sources of information, (b) involving multiple methods to obtain information, (c) using a multidisciplinary approach in reviewing screening information and making referral decisions, and (d) conducting various screening activities throughout the year. Screening is perceived as a necessary, but not sufficient process for meeting children's needs.

Working with young children is another program structural consistency. Young children were children in kindergarten through third grades, but recently, PMHP included children in preschool programs. Because PMHP is a prevention program for children at risk of developing school adjustment problems, older children who might experience various crisis situations, children with disabilities, and others might receive PMHP services. Those children who are diagnosed as seriously emotionally disturbed or behaviorally disordered, however, are not appropriate for PMHP. PMHP is a prevention program targeted toward the population of young children at risk for school adjustment difficulties, not a treatment program for children with serious emotional disturbances or behavior disorders.

A third, and central, component to PMHP is the use of nonprofessionals to provide direct, on-going, support services to children. People used as nonprofessional child-associates include: volunteers, (e.g., college students, foster grandparents, Mental Health Association members) and part-time employees (e.g., successful parents working as aides). Almost all child associates are recruited and selected for their pre-existing care-giving abilities, and characteristics of warmth, empathy, and benevolent firmness that are typically associated with successful therapeutic outcomes. Initially, PMHP used child associates because of the limited availability and high cost of professionals. However, research suggests that nonprofessionals are no less effective than professionals in producing positive therapeutic outcomes (Berman & Norton, 1985; Durlack, 1979; Hattie, Sharpley, & Rogers, 1984). The actual therapeutic approaches child associates use to work with children vary by treatment unit (individual or group), and the intervention orientation (nondirective to behavioral) of the supervising professional. PMHP encourages variations in approach to meet the specific needs of school districts.

The fourth common structural strand includes changes in professional roles. Such activities include selection, training, and supervision of nonprofessional child associates and consultation resource activities with school personnel and parents. Graduate schools often ignore supervision in professional training (Knoff, 1986), so further training may be necessary. In contrast, most graduate programs include training in consultation, and so PMHP professionals are well-prepared for consultation activities (e.g., assignment, progress, end-of-program conferences), which lead to additional unstructured consultation meetings. In many ways, PMHP structures promote alternate professional roles for mental-health professionals.

The following example summarizes how a PMHP program might operate during a school year. The program begins in September when staff are introduced to PMHP as a prevention program for children "at risk" for school adjustment difficulties. For schools where additional training modules have been completed (e.g., crisis training, planned short-term intervention, working with acting-out children), children appropriate for those services are also described. Timelines for completing various programmatic steps are provided. PMHP behavior observations typically occur in 3 to 4 weeks. Teacher and child ratings, and any direct screening, occur at 4 to 6 weeks into the school year. Child associates assist with the screening process.

After the initial screening procedures are completed, an assignment conference involving the PMHP team (mental-health professional(s), child associates, principal, and teacher) meet to discuss and review the screening data and any other pertinent information. School professionals contact the parents, describe the program, indicate which goals have been suggested for the child, and request parent's written permission for the child to become involved. During the assignment conferences, every targeted student is discussed, and then specific goals are developed. While teachers attend the assignment conferences, a substitute teacher covers their class.

Child associates see targeted children one to three times per week in a "play room" stocked with various play materials. Mental-health professionals supervise child associates 1/2 to 1 hour per week, either individually or in a group. Child-associate activities range from establishing behavioral contracts to active listening, depending on the child's goals and the associate's training.

Formal progress conferences are held mid-way between program initiation and termination; informal consultations occur as needed. During these conferences, adults review goals, modify intervention strategies, or involve others in the child's treatment plan. Children who were not initially selected, but who show needs, might enter the program, whereas those children meeting their goals exit the program.

Evaluation Results

Both formative and summative program evaluations have occurred throughout PMHP's history. An array of studies involving various samples, dependent variables, sophistication of experimental design, and methods of analysis are available (e.g., Cowen et al., 1975; Cowen, Weissberg et al., 1983; Weissberg, Cowen, Lotyczewski, & Gesten, 1983) and by others (Durlak, 1977; Kirschenbaum, 1979; Kirschenbaum, DeVoge, Marsh, & Steffen, 1980; Rickel, Dyhdalo, & Smith, 1984; Sandler, Duricko, & Grande, 1975). The preponderance of reported outcomes suggest that PMHP decreases school adjustment problems, and increases behaviors associated with school competence. Although long-term (i.e., longer than 5 years) follow-up studies are not available, short- to intermediate-term follow-up studies report that early program gains are maintained over time (Chandler, Weissberg, Cowen, & Guare, 1984; Cowen, Dorr, Trost, & Izzo, 1972; Lorion, Cohen, & Caldwell, 1976).

There are many PMHP formative evaluations. Terrell, McWilliams, and Cowen (1972) reported that child associates can work as effectively with small groups of children as they can with individuals. Lorion, Cowen, and Caldwell (1974) evaluated the relative effectiveness of PMHP in working with three types of children: acting-out, shy-anxious, and learn-ing disabled. PMHP was more effective with shy-anxious than acting-out children. Following this result, a limit-setting method for dealing with acting-out youngsters was successfully developed and implemented (Cowen, Orgel, Gesten, & Wilson, 1979).

Felner and his colleagues (e.g., Felner, Ginter, Boike, & Cowen, 1981; Felner, Stolberg, & Cowen, 1975) reported that children experiencing stressful life events, such as death of a family member or parental divorce, had more serious school adjustment difficulties than noncrisis peers. A specific crisis intervention program successfully addressed the needs of students in crisis (Felner, Norton, Cowen, & Farber, 1981). Lorion, Cowen, and Kraus (1974) explored the regularities and efficacies of various program practices and discovered that multiple sessions per week were no more effective than seeing children once per week in reducing school adjustment difficulties. Although children tended to be seen for an entire school year (Lorion et al., 1974), Winer, Weissberg, and Cowen (1988) found short-term intervention is as effective as full-year intervention for reducing problem behaviors. These formative evaluations have guided changes within PMHP practices.

Generalization of results across settings, providers, and behaviors has also been evaluated via direct evidence (e.g., Cowen, Weissberg et al., 1983) and surveys (Cowen, Davidson, & Gesten, 1980; Cowen, Spinell, Wright, & Weissberg, 1983). Highlights of these results include: successful program implementations in large, small, urban, suburban, and rural districts with African American, Hispanic, Asian, and Caucasian populations; successful use of a wide range of child associates; and the proliferation of diverse theoretical intervention perspectives across various treatment formats. In sum, the flexibility of the PMHP structural model accepts the infusion of local practices and procedures allowing for widespread application of PMHP.

PMHP is not without limitations, some of which have been described previously (Cowen et al., 1975). Most important is PMHP's lack of long-term longitudinal follow-up studies. Although short-term effectiveness is well-documented, no studies examine long-term results. Differential outcomes of working with acting-out or shy-anxious children have been documented, but differential effects for other groups of "at-risk" children (e.g., poor interpersonal relationships, limited frustration tolerance, poor self-esteem) have not been evaluated. One reason for inattention to differential outcomes is the lack of clear understanding regarding "children at risk for school adjustment difficulties." Although flexibility in targeting children at risk may facilitate program adaption, no clear understanding of which children should (and should not) receive PMHP interventions exists. PMHP has adopted a traditional medical model (i.e., aimed at treating the child) rather than working with environmental factors, such as families and parents. As such, PMHP has not systematically explored the potential impact of environmental interventions focused on these factors. Finally, despite PMHP's flexible structure, PMHP essentially recapitulates traditional treatment models of service delivery—it just targets them toward young children. Therefore, many criticisms and limitations of PMHP also apply to traditional treatment approaches.

The School Transitional Environment Project (STEP)

STEP aims to ease the transitional developmental crisis of moving from elementary to middle- or junior-high school, and/or from middle- or junior-high school to high school. It does so by decreasing the school's environmental complexity, and by increasing the school's responsiveness to children's needs via personalized social support (Felner, Ginter, & Primavera, 1982; Felner & Adan, 1988). STEP wants to prevent school failure caused by unsuccessful transitions.

Background

STEP assumes that school transitions constitute major life transitions, which either enhance or retard students' psychological, social, academic, and behavioral functioning. Felner and his colleagues (Felner & Adan, 1988; Felner et al., 1993; Felner et al., 1983; Felner, Primavera, & Cauce, 1981) note school transitions often precede significant decreases in academic functioning and psychological

health, and increased substance abuse, delinquency, and dropout rates. Recognizing these circumstances, Felner et al. (1982) and Felner and Adan (1988) targeted the transition of adequately coping students in STEP. Students with difficulties in personal, social, or academic areas were not targeted. Essentially, STEP was designed for students who were reasonably successful, as evidenced by past school functioning, but whose susceptibility for difficulties increased because of the transition from one school organizational pattern to another.

STEP program authors considered specific school characteristics in program development. One characteristic was the school's environmental complexity. Schools with higher levels of administrative disorganization, those with new students entering from many feeder schools, and those presenting new social demands were considered complex. A second characteristic was limited support services availability. A third characteristic was school size—the larger the school, the less attention to individual student by the school staff, and thus, less social support for effective transition resolution. STEP attempts to reduce the stress of educational/developmental transitions by reducing school complexity and increasing social support.

Program Description

STEP has three major components. First, it organizes the school environment into STEP "units," which are groups of four to five homerooms. Students assigned to STEP units have the same homeroom and attend basic academic subjects, such as English, Mathematics, Social Studies, Science, and Health, together. To increase social familiarity and reduce setting complexity, STEP classrooms are located near one another. Felner and Adan (1988) suggest such an arrangement makes schools less overwhelming, more familiar, less stressful, and more comfortable to new incoming students than traditional arrangements.

The second STEP component restructures homeroom periods. Homeroom teachers have typically done little more than take daily attendance. In the STEP program, homeroom teachers assume additional responsibilities, including: follow-up suspected truancy, major guidance responsibilities (e.g., choosing classes, providing brief counseling for various problems), and developing a cohesive, supportive classroom identity. Homeroom teachers are helped to assume these roles by brief training and ongoing consultation.

The third STEP component is an interdisciplinary team approach to solving problems. Teachers within a STEP unit meet regularly to coordinate assessment of students' functioning, provide appropriate referrals, and request additional consultation and assistance from other school personnel. Essentially, STEP unit teachers assume responsibility for meeting or managing all of the needs in their unit, rather than relying on school-wide administration and support.

In sum, the STEP program provides an instructional model, similar to that of many middle schools, in which students receive their primary educational needs from a core group of four to five teachers. Teachers' academic responsibilities are maintained, while administrative and counseling activities are increased. By making each STEP unit relatively small, responsibility for unit members is enhanced. Additional roles and responsibilities characterize the operation of a "small school" (Barker & Gump, 1964).

Evaluation Results

The initial STEP evaluation (Felner et al., 1982) assessed changes in academic performance, self-esteem, school absenteeism, perceptions of school environment, and social support over one school year. When compared with a matched no-treatment control group, STEP students obtained significantly better results for all the above variables. Thus, STEP apparently prevented many problems from occurring.

Felner and Adan (1988) summarized follow-up results from the initial STEP implementation described above and additional STEP implementations. Academic grades, achievement test data, attendance statistics, and information on those students who graduated, transferred, or dropped out of school were obtained for over 90% of the initial cohort. Results showed: (a) 43% of regular students (controls) versus 21% of STEP students dropped out of school; (b) STEP students had significantly higher grades and fewer absences than controls; and (c)

low-achieving students in STEP (i.e., those at risk of failure or dropout) had higher high school graduation rates than controls.

STEP programs have replicated positive outcomes across settings (middle- and high schools; urban, suburban, and rural schools), student characteristics (SES, minority status), and have been maintained over time (Felner & Adan, 1988; Felner et al., 1993). Although it adopts a primary prevention philosophy (i.e., it aims to help all children, not just those at-risk), STEP also enhances educational outcomes and reduces school failure for traditionally at-risk students (e.g., minority, poor, urban youth) (Felner et al., 1993).

STEP reduces transitional stressors by reducing the movement patterns of students, and by increasing teachers' and students' responsibilities to each other. These changes in school environments promote school success. Therefore, STEP alters a potentially harmful situation, and provides additional social support to students during a particularly stressful life event (i.e., school transitions). Although STEP has not been replicated with all potential target groups, the results of available studies suggest STEP is an effective primary prevention intervention.

Life Skills Training (LST)

LST is an example of a substance abuse prevention program (Botvin, 1983, 1986; Botvin, Baker, Renick, Filazzola, & Botvin, 1984; Botvin & Eng, 1982; Botvin, Eng, & Williams, 1980; Botvin & McAlister, 1981; Botvin & Tortu, 1988) designed for junior-high school students. Students are taught to resist peer influences to smoke, drink, or use drugs, and peer pressure in general (Botvin, 1983; Botvin & Tortu, 1988). That is, LST develops individual competencies such as social skills and decision-making in the context of drug prevention efforts.

Background

Botvin and his colleagues (Botvin & McAlister, 1981; Millman & Botvin, 1983) have concluded that internal factors indicative of high-risk individuals for alcohol and substance abuse include: low self-esteem, aggression associated with shy-anxious behaviors, high anxiety and nervousness, passivity, lack of assertiveness, and an external locus of control. Also, external social factors, such as the attitudes and behaviors of family and friends, and portrayal of drugs in the popular media, can affect children's use and abuse of various substances (Botvin & Tortu, 1988). Low grades and associated school failure (e.g., dropouts) are also associated with increased potential for substance use and abuse (Jessor, 1982). Botvin (1983) attempts to enhance students' resistance to factors associated with substance use and abuse by teaching them new intrapersonal and interpersonal skills.

Botvin and Tortu (1988) argue that seventh, eighth, and ninth graders should be targeted for intervention because children in these grades actively experiment with various substances, behaviors, life styles, and values. This experimentation is a predictable developmental period that allows for the influence of positive and negative informational and experiential events. Furthermore, students at this age have a propensity to engage in behaviors that are risk-taking, health-compromising, peer-group patronizing, and argumentative. These behaviors increase the likelihood that they will ignore established rules, and also increases the use of rationalizations for self-serving behaviors (Botvin & Tortu, 1988).

LST aims to help students learn how to resist social pressures, to reduce their motivation to use various substances, and to increase their overall personal competence via the development and promotion of effective individual and peer social skills. Because the LST program uses positive information, it avoids the backlash induced by "scare tactics." Instead, LST attempts to impart knowledge appropriate for "here and now" orientation of most young adolescents. LST stresses the short-term, not long-term, consequences of substance abuse.

Program Description

Botvin and Tortu (1988) summarize LST's five major components. The first component is general information about the "gateway" substances (i.e., tobacco, alcohol, and marijuana). This component increases students' knowledge regarding short-term effects of these commonly available substances. The second component provides strategies for responsi-

ble decision-making, and illustrates how advertisers attempt to persuade consumers to use their products. The third component addresses self-perceptions via an 8-week self-improvement project. This component provides information on how to approach a goal, and it provides direct life experiences for goal acquisition. The fourth component teaches basic relaxation techniques for anxieties in social situations. Real-life practice is encouraged to promote skill generalization. The fifth component provides skills for establishing and maintaining relationships through communication, initiation, and assertiveness training. The social-learning perspective of the program encourages students to practice behaviors in different situations and settings. In addition to the components outlined above, additional booster curricula are available for eighth and ninth grades. Observation, practice, and continued learning of refusal and social skills are emphasized (Botvin & Tortu, 1988). These five components, and booster sessions, are delivered in a series of lessons typically provided in students' health or science classes (see also Dusenbury & Botvin, 1992).

Evaluation Results

LST program evaluations focus on cigarette (Botvin et al., 1980; Botvin & Eng, 1982; Botvin et al., 1984), alcohol (Botvin & Tortu, 1988; Botvin et al., 1984) and marijuana use (Botvin et al., 1984). These evaluations are often conducted in suburban New York or New York City public schools. Botvin and his colleagues use unusually rigorous evaluation designs including random assignment to treatment and control groups. Also, they supplement self-reports and other paper and pencil tasks with direct measures of drug use, such as collecting random saliva samples. Overall, treatment groups have 40–75% fewer new cigarette smokers than no-treatment controls after initial, 3-month, and 1-year follow-up studies. In one large study, Botvin et al. (1984) found that peer-led LST group members, when compared to control groups, engaged in cigarette and marijuana smoking significantly less often. These results, however, did not generalize to teacher-led groups. One problem associated with the teacher-led groups was treatment integrity. Teachers did not follow the LST curriculum as carefully as did peer leaders, which may have degraded the quality of their program implementation (Botvin & Tortu, 1988).

In summary, Botvin and his colleagues have systematically assessed the background and etiological factors related to substance abuse. From that generative research, they have developed the LST program for middle-school or junior-high school students. Although Botvin and his colleagues are continuing to research and evaluate their program (Botvin & Tortu, 1988; Dusenbury & Botvin, 1992), LST has not been replicated in many different locations, nor has it addressed drugs other than the incidence of "gateway" drugs. Nonetheless, Botvin's work is an example of a well-conceived and well-researched primary prevention program.

PREVENTION RESOURCES

Many psychologists seek information about how to prevent a specific disorder. The examples in the preceding section illustrate how theoretical orientations and generative knowledge bases guide intervention activities, which are further refined through objective formative and summative evaluation. However, many psychologists seek specific information regarding the "state of the art" with respect to prevention of a wider range of disorders than are covered in the preceding examples.

To address this need, we summarize resources to get practitioners started in prevention. Specifically, Figure 16.3 contains a list of recent literature reviews and sample resource organizations by target category. We encourage readers to supplement this list via current literature searches, and by contacting appropriate resource organizations for current information.

BARRIERS TO SUCCESSFUL PREVENTION WORK WITH CHILDREN

Problems with Prevention

Despite the success of prevention efforts, psychologists still devote little energy towards prevention (Reschly & Wilson, 1995). Certainly, prevention efforts are worthy, and well within the domain of psychological practice. Ethical standards and practice guidelines promulgated by professional associations (e.g., American Psychological Association, 1992; National Association of School Psychologists, 1992) place the welfare of the client (child) above all other concerns, and consequently specify prevention as a major service to be delivered by psychologists. Why, then, do psychologists resist prevention-oriented activities? We suggest there are at least two domains to consider in answering this question: (a) personal characteristics of psychologists, and (b) systemic factors. We conclude this discussion with suggestions for overcoming barriers to effective prevention work.

Personal Factors

The personal characteristics of psychologists influence whether, and how well, they engage in prevention activities. Affective factors play a role in motivating or inhibiting professionals from engaging in prevention. Generally, prevention is a risky activity, in that psychologists have lower self-efficacy for prevention than for treatment/rehabilitative services. Psychologists also risk rejection when they initiate services, thus discouraging proactive or preventive service delivery. Also, because few systems specifically request psychologists to engage in prevention (see below), psychologists may fill their schedule of services with other activities (i.e., they do not value prevention sufficiently to prioritize it over other service delivery demands) (Braden, 1988). These beliefs reduce the likelihood that psychologists will initiate and maintain prevention-oriented work.

A second personal domain relates to the knowledge, skills, and abilities (KSAs) for conducting prevention work. Despite the recommendation that psychologists engage in prevention work, professional organizations do not mandate "training" in prevention KSAs (e.g., National Association of School Psychologists, 1994; Office of Program Consultation and Accreditation 1996). Consequently, most psychologists receive little or no formal training in prevention. Given the lack of coverage in most graduate training curricula, and the limited experiences trainees receive during internships, many psychologists accurately perceive their KSAs

Prevention Resources

Prevention/Promotion Target Agencies (Internet address)	Literature Reviews

Drug Abuse

Internet Substance Abuse Resources

http://freenet.vcu.educ/health/vatc/internet.html

The National Clearinghouse for Alcohol and Drug Information

http://www.health.org/

The SubstanceAbuse and Mental Health Services

Administration http://www.samhsa.gov/

Research and Intervention: Preventing Substance Abuse in
   Higher Education

http://www.ed.gov/pubs/PreventingSubstanceAbuse/index.html

National Institute on Drug Abuse http://www.nida.nih.gov/

Center for Education and Drug Abuse

http://www.pit.edu/~mmv/cedar.html

Bailey, G. W. (1990). Current perspectives on substance abuse in youth. *Journal of the American Academy of Child and Adolescent Psychiatry, 28*(2), 151–162; Bruvold, W. H. (1990). A meta-analysis of the California school-based risk reduction program. *Journal of Drug Education, 20*(2), 139–152; Hawkins, J. D., Catalano, R. F., & Miller, J. Y. (1992).Risk and protective factors for alcohol and other drug problems in adolescence and early adulthood: Implications for substance abuse prevention. *Psychological Bulletin, 112*(1), 64–105; Logan, B. N. (1991). Adolescent substance abuse prevention: An overview of the literature. *Family and Community Health, 13*(4), 25–36; Swaim, R. C. (1991). Childhood risk factors and adolescent drug and alcohol abuse. *Educational Psychology Review, 3*(4), 363–398.

Juvenile Delinquency

Office of Juvenile Justice and Delinquency Prevention

http://www.iir.com/nygc/nygc.htm

U.S. Dept. of Justice http://justice2.usdoj.gov/

Feldman, P. (1989). Applying psychology to the reduction of juvenile offending and offences: Methods and results. *Issues in Criminological and Legal Psychology, 14,* 3–32; Yoshikawa, H. (1994). Prevention as cumulative protection: Effects of early family support and education on chronic delinquency and its risks. *Psychological Bulletin, 115*(1), 28–54.

Suicide

Suicide Awareness/Voices in Education http://www.save.org/

Baker, F. M. (1990). Black youth suicide: Literature review with a focus on prevention. *Journal of the National Medical Association, 82*(7), 495–507; Ladame, F., & Wagner, P. (1994). Adolescence and suicide: An update of recent literature. *European Psychiatry, 9*(Suppl 2), 211S-217S; Shaffer et al., (1988). Preventing teenage suicide: A critical review. *Journal of the American Academy of Child and Adolescent Psychiatry, 27*(6), 675–687.

General Psychiatric Disorders

The Wisconsin Clearinghouse http://www.uhs.wisc.edu/wch/

At-Risk Children and Youth

http://www.ncrel.org/sdrs/areas/un0cont.htm

Center for Prevention Research

http://www.uky.edu/RGS/PreventionResearch/welcome.html

National Institute on the Education of At-Risk Students

http://www.ed.gov/offices/OERI/At-Risk/

McGuire, J., & Earls, F. (1991). Prevention of psychiatric disorders in early childhood. *Journal of Child Psychology and Psychiatry and Allied Disciplines, 32*(1), 129–152.

School Drop-Out

Guide to U.S. Department of Education Programs

http://www.ed.gov/pub/GuideEDPgm/

Muha, D. G., & Cole, C. (1990). Dropout prevention and group counseling: A review of the literature. High School Journal, 74(2), 76–80.

Child Abuse

Children's Defense Fund

http://www.tmn.com/cdf/index.html

Berrick, J. D., & Barth, R. P. (1992). Child sexual abuse prevention: Research review and recommendations. Social Work Research and Abstracts, 28(4), 6–15; Carroll, L. A., Miltenberger, R. G., O'Neill, H. K. (1992). A review and critique of research evaluating child sexual abuse prevention programs.

Figure 16.3. Prevention resources by target area.

Child Abuse, continued

Education and Treatment of Children, 15(4), 335–354; Wolfe, D. A., Reppucci, N. D., Hart, S. (1994). Child abuse prevention: Knowledge and priorities. *Journal of Clinical Child Psychology,* 24(Suppl), 5–22.

Unprotected Sexual Activity

Planned Parenthood http://www.ppca.org/ppcasti.html

HIV Infoweb http://www.jri.org/infoweb/

van der Pligt, J., & Richard, R. (1994). Changing adolescents' sexual behaviour: Perceived risk, self-efficacy and anticipated regret. Patient Education and Counseling, 23(3), 187–196.

Violence

Partners Against Violence http://www.pavnet.org/

Peace Studies and Conflict Research
http://csf.Colorado.EDU/peace/index.html

Hampton, R. L., Jenkins, P., & Gullotta, T. P. (1996). Preventing violence in America. Thousand Oaks, CA: Sage Publications; Larsen, J. (1994). Violence prevention in the schools: A review of selected programs and procedures. School Psychology Review, 21(2), 151–164.

Figure 16.3., continued   Prevention resources by target area.

for prevention as being insufficient to the task. This, in turn, leads to two problems: (a) avoidance of prevention work and (b) prevention work with an unnecessarily high degree of failure. Professional ignorance of prevention promotes "the myth…that a technology of primary prevention is missing" (Zins et al. 1988, pp. 544–555). When psychologists do engage in prevention work, their lack of KSAs may lead to unrealistic time perspectives for intervention effects, inflated expectations for program goals, unrealistic demands on human and financial resources, and psychologically simplistic program content (Cowen, 1980, 1982b; Hightower, 1988; Lorion, 1983; Sarason, 1986). Thus, psychologists may need to address affective (i.e., attitudes, beliefs) and cognitive (i.e., KSAs) factors to enhance and increase prevention work.

System Factors

Funding mechanisms, reinforcement contingencies, and organizational structures also inhibit psychologists' involvement in prevention. In schools, categorically-oriented funding mechanisms create an unrelenting demand for psychologists to declare children eligible for special education. Often, schools with many children in special education are given more money than schools with few children in special education. This funding method reinforces the psychologist's role as gatekeeper for special programs, and it discourages prevention programs by

withholding resources from schools that successfully prevent school failure. Nonschool agencies, such as clinics, are also driven by funding mechanisms that reward treatment services (e.g., third-party payments for therapy) or symptom-specific interventions (e.g., grants or contracts for specific problems). Even research for demonstration programs suffers from a funding structure that discourages longitudinal work (i.e., most programs are funded in cycles of 1–3 years).

Cost is a major concern to most systems. Although proponents of prevention often claim that prevention is cost effective (i.e., prevention is cheaper than treatment), this is not necessarily true. First, there is the issue of which system bears the costs, and which one earns the benefits. For example, it might be true that prevention of drug abuse might be cheaper to society (e.g., health-care costs, lost work, prison costs) than treatment, yet the systems responsible for prevention (e.g., schools) may recoup few of the benefits (e.g., schools do not receive reimbursement from private health providers for reducing health costs). Second, the assumption that prevention is cheaper than treatment (i.e., "An ounce of prevention is worth a pound of cure") may be inaccurate. Russell (1986) examines the cost of prevention versus treatment for common diseases, and concludes that prevention may cost the same or more than treatment. However, he also notes that quality of life is greater when diseases are prevented rather than treated, and so prevention may be justified even if it costs more than treatment. In contrast, Groth and Shumaker (1995) counter that prevention programs addressing some diseases and conditions (e.g., smoking cessation) can be cost effective. Although cost-benefit ratios for prevention programs are controversial, no one argues that effective prevention programs enhance the quality of life for those served.

Another issue related to prevention cost is the issue of payment for services. Traditional health plans in the United States were directed toward hospital services, and may have inadvertently discouraged (nonhospital) prevention efforts. It is not clear whether the shift to managed care plans may discourage or encourage prevention programs. On the one hand, managed care plans often cut costs by reducing the services provided to clients. In this context, prevention is a service that can often be eliminated with little consumer complaint, and so managed care may discourage prevention work. On the other hand, some argue that in mature managed care markets, providers will have to compete with each other for customers. Prevention programs may improve plan profitability by increasing customer satisfaction while concurrently decreasing expensive health-care services. Although some scenarios are encouraging (e.g., some health maintenance organizations in Minneapolis have begun aggressively recruiting clients for smoking cessation programs), it is not clear whether prevention will thrive or wither under managed care. However, it is increasingly clear that traditional forms of treatment (i.e., multiple hourly office visits for one-to-one psychotherapies) are withering under managed care, which could encourage psychologists to consider offering alternative, proactive, preventive services.

Systemic reinforcement contingencies also discourage psychologists from engaging in preventive efforts. In schools, the refer-test-place sequence maintains a negative reinforcement schedule for teachers to refer children (i.e., school psychologists negatively reinforce teacher requests by removing difficult children from the classroom). Agency-based psychologists also find themselves in a milieu where treatment of problems, rather than their prevention, are rewarded by personal interest, collegial support (e.g., case conferences), and the implicit

promise of "fixing the child." Paradoxically, some successful prevention programs fail to garner reinforcement because they may result in nonevents. It is impossible to observe something that does not occur, and consequently, it is difficult to attribute nonevents (e.g., the lack of depression cases, no suicides) to the presence of the prevention program, especially in situations where there is no prior history of maladaptive behaviors.

Another barrier to prevention is the lack of proximity between mental-health professionals and children. The physical distance between mental-health professionals (especially those in nonschool agencies) and children discourages prevention efforts. Only people in need of direct treatment for a condition, and who have the money to pay for it, overcome the barriers and enter the agency. Even mental-health professionals employed by school districts shuttle between many schools, spending a day a week at a school in borrowed space and may have other primary roles to fulfill (e.g., testing). These factors erode the mental-health professionals ability to influence prevention-oriented activities. Judicious use of expert and referent power may increase the ability of mental-health professionals to create and maintain prevention programs, but it is an uphill battle that is complicated by limited physical proximity, few resources, and a lack of administrative sanction.

Beyond the "passive" constraints in many systems, prevention programs are sometimes the object of direct attacks. Some groups in society object to preventive efforts with children, especially prevention programs in public settings. The Citizens Commission on Human Rights (CCHR), a group "established in 1969 by the Church of Scientology to investigate and expose psychiatric violations of human rights" (quote from CCHR letterhead), actively opposes mental-health promotion and mental illness prevention efforts with children (CCHR, 1996). Some religious groups view mental-health initiatives, such as encouraging coping strategies or building self-esteem, as efforts to impose alien values on their children. In response to these concerns, the U.S. Congress passed legislation aimed at eliminating uninformed participation in psychological research and treatment programs in schools.

Although it appears reasonable to insist on informed consent for participation in prevention programs, many primary preventive efforts (e.g., STEP school restructuring) must include all of the children at a site. Just as fluoridation of water to prevent dental carries affects everyone, systemic changes to enhance mental health or prevent mental illness may affect an entire population. It is not clear whether conservative challenges under federal legislation could be used to stop primary prevention programs, but it is a possibility.

Responses to Obstacles

The critique of obstacles to prevention activities implies a number of actions for the future. Training programs should consider explicitly training students in prevention activities. Appropriate coursework, practice, and supervised field experiences could be combined to promote mental-health professionals KSAs, self-confidence, and motivation to pursue prevention work. Professional organizations could help prevention work by developing appropriate training standards, and by working with regulatory agencies, third-party providers, and legislative bodies to reduce prohibitions and increase incentives for prevention efforts.

The research community must work together with health and education agencies to build an accurate database justifying the costs of preventive work. This chapter contains a wealth of literature demonstrating the value of prevention, yet little of the research specifically includes fiscal considerations. Systems need accurate, realistic appraisals of the costs and potential benefits of prevention programs to make informed and effective allocation of limited resources (see Mrazek & Haggerty, 1994). Likewise, prevention researchers must be honest in appraising their work. Too often, researchers claim success on the basis of attitude or knowledge changes, rather than basing claims on actual changes in problem incidence or prevalence (see Berrick & Barth, 1992; Bruvold, 1990 for relevant reviews).

Government policy is another arena that must address prevention and mental-health promotion efforts. Current policies are often conflicted. For example, the U.S. Surgeons General have an unwavering and distinguished commitment to smoking cessation, whereas Congress continues to vote financial subsidies to tobacco farmers. Likewise, recent efforts to encourage prevention (e.g., U.S. Preventive Services Task Force, 1996) are inconsistent with budget cutbacks and regulations prohibiting primary prevention efforts. Finally, there are no national policies for promoting mental health, even among the most advanced health-care systems in the world (Tutor, 1996).

Finally, we believe psychologists must examine their own values and behaviors related to prevention. Realistically, many systems fail to encourage—or actively discourage—prevention efforts. Also, many psychologists lack the KSAs needed for effective prevention work. Yet, just as realistically, many psychologists favor the more immediate (and in some cases, material) rewards of treatment over the delayed (and often less lucrative) rewards of prevention. We encourage psychologists to reconsider treatment-oriented activities and priorities with the goal of increasing time spent on prevention. Although we can cite lofty and pious reasons for our suggestion, we also note that prevention services may be of greater value to cost-conscious health plans than traditional treatments.

CONCLUSION

Prevention and treatment paradigms for children have several important significant common elements. Both share a common heritage from the child guidance movement through the mid 1950s. Historically, the two approaches have had more years in common than years separate. Both approaches rest on common theories (e.g., learning, personality, social, developmental, systems), generative knowledge bases, experimental methodologies, and research methods. Treatment and prevention share the goals of modifying perceptions, thinking, behaviors, environments, or systems that limit individuals functioning (Strayhorn, 1988). Finally, professionals in prevention or treatment, must be able to define or diagnose problems, innovate designs to address those problems, evaluate the efficacy and effectiveness of interventions, and disseminate and/or use the acquired information in real-life situations.

Differences between prevention and treatment start with their definitions. Preventive interventions characteristically target populations rather than troubled individuals, and do so earlier than treatment in the cycle of unfolding problems. Indeed, timing interventions to occur before difficulties become chronic is a hallmark that distinguishes prevention from treatment. Whereas the individual is the prime focus of treatment, prevention programs are more likely to target combinations of individual, environmental, and systemic features. Whereas those involved in treating individuals must observe, diagnose, and implement treatment plans for clients, prevention professionals must be able to diagnose, plan, and intervene with larger, more complex, systems. Finally, relevant intervention outcomes are different in the two approaches. Those who treat have the goal of "curing" a problem, and thus reducing existing cases by at least one. For prevention, the goal is to change incidence either by enhancing competence or decreasing problems in a targeted population. In the societal sense, treatment has had, and will continue to have, valuable but limited potential; by contrast, prevention's potential has yet to be realized.

REFERENCES

Albee, G. W. (1959). *Mental health manpower trends.* New York: Basic Books.

Albee, G. W. (1982). Preventing psychopathology and promoting human potential. *American Psychologist, 37,* 1043–1050.

Albee, G. W. (1986). Lessons from observations on the primary prevention of psychopathology. *American Psychologist, 41,* 891–898.

Albee, G. W. (1994). The fourth revolution. In D.R. Trent and C. Reed (eds.), *Promotion of mental health,* vol. 3 (pp. 1–16). Aldershot, UK: Avebury.

Albee, G. W., & Joffe, J. M. (Eds.). (1977). *The primary prevention of psychopathology: The issues.* Hanover, NH: University Press of New England.

American Psychological Association (1992). Ethical principles of psychologists. *American Psychologist, 36,* 633–638.

Anderson, L. S., Cooper, S., Hassol, L., Klein, D. C., Rosenblum, G., & Bennett, C. C. (1966). *Community psychology: A report of the Boston conference on the education of psychologists for community mental health.* Boston, MA: Boston University.

Barker, R. G., & Gump, P. (1964). *Big school, small school.* Stanford, CA: Stanford University Press.

Berman, J. S., & Norton, N. C. (1985). Does professional training make a therapist more effective? *Psychological Bulletin, 98,* 401–407.

Berrick, J. D., & Barth, R. P. (1992). Child sexual abuse prevention: Research review and recommendations. *Social Work Research and Abstracts, 28*(4), 6–15.

Bloom, B. L. (1977). *Community mental health: A general introduction.* Monterey, CA: Brooks/Cole.

Bloom, B. L. (1979). Prevention of mental disorders: Recent advances in theory and practice. *Community Mental Health Journal, 15,* 179–191.

Botvin, G. J. (1983). *Life Skills Training: Teacher's manual.* New York: Smithfield Press.

Botvin, G. J. (1986). Substance abuse prevention research: Recent developments and future directions. *Journal of School Health, 56,* 369–374.

Botvin, G. J., Baker, E., Renick, N., Filazzola, A. D., & Botvin, E. M. (1984). A cognitive-behavioral approach to substance abuse prevention. *Addictive Behaviors, 9,* 137–147.

Botvin, G. J., & Eng, A. (1982). The efficacy of a multicomponent approach to the prevention of cigarette smoking. *Preventive Medicine, 11,* 199–211.

Botvin, G. J., Eng, A., & Williams, C. L. (1980). Preventing the onset of cigarette smoking through Life Skills Training. *Preventive Medicine, 9,* 135–143.

Botvin, G. J., & McAlister, A. (1981). Cigarette smoking among children and adolescents: Causes and prevention. In C. B. Arnold (Ed.), *Annual review of disease prevention* (pp. 222–249). New York: Springer.

Botvin, G. J., & Tortu, S. T. (1988). Preventing adolescent substance abuse through Life Skills Training. In R. H. Price, E. L. Cowen, R. P. Lorion, & J. Ramos-McKay (Eds.), *Fourteen ounces of prevention: A casebook for practitioners* (pp. 98–110). Washington, DC: American Psychological Association.

Bower, E. M. (1977). Mythologies, realities and possibilities in primary prevention. In G. W. Albee & J. M. Joffe (Eds.), *Primary prevention of psychopathology,* Vol. I: The issues (pp. 24–41). Hanover, NH: University Press of New England.

Bower, E. M. (1978). Early periodic screening diagnosis and treatment: Realities, risks, and possibilities. *American Journal of Orthopsychiatry, 48,* 114–130.

Braden, J. P. (1988). *Irrational beliefs of school psychologists: Why I can't (won't) do prevention work.* Paper presented at the annual Convention of the National Association of School Psychologists, Chicago, IL.

Brody, N., & Crowley, M. J. (1995). Environmental (and genetic) influences on personality and intelligence. In D. H. Saklofske & M. Zeidner (Eds.), International handbook of personality and intelligence (59–80). New York: Plenum Press.

Bruvold, W. H. (1990). A meta-analysis of the California school-based risk reduction program. *Journal of Drug Education, 20*(2), 139–152.

Caplan, G. (1964). Principles of preventive psychiatry. New York: Basic Books.

Caplan, G. In N. M. Lambert (Ed.), *The protection and promotion of mental health in schools.* (Public Health Service Publication No. 1226). Washington, DC: U.S. Government Printing Office.

Chandler, C., Weissberg, R. P., Cowen, E. L., & Guare, J. (1984). The long-term effects of a school-based secondary prevention program for young maladapting children. *Journal of Consulting and Clinical Psychology, 52,* 165–170.

Citizens Commission on Human Rights (1996). *Destroying lives: Psychiatry education's ruin.* Los Angeles, CA: Church of Scientology.

Cowen, E. L. (1980). The wooing of primary prevention. *American Journal of Community Psychology, 8,* 258–284.

Cowen, E. L. (1982a). Primary prevention research: Barriers, needs and opportunities. *Journal of Primary Prevention, 2,* 131–137.

Cowen, E. L. (1982b). The special number: A compleat roadmap. In E. L. Cowen (Ed.), Research in primary prevention in mental health. *American Journal of Community Psychology, 10,* 239–250.

Cowen, E. L. (1983). Primary prevention in mental health: Past, present and future. In R. D. Felner, L. Jason, J. Moritsugu, & S. S. Farber (Eds.), *Preventive psychology: Theory, research and practice in community interventions* (pp. 11–25). New York: Pergamon Press.

Cowen, E. L. (1986). Primary prevention in mental health: A decade of retrospect and a decade of prospect. In M. Kessler & S. E. Goldston (Eds.), *A decade of progress in primary prevention* (pp. 3–42). Hanover, NH: University Press of New England.

Cowen, E. L., Davidson, E. R., & Gesten, E. L. (1980). Program dissemination and the modification of delivery practices in school mental health. *Professional Psychology, 11,* 36–47.

Cowen, E. L., Dorr, D. A., Trost, M. A., & Izzo, L. D. (1972). A follow-up study of maladapting school children seen by nonprofessionals. *Journal of Consulting and Clinical Psychology, 39,* 235–238.

Cowen, E. L., & Hightower, A. D. (1989). The Primary Mental Health Project: Thirty years after. *Prevention in Human Services, 6*(2), 225–257.

Cowen, E. L., & Hightower, A. D. (1990). The Primary Mental Health Project: Alternative approaches in school-based prevention interventions. In T. B. Gutkin & C. R. Reynolds (Eds.), *The handbook of school psychology* (2nd ed., pp. 775–795). New York: Wiley.

Cowen, E. L., Orgel, A. R., Gesten, E. L., & Wilson, A. B. (1979). The evaluation of an intervention program for young school children with acting-out problems. *Journal of Abnormal Child Psychology, 7,* 381–396.

Cowen, E. L., Spinell, A., Wright, S., & Weissberg, R. P. (1983). Continuing dissemination of a school-based early detection and prevention model. *Professional Psychology, 14,* 118–127.

Cowen, E. L., Zax, M., Izzo, L. D., & Trost, M. A. (1966). Prevention of emotional disorders in the school setting: A further investigation. *Journal of Consulting Psychology, 30,* 381–387.

Cowen, E. L., et al. (1975). *New ways in school mental health: Early detection and prevention of school maladaptation.* New York: Human Sciences Press.

Cowen, E. L., Weissberg, R. P., Lotyczewski, B. S. (1983). Validity generalization of school-based preventive mental health program. *Professional Psychology, 14,* 613–623.

Cowen, E. L., Trost, M. A., Izzo, L. O., Lorion, R. P., Dorr, D., & Isaacson, R. V. (1996). *School-based prevention for children at risk: The Primary Mental Health Project.* Washington, DC: American Psychological Association.

Cronbach, L. J., & Meehl, P. F. (1955). Construct validity in psychological tests. *Psychological Bulletin, 52,* 281–302.

Davidson, W. S., & Redner, R. (1988). The prevention of juvenile delinquency: Diversion from the juvenile justice system. In R. H. Price, E. L. Cowen, R. P. Lorion, & J. Ramos-McKay (Eds.), *Fourteen ounces of prevention: A casebook for practitioners* (pp. 123–128). Washington, DC: American Psychological Association.

Durlak, J. A. (1977). Description and evaluation of a behaviorally oriented, school-based preventive mental health program. *Journal of Consulting and Clinical Psychology, 45,* 27–33.

Durlak, J. A. (1979). Comparative effectiveness of paraprofessional and professional helpers. *Psychological Bulletin, 86,* 80–92.

Dusenbury, L., & Botvin, G. J. (1992). Applying the competency enhancement model to substance abuse prevention. In M. Kessler, S. E. Goldston, & J. M. Joffe (Eds),. *The present and future of prevention: In honor of George W. Albee.* Newbury Park, CA: Sage Publications.

Felner, R. D., & Adan, A. M. (1988). The School Transition Environment Project: An ecological intervention and evaluation. In R. H. Price, E. L. Cowen, R.

P. Lorion, & J. Ramos-McKay (Eds.), *Fourteen ounces of prevention: A casebook for practitioners* (pp. 111–122). Washington, DC: American Psychological Association.

Felner, R. D., Brand, S., Adan, A. M., Mulhall, P. F., (1993). Restructuring the ecology of the school as an approach to prevention during school transitions: Longitudinal follow-ups and extensions of the School Transitional Environment Project (STEP). *Prevention in Human Services, 10*(2), 103–136.

Felner, R. D., Ginter, M. A., Boike, M. F., & Cowen, E. L. (1981). Parental death or divorce and the school adjustment of young children. *American Journal of Community Psychology, 9,* 181–191.

Felner, R. D., Ginter, M., & Primavera, J. (1982). Primary prevention and school transitions: Social support and environmental structure. *American Journal of Community Psychology, 10,* 277–290.

Felner, R. D., Jason, L. A., Moritsugu, J. N., & Farber, S. S., (Eds.). (1983). *Preventive psychology: Theory, research and practice.* New York: Pergamon Press.

Felner, R. D., Norton, P. L., Cowen, E. L., & Farber, S. S. (1981). A prevention program for children experiencing life crisis. *Professional Psychology, 12,* 446–452.

Felner, R. D., Primavera, J., & Cauce, A. M. (1981). The impact of social transitions: A focus for preventive efforts. *American Journal of Community Psychology, 9,* 449–459.

Felner, R. D., Stolberg, A. L., & Cowen, E. L. (1975). Crisis events and school mental health referral patterns of young children. *Journal of Consulting and Clinical Psychology, 43,* 305–310.

Glidewell, J. C., & Swallow, C. S. (1969). The prevalence of maladjustment in elementary schools: A report prepared for the Joint Commission on the Mental Health of Children. Chicago: University of Chicago Press.

Goldston, S. E. (1987). *Concepts of primary prevention: A framework for program development.* California Department of Mental Health, Office of Prevention.

Gresham, F. M., Gansle, K. A., Noell, G. H., Cohen, S., & Rosenblum, S. (1993). Treatment integrity of school-based behavioral intervention studies: 1980–1990. *School Psychology Review, 22*(2), 254–272

Groth, M. G., & Schumaker, J. (1995). Psychologists in disease prevention and health promotion: A review of the cost effectiveness literature. *Psychology: A Journal of Human Behavior, 32*(1), 1–10.

Gump, P. V. (1980). The school as a social situation. In M. R. Rosenzweig & L. W. Porter (Eds.), *Annual Review of Psychology, 31,* 553–582.

Hattie, J. A., Sharpley, C. F., & Rogers, H. J. (1984). Comparative effectiveness of professional and para-

professional helpers. *Psychological Bulletin, 95,* 534-541.

Herrnstein, R. J., & Murray, C. (1994). *The bell curve: Intelligence and class structure in American life.* New York: Free Press.

Hightower, A. D. (1988, April). Prevention program development: The pragmatics. In A. D. Hightower (Chair) *The nuts and bolts of implementing a prevention program.* Symposium conducted at the NASP annual meeting, Chicago, IL.

Insel, P. M., & Moos, R. H. (1974). Psychosocial environments: Expanding the scope of human ecology. *American Psychologist, 29,* 179–188.

Iscoe, I., & Spielberger, C. D. (Eds.). (1970). *Community psychology: Perspectives in training and research.* New York: Appleton-Century-Crofts.

Jessor, R. (1982). Critical issues in research on adolescent health promotion. In T. Coates, A. Petersen, & C. Perry (Eds.), *Promoting adolescent health: A dialog on research and practice* (pp. 447–46). New York: Academic Press.

Joffe, J. M., Albee, G. N., & Kelly, L. D. (Eds.). (1984). *Readings in primary prevention of psychopathology.* Hanover, NH: University Press of New England.

Kagan, J. (1994). *Galen's prophecy: Temperament in human nature.* New York: BasicBooks.

Kellam, S. G., Branch, J. D., Agrawal, K. C., & Ensminger, M. E. (1975). *Mental health and going to school: The Woodlawn program of assessment, early intervention, and evaluation.* Chicago: University of Chicago Press.

Kelly, J. G. (1988). *A guide to conducting prevention research in the community: First steps.* New York: Haworth Press.

Kennedy, J. F. (1963). *Message from the President of the United States relative to mental illness and mental retardation.* (88th Congress, 1st Session, U. S. House of Representatives Document #58). Washington, DC: U. S. Government Printing Office.

Keogh, B. K., & Becker, L. D. (1973). Early detection of learning problems: Questions, cautions and guidelines. *Exceptional Children, 40,* 5–11.

Kessler, M., & Albee, G. W. (1975). Primary prevention. In M. R. Rosenzweig & L. W. Porter (Eds.), *Annual Review of Psychology, 26,* 557–591.

Kessler, M., & Goldston, S. E. (Eds.). (1986). *A decade of progress in primary prevention.* Hanover, NH: University Press of New England.

Kirschenbaum, D. (1979). Social competence intervention and evaluation in the inner city: Cincinnati's Social Skills Development Program. *Journal of Consulting and Clinical Psychology, 47,* 778–780.

Kirschenbaum, D., DeVoge, J. B., Marsh, M. E., & Steffen, J. J. (1980). Multimodal evaluation of therapy vs. consultation components in a large inner-city early intervention program. American Journal of Community Psychology, 8, 587–601.

Klein, D. C., & Goldston, S. E. (Eds.). (1977). Primary prevention: An idea whose time has come. Washington, DC: U.S. Government Printing Office, DHEW Publication No. (ADM) 77–447. Washington, DC.

Knoff, H. M. (1986). Supervision in school psychology: The forgotten or future path to effective services? School Psychology Review, 15, 529–545.

Kuhn, T. S. (1970). The structure of scientific revolutions (2nd ed.). Chicago: University of Chicago Press.

Light, J. G., & DeFries, J. C. (1995). Comorbidity of reading and mathematics disabilities: Genetic and environmental etiologies. Journal of Learning Disabilities, 28(2), 96–106.

Lorion, R. P. (1983). Evaluating preventive interventions: Guidelines for the serious social change-agent. In R. D. Felner, L. A. Jason, J. N. Moritsugu, & S. S. Farber (Eds.), Preventive psychology: Theory, research and practice (pp. 251–268). New York: Pergamon Press.

Lorion, R. P., Caldwell, R. A., & Cowen, E. L. (1976). Effects of a school mental health project: A one-year follow-up. Journal of School Psychology, 14, 56-63.

Lorion, R. P., Cowen, E. L., & Caldwell, R. A. (1974). Problem types of children referred to a school based mental health program: Identification and outcome. Journal of Consulting and Clinical Psychology, 42, 491–496.

Lorion, R. P., Cowen, E. L., & Kraus, R. M. (1974). Some hidden "regularities" in a school mental health program and their relation to intended outcomes. Journal of Consulting and Clinical Psychology, 42, 346-352.

Lorion, R. P., & Lounsbury, J. W. (1981). Conceptual and methodological considerations in evaluating preventive interventions. In W. R. Task & G. Stahler (Eds.), Innovative approaches to mental health evaluations. NY: Academic Press.

Lorion, R. P., Tolan, P. H., & Wahler, R. G. (1987). Prevention. In H. C. Quay (Ed.) Handbook of juvenile delinquency (pp. 383–416). New York: Wiley.

Lynn, R. (1995). Cross-cultural differences in intelligence and personality. In D. H. Saklofske & M. Zeidner (Eds.), International handbook of personality and intelligence (pp. 107–124). New York: Plenum Press.

Maccoby, N., & Altman, D. G. (1988). Disease prevention in communities: The Stanford Heart Disease Prevention Program. In R. H. Price, E. L. Cowen, R. Lorion, & J. Ramos-McKay (Eds.), Fourteen ounces of prevention: A casebook for practitioners (pp.

165–174). Washington, DC: American Psychological Association.

Millman, R. B., & Botvin, G. J. (1983). Substance use, abuse, and dependence. In M. D. Levine, W. B. Carey, A. C. Crocker, & R. T. Gross, (Eds), Developmental behavioral pediatrics (pp. 683–708). Philadelphia: Saunders

Moos, R. H. (1974). Evaluating treatment environments: A social ecological approach. New York: Wiley.

Mrazek, P. J., & Haggerty, R. J. (Eds.). (1994). Reducing risks for mental disorders: Frontiers for preventive intervention research (Committee on Prevention of Mental Disorders, Division of Biobehavorial Sciences and Mental Disorders, Institute of Medicine). Washington, DC: National Academy Press.

Munoz, R. F., Snowden, L. F., & Kelly, J. G. (Eds.).(1979). Social and psychological research in community settings. San Francisco: Jossey-Bass.

Namir, S., & Weinstein, R. S. (1982). Children: Facilitating new directions. In L. R. Snowden (Ed.), Reaching the underserved: Mental health needs of neglected populations (pp. 43–73). Beverly Hills: Sage Publications.

National Association of School Psychologists. (1992). Professional conduct manual. Washington, D.C.: Author.

National Association of School Psychologists (1994). Standards for training and field placement programs in school psychology. Washington, DC: Author.

Neisser, U., et al. (1996). Intelligence: Knowns and unknowns. American Psychologist, 51(2), 77–101.

Office of Program Consultation and Accreditation (1996). Guidelines and principles for accreditation of programs in professional psychology. Washington, DC: American Psychological Association.

Paget, K. D. (1991). Early intervention and treatment acceptability: Multiple perspectives for improving service delivery in home settings. Topics in early childhood special education, 11(2), 1–17.

President's Commission on Mental Health (1978). Report to the President (Vol. 1). Washington, DC: U. S. Government Printing Office, Stock No. 040-000-00390-8.

Prevention Task Panel Report (1978). Task Panel reports submitted to the President's Commission on Mental Health (Vol. 4, pp. 1822–1863). Washington, DC: U.S. Government Printing Office, Stock No. 040-000-00393-2.

Price, R. H. (1983). The education of a prevention psychologist. In R. D. Felner, L. A. Jason, J. N. Moritsugu, & S. S. Farber (Eds.), Preventive psychology: Theory, research and practice (pp. 290–296). New York: Pergamon Press.

Price, R. H. (1986). Education for prevention. In M. Kessler & S. E. Goldston (Eds.), *A decade of progress in primary prevention* (pp. 289–306). Hanover, NH: University Press of New England.

Price, R. H., Cowen, E. L., Lorion, R. P., & Ramos-McKay, J. (Eds.). (1988). *Fourteen ounces of prevention: A casebook for practitioners.* Washington, DC: American Psychological Association.

Price, R. H., & Smith. S. S. (1985). *A guide to evaluating prevention programs in mental health.* Rockville, MD: National Institute of Mental Health.

Rappaport, J. (1987). *Community psychology: Values, research, and action.* New York: Holt, Rinehart, & Winston.

Reschly, D. J., & Wilson, M. S. (1995). School psychology practitioners and faculty: 1986 to 1991–92 trends in demographics, roles, satisfaction, and system reform. *School Psychology Review, 24*(1), 62–80.

Rickel, A. U., Dyhdalo, L. L., & Smith, R. L. (1984). Prevention with preschoolers. In M. C. Roberts & L. Peterson (Eds.), *Prevention of problems in childhood: Psychological research and applications* (pp. 74-102). New York: Wiley.

Roberts, M. C., & Peterson, L. (Eds.). (1984). *Prevention of problems in childhood: Psychological research and applications.* New York: Wiley.

Rowe, D. C. (1994). *The limits of family influence: Genes, experience, and behavior.* New York: Guilford.

Russell, L. B. (1986). *Is prevention better than cure?* Washington, DC: Brookings Institute.

Rutter, M. (1987). Psychosocial resilience and protective mechanisms. American Journal of Orthopsychiatry, 57(3), 316-331.

Sameroff, A. J., & Chandler, M. J. (1975). Reproductive risk and the continuum of caretaking casualty. In F. D. Honowitz, M. Heatherington, S. Scarr-Salapatek, & G. Siegel (Eds.), *Review of child development research* (Vol. 4, pp. 187–244). Chicago: University of Chicago Press.

Sandler, I. N., Duricko, A., & Grande, L. (1975). Effectiveness of an early secondary prevention program in an inner city elementary school. *American Journal of Community Psychology, 3,* 23–32.

Sarason, S. B. (1986, August). *And what is the public interest?* Paper presented at the American Psychological Association annual convention, Washington, DC.

Seligman, M. E. P. (1995). *The optimistic child.* Boston, MA: Houghton Mifflin.

Spaulding, J., & Balch, P. (1983). A brief history of primary prevention in the twentieth century. *American Journal of Community Psychology, 11,* 59–80.

Strayhorn, J. M. (1988). *The competent child: An approach to psychotherapy and preventive mental health.* New York: Guilford.

Task Panel Report: Learning failure and unused learning potential (1978). *Task panel reports submitted to the President's commission on mental health* (Vol. 3, pp. 661–704). Washington, DC: U.S. Government Printing Office, Stock No. 040-000-00392-4.

Terrell, D. L., McWilliams, S. A., & Cowen, E. L. (1972). Description and evaluation of group-work training for nonprofessional aides in a school mental health program. *Psychology in the Schools, 9,* 70–75.

Tudor, K. (1996). *Mental health promotion: Paradigms and practice.* London: Routledge.

U.S. Department of Justice (1995). *Solving youth violence: Partnerships that work:* National conference proceedings. Washington, DC: Author.

U.S. Preventive Services Task Force (1996). *Guide to clinical preventive services: Report of the U.S. Preventive Services Task Force* (2nd ed). Baltimore, MD: Williams & Wilkins.

Weissberg, R. P., Cowen, E. L., Lotyczewski, B. S., & Gesten, E. L. (1983). The primary mental health project: Seven consecutive years of program outcome research. *Journal of Consulting and Clinical Psychology, 51,* 100–107.

Whitney, G. L. (1994). *Behavior: genetics. In The encyclopedia of psychology.* New York: Plenum Press.

Winer, J. I., Weissberg, R. P., & Cowen, E. L. (1988). Evaluation of a planned short-term intervention for school children with focal adjustment problems. *Journal of Child Clinical Psychology, 17,* 106–115.

Winett, R. A., Riley A. W., King, A. C., & Altman, D. G. (1989). Prevention in mental health: A proactive—developmental—ecological perspective. In T. H. Ollendick & M. Hersen (Eds.), Handbook of child psychopathology (2nd ed., pp. 499–521). New York: Plenum Press.

Zax, M., & Specter, G. A. (1974). *An introduction to community psychology.* New York: Wiley.

Zins, J. E., Conyne, R. K., & Ponti, C. R. (1988). Primary prevention: Expanding the impact of psychological services in schools. School Psychology Review, 17, 542–549.

CHAPTER 17

INFORMED CONSENT, CONFIDENTIALITY, AND DUTY TO REPORT LAWS IN THE CONDUCT OF CHILD THERAPY

Mark B. DeKraai
Bruce D. Sales
Susan R. Hall

In child therapy, it is the parent or legal guardian in most cases who is the client of the services, even though the child is the patient. This occurs because the law presumes the minor-child is incompetent, which means that the child lacks the requisite legal capacity to consent to or refuse services, or to hold the right to confidentiality in regard to any information that he or she divulges during therapy. Rather, it is the parent or legal guardian who holds these rights. Thus, child therapy presents the opportunity for potentially serious conflicts of interest between the child, parent, and therapist.

Because the American Psychological Association's Ethical Principles and Code of Conduct (American Psychological Association [APA], 1992) provides little guidance on how to respond to such issues (see e.g., Section 1.21, which only tells psychologists to clarify their relationships with all parties), and because these topics present legal and therapeutic issues that are not likely to be known or understood simply by considering the way the law regulates therapy with adults, this chapter will focus on these complex interrelated legal-therapeutic topics. The chapter starts with a consideration of informed consent for child therapy, moves to an analysis of confidentiality of information within child therapy, and concludes with a discussion of one of the most prominent laws that supersedes confidentiality—mandatory reporting laws.

INFORMED CONSENT

The concept of consenting to services is based on the notion of respect for individual autonomy, such that individuals should have the authority to decide what happens to their bodies. The doctrine originated and found its early refinement in the context of medical surgery (*Schloendorff v. Society of New York Hospital*, 1914/1957; *Canterbury v. Spence*, 1972). With regard to psychotherapy, "informed consent" as it is commonly referred to in the literature and law, applies to client decisions regarding whether to engage in therapy, what happens during the course of therapy, and what information to allow the therapist to disclose to others. In other words, apart from certain legal exceptions (e.g., such as in the provision of certain emergency treatments or in involuntary civil commitment), a client cannot be given therapy and cannot be required to engage in particular conduct, or disclose particular information while in therapy, without his or her informed consent. Furthermore, apart from the exceptions discussed later in this chapter, a therapist cannot legally disclose information obtained in therapy without the client's informed consent. Actions taken by the therapist, such as releasing confidential information, without the informed consent of the client, may result in professional liability.

To satisfy the doctrine of informed consent, the consent must be *voluntary, knowing,* and *competent* (Brakel, Parry, & Weiner, 1985). To meet the criterion of voluntariness, the consent decision must be the product of free choice and cannot be the result of factors such as threat, fraud, or duress. Stricter standards are likely to apply to children as opposed to adults in those limited circumstances (discussed below) when a child has the legal right to consent. For example, in an analogous situation involving waiver to the right against self-incrimination, the U.S. Supreme Court suggested that special care should be taken to ensure that a waiver by a child is voluntary (*In re Gault,* 1967). However, the Court has never articulated these special standards for the therapeutic context.

The second criterion, knowing, primarily concerns the type of information about therapy that the therapist should provide to the client. The therapist must disclose the nature of the proposed treatment and the foreseeable risks and benefits that may result from it. For example, the therapist should disclose the nature of the diagnosis or evaluation of the problem, the prognosis of the problem without therapy, the nature and goals of the specific treatment techniques, the efficacy of the treatment techniques when outcome studies are available, the projected length of treatment, and the limits of confidentiality (see Keith-Spiegel & Koocher, 1985; Simon, 1987).

Traditionally, the legal standard for meeting this criterion revolved around some standard measure of professional behavior. In other words, the information that a professional was required to disclose depended on information normally disclosed by other professionals practicing the same type of treatment (see *Natanson v. Kline,* 1960). Under this rule, an aggrieved client who brought a malpractice action was required to show that professional standards were not met—a requirement that had proved difficult for client/litigants to meet (Brakel et al., 1985). Although this rule is still the law in some states, a new standard has emerged. The "reasonable patient or client" standard requires the professional to disclose information that a reasonable client would need in order to make informed decisions concerning the treatment procedure (*Canterbury v. Spence,* 1972; *Largey v. Rothman,* 1988). The basis for this change in legal standards is the idea that it is the client, not the therapist, who has the prerogative of deciding what is in the best interests of the client/patient. Under this standard, therapists must disclose the information that they know or reasonably should know would influence client decisions.

The third criterion, competency, is perhaps the most relevant to child therapy. While there is no single theory or definition of competency, it is generally recognized that competency includes at least a factual understanding of the illness and treatment alternatives, including their risks and benefits, and the capacity for rational decision-making (Redding, 1993). Indeed, the general trend in both law and medicine is toward developing a notion of variable or situation-specific competence (Macklin, 1982). In most cases, a person is presumed competent to consent; that is, he or she has the necessary cognitive capacity to give a legally valid consent to treatment. At common law, however, children were presumed incompetent to consent (Rozovsky, 1995). They were thought to lack the necessary mental capacity to consent because of the nature of their inexperience and immaturity.

Over the past decade, however, a sizable and convincing body of empirical research suggests that children have more competence than what has been recognized by the legal system. Further evidence suggests that allowing children to participate in the treatment decision-making process may improve not only their attitudes toward therapy but also the effectiveness of treatments (Redding, 1993). Thus, it should not be surprising that there are exceptions to this blanket presumption.

The first exception to the presumption of a minor's incompetency is the mature minor doctrine. This doctrine was initially carved out by courts, but a few states have codified the rule in statute. Generally, the doctrine holds that in certain situations a minor may be deemed mature enough to give competent consent. The doctrine is typically applied where the minor is near the age of majority and is able to comprehend the nature and impact of the treatment (Wadlington, 1983). The complexity of the therapy and the risks involved are also likely to be considered in applying the rule (Rozovsky, 1995). As Ehrenreich and Melton (1983) point out, the courts have not clearly articulated the standards used to determine whether a minor is mature.

A second exception is the emancipated minor doctrine. Under this doctrine, minors are deemed capable of consenting to treatment if they have become independent from their parents. Factors to consider in determining emancipation include marriage, service in the armed forces, head of a household, employment, and living on one's own (Rozovsky, 1995). Generally, emancipation is considered on a case-by-case basis; however, in many states the issue of emancipation is controlled by statute.

A third category of exceptions, if it is one at all, is more diffuse. Some of these laws allow minors to consent to most treatments (Ehrenreich & Melton, 1983). Others are more restrictive and pertain only to specific types of therapy, such as treatment for substance abuse, or to certain aspects of therapy, such as consent for the release of confidential information. Still other statutes allow minors to consent to certain medical procedures that may include certain types of therapy; however, these "medical-care" consent statutes have their own restrictions and may apply only to specific situations such as emergency care, routine procedures, or where a guardian or parent is not immediately available (Rozovsky, 1995).

Finally, although not technically an exception, consent statutes generally provide an age limit above which a child can give valid consent. Generally, this age can range from 12 to 18. The Colorado statute illustrates this point:

[A] minor eighteen years of age or older, or a minor fifteen years of age or older who is living separate and apart from his parent, parents, or legal guardian, with or without the consent of his parent, parents, or legal guardian, and is managing his own financial affairs, regardless of the source of his income...may give consent. (Colo. Rev. Stat., 1996).

Not only may a child be incompetent to consent because of age, he or she may be incapable of consenting because of mental illness or deficiency. This problem has been referred to as double incompetency (Koocher, 1983). Generally, a person is not deemed incapable of consenting merely because he or she is undergoing therapy for a mental illness (e.g., *Wilson v. Lehman,* 1964). An individual is usually presumed competent unless adjudicated incompetent. Therefore, if a child falls under an exception to the presumption of child incompetency (e.g., emancipation), the therapist can presume that the child can provide legal consent unless the child has been declared legally incompetent.

If a child is not legally competent, who can consent to the minor's treatment? Traditionally, parents have had the authority for consenting on behalf of their minor children (Howell, 1995), but many states have enacted laws that give other persons, such as guardians or relatives, the authority to consent on behalf of minors. The Georgia law (subsection (a), items 2 through 6 of Ga. Code Ann. 31-9-2 (1997)) provides an example of a statute giving certain individuals the authority to consent to medical treatment:

2. *In the absence or unavailability of a living spouse, any parent, whether an adult or a minor, for his minor child;*

3. *Any married person, whether an adult or a minor, for himself and for his spouse;*

4. *Any person temporarily standing in loco parentis, whether formally serving or not, for the minor under his care; and any guardian, for his ward;*

5. *Any female, regardless of age or marital status, for herself when given in connection with pregnancy, or the prevention thereof, or childbirth;*

6. *Upon the inability of any adult to consent for himself and in the absence of any person to consent*

under paragraphs (2) through (5) of this subsection the following persons in the following order of priority:

a. Any adult child for his parents;

b. Any parent for his adult child;

c. Any adult for his brother or sister; or

d. Any grandparent for his grandchild.

The traditional standard for substitute consent is the best interests of the child. In other words, when a child is legally incapable of consenting to therapy or disclosure of information, a substitute decision maker, such as a parent or guardian, must make decisions that are in the child's best interests, which is defined by what a reasonable person would say. A second standard that has developed in recent years is substituted judgment, which requires the substitute decision maker to act as the client would act if he or she were competent. A third and more recent standard is a combination of the best interests and substituted judgment standards (Parry, 1987a, 1987b).

In certain circumstances, there may be a conflict of interest between the substitute decision maker and the minor-patient, and the substitute decision maker may have difficulty acting in the best interests of the patient or as the patient would act if competent. Consider a case reported by Weinapple and Perr (1981), in which a mother directed the disclosure of her son's psychotherapeutic records for use in a child custody proceeding. In this case, the consent for disclosure was designed more for the benefit of the mother than of the child. Although the trial court held that the minor-patient, who was 14 years old, had the capacity to refuse to consent to disclosure, a similar situation could occur in which a patient would be declared incompetent to consent. In such a case, where there is a conflict of interest on the part of the parent or guardian, courts tend to appoint a *guardian ad litem* (a person appointed by the court to represent the interests of the child in a litigation) to determine whether the directed disclosure is in the best interests of the minor (*In re Commitment of J. C. G.,* 1976).

Occasionally, the state may intervene on behalf of a child when the substitute decision maker does not follow the legal standards. State intervention typically occurs when parents refuse to consent to a medical procedure necessary to save the life of their child. Less common are situations where the state intervenes because parents have refused to give consent for their children to undergo mental-health treatment (Ehrenreich & Melton, 1983).

In summary, apart from involuntary or emergency treatment, the therapist must obtain informed consent to provide therapy to a child. The consent must be voluntary, knowing, and competent. To ensure that the consent is voluntary, the therapist should assess whether the consent is a product of fraud, threat, or duress. To ensure that the decision is knowing, the therapist must reveal enough information to allow the patient or substitute decision maker to make an informed decision. The therapist should discuss the potential benefits of therapy and the potential for alleviation of the presenting problem. Where outcome studies are available, they also should be discussed. Finally, risks attendant to therapy should be discussed, including the potential for disclosure of sensitive information.

To ensure that the consent is competent, the therapist must become informed about the relevant laws in the particular jurisdiction. In reviewing these laws, the therapist should determine: what is the age of majority, whether the jurisdiction has mature minor or emancipated minor laws, whether the jurisdiction has enacted minor consent statutes, and any specific conditions in the application of these statutes. The therapist should also attend to whether a substitute decision maker is using proper legal standards in consenting on behalf of a minor. In general, a therapist should not take action that would be contrary to the interests of the minor, even if requested to do so by a parent or guardian.

CONFIDENTIALITY

There are several arguments to support the importance of confidentiality in the therapeutic process. Some assert that the confidentiality of information disclosed in therapy is important to protect the interests of the client. Not to do so, for example, may result in therapeutic information subsequently being used against the client (Winslade, 1982); often information revealed in therapy, if disclosed, could adversely affect a client's legal status, relationships, and so forth. Another interest is the avoidance of embarrassment or stigmatization. Often, information revealed in therapy will be of such a nature that if disclosed to the public it would cause a devaluation of the person (Denkowski & Denkowski, 1982; Friedlander, 1982). Confidentiality of this information, then, maintains the client's dignity (Appelbaum, Kapen, Walters, Lidz, & Roth, 1984). Indeed, many studies show that clients are concerned about the release of stigmatizing confidential information (Jensen, McNamara, & Gustafson, 1991; McGuire, Toal, & Blau, 1985; Appelbaum et al., 1984; Schmid, Appelbaum, Roth, & Lidz, 1983; Lindenthal & Thomas, 1982a, 1982b). Finally, some argue that without confidentiality, psychotherapy is rendered less effective or possibly even ineffective (Shwed, Kuvin, & Baliga, 1979; Siegal, 1979; Laurence, 1984; Epstein, Steingarten, Weinstein, & Nashel, 1977; Hollender, 1965)—an assertion that is accepted by the majority of mental-health professionals (Jagim, Wittman, & Noll, 1978; Suarez & Balcanoff, 1966; Wise, 1978). This argument is based on at least five assumptions. Absent confidentiality: (1) potential clients will not seek out psychotherapy; (2) potential clients will be reluctant to enter therapy, thus causing a delay in required assistance; (3) clients already in therapy will be more likely to terminate therapy prematurely; (4) clients will be reluctant to divulge essential information, thereby rendering therapy ineffectual; and (5) therapists will employ procedures that are detrimental to the therapeutic process (e.g., they may be reluctant to keep written records) (DeKraai & Sales, 1984; Shuman & Weiner, 1982). As Trempor (1984) points out, however, the first three assumptions are probably less relevant to younger children, who seldom initiate therapy or decide when to terminate.

Although most therapists agree that confidentiality is important, there are a number of threats to confidentiality of information revealed by clients in general and minor clients in particular. The major threats are searches, subpoenas, breach of confidence, and access requirements.

Search and Seizure

Searches and seizures present a significant threat to the privacy of psychotherapy, since "under existing law, valid warrants may be issued to search any property, whether or not occupied by a third party, at which there is probable cause to believe that fruits, instrumentalities, or evidence of a crime will be found" (emphasis in original) (*Zurcher v. Stanford Daily*, 1978, p. 554). Law enforcement officers may engage in such practices in a number of cases. First, the government might suspect the therapist of committing a crime against the state or a third party. For example, the therapist might be accused of submitting false insurance claims, thus attempting to defraud an insurance company (*Hawaii Psychiatric Society v. Ariyoshi*, 1979; *McKirdy v. Superior Court*, 1982; *People v. Blasquez*, 1985; *Reynaud v. Superior Court*, 1982). Second, the state might suspect the therapist of committing a crime against a client (e.g., *Burrows v. Superior Court*, 1974; *State v. Tsavaris*, 1980/1981; *State v. Byrd*, 1990). Third, information given to the therapist during therapy may be considered evidence to a crime committed by the client which is unrelated to therapy (*In re Gartley*, 1985/1987). Fourth, a client might be suspected of a crime in connection with the therapy, such as fraudulent collection of unemployment compensation (*Doe v. Harris*, 1982/1988). Fifth, both the therapist and the client may be suspected of complicity in a crime (*Commonwealth v. Santner*, 1982/1984; Nye, 1980). Sixth, a client in therapy might reveal information about criminal activities of a third party. This situation is particularly relevant to juveniles who reveal their parents' child-, spouse-, or grandparent-abusing activities. Hence, numerous scenarios exist for search and seizure in the therapist's office. But is a search of the therapeutic files truly pernicious?

Many factors exist that make the search more damaging than other forms of confidential information disclosure. Irrelevant but confidential information may be examined during a search in an effort to identify relevant documents. Bloom (1980) calls this examination of nonsuspect third-party files a "rummaging effect." A search also can disrupt normal business operations. Therapy sessions may have to be canceled, secretaries and other employees may be prevented from working, and office space and files may be restricted from use. In addition, a search can damage a therapist's reputation. A search is a relatively public event; clients in the office and people on the street will be aware of it, with the result that the therapist may be stigmatized. Relatedly, the search may damage clients' reputations, since law enforcement officials may become aware of the names of various clients when a search is conducted. This result may be particularly onerous to clients who are politicians, lawyers, or other highly visible people in the community. Finally, the disclosure is government-forced, with little or no opportunity for discussion. Unlike other court-ordered disclosures, no opportunity is allowed for adversarial dispute of the forced disclosure until after the intrusion has occurred, the premises have been searched, and the materials have been seized.

Generally, when presented with a valid search warrant, the therapist has few options in attempting to safeguard the confidentiality of client information. Notwithstanding, there are some guidelines that he or she can follow to minimize the intrusion. First, the therapist should contact an attorney immediately, since he or she is in the best position to prevent a search or seek an injunction to stop a search in progress. Note, however, that there is no requirement for the searching officers to wait for an attorney to review the warrant, supervise the search, or take action to stop the search. Second, the therapist should offer to produce the requested documents. This action will protect the confidentiality of irrelevant client files from the rummaging effect. Yet, if searching officers believe the presented documents to be incomplete, they may search the irrelevant files anyway. Finally, the therapist should request that the documents be sealed until proceedings can be initiated to determine whether the information should be disclosed. In most states, however, the searching officers would not be required to comply with this request.

California is one of the few states to provide a system of search-and-seizure protections to assure the confidentiality of particularly sensitive information such as client files (Cal. Penal Code, 1982). The state provides statutorily for a special master (a person appointed by a court to act as its representative) to be appointed to accompany the searching officers when the search involves evidence in the possession of an attorney, a physician, a psychotherapist, or a clergyperson who is not suspected of engaging in illegal activities. The master is required to request that the desired items be relinquished voluntarily. Only on refusal to comply with the request will a search be conducted. When the psychotherapist or other professional requests the maintenance of confidentiality for particular items, the master is required to seal those items. If the therapist is not present during the search and cannot be located, the master is given the discretion to decide which documents appear to be privileged and to seal those items. The California statute further provides for a hearing regarding return of seized documents on the ground that the warrant of search was constitutionally deficient or that the documents are privileged (see following section). The hearing is to be conducted within three days of service of the warrant unless this is impractical.

Subpoena

Therapists are frequently required by law to testify in court as to matters that would normally be considered confidential by both the therapist and the patient. The most common method for courts to require such disclosure is through a subpoena. There are two types—the *subpoena ad testificandum,* which requires a witness to appear before the issuing court or magistrate and give testimony, and the *subpoena duces tecum,* which requires a witness to produce documents or records in his or her possession at a legal proceeding. The legal authority for a court's subpoena power is usually found in a statute or court rule of the jurisdiction. Generally, all persons within the court's jurisdiction are subject to this power. Failure to comply with a subpoena (i.e., to reveal client information to the court) may result in criminal sanction such as fine or imprisonment.

A therapist cannot defend against a subpoena by asserting that the information is protected by confidentiality law, because the law of confidentiality does not apply to legal proceedings. Early common law held that the courts' need to have all evidence available to resolve a dispute outweighed the therapists' and patients' need for confidentiality. Thus, state legislatures enacted privileged communications statutes to provide the needed protection in legal proceedings for information revealed during the course of therapy (DeKraai & Sales, 1982). In a jurisdiction with a privileged communications law that applies to communications between a therapist and a client, the disclosure of such communications may not be compelled in a legal proceeding.

These laws are not absolute however. First, the professions that are covered by the privilege varies across jurisdictions and is an issue of debate (Herlihy & Sheeley, 1987). While many states provide privileges for communications between patients and psychologists or psychiatrists, only some provide privileges for other types of therapists (Smith-Bell & Winslade, 1996). This is in contrast to much of the literature that proposes extending privileges to other therapists (Stroube, 1979) such as social workers (Delgado, 1973), school guidance counselors (Robinson, 1974), and rape crisis counselors (Appelbaum & Roth, 1981; Laurence, 1984; Scarmeas, 1982; Stouder, 1982; Williamson, 1984).

Second, even if all professionals that could be considered psychotherapists were included under a psychotherapist-client privilege (see Nye, 1979; Knapp & VandeCreek, 1985), there would still exist a serious threat to confidentiality. Nonprofessionals (e.g., secretaries, clerks, direct-care technicians, graduate student interns) often have access to psychotherapeutic information and could be compelled to reveal the information under most privileges (*Myers v. State,* 1984; *Lipsey v. State,* 1984; but see *State v. Miller,* 1985/1986). This had led some to suggest that the locus of the privilege and the responsibility for confidentiality should lie with the facility or program rather than a specific professional (Hague, 1983; Kenny, 1982).

Third, another gap in these laws concerns the type of information that is privileged. Generally, information must be confidential and revealed in the context of a professional relationship to be privileged. As Shah (1969) points out, this requirement would not cover the fact that the person has or is currently undergoing psychotherapy. Unfortunately, even in today's society where participation in psychotherapy is less stigmatizing than in the past, clients may be reluctant to seek out therapy if they believe this fact will be disclosed.

Fourth, traditionally, courts did not consider communications confidential if made in the pres-

ence of third parties (e.g., *United States v. Blackburn,* 1971/1972). Hence, family or group therapy communications are not confidential unless specifically made so in the law. For example, the Supreme Court of Minnesota extended the psychotherapist-patient privilege to group therapy when group sessions are a necessary and integral part of a patient's diagnosis and treatment because the confidentiality of communications made during such sessions is essential to maintaining its effectiveness as a therapeutic tool (*State v. Andring,* 1984).

Fifth, even if the information meets the above requirements and thereby falls under the therapist-client privilege, the disclosure of such information may be required if it falls under an exception to the privilege. Many psychotherapists have argued that the privilege should be absolute; in other words, communications made to a therapist in the context of a professional relationship should never be allowed to be revealed in a legal proceeding (Everstine et al., 1980). In most jurisdictions, however, this position has not been adopted, and exceptions have been carved out where the need for information is deemed to outweigh the interests of clients. Some of the most common exceptions include: (a) where a therapist has been appointed by a court to examine a party to a legal proceeding, (b) where a client raises his or her mental state as a claim or defense in a legal proceeding, (c) where a therapist determines that a client requires hospitalization for a mental or emotional disorder, and (d) where a client brings an action for malpractice against the therapist.

Another exception that is gaining increasing popularity is the child-custody exception (see Malmquist, 1994; Beigler, 1972; *Dawes v. Dawes,* 1984; Guernsey, 1981; *In re Adoption of Embick,* 1986; Knapp & VandeCreek, 1985, 1987). The competing interests involved with this exception essentially revolve around the assumption that the court's interest in reaching a proper custody determination outweighs the privacy of the parents and children. This exception generally applies to communications made between either a therapist and parents (*In re Adoption of B. G. S.,* 1992) or a therapist and child (*In re M. C.,* 1986).

Sixth, there are specific limits to who may assert and who may waive the privilege. Generally, the privilege belongs to the client and only the client may assert or waive the privilege (e.g., *Fitzgibbon v. Fitzgibbon*, 1984). In the case of the minor-child, the parent, rather than the minor, is typically the client and therefore holds the authority to assert or waive the privilege. As a general rule however, if a privilege statute gives a minor client the authority to assert the privilege (Ehrenreich & Melton, 1983), or if the child has the capacity to provide competent consent (Weinapple & Perr, 1981), then the privilege belongs to the child rather than the parents. Yet, minor clients should be informed that they may not have the ability to assert or waive the privilege.

In summary, therapists should become aware of the laws in their jurisdiction that safeguard confidential information from disclosure through subpoenaed testimony or record production. If presented with a subpoena, the therapist should consult an attorney. If a parent attempts to assert or waive the privilege on behalf of a minor-child and the therapist disagrees with the decision, the therapist should raise the issue of potential parental conflict of interest with the court. In such a situation, a court may appoint a guardian *ad litem* to represent the best interests of the child, or the court may decide whether a privilege should be waived. It should be kept in mind that even in situations where the therapist believes information should remain confidential, if a court orders the therapist to testify, he or she must do so or face criminal penalties.

Breach of Confidence

Some commentators have argued that all information disclosed in psychotherapy should be confidential even if the client consents to its release (Dubey, 1974). Others have argued that clients should have control over release of their records (Coleman, 1984; Keith-Spiegel & Koocher, 1985; Rosen, 1977). With child therapy, however, the issue of the child's competency to waive confidentiality arises, just as it does with consent to treatment and with the assertion or waiver of privileged communications.

Even without consent, however, the law allows a variety of individuals and entities (e.g., consulting therapists, the client's family, student interns, treatment staff, clerical staff, government agencies, and insurance agencies) to obtain legitimate access to psychotherapeutic information under certain circumstances. This result occurs for several reasons. For instance, not all information can legally be kept confidential. As already noted, information indicating that clients are participating in therapy is generally considered nonconfidential (Shah, 1969). In addition, for information to be considered confidential, it must have been disclosed in the context of a professional relationship. Also, laws designed to protect the confidentiality of psychotherapeutic information often allow persons with access to the information to disclose it to specified persons or entities without incurring liability. These laws allow disclosure to treatment professionals other than the treating therapist, treatment facilities, certain state agencies, law enforcement officials, insurance agencies, attorneys, guardians, and families or clients (Moore, 1994; DeKraai & Sales, 1984). For example, Virginia's statute allows professionals to disclose the following information to a patient's third-party payor or insurance company:

1. *The patient's name and the contract or policy number;*
2. *The date the patient was admitted to a treatment facility or the date the patient began receiving mental health, mental retardation or substance abuse services;*
3. *The date of the onset of the patient's illness;*
4. *The date the patient was discharged from the treatment facility or the date the services terminated, if known;*
5. *The diagnosis, with brief information substantiating the diagnosis;*
6. *A brief description of the services provided such patient, including type of therapy, medications ordered and administered, and number of hours spent in individual, group, or family treatment, recreational therapy, or rehabilitative activities;*
7. *Status of the patient, whether in-patient or out-patient; and*
8. *The patient's relationship to the contract subscriber or policyholder.* (Va. Code Ann. § 37.1-226, Michie 1997)

Virginia's statute provides for such disclosure only when the patient has submitted a bill to the third party, based on the theory that the patient has thus consented to revealing the above information. Yet, some commentators advocate that managed-care entities should take a more active role in protecting and providing for patients' reasonable expectations of confidentiality (Corcoran & Winslade, 1994).

Given the breadth of access to psychotherapeutic information, many states have enacted laws that provide mechanisms for protection or redress against unauthorized or threats of unauthorized voluntary disclosures by persons or who have legitimate access to confidential information (DeKraai & Sales, 1984). Most of these nondisclosure laws are found in the professional sections of state codes that cover specific psychotherapeutic professions (e.g., psychologists, psychiatrists, social workers). These provisions vary considerably, resulting in disparate protection among different types of therapists. Other nondisclosure laws are limited to specific types of clients (e.g., persons with developmental disabilities, persons treated for substance abuse) or to a specific type of agency (e.g., community mental-health programs, state supported mental retardation programs). In these latter two situations, the existence and level of protection against breaches of confidentiality will vary across psychotherapeutic situations.

In addition to statutory remedies for illegal voluntary disclosures, there are at least five common law tort remedies (see generally Lamb, 1983; Newman, 1981; Egar, 1976):

1. breach of confidence, which is an action for malpractice that requires the client to show the existence of a professional duty to maintain confidentiality, breach of that duty, and injury resulting from the breach (see generally, Vickery, 1982);
2. breach of contract, which is an action based on the theory that an implied or expressed contract exists between therapists and clients and that this contract has been violated (Feldman & Ward, 1979);

3. breach of a fiduciary duty, which is an action based on the theory that clients have placed trust and reliance upon the therapist who is then obligated to act in the best interests of the client (Turner & Thomason, 1970),
4. breach of privacy,[1] which is an action based on the right of the individual to be free from unwarranted disclosure of one's private life; and
5. defamation, which is an action that is available if the disclosure of information subjects the client to public ridicule or shame (DeKraai & Sales, 1984).

Concurrent with the variations in the laws found across different jurisdictions, the penalties for wrongful disclosure also vary by state. Some laws provide for license revocation for specific types of professions. Other laws allow civil damages including actual and punitive damages. Still other laws impose criminal sanctions for wrongful disclosure (i.e., fines and/or imprisonment).

In conclusion, in addition to knowing the laws governing consent, the therapist should know whether confidentiality statutes exist in the jurisdiction, the types of therapists and clients included in the statutes, the penalties for wrongful disclosure, and who may have access without client consent. In addition, therapists should inform others with access to confidential information (e.g., secretaries, interns, other clients) of their duty to protect the information. Finally, therapists should inform their clients of the potential for disclosure, including the persons who will have access to the information and the remedies for breach of confidences.

Parental Access to Information

The desire of the parents to access psychotherapeutic information presents a special challenge to therapists. Often disclosure of this information will be beneficial to the therapeutic process (Simon, 1987).

---

1 The concept of privacy can be understood as an individual's right to limit others' access in certain respects (Gavison, 1980), such as limiting the access of others to one's body or mind. Although there is a recognized constitutional right to privacy (*Griswold v. Connecticut,* 1965), the scope of that right is narrow. Indeed, the U.S. Supreme Court held that there is no federal constitutional right to informational privacy for medical records (*Whalen v. Roe,* 1977). As a result, it is unlikely that therapeutic communications would be protected under federal right to privacy. Yet, a few federal appellate and state courts have recognized a constitutional right to privacy for the psychotherapeutic relationship (Smith-Bell & Winslade, 1996).

When it is, the child's privacy interests are not compromised if the therapist explains the reason for disclosure and the child consents. A more difficult situation occurs when parents wish access to information that the minor-child wishes to remain confidential.

Generally, if parents are the legal substitute decision makers and have consented to treatment, they have a legal right as the client of the services to access the child's therapeutic records. Another rationale for such parental access is that because parents have the authority to consent to release of the child's therapeutic records to other persons or entities (e.g., insurance companies), the parents need to be aware of the content of the records in order to make an informed decision about disclosure (Ehrenreich & Melton, 1983).

Where the child has the capacity to consent, whether or not he or she is legally entitled to do so, the issue of parental access is less clear. One of the few cases that have addressed this issue indicates the parents may be denied access where disclosure would be contrary to the interest of the child and where a child is promised confidentiality. In *State in the Interest of D. G.* (1980), a father requested the therapeutic records of his 15-year-old daughter. The daughter had been adjudged as in need of supervision, placed in foster care, and provided mental-health services. The daughter had been promised confidentiality and her therapist testified that it would not be in the child's best interests to allow the parents access to the records. The parents, on the other hand, argued that they were interested in the welfare of their daughter and wanted the records so as to gain insight into their daughter's problems. The New Jersey appellate court denied access holding that in spite of state law which apparently allows access to parents, the decision to release the information rests with the discretion of the court. Because the client was promised confidentiality and the available evidence indicated hostility between the father and daughter, the court in its discretion would not allow disclosure to the parents.

In sum, when parents request access to their child's therapeutic records, the therapist should assess whether disclosure is in the best interests of the child. If the child has the capacity to consent and

desires confidentiality, or if the child does not have the capacity to consent and disclosure would not be in the best interests of the child, the therapist should deny parental access. There are a number of legal theories on which parents may seek access in a court of law (e.g., Madden, 1982). The court will then determine whether access should be granted.

REPORTING LAWS

Reporting laws operate like an exception to confidentiality. However, whereas an exception means that information is not confidential, a reporting law supersedes otherwise confidential information and imposes an affirmative duty on therapists to disclose specific knowledge obtained in therapy. Failure by the therapist to reveal information under these circumstances may lead to liability. These laws are based on the premise that the privacy of information revealed in therapy is outweighed by society's need to secure the physical safety of its members. There are two major types of reporting laws: dangerous-person reporting laws and child-abuse reporting laws.

Dangerous-Person Reporting Laws

The courts in some states have established a dangerous-person reporting requirement or a duty to warn for therapists. The most famous case to establish such a mandate was *Tarasoff v. Regents of University of California* (1974/1976). In this case the California Supreme Court held that when the therapist knows or reasonably should know that a client poses a threat to a third party, the therapist has a duty to take reasonable action to protect the potential victim. Although this action could include such measures as initiating emergency commitment procedures, the most common duty, as discussed in *Tarasoff* and subsequent court cases, includes warning the potential victim of the client's threats. Failure to warn the victim in these situations will result in civil liability if the client harms the victim. It is evident that dangerous-person reporting laws directly conflict with confidentiality. In recognizing this conflict, the *Tarasoff* court found that the interests in effective treatment and individual privacy are outweighed by society's interest in the safety of its citizens. Subsequent cases in California and other states have followed the *Tarasoff* doctrine (Leong, Eth, & Silva, 1994; Beck, 1985; George, 1985; Knapp & VandeCreek, 1982).

Some states have adopted statutory rules that impose a duty to warn in situations similar to that addressed in *Tarasoff* (See Cal. Civ. Code, 1995; Colo. Rev. Stat., 1997; Del. Code Ann., 1996; Fla. Stat. Ann., 1997; Idaho Code, 1997; Ind. Code., 1997; Ky. Rev. Stat. Ann., 1996; La. Rev. Stat. Ann., 1996; Minn. Stat., 1996; Mont. Code Ann., 1996; Neb. Rev. Stat., 1996; N.H. Rev. Stat. Ann., 1995; N.J. Stat. Ann., 1997; Utah Code Ann., 1997; Wash. Rev. Code Ann., 1996). These statutes have generally limited the duty to instances in which a patient has communicated a serious threat of physical violence against a readily identifiable victim (*Bradley v. Ray*, 1995).

For the most part, the commentary on the duty-to-warn laws has been critical and has included the following observations:

1. the laws are based on the faulty presumption that psychotherapists can accurately predict dangerousness (Gurevitz, 1977; Latham, 1975; Merton, 1982; Stone, 1976) when the evidence is to the contrary (e.g., Cocozza & Steadman, 1976; Monahan, 1981; APA, ad hoc Committee on Legal Issues, 1985);
2. an incorrect judgment could lead to liability for breach of confidence (Cohen, 1978; Roth & Meisel, 1977); hence, therapists may overpredict or underpredict dangerousness to avoid liability (Bersoff, 1976; Stone, 1976);
3. therapists might become reluctant to engage in therapy with potentially dangerous clients and clients may become reluctant to reveal their dangerous urges to therapists; psychotherapy will thereby become negatively affected, increasing the danger to society (Noll, 1976; Sloan & Klein, 1977; Stone, 1976);
4. warning a potential victim may cause unnecessary mental distress for the person (Griffith & Griffith, 1978); and
5. disclosure of a dangerous client's intentions may threaten the therapist's safety (Sloan & Klein, 1977).

Yet, not all of the commentary concerning *Tarasoff* has been negative. It has been argued that:

1. psychotherapists should have a duty to society and the potential victim as well as the client, and that warning the potential victim may fulfill this duty by preventing injury or death (Fleming & Maximov, 1974; Glassman, 1975; Kaplan, 1975; Leonard, 1977);
2. the legal duty to warn is in accordance with current ethical standards adopted by the psychotherapeutic professions (Kaplan, 1975). In one recent survey of therapists, 97.5% said that they would warn a potential victim of threatened harm regardless of legal liability (Rosenhan, Teitelbaum, Teitelbaum, & Davidson, 1993);
3. dangerous-person reporting laws will benefit not only society but the psychotherapeutic process as well. Wexler (1979, 1981), for example, suggests that these laws will facilitate the use of joint and family therapy where both the client and the potential victim are included;
4. there is no clear evidence that these types of laws will have a negative impact on psychotherapy (Seligman, 1977; Givelber, Bowers, & Blitch, 1984, 1985; Beck, 1982; but see Wise, 1978); and
5. although therapists now contend that they cannot predict dangerousness, they contended just the opposite for years and, in fact, still are involved in the prediction of dangerousness in various legal arenas (e.g., civil commitment, termination of parental rights) (Ayres & Holbrook, 1975; Seligman, 1977).

Regardless of the academic commentary on the desirability of this type of law, courts continue to define and refine the requirements for imposing a duty to report and liability for failure to do so. These requirements include:

Special relationship. A special relationship must exist between the client and the therapist before a duty to warn arises. Generally a therapeutic relationship will satisfy this condition (*Tarasoff v. Regents of University of California*, 1974/1979; *McIntosh v. Milano*, 1979; *Abernathy v. United States*, 1985). Yet, the individual facts of a case and a state's statutes should be considered. In a recent state court case, *Boulanger v. Pol* (1995), the Kansas Supreme Court held that the relationship between a psychiatrist and a voluntary patient at an intermediate mental-health-care facility was not a special relationship that would create an affirmative duty to warn a third party or to involuntarily commit the patient.

Type of danger. Most cases have involved a threat to the physical safety of a third person (e.g., *Tarasoff v. Regents of University of California,* 1974/1976; *McIntosh v. Milano,* 1979; *Lipari v. Sears, Roebuck & Co.,* 1980; *Shaw v. Glickman,* 1980). Other cases have raised the issue of a duty to warn third persons when a client poses a physical danger to self (e.g., *Bellah v. Greenson,* 1978). Yet, the *Bellah* court decided that disclosure is not mandatory in cases involving self-inflicted harm, suicide, or property damage (Rosenhan, Teitelbaum, Teitelbaum, & Davidson, 1993). Finally, one case found a duty to warn even where the threat involved property damage. In *Peck v. Counseling Service of Addison County, Inc.* (1985), a therapist learned of a minor-client's desire to burn down his father's barn. The therapist did not warn the father, and the client subsequently did in fact set fire to the barn. The Supreme Court of Vermont adopted the *Tarasoff* reasoning and held the therapist liable for failing to warn the father of his son's intentions. The court failed to note the distinction between the harm inflicted in the *Tarasoff* case (murder) and the harm committed in the case before it (barn burning).

Victim's preexisting knowledge. In *In re Estate of Votteler* (1982), the Supreme Court of Iowa held that the *Tarasoff* doctrine should not extend to a situation where the potential victim is aware of the danger (see also *Hinkelman v. Borgess Med. Cen.,* 1987; *Wagshall v. Wagshall,* 1989).

Therapist's knowledge of the danger. In Tarasoff the therapist had determined that his client posed a threat to a third party. But is actual knowledge of serious and imminent danger a requisite for the duty to arise? Courts have found that a duty to warn an intended victim exists even where the therapist may not have actual knowledge of the danger. Although

a slight suspicion that the client may pose a threat will not create a duty to warn, the therapist will be held to the standards of the psychotherapeutic profession in determining whether he or she should have known of the danger (*Tarasoff v. Regents of University of California,* 1974/1976; *Canon v. Thumudo,* 1988; *Lipari v. Sears, Roebuck & Co.,* 1980). Therefore, if actual knowledge cannot be shown, whether the therapist should have predicted the danger is a question of fact that must be determined at trial.

Identifiability of the victim(s). To whom should the duty to warn be extended? Generally the duty extends to readily identifiable and foreseeable victims (*Doyle v. United States,* 1982; *Chrite v. United States,* 1983). Although the intended victim need not be specifically named, he or she must be a member of a distinct group of identifiable potential victims (*Mavroudis v. Superior Court,* 1980; *Jablonski by Pahls v. United States,* 1983; *Hedlund v. Superior Court,* 1983). Courts have held that the duty to warn does not extend to members of a large amorphous public or to a potential victim who is in no greater danger than any other member of the public (*Brady v. Hopper,* 1983/1984; *Cairl v. State,* 1982; *Leedy v. Hartnett,* 1981/1982; *Thompson v. County of Alameda,* 1980).

However, one case deviates from this line of authority and created a cause of action even for victims who were not readily identifiable. In *Schuster v. Altenberg* (1988), a minor-patient's family brought suit against a psychiatrist for failure to warn the patient of a medication's side effects, failure to warn the patient's family of her dangerousness, and failure to seek commitment of the patient. The plaintiffs sought damages for injuries and medical expenses resulting from a car accident in which the patient was killed and her sister seriously injured. It was alleged that the medication's side effects caused the patient to have the accident. The Wisconsin Supreme Court held that the duty to warn was not limited to specific threats against an identified person and that the cause of action is based on whether the therapist took action that conforms to accepted standards of care.

In summary, the duty to warn is receiving attention in the nation's courts as third-party victims bring suit against therapists for the actions of their patients. Thus, it is important for therapists to determine if their state has such a law, and what are its requirements. In general, a therapist may defend against such a civil lawsuit using the following assertions: (a) no therapeutic relationship existed; (b) the patient did not pose a serious threat; (c) the victim knew of the threat; (d) under existing professional standards, a therapist could not have predicted the danger; and (e) the victim was not a member of a readily identifiable and foreseeable group for which the threat of danger was significantly greater than for others.

Child-Abuse Reporting Laws

Child-abuse reporting laws are designed to facilitate the detection of abuses toward persons who are unable or unlikely to report the abuse themselves. Although some abuse reporting laws apply to particularly vulnerable adults such as the elderly or persons with a developmental disability (DeKraai & Sales, 1984), the most visible of these laws apply only to children (see Fraser, 1978; Guyer, 1982). Mandatory child-abuse reporting laws exist in all 50 states, and their purpose is to protect children from maltreatment that threatens them both physically and psychologically (Levine, 1993).

Statutes vary across states regarding what type of abuse is reportable. Laws usually require specified persons to report to state authorities nonaccidental physical injury, neglect, sexual abuse, and mental or emotional harm of persons in the protected class. Under most statutes, the reporter does not need proof of the maltreatment to report abuse (Smith-Bell & Winslade, 1996). Instead, an individual must have a "reasonable suspicion" that the defined abuse has occurred for the reporting requirement to take effect (Smith & Meyer, 1984).

Although early reporting laws required only physicians to report abuse, recent laws have increasingly included other persons such as therapists (Hurley, 1985). For example, California's mandatory child-abuse reporting law includes psychologists, social workers, and marriage, family, and child counselors in the definition of health-care practitioners who have a duty to report (Ebert, 1992).

Some laws are so broad that they require "any person" to report child abuse. These laws are particularly problematic for group or family therapy. In this situation, all of the participants in therapy may have a duty to report abuse (Smith & Meyer, 1984).

Legislators have attempted through various legal mechanisms to encourage therapists to comply with the law. All states grant the therapist immunity from civil or criminal liability for good-faith reporting (Smith-Bell & Winslade, 1996); that is, a civil or criminal action may not be brought against a therapist for breaching a client's confidences by reporting the abuse (*Awkerman by Awkerman v. Tri-County Orthopedic Group, P.C.,* 1985). Also, many state evidence codes explicitly recognize that testimony given under a mandatory child-abuse reporting law is an exception to the client's confidentiality and privilege communications rights (Smith-Bell & Winslade, 1996). In addition, some statutes impose civil or criminal liability for failure to report the abuse (DeKraai & Sales, 1984; Mazura, 1977; *Landeros v. Flood,* 1976). Thus, these laws are based on the belief that the interest in protecting the harmed individual outweighs the interest in therapeutic confidentiality (Cunningham, 1984; Weisberg & Wald, 1984).

Pesce v. J. Sterling Morton High School, District 201, Cook County, Illinois (1987) illustrates the conflict between maintaining confidentiality and disclosing possible child abuse. In this case, a student (A) contacted a school psychologist (SP) and expressed concerns about her friend, another student (B). A showed SP a note written by B that indicated suicidal thoughts and a confusion about his (B's) sexual preferences. A also informed SP that something sexual had occurred between B and a male faculty member. SP encouraged A to have B come in for counseling. As a result of this recommendation, B contacted SP, and SP informed B that his communications with SP would be confidential. Subsequently, B denied having suicidal thoughts and stated that nothing sexual had occurred with the teacher; however, B said that the teacher had shown him some "pictures" while he was at the teacher's house. B also told SP that he wanted assistance in resolving his confusion about sexual preferences, and SP arranged for counseling from a therapist (T).

In making a decision about whether to disclose the possible sexual abuse, SP contacted an attorney and a psychologist and consulted state laws, school guidelines, and professional/ethical guidelines; SP decided not to disclose the information. Later, however, SP met with B and T and discussed the idea of revealing the information. During the discussion, B disclosed that he had engaged in sex with the teacher. The student agreed that the information should be revealed, and SP contacted school authorities.

Subsequently, the school board held a hearing where it suspended and demoted SP for failing to promptly report the sexual abuse. SP challenged the school board's action in state court, arguing that state child-abuse reporting requirements violated the constitutional right to privacy. The court of appeals held that the compelling interest of the state in preventing child abuse outweighed the privacy interests. As stated by the court:

> Of critical importance here is the fact that the state is acting to protect one of the most pitiable and helpless classes in society—abused children....The compelling interest of the state reflects several characteristics special to abused children: they often may be unaware of their own abuse or injury; they may often be unable to report abuse; the effects of abuse may be invisible to third parties; abused children can carry physical and emotional scars for a lifetime; and of course the state bears a special responsibility to protect children who are considered unable voluntarily to choose their own course of action. (pp. 797–798).

Partially because of situations like the one presented in this case, many therapists have been critical of abuse reporting laws. Criticisms also have been levied based on other grounds, including:

1. that therapists may not be aware of the law's requirements. If they are not, the law is likely to be marginally effective (see, e.g., Swoboda, Elwork, Sales, & Levine, 1978). Recent research, however, suggests that practitioners are aware of the duty to report (Crenshaw, Lichtenberg, & Bartell, 1993; Beck & Ogloff, 1995);

2. even if aware of the law, psychotherapists may not be willing to breach confidentiality in order to report the abuse. In fact, research suggests that

professionals' adherence to reporting laws may depend on factors such as the type of abuse and the degree of certainty or confidence they have that the abuse occurred (Beck & Ogloff, 1995; Kalichman, Craig, & Follingstad, 1990; see also Muehleman & Kimmons, 1981). In addition, many professionals often fail to report identified child maltreatment because they believe that the child protection system will not provide the help needed by a family that is trying to cope with the violence (APA, 1996);

3. even if the report is filed, patients may not be willing to testify against the abuser which negates the value of the report (Thurman, 1984). In fact this does occur, although alternative courtroom procedures and statutes have been enacted to protect child victims from the trauma of testifying against their abusers, which may increase the number of children who testify (Hall, 1995); and

4. abuse reporting laws may not be as good as respecting confidentiality requirements for meeting society's interest in ultimately protecting children and dependent adults from abuse. Sherlock and Murphy (1984) point out that therapy for the abuser might more effectively protect society's interests in the long run than reporting the abuse. Their assumption is that mandatory reporting will favor a criminal justice response and preclude beneficial therapy for the abuser. Yet, effective therapy for offenders and victims may include reporting abuse (Levine, 1993). In one study, Watson and Levine (1989) evaluated 65 child abuse cases and found that the psychotherapeutic relationship can survive and occasionally benefit from a therapist's confrontation and reporting of a patient's abusive behavior. Additionally, the failure to report abuse was found to be antitherapeutic in a program for torture survivors (Van Eenwyk, 1990).

Moreover, therapists should become aware of the laws in their jurisdiction regarding abuse reporting. They should know who has a duty to report, what types of abuse are required to be reported, to whom the case should be reported, and whether there is immunity for good-faith reporting. In addition, therapists should inform their patients of the therapists reporting obligations when child abuse is disclosed during therapy.

CONCLUSION

In conclusion, informed consent, confidentiality, and reporting laws are particularly relevant to the field of child therapy. Therapists have a duty to understand the laws in these areas so as to protect themselves from possible legal disabilities, as well as to protect the interests of their clients. Although this chapter provides an analysis of the relevant legal issues pertaining to these areas, we recommend that psychologists become knowledgeable about the particular laws that apply in their jurisdiction. We further recommend that the therapist consult an attorney should a legal issue arise.

REFERENCES

Abernathy v. United States, 773 F.2d 184 (8th Cir. 1985).

American Psychological Association, ad hoc Committee on Legal 'issues. (1985, August). *Duty to protect: Legislative alert.* Washington, DC: Author.

American Psychological Association (1992). Ethical principles and code of conduct. *American Psychologist, 47,* 1597–1611.

American Psychological Association (1996). *Report of the American Psychological Association Presidential Task Force on Violence and the Family.* Washington, DC: Author.

Appelbaum, P. S., Kapen, G., Walters, B., Lidz, C., & Roth, L. H. (1984). Confidentiality: An empirical test of the utilitarian perspective. *Bulletin of the American Academy of Psychiatry and the Law, 12,* 109–116.

Appelbaum, P. S., & Roth, L. H. (1981). In the matter of PAAR: Rape problems and matters of confidentiality. *Hospital and Community Psychiatry, 32,* 461–462.

Awkerman by Awkerman v. Tri-County Orthopedic Group, P.C., 143 Mich. App. 722, 373 N.W.2d 204 (1985).

Ayers, R. J., Jr., & Holbrook, J. T. (1975). Law, psychotherapy, and the duty to warn: A tragic trilogy. *Baylor Law Review, 27,* 677–705.

Beck, J. C. (1982). When the patient threatens violence: An empirical study of clinical practice after *Tarasoff. Bulletin of the American Academy of Psychiatry and Law, 10,* 189–201.

Beck, J. C. (1985). *The potentially violent patient and the Tarasoff decision in psychiatric practice.* Washington, DC: American Psychiatric Press.

Beck, K. A., & Ogloff, J. R. P. (1995). Child abuse reporting in British Columbia: Psychologists' knowledge of and compliance with the reporting law. *Professional Psychology: Research and Practice, 26*(3), 245–251.

Beigler, J. S. (1972). The 1971 amendment of the Illinois statute on confidentiality: A new development in privilege law. *American Journal of Psychiatry, 129,* 311–315.

Bellah v. Greenson, 81 Cal. App. 3d 614, 146 Cal. Rptr. 535 (1978).

Bersoff, D. N. (1976). Therapists as protectors and policemen: New roles as the result of *Tarasoff? Professional Psychology, 7,* 267–273.

Bloom, L. H., Jr. (1980). The law office search: An emerging problem and some suggested solutions. *Georgetown Law Journal, 69,* 1–100.

Boulanger v. Pol, 258 Kan. 289, 900 P.2d 823 (1995).

Bradley v. Ray, 904 S.W.2d 302 (Mo. Ct. App. 1995).

Brady v. Hopper, 570 F. Supp. 1333 (D. Colo. 1983), aff'd, 751 F.2d 329 (10th Cir. 1984).

Brakel, S. J., Parry, J., & Weiner, B. A. (1985). *The mentally disabled and the law* (3rd ed.). Chicago: American Bar Foundation.

Burrows v. Superior Court, 13 Cal. 3d 238, 529 P.2d 590, 118 Cal. Rptr. 166 (1974).

Cairl v. State, 323 N.W.2d 20 (Minn. 1982).

Cal. Civ. Code § 43.92 (West 1995).

Cal. Penal Code § 1524 (West 1982).

Canon v. Thumudo, 430 Mich. 326, 422 N.W.2d 688 (1988).

Canterbury v. Spence, 464 F.2d 772, 150 U.S.App.D.C. 263 (1972), *cert. denied, Spence v. Canterbury,* 409 U.S. 1064 (1972).

Chrite v. United States, 564 F. Supp. 341 (E.D. Mich. 1983).

Cocozza, J., & Steadman, H. (1976). The failure of psychiatric predictions of dangerousness: Clear and convincing evidence. *Rutgers Law Review, 29,* 1048–1101.

Cohen, R. N. (1978). Tarasoff v. Regents of the University of California: The duty to warn: Common law and statutory problems for psychotherapists. *California Western Law Review, 14,* 153–182

Coleman, V. (1984). Why patients should keep their own records. *Journal of Medical Ethics, 10,* 27–28.

Colo. Rev. Stat. § 13–21–117 (1997).

Colo. Rev. Stat. § 13-22-103 (1996).

Commonwealth v. Santner, 308 Pa. Super. 67, 454 A.2d 24 (1982), *cert. denied, Pennsylvania v. Santer,* 468 U.S. 1217 (1984).

Corcoran, K., & Winslade, W. J. (1994). Eavesdropping on the 50-minute hour: Managed mental health care and confidentiality. *Behavioral Sciences and the Law, 12*(4), 351–365.

Crenshaw, W. B., Lichtenberg, J. W., & Bartell, P. A. (1993). Mental health providers and child sexual abuse: A multivariate analysis of the decision to report. *Journal of Child Sexual Abuse, 2*(4), 19–42.

Cunningham, C. D., Jr. (1984). Vanishing exception to the psychotherapist-patient privilege: The child abuse reporting act. *Pacific Law Journal, 16,* 335–352.

Dawes v. Dawes, 454 So.2d 311 (La. App. 1984), *writ denied,* 457 So.2d 18 (1984).

DeKraai, M. B., & Sales, B. D. (1982). Privileged communications of psychologists. *Professional Psychology: Research and Practice, 13,* 372–388.

DeKraai, M. B., & Sales, B. D. (1984). Confidential communications of psychotherapists. *Psychotherapy, 21,* 293–318.

Del. Code Ann. tit. 16, § 5402 (1996).

Delgado, R. (1973). Underprivileged communications: Extension of the psychotherapist privilege to patients of psychiatric social workers. *California Law Review, 61,* 1050–1071.

Denkowski, K. M., & Denkowski, G. C. (1982). Client-counselor confidentiality: An update of rationale, legal status, and implications. *The Personnel and Guidance Journal, 60,* 371–375.

Doe v. Harris, 696 F.2d 109 (D.C. Cir. 1982), *jmt aff'd in part & rev'd in part, Doe v. Stephens,* 851 F.2d 1457, 271 U.S.App.D.C. 230 (1988).

Doyle v. United States, 530 F. Supp. 1278 (C.D. Cal. 1982).

Dubey, J. (1974). Confidentiality as a requirement of the therapist: Technical necessities for absolute privilege in psychotherapy. *American Journal of Psychiatry, 131,* 1093–1096.

Ebert, B. W. (1992). Mandatory child abuse reporting in California: Special section: American Academy of Forensic Psychology. *Forensic Reports, 5*(4), 335–350.

Egar, D. L. (1976). Psychotherapist's liability for extrajudicial breaches of confidentiality. *Arizona Law Review, 18,* 1061–1094.

Ehrenreich, N. S., & Melton, G. B. (1983). Ethical and legal issues in the treatment of children. In C. E. Walker & M. C. Roberts (Eds.), *Handbook of clinical child psychology* (pp. 1285–1305). New York: John Wiley & Sons.

Epstein, G. N., Steingarten, J., Weinstein, H. D., & Nashel, H. M. (1977). Panel report: Impact of law on the practice of psychotherapy. *Journal of Psychiatry and Law, 5,* 7–40.

Everstine, L., Everstine, D. S., Heymann, G. M., True, R. H., Frey, D. H., Johnson, H. G., & Seiden, R. H. (1980). Privacy and confidentiality in psychotherapy. *American Psychologist, 35,* 828–840.

Feldman, S. R., & Ward, T. M. (1979). Psychotherapeutic injury: Reshaping the implied contract as an alternative to malpractice. *North Carolina Law Review, 58,* 63–96.

Fitzgibbon v. Fitzgibbon, 197 N.J. Super. 63, 484 A.2d 46 (1984).

Fla. Stat. Ann. § 455.671 (West 1997) [previously Fla. Stat. Ann. § 455.2415 (West 1994)].

Fleming, J. G., & Maximov, B. (1974). The patient or his victim: The therapist's dilemma. *California Law Review, 62,* 1025–1068.

Fraser, B. G. (1978). A glance at the past, a gaze at the present, a glimpse at the future: A critical analysis of the development of child abuse reporting statutes. *Chicago-Kent Law Review, 54,* 641–686.

Friedlander, W. J. (1982). A basis of privacy and autonomy in medical practice. *Social Science and Medicine, 16,* 1709–1718.

Ga. Code Ann. § 31-9-2 (1997) [previously Ga. Code Ann. § 88-2904 (1986)].

Gavison, R. (1980). Privacy and the limits of the law. *Yale Law Journal, 89,* 421–472, cited in Smith-Bell, M., & Winslade, W. J. (1994). Confidentiality in the psychotherapeutic relationship. In B. D. Sales & D. W. Shuman (Eds.), *Law, mental health, and mental disorder* (pp. 62–75). Pacific Grove, CA: Brooks/Cole.

George, J. C. (1985). Hedlund paranoia. *Journal of Clinical Psychology, 41,* 291–294.

Givelber, D. J., Bowers, W. J., & Blitch, C. L. (1984). Tarasoff, myth and reality: An empirical study of private law in action. *Wisconsin Law Review, 1984,* 443–497.

Givelber, D. J., Bowers, W. J., & Blitch, C. L. (1985). The Tarasoff controversy: A summary of findings from an empirical study of legal, ethical, and clinical issues. In J. C. Beck (Ed.), *The potentially violent patient and the Tarasoff decision in psychiatric practice* (pp. 35–57). Washington, DC: American Psychiatric Press.

Glassman, M. S. (1975). Psychotherapist has a duty to warn an endangered victim whose peril was disclosed by communications between the psychotherapist and patient. *University of Cincinnati Law Review, 44,* 368–375.

Griffith, E. J., & Griffith, E. E. H. (1978). Duty to third parties, dangerousness, and the right to refuse treatment: Problematic concepts for psychiatrist and lawyer. *California Western Law Review, 14,* 241–274.

Griswold v. Connecticut, 381 U.S. 479 (1965).

Guernsey, T. F. (1981). The psychotherapist-patient privilege in child placement: A relevancy analysis. *Villanova Law Review, 26,* 955–996.

Gurevitz, H. (1977). *Tarasoff:* Protective privilege versus public peril. *American Journal of Psychiatry, 134,* 289–292.

Guyer, M. J. (1982). Child abuse and neglect statutes: Legal and clinical implications. *American Journal of Orthopsychiatry, 52,* 73–81.

Hague, W. W. (1983). The psychotherapist-patient privilege in Washington: Extending the privilege to community mental health clinics. *Washington Law Review, 58,* 565–586.

Hall, S. R. (1995, September 30). *A multidisciplinary manual for the use of televised alternative procedures (videotaped interviews and videotaped and closed-circuit testimony) with victim and non-victim child witnesses.* Phoenix, AZ: Governor's Division for Children.

Hawaii Psychiatric Society v. Ariyoshi, 481 F. Supp. 1028 (D. Hawaii 1979).

Hedlund v. Superior Court, 34 Cal. 3d 695, 669 P.2d 41, 194 Cal. Rptr. 805 (1983).

Herlihy, B., & Sheeley, V. L. (1987). Privileged communication in selected helping professions: A comparison among statutes. *Journal of Counseling and Development, 65,* 479–483.

Hinkelman v. Borgess Med. Cen., 157 Mich. App. 314, 403 N.W.2d 547 (1987).

Hollender, M. (1965). Privileged communication and confidentiality. *Diseases of the Nervous System, 26,* 169–175.

Howell, S. D. (1995). *Psychotherapy and the law. Alabama Lawyer, 56,* 44–49.

Hurley, M. M. (1985). Comment. Duties in conflict: Must psychotherapists report child abuse inflicted by clients and confided in therapy? *San Diego Law Review, 22,* 645–668.

Idaho Code §§ 6-1902, 6-1903 (1997).

Ind. Code. §§ 34–4–12. 4–1, 34–4–12. 4–4 (1997).

In re Adoption of B. G. S., 418 Pa. Super 588, 614 A.2d 1161 (1992).

In re Adoption of Embick, 351 Pa. Super. 491, 506 A.2d 455 (1986).

In re Commitment of J. C. G., 144 N.J. Super. 579, 366 A.2d 733 (1976).

In re Estate of Votteler, 327 N.W.2d 759 (Iowa, 1982).

In re Gartley, 341 Pa. Super. 350, 491 A.2d 851 (1985),

order aff'd sub nom, In Re Search Warrant B-21778, 513 Pa. 429, 521 A.2d 422 (1987).

In re Gault, 387 U.S. 1 (1967).

In re M. C., 391 N.W.2d 674 (S.D. 1986).

Jablonski by Pahls v. United States, 712 F.2d 391 (9th Cir. 1983).

Jagim, R. D., Wittman, W. D., & Noll, J. O. (1978). Mental health professional attitudes toward confidentiality, privilege, and third-party disclosure. *Professional Psychology, 9,* 458–466.

Jensen, J. A., McNamara, J. R., & Gustafson, K. E. (1991). Parents' and clinicians' attitudes toward the risks and benefits of child psychotherapy: A study of informed-consent content. *Professional Psychology: Research and Practice, 22*(2), 161–170.

Kalichman, S. C., Craig, M. E., & Follingstad, D. R. (1990). Professionals' adherence to mandatory child abuse reporting laws: Effects of responsibility attribution, confidence ratings, and situational factors. *Child Abuse and Neglect, 14*(1), 69–77.

Kaplan, R. B. (1975). *Tarasoff v. Regents of the University of California:* Psychotherapists, policemen and the duty to warn—an unreasonable extension of the common law? *Golden Gate University Law Review, 6,* 229–248.

Keith-Spiegel, P., & Koocher, G. P. (1985). *Ethics in psychology: Professional standards and cases.* New York: Random House.

Kenny, D. J. (1982). Confidentiality: The confusion continues. *Journal of Medical Ethics, 8,* 9–11.

Knapp, S. J., & VandeCreek, L. (1982). *Tarasoff:* Five years later. *Professional Psychology, 13*(3), 511–516.

Knapp, S. J., & VandeCreek, L. (1985). Psychotherapy and privileged communications in child custody cases. *Professional Psychology: Research and Practice, 16*(3), 398–407.

Knapp, S. J., & VandeCreek, L. (1987). *Privileged communications in the mental health professions.* New York: Van Nostrand Reinhold.

Koocher, G. P. (1983). Competence to consent: Psychotherapy. In G. B. Melton, G. P. Koocher, & M. J. Saks (Eds.), *Children's competence to consent* (pp. 111–128). New York: Plenum Press.

Ky. Rev. Stat. Ann. §§ 202A.400, 645.270 (Baldwin 1996).

Landeros v. Flood, 17 Cal. 3d 399, 551 P.2d 389, 131 Cal. Rptr. 69 (1976).

La. Rev. Stat. Ann. § 9:2800.2 (West 1996).

Largey v. Rothman, 110 N.J. 204, 540 A.2d 504 (1988).

Lamb, L. E. (1983). To tell or not to tell: Physician's liability for disclosure of confidential information about a patient. *Cumberland Law Review, 13,* 617–637.

Latham, J. A., Jr. (1975). Liability of psychotherapists for failure to warn of homicide threatened by patient. *Vanderbilt Law Review, 28,* 631–640.

Laurence, M. (1984). Rape victim-crisis counselor communications: An argument for an absolute privilege. *University of California, Davis Law Review, 17,* 1213–1245.

Leedy v. Hartnett, 510 F. Supp. 1125 (M.D. Pa. 1981), aff'd, 676 F.2d 686 (3rd Cir. 1982).

Leonard, J. B. (1977). A therapist's duty to potential victims: A nonthreatening view of *Tarasoff. Law and Human Behavior, 1,* 309–317.

Leong, G. B., Eth, S., & Silva, J. A. (1994). "Tarasoff" defendants: Social justice or ethical decay? *Journal of Forensic Sciences, 39*(1), 86–93.

Levine, M. (1993). A therapeutic jurisprudence analysis of mandated reporting of child maltreatment by psychotherapists. *New York Law Journal of Human Rights, 10,* 711–738.

Lindenthal, J. J., & Thomas, C. S. (1982a). Psychiatrists, the public and confidentiality. *The Journal of Nervous and Mental Disease, 170,* 319–323.

Lindenthal, J. J., & Thomas, C. S. (1982b). Consumers, clinicians, and confidentiality. *Social Science and Medicine, 16,* 333–335.

Lipari v. Sears, Roebuck & Co., 497 F. Supp. 185 (D.C. Neb. 1980).

Lipsey v. State, 170 Ga. App. 770, 318 S.E.2d 184 (1984).

Macklin, R. (1982). Some problems in gaining informed consent from psychiatric patients. *Emory Law Journal, 31,* 345–374.

Madden, J. M. (1982). Patient access to medical records in Washington. *Washington Law Review, 57,* 697–713.

Malmquist, C. P. (1994). Psychiatric confidentiality in child custody disputes. *Journal of the American Academy of Child and Adolescent Psychiatry, 33*(2), 1158–1168.

Mavroudis v. Superior Court, 102 Cal. App. 3d 594, 162 Cal. Rptr. 724 (1980).

Mazura, A. C. (1977). Physicians' liability for failure to diagnose and report child abuse. *Wayne Law Review, 23,* 1187–1201.

McGuire, J. M., Toal, P., & Blau, B. (1985). The adult client's conception of confidentiality in the therapeutic relationship. *Professional Psychology: Research and Practice, 16*(3), 375–384.

McIntosh v. Milano, 168 N.J. Super. 466, 403 A.2d 500 (1979).

McKirdy v. Superior Court, 138 Cal. App. 3d 12, 188 Cal. Rptr. 143 (1982).

Merton, V. (1982). Confidentiality and the "dangerous" patient: Implications of *Tarasoff* for psychiatrists and lawyers. *Emery Law Journal, 31,* 261–343.

Minn. Stat. § 148.975 (1996).

Monahan, J. (1981). *The clinical prediction of violent behavior.* Rockville, MD: National Institute of Mental Health.

Mont. Code Ann. §§ 27-1-1101—1103 (1996).

Moore, S. E. (1994). Confidentiality of child and adolescent treatment records. *Child and Adolescent Social Work Journal, 11*(2), 165–175.

Myers v. State, 251 Ga. 883, 310 S.E.2d 504 (1984).

Muehleman, T., & Kimmons, C. (1981). Psychologist's view on child abuse reporting, confidentiality, life, and the law: An exploratory study. *Professional Psychology, 12,* 631–638.

Natanson v. Kline, 186 Kan. 393, 350 P.2d 1093 (1960).

Neb. Rev. Stat. § 71-1,206.30 (1996).

Newman, S. (1981). Privacy in medical information: A diagnosis. *University of Florida Law Review, 33,* 394–424.

N.H. Rev. Stat. Ann. §§ 329:31, 330-A:22 (1995).

N.J. Stat. Ann. § 2A:62A-16 (West 1997).

Noll, J. O. (1976). The psychotherapist and informed consent. *American Journal of Psychiatry, 133,* 1451–1453.

Nye, S. (1979). Commentary on model law on confidentiality of health and social service records. *American Journal of Psychiatry, 136,* 145–147.

Nye, S. G. (1980). Patient confidentiality and privacy: The federal initiative. *American Journal of Orthopsychiatry, 50,* 649–658.

Parry, J. W. (1987a). A unified theory of substitute consent: Incompetent patient's right to individualized health care decision-making. *Mental and Physical Disability Law Reporter, 11*(6), 378–385.

Parry, J. W. (1986). Psychiatric care and the law of substitute decisionmaking. *Mental and Physical Disability Law Reporter, 11*(3), 152–159.

Peck v. Counseling Service of Addison County, Inc., 146 Vt. 61, 499 A.2d 422 (1985).

People v. Blasquez, 165 Cal. App. 3d 408, 211 Cal. Rptr. 335 (1985).

Pesce v. J. Sterling Morton High School, District 201, Cook County, Illinois, 830 F.2d 789 (7th Cir. 1987).

Redding, R. E. (1993). Children's competence to provide informed consent for mental health treatment. *Washington and Lee Law Review, 50,* 695–753.

Reynaud v. Superior Court, 138 Cal. App. 3d 1, 187 Cal. Rptr. 660 (1982).

Robinson, W. P., III. (1974). Testimonial privilege and the school guidance counselor. *Syracuse Law Review, 25,* 911–952.

Rosen, C. E. (1977). Why clients relinquish their rights to privacy under sign-away pressures. *Professional Psychology, 8,* 17–24.

Rosenhan, D. L., Teitelbaum, T. W., Teitelbaum, K. W., & Davidson, M. (1993). Warning third parties: The ripple effects of *Tarasoff Pacific Law Journal, 24,* 1165–1232.

Roth, L. H., & Meisel, A. (1977). Dangerousness, confidentiality, and the duty to warn. *American Journal of Psychiatry, 134,* 508–511.

Rozovsky, F. A. (1995). 1995 *Supplement, Consent to treatment: A practical guide* (2nd ed., 1990). Boston: Little, Brown.

Scarmeas, C. J. (1982). Rape victim-rape crisis counselor communications: A testimonial privilege. *Dickerson Law Review, 86,* 539–564.

Schloendorff v. Society of New York Hospital, 211 N.Y. 125, 105 N.E. 92 (1914), overruled by Bing v. Thunig, 2 N.Y.2d 656, 143 N.E.2d 3, 163 N.Y.S.2d 3 (1957) (holding that hospitals are not immunized from employees' negligence).

Schmid, D., Appelbaum, P. S., Roth, L. H., & Lidz, C. (1983). Confidentiality in psychiatry: A study of the patient's view. *Hospital and Community Psychiatry, 34,* 353–355.

Schuster v. Altenberg, 144 Wis. 2d 223, 424 N.W.2d 159 (1988).

Seligman, B. X. (1977). Untangling *Tarasoff: Tarasoff v. Regents of the University of California. Hastings Law Journal, 29,* 179–210.

Shah, S. T. (1969). Privileged communications, confidentiality, and privacy: Privileged communications. *Professional Psychology, 1,* 56–59.

Shaw v. Glickman, 45 Md. App. 718, 415 A.2d 625 (1980).

Sherlock, R., & Murphy, W. (1984). Confidentiality and therapy: An agency perspective. *Comprehensive Psychiatry, 25,* 88–95.

Shuman, D. W., & Weiner, M. F. (1982). The privilege study: An empirical examination of the psychotherapist-patient privilege. *North Carolina Law Review, 60,* 893–942.

Shwed, H. J., Kuvin, S. F., & Baliga, R. K. (1979). Medical audit: Crises in confidentiality and the patient-psychiatrist relationship. *American Journal of Psychiatry, 136,* 447–450.

Siegal, M. (1979). Privacy, ethics, and confidentiality. *Professional Psychology, 10,* 249–258.

Simon, R. I. (1987). *Clinical psychiatry and the law.* Washington, DC: American Psychiatric Press.

Sloan, J. B., & Klein, S. B. (1977). Psychotherapeutic disclosures: A conflict between right and duty. *University of Toledo Law Review, 9,* 57–72.

Smith-Bell, M., & Winslade, W. J. (1996). Confidentiality in the psychotherapeutic relationship. In B. D. Sales & D. W. Shuman (Eds.), *Law, mental health, and mental disorder* (pp. 62–75). Pacific Grove, CA: Brooks/Cole.

Smith, S. R., & Meyer, R. G. (1984). Child abuse reporting laws and psychotherapy: A time for reconsideration. *International Journal of Law and Psychiatry, 7,* 351–366.

State v. Andring, 342 N.W.2d 128 (Minn. 1984).

State v. Byrd, 568 So.2d 554 (La. 1990).

State v. Miller, 300 Or. 203, 709 P.2d 225 (1985), *cert. denied, Miller v. Oregon,* 475 U.S. 1141 (1986).

State v. Tsavaris, 382 So. 2d 56 (Fla. Dist. Ct. App. 1980), *aff'd,* 394 So.2d 418 (1981).

State in the Interest of D. G., 174 N.J. Super 243, 416 A.2d 77 (1980).

Stone, A. A. (1976). The *Tarasoff* decision: Suing psychotherapists to safeguard society. *Harvard Law Review, 90,* 358–378.

Stouder, B. (1982). Criminal law and procedure (evidence)—Pennsylvania establishes new privilege for communications made to a rape crisis center counselor—*In re Pittsburgh Action Against Rape,* 494 Pa. 15, 428 A.2d 126 (1981). *Temple Law Quarterly, 55,* 1124–1148.

Stroube, M. K. (1979). The psychotherapist-patient privilege: Are some patients more privileged than others? *Pacific Law Journal, 10,* 801–824.

Suarez, J. M., & Balcanoff, E. J. (1966). Massachusetts psychiatry and privileged communications. *Archives of General Psychiatry, 15,* 619–623.

Swoboda, J. W., Elwork, A., Sales, B. D., & Levine, D. (1978). Knowledge of and compliance with privileged communications and child-abuse-reporting laws. *Professional Psychology, 9,* 448–457.

Tarasoff v. Regents of University of California, 13 Cal. 3d 177, 529 P.2d 553, 118 Cal. Rptr. 129 (1974), vacated, 17 Cal. 3d 425, 551 P.2d 334, 131 Cal. Rptr. 14 (1976).

Thompson v. County of Alameda, 27 Cal. 3d 741, 614 P.2d 728, 167 Cal. Rptr. 70 (1980).

Thurman, R. F. (1984). Incest and ethics: Confidentiality's severest test. *Denver Law Journal, 61,* 619–653.

Trempor, C. (1984). Protection of minors' confidentiality in psychotherapy. In D. N. Weisstub (Ed.), Law and *mental health: International perspectives.* Elmsford, NY: Pergamon Press.

Turner, J. F., & Thomason, J. W. (1970). Physician-patient confidences: Legal effects of computerization of records. *Alabama Lawyer, 31,* 193–202.

United States v. Blackburn, 446 F.2d 1089 (5th Cir. 1971), *cert. denied, Blackburn v. United States,* 404 U.S. 1017 (1972).

Utah Code Ann. § 78-14a-102 (Michie 1997).

Van Eenwyk, J. R. (1990). When laws and values conflict: Comment on Pope and Bajt. *American Psychologist, 45*(3), 399–400.

Vickery, A. B. (1982). Breach of confidence: An emerging tort. *Columbia Law Review, 82,* 1426–1468.

Va. Code Ann. § 37.1-226 (Michie 1997).

Wadlington, W. J. (1983). Consent to medical care for minors: The legal framework. In G. B. Melton, G. P. Koocher, & M. J. Saks (Eds.), *Children's competence to consent* (pp. 57–74). New York: Plenum Press.

Wagshall v. Wagshall, 148 A.D.2d 445, 538 N.Y.S.2d 597 (1989), *appeal dismissed in part rev'd in part,* 74 N.Y.2d 781, 543 N.E.2d 744, 545 N.Y.S.2d 101 (1989).

Wash. Rev. Code Ann. § 71.05.120 (West 1996).

Watson, H., & Levine, M. (1989). Psychotherapy and mandated reporting of child abuse. *American Journal of Orthopsychiatry, 59*(2), 246–256.

Weinapple, M., & Perr, I. N. (1981). The right of a minor to confidentiality: An aftermath of *Bartley v. Kremens.*

Bulletin of the American Academy of Psychiatry and Law, 9, 247–254.

Weisberg, R., & Wald, M. (1984). Confidentiality laws and state efforts to protect abused or neglected children: The need for statutory reform. *Family Law Quarterly, 18,* 143–212.

Wexler, D. B. (1979). Patients, therapists and third parties: The victimological virtues of *Tarasoff. International Journal of Law and Psychiatry, 2,* 1–28.

Wexler, D. B. (1981). *Mental health law: Major issues.* New York: Plenum Press.

Whalen v. Roe, 429 U.S. 589 (1977).

Williamson, K. E. (1984). Confidentiality of sexual assault victim-counselor communication: A proposed model statute. *Arizona Law Review, 26,* 416–488.

Wilson v. Lehman, 379 S.W.2d 478 (Ky. 1964).

Winslade, W. J. (1982). Confidentiality of medical records: An overview of concepts and legal policies. *The Journal of Legal Medicine, 3,* 497–533.

Wise, T. P. (1978). Where the public peril begins: A survey of psychotherapists to determine the effects of *Tarasoff. Stanford Law Review, 31,* 165–190.

Zurcher v. Stanford Daily, 436 U.S. 547 (1978).

AUTHOR INDEX

SUBJECT INDEX